Introduction to Discrete MATHEMATICS

INTRODUCTION to Discrete MATHEMATICS

Wayne M. Dymàček
Washington and Lee University

Henry Sharp, Jr.
Washington and Lee University

Boston, Massachusetts   Burr Ridge, Illinois   Dubuque, Iowa
Madison, Wisconsin   New York, New York   San Francisco, California   St. Louis, Missouri

WCB/McGraw-Hill

A Division of The **McGraw·Hill** Companies

Introduction to Discrete Mathematics

This book is printed on acid-free paper.

1 2 3 4 5 6 7 8 9 0 DOC DOC 9 0 0 9 8 7

ISBN 0-07-018566-2

Publisher: Thomas L. Casson
Sponsoring editor: Jack Shira and Maggie Rogers
Marketing manager: Michelle Sala
Project manager: Terri Wicks
Production supervisor: Michelle Lyon
Designer: Carol Barr
Cover designer: Suzanne Montazer
Compositor: Publication Services, Inc.
Typefaces: Times Roman, Modula, and Gill Sans
Printer: R. R. Donnelley & Sons Company

Grateful acknowledgment is made for use of the following:

Realia *Page 520* ©Monticello/Thomas Jefferson Memorial Foundation, Inc.

Library of Congress Cataloging-in-Publication Data

Dymàček, Wayne M.
    Introduction to discrete mathematics / Wayne M. Dymàček, Henry Sharp, Jr.
        p.   cm.
    Includes bibliographical references and indexes.
    ISBN 0-07-018566-2
    1. Mathematics.   I. Sharp, Henry, 1923–   .   II. Title.
QA39.2.D95   1998
510–dc21   97-5717
                                                                          CIP

http://www.mhhe.com

*I dedicate this book to my children,
Ivy and Julian, and to my wife,
Diana, without whose
encouragement it would not have
been published.*

W. M. D.

*I dedicate this work to the memory
of my long-time friend and
colleague, Trevor Evans, whose
early encouragement whetted an
interest in matters combinatorial.*

H. S.

Contents

Chapter 2   Mathematical Induction   123

Chapter 3   Combinatorics   217

Preface

Audience

In a number of ways *discrete mathematics* is an attractive alternative to the more traditional introductory courses in mathematics offered at many colleges. While calculus and its prerequisites remain at the core of programs in science and engineering, for students in other fields, discrete mathematics can provide an ideal entree to the study of many important mathematical concepts. Its problems are often easy to understand and interesting to think about, yet even at the beginning level their challenge can be substantial. Further, in perhaps no other area of mathematics does "recognition of pattern" and "generalization from special cases" occur with greater frequency and naturalness. Few courses, therefore, can better serve a student population, fragmented by need or interest into those who:

a. enjoy mathematics, whether or not they intend to major in it or a related field; or

b. are curious about a kind of mathematics different from the traditional calculus; or

c. intend to major in a computer-related area for which this material is prerequisite; or

d. intend to major in one of the social sciences which now make regular use of discrete concepts; or, perhaps,

e. wish only to satisfy a general education requirement in mathematics.

We believe that with minor modifications in emphasis the material presented here can be directed toward any one of the student categories noted above.

Prerequisites and Level

This textbook is intended for use on the introductory collegiate level. No prerequisites are assumed beyond three years of secondary level mathematics; in particular, an introduction to the ideas of calculus is not necessary. Because proof plays a central role in mathematics, we do expect a year of high school geometry, not so much for its content as for its maturing effect and for the introduction it provides to the general idea of logical structure.

Approach and Guiding Philosophy

The spiral approach. In the first half of the book, especially, we have used a **spiral** approach to the presentation of ideas. We have avoided the compartmentalization implied by separate chapters on logic, sets, and numbers; these fundamental concepts are developed in parallel to emphasize their interaction with one another. Beginning with very simple results and techniques, the material progresses in a gentle upward spiral of difficulty toward significant problem-solving and theorem-proving capability.

In our view, the essence of the "spiral" approach is: refrain from introducing new definitions, concepts, or extensions until they become critical to the understanding of current material. For example, the ideas of "set," "subset," "membership," and "inclusion" are important from Section 1 on, but *operations* on sets are delayed until Section 15. This is not to imply that "union" and "intersection" could not have been used earlier—rather, that they have not been necessary in conveying the ideas presented up to that point.

Proofs. It has been said that the essence of mathematics is "proof." Certainly, one cannot develop an appreciation of mathematics without coming to grips with the ideas of theorem and proof. In our opinion, any introduction to mathematics must address this issue. We do so early on, primarily in the context of the real number system where many of the theorems proved are related to very simple facts already familiar to those with the anticipated background. Our purpose is that attention remain focused on the proof technique under discussion, and that it not be diverted by concern with algebraic maneuvering. The most important goal in Chapters 1 and 2 is to promote the development of confidence and independence in dealing with proofs. The keys to this development are *example* and *practice*. In order to emphasize just those aspects of logical argument which commonly occur in mathematical reasoning, we have deliberately avoided such technical terminology in logic as "modus ponens," "modus tollens," "tautology," etc. Finally, it is no great exaggeration to observe that Chapters 0 and 1 are designed to set the stage for our presentation of "mathematical induction," a technique of proof which occupies central importance in discrete mathematics as well as in computer science.

Recommendations. Our objectives are consistent with recommendations published in, for example, "The Future of College Mathematics," Springer-Verlag, and "Model Curriculum for a Liberal Arts Degree in Computer Science" by Norman Gibbs and Alan Tucker. Among those objectives are: that the course be designed for the freshman year, that its intellectual level be comparable with introductory calculus, that the concept of "algorithm" be introduced early and illustrated frequently, that the elementary mathematical prerequisites for computer science courses be included, and that there be sufficient material for a two-semester sequence.

In addition, some nationally proposed curricula recommend the inclusion of a unit on probability. We have adopted this recommendation because students often find that probability concepts are fun to think about, and because those concepts reinforce so many of the earlier ideas: enumeration, abstract logical structure, the binomial theorem, inclusion-exclusion, and so on.

Writing Style. We have adopted a "low-key" conversational style of writing. Although theorems and many examples are set apart, definitions and other important concepts are incorporated into the running text to enhance the narrative flow and to present a less formidable appearance. For easy reference, all such terms are highlighted in bold characters at initial occurrence. Also, the end of a displayed proof is indicated by a ■; the end of a displayed example is indicated by a ⬤; the end of a displayed algorithm is indicated by a ▲. Occasionally, an algorithm may be incompletely displayed, and in that case the △ replaces the ▲. Finally, the ✎ is used to mark an illustration that is best read with pencil in hand.

Flexibility

Chapters 0-3. Throughout the preparation of this work, flexibility of design has been a major concern. Enough material is included to occupy a full two-semester sequence. The first half, however, is essentially a self-contained unit which might best be described as *an introduction to mathematics, with a "combinatorial" flavor.* Important themes are: experimentation, recognition of pattern, conjecture, proof, generalization, induction, and enumeration.

We have labeled the first chapter of this book with the number "0," not because its content is either negligible or unimportant, but because its main concern is with the basic vocabulary of words and symbols to which students were introduced at the pre-college level. It is our intent that this material be used selectively to assure a reasonably uniform working knowledge of the basic vocabulary at the beginning of a course. Chapters 0 and 1, together, contain a leisurely but fairly thorough exposure to those common understandings of terms, operations, and ideas upon which the remainder of the text depends. Adaptation of this material, in whatever detail may be necessary to match individual and/or class needs, is both possible and desirable.

The "core" content of the subject is contained in Chapters 0 through 3, and in our own courses we have found that this requires about one term.

Chapter 4. Our students who continue in computer science rarely take a separate course in probability theory; in order to include an introduction to probability in the first term we have most often omitted Sections 18 and 19.

Chapters 4–6. Our experience suggests that Chapters 4 through 6 contain more material than can readily be covered in a second term. Selection, of course, is a matter of particular need or preference. Chapter 4 is essentially independent of the following chapters and may be omitted in whole or part, if desired. Chapter 6 is dependent to a limited extent on the first four sections of Chapter 5. For a course designed mainly as a "survey," the latter sections in each chapter are the more easily omitted.

Features

Numbering System. Discrete mathematics is a fascinating collection of ideas, many of which interact substantially with one another producing a kind of "inner consistency" of combinatorial thinking. To stress this consistency, we have numbered the sections consecutively throughout the book and they are our primary structural units. It is true that sections dealing with related topics *are* gathered into chapters, but this is intended to display the organization of the material and to facilitate selection of content from one course to another. Each section includes a multiplicity of ideas and these are ordered into consecutively numbered (like paragraph 9.3), and relatively compact, paragraphs. Paragraph numbers are displayed in the header to odd-numbered pages, thus location of a reference like "See paragraph 5.12" is essentially trivial. Use of bold-face type directs attention quickly to important concepts.

Theorems, tables, tutorials, and figures are identified (separately) by paragraph label, supplemented by an alphabetic character when more than one instance occurs in a Paragraph. Thus, "Figure 29.2B" refers to the second figure (designated B) in the second paragraph of Section 29. Where appropriate, displayed formulas are numbered consecutively within paragraphs. Reference to display numbers outside the current paragraph is keyed to paragraph number, for example, as (1) in paragraph 11.2. Very simply, all referencing is tied to paragraphs.

Informality. We emphasize that attention to the text is very important, for it is there that fundamental ideas are motivated, defined and interpreted. Our "device" of speaking directly to students is intended to attract their interest. Additionally, in order to encourage thoughtful reading, questions are frequently posed in the running text and only rarely are they meant to be rhetorical; most often they open avenues to a deeper consideration of the ideas at hand. Examples, also, occur frequently, both in the running text and in displayed format. In every case, the intent is to motivate or illustrate some abstract concept, often a definition or a theorem.

Tutorial Boxes. We employ in this textbook a more formal device to attract critical attention to the material as it is read. At appropriate junctures in each Section, the presentation is interrupted by "**Tutorial boxes.**" These in general contain several questions which require a mix of routine calculations with extensions or proofs. They are intended both to confirm and to reinforce the understanding of preceding material, in preparation for new ideas to follow. It is our hope that the Tutorials will be treated as an integral part of reading and study assignments. Answers to all tutorials can be found at the end of the textbook.

Complements. In another departure from customary textbook organization, we have appended to most Sections a special discussion, called a **Complement,** illustrating an important idea in the current Section but at a level somewhat in advance of the main text. We found that students having stronger preparation and/or motivation were attracted by the occasional deeper follow-up topics included in early versions of the notes. Additional encouragement persuaded us to present many more such topics, some of which are among the most important and beautiful results in the field. In general, the Complements are not intended to be an integral part of the main development; none of them is necessary to what we consider to be a perfectly reasonable introduction to discrete mathematics, and they are not referenced in the main body of the text. They *are* intended for use in a selective way to broaden the horizons of those students whose individual backgrounds and abilities permit it. We would like to think, of course, that one or more of the Complements (whether assigned formally or browsed through casually) might ignite enthusiasm for further study of discrete mathematics.

Historical Asides. Historical information about major concepts and trends in mathematics, and about the extraordinary individuals responsible for them, is an important component of mathematical literacy. Inclusion of such information in elementary textbooks, therefore, is a reasonable expectation. Yet, to be realistic, limitations of both space and time intrude. To economize on both, we have avoided biographical sketches as well as extended digressions on cultural context. We have sought a middle ground: retaining in the text an emphasis on learning and doing mathematics; but, where appropriate, making informal reference to people and events of historic interest. These succinct commentaries should not deflect attention from the technical development and, hopefully, will open a window of opportunity for those instructors inclined to more detailed discussion. We would expect that, given encouragement, many students will enjoy exploring a bit of the fascinating story behind such individuals as Pythagoras, Euclid, al-Khwārizmī, Fibonacci, Fermat, Pascal, Euler, and Gauss (not to mention the more modern mathematicians), all of whom have contributed so decisively to the concepts introduced here.

References. Even a casual survey of the QA (= call letters for books in mathematics) shelves in a college library will indicate the abundance of reference material on nearly every topic included in this textbook. Only a few titles from among the many available will be mentioned; these in turn may supply further suggestions, if such are needed. Included at the end of this book is a short list of well-known works "about" mathematics; many of them written by eminent mathematicians attempting to convey to a general audience something of the pleasure, power, and usefulness inherent in mathematical concepts. These books should not be considered "light" reading, but they are (in varying degree) non-technical in the sense that they offer fascinating, accessible glimpses into the world of mathematics. In addition to these suggestions for more general reading, we include a brief list of specialized books or papers which contain information closely related to some of the complements. These references usually are at different levels of difficulty; not all will be equally helpful to individual users. The best advice is to browse among them for appropriate assistance.

Section Overviews. Each section opens with a concise outline of the major concepts to be introduced and/or discussed in that section. Included also is a list of key words, usually to be defined in the text and important enough to require careful study. We have not considered it necessary, or even especially helpful, to provide section or chapter summaries. In essence, these would mainly serve to reiterate information already included in the "Overviews." Beyond that, our use of spiral organization requires frequent reference to earlier discussions, thereby sustaining coherence of the underlying themes in each chapter.

Problem Sets. Every section except the one labeled "zero" contains exercises in two places: the "Tutorial Boxes" inserted in the text, and the "Problem Sets" at the end of the section. There are at least 25 questions in each problem set, often more than 40. These range from routine computations (usually those with the lower number labels) to sequences of questions which taken together amplify ideas barely mentioned in the text. The exercises in between are a more-or-less random mix in difficulty. Incidentally, "difficulty" in discrete mathematics may be difficult to pin down. Problems often yield to different lines of attack: An ingenious idea may reduce the labor manyfold.

Algorithms. In its formative years, computer science relied heavily upon the concept of "Flow Chart," especially as related to the construction of programs. We have adopted here an embryonic form of flow chart to complement the descriptions of many algorithms introduced in the text. We believe that these diagrams will prove helpful in clarifying the general notion of an algorithm, in emphasizing the underlying structure of particular algorithms, and in reducing the "human" perception of an operation to an elemental form suitable for machine implementation. To this end we urge that each flow chart be traced through with numerical (or other appropriate) input as its algorithm is being discussed.

Additional Pedagogy

By its somewhat unusual format of Section plus Complement, this textbook can be adapted to accommodate varying levels of student preparation. For students with limited backgrounds, the reinforcement supplied by the early Sections should ease the transition to new and more complex concepts. For better prepared students who already know many of the elementary facts, Chapter 0 may be omitted and Chapter 1 may be surveyed selectively for a review of proof techniques and for some of the more advanced ideas discussed in the Complements.

Not only is there variability in background to consider, but within any given class there is often a disparity in talent and motivation. It is our hope that the Complements will offer a useful focus for independent study assignments (or, even, for small group projects).

We should remember that discrete mathematics is, first of all, mathematics; as such it has an existence independent of the fact that it is essentially the language of computer science. There are places in the text where computer-related concepts are discussed, but these invariably are included for the special point of view they bring to the mathematical ideas. Our text, however, includes no topics or exercises requiring the use of a personal computer. A hand-held calculator will occasionally be helpful for some of the problems but never necessary to an understanding of the concepts introduced and explored.

Supplements

An Instructor's Solutions Manual is available to adopters of our book. Please contact your WCB/McGraw-Hill sales representative for more information.

Acknowledgments

This textbook has evolved from classroom notes prepared for a course in Discrete Mathematics which was introduced at Washington and Lee University in 1984 and which has been taught at least once each year since that time. Modifications and other improvements have resulted from many suggestions by students, colleagues, and reviewers, to all of whom we acknowledge a debt of gratitude: in particular Professor T. O. Vinson and W. K. Smith and the students in our advanced combinatorics and graph theory courses. Also, we would like to thank the following McGraw-Hill reviewers:

Michael Meck, *Southern Connecticut State University*
Robert Baer, *Miami University, Hamilton*
Jane Edgar, *Brevard Community College*
Kathy Pilger, *Bob Jones University*
George Schultz, *St. Petersburg Junior College*
Robert Beezer, *University of Puget Sound*
Frederick Hoffman, *Florida Atlantic University*
William Krant, *El Paso Community College*

Addresses

Our snail mail address is Washington and Lee University, Department of Mathematics, Lexington, Virginia 24450 and our email address is `wdymacek@wlu.edu`. Any comments, suggestions, or corrections are appreciated.

Wayne M. Dymàček

Henry Sharp, Jr.

A Few Words to the Student

Sections

Forget the long preface! All you need is here. The main structural units in this textbook are the sections; there are forty-one of them, each separated into numbered paragraphs. **All** labeling and referencing is keyed to these paragraphs. To stress the inter-relationship of topics in "discrete mathematics," the text incorporates unusually many backward references. Most often, we expect, current context will be an adequate reminder, but when a reference is actually needed it can be located quickly via the page headings which include a paragraph indicator. For example, to refer to (1) in the third paragraph of Section 7, simply thumb to the page(s) headed 7.3.

Tutorial Boxes

At several places in each section there is a "Tutorial box" which lists questions about the material just discussed. Answering these will help fix the ideas in mind and, also, will help indicate where an idea may be incompletely understood and need reinforcement. The answers to each of these tutorials appears in the answer section of the text.

Questions?

Are you ready? Any introduction to an unfamiliar subject will employ specialized vocabulary (much like a foreign language). This text is no exception, but the early sections relate to the mathematics common to most secondary level programs. The purpose is to allow concentration on concepts and relationships without the handicap of reference to newly defined "things." In consequence, you will explore territory that is already familiar in general; but keenest enjoyment depends on more detailed study of the scenery. There is a paradox here: Out of intellectual effort (which may not be much fun) comes the subtlety of understanding needed to "catch the point" of a clever argument—even to create your own clever argument. And **that,** perhaps surprisingly, **is** fun. There is a sense of pleasure (and also pride) in the sudden recognition of an unexpected twist which solves a problem that seemed hopelessly mired in drudgery. Here is a quick example (which, incidentally, will appear in a later problem set.)

A Problem. A positive integer, like 18, has both 1 and itself as factors, and may have other factors between them. Curiosity asks, how many factors does such a number have? To answer, we can begin with 1 and start testing all the way up to the number. For the number 18, we test:

$$1 \text{ yes,} \quad 2 \text{ yes,} \quad 3 \text{ yes,} \quad 4 \text{ no,} \quad 5 \text{ no,} \quad 6 \text{ yes,} \quad \text{and so on.}$$

Easy enough here and the whole list includes only the six numbers

$$1, \quad 2, \quad 3, \quad 6, \quad 9, \quad 18.$$

A Solution. But, suppose we had looked at the number 8775 (or any other)? Isn't there some less tedious approach than simply examining all smaller numbers one-by-one? So we think, what prime factors does the number 18 have? Since $18 = 2 \cdot 3 \cdot 3 = 2 \cdot 3^2$, consider the product

$$(1 + 2)(1 + 3 + 3^2) = 1 + 2 + 3 + 2 \cdot 3 + 3^2 + 2 \cdot 3^2.$$

Notice that each term on the right is one of the factors of 18; hence the answer to our question is simply the number of such terms. But the number of terms on the right doesn't change if we replace each term on the left by 1

$$(1 + 1)(1 + 1 + 1).$$

This forces each term on the right to be 1, hence the number of such terms is simply $2 \cdot 3 = 6$.

Here then is a clever idea we can use to count the number of factors of 8775 (without testing each smaller positive integer). Since

$$8775 = 3^3 \cdot 5^2 \cdot 13,$$

we get the number of its factors by replacing each term in

$$(1 + 3 + 3^2 + 3^3)(1 + 5 + 5^2)(1 + 13)$$

by 1

$$(1 + 1 + 1 + 1)(1 + 1 + 1)(1 + 1) = 24.$$

Finally, in full generality, if $N = p^a \cdot q^b \cdot \ldots \cdot t^e$, where p, q, $\ldots$, t are different primes, then the number of factors of N is the product

$$(a + 1) \cdot (b + 1) \cdot \ldots \cdot (e + 1),$$

and our question is answered. Now, can you show quickly that 693 has exactly twelve factors? Check your answer, if you like, by listing the factors. Do you need to test integers larger than 26?

About the Authors

Wayne M. Dymáček is a Professor of Mathematics at Washington and Lee University and had previously worked for the National Security Agency. He received his Ph.D. from Virginia Tech, specializing in graph theory, an area in which he has published several papers. He has directed numerous undergraduate students in summer research work, from which several papers have been published or submitted. For eleven years he has helped grade the AP calculus exams and he is currently on the Mathematical Association of America's Committee on Testing.

Henry Sharp, Jr., until his retirement in 1991, was Head of the Mathematics Department at Washington and Lee University. He had taught previously at the Georgia Institute of Technology and, for many years, at Emory University. He received both A.M. and Ph.D. degrees from Duke University and has published a number of papers in various professional journals in the areas of general topology, dimension theory, combinatorics, and graph theory.

Discrete

MATHEMATICS

Introduction

Section 0. Introduction and Preliminary Examples

0.1 *Discrete mathematics* is a relatively recent entry among the various courses now offered at the collegiate level. Although the name is new, it refers to a collection of related concepts, some of which date from antiquity while others are contemporary in origin. Whatever discrete mathematics may be, it shares the basic vocabulary of sets, numbers, and logic developed in the familiar progression in mathematics education from arithmetic through algebra to geometry and beyond. What distinguishes it are the concepts emphasized and the questions asked. In this brief introduction we intend to suggest just a few of the many kinds of problems which may be considered typical of the subject.

   The four examples which follow should be considered as simple "thought experiments," intended primarily to set the stage. Each example raises a very general question which in its simplest cases can be answered after a little thought or after a bit of scribbling on a piece of scratch paper. The discovery and development of techniques required to answer such questions in general is a major goal of this course. But, for the moment, to understand these simple cases is to begin an appreciation of what discrete mathematics is about.

0.2 Our first problem is related to the behavior of certain elementary particles as described in modern physics, but it can be presented in much less forbidding language.

Example 1 Suppose that you have some dollar bills, say n of them, and in a fit of generosity you decide to give them away to the k friends who happen to be with you at the moment. Of course, in purchasing power one bill is just like any other, but the friends are clearly distinguishable from one another. Our question is, "In how many different ways can you carry out this charitable intent?" The answer is given in the following table for small values of n and k.

k / n	1	2	3	4
1	1	2	3	4
2	1	3	6	
3	1	4	10	
4	1	5		

Now, where does this table come from? Indeed, how can you be sure that the entries in the table are correct?

If $k = 1$, then the *one* friend present must receive all the bills, so the first column is correct. But with more than one friend present there are multiple possibilities. You might, for example, divide the bills as evenly as possible among the k friends, or you might choose to give all the bills to one friend and none to the others. In any event, to explore further how the entries might be determined, consider column 2 which corresponds to distributing the dollar bills between two friends (that is, $k = 2$). For convenience, suppose that your two friends are identified by $\mathscr{A}$ and $\mathscr{B}$. Then the possible distributions of n bills (for $n = 1, 2$, and 3) are as follows:

$n = 1$		$n = 2$		$n = 3$	
$\mathscr{A}$	$\mathscr{B}$	$\mathscr{A}$	$\mathscr{B}$	$\mathscr{A}$	$\mathscr{B}$
1	0	2	0	3	0
0	1	1	1	2	1
		0	2	1	2
				0	3

Perhaps you can detect the pattern: If $n = 8$, for example, then the number of distributions is 9. Incidentally, one of the key ideas underlying discrete mathematics is **the search for patterns.** In this example, however, the pattern is not so obvious for larger values of n and k; try verifying the table entry for $n = 3$ and $k = 3$. In paragraph 20.5 we will discover a simple formula for computing these table entries.

0.3

Our second problem has several different interpretations, but it originated in the following way.

Example 1

The product of two numbers x and y is indicated by $x \cdot y$. To find the product of three numbers x, y, and z requires two multiplications; for example, find the product of the first two numbers, then multiply that by the third. This can be indicated by using parentheses: $(x \cdot y) \cdot z$. Without changing the order of the factors, the same product can be computed differently as indicated by $x \cdot (y \cdot z)$, which means that the product of y and z is multiplied by x. Thus, $(3 \cdot 5) \cdot 7 = 15 \cdot 7 = 105$ and $3 \cdot (5 \cdot 7) = 3 \cdot 35 = 105$ are the two allowable ways of finding the product of 3, 5, and 7. [Of course, $(3 \cdot 7) \cdot 5$ produces the same product, but in this example we agree not to interchange the factors.] The question is, "Given n numbers, in how many different ways can the product be determined by inserting parentheses appropriately?" For small values of n these numbers are:

n	2	3	4	5
No. of ways	1	2	5	14

Again, where does the table come from, and how can you be sure that the entries are correct?

To verify the $n = 4$ case, let the four numbers be denoted by w, x, y, and z, and consider the product $w \cdot x \cdot y \cdot z$. Here are the five ways:

$$((w \cdot x) \cdot y) \cdot z, \qquad (w \cdot (x \cdot y)) \cdot z, \qquad (w \cdot x) \cdot (y \cdot z),$$
$$w \cdot ((x \cdot y) \cdot z), \qquad w \cdot (x \cdot (y \cdot z)).$$

To illustrate this, construct these five indicated multiplications for the special case of $w = 2$, $x = 3$, $y = 5$, and $z = 7$. One of them is

$$((2 \cdot 3) \cdot 5) \cdot 7 = (6 \cdot 5) \cdot 7 = 30 \cdot 7 = 210.$$

Note that the final product is the same in every case; what differs are the intermediate products which must be calculated in reaching the final answer.

Verifying the $n = 5$ case is more of a challenge; you might enjoy spending a few minutes trying to discover all the possibilities. What becomes quickly apparent is the desirability of adopting a systematic approach. In paragraph 19.5 we will discover an easy way to compute the entries in this table.

0.4

The preceding examples illustrate questions that begin "How many...?" They are referred to as enumeration questions, and they belong to a part of discrete mathematics called "combinatorics." But other kinds of questions are also important, as represented by our third example.

Example 1

Adjacent to the campus is an ice cream shop which offers eight different flavors. To make a little extra spending money, you have a part-time job behind the counter. Suppose that five of your friends come in for cones, and you know that each of them has certain dislikes among the available flavors. The question is, "Can you serve each one of them an acceptable flavor without duplication?" The answer depends on individual tastes, and by trial and error it could be discovered. But these numbers are relatively small; suppose there were 31 flavors and 20 customers. Now trial and error becomes tedious. Rather than answering the question by trying to produce an actual selection of different flavors, it would be desirable to identify a criterion which would guarantee the existence of an appropriate selection, if one were possible. There is such a criterion, and it is closely related to the following *negative* observation: If the total number of flavors acceptable to some n of the customers is smaller than n, then no selection of different (acceptable) flavors is possible. For example, suppose that your friends like only the following flavors:

$$\mathcal{F}_1 : \quad \text{(peppermint, praline)},$$

$$\mathcal{F}_2 : \quad \text{(praline, pistachio)},$$

$$\mathcal{F}_3 : \quad \text{(peppermint, pistachio)},$$

$$\mathcal{F}_4 : \quad \text{(peppermint, praline, pistachio)},$$

$$\mathcal{F}_5 : \quad \text{(praline, pistachio, peach, pineapple)}.$$

Even though five flavors are favored among your five friends, there is no way the first four can be given different acceptable flavors; hence there must be duplication when all five are served. A more general discussion appears in paragraph 11.6.

0.5   The three examples above share the common characteristic of dealing with one or more finite collections of things. This is a fair, though not totally accurate, observation about discrete mathematics. Certainly, most of what we cover in *this* course is directly concerned with finiteness. Although we have described each of these examples in more or less "homely" language, their applications are important enough that the concepts are known, generally, by the names of the mathematicians or scientists associated with them. The first illustrates what is called "Bose-Einstein statistics," because of the great success in calculating the behavior of photons following techniques suggested by the scientists Satyendra Nathe Bose (1894–1974) and Albert Einstein (1879–1955). The second illustrates "Catalan numbers," named for the mathematician Eugène C. Catalan (1814–1894). The third illustrates the idea of a "system of distinct representatives," based on a famous theorem of the twentieth century mathematician Philip Hall (1904–1982).

0.6   Finally, we consider an example which again asks an enumeration question, but this time the answer will appear in an unusual algebraic form. Before stating the problem, we recall that by dividing $1 - y$ into 1 we can write the symbolic equation

$$\frac{1}{1-y} = 1 + y + y^2 + y^3 + \cdots. \tag{1}$$

We will consider (1) to be a formal expression which simply allows us to replace one side by the other in the example which follows. For the time being, consider the three dots, $\cdots$, as an indication that the addition should be continued in the evident way; thus, the next term on the right-hand side of (1) is y^4.

Example 1

This example is a variation on the question, "In how many ways can you make change for a dollar?" We pose the simpler question, "In how many ways can you make change using only nickels and dimes?" A possible approach to this problem exploits one of the fundamental properties of algebraic manipulation, namely, $x^m \cdot x^n = x^{m+n}$. Suppose we replace y in (1) first by x^5, then by x^{10}, and then rewrite the formula

$$G(x) = \frac{1}{1 - x^5} \cdot \frac{1}{1 - x^{10}} \tag{2}$$

as the product

$$G(x) = (1 + x^5 + x^{10} + x^{15} + x^{20} + \cdots) \cdot (1 + x^{10} + x^{20} + \cdots). \tag{3}$$

Now, consider that terms in the first factor represent nickels (1 means no nickel, x^5 means one nickel, x^{10} means two nickels, etc.) and terms in the second factor represent dimes (1 means no dime, x^{10} means one dime, x^{20} means two dimes, etc.). When these factors are multiplied, (3) can be written as

$$G(x) = 1 + x^5 + 2x^{10} + 2x^{15} + 3x^{20} + 3x^{25} + \cdots. \tag{4}$$

How does this algebraic expression help? You can easily check the following observation by experiment: If you have a pile of nickels and a pile of dimes, then you can produce 5 cents in exactly one way, 10 cents in exactly two ways, 15 cents in exactly two ways, 20 cents in exactly three ways, and 25 cents in exactly three ways. Notice that these numbers are the coefficients of the appropriate powers of x in (4).

The expression $G(x)$ is called a **generating function.** But we should raise a warning flag: $G(x)$ in not a function in the familiar usage of elementary algebra and analysis. We don't substitute numbers for x to find function values $G(x)$! We are using $G(x)$ as an abbreviation for the formula in (2), which can be rewritten as the sum of terms in (4). Note that $G(x)$ contains in succinct form the answers to many questions. For example, the coefficient of x^{100} is the number of ways you can make change for a dollar using only nickels and dimes. Of course the work is a little tedious, but the answer comes after a very routine calculation. You can verify that the answer is 11 by writing out each of the two factors in (3) as far as the term involving x^{100}. Don't multiply all the terms, just those resulting in a product giving x^{100}; for example, $x^{20} \cdot x^{80}$. Again, there appears to be a pattern: one product for each of the following 11 terms in the right-hand factor of (3):

$$1 + x^{10} + x^{20} + x^{30} + x^{40} + x^{50} + x^{60} + x^{70} + x^{80} + x^{90} + x^{100}.$$

Now test the pattern on a \$2 bill; you should discover that there are 21 ways to make change for it using only nickels and dimes. (A \$2 bill is fairly rare; do you know which President's image appears on it?)

The situation becomes more complicated if we allow the use of all coins having smaller value than a dollar. The generating function in this case is

$$H(x) = \frac{1}{1-x} \cdot \frac{1}{1-x^5} \cdot \frac{1}{1-x^{10}} \cdot \frac{1}{1-x^{25}} \cdot \frac{1}{1-x^{50}}, \tag{5}$$

and the coefficient of x^{100} is the number of ways to make change for a dollar. This calculation is again routine but exceedingly tedious by hand (even with a few clever shortcuts). The answer along with a fuller discussion will appear in paragraph 19.4.

Section 1.   Numbers and Sets: Basic Terminology

Overview for Section 1

- Review of basic terminology and notation related to the real number system and to elementary set theory
- Introduction, by example, to one of the important goals of mathematics, that of generalization
- Use of transitivity to emphasize the distinctions between elements, sets, and power sets

Key Concepts: coordinate systems, distance, classification of real numbers, membership, inclusion, set complementation, and set equality

1.1   The usual geometric representation of the real number system is a line on which are marked a point called the **origin** (corresponding to the number 0) and a different point called the **unit** (corresponding to the number 1). A line so marked is called a **number axis,** and two such axes, one horizontal and one vertical which intersect at the origin on each axis, constitute what is called a **rectangular coordinate system,** displayed in Figure 1.1A. On such a coordinate system one can sketch the graphs of linear, quadratic, and other polynomial functions, trigonometric functions, and, of course, many others.

On the axes shown, each point can be labeled by a real number called its **coordinate,** which indicates both distance and direction from the origin to the point.

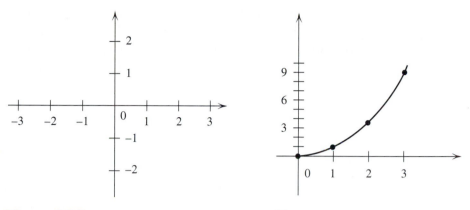

Figure 1.1A   **Figure 1.1B**

Positive coordinates correspond to points to the right of the origin if the axis is horizontal and to points up from the origin if the axis is vertical. *Negative coordinates* correspond to points to the left of the origin (or down). In Figure 1.1A, points having *integer coordinates* are labeled 0 (the origin), 1, −1, 2, −2, and so on; points in between integers correspond to numbers which can be written as fractions or as nonrepeating decimals (more about this in Sections 6 and 7). We should emphasize a critical distinction between the integers and the more inclusive class of real numbers.

- No two *integers* are closer together than one unit. We can find pairs of numbers, for example, $\frac{1}{3}$ and $\frac{2}{3}$, which have no integer between them. (Points with integer coordinates are spaced at "discrete" positions along the axis.)

- *Real numbers* can be found which are as close together as we please. In fact, given any pair of numbers, again, for example, $\frac{1}{3}$ and $\frac{2}{3}$, every number between them is a real number.

This distinction serves as an analogy between discrete and what is often termed "continuous" mathematics. Discrete mathematics deals with questions concerning sets in which the elements are not necessarily related to one another by any intuitive concept of "nearness." The examples in Section 0 illustrate this point; there, we had no interest in whether the elements in question were "close" together. On the other hand, the concept of "nearness" is fundamental in continuous mathematics. Consider the property of area, for example: If the side lengths of two squares are *nearly* the same, then we can be sure that the areas of the squares are *nearly* the same. Much of the traditional secondary school mathematics curriculum is concerned with continuous mathematics. Recall the familiar observation from algebra that the graph of a quadratic polynomial has no breaks or gaps in it; that is, it is continuous. For example, if x represents the side length of a square, then the area is modeled by that part of the graph of $y = x^2$ shown in Figure 1.1B; two points on the horizontal axis which are close together correspond to points on the graph which are close together.

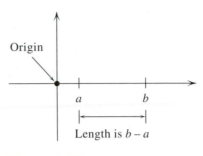

Length is $b - a$

Figure 1.2A

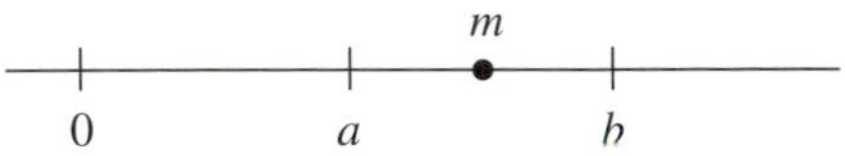

$$m$$

$$0 \qquad a \qquad b$$

Figure 1.2B

1.2 Real numbers are considered to be ordered by the symbol $<$ from smaller to larger. **Positive real numbers** p are those for which $0 < p$ (note that 0 is not a positive number). To say that a is **less than** b ($a < b$) means that there is a positive number p for which $b = a + p$. This number p is called the **difference** $b - a$. If a and b denote different real numbers, then either a is less than b or a is **greater than** b ($a > b$), which means, of course, that $b < a$. All real numbers which lie between a and b constitute what is called an **interval** with **endpoints** a and b. The geometric picture of these ideas is conveniently obtained by considering the horizontal number axis with two points labeled by coordinates a and b; if $a < b$, then the corresponding points are in the order indicated in Figure 1.2A. We will refer to the **length** of the geometric interval between the points labeled a and b as the positive number $b - a$; this number is also called the **distance** between the given points.

Example 1 Assume that $a < b$, and consider the axis in Figure 1.2B with two points having coordinates a and b. How can we find that point which is halfway between a and b? The point having coordinate m which satisfies this condition must be equidistant from a and b. Thus the intervals from a to m and from m to b must have the same length. Hence,

$$m - a = b - m,$$
$$2 \cdot m = a + b,$$
$$m = \frac{a + b}{2}.$$

The coordinate of the midpoint is simply the *arithmetic mean* (or the *average value*) of a and b.

1.3 There is an alternative way to solve the midpoint problem which, it turns out, can be adapted very easily to solve a more general problem which we will investigate in paragraph 29.6. Starting from the origin, one must first get to a, then one must cover one-half of the interval from a to b. Hence,

$$m = a + \left(\tfrac{1}{2} \cdot (b - a)\right) = a - \left(\tfrac{1}{2} \cdot a\right) + \left(\tfrac{1}{2} \cdot b\right)$$

$$= \left(1 - \tfrac{1}{2}\right) \cdot a + \tfrac{1}{2} \cdot b = \frac{a + b}{2}.$$

Suppose we make use of this alternate technique to find the point having coordinate q which is one-fourth of the way from the point a to the point b. Thus, to find q we must first get to a, then cover one-fourth of the interval from a to b; that is,

$$q = a + \tfrac{1}{4} \cdot (b - a) = \left(1 - \tfrac{1}{4}\right) \cdot a + \tfrac{1}{4} \cdot b$$

$$= \tfrac{3}{4} \cdot a + \tfrac{1}{4} \cdot b.$$

Example 1   On a number axis consider the points having coordinates -3 and 9. To find the coordinate of the point q which is one-fourth of the way from -3 to 9, simply compute

$$q = \tfrac{3}{4} \cdot (-3) + \tfrac{1}{4} \cdot 9 = 0.$$

A quick sketch offers geometric confirmation that the origin is the desired point.

Tutorial 1.3

a. Find the coordinate of the point which is one-fourth of the way from the point labeled 9 to the point labeled -3. (*Hint:* Same as Example 1 but with endpoints reversed.)

b. Let a denote the point labeled 9 and let b denote the point labeled -3. Now find the coordinate of the point three-fourths of the way from a to b by finding:

i   The midpoint m of the interval from a to b,

ii Then the midpoint of the interval from m to b.

1.4   We noted in Section 0 that one of the goals of discrete mathematics is to recognize patterns. Another goal is **to form generalizations from special cases.** To illustrate this goal, consider how we might generalize the examples discussed above.

Again, let a and b denote different real numbers, but not necessarily in any given order. Our problem is to find that point on the axis (between the points having coordinates a and b) which lies at a given proportion of the way from a to b. Let t denote any real number between 0 and 1, indicating the "proportion." As before, beginning at the origin, first get to a, then cover t proportion of the way from a to b. Thus, the desired point has as its coordinate

$$w = a + t \cdot (b - a) = a - t \cdot a + t \cdot b = (1 - t) \cdot a + t \cdot b. \tag{1}$$

This formula is the generalization we seek, since each of the situations above is a special case:

- If $t = \frac{1}{2}$, then $w = \left(1 - \frac{1}{2}\right) \cdot a + \frac{1}{2} \cdot b = \frac{1}{2} \cdot (a + b)$.

- If $t = \frac{1}{4}$, then $w = \left(1 - \frac{1}{4}\right) \cdot a + \frac{1}{4} \cdot b = \frac{3}{4} \cdot a + \frac{1}{4} \cdot b$.

Example 1

For various values of a, b, and t, the coordinate w in (1) is given by the following table:

a	b	t	w
-3	9	0.1	$(0.9) \cdot (-3) + (0.1) \cdot 9 = -1.8$
5	-1	0.3	$(0.7) \cdot 5 + (0.3) \cdot (-1) = 3.2$
5	-1	$\frac{1}{3}$	$\frac{2}{3} \cdot 5 + \frac{1}{3} \cdot (-1) = 3$
0	100	0.01	$(0.99) \cdot 0 + (0.01) \cdot 100 = 1.$

1.5

In the past century mathematicians have discovered that it is possible to identify a subject even more basic than arithmetic and geometry: set theory. The language of sets has become pervasive in mathematics; in fact, we have already tacitly used it when we considered the integers and the real numbers in paragraph 1.1. The word "set" is assumed to describe a concept so fundamental (and familiar) that no attempt is made to "define" it further. The intent of the word is suggested by a number of alternatives in everyday usage; for example, a politician might refer to the "population" of a country, or you might refer to your "collection" of CDs, or a doctor might refer to a "family" of diseases. (Also suggestive, but in less common use, is such quixotic terminology as a "pride" of lions, an "exaltation" of larks, a "gaggle" of geese, or a "pod" of seals. These terms are venerable, occurring in *The Book of St. Albans,* printed in 1486. On a more poetic note, you can discover in the final scene of *Hamlet* how Shakespeare refers to a set of angels.) In any event, as the term is used in mathematics, we will assume that a **set** is determined when a plurality (consisting of any number of things) is collected together, either physically or in our imaginations, into a singular object. It is not necessary that the individual things which are collected together be explicitly known; for example, it is acceptable to refer to the "set" of solutions of an equation such as $x^{17} - 1 = 0$.

Example 1

a. You own a number of books which can be referred to collectively as a set called your library.

b. There are 26 things called letters which can be referred to collectively as a set called the English alphabet.

c. The real number system includes a set formed collectively from things, each of which is called a real number. We will use the special symbol $\mathbb{R}$ to denote the set of all real numbers.

1.6

Often, especially in informal usage, a "collective" word is intended to convey a meaning which is subjective (hence ambiguous) in nature; for example, there is unlikely to be general agreement on a "compilation" of favorite movies. We will seek to avoid such a lack of preciseness by imposing the following restriction to our use of the "set" concept: It must be possible (theoretically, at least) to distinguish those things which *are* collected together in the set from those things which *are not*.

Because of this requirement, it is important that the notation for sets be unambiguous and that the terminology of set theory be precise. It is customary to designate sets by boldface capital letters (except for a few special symbols like $\mathbb{R}$). The things which collectively make up the set are called **elements of,** or **members of,** the set, often designated by lowercase letters. When the number of elements is small, the set may be denoted simply by listing the elements, which are then enclosed in braces to emphasize the singular nature of the set.

Example 1

a. The set of principal vowels in the English language is denoted by

$$\mathbf{V} = \{a, e, i, o, u\}.$$

b. The set of digits in the decimal system of numeration is denoted by

$$\mathbf{D} = \{0, 1, 2, 3, 4, 5, 6, 7, 8, 9\}.$$

The special relationship between a set and one of its elements is indicated by the **membership symbol** $\in$ in the following way:

$$a \in \mathbf{V},$$

which means that the thing named by "a" is a member of the set named by "V". This idea is also expressed by the phrase "a is **an element of V**" or by "a **belongs to V**" or by "a is **in V**."

It is often useful to indicate that a given element does not belong to a given set, and for this we use the symbol $\notin$. Thus,

$$8 \notin \mathbf{V}$$

means that the digit 8 is not one of the principal vowels.

1.7

Even though it may be possible to list all the elements in a given set, the list may be inconveniently long or cumbersome. In such a case, the standard shorthand device is three dots, ..., to mean that the list is incomplete and should be continued in accordance with the indicated pattern. For example, we might denote the English alphabet by

$$\mathbf{A} = \{a, b, c, \ldots, z\},$$

omitting from the list most of the 26 elements. Of course, there is always the danger of misunderstanding, so it is important that the notation carry enough information to minimize that possibility. With respect to the set $\mathbf{A}$, above, we can be reasonably certain that

$$p \in \mathbf{A} \qquad \text{whereas} \qquad 3 \notin \mathbf{A}.$$

In mathematics there is frequent occasion to speak of sets for which it is impossible to list all the elements. Perhaps the simplest examples are:

- The set of positive integers, denoted by

$$\mathbb{N} = \{1, 2, 3, \ldots\}$$

- The set of integers, denoted by

$$\mathbb{Z} = \{0, 1, -1, 2, -2, \ldots\}$$

or sometimes listed as

$$\mathbb{Z} = \{\ldots, -2, -1, 0, 1, 2, \ldots\}$$

Following mathematical custom, we will use the two symbols $\mathbb{N}$ and $\mathbb{Z}$ exclusively as defined above. The positive integers are sometimes referred to as the **natural numbers,** hence the symbol $\mathbb{N}$. The symbol $\mathbb{Z}$ derives from the German word for number, which is "zahl." The three dots, already used several times, have the interesting name "ellipsis," which is derived from the same Greek root as the word "ellipse." You might enjoy searching out the reason for these names.

1.8

A list may sometimes be an inadequate way to define a set, so there is another standard device which fits the requirement of nonambiguity. We enclose in braces a symbol called a **variable,** followed by a descriptive phrase called a **predicate:**

$$\{x : \mathscr{P}(x)\}.$$

The variable is often indicated by a lowercase letter (here, x), and the predicate [indicated here by $\mathscr{P}(x)$] is a description of the allowed replacements for that variable. The two are separated by a colon, :, which in other texts may be replaced by a vertical bar, |. This kind of designation for a set is called the **set-builder** notation. To illustrate, the set of even integers may be indicated by the list

$$\mathbb{E} = \{\ldots, -4, -2, 0, 2, 4, 6, \ldots\},$$

or in set-builder notation by

$$\mathbb{E} = \{n : n = 2k, \text{ for } k \in \mathbb{Z}\},$$

which means that $\mathbb{E}$ is the set of *all* things, each of which is twice some integer.

Tutorial 1.8

a. Referring to Example 1 in paragraph 1.6, is there an element of the set **D** which is not also an element of the set $\mathbb{N}$?

b. Find those elements of $\mathbb{E}$ determined by choosing $k = 1, 3, 9, 27$, and their negatives. (Refer to its set-builder notation in paragraph 1.8)

c. Write a set-builder notation for the set $\mathbb{O}$ of odd integers.

1.9   Among the real numbers $\mathbb{R}$, there are some having various special properties: the *positive integers* or *natural numbers* ($\mathbb{N}$), the *integers* ($\mathbb{Z}$), the *even* integers ($\mathbb{E}$), and others to be discussed later. For the moment, we observe that set theory provides a relationship between sets which is well-illustrated in $\mathbb{R}$.

In general, given any sets **S** and **T,** we say that **S** is a **subset** of **T** if each element of **S** is also an element of **T,** and we denote this relationship by

$$S \subseteq T.$$

The symbol $\subseteq$ is called the **inclusion** or **subset** relation which is expressed also by the phrases "**S** is **included in T**" or by "**S** is **contained in T**." This same idea is expressed by

$$T \supseteq S,$$

which means that **T contains S**.

To indicate that **S** is not a subset of **T**, we use

$$\mathbf{S} \not\subseteq \mathbf{T},$$

and we need to think carefully about what this means. To say that $\mathbf{S} \subseteq \mathbf{T}$ means that *each* element in **S** is also in **T**; so, this property fails if we can find even a single element of **S** which does not belong to **T**. Of course, **S** may have many (perhaps all) elements that fail to belong to **T**. But if $\mathbf{S} \not\subseteq \mathbf{T}$, then all we can guarantee is that there is some element x for which $x \in \mathbf{S}$ and $x \notin \mathbf{T}$. Turning to $\mathbb{R}$ for an illustration of these ideas, each of the following is correct:

$$\mathbb{N} \subseteq \mathbb{Z}, \qquad \mathbb{Z} \subseteq \mathbb{R}, \qquad \mathbb{E} \subseteq \mathbb{Z}, \qquad \mathbb{Z} \not\subseteq \mathbb{E}, \qquad \mathbb{N} \not\subseteq \mathbb{E}.$$

1.10 There is an additional subtlety associated with the inclusion relation. If $\mathbf{S} \subseteq \mathbf{T}$, then each element of **S** is also an element of **T**, but nothing more is claimed about **T**. In particular, **T** may contain elements different from those in **S** or it may not. Thus, for example, each of the following is correct:

$$\mathbb{N} \subseteq \mathbb{N}, \qquad \mathbb{N} \subseteq \mathbb{Z}, \qquad \mathbb{Z} \subseteq \mathbb{Z}.$$

It is very important to recognize that the membership symbol $\in$ and the subset symbol $\subseteq$ denote relationships of different kinds; for an arbitrarily given set **A**, it is correct to say that $\mathbf{A} \subseteq \mathbf{A}$, but it is *not* correct to say that $\mathbf{A} \in \mathbf{A}$. We assume as a fundamental principle of set theory that **no set is an element of itself.** The reason for this prohibition is simple; without it we can produce a logical contradiction. (See paragraph 1.16.)

1.11 Any set is the largest possible subset of itself; there is also a unique smallest set, denoted by $\varnothing$, which contains no element at all and is a subset of any set (even of itself). We call $\varnothing$ the **empty set** (or the **null set** or the **void set**). Thus if **A** is any subset of a set **B**, then it is correct to write

$$\varnothing \subseteq \mathbf{A} \subseteq \mathbf{B}.$$

Now assume that **A** and **B** are any sets (neither is necessarily a subset of the other). The **complement** of **A** in **B**, denoted by $\mathbf{B} - \mathbf{A}$, is the set consisting of all elements of **B** which are not also in **A**. In set-builder notation,

$$\mathbf{B} - \mathbf{A} = \{x : x \in \mathbf{B}, x \notin \mathbf{A}\}.$$

To get the complement of **A** in **B**, we simply eliminate from **B** all elements of **A** which happen to belong to **B**. For example, $\mathbb{Z} - \mathbb{N}$ consists of all integers which are not positive; that is, $\mathbb{Z} - \mathbb{N}$ is the set containing 0 and all the negative integers. It should always be clear from context whether the "negative" sign is intended to mean the familiar subtraction of numbers or the complement of sets, defined above. Notice, also, that for any set **A**,

$$\mathbf{A} - \mathbf{A} = \varnothing \qquad \text{and} \qquad \mathbf{A} - \varnothing = \mathbf{A}.$$

Tutorial 1.11

a. Give an argument (in words) to show that if **B** ⊆ **A**, then **B** − **A** = ∅.
b. Give an argument (in words) to show that if **A** − **B** = ∅, then **A** ⊆ **B**.

1.12

Equality between given sets is intended to mean that identically the same elements belong to each set. Thus, to say that **A** = **B** means that both **A** ⊆ **B** and **B** ⊆ **A**.

Example 1

Referring to Example 1 in paragraph 1.6, let us show that

$$\{0\} = \mathbf{D} - \mathbb{N}.$$

Note first that {0} is *not* the empty set; it *is*, in fact, the set containing exactly one element, namely, the number 0. Since $0 \in \mathbf{D}$ and $0 \notin \mathbb{N}$, then $0 \in \mathbf{D} - \mathbb{N}$. This argument shows that $\{0\} \subseteq \mathbf{D} - \mathbb{N}$. Now suppose that $p \in \mathbf{D} - \mathbb{N}$. Then p must be one of the 10 digits, but it must not be a positive integer. So we conclude that $p = 0$, and since $0 \in \{0\}$, we have shown that $\mathbf{D} - \mathbb{N} \subseteq \{0\}$. Together, these two set inequalities prove that $\{0\} = \mathbf{D} - \mathbb{N}$.

1.13

By general agreement, use of the word "set" in mathematics implies that the elements in the set are different from one another. Consider, for example, the polynomial

$$x^3 - 5 \cdot x^2 + 8 \cdot x - 4,$$

which has the following linear factors (you can check this by multiplying)

$$(x - 1) \cdot (x - 2) \cdot (x - 2).$$

Each value of x which reduces one of these linear factors to zero is a **root** of the polynomial equation

$$x^3 - 5 \cdot x^2 + 8 \cdot x - 4 = 0.$$

Although there are three linear factors, the set of roots, nevertheless, has just two elements, {1, 2}.

1.14

Sets may consist of elements which are more complicated than such things as vowels or integers. A set may have other sets as members; for example, we may consider the set consisting of all subsets of a given set.

Example 1

If the set **M** has a small number of elements, then it may be convenient to list the set of all its subsets according to size. Given the set **M** = {a, b, c}, then:

- The 3-element subset is **M**.

- The 2-element subsets are {a, b}, {a, c}, {b, c}.

- The 1-element subsets are {a}, {b}, {c}.

- The 0-element subset is ∅.

This example suggests a combinatorial question, "How many subsets does a given set have?" In the case of **M** above, it's easy to show that the answer is eight just by counting. "Counting" is one of the most important tasks of discrete mathematics, but it isn't often this easy. Suppose, for example, that **M** had been the entire English alphabet and that we wanted to count its subsets. Just to think about listing all the subsets is discouraging, but in fact we will discover later a very simple answer to the general question. (To say that the answer is simple is not to imply that the answer is small: The English alphabet actually has 67,108,864 subsets!)

1.15

The set of all subsets of any set **A** is called the **power set** of **A**, and we will denote it by 2^A. Thus in Example 1 of paragraph 1.14,

$$2^M = \{\varnothing, \{a\}, \{b\}, \{c\}, \{a, b\}, \{a, c\}, \{b, c\}, M\}.$$

The name "power set" and its notation, 2^A, are not simply capricious choices. On the contrary, we will discover in paragraph 16.1 the perfectly natural basis for this terminology. Also, it may seem a bit fussy to put braces around the single elements a, b, and c above, but it turns out to be important that we distinguish between:

- The element a as a member of the set **M**

- The **singleton** set {a} as a subset of the set **M**

Thus it is correct to write

$$a \in M, \qquad \{a\} \subseteq M, \qquad \text{or} \qquad \{a\} \in 2^M,$$

but it is incorrect to write

$$a \subseteq M, \qquad \{a\} \in M, \qquad \text{or} \qquad \{a\} \subseteq 2^M.$$

The distinction between inclusion $\subseteq$ and membership $\in$ is further emphasized in the following observation: If $\mathbf{A} \subseteq \mathbf{B}$ and $\mathbf{B} \subseteq \mathbf{C}$, then it necessarily follows that $\mathbf{A} \subseteq \mathbf{C}$; but even though $a \in \mathbf{A}$ and $\mathbf{A} \in 2^{\mathbf{A}}$, it is *not* true that $a \in 2^{\mathbf{A}}$. Mathematicians describe this distinction by saying that "inclusion" is a *transitive* relationship, while "membership" is *not* a transitive relationship. We will return to this important idea of transitivity in several later sections; for the moment we rely on the following analogy to help clarify the concept.

Example 1

Consider the following two relationships between people:

"is the child of"   and   "is kin to."

You are the child of your mother and she is the child of her mother, but you are not the child of your grandmother. You, your mother, and your maternal grandmother are in different levels with respect to "is the child of," as is indicated in genealogy tables. This situation is like that involving $\in$. If $a \in \mathbf{A}$, then we may think of a, $\mathbf{A}$, and $2^{\mathbf{A}}$ as being on different levels with respect to membership. Again, you are kin to your mother, your mother is kin to her mother, and you also are kin to your maternal grandmother. Like the inclusion relation, these three individuals are on the same level with respect to "is kin to" (that is, generational differences disappear). We observe that "transitivity" can only apply among objects which have parallel status (i.e., are on the same level) with respect to the given relationship.

1.16

Complement: Foundations
As suggested in paragraph 1.5, the concept of "set" lies at the foundation of mathematics. It is, seemingly, primitive and self-evident. So much so that some mathematicians found it irresistibly tempting to describe everything mathematical as a set or in terms of sets. But, it was discovered almost a century ago that "set theory" cannot be used in such a naive, uncritical manner. Contradictions, even very simple ones, could be derived, using accepted rules of logic, from what initially appear to be reasonable assumptions about sets. Here is an example, attributed to the mathematician and philosopher Bertrand Russell (1872–1970).

Suppose that we admit the existence of a "big" set containing *all* sets as its elements. Call this "big" set $\mathbf{U}$ and note that $\mathbf{U} \in \mathbf{U}$. It makes sense, then, to separate all sets into those that are elements of themselves and those that aren't. If you think about it, all sets that we're used to in mathematics are of the latter type. For example, each element of $\mathbb{N} = \{1, 2, 3, \ldots\}$ is a positive integer, but the set $\mathbb{N}$ is not a positive integer; hence $\mathbb{N} \notin \mathbb{N}$. So, it seems reasonable to collect all sets that don't belong to themselves into a set which we will call $\mathbf{B}$:

$$\mathbf{B} = \{\mathbf{A} : \mathbf{A} \text{ is a set and } \mathbf{A} \notin \mathbf{A}\}. \tag{1}$$

Now ask yourself the question, "Does $\mathbf{B}$ belong to $\mathbf{B}$?" The answer, of course, must be either "yes" or "no."

Assume, first, that the answer is "yes." Then $\mathbf{B} \in \mathbf{B}$. But look back at (1) and note that a set belongs to $\mathbf{B}$ if it does not belong to itself, so $\mathbf{B} \notin \mathbf{B}$. Thus, we have a contradiction.

Assume, next, that the answer is "no." Then $\mathbf{B} \notin \mathbf{B}$. But look back at (1) and note that a set belongs to $\mathbf{B}$ if it does not belong to itself, so $\mathbf{B} \in \mathbf{B}$. Again, we have a contradiction.

Thus, our uncritical use of the "set" concept has created a situation in which an apparently reasonable question, which must have a simple "yes" or "no" answer, cannot have either one because of the existence of a contradiction in each case. It turns out that in order to avoid this impossible condition, certain restrictions have to be placed on the existence and behavior of sets. One of the consequences of these restrictions is our claim earlier in this section that no set is a member of itself.

The discovery of such difficulties as that described above was both unexpected and disturbing (for it cast doubt on the logical soundness of mathematics), and it became the motivation for a sustained effort to create an axiomatic foundation for set theory (much in the spirit of Euclidean geometry). During the past 100 years this work resulted in a refined system of axioms that creates a logically sound theory which avoids the earlier contradictions. Although fascinating, this chapter in the history of mathematics is fairly esoteric, and we will bypass it with no more than these few remarks. Applications of set theory encountered in this book lie well within the scope of current theory. Simply as a matter of "cultural" interest we quote from the axioms listed in *Abstract Set Theory* by A. A. Fraenkel:

- Two sets which contain the same members are equal.

- For any set $\mathbf{S}$ and any predicate $\mathscr{P}$ which is meaningful for all members x of $\mathbf{S}$, there exists the set $\overline{\mathbf{S}}$ that contains just those members x of $\mathbf{S}$ which satisfy the predicate $\mathscr{P}$.

- For any two different objects a and b there exists the set that contains just a and b.

- For any set $\mathbf{A}$ of sets there exists the set that contains just the members of the members of $\mathbf{A}$.

- There exists an infinite set.

- Given a set $\mathbf{S}$, there exists the set whose members are all subsets of $\mathbf{S}$.

We have omitted from this listing two of Fraenkel's axioms which are of a more specialized nature but which bear crucially upon advanced mathematics. Our intent here is to list only those axioms which are fairly transparent in meaning and which are consistent with the applications of set theory at this level of discrete mathematics.

Throughout the history of mathematics there have been a number of crises of understanding, all remarkably similar in broad outline. Prior to each crisis there was a long period of development based on generally accepted ideas with which mathematicians had become comfortable. Then, suddenly, a discovery was made which seemed paradoxical in the sense that it violated currently held beliefs. There followed a period of intense analysis and adaptation through which the discipline became richer in content and more subtle in application than had been previously suspected.

A very early example of such a crisis dates from the fifth century B.C. Rational numbers (which are quotients of integers) were familiar to the Greek mathematicians and philosophers, who sometimes incorporated the idea of number into their speculations about the natural world. The discovery of the existence of "irrational" numbers [attributed to Pythagoras (ca. 580 B.C.)] probably came as a culture shock, forcing the ancient thinkers to reevaluate not only mathematics as it then existed but philosophy as well. Another example, much later in time, came early in the nineteenth century with the independent discovery of non-Euclidean geometry, almost simultaneously by János Bolyai (1802–1860), Nicolai Ivanovich Lobachevsky (1792–1856), and Carl Friedrich Gauss (1777–1855). Again the new discovery not only had great impact on the development of mathematics but beyond that on both physics and philosophy. The "Russell paradox" which dates from the early part of this century was symptomatic of another such crisis. Although research on the foundations of mathematics has continued since that time, the best answers may not yet have been discovered. Subtle, even dramatic, modifications may arise in the future, leading to a deeper, clearer understanding of mathematics and its role in the development of science than we have today.

Problems for Section 1

1. Find the midpoint of the interval with endpoints (a) $a = \frac{1}{2}, b = 3$; (b) $a = 0$, $b = 3$; (c) $a = -2, b = 3$; (d) $a = -10$, $b = 3$.

2. Suppose that $a = 2$. Find b if the midpoint of the interval from a to b is (a) $m = \frac{7}{2}$, (b) $m = 22$.

3. Suppose that the midpoint of an interval is $-\frac{5}{2}$. Find the endpoints if the interval is of length (a) 10, (b) $\frac{1}{2}$.

4. Find the point that is one-third of the way from a to b in each part of Problem 1.

5. Find the point that is three-fourths of the way from a to b in each part of Problem 1.

6. For each of the following intervals, find the two points which subdivide the interval into thirds: (a) $a = \frac{1}{3}, b = \frac{7}{3}$; (b) $a = -2, b = 0$; (c) $a = -9, b = -6$.

7. Describe the position of the point u between a and b if $u = (3a + 2b)/5$.

8. Describe the position of the point v between a and b if $v = (9a + b)/10$.

9. If 5 is midway between a and b and 4 is one-third of the way from a to b, then what are a and b?

10. Answer Problem 9 if 1 and -1 replace 5 and 4, respectively.

11. Sketch the horizontal number axis, mark the origin and a convenient unit. (a) Mark points corresponding to elements in the set $A = \{-4, -2, 0, 2, 4, 6\}$. (b) Show that the following subsets of A contain the same elements: (i) $\{x \in A : -4 < x < 6\}$, (ii) $\{x \in A : -4 < x \le 4\}$, (iii) $\{x \in A : -2 \le x < 6\}$, (iv) $\{x \in A : -2 \le x \le 4\}$, (v) $\{x \in A : -3 < x < 5\}$.

12. What is the set of letters in the state name
(a) MISSISSIPPI, (b) ILLINOIS,
(c) WYOMING?

13. (a) Is {2} an element of { {1}, {2}, {1, 2} } ?
(b) Is {2} a subset of { {1}, {2}, {1, 2} } ?

14. (a) Exhibit the power set of {x, y} (there are
four subsets). (b) Exhibit the elements of
the power set in part (a) which are different
from {x, y}.

15. A subset **B** of the set **A** is called a **proper
subset** of **A** if **B** ≠ **A**. For example, ∅ is
a proper subset of *any* nonempty set. (The
symbol ⊊ is sometimes used in other texts to
indicate proper inclusion, but we will not use
it.) Let **A** = {w, x, y, z}. (a) List each proper
subset **B** of **A**, and indicate those elements
in **A** which are not also in **B**. (b) List each
proper subset of **A** which contains w as an
element.

16. Let **M** = {a, b, c}. (a) List each subset of **M**
which contains c. (b) List each subset of **M**
which fails to contain c. (c) Pair these sets
in an obvious way, and guess a relationship
between the number of subsets of **M** and the
number of subsets of {a, b}.

17. Refer to Problems 15 and 16. (a) What proportion of the subsets of **A** contain w as an
element? (b) What is the relationship between the number of subsets of **A** and the
number of subsets of **M**?

18. To make each of the following statements
correct, what element(s) may (or must) x be
replaced by? (a) {1, 2, x} ⊆ {0, 1, 2},
(b) {a, b, c} ⊆ {x, h, g, d, b, a}, (c) {x} ⊆ ℕ,
(d) x ∈ ℕ.

19. In each of the following, select a value
for x that will make the statement correct. (a) {0, 1, 2, 3} ⊆ {x, 4, 3, 2, 1},
(b) {1, x} ⊆ {1, 10, 100}, (c) x ∈ {p : p is
an integer and $p^2 > 4$}.

20. (a) What is the number of elements in the set
∅? (b) What is the number of elements in

the set {∅}? (c) What is the power set of ∅?
(d) What is the power set of {∅}?

21. Find the complement of **K** in **V** (i.e., **V** − **K**)
if (a) **V** = {a, e, i, o, u} and **K** = {u};
(b) **V** = {a, e, i, o, u} and **K** = {u, v, w}.

22. Find the indicated complements (recall our
agreement about these sets): (a) **D** − {0},
(b) **D** − ℕ, (c) ℕ − **D**, (d) **V** − {u}, (e) **D** − **V**,
(f) **V** − **D**.

23. Let **A** = {1, 2, 3, w, z} and
B = {1, {2}, {3}, {w, z}}. List the elements of
the following sets: (a) **A** − **B**, (b) **B** − **A**.

24. Answer Problem 23 if
A = {∅, 1, {1}, 2, {∅, 2}} and
B = {1, 2, {∅, 1}}.

25. Using **A** and **B** from Problem 23, (a) list the
elements of **B** that are subsets of **A**, (b) list
the subsets of **A** that are also subsets of **B**.

26. Answer Problem 25 using the sets **A** and **B**
in Problem 24.

27. List all the subsets of {a, b, c, d, e} that have
two elements.

28. How else can you describe the set of positive
integers that are less than 1?

29. If **V** = {a, e, i, o, u}, then it is correct to say
that a ∈ **V**. Explain why it is not true that
a ∈ 2^V.

30. Let **B** denote a subset of **V** which is different
from the sets **A** = {a, i} and **C** = {a, e, i, o}.
List the elements in any such set **B** for which
A ⊆ **B** and **B** ⊆ **C**. How many different sets
B satisfy these criteria?

31. Let **A** = {a, b, 1} and **B** = {1, 2, a}. List the
elements in 2^{A-B} and $2^A − 2^B$.

32. For sets **A** and **B** in general, is $2^A − 2^B ⊆ 2^{A-B}$? If so, why? If not, give an example of
sets **A** and **B** for which it is not true.

33. (*Conclusion of Problem 32.*) For any sets **A**
and **B**, show that $2^{A-B} ⊄ 2^A − 2^B$.

34. Making use of transitivity, what conclusion can be drawn from the statements $1 < 8$ and $10 > 8$?

35. Making use of transitivity twice, what conclusion can be drawn from the statements $1 < 3$, $3 < 8$, and $8 < 9$?

Section 2. Structure and Proof: Basic Terminology

Overview for Section 2

- Review of mathematical structure modeled on Euclidean geometry
- Introduction to the idea of "proof"; illustration of a typical form of logical argument
- Different modes of expressing mathematical information (to be used in later sections as motivation for the discussion of various proof techniques)
- Summary of the familiar properties of arithmetic in the real number system

Key Concepts: statement, axiom, definition, theorem, variable, syllogism, and implication

2.1   As has been the case for some 23 centuries, Euclidean geometry remains a classic model of mathematical structure; in it the core concepts are definition, axiom, theorem, and proof. [Modern mathematics does not distinguish between the terms "axiom" and "postulate," as Euclid (ca. 300 B.C.) did.] In more recent years mathematicians have created a similar structure in each of the major areas of mathematics (a familiar one being the real number system). In every case we are concerned with **statements,** also called **propositions,** which are declarative sentences (with subject, verb, and object). It is a fundamental assumption that **a mathematical statement is either true or false, but not both.** This assumption is sometimes referred to as the "law of the excluded middle." It means that a statement (in mathematics) must have exactly one of two possible truth values: true or false; there is no intermediate truth value between the two.

Example 1   The sentence

   The product of two negative real numbers is a positive real number

is an example of a mathematical statement which happens to be true. If in that statement the word "product" is replaced by the word "sum," then the result is the mathematical statement

The sum of two negative real numbers is a positive real number

which is easily recognized to be false.

The sentence

The triangle *ABC* is equilateral

seems to be mathematical, but it cannot be called either true or false without knowing what *ABC* refers to. Hence, lacking further information, it is *not* a mathematical statement.

Finally, the sentence

The temperature outdoors is uncomfortably warm

fails to be a mathematical statement on several grounds. It doesn't seem to have anything to do with mathematics as we know it; furthermore, it expresses a subjective opinion which may vary from one individual to another. Hence, it cannot be called either true or false.

2.2

Euclidean geometry, and any other logical structure, begins with:

- **Primitive terms,** such as

point,   line,   on,

which are undefined but which may be described in ordinary language in an attempt to convey the meaning intended.

- **Axioms,** such as

Two points are on one and only one line

which are statements, assumed to be true, that describe fundamental relationships among the primitive terms.

Beyond this, the mathematical structure is developed and refined through:

- **Definitions** of new terms or concepts, such as

diagonal,   square,   length,

which are based upon the primitive terms or others previously defined.

- **Theorems,** such as

    The diagonals of a square are equal in length

which are statements proved to be true by logical argument based upon the axioms and previously proved theorems.

   It is possible to give logic a formal structure which rests upon carefully defined concepts and rules, similar in many ways to the structure of geometry. We prefer, at this introductory level, to minimize reference to the structure of logic and to build confidence in the use of logical reasoning through the study of many proofs in the familiar setting of real numbers and elementary set theory.

2.3 Recall from paragraph 1.2 that order (or **inequality**) between two real numbers x and y is defined by

$$x < y \qquad \text{means} \qquad y = x + p$$

for some positive number p.

Example 1 Consider the three points with indicated coordinates on the horizontal number axis in Figure 2.3. It is evident, geometrically, that if $-\frac{5}{2}$ is to the left of -2, and if -2 is to the left of $-\frac{1}{2}$, then $-\frac{5}{2}$ is to the left of $-\frac{1}{2}$. This observation translates into numerical statements about inequality. Each of the two statements

$$-\frac{5}{2} < -2 \qquad \text{and} \qquad -2 < -\frac{1}{2}$$

is true, since $-2 = -\frac{5}{2} + \frac{1}{2}$, and $-\frac{1}{2} = -2 + \frac{3}{2}$. Now, we can put these two statements together:

$$-\frac{1}{2} = -2 + \frac{3}{2} = \left(-\frac{5}{2} + \frac{1}{2}\right) + \frac{3}{2} = -\frac{5}{2} + 2,$$

which means that

$$-\frac{5}{2} < -\frac{1}{2}.$$

Figure 2.3

It's easy to find many similar illustrations of the property observed in Example 1:

$$0 < 1 \quad \text{and} \quad 1 < \tfrac{3}{2}, \quad \text{hence } 0 < \tfrac{3}{2},$$

and $\quad -1 < 1 \quad$ and $\quad 1 < 2, \quad$ hence $-1 < 2.$

From these special cases we are led to suppose that whatever real numbers a, b, and c may be chosen,

$$\text{If } a < b \text{ and } b < c, \text{ then } a < c. \tag{1}$$

This is another example of generalization (see paragraph 1.4), and since we can never hope to test all possible special cases, a different approach is required to help us decide whether or not the generalization is true. We will return to this idea for a more detailed treatment in the next section, but on this first pass we note simply that replacing a, b, and c with numbers produces three mathematical statements:

$$a < b, \quad b < c, \quad \text{and} \quad a < c, \tag{2}$$

each of which is either true or false. (As in Example 1, with $a = -\tfrac{5}{2}$, $b = -2$, and $c = -\tfrac{1}{2}$, each of the three statements is true). The letters a, b, and c are called **variables** or **placeholders.**

Example 2

The following table examines the statements in (2) for a few replacement values of a, b, and c:

a	b	c	$a < b$	$b < c$	$a < c$
0	-1	$\tfrac{1}{2}$	False	True	True
1	5	0	True	False	False
-1	0	1	True	True	True

Tutorial 2.3

a. Continue the table in Example 2 for the following choices of a, b, c:

a	b	c
2	0	1
-1	0	$-\tfrac{1}{2}$
$-\pi$	-3	$-\sqrt{2}$

continued on next page

continued from previous page

b. Try (briefly) to make a choice for a, b, c which produces True, True, False (respectively).

2.4

The mathematical intent of (1) in paragraph 2.3 is that if a, b, and c are replaced by real numbers in such a way that

$$a < b \text{ is true} \quad \text{and} \quad b < c \text{ is true,} \tag{1}$$

then it *must* logically follow that

$$a < c \quad \text{is true.}$$

Our task, now, is to construct an argument which verifies this intent, based upon (1) and upon known facts about real numbers. In this situation the argument might go as follows:

$$a < b \quad \text{means that} \quad b = a + p_1 \quad \text{for some positive number } p_1,$$

$$b < c \quad \text{means that} \quad c = b + p_2 \quad \text{for some positive number } p_2.$$

Next, substitute $a + p_1$ for b and use familiar rules of arithmetic to obtain

$$c = b + p_2 = (a + p_1) + p_2 = a + (p_1 + p_2) = a + p_3,$$

where p_3 is the positive number $p_1 + p_2$. By definition,

$$c = a + p_3 \quad \text{means} \quad a < c,$$

which is what we needed to show.

Thus, assuming that a, b, and c represent real numbers, the argument just completed is actually a proof that (1) in paragraph 2.3 is a theorem of arithmetic. This is why, in Tutorial 2.3, you *could not* make a selection which produced the pattern True, True, and False.

This theorem tells us that "less than" is an example of a transitive relationship (see paragraph 1.15); other similar transitive relationships are "less than or equal to," "greater than," and "greater than or equal to."

It is important to observe that our argument above has depended upon some already known facts about numbers; for example, three numbers may be added in different ways to obtain the same sum (called **associativity** of addition), and the sum of two positive numbers is again a positive number (called additive **closure** of the set of positive numbers). In future sections we will be a little more formal in the presentation of proofs, but for brevity we will often use without specific mention such familiar properties of arithmetic as those noted above. As a reminder of some of these properties, paragraph 2.8 is an appendix which contains a brief summary of the structure of arithmetic.

2.5

Just as the number line offers a pictorial representation of inequality, there exists a pictorial representation of the set-theoretic property of inclusion. Referring to paragraph 1.9, the statements

$$\mathbb{E} \subseteq \mathbb{Z} \quad \text{and} \quad \mathbb{Z} \subseteq \mathbb{R},$$

are described in Figure 2.5A by a **Venn diagram,** named for John Venn. In it, the set of real numbers is indicated by the rectangle, the set of integers by an oval inside $\mathbb{R}$, and the set of even integers by a smaller oval inside $\mathbb{Z}$. The intent in Figure 2.5A is that the part of the diagram inside the small oval represents the set of even integers, while the part outside that oval represents the set of real numbers which are *not* even integers. These real numbers include not only the odd integers (which are considered inside the large oval) but all the nonintegers (which are considered outside the large oval).

Venn diagrams frequently are used to illustrate somewhat more complicated relationships among sets.

Example 1

Suppose that we let **L** denote the set of all books cataloged in a particular college library; let **D** denote the set of books in **L** having an author whose name begins with the letter D; let **M** denote the set of books in **L** which have multiple authors. The Venn diagram in Figure 2.5B is intended to illustrate this situation. Note that the ovals representing the sets **D** and **M** subdivide the rectangle into four regions corresponding to the following four possibilities:

1. Books having multiple authors, at least one of whom has a name beginning with the letter D

2. Books having a single author whose name begins with the letter D

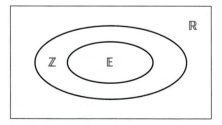

Figure 2.5A

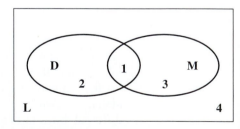

Figure 2.5B

3. Books having multiple authors, none having a name beginning with the letter D

4. Books having a single author whose name does not begin with the letter D

If this textbook belonged to the set **L**, then it would appear in the region labeled **1**. The ideas introduced in this paragraph will be explored more fully in Sections 15 and 18. ●

Again, resorting to generalization, we are led to our earlier observation in paragraph 1.15: Supposing that **A**, **B**, and **C** represent any sets,

$$\text{If } A \subseteq B \text{ and } B \subseteq C, \text{ then } A \subseteq C. \tag{1}$$

Notice the similarity of this statement to that in (1) in paragraph 2.3. As in the previous case, the intent here is that we assume the truth of

$$A \subseteq B \qquad \text{and} \qquad B \subseteq C, \tag{2}$$

then show by logical argument that

$$A \subseteq C \tag{3}$$

must also be true. Again, the argument may depend upon any already established facts. To prove that (3) is a true statement we must show that any element which belongs to **A** also belongs to **C**. To begin the argument, we suppose that $p \in A$. Now use the information provided in (2). Because $A \subseteq B$, it follows that $p \in B$; and because $B \subseteq C$, it follows that $p \in C$. This is what we needed to show, thus (3) is true and (1) qualifies as a mathematical theorem.

2.6

The arguments used to prove (1) in paragraph 2.3 and (1) in paragraph 2.5 illustrate an important principle of logical reasoning:

If

Statement 1 implies the truth of Statement 2,

and if

Statement 2 implies the truth of Statement 3,

then

Statement 1 implies the truth of Statement 3.

For example, from (1) in paragraph 2.5,

$$p \in \mathbf{A}, \qquad \text{therefore} \qquad p \in \mathbf{B},$$

$$p \in \mathbf{B}, \qquad \text{therefore} \qquad p \in \mathbf{C}.$$

So, $\qquad\qquad\qquad p \in \mathbf{A} \qquad \text{implies} \qquad p \in \mathbf{C}.$

(Again, we recognize an occurrence of "transitivity.")

Closely related to this principle is a form of argument called the *syllogism,* which was identified by the Greek philosopher Aristotle (384–322 B.C.) in his study of logic more than 2000 years ago. There are several kinds of syllogism, one of which is illustrated by the following classical argument:

All men are mortal.

Socrates is a man.

Hence, $\qquad\qquad\qquad\qquad\qquad$ Socrates is mortal.

A less classical example of a syllogism is the following adaptation from Lewis Carroll:

All knights who practice riding seldom fall off their horses.

Some knights fall off their horses frequently.

Hence, $\qquad\qquad\qquad$ Some knights fail to practice riding.

A **syllogism,** as in each of these two illustrations, begins with two related sentences which are assumed to be true, followed by a sentence derived logically from the first two. The first two sentences are called the **premises** of the syllogism, while the third sentence is called its **conclusion.** A more detailed description of the concept would take us too far afield; other examples occur in the complement to this section.

Tutorial 2.6

a. Suppose that $a < b$ and that c is a positive number. Prove that $ac < bc$.

b. What conclusion can you draw from the following premises?

All lobsters have claws.

Some crustaceans are lobsters.

2.7   The format of the two earlier mathematical statements, (1) in paragraph 2.3 and (1) in paragraph 2.5, is typical of one of the most frequently occurring modes of expressing mathematical information:

$$\text{If (hypothesis), then (conclusion).} \qquad \textbf{(1)}$$

The "hypothesis" consists of one or more statements, like the premises of a syllogism, and the "conclusion" usually consists of a single statement. If the conclusion is not known to be true, then (1) is often referred to as a **claim.** If, however, we assume that the hypothesis is true and if the conclusion is shown by argument to be a logical consequence of the hypothesis, then (1) qualifies to be called a theorem. The expression given in (1) is called an **implication,** for (1) can be restated

$$\text{(The hypothesis) } implies \text{ (the conclusion.)}$$

Each of the statements, (1) in paragraph 2.3 and (1) in paragraph 2.5, then, is a mathematical theorem in the form of an implication.

2.8   **Appendix** The real number system consists of the set of all real numbers ($\mathbb{R}$), together with the operations of addition ($+$) and multiplication ($\cdot$). The "structure" of the real number system is dictated by the following properties in which we assume that a, b, and c represent real numbers (that is, $a \in \mathbb{R}$, $b \in \mathbb{R}$, $c \in \mathbb{R}$).

Name	Addition	Multiplication
(i) Closure	$(a + b) \in \mathbb{R}$	$(a \cdot b) \in \mathbb{R}$
(ii) Commutative	$(a + b) = (b + a)$	$(a \cdot b) = (b \cdot a)$
(iii) Associative	$(a + b) + c = a + (b + c)$	$(a \cdot b) \cdot c = a \cdot (b \cdot c)$
(iv) Identity	$0 \in \mathbb{R}$ and $(0 + a) = a$	$1 \in \mathbb{R}$ and $(1 \cdot a) = a$
(v) Inverse	$-a \in \mathbb{R}$ and $(a + (-a)) = 0$	If $a \neq 0$, then $1/a \in \mathbb{R}$ and $(a \cdot (1/a)) = 1$
(vi) Distributive	$a \cdot (b + c) = a \cdot b + a \cdot c$	

Notes:

- 0 is called the identity element of addition and 1 is called the identity element of multiplication. No other real numbers satisfy property (iv) above.

- Each $a \in \mathbb{R}$ has one and only one additive inverse, $-a$.

- Each $a \in (\mathbb{R} - \{0\})$ has one and only one multiplicative inverse, $1/a$.

- Multiplication is always done before addition unless overridden by parentheses.

The properties tabulated above are the **algebraic axioms** upon which the arithmetic of real numbers depends. The real number system is richer than this, however, in the sense that it must also satisfy properties of "order" and "completeness."

The **order axioms** are (again, $a \in \mathbb{R}$, $b \in \mathbb{R}$):

(vii) Exactly one of the following holds:

$$a < 0, \qquad a = 0, \qquad 0 < a.$$

(viii) If $0 < a$ and $0 < b$, then $0 < a + b$ and $0 < a \cdot b$.
(ix) $a < b$ means the same thing as $0 < b - a$.

In this chapter we have already made use of words like "closure," "associative," and "order," so it has seemed appropriate here to review the full list of algebraic and order axioms upon which the structure of the real number system depends. But a systematic development of this structure from its axiomatic foundations belongs properly to "continuous" mathematics. In particular, the axiom of completeness cannot be understood without a more detailed study than we will undertake. We note merely that *completeness* provides an axiomatic basis for the existence of irrational numbers such as $\sqrt{2}$ and π, which cannot be expressed as quotients of integers.

It turns out that the full complement of algebraic, order, and completeness axioms is unique to the real number system, and the entire range of computational techniques in arithmetic can be derived as theorems within this structure. Such an ambitious program is not our purpose in this text, nor is it our intention that the axioms listed above be referenced when proofs are given in later sections. We do expect that arguments will be based on computational skills and numerical facts already acquired. The pattern we have in mind has been illustrated several times already and will appear frequently from now on. Models of special importance are proofs of the results listed in the following examples, which are intended to illustrate the variety of forms in which mathematical information actually occurs. These four facts about real numbers are probably already familiar to you. Their proofs require different kinds of argument; each will be used later to motivate the study of a particular technique of proof.

Example 1

If x is an even integer, then the square of x is also an even integer.

The information here is about each element belonging to a specified set. Note that "even" is a property not attributed to the set as a whole but to its individual elements.

Example 2

If **A** is a finite set of integers, then there exists an element in **A** which is larger than any other element in **A**.

The information here is about a particular element in its relation to other elements in a given set.

Example 3
<blockquote>The set of prime numbers is infinite.</blockquote>

The information here is about a set considered as a unit of study. Note that "infinite" is a property attributed not to individual prime numbers but to the set as a whole.

Example 4
<blockquote>The real number $\sqrt{2}$ cannot be expressed as a quotient of two integers.</blockquote>

The information here is about a particular mathematical object without concern for other elements in its set.

2.9

Complement: Whimsical Syllogisms Many people have read and enjoyed two fanciful masterpieces of English literature by Charles L. Dodgson (1832–1898): *Alice's Adventures in Wonderland* and *Through the Looking Glass.* Of course, the author is much better known under his pen name, Lewis Carroll, but it is not so well known that Dodgson studied mathematics at Christ Church College, Oxford University, where he subsequently taught for 27 years. As a professional, he was keenly interested in logic, and several of his other books were intended to popularize the subject. One of those books is *Symbolic Logic,* Part 1 of which was first published by Macmillan and Company in 1897 under the already famous name, Lewis Carroll. The serious intent of the work was disguised to some extent by the recreational flavor of its examples; the author's wonderfully agile imagination produced literally hundreds of lighthearted puzzles to illustrate both correct and flawed logical reasoning. We have selected a number of these puzzles both for your amusement and to challenge your own skill at unraveling hidden meaning. A Venn diagram technique is often helpful in this process, but for the moment we hope that you will enjoy trying a few of these puzzles, reasoning only from the given statements. Answers to the questions are included at the end of the text, but try first to outsmart Dodgson!

Group I. In each of these syllogisms assume that the first two statements are true, then decide whether the conclusion given is logically correct.

1. None but the brave deserve the fair.
   Some braggarts are cowards.
   Some braggarts do not deserve the fair.

2. Some healthy people are fat.
   No unhealthy people are strong.
   Some fat people are not strong.

3. Some holidays are rainy.
   Rainy days are tiresome.
   Some holidays are tiresome.

4. His songs never last an hour.
   A song that lasts an hour is tedious.
       His songs are never tedious.

5. No Professors are ignorant.
   All ignorant people are vain.
       No Professors are vain.

6. No wheelbarrows are comfortable.
   No uncomfortable vehicles are popular.
       No wheelbarrows are popular.

7. Improbable stories are not easily believed.
   None of his stories are probable.
       None of his stories are easily believed.

8. No birds, except peacocks, are proud of their tails.
   Some birds, that are proud of their tails, cannot sing.
       Some peacocks cannot sing.

Group II.   Each of these examples lists two statements which are assumed to be true. In each case, determine the correct conclusion.

9. A prudent man shuns hyenas.
   No banker is imprudent.

10. No fat creatures run well.
    Some greyhounds run well.

11. Umbrellas are useful on a journey.
    What is useless on a journey should be left behind.

12. No one, who exercises self-control, fails to keep his temper.
    Some judges lose their tempers.

13. Some lessons are difficult.
    What is difficult needs attention.

14. No country, that has been explored, is infested by dragons.
    Unexplored countries are fascinating.

15. Canaries, that do not sing loud, are unhappy.
    No well-fed canaries fail to sing loud.

16. All jokes are meant to amuse.
    No act of Parliament is a joke.

Group III.   Recall that in a syllogism the *premises* consist of two statements from which a third statement, called the *conclusion,* logically follows. This idea can be generalized, and in each of the following examples there are more than two premises. Try in each case to deduce the correct conclusion.

17. Babies are illogical.
Nobody is despised who can manage a crocodile.
Illogical persons are despised.

18. No ducks waltz.
No officers ever decline to waltz.
All my poultry are ducks.

19. My gardener is well worth listening to on military subjects.
No one can remember the battle of Waterloo, unless he is very old.
Nobody is really worth listening to on military subjects, unless he can remember the battle of Waterloo.

20. All hummingbirds are richly colored.
No large birds live on honey.
Birds that do not live on honey are dull in color.

21. Nobody, who really appreciates Beethoven, fails to keep silence while the Moonlight Sonata is being played.
Guinea pigs are hopelessly ignorant of music.
No one, who is hopelessly ignorant of music, ever keeps silence while the Moonlight Sonata is being played.

22. The only articles of food, that my doctor allows me, are such as are not very rich.
Nothing that agrees with me is unsuitable for supper.
Wedding cake is always very rich.
My doctor allows me all articles of food that are suitable for supper.

23. No birds, except ostriches, are 9 feet high.
There are no birds in this aviary that belong to anyone but me.
No ostrich lives on mince pies.
I have no birds less than 9 feet high.

24. No kitten, that loves fish, is unteachable.
No kitten without a tail will play with a gorilla.
Kittens with whiskers always love fish.
No teachable kitten has green eyes.
No kittens have tails unless they have whiskers.

25. All writers, who understand human nature, are clever.
No one is a true poet unless he can stir the hearts of men.
Shakespeare wrote *Hamlet.*
No writer, who does not understand human nature, can stir the hearts of men.
None but a true poet could have written *Hamlet.*

26. Animals, that do not kick, are always unexcitable.
Donkeys have no horns.
A buffalo can always toss one over a gate.
No animals that kick are easy to swallow.
No hornless animal can toss one over a gate.
All animals are excitable, except buffaloes.

Problems for Section 2

1. Which of the following are mathematical statements? (*a*) The square of a number between 0 and 1 is also between 0 and 1. (*b*) The square of *x* plus the square of *y* is the square of *z*. (*c*) The square of a number less than zero is less than zero.

2. Which of the following are mathematical statements? (*a*) Alaska is cold. (*b*) A triangle has three sides. (*c*) A square has three sides.

3. Which of the following are mathematical statements? (*a*) In a right triangle, the sum of the squares of the lengths of the legs is equal to the square of the length of the hypotenuse. (*b*) All isosceles triangles are equilateral triangles.

4. Which of the following are mathematical statements? (*a*) The rectangle with vertices *ABCD* is a square. (*b*) The square with vertices *ABCD* is a rectangle.

5. Based on your previous experience, which statements in Problems 1 and 2 do you think are true?

6. Based on your previous experience, which statements in Problems 3 and 4 do you think are true?

7. Assuming $k > 0$, show that if $a < b$, then $a + k < b + k$.

8. Assuming $k > 0$, show that if $a < b$, then $a - k < b - k$.

9. Show that if $0 < a < b$, then $1 < b/a$.

10. Assuming that $k > 0$ and that $a < b$, do you think that $(-k) \cdot a < (-k) \cdot b$? Test your answer by choosing a few different values of k, a, and b.

11. Show that if $a < b$ and $c < d$, then $a + c < b + d$.

12. Suppose that $a < b$ and $c < d$. Choose a number of different values of a, b, c, and d and test (as in Example 2 of paragraph 2.3) the inequality $a - c < b - d$.

13. Show that if $0 < a < b$ and $0 < c < d$, then $a \cdot c < b \cdot d$.

14. Find several values of *a*, *b*, *c*, and *d* for which $a < b$ and $c < d$ are true but $a \cdot c < b \cdot d$ is false. (*Hint:* By Problem 13, some of your selected values must be nonpositive.)

15. If $\mathbf{L} \subseteq \mathbf{M}$ and $\mathbf{K} \subseteq \mathbf{L}$, show that $(\mathbf{L} - \mathbf{K}) \subseteq (\mathbf{M} - \mathbf{K})$.

16. If $\mathbf{L} \subseteq \mathbf{M}$ and $\mathbf{K} \subseteq \mathbf{L}$, show that $(\mathbf{M} - \mathbf{L}) \subseteq (\mathbf{M} - \mathbf{K})$.

17. Recalling notation from paragraphs 1.6 and 1.8, show that $\mathbb{E} - (\mathbb{E} - \mathbf{D}) \subseteq \mathbf{D}$ but that $\mathbb{E} - (\mathbb{E} - \mathbf{D}) \neq \mathbf{D}$.

18. Recalling notation from paragraphs 1.6 and 1.7, show that $\mathbb{N} - (\mathbb{N} - \mathbf{D}) \subseteq \mathbf{D}$ but that $\mathbb{N} - (\mathbb{N} - \mathbf{D}) \neq \mathbf{D}$.

19. Recalling notation from paragraphs 1.7 and 1.8, show that $\mathbb{N} - (\mathbb{N} - \mathbb{E}) \subseteq \mathbb{E}$ but that $\mathbb{N} - (\mathbb{N} - \mathbb{E}) \neq \mathbb{E}$.

20. Let $\mathbf{A} \, \Delta \, \mathbf{B} = \{x : x \text{ is in exactly one of } \mathbf{A} \text{ or } \mathbf{B}\}$. This set is called the **symmetric difference** of the sets **A** and **B**. List the elements in $\mathbf{A} \, \Delta \, \mathbf{B}$ if $\mathbf{A} = \{a, e, i, o, u\}$ and $\mathbf{B} = \{o, p, t, u\}$.

21. (*Continuation of Problem 20.*) List the elements in the symmetric difference, $\mathbf{A} \, \Delta \, \mathbf{B}$, if $\mathbf{A} = \{0, 1, 2, 3, 4, 5, 6, 7, 8, 9\}$ and $\mathbf{B} = \{0, 2, 4, 6, 8\}$.

22. (*Continuation of Problem 20.*) Show that $\mathbb{N} - \mathbb{E} \subseteq \mathbb{N} \, \Delta \, \mathbb{E}$.

23. (*Continuation of Problem 20.*) Show that $\mathbb{E} - \mathbf{D} \subseteq \mathbb{E} \, \Delta \, \mathbf{D}$.

24. (*Conclusion of Problem 20.*) Show in general that $\mathbf{A} - \mathbf{B} \subseteq \mathbf{A} \, \Delta \, \mathbf{B}$.

25. Determine the correct conclusion:
> This problem is easy.
> What is easy requires little effort.

26. Determine the correct conclusion:
> No task that has been completed is lacking in interest.
> Any unfinished task is a challenge.

27. In the Land of Liars and Truthtellers, you encounter two people. You ask the first, "Is either of you a truthteller?" If upon hearing the answer you know the truth, how did that person respond, "yes" or "no"?

28. In the movie, *The Wizard of Oz,* the Scarecrow loudly proclaims the following when he receives his brain: "The sum of the square roots of any two sides of an isosceles triangle is equal to the square root of the remaining side." Is this a mathematical statement? Is this a mathematical fact? Did the Scarecrow really say this or did we just not hear correctly?

CHAPTER 1

Numbers and Proof

Section 3. Implication and Contrapositive

Overview for Section 3

- Examination of a typical form of mathematical theorem called implication (or conditional)
- Illustrations of mathematical proofs using properties of parity, order, and divisibility among the integers
- Introduction to the contrapositive of an implication and its use as an alternative method of proof
- A convenient notation for divisibility

Key Concepts: implication and contrapositive, negation of a statement, parity and divisibility of integers

3.1 Mathematical statements are often **simple** sentences; for example,

$$0 \text{ is a nonnegative integer.}$$

More often, however, several simple sentences are linked in a logical format called a **compound statement** which, itself, is either true or false. In this section we will discuss in greater detail the compound statement called "implication" (see paragraph 2.7):

$$\text{If (hypothesis), then (conclusion).} \tag{1}$$

37

We begin by examining the fact stated in Example 1 of paragraph 2.8 (that the square of an even integer is even). First, however, note that any integer can be divided by 2 in such a fashion that the remainder is either 0 or 1; for example,

$$18 = 2 \cdot 9 + 0 \qquad\qquad 19 = 2 \cdot 9 + 1$$
$$-18 = 2 \cdot (-9) + 0 \qquad -19 = 2 \cdot (-10) + 1.$$

Integers for which this remainder is 0 are called **even;** those for which the remainder is 1 are called **odd.** Thus, in general, any even integer can be expressed in the form $2 \cdot k$ for some integer k; similarly, any odd integer has the form $2 \cdot k + 1$ for some integer k. These representations of even and odd integers will reappear often. The property of being "even" or "odd" attributed to an integer is called its **parity.** Restricting attention, for the moment, to even integers, consider how parity is affected by the operation of squaring. The following table shows some special cases which appear to suggest, in general, that squares of even integers are also even. A convincing argument is simply that if an integer has 2 among its factors, then the square also has 2 as a factor. The details of this argument constitute a proof.

x	0	2	-2	4
x^2	0	4	4	16

THEOREM 3.1

If x is an even integer, then x^2 also is even.

Proof

Let x denote any even integer. Thus, there is an integer k such that $x = 2 \cdot k$. But then

$$x^2 = (2 \cdot k)^2 = (2 \cdot k) \cdot (2 \cdot k) = 2 \cdot 2 \cdot k \cdot k = 2 \cdot (2 \cdot k \cdot k).$$

Since $2 \cdot k \cdot k$ is an integer, x^2 has remainder 0 when divided by 2 and hence is even. ∎

Hereafter, we will adopt the familiar convention of indicating multiplication by adjacency instead of the center dot, unless confusion might result. For example, we will write $2k^2$ instead of $2 \cdot k \cdot k$.

A generalization of this theorem has perhaps already occurred to you: that evenness is preserved when the number is cubed, or raised to the fourth power, or raised to any positive integral power. For if the integer x has 2 as a factor, then so does x^3, x^4, and x^n (for any positive integer n).

Tutorial 3.1

Prove that if x is an even integer, then x^3 also is even.

3.2

In the proof of Theorem 3.1, the hypothesis "x is an even integer" is assumed to be true; hence replacements for x must be integers of the form $2k$. If we were to replace x by an odd integer, then the theorem *offers no evidence* about the parity of x^2, and we cannot make any claim without further investigation. This important point is illustrated in the next example, which describes a different behavior of real numbers and their squares.

Example 1

Assuming that x and y represent real numbers, consider the information about squares given by

$$\text{If } 0 < x < y, \text{ then } 0 < x^2 < y^2. \tag{1}$$

Is this information correct? Look first, at a few special cases.

x	y	Hypothesis $(0 < x < y)$	Conclusion $(0 < x^2 < y^2)$
-1	2	False	True
-1	0	False	False
1	2	True	True

Tutorial 3.2

a. Continue the preceding table for the following paired values of x and y:

x	-2	-2	2	0	5
y	-1	-4	3	9	3

b. Try, briefly, to find values which produce the pattern "True," "False," respectively.

Notice, once again, that when the hypothesis fails, the implication is useless as a prediction of the conclusion, which may sometimes be true, sometimes false. But it turns out that when the hypothesis is true, (1) is a perfect predictor about the conclusion. For example, we know that $0 < \pi < 3.2$; hence we predict with certainty that $\pi^2 < 10.24$. How do we know this? By the following argument which proves that (1) is a theorem. First, by hypothesis, assume that x and y are real numbers for which

$$0 < x < y.$$

Because $x < y$, there is a positive number p for which

$$y = x + p.$$

By the usual rules of arithmetic

$$y^2 = (x + p)^2 = x^2 + 2px + p^2.$$

Because $x > 0$ and $p > 0$,

$$2px + p^2 > 0.$$

Thus, $\qquad\qquad y^2 = x^2 + \text{(a positive number)};$

hence, by definition,

$$x^2 < y^2.$$

Finally, because $x > 0$ and the product of positive numbers is again positive,

$$0 < x^2,$$

which completes the argument. ●

For future reference, we will list the result in Example 1 as the following theorem.

THEOREM 3.2   If x and y are real numbers for which $0 < x < y$, then $0 < x^2 < y^2$.

3.3   There are two general lessons to be drawn from Example 1 of paragraph 3.2.

1. An implication is useful in mathematics only if the hypothesis is true; we are essentially uninterested in any implication having a false hypothesis. Thus, replacements for x and y in the example must be restricted to those numbers for which the inequality $0 < x < y$ holds.

2. We **are** interested in predicting the truth of the conclusion. Hence, the proof of an implication must demonstrate the impossibility of a true hypothesis and false conclusion. Thus, the argument in the example shows that there cannot exist replacements for *x* and *y* which produce a true hypothesis and a false conclusion.

These remarks suggest why the implication

If (hypothesis), then (conclusion)

is said to be:

- *False* when the hypothesis is true but the conclusion is false
- *True* when both the hypothesis and the conclusion are true

After much further practice in mathematical reasoning, we will return to the question of assigning **truth values** [that is, true (T) or false (F)] to this and other compound statements.

There is a special notation generally used in reference to the concept of "implication." Let *p* be an abbreviation for the hypothesis and let *q* be an abbreviation for the conclusion. Then the format

If *p*, then *q*

is abbreviated symbolically by

$$p \rightarrow q \qquad \text{(read "}p\text{ implies }q\text{").}$$

What we have observed so far can be tabulated as follows:

p	*q*	$p \rightarrow q$
True	True	True
True	False	False
False	No Evidence	

3.4

There is a different, often useful, way to state the information given by an implication such as Theorem 3.1, but we need first to introduce a new symbol. To say that an integer is odd means that it is *not* even, and to denote this idea of **negation** we use "~(*x* is even)," which means "it is not true that *x* is even," or "*x* is not even," or "*x* is odd." In general, for any statement *p* we denote its **negation** by

$$\sim p \qquad \text{(read "}not\ p\text{"),}$$

which is interpreted to mean:

- $\sim p$ is true if p is false.
- $\sim p$ is false if p is true.

Tutorial 3.4

a. If p is true, then what is the truth value of $\sim(\sim p)$?

b. If p is false, then what is the truth value of $\sim(\sim p)$?

c. If p is false, then what is the truth value of $\sim(\sim(\sim(\sim p)))$?

Example 1

Assume that x is an integer and that p stands for the statement

$$x \text{ is even.}$$

Here is the tabulation for a few replacements for x:

x	p	$\sim p$	$\sim(\sim p)$
2	True	False	True
1	False	True	False
0	True	False	True
−1	False	True	False

3.5

Again, let x denote an integer and let p stand for the statement "x is even." If q stands for the statement "x^2 is even," then Theorem 3.1 has the abbreviated form

$$p \rightarrow q. \tag{1}$$

Suppose now that x^2 is known to be odd, could x possibly be even? If it were, then (1) requires that x^2 be even. Since x^2 cannot be both even and odd, we must conclude that x is not even. Hence, we have the implication

$$\text{If } x^2 \text{ is odd, then } x \text{ is odd.}$$

This argument generalizes to any mathematical statements p and q. Suppose we are given the implication (1) and suppose that q is known to be false (that is, $\sim q$ is true). If p were true, then (1) requires that q also be true. Since q cannot be both false and true, we must conclude that p is false (that is, $\sim p$ is true). Hence, we have the implication

$$\sim q \rightarrow \sim p. \qquad (2)$$

The argument reverses easily to show that if (2) is known to be true, then (1) must likewise be true. [Briefly, the falsity of q guarantees the falsity of p, by (2); hence if p is known to be true, then q must also be true.] The implication (2) is called the **contrapositive** of the implication (1).

Of course, (2) itself is an implication in which $\sim q$ is the hypothesis and $\sim p$ is the conclusion. You might enjoy thinking about the contrapositive of (2).

What we have discovered about an implication and its contrapositive is that if either one is true, then so is the other. Thus, a proof of either an implication *or* its contrapositive constitutes a proof of both.

Example 1   Consider the following implication from plane geometry:

> If the diagonals of a rectangle intersect at
> right angles, then the rectangle is a square.

The contrapositive is

> If a rectangle is not a square, then its
> diagonals do not intersect at right angles.

You may recall from your earlier course in geometry that the given implication is a theorem; the argument by which it may be proved depends upon which of the two forms, above, is chosen. ●

The importance of the contrapositive derives from the following fact of life: Mathematical theorems in the form of (1) can sometimes be proved more easily when restated in the form of (2), as the next theorem illustrates.

3.6   Recall from arithmetic that if x and y are integers, then x is a **divisor** (or **factor**) of y if there is an integer z such that $y = xz$. We also say that x (or z) **divides** y.

Example 1   The integer 4 is a divisor of

36	since	$36 = 4 \cdot 9,$
-20	since	$-20 = 4 \cdot (-5),$
16	since	$16 = 4 \cdot 4,$
-8	since	$-8 = 4 \cdot (-2),$

$$4 \quad \text{since} \quad 4 = 4 \cdot 1,$$

$$0 \quad \text{since} \quad 0 = 4 \cdot 0.$$

Note especially the last statement, which generalizes to

Any nonzero integer is a divisor of 0.   ●

THEOREM 3.6

If x^2 is divisible by 4, then x is even.

Proof

This implication is in the form $p \to q$, where p denotes "x^2 is divisible by 4," and q denotes "x^2 is even." The contrapositive is $\sim q \to \sim p$, which states in words:

If x is odd, then x^2 is not divisible by 4.

The proof of the contrapositive is especially easy. Since x is odd, we can write $x = 2k + 1$, for some integer k. Hence,

$$x^2 = (2k + 1)^2 = 4k^2 + 4k + 1 = 4(k^2 + k + \tfrac{1}{4}).$$

Since $k^2 + k$ is an integer, $k^2 + k + \tfrac{1}{4}$ is *not* an integer; therefore x^2 is not divisible by 4.   ■

Tutorial 3.6

a. What is the contrapositive of the implication:

If $x > 3$, then $x^2 > 9$.

b. Agreeing to replace $\sim(\sim t)$ by t for any statement t, what is the contrapositive of $(\sim p) \to (\sim q)$?

3.7   Our proof of Theorem 3.6 via its contrapositive consists of an argument which begins with the hypothesis

x is odd,

and continues in a step-by-step sequence of deductions to the conclusion

x^2 is not divisible by 4.

In a similar fashion, the proof of Theorem 3.1 consists of an argument which begins with the hypothesis

$$x \text{ is even}$$

and continues in a step-by-step sequence of deductions to the conclusion

$$x^2 \text{ is even.}$$

The argument pattern, used in the proofs of Theorems 3.6 and 3.1, illustrates what is called **direct** proof. When a theorem is stated in the form of an implication

$$p \to q,$$

there are two possible tracks along which a proof may proceed:

- Prove that statement p implies statement q $(p \to q)$.
- Prove that statement $\sim q$ implies statement $\sim p$ $(\sim q \to \sim p)$.

Either is perfectly acceptable, and which one to use is not always immediately apparent. In any given situation, if one line of argument doesn't seem productive, simply abandon it and try the other.

We close this paragraph with one further example of a direct proof.

THEOREM 3.7

Let a, b, and c be integers. If a divides both b and c, then a divides the integer $b + c$; also, a divides the integer $b - c$.

Remark. The hypothesis consists not only of the divisibility assumption but also of the fact that a, b, and c must be integers (which is necessary in order that our previous definition of "divides" be applicable).

Proof

To say that the integer a divides each of the integers b and c means that there are integers w and z such that

$$b = aw \quad \text{and} \quad c = az.$$

By the distributive law of arithmetic

$$b + c = aw + az = a(w + z),$$

and by closure $w + z$ is an integer denoted, say, by y. Hence

$$b + c = ay,$$

and this means that a is a divisor of the integer $b + c$.
    Similarly, one can show that a divides $b - c$.   ■

3.8
There is a convenient notational abbreviation, often used in discussions of divisibility. If x and y are integers, then to indicate that x is a divisor of y, we use

$$x \mid y,$$

and we read this symbol as "x divides y." Thus in Example 1 of paragraph 3.6, $4 \mid 36$, $4 \mid 0$, $4 \mid (-20)$, etc. To indicate that x is *not* a divisor of y, we use the symbol

$$x \nmid y,$$

and we read it simply "x does not divide y."
    Using this new notation, we can describe parity as follows:

- The integer x is even if $2 \mid x$.
- The integer x is odd if $2 \nmid x$.

Remembering that the letters represent integers, Theorem 3.1 can be restated

$$(2 \mid x) \rightarrow (2 \mid x^2),$$

Theorem 3.6 can be restated

$$(4 \mid x^2) \rightarrow (2 \mid x),$$

and Theorem 3.7 can be restated

$$(a \mid b \text{ and } a \mid c) \rightarrow (a \mid (b + c)) \qquad \text{and} \qquad (a \mid (b - c)).$$

3.9
Complement: Case Studies One of the principal goals of this book is to present models of logical analysis and to provide practice in constructing logically sound arguments. There are a few simple concepts and techniques which underlie almost all mathematical (and other) reasoning. The basic ones are introduced in this chapter through specific applications to familiar properties of the number system. But logical thinking, of course, is not limited to arithmetic, algebra, and geometry. We will illustrate here one of the major logical techniques, applied to a puzzle that you have probably seen before. This technique, which involves the consideration of cases, will reappear frequently.

THEOREM 3.9

Given eight coins which are identical in appearance, suppose that exactly one of them is counterfeit and has been struck from a lighterweight material. If only a beam balance is allowed, then the counterfeit coin can be identified in, at most, two weighings.

Remark. We have chosen to state the puzzle in the form of an implication, and our task is to show that the conclusion (two weighings are sufficient) follows from the several hypotheses about the coins and the beam balance. To begin with, we must agree that the two pans of the beam balance will be level only if each pan holds the same number of true coins. A possible start might be to select two coins arbitrarily, put one on each pan, and if one is lighter than the other, then it must be counterfeit and so has been detected in just a single weighing. The catch is that this does not exhaust the possibilities. Following this approach, it may very well require more than two weighings to complete the task.

The intent of the theorem is not that every possible technique will be successful in either one or two weighings. What it claims is that there is a procedure, quite independent of either luck or personality, which if followed by anyone will necessarily identify the counterfeit coin in two weighings. The proof, then, consists in a direct, constructive argument which proceeds by cases, that is, by identifying and examining each one of the several alternate possibilities at each step in the construction. To complete the proof, we must ensure that *every* possible case is examined. This is not always as easy as it may sound; in certain complex situations even experienced mathematicians have claimed a proof, only to discover later that a crucial alternate case was overlooked. Study the following proof carefully to ensure that every possible case has been considered.

Proof

Label the coins $C_1, C_2, C_3, \ldots, C_8$.

Action 1. Place C_1, C_2, C_3 on one pan and C_4, C_5, C_6 on the other pan. Result: Either the coins balance (call this case 1) or they don't balance (call this case 2).

Case 1. We conclude that the counterfeit coin is not one of those we weighed; hence it is either C_7 or C_8.

Action 2. Place C_7 on one pan and C_8 on the other. Result: The coins do not balance, and the lighter of the two is the counterfeit coin.

Case 2. We conclude that the lighter (higher) of the two pans contains the counterfeit coin. Relabel the three coins in that pan D_1, D_2, D_3.

Action 3. Place D_1 on one pan and D_2 on the other. Result: Either the coins balance (call this case 3) or they don't balance (call this case 4).

Case 3. We conclude that the counterfeit coin is not one of those weighed; hence D_3 is counterfeit.

Case 4.   We conclude that the lighter of D_1 or D_2 is the counterfeit coin.   ■

A number of variations on this theme are interesting to think about.

1. If we are given nine coins, one of which is counterfeit and light, then two weighings suffice to identify it.

2. If we are given eight coins, at *most* one of which is counterfeit and light, then two weighings suffice to determine whether there is a counterfeit coin and, if so, which it is.

3. If we are given eight coins, one of which is counterfeit and *different* in weight from the others, then three weighings suffice to identify it.

The proof above describes a procedure which guarantees the truth of the claim made in the statement of the theorem. That procedure is an example of what is called an *algorithm,* an ancient word derived from the name of an Islamic mathematician, al-Khwārizmī. The concept, however, appears much earlier in the *Elements* of Euclid. As used in contemporary mathematics and computer science, the word refers to a recipe which precisely describes a finite sequence of steps (usually in a computation or in a proof) leading to an identifiable conclusion. Often, an algorithm will involve a sequence of similarly defined operations in which the result of one

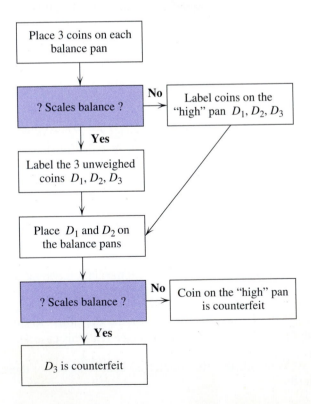

operation may have a significant influence on the result obtained in the succeeding step of the sequence. This concept will be discussed more fully in the next section.

The procedure described in a particular algorithm may often be clarified by a diagram of the steps, called a **flowchart.** We illustrate this idea in the preceding diagram for variation 1 (nine coins, one of which is light). Of course, we must assume that the coins are removed from the pans after each weighing. The idea is to follow the arrows (paying special attention to the decision boxes indicated by shading and question marks) until the 0 coin is determined.

Problems for Section 3

1. Prove the implication: If x is an odd integer, then x^2 also is odd.

2. Let y be any integer. Prove the implication: If x is an even integer, then xy is even.

3. Prove the implication: If x is an odd integer, then x^3 also is odd.

4. Prove the implication: If x and y are each odd integers, then $x + y$ is even.

5. Prove the implication: If x and y are each odd integers, then xy is odd.

6. Pick several integer replacements for x and y to show that the implication, "If $x + y$ is even, then x and y are each odd" fails to be true.

7. Pick several integer replacements for x and y to test whether or not the implication, "If xy is odd, then x and y are each odd" is true. On the basis of your test, what do you think? (This question will be settled in the next section.)

8. Show that if a divides x, then a divides $-x$.

9. Show that if a divides x and a divides $x + y$, then a divides y.

10. Show that if a divides x and a divides $x - y$, then a divides y.

11. State the contrapositive of (a) the implication in Problem 1, (b) the implication in Problem 3.

12. State the contrapositive of (a) the implication in Problem 5, (b) the implication in Problem 7.

13. State the contrapositive of (a) the implication in Problem 2, (b) the implication in Problem 4.

14. State the contrapositive of (a) the implication in Problem 6, (b) the implication in Problem 8.

15. State the contrapositive of the implication: If it is raining, then I will get wet.

16. State the contrapositive of the implication: If $b - a \geq 0$, then $a - b < 0$.

17. Assume $0 < b$ and consider the implication: If $ab \leq cb$, then $a \leq c$. (a) State the contrapositive of this implication. (b) Prove the contrapositive.

18. Assume $0 \leq a$ and consider the implication: If $a^2 \leq 1$, then $a \leq 1$. (a) State the contrapositive of this implication. (b) Prove the contrapositive.

19. Which of the following statements is true? Why? (a) The sum of any three consecutive integers is even. (b) The product of any three consecutive integers is even.

20. Is it true that the sum of any three consecutive integers is divisible by 3? If so, prove it. If not, why not?

21. Show that the sum of any three consecutive odd integers is divisible by 3.

22. Show that the sum of any three consecutive even integers is divisible by 6.

23. Assume that **A** and **B** are each subsets of **M**. Consider the implication: If $A \subseteq B$, then $M - B \subseteq M - A$. (*a*) State the contrapositive of this implication. (*b*) Prove that the contrapositive is true.

24. Show that if x and y are odd integers, then $x^2 + y$ is even. (*Hint:* Use Problems 1 and 4.)

25. Show that if n^5 is odd, then n is odd. (*Hint:* Use the contrapositive.)

26. In this and the next three problems, you will show that no number of the form $4m + 3$ is the sum of two squares. First show that if 2 divides n, then 4 divides n^2.

27. (*Continuation of Problem 26.*) Show that if 2 does not divide n, then $n^2 = 4k + 1$ for some integer k.

28. (*Continuation of Problem 26.*) Show that if u and v are integers, then either 2 divides $u^2 + v^2$ or $u^2 + v^2 = 4k + 1$ for some integer k.

29. (*Conclusion of Problem 26.*) Show that no integer of the form $4m + 3$ is the sum of two squares.

30. Show that if 6 divides n, then 2 divides n and 3 divides n.

31. Show that if 2 divides $3m$, then 2 divides m. (*Hint:* Contrapositive.)

32. (*Conclusion of Problem 31.*) Show that if both 2 and 3 divide n, then 6 divides n. (*Hint:* Since 3 divides n, $n = 3m$ and so 2 divides $3m$.)

33. Show that if x is even, then x^{25} is even.

34. Problem 33 is relatively easy, but to prove the following in a similar manner would be quite difficult: If x is odd, then x^{25} is odd. To prove this, we will use Problem 1 repeatedly. Assuming that x is odd, do the following: (*a*) Let $z = x^2$ and show that z^2 is odd. (Hence, x^4 is odd). (*b*) Show that x^8 is odd. (*c*) Show that x^{16} is odd. (*d*) Using Problem 5, show that $x^{25} = x^{16} \cdot x^8 \cdot x$ is odd.

35. Observe that if n is an integer, then there is another integer k such that exactly one of the following is true: $n = 4k$, $n = 4k + 1$, $n = 4k + 2$, or $n = 4k + 3$. (*a*) Show that if n is even, then either $n = 4k$ or $n = 4k + 2$. (*b*) Show that if n is odd, then either $n = 4k + 1$ or $n = 4k + 3$.

36. Show that if x is odd, then x^2 has a remainder of 1 when divided by 8. [*Hint:* Use Problem 35(*b*).]

37. Show that if xy is odd, then $x + y$ is even. (*Hint:* Use the contrapositive.)

Section 4.   Indirect Proof and Prime Numbers

4.1

The mathematicians of ancient Greece were geometers, primarily. Their understanding of numbers and arithmetic was hindered by the lack of an adequate system of notation; the Arabic numerals in use today were unknown to them. This is not to imply that such a remarkably gifted people were ignorant of arithmetic. Far from it! In this section we explore one of their most beautiful and imaginative creations: a theorem which to this day serves as the typical model of proof by contradiction. In preparation, we need the fact referred to in Example 2 of paragraph 2.8 that a nonempty finite set of integers has a maximum element. The proof of Theorem 4.2, below, which establishes this result, depends upon the concept of **algorithm,** a recurring theme both in discrete mathematics and in computer science. At this point, before we have yet studied an example, it is fair to ask, "What's an algorithm, and what's so special about the idea?" One modern dictionary refers to an algorithm as "a set of rules for solving a problem in a finite number of steps." Under this definition, the quadratic formula, for example, would qualify as an algorithm. We will be a little more restrictive than that in our use of the term. In addition, we assume that the rules include a common set of instructions which is repeated cyclically and which operates in each cycle upon data previously given or previously generated. The algorithm is initiated to achieve some indicated objective, and it must terminate after a finite number of cycles with a response to that objective. The entire process is carefully described so that nothing is left, unintentionally, either to imagination or to chance. As you read through the following algorithm, try to imagine actually performing each instruction as though you were a robot programmed to carry out this routine. What's special, therefore, about an algorithm is its *objectivity.* Applied to the same input data, the Euclidean Algorithm (to be discussed in Section 6) will produce the same result for you, or a computer, as it produced for Euclid.

4.2

Let us agree to call a set **A finite** if it is empty or if there is a positive integer n such that the elements of **A** can be listed as follows:

$$\mathbf{A} = \{a_1, a_2, a_3, \ldots, a_n\}.$$

The elements in the set **A** are **indexed** by the positive integers from 1 through n as subscripts. The intent of the indexing is simply to distinguish one element from another (remember, in a set the elements are different from one another) and also to indicate at a glance the number of elements in **A**. It is not intended that the order of the **indices** (the subscripts) indicate an ordering or ranking among the elements in the set. As an example, suppose we keep in mind the following set

$$\mathbf{A} = \{9, 30, 5, 8, 32, 14\},$$

where $a_1 = 9$, $a_2 = 30, \ldots$, $a_6 = 14$. Our problem is to formalize a procedure which will identify the largest element of **A**. To begin this task, we assume the existence of an imaginary memory **register,** labeled M, which has the property that it can remember only one number at a time. Thus, if we enter a number into M, then whatever number may have been in M before is erased from memory. Consider the following sequence of instructions, and note that unless **A** has at least two elements, there is no need for the algorithm.

ALGORITHM   Maximum Element

Step 1.   Enter a_1 into M. (In our example, 9 is in M.)

Step 2.   Compare a_2 and the number in M. Enter the larger one into M and discard the other. (30 is in M.)

Step 3.   Compare a_3 and the number in M. Enter the larger one into M and discard the other. (30 is still in M.)

. . .

Step n.   Compare a_n and the number in M. Enter the larger one into M and discard the other. (32 is now in M.)

Final Remark.   Since there are no other elements in **A** to compare, the algorithm ends, and the number now in M is the largest element of **A**.   ▲

This algorithm applies to any finite set of real numbers, not simply to integers; hence we have proved the following theorem.

THEOREM 4.2

If **A** is a nonempty finite set of real numbers, then there is an element in **A** which is larger than any other element in **A**.

> ## Tutorial 4.2
>
> Apply the Maximum Element Algorithm to the set of numbers $\{-1, 18, \frac{9}{2}, 19, 0, 21\}$. At each step, indicate which number is in M.

The proof of Theorem 4.2 is called **constructive,** since it outlines a procedure by which the required element can be determined, or constructed, explicitly. Observe that this algorithm is described in terms of a finite list of instructions in which each step is easily understood and results in a specific outcome. Note, also, the cyclic repetition of like steps which eventually terminates with a response to the purpose of the algorithm. Because "algorithm" can have different connotations in different contexts, we do not insist on a precise definition. We are content to observe that the characteristics described above are those generally satisfied by the algorithms to be discussed in this and later sections.

4.3   Very early in the systematic study of mathematics (and probably at some point in your own childhood), it became necessary to cope with the concept of "infinity." If, for example, there were only finitely many positive integers, then by Theorem 4.2 one of them must be the largest, call it L. (You may have once tried to name the largest number you could think of.) Here we face a dilemma. Consider the largest integer plus 1: If $L + 1$ is an integer, then it cannot be greater than L, but if $L + 1$ is greater than L, then it cannot be an integer. Thus if there exists a largest integer, then logic compels us to abandon either a property of *order* (if p is a number, then $p < p + 1$) or a property of *closure* (if p is an integer, then $p + 1$ is also an integer). Since neither alternative is acceptable, we must insist that there is no largest integer. The set of integers, therefore, is not finite; we call such sets **infinite.**

4.4   Multiplicative representation of the positive integers has fascinated mathematicians for more than 2000 years. One of the earliest properties recognized was that many integers greater than 1 could be constructed as products of other "primary" integers. Consider, for example, the integers x on the interval $1 < x < 22$ listed by column in natural order:

2	7	$2 \cdot 2 \cdot 3$	17
3	$2 \cdot 2 \cdot 2$	13	$2 \cdot 3 \cdot 3$
$2 \cdot 2$	$3 \cdot 3$	$2 \cdot 7$	19
5	$2 \cdot 5$	$3 \cdot 5$	$2 \cdot 2 \cdot 5$
$2 \cdot 3$	11	$2 \cdot 2 \cdot 2 \cdot 2$	$3 \cdot 7$

A **prime number,** or **prime,** is a positive integer having no divisor greater than 1 other than itself. The **unit** 1 is not considered a prime; hence the set of primes in the list above is

$$\mathbf{A} = \{2, 3, 5, 7, 11, 13, 17, 19\}.$$

Other numbers in that list illustrate what are called **composites,** that is, positive integers which can be factored into a product of primes, some of which may be repeated, as in

$$15{,}246 = 2 \cdot 3^2 \cdot 7 \cdot 11^2 \qquad \text{or} \qquad 32 = 2^5.$$

Tutorial 4.4

a. For the integers on the interval $21 < x < 32$, write each as a product of prime factors.
b. In **a,** which integer requires the largest number of factors?
c. In **a,** which integer is the largest prime?

Now notice that the smallest prime number 2 is even and that no even number greater than 2 can be prime. Since one of any two consecutive integers is even, among all odd primes no pair can be closer together than two units. If two prime numbers happen to be exactly two units apart, then the pair is called a **prime pair,** among which

$$(3, 5), \qquad (5, 7), \qquad (11, 13), \qquad (17, 19)$$

involve primes in the set **A.** The two primes in a prime pair are often called **twin primes.** Prime numbers as well as twin primes seem to occur fairly erratically among the positive integers. From a list of all primes less than 600, we find

22 primes and 8 prime pairs between   0 and 100,

21 primes and 7 prime pairs between 100 and 200,

16 primes and 4 prime pairs between 200 and 300,

16 primes and 2 prime pairs between 300 and 400,

17 primes and 3 prime pairs between 400 and 500,

16 primes and 1 prime pair between 500 and 600.

Extended counts indicate that the frequency of both primes and prime pairs continues to decrease with size, but the innocuous question, "Are there only finitely many prime pairs?" remains a challenge which after centuries of effort has not yet been answered. The difficulty of this question is all the more surprising in light of Euclid's answer to the corresponding question about primes, "Are there only finitely many prime numbers?" The following theorem is one of the most significant arithmetic achievements of the mathematicians of ancient Greece, and it illustrates a classic proof technique which remains a logical cornerstone of mathematical deduction.

THEOREM 4.4

The set of prime numbers is infinite.

Proof

Assume, on the contrary, that the set of all primes is finite. Then by Theorem 4.2 there exists a largest prime, which we may denote by p. Define q to be the product of the positive integers from 1 to p,

$$q = 1 \cdot 2 \cdot 3 \cdot \cdots \cdot (p - 1) \cdot p.$$

The number $q + 1$ is an integer and is greater than p, hence is not a prime. Now recall that every composite can be constructed as a product of primes, in particular

$$q + 1 \text{ must be divisible by some prime.} \tag{1}$$

But when we divide $q + 1$ by p, or by any prime less than p, there is a remainder of 1. For example,

$$\frac{q + 1}{p} = \frac{q}{p} + \frac{1}{p} = 1 \cdot 2 \cdot 3 \cdot \cdots \cdot (p - 1) + \frac{1}{p},$$

which is not an integer. Thus $q + 1$ is not divisible by p, nor by any prime less than p. Since there are no other primes, we conclude

$$q + 1 \text{ is not divisible by any prime.} \tag{2}$$

Statements (1) and (2) are contradictory, and thus the original assumption must be false; that is, the number of primes must be infinite. ∎

This is the formal proof of the fact referred to in Example 3 of paragraph 2.8.

4.5

The proof technique used for Theorem 4.4 is called *proof by contradiction;* it is based upon our fundamental assumption (paragraph 2.1) that a mathematical statement is either true or false but not both. A mathematical statement s and its negation $\sim s$ are called **contradictory** statements, and our assumption implies that both contradictory statements cannot be true. Thus, if we can construct a true implication of the form

$$r \rightarrow \begin{cases} \text{both } s \\ \text{and } \sim s, \end{cases}$$

then we must conclude that r is false. In outline, proof by contradiction proceeds as follows:

I. Given a mathematical statement p, either

$$p \text{ is true} \qquad \text{or} \qquad \sim p \text{ is true.}$$

II. Assume that $\sim p$ is true, and use this information to identify another mathematical statement s such that the implication

$$\sim p \rightarrow \begin{cases} \text{both } s \\ \text{and } \sim s \end{cases}$$

is true.

III. Conclude that $\sim p$ is false; hence p is true.

Proof by contradiction is often referred to as *indirect proof*, in contrast with the direct proofs which have appeared earlier. Although it was partially disguised, we actually used proof by contradiction in paragraph 4.3 to justify our claim that the set of positive integers is infinite. Suppose we reconsider that argument in order to give another illustration of an indirect proof.

THEOREM 4.5

The set of positive integers is infinite.

Proof

Assume, on the contrary, that the set of positive integers is finite. Then by Theorem 4.2 there exists a largest positive integer which we may call L. By the closure property of the integers, we know that

$$L + 1 \text{ is again a positive integer.} \qquad (1)$$

Since 1 is a positive integer, we know, by the definition of order, that $L + 1$ is greater than L. But, recall that L is the largest positive integer; hence

$$L + 1 \text{ cannot be a positive integer.} \qquad (2)$$

Statements (1) and (2) are contradictory, and both are implied by the assumption that the set of positive integers is finite. Hence, the assumption must be false, so the set of positive integers is infinite. ∎

Tutorial 4.5

Give an indirect proof, as in Theorem 4.5, that the set of even positive integers is infinite.

4.6   Recall that an implication

$$p \rightarrow q$$

is useless as a predictor unless p is true. Thus a proof of its contrapostive

$$\sim q \rightarrow \sim p$$

produces the contradiction that both p and $\sim p$ are true. The assumption that q is false cannot stand, so q must be true. We can think of proof by contrapositive as a proof by contradiction in which the statement contradicted is the hypothesis of the implication. In general, however, a mathematical claim like that in Theorem 4.4 may not be overtly in the form of an implication; hence its indirect proof depends upon identifying some appropriate true statement which can be contradicted.

In the following theorem assume that x represents an integer, and try to identify the role of "contradiction" in its proof.

THEOREM 4.6   If x^2 is even, then x is even.

Proof
The contrapositive is

If x is odd, then x^2 is odd.

Assuming that

$$x \text{ is odd,}$$

then for some integer k,

$$x = 2k + 1.$$

By the usual rules of arithmetic,

$$x^2 = (2k + 1)^2 = 4k^2 + 4k + 1 = (4k^2 + 4k) + 1 = 2(2k^2 + 2k) + 1.$$

By closure, $2k^2 + 2k$ is an integer; call it m. Hence, $x^2 = 2m+1$, which, by definition, means that x^2 is odd. ∎

4.7   **Complement: Recipes and Algorithms** The following is a recipe supposedly taken from a thirteenth century book on Spanish–North African cuisine by an anonymous Spanish Muslim author from Valencia.

> One takes a fat young sheep, skinned and cleaned. It is opened between the two muscles and all that is in its stomach is carefully removed. In its interior one puts a stuffed goose and in the goose's belly a stuffed hen, and in the hen's belly a stuffed young pigeon, and in the pigeon's belly a stuffed thrush and in the thrush's belly another stuffed or fried bird, all of this stuffed and sprinkled with the sauce described for stuffed dishes. The opening is sewn together, the sheep is put in the hot clay oven, or tannur, and it is left until done and crisp on the outside. It is sprinkled with more sauce, and then put in the cavity of a calf which has already been prepared and cleaned. The calf is then stitched together and put in the hot tannur, and left till it is done and crisp on the outside. Then it is taken out and presented.   △

Our description of "algorithm" (following Theorem 4.2) said that the instructions must be easily understood. Is the recipe given above an algorithm? The answer to this question depends upon the reader. For many of us modern-day readers, it is unlikely that we know (or care) how to carefully remove all that is in a sheep's stomach. But for a Spanish Muslim chef, this instruction would have been easily understood. Thus, a set of instructions may be an algorithm for some but not for others. Clearly, each of the steps in this algorithm results in a specific outcome, and the algorithm terminates. (Nothing is put into the fried bird.) The purpose of the algorithm is achieved by providing a meal fit for a royal family.

There exist "arithmetic recipes" which look "algorithmic" but for which it is not known that they terminate. For example, consider the following instructions. Let n be a natural number.

Step 1.   If n is odd, then replace n by $3n + 1$, and if n is even, then replace n by $n/2$.

Step 2.   If $n = 1$, then stop; otherwise go to Step 1.   △

If $n = 18$, then the instructions produce the following list of numbers:

$$18, 9, 28, 14, 7, 22, 11, 34, 17, 52, 26, 13, 40, 20, 10, 5, 16, 8, 4, 2, 1.$$

For $n = 12$, the following list of numbers is produced:

$$12, 6, 3, 10, 5, 16, 8, 4, 2, 1.$$

For small positive integers this process will always terminate, but the number of steps may be large; if $n = 27$, for example, then 70 steps are required and the largest number produced in the sequence is 4616. No one knows whether this "algorithm" terminates for each positive integer.

Perhaps you have wondered about the etymology of the word "algorithm" (or "algorism" in older texts). The Islamic mathematician Muḥammad ibn-Mūsā al-Khwārizmī (ca. 780–850) wrote a mathematics text, *Al-kitāb al-muhtaṣar fī ḥisāb al-jabr wa-l-muqābala*, or *The Condensed Book on the Calculation of Restoring and Comparing.* Our word "algebra" is derived from the word *al-jabr* in the book's title, and the name al-Khwārizmī, after being transliterated from Arabic to Latin to English, became "algorithm." It is fitting that the two words "algebra" and "algorithm" have a common origin in the work of this ancient mathematician. Many of the techniques learned in algebra today are algorithms for the solution of problems in his text.

The Maximum Element Algorithm which proved Theorem 4.2 may be illustrated graphically as in the following flowchart. To be reasonably precise, we need to allow both for the repetition of certain instructions and for the effect that one step may have on the next. It is convenient to think of A and M as the names of registers (or locations in a calculator, for example) which contain numbers. The registers are different in that A may contain many numbers at a time, but M contains only one number at a time. Our flowchart is "dynamic," which means that the contents of both A and M may change as the steps in the algorithm are implemented. So, when we indicate an operation of some kind on A or M, our intent is that the operation apply to the number(s) currently contained in A or M. We begin by assuming that A contains a given finite set of at least two numbers, and the process continues by following the arrows from one box to the next. The algorithm ends when no number remains in register A; at that point the current content of register M is the desired maximum.

Registers: A ⬜ ⬜ M

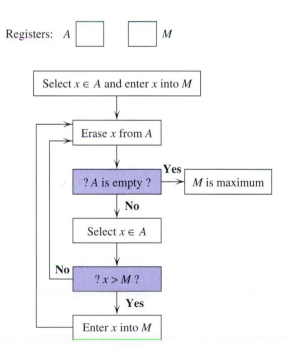

Problems for Section 4

1. Use the algorithm described at the beginning of this section to identify the largest element in the set $\{-15, -18, -13, -30, -28, -12, -20\}$.

2. (a) Construct an algorithm to find the smallest element in the set of numbers $\mathbf{A} = \{a_1, a_2, a_3, \ldots, a_n\}$. (b) Apply this algorithm, step by step, to the set $\mathbf{A} = \{9, 30, 5, 8, 32, 14\}$.

3. Apply your algorithm in Problem 2(a) to the set in Problem 1.

4. Consider the set $\mathbf{A} = \{9, 30, 5, 8, 32, 14\}$. (a) List these elements in order from largest to smallest. (b) Think carefully about how you did this, and describe (at least roughly) how to design an algorithm to order these elements.

5. Give an argument proving that the set of positive integers is infinite, which is similar to that in the text, but considers $2L$ instead of $L + 1$.

6. Prove that there cannot exist a smallest negative integer.

7. (a) List the positive integral divisors of 8 (include both 1 and 8). (b) Think carefully about how you did this, and describe (at least roughly) how to design an algorithm to identify these divisors.

8. (a) List the positive integral divisors of 36. (b) List the pairs of divisors (d_1, d_2) for which $d_1 \le d_2$ and $d_1 d_2 = 36$.

9. (a) List the positive integral divisors of 42. (b) List the pairs of divisors (d_1, d_2) for which $d_1 \le d_2$ and $d_1 d_2 = 42$.

10. (This question is based upon Problems 7, 8, and 9.) (a) In designing an algorithm to identify the positive integral divisors of a positive integer n, is it necessary to test each positive integer less than n? (b) What can

you say about n if the set of its divisors contains an odd number of elements?

11. List the set of all prime numbers less than 50.

12. Eratosthenes (276–194 B.C.) was a Greek mathematician who invented an algorithm (subsequently called **Eratosthenes' sieve**) to identify the prime numbers appearing in a list of all positive integers less than $n + 1$.

Step 1. Mark out 1.

Step 2. Note that 2 is the next smallest unmarked number in the list. Mark out every second number *past* 2.

Step 3. Note that 3 is the next smallest unmarked number in the list. Mark out every third number *past* 3, and note that some numbers, like 6, are marked out again.

. . .

Step k. In general, if k is the next smallest unmarked number in the list, then mark out every kth number *past* k, and note that some numbers may be marked out multiple times.

. . .

Step m. End when $m^2 \ge n$. The unmarked numbers remaining in the list are the desired primes. ▲

Use Eratosthenes' sieve for (a) $n = 50$, (b) $n = 100$.

13. Find all the prime pairs with sum less than 200.

14. Represent each integer x, $37 \le x \le 50$, as a product of primes.

15. As we observed in the text, only eight primes are required in the representation of integers x for which $1 < x < 22$. How many primes are required in the representation of integers x for which $1 < x < 37$?

16. Does the set $A = \{M: M = n^2 + n + 41, n = 0, 1, 2, 3, 4\}$ contain a number which is not prime?

17. (*Continuation of Problem 16.*) Does the set $B = \{M: M = n^2 + n + 41, n = 10, 20, 30, 39\}$ contain a number which is not prime? (*Hint:* Consult the table of primes at the end of this book.)

18. (*Conclusion of Problem 16.*) Show that when $n = 40$, $n^2 + n + 41$ is not prime.

19. What prime numbers can x be replaced by if (*a*) $x^2 \le 289$, (*b*) $x^3 \le 1331$?

20. Find the largest positive integer that divides both 264 and 716. (*Hint:* Express each as a product of primes; then consider all prime factors common to both.)

21. Find the largest positive integer that divides both 306 and 942.

22. Note that the largest positive integer dividing any two prime numbers is 1. Find any two nonprime integers greater than 10 for which this is true.

23. Assume that m and n are positive integers and that $m \le n$. Prove that if $m^2 = n^2$, then $m = n$. (*Hint:* Try the contrapositive.)

24. Prove that an integer cannot be both even and odd.

25. Assuming that x, y, and z are integers, prove that if x is a divisor of y and y is a divisor of z, then x is a divisor of z.

26. Assuming that x and y are integers, prove that if x has a factor that is not also a factor of y, then x is not a divisor of y.

27. Prove that the largest positive integer that divides both n and $n + 1$ is 1. (*Hint:* Problem 9 of Section 3.)

28. Let $A = \{a_1, a_2, \ldots, a_n\}$ be a nonempty set of integers. Let r be a given integer. Give an algorithm that will find the number of elements of A that are divisible by r.

29. Let A and r be as in Problem 28. Give an algorithm that will find the number of elements of A that are less than r. (You may want to think about how to modify your algorithm so that it answers Problem 28 at the same time.)

30. Let n be an odd integer. Show that if n divides $2k$, then n divides k. (*Hint:* Problem 5 of Section 3.)

31. Assuming that a, b, and d are real numbers, prove that if $0 < a < b$ and $a < d$, then $a^2 < bd$.

32. Assume that x and y are integers. Show that if xy is odd, then x and y are both odd. (*Hint:* Assume that at least one of the numbers, say x, is even.)

33. In this and the next five problems you will show that there is no largest prime of the form $4k + 3$. Show that the primes are divided into three sets: $\{2\}$, primes of the form $4k + 1$, and primes of the form $4k + 3$. (Refer to Problem 35 in Section 3.)

34. (*Continuation of Problem 33.*) Show that if each of the integers m and n has remainder 1 when divided by 4, then so does the product mn.

35. (*Continuation of Problem 33.*) As a warm-up for the next three problems, list the first 10 primes of the form $4k + 3$.

36. (*Continuation of Problem 33.*) Assume that $p_1, p_2, \ldots, p_n$ are all the primes of the form $4k + 3$ with $p_1 < p_2 < \cdots < p_n$. (Note, $p_1 = 3$.) Let $q = 4p_1 p_2 \cdots p_n - 1$ and show that p_i does not divide q for $i = 1, 2, \ldots, n$.

37. (*Continuation of Problem 33.*) Show that $q = 4m + 3$ for some integer m and that $q > p_n$. Conclude that q is not prime.

38. (*Conclusion of Problem 33.*) Since q is not prime (Problem 37), all primes that divide it are of the form $4k + 1$ (Problem 36). Using Problem 34, derive a contradiction.

39. Assume that each integer can be expressed as either $6k$, $6k+1$, $6k+2$, $6k+3$, $6k+4$, or $6k+5$. Show that the primes are divided into four sets: $\{2\}$, $\{3\}$, primes of the form $6k+1$, or primes of the form $6k+5$.

40. Following the pattern of argument in Problems 33 to 38, show that there are an infinite number of primes of the form $6k+5$.

41. There are n prison cells in a jail, numbered 1 to n. On day 1, the jailer locks every cell. On day 2, the jailer unlocks every other cell, those numbered $(2, 4, 6, \ldots)$. On day 3, the jailer visits every third cell $(3, 6, 9, \ldots)$, unlocking the locked cells (like cell 3) and locking the unlocked cells (like cell 6). On day 4, the jailer visits every fourth cell, unlocking the locked cells and locking the unlocked cells. He continues this procedure on the kth day by visiting every kth cell and changing whether the cell is locked or unlocked. After n days, which cells are locked? Why? (*Hint:* Try this for $n = 10$.)

42. After Eratosthenes, sieves were little studied until this century. A Norwegian mathematician, Viggo Brun (1885–1978), revived the study of sieves by using them to make amazing progress on the question of whether there are infinitely many twin primes. Stanislav Ulam (1909–1984) also invented a sieve to generate the **lucky numbers,** which have primelike qualities. To generate them, begin with $\mathbb{N}$ and first delete all even positive integers. Since 3 is the second number (after 2 was deleted), delete every third number from those remaining. At the kth stage of this sieve, strike out every mth number, where m is the kth number in the list after the $(k-1)$st stage. (Note: this is a process different from that used in Problem 12.) The first five lucky numbers are 1, 3, 7, 9, 13. List the next 10 lucky numbers.

43. Write an algorithm that produces the first 100 primes of the form $6k+1$ (here $k \in \mathbb{N}$).

44. Write an algorithm that produces the first 100 primes of the form $k^2 + 1$ (here $k \in \mathbb{N}$).

Section 5. Logical Equivalence and Divisibility

Overview for Section 5

- Introduction to the converse of an implication, and distinction between an implication and its converse
- Introduction to logical equivalence using divisibility properties of the integers
- Discussion of the division algorithm with special emphasis on the remainder
- Illustration of the role of counterexample in mathematical argument
- Parity properties of sums and products of integers

Key Concepts: converse of an implication, logical equivalence, division algorithm, counterexample, parity of a sum of integers

5.1

For convenience, let us assume throughout this section that p and q represent mathematical statements and that x represents any integer. Consider the implication

$$\text{If } x > 0, \text{ then } x^2 > 0. \tag{1}$$

This happens to be a mathematical theorem, for we know that the product of positive numbers is positive. (Thus if x is replaced by any positive integer, then x^2 must also be positive.) Now, 9 is a (positive) square integer, and it is a not uncommon error to claim, from (1), that since $x^2 = 9$, then x must be 3; thus assuming that the (reversed) implication

$$\text{If } x^2 > 0, \text{ then } x > 0 \tag{2}$$

also is a theorem. But (2) fails dramatically, because every square integer *is* positive *and* has a negative integral square root.

Given an implication

$$p \to q,$$

the new implication obtained by reversing hypothesis and conclusion

$$q \to p$$

is called its **converse.** Thus, $p \rightarrow q$ and $q \rightarrow p$ are converses of one another [as illustrated in (1) and (2), above]. It is not generally the case that an implication and its converse are *both* true; the fact that one of them is known to be true has no bearing on the truth of the other. This prompts the warning: Just because a mathematical theorem can be expressed as an implication, don't jump to the conclusion that its converse also is a theorem.

Example 1

Consider the following implications (each is true):

a. If a triangle is equilateral, then it is isosceles.

b. If I drive 75 mph, then I am breaking the law in Virginia.

c. If x is a prime number, then $x > 1$.

The converse fails in each case, for there exist:

a. Isosceles triangles which are not equilateral;

b. Laws, unrelated to speeding, that I might break;

c. Positive integers greater than 1 which are not prime.

5.2

Recall that Theorem 3.1 can be stated

$$(x \text{ is even}) \rightarrow (x^2 \text{ is even}),$$

and that Theorem 4.6 can be stated

$$(x^2 \text{ is even}) \rightarrow (x \text{ is even}).$$

These two implications are, in fact, converses of one another. It happens in this case that both of them are true; but remember that each theorem required a separate proof. This is an example of the relatively rare occurrence in mathematics when an implication

$$p \rightarrow q \quad \text{and its converse} \quad q \rightarrow p$$

are both true. When this condition holds, we say that p and q are **logically equivalent,** which means that if either one is true, then both are true. The notation for logical equivalence is

$$p \leftrightarrow q,$$

and the usual way to state this in mathematical language is

$$p \text{ if and only if } q,$$

which is simply an abbreviation for the two statements

$$\text{"}p \text{ if } q\text{"} \qquad \text{and} \qquad \text{"}p \text{ only if } q.\text{"}$$

The correspondence is

$$\text{"}p \text{ if } q\text{" means } q \to p \qquad \text{and} \qquad \text{"}p \text{ only if } q\text{" means } p \to q.$$

Thus, Theorems 3.1 and 4.6 can be combined into the following single statement.

THEOREM 5.2

The integer x is divisible by 2 if and only if x^2 is divisible by 2.

A statement in the form of a logical equivalence

$$p \leftrightarrow q \tag{1}$$

must, like any statement in mathematics, be either true or false but not both. The important point is that if a mathematical statement in the form of (1) can be proved to be true, then it is a theorem; to prove the truth of (1) requires a proof that each one of the implications

$$p \to q \qquad \text{and} \qquad q \to p$$

is true.

5.3

We observed in paragraph 3.1 that when an integer is divided by 2, there may be a remainder of either 0 or 1, and we used this fact to determine the parity of the number. Because remainders provide useful information, it will be helpful to consider the more general situation in which a positive integer a is divided by an integer b greater than 2. The process can be visualized in the following way. Let **A** denote a set which contains exactly a elements. Now, separate the set **A** into as many subsets as possible, each containing exactly b elements and none having elements in common. Suppose there are q such subsets, and note that the remaining elements of **A**, if any, form a subset which has fewer than b elements; let r denote the number of these elements. Recall that these integers have names: a is called the **dividend,** b is called the **divisor,** q is called the **quotient,** r is called the **remainder,** and the relationship between them,

$$a = b \cdot q + r,$$

is called the **division algorithm.** As a simple example, 6 nickels and 4 pennies have a value of 34 cents; that is,

$$34 = 5 \cdot 6 + 4.$$

As we use the division algorithm in this text, we will assume that:

- The integer b must be positive.

- The remainder r must satisfy $0 \leq r < b$.

- The integer a need not necessarily be positive.

The division algorithm supplies useful information in the consideration of other logical equivalences similar to the one stated in Theorem 5.2.

THEOREM 5.3

The integer x is divisible by 3 if and only if x^2 is divisible by 3.

As with Theorem 5.2, the proof of this theorem requires two separate arguments corresponding to the implications (expressed in "divides" notation):

$$(3 \mid x^2) \rightarrow (3 \mid x), \tag{1}$$

and

$$(3 \mid x) \rightarrow (3 \mid x^2). \tag{2}$$

Note that (1) expresses the "if" part of Theorem 5.3, while (2) expresses the "only if" part. Before undertaking either part of the proof, it will be helpful to examine the division algorithm with $b = 3$. If an integer is divided by 3, the result can be expressed in such a way that the remainder is either 0, 1, or 2; for example,

$$12 = 3 \cdot 4 + 0 \qquad 16 = 3 \cdot 5 + 1 \qquad 23 = 3 \cdot 7 + 2$$
$$-12 = 3 \cdot (-4) + 0 \qquad -16 = 3 \cdot (-6) + 2 \qquad -23 = 3 \cdot (-8) + 1$$

Just as division by 2 separated all integers into two subsets (the even integers with remainder 0 and the odd integers with remainder 1), division by 3 separates all integers into three subsets depending upon the remainder. We require that two integers belong to the same subset if each leaves the same remainder when divided by 3. The standard notation for these subsets of $\mathbb{Z}$ is

$$[\mathbf{0}]_3 = \{\ldots, -6, -3, 0, 3, 6, \ldots\} \qquad \text{(note that remainder is 0);}$$
$$[\mathbf{1}]_3 = \{\ldots, -5, -2, 1, 4, 7, \ldots\} \qquad \text{(note that remainder is 1);}$$
$$[\mathbf{2}]_3 = \{\ldots, -4, -1, 2, 5, 8, \ldots\} \qquad \text{(note that remainder is 2).}$$

For convenience, we suggest referring to them verbally as

"class 0"   for $[\mathbf{0}]_3$,

"class 1"   for $[\mathbf{1}]_3$,

"class 2"   for $[\mathbf{2}]_3$.

In more advanced mathematics, the divisor 3 is sometimes called the **modulus,** and these sets are then called **residue classes (mod 3).** This concept lies at the heart of an important chapter in the history of mathematics, much of which was developed before his twentieth birthday by Carl Friedrich Gauss (1777–1855).

5.4

Divisibility and the division algorithm will be of recurring interest in succeeding sections, and the notation introduced above offers an economy of expression which is difficult to resist. Assuming that m is a given integer greater than 1, consider the following equivalences:

a. $x \in [1]_m$.

b. The integer x has a remainder of 1 when divided by m.

c. $x = m \cdot q + 1$ for some integer q.

Although the expressions in equivalences **b** and **c** are more familiar to us at the moment, the abbreviated symbolism in equivalence **a** will be used with some regularity. Recall that we have used the notation $m \mid x$ as an abbreviation for the phrase "m is a divisor of x." Since any multiple of m has remainder 0 when divided by m, $x \in [0]_m$ also means that "m is a divisor of x." It is now easy to recognize that the "class" notation extends in a natural way to provide information beyond simple divisibility. For example,

$$x \in [0]_2 \qquad \text{means} \qquad x = 2 \cdot q \qquad \text{for some integer } q,$$
$$x \in [0]_3 \qquad \text{means} \qquad x = 3 \cdot q \qquad \text{for some integer } q,$$
$$x \in [2]_5 \qquad \text{means} \qquad x = 5 \cdot q + 2 \qquad \text{for some integer } q,$$
$$x \in [1]_9 \qquad \text{means} \qquad x = 9 \cdot q + 1 \qquad \text{for some integer } q,$$
$$x \in [11]_{12} \qquad \text{means} \qquad x = 12 \cdot q + 11 \qquad \text{for some integer } q.$$

Tutorial 5.4

For each of the following statements, indicate whether it is true or false and give a reason:

a. $18 \in [0]_3$, **f.** $100 \in [1]_9$,

b. $4 \mid 18$, **g.** $89 \in [1]_9$,

c. $18 \in [0]_4$, **h.** $9 \in [1]_9$,

d. $28 \in [3]_5$, **i.** $1000 \in [1]_9$.

e. $82 \in [3]_5$,

Making use of this new notation, consider first the claim

$$\text{If } x \in [\mathbf{0}]_3, \text{ then } x^2 \in [\mathbf{0}]_3.$$

The proof is easy. Let $x \in [\mathbf{0}]_3$. Then $x = 3q$ for some integer q. Hence $x^2 = (3q)^2 = 3(3q^2)$. This implies that x^2 is divisible by 3 (that is, the remainder is 0), so $x^2 \in [\mathbf{0}]_3$.

Next consider the claim

$$\text{If } x \in [\mathbf{1}]_3, \text{ then } x^2 \in [\mathbf{1}]_3.$$

The proof is easy. Let $x \in [\mathbf{1}]_3$. Then $x = 3q + 1$ for some integer q. Hence,

$$x^2 = (3q + 1)^2 = (3q)^2 + 2(3q) + 1 = 3(3q^2 + 2q) + 1.$$

This implies that when x^2 is divided by 3, the remainder is 1, so $x^2 \in [\mathbf{1}]_3$.

The pattern seems clear from these two cases, and we confidently assert the claim

$$\text{If } x \in [\mathbf{2}]_3, \text{ then } x^2 \in [\mathbf{2}]_3.$$

Surely this must be a true statement, and its proof must be just as easy as the others—so why bother with the details? Why? Because the details won't work. The claim is false!

Let $x \in [\mathbf{2}]_3$. Then $x = 3q + 2$ for some integer q. Hence,

$$x^2 = (3q + 2)^2 = (3q)^2 + 2 \cdot 2 \cdot (3q) + 4$$
$$= 3(3q^2) + 3(4q) + 3 + 1 = 3(3q^2 + 4q + 1) + 1.$$

Again, the remainder is 1, so x^2 is in $[\mathbf{1}]_3$, *not* in $[\mathbf{2}]_3$.

Moral.   **The details are all-important.**

This little fable illustrates how important restraint is in mathematics.

Moral.   **Resist leaping to conclusions.**

But the story is not over. Have you guessed that the proof of Theorem 5.3 is buried in our fable?

Proof of Theorem 5.3

The set $[\mathbf{0}]_3$ consists exactly of those integers which are divisible by 3. Thus the "only if" part of our theorem can be restated

$$\text{If } x \in [\mathbf{0}]_3, \text{ then } x^2 \in [\mathbf{0}]_3$$

and this we have already shown to be true. The converse statement is

$$\text{If } x^2 \in [\mathbf{0}]_3, \text{ then } x \in [\mathbf{0}]_3$$

and it can be restated in contrapositive form

$$(3 \nmid x) \rightarrow (3 \nmid x^2).$$

But $3 \nmid x$ means simply that $x \in [\mathbf{1}]_3$ or $x \in [\mathbf{2}]_3$, and in either case we have already shown that $x^2 \notin [\mathbf{0}]_3$. ■

5.5 When an integer is divided by 4, the remainder must be one of the numbers 0, 1, 2, or 3. Thus,

$$12 = 4 \cdot 3 + 0 \qquad 17 = 4 \cdot 4 + 1 \qquad 14 = 4 \cdot 3 + 2 \qquad 23 = 4 \cdot 5 + 3$$

$$-12 = 4 \cdot (-3) + 0 \qquad 3 = 4 \cdot 0 + 3 \qquad -14 = 4 \cdot (-4) + 2 \qquad -23 = 4 \cdot (-6) + 1$$

As in the case of division by 3, we may classify the integers into subsets by requiring that two numbers in $\mathbb{Z}$ belong to the same subset if each has the same remainder when divided by 4. The customary notation for these subsets is similar to that used earlier, but the divisor is 4, and we write

$$[\mathbf{0}]_4 = \{\ldots, -8, -4, 0, 4, 8, \ldots\} \qquad \text{(remainder is 0)};$$

$$[\mathbf{1}]_4 = \{\ldots, -7, -3, 1, 5, 9, \ldots\} \qquad \text{(remainder is 1)};$$

$$[\mathbf{2}]_4 = \{\ldots, -6, -2, 2, 6, 10, \ldots\} \qquad \text{(remainder is 2)};$$

$$[\mathbf{3}]_4 = \{\ldots, -5, -1, 3, 7, 11, \ldots\} \qquad \text{(remainder is 3)}.$$

Assuming that the divisor is clearly understood, these subsets also may be referred to verbally by "class 0," "class 1," "class 2," and "class 3," respectively.

In general, any positive integer, say b, may be used as divisor to produce b subsets of $\mathbb{Z}$, among which the set

$$[\mathbf{0}]_b = \{\ldots, -2b, -b, 0, b, 2b, \ldots\}$$

always consists of the multiples of b.

Theorems 5.2 and 5.3 are examples of logical equivalence which look quite similar, and from them we might be tempted to leap to the conclusion that

$$x \text{ is divisible by 4 if and only if } x^2 \text{ is divisible by 4.}$$

But the lesson just learned warns us to proceed with caution. Although it is easy to prove that the implication

$$(4 \mid x) \rightarrow (4 \mid x^2) \tag{1}$$

is a theorem, it happens that the converse is *not* a theorem. The reason is very simple: The converse claims that any integer x for which x^2 is divisible by 4 must itself be divisible by 4. But it's easy to find integers which fail this test; for example,

$$4 \mid 2^2, \quad \text{but} \quad 4 \nmid 2,$$
$$4 \mid 6^2, \quad \text{but} \quad 4 \nmid 6.$$

Actually, to show that the converse of (1) fails to be a theorem, we need to exhibit only *one* integer replacement for x which satisfies the hypothesis but not the conclusion, and any such integer is called a **counterexample.** As shown above, each of 2 and 6 is a counterexample to the claim that

$$(4 \mid x^2) \rightarrow (4 \mid x).$$

Tutorial 5.5

a. Discover for yourself at least four counterexamples, different from 2 and 6, to the claim immediately above.

b. Generalizing from all these counterexamples, try to discover the "numerical" property that each must have.

Counterexamples, which disprove claims (or conjectures), as in the instance above, are an important part of mathematics. Often, they are discovered only at the expense of much time and effort, and, like theorems, they help delineate the boundaries of mathematical truth. Thus, the implication given in (1) is a true statement, but its converse is false.

5.6

In a later section we will need to refer to the parity of a sum of integers; its behavior is quite different from that of a product. If a_1 and a_2 denote integers, then the following table is easy to verify.

a_1	a_2	$a_1 \cdot a_2$	$a_1 + a_2$
Even	Even	Even	Even
Even	Odd	Even	Odd
Odd	Even	Even	Odd
Odd	Odd	Odd	Even

From this table we formulate two logical equivalences:

1. The product $a_1 \cdot a_2$ is even if and only if at least one factor is even.

2. The sum $a_1 + a_2$ is even if and only if both terms are even or both terms are odd.

Theorem 5.6A, below, states the result needed later; it is a generalization of equivalence **2** obtained by considering more than two terms.
    Now, let

$$a_1, a_2, a_3, \ldots, a_n$$

be a finite list of integers (not necessarily all distinct), and let s denote the sum of the n entries in the list

$$s = a_1 + a_2 + a_3 + \cdots + a_n.$$

Under what conditions can we be sure that s is even? By the commutativity of addition, the list can be rearranged so that the odd terms are written first, followed by the even terms:

$$s = (\text{sum of the odd terms}) + (\text{sum of the even terms}) = s_{\text{odd}} + s_{\text{even}}.$$

Almost immediately, we observe that s_{even} is an even integer since, by the distributive law, we can factor a 2 out of each of the even terms; thus 2 is a factor of s_{even}. Now suppose that there are exactly m odd terms in our list, reindexed (if necessary) so that

$$s_{\text{odd}} = a_1 + a_2 + \cdots + a_m.$$

Since each of these odd terms has the form $2k + 1$,

$$s_{\text{odd}} = (2k_1 + 1) + (2k_2 + 1) + \cdots + (2k_m + 1)$$
$$= 2(k_1 + k_2 + \cdots + k_m) + \underbrace{(1 + 1 + \cdots + 1)}_{m \text{ terms}}.$$

It is clear, expressed in this form, that s_{odd} is even if m is even and is odd if m is odd. Thus, we have proved the following logical equivalence.

THEOREM 5.6A
The sum of the entries in any finite list of integers is even if and only if the number of odd entries in the list is even.

As a final remark in this connection, it is clear that equivalence **1** generalizes as follows.

THEOREM
5.6B

The product of the entries in any finite list of integers is even if and only if at least one integer in the list is even.

Tutorial 5.6

Consider a list of integers denoted by a_1, a_2, a_3.

a. Complete the following table of possibilities (there should be eight cases altogether):

Case	a_1	a_2	a_3
1	Even	Even	Even
2	Even	Even	Odd
3	Even	Odd	Even
...	...	...	...

b. In how many cases is at least one integer even?

c. What case corresponds to the claim:

It is not true that at least one integer is even.

d. Use a contrapositive argument to prove that

If $a_1 \cdot a_2 \cdot a_3$ is even, then at least one of the integers is even.

e. Finally, complete the proof of the theorem

$a_1 \cdot a_2 \cdot a_3$ is even if and only if at least one of the entries is even.

5.7

Complement: The Division Algorithm Earlier in this section we referred to the operation of dividing a positive integer a by another positive integer b, and we identified the division algorithm

$$a = b \cdot q + r,$$

with quotient q and remainder r (where $0 \leq r < b$). Here we want to create an algorithm by which q and r can be determined. The procedure to be described shortly is even more basic than that learned in arithmetic, which also has as its primary objective the determination of q and r. Applied to the problem of dividing 947 by 83, for example, the familiar arithmetic technique yields

$$
\begin{array}{r}
11 \\
83 \overline{)\ 947} \\
83 \\
\overline{117} \\
83 \\
\overline{34}
\end{array}
$$

from which we discover that the quotient is 11 with remainder 34. Hence, the result may be expressed

$$947 = 83 \cdot 11 + 34.$$

We will use this numerical example to illustrate the steps in our algorithm. Imagine a very simple machine which can add, subtract, and compare two numbers. Even though the machine cannot divide, we will try first to invent a way that it can be used to find the remainder when 947 is divided by 83. Assume that the machine has places to store numbers (as before, we call them registers). Begin by placing 83 in a register labeled B and 947 in a register labeled A. The number in B will remain unchanged, but A may contain different numbers at different stages throughout the process. Labeling the registers has a definite advantage: It allows us to describe an arithmetic operation without naming the specific numbers involved. For example, $A - B$ means to subtract whatever number is in register B from whatever number is in register A.

Here is a flowchart of an algorithm designed to find the remainder:

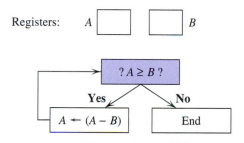

The desired remainder is the value of A when the algorithm ends. Here's why. The machine compares A with B. If A is less than B, then the algorithm ends. If not, then the number $A - B$ is computed and inserted into register A (erasing the number previously in it). Now, the cycle begins again: The machine compares the new number A with B and continues. The first two cycles and the last cycle in our numerical example (these cycles, by the way, are called **loops**) are as follows:

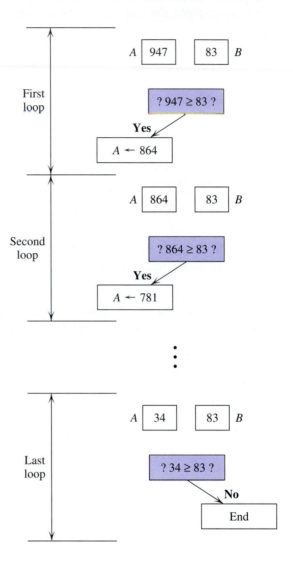

At this point, note that register *A* contains the remainder, 34.

The quotient in this example, already known to be 11, is simply the number of subtractions (i.e., "loops") required before reaching "End." But the algorithm, above, doesn't supply this information. A simple modification, making use of another register labeled *Q*, corrects the deficiency.

Initial assignment: A | 947 | B | 83 | Q | 0 |

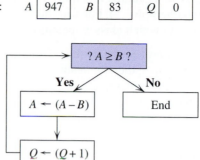

The bottom box means: Add 1 to the current number in register Q; then insert this new number into register Q. Thus, at the end of the first loop, the contents of the registers are

A | 864 | B | 83 | Q | 1 |

and at the end of the second loop, the contents of the registers are

A | 781 | B | 83 | Q | 2 |

Notice that register Q serves as a counter, which records how many times a new difference, $A - B$, is inserted into A; that is, it counts the number of loops before "End." When the algorithm ends, the current contents of the three registers are

A | 34 | B | 83 | Q | 11 |

Thus, $$947 = 83 \cdot 11 + 34.$$

Problems for Section 5

1. In this section, we identified integers belonging to $[0]_3$, $[1]_3$, or $[2]_3$. Determine which class x^3 belongs to for x in each class.

2. Which of the following are theorems?
   (a) $x \in [0]_3$ if and only if $x^3 \in [0]_3$.
   (b) $x \in [1]_3$ if and only if $x^3 \in [1]_3$.
   (c) $x \in [2]_3$ if and only if $x^3 \in [2]_3$.

3. Let the integers be separated into four classes (as in paragraph 5.5). For x in each class, determine to which class x^2 belongs.

4. Let the integers be separated into four classes (as in paragraph 5.5). For x in each class, determine to which class x^3 belongs.

5. (*a*) Give a few examples to show that if an integer is divided by 5, then the result can be expressed so that the remainder is 0, 1, 2, 3, or 4. Include both positive and negative integers among your examples. (*b*) As before, let $x \in [r]_5$ if $x = 5 \cdot k + r$. If $x \in [2]_5$, determine the class to which (i) x^2 belongs, (ii) x^3 belongs, (iii) x^4 belongs.

6. Prove the theorem: The integer x is divisible by 5 if and only if x^2 also is divisible by 5.

7. Consider the following claim: The integer x is divisible by 8 if and only if x^2 also is divisible by 8. Note the similarity between this statement and the preceding one. Is a proof really necessary? Maybe you should try one!

8. (*a*) Prove the implication: If x is the sum of any five consecutive integers, then x is divisible by 5. (*b*) Prove the implication: If x is divisible by 5, then there are five consecutive integers with x as their sum.

9. What is the converse of each implication? (*a*) If it is raining, then I will get wet. (*b*) If $b - a \geq 0$, then $a - b < 0$ (assume that a and b are real numbers).

10. Express both the converse and the contrapositive of each implication as given. (*a*) $p \rightarrow q$, (*b*) $p \rightarrow \sim q$, (*c*) $\sim p \rightarrow q$, (*d*) $\sim p \rightarrow \sim q$.

11. Express each of the following as an implication (using the "arrow" notation). (*a*) $\sim p$ if q, (*b*) p only if $\sim q$, (*c*) q if p, (*d*) $\sim q$ only if p.

12. The logical equivalence $p \leftrightarrow q$ sometimes appears in mathematical literature as follows: p is a necessary and sufficient condition for q. This statement is a short form for two statements: (i) p is a necessary condition for q, (ii) p is a sufficient condition for

q. Each of statements (i) and (ii) can be expressed as an implication. Give the "arrow" notation for each.

13. Find at least two counterexamples (if possible) for each statement. (*a*) All prime numbers are odd. (*b*) No prime number is greater than 300. (*c*) Every integer divisible by 6 is also divisible by 3. (*d*) Every integer divisible by 3 is also divisible by 6.

14. (*a*) What is the converse of the implication: If 5 is a divisor of n, then 5 is a divisor of $2n$? (*b*) Is the implication a logical equivalence? (*Hint:* Is the converse also a theorem? Refer to Problem 30 of Section 4.)

15. (*a*) What is the converse of the implication: If 3 is a divisor of n, then 3 is a divisor of $2n$? (*b*) Is the implication a logical equivalence? (See the hint in Problem 14.)

16. (*a*) What is the converse of the implication: If 6 is a divisor of n, then 6 is a divisor of $2n$? (*b*) Is the implication a logical equivalence?

17. What is the theorem suggested by Problems 14, 15, and 16?

18. Let x and y denote two integers such that the product xy is divisible by 3. (*a*) List several values of x and y which satisfy this condition. (*b*) Prove that at least one of x or y is divisible by 3. (*Hint:* Consider an indirect proof.)

19. Suppose that neither of the integers x and y is divisible by 3. Prove that if $x + y$ is divisible by 3, then x and y belong to different classes.

20. Suppose that neither of the integers x and y is divisible by 3. Is the following logical equivalence true? In order that $x + y$ be divisible by 3 it is necessary and sufficient that x and y belong to different classes. (See Problem 12.)

21. Suppose that p is a prime larger than 3. Prove that exactly one number in the set $\{p, p + 2, p + 4\}$ is divisible by 3. (*Hint:* Since p is not divisible by 3, it must belong to $[1]_3$ or $[2]_3$.)

22. Here is a familiar bit of folklore: If it ain't broke, don't fix it. (*a*) Re-express this so that it becomes an implication in "good" English. (Remember that both hypothesis and conclusion must be statements.) (*b*) What is the contrapositive of your implication? (*c*) What is the converse of your implication?

23. Here is another familiar saying: If the shoe fits, wear it. (*a*) Why doesn't this saying satisfy the definition of an implication? (*b*) Spend a few minutes thinking about what this saying means; then try to express it as an implication.

24. Here is a quotation from Shelley: "If Winter comes, can Spring be far behind?" (*a*) Consider what you think the poet intends, and convert this question into an implication. (*b*) What is the converse of your implication?

25. Here is a line spoken by (Jack) Falstaff in *Henry IV,* Part I: "If there were not two or three and fifty upon poor old Jack, then I am no two-legged creature." (*a*) What is Falstaff saying? Express it as an implication. (*b*) What is the contrapositive of your implication? (*c*) What is the converse of the contrapositive?

26. Prove or disprove: x is divisible by 6 if and only if x^2 is divisible by 6. (*Hint:* Recall Problems 30 to 32 in Section 3.)

27. Show that 12 divides n if and only if 3 divides n and 4 divides n. (*Hint:* If $3k = 4m$, then k is even, so $3r = 2m$.)

28. Let p be the statement: If x is an odd prime, then x is of the form $4n + 1$ or $4n + 3$. Show that one of the following is logically equivalent to p. (*a*) If x is not of the form $4n + 1$

and not of the form $4n + 3$, then x is not an odd prime. (*b*) If x is not of the form $4n + 1$ *or* not of the form $4n + 3$, then x is not an odd prime.

29. Show that if integers x and y are both even, then $x^2 + 3y^2$ is also even.

30. Show that if integers x and y are both odd, then $x^2 + 3y^2$ is even.

31. Problems 29 and 30 can be combined as follows: If x and y are of the same parity, then $x^2 + 3y^2$ is even. State both the contrapositive and the converse of this implication.

32. (*Conclusion of Problem 31.*) Show that integers x and y are of the same parity if and only if $x^2 + 3y^2$ is even.

33. Show that xy is odd if and only if the integers x and y are both odd. (*Hint:* Refer to Problem 5 in Section 3 and to the table in paragraph 5.6.)

34. If the following is true, prove it; if not, why not? The integers x and y are of the same parity if and only if x and xy are of the same parity. (*Hint:* First, make a table.)

35. Suppose that m is odd. Show that 2 divides mk if and only if 2 divides k.

36. Suppose m is in $[1]_3$. Show that if 3 divides mk, then 3 divides k. (*Hint:* Write $m = 3r + 1$ and $mk = 3s$ for some integers r and s.)

37. (*Continuation of Problem 36.*) Suppose m is in $[2]_3$. Show that if 3 divides mk, then 3 divides k.

38. (*Conclusion of Problem 36.*) Show that if 3 does not divide m, then 3 divides mk if and only if 3 divides k.

39. Is $1 + 1 \cdot 2 \cdot 3 \cdot \cdots \cdot (n - 1) \cdot n$ prime for all $n \in \mathbb{N}$? Try a few replacement values for the integer n. Do you think the answer is "yes"?

40. Is $2^n - 1$ prime for all integers $n \geq 1$? No, it isn't. Find three counterexamples.

41. Is $2^p - 1$ prime for all primes p? No, it isn't. Find a counterexample.

42. Is $2^n + 1$ prime for all $n \geq 0$?

43. Is $2^{2^n} + 1$ prime for all $n \geq 0$? (*Hint:* Replace n by 0, 1, 2, and 3. Make a guess, then consult a number theory book and look up Fermat primes or Fermat numbers.)

Section 6. Rationals, Pigeons, and Euclid

Overview for Section 6

- Introduction to rational numbers and to rational fractions with relatively prime numerator and denominator
- Rational numbers as terminating or periodic decimals
- Applications of the Pigeonhole Principle
- Use of the Euclidean Algorithm to determine the greatest common divisor of two integers
- Construction of a flowchart to illustrate the Euclidean Algorithm

Key Concepts: relatively prime integers, rational numbers, terminating or periodic decimals, Pigeonhole Principle, greatest common divisor, Euclidean Algorithm

6.1

Numbers which can be expressed in the form a/b, where a and b are any integers except that $b \neq 0$, are called **rational,** and we will frequently refer to a/b as a **rational fraction.** Because rational numbers can be expressed as quotients of integers, the set of all rational numbers is denoted by the special symbol $\mathbb{Q}$. Any integer can be expressed as a quotient (for example $7 = \frac{7}{1}$); hence $\mathbb{Z} \subset \mathbb{Q}$. Furthermore, each rational number is also a real number; hence $\mathbb{Q} \subset \mathbb{R}$.

In this section we will examine in some detail what happens when an integer a is divided by another integer b. We dispose first of those considerations which are reasonably obvious so as to focus on other aspects of the question which require careful thought. At each succeeding step in the listing below we avoid the special cases previously considered.

- If at least one of the integers is 0, then note: $a/0$ is undefined for all a, and $0/b = 0$ for all $b \neq 0$.

- If either a or b is negative, then note: $a/b < 0$ if exactly one of the integers is negative; $a/b > 0$ if both integers are negative.

- If $a \geq b$, then note: a/b has an integral part and a proper fractional part. For example, $\frac{38}{7} = 5 + \frac{3}{7}$, where 5 is the integral part and $\frac{3}{7}$ is the proper fractional part.

- If a and b share a common factor, then note: The common factor can be canceled without affecting the quotient. For example, if $a = a' \cdot c$ and $b = b' \cdot c$, then

$$\frac{a}{b} = \frac{a' \cdot c}{b' \cdot c} = \frac{a'}{b'} \cdot \frac{c}{c} = \frac{a'}{b'}.$$

Because of this last result, a given rational number always has many fractional representations (for example, $\frac{3}{7} = \frac{6}{14} = \frac{-3}{-7} = \cdots$); hence it is reasonable to assume for our investigation that a and b have no common factor (other than 1). We describe this relationship between a and b by saying that they are **relatively prime.** Of course, any two different prime numbers are relatively prime, but it is not necessary that either a or b be prime in order that the pair be relatively prime. For example, 15 and 17 are relatively prime, as are 15 and 16. Finally, we have stripped away the inessentials and have reduced the question to its real intent:

> What, of intellectual interest, can be discovered by studying the quotient a/b of relatively prime integers, where $0 < a < b$?

6.2   The familiar division technique learned in elementary arithmetic converts a rational fraction into decimal form. To illustrate, consider the fraction $\frac{3}{8}$.

$$
\begin{array}{r}
0.375 \\
8 \overline{)\,3.000} \\
\underline{2\,4} \\
60 \\
\underline{56} \\
40 \\
\underline{40} \\
0
\end{array}
$$

We digress briefly to indicate how this technique makes repeated use of the division algorithm (paragraph 5.3). The divisor is 8, and at each step after the first, the algorithm is applied to the preceding remainder multiplied by 10. Note that the algorithm is applied four times:

$$3 = 8 \cdot 0 + 3, \qquad 60 = 8 \cdot 7 + 4,$$
$$30 = 8 \cdot 3 + 6, \qquad 40 = 8 \cdot 5 + 0.$$

Now, put these together in reverse order:

$$4 = 8 \cdot \frac{5}{10};$$

hence

$$60 = 8 \cdot 7 + 8 \cdot \frac{5}{10}.$$

$$6 = 8 \cdot \frac{7}{10} + 8 \cdot \frac{5}{10^2};$$

hence

$$30 = 8 \cdot 3 + 8 \cdot \frac{7}{10} + 8 \cdot \frac{5}{10^2}.$$

$$3 = 8 \cdot \frac{3}{10} + 8 \cdot \frac{7}{10^2} + 8 \cdot \frac{5}{10^3}.$$

Finally, divide by 8 to obtain

$$\frac{3}{8} = \frac{3}{10} + \frac{7}{10^2} + \frac{5}{10^3} = 0.375.$$

This example illustrates the fact that if the remainder at any step is 0, then the algorithm ends, since a/b then has a **terminating** decimal representation. Consider now the two following examples which are not terminating:

```
    0.142857...              0.815...
7 ) 1.000000...      330 ) 269.000...
    7                      264 0
   ___                     ____
    30                      5 00
    28                      3 30
   ___                     ____
     20                     1 700
     14                     1 650
    ___                    _____
      60                      500
      56
     ___
      40
      35
     ___
       50
       49
      ___
       10
```

These illustrate the condition that no remainder is 0. If, in general, the divisor is b, then there are only $b - 1$ nonzero remainders possible; hence there *must* be a repetition of remainder within the first b steps. The algorithm then ends since no new information is generated by a continuation. The string of decimals between the repetitions is iterated ad infinitum. In this situation a/b is said to have a **periodic** (or **repeating**) decimal representation, and the number of digits in the repeating string is called the **period** of the decimal. Note that the period may be less than $b - 1$ but cannot exceed it. For example,

$$\tfrac{1}{7} = 0.142857142857\ldots \qquad \text{and} \qquad \tfrac{269}{330} = 0.81515\ldots.$$

In the first the period is 6; in the second the period is 2. As a notational convenience we adopt the usual practice of placing a bar over the first repeating string of digits to indicate a periodic decimal. Thus, these two periodic decimals may also be written

$$\tfrac{1}{7} = 0.\overline{142857} \qquad \text{and} \qquad \tfrac{269}{330} = 0.8\overline{15}.$$

Tutorial 6.2

a. Find the decimal representation of the rational fraction $\tfrac{7}{8}$. Is it terminating or periodic?

b. Find the decimal representation of the rational fraction $\tfrac{8}{45}$. Is it terminating or periodic?

6.3

If a rational fraction a/b has no 0 remainder, then the algorithm must end in not more than b steps. In the rational fraction $\tfrac{1}{7}$, for example, the first six steps involved all possible nonzero remainders in the order 1, 3, 2, 6, 4, and 5. Thus the seventh step must produce one of the remainders previously obtained, in this case "1." This argument depends on a logical principle so obvious that we are tempted to ignore it completely. But it is worth explicit discussion because there are surprisingly important applications and extensions of the principle in discrete mathematics.

The Pigeonhole Principle

If you have more pigeons than pigeonholes, then at least two pigeons must roost in the same pigeonhole.

Example 1

The Pigeonhole Principle is often illustrated by the following problem, which you may have seen before.

> Prove that there are at least two people in New York City having exactly the same number of hairs on their heads.

A little research in physiology texts reveals that the number of hairs on a human scalp averages about 400 per square centimeter. Hence, we will assume that the total number of hairs on any head does not exceed 150,000. But since there are far more residents of New York City than that, it is impossible that they all have different numbers of hairs on their heads. (We will see a bit later in this section that there must be at least 47 inhabitants of the city who have the same number of hairs on their heads!)

In a similar way, one can reason that there are at least two pine trees in the state of Maine that have exactly the same number of needles. The use of the Pigeonhole Principle in answering such questions certainly beats a person-by-person or a tree-by-tree search for a matching pair. But the trade-off is total uncertainty in identifying specific individuals having the desired characteristics. A proof of this type is essentially different from the constructive proof of Theorem 4.2 (for example). In contrast, it is called **existential** for it guarantees the existence of the objects claimed without offering a clue about how to construct or discover such objects.

Tutorial 6.3

Suppose that an instructor wishes to assign each class member exactly one problem at the end of this section. How large must the class be to ensure that at least two class members are assigned the same problem?

6.4   Our work so far in this section has proved an important property of rational numbers.

THEOREM 6.4A   Any rational fraction *a/b* has a decimal representation which is either terminating or periodic.

Notice that use of the Pigeonhole Principle in the proof merely assures that remainders must begin to repeat at some step in the process; it offers no information about the period of the decimal representation (beyond the fact that it cannot exceed the denominator).

Theorem 6.4A suggests, but leaves unanswered, the question, "Can any terminating or periodic decimal be represented by a rational fraction?" We observe, immediately, that a terminating decimal can be represented as a rational fraction; simply multiply on each side by an appropriate power of 10 to convert the right-hand side to an integer. For example, if

$$x = 0.375,$$

then multiply by 10^3

$$1000x = 375.$$

Now solve for x, obtaining $x = \frac{375}{1000}$. It is customary to cancel common factors so that the numerator and denominator are relatively prime; thus x has the representation

$$x = \tfrac{3}{8} \qquad \text{(note that 125 is the common factor)}.$$

Consider next the periodic decimal

$$x = 0.142857142857\ldots = 0.\overline{142857}.$$

If, as in this case, the repeating string of digits begins at the decimal point, multiply on both sides by a power of 10 sufficient to move the decimal point exactly one period to the right. In this problem the period is 6; hence multiply by 10^6:

$$10^6 x = 142857.\overline{142857} = 142857 + 0.\overline{142857}$$
$$= 142857 + x,$$
$$(10^6 - 1) \cdot x = 142857,$$
$$x = \tfrac{142857}{999999} = \tfrac{1}{7} \qquad \text{(note that the numerator is the common factor)}.$$

Finally, consider the periodic decimal

$$x = 0.81515\ldots = 0.8\overline{15}.$$

If, as in this case, the repeating string of digits does not begin at the decimal point, then multiply first on both sides by a power of 10 sufficient to move the decimal point to the beginning of the repeating string:

$$10x = 10 \cdot 0.8\overline{15} = 8.\overline{15}.$$

Now, as in the preceding case, multiply again on both sides by a power of 10 sufficient to move the decimal point exactly one period to the right:

$$100(10x) = 1000x = 815.\overline{15}.$$

Since
$$10x = 8.\overline{15},$$

we have
$$1000x = 807 + 8.\overline{15} = 807 + 10x.$$

Hence,
$$990x = 807,$$

or
$$x = \tfrac{807}{990} = \tfrac{269}{330}.$$

The arguments given above generalize readily, and they illustrate the procedure by which we can construct the rational fraction which corresponds to any given periodic decimal. Hence, Theorem 6.4A turns out to be reversible, and we can claim the logical equivalence of rational fractions and terminating or periodic decimals.

THEOREM 6.4B | A number is rational if and only if it has a terminating or periodic decimal representation.

Tutorial 6.4

Find the rational fraction corresponding to the periodic decimal 0.18.

6.5 The fraction $\frac{142857}{999999}$ referred to earlier in this section was generated from the decimal representation of $\frac{1}{7}$. Thus, we knew in advance that cancellation of all common divisors in 142,857 and 999,999 would reduce that fraction to its lowest form, $\frac{1}{7}$, in which numerator and denominator are relatively prime. But without prior information, it may be very tedious to determine the **greatest common divisor** (gcd) which must be canceled in order to reduce a given fraction to its lowest form. For example, what is the lowest form of the fraction $\frac{2873}{15067}$? Of course, trial and error beginning with the smaller primes will eventually produce the result. But this is not a very exciting method and, in general, is likely to be quite tedious. It turns out, however, that there is a very important procedure, known to Euclid and now called the **Euclidean Algorithm,** which produces the gcd of two positive integers. We look first at an example.

Example 1 Find the gcd of the two integers 2873 and 15,067. We make repeated use of the division algorithm:

$$15067 = 2873 \cdot 5 + 702,$$
$$2873 = 702 \cdot 4 + 65,$$
$$702 = 65 \cdot 10 + 52,$$
$$65 = 52 \cdot 1 + 13,$$
$$52 = 13 \cdot 4 + 0.$$

[This is an example of an algorithm which predates by many centuries al-Khwārizmī (see paragraphs 3.9 and 4.7)]. The smallest nonzero remainder, 13, is the desired gcd of 2873 and 15067. We justify this claim in the following argument. Let d be the gcd of 2873 and 15067.

Since $15067 - (2873 \cdot 5) = 702,$ d is a divisor of 702.

Since $2873 - (702 \cdot 4) = 65,$ d is a divisor of 65.

Since $702 - (65 \cdot 10) = 52,$ d is a divisor of 52.

Since $65 - (52 \cdot 1) = 13,$ d is a divisor of 13.

Hence, $d \leq 13$. But, now, 13 is a divisor of 52, hence of 65, hence of 702, hence of 2873, hence of 15,067. This shows that 13 is a common divisor of 2873 and 15,067; hence $13 \leq d$. These two inequalities show that $d = 13$.

Finally, since $2873 = 13 \cdot 221$ and $15,067 = 13 \cdot 1159$, $\frac{221}{1159}$ is the lowest form of the rational fraction $\frac{2873}{15067}$.

Tutorial 6.5

a. Use the Euclidean Algorithm to find the gcd of the integers 105 and 1386.

b. Express the fraction $\frac{105}{1386}$ in its lowest form.

6.6   Our problem now is to describe the Euclidean Algorithm in general: It will begin with positive integers a and b, $b < a$, and will produce the greatest common divisor of the two numbers. As indicated in Example 1 of paragraph 6.5, the division algorithm is used multiple times, and it will be convenient to identify each use by subscripts.

First, apply the division algorithm to a and b, obtaining quotient q_1 and remainder r_1:

$$a = b \cdot q_1 + r_1.$$

Next, apply the division algorithm to b and r_1, obtaining quotient q_2 and remainder r_2:

$$b = r_1 \cdot q_2 + r_2.$$

Next, apply the division algorithm to r_1 and r_2, obtaining quotient q_3 and remainder r_3:

$$r_1 = r_2 \cdot q_3 + r_3.$$

The procedure continues until the new remainder is 0. The smallest nonzero remainder is then the desired gcd. If k is a positive integer for which $r_k > 0$ and $r_{k+1} = 0$, then the full display is

$$a = b \cdot q_1 + r_1,$$
$$b = r_1 \cdot q_2 + r_2,$$
$$r_1 = r_2 \cdot q_3 + r_3,$$
$$\vdots$$
$$r_{k-2} = r_{k-1} \cdot q_k + r_k,$$
$$r_{k-1} = r_k \cdot q_{k+1} + r_{k+1}.$$

By the properties of the division algorithm,

$$r_1 > r_2 > r_3 > \cdots > r_k > 0,$$

hence the algorithm must end in not more than $r_1 + 1$ steps.

The proof in Example 1 of paragraph 6.5 that 13 was the required gcd generalizes without complication. The idea is to show that r_k is a common divisor of a and b and that no number greater than r_k is a common divisor of a and b. Central to this argument is the fact that sums and differences of numbers divisible by m are themselves divisible by m (see Theorem 3.7).

6.7 Finally, we consider the question of how a machine might be designed to implement the Euclidean Algorithm. We will assume that it has registers where numbers may be stored and that it can perform both division of one integer by another and comparison of one integer with another. The following flowchart illustrates the structure of the procedure. As the initial assignment, insert the positive integer a in register N, and insert the positive integer b in register M.

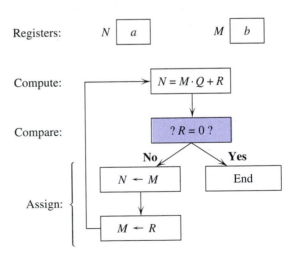

The meaning of the "assign" boxes is:

- Current number in register M is inserted in register N.
- Current remainder is then inserted in register M.

The order in which these assign operations is carried out is "noncommutative." Thus, if R is assigned to M first, then the previous content of M is erased. Hence when M is assigned to N, both N and M wind up containing R; not at all what is needed!

Moral.   **The sequencing of operations in an algorithm is critical.**

As its first step, the machine determines q and r so that

$$a = b \cdot q + r,$$

which is possible because it knows how to "divide." As its second step, the machine decides whether or not r is 0; possible this time because it knows how to "compare" numbers. It then proceeds to reassign b and r (if a second loop is necessary) and prepares to pick up the new entries in registers N and M for the next loop. At the beginning of each succeeding loop the machine computes the new formula $N = M \cdot Q + R$, compares R with 0, and continues. After some finite number of loops the remainder will be 0, and the algorithm ends. At that point, the current number in register M is the gcd of a and b.

6.8

Complement: Floors and Ceilings

The Pigeonhole Principle is a very simple version of an important class of problems having to do with **minimization:** Given some appropriate objective, we seek the minimum-sized set which will guarantee that objective. For example, if one has the same number of pigeons and pigeonholes, even though most of the possible roosting patterns place more than one pigeon in some pigeonhole, we cannot guarantee that *every* pattern does so. It takes, however, only *one* additional pigeon to ensure that at least two birds are in some hole, no matter what the distribution. Now, it's a common mistake to jump to the conclusion that *two* additional pigeons will guarantee three birds in some hole. But, unless there is only one pigeonhole, it is easy to find a distribution in which two holes contain two birds each and the rest have one bird each. Suppose that our objective is to have at least three pigeons in some pigeonhole, *regardless* of the distribution. Then we must ensure that the average number of pigeons per pigeonhole is greater than 2 (not necessarily 3 or more, but any real number greater than 2). If a bookcase in your room has four shelves and if you load eight books into it, then the average number of books per shelf is 2, and it's possible to avoid a distribution in which some shelf contains three books. If, however, nine books are loaded into the book case, then the average number of books per shelf is 2.25, and it's no longer possible to avoid having at least three books on one shelf.

We may formalize these considerations in the following:

Generalized Pigeonhole Principle

If **A** denotes a set containing m elements, each of which belongs to exactly one of n subsets of **A**, then at least one of those subsets contains at least m/n elements.

Notice that m/n is simply the average number of elements per subset. At the risk of belaboring the obvious, suppose that the subsets are labeled $1, 2, \ldots, n$, and suppose that m_i is the number of elements in the subset labeled i. If for each i, $m_i < m/n$, then

$$m = m_1 + m_2 + \cdots + m_n < \underbrace{\frac{m}{n} + \frac{m}{n} + \cdots + \frac{m}{n}}_{n \text{ terms}} = m.$$

Since no number is less than itself, this is a contradiction; hence at least one subset must contain at least m/n elements.

Example 1

Suppose that you are one of 12 students in a seminar, and suppose that the instructor brings a box of doughnuts to share with the class. If the box contains a baker's dozen, then a possible distribution is one doughnut to each of the 13 individuals present. Just one additional doughnut in the box (making a total of 14) is enough to guarantee that at least one person gets more than one doughnut (Shall we assume it to be the instructor?). If the box, however, contains 27 doughnuts, then the average is $\frac{27}{13}$ (which is slightly larger than 2.07); hence by the generalized Pigeonhole Principle at least one individual must have more than 2.07 doughnuts. When we speak of "doughnuts" (or "pigeons" or "elements" in this context), we will assume that they come in "wholes" so that "more than 2.07" really means "at least 3."

Although m/n is a perfectly good rational number, in the context of discrete mathematics its fractional part (if any) may not be meaningful. Two special symbols have been devised to suppress fractional parts, called **floor** and **ceiling,** denoted by $\lfloor x \rfloor$ and $\lceil x \rceil$, respectively. Here's how to find them. Let x denote any real number, and think of x as it appears on a vertically drawn number axis. Then, if x is an integer,

$$\begin{cases} \text{floor}(x) = \lfloor x \rfloor = x, \\ \text{ceiling}(x) = \lceil x \rceil = x; \end{cases}$$

and if x is not an integer,

$$\begin{cases} \text{floor}(x) \text{ is the next integer below } x, \\ \text{ceiling}(x) \text{ is the next integer above } x. \end{cases}$$

Thus, if x is any real number, then $\lfloor x \rfloor$ is the greatest integer less than or equal to x, and $\lceil x \rceil$ is the smallest integer greater than or equal to x.

Example 2

x	0	1	-1	$\sqrt{2}$	$-\sqrt{2}$	π	$-\pi$	$\frac{49}{3}$	$-\frac{49}{3}$	43.9	-43.9
$\lfloor x \rfloor$	0	1	-1	1	-2	3	-4	16	-17	43	-44
$\lceil x \rceil$	0	1	-1	2	-1	4	-3	17	-16	44	-43

The notation used above for "floor" and "ceiling" has been widely adopted, especially in computer science. In mathematics, the "greatest integer function" is a more traditional name for the concept which we have described as "floor," and it is usually denoted by $[x]$. This is a nice example of a function which is defined on the entire real axis but has only integer values. From the appearance of its graph (Figure 6.8A) it is called a step function. You should examine this graph very carefully; then sketch the corresponding graph for the ceiling function.

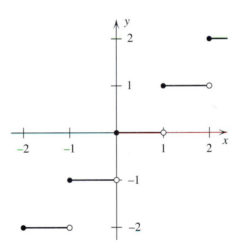

Figure 6.8A   Graph of $\lfloor x \rfloor$, or the greatest integer function, $[x]$.

From a careful study of the table in Example 2, it should be clear that there is a regular relationship between the floor and ceiling functions.

THEOREM
6.8

For any real number x,

$$\lceil x \rceil = -\lfloor -x \rfloor.$$

Proof

If x is an integer, then so is $-x$; hence $\lfloor -x \rfloor = -x$, and

$$-\lfloor -x \rfloor = -(-x) = x = \lceil x \rceil.$$

If x is not an integer, then suppose x satisfies the inequality

$$m < x < m + 1,$$

where m is an integer. Thus $\lfloor x \rfloor = m$ and $\lceil x \rceil = m+1$. Negating the inequality yields $-m - 1 < -x < -m$. Hence $\lfloor -x \rfloor = -m - 1$, and so

$$-\lfloor -x \rfloor = -(-m - 1) = m + 1 = \lceil x \rceil. \qquad \blacksquare$$

Returning to the statement of the generalized Pigeonhole Principle, observe that at least one of the subsets must contain at least $\lceil m/n \rceil$ elements.

Example 3

You have a square dartboard measuring 1 foot on a side. You throw nine darts, all of which hit the board. Why is it that at least three of the darts cannot be separated from one another by more than $(\sqrt{2})/2$ feet? Divide the board into four equal squares, $\frac{1}{2}$ foot on a side (as in Figure 6.8B). Then at least $\lceil \frac{9}{4} \rceil = 3$ darts fall in the same smaller square, hence cannot be farther apart than the diagonal of the square, which is $(\sqrt{2})/2$ feet.

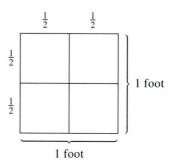

Figure 6.8B

Finally, here is a somewhat more elaborate application.

Example 4

A gambler (G) offers the following game to a sucker (S). G antes 40 $1 bills to the pot, and S adds 15 $1 bills. S gets to keep the entire pot if the bills can be arranged in 10 piles around a circle subject to two conditions:

a. All piles contain different numbers of bills.

b. No three consecutive piles contain more than 16 bills.

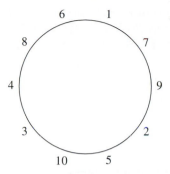

Figure 6.8C

See Figure 6.8C for an attempt by S. Why is it that G is really not gambling—S cannot win the pot?

S soon discovers that the piles must contain 1, 2, 3, 4, 5, 6, 7, 8, 9, and 10 bills, since the sum is $55. Now, think about condition **b**. There are exactly 10 sets of three consecutive piles [in Figure 6.8C they are (1, 7, 9), (7, 9, 2), (9, 2, 5), etc.]. But *we note that if we add up all the different sums from all 10 sets of three consecutive piles, the grand total is 165*: because in this process, each bill is counted exactly three times. Now think of 165 pigeons and 10 pigeonholes (pigeonhole = set of three consecutive piles). Some pigeonhole must contain $\lceil \frac{165}{10} \rceil = 17$ pigeons.

A closing note is in order. The generalized Pigeonhole Principle guarantees that there are three consecutive piles with at least 17 bills in them; it provides no evidence beyond that. Possibly, however, a slightly stronger claim is true. All the examples that we have constructed so far have three consecutive piles with at least 18 bills in them. Can this observation be proved? We don't know the answer. ⬤

Problems for Section 6

1. Find the equivalent rational fraction with relatively prime numerator and denominator. (*a*) $\frac{9}{15}$, (*b*) $\frac{32}{48}$, (*c*) $\frac{19}{57}$, (*d*) $\frac{26}{169}$, (*e*) $\frac{35}{63}$, (*f*) $\frac{289}{323}$.

2. Find the equivalent rational fraction with relatively prime numerator and denominator. (*a*) $\frac{259}{333}$, (*b*) $\frac{330}{484}$, (*c*) $\frac{231}{1820}$.

3. Find a periodic decimal expansion and state its period. (*a*) $\frac{9}{11}$, (*b*) $\frac{18}{37}$, (*c*) $\frac{68}{165}$, (*d*) $\frac{22}{111}$.

4. Find a periodic decimal expansion and state its period. (*a*) $\frac{3}{13}$, (*b*) $\frac{14}{39}$, (*c*) $\frac{5}{13}$.

5. Find the decimal expansion and period of $n/7$ for $n = 1, 2, 3, 4, 5, 6$.

6. Find a fraction representing the periodic decimal. (*a*) 0.1111..., (*b*) 0.2222..., (*c*) 0.5555..., (*d*) 0.8888....

7. Find a fraction representing the periodic decimal. (*a*) 0.1313..., (*b*) 0.241313..., (*c*) 0.123123..., (*d*) 0.011001100110....

8. Find a fraction representing the periodic decimal. (*a*) 0.999..., (*b*) 0.0999..., (*c*) 0.3999..., (*d*) 0.127999....

9. Extrapolating from Problem 8, express each terminating decimal as a periodic decimal. (*a*) 0.013, (*b*) 0.21, (*c*) 0.375, (*d*) 0.81999.

10. Extrapolating from Problems 8 and 9, show that r is rational if and only if r has a periodic decimal expansion. (Refer to Theorem 6.4B.)

11. Let d represent a digit. If the denominator of x is 1111, then find d when (a) $x = 0.015d015d\ldots$, (b) $x = 0.017d017d\ldots$.

12. How many students must a class have to guarantee that (a) at least two students have the same birth month and (b) at least three students have the same birth month?

13. You have 14 pigeons and 12 pigeonholes. (a) Does this guarantee that at least two pigeonholes have more than one occupant? (b) Same question if, in addition, no pigeonhole can hold more than two pigeons.

14. Eight individuals share a sack of doughnuts. How many doughnuts must there be to guarantee that at least one indiviual has four doughnuts?

15. A rural mail route has exactly 143 boxes. How many letters must be delivered on this route to guarantee that some box will receive at least three letters?

16. A man has six black socks and six blue socks in a drawer. How many must he pick (in the dark) to guarantee a matching pair? How many must he pick to guarantee a blue pair?

17. Find five nonprime positive integers, each of which is relatively prime to 9.

18. List all the positive integers less than 30 which are relatively prime to 6.

19. List all the positive integers which are less than 30 and relatively prime to 30. What do you observe about these numbers?

20. Find the least integer n for which it is true that there are exactly five nonprime positive integers, each of which is less than n and relatively prime to n. (The answer isn't 11 since $\{1, 4, 6, 8, 9, 10\}$ contains six nonprime integers.)

21. Use the Euclidean Algorithm to show that 260 and 33 are relatively prime.

22. Of course, you could have answered Problem 21 more easily by factoring each number. For the numbers 2717 and 1369, however, it will probably be easier to show that they are relatively prime by the Euclidean Algorithm.

23. Use the Euclidean Algorithm to find the gcd of 420 and 270.

24. Use the Euclidean Algorithm to find the gcd of 1820 and 231.

25. Use the Pigeonhole Principle to show that for any 11 positive integers, the difference between some two of them is divisible by 10. (*Hint:* Consider the unit's digit of the numbers with the pigeonholes being the digits $0, 1, \ldots, 9$.)

26. Given any 11 integers (positive, negative, or zero), is it true that the difference of some two of them is divisible by 10?

27. There were seven students who always compared their discrete test grades. They discovered that either the sum of two grades or the difference of two grades was always divisible by 10. Use the Pigeonhole Principle to show that for any seven positive integers, either the sum of two or the difference of two is divisble by 10. (*Hint:* The pigeonholes are $\{0\}$, $\{5\}$, $\{1, 9\}$, $\{2, 8\}$, $\{3, 7\}$, $\{4, 6\}$. Again consider the unit's digit of the numbers.)

28. (*Conclusion of Problem 27.*) Find a set of six positive integers so that neither the sum of two nor the difference of two is divisible by 10.

29. You have an equilateral-triangular dartboard of side 2 feet. Show that if you throw five darts at the board, two of them are within 1 foot of each other.

30. What is the least number of cards that must be drawn from a deck of 52 cards to ensure that two are from the same suit? Why?

31. Prove that your bank statement for any 10-year period will have, at least twice, exactly the same number of cents in its monthly balance.

32. Use common sense and the Pigeonhole Principle to show that during the last year at least 10 people in the United States earned the same income, to the penny. (*Hint:* The U.S. population is over 200,000,000, and over half the population earned less than $100,000.00.)

33. Find a string of 20 zeroes and ones with exactly 11 ones such that no 2 ones are exactly 3 apart in the list. (*Hint:* One such string starts 111000....)

34. In any list of 19 zeroes and ones with exactly 12 ones show that at least 2 of the ones are exactly 3 apart in the list. (*Hint:* If $a_1a_2a_3a_4a_5\ldots$ is such a string, place a duplicate of it underneath the original string but offset by 3.

$$a_1a_2a_3a_4a_5\ldots$$
$$\quad\quad a_1a_2a_3a_4a_5\ldots$$

If there are 2 ones in a column, then these 2 ones are 3 apart in the original string. How many ones are in both strings, and how many columns are there?

35. With discrete mathematics being such a popular course, there are usually long lines of students waiting to sign up for the course at registration time. Observing the line of 80 students, we noticed that there were 45 women and 35 men in line. It was also the case that at least 2 of the women were 9 apart in the line. One more man broke into the line, and then no 2 women were 9 apart. Find such a line. (Women at positions 14 and 23 are 9 apart; women can, of course, be closer than 9 apart.)

36. Show that in a line with 45 women and 35 men, 2 women must be 9 apart in the line. (*Hint:* Consider Problem 34.)

37. Let $x = 69.999\ldots$, $y = 0.0142857142857\ldots$, $z = 0.444\ldots$, and $w = 1.555\ldots$. Write $(x+y)/(z+w)$ as a rational fraction in lowest terms. (*a*) To convert $10y$ to a rational fraction, consult Problem 5. (*b*) Note also that $z + w = 1.999\ldots$ and use Problem 8 to convert $z + w$ and x to rational fractions.

38. Let $x = 14.999\ldots$, $y = 0.0333\ldots$, $z = 1.777\ldots$, and $w = 0.222\ldots$. Write $(x+y)/(z+w)$ as a rational fraction in lowest terms.

39. One of the most infamous alphanumeric puzzles is the following:

$$\frac{EVE}{DID} = 0.\overline{TALKTALK}\ldots$$

Here each letter is a different digit, and the fraction on the left is in lowest terms. Find the digit associated with each letter.

40. One of your friends writes down 26 of the integers in the set $\{1, 2, 3, 4, \ldots, 50\}$. Show that there must be two of your friend's integers so that one of the two divides the other. (*Hint:* Let the pigeonholes be labeled by $1, 3, 5, \ldots, 49$. Put the number n into pigeonhole q, where $n = 2^e q$ with q odd. For example, both $24 = 2^3 \cdot 3$ and $48 = 2^4 \cdot 3$ go into pigeonhole 3.)

41. Note that if $x = 0.\overline{a_1a_2\ldots a_k}$, then

$$x = \frac{a_1a_2\ldots a_k}{10^k - 1}.$$

Find a similar expression for x if
(*a*) $x = 0.b_1b_2\ldots b_r\overline{a_1a_2\ldots a_k}$,
(*b*) $x = 0.a_1a_2\ldots a_k$.

42. Using the Euclidean Algorithm it can be shown that if $\gcd(a, b) = 1$, then there are integers x and y such that $ax + by = 1$. For example, $\gcd(28, 9) = 1; 28 = 9 \cdot 3 + 1$, and so $1 = 1 \cdot 28 + (-3) \cdot 9$. For another example consider 28 and 15.

$$28 = 15 \cdot 1 + 13 \qquad \text{(Step 1)}$$
$$15 = 13 \cdot 1 + 2 \qquad \text{(Step 2)}$$
$$13 = 2 \cdot 6 + 1. \qquad \text{(Step 3)}$$

So gcd(28, 15) = 1. Now

$$1 = 13 - (2 \cdot 6) \qquad \text{(Step 3)}$$

$$= 13 - ((15 - 13) \cdot 6) \qquad \text{(Step 2)}$$
$$= (7 \cdot 13) - (6 \cdot 15) \qquad \text{(Simplify)}$$
$$= (7(28 - 15)) - (6 \cdot 15) \qquad \text{(Step 1)}$$
$$= (7 \cdot 28) - (13 \cdot 15). \qquad \text{(Simplify)}$$

Thus $1 = 28x + 15y$, where $x = 7$ and $y = -13$. Find x and y such that $2717x + 1369y = 1$.

Section 7.   Irrationals and One-to-One Correspondence

Overview for Section 7

- Introduction of nonterminating, nonperiodic decimals
- Proof that $\sqrt{2}$ is not a rational fraction
- Geometric technique for locating $\sqrt{2}$ and $\sqrt{3}$ on the real number axis; decimal approximations
- One-to-one correspondence between real numbers and points on the real number axis
- Applications of the Fundamental Theorem of Arithmetic (FTOA)

Key Concepts: irrational numbers, one-to-one correspondence, decimal approximation to certain irrationals, Fundamental Theorem of Arithmetic

7.1   Return to the number axes mentioned in paragraph 1.1 on which we had marked several points with integer coordinates. Of course, it is easy to imagine that rational fractions also can be used as coordinates of points on an axis; for example, $\frac{1}{2}$ is the coordinate of the midpoint of the interval between the origin and the point labeled 1, and $-\frac{1}{3}$ is the coordinate of the point which is one-third of the way from the origin to the point labeled -1. If we continue to mark points with rational fraction coordinates, it soon appears that these points occur everywhere on the axis. (Try marking just 20 such points in the unit interval.) But this is an illusion: One of the most fascinating chapters in the history of mathematics deals with the paradoxical nature of the set of real numbers. The story is a long one, and in this section we take only the first steps along the way. The full story belongs to another branch of mathematics, but we will touch on it once again in paragraph 15.6.

We know from the preceding section that all rational fractions are represented by decimals which are either terminating or periodic. With a little imagination it is possible to describe decimals which are neither terminating nor periodic; for example,

$$x_1 = 0.12345678910111213\ldots$$

or
$$x_2 = 0.101001000100001000001\ldots.$$

The pattern in each case seems clear enough; what is not so clear is the meaning ascribed to x_1, for example. Once again, the full story belongs elsewhere, but in brief x_1 is assumed to designate a real number which lies

Between the rational numbers 0.1 and 0.2,

Between the rational numbers 0.12 and 0.13,

Between the rational numbers 0.123 and 0.124,

and so on, to any desired approximation. (The "completeness axiom" referred to in paragraph 2.8 is at work here.)

Tutorial 7.1

Construct a nonterminating, nonperiodic decimal on each of the following three intervals:
a. Between 1 and 2,
b. Between −1 and 0,
c. Between 0 and 1.

Nonterminating, nonperiodic decimals are called **irrational numbers,** and they together with the rational numbers (which include, of course, the integers) are called the set of **real numbers.** It is a fundamental property of mathematics that each real number identifies a position on the number axis (in the familiar ordering), and that each point on the number axis is identified with a particular real number. This is an example of a **one-to-one correspondence** between two sets. Explicitly, if **A** denotes the set of all points on the number line and if $\mathbb{R}$ denotes the set of all real numbers, then to each point in **A** corresponds exactly one number in $\mathbb{R}$ (called its coordinate) and to each number in $\mathbb{R}$ corresponds exactly one point in **A**.

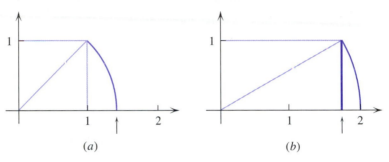

(a)   (b)

Figure 7.2

7.2

Because irrational numbers are located only approximately between given rational numbers, one might ask whether a geometrically precise location for any irrational number can be determined. Consider for example, the two geometric constructions in Figure 7.2 (the axes are perpendicular to one another, and the arcs are parts of circles centered at the origin). In Figure 7.2a, the arrow indicates the point in which the circular arc intersects the horizontal axis; in Figure 7.2b, the arrow indicates the intersection of a vertical segment with the horizontal axis. These points on the axis correspond to real numbers, and an application of the Pythagorean Theorem in each case shows that the real numbers are $\sqrt{2}$ in (a) and $\sqrt{3}$ in (b).

Having identified points corresponding to $\sqrt{2}$ and $\sqrt{3}$, it is appropriate to ask, "What kind of numbers are they, rational or irrational?" Look back at Example 4 in paragraph 2.8. If, indeed, the statement in that example is a theorem, then $\sqrt{2}$ must be an irrational number. Recall that rational numbers are characterized as quotients of integers. Since we have agreed that $\sqrt{2}$ is a real number, we may show that it is irrational simply by proving that it cannot be rational.

Tutorial 7.2A

a. Label the appropriate triangles in Figure 7.2 to show that the arrows indicate points corresponding to $\sqrt{2}$ and $\sqrt{3}$.

b. Using a straightedge and compass, give a geometric construction (as in Figure 7.2) which determines the point on the horizontal axis corresponding to the real number $\sqrt{5}$.

THEOREM 7.2

The number $\sqrt{2}$ is not a rational fraction.

Proof

(This is another example of proof by contradiction.) Assume that $\sqrt{2}$ *can* be represented as a quotient of two integers p/q. Of course, we may cancel out any common factors in numerator and denominator, so it is reasonable to assert that

The integers p and q are relatively prime.　　　　　**(1)**

Thus, by assumption, $\sqrt{2} = p/q$, and now squaring both sides yields

$$2 = \frac{p^2}{q^2} \qquad \text{or} \qquad p^2 = 2q^2.$$

This says that p^2 is even, and by Theorem 5.2, p must also be even. So we can write $p = 2k$, and it follows that $p^2 = 4k^2$. But p^2 also equals $2q^2$, so $2q^2 = 4k^2$ from which $q^2 = 2k^2$. This says that q^2 is even, and again by Theorem 5.2, q must also be even. Hence it follows that p and q both have 2 as a common factor, and

The integers p and q are not relatively prime.　　　　　**(2)**

Statements (1) and (2) are contradictory. The original assumption, therefore, must be false; hence $\sqrt{2}$ *cannot* be represented as a quotient of two integers. ∎

Tutorial 7.2B

It will be good practice to prove that $\sqrt{3}$ is irrational. The proof is almost identical with the one above: use "divisible by 3" in place of "even," and refer to Theorem 5.3.

7.3　There remains a question. Since $\sqrt{2}$ is irrational, its decimal representation must be nonterminating and nonperiodic. Thus we can never write out (or, indeed, know) its decimal representation in full. But we *can* approximate it to any reasonable accuracy by making use of the order properties of real numbers. The fact needed is stated in the following theorem, which (among positive numbers) is the converse of Theorem 3.2.

THEOREM 7.3

If x and y are positive real numbers for which $x^2 < y^2$, then $x < y$.

Proof

Since $x^2 < y^2$,

$$0 < y^2 - x^2 = (y - x)(y + x). \tag{1}$$

Because x and y are positive, so is $y + x$ and $1/(y + x)$. Multiplying both sides of (1) by $1/(y + x)$, we find $0 < y - x$, which means $x < y$. ∎

Example 1

Let $x^2 = 9$ and $y^2 = 16$; hence $x^2 < y^2$. From (1),

$$0 < y^2 - x^2 = (y - x)(y + x),$$
$$0 < 16 - 9 = (4 - 3)(4 + 3).$$

Certainly $3 < 4$, as required by Theorem 7.3, but suppose we had factored $16 - 9$ as follows:

$$0 < 16 - 9 = ((-4) - 3)((-4) + 3).$$

It is certainly *not* the case that $3 < -4$. This error results from thinking of x as 3 ($3^2 = 9$) and of y as -4 ($(-4)^2 = 16$), in violation of the condition that x and y be positive. Note, once again, that unless the hypothesis is true, an implication (such as Theorem 7.3) is useless as a predictor of the conclusion.

Example 2

To find the first four decimals in $\sqrt{2}$ we begin by observing from Figure 7.2a that $\sqrt{2}$ is about 1.4. Since $(1.4)^2 = 1.96$, it follows that $1.4 < \sqrt{2}$, but not by much. Since, also, a quick calculation shows that

$$(1.41)^2 = 1.9881 \quad \text{and} \quad (1.42)^2 = 2.0164,$$

we must have

$$1.41 < \sqrt{2} < 1.42.$$

Similarly, by trial and error, we find

$$1.414 < \sqrt{2} < 1.415,$$

and

$$1.4142 < \sqrt{2} < 1.4143.$$

Hence the required answer is 1.4142. To indicate how close this approximation is note that $2 - (1.4142)^2 < 0.00004$ and $(1.4143)^2 - 2 < 0.00025$. Thus, 1.4142 is a closer approximation than 1.4143.

We might refer to this technique as "squeezing down" on the answer. It works in this case because of the property stated in Theorem 7.3.

Tutorial 7.3

a. Show that $\sqrt{3}$ is between 1.73 and 1.74.
b. Which one of those decimals is the closer approximation?

7.4   At the beginning of this section we illustrated the very important idea of one-to-one correspondence. In general, two sets **A** and **B** are in **one-to-one correspondence** if it is possible to pair off the elements (one from **A** with one from **B**) in such a way that no elements are left over in either set and no element in either set is used more than once. We will return to this idea many times in later sections, both in reference to infinite sets (as here) but especially to finite sets. One-to-one correspondence turns out to be the natural tool to use in deciding whether two sets have the same number of elements when a simple count of the elements is impractical. Some further illustrations appear in Example 1; more detailed discussion is best postponed until the need arises.

Example 1

a. If $\mathbf{A} = \{1, 2, 3\}$ and $\mathbf{B} = \{a, b, c\}$, then a possible one-to-one correspondence is given by the pairing

$$(1, a), (2, b), (3, c).$$

b. If $\mathbf{A} = \{1, 2, 3\}$ and $\mathbf{B} = \{a, b, c, d\}$, then no such pairing is possible without having an element of **B** left over or using an element of **A** twice. Thus there exists no one-to-one correspondence between **A** and **B**.

c. If $\mathbf{A} = \{1, 2, 3, 4, \ldots\}$ and $\mathbf{B} = \{1, 3, 5, 7, \ldots\}$, then a possible pairing is

$$(1, 1), (2, 3), (3, 5), (4, 7), \ldots, (n, 2n - 1), \ldots$$

where $n \in \mathbb{N}$. Note that the second coordinate is always 1 less than twice the first coordinate.

d. If $\mathbf{A} = \{0, 1, 2, 3, \ldots\}$ and $\mathbf{B} = \{1, 3, 5, 7, \ldots\}$, then a possible pairing is

$$(0, 1), (1, 3), (2, 5), (3, 7), \ldots, (n, 2n + 1), \ldots$$

where n is a nonnegative integer. Note that the second coordinate is always 1 more than twice the first coordinate.

e. If a commercial airliner is flying at full capacity, then there is a one-to-one correspondence between the set of passengers and the set of seats in the passenger compartments.

7.5

The set of all positive integers can be separated into three subsets:

The unit	{1},
The primes	{2, 3, 5, 7, 11, ...},
The composites	{4, 6, 8, 9, 10, ...}.

Any composite number can be factored into a product of prime numbers. Some of the primes may be repeated, as in

$$15{,}246 = 2 \cdot 3^2 \cdot 7 \cdot 11^2 \qquad \text{or} \qquad 32 = 2^5.$$

Suppose we agree in this section to express composites as products of primes without exponents greater than 1; so each prime factor is listed separately, as in

$$15{,}246 = 2 \cdot 3 \cdot 3 \cdot 7 \cdot 11 \cdot 11 \qquad \text{or} \qquad 32 = 2 \cdot 2 \cdot 2 \cdot 2 \cdot 2.$$

It seems quite clear that there is no other possible way of expressing these composites as products of primes (except for a rearrangement of the factors). This observation is true in general, but the proof, which is given in most texts on number theory, is quite subtle. Because the result is so important in problems relating to factorization, it is often referred to as the **Fundamental Theorem of Arithmetic** (abbreviated FTOA).

THEOREM 7.5A (FTOA)

A positive integer greater than I is either a prime or can be factored into a product of primes in one and only one way (except for rearrangement of the factors).

We will not include a proof of this theorem here. What it says, essentially, is that if t is a composite number and if

$$t = p_1 p_2 \cdots p_n \qquad \text{and} \qquad t = q_1 q_2 \cdots q_m$$

where each of the factors is a prime, then there is a one-to-one correspondence between the p factors and the q factors under which the corresponding factors are identical. This implies that $m = n$ and that the q factors are simply a rearrangement of the p factors. Thus, in any factorization of a composite number into a product of primes without exponents greater than 1, each prime must occur the same number of times.

The result just stated can be made the basis of a second proof that $\sqrt{2}$ is not a rational number. More importantly, this new method of proof generalizes immediately to a wide class of comparable results.

Alternate Proof of Theorem 7.2

Again, assume that $\sqrt{2}$ can be represented as a quotient of integers (they need not be considered relatively prime), $\sqrt{2} = r/s$, or $2s^2 = r^2$. Note that if any prime p appears among the factors of a number t, then p necessarily appears an even number of times among the factors of t^2. Thus the prime 2 must appear an even number of times among the factors of r^2 and of s^2. By FTOA, the composite numbers $2s^2$ and r^2 must have the same prime factorization. But the prime number 2 appears an odd number of times in the factorization of $2s^2$ and an even number of times in the factorization of r^2, so we have a contradiction.   ■

What about the generalization? Let x be any positive integer which has a prime factorization in which some prime number, say p, occurs an odd number of times. Then $\sqrt{x}$ is not a rational number, and the proof is almost identical to that above. Note that such numbers x include all primes as well as composites like 6, 10, 12, 200, etc. For example, to show that $\sqrt{12}$ is not rational, assume that it is:

$$\sqrt{12} = \frac{r}{s}.$$

Then $\qquad\qquad 12s^2 = r^2 \qquad$ or $\qquad 2 \cdot 2 \cdot 3s^2 = r^2.$

Now, it's clear that the prime number 3 appears a different number of times in the factorizations of $12s^2$ and r^2, which contradicts FTOA. Here is the formal statement of the generalization.

THEOREM 7.5B If x is any positive integer which has a prime factorization in which some prime occurs an odd number of times, then $\sqrt{x}$ is not a rational number.

Tutorial 7.5

Construct the proof of Theorem 7.5B. It will be almost identical to the proof, above, that $\sqrt{12}$ is not rational.

7.6

Complement: The Golden Section In paragraph 7.2 we considered the geometric determination of line segments having irrational lengths $\sqrt{2}$, $\sqrt{3}$, and $\sqrt{5}$. The figures were set, for convenience, in a rectangular coordinate system (as in Figure 7.2), but this was unnecessary. The ancient Greeks already had learned to construct such segments using only the classical tools of straightedge and compass. In fact, they could construct the square root of any positive integer (compare with Problems 28 and 29 in Section 11). But other problems, surprisingly simple in statement, eluded their every effort. For example, they could easily bisect an arbitrarily given angle, but they were unable to discover how to trisect it. They **did** know that the trisection problem could be solved through the use of slightly more sophisticated instruments, but the "mystique" of geometry via straightedge and compass persisted as a dominant theme in geometry, and the trisection problem remained unresolved for the next two *millennia*. Finally, by the nineteenth century, mathematicians had discovered how to describe geometric operations in algebraic terms, and they were then able to prove that the problem of trisecting an arbitrarily given angle **could not** be solved using straightedge and compass alone. This interplay between geometry and algebra is a fascinating chapter in the history of mathematics and is fundamental to what we have called "continuous" mathematics.

We return now to another important (and positive) accomplishment of Greek mathematics. More than 25 centuries ago they solved the problem referred to as dividing a line segment into "extreme and mean ratio": Given a line segment AB,

divide it by a point C in such a way that the ratios AB/AC and AC/CB are equal.

Why were they interested in this problem? One reason is suggested by constructing a rectangle on the segment AB of height AC, as in Figure 7.6A. To Greek artists and builders, the proportions of this rectangle were especially pleasing aesthetically; its shape appears repeatedly among the surviving examples of their work (including the Parthenon in Athens). Indeed, throughout succeeding centuries, in art and architecture (and in "primitive" science) the extreme and mean ratio retained its influential role. In the Renaissance it was referred to as the "divine proportion," and in the nineteenth century it became known as the "golden section."

The solution to the original problem which actually appears in Euclid's *Elements* determines the point C on the given segment AB in such a way that the square with side AC has the same area as the rectangle with sides AB and BC. We will give an argument which, in a modest way, suggests how algebra can be made to interact with geometry. To simplify computation, we will assume that the given segment AB has unit length, and we will let x denote the (unknown) length of segment AC (Figure 7.6B). The condition to be satisfied by the position of C is

$$\frac{1}{x} = \frac{x}{1-x},$$

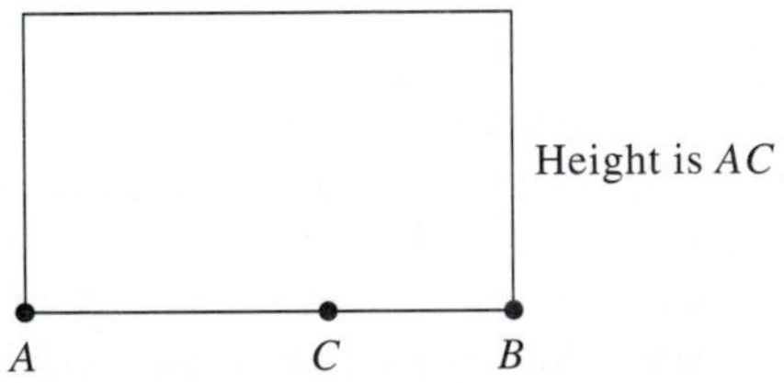

Height is AC

Figure 7.6A

Figure 7.6B

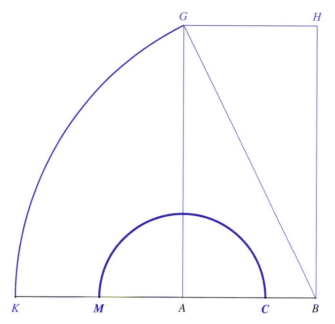

Figure 7.6C

which translates into the quadratic equation

$$x^2 + x - 1 = 0.$$

The solution, by the quadratic formula, is

$$x = \frac{\sqrt{5} - 1}{2},$$

where we have chosen the positive root so that the length AC is a positive number. The problem we now face is to construct the segment AC of length x by means of straightedge and compass only.

Step 1. On AB as a base, construct a rectangle $AGHB$ of height 2 (double the line segment AB). From Figure 7.6C, it is clear that the diagonal BG is of length $\sqrt{5}$.

Step 2. Let the circular arc with center B and radius BG intersect the line BA at K. Observe that the segment KA has length $\sqrt{5} - 1$.

Step 3. Bisect the segment KA at M, and let the circle with center A and radius AM intersect AB at C. Observe that the segment AC has length $(\sqrt{5} - 1)/2$; and the construction is completed.

By one of those small "miracles" that occur so unexpectedly (yet, not so infrequently) in mathematics, the construction above is intimately related to another of

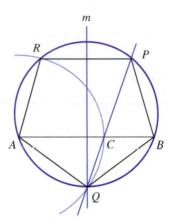

Figure 7.6D

the jewels in Greek geometry:

> to construct (with straightedge and compass
> only) a regular pentagon (a polygon of five
> equal sides inscribed in a circle).

This is a much less intuitive construction, for example, than the equilateral triangle, the square, or the regular hexagon (all of which can be found easily in terms of the diameter and radius of the circle). The key result, here, is that if C divides the line segment AB into extreme and mean ratio, then the segment AC is the side length of a regular pentagon inscribed in a circle determined as follows: Let m denote the perpendicular bisector of the given segment AB. With AC as the radius, construct a circular arc with center at A and let it intersect the line m at Q (see Figure 7.6D). The three points A, Q, and B determine a circle which intersects the previously drawn arc at R. Finally, the line QC intersects the circle at P, completing the regular pentagon having vertices A, Q, B, P, and R.

Problems for Section 7

1. Of course, we know that $\sqrt{4}$ is rational. Nevertheless, as in the text, attempt to prove that $\sqrt{4}$ is not rational. Where does the proof disintegrate?

2. Use the Fundamental Theorem of Arithmetic (FTOA) to show that $\sqrt[3]{2}$ is not rational.

3. Prove that $\sqrt[3]{3}$ is not rational.

4. If p is a prime, use FTOA to show that $\sqrt[3]{p}$ is not rational.

5. Show that $\sqrt[3]{4}$ is not rational.

6. Referring to Problems 2 to 5 and Theorem 7.5B, state a theorem describing which integers have nonrational cube roots.

7. Prove that if $0 < x < y$, then $0 < x^3 < y^3$.
   (*Hint:* Multiply $0 < x^2 < y^2$ by x and
   $0 < x < y$ by y^2.)

8. (*a*) Verify that $(y-x)(x^2+xy+y^2) = y^3 - x^3$
   by multiplying out the left-hand side.
   (*b*) Use part (*a*) to prove that if $0 < x < y$,
   then $0 < x^3 < y^3$.

9. Verify that $(y - x)(x^4 + x^3y + x^2y^2 + xy^3 + y^4) = y^5 - x^5$, and use this fact to show that
   if $0 < x < y$, then $0 < x^5 < y^5$.

10. Find the first four decimals in $\sqrt{3}$. Confirm
    your answer with inequalities.

11. Find the first four decimals in $\sqrt{5}$. Confirm
    your answer with inequalities.

12. Find the first three decimals in $\sqrt[3]{2}$. Confirm
    your answer with inequalities.

13. Find the first three decimals in $\sqrt[3]{3}$. Confirm
    your answer with inequalities.

14. Are the following sets in one-to-one corre-
    spondence (why or why not): **A** is the set
    of fingers on one hand and **B** is the starting
    lineup for the Chicago Bulls?

15. Are the following sets in one-to-one cor-
    respondence (why or why not): The set of
    positive integers $\mathbb{N}$ and $\mathbf{B} = \{n^2 : n \in \mathbb{N}\}$?

16. Describe a one-to-one correspondence be-
    tween the set of all positive multiples of 2
    and the set of all positive multiples of 3.

17. Describe a one-to-one correspondence be-
    tween the set of all negative integers and the
    set of all even positive integers.

18. Show that $\mathbb{N}$ and $\mathbb{Z}$ are in one-to-one corre-
    spondence. (*Hint:* Use Example 1, part **d**, in
    paragraph 7.4 and Problem 17.)

19. Consider the set $\mathbf{M} = \{a, b, c, d, e\}$. We will
    learn later that there are exactly 32 subsets
    of **M**, including the 0-element set $\varnothing$ and
    the 5-element set **M**. Describe a one-to-one
    correspondence between the subsets of **M**
    containing an even number of elements and

the subsets of **M** containing an odd number
of elements.

20. As in the previous problem, let
    $\mathbf{M} = \{a, b, c, d, e\}$. Describe a one-to-one
    correspondence between the subsets of **M**
    containing the element e and the subsets of
    M not containing e.

21. In Problems 21 to 27, you will show that the
    nth root of a prime is not rational. To start,
    show that $\sqrt[4]{2}$ is not rational.

22. For another warm-up, show that $\sqrt[5]{2}$ is not
    rational.

23. Using FTOA, show that if p is prime, then
    $\sqrt[4]{p}$ is not rational.

24. Using FTOA, show that if p is prime, then
    $\sqrt[5]{p}$ is not rational.

25. Using FTOA, show that $\sqrt[n]{2}$ is not rational if
    $n > 1$.

26. Using FTOA, show that $\sqrt[n]{3}$ is not rational if
    $n > 1$.

27. Using FTOA, show that if p is prime, then
    $\sqrt[n]{p}$ is not rational, where n is a positive inte-
    ger greater than 1.

28. Recall that $\log_{10} y = x$ means that $10^x = y$.
    For example, $\log_{10} 100 = 2$ since $10^2 = 100$. To show that $z = \log_{10} 2$ is not rational,
    assume that z is rational and so $z = m/n$.
    (*a*) Why is $m < n$? (*b*) Raise both sides of
    the equation $10^{(m/n)} = 2$ to the nth power.
    (*c*) Use FTOA to show that there are differ-
    ent numbers of 2s in the factorization of each
    side of the equation in (*b*).

29. Following Problem 28, show that $\log_{10} 3$ is
    not rational.

30. Show that $\log_{10} 9$ is not rational.

31. As you may recall, $\log_{10} 9 = \log_{10}(3^2) = 2 \cdot \log_{10} 3$. Since we know that $\log_{10} 3$ is
    not rational, could we use this to show that
    $\log_{10} 9$ is not rational? Indeed so. Show that

if r is a rational number different from 0 and x is irrational, then $r \cdot x$ is not rational. (This would show that $\log_{10} 9$ is not rational since 2 is rational and $\log_{10} 3$ is not rational.)

32. If x and y are irrational, is it possible for $x + y$ to be rational? Why?

33. If x and y are irrational, is it possible for $x \cdot y$ to be rational? Why?

34. If x is rational and y is irrational, is it possible for $x + y$ to be rational? Why?

35. The three most used bases for logarithms are 2, e, and 10. We will not concern ourselves with base e. But $\log_2 x$ is important for computer science. Show that $\log_2 10$ is not rational. (*Hint:* Suppose $\log_2 10 = r/s$, and hence $2^{(r/s)} = 10$. Raise both sides to the sth power and derive a contradiction.)

36. List four values of x for which $\log_{10} x$ is rational.

37. List four values of x for which $\log_2 x$ is rational.

38. Show that if $2^x = 3$, then x is not rational.

39. Let **A**, **B**, and **C** be sets. Show that if there is a one-to-one correspondence between **A** and **B** and if there is a one-to-one correspondence between **B** and **C**, then there is also a one-to-one correspondence between **A** and **C**. (This is another example of transitivity.)

40. For this problem you will need the definition of $\lfloor x \rfloor$ which appears in paragraph 6.8. Referring to Problem 18, verify that the pairing $(n, (-1)^n \cdot \lfloor n/2 \rfloor)$, for $n \in \mathbb{N}$, gives a one-to-one correspondence between the set of positive integers and the set of all integers.

41. Exhibit a one-to-one correspondence between the set of all odd integers and the set of all cubes. (Refer to Problem 39.)

42. Observe that if r is a rational number and s is an irrational number, then $(r + s)/2$ is not rational. Show that $(r + s)/2$ is between r and s and hence, between any rational number and any irrational number, there is an irrational number.

Section 8.   Positional Notation and Binary Arithmetic

Overview for Section 8

• Introduction to the binary system of notation and to binary arithmetic
• Algorithmic conversion of any base 10 integer to another base
• Special technique for quick binary-hexadecimal conversion

Key Concepts: positional notation (decimal, binary, and hexadecimal), binary arithmetic, decimal-binary conversion algorithm

8.1

Select any positive integer; form another integer by rearranging its digits in any order; subtract the smaller integer from the larger. The difference is always divisible by 9. Here are a few examples.

Integer	Rearrangement	Difference
5119	1591	$3528 = 392 \cdot 9$
238	382	$144 = 16 \cdot 9$
84	48	$36 = 4 \cdot 9$

The question is, "Why?"

Look first at the number 84. The notation means 8 *tens* plus 4 *ones*; that is, $84 = 8 \cdot 10 + 4 \cdot 1$. This result can be rewritten

$$84 = 8 \cdot (9 + 1) + 4 = 8 \cdot 9 + (8 + 4) = 8 \cdot 9 + 12.$$

Next, look at the number 238. The notation means 2 *hundreds* plus 3 *tens* plus 8 *ones*; that is,

$$238 = 2 \cdot 10^2 + 3 \cdot 10 + 8 \cdot 1.$$

This result can be rewritten

$$238 = 2 \cdot (9 + 1)(9 + 1) + 3 \cdot (9 + 1) + 8,$$
$$= 2 \cdot 9^2 + 2 \cdot 2 \cdot 9 + 2 \cdot 1 + 3 \cdot 9 + 3 \cdot 1 + 8,$$
$$= 2 \cdot 9^2 + 4 \cdot 9 + 3 \cdot 9 + (2 + 3 + 8),$$
$$= (18 + 4 + 3) \cdot 9 + 13.$$

What we notice from these two cases is that each number can be expressed as a multiple of 9 *plus* the sum of its digits:

$$84 = 8 \cdot 9 + 12,$$
$$238 = 25 \cdot 9 + 13.$$

It's easy to check that the same result holds in the case of 5119:

$$5119 = 567 \cdot 9 + 16.$$

These three special cases suggest that a similar statement might be true for any positive integer. The proof techniques discussed so far, however, are not appropriate to the task of proving such a generalization. New machinery, to be developed shortly, is needed, and in Section 10 we will be able to prove the following theorem, which states that the expected generalization is true.

> Any positive integer can be expressed as a multiple of 9 plus the sum of its digits.

Tutorial 8.1

a. Reverse the digits in the integer $x = 123,456,789$ to obtain a new integer y.

b. Show by division that 9 divides $y - x$.

c. Use the preceding theorem to show that 9 divides $y - x$.

Based upon this theorem, the answer to our original question is easy. For example,

$$5119 = m \cdot 9 + (5 + 1 + 1 + 9)$$

$$1591 = k \cdot 9 + (1 + 5 + 9 + 1), \quad \text{and the difference is}$$

$$3528 = m \cdot 9 - k \cdot 9 = (m - k) \cdot 9.$$

The difference of the two numbers is divisible by 9 because the two sums of digits are the same; hence they cancel out when one number is subtracted from the other.

8.2

As illustrated in the preceding paragraph, the notation for positive integers combines digits with position. In our familiar **decimal** system (with 10 as the **base**), the counting groups are powers of 10: *units* (10^0), *tens* (10^1), *hundreds* (10^2), *thousands* (10^3), etc. The notation is designed to tell us how many of each group to take. The "zero," by the way, was invented to protect position; for example

$$41,038 = 4 \cdot 10^4 + 1 \cdot 10^3 + 0 \cdot 10^2 + 3 \cdot 10^1 + 8 \cdot 10^0.$$

The idea underlying this system of numeration is independent of the *base* used. Although familiarity might suggest otherwise, there appears to be no reason behind the choice of 10 as the base more compelling than the physiological observation that people normally have 10 fingers (digits). Throughout recorded history, many other bases have been used, among them 12, 20, and 60. Remnants of these linger in common usage: a dozen eggs—four score years and ten—60 seconds in a minute. But electronic computers have no fingers, in spite of the fact that they are referred to as *digital* machines! So, what base is best for them? The first such machines were built some 50 years ago, and they were primitive by today's standards. Improvements in technology have enormously increased the power and convenience of computers; but the underlying logic remains dependent upon electronic components which can distinguish between two states, often modeled by the flow of electric current (like a light switch, for example, either on or off). We may think of a number being represented electronically by such components (called **flip-flops**) arrayed to correspond with positional notation. Since each flip-flop has only two states, it can distinguish between only two "digits." Thus the numeration system most suitable to electronic computing is like one which might have been invented by beings who had only two fingers instead of ten. In this "two-finger" system, the only "digits" are 0 and 1; they are called **bits** (*binary* dig*its*), and numbers are constructed by grouping into powers of 2: *units* (2^0), *twos* (2^1), *fours* (2^2), *eights* (2^3), etc. This produces the **base 2** notation, which is designed to identify the necessary powers of 2. For example, since decimal 13 is $8 + 4 + 1$, it can be written in base 2 notation as

$$13 = 1 \cdot 2^3 + 1 \cdot 2^2 + 0 \cdot 2^1 + 1 \cdot 2^0 = 1101.$$

Notice how important the 0 is to the correct interpretation of those bits on its left. The base 2 system is often called the **binary** system, and the first 16 positive integers have the following binary equivalents:

1	2	3	4	5	6	7	8
1	10	11	100	101	110	111	1000
9	10	11	12	13	14	15	16
1001	1010	1011	1100	1101	1110	1111	10000

(1)

Further, the addition and multiplication tables in binary are as simple as possible.

+	0	1
0	0	1
1	1	10

·	0	1
0	0	0
1	0	1

The only momentary surprise is the entry 10 in the addition table. But, of course, $1 + 1 = 2$ and

$$2 = 1 \cdot 2^1 + 0 \cdot 2^0 = 10$$

in binary notation. The *general rule for addition in binary* is: When two integers expressed in binary notation are added, the sum of two 1s is given by a 0 in that position and a carry of 1 to the next position on the left. For example, consider the sums

$$
\begin{array}{r}
1101 \\
101 \\
\hline
10010
\end{array}
\qquad \text{and} \qquad
\begin{array}{r}
110 \\
11 \\
1011 \\
100 \\
\hline
11000
\end{array}
$$

For comparison, these sums in decimal notation are

$$
\begin{array}{r}
13 \\
5 \\
\hline
18
\end{array}
\qquad \text{and} \qquad
\begin{array}{r}
6 \\
3 \\
11 \\
4 \\
\hline
24
\end{array}
$$

8.3 Given an integer in binary notation, it is easy to determine the corresponding decimal form: Simply add the indicated powers of 2. Thus, 10010 in binary notation means

$$1 \cdot 2^4 + 0 \cdot 2^3 + 0 \cdot 2^2 + 1 \cdot 2 + 0 = 16 + 2 = 18.$$

Tutorial 8.3A

a. Let $x = 1101001$ be an integer in binary notation. Write x as a sum of powers of 2.
b. What is the decimal notation for x?
c. If the binary representation of an integer ends in 1, can that integer be even?

But what about the opposite problem? Is there a convenient way to find the binary representation of an integer expressed in decimal notation? There is, and it depends upon the following (general) algorithm which converts a decimal integer to its representation in *any* base m. Our problem is to express the decimal integer n as a sum of powers of m. For example, 12,031 in base m means

$$1 \cdot m^4 + 2 \cdot m^3 + 0 \cdot m^2 + 3 \cdot m + 1.$$

(Note that each coefficient must be less than m.) Now let n denote a positive integer and let m denote an integer such that $m > 1$. Using the division algorithm we may write

$$n = m \cdot q + r,$$

where q is the quotient and r is the remainder, which must be one of the numbers $0, 1, \ldots, m-1$. Now we construct an algorithm for determining the entries in this array of boxes:

...   3   2   1   0

ALGORITHM   Base Conversion

Step 1. Divide n by m, obtaining quotient q and remainder r. Enter r in the box labeled 0.

Step 2. Divide q by m, obtaining a new quotient and a new remainder. Enter new remainder in the box labeled 1.

Step 3. Divide new quotient by m, obtaining a new quotient and a new remainder. Enter new remainder in the box labeled 2.

...   Continue until new quotient is 0.

Step k. End.   ▲

The flowchart for this algorithm is as follows (note that M is constant):

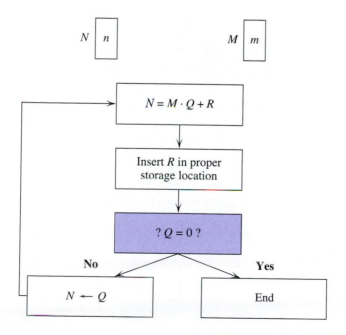

Example 1

Apply this algorithm with $n = 1984$ and $m = 10$.

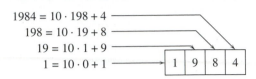

$$1984 = 10 \cdot 198 + 4$$
$$198 = 10 \cdot 19 + 8$$
$$19 = 10 \cdot 1 + 9$$
$$1 = 10 \cdot 0 + 1$$

| 1 | 9 | 8 | 4 |

Surprise! What we have generated is the decimal notation for the integer 1984. ●➤

This is not a very exciting example, perhaps, but it *does* suggest the answer we're after. The number m turns out to be the new base.

Example 2

Try the Base Conversion Algorithm again with $n = 21$ and $m = 2$.

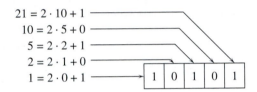

$$21 = 2 \cdot 10 + 1$$
$$10 = 2 \cdot 5 + 0$$
$$5 = 2 \cdot 2 + 1$$
$$2 = 2 \cdot 1 + 0$$
$$1 = 2 \cdot 0 + 1$$

| 1 | 0 | 1 | 0 | 1 |

This time, what we have generated is the binary representation of the number 21, that is,

$$21 = 1 \cdot 2^4 + 0 \cdot 2^3 + 1 \cdot 2^2 + 0 \cdot 2^1 + 1 \cdot 2^0.$$ ●➤

Tutorial 8.3B

a. Use the Base Conversion Algorithm to find the binary representation of the integer 88.

b. If an integer is divisible by 8, what can you claim about its binary representation?

8.4

Although other bases than 10 or 2 have been used in developing systems of numeration, few of them have much more than historical interest. We will look very briefly at just one of them, which also has ties to computing.

Example 1

Try the Base Conversion Algorithm one more time with $n = 391$ and $m = 16$.

$$391 = 16 \cdot 24 + 7$$
$$24 = 16 \cdot 1 + 8$$
$$1 = 16 \cdot 0 + 1$$

| 1 | 8 | 7 |

This time we have generated the representation of 391 in a system of numeration with base 16, called the **hexadecimal** (or **hex**, for short) system:

$$391 = 1 \cdot 16^2 + 8 \cdot 16^1 + 7 \cdot 16^0.$$

Thus, the number 391 has 187 as its hex representation.

In Example 1 the base is 16, which is 2^4. Because of this, one would expect to find a direct relationship between the hex and binary systems. To discover the connection, we need to examine the binary representation of 391. Hence, again apply the Base Conversion Algorithm, this time with $n = 391$ and $m = 2$.

$$391 = 2 \cdot 195 + 1$$
$$195 = 2 \cdot 97 + 1$$
$$97 = 2 \cdot 48 + 1$$
$$48 = 2 \cdot 24 + 0$$
$$24 = 2 \cdot 12 + 0$$
$$12 = 2 \cdot 6 + 0$$
$$6 = 2 \cdot 3 + 0$$
$$3 = 2 \cdot 1 + 1$$
$$1 = 2 \cdot 0 + 1$$

Thus the binary representation of 391 is 110000111. Now group the binary bits in strings of length 4, from the right. Because there are 9 bits, we precede the leftmost 1 with three 0s to form a string of length 4:

Binary	0001	1000	0111
Hex	1	8	7

Now, note that each string of four bits produces a hex digit, and these three are exactly the hex representation of 391.

Tutorial 8.4

If the hex representation of an integer ends in 0, what can you claim about its binary representation?

8.5

A system of numeration based on 8, called **octal,** also is used in computer science. The basic idea is no different—simply group in powers of 8. Thus,

$$391 = 6 \cdot 8^2 + 0 \cdot 8^1 + 7 \cdot 8^0;$$

hence the octal representation of 391 is 607.

A fuller discussion of these systems of numeration is more appropriate to a course in computer science, but a few general remarks are in order here before moving on.

1. In the hex system we have ignored an important detail: hex "digits" may be larger than 9; thus symbols for them must be agreed on. (Although no longer in use, one of the very early computer systems used the letters K for the hex digit 10, S for 11, N for 12, J for 13, F for 14, and L for 15. The letters formed an acronym for the phrase "king-sized numbers just for laughs.") The generally accepted notation for hex digits today is: A for 10, B for 11, C for 12, D for 13, E for 14, and F for 15. This is the notation we will use; thus, for example, the hex number F9D means

$$F \cdot 16^2 + 9 \cdot 16^1 + D \cdot 16^0,$$

or

$$15 \cdot 256 + 9 \cdot 16 + 13 \cdot 1,$$

which is 3997 in decimal notation. The binary notation for F9D is determined easily from the binary equivalents listed in (1) in paragraph 8.2:

F	9	D
1111	1001	1101.

Thus F9D in hex is 111110011101 in binary.

2. In the language of computer science, a pair of hex digits (that is, a string of eight bits) is called a **byte.** Although, as we have seen, the bit is a natural unit in the number system for digital machines, the byte has become a natural unit of information in the language of computers. It is through bytes that the computer recognizes alphabetic (and other) characters.

3. We have imposed no restriction on the number of bits available to represent an integer. This is no longer feasible when computations are carried out on a calculator, or even on a computer. In any practical situation, the limitation on the number of positions available may introduce what are called "round-off" errors; especially in large-scale calculations.

4. We have avoided completely the problem of negative numbers. This is addressed in computer arithmetic by the designation of a "sign bit," which further complicates the representation of a number.

5. Finally, because strings of "digits," such as 101, make sense in different systems of numeration, we will minimize the chance of confusion by adopting the following convention: **Numbers which appear hereafter are to be considered decimal, unless there is a specific indication to the contrary.** Frequently, a subscript is used to indicate the intended base. Thus, $(11001)_2$ means that 11001 is the binary representation of the number 25.

Example 1

$$101 = 1 \cdot 10^2 + 0 \cdot 10^1 + 1 \cdot 10^0;$$
$$(101)_2 = 1 \cdot 2^2 + 0 \cdot 2^1 + 1 \cdot 2^0 = 5;$$
$$(101)_{16} = 1 \cdot 16^2 + 0 \cdot 16^1 + 1 \cdot 16^0 = 257;$$
$$(1D)_{16} = 1 \cdot 16^1 + D \cdot 16^0 = 16 + 13 = 29;$$
$$(AA)_{16} = A \cdot 16^1 + A \cdot 16^0 = 10 \cdot 16 + 10 = 170 = (10101010)_2;$$
$$(B0C)_{16} = B \cdot 16^2 + 0 \cdot 16^1 + C \cdot 16^0 = 11 \cdot 256 + 0 + 12 \cdot 16^0,$$
$$= 2828 = (101100001100)_2.$$

8.6

Complement: Subtraction in Binary Additions can be performed by digital machines via simple electronic circuitry which combines the information in arrays of zeroes and ones according to the general rule stated earlier in this section. Now, machines produce complicated arithmetic results by reducing them to the very simplest operations performed millions of times, essentially at the speed of light. Any shortcuts, therefore, in either technique or internal circuitry may save great amounts of time and money. The wizards who first designed computers had this in mind, and they were particularly ingenious in teaching computers to subtract. This is not a course in computer arithmetic, but we digress briefly to describe the underlying mathematical idea because of its intrinsic interest.

Assume that x and y are positive integers expressed in binary notation. If $x < y$, our goal is to determine $y - x$. Consider, for example, $y = 110101$ and $x = 100110$. First, we attempt subtraction by brute force (remembering to borrow in binary). Sequentially, the steps are

110101	1100 10-	101 10- -
100110	1001 1-	100 1- -
... 1	... 11	001 111

The problem lies with the potentially necessary "borrowing" required to carry out subtraction in general. The first borrow, above, was from the next column over, but the second was from two columns over. The bookkeeping required to keep track of all this electronically is not impossible, but it is certainly an undesirable complication. In the interest of economy, then, we search for a different and better procedure.

Let x denote a string of bits, $x = b_1 b_2 b_3 \ldots b_n$, in which for each i, b_i is either 0 or 1. (Note that the leading bit may be either 0 or 1.) The **complement** $\bar{x}$ of x is the string obtained by replacing each 0 in x by 1 and each 1 in x by 0. Thus,

$\bar{x} = t_1 t_2 t_3 \ldots t_n$, in which for each i, $t_i = 1 - b_i$. For example,

$$x = 1111 \qquad \bar{x} = 0000,$$

$$x = 001011 \qquad \bar{x} = 110100.$$

THEOREM 8.6

If $x = b_1 b_2 \ldots b_n$ is a string of n bits, then $x + \bar{x} + 1$ is the binary representation of 2^n.

Proof

Note that

$$x + \bar{x} = \underbrace{11 \ldots 11}_{n \text{ ones}}.$$

In binary notation this is the number

$$1 \cdot 2^{n-1} + 1 \cdot 2^{n-2} + \cdots + 1 \cdot 2^1 + 1 \cdot 2^0.$$

Adding 1 to this number yields the next higher power of 2,

$$\underbrace{100 \ldots 00}_{n \text{ zeroes}}. \qquad \blacksquare$$

Now consider the problem of subtracting x from y, where $x \le y$. Let 2^{m-1} be the highest power of 2 in y, and let 2^{k-1} be the highest power of 2 in x. Thus the number of bits in y is m, and the number of bits in x is k, and $k \le m$. Now we will rewrite x, if necessary, with $m - k$ leading 0s so that the number of bits in x and y is the same. From Theorem 8.6,

$$x + \bar{x} + 1 = 2^m;$$

hence

$$x = 2^m - \bar{x} - 1,$$

and

$$y - x = y + \bar{x} + 1 - 2^m. \qquad (1)$$

Formula (1) is the key. To find $y - x$ simply

- Adjoin to x whatever leading 0s may be necessary (so that x and y have the same number of bits).

- Find the complement $\bar{x}$ of x.

- Add y, $\bar{x}$, and 1.

- From that sum subtract 2^m.

It turns out that each of these is a very simple operation electronically; hence the problem of machine subtraction is solved. The first three tasks are perfectly straight-forward and lead to the sum $S = y + \bar{x} + 1$. The fourth task is equally simple, but to describe it we must first observe that

$$2^m < S < 2^{m+1}. \tag{2}$$

Formula (2) follows easily from the facts that $x < y$ and $y < 2^m$,

$$2^m = x + \bar{x} + 1 < y + \bar{x} + 1 = y + 2^m - x < 2^m + 2^m = 2^{m+1}.$$

Finally, to subtract 2^m from S, simply erase the leading 1 in the binary representation of S.

Return, now, to the earlier example,

$$y = 110101 \qquad \text{and} \qquad x = 100110.$$

Note that x and y already have the same number of bits, thus $\bar{x} = 011001$.

$$
\begin{array}{r}
110101 \\
011001 \\
1 \\
\hline
1001111
\end{array}
$$
$= S$;   hence $y - x = 1111$.

Here are two more examples:
Let $y = 1001100$ and $x = 1101$. Rewrite x as 0001101; thus $\bar{x} = 1110010$.

$$
\begin{array}{r}
1001100 \\
1110010 \\
1 \\
\hline
10111111
\end{array}
$$
$= S$;   hence $y - x = 111111$.

Let $y = 10100100$ and $x = 101$. Rewrite x as 00000101; thus $\bar{x} = 11111010$.

$$
\begin{array}{r}
10100100 \\
11111010 \\
1 \\
\hline
110011111
\end{array}
$$
$= S$;   hence $y - x = 10011111$.

The procedure we have outlined above is sometimes called subtraction by **two's complement.** The idea, in general, is not limited to binary notation. In the decimal system, a similar procedure is referred to by the name **ten's complement.** In it, each digit d_i is replaced by $9 - d_i$. Consider the subtraction in decimal notation (first by borrowing, then by ten's complement):

$$
\begin{array}{r}
81053 \\
-\ 09021 \\
\hline
72032
\end{array}
\qquad
\begin{array}{r}
81053 \\
+\ 90978 \\
\hline
172031
\end{array}
$$

$$
\begin{array}{r}
+\qquad 1 \\
\hline
72032
\end{array}
\qquad \text{and erase the leading 1.}
$$

As suggested in paragraph 8.2, the idea of different bases for systems of numeration is a very old one. The decimal system, which is in almost universal use today, is often referred to as the "Arabic" system, but it should more properly be called the "Hindu-Arabic" system. Hindu mathematicians, perhaps as early as A.D. 600, were using such a system. Later, it was learned by Arabian mathematicians and was transmitted by them to Europe, where it came into general use about 500 years ago. The binary system was discussed by Gottfried Wilhelm Leibniz, one of the inventors of calculus, but was little more than a curiosity until the invention of digital computers. The idea of complementing a number is also old. It was used, in fact, by Blaise Pascal in a mechanical calculating machine which he invented at the age of 19.

Problems for Section 8

1. Rearrange the digits of the following numbers and show that the difference is divisible by 9 (your quotient may be either positive or negative): (a) 392, (b) 100, (c) 38,902, (d) 1,044,761.

2. Consider the positive integer $x = 843$. Find a rearrangement y of the digits in x, such that $x - y$ is divisible by 9^2.

3. Consider the positive integer $x = 4932$. Let y denote a rearrangement of its digits. Find y if either $x - y$ or $y - x$ is $9 \cdot 282$.

4. Show that 104 and 7115 have the same remainder when divided by 9. [*Hint:* Write each in the form $9 \cdot k +$ (sum of digits). It is not necessary to evaluate k.]

5. Answer without actually carrying out the division. Show that each number has the same remainder when divided by 9: (i) 422, (ii) 6155, (iii) 8882.

6. For any positive integer n let $s(n)$ denote the sum of its digits. Assuming the theorem in paragraph 8.1, prove that if k and m are positive integers for which $s(k) = s(m)$, then $k - m$ is divisible by 9.

7. (*Continuation of Problem 6.*) Show that $13,638 - 948$ is divisible by 9.

8. (*Continuation of Problem 6.*) Is it true that the difference between any two of the three integers 4812, 3534, and 69 is divisible by 9?

9. (*Continuation of Problem 6.*) Suppose that $s(n) - s(m)$ is divisible by 9. Is it true that $n - m$ is divisible by 9?

10. (*Conclusion of Problem 6.*) Test for divisibility by 9: (a) $7196 - 3812$, (b) $7196 - 1211$.

11. Convert the following binary numbers to decimal form: (a) 110001, (b) 111111, (c) 10001, (d) 101010.

12. Convert the following binary numbers to decimal form: (a) 110101, (b) 10011101001.

13. Convert the following hex numbers to decimal form: (a) $(4F)_{16}$, (b) $(DD)_{16}$.

14. Convert the hex number $(12AF)_{16}$ to decimal form.

15. Convert the following decimal integers to binary form: (a) 97, (b) 26, (c) 321.

16. Convert the following decimal integers to binary form: (a) 137, (b) 573, (c) 1382.

17. Convert the decimal integer 137 to (a) binary form, (b) hex form, (c) octal form.

18. Convert the decimal integer 2001 to (a) binary form, (b) hex form, (c) octal form.

19. Discuss the relationship between the three representations in either Problem 17 or Problem 18.

20. Add in binary and check in decimal:
(a) 10011   (b) 10011
     101   1010
    1011   110
                  11

21. Add in binary and check in decimal:
(a) 110001   (b) 11
   10001   111
  111111   100
             10
              1
          101

22. The usual multiplication algorithm works even more simply in binary than in decimal. Consider the following product.

$$
\begin{array}{r}
11001 \\
1011 \\
\hline
11001 \\
11001 \\
11001 \\
\hline
100010011
\end{array}
$$

Show that the product is correct by converting each factor and the answer to decimal form and multiplying in decimal.

23. Multiply 10011 by 10101 in binary arithmetic.

24. Multiply 110111 by 11011 in binary arithmetic.

25. Square the binary number 110101.

26. Convert the decimal number 182 to base 7.

27. Convert the decimal number 182 to base 3.

28. It is important to know that 1 kilobyte is 2^{10} bytes. Compute 2^k for $k = 0, 1, 2, \ldots, 10$.

29. Since 1 megabyte is 2^{20} bytes and $2^{20} = (2^{10})^2$, compute the decimal form of 2^{20}.

30. Show that a positive integer is even or odd, depending upon whether its binary representation ends in 0 or 1.

31. Show that n is odd if and only if 1 appears an odd number of times in the base 3 expansion of n.

32. (a) How many 9s are in the decimal expansion of $10^3 - 1$? (b) How many 1s are in the binary expansion of $2^3 - 1$? (c) How many 1s are in the binary expansion of $2^n - 1$? (d) How many 1s are in the binary expansion of $128^{13} - 1$?

33. Recall from Problem 6 that $s(n)$ is the sum of the digits of n. For each positive integer n, let $s_9(n)$ be the result of the following algorithm: **Step 0:** Start with $m = n$. **Step 1:** Compute $s(m)$. **Step 2:** If $s(m) > 9$, then let m be $s(m)$ and repeat Step 1. If $s(m) = 9$, then let $s_9(n) = 0$ and stop. If $s(m) < 9$, then let $s_9(n) = s(m)$ and stop. ▲

For $n = 98476$, $s(n) = 34$. Since $34 > 9$, we compute $s(34) = 7$. Since $s(7) < 9$, $s_9(98476) = 7$. Compute $s_9(n)$ for

(a) $n = 99$, (b) $n = 10986$, (c) $n = 1492$, (d) $n = 198919896213$.

34. (*Continuation of Problem 33.*) We will not prove this now, but $s_9(n)$ is simply the remainder when n is divided by 9. Verify this for the numbers in Problem 33.

35. (*Continuation of Problem 33.*) Computing $s_9(n)$ is called "casting out nines"; it is an ancient technique for determining the remainder when n is divided by 9. A "quick and dirty" procedure is to sum the digits from the left, subtracting 9 whenever the sum is at least 9. Note that 9s, 0s, and digits summing to 9 can be passed over. For example, let $n = 561459048$.

	Cast out 9?	Result
$5 + 6 = 11$	Subtract 9	2
$2 + 1 = 3$	. . .	3
$3 + (4 + 5)$	9	3
$3 + 9$	9	3
$3 + 0$	. . .	3
$3 + 4 = 7$	. . .	7
$7 + 8 = 15$	Subtract 9	6

Hence, $s_9(561459048) = 6$. Casting out 9s, compute $s_9(n)$ for (a) $n = 253467$, (b) $n = 909187$, (c) $n = 357883$, (d) $n = 42357871$.

36. (*Continuation of Problem 33.*) Here are two equations concerning s_9. For n and m in $\mathbb{N}$, (1) $s_9(n + m) = s_9(s_9(n) + s_9(m))$ and (2) $s_9(n \cdot m) = s_9(s_9(n) \cdot s_9(m))$. (They are easier to compute than to write.) For example, $s_9(287 + 974) = s_9(1261) = 1$; and $s_9(287) = 8$, $s_9(974) = 2$, and so $s_9(287) + s_9(974) = 10$. But $s_9(10) = 1$ which verifies the first equation. Verify both equations for (a) $n = 42$, $m = 86$; (b) $n = 297$, $m = 123$; (c) $n = 1482$, $m = 1521$; (d) $n = 567$, $m = 765$.

37. (*Continuation of Problem 33.*) By the Pigeonhole Principle, a number having all its digits distinct must have fewer than 11 digits. Prove that no number having exactly 10 distinct digits can be prime. [*Hint:* For such a number n, compute $s_9(n)$.]

38. (*Continuation of Problem 33.*) Casting out nines is a useful, but not a perfect check on arithmetical calculations. For example, does $57 \times 42 = 2294$? Now $s_9(57 \times 42) = s_9(3 \times 6) = 0$ and $s_9(2294) = 8$. Can $8 = 0$? No. So $57 \times 42 \neq 2294$. Using s_9, check the following products: (a) $284 \times 695 = 196381$, (b) $5478 \times 9874 = 54086772$, (c) $5744 \times 2587 = 14859728$, (d) $2762 \times 1992 = 5501004$. Now check these with your calculator.

39. (*Continuation of Problem 33.*) Find d by computing s_9 for each of the three numbers in the following product: $6666666 \times 6666666 = 444444d5555556$.

40. (*Conclusion of Problem 33.*) If $2d99561 = (3(523 + d))^2$, then what is d?

41. It is also possible to convert fractions to binary: for example, just as $\frac{1}{10} = 10^{-1} = 0.1$ and $1\frac{1}{10} = 1.1$, then $\frac{1}{2} = (0.1)_2$ and $\frac{3}{2} = (1.1)_2$. Convert the following to binary: (a) $\frac{1}{4}$, (b) $\frac{1}{8}$, (c) $\frac{3}{4} = \frac{1}{2} + \frac{1}{4}$, (d) $13\frac{5}{8}$.

42. Convert these binary numbers to fractional decimal form: (a) $(10.01)_2$, (b) $(0.01101)_2$, (c) $(1.111)_2$, (d) $(101.101)_2$.

43. Since

$$\frac{a}{2} + \frac{b}{4} + \frac{c}{8} + \frac{d}{16} = \frac{1}{16} \cdot (8a + 4b + 2c + d),$$

$$(0.abcd)_2 = \frac{8a + 4b + 2c + d}{16}$$

$$= \frac{(abcd)_2}{16} = 0.(abcd)_{16}.$$

For example, $(.1001)_2 = \frac{1}{2} + \frac{0}{4} + \frac{0}{8} + \frac{1}{16} = \frac{1}{16} \cdot (8 + 0 + 0 + 1) = \frac{9}{16} = (.9)_{16}$.

Also $(.1101)_2 = \frac{13}{16} = (.D)_{16}$. Convert the following from binary to hexadecimal: (a) $(11.0111)_2$, (b) $(.01001110)_2$, (c) $(10110110.01101011)_2$.

44. What is $\frac{2}{3}$ in binary? Let $\frac{2}{3} = (0.a_1a_2a_3a_4\ldots)_2$. Since $\frac{2}{3} > \frac{1}{2}$, $\frac{2}{3} = (0.1a_2a_3a_4\ldots)_2$. Since $\frac{2}{3} - \frac{1}{2} = \frac{1}{6}$ and $\frac{1}{6} < \frac{1}{4}$, $\frac{2}{3} = (0.10a_3a_4\ldots)_2$. But

$\frac{1}{6} - \frac{1}{8} = \frac{1}{24}$, and so $\frac{2}{3} = (0.101a_4\ldots)_2$. Find the next three "digits" in this binary expansion. Can you write $\frac{3}{5}$ in binary?

45. In what bases b ($b < 10$) can an even positive integer have an odd unit's digit?

46. In base 3, show that n is divisible by 3 if and only if the unit's digit is 0.

CHAPTER 2

Mathematical Induction

Section 9. Quantified Statements and Their Negations

Overview for Section 9

- Introduction to predicates and quantifiers
- Examples of universally quantified statements
- Examples of existentially quantified statements
- How quantified statements are negated
- Examples of doubly quantified statements

Key Concepts: universal and existential quantification, negation of quantified statements, doubly quantified statements

9.1   Much of algebra is concerned with the study of equations such as

$$x^3 - 3x^2 - 2x + 6 = 0. \qquad \qquad (1)$$

There is always a restriction, often implicitly understood, on the allowed replacements for the variable. The set of allowed replacements is called the **universe,** denoted in general by **S**, which is separated by (1) into two complementary subsets consisting of those elements for which the equation is true and those for which it is false. Note that (1) by itself is neither true nor false; thus it is not a mathematical statement. Its left-hand side can be thought of as a pattern of operations (formula) to be applied to elements of **S**, and we will refer to (1) as a **predicate** in x (the term "open sentence" is also used for such expressions). In this paragraph, we will limit our concern to only two choices for the universe: $\mathbb{R}$ and $\mathbb{N}$. If **S** is the set of all real numbers, then choosing to replace x with 1 and $\sqrt{2}$ we obtain, respectively, the false statement

$$1^3 - 3 \cdot 1^2 - 2 \cdot 1 + 6 = 0,$$

and the true statement

$$(\sqrt{2})^3 - 3 \cdot 2 - 2 \cdot \sqrt{2} + 6 = 0.$$

It turns out that (1) is a true statement if x is replaced by any one of the three numbers $\sqrt{2}, -\sqrt{2}, 3$ and is false for all other real number replacements for x. If, however, the universe is limited to the set of all positive integers, then (1) is a true statement if x is replaced by 3 and is false for all other positive integral replacements for x.

   The set-builder notation, referred to in paragraph 1.8, is designed to utilize predicates similar to (1). It offers a precise way to specify a set of objects, without actually naming the objects. The value of this technique is more apparent in situations which are less immediate than the example at hand. But to continue, for illustrative purposes, if $\mathbb{R}$ denotes the set of real numbers and if $\mathbb{N}$ denotes the set of positive integers, then (1) may be used to identify the following sets which consist of elements in the universe for which the equation is true:

$$\{x \in \mathbb{R} : x^3 - 3x^2 - 2x + 6 = 0\} = \{\sqrt{2}, -\sqrt{2}, 3\}$$

and
$$\{x \in \mathbb{N} : x^3 - 3x^2 - 2x + 6 = 0\} = \{3\}.$$

More generally, if $\mathcal{P}(x)$ denotes a predicate, like (1) for example, then $\{x \in \mathbf{S} : \mathcal{P}(x)\}$ is exactly the set of elements $a \in \mathbf{S}$ for which $\mathcal{P}(a)$ is a true statement.

9.2

In most applications, this set-builder notation will identify a *proper* subset of the universe; that is, the predicate will be true for some elements in the universe and false for others. There is a special case of this idea, however, which arises when the predicate turns out to be true for every element in the universe. Here is a very simple illustration which follows from the observation that one of every pair of consecutive positive integers n and $n + 1$ is even:

$$\{n \in \mathbb{N} : n(n + 1) \text{ is even}\} = \mathbb{N}. \tag{1}$$

The information conveyed in (1) may be reformulated as follows:

$$\text{For each positive integer } n, \ n^2 + n \text{ is even.}$$

In this chapter we will be concerned with a number of mathematical theorems which are expressed in just such language. Let **S** be the universe and let $\mathcal{P}(x)$ denote a predicate which is either true or false when x is replaced by an element of **S**. To claim that $\mathscr{P}(x)$ is, in fact, true for each element in the universe, we write what is called a **universally quantified statement.**

$$\text{For each } x \in \mathbf{S}, \quad \mathscr{P}(x). \tag{2}$$

It has become customary in logic to use the inverted A, namely, $\forall$, as a **universal quantifier;** hence (2) has the abbreviated form

$$\forall x \in \mathbf{S}, \quad \mathscr{P}(x). \tag{2'}$$

The rather pretentious phrase "universal quantifier" may be loosely justified as attributing a described property to *all* members of a given universe. Theorems of the sort stated in Example 1 of paragraph 2.8,

$$\text{The square of an even integer is even}$$

may be expressed in the form of universally quantified statements. That theorem was proved in paragraph 3.1, and if $\mathbb{E}$ denotes the set of all even integers, then Theorem 3.1 has the concise form

$$\forall x \in \mathbb{E}, \quad x^2 \in \mathbb{E}. \tag{3}$$

Tutorial 9.2

a. Translate the statement "Every even integer has an even cube" into a form similar to (3).
b. Let $\mathbb{O}$ denote the set of odd integers. Prove the theorem: $\forall x \in \mathbb{O}, \quad x^3 \in \mathbb{O}$.

9.3 Because it is impossible to find an even integer which fails to have an even square, (3) in paragraph 9.2 is a true statement. In general, however, a claim expressed by

$$\forall x \in \mathbf{S}, \quad \mathscr{P}(x) \tag{1}$$

is a mathematical statement which may in fact be false; in which case its negation is a theorem. In paragraph 3.4 we considered the relationship between a (simple) mathematical statement, denoted there by p, and its negation, denoted by $\sim p$. Here, we are concerned with a more complex statement, and one of our problems is how to interpret the negation of (1):

$$\sim (\forall x \in \mathbf{S}, \quad \mathscr{P}(x)). \tag{2}$$

As we observed at the beginning of paragraph 9.2, if x is replaced by a particular element in the universe, say $a \in \mathbf{S}$, then $\mathcal{P}(a)$ is a (simple) mathematical statement which, itself, is either true or false. In a sense, then, we may think of (1) as an abbreviation for a set of mathematical statements in the form $\mathcal{P}(a)$, one for each $a \in \mathbf{S}$. In order that (1) be true, *every* statement $\mathcal{P}(a)$ in the set must, individually, be true. Thus (1) is false if there exists a single element, say y in $\mathbf{S}$, for which $\mathcal{P}(y)$ is false. If such an element can be discovered, it is called a counterexample (see paragraph 5.5) to the claim that (1) is true, and its existence is indicated in symbolic form by

$$\exists y \in \mathbf{S}, \quad (\sim \mathcal{P}(y)). \tag{3}$$

The backward E is read "there exists" and is called the **existential quantifier.** Thus (3) is the abbreviation for the following **existentially quantified statement:**

There exists an element y in $\mathbf{S}$ for which $\mathcal{P}(y)$ is false.

The argument above demonstrates the following important relationships:

- If the universally quantified statement (1) is true, then the existentially quantified statement (3) is false.

- If the universally quantified statement (1) is false, then the existentially quantified statement (3) is true.

Thus, (3) is the negation of (1), and we can write

$$\sim(\forall x \in \mathbf{S}, \quad \mathcal{P}(x)) \leftrightarrow \exists x \in \mathbf{S}, \quad (\sim \mathcal{P}(x)).$$

Example 1   Consider the statement:

All rational numbers have positive squares.

This can be expressed symbolically as

$$\forall q \in \mathbb{Q}, \quad q^2 > 0, \tag{4}$$

(where $\mathbb{Q}$ denotes the set of rational numbers). The negation of (4) is

$$\exists q \in \mathbb{Q}, \quad q^2 \leq 0. \tag{5}$$

Two quick reminders may be in order here. First, the same variable q is used in each of statements (4) and (5), but this is not important. Different letters could have been chosen; for example, "$\exists x \in \mathbb{Q}, x^2 \leq 0$" has exactly the same meaning as the statement in (5). Second, notice that the negation of the predicate "$q^2 > 0$" is *not* "$q^2 < 0$." To say that a real number is not positive means that the number may be either zero or negative. Thus, the negation of (4) may be stated:

There is a rational number with a square that is either zero or negative.

We noted in paragraph 9.2 that the same information is conveyed by the two statements

$$\{n \in \mathbb{N} : n^2 + n \text{ is even}\} = \mathbb{N}$$

and
$$\forall n \in \mathbb{N} : n^2 + n \text{ is even.}$$

Similarly, the claim made by the existentially quantified statement (5) can be expressed in terms of sets,

$$\{q \in \mathbb{Q} : q^2 \leq 0\} \neq \varnothing. \tag{6}$$

Neither of the statements (5) or (6) makes any claim beyond the existence of *at least one* rational number with a nonpositive square. In particular, no clue is offered as to which element(s), or how many, may actually satisfy the given condition. We may recall, however, from previous experience with real numbers that any nonzero real number has a positive square. The set described in (6), therefore, must be the singleton set

$$\{q \in \mathbb{Q} : q^2 \leq 0\} = \{0\}.$$

Tutorial 9.3

a. Consider the universally quantified statement "$\forall x \in \mathbb{Z}, \quad 1 - x^2 \leq 0$." State its negation, and decide which of the two quantified statements is true.

b. State the negation of "Every dog must have its day."

9.4 Suppose, now, that we reconsider our discussion in paragraph 9.3 but begin this time with the existential quantifier. Given the predicate $\mathcal{P}(x)$, consider the statement

$$\exists x \in \mathbf{S}, \quad \mathcal{P}(x) \tag{1}$$

which is true provided we can find at least one element a in $\mathbf{S}$ for which $\mathcal{P}(a)$ is true. In this case, $\mathcal{P}(x)$ cannot be false for every element in $\mathbf{S}$, which means that the universally quantified statement

$$\forall x \in \mathbf{S}, \quad (\sim\mathcal{P}(x)) \tag{2}$$

is false. Similarly, it follows that if (1) is false, then (2) is true. Thus, (2) is the logical negation of (1), and we can write

$$\sim(\exists x \in \mathbf{S}, \quad \mathcal{P}(x)) \leftrightarrow \forall x \in \mathbf{S}, \quad (\sim\mathcal{P}(x)). \tag{3}$$

The following table summarizes the relationship between quantified statements and their negations:

Quantified statement	Its negation
$\forall x \in \mathbf{S}, \quad \mathcal{P}(x)$	$\exists x \in \mathbf{S}, \quad (\sim\mathcal{P}(x))$
$\exists x \in \mathbf{S}, \quad \mathcal{P}(x)$	$\forall x \in \mathbf{S}, \quad (\sim\mathcal{P}(x))$

If x is replaced by any element in the universe, $\mathcal{P}(x)$ becomes a simple statement, and it follows that $\sim(\sim(\mathcal{P}(x)))$ is logically equivalent to $\mathcal{P}(x)$. Thus, if each of the negations in the table above is itself negated, the resulting statement is exactly the original quantified statement.

Example 1   **a.** The statement

>   Every real number has a nonnegative square

has the negation

>   Some real number has a negative square.

b. The statement

>   There exists an even prime number

has the negation

>   Every prime number is odd.

c. The statement

>   All roads lead to Rome

has the negation

>   Some road does not lead to Rome.

d. The statement

>   Some people are born lucky

has the negation

No one is born lucky.　　　　●

The statements in parts (c) and (d) of Example 1 are hardly mathematical, but they do illustrate quantification in ordinary discourse. Perhaps you have noticed a problem: The English language is sometimes imprecise in meaning. For example, the negation in part (d) could be read

All people are born unlucky.

Is this really what is intended? Is the negation of "lucky" "unlucky?" It may be worth thinking about for a moment.

The mathematical statements in parts (a) and (b) of Example 1 may be expressed in the following symbolic form, where $\mathbb{R}$ denotes the set of all real numbers and $\mathbb{P}$ denotes the set of all primes:

$$\forall x \in \mathbb{R}, \quad x^2 \geq 0 \qquad \text{and} \qquad \exists x \in \mathbb{R}, \quad x^2 < 0.$$

$$\exists x \in \mathbb{P}, \quad x \text{ is even} \qquad \text{and} \qquad \forall x \in \mathbb{P}, \quad x \text{ is odd.}$$

In each of these pairs, the first statement is true and its negation is false. In these special cases, it is clear that the negation of the negation *is* the original quantified statement. For example,

$$\sim(\exists x \in \mathbb{R}, \quad x^2 < 0)$$

means

$$\forall x \in \mathbb{R}, \quad \sim(x^2 < 0), \qquad \text{or} \qquad \forall x \in \mathbb{R}, \quad x^2 \geq 0.$$

As often happens in mathematics, an idea may be described in more than one way. Following are several different phrases which express the meaning of $\forall$ and $\exists$:

$\forall x \in \mathbf{S}$	$\exists x \in \mathbf{S}$
For each x in $\mathbf{S}$	For some x in $\mathbf{S}$
For every x in $\mathbf{S}$	There is an x in $\mathbf{S}$
For all x in $\mathbf{S}$	There exists an x in $\mathbf{S}$
For any x in $\mathbf{S}$	For at least one x in $\mathbf{S}$

Tutorial 9.4

Assume that the existentially quantified statement in (1) is false. Write out the argument that the statement in (2) is true.

9.5 Mathematical statements often are more complicated than those included in Example 1 of paragraph 9.4; some, in fact, require both kinds of quantification. For example, consider the statement:

For each rational number r there is an integer m such that $m \cdot r$ is an integer.

To quantify this we write ($\mathbb{Q}$ = rationals, $\mathbb{Z}$ = integers)

$$\forall r \in \mathbb{Q}, \quad \exists m \in \mathbb{Z}, \quad m \cdot r \in \mathbb{Z}. \tag{1}$$

(Note that there is an implicit "such that" after "$\exists m \in \mathbb{Z}$.") A statement written in this form is easy to negate since we know how to negate both $\forall$ and $\exists$. We observe first that "$\exists m \in \mathbb{Z}, m \cdot r \in \mathbb{Z}$" is the predicate corresponding to the quantifier "$\forall r \in \mathbb{Q}$." Thus the negation of (1) is

$$\exists r \in \mathbb{Q}, \quad (\sim(\exists m \in \mathbb{Z}, \quad m \cdot r \in \mathbb{Z}));$$

hence $\quad\quad\quad\quad \exists r \in \mathbb{Q}, \quad (\forall m \in \mathbb{Z}, \quad m \cdot r \notin \mathbb{Z})),$

and finally,

$$\exists r \in \mathbb{Q}, \quad \forall m \in \mathbb{Z}, \quad m \cdot r \notin \mathbb{Z}. \tag{2}$$

In words this statement reads:

There is a rational number r so that $m \cdot r$ is not an integer for all integers m.

Because rational numbers can be written as fractions, it should be clear that statement (1) is true and its negation in (2) is false.

Example 1 Recalling the notation introduced in paragraph 5.3,

$$a \in [1]_9$$

means that a is an integer which has the remainder 1 when divided by 9. This can be expressed as an existentially quantified statement,

$$\exists q \in \mathbb{Z}, \quad a = 9 \cdot q + 1.$$

Choosing $a = -35$, for example, the quotient q is -4,

$$-35 = 9(-4) + 1.$$

Now, consider the doubly quantified statement

$$\forall x \in \mathbb{Z}, \quad \exists q \in \mathbb{Z}, \quad x = 9 \cdot q + 1. \tag{3}$$

Is this statement true or false? The answer is not difficult, but suppose we construct the negation of (3) for practice. It is

$$\exists x \in \mathbb{Z}, \quad \sim(\exists q \in \mathbb{Z}, \quad x = 9 \cdot q + 1),$$

or

$$\exists x \in \mathbb{Z}, \quad \forall q \in \mathbb{Z}, \quad x \neq 9 \cdot q + 1. \tag{4}$$

Replacing x by 18 (one of many possibilities), it is clear that

$$18 \neq 9 \cdot q + 1,$$

for $q = 1$, $q = 2$, or any other replacement for q. Therefore (4) is true and (3) is false.   ●

In statements which involve two or more quantifiers, it may seem natural to suppose that the order in which they are expressed is immaterial. Returning to (2), what difference can there be, for example, between

$$\exists r \in \mathbb{Q}, \quad \forall m \in \mathbb{Z}, \quad m \cdot r \notin \mathbb{Z},$$

and

$$\forall m \in \mathbb{Z}, \quad \exists r \in \mathbb{Q}, \quad m \cdot r \notin \mathbb{Z}?$$

The answer is that they have totally different meanings. We know that the first statement is false [since it is the negation of (1) which is true]; but think about the other. It says:

> No matter what positive integer you may happen to choose, you can then find a rational number such that the product of the two numbers is not an integer.

But this is clearly true, for if m is any integer, then pick r to be the reciprocal of any prime that is not a divisor of m. For example, if $m = -894$, then an acceptable choice for r is $\frac{1}{5}$:

$$(-894) \cdot \left(\tfrac{1}{5}\right) = \left(-178\tfrac{4}{5}\right) \notin \mathbb{Z}.$$

Moral. **The "order of events" in multiply quantified statements is critically important.**

The most reasonable advice, perhaps, is simply to think carefully about the intent of the statement.

9.6 Complement: Ramsey Numbers

Sociologists are often concerned with the study of interactions among human beings both within and between sets of various sizes. We consider now a very special human relationship, that of "acquaintance." Suppose we agree that any two humans either are acquainted with one another or are strangers to one another. Then we may call a set **H** of humans a **clique** if each member of **H** is acquainted with each other member of that set. Similarly, we may call a set **K** of humans an **anticlique** if each member of **K** is a stranger to each other member of that set. Agreeing that it takes two to be acquainted, it is clear that any clique must contain at least two members and may contain more; similarly for any anticlique.

Related to these concepts is a very interesting and exceptionally difficult mathematical problem based upon a remarkable theorem by Frank Plumpton Ramsey (1903–1930). (Incidentally, his brother, Arthur Michael Ramsey, was the Archbishop of Canterbury from 1961 to 1974.) Ramsey's Theorem, which involves an interesting variation on the theme of universal quantification, is a deep generalization of the Pigeonhole Principle. We will discuss here only a few special cases; these, nevertheless, incorporate the main idea of the theorem.

Suppose that p and q are given positive integers, both greater than 1. Ramsey's Theorem asserts that:

For all sufficiently large positive integers n, every set of n humans contains either a clique of size p or an anticlique of size q.

To clarify the meaning, suppose we agree that if a set contains a clique (or an anticlique) of size k, for example, then it also contains cliques (or anticliques) of each size less than k. Thus, to claim that a set contains a clique of size p does not imply that it fails to contain one of larger size. Given any set consisting of exactly four humans, the various possibilities are that the set contains:

1. A clique of size 4
2. A clique of size 3, but none larger
3. A clique of size 2, but none larger
4. No clique of any size

To illustrate these possibilities, suppose that the members of the set are named $\mathcal{A}$, $\mathcal{B}$, $\mathcal{C}$, $\mathcal{D}$. It may happen that:

1. Each individual is acquainted with all the others.
2. $\mathcal{A}$, $\mathcal{B}$, and $\mathcal{C}$ are acquainted with one another, while $\mathcal{D}$ is a stranger to at least one of them.

3. $\mathcal{A}$ and $\mathcal{B}$ are acquainted, while $\mathcal{C}$ is a stranger to $\mathcal{A}$, and $\mathcal{D}$ is a stranger to $\mathcal{B}$.

4. No two of them are acquainted.

Now, consider the following situation. Let $\mathbf{H} = \{\mathcal{A}, \mathcal{B}, \mathcal{C}, \mathcal{D}, \mathcal{E}\}$ be a set of five humans, and suppose that $\mathcal{A}$ is acquainted only with $\mathcal{E}$ and $\mathcal{B}$, $\mathcal{B}$ is acquainted only with $\mathcal{A}$ and $\mathcal{C}$, $\mathcal{C}$ is acquainted only with $\mathcal{B}$ and $\mathcal{D}$, $\mathcal{D}$ is acquainted only with $\mathcal{C}$ and $\mathcal{E}$, and, finally, $\mathcal{E}$ is acquainted only with $\mathcal{D}$ and $\mathcal{A}$. Thus $\mathbf{H}$ contains a clique of size 2, but none larger. What about anticliques? There is at least one of size 2, and with a little checking you can show that there cannot be one of size 3. Thus there exists an acquaintance pattern among five people in which the largest clique is of size 2 and the largest anticlique is also of size 2.

Consider next the version of Ramsey's Theorem with $p = q = 3$:

5. For all sufficiently large positive integers n, every set of n humans contains either a clique of size 3 or an anticlique of size 3.

We need to interpret the rather peculiar quantification, "for all sufficiently large positive integers $n, \ldots$." It doesn't say, "for all positive integers...," and it doesn't say, "for some big positive integers...," and it doesn't give any clue as to how large the positive integers must be. What it really means is the following: There exists some (very likely unknown) positive integer r such that the integers n we are concerned with are those and only those which are larger than or equal to r.

And now for the Ramsey statement labeled **5,** we want to know, "What is the size of the integer r for which every set of r, or more, humans contains either a clique or an anticlique of size 3?" It can't be 4 because we've seen an example of a set of size 4 which has neither a clique nor an anticlique of size 3. Furthermore, it can't be 5 because we've just seen a counterexample. We will prove in Theorem 37.5 that r can, in fact, be as small as 6, so the following is true: For all positive integers $n \geq 6$, every set of n humans contains either a clique of size 3 or an anticlique of size 3.

Notice in the original statement of Ramsey's Theorem that the smallest possible value that n may have depends on our choice of p and q. We will denote this smallest value by $r(p, q)$, and we call it a **Ramsey number.** It isn't hard to show that $r(2, 2) = 2$, $r(3, 2) = 3$, $r(4, 2) = 4$, and, in fact, $r(p, 2) = p$ for all $p \geq 2$ (see Example 1 below). By the fact referred to immediately above as Theorem 37.5, $r(3, 3) = 6$. In general, it turns out that $r(p, q)$ is known for just a few other values of p and q. These calculations are exceedingly difficult, and the evaluation of Ramsey numbers, not included in the table below, remains an unsolved problem.

Example 1

Suppose a discrete mathematics class has p students. If each student is acquainted with every other student, then the class is a clique of size p. If, however, there are two students who are not acquainted, then these two form an anticlique of size 2. This means that $r(p, 2) = p$ for $p \geq 2$.

Likewise, $r(2, p) = p$ since either every student in the class is not acquainted with any other student in the class (making the class an anticlique of size p) or two students are acquainted (making these two students a clique of size 2).

p \ q	2	3	4	5	6	7	8	9	10
2	2	3	4	5	6	7	8	9	10
3	3	6	9	14	18	23	28	36	
4	4	9	18	25					
5	5	14	25						
6	6	18							
7	7	23							
8	8	28							
9	9	36							
10	10								

Table of known Ramsey numbers (1997)

Problems for Section 9

1. Identify with a list the elements belonging to each of the following sets: (a) $\{x \in \mathbb{R}: x^2 - 2x - 3 = 0\}$, (b) $\{x \in \mathbb{N}: x^2 - 7x - 10 = 0\}$, (c) $\{x \in \mathbb{N}: x^2 + 2x - 3 = 0\}$.

2. Describe in another way each of the following sets: (a) $\{x \in \mathbb{R}: x^2 - 1 = 0\}$, (b) $\{x \in \mathbb{R}: x^2 = 0\}$, (c) $\{x \in \mathbb{R}: x^2 + 1 = 0\}$.

3. Give an argument to suggest that $\{x \in \mathbb{N}:$ there is a prime p such that $p > x\} = \mathbb{N}$.

4. Give a counterexample to the claim: $\{x \in \mathbb{N}:$ there is a prime p such that $p < x\} = \mathbb{N}$.

5. If $\mathbb{P}$ denotes the set of all prime numbers, express each of the following quantified statements symbolically: (a) All prime numbers are odd. (b) No prime number is greater than 300. (c) Which, if either, of these statements is true?

6. If $\mathbb{N}$ denotes the universe, express each of the following symbolically: (a) Every inte-ger divisible by 6 is also divisible by 3. (b) Some integer divisible by 3 is also divisible by 6. (c) Which, if either, of these statements is true?

7. State the negation of each of the following: (a) Every real number is rational. (b) Some real number is rational.

8. State the negation of the following: No real number is rational.

9. State the negation of each of the following: (a) Some Senators are lawyers. (b) All scientists enjoy mathematics.

10. Consider the following familiar quotation: None but the brave deserves the fair. (a) Interpret this in quantified form. (Be careful, this statement does not mean that every brave person deserves a fair person.) (b) State its negation.

11. Consider this claim: The sum of three consecutive integers, the first of which is even,

is not divisible by 6. (*a*) Restate the claim explicitly as a universally quantified statement. (*b*) List three particular cases illustrating this condition. (*c*) Prove the claim.

12. Let $\mathbb{E}' = \{n \in \mathbb{N}: n$ is even and $n > 2\}$ and let $\mathbb{P}$ be the set of primes. Goldbach's Conjecture (Christian Goldbach, 1690–1764) can be expressed symbolically as $\forall n \in \mathbb{E}'$, $\exists p_1, p_2 \in \mathbb{P}$, $p_1 + p_2 = n$. Express this conjecture and its negation in words.

13. Consider the claim: The product of any three consecutive integers is divisible by 6. (*a*) Restate the claim explicitly as a universally quantified statement. (*b*) List three particular cases illustrating this condition. (*c*) Prove the claim.

14. Consider the claim: The product of any three consecutive even integers is divisible by 48. (*a*) Restate the claim explicitly as a universally quantified statement. (*b*) List three particular cases illustrating this condition. (*c*) Prove this claim.

15. Express symbolically: (*a*) For all primes p and for all natural numbers a, p divides the difference of a^p and a. (*b*) Express the negation in words and symbols.

16. The proposition "any child can assemble it" has the logical structure $\forall x \in \mathbf{S}$, $p(x)$. (*a*) What is $\mathbf{S}$? (*b*) What is $p(x)$?

17. The statement "No one will be admitted unless over 18 years of age" has the structure $\forall x \in \mathbf{S}$, $p(x) \to q(x)$. (*a*) What is $\mathbf{S}$? (*b*) What is $p(x)$? (*c*) What is $q(x)$?

18. Let $\mathbf{S}$ be the set of all people, let $p(x)$ be "x brushes regularly," let $q(x)$ be "x sees his

dentist," and let $r(x)$ be "x has no cavities." (*a*) Translate into English: $\forall x \in \mathbf{S}$, $(p(x)$ and $q(x)) \to r(x)$. (*b*) What do you think is the negation of this statement?

19. State the negation of each of the following without using negative words: (*a*) There is a natural number that is even. (*b*) Every natural number is even.

20. Express each statement in Problem 19 symbolically.

21. Let $\mathbb{N}' = \{n \in \mathbb{N}: n > 1\}$. As usual, let $\mathbb{P}$ be the set of primes. (*a*) Express symbolically: Every natural number larger than 1 is divisible by some prime. (*b*) Express the negation of this statement symbolically and in words.

22. Let x be a real number. Express the following statement symbolically: For all natural numbers n, there is a rational number r such that the absolute value of the difference of x and r is less than the reciprocal of n.

23. State the following in words: $\forall n \in \mathbb{N}$, $\exists x \in \mathbb{R}$, $x^n - 1 = 0$. Give the negation in symbols. Which of the two is a true statement?

24. Let $\mathbf{S} \subseteq \mathbb{R}$. Then x is a **cluster point** of $\mathbf{S}$ if $\forall$ positive $e \in \mathbb{R}$, $\exists s \in \mathbf{S}$, $0 < |x - s| < e$. Express this definition in words.

25. Let $\mathbf{S} \subseteq \mathbb{R}$. Then x is a **boundary point** of $\mathbf{S}$ if $\forall$ positive $e \in \mathbb{R}$, $\exists s \in \mathbf{S}$, $z \in \mathbb{R} - \mathbf{S}$, $|x - s| < e$ and $|x - z| < e$. Express this definition in words.

26. Refer to Problem 12 to express "$\exists p_1, p_2 \in \mathbb{P}$, $\forall n \in \mathbb{E}'$, $p_1 + p_2 = n$" in words. Why is this quite different from Goldbach's Conjecture?

Section 10.   Well-Ordering Axiom

Overview for Section 10

- Motivation for the Well-Ordering Axiom (WOA)
  - Illustrations of proofs by WOA
- Introduction to summation notation and index variables
  - Description of telescopic sums
  - Introduction to triangular numbers

Key Concepts: Well-Ordering Axiom, summation notation and its properties, telescopic sums, triangular numbers

10.1

In Section 9 we observed that quantified statements share with all mathematical statements the property of being either true or false, but not both. The following statement [(3) in Example 1 of paragraph 9.5],

$$\forall x \in \mathbb{Z}, \quad \exists q \in \mathbb{Z}, \quad x = 9 \cdot q + 1,$$

illustrates a false universally quantified statement. It can be expressed more concisely in our "class" notation,

$$\forall x \in \mathbb{Z}, \quad x \in [\mathbf{1}]_9,$$

which makes the nonsensical claim that *every* integer has remainder 1 when divided by 9. We now consider a statement which is very similar in form to that one:

$$\forall n \in \mathbb{N}, \quad 10^n \in [\mathbf{1}]_9. \tag{1}$$

This cryptic message makes the claim that *every* positive integral power of 10 has a remainder 1 when divided by 9. Is this claim true or false?

Suppose we denote by $\mathcal{P}(n)$ the predicate in (1),

$$10^n \in [\mathbf{1}]_9,$$

which means that there is an integer q for which

$$10^n = 9 \cdot q + 1.$$

We may consider this to represent a collection of infinitely many simple statements, one for each positive integer n:

$$\mathcal{P}(1): \quad 10^1 = 9 \cdot 1 + 1 \qquad \text{(here } q \text{ is 1)},$$

$$\mathcal{P}(2): \quad 10^2 = 9 \cdot 11 + 1 \qquad \text{(here } q \text{ is 11)},$$

$$\mathcal{P}(3): \quad 10^3 = 9 \cdot 111 + 1 \qquad \text{(here } q \text{ is 111), and so on.}$$

Thus far, each one of these simple statements is true, so we have found no immediate counterexample. But the set $\mathbb{N}$ is infinite; hence there is no hope of guaranteeing the truth of (1) by continuing to examine the simple statements $\mathcal{P}(4), \mathcal{P}(5), \mathcal{P}(6), \ldots$. We must be cleverer than that!

Of course, (1) must be either true or false, and since the route to a direct proof appears to be impractical, we try an indirect argument. Assume that

$$(1) \text{ is false.} \tag{2}$$

From Section 9 we know how to negate a universally quantified statement: It is only necessary that there exist a single counterexample. Thus, if (2) is correct, then there must exist some $k \in \mathbb{N}$ for which 10^k does not have remainder 1 when divided by 9. Since we already know that $10^1 = 9 \cdot 1 + 1$, it must be the case that $k > 1$. (In fact, from the illustrations above we know that $k > 3$.) Now observe that we could assign T (true) or F (false) to each positive integer from 1 to k depending on whether the simple statement $\mathcal{P}(n)$ is true or false when n is replaced by that integer. Thus, from what we know so far, the assignment looks like

$$\begin{array}{ccccc} 1 & 2 & 3 & \cdots & k \\ T & T & T & \cdots & F. \end{array}$$

We don't know what happens between 3 and k, but it seems reasonable to assume that we could check out each case and determine:

$$\text{There is a } \textit{smallest} \text{ integer } j \text{ for which } \mathcal{P}(j) \text{ is false.} \tag{3}$$

Thus, the assignment must look like this (all assignments before the jth are T)

$$\begin{array}{cccc} 1 & \cdots & j-1 & j \\ T & \cdots & T & F \end{array}$$

where $j \leq k$ and $j - 1 \in \mathbb{N}$. This implies that

$$10^{j-1} \in [\mathbf{1}]_9 \qquad \text{and that} \qquad 10^j \notin [\mathbf{1}]_9.$$

We will now show that these two statements are contradictory. By the first one, there exists an integer q for which $10^{j-1} = 9 \cdot q + 1$, and since $10^j = 10^{j-1} \cdot 10$, we can write

$$10^j = (9 \cdot q + 1) \cdot 10,$$
$$= (9 \cdot q + 1) \cdot (9 + 1),$$
$$= 81 \cdot q + 9 \cdot q + 9 \cdot 1 + 1.$$

Thus, $10^j = 9 \cdot Q + 1,$ where $Q = 9 \cdot q + q + 1.$

Because q is an integer, so is Q, and this implies that $10^j \in [\mathbf{1}]_9$, which flatly contradicts the earlier claim that $\mathcal{P}(j)$ is false. We have reached the classical impasse in a proof by contradiction; hence one of our two assumptions (2) or (3) must be false. We conclude that (2) is the one to go because claiming that (3) is false would violate one of our intuitive understandings about integers: that we can examine a finite set of them one at a time, as we did, for example, in the proof of Theorem 4.2. This perception is so fundamental that it is incorporated among the axioms upon which we base the construction of our number system. It is called the **Well-Ordering Axiom.**

Well-Ordering Axiom

If **A** is any nonempty subset of the set of positive integers, then among the elements of **A** there is a smallest one.

Tutorial 10.1

Let $\mathbf{A} = \{x \in \mathbb{N} : x^2 - 4x - 5 > 0\}$.
a. Show that $\mathbf{A} \neq \varnothing$ by exhibiting an element in **A**.
b. Identify the smallest element in **A**.

10.2   We have the tools at hand, now, to give a formal proof that (1) in paragraph 10.1 is true.

THEOREM 10.2A   For each $n \in \mathbb{N}$, $10^n \in [\mathbf{1}]_9$.

Proof

Let $\mathcal{P}(n)$ denote the predicate $10^n \in [\mathbf{1}]_9$. Assume that the theorem is false; hence there is some element $k \in \mathbb{N}$ for which $\mathcal{P}(k)$ is false. Let

$$\mathbf{A} = \{a \in \mathbb{N} : \mathcal{P}(a) \text{ is false}\}.$$

Since $k \in \mathbf{A}$, $\mathbf{A}$ is nonempty, and by the Well-Ordering Axiom there is a smallest integer, call it j, for which $\mathcal{P}(j)$ is false. By testing, we found that $\mathcal{P}(1)$ is true, and so we know that $j > 1$. Hence $j - 1 \in \mathbb{N}$, and it follows that $\mathcal{P}(j - 1)$ is true and $\mathcal{P}(j)$ is false, so

$$10^{j-1} \in [\mathbf{1}]_9 \qquad \text{and} \qquad 10^j \notin [\mathbf{1}]_9.$$

But by the argument already given,

$$10^j = 10^{j-1} \cdot 10 = (9 \cdot m + 1)(9 + 1) = 9 \cdot Q + 1,$$

which contradicts the claim that $10^j \notin [\mathbf{1}]_9$. Hence our assumption (that the theorem is false) must itself be false; so the theorem is true. ∎

Note that there is nothing new in the technique of proof used here. Of course, we do have a new explicitly stated axiom, but the ideas are familiar: counterexample and proof by contradiction. For such a simple and intuitively evident property, the Well-Ordering Axiom is surprisingly powerful. It turns out to be one of the principal tools in nearly every branch of mathematics, but especially in discrete mathematics and in computer science. It will be the foundation of many of our most important results. The examples and theorems in this section and the next will hint at the variety of its applications. For brevity in reference, we will sometimes write WOA instead of Well-Ordering Axiom.

We are in a position now to pick up the thread left dangling in paragraph 8.1 where we stated, but did not prove, that any positive integer can be expressed as a multiple of 9, plus the sum of its digits. The proof is based on Theorem 10.2A.

THEOREM 10.2B

$\forall n \in \mathbb{N}$, n is a multiple of 9, plus the sum of its digits.

Proof

Any positive integer n has a representation in the decimal system as follows:

$$n = d_k \cdot 10^k + d_{k-1} \cdot 10^{k-1} + \cdots + d_2 \cdot 10^2 + d_1 \cdot 10^1 + d_0 \cdot 10^0 \qquad (1)$$

where each d_i is a digit and $d_k \neq 0$. By Theorem 10.2A, each power of 10 has remainder 1 when divided by 9. Hence we can write $10^i = 9m_i + 1$, $0 \leq i \leq k$. Substituting into (1),

$$
\begin{aligned}
n &= d_k \cdot (m_k \cdot 9 + 1) + d_{k-1} \cdot (m_{k-1} \cdot 9 + 1) + \cdots \\
&\quad + d_2 \cdot (m_2 \cdot 9 + 1) + d_1 \cdot (m_1 \cdot 9 + 1) + d_0, \\
&= 9(d_k \cdot m_k + d_{k-1} \cdot m_{k-1} + \cdots + d_2 \cdot m_2 + d_1 \cdot m_1) \\
&\quad + (d_k + d_{k-1} + \cdots + d_2 + d_1 + d_0)
\end{aligned}
$$

and this is the result desired. ∎

Example 1

Following the procedure in the proof above, we express 328 as a multiple of 9, plus 13 (the sum of its digits).

$$328 = 3 \cdot (100) + 2 \cdot (10) + 8,$$
$$= 3 \cdot (99 + 1) + 2 \cdot (9 + 1) + 8,$$
$$= 3 \cdot 99 + 2 \cdot 9 + 3 + 2 + 8,$$
$$= 9 \cdot (33 + 2) + (3 + 2 + 8).$$

10.3

In the proof of Theorem 10.2B, the notation for the sum of the digits is both awkward and lengthy. Mathematicians have invented a very handy abbreviation for this,

$$\sum_{i=0}^{k} d_i = d_0 + d_1 + \cdots + d_k.$$

The Greek capital letter sigma (Σ) means to sum, or add together, all terms that look like d_i, where the **index variable** i is replaced successively by integers from 0 to k (inclusive). Other specific illustrations of this **summation notation** are

$$\sum_{i=0}^{3} d_i = d_0 + d_1 + d_2 + d_3,$$

$$\sum_{i=6}^{8} d_i = d_6 + d_7 + d_8,$$

$$\sum_{i=0}^{5} (2i + 1) = 1 + 3 + 5 + 7 + 9 + 11.$$

A summation, in general, may be represented as in (1) below, where we assume that $f(i)$ stands for some number for each i on the interval $a \le i \le b$. (To get the preceding summation, let $a = 0$, $b = 5$, and $f(i) = 2i + 1$.)

$$\sum_{i=a}^{b} f(i) = f(a) + f(a + 1) + \cdots + f(b). \tag{1}$$

Here are some important general observations about the summation indicated in (1):

• The index letter is a "dummy" variable; it does not appear on the right-hand side. The particular letter used is not important; j and k are other frequent choices.

• The limits of summation range between $i = a$ and $i = b$; so we require that $a \le b$. Note that the number of terms in the sum is $b + 1 - a$. For example, $\sum_{i=2}^{4} i^2 = 4 + 9 + 16$ has $(4 + 1 - 2) = 3$ terms.

- In the special case that $b = a$, we agree that there is just one term, namely, $f(a)$. For example, $\sum_{i=1}^{1} i^2 = 1^2 = 1$.

- If $f(i)$ is a constant c, then $\sum_{i=a}^{b} f(i) = \sum_{i=a}^{b} c = (b+1-a) \cdot c$. For example, if $f(i) = 5$, then

$$\sum_{i=2}^{7} f(i) = \sum_{i=2}^{7} 5 = 5 + 5 + 5 + 5 + 5 + 5 = 6 \cdot 5 = 30.$$

Tutorial 10.3

a. Referring to (1), write each of the following as a sum:

$$\sum_{i=1}^{9} (2i + 3), \qquad \sum_{i=1}^{3} (2i + 3), \qquad \sum_{i=4}^{9} (2i + 3).$$

b. By writing as a summation and by grouping the terms appropriately, show that

$$\sum_{i=1}^{9} a_i = \sum_{i=1}^{3} a_i + \sum_{i=4}^{9} a_i.$$

Example 1

This example is somewhat more complicated than many others; it has been chosen to illustrate a special, but often useful, property of summations. Suppose you encountered the sum

$$\frac{1}{63} + \frac{1}{99} + \frac{1}{143} + \frac{1}{195} + \frac{1}{255} + \frac{1}{323}. \tag{2}$$

With a hand calculator you may easily discover that this sum is approximately 0.045. Your calculator may possibly *not* tell you that this sum is exactly $\frac{6}{133}$. Adding fractions, of course, is a standard technique of arithmetic, and you can obtain the answer that way. Suppose, however, we consider the sum a moment or two and attempt to write it in slightly different form. After some experimentation we discover that each denominator is a product of consecutive odd integers; hence (2) can be expressed as follows:

$$\frac{1}{7 \cdot 9} + \frac{1}{9 \cdot 11} + \frac{1}{11 \cdot 13} + \frac{1}{13 \cdot 15} + \frac{1}{15 \cdot 17} + \frac{1}{17 \cdot 19}.$$

Since for each $i \in \mathbb{N}$, $2i - 1$ and $2i + 1$ represent consecutive odd integers, each term in the summation has the form

$$f(i) = \frac{1}{(2i - 1)(2i + 1)}.$$

In sigma notation, (2) can be written

$$\sum_{i=4}^{9} \frac{1}{(2i - 1)(2i + 1)}. \tag{3}$$

Now it turns out that

$$\frac{1}{(2i - 1)(2i + 1)}$$

can be expressed differently using a technique called *partial fraction decomposition:*

$$\frac{1}{(2i - 1)(2i + 1)} = \frac{A}{2i - 1} + \frac{B}{2i + 1}$$

where $\qquad A = \frac{1}{2} \qquad$ and $\qquad B = -\frac{1}{2}.$

Thus, $\qquad \dfrac{1}{(2i - 1)(2i + 1)} = \dfrac{1}{2(2i - 1)} - \dfrac{1}{2(2i + 1)}.$

Consider next the (general) sum,

$$\sum_{i=1}^{n} \frac{1}{(2i - 1)(2i + 1)}$$

$$= \sum_{i=1}^{n} \left(\frac{1}{2(2i - 1)} - \frac{1}{2(2i + 1)} \right)$$

$$= \left(\frac{1}{2 \cdot 1} - \frac{1}{2 \cdot 3} \right) + \left(\frac{1}{2 \cdot 3} - \frac{1}{2 \cdot 5} \right) + \left(\frac{1}{2 \cdot 5} - \frac{1}{2 \cdot 7} \right) + \cdots$$

$$+ \left(\frac{1}{2 \cdot (2n - 3)} - \frac{1}{2 \cdot (2n - 1)} \right) + \left(\frac{1}{2 \cdot (2n - 1)} - \frac{1}{2 \cdot (2n + 1)} \right). \tag{4}$$

Note that the second term in each pair cancels the first term in the following pair, except for the very last term. Thus, (4) simplifies to

$$\sum_{i=1}^{n} \frac{1}{(2i-1)(2i+1)} = \frac{1}{2 \cdot 1} - \frac{1}{2 \cdot (2n+1)}$$

$$= \frac{1}{2} \cdot \left(1 - \frac{1}{2n+1}\right)$$

$$= \frac{2n}{2 \cdot (2n+1)} = \frac{n}{2n+1}. \qquad (5)$$

Because this summation collapses (by cancellation) to the difference of the first and last terms, it is sometimes called **telescopic,** and its final, simple expression is called the **closed form** of the sum. Hence, $n/(2n+1)$ is the closed form of the summation indicated in (4). Now we know that

$$\sum_{i=1}^{9} \frac{1}{(2i-1)(2i+1)} = \frac{9}{2 \cdot 9 + 1} = \frac{9}{19}.$$

Unfortunately, this is not what is required in (3), but it is close. We may group the terms in this sum in the following helpful way (see Tutorial 10.3):

$$\sum_{i=1}^{9} \frac{1}{(2i-1)(2i+1)} = \sum_{i=1}^{3} \frac{1}{(2i-1)(2i+1)} + \sum_{i=4}^{9} \frac{1}{(2i-1)(2i+1)}.$$

Hence,

$$\frac{9}{19} = \frac{3}{7} + \sum_{i=4}^{9} \frac{1}{(2i-1)(2i+1)},$$

or

$$\sum_{i=4}^{9} \frac{1}{(2i-1)(2i+1)} = \frac{9}{19} - \frac{3}{7} = \frac{63 - 57}{133} = \frac{6}{133}.$$

10.4

It is not unusual to see triangular arrangements of bowling pins or stacked cannon balls, as in Figure 10.4. Note that the number of objects in such an arrangement is $\sum_{i=1}^{n} i$, where n is the number of objects on any side. These numbers are called the

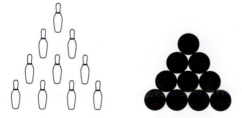

Figure 10.4

triangular numbers and are denoted by t_n. So, by counting, $t_1 = 1, t_2 = 3, t_3 = 6,$ $t_4 = 10$ (illustrated in Figure 10.4), etc.

Tutorial 10.4

a. Evaluate t_5, t_6, t_7, t_8.
b. Give a geometric argument (using a diagram similar to Figure 10.4) that $t_8 - 2 \cdot t_4$ is a perfect square.

It isn't hard to verify that t_8 is 36, but what is the number t_{500}? A direct count may take considerable time. Is there an easy way? Consider t_8, and instead of simply adding the eight integers, we write t_8 in the following two ways and then add:

$$
\begin{aligned}
t_8 &= 1 + 2 + 3 + 4 + 5 + 6 + 7 + 8 \\
t_8 &= 8 + 7 + 6 + 5 + 4 + 3 + 2 + 1 \\
\hline
2 \cdot t_8 &= 9 + 9 + 9 + 9 + 9 + 9 + 9 + 9.
\end{aligned}
$$

Thus $2 \cdot t_8 = 8 \cdot 9$, and so $t_8 = (8 \cdot 9)/2 = 36$. Note especially that there are 8 columns, each summing to 8 plus 1. This idea of adding a list of numbers in two different ways turns out to be an exceptionally useful tool: To get $2 \cdot t_8$ we add across first, then down; to get $8 \cdot 9$ we add down first, then across. Perhaps this same idea will work with the other sum. Writing t_{500} in its natural order and in reverse order gives

$$
\begin{aligned}
t_{500} &= 1 + 2 + 3 + \cdots + 499 + 500 \\
t_{500} &= 500 + 499 + 498 + \cdots + 2 + 1 \\
\hline
2 \cdot t_{500} &= 501 + 501 + 501 + \cdots + 501 + 501.
\end{aligned}
$$

Thus, $2 \cdot t_{500} = 500 \cdot 501$. Hence, $t_{500} = (500 \cdot 501)/2 = 125{,}250$. Note that there are 500 columns, each summing to 500 plus 1. Is this really the right sum? From all the evidence so far, we propose the following theorem about all the triangular numbers t_n.

THEOREM 10.4A

$$
\forall n \in \mathbb{N}, \quad \sum_{i=1}^{n} i = \frac{n(n+1)}{2}.
$$

Proof

For simplicity, we omit some of the detail included in the proof of Theorem 10.2A. Let $\mathcal{P}(n)$ denote the given predicate, and assume that the theorem is false. By the

Well-Ordering Axiom there is a smallest integer j for which $\mathcal{P}(j)$ is false. We ask, can $j = 1$? Test:

$$\sum_{i=1}^{1} i = \frac{1 \cdot 2}{2}.$$

Note that each side is 1; hence $\mathcal{P}(1)$ is true and we must have $j > 1$. Thus, $j - 1$ is a positive integer, and note that $\mathcal{P}(j - 1)$ is true but that $\mathcal{P}(j)$ is false, which means

$$\sum_{i=1}^{j-1} i = \frac{(j-1) \cdot j}{2},$$

$$\sum_{i=1}^{j} i \neq \frac{j \cdot (j+1)}{2}. \tag{1}$$

Now observe that

$$\sum_{i=1}^{j} i = (1 + 2 + \cdots + (j-1)) + j = \left(\sum_{i=1}^{j-1} i\right) + j,$$

or $\quad \displaystyle\sum_{i=1}^{j} i = \frac{(j-1) \cdot j}{2} + j = \frac{j^2 - j + 2j}{2} = \frac{j^2 + j}{2} = \frac{j \cdot (j+1)}{2}. \tag{2}$

Since (1) and (2) contradict each other, our initial assumption must be false; hence the theorem is true. ∎

Example 1   The triangular numbers are constructed by the following scheme:

$$t_1 = 1, \qquad t_2 = t_1 + 2 = 3, \qquad t_3 = t_2 + 3 = 6, \qquad t_4 = t_3 + 4 = 10, \text{ etc.}$$

Consider what happens when these numbers are squared:

$t_1^2 = 1,$

$t_2^2 = (t_1 + 2)^2 = t_1^2 + 2 \cdot 2 \cdot t_1 + 2^2 = 1^2 + 2(2 + 2) = 1^3 + 2^3,$

$t_3^2 = (t_2 + 3)^2 = t_2^2 + 2 \cdot 3 \cdot t_2 + 3^2 = (1^3 + 2^3) + 3(6 + 3) = 1^3 + 2^3 + 3^3,$

$t_4^2 = (t_3 + 4)^2 = t_3^2 + 2 \cdot 4 \cdot t_3 + 4^2 = (1^3 + 2^3 + 3^3) + 4(12 + 4)$
$\quad = 1^3 + 2^3 + 3^3 + 4^3.$

Although we have produced no geometric motivation for this result, the evidence of these few cases suggests that the square of the nth triangular number is the sum of the first n cubes. A typical argument based on WOA proves that this conjecture is correct.   ●

THEOREM 10.4B

$$\forall n \in \mathbb{N}, \quad t_n^2 = \sum_{i=1}^{n} i^3.$$

Sketch of Proof

By WOA, identify $j > 1$ such that

$$t_{j-1}^2 = \sum_{i=1}^{j-1} i^3 \qquad \text{and} \qquad t_j^2 \neq \sum_{i=1}^{j} i^3.$$

This implies that

$$t_j^2 \neq t_{j-1}^2 + j^3.$$

But, using Theorem 10.4A, this contradicts the fact that

$$t_j^2 = (t_{j-1} + j)^2 = t_{j-1}^2 + 2jt_{j-1} + j^2$$

$$= t_{j-1}^2 + 2j\frac{(j-1)\cdot j}{2} + j^2 = t_{j-1}^2 + j^3. \qquad ■$$

10.5   **Complement: Mean Values** In paragraph 1.2 we mentioned briefly the arithmetic mean of two real numbers, denoted here by a_1 and a_2:

$$\frac{a_1 + a_2}{2} = a \qquad \text{or} \qquad a_1 + a_2 = a + a. \tag{1}$$

We observe that the **arithmetic mean** a is a constant which when added to itself produces the same sum as a_1 and a_2. Assuming now that a_1 and a_2 are positive real numbers, we define the geometric mean in precisely the same way except that "addition" is replaced by "multiplication": The **geometric mean,** denoted by g, is that positive constant which when multiplied by itself produces the same product as a_1 and a_2. Thus,

$$a_1 \cdot a_2 = g \cdot g \qquad \text{or} \qquad g = \sqrt{a_1 \cdot a_2}. \tag{2}$$

The algebraic conditions (1) and (2) have nice geometric interpretations. In Figure 10.5A we observe that the arithmetic mean of two numbers corresponds to the midpoint of the interval determined by those numbers. Now, notice that (2) involves products; hence we expect the geometric interpretation to be areas: We think of $a_1 \cdot a_2$ as the area of a rectangle R having side lengths a_1 and a_2, and g^2 as the area of a square S of side length g. The commutative laws imply that we can write the given

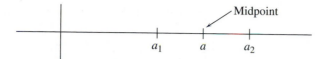

Figure 10.5A

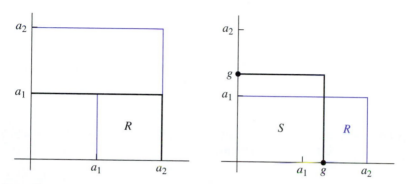

Figure 10.5B

numbers in either order, and for convenience we will assume that

$$0 < a_1 \le a_2.$$

It is clear from Figure 10.5B that

$$a_1^2 \le a_1 \cdot a_2 \le a_2^2.$$

The geometric mean corresponds to a point between a_1 and a_2 for which the area of the square S with side g is exactly the area of the rectangle R. Equation (2) tells us how to calculate g,

$$g = \sqrt{a_1 \cdot a_2},$$

but it doesn't tell us where on the interval it lies relative to the arithmetic mean a. The answer is suggested in Figure 10.5C, which shows that the area of the square of side length a is larger than the area of the rectangle R by exactly the shaded area. Because a is the midpoint of the interval from a_1 to a_2, $(a_2 - a) = (a - a_1)$; therefore from Figure 10.5C, $a_2 = a_1 + 2(a - a_1)$. Again from Figure 10.5C, we have

$$\begin{aligned} a^2 &= a_1^2 + 2a_1 \cdot (a - a_1) + (a - a_1)^2, \\ &= a_1 \cdot (a_1 + 2(a - a_1)) + (a - a_1)^2, \\ &= a_1 \cdot a_2 + (a - a_1)^2. \end{aligned}$$

Hence, the arithmetic mean is too big; its square exceeds $a_1 \cdot a_2$ by $(a - a_1)^2$, and we conclude that the geometric mean is between a_1 and a.

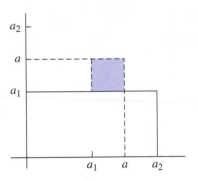

Figure 10.5C

If a_1 and a_2 are any positive real numbers, then the geometric mean does not exceed the arithmetic mean:

$$\sqrt{a_1 \cdot a_2} \leq \frac{a_1 + a_2}{2} \qquad \text{or} \qquad a_1 \cdot a_2 \leq \left(\frac{a_1 + a_2}{2}\right)^2. \tag{3}$$

Consider, next, how we might generalize these mean values. It seems clear enough how we should define the **arithmetic mean** of three real numbers: simply as the average value

$$a = \frac{a_1 + a_2 + a_3}{3} \qquad \text{or} \qquad 3a = a_1 + a_2 + a_3. \tag{4}$$

Again, mimicking this definition with addition replaced by multiplication, we define the **geometric mean** of three positive real numbers as that positive constant which when cubed produces the same product as a_1, a_2, a_3,

$$g^3 = a_1 \cdot a_2 \cdot a_3 \qquad \text{or} \qquad g = \sqrt[3]{a_1 \cdot a_2 \cdot a_3}. \tag{5}$$

Suppose we compare a and g for several choices of a_1, a_2, and a_3. (Here, a calculator will be very useful.)

a_1	a_2	a_3	g	a
1	2	3	1.817	2
5	8	9	7.114	7.333
8	8	11	8.896	9
10	10	10	10	10
21	30	33	27.497	28

In every case, we note that

$$g = \sqrt[3]{a_1 \cdot a_2 \cdot a_3} \leq \frac{a_1 + a_2 + a_3}{3} = a. \tag{6}$$

It turns out that (6) holds for any positive real numbers a_1, a_2, a_3; but more is true: We may generalize (6) to any finite list of positive real numbers $a_1, a_2, a_3, \ldots, a_n$.

Corresponding to the sigma abbreviation for a sum of several terms, there is an abbreviation for the product of several factors: the Greek capital letter Π. Thus, for example,

$$\sum_{i=1}^{5} a_i = a_1 + a_2 + a_3 + a_4 + a_5, \qquad \prod_{i=1}^{5} a_i = a_1 \cdot a_2 \cdot a_3 \cdot a_4 \cdot a_5;$$

$$\sum_{i=2}^{4} i^2 = 2^2 + 3^2 + 4^2, \qquad \prod_{i=2}^{4} i^2 = 2^2 \cdot 3^2 \cdot 4^2.$$

Now, we can state succinctly the theorem which generalizes Theorem 10.5A.

THEOREM 10.5B

$\forall n \in \mathbb{N}$, if $a_1, a_2, \ldots, a_n$ is any list of positive real numbers, then

$$\left(\prod_{i=1}^{n} a_i \right)^{1/n} \leq \frac{1}{n} \cdot \left(\sum_{i=1}^{n} a_i \right). \tag{7}$$

Remark. If $n = 1$, then (7) reduces to $a_1 \leq a_1$, which is trivially true, and if $n = 2$, then (7) reduces to (3), which has already been proved. The proof of Theorem 10.5B must consist in showing that all remaining entries in the following table are T (true):

n	1	2	3	4	5	6	7	8	$\cdots$
Predicate	T	T							$\cdots$

(8)

This appears to be a typical application of WOA in which we assume the theorem false and let k be the least integer for which (7) fails. Then we expect to derive a contradiction from the fact that (7) holds for $n = k - 1$ and fails for $n = k$. The trouble is that exceptional complications arise in this scenario. There is a more tractable approach which illustrates an alternative method of assuring that every entry in (8) is T. We will use a two-stage proof; first showing that every entry in (8) corresponding to a power of 2 is T, then showing that if any entry is T, then so is its predecessor.

**LEMMA
10.5A**

$\forall m \in \mathbb{N}$, any list of 2^m positive real numbers satisfies (7).

Proof

Assuming the statement of the theorem is false, by WOA there is a smallest integer k and a list of 2^k positive real numbers for which

$$\left(\prod_{i=1}^{2^k} a_i \right)^{1/2^k} > \frac{1}{2^k} \cdot \left(\sum_{i=1}^{2^k} a_i \right),$$

or

$$\frac{1}{2^k} \cdot \left(\sum_{i=1}^{2^k} a_i \right) < \left(\prod_{i=1}^{2^k} a_i \right)^{1/2^k}. \tag{9}$$

Because of Theorem 10.5A, we know that $k > 1$; hence any list of 2^{k-1} positive real numbers must satisfy (7). Now, pairing adjacent factors and using (3),

$$\prod_{i=1}^{2^k} a_i = (a_1 a_2)(a_3 a_4) \cdots (a_{2^k-1} \cdot a_{2^k}) \leq \prod_{i=1}^{2^{k-1}} b_i^2, \tag{10}$$

where $b_1 = (a_1 + a_2)/2$, $b_2 = (a_3 + a_4)/2$, and so on. We will assume that if p is any positive integer and if $0 \leq u \leq v$, then $u^{(1/p)} \leq v^{(1/p)}$. Hence from (10) it follows that

$$\left(\prod_{i=1}^{2^k} a_i \right)^{1/2^k} \leq \left(\prod_{i=1}^{2^{k-1}} b_i^2 \right)^{1/2^k} = \left(\prod_{i=1}^{2^{k-1}} b_i \right)^{1/2^{k-1}}. \tag{11}$$

Because (7) holds for the list $b_1, b_2, \ldots, b_{2^{k-1}}$,

$$\left(\prod_{i=1}^{2^{k-1}} b_i \right)^{1/2^{k-1}} \leq \frac{1}{2^{k-1}} \cdot \left(\sum_{i=1}^{2^{k-1}} b_i \right)$$

$$= \frac{1}{2^{k-1}} (b_1 + b_2 + \cdots + b_{2^{k-1}})$$

$$= \frac{1}{2^{k-1}} \left(\frac{a_1 + a_2}{2} + \frac{a_3 + a_4}{2} + \cdots + \frac{a_{2^k-1} + a_{2^k}}{2} \right)$$

$$= \frac{1}{2^k} \cdot \left(\sum_{i=1}^{2^k} a_i \right). \tag{12}$$

From (9), (11), and (12) we obtain the contradiction

$$\frac{1}{2^k} \cdot \left(\sum_{i=1}^{2^k} a_i \right) < \frac{1}{2^k} \cdot \left(\sum_{i=1}^{2^k} a_i \right).$$

∎

LEMMA 10.5B

If (7) holds for any list of n positive real numbers, then (7) also holds for any list of $n - 1$ positive real numbers.

Proof

Let $b_1, b_2, \ldots, b_{n-1}$ be any list of positive real numbers. Define

$$a_1 = b_1, \; a_2 = b_2, \; \ldots, \; a_{n-1} = b_{n-1}, \; a_n = \frac{1}{n-1} \cdot \left(\sum_{i=1}^{n-1} b_i \right).$$

Thus

$$\frac{1}{n} \cdot \left(\sum_{i=1}^{n} a_i \right) = \frac{1}{n} \cdot \left((b_1 + b_2 + \cdots + b_{n-1}) + \frac{1}{n-1} \cdot (b_1 + b_2 + \cdots + b_{n-1}) \right)$$

$$= \frac{1}{n-1} \cdot \left(\sum_{i=1}^{n-1} b_i \right) \qquad \text{(Why does this follow?)}$$

$$= a_n.$$

Further, since (7) holds for any list of n positive real numbers,

$$\prod_{i=1}^{n} a_i \leq \left(\frac{1}{n} \cdot \sum_{i=1}^{n} a_i \right)^n = a_n^n;$$

hence,

$$\prod_{i=1}^{n-1} a_i \leq a_n^{n-1}.$$

Now recall that $a_i = b_i$ for $i = 1$ to $n - 1$. Thus,

$$\left(\prod_{i=1}^{n-1} b_i \right) \leq a_n^{n-1} = \left(\frac{1}{n-1} \cdot \left(\sum_{i=1}^{n-1} b_i \right) \right)^{n-1}.$$

∎

Proof of Theorem 10.5B

Let n be any positive integer, and let m be the least integer for which $n \leq 2^m$. By Lemma 10.5A, the entry in (8) corresponding to 2^m is T. By repeated use of

Lemma 10.5B (if necessary), the entries for $2^m - 1, 2^m - 2, \ldots$ are all T; hence the entry corresponding to n must be T. ∎

Problems for Section 10

1. (a) Express $2 + 4 + 6 + \cdots + 200$ in sigma notation. (b) Express $2 + 4 + 6 + \cdots + 2n$ in sigma notation.

2. Evaluate the sums: (a) $\sum_{i=1}^{5} i$, (b) $\sum_{i=1}^{5} i^2$,

   (c) $\sum_{i=1}^{5} i^3$.

3. Evaluate the sums: (a) $\sum_{j=0}^{1} (2j + 1)$,

   (b) $\sum_{j=0}^{7} (2j + 1)$, (c) $\sum_{j=1}^{7} (2j + 1)$.

4. Evaluate $\sum_{k=1}^{n} (k^2 - k)$ for (a) $n = 1$,
   (b) $n = 3$, (c) $n = 8$.

5. Express the following in sigma notation:
   (a) $\frac{1}{2} + \frac{1}{4} + \frac{1}{6} + \frac{1}{8} + \frac{1}{10}$, (b) $\frac{1}{2} + \frac{1}{4} + \frac{1}{8} + \frac{1}{16}$.

6. Write out the six terms in each sum and compute the sum: (a) $\sum_{i=1}^{6} (-i)$, (b) $\sum_{j=0}^{5} (-j)$,

   (c) $\sum_{i=1}^{6} (-1)^i$, (d) $\sum_{j=0}^{5} (-1)^j$, (e) $\sum_{i=1}^{6} (-1)^i \cdot i$,

   (f) $\sum_{j=0}^{5} (-1)^j (2j + 1)$.

7. Explain why (a) $\sum_{i=1}^{6} i^2 = \left(\sum_{i=1}^{5} i^2 \right) + 36$,

   (b) $\sum_{i=1}^{k+1} i^2 = \left(\sum_{i=1}^{k} i^2 \right) + (k + 1)^2$.

8. Explain why (a) $\sum_{i=1}^{4} \frac{1}{i(i + 1)} =$

   $\left(\sum_{i=1}^{3} \frac{1}{i(i + 1)} \right) + \frac{1}{20}$,

   (b) $\sum_{i=1}^{k} \frac{1}{i(i + 1)} = \left(\sum_{i=1}^{k-1} \frac{1}{i(i + 1)} \right)$

   $+ \frac{1}{k(k + 1)}$.

9. Evaluate: (a) $\sum_{i=1}^{5} (i + 2)$, (b) $\sum_{i=1}^{5} i$, (c) $\sum_{i=1}^{5} 2$.
   Note: The answers to parts (b) and (c) sum to part (a).

10. By using (5) in paragraph 10.3 evaluate the following: (a) $\sum_{i=1}^{50} \frac{1}{(2i - 1)(2i + 1)}$,

    (b) $\sum_{i=25}^{50} \frac{1}{(2i - 1)(2i + 1)}$.

11. Show that (a) $\sum_{i=1}^{20} \frac{1}{(4i^2 - 1)} =$

    $\left(\sum_{i=1}^{19} \frac{1}{(4i^2 - 1)} \right) + \frac{1}{1599}$, (b) $\sum_{i=1}^{20} \frac{1}{(4i^2 - 1)} =$

    $\frac{19}{39} + \frac{1}{1599}$.

    [*Hint:* $4i^2 - 1 = (2i + 1)(2i - 1)$ and use (5) in paragraph 10.3.]

12. Express the following sums with sigma notation: (a) $1 + 3 + 5 + 7 + 9$,
    (b) $1 + 3 + 5 + 7 + \cdots + 101$.

13. Compute: (a) $\sum_{i=1}^{10} (-1)^i \cdot i$, (b) $\sum_{i=1}^{1000} (-1)^i \cdot i$.

14. If $\sum_{i=1}^{n} f(i) = 87$ and $f(n+1) = 45$, then what is $\sum_{i=1}^{n+1} f(i)$?

15. If $f(20) = 6$, $\sum_{i=1}^{50} f(i) = 247$, and $\sum_{i=20}^{50} f(i) = 147$, then what is $\sum_{i=1}^{20} f(i)$?

16. Using Theorem 10.4A, compute: (a) $\sum_{i=1}^{10} i$, (b) $\sum_{i=1}^{20} i$, (c) $\sum_{i=1}^{100} i$.

17. Using Theorem 10.4A, compute: (a) $\sum_{i=50}^{100} i$, (b) $\sum_{i=1}^{10} 2i$, (c) $\sum_{i=1}^{10} (2i + 3)$.

18. Using Theorem 10.4A, what is a formula for (a) $\sum_{i=1}^{n} 2i$, (b) $\sum_{i=1}^{n} (2i + 1)$, (c) $\sum_{i=1}^{n} (2i - 1)$?

19. Write the following in sigma notation:
(a) $\frac{1}{2} - \frac{1}{4} + \frac{1}{8} - \frac{1}{16}$, (b) $1 - \frac{1}{2} + \frac{1}{4} - \frac{1}{8} + \frac{1}{16} - \frac{1}{32}$,
(c) $\frac{1}{2} - \frac{1}{4} + \frac{1}{16} - \frac{1}{256}$.

20. Is it true that every positive integral power of 10 has the remainder 1 when divided by 3? Prove that for all $n \in \mathbb{N}$, $3 \mid (10^n - 1)$.

21. (*Continuation of Problem 20.*) Following the proof of Theorem 10.2B, show that for all $n \in \mathbb{N}$, n is a multiple of 3 plus the sum of the digits of n.

22. (*Conclusion of Problem 20.*) Show that 3 divides n if and only if 3 divides the sum of the digits of n.

23. Is it true that every positive integral power of 10 has the remainder 3 when divided by 7?

24. (*a*) Identify any five different subsets of $\mathbb{N}$, some finite, some infinite, and indicate the smallest element in each, if it exists. (*b*) What is the only condition under which the smallest element will not exist? (*c*) Try very hard to discover a nonempty subset of $\mathbb{N}$ which violates the Well-Ordering Axiom.

In each of the next seven problems, first test the predicate $\mathcal{P}(n)$ for correctness for $n = 1, 2$, and 3, then prove that $\mathcal{P}(n)$ is true for all $n \in \mathbb{N}$ by using the Well-Ordering Axiom.

25. For $n \in \mathbb{N}$, $\sum_{i=1}^{n} i^2 = \frac{n(n+1)(2n+1)}{6}$.

26. For $n \in \mathbb{N}$, $\sum_{i=1}^{n} i^3 = \frac{n^2(n+1)^2}{4}$.

27. For $n \in \mathbb{N}$, $\sum_{i=1}^{n} \frac{1}{i(i+1)} = \frac{n}{n+1}$.

28. For $n \in \mathbb{N}$, $\sum_{i=1}^{n} 3^i = \frac{3^{n+1} - 3}{2}$.

29. For $n \in \mathbb{N}$, $\sum_{i=1}^{n} i(i+1) = \frac{n(n+1)(n+2)}{3}$.

30. For $n \in \mathbb{N}$, $\sum_{i=1}^{n} \frac{1}{4i^2 - 1} = \frac{n}{2n+1}$. [This is (5) in paragraph 10.3.]

31. For $n \in \mathbb{N}$, $\sum_{i=1}^{n} (2i - 1)^2 = \frac{n(4n^2 - 1)}{3}$.

32. Referring to Problem 26, show that $\forall n \in \mathbb{N}$, n^3 is the difference of two squares.
$$\left[Hint: n^3 = \left(\sum_{i=1}^{n} i^3 \right) - \left(\sum_{i=1}^{n-1} i^3 \right). \right]$$

Section 11.   Consequences of the Well-Ordering Axiom

11.1   In paragraph 10.4 we introduced the **triangular** numbers, which can be constructed like pyramids. By Theorem 10.4A, the triangular number built on a base of length n is $(n(n+1))/2$. The triangular number $t_5 = 15$ is illustrated in Figure 11.1A. On similar geometric evidence we can identify a property of **square** numbers which seems to hold generally. Consider Figure 11.1B, which illustrates squares built on bases of

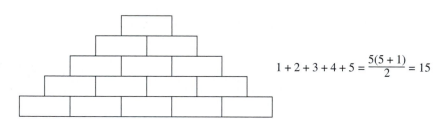

$$1 + 2 + 3 + 4 + 5 = \frac{5(5+1)}{2} = 15$$

Figure 11.1A

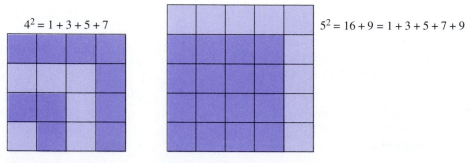

$4^2 = 1 + 3 + 5 + 7$

$5^2 = 16 + 9 = 1 + 3 + 5 + 7 + 9$

Figure 11.1B

lengths 4 and 5. It seems clear that squares of positive integers can be constructed as sums of consecutive odd integers, and by the Well-Ordering Axiom this conjecture can be proved in general. As before, we will use $\mathcal{P}(n)$ as an abbreviation for the indicated predicate.

THEOREM 11.1

$$\forall n \in \mathbb{N}, \quad \sum_{i=1}^{n}(2i - 1) = n^2.$$

Proof

Assume the theorem false; then

$$\{x \in \mathbb{N} : \mathcal{P}(x) \text{ is false}\} \neq \varnothing.$$

By the Well-Ordering Axiom there is a smallest integer j for which $\mathcal{P}(j)$ is false. Note that $\mathcal{P}(1)$ is true, since

$$\sum_{i=1}^{1}(2i - 1) = 1 = 1^2.$$

Thus, $j > 1$ and $(j - 1) \in \mathbb{N}$. Hence,

$$\sum_{i=1}^{j-1}(2i - 1) = (j - 1)^2,$$

but

$$\sum_{i=1}^{j}(2i - 1) \neq j^2.$$

So,

$$j^2 \neq \sum_{i=1}^{j}(2i - 1) = \sum_{i=1}^{j-1}(2i - 1) + (2j - 1) = (j - 1)^2 + (2j - 1),$$

and thus $j^2 \neq j^2$. By this contradiction our assumption must be wrong; hence the theorem is true. ∎

Tutorial 11.1

a. What odd number must be added to 9^2 to produce 10^2?

continued on next page

continued from previous page

b. Make a list of the first 10 triangular numbers $t_1, t_2, t_3, \ldots, t_{10}$.

c. Note that 10^2 can also be produced as the sum of two consecutive triangle numbers. Give a geometric argument in support of this fact.

11.2   As originally stated in paragraph 10.1, the Well-Ordering Axiom applies to the set of positive integers. There are many other sets of integers, however, which behave in a similar fashion. Let t be an integer and define

$$\mathbb{W}_t = \{x \in \mathbb{Z} : t \leq x\}. \tag{1}$$

For example,

$$\mathbb{W}_{-3} = \{-3, -2, -1, 0, 1, 2, \ldots\},$$
$$\mathbb{W}_0 = \{0, 1, 2, 3, \ldots\},$$
$$\mathbb{W}_1 = \mathbb{N},$$
$$\mathbb{W}_5 = \{5, 6, 7, \ldots\}.$$

Each of these sets has the property that any nonempty subset contains a smallest element. Strictly speaking, a claim like this one should be subject to proof. But the claim is hardly less evident than the Well-Ordering Axiom itself; hence we will simply assume that WOA extends to such sets. But, we must exercise caution and not assume too much. It is certainly not the case that every nonempty subset of $\mathbb{Z}$ has a smallest element; for example,

$$\{\ldots, -3, -2, -1, 0\}$$

doesn't. We note, furthermore, that WOA does not apply to the set of rational numbers; for example,

$$\{\tfrac{1}{2}, \tfrac{1}{3}, \tfrac{1}{4}, \tfrac{1}{5}, \ldots\}$$

is a nonempty subset of $\mathbb{Q}$ which has no smallest element.

The motivation for our preceding discussion is simple: There are situations in which the most natural universe is of the form $\mathbb{W}_t$ rather than $\mathbb{N}$.

Example 1   To consider the relationship between n^2 and 2^n, suppose we test the truth of the inequality

$$n^2 < 2^n$$

for small values of n, as displayed in the following table. It is clear that the inequality fails for some positive integers, but the information in the table does seem to support a conjecture that the inequality holds for integers in $\mathbb{W}_5$.

n	n^2	2^n	$n^2 < 2^n$
0	0	1	T
1	1	2	T
2	4	4	F
3	9	8	F
4	16	16	F
5	25	32	T
6	36	64	T

THEOREM 11.2

$$\forall n \in \mathbb{W}_5, \quad n^2 < 2^n.$$

Proof

Assume the theorem false: then

$$\{x \in \mathbb{W}_5 : \mathcal{P}(x) \text{ is false}\} \neq \varnothing.$$

Thus, there is a smallest element j in $\mathbb{W}_5$ for which $\mathcal{P}(j)$ is false, which means that $j^2 \geq 2^j$. Note that $\mathcal{P}(5)$ is true, since $25 < 32$. So, $j > 5$ and $(j - 1) \in \mathbb{W}_5$. Since $\mathcal{P}(j - 1)$ is true and $\mathcal{P}(j)$ is false,

$$(j - 1)^2 < 2^{j-1} \qquad \text{but} \qquad 2^j \leq j^2.$$

Hence,
$$2(j - 1)^2 < 2^j \leq j^2,$$
$$2j^2 - 4j + 2 < j^2,$$
$$j^2 - 4j + 2 < 0,$$
$$j(j - 4) + 2 < 0,$$

which is a contradiction because $j > 5$. ∎

Tutorial 11.2

a. Consider the relationship between n^3 and 2^n by constructing a table (as in Example 1) for $n \leq 10$.

b. State a conjecture, similar to Theorem 11.2, which you think may be provable.

11.3 Divisibility questions, also, are an easy target for WOA. Consider again divisibility by 3 (as in paragraph 5.3), remembering that $[2]_3$ denotes the set of all those integers which have remainder 2 when divided by 3. Observe now that the first few odd powers of 2 can be written

$$2^1 = 3 \cdot 0 + 2,$$
$$2^3 = 3 \cdot 2 + 2,$$
$$2^5 = 3 \cdot 10 + 2,$$
$$2^7 = 3 \cdot 42 + 2.$$

Again, the evidence of a few cases seems persuasive, and we are led to conjecture that all odd powers of 2 belong to $[2]_3$.

THEOREM 11.3

$$\forall n \in \mathbb{W}_0, \quad 2^{2n+1} \in [2]_3.$$

Proof

Assume the theorem false; then

$$\{x \in \mathbb{W}_0 : \mathcal{P}(x) \text{ is false}\} \neq \varnothing,$$

where $\mathcal{P}(x)$ denotes the predicate $2^{2n+1} \in [2]_3$. Thus there is a smallest element j in $\mathbb{W}_0$ for which $\mathcal{P}(j)$ is false, which means that

$$2^{2j+1} \notin [2]_3. \tag{1}$$

Note that $\mathcal{P}(0)$ is true, since $2^1 = 3 \cdot 0 + 2$. So, $j > 0$ and $(j - 1) \in \mathbb{W}_0$. Since $\mathcal{P}(j - 1)$ is true, $2^{2(j-1)+1} = 3 \cdot Q + 2$ for some integer Q. Thus,

$$2^{2j-2+1} = 2^{2j-1} = 3Q + 2,$$

and $$4(2^{2j-1}) = 4(3Q + 2) = 12Q + 8 = 12Q + 6 + 2,$$

$$2^{2j+1} = 3(4Q + 2) + 2,$$

which contradicts (1). ■

11.4 Sometimes even the most evident properties of the real number system involve unsuspected applications of the Well-Ordering Axiom. Our next examples illustrate this subtle control exercised by WOA.

Example 1   We are often aware of a fact about numbers without being aware of *why* we know it. For example, it is perfectly obvious from the picture of the x axis

that there is no integer strictly between 0 and 1. But how do we know this? Whatever answer we give must refer to the axioms and theorems which govern the behavior of the real number system. In addition to the Well-Ordering Axiom, we will need two simple facts:

1. If a is an integer, then a^2 is also an integer.

2. If x is any real number such that $0 < x < 1$, then

$$0 < x^2 < x < 1.$$

By the Well-Ordering Axiom, the set of all positive integers must contain a smallest element, call it s. From fact **1** we know that s^2 is an integer. Furthermore, if $0 < s < 1$, then from fact **2** we know that

$$0 < s^2 < s < 1.$$

But this shows that s^2 is a smaller positive integer than s, which is a contradiction. We are forced then to conclude that $s \geq 1$. ●

Example 2   In paragraph 7.5 we stated without proof the Fundamental Theorem of Arithmetic. We are now able to give a partial proof: that any positive integer greater than 1 is either a prime or a product of primes. If not, then by the Well-Ordering Axiom there is a smallest positive integer greater than 1, call it s, which is neither. Since s is not prime, it must be composite and hence can be written as a product of two positive integers both smaller than s,

$$s = p \cdot q.$$

Since each of p and q is smaller than s and s is the smallest integer that cannot be written as a product of primes, each of p and q is either a prime or can be written as a product of primes. Hence s, itself, can be written as a product of primes. This contradiction proves that there cannot be any exception to the claim that each positive integer greater than 1 is either a prime or a product of primes.

We will omit a proof that the factorization, guaranteed above, *is unique*. ●

Example 3   In paragraph 7.5, we used FTOA to prove that $\sqrt{2}$ is not a rational number. It should be no surprise to observe that we may prove the same result using the Well-Ordering Axiom directly. Thus, if $\sqrt{2} = p/q$, where p and q are positive integers, then the set

$\mathbf{A} = \{a \in \mathbb{N} : a\sqrt{2}$ is an integer$\}$ is nonempty [see (1) in paragraph 9.5]. By WOA there is a smallest integer $k \in \mathbf{A}$. Recall from arithmetic that

$$1 < \sqrt{2} < 2;$$

hence

$$k < k\sqrt{2} < 2k,$$

and

$$0 < k\sqrt{2} - k < k.$$

So, $k\sqrt{2} - k$ is a positive integer smaller than k. Note that $(k\sqrt{2} - k) \cdot \sqrt{2}$ is also an integer (Why?). Hence $(k\sqrt{2} - k) \in \mathbf{A}$, which contradicts the fact that k is the smallest element of $\mathbf{A}$.   ●

11.5

In paragraph 5.3 we used the division algorithm

$$a = b \cdot q + r,$$

in which the quotient is q and the remainder r satisfies

$$0 \le r < b.$$

There, we tacitly assumed that such an r can always be found (i.e., the division algorithm would end). Now, we can prove via Well-Ordering that the tacit assumption is correct.

THEOREM 11.5

Let a and b denote positive integers. Then there exist integers q and r such that

$$a = b \cdot q + r, \qquad \text{where } 0 \le r < b.$$

Proof

Suppose that a and b are positive integers and that we wish to find q and r, as above. We consider separately the three possibilities: $a < b$, $a = b$, and $a > b$. If $a < b$, then $a = b \cdot 0 + a$ (hence $q = 0$ and $r = a$). If $a = b$, then $a = b \cdot 1 + 0$ (hence $q = 1$ and $r = 0$). Finally, we assume that $a > b$. For each positive integer n, the number $a - b \cdot n$ is again an integer. Let $\mathbf{M}$ be the subset of all these integers which are positive:

$$\mathbf{M} = \{m : m = a - b \cdot n, n \in \mathbb{N}, \text{ and } m > 0\}.$$

Since $(a - b \cdot 1) \in \mathbf{M}$, we know that $\mathbf{M}$ is a nonempty subset of the positive integers; hence by the Well-Ordering Axiom, $\mathbf{M}$ contains a smallest integer, call it k. Because

$k \in \mathbf{M}$, there is an integer $n' \in \mathbb{N}$ such that

$$a = b \cdot n' + k \qquad \text{and} \qquad k > 0.$$

Furthermore, if $k > b$, then

$$a = b \cdot n' + b + (k - b) = b \cdot (n' + 1) + (k - b),$$

where $k - b > 0$. But this says that $(k - b) \in \mathbf{M}$, which contradicts the fact that k is the smallest element in $\mathbf{M}$. We must conclude, then, that $k \leq b$; hence,

$$a = b \cdot q + r = \begin{cases} b \cdot n' + k, & \text{if } k < b; \\ b \cdot (n' + 1) + 0, & \text{if } k = b. \end{cases}$$ ∎

11.6   Complement: Systems of Distinct Representatives

Consider a set of n lines in the plane, denoted by $\mathbf{L}_1, \mathbf{L}_2, \ldots, \mathbf{L}_n$. Although these lines may intersect in various ways, it is always possible to select another line $\mathbf{L}$ which is not parallel to any of the lines $\mathbf{L}_i$ and does not contain a point in which any of them intersect. (See Figure 11.6 for an illustration when $n = 3$.) Let the line $\mathbf{L}$ intersect each of the lines $\mathbf{L}_i$ at the point p_i, and note that these points are all distinct from one another. In geometry, the line $\mathbf{L}$ is called a **transversal** of the given family of lines. Each point p_i may be taken as a **representative** (or as a **label**) for its line $\mathbf{L}_i$, and the set $\{p_1, p_2, \ldots, p_n\}$ is an example of a system of distinct representatives.

There is an analog of this situation in discrete mathematics. Suppose we are given any finite family $\mathscr{A}$ of n finite sets $\mathbf{A}_1, \mathbf{A}_2, \ldots, \mathbf{A}_n$. Without the power of geometry to fall back on, we have no device (like the transversal $\mathbf{L}$) to guide us in the selection of a system of distinct representatives for the family $\mathscr{A}$. If each set is nonempty, then for each i we can simply choose an element $a_i \in \mathbf{A}_i$, and these elements serve as representatives of their sets. But the interesting question is, "Can these elements be chosen so that they are all distinct from one another?"

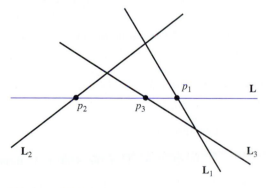

Figure 11.6

Recall that in paragraph 0.4 we considered a special case of Philip Hall's Theorem on systems of distinct representatives, in which his concern was unambiguous representation.

Let $\mathcal{A} = \{A_1, A_2, \ldots, A_n\}$ be a finite collection of sets. Assume that each of these sets is finite, but they need not have the same number of elements and they may overlap in any way. Any selection of a single element from each set without duplication is called a system of distinct representatives for the collection $\mathcal{A}$. We will abbreviate this concept by SDR.

An SDR is sometimes referred to as a **transversal** of its family $\mathcal{A}$ because it is a kind of finite analog of the geometric transversal. Just as in the geometric situation, there may exist many different transversals for a given family. Our only concern here, however, is with conditions which guarantee that at least one SDR exists.

If any one of the sets in the given family $\mathcal{A}$ is empty, then no element is available to represent that set; hence no SDR can exist. To avoid this trivial situation we assume that each set A_i is nonempty. But the following simple example shows that this condition is not enough (compare with Example 1 in paragraph 0.4).

Example 1

Let the collection $\mathcal{A} = \{A_1, A_2, A_3, A_4, A_5\}$ consist of the sets $A_1 = \{1, 2\}$, $A_2 = \{2, 3\}$, $A_3 = \{1, 3\}$, $A_4 = \{1, 2, 3\}$, and $A_5 = \{2, 3, 4, 5\}$. Even though there are at least two choices of representative for each set, a little trial and error shows that whatever distinct representatives may be selected for sets A_1, A_2, and A_3, there can be no distinct representative selected from A_4. This is because the number of sets in the subcollection $\{A_1, A_2, A_3, A_4\}$ is 4, while the total number of elements belonging to any of A_1, A_2, A_3, or A_4 is 3, since each is a subset of $\{1, 2, 3\}$. ●

In what follows it will be helpful to anticipate some notation that will be discussed more thoroughly in paragraph 15.1. First, if A and B are sets, then the **union** of A and B is

$$A \cup B = \{x : x \in A \text{ or } x \in B\}.$$

Second, if A is a finite set, then we denote the number of elements of A by $|A|$.

Example 2

In Example 1, $A_1 \cup A_2 \cup A_3 \cup A_4 = \{1, 2, 3\}$, and so $|A_1 \cup A_2 \cup A_3 \cup A_4| = 3$. To conserve space, this union is sometimes denoted $\cup A_i$. If $\mathcal{B} = \{A_1, A_2, A_3, A_4\}$, then $\cup A_i$ can be written also as $\cup \mathcal{B}$. In general, the "$\cup$" in front of a family of sets denotes the union of all the sets in the family. ●

Example 1 implies that if an SDR for any family $\mathcal{A}$ is to exist, then the following is a *necessary* condition:

$$\text{For any subfamily } \mathcal{B} \text{ of } \mathcal{A}, \ |\mathcal{B}| \leq |\cup \mathcal{B}|. \qquad (\mathcal{H})$$

This condition may be translated, "any k of the sets in $\mathcal{A}$ must contain between them at least k elements." A trivial illustration of a family which satisfies $(\mathcal{H})$ is any collection of mutually disjoint sets.

Example 3 The military alphabet is an SDR illustrating this situation. It is a selection of words representing the sets of words having the same initial letter (hence representing that letter). The intent, of course, is to enhance the accuracy of verbal communication by identifying unambiguously those letters which sound alike in speech. This SDR changes from time to time, but currently its first few elements are alpha, bravo, charlie, delta, and echo.

But a requirement that the sets be mutually disjoint is much too strong. The answer discovered by Philip Hall is both elegant and unexpected: condition $(\mathcal{H})$ is *sufficient*. This statement means that if there is no bar to the construction of an SDR through some failure of $(\mathcal{H})$, as in Example 1, then no unforeseen subtlety can arise to prevent its existence.

Hall's original proof of the theorem was elementary in the sense that it involved only an application of mathematical induction, but the technique was quite involved. Since its publication in 1935, there have been numerous other proofs given, some much simpler than the original. One of the simplest proofs is due to P. R. Halmos and H. E. Vaughan; our proof is a slight modification of it.

Let $\mathcal{A}$ be a finite family of finite sets. The set $\mathbf{A} \in \mathcal{A}$ is called a **minimal** set of $\mathcal{A}$ if for all $\mathbf{B} \in \mathcal{A}$, $|\mathbf{A}| \le |\mathbf{B}|$. Note that if $\mathcal{A}$ is nonempty and contains only finite sets, then $\mathcal{A}$ has a minimal set. To see this, let

$$\mathbf{S} = \{n \in \mathbb{N}: \exists \mathbf{A} \in \mathcal{A} \text{ with } |\mathbf{A}| = n\}.$$

Since $\mathcal{A}$ is nonempty, the set $\mathbf{S}$ is nonempty, and so by WOA $\mathbf{S}$ has a least element. Hence there is a set in $\mathcal{A}$ which has this number of elements and so is a minimal set. In Example 1, $\mathbf{A}_1$, $\mathbf{A}_2$, and $\mathbf{A}_3$ are minimal sets in $\mathcal{A}$.

THEOREM 11.6 A finite family of finite sets has an SDR if and only if it satisfies the condition $(\mathcal{H})$.

Remark. We know already that $(\mathcal{H})$ is a necessary condition for the existence of an SDR, so we need only prove that $(\mathcal{H})$ implies an SDR. Note, also, that $(\mathcal{H})$ is inherited by any subfamily of a family which satisfies $(\mathcal{H})$.

Proof

We will use the Well-Ordering Axiom. Supposing the theorem false, there must be some collection of sets for which $(\mathcal{H})$ holds but for which there is no SDR. By WOA there is a smallest integer n for which there is a collection of n finite sets

$$\mathcal{A} = \{\mathbf{A}_1, \mathbf{A}_2, \dots, \mathbf{A}_n\}$$

satisfying $(\mathcal{H})$ but having no SDR. Observe that $n > 1$, for any single, nonempty set has an SDR. (In fact, any element in that set can be selected to represent the set.)

Let A_1 be a set in the family and let p be one of its members. Now erase p from each of the sets $A_2, \ldots, A_n$ to which it belongs, and put

$$\mathcal{A}' = \{A_2', A_3', \ldots, A_n'\}$$

where $A_i' = A_i - \{p\}$. If $\mathcal{A}'$ satisfied $(\mathcal{H})$, then since it has fewer than n sets, it would have an SDR (not including the point p). So, that SDR together with p selected from A_1 would produce an SDR for $\mathcal{A}$, which is forbidden. Thus there is some subfamily $\mathcal{B}'$ of $\mathcal{A}'$ for which $|\mathcal{B}'| > |\cup \mathcal{B}'|$. If we were to adjoin p to the sets in $\mathcal{B}'$, then $(\mathcal{H})$ holds for the corresponding subfamily $\mathcal{B}$. Also $|\mathcal{B}'| = |\mathcal{B}|$ and $\cup\mathcal{B} = \cup\mathcal{B}' \cup \{p\}$. Since $\mathcal{B}$ is a subfamily of $\mathcal{A}$,

$$|\mathcal{B}| \leq |\cup \mathcal{B}| = |\cup \mathcal{B}'| + 1 < |\mathcal{B}'| + 1 = |\mathcal{B}| + 1$$

and so

$$|\mathcal{B}| = |\cup \mathcal{B}|.$$

This implies that each element in $\cup\mathcal{B}$ appears in the SDR guaranteed for $\mathcal{B}$ by WOA. Erase all the elements in $\cup\mathcal{B}$ from the remaining sets in $\mathcal{A}$. The resulting family has fewer than n sets and also must satisfy $(\mathcal{H})$ [for otherwise the assumption that $\mathcal{A}$ satisfies $(\mathcal{H})$ would fail]. Thus, the remaining sets must have an SDR, which coupled with the SDR for $\mathcal{B}$ produces an SDR for $\mathcal{A}$, contrary to the fact that $\mathcal{A}$ has no SDR. ∎

Problems for Section 11

In each of the next four problems, first test the predicate $\mathcal{P}(n)$ for correctness for $n = 1, 2,$ and 3, then prove that $\mathcal{P}(n)$ is true for all $n \in \mathbb{N}$ by using the Well-Ordering Axiom.

1. For $n \in \mathbb{N}$, $4^n - 1$ is divisible by 3.

2. For $n \in \mathbb{N}$, $5^n - 1$ is divisible by 4.

3. For $n \in \mathbb{N}$, $3^{2n} - 1$ is divisible by 8.

4. For $n \in \mathbb{N}$, $8^{2n} - 1$ is divisible by 9.

5. Let x be an odd integer. Show that for $n \in \mathbb{N}$, x^n is odd.

6. It is a fundamental principle of arithmetic that the product of any two positive numbers is positive. In particular then, $x^2 > 0$ if $x > 0$. Prove: For $n \in \mathbb{N}$, if $x > 0$, then $x^n > 0$.

7. Consider the predicate $\mathcal{P}(n)$: $n^2 > 5n + 3$. (a) Show that $\mathcal{P}(n)$ is false for

$n = 1, 2, 3, 4, 5$. (b) Show that $\mathcal{P}(n)$ is true for $n = 6, 7, 8, 9, 10$.

8. (Continuation of Problem 7.) You will show that: $\forall n \in \mathbb{W}_6$, $\mathcal{P}(n)$. (a) State this in words. (b) State the negation of this in words and symbols.

9. (Continuation of Problem 7.) Let $S = \{n \in \mathbb{W}_6: \mathcal{P}(n)$ is false $\}$. So if $n \in S$, then $n^2 \leq 5n + 3$. (a) Show that $6 \notin S$. (b) If $S \neq \emptyset$, then by WOA, S has at least element j. Why is $(j - 1)$ in $\mathbb{W}_6$? State what it means for j to belong to S and $j - 1$ not to belong to S.

10. (Conclusion of Problem 7.) Notice that $\sim\mathcal{P}(j)$ is the inequality $j^2 \leq 5j + 3$. (a) Since $(j - 1) \in S$, express $\mathcal{P}(j - 1)$ as an inequality. (b) Combine the inequalities $\mathcal{P}(j - 1)$ and $\sim\mathcal{P}(j)$ and solve for j. Is j in $\mathbb{W}_6$? Your answer should be "no." Since

$j \notin \mathbb{W}_6$, you have a contradiction. So $\mathbf{S} = \varnothing$, and $\mathcal{P}(n)$ is true for all $n \in \mathbb{W}_6$.

11. Show that for all $n \geq 11$, $n^2 - n - 100 > 0$.

12. Show that for all $n \geq 3$, $n^2 > 2n + 1$.

13. Using Problem 12, show that for all $n \geq 6$, $2^n > (n + 1)^2$.

14. Let $\mathbf{T} = \{m\colon m = 2a + 5b \text{ for } a, b \in \mathbb{W}_0\}$. (a) List 10 elements of $\mathbf{T}$. (b) What is the smallest positive integer not in $\mathbf{T}$? What do you think is the largest integer not in $\mathbf{T}$? (c) Show that 5, 6, 7, and 8 are in $\mathbf{T}$.

15. (Continuation of Problem 14.) Let $\mathbf{S} = \{m \in \mathbb{W}_8\colon m \notin \mathbf{T}\}$. (a) Assume $\mathbf{S}$ is not empty. Why does $\mathbf{S}$ have a least element j? (b) Now $j \neq 2a + 5b$ for all nonnegative integers a and b but $j - 1 = 2a' + 5b'$ for some $a', b' \in \mathbb{W}_0$. Why?

16. (Continuation of Problem 14.) (a) If $b' = 0$, then why is $a' > 2$? (b) Let $a = a' - 2$ and let $b = 1$. Show that $2a + 5b = j$.

17. (Conclusion of Problem 14.) (a) If $b' > 0$, let $a = a' + 3$ and $b = b' - 1$. Show that $j = 2a + 5b$. (b) Conclude that $j \notin \mathbf{S}$. (c) Conclude that $\mathbf{S}$ is empty. (d) Conclude that the only integers that can't be written as $2a + 5b$ are 1 and 3.

18. For $n \in \mathbb{W}_2$, show that

$$(1 - \tfrac{1}{4})(1 - \tfrac{1}{9})(1 - \tfrac{1}{16})\cdots\left(1 - \frac{1}{n^2}\right) = \frac{n + 1}{2n}.$$

19. For $n \in \mathbb{W}_2$, show that

$$\frac{2^2}{1\cdot 3} \cdot \frac{3^2}{2\cdot 4} \cdot \frac{4^2}{3\cdot 5} \cdots \frac{n^2}{(n-1)(n+1)} = \frac{2n}{n+1}.$$

20. Let $a, b \in \mathbb{N}$ and let $d = \gcd(a, b)$. In this and the next two problems you will show that there are integers x and y such that $ax + by = d$. (See Problem 42 in Section 6.) (a) Show that $\mathbf{S} = \{m \in \mathbb{N}\colon m = ax + by, x, y \text{ in } \mathbb{Z}\}$ is not empty. By WOA,

$\mathbf{S}$ has a least element j; hence $j = ax + by$. (b) By the division algorithm there are integers q and r such that $a = q \cdot j + r, 0 \leq r < j$. Solve for r and substitute $ax + by$ for j.

21. (Continuation of Problem 20.) (a) If $r > 0$, then by Problem 20, $r \in \mathbf{S}$. Why is this a contradiction? (b) Conclude that $r = 0$, and so j divides a. Show that j must also divide b. (c) Conclude that $j \leq d$.

22. (Conclusion of Problem 20.) (a) Show that d divides j. Remember that $j \in \mathbf{S}$. (b) Conclude that $d = j$, and hence $d = ax + by$ for some integers x and y.

23. When Godfrey Harold Hardy (1877–1947) (famous English mathematician) was visiting Srinivasa Ramanujan (1887–1920) (famous Indian mathematician) who was ill, Hardy remarked that he had ridden in taxicab no. 1729, and thought that the number was dull and hoped that it was not an unfavorable omen. Ramanujan reflected and replied that it was a very interesting number, since 1729 is the smallest integer expressible as the sum of two cubes in two different ways. Verify Ramanujan's assertion (begin by making a list of the first 12 cubes).

24. **Theorem.** All numbers are interesting. **Proof.** Let $\mathbf{S} = \{n \in \mathbb{N}\colon n \text{ is not interesting}\}$. Use Well-Ordering to show that if $\mathbf{S}$ is not empty, then a contradiction arises. (Hint: Isn't the smallest number of any set interesting?)

25. Compute the sum of all the odd numbers between 500 and 1000.

26. (a) Compute the sum of the 50 smallest odd positive integers. (b) Compute the sum of the next 50 smallest odd positive integers.

27. Compute $\sum_{i=1}^{100}(-1)^i(2i - 1)$. (Hint: Pair the summands.)

28. Suppose that a segment of unit length is given in the plane. Using only a straightedge and compass, invent a geometric algorithm for marking successively on a horizontal line the lengths $1, \sqrt{2}, \sqrt{3}, \sqrt{4}, \sqrt{5}, \sqrt{6}, \sqrt{7}$, and $\sqrt{8}$. (See accompanying figure for a hint.)

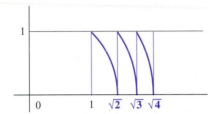

29. Problem 28 seems to suggest that the positive square root of any positive integer can be constructed using only a straightedge and compass. State this observation in the form of a theorem, and attempt a proof via WOA.

Consider Boethius's Table as found in Robert D. Stevick's *The Earliest Irish and English Book-arts: Visual and Poetic Forms before* A.D. *1000.* The jth entry in the first row is 2^{j-1} and the jth entry on the diagonal is 3^{j-1}. Any other entry is double the entry immediately to its left.

1	2	4	8	16	32	64	...
	3	6	12	24	48	96	...
		9	18	36	72	144	...
			27	54	108	216	...
				81	162	324	...
					243	486	...
						729	...
							...

30. Show that the entry in row i, column j of Boethius's Table is $2^{j-1}3^{i-1}$. To do this, consider i to be a fixed integer and use WOA on j.

31. *(Continuation of Problem 30.)* Show that the **arithmetic mean** (the average) of two consecutive row entries is the number below the smaller number.

32. *(Continuation of Problem 30.)* Show that the harmonic mean of two consecutive row entries is the number above the larger number. [The **harmonic mean** of two numbers a and b is $(2ab)/(a + b)$.]

33. *(Continuation of Problem 30.)* Show that the geometric mean of the entry in row i, column j and the entry in row $(i + 2m)$, column $(j + 2m)$ is the entry midway between them; namely the one in row $(i + m)$, column $(j + m)$. (The **geometric mean** of the two numbers a and b is $\sqrt{a \cdot b}$.)

34. *(Continuation of Problem 30.)* Show that the harmonic mean of any two numbers a and b is the ratio of the square of the geometric mean to the arithmetic mean.

35. Let $t \in \mathbb{Z}$. Use the following steps to show that every nonempty subset of $\mathbb{W}_t$ contains a least element. (*a*) Assume that **A** is a nonempty subset of $\mathbb{W}_t$, and let **B** $= \{k + 1 - t : k \in \textbf{A}\}$. Show that **B** is nonempty. (*b*) Let $x \in$ **B** and show that $x \in \mathbb{N}$. (*c*) Use WOA to show that **B** contains a least element. (*d*) Conclude that **A** contains a least element.

Section 12.   Principle of Mathematical Induction

12.1   Consider the general, universally quantified statement

$$\forall n \in \mathbb{N}, \quad \mathscr{P}(n)$$

in which $\mathscr{P}(n)$, as usual, denotes some predicate. Examining the proofs of Theorems 10.2A and 10.4A, notice that in each case we established two critical facts:

- $\mathscr{P}(1)$ is true.

- For $j > 1$, it cannot happen that $\mathscr{P}(j - 1)$ is true while $\mathscr{P}(j)$ is false.

As indicated in paragraph 10.1, the situation may be described by a table

n	1	2	3	4	$\cdots$	k	$\cdots$
$\mathscr{P}(n)$							

(1)

in which the kth entry is T or F depending upon whether the simple statement $\mathscr{P}(k)$ is true or false. What is shown in those proofs is that the pattern

T	F

(2)

cannot appear as entries in this table (for if they do, a contradiction ensues). Thus, if the table contains any F at all, the pattern can only be:

- Every entry F.

- The initial entries are F's, followed by all T's.

In either of these cases note that the first entry is F. Thus, if we can show that the first entry *must* be T, then all entries must be T.

The analysis above suggests an alternate technique for proving that every entry in (1) is T. Consider the implication:

$$\text{If } \mathcal{P}(k) \text{ is true, then } \mathcal{P}(k+1) \text{ is true.} \tag{3}$$

To prove the truth of an implication $p \to q$, we assume that the hypothesis is true and, on that basis, show that the conclusion necessarily follows. Note carefully that this argument does *not* prove that q is true; it merely proves that q cannot be false when p is true. Thus, if we can prove the truth of the implication (3), then we know that the T followed by F pattern in (2) cannot occur in (1). As before, to guard against *any* F entry in the table we need only show in addition that the first entry must be T. The outline of this argument is often expressed as follows, where $\mathcal{P}(n)$ denotes a predicate.

Suppose that:

a. $\mathcal{P}(1)$ is true,

b. If $\mathcal{P}(k)$ is true, then $\mathcal{P}(k+1)$ is true;

then for every $n \in \mathbb{N}$, $\mathcal{P}(n)$ is true.

Condition **b** guarantees that the pattern in (2) cannot occur, and condition **a** guarantees that the leading entry is T; thus no F can occur in the table. This is often referred to as the Principle of Mathematical Induction. There is an equivalent statement of the principle in terms of sets of positive integers, and we will use it frequently in this form.

Principle of Mathematical Induction

Let $\mathbf{M} \subseteq \mathbb{N}$.

If

a. $1 \in \mathbf{M}$,

b. If $k \in \mathbf{M}$, then $(k+1) \in \mathbf{M}$,

then $\mathbf{M} = \mathbb{N}$.

12.2 For those who have studied mathematical induction previously, the proofs of Theorems 10.2A and 10.4A should have seemed (at least vaguely) familiar. Although this may be surprising, it is no accident. We will show in the Complement (paragraph 12.6) that the Well-Ordering Axiom and the Principle of Mathematical Induction are logically equivalent. We would expect, therefore, similarities of technique and concept. Indeed, it is customary to refer to either technique as a proof by mathematical induction. There are, however, occasions when the peculiarities of a specific problem may adapt more readily to one of the forms than the other. Incidentally, we will sometimes refer to the Principle of Mathematical Induction by the abbreviation PMI.

Example 1

Applications of PMI often make use of summation properties such as:

$$\sum_{i=1}^{10} i = (1 + 2 + 3 + 4 + 5 + 6 + 7 + 8 + 9) + 10 = \sum_{i=1}^{9} i + 10.$$

$$\sum_{i=1}^{k+1} i = (1 + 2 + \cdots + k) + (k + 1) = \sum_{i=1}^{k} i + (k + 1).$$

$$\sum_{i=1}^{10} (2i + 1) = \sum_{i=1}^{9} (2i + 1) + (2(10) + 1)$$

$$= (3 + 5 + 7 + 9 + 11 + 13 + 15 + 17 + 19) + 21.$$

$$\sum_{i=1}^{k+1} (2i + 1) = \sum_{i=1}^{k} (2i + 1) + (2(k + 1) + 1)$$

$$= \sum_{i=1}^{k} (2i + 1) + (2k + 3).$$

To illustrate how the Principle of Mathematical Induction is applied, we return to Theorem 10.4A, which says that the sum of the first n positive integers is $(n(n+1))/2$.

Proof of Theorem 10.4A by PMI

Let

$$\mathbf{M} = \left\{ n \in \mathbb{N}: \sum_{i=1}^{n} i = \frac{n(n + 1)}{2} \right\},$$

and let $\mathcal{P}(n)$ denote the predicate. To claim by the Principle of Mathematical Induction that $\mathcal{P}(n)$ is true for every positive integer n, we must show that $\mathbf{M} = \mathbb{N}$. To do this we demonstrate that **a** $\mathcal{P}(1)$ is true, which means that $1 \in \mathbf{M}$, and **b** if $\mathcal{P}(k)$ is true, then $\mathcal{P}(k + 1)$ is true, which means that if $k \in \mathbf{M}$, then $(k + 1) \in \mathbf{M}$.

a. $\mathcal{P}(1)$ is true, since

$$\sum_{i=1}^{1} i = 1 = \frac{1(1 + 1)}{2}.$$

Thus $1 \in \mathbf{M}$.

b. In this part, keep in mind that we are *not* trying to prove that either $\mathcal{P}(k)$ is true or $\mathcal{P}(k+1)$ is true. We are merely trying to prove that the implication

$$\mathcal{P}(k) \rightarrow \mathcal{P}(k+1)$$

is true. To accomplish this, we must assume that $\mathcal{P}(k)$ *is* true, then show that $\mathcal{P}(k+1)$ *must* also be true. Observe, first, that $\mathcal{P}(k)$ is

$$\sum_{i=1}^{k} i = \frac{k(k+1)}{2}$$

and that $\mathcal{P}(k+1)$ is

$$\sum_{i=1}^{k+1} i = \frac{(k+1)(k+2)}{2}.$$

Since

$$\sum_{i=1}^{k+1} i = \left(\sum_{i=1}^{k} i \right) + (k+1),$$

and since $\mathcal{P}(k)$ is true, we can replace

$$\sum_{i=1}^{k} i \qquad \text{by} \qquad \frac{k(k+1)}{2};$$

hence

$$\sum_{i=1}^{k+1} i = \frac{k(k+1)}{2} + (k+1),$$

$$= \frac{k(k+1)}{2} + \frac{2(k+1)}{2} = \frac{(k+1)(k+2)}{2},$$

which is exactly the statement $\mathcal{P}(k+1)$. Hence, if $k \in \mathbf{M}$, then $(k+1) \in \mathbf{M}$. Now the Principle of Mathematical Induction guarantees that $\mathbf{M} = \mathbb{N}$, and thus $\mathcal{P}(n)$ is true for all $n \in \mathbb{N}$. ∎

Tutorial 12.2

Determine a_n in each of the following equations.

a. $\displaystyle\sum_{i=1}^{9} (2i - 1) = \sum_{i=1}^{8} (2i - 1) + a_n.$

continued on next page

continued from previous page

b. $\displaystyle\sum_{i=1}^{16}\frac{i(i+1)}{2} = \sum_{i=1}^{15}\frac{i(i+1)}{2} + a_n.$

c. $\displaystyle\sum_{i=1}^{n}\frac{i(i+1)}{2} = \sum_{i=1}^{n-1}\frac{i(i+1)}{2} + a_n.$

12.3   Many fascinating relationships involving sums have been discovered. Consider, for example, the following:

$$\frac{1}{1\cdot 2}, \qquad \frac{1}{1\cdot 2}+\frac{1}{2\cdot 3}, \qquad \frac{1}{1\cdot 2}+\frac{1}{2\cdot 3}+\frac{1}{3\cdot 4}, \qquad \frac{1}{1\cdot 2}+\frac{1}{2\cdot 3}+\frac{1}{3\cdot 4}+\frac{1}{4\cdot 5}.$$

A little computation shows that these sums equal, respectively,

$$\frac{1}{2}, \qquad \frac{2}{3}, \qquad \frac{3}{4}, \qquad \frac{4}{5}.$$

A reasonable prediction for the next sum appears to be $\frac{5}{6}$. Can a pattern of such regularity (and predictability) be accidental? At the moment we don't know, but it seems reasonable to guess that the expected result will hold for sums of any number of terms. To be certain, however, we prove it via mathematical induction.

THEOREM 12.3

For each $n \in \mathbb{N}$,

$$\sum_{i=1}^{n}\frac{1}{i(i+1)} = \frac{n}{n+1}.$$

Proof

Denote by $\mathcal{P}(n)$ the predicate

$$\sum_{i=1}^{n}\frac{1}{i(i+1)} = \frac{n}{n+1}.$$

We must show that $\mathbf{M} = \{n \in \mathbb{N}: \mathcal{P}(n) \text{ is true}\}$ is the set of natural numbers.

a. $\mathcal{P}(1)$ has exactly one term on the left-hand side, $\frac{1}{2}$, which is equal to the right-hand side; hence $\mathcal{P}(1)$ is true. Thus $1 \in \mathbf{M}$.

b. Assume that $\mathcal{P}(k)$ is true, that is,

$$\sum_{i=1}^{k}\frac{1}{i(i+1)} = \frac{k}{k+1}.$$

Now, observe that

$$\sum_{i=1}^{k+1} \frac{1}{i(i+1)} = \sum_{i=1}^{k} \frac{1}{i(i+1)} + \frac{1}{(k+1)(k+2)},$$

$$= \frac{k}{k+1} + \frac{1}{(k+1)(k+2)} = \frac{k(k+2)+1}{(k+1)(k+2)},$$

$$= \frac{(k+1)^2}{(k+1)(k+2)} = \frac{k+1}{k+2},$$

which shows that $\mathcal{P}(k+1)$ is true. Thus, if $k \in \mathbf{M}$, then $(k+1) \in \mathbf{M}$. By the Principle of Mathematical Induction, $\mathbf{M} = \mathbb{N}$. ■

Tutorial 12.3

Consider the summation $\sum_{i=1}^{n} \frac{2}{4i^2 - 1}$.

a. Compute (as a fraction) this sum for each of the following values of n: 1, 2, 3, 4.

b. Guess at a generalization which you believe is provable.

Example 1   Let $f(i) = 1/2^i$ for all positive integers i. Considering the sums

$$\sum_{i=1}^{2} f(i) = \frac{1}{2^1} + \frac{1}{2^2} = \frac{3}{2^2} = \frac{2^2 - 1}{2^2},$$

and

$$\sum_{i=1}^{3} f(i) = \sum_{i=1}^{2} f(i) + \frac{1}{2^3} = \frac{7}{2^3} = \frac{2^3 - 1}{2^3},$$

we are led to conjecture that, in general,

$$\sum_{i=1}^{k+1} f(i) = \sum_{i=1}^{k} f(i) + \frac{1}{2^{k+1}} = \frac{2^{k+1} - 1}{2^{k+1}}.$$

Admittedly, the evidence is slender at this point, but the conjecture is true, and an inductive proof can be given. Observe that for any positive integer k, the sum is strictly less than 1 but that it differs from 1 by only $1/2^{k+1}$. Thus, for $k = 99$ the sum differs from 1 by only $1/2^{100}$ (which is an incomprehensibly small number).

This observation lies behind the claim (made in other mathematics courses) that

$$\frac{1}{2^1} + \frac{1}{2^2} + \frac{1}{2^3} + \frac{1}{2^4} + \cdots = 1.$$

12.4

As another illustration of the Principle of Mathematical Induction we prove a result about real numbers, and the argument will depend upon certain well-known properties of numbers and inequalities.

THEOREM 12.4 Let x and y denote any pair of real numbers for which $0 < x < y$. For each $n \in \mathbb{N}$, $0 < x^n < y^n$.

Proof

Consider x and y to be fixed real numbers subject to the hypothesis that $0 < x < y$. Let $\mathcal{P}(n)$ denote the predicate

$$0 < x^n < y^n,$$

and let $\mathbf{M} = \{n \in \mathbb{N} : \mathcal{P}(n) \text{ is true}\}$.

a. Now $\mathcal{P}(1)$ is true by hypothesis, and so $1 \in \mathbf{M}$.

b. Assume next that $k \in \mathbf{M}$; hence $0 < x^k < y^k$. Since both x^k and y are positive, multiplying an inequality by either will not reverse the inequality. So multiply $0 < x < y$ by x^k to get

$$0 < x^{k+1} < yx^k$$

and multiply $0 < x^k < y^k$ by y to get

$$0 < yx^k < y^{k+1}.$$

Combining these two inequalities yields

$$0 < x^{k+1} < yx^k < y^{k+1}.$$

Thus, $\mathcal{P}(k + 1)$ is true, and so $(k + 1) \in \mathbf{M}$. By PMI, $\mathbf{M} = \mathbb{N}$ and $\mathcal{P}(n)$ is true for all $n = \mathbb{N}$. ∎

Before ending this discussion, we compare once again the two methods of proof involving the Well-Ordering Axiom and the Principle of Mathematical Induction.

• In WOA we consider the set

$$\{n \in \mathbb{N} : \mathcal{P}(n) \text{ is false}\},$$

and we show that this set is empty by assuming the contrary, then producing a contradiction.

• In PMI, we consider the set

$$\{n \in \mathbb{N} : \mathcal{P}(n) \text{ is true}\},$$

and we show that this set is $\mathbb{N}$ by proving parts **a** and **b** of PMI.

Which of these two methods should be used in any given situation depends sometimes upon the nature of the problem, but more often it is a matter of technical indifference, and the choice is dictated by one's mathematical taste or experience.

We observed in paragraph 11.2 that WOA could be extended to more general subsets of $\mathbb{Z}$ than $\mathbb{N}$. Similarly, PMI can be adapted to subsets of $\mathbb{Z}$ of the form

$$\mathbb{W}_t = \{x \in \mathbb{Z} : t \le x\}$$

for any fixed $t \in \mathbb{Z}$. We need only modify the principle as follows:

Modified Principle of Mathematical Induction

Let $\mathbf{M} \subseteq \mathbb{W}_t$.

If

a. $t \in \mathbf{M}$,

b. If $k > t$ and $k \in \mathbf{M}$, then $(k + 1) \in \mathbf{M}$,

then $\mathbf{M} = \mathbb{W}_t$.

For example, Theorem 11.2 can be proved as outlined in the following tutorial.

Tutorial 12.4

Let $\mathcal{P}(n)$ be the predicate: $n^2 < 2^n$. Define $\mathbf{M} = \{n \in \mathbb{W}_5 : \mathcal{P}(n) \text{ is true}\}$. Show:

a. $5 \in \mathbf{M}$.

b. If $k > 5$ and $k \in \mathbf{M}$, then $(k + 1) \in \mathbf{M}$.

(*Hint:* Use the fact that $2k + 1 < k^2$ for $k \in \mathbb{W}_5$, Problem 12 in Section 11.)

12.5

A positive integer which reads the same both left to right and right to left is called a **palindrome**: for example, 12321 or 7887. Palindromes occur occasionally on the odometers of automobiles, but the concept is not one of central importance in the theory of arithmetic or of mathematics in general. Nevertheless, there is an entertaining property associated with these numbers: that every palindrome having an even number of digits is divisible by 11. Try it for 7887 and 138831 (again, don't jump too quickly to the conclusion these special cases might suggest).

Tutorial 12.5

a. Find the quotient in each case: $\frac{7887}{11}$, $\frac{138831}{11}$.
b. What observation about the quotient is suggested by part **a**?
c. Find the quotient of $\frac{210012}{11}$.

The argument will depend on the following observation, which offers a good illustration of PMI: If 1 is added to any odd power of 10, the result is always divisible by 11. Before trying a proof, suppose we test the first few instances:

$$10^1 + 1 = 11,$$
$$10^3 + 1 = 1001 = 11 \cdot 91,$$
$$10^5 + 1 = 100001 = 11 \cdot 9091.$$

THEOREM 12.5

$$\forall n \in \mathbb{N}, \quad 11 \mid (10^{2n-1} + 1).$$

Proof

Denote the predicate $11 \mid (10^{2n-1} + 1)$ by $\mathcal{P}(n)$, and let $\mathbf{M} = \{n \in \mathbb{N} : \mathcal{P}(n) \text{ is true}\}$. Again, we must show parts **a** and **b** of PMI.

a. Note that $\mathcal{P}(1)$ is the statement $11 \mid (10^1 + 1)$, which is true since 11 does divide 11. Thus, $1 \in \mathbf{M}$.

b. Now assume that $\mathcal{P}(k)$ is true, which means that

$$10^{2k-1} + 1 = 11 \cdot m, \qquad \text{for some integer } m.$$

Next consider

$$10^{2(k+1)-1} + 1 = 10^{2k+1} + 1 = 10^2 \cdot 10^{2k-1} + 1,$$
$$= 10^2 \cdot 10^{2k-1} + 10^2 - 10^2 + 1.$$

The last step does not change the expression since $10^2 - 10^2 = 0$, but this "trick" of adding and subtracting the same thing allows us to use the assumption about $\mathcal{P}(k)$ as follows:

$$10^{2(k+1)-1} + 1 = 10^2(10^{2k-1} + 1) - 10^2 + 1 = 10^2(11 \cdot m) - 99,$$
$$= 11(10^2 \cdot m - 9).$$

Since $10^2 m - 9$ is an integer, this shows that 11 divides the left-hand side and that $\mathcal{P}(k+1)$ is true. Since $k \in \mathbf{M}$ implies $(k+1) \in \mathbf{M}$, by PMI, $\mathbf{M} = \mathbb{N}$. ∎

Not all palindromes are divisible by 11; you can discover counterexamples easily, but (of course) they all have an odd number of digits. To prove our earlier claim about palindromes, consider an arbitrary one having $2n$ digits,

$$z = d_1 d_2 \ldots d_n d_n \ldots d_2 d_1,$$

where each d_i is one of the ten digits and $d_1 \neq 0$. Since z is a positive integer, its meaning (in the decimal system) is

$$z = d_1 \cdot 10^{2n-1} + d_2 \cdot 10^{2n-2} + \cdots + d_n \cdot 10^{n-1} + \cdots + d_2 \cdot 10 + d_1.$$

Now, we can rewrite this as

$$z = (d_1 \cdot 10^{2n-1} + d_1) + (d_2 \cdot 10^{2n-2} + d_2 \cdot 10) + \cdots + (d_n \cdot 10^n + d_n \cdot 10^{n-1}),$$
$$= d_1 \cdot (10^{2n-1} + 1) + 10 d_2 \cdot (10^{2n-3} + 1) + \cdots + 10^{n-1} d_n \cdot (10 + 1).$$

Finally, note that each factor in parentheses is 1 plus an odd power of 10 and hence by Theorem 12.5 is divisible by 11. So, therefore, is z. Keeping track of all these powers of 10 is a bit tedious, so here's a numerical illustration of the steps indicated above. Consider the palindrome 138831.

$$138831 = 1 \cdot 10^5 + 3 \cdot 10^4 + 8 \cdot 10^3 + 8 \cdot 10^2 + 3 \cdot 10 + 1,$$
$$= 1(10^5 + 1) + 3(10^4 + 10) + 8(10^3 + 10^2),$$
$$= 1(10^5 + 1) + 30(10^3 + 1) + 800(10 + 1),$$
$$= 1(11 \cdot 9091) + 30(11 \cdot 91) + 800(11),$$
$$= 11 \cdot (9091 + 2730 + 800),$$
$$= 11 \cdot (12621).$$

12.6   **Complement: Equivalence of WOA and PMI** To show that the Well-Ordering Axiom and the Principle of Mathematical Induction are logically equivalent, we must prove two implications: WOA → PMI and PMI → WOA.

First, assume the Well-Ordering Axiom. Let $\mathbf{M} \subseteq \mathbb{N}$ be such that:

a. $1 \in \mathbf{M}$.

b. If $n \in \mathbf{M}$, then $(n + 1) \in \mathbf{M}$.

We must show that $\mathbf{M} = \mathbb{N}$. If $\mathbf{M} \neq \mathbb{N}$, then the set $\mathbf{S} = \{n \in \mathbb{N} : n \notin \mathbf{M}\}$ is not empty. By WOA, $\mathbf{S}$ has a least element which we denote by j. Now, recall that in Example 1 of paragraph 11.4 we proved (via WOA) that there is no integer strictly between 0 and 1. Since $j \in \mathbf{S} \subseteq \mathbb{N}$, $j \geq 1$, but $j \neq 1$ because $1 \in \mathbf{M}$. We conclude that $j > 1$; hence $(j - 1) \in \mathbb{N}$. Because j is the least element in $\mathbf{S}$, $(j - 1) \notin \mathbf{S}$ which implies that $(j - 1) \in \mathbf{M}$. Thus, by **b** above, $(j - 1) + 1 = j \in \mathbf{M}$. This contradicts the fact that $j \in \mathbf{S}$. Therefore, $\mathbf{S}$ is empty and $\mathbf{M} = \mathbb{N}$. This proves that WOA $\rightarrow$ PMI. ∎

Next, assume the Principle of Mathematical Induction. We must show that any nonempty subset of the set of positive integers has a smallest element. The proof in this direction is a bit more involved, and one of the difficulties is that we must take care to use only properties that have not been proved on the basis of WOA. In particular, we will need the "suspect" fact: If n is any positive integer, then there is no positive integer strictly between $(n - 1)$ and n. (This property, incidentally, is the basis for our remarks in paragraph 1.1 on the distinction between integers and real numbers.) To remove suspicion, we digress to prove this fact by PMI.

LEMMA 12.6A $\forall n \in \mathbb{N}$, if $x \in \mathbb{R}$ and $(n - 1) < x < n$, then x is not an integer.

Proof

Let $\mathcal{P}(n)$ denote the predicate:

> If $x \in \mathbb{R}$ and $(n - 1) < x < n$, then x is not an integer

and let $\mathbf{M} = \{n \in \mathbb{N} : \mathcal{P}(n) \text{ is true}\}$.

a. Consider $\mathcal{P}(1)$, which says:

> If $x \in \mathbb{R}$ and $0 < x < 1$, then x is not an integer.

The intent of $\mathcal{P}(1)$ is that there is no positive integer less than 1, so we will prove by PMI that

$$\forall m \in \mathbb{N}, \qquad m \geq 1.$$

Let $\mathbf{M}_1 = \{m \in \mathbb{N} : m \geq 1\}$ and note that $1 \in \mathbf{M}_1$ since $1 \geq 1$. Now assume that $k \in \mathbf{M}_1$, which means that $k \geq 1$. Thus,

$$k + 1 \geq 1 + 1 \geq 1,$$

hence $(k + 1) \in \mathbf{M}_1$. By PMI, $\mathbf{M}_1 = \mathbb{N}$, so $\mathcal{P}(1)$ is true. This proves that $1 \in \mathbf{M}$.

b. Assume that $\mathcal{P}(k)$ is true; hence $k \in \mathbf{M}$. This means:

If $x \in \mathbb{R}$ and $(k-1) < x < k$, then x is not an integer.

If m were an integer and $k < m < k+1$, where we assume that $k > 0$, then $m-1$ is an integer and we have $k-1 < m-1 < k$. This contradicts $\mathcal{P}(k)$, so $\mathcal{P}(k+1)$ is true and $(k+1) \in \mathbf{M}$. By PMI, $\mathbf{M} = \mathbb{N}$. ■

Now, let $\mathbf{S}$ be any nonempty subset of $\mathbb{N}$ and suppose that $n \in \mathbf{S}$. We need to show that $\mathbf{S}$ has a least element. Note that if $n = 1$, then $\mathbf{S}$ has a least element (by Lemma 12.6A). But if $n \neq 1$, then we can make no such claim, and it appears that we will need another argument based on PMI. Consider the following predicate which we will denote by $\mathcal{P}_1(n)$:

If $\mathbf{A} \subseteq \mathbb{N}$ and if $m \in \mathbf{A}$, with $m \leq n$, then $\mathbf{A}$ has a least element.

LEMMA 12.6B

$\forall n \in \mathbb{N}, \quad \mathcal{P}_1(n)$ is true.

Proof

Let $\mathbf{M} = \{n \in \mathbb{N} : \mathcal{P}_1(n) \text{ is true}\}$.

a. By Lemma 12.6A, $1 \in \mathbf{M}$.

b. Assume that $k \in \mathbf{M}$, and consider $\mathcal{P}_1(k+1)$:

If $\mathbf{A} \subseteq \mathbb{N}$ and $m \in \mathbf{A}$, with $m \leq k+1$, then $\mathbf{A}$ has a least element.

Let $\mathbf{A}$ satisfy the hypothesis of $\mathcal{P}_1(k+1)$. Suppose that $m \in \mathbf{A}$ and $m < k+1$. By Lemma 12.6A, there is no integer strictly between k and $k+1$. Hence, $m \leq k$. Since $k \in \mathbf{M}$, $\mathbf{A}$ has a least element. On the other hand, if no element of $\mathbf{A}$ is less than $k+1$, then $(k+1) \in \mathbf{A}$ and $k+1$ is the least element in $\mathbf{A}$. In either case, therefore, $\mathbf{A}$ has a least element and $(k+1) \in \mathbf{M}$. By PMI, $\mathbf{M} = \mathbb{N}$. ■

Finally, observe that if $\mathbf{S}$ is any nonempty subset of $\mathbb{N}$, then some positive integer n is in $\mathbf{S}$; hence $\mathcal{P}_1(n)$ guarantees that $\mathbf{S}$ has a least element. This completes the proof that PMI $\to$ WOA. ■

Once again, we stress an important fact about implication. The argument given here does not prove that either WOA or PMI is true. It merely proves that neither one can be true unless the other one is true also. It is possible to assume either one as an axiom describing the behavior of our familiar real number system. Instead of assuming WOA (as in paragraph 10.1), we could have based our development of mathematical induction on PMI. (In fact, most other textbooks tend to favor that approach, but we believe the one chosen here is more natural.) As a final observation, without WOA or some comparable condition the resulting number system fails to be the one with which we are familiar.

Problems for Section 12

Remark. Many of the problems in the preceding two problem sets may be proved by use of the Principle of Mathematical Induction. It is recommended that at least a few of these be tried to emphasize the similarities (as well as differences) in the WOA and PMI proof techniques. The following seven statements should be proved by PMI.

1. For $n \in \mathbb{N}$,

$$\sum_{i=1}^{n}(2i - 1) \cdot 2i = \frac{n(n + 1)(4n - 1)}{3}.$$

2. For $n \in \mathbb{N}$,

$$\sum_{i-1}^{n}(2i - 1)^3 = n^2(2n^2 - 1).$$

[*Hint:* $(2n + 1)^3 = 8n^3 + 12n^2 + 6n + 1$ and $2n^4 + 8n^3 + 11n^2 + 6n + 1 = (n + 1)^2(2n^2 + 4n + 1).$]

3. For $n \in \mathbb{N}$,

$$\sum_{i=1}^{n}(2i)^3 = 2n^2(n + 1)^2.$$

4. For $n \in \mathbb{N}$,

$$\sum_{i=1}^{n}(2i)(2i + 1)(2i + 2) = 2n(n + 1)^2(n + 2).$$

5. For $n \in \mathbb{N}$,

$$\sum_{i=1}^{n}\frac{1}{(2i + 1)(2i + 3)} = \frac{n}{3(2n + 3)}.$$

6. For $n \in \mathbb{N}$,

$$\sum_{i=1}^{n}i \cdot 2^{i-1} = (n - 1)2^n + 1.$$

7. For $n \in \mathbb{N}$, $n^5 - n$ is divisible by 5. [*Hint:* $(n + 1)^5 = n^5 + 5n^4 + 10n^3 + 10n^2 + 5n + 1.$]

8. In Theorem 10.4A we determined a formula for the sum of the first n positive integers. Now, determine a formula for (and prove it by PMI) the sum of the first n even positive integers.

9. Determine and prove a formula for the sum of the first n positive multiples of 3.

10. Refer to Problem 29 in Section 10. The following can be proved. For $n \in \mathbb{N}$,

$$\sum_{i=1}^{n}i(i + 1)(i + 2) = \frac{n(n + 1)(n + 2)(n + 3)}{4}.$$

And for $n \in \mathbb{N}$,

$$\sum_{i=1}^{n}i(i + 1)(i + 2)(i + 3)$$

$$= \frac{n(n + 1)(n + 2)(n + 3)(n + 4)}{5}.$$

What pattern suggests itself?

Remark. Mathematical induction offers a natural opportunity for experimentation and discovery. The next three problems are intended to exploit this feature. You should (1) examine the statement in a number of special cases (i.e., for small values of n), (2) try to discover an appropriate general formula, and (3) use mathematical induction to prove, if possible, your conjecture. If you find a counterexample, simply return to the problem for a more careful analysis.

11. What is the maximum number of points in which n lines in the plane may intersect? (Recall from geometry that two distinct lines may intersect in, at most, one point.)

12. One line divides the plane into two parts (separated by the line). Two lines divide the plane into three parts (if the lines are parallel) or four parts (if the lines are not parallel). Three lines divide the plane into a maximum of seven parts (no two lines are parallel and the three are not concurrent). Find the maximum number of parts into which n lines divide the plane.

13. Consider a set of n points on a circle. Joining adjacent points produces an n-sided polygon. Any line joining nonadjacent points is called a diagonal. Find the number of diagonals in this polygon.

14. (a) What is the quotient and remainder when $x^2 + 1$ is divided by $x - 1$? (b) What is the quotient and remainder when $x^3 + 1$ is divided by $x - 1$? (c) What is the quotient and remainder when $x^4 + 1$ is divided by $x - 1$? (d) What do you suppose the quotient and remainder are when $x^n + 1$ is divided by $x - 1$? (e) Using PMI or WOA, prove your assertion.

15. Prove, using PMI, $\forall n \in \mathbb{N}, 2^{n+4} > (n + 4)^2$. (Note that this is the same as Theorem 11.2.)

16. Show that for all $n \in \mathbb{N}, 64 \mid (9^n - 8n - 1)$. [*Hint:* Verify $9^{n+1} - 8(n + 1) - 1 = 9(9^n - 8n - 1) + 64n$.]

17. Show that for all $n \in \mathbb{N}, 4 \mid (7^{2n-1} + 1)$.

18. Show that for all $n \in \mathbb{N}, \left(1 + \frac{1}{2}\right)^n \geq 1 + n/2$.

19. Show that for all $n \in \mathbb{N}, \left(1 + \frac{2}{3}\right)^n \geq 1 + 2n/3$.

20. Show that for all $n \in \mathbb{N}, \left(1 + \frac{5}{2}\right)^n \geq 1 + 5n/2$.

21. Clearly Problems 18, 19, and 20 are telling us something. Let $x > -1$. Prove that $\forall n \in \mathbb{N}, (1 + x)^n \geq 1 + nx$. (This is called Bernoulli's Inequality.)

22. If $x < -3$, you will show that $(1 + x)^3 < 1 + 3x$. Hence, Bernoulli's Inequality is not true for $n = 3$ and $x < -3$. (a) Verify that $(1 + x)^3 = 1 + 3x + 3x^2 + x^3$. (b) If $x < -3$, then $x + 3 < 0$. Multiply both sides by the positive quantity x^2. (c) Add $1 + 3x$ to both sides of the inequality resulting from part (b) to get the desired result.

23. (This problem anticipates Section 13. It should be attempted only by those having a prior acquaintance with the function concept.) Suppose that a certain function f satisfies the condition $f(a + b) = f(a) + f(b)$ for all real numbers a and b. Use PMI or WOA to show that for all positive integers $n, f(n) = n \cdot f(1)$.

24. Show that for all $n \in \mathbb{N}, 5 \mid (2^{2n-1} + 3^{2n-1})$. [*Hint:* $2^{2n+1} + 3^{2n+1} = 4 \cdot 2^{2n-1} + 9 \cdot 3^{2n-1} = 4(2^{2n-1} + 3^{2n-1}) + 5 \cdot 3^{2n-1}$.]

25. Use WOA or PMI to show that for all $n \in \mathbb{N}$, if a set has n elements, then it has $n(n - 1)/2$ subsets that contain two elements each.

26. Show that for all $n \in \mathbb{N}, 11 \mid (10^{2n} - 1)$.

27. (*Continuation of Problem 26.*) Let $n = d_r d_{r-1} \ldots d_2 d_1 d_0$, where each d_i is a digit and $d_r \neq 0$. Let

$$s^*(n) = \sum_{i=0}^{r}(-1)^i d_i$$
$$= d_0 - d_1 + d_2 - d_3 + \cdots.$$

Compute $s^*(n)$ for (a) $n = 33$, (b) $n = 286$, (c) $n = 1234567$, (d) $n = 7654321$, (e) $n = 1819171625$, (f) $n = 5261719181$.

28. (*Continuation of Problem 26.*) If $n = d_r d_{r-1} \ldots d_2 d_1 d_0$, then $n = \sum_{i=0}^{r} d_i \cdot 10^i$. If i is even, then write 10^i as $(10^i - 1) + 1$, and if i is odd, write 10^i as $(10^i + 1) - 1$. Show that

$$n = \sum_{i \text{ even}} d_i(10^i - 1)$$
$$+ \sum_{i \text{ odd}} d_i(10^i + 1) + \sum_{i=0}^{r}(-1)^i d_i.$$

29. (*Continuation of Problem 26.*) Using Problems 26 and 28 and Theorem 12.5, show that $11 \mid (n - s^*(n))$ for all $n \in \mathbb{N}$.

30. (*Continuation of Problem 26.*) For each $n \in \mathbb{N}$, let $s_{11}(n)$ be the output of the following algorithm (called "casting out 11s"; cf. Problem 35 in Section 8):

Step 0: Start with $m = n$.
Step 1: Compute $s^*(m)$.
Step 2: If $s^*(m) > 10$, then let m be $s^*(m)$ and repeat step 1. If $0 \leq s^*(m) \leq 10$, then $s_{11}(n) = s^*(m)$ and the algorithm ends. If $s^*(m) < 0$, then go to step 3.
Step 3: Let $s^*(m)$ be $s^*(m) + 11$. Go to step 2.   ▲

Compute $s_{11}(n)$ for each part of Problem 27.

31. (*Continuation of Problem 26.*) Show that if $s_{11}(n) = n - 11m$ for some integer m, then $s_{11}(n)$ is the remainder resulting from dividing n by 11.

32. (*Conclusion of Problem 26.*) Show that for all $n \in \mathbb{N}$, $s_{11}(n)$ is the remainder resulting from dividing n by 11.

33. Each recently published book has a 10-digit International Standard Book Number (ISBN). Find five examples.

34. (*Continuation of Problem 33.*) Let $a_1 a_2 a_3 \ldots a_{10}$ be the ISBN of a book. If $n = \sum_{i=1}^{9} i \cdot a_i$, then $s_{11}(n) = a_{10}$. *Note:* If $s_{11}(n) = 10$, then $a_{10} = $ X. Verify that the five ISBNs you found satisfy this relation, and also verify that the following are ISBNs: (*a*) 0-53492-373-9, (*b*) 0-205-04814-5, (*c*) 0-471-61198-0.

35. (*Continuation of Problem 33.*) Show that the following cannot be ISBNs: (*a*) 0-521-38534-8, (*b*) 0-472-86737-3, (*c*) 0-388-96126-7.

36. (*Conclusion of Problem 33.*) It is easy to mentally compute $s_{11}(n)$, where $n = \sum_{i=1}^{9} i \cdot a_i$. You simply need to cast out 11s

as you proceed. The following are the steps used for the ISBN in Problem 34(*a*). Note that in each step, the 11s are cast out.

	Total	
$1 \cdot 0$		0
$+ 2 \cdot 5$	$0 + 10 = 10 =$	-1
$+ 3 \cdot 3$	$-1 + 9 = 8 =$	8
$+ 4 \cdot 4$	$8 + 16 = 24 =$	2
$+ 5 \cdot 9$	$2 + 45 = 47 =$	3
$+ 6 \cdot 2$	$3 + 12 = 15 =$	4
$+ 7 \cdot 3$	$4 + 21 = 25 =$	3
$+ 8 \cdot 7$	$3 + 56 = 59 =$	4
$+ 9 \cdot 3$	$4 + 27 = 31 =$	-2.

Since $-2 + 11 = 9$, the last digit in the number is 9. If you practice doing this, then you will be ready to "read minds." Tell a friend to give you the first nine digits of an ISBN and to concentrate on the last digit. Pretend to read your friend's mind while computing the tenth digit. We suspect that your friend will be quite amazed.

37. Find z if the following is a valid ISBN: 0-06-2z5503-X.

There are, of course, many statements which appear initially to be provable by PMI but which turn out to be false: either part **a** or part **b** fails to hold. Consider, for example, the following problems.

38. Can PMI be used to show that "$\forall n \in \mathbb{N}$, $n = n + 1$" is a theorem? Observe that part **b** holds, but does part **a** hold also?

39. Is it true that $\forall n \in \mathbb{N}$, $1 + 3 + \cdots + (2n - 1) = n^3 - 5n^2 + 11n - 6$?

40. Is it true that $\forall n \in \mathbb{N}$, $2 + 4 + \cdots + 2n = n^3 - 5n^2 + 12n - 6$?

41. Consider the claim: $\forall n \in \mathbb{N}$, $2^n < (n + 1)^3$. (*a*) Test the inequality for $n = 1, 2, 3, 4, 5$, and 6. (*b*) Attempt a proof via PMI. (*c*) Test the inequality for $n = 11$.

Section 13. Functions and Sequences

Overview for Section 13

- Definitions and examples related to the concept of function
- Functions and graphs
- Special functions called sequences
- Lists, n-tuples, and inductive definition
- Definition of factorial function
- Recurrence formulas and the Fibonacci sequence

Key Concepts: orderd pair, relation, domain, range, function, independent and dependent variables, sequence and its graph, n-tuple, factorial sequence, recurrence, Fibonacci sequence

13.1

In earlier sections we have often made use of expressions like $2x + 1$ or $n(n + 1)/2$, each of which dictates a pattern of arithmetic operations on replacements for the variable x or n. It is convenient to establish a generic representation for such expressions, and the one most frequently used is $f(x)$ or $f(n)$. It may be helpful to think of "f" as a formula, or recipe, which results in various outputs depending upon the input chosen as a replacement for the variable.

Example 1

Consider the formula $f(n) = 2^n$, and suppose we agree to replace n only by integers. Then we can construct the following table of paired values:

Input	-2	-1	0	1	2
Output	$\frac{1}{4}$	$\frac{1}{2}$	1	2	4

There is an "order of events" implied here: First, choose the replacement for n; second, compute the output value paired with that choice. For example, choosing the input value 26 results in the output value 67,108,864 (we met this number in paragraph 1.14).

To formalize this concept of paired values, we introduce the symbol (u, v) to denote an **ordered pair**; u is the **first coordinate** and v is the **second coordinate** of the ordered pair. Ordered pairs (u_1, v_1) and (u_2, v_2) are **different** if either

$$u_1 \neq u_2,$$

(1)

or   if $u_1 = u_2$, then $v_1 \neq v_2$.   **(2)**

Thus, $(u_1, v_1) = (u_2, v_2)$ provided both $u_1 = u_2$ and $v_1 = v_2$. Any set **R** of ordered pairs is called a **relation** (so named because it establishes a pairing or relationship between first and second coordinates). The set of all first coordinates is called the **domain** of the relation; the set of all second coordinates is called the **range** of the relation.

Example 2

Consider the relation

$$\mathbf{R} = \{(1, 2), (3, 4), (3, 2)\}.$$

The domain of **R** is $\{1, 3\}$, and the range of **R** is $\{2, 4\}$. (Recall our agreement that the elements in a set must be different from one another.) Note, especially, the use of *parentheses* in the notation for an ordered pair, as in $(1, 2)$, and the use of *braces* in the notation for a set, as in $\{1, 3\}$. In this relation the element 2 in the range is related to two different elements in the domain, and the element 3 in the domain is related to two different elements in the range.

13.2

A substantial proportion of mathematics is devoted to the study of relations of various sorts; the concept is at once extremely general and extremely important. We will return to the study of relations in Chapter 5; for the time being we focus attention on one of the most fundamental concepts in all of mathematics. A **function** is the special sort of relation obtained when there is a *unique* second coordinate corresponding to each first coordinate. Thus a function is characterized by the property that no element in the domain is related to two different elements in the range. [No two ordered pairs in a function differ by virtue of condition (2) in paragraph 13.1.] The relation **R** in Example 2 of paragraph 13.1 is not a function, but if the ordered pair $(3, 2)$ is replaced by the ordered pair $(2, 2)$, then the resulting relation is a function with domain $\{1, 2, 3\}$ and range $\{2, 4\}$. Functions are often designated by lowercase letters such as f, g, or h. If u is in the domain of f, and if $(u, v) \in f$, then we write $f(u) = v$. Thus, from Example 1 in paragraph 13.1, $f(0) = 1$ and $f(26) = 67,108,864$. The importance of the function concept rests on the unambiguous assignment of each **function value** $f(u)$. The symbol u, representing first coordinates, is called the **independent variable,** and the symbol v, representing second coordinates, is called the **dependent variable.** In the table of Example 1 in paragraph 13.1, the inputs are values of the independent variable (in this case, n), and they are chosen from the domain $\mathbb{Z}$. In that example, f is a function and the outputs are function values, which belong to the range of the function.

Example 1

We may use the same formula as in Example 1 of paragraph 13.1, $f(n) = 2^n$, to define many functions. If we choose the domain to be:

- $\{0, 1, 2, 3, 4, 5, 6\}$, then $f = \{(0, 1), (1, 2), (2, 4), (3, 8), (4, 16), (5, 32), (6, 64)\}$.

- $\{5\}$, then $f = \{(5, 32)\}$.

- $\{0, 1, 2, 3, \ldots\}$, then $f = \{(0, 1), (1, 2), (2, 4), (3, 8), \ldots\}$.

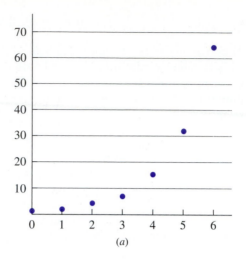

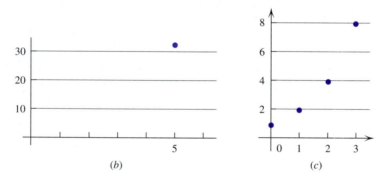

Figure 13.2

The functions defined in this example may be pictured as graphs by plotting ordered pairs on a rectangular coordinate system (see Figure 13.2). Because the domains are subsets of the set of integers, the graphs consist of "discrete" points, one for each element in the domain. In the three parts of this figure we have retained the same horizontal scale, but note that the vertical scales differ considerably. (Resist the temptation to connect these points in a smooth curve! Why? Because this would imply the existence of function values corresponding to real numbers *not* belonging to the domains allowed in this example.)

Example 2 Let $f(n) = n^2$. If we choose the domain to be:

- $\{0, 1, 2, 3, 4, 5, 6\}$, then $f = \{(0, 0), (1, 1), (2, 4), (3, 9), (4, 16), (5, 25), (6, 36)\}$.
- $\{-2, -1, 1, 2, 3, \}$, then $f = \{(-2, 4), (-1, 1), (1, 1), (2, 4), (3, 9)\}$.
- $\mathbb{N}$, then $f = \{(1, 1), (2, 4), (3, 9), (4, 16), \ldots\}$.

For practice, on the same rectangular coordinate system, sketch the graphs of the functions defined by the formulas in Examples 1 and 2 with domain {0, 1, 2, 3, 4, 5, 6}. Compare with Example 1 in paragraph 11.2.   ●

Tutorial 13.2

a. As in Example 2, suppose that $f(n) = n^2$. If the domain of f is $\mathbb{Z}$, construct the table of function values corresponding to $-4 \le n \le 4$.

b. For the function described in part **a**, the range is not $\mathbb{Z}$ but a subset of $\mathbb{Z}$. What is the range?

Example 3

Let x be a real number satisfying $-1 \le x \le 1$. Let $w(x)$ be the y value(s) determined by the equation $x^2 + y^2 = 1$. One should be alert to the fact that equations or formulas do not always determine functions. Here, $w(0) = 1$ and $w(0) = -1$ since both $0^2 + 1^2 = 1$ and $0^2 + (-1)^2 = 1$. Because it does not uniquely assign a y value to each x value, w is *not* a function. However, w *is* a relation which contains infinitely many ordered pairs, either one or two for each real number in the domain $\{x \in \mathbb{R} : -1 \le x \le 1\}$. Some of these ordered pairs are $(-1, 0)$; $(0, -1)$; $(0, 1)$; $(1, 0)$; $(-1/\sqrt{2}, -1/\sqrt{2})$; $(-1/\sqrt{2}, 1/\sqrt{2})$; $(1/\sqrt{2}, -1/\sqrt{2})$; $(1/\sqrt{2}, 1/\sqrt{2})$.   ●

13.3

As suggested in the preceding examples, to identify a function we need to know:

- The domain.
- How to assign (unique) second coordinates.

The domain need not necessarily be a subset of the integers. If, however, the domain is the set $\mathbb{N} = \{1, 2, \ldots\}$, then the function is called a **sequence;** the function values are indexed by the positive integers, sequentially, into a first, a second, a third, and so on. It is convenient, therefore, to indicate a sequence in subscript notation as follows:

$$(a_1, a_2, a_3, \ldots).$$

This is an abbreviation for the more precise notation of a function as a set of ordered pairs

$$\{(1, a_1), (2, a_2), (3, a_3), \ldots\}.$$

Thus, the sequence defined by the formula 2^{-n} is

$$\{(1, \tfrac{1}{2}), (2, \tfrac{1}{4}), (3, \tfrac{1}{8}), \ldots\},$$

which is abbreviated to

$$\left(\tfrac{1}{2}, \tfrac{1}{4}, \tfrac{1}{8}, \ldots\right).$$

Often, especially in discrete mathematics, we are concerned with finite "sequences": functions in which the domain is $\{1, 2, \ldots, n\}$ for some positive integer n. These are indicated in subscript notation as follows:

$$(a_1, a_2, \ldots, a_n);$$

again, an abbreviation for

$$\{(1, a_1), (2, a_2), \ldots, (n, a_n)\}.$$

Such an expression is often called a **finite indexed list** or an ***n*-tuple,** indicating that the entries in the list are arranged into a first coordinate, a second coordinate, $\ldots$, an nth coordinate. The entries, or coordinates, need not be distinct; for example,

$$(1, 0, 1, 0, 1)$$

is an indexed list with five entries. Occasionally, an n-tuple may be referred to as a "linear array" or as a "sequence," but we will avoid such terminology for the most part. (In computer science, the word "array" has a similar but somewhat more technical connotation.)

In general, a function is more than simply a formula (or a rule) designed to identify function values. The domain is essential, and, unless it is known from context, any notation chosen to designate a function must carry a specification of the domain. The range is less important, for if we know the domain and how to find function values, then the range is unambiguously determined. We will often use the following notation:

$$f\colon \mathbf{D} \to \mathbf{E}. \tag{1}$$

This is read, "f maps $\mathbf{D}$ into $\mathbf{E}$" or "f is a function on $\mathbf{D}$ to $\mathbf{E}$." It means:

- f is a function.
- $\mathbf{D}$ *is* the domain of f.
- $\mathbf{E}$ *contains* the range of f.

The set $\mathbf{E}$ is sometimes called the **codomain** of the function f; it is simply a convenient indicator of where the function values may lie. For example, the notation

$$f\colon \mathbf{D} \to \mathbb{R}$$

suggests that f is a function with domain **D** and with real number function values. It does not suggest that *every* real number is a function value.

Example 1 If $f(n) = 2^n$, then $f: \mathbb{N} \to \mathbb{N}$ denotes the sequence $\{(1, 2), (2, 4), (3, 8), \ldots\}$. The domain of f is $\mathbb{N}$, which means that there is a function value for each positive integer. Moreover, each function value is a positive integer, but the range is not all of $\mathbb{N}$, it is the subset $\{2, 4, 8, \ldots\}$ of $\mathbb{N}$.

13.4 The Principle of Mathematical Induction is a vital tool for two different purposes: It may be used in the proof of certain theorems, and it may be used in defining certain sequences. In Theorem 10.4A we considered the sum of the first n positive integers. We may equally well consider products of the first n positive integers. For example,

$$f(1) = 1, \qquad f(2) = 1 \cdot 2, \qquad f(3) = 1 \cdot 2 \cdot 3, \qquad f(4) = 1 \cdot 2 \cdot 3 \cdot 4, \text{ and so on.}$$

This "and so on" is an abbreviation for the following **inductive definition:**

$$f(1) = 1, \tag{1}$$

and $$f(n) = f(n - 1) \cdot n \text{ for } n \in \mathbb{N} \text{ and } n > 1. \tag{2}$$

Observe that

$$f(2) = f(2 - 1) \cdot 2 = f(1) \cdot 2 = 1 \cdot 2,$$
$$f(3) = f(2) \cdot 3 = 1 \cdot 2 \cdot 3,$$
$$f(4) = f(3) \cdot 4 = 1 \cdot 2 \cdot 3 \cdot 4.$$

Mathematical induction guarantees that there is no positive integer for which f fails to be determined. (For if there were, then there would be a smallest, and we immediately reach a contradiction.)

The special sequence just defined occurs with great frequency in mathematics; hence a convenient name and abbreviation is desirable. We call it the **factorial sequence** and denote its formula by $f(n) = n!$. Thus,

$$1! = 1; \qquad 2! = 2; \qquad 3! = 6; \qquad \ldots \qquad 8! = 40{,}320; \qquad \ldots.$$

Example 1 Both for practice and for later reference, here are some examples of operations with factorials.

- $\dfrac{8!}{6!} = \dfrac{8 \cdot 7 \cdot 6 \cdot 5 \cdot 4 \cdot 3 \cdot 2 \cdot 1}{6 \cdot 5 \cdot 4 \cdot 3 \cdot 2 \cdot 1} = 8 \cdot 7.$

- $2^5 \cdot 5! = 2 \cdot 5 \cdot 2 \cdot 4 \cdot 2 \cdot 3 \cdot 2 \cdot 2 \cdot 2 \cdot 1 = 10 \cdot 8 \cdot 6 \cdot 4 \cdot 2.$ (This is the product of the first five even positive integers.)

- $(2n)! = (2n)(2n-1)(2n-2)\cdots 3\cdot 2\cdot 1$. (This is the product of the first $2n$ positive integers. It is *not* $2\cdot n!$.)

- $\dfrac{10!}{2^5\cdot 5!} = \dfrac{10\cdot 9\cdot 8\cdot 7\cdot 6\cdot 5\cdot 4\cdot 3\cdot 2\cdot 1}{10\cdot 8\cdot 6\cdot 4\cdot 2} = 9\cdot 7\cdot 5\cdot 3\cdot 1$. (This is the product of the first five odd integers.)

Tutorial 13.4

a. Evaluate each of the following to show that they are not the same: $8! - 5!$ and $(8-5)!$.

b. Evaluate each of the following to show that they are not the same: $(4!)\cdot(3!)$ and $(4\cdot 3)!$.

c. Write a factorial formula for the product of the first 10 even positive integers.

13.5

Inductive definitions need not, as in the previous illustration, depend solely on *one* value to determine the next. A classic example was described by an Italian mathematician, Leonardo of Pisa (ca. 1170–1240, and is referred to today as Fibonacci) almost eight centuries ago. The problem he was concerned with required that, for $n > 2$,

$$f(n) = f(n-1) + f(n-2). \tag{1}$$

In general, a formula like (1), or like (2) in paragraph 13.4, is called a **recurrence;** its purpose is to specify how function values are computed on the basis of previously determined values. Note that (1) establishes the pattern of computation, but it gives no clue as to how to begin the sequence. As an independent piece of information, **initial values** (or **value**) must be assigned. Note that (1) in paragraph 13.4 assigns an initial value to the recurrence given in (2) in paragraph 13.4. Different sequences will result from different choices of initial values. Fibonacci was interested especially in the sequence with initial values

$$f(1) = f(2) = 1. \tag{2}$$

The sequence generated by (1) and (2) is called the **Fibonacci sequence,** and we denote $f(n)$ by F_n. The first few terms in the Fibonacci sequence are

$$F_1 = 1, \quad F_3 = F_2 + F_1 = 2, \quad F_5 = 3 + 2 = 5,$$
$$F_2 = 1, \quad F_4 = 2 + 1 = 3, \quad F_6 = 5 + 3 = 8.$$

The sequence idea is quite natural; in fact, the arithmetic and geometric progressions which appear in secondary school algebra courses are examples of sequences. (See Problems 9 and 14 for a brief refresher.) The arithmetic progression with initial term 1, and common difference 2, is denoted by

$$1, 3, 5, 7, \ldots,$$

which has the more formal representation as a set of ordered pairs $\{(1, 1), (2, 3), (3, 5), (4, 7), \ldots\}$. It is possible to discover a formula for the sum of the first k terms in a progression (see Problems 13 and 18). Applying that formula to this example, we find that the sum of the first k terms is given by

$$1 + 3 + 5 + \cdots + (2k - 1) = k^2.$$

This, of course, is exactly the result proved in Theorem 11.1. For sequences which are not generated quite as simply as progressions, the sum of the first k terms remains an interesting problem, but the formula may not turn out to be so simple.

Consider, for example, the Fibonacci sequence $(F_1, F_2, F_3, \ldots)$ and denote the sum of the first n Fibonacci numbers by S_n:

$$S_n = F_1 + F_2 + \cdots + F_n. \tag{3}$$

Now construct the following table relating these numbers:

n	1	2	3	4	5	6	7	8	$\cdots$
F_n	1	1	2	3	5	8	13	21	$\cdots$
S_n	1	2	4	7	12	20	33	54	$\cdots$

Tables, often, are very helpful in discovering patterns, and this one is no exception. The pattern will be clear if we simply add 1 to each S_n:

$$2 \quad 3 \quad 5 \quad 8 \quad 13 \quad 21 \quad 34 \quad 55 \quad \ldots.$$

Note that we seem to be generating the Fibonacci sequence values corresponding to $n + 2$. We wonder, of course, whether this is true in general, and the answer comes from an application of mathematical induction.

THEOREM 13.5

Let $(F_1, F_2, F_3, \ldots)$ denote the Fibonacci sequence, and let S_n be the sum indicated in (3). For each $n \in \mathbb{N}$,

$$1 + S_n = F_{n+2}.$$

Proof

Denote by $\mathcal{P}(n)$ the predicate $1 + S_n = F_{n+2}$. Let $\mathbf{M} = \{n \in \mathbb{N} : \mathcal{P}(n) \text{ is true}\}$. Now $\mathcal{P}(1)$ is true since $1 + S_1 = 2 = F_3 = F_{1+2}$, and so $1 \in \mathbf{M}$. Next assume that $k \in \mathbf{M}$; hence $\mathcal{P}(k)$ is true,

$$1 + S_k = F_{k+2}. \tag{4}$$

Making use of (4) we must show that $\mathcal{P}(k + 1)$ is true. From (3) we can write

$$S_{k+1} = \sum_{i=1}^{k+1} F_i = S_k + F_{k+1}.$$

Thus it follows that

$$1 + S_{k+1} = 1 + S_k + F_{k+1} = F_{k+2} + F_{k+1}.$$

From the recursion in (1),

$$1 + S_{k+1} = F_{k+3} = F_{k+1+2},$$

which shows that $\mathcal{P}(k + 1)$ is true. Hence $(k + 1) \in \mathbf{M}$, and so by PMI, $\mathbf{M} = \mathbb{N}$. ∎

Because the Principle of Mathematical Induction and the Well-Ordering Axiom are logically equivalent, we could have used WOA equally well in this proof. For practice, and to illustrate again the subtle difference in technique, we include here a second proof of Theorem 13.5.

Proof by WOA

If the theorem is false, then there is a smallest positive integer, call it j, for which $\mathcal{P}(j)$ fails. Note that

$$1 + S_1 = 2 = F_3,$$

hence $\mathcal{P}(1)$ is true, so $j > 1$. Since $\mathcal{P}(j - 1)$ is true and $\mathcal{P}(j)$ is false, both of the following are correct:

$$1 + S_{j-1} = F_{j-1+2} = F_{j+1}, \qquad \text{and} \qquad 1 + S_j \neq F_{j+2}.$$

We know that
$$S_j = S_{j-1} + F_j;$$

hence
$$1 + (S_{j-1} + F_j) \neq F_{j+2},$$
$$(1 + S_{j-1}) + F_j \neq F_{j+2},$$
$$F_{j+1} + F_j \neq F_{j+2}.$$

This last condition contradicts the recurrence formula (1). (To see this, replace n with $j + 2$.) Thus our assumption that the theorem is false is itself false, so the theorem is true.   ■

Tutorial 13.5

a. Find the first 20 terms in the Fibonacci sequence.

b. Making use of Theorem 13.5, evaluate
$$F_1 + F_2 + \cdots + F_{12}.$$

c. Test your answer to part **b** by adding
$$F_1 + F_2 + \cdots + F_{12}.$$

13.6

When a sequence is defined by recursion, we may not know a simple formula by which the nth term can be computed (there may not even exist such a formula). We may find it necessary, however, to approximate the nth term, or at least to place some cap on just how large that term might be. Although, for example, it isn't too time-consuming to complete the Fibonacci sequence through F_{20}, could we have predicted beforehand something about its size: is it less than 10,000 or perhaps even less than 1000?

A useful prediction about the nth term of any such sequence often requires a proof by induction. To use PMI, we must have a recursion which defines the nth sequence value in terms of its immediate predecessor. But the Fibonacci sequence is not of that type (it requires two preceding terms). In such cases WOA offers an appropriate strategy, but there exists also an alternate version of PMI, often called the

Second Principle of Mathematical Induction

Let $\mathbf{M} \subseteq \mathbb{N}$.

If

a. $1 \in \mathbf{M}$,

b. If $\{1, 2, \ldots, k\} \subseteq \mathbf{M}$, then $(k + 1) \in \mathbf{M}$,

then $\mathbf{M} = \mathbb{N}$.

It can be shown that this Second Principle of Mathematical Induction (abbreviated, SPMI) is logically equivalent to the original PMI (and, hence, to WOA). Assuming that $\mathcal{P}(n)$ is a predicate, SPMI says, in effect, that if $\mathcal{P}(1)$ is true and if $\mathcal{P}(k + 1)$ is true whenever $\mathcal{P}(1), \mathcal{P}(2), \ldots, \mathcal{P}(k)$ are true, then $\mathcal{P}(n)$ is true for every positive integer. Making use of SPMI, we can prove an unexpected result about Fibonacci numbers.

<table>
<tr><td>**THEOREM**
13.6</td><td>$$\forall n \in \mathbb{N}, \quad F_{n+1} < (\tfrac{7}{4})^n.$$</td></tr>
</table>

Proof

Let $\mathcal{P}(n)$ denote the predicate

$$F_{n+1} < (\tfrac{7}{4})^n.$$

Define $\mathbf{M} = \{ n \in \mathbb{N} : \mathcal{P}(n) \text{ is true} \}$. Observe that $\mathcal{P}(1)$ is true, since $F_2 = 1 < (\tfrac{7}{4})^1$, and $\mathcal{P}(2)$ is true since

$$F_3 = 2 < (\tfrac{7}{4})^2 = \tfrac{49}{16}.$$

Now, let $k > 2$ and assume that $\{1, 2, \ldots, k\} \subseteq \mathbf{M}$. In particular, then, we are assuming that $\mathcal{P}(k)$ and $\mathcal{P}(k-1)$ are true, so

$$F_{k+1} < (\tfrac{7}{4})^k \qquad \text{and} \qquad F_k < (\tfrac{7}{4})^{k-1}.$$

Finally, we must consider $\mathcal{P}(k+1)$, which claims that

$$F_{k+2} < (\tfrac{7}{4})^{k+1}.$$

The following argument shows that the claim is true,

$$F_{k+2} = F_{k+1} + F_k < (\tfrac{7}{4})^k + (\tfrac{7}{4})^{k-1} = (\tfrac{7}{4})^{k-1}(\tfrac{7}{4} + 1),$$

so

$$F_{k+2} < (\tfrac{7}{4})^{k-1}(\tfrac{11}{4}) < (\tfrac{7}{4})^{k-1}(\tfrac{7}{4})^2 = (\tfrac{7}{4})^{k+1}.$$

Thus, $(k+1) \in \mathbf{M}$, and the theorem is true. ∎

13.7 Earlier in this section we were given the recurrence formulas for the factorial function and the Fibonacci sequence. Now, we consider the reverse situation: Given the description of a sequence, we attempt to find both the recurrence and the initial values which produce that sequence. To illustrate, consider the specific sequence denoted by g, where for each positive integer n, $g(n)$ is the number of prime factors of n including repetitions of the same prime (see Theorem 7.5A). Since 1 has no prime factor, we put $g(1) = 0$. For each prime p we put $g(p) = 1$. Each composite integer n has a prime factor, say p, and can be written $n = p \cdot m$ for some positive integer m less than n. Thus n will have one more prime factor than m. Hence, the function g can be described by

$$g(1) = 0;$$
$$g(p) = 1, \qquad \text{if } p \text{ is a prime};$$
$$g(n) = 1 + g(m), \qquad \text{if } n = p \cdot m \text{ and } p \text{ is some prime}.$$

Finally, we observe that the special definition for $g(p)$ is unnecessary, since $g(p) = g(p \cdot 1) = 1 + g(1) = 1$. Hence the desired representation is

$$g(1) = 0,$$

$$g(p \cdot m) = 1 + g(m), \qquad \text{for } p \text{ a prime.}$$

It is an easy exercise to compute the following table of values:

n	1	2	3	4	5	6	7	8	9
$g(n)$	0	1	1	2	1	2	1	3	2

The construction of this table raises a very subtle point. The value $g(6)$, for example, can be computed in two different ways:

$$g(6) = \begin{cases} g(2 \cdot 3) = 1 + g(3), \\ g(3 \cdot 2) = 1 + g(2). \end{cases}$$

Since $g(3) = g(2) = 1$, there is no question that $g(6) = 2$. But suppose we consider $g(210)$. We can write, for example,

$$g(210) = \begin{cases} g(2 \cdot 105) = 1 + g(105), \\ g(3 \cdot 70) = 1 + g(70), \\ g(5 \cdot 42) = 1 + g(42). \end{cases}$$

How do we know that $g(210)$ is *well-defined*; that is, how do we know that the same number will be computed in each of these possible formulas? We will leave this consideration, in general, to a more advanced course. Here, we simply raise a warning flag: that care must be exercised in defining and computing functions by recursion. For those who continue with courses in computer science, the issue will recur in questions related to the implementation of algorithms.

As a final remark, however, we should note that the function g defined above is necessarily well-defined because of FTOA. Observe, for example, that $105 = 3 \cdot 5 \cdot 7, 70 = 2 \cdot 5 \cdot 7$, and $42 = 2 \cdot 3 \cdot 7$; hence in this instance

$$g(105) = g(70) = g(42) = 3.$$

13.8

Complement: Recursion

The idea of "inductive" definition was introduced in this section via the factorial function, which is defined by the following procedure, which we will refer to as P_f:

$$f(1) = 1,$$

and for each positive integer $n > 1$,

$$f(n) = f(n - 1) \cdot n.$$

This procedure is actually an endless "algorithm," which computes factorial function values beginning with 1 and continuing sequentially into the set $\mathbb{N}$. In real time, the production of this sequence ends with some, perhaps indefinite, positive integer; but, theoretically, P_f defines the entire sequence which begins:

n	1	2	3	4	5	6	7	$\cdots$
$f(n)$	1	2	6	24	120	720	5040	$\cdots$

Each new function value corresponding to $n > 1$ is obtained by multiplying the immediately preceding function value by n; thus,

$$f(6) = 120 \cdot 6 = 720,$$

and
$$f(7) = 720 \cdot 7 = 5040.$$

Note the ease with which each new function value can be computed, because the previous one is already known.

Suppose, however, that the previous one is not known. We begin again, assuming that no function values, other than $f(1)$, are known. Our problem is to compute $f(n)$ for some chosen n; for example, if $n = 8$, then P_f says

$$f(8) = f(7) \cdot 8.$$

But, we don't know $f(7)$; hence we must again invoke P_f which says

$$f(7) = f(6) \cdot 7.$$

But, we don't know $f(6)$; hence we must again invoke $P_f, \ldots$. This continuing return to the procedure P_f is described in computer science as "recursive calling." In a sense, the procedure must refer to (or call) itself in attempting to compute the required value. In our illustration, the final call is in the computation

$$f(2) = f(1) \cdot 2,$$

for $f(1)$ is known; and because of that, $f(1)$ is called the "stopping" value for the procedure which computes $f(n)$. The procedure itself is called "recursive" because of its self-reference.

In mathematics, it is customary to recognize a small distinction between inductive definition, as in the factorial function, and recursive definition, which is the more general concept.

We will give only a brief description of the general concept since it will not be needed in our later work. The essential difference is that:

- Inductive definition proceeds serially with respect to integer order, beginning with $f(1)$, then to $f(2)$, $f(3)$, $\ldots$, in sequence.

- Recursive definition proceeds serially with respect to "precedence"; that is, a given function value may be defined in terms of *any* already determined function values.

Any inductively defined function is also recursively defined, but the reverse is not true. There exist recursively defined functions g for which some function values $g(n)$ depend on already determined values $g(m)$, where $m > n$.

Example 1

For each $n \in \mathbb{N}$, define the formula $g(n)$ by

$$g(1) = 1;$$

$$g(n) = \begin{cases} 0, & \text{if } n \text{ is a prime;} \\ 1 + g(n + 1), & \text{if } n \text{ is neither 1 nor a prime.} \end{cases}$$

In this example, g counts the number of units from n to the smallest prime greater than or equal to n. Here are the first few function values.

$$g(1) = 1, \qquad g(2) = 0, \qquad g(3) = 0,$$

$$g(4) = 1 + g(5) = 1,$$

$$g(5) = 0,$$

$$g(6) = 1 + g(7) = 1,$$

$$g(7) = 0,$$

$$g(8) = 1 + g(9) = 1 + 1 + g(10) = 1 + 1 + 1 + g(11) = 3,$$

$$g(9) = 1 + g(10) = 1 + 1 + g(11) = 2,$$

$$g(10) = 1 + g(11) = 1,$$

$$g(11) = 0.$$

Pictured in Figure 13.8 is the flowchart which illustrates the computations required. We use three registers:

- N is the current value of n.
- M is the function value.
- N^* is an auxiliary register needed only in an inner loop.

For each n, the "print" command is activated only when the M register holds the current g value $g(n)$. As the algorithm iterates, the print box produces the sequence of g values which follow $g(1)$. It may be of interest to use the flowchart in Figure 13.8 to fill out the accompanying table (the values should coincide with those above).

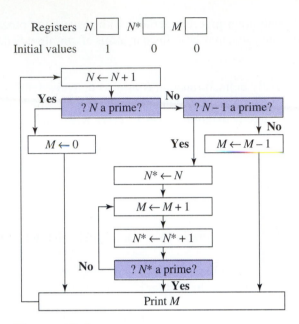

Registers N [ ] N^* [ ] M [ ]

Initial values   1   0   0

Figure 13.8

n	1	2	3	4	5	6	7	8	9	10	11	$\cdots$
$g(n)$	1											$\cdots$

Problems for Section 13

1. Specify the domain and range of each of the following relations.
   (a) $\{(0, 0), (0, 1), (1, 1), (1, 2), (2, 2)\}$;
   (b) $\{(0, 0), (0, 1), (1, -1), (0, 2), (0, -2), (0, 3), (0, -3)\}$; (c) $\{(a, 1), (b, 0), (c, 0), (d, 0), (e, 1)\}$;
   (d) $\{(x, y): x \in \mathbb{N}, y \in \mathbb{N}, y > x\}$.

2. Let $\mathbf{M} = \{a, b, c, d, e\}$ and $\mathbf{V} = \{a, e, i, o, u\}$. List all ordered pairs in the relation $\{(x, y): x \in \mathbf{M}, y \in \mathbf{V}, y$ does not follow x in alphabetic order$\}$.

3. The **inverse** of the relation $\mathbf{R}$, denoted $\mathbf{R}^{-1}$, is $\{(y, x): (x, y) \in \mathbf{R}\}$. Give the inverse of each relation in Problems 1 and 2.

4. Is the relation $\mathbf{R} = \{(a, b), (b, c), (a, c)\}$ a function? Explain your answer.

5. A famous and useful function in the theory of numbers (called the **Euler phi function**) (named after Leonhard Euler) is defined as follows: For each positive integer n, $\phi(n)$ denotes the number of elements in the set $1, 2, 3, \ldots, n$ which are relatively prime to n. Thus $\phi(1) = \phi(2) = 1$ and $\phi(3) = \phi(4) = 2$. (a) Find $\phi(k)$ for $k = 5, 6, 7, 8, 9, 10$. (b) If p is a prime, then show that $\phi(p) = p - 1$. (c) Show that $\phi(12) = \phi(3) \cdot \phi(4) \neq \phi(2) \cdot \phi(6)$, and $\phi(20) = \phi(4) \cdot \phi(5) \neq$

$\phi(2) \cdot \phi(10)$. **Remark.** Part (c) suggests the following theorem that is proved in more advanced courses: $\phi(a \cdot b) = \phi(a) \cdot \phi(b)$ if and only if a and b are relatively prime.

The next two problems are concerned with **lattice points,** that is, ordered pairs in which each coordinate is an integer.

6. On a rectangular coordinate system, mark a few of the lattice points corresponding to the relation $\mathbf{Z} = \{(x, y): x \text{ is even, } y \text{ is odd and less than } x\}$.

7. Let $\mathbf{R}$ denote the relation: $\{(x, y): 0 < x < 10, 0 < y < 10, \text{ and } x - y \text{ is a positive perfect square}\}$. List five elements in $\mathbf{R}$, and decide whether or not $\mathbf{R}$ is a function.

8. List six pairs in the relation $\mathbf{W} = \{(x, y): x \text{ won a World Series over } y\}$. (Consult a world almanac in your library, if necessary.)

9. Let a and d represent nonzero constants. An **arithmetic progression** is a sequence defined inductively by $f(1) = a$ (the initial value), $f(n) = d + f(n-1)$ for $n \in \mathbb{N}$ and $n > 1$ (the recurrence). Here d is called the **common difference.** List the first 10 terms in the arithmetic progression determined by (a) $a = 1, d = 1$; (b) $a = 3, d = 5$; (c) $a = -5, d = -2$.

10. Define an arithmetic progression as follows: $f(1) = 2$ and for $n > 1$, $f(n) = -7 + f(n-1)$. (a) Evaluate $f(m)$ for $m = 2, 3, 4,$ and 20. (b) Determine a simple formula for $f(n)$.

11. Use induction to show that for the arithmetic progression with initial value a and common difference d, $f(n) = a + d \cdot (n-1)$.

12. For the following a and d, find a formula for the nth term of an arithmetic progression with initial value a and common difference d. (*Hint:* Use Problem 11.) (a) $a = 1, d = 1$; (b) $a = 3, d = 5$; (c) $a = -5, d = -2$; (d) $a = 2, d = -7$.

13. Consider $\sum_{k=1}^{n}(a + d \cdot (k - 1))$ and rewrite this as two sums, $\sum_{k=1}^{n} a + d \cdot \sum_{k=1}^{n}(k - 1)$. (a) Why is $\sum_{k=1}^{n}(k - 1) = \sum_{k=1}^{n-1} k$?

(b) Using Theorem 10.4A, show that if $f(1) = a$ and $f(k) = d + f(k - 1)$, then $\sum_{k=1}^{n} f(k) = n \cdot (a - d) + \dfrac{d \cdot n \cdot (n + 1)}{2}$.

14. Let a and r represent nonzero constants. A **geometric progression** is a sequence defined inductively by $f(1) = a$ (initial value) and $f(n) = r \cdot f(n-1)$ for $n \in \mathbb{N}$ and $n > 1$ (the recurrence). Here r is called the **common ratio.** List the first five terms in the geometric progression determined by (a) $a = 1, r = 1$; (b) $a = 1, r = \frac{1}{2}$; (c) $a = 3, r = -2$.

15. Define a geometric progression as follows: $f(1) = 3$ and for $n > 1$, $f(n) = 5 \cdot f(n-1)$. (a) Evaluate $f(m)$ for $m = 2, 3, 4,$ and 10. (b) Determine a simple formula for $f(n)$. (c) What is the sum of the first five terms?

16. Use induction to show that for the geometric progression with initial value a and common ratio r, the nth term is $f(n) = a \cdot r^{n-1}$.

17. For the following geometric progressions, find a formula for $f(n)$ and determine the sum of the first five terms. (a) $a = 1, r = 1$; (b) $a = 1, r = \frac{1}{2}$; (c) $a = 3, r = -2$; (d) $a = 1, r = -1$.

18. Use induction to show that for the geometric progression $f(1) = a$, $f(n) = r \cdot f(n-1)$, $n > 1$, that

$$\sum_{k=1}^{n} f(k) = \sum_{k=1}^{n} ar^{k-1} = a \sum_{k=0}^{n-1} r^k = a \cdot \frac{r^n - 1}{r - 1}.$$

19. Compute the following sums using Problem 18. (a) $\displaystyle\sum_{k=0}^{n-1}(-1)^k$,

(b) $\displaystyle\sum_{k=0}^{n-1}\left(\frac{1}{2}\right)^k$, (c) $\displaystyle\sum_{k=1}^{n-1}\frac{1}{3^k}$, (d) $\displaystyle\sum_{k=0}^{n-1}\frac{(-1)^k}{5^k}$.

20. Define a sequence g as follows: $g(1) = 1$, $g(2) = -1$, and for $n > 2$, $g(n) = g(n-2) - g(n-1)$. Write out the first 10 terms of this sequence.

21. Define a sequence g as follows: $g(1) = 1$, $g(2) = 3$, and for $n > 2$, $g(n) = 3 \cdot g(n-1) - 2 \cdot g(n-2)$. Write out the first 10 terms of this sequence and guess at a simple formula for $g(n)$.

22. Define a sequence f as follows: $f(1) = 1$, $f(2) = 2$, $f(3) = 5$, and for $n > 3$, $f(n) = f(n-3) + 2 \cdot f(n-2) + 3 \cdot f(n-1)$. Write out the first seven terms of this sequence.

23. List the first five terms of the sequence, $f(1) = 2$, $f(n) = 6 - f(n-1)$, for $n > 1$. Prove that $f(n) = 3 + (-1)^n$.

24. Evaluate: (a) 8!, (b) 10!, (c) 12!, (d) $\dfrac{7!}{3!}$, (e) $\dfrac{5!}{4!}$, (f) $\dfrac{20!}{17!}$.

25. Evaluate: (a) $\dfrac{52!}{3! \cdot 49!}$, (b) $\dfrac{52!}{4! \cdot 48!}$, (c) $\dfrac{52!}{5! \cdot 47!}$.

26. Show that (a) $5! + 7! \neq 12!$, (b) $18! - 9! \neq 9!$, (c) $5! - 3! \neq 2!$.

27. Show by algebraic computation (not induction) that for $n > 2$, $n! - (n-2)! = (n^2 - n - 1) \cdot (n-2)!$.

28. (a) Compute: $\dfrac{3!}{2!1!}$, $\dfrac{4!}{2!2!}$, $\dfrac{5!}{2!3!}$, $\dfrac{6!}{2!4!}$.
(b) Is there a simpler expression for
$\dfrac{n!}{2!(n-2)!}$? Where has this number appeared earlier?

29. Express using factorials: (a) the product of the first eight even positive integers, (b) the product of the first eight odd positive integers.

30. (a) Write $2^2 \cdot 3^2 \cdot 4^2 \cdots 50^2$ using factorials.
(b) Write $3 \cdot 6 \cdot 9 \cdot 12 \cdots 99$ using factorials.

31. Prove that for all $n \in \mathbb{N}$,

$$\sum_{k=1}^{n} k(k!) = (n+1)! - 1.$$

32. (a) Modeling your argument on the proof of Theorem 13.6, prove that $\forall n \in \mathbb{N}$, $F_{n+1} < \left(\frac{5}{3}\right)^n$. (b) Why does this proof fail if $\frac{5}{3}$ is replaced by $\frac{8}{5}$?

Note. In the subsequent problems, let $F_0 = 0$ and $F_{-1} = 1$.

33. Show that $F_1 + F_3 + \cdots + F_{2n-1} = F_{2n}$.

34. Consider a Fibonacci-like sequence defined by (1) in paragraph 13.5 but with the initial conditions $f(1) = 1$ and $f(2) = 3$.
(a) Write out the first seven terms in this sequence. (b) Determine a formula, like that in Theorem 13.5, for the sum of the first n terms of this sequence.

35. Let $f(1) = a$, $f(2) = b$, and $f(n) = f(n-1) + f(n-2)$ for $n > 2$. Show that for all $n \in \mathbb{N}$,

$$\sum_{k=1}^{n} f(k) = f(n+2) - f(2).$$

36. For the sequence defined in Problem 35, show that for all $n \in \mathbb{N}$, $f(n) = a \cdot F_{n-2} + b \cdot F_{n-1}$.

37. Show that for all $n \in \mathbb{N}$, $F_{n+1}^2 - F_n^2 = F_{n+2} \cdot F_{n-1}$. [*Hint:* Don't use induction, and recall that $a^2 - b^2 = (a+b) \cdot (a-b)$.]

38. Show that for all $n \in \mathbb{N}$, $F_{n+1}F_{n-1} - F_n^2 = (-1)^n$. Here are three hints. (i) Use PMI. (ii) $F_{n+2}F_n - F_{n+1}^2 = (F_{n+1} + F_n)F_n - F_{n+1}^2$.

(iii) Rewrite (ii), factor out F_{n+1}, and remember that $F_{n+1} - F_n = F_{n-1}$.

39. In the next three problems we are concerned with the identity

$$F_{n+m} = F_{m-1}F_n + F_mF_{n+1}. \quad (1)$$

(*a*) Remembering that $F_0 = 0$, show that (1) is true for $m = 1$. (*b*) Show that (1) is true for $m = 2$.

40. Let n denote a *fixed* positive integer. Show by induction on m that (1) in Problem 39 is true for *all* $m \in \mathbb{N}$.

41. Using (1) in Problem 39, show that $F_{n+1}^2 + F_n^2 = F_{2n+1}$ for all $n \in \mathbb{N}$.

42. Show that $\forall n \in \mathbb{N}$,

$$\sum_{i=1}^{n} F_{2i} = F_{2n+1} - 1.$$

43. Show that $\forall n \in \mathbb{N}$,

$$\sum_{i=1}^{n} F_i^2 = F_n \cdot F_{n+1}.$$

44. Show that $\forall n \in \mathbb{N}$,

$$\sum_{i=1}^{2n} F_i \cdot F_{i-1} = F_{2n}^2.$$

(*Hint:* Note that

$$\sum_{i=1}^{2(n+1)} F_i \cdot F_{i-1} = \sum_{i=1}^{2n} F_i \cdot F_{i-1} + F_{2n+1} \cdot F_{2n}$$
$$+ F_{2n+2} \cdot F_{2n+1}.)$$

45. Compute F_{n+1}/F_n for $n = 1, 2, 3, \ldots, 10$. It can be shown that for n large,

$$\frac{F_{n+1}}{F_n} \approx \frac{1 + \sqrt{5}}{2}.$$

Use your calculator to compare F_{n+1}/F_n to $(1 + \sqrt{5})/2$ for $n = 8, 9,$ and 10.

Section 14. Inductive versus Deductive Logic

Overview for Section 14

- Discussion of inductive logic
- Comparison of inductive and deductive logic
- Introduction to the logical connectives: disjunction, conjunction, equivalence, and implication
- Construction of truth tables
- Examination of the De Morgan Laws

Key Concepts: inductive and deductive logic, disjunction, conjunction, equivalence, implication, truth tables, De Morgan Laws, "necessary and sufficient" terminology

14.1

The name "mathematical induction" is subject to misinterpretation based upon the philosophical distinction between inductive and deductive logic. The term "inductive reasoning" (or "inductive logic") is used in philosophy to describe the process of reaching general conclusions based upon the study of individual cases. This is the classic methodology of the experimental and observational sciences. Both mythology (in primitive societies) and the natural sciences (in more modern times) offer a continuous application of inductive reasoning. We can view them, somewhat loosely, as examples of a process that is at least partially algorithmic. In outline, here is how it works.

Let Φ denote some phenomenon which is not understood but about which observational data have been collected and recorded. The objective is to explain Φ, and the controlling assumption is that there must be consistency between the explanation of Φ and the observed data about Φ.

- A theoretical framework is hypothesized to account for the accumulated data.
- From the theory, predictions about Φ are inferred.
- Predictions are tested against new experimental and/or observational evidence.
- Discrepancies between prediction and evidence demand restructuring of the theoretical framework.

In this spiral progression, theories about the behavior of Φ are continually refined (or completely revised) to account for newly accumulated and more accurate observed data about Φ.

Example 1

Let Φ denote the spatial relationship between the earth and other astronomical objects. By the period of classical Greek civilization, enough observational data had been recorded to support the so-called Ptolemaic theory, named for Claudius Ptolemy (ca. A.D. 150). The hypothesis was that the earth is spherical but fixed in space, and that the stars, sun, moon, and planets revolve about it in spherical shells concentric with the earth. Over centuries of time, experimental devices were constructed to improve the accuracy of astronomical observations. Astronomers were forced to add more and more refinements to the Ptolemaic theory to account for the new data. In the mid-sixteenth century, after roughly 1400 years, increasing complexity of that theory forced a complete change in astronomical thought, now known as the Copernican theory after its originator Nicolaus Copernicus (1473–1543). In it, the sun is fixed and planets, including the earth, revolve about it. At first, the nature of the planetary orbits was uncertain; it was assumed that orbits were circular. Again, accumulated data supported a revision of the theory. This time, due to Johannes Kepler (1571–1630), it was shown that the orbits are not circular but elliptic with the sun at one focus of the ellipse. This modification in Φ occurred about the year 1600. Later in the seventeenth century, the invention of calculus [by Sir Isaac Newton (1642–1727) and Gottfried Wilhelm Leibniz (1646–1716)] and the discovery of the law of gravitation (by Newton) provided analytical tools upon which much of modern astronomy is based. It is now known that the sun is not stationary but revolves (along with the entire solar system) about the center of a massive collection of stars called the Milky Way galaxy, which, in turn, is but one of a multitude of other galaxies. As an exciting and very active science, astronomy continues to evolve in this same kind of inductive interplay between observation and theory.

14.2

What about the potential confusion referred to at the beginning of paragraph 14.1? The Principle of Mathematical Induction is not induction at all! It is a tool of deductive logic; conclusions obtained by its use are as rigorously correct as any others in mathematics. We often, however, use the evidence of a number of special cases to infer a general (or universally quantified) statement, as illustrated in Example 1 of paragraph 10.4 and in the following two examples. This is inductive reasoning: proceeding from the particular to the general. But at this point the similarity ends. Within the context to which inductive reasoning alone applies, there is no test of the absolute truth of the general theory. As in Example 1 of paragraph 14.1, the general theory is subject to continuing modification. But the essence of mathematical induction is the existence of a *deductive* test which guarantees the truth of the general theorem (within the axiomatic structure of mathematics). This test, of course, is the Principle of Mathematical Induction, or the equivalent Well-Ordering Axiom.

Example 1

Much of the discussion in Section 8 was based upon the representation of integers in terms of powers of 2. Recalling that $2^0 = 1$, consider the following sums:

$$1 + 2 = \quad 3 = 2^2 - 1,$$
$$1 + 2 + 2^2 = \quad 7 = 2^3 - 1,$$
$$1 + 2 + 2^2 + 2^3 = 15 = 2^4 - 1,$$
$$1 + 2 + 2^2 + 2^3 + 2^4 = 31 = 2^5 - 1.$$

These individual cases offer impressive evidence in favor of a conjecture to the effect that

$$\forall n \in \mathbb{N}, \quad \sum_{i=0}^{n} 2^i = 2^{n+1} - 1. \tag{1}$$

It is important at this point not to claim that (1) is true; such a claim can only be justified by proof (not by the correctness of any number of special cases). As it happens, (1) *is* a true statement, hence qualifies to be called a theorem. The proof is a perfectly straightforward application of WOA or PMI, and we omit it here. An interesting comparison follows from the observation that for any particular choice of *n*, we are dealing with the sum of a geometric progression (refer to Problem 18 in Section 13).

As illustrated in Example 1, inductive reasoning can be useful in mathematics only as a guide in the formulation of conjectures inferred from a number of particular cases and subject to verification by the methods of deductive logic. But a conjecture, once made, may very well be false. There is no assurance that our first guess (or even the first few guesses) will be correct. Cautious optimism is a necessity, and also perseverance in the search for the correct generalization. (The generalization can be claimed correct only if it can be proved.) The next example is a very nice illustration of this problem (see the article by L. Moser listed in the references).

Example 2   Choose n points on the circumference of a circle so that no three of the lines determined by these points intersect at a point inside the circle. Let $f(n)$ denote the number of regions into which these lines subdivide the interior of the circle. Thus, f is a sequence, and its first few values can be determined experimentally as in Figure 14.2. The evidence seems clear that our conjecture should be

$$\forall n \in \mathbb{N}, \quad f(n) = 2^{n-1}. \tag{2}$$

Now, trouble begins. Although we've already determined that $2^0 = f(1)$, PMI also requires that we prove the truth of the implication:

$$\text{If } f(k) = 2^{k-1}, \text{ then } f(k+1) = 2^k.$$

But, try as we may, the implication cannot be proved. Reconsidering the conjecture, suppose we have a big circle (say 1 foot in diameter) with 101 points on the circumference. It's clear that the lines are likely to subdivide the interior into a huge number of very small regions, but is that number likely to be as large as 2^{100}? As it happens $2^{100} > 10^{30}$, and this number is far larger than the number of atoms in a balloon of diameter 1 foot filled with hydrogen. Are we really likely to have regions smaller on the average than hydrogen atoms? In reality, $f(n)$ must decrease

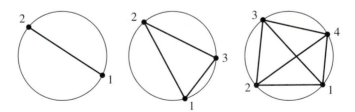

Number of points n	Number of lines	Number of regions $f(n)$
1	0	$1 = 2^0$
2	1	$2 = 2^1$
3	3	$4 = 2^2$
4	6	$8 = 2^3$

Figure 14.2

significantly from 2^{n-1} as n increases. It is easy to show (experimentally) that $n = 6$ is where the deviation begins:

$$f(5) = 2^{5-1}, \qquad \text{but} \qquad f(6) < 2^{6-1}.$$

With a counterexample in hand, the search continues for the correct conjecture. Both the search and the proof turn out to be quite difficult, and we will abandon this example for the time being, returning to it in paragraph 17.4.

Tutorial 14.2

Referring to Example 2:
a. Verify, experimentally, that $f(5) = 16$.
b. Find $f(6)$ experimentally.

14.3 Whereas inductive reasoning argues from the particular to the general, we may characterize "deductive logic" as arguing from the general to the particular. That is, a general system of axioms and definitions is established and the resulting structure is explored through individual theorems and examples. Euclidean geometry is the classic example of such a deductive structure. Proofs of the sort we have concentrated on in prior sections are the hallmark of deductive logic. For the most part, these proofs have corresponded to very simple statements; but often more complex statements are met in mathematics, computer science, and in nearly all other aspects of communication. To understand and analyze them, it is necessary to begin a more detailed and systematic treatment of deductive logic.

Let p and q denote simple statements to each of which the condition "true" or "false" can be assigned. For example:

- "$\sqrt{2}$ is an irrational number" is true.

- "4 is a prime number" is false.

- "$8 \leq 9$" is true.

- "3^2 is an even integer" is false.

Logical assertions of more complicated format are created using negation and the **logical connectives** called:

- **Disjunction:** p or q;

- **Conjunction:** p and q.

The symbolic abbreviation for disjunction is $p \vee q$, and its meaning is "either p or q or both." The symbolic abbreviation for conjunction is $p \wedge q$, and its meaning is "both p and q."

p	q	$p \vee q$	$p \wedge q$
T	T	T	T
T	F	T	F
F	T	T	F
F	F	F	F

Table 14.3

The possible **truth values** [that is, T (for true) and F (for false)] which can be assigned to the statements p and q determine the truth value of the connective, as indicated in Table 14.3. Note that disjunction is false if both p and q are false and is true otherwise; and conjunction is true if both p and q are true and is false otherwise. This assignment of truth values is quite natural: the claim that "p *or* q is true" should be false only when neither p nor q is true; the claim that "p *and* q are true" should be true only when neither p nor q is false.

Example 1

The statement:

"4 is a prime number and $8 \leq 9$" is false,

"4 is a prime number or $8 \leq 9$" is true,

"$\sqrt{2}$ is an irrational number and $8 \leq 9$" is true,

"4 is a prime number or $\sqrt{2}$ is a rational number" is false,

"$\sqrt{2}$ is an irrational number or $8 \leq 9$" is true.

The English language admits an **exclusive** use of the word "or": either p or q but not both. In mathematics, however, the unmodified "or" should always be interpreted in the **inclusive** sense: either p or q or both (as illustrated in the final statement in Example 1). The truth table for disjunction ensures this inclusive interpretation of "or." Nevertheless, there are some (relatively rare) occasions in mathematics which require the exclusive interpretation of "or," and specific indication must be given. Recall, for example, our fundamental assumption that mathematical statements must be true or false *but not both*. We will see a bit later in Table 14.6C an unexpected, alternative expression for the exclusive use of "or."

14.4

Negation, which we denote by $\sim p$ (as in paragraph 3.4), reverses the truth value assigned to p. As we observed earlier, the negation of a negation simply returns to the original statement; hence $\sim(\sim p)$ and p have the same truth value. The negation of a disjunction or the negation of a conjunction is a more complicated issue, which we consider next.

One of the assets of the symbolic representation is that certain operations can be performed routinely (almost without thought). As a first step toward the negation of disjunction, simply reverse the truth values given in Table 14.3, as shown in Ta-

p	q	$\sim p$	$\sim q$	$\sim(p \vee q)$	$(\sim p) \wedge (\sim q)$
T	T	F	F	F	F
T	F	F	T	F	F
F	T	T	F	F	F
F	F	T	T	T	T

Table 14.4A

ble 14.4A. This is correct, but hardly enlightening—we can do better. To say that the disjunction $p \vee q$ is true means that at least one of the statements p and q is true. Thus the negation of this disjunction means that *both p and q* must be false (i.e., the conjunction of $\sim p$ and $\sim q$). This clue leads directly to a very important logical principle, one of the two that are known as the **De Morgan Laws** [Augustus De Morgan (1806–1871)]. The two logical formulas (final two columns in Table 14.4A)

$$\sim(p \vee q) \qquad \text{and} \qquad (\sim p) \wedge (\sim q)$$

have precisely the same truth value in each possible case; hence they are called **logically equivalent.** This means, of course, that one of the formulas is true if and only if the other formula is true. (Recall the discussion of logical equivalence in paragraph 5.2.)

Example 1

If p is "4 is a prime number " and if q is "3^2 is an even integer," then $\sim(p \vee q)$ becomes:

It is not true that either 4 is a prime number or 3^2 is an even integer.

And $(\sim p) \wedge (\sim q)$ becomes:

4 is not a prime number and 3^2 is not an even integer.

A little thought convinces us that both statements are true.

Tutorial 14.4

a. Is the negation of the following statement true or false?

41 is a prime number or 43 has a divisor less than 7.

b. Use the appropriate line in Table 14.4A to confirm your answer.

p	q	$\sim p$	$\sim q$	$\sim(p \wedge q)$	$(\sim p) \vee (\sim q)$
T	T	F	F	F	F
T	F	F	T	T	T
F	T	T	F	T	T
F	F	T	T	T	T

Table 14.4B

The first De Morgan Law in Table 14.4A tells us how to negate disjunction. Now, we construct the truth table for the other De Morgan Law which tells us how to negate conjunction.

Consider the negation of the conjunction, $p \wedge q$. We will get at the idea by supposing that $p \wedge q$ is true, then asking for the meaning of $\sim(p \wedge q)$. In words, "it is false that both p is true and q is true." But this means that at least one of p or q must be false; that is, "p is false or q is false." Hence we expect logical equivalence between the formulas

$$\sim(p \wedge q) \quad \text{and} \quad (\sim p) \vee (\sim q).$$

Consider, for example, the second row in Table 14.4B. The negations of p and q are immediate. By the second row of Table 14.3, the conjunction of T and F statements is F, so its negation is T. By the third row of Table 14.3, the disjunction of F and T statements is T also. Now, follow across each row in Table 14.4B and observe that the truth value for each of the two formulas (final two columns) is, in fact, the same.

14.5

Our old friend's implication ($p \rightarrow q$) and equivalence ($p \leftrightarrow q$) may also be considered logical connectives and may be analyzed via truth tables just as we have done for disjunction and conjunction.

To say that statements p and q are logically equivalent should mean that they have the same truth value; that is, equivalence should be true when both p and q are true or when both are false (Table 14.5A). In paragraph 5.2 we observed that logical equivalence is sometimes indicated by using the "if and only if" language. Among integers, for example,

p	q	$p \leftrightarrow q$
T	T	T
T	F	F
F	T	F
F	F	T

Table 14.5A

$$5 \mid n \text{ if and only if } 5 \mid n^2. \tag{1}$$

This same idea of logical equivalence is expressed in the frequently used terminology,

$$p \text{ is a necessary and sufficient condition for } q.$$

In this language (1) can be restated:

$$5 \mid n \text{ is a necessary and sufficient condition for } 5 \mid n^2. \tag{2}$$

The relationships among these several terminologies are shown in the following table:

$p \leftrightarrow q$	$p \rightarrow q$	$q \rightarrow p$
p if and only if q	p only if q	p if q
p is a necessary and sufficient condition for q	p is sufficient for q	p is necessary for q

Occasionally, there is a grammatical problem with the language use in (2), and in such instances (2) may be restated:

In order that $5 \mid n^2$, it is necessary and sufficient that $5 \mid n$.

Perhaps the safest guide through this duplicate terminology is simply to think carefully about the meaning of the language used.

Implication is a little more subtle. Because it is never used in practice except under the assumption that the hypothesis p is true, it would be reasonable to assign its truth values as shown in Table 14.5B. But simply leaving the table in this incomplete state is unsatisfactory, not only for aesthetic reasons but because it may lead to problems in the analysis of more complicated statements. So, how do we proceed? There are four possible ways to replace the dashes in Table 14.5B (top to bottom):

$$\begin{array}{ccccc} \text{T} & \text{T} & \text{F} & & \text{F} \\ \text{T} & \text{F} & \text{T} & \text{and} & \text{F} \end{array}.$$

p	q	$p \rightarrow q$
T	T	T
T	F	F
F	T	–
F	F	–

Table 14.5B

p	q	$p \rightarrow q$
T	T	T
T	F	F
F	T	T
F	F	T

Table 14.5C

The assignment

$$F$$
$$T$$

can be eliminated immediately, for this would indicate no difference between implication and equivalence (and we know that they are quite different logically). Recall that $p \leftrightarrow q$ means $p \rightarrow q$ and $q \rightarrow p$; equivalence is the conjunction of two implications. Hence, $p \leftrightarrow q$ and $(p \rightarrow q) \wedge (q \rightarrow p)$ should have the same truth values for all possible values of p and q. Of the three remaining possible assignments, only one satisfies this condition, and we agree to complete Table 14.5B as shown in Table 14.5C.

Example 1

We construct the truth table which shows that the above assignment leads to the same truth values for $p \leftrightarrow q$ and $(p \rightarrow q) \wedge (q \rightarrow p)$.

p	q	$p \rightarrow q$	$q \rightarrow p$	$(p \rightarrow q) \wedge (q \rightarrow p)$	$p \leftrightarrow q$
T	T	T	T	T	T
T	F	F	T	F	F
F	T	T	F	F	F
F	F	T	T	T	T

Note that the assignment of truth values in the column for $q \rightarrow p$ is based on Table 14.5C, remembering that q is the hypothesis and p the conclusion. Thus the column entry is F only when q is T and p is F.

Tutorial 14.5

Assume the other two possible ways of completing Table 14.5B, and in each case show that the logical equivalence (in Example 1) fails.

14.6

By the choice made in Table 14.5C it should be emphasized that if p is false, then $p \rightarrow q$ is true, regardless of whether q is true or false. For example, both the following implications are true:

If $0 = 1$, then $\sqrt{2}$ is rational.

If $0 = 1$, then $4 + 5 = 9$.

Thus, if p is false, then the implication is useless as a predictor of q. But this is really a technicality; it should always be remembered that when a theorem is stated as an implication

$$(\text{hypothesis}) \rightarrow (\text{conclusion}),$$

we tacitly assume the truth of the hypothesis. Hence the theorem is a perfect predictor of the conclusion.

Since both implication and logical equivalence have truth tables, each can also be negated (as displayed in Table 14.6A). The columns labeled A_2 and B_2 are obtained routinely from A_1 and B_1 by changing truth values. There is a more interesting problem, however, if we search for different formulas for these negations.

Compare the column A_2 with that for $p \wedge q$ in Table 14.3. Notice that we need only interchange the T and F in the first two rows. This can be done by simply changing q to $\sim q$ as in Table 14.6B. Thus, $\sim(p \rightarrow q)$ and $p \wedge (\sim q)$ are logically equivalent statements. One can reason about this as follows: In order that $p \rightarrow q$ fail, it must happen that p is true *and* q is false, that is, we must have the conjunction of p and (not q).

The negation of logical equivalence is especially interesting because its truth table (column B_2 in Table 14.6A) is exactly what we might expect for the "exclusive or," that is, true when either p or q is true but not when both are true or both false. In Table 14.6C, we show that this can be stated as $(p \vee q) \wedge (\sim(p \wedge q))$.

In our final example of the construction of truth tables we will prove the logical equivalence of an implication and its contrapositive (paragraph 3.5). To do this, we

		A_1	A_2	B_1	B_2
p	q	$p \rightarrow q$	$\sim(p \rightarrow q)$	$p \leftrightarrow q$	$\sim(p \leftrightarrow q)$
T	T	T	F	T	F
T	F	F	T	F	T
F	T	T	F	F	T
F	F	T	F	T	F

Table 14.6A

p	q	$\sim q$	$p \wedge (\sim q)$
T	T	F	F
T	F	T	T
F	T	F	F
F	F	T	F

Table 14.6B

p	q	$p \wedge q$	$\sim(p \wedge q)$	$p \vee q$	$(p \vee q) \wedge (\sim(p \wedge q))$
T	T	T	F	T	F
T	F	F	T	T	T
F	T	F	T	T	T
F	F	F	T	F	F

Table 14.6C

p	q	$p \rightarrow q$	$\sim q$	$\sim p$	$(\sim q) \rightarrow (\sim p)$
T	T	T	F	F	T
T	F	F	T	F	F
F	T	T	F	T	T
F	F	T	T	T	T

Table 14.6D

must show that the two statements share the same truth table, and this is demonstrated in Table 14.6D.

14.7   **Complement: Truth Tables** Truth tables may be constructed for complicated expressions involving any number of simple statements. Looking at one, two, and three simple statements only, the possible truth value assignments are given in Tables 14.7A and 14.7B. In each of these tables, consider what happens when T is replaced by 0 and F by 1.

(1)	(2)		(3)		
p	p	q	p	q	r
T	T	T	T	T	T
F	T	F	T	T	F
	F	T	T	F	T
	F	F	T	F	F
			F	T	T
			F	T	F
			F	F	T
			F	F	F

Table 14.7A

(1)	(2)		(3)		
0	0	0	0	0	0
1	0	1	0	0	1
	1	0	0	1	0
	1	1	0	1	1
			1	0	0
			1	0	1
			1	1	0
			1	1	1

Table 14.7B

Base 10	Base 2
0	0
1	1
2	1 0
3	1 1
4	1 0 0
5	1 0 1
6	1 1 0
7	1 1 1

Table 14.7C

Notice the similarity between Table 14.7B(3) and the numbers 0 to 7 in binary. The rows in Table 14.7B(3) and Table 14.7C are the same except for the leading zeroes. So the ith row of Table 14.7B(3) corresponds to the number i in binary. (Here the first row is called the zeroth row.) In fact, the number of rows in a truth table for n statements is 2^n, and the ith row of the truth table corresponds (T to 0, F to 1) to the number i in binary for $0 \leq i \leq 2^n - 1$. (We will see another table like this in paragraph 16.1.)

Here is a puzzle that is solved easily using truth tables. Suppose you have cards that have a letter on one side and an integer on the other side. Four of the possible such cards are pictured below:

I	M	8	3

Someone now tells you:

If a vowel is on one side of a card, then an even number is on the other side of the card. **(1)**

Our question is, "For the cards above, what is the minimum number of cards that have to be turned over to verify the conditional (1)?"

To analyze this, consider the following two statements:

p :   A vowel is on one side of the card.

q :   An even number is on one side of the card.

The truth table for $p \to q$ is:

p	q	$p \rightarrow q$
T	T	T
T	F	F
F	T	T
F	F	T

For the card with the letter **M** on it, p is false. Thus $p \rightarrow q$ must be true regardless of what is on the other side of the card. You do not need to turn this card over. For the card with the number **8** on it, q is true. Again, by looking at the truth table we see that $p \rightarrow q$ must be true, and you do not have to turn this card over. Now p is true for the card with the letter **I** on it. But to determine if $p \rightarrow q$ is true, we must know whether q is true. Hence this card must be turned over. For the card with the number **3,** q is false. Again this card must be turned over to determine if p is false. Hence only two of these cards must be turned over to determine the truth value of (1) for all four cards.

Example 1 In paragraph 5.3 we separated the integers into three classes, depending upon the remainder under division by 3. We also showed:

$$\text{If } x^2 \in [1]_3, \text{ then } x \in [1]_3 \text{ or } x \in [2]_3. \tag{2}$$

Let p, q, and r be the following statements:

$$p: x^2 \in [1]_3, \qquad q: x \in [1]_3, \qquad r: x \in [2]_3,$$

and examine the truth table in Table 14.7D. Note that if q is true, then $p \rightarrow (q \vee r)$ is also true. Hence, in a proof of $p \rightarrow (q \vee r)$ we can always assume that one of q or

p	q	r	$q \vee r$	$p \rightarrow (q \vee r)$
T	T	T	T	T
T	T	F	T	T
T	F	T	T	T
T	F	F	F	F
F	T	T	T	T
F	T	F	T	T
F	F	T	T	T
F	F	F	F	T

Table 14.7D

r is false, and then we need only show that the other is true. The following is a proof of (2) based on this procedure.

Proof of (2)

Suppose that $x^2 \in [\mathbf{1}]_3$. If $x \in [\mathbf{1}]_3$, then we are done. So suppose that $x \notin [\mathbf{1}]_3$, and hence either $x \in [\mathbf{0}]_3$ or $x \in [\mathbf{2}]_3$. If $x \in [\mathbf{0}]_3$, then clearly $x^2 \in [\mathbf{0}]_3$, and hence this forces x to be in $[\mathbf{2}]_3$.   ∎

Note that the contrapositive of (2) is:

$$\text{If } x \notin [\mathbf{1}]_3 \text{ and } x \notin [\mathbf{2}]_3, \text{ then } x^2 \notin [\mathbf{1}]_3.$$

This can be written:

$$\text{If } x \in [\mathbf{0}]_3, \text{ then } x^2 \notin [\mathbf{1}]_3.$$

Admittedly, in this case, the contrapositive is easy to prove, but nevertheless, this method of proving $p \rightarrow (q \vee r)$ is quite useful.

As another example, we will show that if x, y, and z are positive integers, then if x divides y, then either x does not divide z or x divides $y + z$.

Proof

Suppose that x divides y. If x does not divide z, then we are done. So suppose that x divides z. Hence x divides y and x divides z, and by Theorem 3.7, x divides $y + z$.   ∎

Problems for Section 14

1. Look up "induction" (or "inductive reasoning") in an encyclopedia and briefly describe an application of inductive reasoning to science which is different from that in Example 1 of paragraph 14.1.

2. Consider the product of any five consecutive positive integers. (*a*) List three particular illustrations. (*b*) We know already that such a product is divisible both by 2 and by 3. Try to determine the "best" divisibility claim you can make about any such product. (*Hint:* Refer to Problem 13 of Section 9.) (*c*) State your claim as a universally quantified statement and prove it.

3. Consider statement (1) in Example 1 of paragraph 14.2. For $n = 1, 2, 3$, and 4, express each side as a number in binary notation. Prove the theorem and explain how it can be interpreted as a simple fact in binary arithmetic.

4. (*a*) Compute the following sums: $1 + 5$; $1 + 5 + 9$; $1 + 5 + 9 + 13$; $1 + 5 + 9 + 13 + 17$. (*b*) Predict the sum, for $n \in \mathbb{N}$, of $1 + 5 + 9 + \cdots + (4n - 3)$. (*Hint:* Use Theorem 10.4A.) (*c*) Prove that your prediction is correct.

5. Consider the statements labeled p: "9 and 11 is a prime pair" and q: "$\sqrt{13}$ is an irrational number." (*a*) Express in words the disjunction and the conjunction of these statements. (*b*) Which of these two is a true statement?

6. Consider the statement labeled *r*: "No even integer is divisible by 3." Referring to *p* and *q* in Problem 5, express in words:
(*a*) $(p \wedge q) \vee r$. Is this a true statement?
(*b*) $p \vee (q \wedge r)$. Is this a true statement?

7. For integers *x*, let *p* denote the statement "$x > 3$," and let *q* denote the statement "*x* and $x + 2$ is a prime pair." (*a*) State the conjunction $p \wedge q$ in words. (*b*) Consider several special cases, and determine whether the truth of $p \wedge q$ implies "$6 \mid (x + 1)$."

8. Construct the truth tables for $p \vee (\sim p)$ and for $p \wedge (\sim p)$.

9. Construct the truth table for $\sim(p \wedge \sim q)$.

10. Construct the truth table for $\sim(p \vee \sim q)$.

11. Construct the truth tables for $(\sim p) \vee q$ and for $((\sim p) \vee q) \wedge (p \vee (\sim q))$.

12. The truth table corresponding to three statements *p*, *q*, *r* requires eight rows. Construct the truth table for $(\sim(p \wedge q)) \vee r$.

13. Construct the truth table for $(\sim p \vee q) \wedge (\sim q \vee r)$.

14. Construct the truth table for $p \wedge (q \vee (p \vee r))$.

15. (*a*) Use a De Morgan Law to show that $\sim(\sim p \vee q) \vee p$ is equivalent to *p*. (*b*) Use truth tables to show that $\sim(\sim p \vee q) \vee p$ is equivalent to *p*.

16. Show that $p \vee q$ is not equivalent to $\sim((\sim p \vee q) \vee q)$.

17. Use De Morgan Laws to show that the following are equivalent: $(\sim p \vee \sim q) \wedge r$ and $\sim((p \wedge q) \vee \sim r)$.

18. Use truth tables to show that the statements in Problem 17 are equivalent.

19. Use truth tables to prove that $(q \rightarrow p) \rightarrow p$ is equivalent to $p \vee q$.

20. Construct the truth table for $p \wedge (\sim q \rightarrow (r \vee p))$.

21. Consider the statements *p*: "4 is prime" and *q*: "16 is a perfect square." Which of the following are true? (*a*) $p \vee q$, (*b*) $p \wedge q$, (*c*) $p \rightarrow q$, (*d*) $q \rightarrow p$, (*e*) $p \leftrightarrow q$.

22. Repeat Problem 21 with these statements: *p*: "3 is prime," *q*: "16 is a perfect square."

23. Repeat Problem 21 with these statements: *p*: "4 is prime," *q*: "17 is a perfect square."

24. Let $\mathbb{Q}$ be the rational numbers. Consider the statement *s*: There are irrational numbers *x* and *y* such that x^y is rational. (*a*) Express this statement with the symbols $\exists$ and $\forall$. (*b*) Express the negation of this statement in both words and symbols.

25. (*Continuation of Problem 24.*) Now consider the following three statements:

$$p : \sqrt{2} \in \mathbb{Q}, \qquad q: (\sqrt{2})^{\sqrt{2}} \in \mathbb{Q},$$

$$r: \left((\sqrt{2})^{\sqrt{2}}\right)^{\sqrt{2}} \in \mathbb{Q}.$$

(*a*) Which one of these have we proven false? (*b*) Simplify $\left((\sqrt{2})^{\sqrt{2}}\right)^{\sqrt{2}}$ to show that *r* is true.

26. (*Continuation of Problem 24.*) (*a*) Show that if *q* is true, then *s* is true. (*b*) Show that if *q* is false, then since *r* is true, so is *s*.

27. (*Conclusion of Problem 24.*) In part (*a*), let *q* and *s* be any statements. (*a*) Construct a truth table for $(q \rightarrow s) \wedge ((\sim q) \rightarrow s)$. Observe that $(q \rightarrow s) \wedge ((\sim q) \rightarrow s)$ is equivalent to *s*. (*b*) Now consider the statements *q* and *s* from Problems 24 and 25. In Problem 26 you showed that $(q \rightarrow s) \wedge ((\sim q) \rightarrow s)$ is true. Conclude that *s* is true. [Note that you still do *not* know whether $(\sqrt{2})^{\sqrt{2}}$ is rational, and it is beyond the scope of this text to prove that it is not.]

28. Show that $(p \vee (\sim p)) \rightarrow q$ is equivalent to $(p \rightarrow q) \wedge ((\sim p) \rightarrow q)$.

29. Find two combinations of the statements p, q, and r using $\vee$, $\wedge$, and $\sim$ so that (a) there is exactly one T in the column for one combination, (b) there are exactly two T's in the column for the other combination.

30. Repeat Problem 29 except that the column for the combinations should have (a) exactly three T's, (b) exactly four T's.

31. If p is a prime, then the sum of all the numbers that divide p is simply $p + 1$. Find the sum of all the numbers that divide (a) 2^n for $n = 1, 2, 3, 4$; (b) 3^n for $n = 1, 2, 3, 4$; (c) 5^n for $n = 1, 2, 3, 4$.

32. Using Problem 18 in Section 13, show that the sum of all divisors of (a) 2^n is $2^{n+1} - 1$, (b) 3^n is $(3^{n+1} - 1)/2$, (c) 5^n is $(5^{n+1} - 1)/4$.

33. For a prime p and for all $n \in \mathbb{N}$, show that the sum of all divisors of p^n is $(p^{n+1} - 1)/(p - 1)$. (See Problem 32.)

34. (a) Find all the divisors of 220 and compute the sum of those less than 220. (b) Find all the divisors of 284 and compute the sum of those less than 284.

35. A pair of numbers whose proper divisors sum to each other is called an **amicable pair**. The pair 220 and 284 is the smallest such pair. Verify that the following pairs

are also amicable. (a) $1184 = 2^5 \cdot 37$ and $1210 = 2 \cdot 5 \cdot 11^2$ (discovered in 1886 by a 16-year-old Italian boy). (b) $17{,}296 = 2^4 \cdot 23 \cdot 47$ and $18{,}416 = 2^4 \cdot 1151$.

36. Let U_n be the unit's digit in $\sum_{k=1}^{n} k!$. (a) Compute U_n for $n = 1, 2, 3, 4$, and 5. (b) What is U_{99}? Why? (c) What is U_n? Why?

37. (a) Show that $\gcd(F_n, F_{n+1}) = 1$ for $n = 1, 2, 3, 4, 5$. (Here F_n is the nth Fibonacci number.) (b) Using WOA or PMI, show that $\gcd(F_n, F_{n+1}) = 1$ for all $n \in \mathbb{N}$.

38. (a) Note that $F_3 = 2$. What are the subscripts of the Fibonacci numbers that 2 divides? (*Hint:* $2 \mid F_6$ and $2 \mid F_9$.) (b) Noting that $F_4 = 3$, what are the subscripts of the Fibonacci numbers that 3 divides? (c) Noting that $F_5 = 5$, what are the subscripts of the Fibonacci numbers that 5 divides? (d) What is your conjecture?

39. Compute the gcd of the following pairs of Fibonacci numbers. (a) F_3, F_6; (b) F_4, F_6; (c) F_8, F_{12}; (d) F_9, F_{12}; (e) F_6, F_{12}.

40. Assuming your conjecture in Problem 38 is true and using Problem 39, what do you conjecture about $\gcd(F_m, F_n)$?

41. Amplifying a remark of John Hancock, Benjamin Franklin said, "we must all hang together or ... we shall all hang separately." This is in the form of a disjunction, but was that Franklin's intent? What do you think?

CHAPTER 3

Combinatorics

Section 15. Sets and Counting

Overview for Section 15

- Binary operations on sets: union and intersection
- Discussion of "size" or "cardinality" of sets
- Introduction to three Fundamental Counting Principles
- Discussion of the Cartesian product of sets
- Classification and enumeration of certain functions on finite sets
- Return to the factorial function

Key Concepts: union, intersection, disjoint sets, cardinality, Fundamental Counting Principles I, II, and III, Cartesian products, constant functions, one-to-one functions

15.1 Addition, in arithmetic, is an example of a *binary operation* on numbers: Given two numbers, addition creates a new number called the sum. Multiplication is another example of a binary operation on numbers. This concept of binary operation is not restricted to numbers but can be defined in many other contexts. In this section, we will study several such operations defined on sets.

Let **A** and **B** denote any sets. The **union** of **A** and **B** is the new set

$$\mathbf{A} \cup \mathbf{B} = \{x: \ x \text{ belongs to at least one of the sets } \mathbf{A}, \mathbf{B}\}.$$

The **intersection** of **A** and **B** is the new set

$$A \cap B = \{x: \; x \text{ belongs to both sets } \mathbf{A}, \mathbf{B}\}.$$

Example 1   **a.** If $\mathbf{A} = \{a, b, c\}$ and $\mathbf{B} = \{a, e, i, o, u\}$, then

$$\mathbf{A} \cup \mathbf{B} = \{a, b, c, e, i, o, u\} \qquad \text{and} \qquad \mathbf{A} \cap \mathbf{B} = \{a\}.$$

b. If **A** is the set of all even integers and if **B** is the set of all odd integers, then

$$\mathbf{A} \cup \mathbf{B} = \mathbb{Z} \qquad \text{and} \qquad \mathbf{A} \cap \mathbf{B} = \varnothing.$$

c. For any set $\mathbf{A}$, $\mathbf{A} \cup \mathbf{A} = \mathbf{A}$ and $\mathbf{A} \cap \mathbf{A} = \mathbf{A}$.

The relationship between union and intersection is described in the following theorem.

THEOREM 15.1

Let **S** be any set and let **A** and **B** denote subsets of **S**. Then

$$\varnothing \subseteq \mathbf{A} \cap \mathbf{B} \subseteq \mathbf{A} \subseteq \mathbf{A} \cup \mathbf{B} \subseteq \mathbf{S}. \tag{1}$$

Proof

a. The empty set is a subset of any set.

b. If $x \in \mathbf{A} \cap \mathbf{B}$, then $x \in \mathbf{A}$ and **B**; hence $x \in \mathbf{A}$.

c. If $x \in \mathbf{A}$, then x is in at least one of the sets $\mathbf{A}, \mathbf{B}$; hence $x \in \mathbf{A} \cup \mathbf{B}$.

d. Since $\mathbf{A}, \mathbf{B}$ each are contained in $\mathbf{S}$, $\mathbf{A} \cup \mathbf{B} \subseteq \mathbf{S}$.

Suppose we consider Theorem 15.1 as it relates to each of the three parts of Example 1.

a. If **S** denotes the set of all letters in the alphabet, then (1) says

$$\varnothing \subseteq \{a\} \subseteq \{a, b, c\} \subseteq \{a, b, c, e, i, o, u\} \subseteq \mathbf{S}.$$

Notice that we might just as well have begun with the set names interchanged; hence (1) also says

$$\varnothing \subseteq \{a\} \subseteq \{a, e, i, o, u\} \subseteq \{a, b, c, e, i, o, u\} \subseteq \mathbf{S}.$$

These set inequalities illustrate an important concept: The set **K** is a **proper subset** of the set **M** if $\mathbf{K} \subseteq \mathbf{M}$ and $\mathbf{K} \neq \mathbf{M}$. Thus if we erase from the set **M** at least one of its elements, then what remains is a proper subset. For example, $\{a\}$ is a proper subset of $\{a, b, c\}$.

b. If $\mathbf{S} = \mathbb{Z}$, and if $\mathbb{E}$ denotes the set of all even integers and $\mathbb{O}$ denotes the set of all odd integers, then (1) says

$$\varnothing \subseteq \mathbb{E} \cap \mathbb{O} \subseteq \mathbb{E} \subseteq \mathbb{E} \cup \mathbb{O} \subseteq \mathbb{Z}.$$

Since $\mathbb{E} \cap \mathbb{O} = \varnothing$ and $\mathbb{E} \cup \mathbb{O} = \mathbb{Z}$, this inequality reduces to

$$\varnothing \subseteq \mathbb{E} \subseteq \mathbb{Z}.$$

This set inclusion illustrates another important concept: Two sets $\mathbf{K}$ and $\mathbf{M}$ are called **disjoint** if they have no element in common, that is, if $\mathbf{K} \cap \mathbf{M} = \varnothing$. The sets $\mathbb{E}$ and $\mathbb{O}$, of course, are disjoint.

c. If $\mathbf{S} = \mathbf{A}$, then (1) says

$$\varnothing \subseteq \mathbf{A} \cap \mathbf{A} \subseteq \mathbf{A} \subseteq \mathbf{A} \cup \mathbf{A} \subseteq \mathbf{S},$$

which reduces to

$$\varnothing \subseteq \mathbf{A}.$$

This set inclusion illustrates the fact that (1) applies even in the most special (trivial) situations. If $\mathbf{A} = \varnothing$, for example, (1) is a triviality, and no one of the sets is a proper subset of another. If $\mathbf{A} \neq \varnothing$, then $\varnothing$ is a proper subset of $\mathbf{A}$, and $\mathbf{A} \cap \mathbf{A}$ is a subset, but not a proper subset, of $\mathbf{A}$. Furthermore, no nonempty set can be disjoint from itself, but any set is always disjoint from $\varnothing$.

These latter observations have been included for the sake of completeness; true but not terribly exciting or even unexpected. We will look next at another, almost equally evident, observation which (in the hands of genius) led to one of the most exciting developments in modern mathematics. (Refer to paragraph 15.6.)

15.2

In paragraph 7.1 we introduced the notion of one-to-one correspondence. Recall that the sets $\mathbf{A}$ and $\mathbf{B}$ are in one-to-one correspondence if the elements of $\mathbf{A}$ can be paired with those of $\mathbf{B}$ in such a way that no element (in either set) is left out and no element appears in more than one pair. Two sets are said to have the **same number of elements,** or to be of the **same size,** if there exists a one-to-one correspondence between them. This idea is perfectly general, applying to any sets whether finite or infinite. We will be concerned mainly with finite sets, but occasionally we must consider infinite sets (such as $\mathbb{N}$ or $\mathbb{R}$), and in this context we say that two sets have the **same cardinality** if there is a one-to-one correspondence between them. (This term derives from "cardinal number" in elementary arithmetic. Other terms sometimes used for "cardinality" are **power** and **order.**) "Cardinality" is the more general term, and when used to describe a finite set it refers to the number of elements in that set. In either case, it is customary to use the symbol $|\mathbf{A}|$ to denote the number of elements in, or the cardinality of, the set A. Because of the similarity, it is important not to confuse this set theoretic use of $|A|$ with the absolute value symbol as used in arithmetic.

Example 1

a. If $A = \{a, e, i, o, u\}$, then $|A| = 5$.

b. If A is a singleton set, then $|A| = 1$.

c. If A and B are disjoint, then $|A \cap B| = |\varnothing| = 0$.

THEOREM 15.2

If S is a finite set and if A and B are subsets of S, then

$$|\varnothing| \leq |A \cap B| \leq |A| \leq |A \cup B| \leq |S|.$$

We will assume that the truth of this theorem is evident. It is based on Theorem 15.1 and the argument that if M and N are two sets for which $M \subseteq N$ and if we can list the elements of N as $\{x_1, x_2, \ldots, x_n\}$, then no subset of N can contain more than these elements. Theorems 15.1 and 15.2 are obviously similar, but they are intended to emphasize the important distinction that "$\leq$" is a relationship between numbers while "$\subseteq$" is a relationship between sets. The use of symbols must always be consistent; for example, it is *incorrect* to use

$$|M| \subseteq |N| \qquad \text{or} \qquad M \leq N,$$

but it is correct to use

$$|M| \leq |N| \qquad \text{or} \qquad M \subseteq N.$$

15.3

Throughout the remainder of this section we will assume that S is a finite set and that A and B are subsets of S. One of the most important aspects of discrete mathematics deals with the problem of enumerating various sets. Although most of the interesting applications require sophisticated analysis, and are often subtle beyond belief, the techniques rest ultimately upon a few very simple rules which we will call **Fundamental Counting Principles** (abbreviated **FCP**).

FCP I

If $A \cap B = \varnothing$, then $|A \cup B| = |A| + |B|$.

This one is immediately evident: Simply count the elements in one set followed by those in the other set. For example, if A is the set of prime factors of 154 and if B is the set of prime factors of 15, then $|A \cup B| = |A| + |B| = 3 + 2 = 5$. This principle, while simple, will occur often in the sequel.

Tutorial 15.3A

Here is the outline of another argument that

$$|\mathbf{A}| \leq |\mathbf{A} \cup \mathbf{B}|.$$

a. Note that $\mathbf{A} \subseteq \mathbf{A} \cup \mathbf{B}$. Why?

b. Let $\mathbf{C}$ denote the complement of $\mathbf{A}$ in $\mathbf{A} \cup \mathbf{B}$. Show that $\mathbf{A} \cup \mathbf{B} = \mathbf{A} \cup \mathbf{C}$.

c. Why is it true that you can apply FCP I to $\mathbf{A} \cup \mathbf{C}$?

d. Observe that $|\mathbf{C}| \geq 0$; hence $|\mathbf{A}| = |\mathbf{A} \cup \mathbf{B}| - |\mathbf{C}| \leq |\mathbf{A} \cup \mathbf{B}|$. Under what condition is $|\mathbf{A}| = |\mathbf{A} \cup \mathbf{B}|$?

We have already had occasion to use the ordered-pair concept in paragraph 13.1. Again, consider the sets $\mathbf{A}$ and $\mathbf{B}$, and assume them to be nonempty. We define the **Cartesian product** (or **product**) of $\mathbf{A}$ and $\mathbf{B}$ by

$$\mathbf{A} \times \mathbf{B} = \{(x, y): \ x \in \mathbf{A} \text{ and } y \in \mathbf{B}\}.$$

Note that an element of $\mathbf{A} \times \mathbf{B}$ is an *ordered pair*; it need not be an element of either $\mathbf{A}$ or $\mathbf{B}$.

Example 1   If $\mathbf{A} = \{a, b, c\}$ and $\mathbf{B} = \{a, e, i, o, u\}$, then

$$\begin{aligned}
\mathbf{A} \times \mathbf{B} = \{ & (a, a), \ (a, e), \ (a, i), \ (a, o), \ (a, u), \\
& (b, a), \ (b, e), \ (b, i), \ (b, o), \ (b, u), \\
& (c, a), \ (c, e), \ (c, i), \ (c, o), \ (c, u)\}.
\end{aligned}$$

There are two important distinctions to be emphasized between the Cartesian product and the earlier operations of union and intersection.

- If $\mathbf{A} \subseteq \mathbf{S}$ and $\mathbf{B} \subseteq \mathbf{S}$, then $\mathbf{A} \cup \mathbf{B} \subseteq \mathbf{S}$ and $\mathbf{A} \cap \mathbf{B} \subseteq \mathbf{S}$, but not so for $\mathbf{A} \times \mathbf{B}$; in Example 1, if $\mathbf{S} = \mathbf{A} \cup \mathbf{B}$, then $\mathbf{S} \cap (\mathbf{A} \times \mathbf{B}) = \varnothing$.

- The operations of union and intersection are *commutative*; that is, $\mathbf{A} \cup \mathbf{B} = \mathbf{B} \cup \mathbf{A}$ and $\mathbf{A} \cap \mathbf{B} = \mathbf{B} \cap \mathbf{A}$. But, again, not so for $\mathbf{A} \times \mathbf{B}$. To obtain $\mathbf{B} \times \mathbf{A}$, we must interchange coordinates of all ordered pairs in $\mathbf{A} \times \mathbf{B}$. The resulting set of ordered pairs is of the same size, but in general its elements are different. Note in Example 1 that the intersection of $\mathbf{A} \times \mathbf{B}$ and $\mathbf{B} \times \mathbf{A}$ is nonempty, (a, a) is in both, but each contains many ordered pairs not in the other.

As is displayed in Example 1, the set $\mathbf{A} \times \mathbf{B}$ can be expressed as the union of three disjoint sets, each the same size as $\mathbf{B}$. Thus by FCP I,

$$|A \times B| = 5 + 5 + 5 = 3 \cdot 5 = 15.$$

This observation is generalized in our second FCP. It is easy to see that $A \times B$ can be written as $|A|$ rows of $|B|$ ordered pairs each.

FCP II

If A and B are nonempty sets, then

$$|A \times B| = |A| \cdot |B|.$$

If either A or B is empty, then by convention we say that $A \times B$ is empty, so $|A \times B| = 0$.

Example 2

Let D denote the set of 10 digits $0, 1, \ldots, 9$ and let D' denote the set of nonzero digits. Then $|D' \times D| = 90$. Note that each ordered pair in $D' \times D$ corresponds to a two-digit positive integer. Thus there are 90 positive integers x for which $10 \leq x \leq 99$. ●

Tutorial 15.3B

Let $A = \{0, 1\}$ and let $B = \{x, y, z\}$.
a. By listing elements in the two sets $A \times B$ and $B \times A$, show that $|A \times B| = |B \times A|$, although $A \times B \neq B \times A$.
b. List the elements in $A \times A$ and $B \times B$.
c. Is it true that $|A \times A| = |B \times B|$?

Suppose now that we want to determine the number of two-digit positive integers in which the digit is not repeated. We must consider the proper subset of $D' \times D$ obtained by erasing the ordered pairs $(1, 1)$, $(2, 2)$, and so on. The answer, of course, is $90 - 9 = 81$, but FCP II does not apply in this case; we must modify it slightly. Let $A = \{a_1, a_2, \ldots, a_n\}$, and suppose that for each $a_i \in A$ there is determined a set B_i. The sets B_i may differ from one another (this is what keeps FCP II from applying), but we will assume that

$$|B_1| = |B_2| = |B_3| = \cdots = |B_n| = m.$$

Now, let W denote the following set of ordered pairs.

$$W = \{(a_i, b): a_i \in A \text{ and } b \in B_i\}.$$

Using the notation just described, our third FCP is

FCP III

$$|\mathbf{W}| = |\mathbf{A}| \cdot |\mathbf{B}_i| = n \cdot m.$$

Example 3

Return to the preceding discussion and consider the selection of a two-digit number with nonrepeating digits. If the first digit chosen is 1, then the second digit must be chosen from the set

$$\mathbf{B}_1 = \{0, 2, 3, 4, 5, 6, 7, 8, 9\};$$

if the first digit chosen is 2, then the second digit must be chosen from the set $\mathbf{B}_2 = \{0, 1, 3, 4, 5, 6, 7, 8, 9\}$; and so on. Since for each i, $|\mathbf{B}_i| = 9$, $|\mathbf{W}| = 9 \cdot 9 = 81$ by FCP III.

Example 4

In some colleges the normal load for a student is four courses per term. For example, consider the set $\mathbf{A} = \{\text{Fred, Barbara, Holly}\}$. Suppose the courses taken are

$$\mathbf{B}_{\text{Fred}} = \{\text{discrete, English literature, U.S. history, art}\},$$

$$\mathbf{B}_{\text{Barbara}} = \{\text{discrete, French, politics, music}\},$$

$$\mathbf{B}_{\text{Holly}} = \{\text{discrete, German, economics, biology}\}.$$

If $\mathbf{W} = \{(a, b): a \in \mathbf{A}, b \in \mathbf{B}_a\}$, then by FCP III, $|\mathbf{W}| = 3 \cdot 4 = 12$. Note that $|\mathbf{W}|$ is not the number of courses taken by these students (since the "discrete" course is duplicated). Rather think of $|\mathbf{W}|$ as the number of course grades received by these students.

Example 5

The reading list in your literature course includes 11 novels. One of your assignments is to read two novels by the end of the term. Any particular way of completing this assignment may be considered an ordered pair (first novel read, second novel read). The number of ways you can fill the first coordinate is 11, and for each of them the number of ways you can fill the second coordinate is 10; hence (by FCP III) the total number of such ordered pairs is $11 \cdot 10 = 110$. Notice that the class size would have to be at least 111 to guarantee that at least two students read the same two novels in the same order.

15.4

The previous examples are both simple and not very surprising, but the power of these counting principles becomes more obvious when they are applied sequentially, as illustrated in the following discussion.

Let $\mathbf{A} = \{a_1, a_2, \ldots, a_n\}$ and let $\mathbf{B} = \{b_1, b_2, \ldots, b_m\}$ so that $|\mathbf{A}| = n$ and $|\mathbf{B}| = m$. Assume that each of these numbers is greater than zero. We can define many functions of the form

$$f: \mathbf{A} \to \mathbf{B}, \tag{1}$$

all of them having $\mathbf{A}$ as domain, but the range of each one will be some subset of $\mathbf{B}$ [compare with (1) in paragraph 13.3]. Among the simplest such functions are the **constant functions** in which the range is a singleton; for example, for each $a_i \in \mathbf{A}$, let $f(a_i) = b_1$. Thus there are m different constant functions, one for each element in $\mathbf{B}$, but these are only a few of the possible functions. The more general question is, "How many functions f are there altogether?" Consider first, functions of the form

$$f = \{(a_1, \quad), (a_2, \quad)\}.$$

Each ordered pair (b_i, b_j) in the set $\mathbf{B} \times \mathbf{B}$ provides the second coordinates in f:

$$\{(a_1, b_i), (a_2, b_j)\}.$$

Hence, there is a one-to-one correspondence between the pairs in $\mathbf{B} \times \mathbf{B}$ and the functions f. For f of the form

$$f = \{(a_1, \quad), (a_2, \quad), (a_3, \quad)\},$$

the set of ordered triples, $\mathbf{B} \times \mathbf{B} \times \mathbf{B}$, provides second coordinates for the ordered pairs in f. In general, the set of ordered n-tuples $\underbrace{\mathbf{B} \times \mathbf{B} \times \cdots \times \mathbf{B}}_{n \text{ factors}}$ provides second coordinates for the ordered pairs in

$$f = \{(a_1, \quad), \underset{\mathbf{B}}{} \times (a_2, \quad), \underset{\mathbf{B}}{} \times (a_3, \quad), \underset{\mathbf{B}}{} \times \cdots \times (a_n, \quad)\}. \underset{\mathbf{B}}{} \tag{2}$$

By a repeated use of FCP II, the total number of such n-tuples is

$$\underbrace{|\mathbf{B}| \cdot |\mathbf{B}| \cdots |\mathbf{B}|}_{|\mathbf{A}| \text{ times}} = |\mathbf{B}|^{|\mathbf{A}|} = m^n.$$

The argument in detail uses mathematical induction, but the result seems transparent enough that we omit the proof.

Again consider the sets $\mathbf{A}$ and $\mathbf{B}$, as described above, but now assume that $m < n$. To construct a function f we must assign an element of $\mathbf{B}$ to each of the ordered pairs in (2). The Pigeonhole Principle demands that some element in $\mathbf{B}$ be assigned to two different ordered pairs in f. Hence, in this case, the function must have the property that some second coordinate is repeated. If, on the other hand, $m \geq n$, then it is possible to construct functions in which no second coordinate is repeated. A function with this important property is called **one-to-one.** Such a function establishes what we have called a one-to-one correspondence between the domain and the range of f.

Note that if $m = n$, then the correspondence is between **A** and **B**, but if $m > n$, then the correspondence is between **A** and a subset of **B**. Now we consider the question, "If $m \geq n$, how many one-to-one functions f are there?" Again, the form of such a function is given by (2), but this time the second coordinates may not be chosen arbitrarily from **B**. In fact, having chosen b_1 in (a_1, b_1), the choice for b_2 must avoid b_1. Having chosen b_1 and b_2, the choice for b_3 must avoid both b_1 and b_2. We can formalize this argument as follows. For each $b_i \in \mathbf{B}$, let $\mathbf{B}_i = \mathbf{B} - \{b_i\}$. Then the set $\mathbf{W}_1 = \{(b_i, b') : b_i \in \mathbf{B}, b' \in \mathbf{B}_i\}$ provides second coordinates for the ordered pairs in

$$f = \{(a_1, b_i), (a_2, b')\}.$$

By FCP III, there are $|\mathbf{B}| \cdot |\mathbf{B}_i| = m(m - 1)$ such functions. Now consider functions of the form

$$f = \{(a_1, \quad), (a_2, \quad), (a_3, \quad)\}.$$

For $(b_i, b_j) \in \mathbf{W}_1$, let $\mathbf{B}_{ij} = \mathbf{B} - \{b_i, b_j\}$, and put $\mathbf{W}_2 = \{((b_i, b_j), b') : (b_i, b_j) \in \mathbf{W}_1, b' \in \mathbf{B}_{ij}\}$. Again, by FCP III, $\mathbf{W}_2$ has $|\mathbf{W}_1| \cdot |\mathbf{B}_{ij}| = |\mathbf{B}| \cdot |\mathbf{B}_i| \cdot |\mathbf{B}_{ij}| = m(m - 1)(m - 2)$ ordered triples, each of which provides second coordinates for the ordered pairs in f. Similarly, repeated use of FCP III leads to the following number of one-to-one functions, which for abbreviation we denote by the symbol $(m)_n$,

$$(m)_n = m \cdot (m - 1) \cdot (m - 2) \cdots (m - n + 1).$$

As before, the proof requires mathematical induction; again we will omit it because the result is transparent: there are m choices for b_1, $(m - 1)$ choices for b_2, $(m - 2)$ choices for b_3, and so on, for each of the n second coordinates required.

Note that there must be exactly n factors in this product. In the event that m and n are the same, this number is simply a factorial:

$$(m)_m = m!.$$

If $m > n$, we can still write the number using factorials in a very simple way. Observe that

$$m! = m \cdot (m - 1) \cdots (m - n + 1) \cdot (m - n) \cdot (m - n - 1) \cdots 2 \cdot 1$$
$$= m \cdot (m - 1) \cdots (m - n + 1) \cdot (m - n)!$$
$$= (m)_n \cdot (m - n)!.$$

Hence,
$$(m)_n = \frac{m!}{(m - n)!}.$$

15.5

In the preceding development we presented a number of facts, which are summarized in the following theorem.

THEOREM 15.5

Let **A** and **B** denote nonempty sets for which $|\mathbf{A}| = n$ and $|\mathbf{B}| = m$.
a. The number of functions $f: \mathbf{A} \to \mathbf{B}$ is m^n.
b. The number of constant functions $f: \mathbf{A} \to \mathbf{B}$ is m.
c. The number of one-to-one functions $f: \mathbf{A} \to \mathbf{B}$ is
   i. 0, if $m < n$,
   ii. $m!$, if $m = n$,
   iii. $\dfrac{m!}{(m-n)!}$, if $m > n$.

Example 1

Let $\mathbf{A} = \{0, 1\}$ and let $\mathbf{B} = \{a, b, c\}$. Here $n = 2$ and $m = 3$. Hence the number of functions $f: \mathbf{A} \to \mathbf{B}$ is $3^2 = 9$, and the number of one-to-one functions is

$$(3)_2 = \frac{3!}{(3-2)!} = \frac{3!}{1!} = 3! = 6.$$

It will be good practice to list these functions. We indicate below the possible selections of the second coordinates.

$$f = \{(0, \quad), (1, \quad)\}$$

a	a
a	b
a	c
b	a
b	b
b	c
c	a
c	b
c	c

Note that there are nine possibilities altogether, but only six of them have no repeated coordinates.

Tutorial 15.5

Let $\mathbf{A} = \{1, 2, 3\}$ and let $\mathbf{V} = \{a, e, i, o, u\}$.
a. How many functions $f: \mathbf{A} \to \mathbf{V}$ are there? Give an example of one constant function and one nonconstant function.
b. How many one-to-one functions $f: \mathbf{A} \to \mathbf{V}$ are there? Give examples of two such functions.

Example 2   Let $B = \{p_1, p_2, \ldots, p_{25}\}$ be the set of 25 players on a baseball team and let

$$P = \{\text{catcher, pitcher, first baseman, second baseman, third baseman,}$$
$$\text{shortstop, left field, right field, center field}\}$$

be the set of the nine positions. What exactly is the significance of functions $f\colon B \to P$ or of functions $g\colon P \to B$? To answer these questions, suppose we ask yet two more questions:

a. What position does each player play best?

b. Who plays what position best?

The answer to question **a** is a function from **B** into **P**; for example,

$$f = \{(p_1, \text{catcher}), (p_2, \text{catcher}), (p_3, \text{first baseman}), (p_4, \text{shortstop}), \ldots\}.$$

Thus players 1 and 2 play best as catchers and player 3 plays best at first. Similarly, the answer to question **b** is a function from **P** into **B**; for example,

$$g = \{(\text{catcher}, p_1), (\text{pitcher}, p_{25}), (\text{first baseman}, p_3), (\text{second baseman}, p_8),$$
$$(\text{third baseman}, p_8), (\text{shortstop}, p_8), \ldots\}.$$

Note that it is possible for one player to be the best on the team at two different positions. In our example, the best player at second, short, and third is player 8, p_8.

The total number of answers to question **a** is the number of functions $f\colon B \to P$, or $9^{25} \approx 7 \times 10^{23}$. The number of answers to question **b** is the number of functions $g\colon P \to B$, or $25^9 \approx 3.8 \times 10^{12}$, a much smaller number than 9^{25}.

There are obviously no one-to-one functions from **B** into **P** since $|B| > |P|$, but there are one-to-one functions from **P** into **B**. This, of course, is necessary because each time a game is played, the manager chooses one of these one-to-one functions as his starting lineup. It is sometimes suggested that a manager should try all possible starting lineups to see which is the best. In this example, there are

$$(25)_9 = \frac{25!}{(25-9)!} = \frac{25!}{16!} = 741,354,768,000$$

possible lineups and, obviously, no manager can try them all.

Example 3   Suppose that your favorite pizza restaurant offers 12 different toppings, any combination of which you can order. You plan to eat a pizza a day (it keeps the doctor away) and wonder how long it would take until you have tried all the possible combinations. To solve this, just think of your pizza as a function, with its domain as the set of toppings and its range as the set {ordered, not ordered}. For example, you order a pizza with sausage and pepperoni but no olives or anchovies. Then your function pizza would be {(sausage, ordered), (pepperoni, ordered), . . . , (olives, not ordered), (anchovies, not ordered), . . .}

where the " . . . " indicate the other toppings. There are two constant functions: one is a plain pizza (all second coordinates are "not ordered"), and the other includes all 12 toppings (all second coordinates are "ordered"). The domain of our pizza functions has 12 elements, and the range has only 2 elements. By part **a** of Theorem 15.5, there are 2^{12} different pizzas. Since $2^{12} = 4096$, if you ate one pizza a day, it would take over *eleven* years to try each one of the different combinations. Bon appetit!   ⬤

15.6   **Complement: Transfinite Sets** Modern set theory begins with the nineteenth century mathematician Georg Cantor (1845–1918). Although the basic ideas were already in place, Cantor, beginning about 1870, essentially created a new branch of mathematics. His ideas were astonishingly original, almost heretical, and they aroused among his contemporary mathematicians a "storm" of admiration and protest. He was, and remains, one of the most influential mathematicians who ever lived. We will consider a small fragment of his research related to infinite sets. Intuitively, one might think that there is little need to define "infinite"; surely the idea is evident, and surely a set is either infinite or not and there is little to distinguish one infinite set from another. Not so! Cantor used a simple, intrinsic characterization of infinite sets and showed that it is possible to distinguish infinite sets by "size."

The key idea is that of one-to-one correspondence, already thoroughly familiar in Cantor's day. Recall that two sets are in one-to-one correspondence if the elements in the sets can be paired off in such a way that all are used and none in either set is used more than once. For convenience in notation, suppose we denote by **A** ~ **B** the fact that **A** and **B** are in one-to-one correspondence (**A** is equivalent to **B**). For example, remembering that **V** denotes the set of principal vowels, then

$$\mathbf{V} \sim \{2, 3, 5, 7, 11\} \sim \{*, \&, \cent, \%, \#\}.$$

Notice in this example of one-to-one correspondence that it has not been necessary to mention the number of elements in the sets. In fact, it is easy to imagine one-to-one correspondences in which the number of elements in the sets is unknown. Suppose, for example, that you are unable to find a space in your favorite parking lot. Then there is a one-to-one correspondence between the set of spaces and the set of autos in them.

Given a finite set, like any of those mentioned above, intuition tells us that there is no possible way to establish a one-to-one correspondence between the set and any of its *proper* subsets. For example, if we erase from **V** any one of its elements, say u, then any function $f: \mathbf{V} \to \{a, e, i, o\}$ must assign the same function value to at least two elements in the domain. (Note that the Pigeonhole Principle is at work here.) But for $\mathbb{N}$, the set of all positive integers, the situation is different: Suppose we relate each element in $\mathbb{N}$ with its immediate successor. Thus if $\mathbb{W}_2$ denotes the set of all positive integers greater than 1, then the function $f: \mathbb{N} \to \mathbb{W}_2$,

$$\{(1, 2), (2, 3), (3, 4), \ldots, (n, n + 1), \ldots\},$$

establishes a one-to-one correspondence between $\mathbb{N}$ and its proper subset $\mathbb{W}_2$. This distinction can be made the basis for a definition of infinite sets. A set $\mathbf{M}$ is called **infinite** if there is some proper subset $\mathbf{M}_1$ of $\mathbf{M}$ which is in one-to-one correspondence with $\mathbf{M}$. Otherwise, the set $\mathbf{M}$ is called **finite.**

Note that this definition of finite set does not depend upon comparison with a "standard" set like the subset $\{1, 2, \ldots, n\}$ of $\mathbb{N}$ (recall paragraph 4.2). Among finite sets, it is clear that $\mathbf{A} \sim \mathbf{B}$ means that $\mathbf{A}$ and $\mathbf{B}$ have the same number of elements, hence have the same size. As indicated in paragraph 15.2, we will refer to size (or number of elements) as the cardinality of the set, and we will denote the cardinality of the set $\mathbf{A}$ by $|\mathbf{A}|$. So, $\mathbf{A} \sim \mathbf{B}$ means $|\mathbf{A}| = |\mathbf{B}|$.

The cardinality (cardinal, in brief) of any finite set is some positive integer, but no positive integer is sufficiently large to be the cardinal of the set $\mathbb{N}$. Cantor called $|\mathbb{N}|$ a transfinite number, and he was able to show that no infinite set has a cardinal less than that. Since there are no smaller cardinals of infinite sets than $|\mathbb{N}|$, we might ask whether there are any infinite sets with larger cardinal; or indeed are all infinite sets of the same size? Using only proof techniques already familiar to us, we can show that there *is* a set of larger cardinal than $|\mathbb{N}|$; and even more surprising, we can show that given any infinite set $\mathbf{A}$ at all, there exists a set having cardinal greater than $|\mathbf{A}|$. So among Cantor's transfinite cardinals there is an unending sequence, each one larger than all the preceding ones.

THEOREM 15.6

If $2^{\mathbb{N}}$ is the power set of $\mathbb{N}$, then $|\mathbb{N}| \neq |2^{\mathbb{N}}|$.

Proof

We must show that there is no one-to-one correspondence between $\mathbb{N}$ and $2^{\mathbb{N}}$. Suppose, on the contrary, that there were. Then we can pair the elements in $\mathbb{N}$ and $2^{\mathbb{N}}$ as follows:

$$(1, \mathbf{A}_1), (2, \mathbf{A}_2), (3, \mathbf{A}_3), \ldots,$$

where the sets $\mathbf{A}_i$ must include all the subsets of $\mathbb{N}$. Thus,

No subset of $\mathbb{N}$ fails to appear in the list above.   **(1)**

Now examine the pair $(1, \mathbf{A}_1)$. Since $\mathbf{A}_1 \subseteq \mathbb{N}$, the element 1 either is in $\mathbf{A}_1$ or it isn't. If it isn't, put 1 in a new set we will call $\mathbf{B}$. Next examine the pair $(2, \mathbf{A}_2)$, and again note that 2 either is in $\mathbf{A}_2$ or it isn't. If it isn't, put 2 in $\mathbf{B}$. Continue, and notice that we have defined a subset $\mathbf{B}$ of $\mathbb{N}$ as follows:

$$\mathbf{B} = \{k \in \mathbb{N} : k \notin \mathbf{A}_k\}.$$

By condition (1), the set $\mathbf{B}$ must appear somewhere in our list, so there is a positive integer j such that $(j, \mathbf{B})$ is in the original list. In our earlier notation, $\mathbf{B} = \mathbf{A}_j$. Now, ask yourself, "Does j belong to $\mathbf{B}$?" Of course, either it does or it doesn't. But in either case, we reach a contradiction; hence we must conclude that $\mathbb{N} \sim 2^{\mathbb{N}}$ is false. ∎

Final Remark.   Cantor's theory establishes an "order" among cardinal numbers. In brief, $|A| \leq |B|$ means that **A** is equivalent to some subset of **B**. Strict inequality requires, in addition, that **A** and **B** are not equivalent. Thus, if you can find a one-to-one correspondence between $\mathbb{N}$ and a subset of $2^{\mathbb{N}}$, then you can show by Theorem 15.6 that the cardinal of $\mathbb{N}$ is less than that of $2^{\mathbb{N}}$. As a hint, refer to Example 1 of paragraph 1.14.

Problems for Section 15

1. Let $A = \{x : x \text{ is a prime factor of } 858\}$ and let $B = \{x : x \text{ is a prime factor of } 924\}$. List the elements in each set: (a) $A \cup B$, (b) $A \cap B$, (c) $A - B$, (d) $B - A$.

2. Let **S** be a given set containing **A** and **B** as subsets. Denote the complements of **A** and **B** in **S** by $\overline{A}$ and $\overline{B}$. Show that (a) $A - B = A \cap \overline{B}$, (b) $B - A = \overline{A} \cap B$.

3. Let $A = \{0, 1, 2\}$ and let $B = \{a, b\}$. List the elements in the sets (a) $A \times B$, (b) $B \times A$.

4. Let **A** denote the set of letters in the name WASHINGTON and let **B** denote the set of letters in the name JEFFERSON. (a) List the elements in the sets $A \cup B$ and $A \cap B$. (b) How many elements are in the set $A \times B$? List a few of them.

5. Let **A** and **B** denote the sets described in Problem 4. (a) Find an element in $(A \times B) - (B \times A)$. (b) Find an element in $(B \times A) - (A \times B)$. (c) List the elements in the sets $(A \times B) \cap (B \times A)$.

6. Let $S = \{s_1, s_2, s_3, \ldots, s_8\}$. Note that $|\varnothing| = 0$ and $|S| = 8$. Find any subsets **A** and **B** of **S** such that $|\varnothing| < |A \cap B| < |A| = |A \cup B| < |S|$.

7. (*Continuation of Problem 6.*) Find any subsets **A** and **B** such that $0 = |A \cap B| < |B| = |A| < |A \cup B|$.

8. (*Conclusion of Problem 6.*) Is it possible to find sets **A** and **B** such that
(a) $0 = |A \cap B| < |A| = |A \cup B|$?
(b) $0 = |A \cap B| < |B| < |A| = |A \cup B|$?

9. Let $S = \{1, 2, 3, \ldots, 20\}$, and for any subset **A** of **S** let $S - A = \overline{A}$. List the elements in each of these sets if $A = \{3, 6, 9, 12, 15, 18\}$ and $B = \{7, 8, 9, 10, 11, 12, 13\}$: (a) $\overline{A \cup B}$, (b) $\overline{A \cap B}$, (c) $\overline{A} \cup \overline{B}$, (d) $\overline{A} \cap \overline{B}$. (e) Do you notice anything unusual about these sets?

10. Let **A** be the set of primes less than 10 and let $B = \{1, 2, 3, 4, 5\}$. Let $R \subseteq A \times B$ be such that if $(a, b) \in R$, then $a \cdot b$ is a Fibonacci number. (a) Compute $|A \times B|$. (b) List the elements of **R**. (c) Is **R** a function? Why or why not?

11. Let **A** be the odd numbers between 2 and 20, let $B = \{2, 4, 6, 8\}$, and let $R = \{(a, b) : (a, b) \in A \times B \text{ and } a + b \text{ is Fibonacci}\}$. (a) Compute $|A \times B|$. (b) List the elements of **R**. (c) Is **R** a function? Why or why not?

12. Let $f(x)$ define a function which has exactly four distinct roots, all of which are positive, and let $g(x)$ define a function which has exactly three distinct roots, all of which are negative. How many distinct roots does the function defined by $f(x) \cdot g(x)$ have?

13. Why doesn't FCP I apply in enumerating the union of the sets **A** and **B** if **A** is the set of even integers between 0 and 10 (inclusive) and if **B** is the set of prime numbers less than 10?

14. A password consists of two different letters followed by four different digits. How many possible passwords are there?

15. How many positive integers have a four-place representation (no leading zeros) (*a*) in base 10, (*b*) in base 2, (*c*) in base 16? (*d*) How many four-place representations are there of each type if the leading places can be zero?

16. Of a group of 20 individuals, suppose that 8 were born in Alabama, 5 were born in Alaska, 4 were born in Arizona, and 3 were born in Arkansas. In how many ways can four people be selected from this group so that each state is represented?

17. A traveling salesman must visit each of seven cities, once only. In how many ways can he arrange his journey?

18. Let $A_0, A_1, A_2, \ldots, A_n$ be nonempty, finite sets having cardinalities $p_0, p_1, p_2, \ldots, p_n$, respectively, and assume that $A_i \cap A_j = \emptyset$ for each $i \neq j$. By mathematical induction, prove that for each $n \in \mathbb{N}$, the cardinality of the union of all the sets A_i is the sum of the cardinalities p_i.

19. Let n be a positive integer, and let $A_0, A_1, A_2, \ldots, A_n$ be nonempty, finite sets having cardinalities $p_0, p_1, p_2, \ldots, p_n$, respectively. Define $A_0 \times A_1 \times A_2 \times \cdots \times A_n$ inductively, and prove that its cardinality is the product of the cardinalities p_i.

20. If $n \in \mathbb{N}$, let $\tau(n)$ be the number of positive divisors of n. For example, $\tau(2) = 2$ since 1 and 2 divide 2, and $\tau(6) = 4$ since 1, 2, 3, and 6 divide 6. Compute (*a*) $\tau(12)$, (*b*) $\tau(15)$, (*c*) $\tau(19)$, (*d*) $\tau(30)$.

21. (*Continuation of Problem 20.*) (*a*) Show that if p is prime, then $\tau(p) = 2$. (*b*) Show that if p is prime and $a \in \mathbb{N}$, then $\tau(p^a) = a + 1$.

22. (*Continuation of Problem 20.*) Let $n = p^a q^b$, where p and q are different primes and a and b are positive integers. (*a*) Show that if d divides n, then $d = p^{a'} q^{b'}$, where $0 \leq a' \leq a$ and $0 \leq b' \leq b$. (*b*) Let $A = \{0, 1, \ldots, a\}$ and $B = \{0, 1, \ldots, b\}$. What is $|A \times B|$? (*c*) Using (*a*) and (*b*), show that $\tau(n) = (a + 1) \cdot (b + 1)$.

23. (*Conclusion of Problem 20.*) If $n = p_1^{e_1} p_2^{e_2} \cdots p_r^{e_r}$, where the p_i's are distinct primes and all the e_i's are positive, then using the result in Problem 19, show that $\tau(n) = (e_1 + 1) \cdot (e_2 + 1) \cdots (e_r + 1)$.

24. (*a*) How many nonnegative integers less than 10 do not have 1 as a digit? (*b*) How many nonnegative integers less than 100 do not have 1 as a digit? (*c*) How many nonnegative integers less than 1000 do not have 1 as a digit?

25. (*a*) How many nonnegative integers less than 1000 do not have 3 as a digit? (*b*) How many nonnegative integers less than 1000 do not have either 3 or 5 as a digit?

26. Show that the following sets have the same cardinality: $A = \{x : x \text{ is a prime factor of 84}\}$, $B = \{x : x \text{ is a vowel in the word "mathematics"}\}$.

27. How many elements are there in each of the following sets? (*a*) $\emptyset$, (*b*) $\{\emptyset\}$, (*c*) $\{\emptyset, \{\emptyset\}\}$, (*d*) $\{\emptyset, \{\emptyset\}, \{\emptyset, \{\emptyset\}\}\}$.

28. Show that the set of even positive integers and the set of odd positive integers have the same cardinality.

29. A class has 21 students, each of whom will earn one of the grades A, B, C, D, or F. (*a*) How many functions are there from the set of students to the set of grades? (*b*) Is it possible for any such function to be one-to-one? Why?

30. Let **A** denote the set of letters in the alphabet and let **D** denote the set of digits. Thus $|\mathbf{A}| = 26$ and $|\mathbf{D}| = 10$. (*a*) How many functions are there of each type? (i) $f: \mathbf{A} \to \mathbf{D}$, (ii) $f: \mathbf{D} \to \mathbf{A}$. (*b*) How many one-to-one functions are there of each type? (i) $f: \mathbf{A} \to \mathbf{D}$, (ii) $f: \mathbf{D} \to \mathbf{A}$.

31. How many constant functions are there of each type of function in Problems 29 and 30?

32. Let $A = \{1, 2, 3, 4\}$. How many functions $f: A \to A$ are there which are not one-to-one?

33. Let $\mathbf{A} = \{1, 2, 3, 4, 5, 6, 7, 8\}$ and let $\mathbf{B}$ denote any set. Recall that if $f: \mathbf{A} \rightarrow \mathbf{B}$ is a function, then the domain is $\mathbf{A}$ and the range is contained in $\mathbf{B}$. If, in fact, the range of f is all of $\mathbf{B}$, then f is called an **onto** function. Now consider three statements: (i) $\mathbf{B}$ contains eight elements, (ii) $\mathbf{B}$ contains at most eight elements, and (iii) $\mathbf{B}$ contains at least eight elements. Which of these three statements gives the most accurate information about $\mathbf{B}$: (a) If f is one-to-one and onto? (b) If f is one-to-one? (c) If f is onto?

34. Let $\mathbf{A}$ be a finite set of cardinality $n > 0$; that is, $|\mathbf{A}| = n$. How many functions are there from $\mathbf{A}$ into, but not onto, itself?

35. Suppose that $\mathbf{A}$ is a non-empty finite set. Prove that the function $f: \mathbf{A} \rightarrow \mathbf{A}$ is onto if and only if it is one-to-one.

36. Let $\mathbf{T} = \{T_1, T_2, \ldots, T_n\}$ be a set of towns. (Here, $n \geq 2$.) We say that T_i and T_j are connected if there is a direct flight from T_i to T_j or from T_j to T_i. (Note that no town is connected to itself.) Let $f(T_i)$ be the number of towns connected to T_i. Hence f is a function mapping $\mathbf{T}$ into $\{0, 1, 2, \ldots, n-1\}$. Show that f cannot be one-to-one.

37. Let $\mathbf{E}$ be a set of 15 elephants and $\mathbf{G}$ be a set of 16 grapes. There are two types of functions associated with these sets: $f: \mathbf{E} \rightarrow \mathbf{G}$ and $g: \mathbf{G} \rightarrow \mathbf{E}$. (a) How many constant functions are there of each type? (b) How many one-to-one functions are there of each type? (c) How many functions of each type are there in all? (d) Imagine that you are making up a test and that you want parts (a), (b), and (c) to be one of your questions. Invent a story for which the answers to parts (a), (b), and (c) would be required. (Elephants and grapes do not have to be used as the elements in your sets.)

38. When the local ice cream shop opened, it offered six toppings that could be put on its sundaes, and its customers could choose as many or as few of the toppings as they pleased. Eating one sundae each Sunday, how many Sundays will it take to try each topping combination?

39. (*Continuation of Problem 38.*) On Super Bowl Sunday, the local ice cream shop offered its SuperSundae. The customer could choose any subset of the 12 different kinds of ice cream sold and any subset of the 6 toppings. How many different SuperSundaes are there given so that at least one flavor of ice cream and at least one topping must be chosen?

40. (*Conclusion of Problem 38.*) How many different SuperSundaes are there if at least two flavors of ice cream and at least two toppings must be chosen?

41. Let's return to Example 1 of paragraph 0.2 where you were giving n \$1 bills to at most k of your friends. Denote the number of ways of doing this by $g(n, k)$. (a) Show that $g(n, 1) = 1$ for $n \geq 1$. (b) Show that $g(1, k) = k$ for $k \geq 1$. (c) Show that $g(n, 2) = n + 1$ for $n \geq 1$.

42. (*Conclusion of Problem 41.*) Suppose that one of your k friends is Ivy. (a) Show that there are $g(n, k-1)$ ways to give your n \$1 bills so that Ivy gets none. (b) Show that there are $g(n-1, k)$ ways to give your n \$1 bills so that Ivy gets at least one. (c) Using FCP I, show that $g(n, k) = g(n, k-1) + g(n-1, k)$. (d) What is $g(5, 5)$?

43. If $\mathbf{A} \cap \mathbf{B} \neq \varnothing$, then show that $(\mathbf{A} \times \mathbf{B}) \cap (\mathbf{B} \times \mathbf{A}) = (\mathbf{A} \cap \mathbf{B}) \times (\mathbf{A} \cap \mathbf{B})$.

44. Let $\mathbf{A}$ be a finite set and define $\mathscr{F} = \{(\mathbf{B}, \mathbf{C}) : \mathbf{B} \subseteq \mathbf{A}, \mathbf{C} \subseteq \mathbf{A}, \mathbf{B} \cap \mathbf{C} = \varnothing\}$. List the nine elements in $\mathscr{F}$ if $\mathbf{A} = \{a, b\}$.

45. (*Conclusion of Problem 44.*) Let $\mathbf{A} = \{a_1, a_2, a_3, \ldots, a_n\}$. Show that $\mathscr{F}$ has 3^n elements by considering functions from $\mathbf{A}$ into $\{0, 1, 2\}$. *Hint:* Put an element into $\mathbf{B}$ if it is mapped onto 1 and into $\mathbf{C}$ if it is mapped onto 2.

Section 16.   Permutations and Combinations

16.1

Look back at Example 1 of paragraph 15.5 and consider what happens if we reverse the roles of domain and range:

$$g : \mathbf{B} \to \mathbf{A}, \qquad \text{where } \mathbf{B} = \{a, b, c\} \text{ and } \mathbf{A} = \{0, 1\}.$$

By Theorem 15.5, part **a**, there are 2^3 such functions, each assigning 0 or 1 to elements of **B**. We list them in Table 16.1. Each of these functions corresponds to a particular subset of **B**, identified as those elements for which the function value is 1. These corresponding subsets are also listed, and notice that we have generated the power set of **B** (refer to paragraph 1.15).

$\mathbf{B} = \{a,$	$b,$	$c\}$	Subset
0	0	0	$\varnothing$
0	0	1	$\{c\}$
0	1	0	$\{b\}$
0	1	1	$\{b, c\}$
1	0	0	$\{a\}$
1	0	1	$\{a, c\}$
1	1	0	$\{a, b\}$
1	1	1	$\{a, b, c\} = \mathbf{B}$

Table 16.1

This is more than a coincidence, of course. For *any* set **B**, a function

$$g : \mathbf{B} \to \{0, 1\}$$

is called a **characteristic function** on **B**. There is a one-to-one correspondence between the set of all characteristic functions on **B** and the set of all subsets of **B**: a given characteristic function g corresponding to that subset of **B** described by $\{x \in \mathbf{B} : g(x) = 1\}$. If $|\mathbf{B}| = m$, then the number of characteristic functions on **B** is 2^m (by part **a** of Theorem 15.5); hence the total number of subsets of **B**, including **B** and $\emptyset$, is 2^m. In Example 3 of paragraph 15.5, the pizzas were essentially characteristic functions on the set of toppings.

Using the notation introduced in paragraph 1.15, we denote the power set of **B** by $2^{\mathbf{B}}$. The rationale for this notation is suggested by the enumeration formula stated in Theorem 16.1. Again, keep in mind that an element of $2^{\mathbf{B}}$ is a subset of **B**.

THEOREM 16.1

For all nonnegative integers m, if **B** is a set such that $|\mathbf{B}| = m$, then

$$|2^{\mathbf{B}}| = 2^{|\mathbf{B}|} = 2^m.$$

Proof

Instead of resorting to the "characteristic function" model noted above, suppose we illustrate once again an inductive argument. The claim is clearly true for "very small" sets:

If $\mathbf{B} = \emptyset$,   then $2^{\mathbf{B}} = \{\emptyset\}$,   so $|2^{\mathbf{B}}| = 2^0 = 1$.

If $\mathbf{B} = \{a\}$,   then $2^{\mathbf{B}} = \{\emptyset, \{a\}\}$,   so $|2^{\mathbf{B}}| = 2^1 = 2$.

Now, assume that the claim is true for any set **B** for which $|\mathbf{B}| = k$ (we may assume that $k > 1$). Let **B**′ be a set for which $|\mathbf{B}'| = k + 1$, let $x \in \mathbf{B}'$, and let $\mathbf{B} = \mathbf{B}' - \{x\}$. For each subset **A** of **B**, let $\mathbf{A}' = \mathbf{A} \cup \{x\}$. Then

$$2^{\mathbf{B}'} = \{\mathbf{A} : \mathbf{A} \subseteq \mathbf{B}\} \cup \{\mathbf{A}' : \mathbf{A} \subseteq \mathbf{B}\}.$$

By FCP I,

$$|2^{\mathbf{B}'}| = |2^{\mathbf{B}}| + |2^{\mathbf{B}}| = 2 \cdot 2^k = 2^{k+1} = 2^{|\mathbf{B}'|}. \quad \blacksquare$$

From this theorem it follows that there are $2^5 = 32$ subsets of **V** (the vowels), and there are $2^{26} = 67,108,864$ subsets of the English alphabet (see Example 1 of paragraph 13.1).

16.2

For future reference we will need more detailed information about subsets than simply the enumeration of the power set. For example, how many subsets of **B** are there of size k for $0 \leq k \leq m$? **Combinatorial mathematics** is that branch of discrete mathematics which deals with questions, like this one, related to the enumeration of sets or collections of sets subject to given conditions. There is a simple strategy for enumeration which is successful in a suprising number and variety of situations. For example, in paragraph 10.4 we applied it to the problem of enumerating triangular numbers. In essence, the strategy says:

> To count objects of a certain class, describe the class in two different ways, leading to two different enumeration formulas. Then equate the formulas. **(1)**

The answer to our question about the enumeration of k-element subsets involves a classic application of this technique. But to understand the argument, we must first build a little machinery.

In paragraph 13.3 we introduced the idea of an n-tuple, which can be thought of as a function with domain $\{1, 2, \ldots, n\}$ into some range. Thus, the ordered pairs in the function might be listed as

$$\{(1, b_1), (2, b_2), \ldots, (n, b_n)\}.$$

In this very general notation, it is customary to recognize that the subscripts indicate position in the list, which is an indication also of domain element. Hence, the function may be abbreviated in the familiar form

$$(b_1, b_2, \ldots, b_n), \tag{2}$$

in which the entry b_i is called the **ith coordinate.**

If the coordinates in (2) are all different from one another, then any rearrangement of the coordinates may be considered a different n-tuple and, therefore, a different function on the domain $\{1, 2, \ldots, n\}$.

Example 1   Consider the 5-tuple (sometimes referred to as a *quintuple*)

$$\{(1, a), (2, e), (3, i), (4, o), (5, u)\}.$$

In abbreviated form we may write this as (a, e, i, o, u), and among its many possible rearrangements are (a, e, i, u, o), (e, a, o, i, u), and (u, o, i, e, a). These, in fact, are one-to-one functions of the sort discussed in paragraph 15.4, and we discovered there that the number of such functions is $(5)_5 = 5! = 120$. Attempting to write them all out is the best incentive toward recognizing the need for a systematic approach. One possibility is to rearrange from the right, always leaving as many of the leftmost coordinates fixed as possible. Such a listing would begin

(a, e, i, o, u), (a, e, i, u, o), (a, e, o, i, u), (a, e, o, u, i), (a, e, u, i, o), (a, e, u, o, i), ...

16.3   The rearrangements illustrated in Example 1 of paragraph 16.2 are called *permutations*. They may be considered special cases of a more general idea. The letters chosen happen to be the vowels, but it might be of interest to consider arrangements consisting of any letters of the alphabet. Involved here is a two-step process: First select any n elements from a given set (for example, {a, h, t, w} from the alphabet), then arrange these n elements into an n-tuple [for example, (w, h, a, t), or (t, h, a, w), or (w, t, h, a)]. In this way we obtain permutations of *some* of the elements in a given set. This idea is an especially simple one, but to be precise we should state it more formally: Given the set **B**, a **permutation** is a one-to-one function

$$g : \{1, 2, \ldots, n\} \to \mathbf{B}.$$

Again, the usual designation for such a permutation is

$$(b_1, b_2, \ldots, b_n),$$

where the coordinates are elements selected from the set **B**.

In the definition above we have tacitly assumed that there are "enough" elements in **B**. Assuming that $|\mathbf{B}| = m$, recall from part **c** of Theorem 15.5 that no one-to-one function (hence no permutation) exists if $|\mathbf{B}| < n$. Furthermore, if $|\mathbf{B}| \geq n$, then the number of permutations is

$$
\begin{aligned}
(m)_n &= \frac{m!}{(m - n)!}, && \text{if } m > n, \\
&= m!, && \text{if } m = n.
\end{aligned}
\tag{1}
$$

Incidentally, this is the second time we have had to separate this kind of enumeration into two cases. We could combine both cases into one if it were true that $m!/(m - n)! = m!$, when $m = n$. But for this to be so, we must have $(m - m)! = 1$. Looking back at paragraph 13.4, recall that the factorial function was defined only for positive integer values of n. This means that we may define $0!$ in any convenient way. To simplify this and many future combinatorial calculations, we agree to extend the domain of the factorial function to include 0 by defining $0! = 1$. Note that the inductive definition of the factorial function can now be given by

$$
\begin{aligned}
0! &= 1, \\
n! &= n \cdot (n - 1)! && \text{for all } n \in \mathbb{N}.
\end{aligned}
\tag{2}
$$

Further, the two formulas in (1) above can be combined into the single formula

$$(m)_n = \frac{m!}{(m - n)!} \qquad \text{for all } n \leq m. \tag{3}$$

Example 1

Among the permutations of five letters of the English alphabet are (a, b, c, d, e), ..., (p, o, n, m, l), ..., (v, w, x, y, z). It is clear that there are *many* of them, but how many? The number of permutations of five letters of the alphabet is simply the number of one-to-one functions

$$g : \{1, 2, 3, 4, 5\} \to \mathbf{B}, \qquad \text{where } |\mathbf{B}| = 26.$$

By (3), the number of such functions (i.e., permutations) is

$$(26)_5 = \frac{26!}{(26-5)!} = \frac{26!}{21!} = 26 \cdot 25 \cdot 24 \cdot 23 \cdot 22 = 7{,}893{,}600.$$

A convenient way to remember this enumeration is to think of constructing the permutations by filling the coordinate blanks in

$$(\underline{\hspace{1cm}}, \underline{\hspace{1cm}}, \underline{\hspace{1cm}}, \underline{\hspace{1cm}}, \underline{\hspace{1cm}}).$$

There are 26 ways of selecting the first coordinate, after which there are 25 ways of selecting the second coordinate, and so on. The total number is, therefore,

$$26 \cdot 25 \cdot 24 \cdot 23 \cdot 22 = 7{,}893{,}600.$$

Tutorial 16.3

a. List all six of the permutations of the elements in the set $\{x, y, z\}$.

b. How many permutations are there of three elements from the set $\{5, 6, 7, 8, 9\}$?

c. Thinking of each permutation in part **b** as a three-digit integer, how many of them are odd numbers?

16.4

The enumeration of permutations, described above, is the "machinery" prerequisite to the solution of our earlier problem: If $|\mathbf{B}| = m$ and if k is any integer for which $0 \le k \le m$, how many subsets of $\mathbf{B}$ are there of size k? The answer will come from an application of the enumeration technique described in (1) in paragraph 16.2, not to subsets but to permutations.

Let $\mathbf{B}$ denote a set with m elements and let $\mathbf{K}$ denote the set of all permutations of k elements of $\mathbf{B}$, where $0 \le k \le m$. From (3) in paragraph 16.3,

$$|\mathbf{K}| = (m)_k = \frac{m!}{(m-k)!}.$$

Now, we must describe and enumerate $\mathbf{K}$ in a different way. For convenience, let us refer to a subset of $\mathbf{B}$ containing k elements as a **k-element subset** of $\mathbf{B}$ (or **k-set** of $\mathbf{B}$). Corresponding to any k-set of $\mathbf{B}$, call it $\mathbf{H}_k$, there are $(k)_k = k!$ permutations of $\mathbf{H}_k$. We don't yet know how many k-sets of $\mathbf{B}$ there are, but the usual notation for the *number* of such subsets is $\binom{m}{k}$. (A convenient way to read this notation is "m choose k.") For each of these $\binom{m}{k}$ subsets there are $k!$ permutations. But these account for *all* the permutations belonging to **K**. Hence by FCP III,

$$|\mathbf{K}| = \binom{m}{k} \cdot k!. \tag{1}$$

From the two enumerations of the set **K**,

$$\binom{m}{k} \cdot k! = \frac{m!}{(m-k)!};$$

hence

$$\binom{m}{k} = \frac{m!}{(m-k)! \cdot k!}. \tag{2}$$

This is the answer to our question about the number of k-sets of **B**. [Without this interpretation of (2), it would be difficult to prove that $\dfrac{m!}{(m-k)!k!}$ is an integer. But knowing that $\binom{m}{k}$ counts a finite number of objects, it necessarily must be a nonnegative integer.] It is traditional to:

- Refer to $(m)_k$ as the number of **permutations of m things taken k at a time.**

- Refer to $\binom{m}{k}$ as the number of **combinations of m things taken k at a time.**

Tutorial 16.4

a. Let $\mathbf{A} = \{a_1, a_2, \ldots, a_n\}$. By actually listing all 3-element subsets of **A**, complete the table:

n	2	3	4	5
No. of 3-sets of **A**				

b. Check your answers in part **a** by use of (2).
c. Show, by canceling common factors, that $\binom{15}{5}$ is an integer.

16.5   The interpretation of $\binom{m}{k}$ as the number of k-sets of an m-set leads directly to a recursion formula of wide usefulness. We again use the technique of enumerating a set in two different ways.

Let $\mathbf{A} = \{a_1, a_2, \ldots, a_m, a_{m+1}\}$ be a set of size $m + 1$. The number of k-sets of **A** is $\binom{m+1}{k}$. Now we enumerate these subsets in another way. Pick any element in **A**, say a_{m+1}, and write **A** as the union of an m-element set and a singleton set

$$\mathbf{A} = \mathbf{A'} \cup \{a_{m+1}\}, \qquad \text{where} \quad \mathbf{A'} = \{a_1, a_2, \ldots, a_m\}.$$

Now any k-set of **A** belongs to one of two types:

- It contains the element a_{m+1}.
- It does not contain a_{m+1}.

There are $\binom{m}{k-1}$ subsets of the first type, since those elements different from a_{m+1} must form a $(k-1)$-set of **A'**; and there are $\binom{m}{k}$ subsets of the second type, since all k of the elements must be selected from **A'**. By FCP I we have

$$\binom{m+1}{k} = \binom{m}{k-1} + \binom{m}{k}. \tag{1}$$

The correctness of (1) has now been established, but by (2) in paragraph 16.4 it can be reexpressed as an algebraic formula

$$\frac{(m+1)!}{(m+1-k)!\,k!} = \frac{m!}{(m-k+1)!\,(k-1)!} + \frac{m!}{(m-k)!\,k!}, \tag{2}$$

the correctness of which is, perhaps, not so obvious. It turns out that (2) is easy to verify for small values of m and k: Try it for $m = 6$ and $k = 3$. You should find

$$\binom{7}{3} = 35 = 15 + 20 = \binom{6}{2} + \binom{6}{3}.$$

The algebraic verification of (2) is a good exercise to test your understanding of factorials (see Problem 11). Compute the sum

$$\frac{m!}{(m-k+1)!\,(k-1)!} + \frac{m!}{(m-k)!\,k!},$$

being careful with the common denominator, and show that it is equal to

$$\frac{(m+1)!}{(m+1-k)!\,k!}.$$

Example 1   For practice and for future reference, here are some special cases:

$$\binom{m}{0} = \binom{m}{m} = 1, \qquad \binom{m}{1} = \binom{m}{m-1} = m, \qquad \binom{m}{2} = \binom{m}{m-2} = \frac{m(m-1)}{2}.$$

In general,

$$\binom{m}{k} = \binom{m}{m-k} = \frac{m!}{(m-k)!k!}.$$

An alternate way to recognize the equality of $\binom{m}{k}$ and $\binom{m}{m-k}$ is to note that each particular k-element subset identifies also a particular $(m-k)$-element subset (namely, its complement). See Problem 12 in this section.   ●

Tutorial 16.5

Verify (1) for the case $m = 11$ and $k = 4$ in two ways:

a. Compute $\binom{12}{4}, \binom{11}{3}, \binom{11}{4}$ separately.

b. Find a common denominator, and add $\dfrac{11!}{8!3!} + \dfrac{11!}{7!4!}$.

16.6   Enumeration by permutations and by combinations is an indispensable concept in discrete mathematics, but it may be difficult to determine, in a given application, just which one of the formulas to use. The right choice depends upon whether "order" is important in distinguishing the objects being counted. For example, suppose that 3 people are to be elected from a field of 10 candidates. If we are concerned only with the identity of those elected, then the result can be reported simply as a 3-element subset of the set of candidates. Hence there are $\binom{10}{3} = 120$ different possible outcomes of the election. But if the 3 individuals elected are to serve terms of 1, 2, and 3 years (to be determined by lot, perhaps), then those elected can be ranked (or ordered) depending upon the length of term. Thus a given set of 3 people proliferates into 6 different rankings ($6 = 3!$), and the total number of outcomes is $120 \cdot 6 = 720$. Explicitly, when order is indifferent, the number of outcomes is the number of *combinations* of 10 things taken three at a time (that is, 120); but when order is essential, the number of outcomes is the number of *permutations* of 10 things taken three at a time (that is, 720).

Example 1   Consider a class with 20 discrete mathematics students. As an experiment, each week the instructor randomly chooses 5 students and assigns the first student chosen 10 homework problems; the second, 8 problems; the third, 6 problems: the fourth, 4 problems; and the fifth, only 2 problems. Here order is important, and so we think permutations. There are $(20)_5$ ways of choosing these students.

This is not a very democratic procedure, and so during the later weeks of the term the instructor randomly chooses 5 students, assigning each of them 10 problems. Here the order of the students chosen doesn't matter, and so we think combinations. Hence there are $\binom{20}{5}$ ways of choosing these students. Now $(20)_5 = 1{,}860{,}480$

and $\binom{20}{5} = 15{,}504$, and we see again that there are many more ways when order is important.

Example 2

Five different lines are drawn in a plane in such a way that no two are parallel and no three are concurrent. How many points of intersection are there?

The given conditions are intended to ensure that each pair of lines intersects in a point distinct from all the others. Thus, the points of intersection are in one-to-one correspondence with the pairs of lines. The number of such pairs is $\binom{5}{2} = 10$, and this is the number of points of intersection. Note that for a given pair of lines, "order" is immaterial since the pair determines a single point. We are dealing, therefore, with combinations.

Example 3

Five different teams have qualified to participate in a playoff tournament to determine the conference champion and runner-up. How many possible playoff outcomes are there?

The competition is designed to eliminate three of the teams, and the remaining two teams play for the championship. Of course, there are $\binom{5}{2}$ ways to determine the finalists, but now order is important since the champion might be either one of the two finalists. We are dealing, therefore, with permutations, and the answer is

$$(5)_2 = \frac{5!}{(5-2)!} = 5 \cdot 4 = 20.$$

16.7

As another illustration of the counting strategy described in (1) in paragraph 16.2, we now prove an important identity.

THEOREM 16.7

For any positive integer n,

$$\binom{n}{0} + \binom{n}{1} + \binom{n}{2} + \cdots + \binom{n}{n} = 2^n.$$

Proof

In paragraph 16.1 we noted that the characteristic functions on a set $\mathbf{B}$ are in one-to-one correspondence with the subsets of $\mathbf{B}$. If $|\mathbf{B}| = n$, then the number of subsets of $\mathbf{B}$ is 2^n. But any subset of $\mathbf{B}$ must have k elements for some $0 \leq k \leq n$. Thus we may enumerate the set of all subsets of $\mathbf{B}$ in a second way by counting the number of subsets of each possible size and adding. Since $\binom{n}{k}$ is the number of k-sets of $\mathbf{B}$, we obtain the required equation. ∎

Applying Theorem 16.7 in the special case $n = 4$, we calculate

$$\binom{4}{0} + \binom{4}{1} + \binom{4}{2} + \binom{4}{3} + \binom{4}{4} = \frac{4!}{0!4!} + \frac{4!}{1!3!} + \frac{4!}{2!2!} + \frac{4!}{3!1!} + \frac{4!}{4!0!}$$

$$= 1 + 4 + 6 + 4 + 1 = 16 = 2^4.$$

16.8

Complement: Poker The card game poker can be traced back to the seventeenth century German card game pochen. (Appropriately, "pochen" is a German verb meaning "to bluff.") From Germany, the game traveled to France and assumed the name pogue. French colonists carried the game to the Louisiana Territories, and there the name was corrupted to poker. The Mississippi was (and is) the gateway to the Midwest, and it carried much, including poker, to the central United States.

Poker is played with the standard *deck* (pack) of 52 cards, divided into four *suits* of 13 *ranks*. The English names of the suits are derived from either the French name of the suit or the design of the suit. The traditional suit descriptions are listed in Table 16.8A.

For our purposes the ranks are (from high card to low card) ace, king, queen, jack (knave), 10, 9, 8, 7, 6, 5, 4, 3 (trey), 2 (deuce). (In some poker games the ace can also be used as a 1. In our game, the ace is always higher than a king and there are no wild cards.) A typical poker hand consists of five cards. First, there are $\binom{52}{5} =$ 2,598,960 poker hands in the standard deck. These hands are ranked as shown in Table 16.8B, with the understanding that each hand contains no hand ranked above it. For example, a royal flush is not considered a straight flush, and no straight flush is considered a plain flush.

English		French	German	Spanish	Italian
Spade	♠	Pique	Grün	Espada	Spada
Heart	♡	Coeur	Herz	Copa	Coppa
Diamond	◇	Carreau	Schelle	Oro	Denaro
Club	♣	Trefle	Eichel	Basto	Bastone

Table 16.8A Poker suits

Royal flush	A, K, Q, J, 10 of one suit. Example: A♣, K♣, Q♣, J♣, 10♣
Straight flush	Five consecutive ranks of one suit. Example: 9♡, 8♡, 7♡, 6♡, 5♡
Four of a kind	All cards of one rank and a fifth card. Example: 6♡, 6◇, 6♠, 6♣, K◇
Full house	Three of one rank and a pair of another rank. Example: K♡, K◇, K♠, 2♣, 2◇
Flush	Five cards of one suit. Example: K, 10, 9, 4, 2 of ♡
Straight	Five ranks in succession regardless of suit. Example: J♡, 10◇, 9◇, 8♠, 7♣
Three of a kind	Three cards of one rank and two other cards of two other ranks. Example: 8♡, 8◇, 8♠, K◇, 5♡
Two pairs	Example: 8♡, 8◇, 6♣, 6♡, K♠
One pair	Example: 7◇, 7♡, K◇, 8◇, 2♣
Nothing	Example: A♡, 8◇, 6♣, 5◇, 2♡

Table 16.8B Poker ranking

There are just four royal flushes in a deck of cards. To count the straight flushes in a suit, we note that the low card in a straight can range from a deuce to a 10, nine possibilities. But we have already counted the royal flush, and since we must choose one of the four suits, the number of straight flushes is

$$(9 - 1) \cdot \binom{4}{1} = 32.$$

For the number of four of a kind's, we first choose the rank and then choose any of the remaining 48 cards,

$$\binom{13}{1} \cdot 48 = 624.$$

For a full house, choose the two ranks (order is important since {J$\heartsuit$, J$\diamondsuit$, J$\spadesuit$, 9$\heartsuit$, 9$\diamondsuit$} is different from {9$\heartsuit$, 9$\diamondsuit$, 9$\clubsuit$, J$\heartsuit$, J$\diamondsuit$}), and then choose the three suits for the three of a kind and the two suits for the pair. The number is

$$(13)_2 \cdot \binom{4}{3} \cdot \binom{4}{2} = 3744.$$

For the flushes, first choose a suit, and then choose any of the five cards from the 13 in the suit. This gives

$$\binom{4}{1} \cdot \binom{13}{5}$$

which, however, also includes the royal and straight flushes. Since there are nine royal and straight flushes, the correct number is

$$\binom{4}{1} \cdot \left[\binom{13}{5} - 9 \right] = 5112.$$

To count the straights we first count the straights consisting of the ranks 6, 7, 8, 9, 10. There are four ways to choose the 6, four ways to choose the 7, and so forth, and hence by FCP II, there are 4^5 of these straights. Once again we have counted straight flushes and must subtract 4, one for each suit. Hence, the total number of plain straights consisting of the ranks 6, 7, 8, 9, 10, is $4^5 - 4$. Therefore, the total number of straights is $4^5 - 4$ times the number of lowest ranks possible for a straight. These lowest ranks are 2, 3, ..., 10, and so the number of straights is

$$(4^5 - 4) \cdot 9 = 9180.$$

For three of a kind's, first choose the rank for the three of a kind, then the three suits, then choose the ranks for the other two cards, and finally choose the suits for these two cards. The result is

$$\binom{13}{1} \cdot \binom{4}{3} \cdot \binom{12}{2} \cdot \binom{4}{1} \cdot \binom{4}{1} = 54{,}912.$$

The procedure for counting the hands with two pairs is similar. First choose the ranks for the pairs, choose the suits for each pair, and then choose one of the remaining 44 cards. This yields

$$\binom{13}{2} \cdot \binom{4}{2} \cdot \binom{4}{2} \cdot \binom{44}{1} = 123{,}552.$$

To count the number of hands with one pair, first choose the rank for the pair, choose the suits for the pair, choose the ranks for the remaining three cards, and finally choose a suit for each of these ranks. Hence, the number of hands containing one pair is

$$\binom{13}{1} \cdot \binom{4}{2} \cdot \binom{12}{3} \cdot \binom{4}{1} \cdot \binom{4}{1} \cdot \binom{4}{1} = 1{,}098{,}240.$$

Customarily, the number of hands with nothing in them would be computed by adding all the above together and subtracting from $\binom{52}{5}$. But let's calculate this directly. First we need five distinct ranks, $\binom{13}{5}$ ways, but not wanting a straight we must subtract nine, $\binom{13}{5} - 9$. For each rank chosen, there are four possible suits. By FCP II we have 4^5 possibilities, but four of these are flushes, giving us $4^5 - 4$. The total number of "nothing" hands is, therefore,

$$\left[\binom{13}{5} - 9\right] \cdot [4^5 - 4] = 1{,}303{,}560.$$

Adding the number of all these hands together gives $\binom{52}{5}$, as expected.

Problems for Section 16

1. Let $V = \{a, e, i, o, u\}$. List the ordered pairs in the characteristic function corresponding to each of the subsets. (a) $\{e\}$; (b) $\{i, o, u\}$; (c) $\varnothing$; (d) V.

2. Let $S = \{1, 2, 3, \ldots, n\}$, let A be any subset of S, and let $f\colon S \to \{0, 1\}$ be the characteristic function corresponding to A. Show

that

$$|A| = \sum_{i=1}^{n} f(i).$$

3. List (in a convenient tabulation) all possible functions $f\colon \{a, b, c, d\} \to \{0, 1\}$ and by each indicate its corresponding subset.

4. How many subsets of the alphabet are there? How many of these subsets contain exactly 25 letters?

5. Prove that for each $n \in \mathbb{N}$, if $|\mathbf{A}| = n$, then $|2^{\mathbf{A}}| = 2^n$ by exhibiting a one-to-one correspondence between $2^{\mathbf{A}}$ and the set of characteristic functions on $\mathbf{A}$.

6. Find the number of permutations of 26 things taken 3 at a time.

7. (*Continuation of Problem 6.*) Computer keyboards have inherited from typewriters the arrangement of alphabetic characters into three rows: 10 in the upper row, 9 in the middle row, and 7 in the lower row. Find the number of permutations of the letters in each row taken three at a time.

8. (*Continuation of Problem 6.*) Let a permutation on three letters be obtained by striking one key in each row. This can be done in 630 ways. Why? Now for each such selection, the three letters may be permuted among themselves. What is the total number of permutations on three letters obtained in this way?

9. (*Continuation of Problem 6.*) Consider now permutations on three letters in which two rows only are represented. In this case, two letters are selected from one row, and the remaining letter may come from either of the other rows. What is the number of such permutations in which two letters are selected (*a*) from the upper row, (*b*) from the middle row, (*c*) from the lower row?

10. (*Conclusion of Problem 6.*) Explain the fact that the answers to all parts of Problems 7, 8, and 9 add up to the answer to Problem 6.

11. Carry out in detail the arithmetic proof of (2) in paragraph 16.5.

12. Show that $\dbinom{m}{k} = \dbinom{m}{m-k}$ both arithmetically and by counting the same set in two different ways.

13. On a sheet of paper mark five points, no three on the same line. Let a straight line be determined by any two of these points. (*a*) How many such lines can be drawn? (*b*) How many such lines can be drawn if you begin with 12 points instead of 5?

14. Compute (*a*) $(101)_3$, (*b*) $\dbinom{101}{3}$, (*c*) $\dbinom{101}{4}$.

15. (*a*) Show that

$$\binom{101}{4} = \frac{98}{4} \cdot \binom{101}{3}.$$

(*b*) Show, in general, that

$$\binom{n}{k+1} = \frac{n-k}{k+1} \cdot \binom{n}{k}.$$

16. In how many ways can two students be chosen from a class of 18?

17. In how many ways can two students be chosen from a class of 18 if one of them receives an A and the other receives a B?

18. Twelve runners compete in a 100-yard dash. Assuming no ties, in how many ways can the first-, second-, and third-place winners be determined?

19. Twelve books that you haven't yet read are on a shelf in your library. In how many ways can you select three of them to take along on your vacation?

20. Assume that the U.S. Senate has 53 Republicans and 47 Democrats. A committee of seven senators is to consist of four Republicans and three Democrats. How many such committees are possible?

21. (*a*) In how many ways can six people arrange themselves in a row containing six seats? (*b*) In how many ways can six people arrange themselves in chairs around a circular table? (Distinguish these arrangements only by relative order.)

22. According to legend, a table on display in Winchester, England, is supposed to be the original *Round Table* of King Arthur. It has spaces marked off for 25 seats. In how many ways might the Knights have seated themselves around this table? (Again, distinguish these arrangements only by relative order.)

23. (*a*) In how many ways can a committee of five be chosen from 10 eligible individuals? (*b*) How is this number changed if two of the individuals desire to serve together on the committee or not at all?

24. The decimal representation of a positive integer is to contain six of the nine nonzero digits, none repeated. How many such numbers are there?

25. A positive integer has a six-place binary representation in which exactly three places are occupied by a 1. (*a*) In how many such numbers do the bits alternate? (*b*) In how many such numbers are the 0s grouped together?

26. (*a*) Express $10! - (10)_8$ as simply as possible using only one factorial. (*b*) Express $n! - (n)_{n-2}$ as simply as possible using only one factorial.

27. Show that $\binom{n}{0} + \binom{n+1}{1} + \binom{n+2}{2} - \binom{n+3}{2} = 0$.

28. Let $P_n = \sum_{i=0}^{n}(n)_i$. (*a*) Compute P_n for $n = 0, 1, 2, 3, 4$. (*b*) Show that $P_n = n \cdot P_{n-1} + 1$.

29. The letters in the word "boo" can be arranged in three different ways: boo, obo, oob. List the 12 different looking arrangements of the letters in "book."

30. (*Continuation of Problem 29.*) There are $4! = 24$ different arrangements of the letters in "tore." (*a*) List all the different arrangements of the letters in "tort." (*b*) List all the different arrangements of the letters in "toot."

31. (*Continuation of Problem 29.*) Note that tore and eort become the same if "e" is replaced by "t." Show that the number of arrangements of the letters of "tort" is simply $\dfrac{4!}{2!}$. Similarly show that the number of different looking arrangements of "toot" is $\dfrac{4!}{2!2!}$.

32. (*Continuation of Problem 29.*) Show that the number of different arrangements of (*a*) "feeder" is $\dfrac{6!}{3!}$, (*b*) "effete" is $\dfrac{6!}{3!2!}$.

33. (*Conclusion of Problem 29.*) "Humuhumunukunukuapuaa" is a Hawaiian word for fish. How many different looking arrangements are there of the letters in this word? (Treat the capital H just like the lowercase h.)

34. A student wants to take four courses. She has 11 courses to choose from: 6 sophomore level and 5 freshman level. Each course is available at 8, 9, 10, and 11 A.M. (*a*) If the student wants to take 2 freshman and 2 sophomore courses, how many choices does she have? (*b*) If she wants to alternate these courses, freshman, sophomore, freshman, sophomore, how many choices does she have?

35. Suppose that 10 points are marked in the plane, and that no three of them lie on the same line. How many triangles can be drawn if the vertices must belong to this set of 10 points?

36. (*Continuation of Problem 35.*) Given 10 points, no 3 of them on a line, with 6 of them red and 4 of them blue. (*a*) How many triangles are there with all red vertices? (*b*) How many triangles are there with all blue vertices? (*c*) How many triangles are there with exactly one red vertex?

37. (*Conclusion of Problem 35.*) Given 12 points, no 3 of them on a line with 6 red, 4 blue, and 2 green points. (*a*) How many triangles have vertices all the same color? (b) How many triangles have vertices with each vertex a different color? (c) How many triangles have at least one green vertex?

38. A lacrosse team has 10 players: 1 goalie, 3 defense, 3 middies, and 3 attack. Consider a squad with just 16 players: 5 defense, 1 goalie, 6 middies, and 4 attack. How many starting lineups are there?

39. (*Conclusion of Problem 38.*) On many teams, the defense and attack are further specialized into left, right, and crease. If this is the case, then how many starting lineups are there? (*Hint:* This problem involves both permutations and combinations.)

Poker Hand Problems. In the complement to this section (paragraph 16.8) we discussed poker hands. For these problems, you only need to know that a deck of cards consists of 52 cards of 4 suits, 2 of which are red and the other 2 are black. There are 13 ranks, 4 cards in each rank with 1 from each suit. The ranks are ordered (low card to high), 2, 3, 4, 5, …, 10, jack, queen, king, ace. A poker hand consists of 5 cards of the 52 in the deck.

40. (a) How many poker hands consist of one card of one color and four cards of the other color? (b) How many poker hands consist of two cards of one color and three cards of the other color? (c) How many poker hands consist of all cards with the same color?

41. (a) How many poker hands consist of one card of one suit and four cards of another suit? (b) How many poker hands consist of two cards of one suit and three cards of another suit? (c) How many poker hands consist of all cards of the same suit?

42. (a) How many poker hands have exactly one queen? (b) How many poker hands have exactly two queens? (c) How many poker hands have exactly three queens? (d) How many poker hands have exactly four queens?

43. (a) How many poker hands have no queens? (b) How many poker hands have at least two queens?

44. A four flush is a poker hand consisting of four cards of one suit and a fifth card of another suit, but containing no pairs. How many four flushes are there in a deck of cards?

Section 17. Binomial Theorem

Overview for Section 17

- Introduction to the Binomial Theorem
- Determination of binomial coefficients
  - Display of Pascal's triangle
- Applications of the Binomial Theorem

Key Concepts: binomial expansion, binomial coefficient, Binomial Theorem, Pascal's triangle

17.1

In paragraph 8.1 we found it helpful to write 10^2 in the form $(9 + 1)^2$. A sum of two terms is often called a **binomial,** and we will discover many other applications in later sections for powers of binomials.

Assume that x and y represent unknown but fixed numbers. Our problem is to compute the power $(y + x)^m$ for any $m \in \mathbb{N}$. By actual calculation, we can verify the following **binomial expansions:**

$$m = 0 : \qquad (y + x)^0 = 1,$$
$$m = 1 : \qquad (y + x)^1 = y + x,$$
$$m = 2 : \qquad (y + x)^2 = y^2 + 2yx + x^2,$$
$$m = 3 : \qquad (y + x)^3 = y^3 + 3y^2x + 3yx^2 + x^3.$$

Based on these special cases, we predict the following behavior.

- There are $m + 1$ terms in the expansion, one for each power of x from x^0 to x^m.

- In each term the sum of the exponents of y and x is m (the factors $x^0 = y^0 = 1$ are omitted in the extreme terms).

- Each term is of the form $C(m, k) \cdot y^{m-k}x^k$, in which the coefficient $C(m, k)$ depends on both m and k.

It appears, thus, that

$$(y + x)^m = C(m, 0) \cdot y^m + C(m, 1) \cdot y^{m-1}x + C(m, 2) \cdot y^{m-2}x^2 + \cdots + C(m, m) \cdot x^m,$$

or in sigma notation,

$$(y + x)^m = \sum_{k=0}^{m} C(m, k) \cdot y^{m-k}x^k. \tag{1}$$

Before proceeding further, we must evaluate the coefficients $C(m, k)$. Once again, we need evidence about the general pattern, and by examining the special case

$$(y + x)^3 = C(3, 0) \cdot y^3 + C(3, 1) \cdot y^2x + C(3, 2) \cdot yx^2 + C(3, 3) \cdot x^3,$$

we will discover an important clue about the nature of these coefficients. Write

$$(y + x)^3 = (y + x) \cdot (y + x) \cdot (y + x),$$

and recall that a term in this expansion is obtained by selecting one letter from each of these three factors, then forming their product. Because there are two choices in each factor, there should be $2^3 = 8$ terms altogether. The familiar multiplication algorithm computes these terms automatically:

- $(y + x) \cdot (y + x) = y^2 + yx + xy + x^2$

- $(y + x) \cdot (y + x)^2 = (y + x) \cdot (y^2 + yx + xy + x^2)$
  $$= y^3 + y^2x + yxy + yx^2 + xy^2 + xyx + x^2y + x^3.$$

Finally,

$$(y + x)^3 = y^3 + 3y^2x + 3yx^2 + x^3,$$

because the rules of arithmetic allow us to combine terms with like powers of x and y. Observe that the sum of the coefficients, $1 + 3 + 3 + 1 = 8$, actually counts the original number of terms. Thus, for example, $C(3, 2) = 3$ is the number of terms in the original expansion which have x^2 as a factor. It will be helpful to tabulate this entire computation, as in Table 17.1. If we replace y by 0 and x by 1, the similarity between this table and Table 16.1 is striking: The three terms involving x^2, for example, correspond to the three 2-element subsets. Thus, $C(3, 2)$ turns out to be the number of 2-element subsets of a 3-element set. Because this special case doesn't appear to be exceptional, we are led to predict, in general, that

$$C(m, k) = \binom{m}{k}.$$

Selections			
$(y + x)$	$(y + x)$	$(y + x)$	*Term*
y	y	y	y^3
y	y	x	y^2x
y	x	y	y^2x
y	x	x	yx^2
x	y	y	y^2x
x	y	x	yx^2
x	x	y	yx^2
x	x	x	x^3

Table 17.1

> ## Tutorial 17.1
>
> **a.** Expand $(y + x)^4$ as follows:
>   **i.** Find the product $y(y^3 + 3y^2x + 3yx^2 + x^3)$.
>   **ii.** Find the product $x(y^3 + 3y^2x + 3yx^2 + x^3)$.
>   **iii.** Then add (remembering to combine like powers).
> **b.** Find the coefficient of y^3x in part **i**, in part **ii**, and in part **iii**. [Compare with (1) in paragraph 16.5.]

17.2

The pieces, finally, are all in place, and we can prove the most important result of elementary discrete mathematics, the **Binomial Theorem.**

THEOREM 17.2

If m is a nonnegative integer, then

$$(y + x)^m = \sum_{k=0}^{m} \binom{m}{k} y^{m-k} x^k. \tag{1}$$

Proof

We will use the Principle of Mathematical Induction. Let $\mathcal{P}(m)$ denote the predicate [indicated by (1)]. Let $\mathbf{M} = \{m \in \mathbb{N} : \mathcal{P}(m) \text{ is true}\}$. We show, first, that both $\mathcal{P}(0)$ and $\mathcal{P}(1)$ are true (although only $\mathcal{P}(0)$ is necessary).

- $1 = (y + x)^0 = \sum_{k=0}^{0} \binom{0}{k} y^{0-k} x^k = \binom{0}{0} y^0 x^0 = 1;$ hence $0 \in \mathbf{M}$.

- $(y + x)^1 = \sum_{k=0}^{1} \binom{1}{k} y^{1-k} x^k = \binom{1}{0} y^1 x^0 + \binom{1}{1} y^0 x^1 = y + x;$ hence $1 \in \mathbf{M}$.

Next, for $j > 1$ assume that $j \in \mathbf{M}$, which means that $\mathcal{P}(j)$ is true and that

$$(y + x)^j = \sum_{k=0}^{j} \binom{j}{k} y^{j-k} x^k.$$

Finally, on the basis of our assumption, we must show that $\mathcal{P}(j + 1)$ is true. Thus, we must calculate

$$(y + x)^{j+1} = (y + x) \cdot (y + x)^j$$

$$= (y + x) \cdot \Big(y^j + \cdots + \underbrace{\binom{j}{k-1} y^{j-k+1} x^{k-1}}_{\alpha} + \underbrace{\binom{j}{k} y^{j-k} x^k}_{\beta} + \cdots + x^j \Big).$$

To complete the calculation, we multiply each term in $(y + x)^j$ by y, then by x, then combine like terms. To find the general term involving x^k, combine the two terms obtained by multiplying α by x and β by y. Hence,

$$(y + x)^{j+1} = \cdots + \binom{j}{k-1} y^{j-k+1} x^k + \binom{j}{k} y^{j-k+1} x^k + \cdots$$

$$= \cdots + \left(\binom{j}{k-1} + \binom{j}{k}\right) y^{j+1-k} x^k + \cdots .$$

By (1) in paragraph 16.5,

$$\binom{j}{k-1} + \binom{j}{k} = \binom{j+1}{k};$$

hence

$$(y + x)^{j+1} = \sum_{k=0}^{j+1} \binom{j+1}{k} y^{j+1-k} x^k,$$

since the smallest power of x is x^0 (in the term y^{j+1}) and the largest power of x is x^{j+1} (in the term x^{j+1}). Thus $(j+1) \in \mathbf{M}$ and by PMI, $\mathbf{M} = \mathbb{N}$; hence the theorem is proved. ■

Tutorial 17.2

Using the predicate (1) in Theorem 17.2, write out the summations:

a. $(y + x)^2 = \sum_{k=0}^{2} \binom{2}{k} y^{2-k} x^k.$

b. $(y + x)^3 = \sum_{k=0}^{3} \binom{3}{k} y^{3-k} x^k.$

c. $(y + x)^4 = \sum_{k=0}^{4} \binom{4}{k} y^{4-k} x^k.$

17.3   Because of this theorem, the numbers $\binom{m}{k}$ are called **binomial coefficients.** By the recursion relation, (1) in paragraph 16.5, they can be tabulated systematically in a triangular array, called **Pascal's triangle** (Table 17.3A). The initial condition is $\binom{m}{0} = \binom{m}{m} = 1$ for $m = 0, 1, 2, \ldots$. All other entries are obtained as the sum of two numbers in the preceding row, immediately above and to the left of the given entry ($3 + 1 = 4$, for example). Incidentally, it does no harm (and is helpful under some conditions) to assign the value 0 to $\binom{m}{k}$ when $k > m$. Thus in Table 17.3A, the dashes may be replaced with 0s. An even more suggestive display of Pascal's triangle appears in Table 17.3B. In each row, the extreme entries are 1, and all other entries are obtained by adding the two nearest neighbors in the preceding row. Observe that

			k			
m	0	1	2	3	4	5
0	1	–	–	–	–	–
1	1	1	–	–	–	–
2	1	2	1	–	–	–
3	1	3	3	1	–	–
4	1	4	6	4	1	–
5	1	5	10	10	5	1

Table 17.3A Pascal's triangle

```
              1
            1   1
          1   2   1
        1   3   3   1
      1   4   6   4   1
              ...
```

Table 17.3B

the sums of the entries in these rows are (from the top) 1, 2, 4, 8, 16, ... These sums are the appropriate powers of 2 assured by Theorem 16.1. Note especially that if each of x and y in Theorem 17.2 is replaced by 1, then that theorem simply reproduces Theorem 16.1.

Example 1 Expand $(2 + x)^5$. By the Binomial Theorem,

$$(2 + x)^5 = \sum_{k=0}^{5} \binom{5}{k} 2^{5-k} x^k$$

$$= \binom{5}{0} 2^5 + \binom{5}{1} 2^4 x + \binom{5}{2} 2^3 x^2 + \binom{5}{3} 2^2 x^3 + \binom{5}{4} 2 x^4 + \binom{5}{5} x^5$$

$$= 32 + 80x + 80x^2 + 40x^3 + 10x^4 + x^5.$$

Example 2 Find that term involving x^5 in each of the following expansions:

a. $(2 + x)^8$.

b. $(2 - x)^8$.

c. $\left(\dfrac{y}{3} + 2x\right)^{15}$.

By the Binomial Theorem,

a. $(2 + x)^8 = \displaystyle\sum_{k=0}^{8} \binom{8}{k} 2^{8-k} x^k.$

b. $(2 - x)^8 = (2 + (-x))^8 = \displaystyle\sum_{k=0}^{8} \binom{8}{k} 2^{8-k} (-x)^k.$

c. $\left(\dfrac{y}{3} + 2x\right)^{15} = \displaystyle\sum_{k=0}^{15} \binom{15}{k} \left(\dfrac{y}{3}\right)^{15-k} (2x)^k.$

In each case, choose $k = 5$ to obtain the required term:

a. $\binom{8}{5} 2^3 x^5 = 448x^5.$

b. $\binom{8}{5} 2^3 (-x)^5 = -448x^5.$

c. $\binom{15}{5} \left(\dfrac{y}{3}\right)^{10} (2x)^5 = 3003 y^{10}(3^{-10})2^5 x^5 = \dfrac{96096}{59049} y^{10} x^5.$

Tutorial 17.3

Find the term involving x^4 in

a. $(1 + x)^6.$
b. $(1 - x)^6.$

17.4

Moser's Problem We return to Moser's problem (Example 2 in paragraph 14.2). On a circle mark n points and connect the $\binom{n}{2}$ pairs of points with line segments. Let the points be placed so that no three of the line segments intersect in a point inside the circle. The problem is to determine $f(n)$, the number of regions into which the interior of the circle is subdivided by the $\binom{n}{2}$ line segments. In Example 2 of paragraph 14.2, we observed that for $n < 6$ we were led to predict that $f(n) = 2^{n-1}$. To test this prediction (or any other), we need to discover the relationship between $f(n)$ and $f(n+1)$. Again the first step is to search for a pattern by considering several special cases.

a. Look at the case $n = 3$, for which $f(3) = 4$ (see Figure 17.4A).
   i. After adjoining the new point 4, there are three new line segments between 4 and each of the old points. The old region adjacent to 4 is subdivided into four new regions, so there is a net gain of three.
   ii. Now look at the new line segments. One of them intersects an old line segment inside the circle at a point which we will call a *crossing point*. There is one

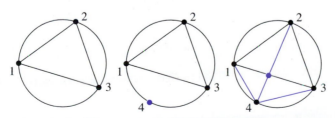

Figure 17.4A

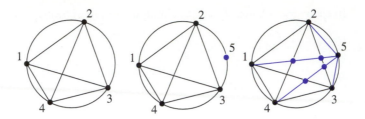

Figure 17.4B

crossing point, and it corresponds to the subdivision of one old region into two new regions, for a net gain of one. Hence,

$$f(3 + 1) = f(3) + 3 + 1,$$
$$f(4) = f(3) + 4 = 8.$$

b. Look at the case $n = 4$, for which $f(4) = 8$ (see Figure 17.4B).
  i. After adjoining the new point 5, there are four new line segments between 5 and each of the old points. The old region adjacent to 5 is subdivided into five new regions, so there is a net gain of four.
  ii. Again, call a point in which a new line segment intersects an old line segment inside the circle a crossing point. There are four crossing points, and each one corresponds to the subdivision of one old region into two new regions, for a net gain of four regions. Hence,

$$f(4 + 1) = f(4) + 4 + 4,$$
$$f(5) = f(4) + 8 = 16.$$

The pattern described above holds in general: At each stage the new regions are of two types: those adjacent to the new point or those corresponding to crossing points. The net gain from those of the first type is always just the number of old points. The net gain from those of the second type is simply the number of crossing points. Now, notice that each crossing point can be identified by a triple of old points consisting of the two endpoints of its old line segment and the old endpoint of its new line segment. Each such triple corresponds to exactly one crossing point, so the number of crossing points is $\binom{n}{3}$. Hence, for $n > 2$,

$$f(n + 1) = f(n) + n + \binom{n}{3} = f(n) + \binom{n}{1} + \binom{n}{3}. \qquad \textbf{(1)}$$

Returning to our first prediction that $f(n) = 2^{n-1}$, note that

$$f(6) = f(5) + \binom{5}{1} + \binom{5}{3} = 2^{5-1} + 5 + 10 = 16 + 15 = 31.$$

Since this is not $2^{6-1} = 32$, we must admit that the first prediction fails.

To try to discover the correct prediction, we again look for patterns. Since $f(3) = 2^2 = 4$, by the Binomial Theorem we can write

$$f(3) = \binom{2}{0} + \binom{2}{1} + \binom{2}{2} = \binom{3}{0} + \binom{3}{2}.$$

Using (1) and the facts that $\binom{m}{0} = \binom{m+1}{0}$ and $\binom{m}{k} + \binom{m}{k+1} = \binom{m+1}{k+1}$ gives the following four values of f:

$$f(4) = f(3) + \binom{3}{1} + \binom{3}{3} = \binom{3}{0} + \binom{3}{1} + \binom{3}{2} + \binom{3}{3} = \binom{4}{0} + \binom{4}{2} + \binom{4}{4},$$

$$f(5) = f(4) + \binom{4}{1} + \binom{4}{3} = \binom{4}{0} + \binom{4}{1} + \binom{4}{2} + \binom{4}{3} + \binom{4}{4} = \binom{5}{0} + \binom{5}{2} + \binom{5}{4},$$

$$f(6) = f(5) + \binom{5}{1} + \binom{5}{3} = \binom{5}{0} + \binom{5}{1} + \binom{5}{2} + \binom{5}{3} + \binom{5}{4} = \binom{6}{0} + \binom{6}{2} + \binom{6}{4},$$

$$f(7) = f(6) + \binom{6}{1} + \binom{6}{3} = \binom{6}{0} + \binom{6}{1} + \binom{6}{2} + \binom{6}{3} + \binom{6}{4}.$$

So, the pattern repeats, and it seems clear that we should predict

$$f(n) = \sum_{k=0}^{4} \binom{n-1}{k}. \qquad (2)$$

For this formula to make sense when the values of n are small, we must agree that $\binom{m}{k} = 0$ when $k > m$ and also that $\binom{0}{0} = 1$; see the text discussing Table 17.3A.

It turns out that this prediction is correct, and the proof is a straightforward application of mathematical induction. The details of the argument are included in the problems for this section.

As a final comment on this example, note that $f(n)$ includes at most the first five terms in the binomial expansion of $(1+1)^{n-1} = 2^{n-1}$. Hence, for large n, $f(n)$ is very much less than 2^{n-1} which is the sum of *all* binomial coefficients $\binom{n-1}{k}$ for $k = 0, 1, 2, \ldots, n-1$. ●

17.5

Complement: Binomial Series The first few terms of the binomial expansion suggest a general pattern which can be observed most easily by considering the special case of Theorem 17.2 with $y = 1$:

$$(1+x)^m = 1 + \frac{m}{1} \cdot x + \frac{m}{1} \cdot \frac{m-1}{2} \cdot x^2 + \frac{m}{1} \cdot \frac{m-1}{2} \cdot \frac{m-2}{3} \cdot x^3 + \cdots + x^n.$$

Now, look carefully at the way each coefficient (after the first) depends upon that of the preceding term. To find the coefficient of x^k simply multiply the coefficient of

x^{k-1} by the factor

$$\frac{m - (k - 1)}{k}.$$

Hence, at each step the new *factor* is the previous *factor* with its numerator decreased by 1 and its denominator increased by 1. Thus, for example,

$$\text{If } k = 1, \text{ multiply 1 by } \frac{m}{1}.$$

$$\text{If } k = 2, \text{ multiply } \frac{m}{1} \text{ by } \frac{m-1}{2}.$$

$$\text{If } k = 3, \text{ multiply } \frac{m}{1} \cdot \frac{m-1}{2} \text{ by } \frac{m-2}{3}.$$

Although this may seem a bit complicated, notice how easy it is to determine the coefficients a_k in

$$(1 + x)^6 = 1 + a_1 x + a_2 x^2 + a_3 x^3 + a_4 x^4 + a_5 x^5 + a_6 x^6.$$

Simply, begin with $a_1 = \frac{6}{1}$, then

$$a_2 = \frac{6}{1} \cdot \frac{5}{2}, \qquad a_3 = \frac{6}{1} \cdot \frac{5}{2} \cdot \frac{4}{3}, \qquad a_4 = \frac{6}{1} \cdot \frac{5}{2} \cdot \frac{4}{3} \cdot \frac{3}{4},$$

$$a_5 = \frac{6}{1} \cdot \frac{5}{2} \cdot \frac{4}{3} \cdot \frac{3}{4} \cdot \frac{2}{5}, \qquad a_6 = \frac{6}{1} \cdot \frac{5}{2} \cdot \frac{4}{3} \cdot \frac{3}{4} \cdot \frac{2}{5} \cdot \frac{1}{6}.$$

These numbers are

$$a_1 = 6, \qquad a_2 = 15, \qquad a_3 = 20, \qquad a_4 = 15, \qquad a_5 = 6, \qquad a_6 = 1.$$

Since the numerators are decreasing by 1 each time,

$$a_7 = a_6 \cdot \frac{0}{7} = 0,$$

and now all succeeding coefficients must also be 0.

What we have described here is an algorithm that for positive integers m creates sequentially the binomial coefficients.

$$a_1 = \binom{6}{1}, \qquad a_2 = \binom{6}{2}, \qquad a_3 = \binom{6}{3}, \qquad a_4 = \binom{6}{4}, \qquad a_5 = \binom{6}{5}, \qquad a_6 = \binom{6}{6}.$$

But the algorithmic procedure is quite independent of the fact that m is a positive integer. Suppose, for example, we choose to replace m by the number -1. Then

$$a_1 = \frac{-1}{1}, \qquad a_2 = \frac{-1}{1} \cdot \frac{-2}{2}, \qquad a_3 = \frac{-1}{1} \cdot \frac{-2}{2} \cdot \frac{-3}{3}, \qquad a_4 = \frac{-1}{1} \cdot \frac{-2}{2} \cdot \frac{-3}{3} \cdot \frac{-4}{4},$$

and hence, $a_1 = -1, a_2 = 1, a_3 = -1$, and $a_4 = 1$. So, we obtain the formal representation

$$(1 + x)^{-1} = 1 - x + x^2 - x^3 + x^4 - \cdots. \tag{1}$$

This formula is also obtained from (1) in paragraph 0.6 by replacing y with $-x$. It may be described as a *formal series*, or more precisely, as a *binomial series*. Notice, especially, that no factor in the numerator is ever 0; hence this series does not terminate like the binomial expansion does. Because of this fact, we must again issue a warning. Replacing x by 1, what are we to make of the formula

$$\frac{1}{1+1} = 1 - 1 + 1 - 1 + 1 - \cdots?$$

For the moment we will not try to assign a meaning to that expression. But we note that for some values of x a reasonable interpretation of (1) can be given. For example, replacing x by $-\frac{1}{10}$ we find

$$\frac{1}{1-\frac{1}{10}} = \frac{10}{9} = 1 + \frac{1}{10} + \frac{1}{10^2} + \frac{1}{10^3} + \frac{1}{10^4} + \cdots = 1.1111\ldots,$$

which is the decimal representation of the rational number

$$\frac{1}{1-\frac{1}{10}} = \frac{10}{9} = 1 + \tfrac{1}{9}.$$

As a second example, we will consider the binomial series which results from the choice $m = \frac{1}{2}$. Let

$$(1 + x)^{1/2} = \sqrt{1+x} = 1 + a_1 x + a_2 x^2 + a_3 x^3 + a_4 x^4 + \cdots,$$

and again compute the coefficients by the algorithm:

$$a_1 = \tfrac{1}{2}, \qquad a_2 = \frac{1}{2} \cdot \frac{\frac{1}{2}-1}{2}, \qquad a_3 = \frac{1}{2} \cdot \frac{\frac{1}{2}-1}{2} \cdot \frac{\frac{1}{2}-2}{3},$$

$$a_4 = \frac{1}{2} \cdot \frac{\frac{1}{2}-1}{2} \cdot \frac{\frac{1}{2}-2}{3} \cdot \frac{\frac{1}{2}-3}{4}.$$

These coefficients are $a_1 = \tfrac{1}{2}, a_2 = -\tfrac{1}{8}, a_3 = \tfrac{1}{16}, a_4 = -\tfrac{5}{128}.$

Example 1

If you have a calculator, use it to approximate $\sqrt{29}$; the answer should be 5.38516 (approximately). It turns out that we can confirm this by using the binomial series for $(1 + x)^{1/2}$. Note that

$$\sqrt{29} = \sqrt{25+4} = \sqrt{25\left(1 + \tfrac{4}{25}\right)} = 5\sqrt{1+0.16}.$$

So,
$$\sqrt{29} = 5(1 + \tfrac{1}{2} \cdot (0.16) - \tfrac{1}{8} \cdot (0.16)^2 + \tfrac{1}{16} \cdot (0.16)^3 - \cdots)$$
$$= 5(1 + 0.08 - 0.0032 + 0.000256 - \cdots)$$
$$\approx 5(1.077056)$$
$$\approx 5.38528.$$

For later use we need to derive a formula for the coefficients $a_1, a_2, \ldots, a_k, \ldots$ in the binomial series for $(1 + x)^{1/2}$. To discover the pattern we write them out as follows:

$$a_1 = \tfrac{1}{2},$$

$$a_2 = a_1 \cdot \frac{-\tfrac{1}{2}}{2} = -\frac{1}{2 \cdot 4},$$

$$a_3 = a_2 \cdot \frac{-\tfrac{3}{2}}{3} = \frac{1 \cdot 3}{2 \cdot 4 \cdot 6},$$

$$a_4 = a_3 \cdot \frac{-\tfrac{5}{2}}{4} = -\frac{1 \cdot 3 \cdot 5}{2 \cdot 4 \cdot 6 \cdot 8},$$

$$a_5 = a_4 \cdot \frac{-\tfrac{7}{2}}{5} = \frac{1 \cdot 3 \cdot 5 \cdot 7}{2 \cdot 4 \cdot 6 \cdot 8 \cdot 10}.$$

Recalling Example 1 of paragraph 13.4, we can write the product of the first k even integers as $2^k(k!) = 2 \cdot 4 \cdot 6 \cdots (2k)$, and we can write the product of the first k odd integers as

$$\frac{(2k)!}{2^k \cdot (k!)} = 1 \cdot 3 \cdot 5 \cdots (2k - 1).$$

From the pattern developed above, the coefficient a_k $(k > 1)$ is the product of the first $k - 1$ odd integers divided by the product of the first k even integers. Hence,

$$a_k = \frac{\dfrac{(2k-2)!}{2^{k-1}(k-1)!}}{2^k(k!)} = \frac{(2k-2)!}{2^{2k-1}(k-1)!(k!)},$$

where the sign is positive if k is odd and negative if k is even. Since $k!$ can be expressed as $k \cdot (k - 1)!$, we can rewrite a_k as

$$\frac{1}{2^{2k-1} \cdot k}\binom{2k-2}{k-1}.$$

Finally,

$$(1 + x)^{1/2} = 1 + \tfrac{1}{2} \cdot x + \sum_{k=2}^{\infty} \frac{(-1)^{k-1}}{2^{2k-1} \cdot k}\binom{2k-2}{k-1}x^k. \tag{2}$$

Binomial series, among others, are studied in the branch of continuous mathematics called *calculus*. The chief problem is concerned with identifying those values of x for which the series can be evaluated. It can be shown, for example, that the series designated earlier by (1) can be evaluated for any real number x satisfying $-1 < x < 1$.

Problems for Section 17

1. Tabulate the first 10 lines of Pascal's triangle.

2. What is the middle number in the twelfth line of Pascal's triangle? (*Hint:* This line starts with 1, 12, ...)

3. Expand $(y + x)^6$. Write out the sum in detail and also in sigma notation.

4. Expand $(y - x)^6$ as in Problem 3. Note the difference.

5. Expand as in Problem 3. (*a*) $(1 + x)^2$, (*b*) $(1 + x)^3$, (*c*) $(1 + x)^7$, (*d*) $(1 + x)^8$.

6. In the expansions in Problem 5, the number of terms is 1 more than the exponent. Hence, if m is an even integer, there is a unique middle term in the expansion. By analogy with your results in Problem 5(*a*) and (*d*), find the middle term in the following expansions (leave your answer in terms of a binomial coefficient): (*a*) $(1 + x)^{26}$, (*b*) $(1 - x)^{26}$.

7. In each part of Problem 5, replace x by 1. Interpret your results in relation to Problem 5 in Section 16.

8. Expand and simplify: $(x + 2y)^6$.

9. Find the term involving $x^{5/2}$ in $\left(\sqrt{y} - \sqrt{x}\right)^7$.

10. Find the coefficient of $a^{12}b^3$ in the expansion of $(2a - 3b)^{15}$.

11. Expand and simplify: $((1 + x) + y)^3$.

12. By combining like terms, we note that the expansion of $(y + x)^3$ contains four distinct terms. How many terms does $(y + x + w)^3$ contain? [*Hint:* Observe that

$$(y + x + w)^3 = ((y + x) + w)^3$$
$$= \sum_{k=0}^{3} \binom{3}{k}(y + x)^{3-k}w^k.]$$

In each of the next three problems, find the numerical value to three decimal places. [*Hint:* Express each in the form $(1 + 1/n)^n$.]

13. $(1.25)^4$

14. $(1.2)^5$

15. $(1.1)^{10}$

16. Assume that n, r, and k are integers which satisfy $0 \le k \le r \le n$. Show that

$$\binom{n}{r} \cdot \binom{r}{k} = \binom{n}{k} \cdot \binom{n-k}{r-k}.$$

17. The **constant term** in an expression involving x is the term with no x in it. For example, in $x^3 + 6x - 4$, the constant term is -4 and in $3x^2 + 6x + \frac{1}{2} + 1/x^2 - 1/(6x^3)$, the constant term is $\frac{1}{2}$. (*a*) What is the constant term in the expansion of $(x + 1/x)^6$? (*b*) Is there a constant term in the expansion of $(x + 1/x)^5$?

18. Use the Binomial Theorem to show that if n is any positive integer, then $(2 + \sqrt{2})^n + (2 - \sqrt{2})^n$ is an integer.

19. Show that

$$\sum_{k=0}^{6} (-1)^k \binom{6}{k} = 0.$$

[*Hint:* Expand $(y - x)^6$ and then let $x = y = 1$.]

20. Examine the first few rows of Pascal's triangle to predict the relationship between

$$U = \sum_{k \text{ odd}} \binom{m}{k} \quad \text{and} \quad V = \sum_{k \text{ even}} \binom{m}{k}.$$

For example, with $m = 3$,

$$U = \binom{3}{1} + \binom{3}{3} \quad \text{and} \quad V = \binom{3}{0} + \binom{3}{2}.$$

21. Use the Binomial Theorem to show that if n is any positive integer, then

$$\sum_{k=0}^{n}(-1)^k\binom{n}{k} = 0.$$

22. Use Problem 21 to show that

$$\binom{100}{0} + \binom{100}{2} + \cdots + \binom{100}{100}$$
$$= \binom{100}{1} + \binom{100}{3} + \cdots + \binom{100}{99}.$$

23. Indicated in the figures below, there are four paths from A to C (each step in the path moves either to the letter to the right or the letter above):

```
C           C
B C         B C
A B C       A B C


  C           C
B C         B C
A B C       A B C
```

How many paths are there from A to G in the following figure?

```
G
F G
E F G
D E F G
C D E F G
B C D E F G
A B C D E F G
```

24. Consider Pascal's triangle in Table 17.3A, with each dash replaced by a zero. Let c_n be the sum of the first three numbers in row n (n starts at 0). Find a recursive formula and a closed form for the c_n's.

25. In Moser's Problem, paragraph 17.4, we claimed that the sequence $f(n)$, $n > 4$, is obtained by adding together the first five numbers in row $(n - 1)$ of Pascal's triangle.

Show first that

$$\sum_{k=0}^{4}\binom{n-1}{k} = \binom{n}{0} + \binom{n}{2} + \binom{n}{4}.$$

26. (*Conclusion of Problem 25.*) Using (1) in paragraph 17.4, show that for all $n \in \mathbb{N}$,

$$f(n) = \sum_{k=0}^{4}\binom{n-1}{k}.$$

27. Build a triangle similar to Pascal's, using the same recursion formula but replacing all 1s with 2s. Construct the first five rows, and predict the relationship between these numbers and those in Pascal's triangle.

28. You are going to prove the result in Problem 16 by referring to Girl Scouts. Suppose there are n Girl Scouts in the troop. (*a*) Choose r of these Girl Scouts to sell cookies with k of the r selling Thin Mints and the remaining $r - k$ selling Samoas. In how many ways can this be done? (*b*) Choose from the n Girl Scouts the k girls who will be forced to sell Thin Mints and then choose from the remaining $n - k$ Girl Scouts the $r - k$ who are lucky enough to sell Samoas. In how many ways can this be done? (*c*) Why must the answers to (*a*) and (*b*) be equal?

29. Verify that

$$\sum_{k=0}^{m}\binom{n+k}{n} = \binom{m+n+1}{n+1}$$

for $m = 4, 5, 6$ and $n = 3$.

30. Consider the row of Pascal's triangle that begins 1   15   105   455   1365. (*a*) If $\binom{m}{k} = 1365$, then what are m and k? (*b*) What are the first five numbers in the row above and the row below this row?

31. Use Problem 16 to show that

$$\sum_{r=k}^{n}\binom{n}{r}\cdot\binom{r}{k} = \binom{n}{k}\cdot 2^{n-k}.$$

[*Hint:* Substitute $\binom{n}{k} \cdot \binom{n-k}{r-k}$ for $\binom{n}{r} \cdot \binom{r}{k}$ and note that $\binom{n}{k}$ is a constant with respect to r.]

32. In the formula

$$(y + x)^n = \sum_{k=0}^{n} \binom{n}{k} \cdot y^{n-k} x^k,$$

substitute (*a*) 1 for y and 2 for x, (*b*) 1 for y and 3 for x, (*c*) 1 for y and 4 for x.

33. Using your answers from Problem 32 as a guide, show that

$$\sum_{k=0}^{n} \binom{n}{k} \cdot 3^{2n} = 10^n.$$

(*Hint:* $3^{2n} = 9^n$.)

34. If $m < k$, then $\binom{m}{k} = 0$. Let $G_n = \sum_{k=0}^{n} \binom{n-k}{k}$. (*a*) Compute G_n for $n = 0$, 1, 2, 3, 4, and 5. (*b*) What familiar numbers are the G_n's?

35. Let α be any real number. Let $(\alpha)_0 = 1$ and for any positive integer k, define $(\alpha)_k = \alpha \cdot (\alpha - 1) \cdot (\alpha - 2) \cdots (\alpha - k + 1)$. Compute $(\alpha)_k$ for $k = 1, 2, 3, 4$ and for (*a*) $\alpha = -2$, (*b*) $\alpha = \frac{1}{2}$, (*c*) $\alpha = -\frac{1}{2}$.

36. (*Continuation of Problem 35.*) Let α be any real number. For any nonnegative integer k, let $\binom{\alpha}{k} = \frac{(\alpha)_k}{k!}$. If $\alpha \in \mathbb{N}$ and $k > \alpha$ then show that both $(\alpha)_k$ and $\binom{\alpha}{k}$ are 0.

37. (*Continuation of Problem 35.*) Compute $\binom{\alpha}{0}, \binom{\alpha}{1}, \binom{\alpha}{2}, \binom{\alpha}{3}$ for $\alpha = 1, \alpha = \frac{1}{2}, \alpha = -1$, and $\alpha = -\frac{1}{2}$.

38. (*Conclusion of Problem 35.*) (*a*) Compute $\binom{\alpha}{1}$ for all α. (*b*) Find a formula for $\binom{-2}{k}$ in terms of k.

39. Let p be a positive integer and let k be an integer satisfying $0 < k < p$. (*a*) Find two examples to show that if p is *not* a prime, then p need not divide $\binom{p}{k}$. (*b*) Find two examples to show that if p *is* a prime, then p may divide $\binom{p}{k}$. (*c*) Prove that if p is a prime, then p *must* divide $\binom{p}{k}$.

40. (*Continuation of Problem 39.*) Let n be a positive integer. Does 7 divide $n^7 - n$ for each of the integers $n = 2, 3, 6, 7, 10$?

41. (*Continuation of Problem 39.*) Prove that for all $n \in \mathbb{N}$, 7 divides $n^7 - n$. [*Hint:* Use induction and part (*c*) in Problem 39.]

42. (*Conclusion of Problem 39.*) Use induction to show that if p is a prime, then for all $n \in \mathbb{N}$, $p \mid (n^p - n)$.

43. Referring to Example 1 in paragraph 0.1 and Problems 41 and 42 of Section 15, show that $g(n, k) = \binom{n+k-1}{n}$. (*Hint:* Consider the part of Table 17.3A below the diagonal of 1s.)

44. There is also a Binomial Theorem which is useful in advanced mathematics, where it can be shown that for $\alpha \in \mathbb{R}$,

$$(1 + x)^\alpha = \sum_{k=0}^{\infty} \binom{\alpha}{k} \cdot x^k.$$

You may recall that Professor Moriarty was one of the major villains in the Sherlock Holmes stories by Sir Arthur Conan Doyle (1859–1930). About him Holmes said, admiringly, "At the age of twenty-one he wrote a treatise upon the binomial theorem, which has had a European vogue." The final problem in this set is to discover the name of the short story from which the quotation above was taken. If you read that story you will find that it has nothing to do with mathematics, but you may enjoy it anyway!

Section 18.   Inclusion-Exclusion

Overview for Section 18

- Introduction to Venn diagrams
- Application of Venn diagrams in enumeration
- Explanation of distributive laws in set theory
- Definition of partition
- Discussion of simple inclusion-exclusion relations
- Definition of the greatest integer function (or floor function)

Key Concepts: Venn diagrams, distributive laws, partition, inclusion-exclusion relations, greatest integer function

18.1   Set theory is much more than a descriptive language designed to help make precise our understanding of mathematical structures such as the real number system. It, too, has a well-defined structure (in some ways quite unlike others we have met) which is based upon the key ideas of union, intersection, and complement. Among the many applications of set theory is the one discussed later in this section, which turns out to be an indispensable tool in the solution of many complicated combinatorial problems.

The concept of a *Venn diagram*, named for John Venn (1834–1923), is useful in examining the relationships between union, intersection, and complement. Let $\mathbf{S}$ denote a nonempty set which we will refer to here as the *universe*, and let $\mathbf{S}$ be represented pictorially as the interior of a rectangle. We will assume that all sets under consideration are subsets of this universe $\mathbf{S}$. Any set $\mathbf{A}$ may be represented pictorially by an oval inside the rectangle. Thus $\mathbf{A}$ separates $\mathbf{S}$ into two disjoint pieces, $\mathbf{A}$ and the complement of $\mathbf{A}$, which we denote $\overline{\mathbf{A}}$. In the Venn diagram of Figure 18.1, $\overline{\mathbf{A}}$ is the shaded region, and note that

$$\mathbf{A} \cap \overline{\mathbf{A}} = \varnothing \qquad \text{and} \qquad \mathbf{A} \cup \overline{\mathbf{A}} = \mathbf{S}. \tag{1}$$

There is a remarkably close relationship between set theory and the symbolic treatment of logical reasoning (see Section 14). For example, "$x \in \mathbf{A}$" is a true statement if and only if "$x \in \overline{\mathbf{A}}$" is false. Thus, complement and negation are linked by the condition that for any x in the universe, the two statements

$$x \in \overline{\mathbf{A}} \qquad \text{and} \qquad \sim(x \in \mathbf{A})$$

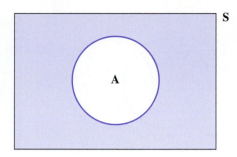

Figure 18.1

are equivalent. Similarly:

- Union   corresponds to   disjunction.
- Intersection   corresponds to   conjunction.

Thus, for an element $x \in \mathbf{S}$:

- $x \in (\mathbf{A} \cup \mathbf{B})$ if and only if $(x \in \mathbf{A}) \vee (x \in \mathbf{B})$.
- $x \in (\mathbf{A} \cap \mathbf{B})$ if and only if $(x \in \mathbf{A}) \wedge (x \in \mathbf{B})$.

18.2 The De Morgan Laws (Tables 14.4A and 14.4B) have a natural set-theoretic interpretation.

THEOREM 18.2

If **S** is the universe and if **A** and **B** are subsets of **S**, then
a. $\overline{\mathbf{A} \cup \mathbf{B}} = \overline{\mathbf{A}} \cap \overline{\mathbf{B}}$.
b. $\overline{\mathbf{A} \cap \mathbf{B}} = \overline{\mathbf{A}} \cup \overline{\mathbf{B}}$.

Proof

a. Assume that $x \in \overline{\mathbf{A} \cup \mathbf{B}}$. If $x \in \mathbf{A}$, then $x \in \mathbf{A} \cup \mathbf{B}$, which contradicts the assumption. Thus $x \notin \mathbf{A}$. If $x \in \mathbf{B}$, then $x \in \mathbf{A} \cup \mathbf{B}$, which contradicts the assumption. Thus $x \notin \mathbf{B}$. Hence $x \in \overline{\mathbf{A}} \cap \overline{\mathbf{B}}$. This proves that $\overline{\mathbf{A} \cup \mathbf{B}} \subseteq \overline{\mathbf{A}} \cap \overline{\mathbf{B}}$.
  Now assume that $x \in \overline{\mathbf{A}} \cap \overline{\mathbf{B}}$. Then $x \in \overline{\mathbf{A}}$, so $x \notin \mathbf{A}$. Also, $x \in \overline{\mathbf{B}}$, so $x \notin \mathbf{B}$. Hence $x \notin \mathbf{A} \cup \mathbf{B}$; therefore $x \in \overline{\mathbf{A} \cup \mathbf{B}}$. This proves that $\overline{\mathbf{A}} \cap \overline{\mathbf{B}} \subseteq \overline{\mathbf{A} \cup \mathbf{B}}$.
  Both conditions now imply that $\overline{\mathbf{A} \cup \mathbf{B}} = \overline{\mathbf{A}} \cap \overline{\mathbf{B}}$.

b. The proof of part **b** is similar. We omit it here but illustrate the situation via the Venn diagrams in Figure 18.2. Note that the shaded areas are the same. ∎

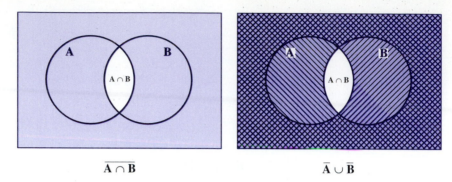

$\overline{A} \cap \overline{B}$ $\overline{A} \cup \overline{B}$

Figure 18.2

Tutorial 18.2A

a. Prove, as in part **a** of Theorem 18.2, that $\overline{A \cap B} \subseteq \overline{A} \cup \overline{B}$.

b. Let $S = \{u, v, w, x, y, z\}$, $A = \{u, v, x, y\}$, and $B = \{w, x, y, z\}$. Verify Theorem 18.2 in this special case.

Example 1

Let **S** denote the set of positive integers less than or equal to 300. How many elements in **S** are not divisible by 3 or are not divisible by 5?

Let **M** denote the set of elements in **S** that are not divisible by 3 or are not divisible by 5. We need to think carefully about **M**. The membership test that we apply to an element x is "$x \in M$ if x is not divisible by 3 or if x is not divisible by 5". Note that 1, 3, and 5 (for example) pass the test because 1 is not divisible by 3 or by 5, 3 is not divisible by 5, and 5 is not divisible by 3. Now let

$$A = \{x \in S: \ x \text{ is divisible by 3}\},$$

$$B = \{x \in S: \ x \text{ is divisible by 5}\}.$$

Our question, then, is, "How many elements are in $\overline{A} \cup \overline{B}$?" By one of the De Morgan Laws, $\overline{A} \cup \overline{B} = \overline{A \cap B}$, and the latter set is easy to enumerate. Note that $x \in A \cap B$ if x is divisible both by 3 and by 5; that is, x is divisible by 15. Each fifteenth member of **S** is divisible by 15; hence

$$|A \cap B| = \tfrac{300}{15} = 20.$$

Because any set and its complement are disjoint, by FCP I

$$|S| = |A \cap B| + |\overline{A \cap B}|.$$

Therefore,
$$|\overline{A \cap B}| = |S| - |A \cap B|$$
$$= 300 - 20$$
$$= 280.$$

Tutorial 18.2B

Suppose that the question in Example 1 is phrased, "How many elements in **S** are not divisible by either 3 or 5?" Suppose, further, that we interpret this to mean those elements in **S** which are divisible by neither 3 nor 5. What set do we need to enumerate, and what is its alternate De Morgan form?

18.3   Venn diagrams are useful in exploring other relationships between union and intersection. Let **A**, **B**, and **C** denote three subsets of the universe **S**, and consider the expression **A** ∩ **B** ∪ **C**. The Venn diagrams in Figure 18.3A illustrate the ambiguity in this expression; the shaded regions differ depending on where we insert the parentheses.

Even though **A** ∩ (**B** ∪ **C**) ≠ (**A** ∩ **B**) ∪ **C**, each of the expressions, separately, does lead to a general law of set theory called a *distributive law*. The distributive law of arithmetic asserts that if x, y, and z are any real numbers, then

$$x \cdot (y + z) = x \cdot y + x \cdot z. \tag{1}$$

Here is one of the set-theoretic results:

THEOREM 18.3A

If **A**, **B**, and **C** are sets, then

$$\mathbf{A} \cap (\mathbf{B} \cup \mathbf{C}) = (\mathbf{A} \cap \mathbf{B}) \cup (\mathbf{A} \cap \mathbf{C}). \tag{2}$$

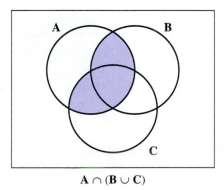

A ∩ (**B** ∪ **C**)

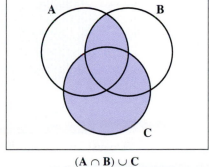

(**A** ∩ **B**) ∪ **C**

Figure 18.3A

Proof

If $p \in A \cap (B \cup C)$, then $p \in A$ and $p \in (B \cup C)$. Thus either $p \in B$ or $p \in C$; hence either $p \in (A \cap B)$ or $p \in (A \cap C)$. In either case

$$A \cap (B \cup C) \subseteq (A \cap B) \cup (A \cap C).$$

The proof of the reverse inclusion is equally simple and is deferred to the problems at the end of this section. ∎

From the similarity between (1) and (2), one might easily infer that sets under the operations of intersection and union behave like numbers under the operations of multiplication and addition. But, again, don't leap before you look!

Recall from arithmetic that in equation (1) it is not possible to interchange the operations; in general,

$$x + (y \cdot z) \neq (x + y) \cdot (x + z).$$

For example,

$$2 + (3 \cdot 5) \neq (2 + 3) \cdot (2 + 5).$$

But in set theory the situation is different. Return to (2) and simply interchange the operations on each side. The result is

$$A \cup (B \cap C) \quad \text{and} \quad (A \cup B) \cap (A \cup C).$$

The Venn diagrams for each of these are shown in Figure 18.3B. The shaded regions are identical in both Venn diagrams; hence we conclude that it must be possible to prove the following:

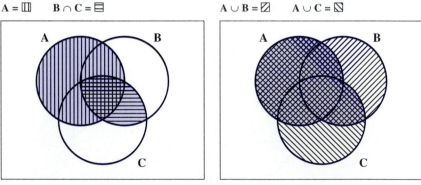

$A \cup (B \cap C) =$ shaded $= (A \cup B) \cap (A \cup C)$

Figure 18.3B

THEOREM 18.3B	If **A**, **B**, and **C** are sets, then

$$\mathbf{A} \cup (\mathbf{B} \cap \mathbf{C}) = (\mathbf{A} \cup \mathbf{B}) \cap (\mathbf{A} \cup \mathbf{C}). \qquad (3)$$

The proof of Theorem 18.3B is quite similar to that of Theorem 18.3A and is omitted here (see Problem 12). The important lesson of Theorems 18.3A and 18.3B is that in set theory (unlike arithmetic) *both* possible distributive laws are valid.

Example 1   Let $\mathbf{S} = \{1, 2, 3, \ldots, 15\}$, and let $\mathbf{A} = \{x \in \mathbf{S}: 3 \mid x\}$, $\mathbf{B} = \{x \in \mathbf{S}: 5 \mid x\}$, $\mathbf{C} = \{x \in \mathbf{S}: x \text{ is prime}\}$. Explicitly, $\mathbf{A} = \{3, 6, 9, 12, 15\}$, $\mathbf{B} = \{5, 10, 15\}$, and $\mathbf{C} = \{2, 3, 5, 7, 11, 13\}$. Then, referring to (2):

$$\mathbf{A} \cap (\mathbf{B} \cup \mathbf{C}) = \{3, 6, 9, 12, 15\} \cap \{2, 3, 5, 7, 10, 11, 13, 15\},$$

$$(\mathbf{A} \cap \mathbf{B}) \cup (\mathbf{A} \cap \mathbf{C}) = \{15\} \cup \{3\},$$

so $$\mathbf{A} \cap (\mathbf{B} \cup \mathbf{C}) = (\mathbf{A} \cap \mathbf{B}) \cup (\mathbf{A} \cap \mathbf{C}) = \{3, 15\}.$$

Further, referring to (3),

$$\mathbf{A} \cup (\mathbf{B} \cap \mathbf{C}) = \{3, 6, 9, 12, 15\} \cup \{5\},$$

and

$$(\mathbf{A} \cup \mathbf{B}) \cap (\mathbf{A} \cup \mathbf{C}) = \{3, 5, 6, 9, 10, 12, 15\} \cap \{2, 3, 5, 6, 7, 9, 11, 12, 13, 15\}.$$

So, $$\mathbf{A} \cup (\mathbf{B} \cap \mathbf{C}) = (\mathbf{A} \cup \mathbf{B}) \cap (\mathbf{A} \cup \mathbf{C}) = \{3, 5, 6, 9, 12, 15\}.$$

Tutorial 18.3

a. If $\mathbf{B} \subseteq \mathbf{C}$, then both Theorems 18.3A and 18.3B reduce to trivial forms. What are they?

b. If $\mathbf{A} = \{u, v, x, z\}$, $\mathbf{B} = \{w, x, y, z\}$, and $\mathbf{C} = \{t, u, x, z\}$, verify both (2) and (3).

18.4   A **partition** of any set $\mathbf{M}$ is a collection of nonempty subsets $\mathbf{M}_1, \mathbf{M}_2, \ldots, \mathbf{M}_n$ with the properties that:

- $\mathbf{M}$ is the union of all the subsets.
- Each two of the subsets are disjoint from one another.

A	B	*Part*	*Description*
0	0	$\overline{A} \cap \overline{B}$	*x* not in **A** and not in **B**
0	1	$\overline{A} \cap B$	*x* in **B**, but not in **A**
1	0	$A \cap \overline{B}$	*x* in **A**, but not in **B**
1	1	$A \cap B$	*x* in **A** and in **B**

Table 18.4

From (1) in paragraph 18.1, any set **A** partitions **S** into **A** and $\overline{A}$. Two subsets **A** and **B** partition **S** into four parts (or subsets) displayed in Table 18.4 (where, for example, $x \in A$ is indicated by 1 and $x \in \overline{A}$ is indicated by 0). Depending upon the relationships of **A**, **B**, and **S**, one or more of these subsets may be empty. These four disjoint subsets are shown in the Venn diagram of Figure 18.4. The actual partition may be indicated as in the formula

$$\mathbf{S} = (\mathbf{A} \cap \mathbf{B}) \cup (\mathbf{A} \cap \overline{\mathbf{B}}) \cup (\overline{\mathbf{A}} \cap \mathbf{B}) \cup (\overline{\mathbf{A}} \cap \overline{\mathbf{B}}). \tag{1}$$

We know that

$$\mathbf{S} = (\mathbf{A} \cup \mathbf{B}) \cup (\overline{\mathbf{A} \cup \mathbf{B}}), \tag{2}$$

and by one of the De Morgan Laws, $\overline{\mathbf{A} \cup \mathbf{B}} = \overline{\mathbf{A}} \cap \overline{\mathbf{B}}$, so from (1) and (2) we have

$$\mathbf{S} = ((\mathbf{A} \cap \mathbf{B}) \cup (\mathbf{A} \cap \overline{\mathbf{B}}) \cup (\overline{\mathbf{A}} \cap \mathbf{B})) \cup (\overline{\mathbf{A} \cup \mathbf{B}}),$$

and

$$\mathbf{A} \cup \mathbf{B} = (\mathbf{A} \cap \mathbf{B}) \cup (\mathbf{A} \cap \overline{\mathbf{B}}) \cup (\overline{\mathbf{A}} \cap \mathbf{B}). \tag{3}$$

Each of the sets **A** and **B** can also be represented in partitioned form:

$$\mathbf{A} = (\mathbf{A} \cap \mathbf{B}) \cup (\mathbf{A} \cap \overline{\mathbf{B}}), \tag{4}$$

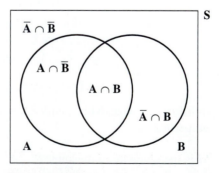

Figure 18.4

$$\mathbf{B} = (\mathbf{A} \cap \mathbf{B}) \cup (\overline{\mathbf{A}} \cap \mathbf{B}). \tag{5}$$

Each of these equations, by FCP I, yields a corresponding enumeration equation; for example,

$$|\mathbf{A}| = |\mathbf{A} \cap \mathbf{B}| + |\mathbf{A} \cap \overline{\mathbf{B}}| \quad \text{or} \quad |\mathbf{A} \cap \overline{\mathbf{B}}| = |\mathbf{A}| - |\mathbf{A} \cap \mathbf{B}|,$$

$$|\mathbf{B}| = |\mathbf{A} \cap \mathbf{B}| + |\overline{\mathbf{A}} \cap \mathbf{B}| \quad \text{or} \quad |\overline{\mathbf{A}} \cap \mathbf{B}| = |\mathbf{B}| - |\mathbf{A} \cap \mathbf{B}|.$$

Hence, from (3),

$$|\mathbf{A} \cup \mathbf{B}| = |\mathbf{A} \cap \mathbf{B}| + (|\mathbf{A}| - |\mathbf{A} \cap \mathbf{B}|) + (|\mathbf{B}| - |\mathbf{A} \cap \mathbf{B}|),$$

or

$$|\mathbf{A} \cup \mathbf{B}| = |\mathbf{A}| + |\mathbf{B}| - |\mathbf{A} \cap \mathbf{B}|. \tag{6}$$

Equation (6) is the simplest case of what are called the **inclusion-exclusion relations.** We can think of (6) in the following way: To count the number of elements in $\mathbf{A} \cup \mathbf{B}$, we must include all the elements of $\mathbf{A}$, together with all the elements of $\mathbf{B}$, but this counts elements in $\mathbf{A} \cap \mathbf{B}$ twice; hence they must be excluded once from the count.

Example 1

Consider again Example 1 in paragraph 18.2, where $\mathbf{S} = \{x \in \mathbb{N}: x \le 300\}$, $\mathbf{A} = \{x \in \mathbf{S}: 3 \mid x\}$, $\mathbf{B} = \{x \in \mathbf{S}: 5 \mid x\}$. Suppose we wish to enumerate the elements of $\mathbf{S}$ which are divisible either by 3 or by 5. We want to evaluate $|\mathbf{A} \cup \mathbf{B}|$, and by (6)

$$|\mathbf{A} \cup \mathbf{B}| = |\mathbf{A}| + |\mathbf{B}| - |\mathbf{A} \cap \mathbf{B}|.$$

Every third element in $\mathbf{S}$ is divisible by 3; hence $|\mathbf{A}| = \frac{300}{3} = 100$. Similarly, $|\mathbf{B}| = \frac{300}{5} = 60$, and $|\mathbf{A} \cap \mathbf{B}| = \frac{300}{15} = 20$. Thus,

$$|\mathbf{A} \cup \mathbf{B}| = 100 + 60 - 20 = 140.$$

Making use of this evaluation, we can now determine the number $|\overline{\mathbf{A}} \cup \overline{\mathbf{B}}|$ by inclusion-exclusion,

$$\begin{aligned}
|\overline{\mathbf{A}} \cup \overline{\mathbf{B}}| &= |\overline{\mathbf{A}}| + |\overline{\mathbf{B}}| - |\overline{\mathbf{A}} \cap \overline{\mathbf{B}}| \\
&= (|\mathbf{S}| - |\mathbf{A}|) + (|\mathbf{S}| - |\mathbf{B}|) - |\overline{\mathbf{A} \cup \mathbf{B}}| \\
&= 200 + 240 - (|\mathbf{S}| - |\mathbf{A} \cup \mathbf{B}|) \\
&= 200 + 240 - 160 \\
&= 280 \quad \text{(as in Example 1 of paragraph 18.2).}
\end{aligned}$$

18.5

The general inclusion-exclusion formula counts the number of elements in the union of n sets. To discover the pattern, we use (6) in paragraph 18.4 to generate the formula for the union of three sets. It will be helpful (at first) to let $\mathbf{D} = \mathbf{A} \cup \mathbf{B}$.

$$|\mathbf{A} \cup \mathbf{B} \cup \mathbf{C}| = |\mathbf{D} \cup \mathbf{C}|$$
$$= |\mathbf{D}| + |\mathbf{C}| - |\mathbf{D} \cap \mathbf{C}|$$
$$= |\mathbf{A} \cup \mathbf{B}| + |\mathbf{C}| - |(\mathbf{A} \cup \mathbf{B}) \cap \mathbf{C}|$$
$$= |\mathbf{A}| + |\mathbf{B}| - |\mathbf{A} \cap \mathbf{B}| + |\mathbf{C}| - |(\mathbf{A} \cap \mathbf{C}) \cup (\mathbf{B} \cap \mathbf{C})|$$
$$= |\mathbf{A}| + |\mathbf{B}| + |\mathbf{C}| - |\mathbf{A} \cap \mathbf{B}|$$
$$- (|\mathbf{A} \cap \mathbf{C}| + |\mathbf{B} \cap \mathbf{C}| - |(\mathbf{A} \cap \mathbf{C}) \cap (\mathbf{B} \cap \mathbf{C})|)$$

and finally,

$$|\mathbf{A} \cup \mathbf{B} \cup \mathbf{C}| = |\mathbf{A}| + |\mathbf{B}| + |\mathbf{C}| - |\mathbf{A} \cap \mathbf{B}| - |\mathbf{A} \cap \mathbf{C}| - |\mathbf{B} \cap \mathbf{C}| + |\mathbf{A} \cap \mathbf{B} \cap \mathbf{C}|. \quad \textbf{(1)}$$

The Venn diagram in Figure 18.5 displays the union $\mathbf{A} \cup \mathbf{B} \cup \mathbf{C}$ in partitioned form, and in Table 18.5 this is related to the inclusion-exclusion formula (1). Note that $\mathbf{A} \cup \mathbf{B} \cup \mathbf{C}$ is partitioned into the seven mutually disjoint subsets indicated in Figure 18.5. In the following tabulation we will work through (1) and will indicate at each step which subsets are included ($+1$) or excluded (-1) from the total (see Table 18.5). The fact that the total in each column is 1 tells us that each subset in the partition has been counted a net total of once in (1); hence the formula accurately enumerates $\mathbf{A} \cup \mathbf{B} \cup \mathbf{C}$.

Tutorial 18.5

Construct a table similar to Table 18.5 for the inclusion-exclusion formula (6) in paragraph 18.4.

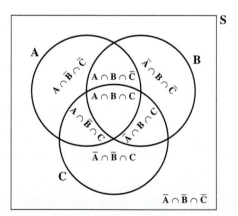

Figure 18.5

	$A\cup B\cup C$	$A\cap\bar{B}\cap\bar{C}$	$A\cap B\cap\bar{C}$	$A\cap\bar{B}\cap C$	$A\cap B\cap C$	$\bar{A}\cap B\cap\bar{C}$	$\bar{A}\cap B\cap C$	$\bar{A}\cap\bar{B}\cap C$
Add $|A|$	+1	+1	+1	+1				
Add $|B|$			+1		+1	+1	+1	
Add $|C|$				+1	+1		+1	+1
Subtract $|A\cap B|$			−1		−1			
Subtract $|A\cap C|$				−1	−1			
Subtract $|B\cap C|$					−1		−1	
Add $|A\cap B\cap C|$					+1			
Total	1	1	1	1	1	1	1	

Table 18.5

The union of four sets is partitioned into 15 mutually disjoint subsets, and the inclusion-exclusion formula for that union can be expressed in the following symbolic way:

$$|A\cup B\cup C\cup D| = \Sigma_1|X| - \Sigma_2|X\cap Y|$$
$$+ \Sigma_3|X\cap Y\cap Z| - \Sigma_4|X\cap Y\cap Z\cap W|. \quad (2)$$

- In Σ_1 there are $\binom{4}{1}$ = 4 terms, and X can be replaced by any of the sets A, B, C, D.

- In Σ_2 there are $\binom{4}{2}$ = 6 terms, and X and Y can be replaced by any pair of the sets A, B, C, D.

- In Σ_3 there are $\binom{4}{3}$ = 4 terms, and X, Y, and Z can be replaced by any triple of the sets A, B, C, D.

- In Σ_4 there is $\binom{4}{4}$ = 1 term, and X, Y, Z, and W must be replaced by A, B, C, D.

Formula (2) suggests the pattern of the general inclusion-exclusion formula which enumerates the union of n sets. Both its statement and its proof (by mathematical induction or by the Binomial Theorem) are fairly complicated. We will not pursue the generalization at this time.

Example 1 As in Example 1 of paragraph 18.4, let $S = \{1, 2, 3, \ldots, 300\}$. How many numbers in S are divisible by either 3, 5, or 7? Let

$$A = \{x \in S: 3\mid x\}, \qquad B = \{x \in S: 5\mid x\}, \qquad C = \{x \in S: 7\mid x\}.$$

The answer to our question is $|A \cup B \cup C|$, and we must use (1). To compute $|C|$ we need the quotient resulting from dividing 300 by 7, namely, 42. We make use here of an idea you may have encountered in an earlier course: the **greatest integer function.** Given a real number x, the greatest integer in x is that integer n for which $n \leq x < n + 1$. This number is often denoted $[x]$, but we will use the slightly different notation $\lfloor x \rfloor$, called the *floor* of x (introduced in paragraph 6.8). For example,

$$\lfloor \pi \rfloor = 3, \qquad \lfloor -\pi \rfloor = -4, \qquad \lfloor -1 \rfloor = -1, \qquad \lfloor \tfrac{300}{7} \rfloor = 42.$$

We also have

$$|A| = \lfloor \tfrac{300}{3} \rfloor = 100, \qquad |B| = \lfloor \tfrac{300}{5} \rfloor = 60, \qquad |C| = \lfloor \tfrac{300}{7} \rfloor = 42,$$

$$|A \cap B| = \lfloor \tfrac{300}{15} \rfloor = 20, \qquad |A \cap C| = \lfloor \tfrac{300}{21} \rfloor = 14,$$

$$|B \cap C| = \lfloor \tfrac{300}{35} \rfloor = 8, \qquad |A \cap B \cap C| = \lfloor \tfrac{300}{105} \rfloor = 2.$$

Hence,

$$|A \cup B \cup C| = 100 + 60 + 42 - 20 - 14 - 8 + 2 = 162. \qquad \bullet$$

18.6

Complement: Derangements Four students, Anne, Bob, Carol, and Dwayne, turn in their discrete mathematics tests without putting their names on them. The tests are graded and handed back to these four students randomly. In how many different ways can this be done so that no student receives his or her own test? For example, here are two ways this could happen:

Student	Test received	Test received
Anne	Bob	Carol
Bob	Anne	Dwayne
Carol	Dwayne	Bob
Dwayne	Carol	Anne

For convenience, let's denote each student by his or her initial. Then the data in the example would be arranged as:

Student	Test received	Test received
A	B	C
B	A	D
C	D	B
D	C	A

Note that what we are interested in are permutations of the four letters A, B, C, D. Recall from paragraph 16.3 that there are $4! = 24$ permutations of these letters. It is traditional in instances like this to call these permutations **arrangements.** A **fixed point** in an arrangement is a letter which remains in its original position, and a **derangement** is an arrangement with no fixed points. We will use inclusion-exclusion to count the number of derangements (denoted by d_4) of four letters and thus answer our question.

Well, actually we will count the number of arrangements which are *not* derangements. Hence, we will count the number of arrangements with at least one fixed point, denoted by s_4, and then subtract it from $4!$ to find d_4.

To help in counting these arrangements, all $4! = 24$ arrangements are given in Table 18.6. For example, in line 9, $BCAD$ means that Anne received Bob's test, Bob received Carol's, Carol received Anne's, and Dwayne received his own test. Hence for this arrangement, Dwayne is a fixed point. Note that the two derangements given as examples are lines 8 and 18. In fact, the nine derangements appear on lines 8, 10, 11, 14, 17, 18, 19, 23, and 24.

Now we have answered our original question but in a somewhat unsatisfactory way. It would be difficult to list all arrangements to find the number of derangements if there were 10 students ($10! = 3,628,800$ arrangements) and impossible if there were 30 students ($30! \approx 2.65 \times 10^{32}$). Hence, we will use inclusion-exclusion to find s_4, and from that it will be easy to see how the formula generalizes.

How many arrangements have at least one fixed point? This is easy to answer. For if A were fixed, then there are $(4 - 1)! = 3!$ ways to arrange the other three letters. If A were not fixed, then any of the other three letters could be, and so we conclude that there are $\binom{4}{1} \cdot (4 - 1)!$ arrangements with at least a single fixed point. But wait, $\binom{4}{1} \cdot (4 - 1)! = 4 \cdot 6 = 24$, and not every arrangement has at least one fixed point.

This is very true. For example, the arrangement in line 7 has been counted twice, once for C being fixed and once for D being fixed. Similarly, the arrangements in lines 2, 3, 6, 15, and 22 have also been counted twice, and the first arrangement has been counted four times!

We now need to subtract from $\binom{4}{1} \cdot (4 - 1)!$ the number of arrangements with at least two fixed points. First, there are $\binom{4}{2}$ ways of choosing the two letters that must be fixed: $AB, AC, AD, BC, BD,$ and CD. Second, once the two fixed letters are chosen, there are $(4-2)!$ ways to arrange the remaining two letters. Hence, there are $\binom{4}{2} \cdot (4 - 2)! = 6 \cdot 2 = 12$ arrangements with at least two fixed points which gives

$$\binom{4}{2} \cdot (4 - 1)! - \binom{4}{2} \cdot (4 - 2)! = 24 - 12 = 12$$

arrangements with at least one fixed point.

Line	Arrangements (permutations)	One letter fixed	Two letters fixed	Three letters fixed	Four letters fixed
1	A B C D	A B C D	AB AD BD / AC BC CD	ABC ACD / ABD BCD	ABCD
2	A B D C	A B	AB		
3	A C B D	A D	AD		
4	A C D B	A			
5	A D B C	A			
6	A D C B	A C	AC		
7	B A C D	C D	CD		
8	B A D C				
9	B C A D	D			
10	B C D A				
11	B D A C				
12	B D C A	C			
13	C A B D	D			
14	C A D B				
15	C B A D	B D	BD		
16	C B D A	B			
17	C D A B				
18	C D B A				
19	D A B C				
20	D A C B	C			
21	D B A C	B			
22	D B C A	B C	BC		
23	D C A B				
24	D C B A				
Total	24	24	12	4	1

$$s_4 = 24 - 12 + 4 - 1 = 15$$
$$d_4 = 4! - s_4 = 24 - 15 = 9$$

Table 18.6

The reason 12 is not our answer is because arrangement 1 has been counted as six different arrangements (for it has AB, AC, AD, BC, BD, and CD fixed), and so far we have counted it four times for at least one fixed point and subtracted it six times for having at least two fixed points; hence it has been counted $4 - 6 = -2$ times. How are we to rectify this mistake? Observe that we have included all permutations with at least one fixed point, excluded all arrangements with at least two fixed points, and hence, we must include the arrangements with at least three fixed points. But there are just $\binom{4}{3} \cdot (4 - 3)! = 4$ of these. (Arrangement 1 counted four times for ABC, ABD, ACD, BCD.) So at this stage there are

$$\binom{4}{1} \cdot (4 - 1)! - \binom{4}{2} \cdot (4 - 2)! + \binom{4}{3} \cdot (4 - 3)! = 24 - 12 + 4 = 16$$

arrangements with at least one fixed point. This is just one too many, and it is clear that we must exclude those arrangements with four fixed points. There is only one of these, of course, but we write 1 as $\binom{4}{4} \cdot (4 - 4)!$. Hence, the number of arrangements with at least one fixed point is

$$s_4 = \binom{4}{1} \cdot (4 - 1)! - \binom{4}{2} \cdot (4 - 2)! + \binom{4}{3} \cdot (4 - 3)! - \binom{4}{4} \cdot (4 - 4)! = 15.$$

Note in particular that arrangement 1 is added four times (for single fixed points), subtracted six times (for double fixed points), added four times (for triples), and subtracted once more because all four letters are fixed. Likewise, arrangement 2 is counted just once because it is first counted twice because A and B are fixed and then subtracted once because the pair AB is fixed. Thus, we can compute d_4 without counting.

$$d_4 = 4! - s_4$$

$$= 4! - \left[\binom{4}{1} \cdot (4 - 1)! - \binom{4}{2} \cdot (4 - 2)! + \binom{4}{3} \cdot (4 - 3)! - \binom{4}{4} \cdot (4 - 4)! \right].$$

Writing the binomial coefficients in terms of factorials yields

$$d_4 = 4! - \frac{4!}{1!(4 - 1)!} \cdot (4 - 1)! + \frac{4!}{2!(4 - 2)!} \cdot (4 - 2)!$$

$$- \frac{4!}{3!(4 - 3)!} \cdot (4 - 3)! + \frac{4!}{4!(4 - 4)!} \cdot (4 - 4)!$$

$$= 4! - \frac{4!}{1!} + \frac{4!}{2!} - \frac{4!}{3!} + \frac{4!}{4!} = 24 - 24 + 12 - 4 + 1 = 9. \qquad (1)$$

Factoring out 4! from each term in (1) gives

$$d_4 = 4! \cdot \left(1 - \frac{1}{1!} + \frac{1}{2!} - \frac{1}{3!} + \frac{1}{4!} \right).$$

The reason for writing d_4 this way is because it generalizes immediately to the number of derangements on n letters. If d_n is the number of arrangements of n letters with no fixed points, then

$$d_n = n! \cdot \left(1 - \frac{1}{1!} + \frac{1}{2!} - \frac{1}{3!} + \cdots + \frac{(-1)^n}{n!}\right).$$

You may recall from another course in mathematics that there is an irrational number denoted by e which occurs in an essential way in the study of natural logarithms. This number has the approximate value $e \approx 2.718281828459$, and its reciprocal has the approximate value $1/e \approx 0.36787944117$. By one of those fascinating quirks which unexpectedly surface in mathematics from time to time, the number $1/e$ is approximated by

$$1 - \frac{1}{1!} + \frac{1}{2!} - \frac{1}{3!} + \cdots + \frac{(-1)^n}{n!}. \tag{2}$$

Below we give values for the expression (2) for various values of n. Note how closely these values agree with $1/e$ for $n \geq 6$.

n	Values of (2)
4	0.375
6	0.368055555556
8	0.367881944445
10	0.367879464286
15	0.367879441171

To conclude, the number of derangements of n letters is

$$d_n = n!\left(1 - \frac{1}{1!} + \frac{1}{2!} - \frac{1}{3!} + \cdots + \frac{(-1)^n}{n!}\right) \approx \frac{n!}{e}.$$

Since there are $n!$ arrangements (permutations) in all, this result tells us that slightly more than one-third of them are derangements. Hence, if test papers are randomly returned to a class of 10 students (or if test papers are randomly returned to a class of 100 students), the chances are better than 1 in 3 that not a single student receives his or her own paper.

Problems for Section 18

1. Consider the set of digits $\mathbf{D} = \{0, 1, 2, \ldots, 9\}$. If $\mathbf{A}$ is the set of even digits in $\mathbf{D}$ and if $\mathbf{B}$ is the set of primes in $\mathbf{D}$, show that (a) $\mathbf{A} = (\mathbf{A} \cap \mathbf{B}) \cup (\mathbf{A} \cap \overline{\mathbf{B}})$, (b) $\overline{\mathbf{A} \cap \mathbf{B}} = \overline{\mathbf{A}} \cup \overline{\mathbf{B}}$, (c) $|\overline{\mathbf{A} \cup \mathbf{B}}| = 2$.

2. Let $\mathbf{A} = \{a, b, c, d\}$, $\mathbf{B} = \{a, e\}$, $\mathbf{C} = \{b, f\}$ be subsets of $\mathbf{S} = \{a, b, c, d, e, f, g, h\}$. Find (a) $\overline{\mathbf{A}}$, (b) $\overline{\mathbf{B}}$, (c) $\overline{\mathbf{A} \cup \mathbf{B}}$, (d) $\mathbf{A} - \mathbf{B}$, (e) $\mathbf{B} - \mathbf{A}$, (f) $\overline{\mathbf{A}} \cap \overline{\mathbf{B}}$.

3. Recall that an ordered pair of real numbers is a **lattice point** if each coordinate is an integer. Let $\mathbf{A}$ denote the set of lattice points with positive first coordinate, and let $\mathbf{B}$ denote the set of lattice points with positive second coordinate. Relative to the usual rectangular coordinate system, describe each of the relations. (a) $\mathbf{A} \cap \mathbf{B}$, (b) $\mathbf{A} \cup \mathbf{B}$, (c) $\overline{\mathbf{A}} \cap \overline{\mathbf{B}}$ (d) $\overline{\mathbf{A} \cup \mathbf{B}}$.

4. Show that $\overline{\mathbf{A} \cup \mathbf{B}} = \overline{\mathbf{A}} \cap \overline{\mathbf{B}}$.

5. Show that $\overline{\mathbf{A} \cap \overline{\mathbf{B}}} = \overline{\mathbf{A}} \cup \mathbf{B}$.

6. Show that $\overline{(\mathbf{A} \cap \mathbf{B}) \cup \mathbf{C}} = (\overline{\mathbf{A}} \cup \overline{\mathbf{B}}) \cap \overline{\mathbf{C}}$.

7. Show that $\overline{\mathbf{A} \cap (\mathbf{B} \cup \mathbf{C})} = \overline{\mathbf{A}} \cup (\overline{\mathbf{B}} \cap \overline{\mathbf{C}})$.

8. Describe three sets $\mathbf{A}$, $\mathbf{B}$, and $\mathbf{C}$ which illustrate the fact that $(\mathbf{A} \cap \mathbf{B}) \cup \mathbf{C} \neq \mathbf{A} \cap (\mathbf{B} \cup \mathbf{C})$.

9. Consider the following statement: "If $\mathbf{A} \cup \mathbf{B} = \mathbf{A} \cup \mathbf{C}$, then $\mathbf{B} = \mathbf{C}$." (a) Show that, in general, this statement is false. (b) Is the statement necessarily true if $\mathbf{B} \cap \mathbf{C} = \varnothing$? (c) Is the statement necessarily true if $\mathbf{A} \cap (\mathbf{B} \cup \mathbf{C}) = \varnothing$?

10. Prove part **b** of Theorem 18.2 by showing that $\overline{\mathbf{A} \cap \mathbf{B}} = \overline{\mathbf{A}} \cup \overline{\mathbf{B}}$. (See Tutorial 18.2A.)

11. Complete the proof of Theorem 18.3A by showing that $(\mathbf{A} \cap \mathbf{B}) \cup (\mathbf{A} \cap \mathbf{C}) \subseteq \mathbf{A} \cap (\mathbf{B} \cup \mathbf{C})$.

12. Prove Theorem 18.3B by showing that $\mathbf{A} \cup (\mathbf{B} \cap \mathbf{C}) = (\mathbf{A} \cup \mathbf{B}) \cap (\mathbf{A} \cup \mathbf{C})$.

13. If $\mathbf{A}$ and $\mathbf{B}$ are subsets of $\mathbf{S}$, indicate each of the following sets by shading a Venn diagram: (a) $\overline{\mathbf{A}} \cup \overline{\mathbf{B}}$, (b) $\overline{\mathbf{A} \cap \mathbf{B}}$, (c) $\overline{\mathbf{A}} \cap \overline{\mathbf{B}}$, (d) $\overline{\mathbf{A} \cup \mathbf{B}}$.

14. If $\mathbf{A}$ and $\mathbf{B}$ are subsets of $\mathbf{S}$, indicate each of the following sets by shading a Venn diagram: (a) $(\mathbf{A} - \mathbf{B}) \cup (\mathbf{B} - \mathbf{A})$, (b) $(\mathbf{A} \cup \mathbf{B}) - (\mathbf{A} \cap \mathbf{B})$. (See Problem 20 in Section 2.)

15. Assume that $\mathbf{A}$, $\mathbf{B}$, and $\mathbf{C}$ are subsets of a set $\mathbf{S}$. Sketch Venn diagrams suggesting that $(\mathbf{A} \cup \mathbf{B}) \cap \mathbf{C} = (\mathbf{A} \cap \mathbf{C}) \cup (\mathbf{B} \cap \mathbf{C})$.

16. Assume that $\mathbf{A}$, $\mathbf{B}$, and $\mathbf{C}$ are subsets of a set $\mathbf{S}$. Sketch Venn diagrams suggesting that $(\mathbf{A} \cap \mathbf{B}) \cup \mathbf{C} = (\mathbf{A} \cup \mathbf{C}) \cap (\mathbf{B} \cup \mathbf{C})$.

17. Sketch a special Venn diagram which suggests that $(\mathbf{A} \cup \mathbf{B}) \cap \overline{\mathbf{C}}$ is empty.

18. Sketch a special Venn diagram which suggests that $\mathbf{A} \cap \mathbf{B} \neq \varnothing$, $\mathbf{B} \cap \mathbf{C} \neq \varnothing$, $\mathbf{A} \cap \mathbf{C} \neq \varnothing$, and that $\mathbf{A} \cap \mathbf{B} \cap \mathbf{C} = \varnothing$.

19. Let $\mathbf{A}$, $\mathbf{B}$, and $\mathbf{C}$ denote mutually disjoint subsets of a set $\mathbf{S}$. Sketch Venn diagrams which suggest that (a) $\{\mathbf{A}, \mathbf{B}, \mathbf{C}\}$ is a partition of $\mathbf{S}$; (b) $\{\mathbf{A}, \mathbf{B}, \mathbf{C}\}$ is not a partition of $\mathbf{S}$.

20. Construct a partition of the alphabet into five subsets as nearly equal in size as possible.

21. The set of positive integers may be partitioned into three subsets as follows: the unit $\{1\}$, the primes, and the composites. List the 10 smallest composite numbers. (This is not a trick question, just an easy one.)

22. As in paragraph 5.3, let $[r]_3$ denote the set of all integers which have remainder r when divided by 3. (a) Show that $\{[0]_3, [1]_3, [2]_3\}$ is a partition of the set of integers. (b) Let $x \in [1]_3$ and let $y \in [2]_3$. Show that no matter what representatives x and y you choose, $x + y$ is always in $[0]_3$.

23. Let $[r]_5$ denote the set of all integers which have remainder r when divided by 5. Show that $\{[0]_5, [1]_5, [2]_5, [3]_5, [4]_5\}$ is a partition of the set of integers.

24. Let $\mathscr{F}$ denote the set of all functions $f: \{a, b, c\} \to \{a, b, c\}$. (a) Find a partition of $\mathscr{F}$ into three equal parts. (b) Let $\mathbf{F}_1$ denote those functions in $\mathscr{F}$ that are one-to-one. Let $\mathbf{F}_2$ denote those functions in $\mathscr{F}$ that are constant. Let $\mathbf{F}_3$ denote the remaining functions in $\mathscr{F}$. Show that $\{\mathbf{F}_1, \mathbf{F}_2, \mathbf{F}_3\}$ is a partition of $\mathscr{F}$, and display any four of the functions in $\mathbf{F}_3$.

25. Let $\mathcal{F}$ be as in Problem 24 and let $\mathbf{F}_a = \{f \in \mathcal{F}: f(a) = a\}$, $\mathbf{F}_b = \{f \in \mathcal{F}: f(b) = b\}$, and $\mathbf{F}_c = \{f \in \mathcal{F}: f(c) = c\}$. (a) Is $\{\mathbf{F}_a, \mathbf{F}_b, \mathbf{F}_c\}$ a partition of $\mathcal{F}$? (b) What is $|\mathbf{F}_a|$?

26. How many numbers between 1 and 700 (inclusive) are divisible by either 5 or 7?

27. How many numbers between 1 and 1000 (inclusive) are not divisible by 2 or are divisible by 5?

28. How many numbers between 1 and 300 (inclusive) are not divisible by 2 or are not divisible by 5?

29. How many numbers between 1 and 500 (inclusive) (a) are not divisible by both 7 and 11, (b) are divisible by neither 7 nor 11? (See Tutorial 18.2B.)

30. Let $\mathbf{S} = \{n \in \mathbb{N}: 1 \le n \le 300\}$. (a) How many numbers in $\mathbf{S}$ are perfect squares or are divisible by 5? (b) How many numbers in $\mathbf{S}$ are perfect squares or are not divisible by 5?

31. Let $\mathbf{S} = \{n \in \mathbb{N}: 1 \le n \le 276\}$. (a) Show that $|\{x \in \mathbf{S}: 3 \mid x\}| = 92$. (b) How many numbers in $\mathbf{S}$ are divisible by 3 or 7 or 13? (c) How many numbers in $\mathbf{S}$ are not divisible by 3 and by 7 and by 13?

32. How many integers in the set $\{1, 2, \ldots, 600\}$ are divisible by 3 or by 5 or by 7?

33. How many integers in the set $\{1, 2, \ldots, 600\}$ are divisible by 3 or by 5, but not by 7?

34. How many integers in the set $\{1, 2, \ldots, 600\}$ are divisible by 3, 5, 7, or 13?

35. Among 120 students, 90 take mathematics and 72 take history. If 10 students take neither, how many take both?

36. Among 36 students, most take discrete mathematics, calculus, and computer science. Twenty take discrete mathematics, 16 take calculus, and 7 take both discrete mathematics and calculus (some of whom also take computer science). Seven take both computer science and discrete mathematics, and 4 of these take all three courses. The number of students who take just computer science is the same as the number that take both computer science and calculus. How many of these students take no computer science or mathematics courses if there are 11 students taking computer science?

37. In a group of 25 foreign language students, 14 take Spanish, 12 take French, 6 take both Spanish and French, 5 take both German and Spanish, and 2 of these students take all three languages. The 6 who take German also take either Spanish or French. How many fail to take German, French, or Spanish?

38. A zip code is a sequence of five digits in which any digit may be repeated any number of times (for example, 00123 or 24450). Let $\mathbf{S}$ denote the set of zip codes in which only odd digits appear. Let $\mathbf{T}$ denote the subset of $\mathbf{S}$ consisting of those zip codes that contain each of the digits 1, 3, and 7. (a) Find $|\mathbf{S}|$. (b) List any five elements in $\mathbf{T}$.

39. (*Continuation of Problem 38.*) Now define three subsets of $\mathbf{S}$ as follows: $\mathbf{A}$ is the set of zip codes that contain at least one 1. $\mathbf{B}$ is the set of zip codes that contain at least one 3. $\mathbf{C}$ is the set of zip codes that contain at least one 7. (a) What is the relationship between $\mathbf{T}$ and $\mathbf{A} \cap \mathbf{B} \cap \mathbf{C}$? (b) By De Morgan Laws, how else can you write $\overline{\mathbf{A} \cap \mathbf{B} \cap \mathbf{C}}$?

40. (*Conclusion of Problem 38.*) Using Problem 39(b), compute $|\overline{\mathbf{A} \cap \mathbf{B} \cap \mathbf{C}}|$ and evaluate $|\mathbf{T}|$.

41. Recall that in Problem 5 in Section 13 we defined $\phi(n)$ to be the number of integers less than n that are relatively prime to n. For $a \in \mathbb{N}$ and $p \in \mathbb{P}$, let $\mathbf{S} = \{n \in \mathbb{N}: 1 \le n \le p^a\}$ and let $\mathbf{S}_p = \{n \in \mathbf{S}: p \mid n\}$. (a) Compute $|\mathbf{S}_p|$ in terms of p and a. (b) Show that $\gcd(m, p^a) = 1$ if and only if $m \notin \mathbf{S}_p$. (c) Show that $\phi(p^a) = |\mathbf{S}| - |\mathbf{S}_p|$. (d) Conclude from (c) that $\phi(p^a) = p^a - p^{a-1} = p^a \cdot (1 - 1/p)$.

42. (*Continuation of Problem 41.*) Let $\mathbf{S} = \{n \in \mathbb{N}: 1 \le n \le p^a q^b\}$, where p and q are distinct primes. Let $\mathbf{S}_p = \{n \in \mathbf{S}: p \mid n\}$ and $\mathbf{S}_q = \{n \in \mathbf{S}: q \mid n\}$. Compute $|\mathbf{S}_p \cup \mathbf{S}_q|$ in terms of p, q, a, and b.

43. (*Continuation of Problem 41.*) Show that $\gcd(m, p^a q^b) = 1$ if and only if $m \notin \mathbf{S}_p \cup \mathbf{S}_q$.

44. (*Continuation of Problem 41.*) Conclude that $\phi(p^a q^b) = p^a q^b - |\mathbf{S}_p \cup \mathbf{S}_q|$. This answer is usually given as $p^a q^b (1 - 1/p) \cdot (1 - 1/q)$.

45. (*Conclusion of Problem 41.*) If $n = p_1^{e_1} p_2^{e_2} \cdots p_r^{e_r}$, then

$$\phi(n) = n \cdot \left(1 - \frac{1}{p_1}\right) \cdot \left(1 - \frac{1}{p_2}\right) \cdots \left(1 - \frac{1}{p_r}\right)$$

$$= p_1^{e_1} \cdot \left(1 - \frac{1}{p_1}\right) \cdot p_2^{e_2} \cdot \left(1 - \frac{1}{p_2}\right) \cdots$$

$$p_r^{e_r} \cdot \left(1 - \frac{1}{p_r}\right).$$

Compute $\phi(n)$ for (*a*) $n = 24$, (*b*) $n = 60$, (*c*) $n = 100$, (*d*) $n = 3000$, (*e*) $n = 210$, (*f*) $n = 1160$.

Section 19. Generating Functions

Overview for Section 19

- Introduction to and operations with generating functions
- Definition of convolution
- Return to recurrence relations

Key Concepts: indeterminate, generating function, convolution, recurrence relations

19.1 The concept of "generating function" borrows its name, but not its meaning, from Section 13. It is *not* a function in the familiar sense of that term but is simply a formal expression

$$F(x) = a_0 + a_1 x + a_2 x^2 + a_3 x^3 + \cdots. \tag{1}$$

The idea and name date from around 1812. In (1), x is considered just a symbol called an *indeterminate*; it is *not* a variable which is replaced by numbers belonging to some domain. As we will use (1), each coefficient a_n has a combinatorial significance associated with n. In a sense, then, $F(x)$ is a storage facility for combinatorial information.

Example 1 For each nonnegative integer n, let $\mathbf{S}_n$ be a set containing n elements. Let a_n denote the number of elements in the power set of $\mathbf{S}_n$; hence $a_n = 2^n$ as we proved in

Theorem 16.1. Thus we can write

$$F(x) = 2^0 + 2^1 x + 2^2 x^2 + 2^3 x^3 + \cdots = \sum_{k=0}^{\infty} 2^k x^k. \tag{2}$$

As in this example, the right-hand side of (1) may involve an infinite number of terms. Notice how the summation notation is adapted to this situation. Retaining x as an indeterminate, it is often possible to discover a formula for $F(x)$ which can be manipulated algebraically to provide useful combinatorial information or insight. This accounts for the importance of the idea. It happens that there *is* a formula for the generating function in (2), and to find it we must digress briefly to illustrate, in perhaps the simplest possible setting, certain algebraic operations on generating functions. Let

$$z = 1 + y + y^2 + y^3 + \cdots. \tag{3}$$

Now, multiply on each side by y (this may be considered an extended distributive law in which each term on the right-hand side is multiplied by y):

$$yz = y + y^2 + y^3 + \cdots.$$

Since the right-hand side is $z - 1$, we have

$$z - 1 = yz$$
$$z - yz = 1$$

and, finally,

$$z = \frac{1}{1 - y},$$

which is exactly the expression (1) in paragraph 0.6.

Example 2   Continuing Example 1, notice that (2) can be rewritten

$$F(x) = 1 + 2x + (2x)^2 + (2x)^3 + \cdots. \tag{4}$$

The right-hand sides of (3) and (4) are identical if y is replaced by $2x$. Since (3) can be written as $1/(1 - y)$, it follows that (4) can be written as

$$F(x) = \frac{1}{1 - 2x}.$$

19.2   There is an alternate way to derive this formula for $F(x)$ which makes use of information about the coefficients in the form of initial values and a recursion relation. This approach will illustrate the more common situation: The coefficients are unknown, but recursion information is known, and the generating function then becomes the tool by which the coefficients are determined.

Suppose now that we do *not* know a_n, the size of the power set of $\mathbf{S}_n$. In the special case $n = 0$, $\mathbf{S}_0 = \varnothing$, and since $\varnothing$ is the one subset of $\varnothing$, $a_0 = 1$. This is the initial value, and to find the recursion relation, put $\mathbf{S}_{n+1} = \mathbf{S}_n \cup \{a\}$, where $a \notin \mathbf{S}_n$. (Compare this with the proof of Theorem 16.1.) For each subset $\mathbf{B}$ of $\mathbf{S}_n$, both $\mathbf{B}$ and $\mathbf{B} \cup \{a\}$ are subsets of $\mathbf{S}_{n+1}$. This one-to-one correspondence shows that there are twice as many subsets of $\mathbf{S}_{n+1}$ as there are of $\mathbf{S}_n$. Hence, for all n,

$$a_{n+1} = 2a_n \qquad \text{or} \qquad a_{n+1} - 2a_n = 0. \tag{1}$$

Returning to (1) in paragraph 19.1,

$$F(x) = a_0 + a_1 x + a_2 x^2 + a_3 x^3 + \cdots,$$

the idea is to operate algebraically on this formula to produce a new generating function which can be simplified by use of (1). For example, first multiply $F(x)$ by $2x$, then subtract that product from $F(x)$ (remembering to combine like powers of x):

$$F(x) = a_0 + \qquad a_1 x + \qquad a_2 x^2 + \qquad a_3 x^3 + \cdots,$$

$$2x \cdot F(x) = \qquad\qquad 2a_0 x + \qquad 2a_1 x^2 + \qquad 2a_2 x^3 + \cdots,$$

$$F(x) - 2x \cdot F(x) = a_0 + (a_1 - 2a_0)x + (a_2 - 2a_1)x^2 + (a_3 - 2a_2)x^3 + \cdots.$$

Because of the recursion relation (1), and because $a_0 = 1$, this simplifies to

$$F(x) \cdot (1 - 2x) = 1, \qquad \text{or} \qquad F(x) = \frac{1}{1 - 2x}$$

as in Example 2 of paragraph 19.1.

Tutorial 19.2

a. Rewrite each of the following as a summation:

$$F(x) = \frac{1}{1 - 3x},$$

$$G(x) = \frac{1}{1 - x^2},$$

$$H(x) = \frac{1}{1 + x^2}.$$

b. Suppose that $F(x) = a_0 + a_1 x + a_2 x^2 + a_3 x^3 + \cdots$ and $a_0 = 1$, $a_{n+1} = 3a_n$ for all $n \geq 0$. Find $F(x)$.

19.3

As just illustrated, arithmetic operations allow us to create new generating functions from old ones. Let us consider addition and multiplication in a little more detail. Suppose that two generating functions are given:

$$F(x) = a_0 + a_1 x + a_2 x^2 + a_3 x^3 + \cdots = \sum_{i=0}^{\infty} a_i x^i,$$

$$G(x) = b_0 + b_1 x + b_2 x^2 + b_3 x^3 + \cdots = \sum_{i=0}^{\infty} b_i x^i.$$

Addition is immediate (again, remembering that like powers of x combine):

$$F(x) + G(x) = (a_0 + b_0) + (a_1 + b_1)x + (a_2 + b_2)x^2 + \cdots$$

$$= \sum_{i=0}^{\infty} (a_i + b_i)x^i. \tag{1}$$

Multiplication is more complicated but, in principle, is modeled on the familiar rules for multiplying two polynomials. To find the coefficient of x^n in the product

$$F(x) \cdot G(x) = (a_0 + a_1 x + a_2 x^2 + a_3 x^3 + \cdots) \cdot (b_0 + b_1 x + b_2 x^2 + b_3 x^3 + \cdots),$$

consider the sum of all products consisting of one term from $F(x)$ and one term from $G(x)$ whose exponents add up to n. For example, if

$$F(x) = 2 + x + 3x^2 \quad \text{and} \quad G(x) = 3 + 5x + x^2 + x^3,$$

then $$F(x) \cdot G(x) = 6 + 13x + 16x^2 + 18x^3 + 4x^4 + 3x^5.$$

In general, therefore, we can write

$$F(x) \cdot G(x) = a_0 b_0 + (a_0 b_1 + a_1 b_0)x + (a_0 b_2 + a_1 b_1 + a_2 b_0)x^2$$

$$+ (a_0 b_3 + a_1 b_2 + a_2 b_1 + a_3 b_0)x^3 + \cdots + \left(\sum_{i=0}^{n} a_i b_{n-i} \right) x^n + \cdots. \tag{2}$$

Formula (2) is the definition of the product of two generating functions, and it has become customary to distinguish this special kind of multiplication by calling it **convolution.** It turns out to have analogs in many other branches of mathematics.

Example 1

Given two generating functions

$$F(x) = \frac{1}{1-x} = 1 + x + x^2 + x^3 + \cdots$$

and $\quad G(x) = \dfrac{1}{1+x} = \dfrac{1}{1-(-x)} = 1 + (-x) + (-x)^2 + (-x)^3 + \cdots,$

$\qquad\qquad = 1 - x + x^2 - x^3 + \cdots,$

consider the following several operations.

a. $F(x) + F(x) = 2F(x) = 2 + 2x + 2x^2 + 2x^3 + \cdots.$

b. $F(x) + G(x) = \dfrac{1}{1-x} + \dfrac{1}{1+x}$

$\qquad\qquad = \dfrac{(1+x) + (1-x)}{(1-x)(1+x)} = \dfrac{2}{(1-x)(1+x)} = 2F(x) \cdot G(x).$

Note that whether we compute this as a sum by (1) or as a convolution by (2), the result is $2 + 2x^2 + 2x^4 + \cdots.$

c. $F(x) \cdot G(x) = \dfrac{1}{1-x} \cdot \dfrac{1}{1+x} = \dfrac{1}{1-x^2} = 1 + x^2 + x^4 + \cdots,$

which by part **b** is simply the "average" $\frac{1}{2} \cdot (F(x) + G(x)).$

d. $F(x) \cdot F(x) = \left(\dfrac{1}{1-x} \right)^2$

$\qquad\qquad = (1 + x + x^2 + x^3 + \cdots) \cdot (1 + x + x^2 + x^3 + \cdots)$

$\qquad\qquad = 1 + 2x + 3x^2 + 4x^3 + \cdots.$

Tutorial 19.3

With $F(x)$ and $G(x)$ defined as in Example 1:
a. Find the convolution $G(x) \cdot G(x)$.
b. Simplify $F(x) \cdot F(x) - G(x) \cdot G(x)$ algebraically, and express in summation notation.

Example 2

Problem 12 in Section 12 lends itself very nicely to an analysis via generating functions: Find the maximum number of regions into which n lines divide the plane. Let a_n denote the required maximum number of regions into which n lines divide the plane, and consider the generating function

$$F(x) = a_0 + a_1 x + a_2 x^2 + a_3 x^3 + \cdots.$$

The first task is to identify an initial value and a recurrence relation. With zero lines, the plane is not divided at all; hence $a_0 = 1$. Now suppose that some n lines

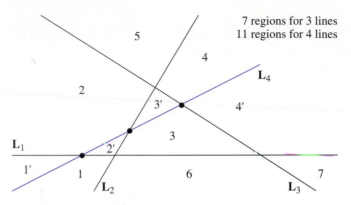

7 regions for 3 lines
11 regions for 4 lines

Figure 19.3

$\mathbf{L_1}, \mathbf{L_2}, \ldots, \mathbf{L_n}$ subdivide the plane into a_n regions. Let $\mathbf{L_{n+1}}$ denote a new line, not parallel to any of the others and not passing through any point in which two other lines intersect. Then $\mathbf{L_{n+1}}$ contains n distinct points of intersection with the lines $\mathbf{L_1}, \mathbf{L_2}, \ldots, \mathbf{L_n}$, and this is the maximum possible number of intersections. These n points subdivide $\mathbf{L_{n+1}}$ into $n + 1$ intervals, each of which divides a previously determined region of the plane into two parts. Hence, $a_{n+1} = a_n + (n + 1)$. Figure 19.3 illustrates this situation for the case $n = 3$.

The desired recurrence relation is

$$a_{n+1} - a_n = n + 1. \tag{3}$$

Now to find the generating function, multiply $F(x)$ by x and subtract:

$$F(x) - x \cdot F(x) = (a_0 + a_1 x + a_2 x^2 + a_3 x^3 + \cdots) - (a_0 x + a_1 x^2 + a_2 x^3 + \cdots)$$
$$= a_0 + (a_1 - a_0)x + (a_2 - a_1)x^2 + (a_3 - a_2)x^3 + \cdots.$$

Because of (3) and the fact that $a_0 = 1$,

$$F(x) \cdot (1 - x) = 1 + x + 2x^2 + 3x^3 + \cdots$$
$$= 1 + x \cdot (1 + 2x + 3x^2 + \cdots)$$
$$= 1 + x \cdot \left(\frac{1}{1 - x}\right)^2$$

by part **d** of Example 1. Finally,

$$F(x) = \frac{1}{1 - x} + \frac{x}{(1 - x)^3} = \frac{x^2 - x + 1}{(1 - x)^3}. \tag{4}$$

19.4   Although Example 2 in paragraph 19.3 does illustrate generating function techniques, it is not particularly efficient from a computational point of view. For example, we know from Figure 19.3 that $a_4 = 11$, but how can we find a_{20}? It is possible to use (4) in paragraph 19.3 to find a_n, in general, but a much more direct procedure is the following. Since $a_0 = 1$ and $a_{n+1} = a_n + (n + 1)$,

$$a_1 = a_0 + 1 = 1 + 1,$$

$$a_2 = 1 + 1 + 2,$$

$$a_3 = 1 + 1 + 2 + 3,$$

and in general,

$$a_n = 1 + 1 + 2 + 3 + \cdots + n = 1 + \frac{n(n + 1)}{2} = \frac{n^2 + n + 2}{2}.$$

The proof here, as in Section 12, involves mathematical induction. Note that we can find a_{20} by a very simple computation:

$$a_{20} = \frac{20^2 + 20 + 2}{2} = 211.$$

We return now to the problem sketched in paragraph 0.6: In how many ways can you make change for a dollar? In the generating function

$$\frac{1}{1 - x^{10}} = 1 + x^{10} + x^{20} + x^{30} + \cdots$$

we may interpret 1 $(= x^0)$ as no dimes, x^{10} as one dime, x^{20} as two dimes, etc. Similarly, in

$$\frac{1}{1 - x^{25}} = 1 + x^{25} + x^{50} + x^{75} + x^{100} + \cdots$$

we may interpret 1 as no quarters, x^{25} as one quarter, x^{50} as two quarters, etc. Convolution turns out to be the critical idea. For example, the sum of terms in

$$\frac{1}{1 - x^{10}} \cdot \frac{1}{1 - x^{25}}$$
$$= (1 + x^{10} + \cdots + x^{50} + \cdots + x^{100} + \cdots) \cdot (1 + x^{25} + x^{50} + x^{100} + \cdots) \quad \textbf{(1)}$$

which involve the power x^{100} is $1 \cdot x^{100} + x^{50} \cdot x^{50} + x^{100} \cdot 1$. This corresponds to the three ways of making a dollar from dimes and quarters only: 4 quarters; 5 dimes plus 2 quarters; and 10 dimes.

The generating function which solves the general problem is

$$\frac{1}{1-x} \cdot \frac{1}{1-x^5} \cdot \frac{1}{1-x^{10}} \cdot \frac{1}{1-x^{25}} \cdot \frac{1}{1-x^{50}}, \tag{2}$$

but to actually produce this multiple convolution is (intolerably) tedious by hand. Since change for a dollar may involve two half-dollars, one half-dollar, or no half-dollars, we will enumerate these cases separately, then add to get the desired number (using FCP I). Furthermore, since pennies must be used in multiples of 5, if we need to produce $5k$ cents using nickels and pennies it can be done in $k+1$ ways: no nickels and all pennies, 1 nickel and the rest pennies, 2 nickels and the rest pennies, $\ldots$, k nickels and no pennies. These 2 observations will allow us to get by with only convolution (1); in detail it is

$$\frac{1}{1-x^{10}} \cdot \frac{1}{1-x^{25}} = 1 + x^{10} + x^{20} + x^{25} + x^{30} + x^{35} + x^{40} + x^{45} + 2x^{50} + x^{55}$$

$$+2x^{60} + x^{65} + 2x^{70} + 2x^{75} + 2x^{80} + 2x^{85} + 2x^{90} + 2x^{95} + 3x^{100} + \cdots . \tag{3}$$

Note, for example, that there are only two ways of making 75 cents with dimes and quarters: three quarters, or one quarter and five dimes. The information is summarized in Table 19.4. The sum of columns A, C, and E is 100 cents ($1) in each case. Columns B, D, and F indicate the number of ways each indicated amount can be produced. The entries in column D are simply the coefficients in (3). Also, an entry in column F is $k+1$, where k is one-fifth the corresponding entry in column E. An entry in column G is the product of the corresponding entries in columns B, D, and F (by FCP II). In the next-to-last line, for example, there are two ways to produce 95 cents using dimes and quarters, and for each of these there are two ways to produce 5 cents using pennies and nickels; hence the entry in column G is 4. The grand total is 292, which is the number of ways you can make change for a dollar.

Example 1

How many ways can you produce a total of n cents? The answer is simply the coefficient of the term involving x^n in the generating function (2). For example, 14 cents can be produced in four ways, shown in the following table:

1¢	5¢	10¢	25¢	50¢
4	2	0	0	0
4	0	1	0	0
9	1	0	0	0
14	0	0	0	0

In Figure 19.4 the expansion of (2) is given for $n \leq 100$ cents.

A	B	C	D	E	F	G
Contributions by half-dollars	# of ways	Contributions by dimes and quarters	# of ways	Contributions by pennies and nickels	# of ways	Total
100¢	1	0¢	1	0¢	1	1
50¢	1	0¢	1	50¢	11	11
50¢	1	10¢	1	40¢	9	9
50¢	1	20¢	1	30¢	7	7
50¢	1	25¢	1	25¢	6	6
50¢	1	30¢	1	20¢	5	5
50¢	1	35¢	1	15¢	4	4
50¢	1	40¢	1	10¢	3	3
50¢	1	45¢	1	5¢	2	2
50¢	1	50¢	2	0¢	1	2
0¢	1	0¢	1	100¢	21	21
0¢	1	10¢	1	90¢	19	19
0¢	1	20¢	1	80¢	17	17
0¢	1	25¢	1	75¢	16	16
0¢	1	30¢	1	70¢	15	15
0¢	1	35¢	1	65¢	14	14
0¢	1	40¢	1	60¢	13	13
0¢	1	45¢	1	55¢	12	12
0¢	1	50¢	2	50¢	11	22
0¢	1	55¢	1	45¢	10	10
0¢	1	60¢	2	40¢	9	18
0¢	1	65¢	1	35¢	8	8
0¢	1	70¢	2	30¢	7	14
0¢	1	75¢	2	25¢	6	12
0¢	1	80¢	2	20¢	5	10
0¢	1	85¢	2	15¢	4	8
0¢	1	90¢	2	10¢	3	6
0¢	1	95¢	2	5¢	2	4
0¢	1	100¢	3	0¢	1	3
						292

Table 19.4

$1 + x + x^2 + x^3 + x^4 + 2x^5 + 2x^6 + 2x^7 + 2x^8 + 2x^9 + 4x^{10} + 4x^{11} + 4x^{12} + 4x^{13} + 4x^{14} + 6x^{15} + 6x^{16} + 6x^{17} + 6x^{18}$

$+ 6x^{19} + 9x^{20} + 9x^{21} + 9x^{22} + 9x^{23} + 9x^{24} + 13x^{25} + 13x^{26} + 13x^{27} + 13x^{28} + 13x^{29} + 18x^{30} + 18x^{31}$

$+ 18x^{32} + 18x^{33} + 18x^{34} + 24x^{35} + 24x^{36} + 24x^{37} + 24x^{38} + 24x^{39} + 31x^{40} + 31x^{41} + 31x^{42} + 31x^{43}$

$+ 31x^{44} + 39x^{45} + 39x^{46} + 39x^{47} + 39x^{48} + 39x^{49} + 50x^{50} + 50x^{51} + 50x^{52} + 50x^{53} + 50x^{54} + 62x^{55}$

$+ 62x^{56} + 62x^{57} + 62x^{58} + 62x^{59} + 77x^{60} + 77x^{61} + 77x^{62} + 77x^{63} + 77x^{64} + 93x^{65} + 93x^{66} + 93x^{67} + 93x^{68}$

$+ 93x^{69} + 112x^{70} + 112x^{71} + 112x^{72} + 112x^{73} + 112x^{74} + 134x^{75} + 134x^{76} + 134x^{77} + 134x^{78} + 134x^{79}$

$+ 159x^{80} + 159x^{81} + 159x^{82} + 159x^{83} + 159x^{84} + 187x^{85} + 187x^{86} + 187x^{87} + 187x^{88} + 187x^{89} + 218x^{90}$

$+ 218x^{91} + 218x^{92} + 218x^{93} + 218x^{94} + 252x^{95} + 252x^{96} + 252x^{97} + 252x^{98} + 252x^{99} + 292x^{100} + \cdots$

Figure 19.4   Generating function for how to make change for n cents.

Tutorial 19.4

In two ways, confirm the coefficient of x^{22} in Figure 19.4. First, complete the table and count entries, and second, use generating functions.

1¢	5¢	10¢
2	0	2

19.5

Complement: Catalan Numbers In Example 1 of paragraph 0.3 we discussed briefly the problem of computing the product of multiple factors

$$x_1 x_2 x_3 \cdots x_n.$$

We will assume that the factors always remain in the same order; since multiplication is a binary operation, it will be performed only on two numbers at a time which we will assume are always adjacent. Our problem is to determine the number of different patterns (of computing intermediate products) which are possible in finding the product of n factors. Because this question was considered and answered by the mathematician Eugene C. Catalan, we call this number (of possible patterns for the product of n factors) a **Catalan number** and denote it by C_n. Hence, we can write the formal expression (or generating function)

$$G(x) = C_0 + C_1 x + C_2 x^2 + C_3 x^3 + C_4 x^4 + \cdots. \tag{1}$$

With zero factors there is no number; hence we agree to put $C_0 = 0$. For later convenience we will put $C_1 = 1$. Recall from paragraph 0.3 that we actually discovered the first few Catalan numbers: $C_2 = 1$, $C_3 = 2$, $C_4 = 5$. To try to get a feeling for what's going on, we review these earlier patterns and construct the pattern for C_5.

Pattern type

$n = 2$: (x_1x_2)
$C_2 = C_1C_1 = 1$

$n = 3$: $((x_1x_2)x_3)$ C_2C_1—1
$(x_1(x_2x_3))$ C_1C_2—1
$C_3 = C_2C_1 + C_1C_2 = 2$

$n = 4$: $((x_1x_2x_3)x_4)$ C_3C_1—2
$((x_1x_2)(x_3x_4))$ C_2C_2—1
$(x_1(x_2x_3x_4))$ C_1C_3—2
$C_4 = C_3C_1 + C_2C_2 + C_1C_3 = 5$

$n = 5$: $((x_1x_2x_3x_4)x_5)$ C_4C_1—5
$((x_1x_2x_3)(x_4x_5))$ C_3C_2—2
$((x_1x_2)(x_3x_4x_5))$ C_2C_3—2
$(x_1(x_2x_3x_4x_5))$ C_1C_4—5
$C_5 = C_4C_1 + C_3C_2 + C_2C_3 + C_1C_4 = 14$

In the display for $n = 4$, for example, the first pattern type is

$$((x_1x_2x_3)\underbrace{}_{C_3} x_4\underbrace{}_{C_1}).$$

That part of the pattern designated C_3 can be reduced to a single number in exactly C_3 ways (as already determined immediately above). Again, projecting ahead to $n = 7$, there are exactly seven pattern types to consider, one of which is

$$((x_1x_2x_3)\underbrace{}_{C_3} (x_4x_5x_6x_7)\underbrace{}_{C_4})).$$

Since there are two ways to compute $(x_1x_2x_3)$ and five ways to compute $(x_4x_5x_6x_7)$, by FCP II this pattern type contributes 10 different ways of computing $(x_1x_2x_3x_4x_5x_6x_7)$. To determine C_7, we must add the contribution of all seven pattern types,

$$C_7 = C_6C_1 + C_5C_2 + C_4C_3 + C_3C_4 + C_2C_5 + C_1C_6.$$

Referring to (2) in paragraph 19.3, it seems clear that convolution is involved here. With this clue, we consider

$$(G(x))^2 = \left(\sum_{k=0}^{\infty} C_k x^k\right) \times \left(\sum_{k=0}^{\infty} C_k x^k\right)$$

$$= C_0 C_0 + (C_1 C_0 + C_0 C_1)x + (C_2 C_0 + C_1 C_1 + C_0 C_2)x^2$$

$$+ (C_3 C_0 + C_2 C_1 + C_1 C_2 + C_0 C_3)x^3 + \cdots + \left(\sum_{j=0}^{k} C_{k-j} C_j\right) x^k + \cdots.$$

Recalling that $C_0 = 0$, this becomes

$$(G(x))^2 = C_2 x^2 + C_3 x^3 + C_4 x^4 + \cdots + C_k x^k + \cdots.$$

By (1), the right-hand side is $G(x) - x$; hence

$$(G(x))^2 - G(x) + x = 0. \tag{2}$$

Whatever $G(x)$ may be, it satisfies the quadratic equation (2), which can be solved for $G(x)$ by the quadratic formula to get

$$G(x) = \frac{1 \pm \sqrt{1 - 4x}}{2}.$$

The final task is the expansion of $\sqrt{1 - 4x}$ by (2) in paragraph 17.5:

$$(1 + (-4x))^{1/2} = 1 + \tfrac{1}{2}(-4x) + \sum_{k=2}^{\infty} \frac{(-1)^{k-1}}{2^{2k-1} \cdot k} \binom{2k-2}{k-1} \cdot (-4x)^k$$

$$= 1 - 2x - \sum_{k=2}^{\infty} \frac{2}{k} \cdot \binom{2k-2}{k-1} \cdot x^k.$$

To avoid negative coefficients, we choose $G(x) = \tfrac{1}{2} - (\sqrt{1 - 4x})/2$; hence

$$G(x) = \tfrac{1}{2} - \tfrac{1}{2} \cdot (1 - 2x - \sum_{k=2}^{\infty} \frac{2}{k}\binom{2k-2}{k-1} \cdot x^k)$$

$$= x + \sum_{k=2}^{\infty} \frac{1}{k}\binom{2k-2}{k-1} \cdot x^k. \tag{3}$$

Comparing (3) with (1), we see that for $k \geq 2$,

$$C_k = \frac{1}{k}\binom{2k-2}{k-1} = \frac{1}{k}\binom{2(k-1)}{k-1}. \tag{4}$$

In some texts, the Catalan numbers are defined by the equivalent formula $\frac{1}{n+1}\cdot\binom{2n}{n}$. Using (4), here is a list of the first 10 Catalan numbers:

$C_1 = 1;$ $C_2 = 1;$ $C_3 = 2;$ $C_4 = 5;$ $C_5 = 14;$ $C_6 = 42;$

$C_7 = 132;$ $C_8 = 429;$ $C_9 = 1430;$ $C_{10} = 4862.$

Problems for Section 19

1. This question involves several modifications of the generating function: $1/(1-y) = 1+y+y^2+y^3+\cdots$. Write the first five terms, then the coefficient of x^n, if y is replaced by (a) $(-x)$, (b) $x/2$, (c) $(1+a)\cdot x$, (d) x^2, (e) $\sqrt{x}$.

2. This question involves several modifications of the generating function: $1/(1-y)^2 = 1 + 2y + 3y^2 + 4y^3 + \cdots$. Write the first five terms, then the coefficient of x^n, if y is replaced by (a) $(-x)$, (b) $x/2$, (c) x^2.

3. (a) Write $1/(1-x)^3$ as

$$\frac{1}{1-x}\cdot\frac{1}{(1-x)^2}.$$

and compute the first five terms. (b) What is the coefficient of x^n? (*Hint:* Consider a diagonal in Pascal's triangle.)

4. (*Continuation of Problem 3.*) (a) Compute the first five terms of $1/(1-x)^4$. (b) What is the coefficient of x^n? (*Hint:* Consider a diagonal in Pascal's triangle.)

5. (*Conclusion of Problem 3.*) Considering Example 1 in paragraph 19.3, what would be the coefficient of x^n in $1/(1-x)^m$?

In Problems 6 to 9, let $F(x) = a_0 + a_1 x + a_2 x^2 + a_3 x^3 + \cdots$. Find a simple formula for F given the coefficients in each problem.

6. Let $a_n = 2$ for all n. Use the extended distributive law.

7. Let $a_n = n$ for all n. Use part **d** in Example 1 of paragraph 19.3.

8. Let $a_n = 3^n$ for all n. This is like Example 2 of paragraph 19.1.

9. Let

$$a_n = \begin{cases} 1, & \text{if } n = k, \\ 0, & \text{if } n \neq k, \end{cases}$$

for some fixed positive integer k.

10. Using $H(x)$ in part **a** of Tutorial 19.2, find a_n for $n = 0, 1, 2, 3,$ and 4 in each of the following:
(a) $\dfrac{1-x}{1+x^2}$, (b) $\dfrac{x^2-x+2}{x^2+1}$.

Let $F(x) = a_0 + a_1 x + a_2 x^2 + a_3 x^3 + \cdots$ for Problems 11 to 14.

11. What is the coefficient of x^n in $F(x) + \dfrac{1}{1-x}$?

12. What is the coefficient of x^n in $F(x) - 2x\cdot F(x)$?

13. What is the coefficient of x^n in $F(x) - 2x\cdot F(x) - \dfrac{1}{1-x}$?

14. What is the coefficient of x^n in

$$F(x) - x \cdot F(x) + \frac{x}{(1-x)^2}?$$

In Problems 15 to 18, determine the generating function corresponding to the given initial value and recurrence relations.

15. $a_0 = 1$, $a_{n+1} = a_n + 1$.

16. $a_0 = 1$, $a_{n+1} = 2a_n$.

17. $a_0 = 2$, $a_{n+1} = -2a_n + 1$.

18. $a_0 = 0$, $a_{n+1} = a_n - n$. Recall that

$$\sum_{n=1}^{\infty} (n \cdot x^n) = \frac{x}{(1-x)^2}.$$

Now we find the generating function $G(x)$ for the Fibonacci sequence $F_1 = F_2 = 1$ and $F_{n+2} = F_{n+1} + F_n$.

19. If $F_0 = 0$, then the Fibonacci series has the form $G(x) = F_0 + F_1 x + F_2 x^2 + F_3 x^3 + \cdots$. Replace F_i by the ith Fibonacci number for $0 \le i \le 10$.

20. (*Continuation of Problem 19.*) (*a*) Compute the first five terms of $G(x) - xG(x) - x^2 G(x)$. (*b*) Find $G(x) - xG(x) - x^2 G(x)$.

21. (*Conclusion of Problem 19.*) (*a*) Find $G(x)$ in closed form. (*b*) Use the quadratic formula to find the roots of the denominator. The larger root is the *golden section* (see paragraph 7.6).

22. In how many ways can you make change for a quarter using only: (*a*) nickels or dimes; (*b*) nickels, dimes, or pennies?

23. In how many ways can you change a $5 bill using only (*a*) $1 bills or half-dollars, (*b*) $1 bills, half-dollars, or quarters?

24. In how many ways can you change a $5 bill using only (*a*) $1 or $2 bills, (*b*) $1 bills, $2 bills, or half-dollars?

25. What is the coefficient of x^n in (*a*) $(1 + x)^n$, (*b*) $(1 + x)^{n+1}$, (*c*) $(1 + x)^{n+2}$, (*d*) $(1 + x)^{n+k}$?

26. (*Continuation of Problem 25.*) Using the geometric series, compute $1 + (1 + x) + (1 + x)^2 + (1 + x)^3 + \cdots + (1 + x)^m$. If you are squeamish about this, let $z = 1 + x$ and compute $1 + z + z^2 + z^3 + \cdots + z^m$. Refer to Problem 18 in Section 13.

27. (*Continuation of Problem 25.*) Compute $(1 + x)^n + (1 + x)^{n+1} + (1 + x)^{n+2} + \cdots + (1 + x)^{n+m}$. [*Hint:* Let $w = (1 + x)^n$ and $z = 1 + x$. You are computing $w + w \cdot z + w \cdot z^2 + w \cdot z^3 + \cdots + w \cdot z^m$.]

28. (*Continuation of Problem 25.*) (*a*) What is the coefficient of x^n in $(1 + x)^n \cdot (1 + x)^{m+1}$? [*Hint:* Write this first as $(1 + x)^{m+n+1}$.] (*b*) What is the coefficient of x^n in

$$\frac{(1 + x)^{m+n+1}}{x}?$$ (*c*) What is the coefficient

of x^n in $\dfrac{(1 + x)^n}{x}$? (*d*) What is the coefficient

of x^n in

$$\frac{(1 + x)^{m+n+1} - (1 + x)^n}{x}?$$

29. (*Conclusion of Problem 25.*) Why must the coefficient of x^n in $(1 + x)^n + (1 + x)^{n+1} + (1 + x)^{n+2} + (1 + x)^{n+3} + \cdots + (1 + x)^{n+m}$ be the same as the coefficient of x^n in your answer from Problem 28(*d*)? Equate these coefficients to get the useful identity

$$\sum_{k=0}^{m} \binom{n + k}{n} = \binom{m + n + 1}{n + 1}.$$

30. This problem is for those who know how to differentiate a polynomial. Using the Binomial Theorem gives

$$(1 + x)^n = \sum_{k=0}^{n} \binom{n}{k} x^k$$

$$= \binom{n}{0} + \binom{n}{1} x^1 + \binom{n}{2} x^2 + \cdots + \binom{n}{n} x^n.$$

(a) Differentiate the far left and the far right sides. (b) Substitute 1 for x to derive

$$n \cdot 2^{n-1} = \sum_{k=1}^{n} k \cdot \binom{n}{k}.$$

(c) If you don't believe in this kind of magic, verify the identity in (b) for $n = 2, 3, 4,$ and 5 and then find another proof.

CHAPTER 4

Probability and Statistics

Section 20.   Probability Computations

Overview for Section 20

- Examples illustrating probability as a ratio
- Experimental frequency ratios
- Outline of problem-solving procedure
- Probability of complementary events

Key Concepts: probability ratio, at random, equally likely, sample space, event, complement

20.1   The systematic study of probability theory has its roots in the seventeenth century, specifically in correspondence between Blaise Pascal (1623–1662) in Paris and Pierre de Fermat (1601–1665) in Toulouse. A French nobleman, much addicted to gambling, had approached Pascal for an explanation of his seemingly paradoxical observations related to a certain game of chance (described in Problems 34 to 36). Pascal solved that problem and, in a subsequent exchange of letters about it and similar questions, he and Fermat established the foundations of probability theory. During more than three centuries since that time, the subject has grown from its frivolous beginning into an impressive structure adequate to deal with some of the most complex questions of modern science. But the elements of the subject are quite simple, arising from the most basic questions one might ask. In the next four sections we will bring together the key ideas as they occur in our examples; only then will we introduce the axiomatic structure upon which probability theory rests.

Roughly speaking, "probability" is a measure of how confident we are that some uncertain event will occur, or perhaps has occurred. "Probability theory" is an intellectual framework constructed to support our assessment of probability. There are two kinds of problems leading to questions about how likely a particular event is to occur. One of these can be described in terms of intervals or areas and is called "continuous"; the other is concerned with finite sets of objects and is termed "discrete." In this book we will deal primarily with discrete probability, but for the sake of contrast we begin with a continuous problem, typical of the kind that can be solved without resorting to advanced mathematical concepts.

Example 1

Two sprinters are about to run the 100-yard dash in a track meet. Based on prior experience we expect each runner to post a time somewhere between 9.5 and 10.3 seconds. Because our timing equipment isn't perfect, if the runners reach the finish line within 0.01 second of one another, then we are unable to distinguish a winner and must call the race a draw. Our question is, "How likely is this race to end in a draw?"

To get an answer to the question, we must build a mathematical model which in some reasonable way describes the possible outcomes of the race and distinguishes from among all of them those which indicate a draw. Here's a way to think about this situation. Label one of the runners X and the other Y, and let x denote the instant that X arrives at the finish line and y denote the instant that Y arrives at the finish line (see Figure 20.1A). Thus, the point with coordinates (x, y) represents one particular way in which the race might end. A point such as (y, y) lying on the line denoted by Δ would indicate a dead heat (X and Y arrive at exactly the same instant). Notice in Figure 20.1A that points close to Δ indicate arrival times close together, while points farther away from Δ indicate more widely separated arrival times. (Incidentally, for points below Δ, Y wins the race and for points above Δ, X wins the race.) Now observe that if Y arrives at a particular instant y and if X arrives at any instant in the interval

$$y - \tfrac{1}{100} < x < y + \tfrac{1}{100},$$

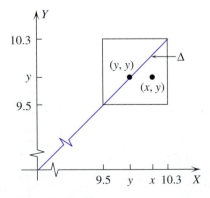

Figure 20.1A

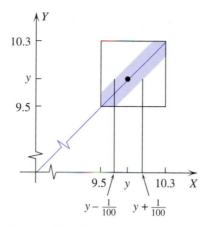

Figure 20.1B

then we must declare the race a draw. The set of all possible such points is indicated by the shaded area of Figure 20.1B.

The set

$$\mathbf{S} = \{(x, y): 9.5 < x < 10.3, 9.5 < y < 10.3\}$$

consists of all points in the square shown in Figure 20.1A, and our assumption is that the actual outcome of the race is described by a point in $\mathbf{S}$ which is no more likely to be in one part of the square than any other. Since each point in the shaded area corresponds to a draw, it seems reasonable to claim that the ratio of the area of the shaded piece in Figure 20.1B to the area of the entire square measures how likely it is that the race ends in a draw. We call this ratio the "probability of a draw," and we calculate it as follows. The total area of $\mathbf{S}$ is $(10.3 - 9.5) \cdot (10.3 - 9.5) = (0.8)^2 = 0.64$. To find the shaded area, we first find the area of *each* unshaded triangle in Figure 20.1B,

$$\tfrac{1}{2} \cdot (0.8 - 0.01)^2 = \tfrac{1}{2} \cdot (0.79)^2 = 0.31 \text{ approximately.}$$

So the shaded area is approximately

$$0.64 - 0.62 = 0.02,$$

and the probability we are looking for is the ratio $(0.02)/(0.64) = 0.03$.   ⬤

We focus now on a discrete problem almost identical, otherwise, to that described in Example 1. In it, we assume that each one of a pair of dice is a small cube marked so that its six faces are distinguished from one another by a different number of dots, from one to six. Thus, when rolled on a horizontal surface, a pair of dice might come to rest with uppermost faces showing (for example) three dots on one die and six dots on the other. (Note that it is customary to refer to a single cube in a pair of dice as a "die.")

Example 2

Suppose you play a game in which a pair of dice is rolled and you win if the two faces showing differ by *at most* 1. The question is, "How likely are you to win?"

To analyze this situation, it will help to think of labeling one of the cubes X and the other cube Y. Then the ordered pair (x, y) will indicate that the X die has the number x showing and the Y die has the number y showing. Of course, the number of such ordered pairs is 36, by FCP II, since the first coordinate can be filled with any one of the six face numbers on the X die, and similarly for the second coordinate. For convenience, we let

$$\mathbf{S} = \{(x, y): x = 1, 2, \ldots, 6 \text{ and } y = 1, 2, \ldots, 6\}$$
$$= \{(1, 1), (1, 2), (1, 3), (1, 4), (1, 5), (1, 6),$$
$$(2, 1), (2, 2), (2, 3), (2, 4), (2, 5), (2, 6),$$
$$\cdots$$
$$(6, 1), (6, 2), (6, 3), (6, 4), (6, 5), (6, 6)\}.$$

The set $\mathbf{S}$ is represented by the marked intersections in Figure 20.1C, and we will assume that when the dice are rolled there is no reason to expect one of these points more than any other. Now notice that you will win if one of the points on or next to the diagonal Δ occurs. The number of those points is 16; hence the ratio $\frac{16}{36}$ is a measure of how likely you are to win the game. As in Example 1, we call this ratio, which is $\frac{4}{9}$, the "probability that you win this game." ⬤

Referring to Example 2, in any given roll of the dice either you win the game or you lose the game, so what does "$\frac{4}{9}$" mean? A possible way to interpret it is as

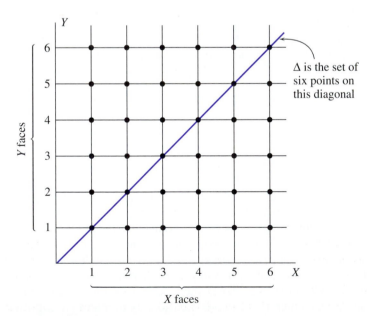

Δ is the set of six points on this diagonal

Figure 20.1C

follows. Let a pair of dice, not biased in any way, be rolled n times, and let m denote the number of times that the faces shown differ by at most 1. Then the ratio m/n should be close to $\frac{4}{9}$ when n is large.

Tutorial 20.1

Is the prediction just made really accurate? You can test it by an actual experiment. Roll a pair of dice 90 times, keeping a record of how often the faces differ by at most 1. As you do this, fill in the following table:

n	1	2	3	4	10	18
m						
m/n						

n	30	50	70	90	...
m					
m/n					

Your ratios for larger values of n should generally be closer to $\frac{4}{9}$ than the others.

20.2 As suggested by the examples above, there are many "chance" occurrences in the real world; and while an individual occurrence may be uncertain, many like occurrences may fall into a predictable pattern. The discipline of mathematical statistics has grown up to study such variability, and probability is the underlying language of statistics. The interpretation of probability involving relative frequency of occurrence offers, in many situations, an opportunity for experimental confirmation of the theory to be developed later. We will concentrate for the time being on describing mathematical models which allow the computation of probabilities based on a few appealingly simple assumptions. Another example will help illustrate this approach.

Example 1 Let **D** represent the set of 52 cards in a well-shuffled deck of playing cards. (See the remark preceding Problem 40 in Section 16.) If a single card is drawn from **D**, then it is reasonable to claim that $\frac{1}{4}$ is the probability of its being a spade (since 13 of the 52 possible cards are spades, there is a 1 in 4 chance of drawing a spade). Now, consider the question, "If a pair of cards is drawn from **D**, what is the probability that both cards are spades?"

As in Example 2 of paragraph 20.1, this one suggests an experiment, called $\mathscr{E}$, which you might perform actually (if you had a deck of cards) or in your imagination.

In either case, we assume that the two cards are drawn **at random,** a phrase intended to mean that a given pair of cards is no more likely to be drawn than any other. In practice, randomness is approximated by drawing from a well-shuffled deck. The answer to our question, above, depends critically upon a careful description of the experiment and its possible outcomes. After a performance of this experiment, you hold in your hand a pair of cards, that is, a 2-element subset of **D**, such as one of the following:

$$\{\text{ace of spades, 2 of hearts}\} \quad \text{or} \quad \{\text{10 of clubs, 4 of clubs}\}. \quad \textbf{(1)}$$

Any such two-element subset is a possible outcome of $\mathscr{E}$; hence the set of all outcomes may be denoted by

$$\mathbf{S} = \{\mathbf{B} \subseteq \mathbf{D} \colon |\mathbf{B}| = 2\}.$$

Note that an element in **S** is *not* one of the cards from **D**. It *is* a two-card subset of **D**.

The size of **S** is easy to find: it is simply the number of subsets of size 2 of a set of size 52; hence

$$|\mathbf{S}| = \binom{52}{2} = 1326.$$

Among the elements of **S**, we are concerned with those which satisfy the condition that both cards are spades: for example, {ace of spades, 10 of spades} or {king of spades, 2 of spades}. For convenience, let **A** denote the subset of **S** consisting of those pairs in which both cards are spades, and note that since **D** contains exactly 13 spades,

$$|\mathbf{A}| = \binom{13}{2} = 78.$$

One of our goals has been to describe the set **S** in such a way that its elements are **equally likely,** a phrase like "at random" intended to mean that each of the possible outcomes is just as likely to occur as any other. Under this assumption, it becomes reasonable to define the probability that an outcome is in **A** to be the ratio $|\mathbf{A}|/|\mathbf{S}|$. Hence, the probability that both cards drawn are spades is

$$\tfrac{78}{1326} = \tfrac{1}{17}.$$

Example 2 of paragraph 20.1 and Example 1 illustrate nicely the sequence of ideas which enter into the computation of discrete probabilities:

- A carefully described experiment, denoted usually by $\mathscr{E}$.

- A description in mathematical terms of the set of all outcomes of $\mathscr{E}$; this set is called the **sample space** of $\mathscr{E}$, denoted usually by **S**.

- The identification of a particular subset of **S** which is of interest.

- The assignment of a number which measures our confidence that a performance of $\mathcal{E}$ will lead to an outcome in the particular subset of interest.

20.3

In general, any subset of **S** is called an **event,** and if the subset we are interested in is denoted by **A,** then the number assigned in the final step of the preceding sequence is called the **probability of A,** and is denoted by $P(\mathbf{A})$. If the experiment is performed and if it produces any outcome that belongs to **A**, then we say that the event **A** has **occurred.**

The schedule of activity suggested in the following diagram will dominate our approach to probability:

$$\mathcal{E} \to \mathbf{S} \to \mathbf{A} \to P(\mathbf{A}). \tag{1}$$

That is, we must understand the experiment, know its sample space, be given an event, and find the probability.

Tutorial 20.3

Return to Example 2 of paragraph 20.1.
a. Describe the experiment $\mathcal{E}$.
b. What is the sample space **S**?
c. Let **A** denote the event that the same number shows on each face. List the elements in **A**.
d. What is the probability of **A**?

Perhaps the most important skill to acquire in analyzing probability questions is the ability to describe the experiment accurately and to identify the sample space completely and unambiguously. Once this has been done, it is often easy to determine the numbers $|\mathbf{S}|$ and $|\mathbf{A}|$, hence to compute $P(\mathbf{A}) = |\mathbf{A}|/|\mathbf{S}|$ (assuming the outcomes to be equally likely). After an experiment has been described, it is often helpful to list several typical outcomes, then to think carefully about the mathematical symbolism required to specify an outcome of the experiment. Notice how this was done in each of the earlier examples. Considering the experiment described in Example 1 of paragraph 20.2, typical elements in **S** are displayed in (1) in paragraph 20.2 and note, in general, that any outcome of $\mathcal{E}$ is simply a 2-element set $\{a, b\}$, where a and b are elements in **D**. Having indicated **S** in this way, it turns out that $|\mathbf{S}|$ is easy to determine. It is intuitively reasonable to assume that the elements of **S** are equally likely; hence we computed the probability of the given event **A** by the ratio $|\mathbf{A}|/|\mathbf{S}|$.

20.4

The experiment $\mathcal{E}$ is not a set, but its sample space $\mathbf{S}$ is a set, and we will assume from this point on that $\mathbf{S}$ is finite. For any event, the probability turns out to be a number between 0 and 1. Probabilities close to 0 represent events that may be considered very unlikely to occur, while those close to 1 represent events that may be considered almost certain to occur. For this reason, it is customary to include the extreme cases: An **impossible** event is assigned probability 0, and a **certain** event is assigned probability 1. Because $\mathbf{S}$ is finite, these extreme cases correspond, respectively, to the events $\varnothing$ and $\mathbf{S}$. [Note, that both $\varnothing$ and $\mathbf{S}$ are subsets of $\mathbf{S}$ and that $P(\varnothing) = |\varnothing|/|\mathbf{S}| = 0$ and $P(\mathbf{S}) = |\mathbf{S}|/|\mathbf{S}| = 1$.]

Example 1

Suppose that two different integers are chosen from the set $\{1, 2, 3, 4, 5\}$. What is the probability that their sum is less than 7? The experiment here is to choose two distinct positive integers less than 6. The sample space consists of all possible such pairs, each of which is an outcome of the experiment:

$$\mathbf{S} = \{\{1, 2\}, \{1, 3\}, \ldots, \{4, 5\}\}.$$

Since there are $\binom{5}{2}$ such outcomes, $|\mathbf{S}| = 10$. To complete our model, we will assume that each of these outcomes is equally likely; hence the probability assignment for each is $\frac{1}{10}$.

The event that the sum is less than 3 is the set $\mathbf{A} = \{\{1, 2\}, \{1, 3\}, \{1, 4\}, \{1, 5\}, \{2, 3\}, \{2, 4\}\}$. The probability that $\mathbf{A}$ occurs is the sum of the individual probabilities which is just the ratio $|\mathbf{A}|/|\mathbf{S}|$; hence $P(\mathbf{A}) = \frac{6}{10}$. The event that the sum is less than 10 is "certain"; hence its probability must be assigned the value 1. Similarly, the event that the sum is less than 3 is "impossible"; hence its probability must be assigned the value 0.

In Example 1, note that there is an occurrence "contrary" to the event $\mathbf{A}$; namely, that the sum is greater than or equal to 7. Denoting this occurrence by the usual symbol for the complement of $\mathbf{A}$ (with respect to $\mathbf{S}$),

$$\mathbf{S} - \mathbf{A} = \overline{\mathbf{A}},$$

it is clear that $\overline{\mathbf{A}}$ also is an event since it is a subset of the sample space. Note that

$$\overline{\mathbf{A}} = \{\{2, 5\}, \{3, 4\}, \{3, 5\}, \{4, 5\}\};$$

hence, $|\overline{\mathbf{A}}| = 4$, and its probability is

$$P(\overline{\mathbf{A}}) = \frac{4}{10} = 1 - \frac{6}{10}.$$

In general, if $\mathbf{A}$ is any event in a sample space $\mathbf{S}$, then the probability of the contrary event is

$$P(\overline{\mathbf{A}}) = 1 - P(\mathbf{A}). \tag{1}$$

Returning to Example 2 in paragraph 20.1, the probability that you will lose the game is $\frac{20}{36}$, which can be written as $1 - \frac{16}{36}$ (that is, 1 minus the probability of winning).

Tutorial 20.4

a. In Example 1 of paragraph 20.1, what is the probability that the race will not end in a draw?

b. In Example 2 of paragraph 20.1, suppose **A** is the event that the faces differ by exactly 1. Describe the event $\overline{\mathbf{A}}$, and find its probability.

c. In Example 1 of paragraph 20.2, describe the event $\overline{\mathbf{A}}$ and find its probability.

Example 2

What is the probability that at least two of four individuals have birthdays falling in the same month? The experiment here consists of determining the birth month of each of four individuals. Identifying them as 1, 2, 3, and 4, we may record the information as an ordered quadruple in which each coordinate is the birth month of that individual. For example, (Dec., Jan., Apr., Oct.) indicates that the individual identified as "1" was born in December, "2" was born in January, and so on. The sample space **S** consists of the set of all possible such quadruples, and by FCP II,

$$|\mathbf{S}| = 12^4 = 20,736.$$

To facilitate the probability assignments, we will make two assumptions: The four individuals are selected randomly, and the 12 months are equally likely as birth months.

The event **A** in question is the set of all quadruples having at least one month repeated among the coordinates. To enumerate **A** directly, we would need to consider quadruples with two repeated months, three repeated months, and four repeated months. This could be done by the principle of inclusion-exclusion, for example, but a much easier procedure is available. The contrary event $\overline{\mathbf{A}}$ turns out to be simple both to describe and to enumerate; it consists of those quadruples in which no month is repeated. Each such quadruple is a permutation of 12 things taken 4 at a time. By (3) in paragraph 16.3,

$$|\overline{\mathbf{A}}| = (12)_4 = \frac{12!}{8!} = 11,880.$$

Referring now to the argument which precedes this example, observe that $P(\mathbf{A})$ and $P(\overline{\mathbf{A}})$ are just numbers; hence (1) can be rewritten $P(\mathbf{A}) = 1 - P(\overline{\mathbf{A}})$. Thus,

$$P(\mathbf{A}) = 1 - \frac{11880}{20736} = \frac{8856}{20736} = \frac{41}{96}$$

is the probability that at least two of the four individuals have the same birth month.

Complement: Occupancy Problems It happens that these introductory probability concepts find a serious application in the effort by modern physicists to explain the experimentally observed behavior of elementary particles such as photons and electrons. According to theory, such particles may exist in any one of a number of states (or energy levels). Consider a collection of k particles, each of which may be found in one of n allowed states, and let a_{nk} denote the number of distinct ways in which the k particles may be distributed among the n states. Since we may think of each particle as occupying its state, this illustrates a fragment of combinatorial mathematics usually referred to as "the occupancy problem." The actual number of distributions depends upon assumed characteristics about the particles, the states, and the kind of occupancy. For example, are particles distinguishable from one another, are states distinguishable from one another, and can states be occupied by more than one particle? If the various distributions (for a particular occupancy problem) may be considered equally likely, then we assign to any one of them the probability $1/a_{nk}$. As a matter of fact, based on this probability assignment, theoretical predictions about certain elementary particles have been verified by experiment. In statistical mechanics, the branch of physics which deals with this sort of question, such probability assignments are called "statistics." We will consider in detail one such assignment, the Bose-Einstein statistics, which was referred to in Example 1 of paragraph 0.2 where the k \$1 bills correspond to particles and your n friends correspond to the states.

Suppose we are given a collection of k photons, indistinguishable from one another, and suppose that any number of them may be in any one of the n distinguishable states. There are several techniques which might be used to calculate the number a_{nk}. One of them involves the use of two-variable generating functions and is outlined in the problem set for this section. We will use here a somewhat simpler technique. The mathematical model which describes this problem must distinguish the n given states but not the k given photons. Consider first the simple case in which $n = 3$ and $k = 3$. Suppose we denote the three photons by asterisks: * * *. Now we need to put them in states identified as number 1, number 2, and number 3. Recall that a horizontal line is divided by two points into three pieces, which can be identified from left to right as first, second, and third. Combining these ideas, the diagram

describes the distribution with one photon in state 1, two photons in state 2, and zero photons in state 3. Every distribution can be described in this way by five marks on a line, three of which are asterisks and the remaining two are dots. Thus a distribution is determined when three of the five marks on the line are selected to be the asterisks.

The number of such distributions is simply $\binom{5}{3}$; hence $a_{3,3} = \binom{5}{3} = 10$, and this is the verification asked for in Example 1 in paragraph 0.2.

This special case is easily generalized to k photons and n states. Recall that only $n - 1$ marks are required to divide the line into n pieces. Placing the k other marks along the line gives us a total of $k + n - 1$ marks. Again, a distribution is determined when we begin with $k + n - 1$ (distinct) marks on a line, then select any k of the marks to be the asterisks (the remaining $n - 1$ marks, of course, are dots). As another example, with six states and four photons we begin with nine marks on the line

then convert any four of these marks to asterisks and the others to dots. Hence,

denotes the distribution with

> 1 photon in state 1,
>
> 0 photons in state 2,
>
> 2 photons in state 3,
>
> 0 photons in state 4,
>
> 1 photon in state 5,
>
> 0 photons in state 6.

In general, since a distribution is determined by choosing any k of the $k + n - 1$ marks, the number of such distributions is

$$a_{nk} = \binom{k + n - 1}{k}.$$

There is no apparent preference in the physical world among these possible distributions; hence it is reasonable to assume them to be equally likely, and the Bose-Einstein statistics yields a probability of

$$\frac{1}{\binom{k + n - 1}{k}}.$$

for any distribution of k photons among n states.

Experimental physicists discovered that the Bose-Einstein probability assignment fails to describe accurately the behavior of certain other elementary particles, for example, the electron. The reason is that the electron behaves according to a different occupancy mode. Electrons are indistinguishable and the states are distinguishable, just as with photons, but it turns out that no state can be occupied by more than one electron. Because of this characteristic, a distribution is completely determined when the states occupied are known. Thus k must not exceed n, and there are $\binom{n}{k}$ possible distributions. If these are equally likely, then the probability of a given distribution is

$$\frac{1}{\binom{n}{k}},$$

and this probability assignment is referred to as the Fermi-Dirac statistics [Enrico Fermi (1901–1954), Paul Dirac (1902–1984)].

Problems for Section 20

In each of the following 12 experiments, describe a sample space **S**, list two typical elements in **S**, and find $|\mathbf{S}|$.

1. Pick a number from 1 to 10, inclusive.

2. Toss a nickel and a dime.

3. Take a ball from an urn containing 50 balls, of which 20 are red.

4. Roll a die.

5. Ask a randomly chosen American his/her birth month.

6. Pick two letters from among a, b, c, and d.

7. Ask a randomly chosen New Englander his/her state of residence (see Figure 34.1A).

8. Pick a card from a deck of 52 playing cards.

9. Of the four aces in a deck of playing cards, pick any three.

10. Make a three-letter "word" by using only a's, b's, and c's. (Consider a word to be a three-letter string xyz in which each of x, y, and z may be replaced by any of the letters a, b, and c.)

11. Same as Problem 10, but do not use any letter more than once.

12. Choose seven members of the U. S. Senate at random to form a committee.

The 12 events listed next refer, respectively, to the 12 experiments listed above. Indicate any special assumptions you make about the sample space, and compute the probability of each.

13. The number is prime.

14. Both coins fall tails.

15. The ball is not red.

16. The number of dots is less than 5.

17. The response is a month without an r in its name.

18. Both letters are consonants.

19. The response is a state which borders Canada.

20. The card is a "face" card (jack, queen, king).

21. Two of the three cards are red.

22. The word *bab* is formed.

23. The word *cab* is formed.

24. Exactly three members are Democrats. (You may find the current composition of the Senate in an almanac.)

In general, sample spaces may be somewhat more complex than those required in the previous problems.

25. You are dealt a hand consisting of exactly three cards from a well-shuffled deck of playing cards. (*a*) Describe a sample space **S** of this experiment, and calculate $|\mathbf{S}|$. (*b*) What is the probability that your hand contains no two cards of the same suit?

26. From a list of 15 people, four are randomly chosen to serve on a committee. (*a*) Describe a sample space **S** of this experiment, and calculate $|\mathbf{S}|$. If eight of the 15 people are male, what is the probability that (*b*) the committee is all female, (*c*) the committee has exactly two females?

27. Six people are randomly selected and their birth months are recorded. (*a*) Describe a sample space **S** of this experiment, and calculate $|\mathbf{S}|$. (*b*) What is the probability that no two were born in the same month? (Assume that birth months are equally likely.)

28. Letters of the alphabet are printed individually on scraps of paper which are thoroughly mixed in a box. A letter is drawn (and its scrap of paper discarded) three times in succession. (*a*) Describe a sample space **S** of this experiment, and calculate $|\mathbf{S}|$. (*b*) What is the probability that no vowel (a, e, i, o, or u) is drawn?

29. Twelve astronauts have taken intensive training for a flight to Mars. Of these, eight have had prior experience on lunar missions. If a crew of four is randomly chosen from this training class, what is the probability that exactly three experienced astronauts will be included?

30. Find the probability that a five-card poker hand will contain exactly k hearts, for each of the values $k = 0, 1, 2, 3, 4, 5$.

31. Six people arrange themselves at random in a row. What is the probability that a given pair of them are next to one another?

32. Six people seat themselves at random around a circular table. What is the probability that a given pair of them are next to one another? (See Problem 21 in Section 16.)

33. Ten individuals, including $\mathcal{A}$ and $\mathcal{B}$, are seated at random around a circular table. What is the probability that $\mathcal{B}$ is seated on $\mathcal{A}$'s left? (See Problem 21 in Section 16.)

34. In this and the next problem you will answer the question that Antoine Gombaud, Chevalier de Méré (1607–1685), posed to Blaise Pascal, who in turn discussed it with Pierre de Fermat. First, you will solve an easier, but related, question. (*a*) Let **S** be the sample space of four rolls of a single die. For example, {1, 3, 2, 3} or {3, 5, 6, 1} would both be in **S**. What is $|\mathbf{S}|$? (*b*) Let's call an element of the sample space that does not contain a 6 a winner. How many winners are there? How many losers (nonwinners) are there? (*c*) What is the probability of winning?

35. (*Continuation of Problem 34.*) The game in which de Méré was interested is similar to the game in Problem 34 but consists in rolling a pair of dice 24 times. In this case, a winner occurs by not getting a pair of 6s on any of the 24 rolls. (*a*) How large is the sample space consisting of 24 rolls of a pair of dice? (*b*) How many winners and losers are there in the sample space? (*c*) What is the probability of winning?

36. (*Conclusion of Problem 34.*) Repeat Problem 35 but with 25 rolls of the pair of dice.

37. A professor and a student are looking for each other, but unless they are both in Robinson Hall within 5 minutes of each other, they will not make contact. If they randomly arrive in Robinson Hall between 3 and 4 P.M., then what is the probability that they will make contact?

38. Repeat Problem 37, but use a digital clock where 3:00, but not 4:00, is included in the possible times and where 3:08 and 3:13 are within 5 minutes of each other.

39. Consider Example 2 of paragraph 20.4, and assume that two of the four individuals are known to be twins (born on the same date). (*a*) What is the probability that at least two of the four individuals have birthdays falling in the same month? (*b*) What is the probability that these four individuals have birthdays falling in at least three different months?

The final three problems in this set relate to paragraph 20.5.

40. As in paragraph 20.5, let a_{ij} be the number of distributions of j particles in i states ($a_{00} = 0$) and let $G(x, y) = \sum_{i=0}\sum_{j=0} a_{ij}x^i y^j$. (*a*) What is a_{0j} for all j? (*b*) What is a_{i0} for all $i \geq 1$? (*c*) Using (*a*) and (*b*), show that $G(x, y) = x + x^2 + x^3 + \cdots + \sum_{n=1}\sum_{k=1} a_{nk}x^n y^k$.

41. (*Continuation of Problem 40.*) (*a*) Show that $a_{nk} = a_{n-1,k} + a_{n,k-1}$, for all $n \geq 1$ and $k \geq 1$. (*b*) Show that $x \cdot G(x, y) = x^2 +$

$x^3 + \cdots + \sum_{n=1}\sum_{k=1} a_{n-1,k}x^n y^k$. (*c*) Show that $y \cdot G(x, y) = \sum_{i=1}\sum_{j=0} a_{ij}x^i y^{j+1} = \sum_{n=1}\sum_{k=1} a_{n,k-1}x^n y^k$. (*d*) Show that $G(x, y) - x \cdot G(x, y) - y \cdot G(x, y) = x$. (*e*) Conclude that

$$G(x, y) = \frac{x}{1 - x - y} = \frac{x}{1 - (x + y)}.$$

42. (*Conclusion of Problem 40.*) (*a*) Using Problem 41(*e*) and (1) in paragraph 0.6, show that $G(x, y) = x + x(x + y) + x(x + y)^2 + x(x + y)^3 + \cdots$. (*b*) What is the degree of each term in $x(x + y)^m$? (*c*) Since a_{nk} is the coefficient of the term $x^n y^k$, show that this coefficient is found in the expansion of $x(x + y)^{n+k-1}$. (*d*) Conclude that

$$a_{nk} = \binom{n + k - 1}{n - 1} = \binom{n + k - 1}{k}.$$

Section 21.   Conditional Probability and Tree Diagrams

Overview for Section 21

- Partition of a sample space
- Discussion and definition of conditional probability given new information
- Introduction to the multiplication rule
- Analysis of experiments by tree diagrams
- Successive drawings with and without replacement

Key Concepts: conditional probability, multiplication rule, tree diagram, branch and branch point, replacement

21.1   As in Example 1 of paragraph 20.2, let **D** denote the set which has as its elements the 52 cards in an ordinary deck of playing cards. If $\mathscr{E}$ denotes the drawing of a single card from **D**, then there are several different sample spaces associated with $\mathscr{E}$; the one chosen depends on the degree of detail required in analyzing the experiment. Some of the possibilities are

$$\mathbf{S}_1 = \mathbf{D},$$
$$\mathbf{S}_2 = \{\text{spade, heart, diamond, club}\},$$
$$\mathbf{S}_3 = \{\text{face, nonface}\},$$
$$\mathbf{S}_4 = \{2, 3, 4, 5, 6, 7, 8, 9, 10, J, Q, K, A\}.$$

For each of these cases, the size is

$$|\mathbf{S}_1| = 52, \qquad |\mathbf{S}_2| = 4, \qquad |\mathbf{S}_3| = 2, \qquad |\mathbf{S}_4| = 13,$$

and a typical outcome is

7 of diamonds for $\mathbf{S}_1$,

Diamond for $\mathbf{S}_2$,

Nonface for $\mathbf{S}_3$,

7 for $\mathbf{S}_4$.

It seems reasonable to assume (if the drawing is from a well-shuffled deck) that the outcomes in each of $\mathbf{S}_1$, $\mathbf{S}_2$, and $\mathbf{S}_4$ are equally likely but that the two outcomes in $\mathbf{S}_3$ are not equally likely. However the likelihoods may be assigned, a crucial requirement in the description of a sample space is that the outcomes represent a *partition* (refer to paragraph 18.4). This means that any performance of the experiment $\mathscr{E}$ must produce a result which corresponds to exactly one of the elements listed in $\mathbf{S}$. Note, for example, that {spade, heart, diamond, face} does not qualify as a sample space for $\mathscr{E}$.

For any choice of $\mathbf{S}$, the probabilities of the outcomes should add up to 1, and the probability of any event should be the sum of the probabilities of the various outcomes in that event. Choosing $\mathbf{S}_2$, for example, it is reasonable to agree that

$$P(\text{spade}) = P(\text{heart}) = P(\text{diamond}) = P(\text{club}) = \tfrac{1}{4},$$

and
$$P(\text{black}) = P(\text{spade}) + P(\text{club}) = \tfrac{1}{4} + \tfrac{1}{4} = \tfrac{1}{2}.$$

On the other hand, if $\mathbf{S}_3$ is chosen, it is reasonable to agree that

$$P(\text{face}) = \tfrac{3}{13} \qquad \text{and} \qquad P(\text{nonface}) = \tfrac{10}{13},$$

because a deck of cards consists of exactly 12 face cards and 40 nonface cards (note that only the jack, queen, and king are face cards). We will consider shortly another example in which the chosen sample space fails to have equally likely outcomes, but there the probability assignment is not so immediately obvious.

Tutorial 21.1

a. Consider the sample space S_1, above. If **B** denotes the event that a black card is drawn, find $P(\mathbf{B})$.

b. Consider the sample space S_4, above. If **F** denotes the event that a face card is drawn, determine both **F** and $P(\mathbf{F})$.

c. In the sample space S_4, is it possible to consider the drawing of a black card an event?

d. Which of the following is acceptable as a sample space for the given experiment $\mathscr{E}$: $S_5 = \{$black, red$\}$; $S_6 = \{$black face, heart face, nonface$\}$; $S_7 = \{$face, black nonface, red nonface$\}$; $S_8 = \{$spade face, club face, heart face, diamond face$\}$?

21.2

Because the probability assigned to an event is sensitive to the amount and kind of information available, we must introduce a refinement called conditional probability. Suppose that **S** is the sample space of an experiment $\mathscr{E}$ and that $P(\mathbf{A})$ is the probability of an event **A** in **S**. If additional, but inconclusive, evidence about $\mathscr{E}$ becomes available, it may be possible to eliminate some of the elements of **S** from consideration and thus (possibly) alter the original probability assignments to obtain a more accurate prediction about the outcome. For example, consider the experiment described in Example 1 of paragraph 20.4. In it, we selected two elements from the set $\{1, 2, 3, 4, 5\}$; hence

$$\mathbf{S} = \{\{1, 2\}, \{1, 3\}, \{1, 4\}, \{1, 5\}, \{2, 3\}, \{2, 4\}, \{2, 5\}, \{3, 4\}, \{3, 5\}, \{4, 5\}\}.$$

The set **A** consisted of the elements in **S** with sum less than 7,

$$\mathbf{A} = \{\{1, 2\}, \{1, 3\}, \{1, 4\}, \{1, 5\}, \{2, 3\}, \{2, 4\}\};$$

therefore, we assigned

$$P(\mathbf{A}) = \tfrac{6}{10}.$$

Now, let **B** denote a second event: that the sum of the pair of numbers is even. Thus,

$$\mathbf{B} = \{\{1, 3\}, \{1, 5\}, \{2, 4\}, \{3, 5\}\} \quad \text{and} \quad P(\mathbf{B}) = \tfrac{4}{10}.$$

Suppose it happens that another party has actually performed the experiment, but refuses to divulge the outcome and will admit only that the sum of the pair of numbers is less than 7. How does this new information affect our assessment of the probability that the sum is even? Since we now know that **A** has occurred, all the points in $\overline{\mathbf{A}}$ can be eliminated, and we are left with a new and smaller sample space. Thus we are no longer concerned with the original event **B** but only with those elements in **B** which are also in **A**, that is

$$\mathbf{B} \cap \mathbf{A} = \{\{1, 3\}, \{1, 5\}, \{2, 4\}\}.$$

Our problem is to determine the probability of **B** restricted by the condition that **A** has occurred; we will denote this "restricted" probability by the special symbol $P(\mathbf{B} \mid \mathbf{A})$, which may be read "the probability of **B** given **A**" or "the probability of **B** conditional upon **A**." Since the new sample space is **A** (and we assume its outcomes to be equally likely):

$$P(\mathbf{B} \mid \mathbf{A}) = \frac{|\mathbf{B} \cap \mathbf{A}|}{|\mathbf{A}|} = \tfrac{3}{6} = \tfrac{1}{2}.$$

Based on the original information available, $\frac{4}{10}$ was a reasonable probability assignment for **B**. With the new information that **A** has occurred, we note that exactly half its elements have an even sum, and our probability assignment for **B** should now reflect this additional evidence, as it does:

$$P(\mathbf{B} \mid \mathbf{A}) = \tfrac{1}{2}.$$

The concept of restricted probability is given the name "conditional probability," and its definition depends upon the important observation that it can be calculated from probabilities relative to the *original* sample space. In the illustration immediately above note that we can write

$$P(\mathbf{B} \mid \mathbf{A}) = \frac{|\mathbf{B} \cap \mathbf{A}|}{|\mathbf{A}|} = \frac{|\mathbf{B} \cap \mathbf{A}|/|\mathbf{S}|}{|\mathbf{A}|/|\mathbf{S}|} = \frac{\tfrac{3}{10}}{\tfrac{6}{10}} = \frac{P(\mathbf{B} \cap \mathbf{A})}{P(\mathbf{A})} = \tfrac{1}{2}.$$

As this special case suggests, the **conditional probability of B given A** is defined in general by the equation

$$P(\mathbf{B} \mid \mathbf{A}) = \frac{P(\mathbf{B} \cap \mathbf{A})}{P(\mathbf{A})}. \tag{1}$$

The "order of events" in the equation defining conditional probability is critical; it is *not* generally true that $P(\mathbf{B} \mid \mathbf{A})$ is the same as $P(\mathbf{A} \mid \mathbf{B})$. For example, from our previous illustration,

$$P(\mathbf{A} \mid \mathbf{B}) = \frac{P(\mathbf{A} \cap \mathbf{B})}{P(\mathbf{B})} = \frac{\tfrac{3}{10}}{\tfrac{4}{10}} = \tfrac{3}{4} \neq P(\mathbf{B} \mid \mathbf{A}).$$

From the previous equations we have what are sometimes called the **multiplication rules:**

$$P(\mathbf{A} \cap \mathbf{B}) = P(\mathbf{B}) \cdot P(\mathbf{A} \mid \mathbf{B}) \qquad \text{and} \qquad P(\mathbf{B} \cap \mathbf{A}) = P(\mathbf{A}) \cdot P(\mathbf{B} \mid \mathbf{A}). \quad \textbf{(2)}$$

But, because the operation of intersection is commutative, $\mathbf{A} \cap \mathbf{B} = \mathbf{B} \cap \mathbf{A}$, and it follows that $P(\mathbf{A} \cap \mathbf{B}) = P(\mathbf{B} \cap \mathbf{A})$; hence

$$P(\mathbf{B}) \cdot P(\mathbf{A} \mid \mathbf{B}) = P(\mathbf{A}) \cdot P(\mathbf{B} \mid \mathbf{A}). \quad \textbf{(3)}$$

Tutorial 21.2

a. If $P(\mathbf{B}) = \frac{1}{2}$ and $P(\mathbf{A} \mid \mathbf{B}) = \frac{2}{3}$, find $P(\mathbf{A} \cap \mathbf{B})$.
b. If $P(\mathbf{B}) = \frac{1}{2}$ and $P(\mathbf{B} \mid \mathbf{A}) = \frac{2}{3}$, why can't you find $P(\mathbf{A} \cap \mathbf{B})$?
c. If $P(\mathbf{B}) = \frac{1}{2}$, $P(\mathbf{A} \mid \mathbf{B}) = \frac{2}{3}$, and $P(\mathbf{B} \mid \mathbf{A}) = \frac{2}{5}$, find $P(\mathbf{A})$.

21.3   One of the traditional illustrations of probability concepts involves the selection of a ball from an urn. The urn simply represents an opaque container, and the ball represents one of a number of similar objects which differ only in some characteristic disguised by the container (say, color). One considers that the contents of the urn are thoroughly mixed so that a drawing from the urn represents a random choice from among the objects it contains.

Example 1   Suppose that there are two urns, I and II, which contain, respectively, four red balls and three green balls (in urn I) and four red balls and five green balls (in urn II). Our experiment is first to pick an urn at random, then to draw a ball from it. The possible outcomes of the experiment are IR, IG, IIR, IIG (where IR, for instance, denotes the outcome in which urn I is chosen and a red ball is taken from it). The sample space is

$$\mathbf{S} = \{\text{IR, IG, IIR, IIG}\}.$$

One might think, initially, that these elements are equally likely, but because the urns differ in content this will turn out not to be the case. Consider the events described as follows:

$$\begin{array}{ll} \textbf{I:} & \text{``urn I is chosen,''} \\ \textbf{II:} & \text{``urn II is chosen,''} \\ \textbf{R:} & \text{``a red ball is drawn,''} \\ \textbf{G:} & \text{``a green ball is drawn.''} \end{array}$$

Written as subsets of the sample space **S**, these are

$$\mathbf{I} = \{IR, IG\},$$
$$\mathbf{II} = \{IIR, IIG\},$$
$$\mathbf{R} = \{IR, IIR\},$$
$$\mathbf{G} = \{IG, IIG\}.$$

Now we must agree on the assignment of probabilities. Since the urn is chosen at random, it is reasonable to assume that

$$P(\mathbf{I}) = P(\mathbf{II}) = \tfrac{1}{2}.$$

Having chosen a particular urn, additional probability assignments depend upon the contents of that urn; hence the following conditional probabilities seem reasonable:

$$P(\mathbf{R} \mid \mathbf{I}) = \tfrac{4}{7} \quad \text{and} \quad P(\mathbf{G} \mid \mathbf{I}) = \tfrac{3}{7},$$
$$P(\mathbf{R} \mid \mathbf{II}) = \tfrac{4}{9} \quad \text{and} \quad P(\mathbf{G} \mid \mathbf{II}) = \tfrac{5}{9}.$$

From these assignments we can compute the probability for each element in **S**. Because probability is associated only with events (which are subsets of **S**), the symbol "$P(IR)$," for example, is inappropriate; it should be "$P(\{IR\})$." But insistence on this technicality seems a bit extreme; hence it is customary to use the simpler notation, agreeing that if $x \in \mathbf{S}$, then $P(x)$ means $P(\{x\})$. Since $\{IR\} = \mathbf{I} \cap \mathbf{R}$ and $\{IG\} = \mathbf{I} \cap \mathbf{G}$, we have by the multiplication rule, (2) in paragraph 21.2,

$$P(IR) = P(\mathbf{I} \cap \mathbf{R}) = P(\mathbf{I}) \cdot P(\mathbf{R} \mid \mathbf{I}) = \tfrac{1}{2} \cdot \tfrac{4}{7} = \tfrac{4}{14},$$

and

$$P(IG) = P(\mathbf{I} \cap \mathbf{G}) = P(\mathbf{I}) \cdot P(\mathbf{G} \mid \mathbf{I}) = \tfrac{1}{2} \cdot \tfrac{3}{7} = \tfrac{3}{14}.$$

Similarly, $P(IIR) = \tfrac{4}{18}$ and $P(IIG) = \tfrac{5}{18}$. One notices that the sum of these four probabilities is 1, as it should be.

Having assigned probabilities to the outcomes in **S**, we may routinely find probabilities of other events, such as

R: "the ball drawn is red,"

$$P(\mathbf{R}) = P(\{IR, IIR\}) = \tfrac{4}{14} + \tfrac{4}{18} = \tfrac{32}{63}.$$

Tutorial 21.3

Refer to Example 1.

a. Suppose **G** is the event that the ball drawn is green. Determine both **G** and $P(\mathbf{G})$.

continued on next page

continued from previous page

b. Verify the given probabilities $P(\text{IIR}) = \frac{4}{18}$ and $P(\text{IIG}) = \frac{5}{18}$.

c. Are the two probabilities in part **b** consistent with our agreement that $P(\text{II}) = \frac{1}{2}$?

21.4

If an experiment consists of multiple stages, then there is a convenient geometric construction which displays both outcomes and probabilities associated with each of the several stages in that experiment. It is called a **tree diagram,** and we illustrate the idea in Figure 21.4, which is based on the experiment described in Example 1 of paragraph 21.3. Reading from left to right, dots in the diagram are called **nodes,** or **branch points,** and the segments incident with a node are called **branches.** Each node in the diagram indicates a particular stage in the history of the experiment. The rightmost nodes represent the various possible outcomes of the experiment; hence they may be considered points in the sample space. The branches (to the right) from intermediate nodes represent the possible choices at that stage, with their appropriate probabilities indicated. By the multiplication rule, the probability of any outcome is the product of the probabilities along the branches leading to that outcome. Thus,

$$P(\text{IIR}) = \frac{1}{2} \cdot \frac{4}{9} = \frac{4}{18}.$$

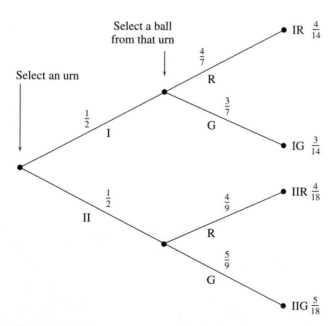

Figure 21.4

As we observed at the end of Example 1 in paragraph 21.3, the event $\mathbf{R} = \{\text{IR, IIR}\}$ has the probability $P(\mathbf{R}) = P(\text{IR}) + P(\text{IIR}) = \frac{32}{63}$.

Example 1

The tree diagram of Figure 21.4 suggests an interesting question. Two paths lead to the event $\mathbf{R}$, that a red ball is drawn: one via urn I, the other via urn II. Suppose it happens that the experiment is performed by someone else, and suppose we are told only that the event $\mathbf{R}$ has occurred. What is the probability that urn I was chosen? We observed earlier that $P(\mathbf{I}) = \frac{1}{2}$, so isn't that the answer to our question? Not necessarily, because this value depends on the assumption that the urns are equally likely. Now we are given the new information that $\mathbf{R}$ has occurred; hence the "equally likely" assumption may no longer be reasonable. What we need is the conditional probability that urn I was chosen given that $\mathbf{R}$ has occurred; that is, $P(\mathbf{I} \mid \mathbf{R})$. From (2) and (3) in paragraph 21.2 we know that

$$P(\text{IR}) = P(\mathbf{I} \cap \mathbf{R}) = P(\mathbf{I}) \cdot P(\mathbf{R} \mid \mathbf{I}) = P(\mathbf{R}) \cdot P(\mathbf{I} \mid \mathbf{R}).$$

But $P(\text{IR}) = \frac{4}{14}$ and $P(\mathbf{R}) = \frac{32}{63}$; hence

$$P(\mathbf{I} \mid \mathbf{R}) = \frac{\frac{4}{14}}{\frac{32}{63}} = \frac{9}{16}.$$

Tutorial 21.4

Refer to Example 1.
a. Find $P(\mathbf{II} \mid \mathbf{R})$.
b. Find $P(\mathbf{I} \mid \mathbf{G})$ and $P(\mathbf{II} \mid \mathbf{G})$.
c. If a node in Figure 21.4 has branches to the right, then the sum of the probabilities on those branches is 1. Why should this be the case?

21.5

The "tree diagram" technique generalizes to experiments consisting of three or more stages. The typical model involves an urn containing balls of various colors: At stage 1 a ball is drawn randomly from the urn and its color recorded; this operation is repeated several times. The problem is to compute the probability of the various colors at each stage. There are two major conditions under which this experiment can be conducted, each leading to quite different probabilities, and each choice models an important physical application. The first is called drawing **with replacement;** that is, the ball drawn at any stage is replaced in the urn before the next draw. Under this agreement, our problem is especially simple: The probabilities remain the same for each successive stage. This model will be explored more fully in Sections 22 and 26. The second condition is called drawing **without replacement;** that is, no ball drawn is replaced. Hence, the contents of the urn change after each draw and so do the probabilities. We will illustrate this situation by a tree diagram in the next example.

Example 1

Consider an urn U which contains three red balls, two white balls, and one blue ball. The experiment $\mathscr{E}$ consists of drawing three balls in sequence from U without replacement, and our problem is to determine the probability that the third draw results in a red ball. The tree diagram in Figure 21.5 displays all possible histories.

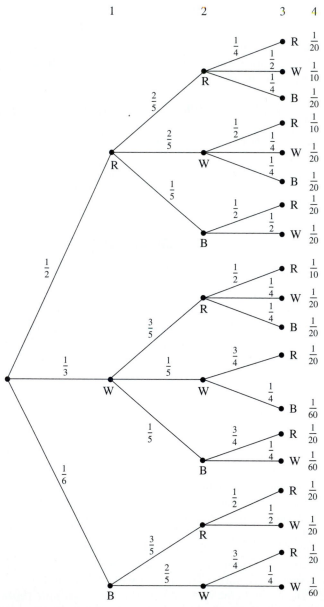

Figure 21.5

Each node in column 1, 2, or 3 indicates the result of the draw at stage 1, 2, or 3 (respectively). A node is omitted if that color is impossible. For example, if a blue ball is drawn at stage 1, then the only later options are red and white (since U contains only one blue ball and drawing is without replacement). The probabilities indicated on each branch are the conditional probabilities which depend, of course, on the history of the experiment up to that stage. Each node in column 3 corresponds to a unique path, along branches joined at intermediate nodes, beginning with the leftmost node. Each such path corresponds to a particular sequence of results at each stage in the experiment, which we have already referred to informally as the experiment's "history." The entry in column 4 next to a node in column 3 is the probability of that particular path through the tree; it is computed as the product of the probabilities on each of the branches (by the multiplication rule). For example, the topmost path corresponds to red on each draw; the probability of that particular history is

$$\tfrac{1}{2} \cdot \tfrac{2}{5} \cdot \tfrac{1}{4} = \tfrac{1}{20}.$$

The sum of the entries in column 4 is 1, which is what we expect. To obtain the probability that $\mathscr{E}$ results in a red ball on the final draw, simply add the probabilities in column 4 next to the R's in column 3:

$$\tfrac{1}{20} + \tfrac{1}{10} + \tfrac{1}{20} + \tfrac{1}{10} + \tfrac{1}{20} + \tfrac{1}{20} + \tfrac{1}{20} + \tfrac{1}{20} = \tfrac{1}{2}.$$

This computation may be referred to as a "sum over histories," which is a phrase borrowed from modern physics.   ●

Disguised in the tree diagram of Figure 21.5 is a property that may not be immediately apparent. The clue is our computation, above, of the probability that the third draw results in a red ball: It is the same as the probability that the *initial* draw results in a red ball. Although this is not an accident, we will refrain from further discussion here. A simple version of this phenomenon will be considered in Problems 25 and 26.

21.6 Complement: Paradoxes

Probability is notoriously deceptive. Even quite simple questions lure the unwary into responses that initially appear eminently logical, yet are demonstrably wrong. We will examine four of these so-called paradoxes here. The ones chosen are classics, which appear with some regularity in probability textbooks, both old and new. At the end of this complement we will refer to a paper which examines this issue.

1. Probability was born in paradox: The Chevalier de Méré had observed that he won more often than he lost when betting on the occurrence of a 6 in 4 tosses of a single die. When the game changed to tossing a pair of dice, he assumed that it should be just as favorable to bet on the occurrence of a double 6 in 24 tosses. Perhaps he reasoned like this: Since a single die has 6 outcomes and a pair of dice has 36 outcomes, then if 4 tosses are sufficient in the first game, 24 tosses should be sufficient in the new game (because the ratios 4:6 and 24:36 are the same). Whatever the case, he discovered that he now lost more frequently than he won! It was at this point that he sought Pascal's help. (Problems 34 to 36 in Section 20 address this issue.) We will look briefly at the simpler game; the new game is analyzed the same way, though its computations are a little more difficult. Let $\mathscr{E}$ be the experiment of tossing a single die four times. Then $\mathbf{S} = \{(x_1, x_2, x_3, x_4): x_i = 1, 2, 3, 4, 5, 6\}$, and $|\mathbf{S}| = 6^4$. Let $\mathbf{A}$ denote the event that at least one value of x_i is 6. The computations for $\overline{\mathbf{A}}$ turn out to be easier, since

$$\overline{\mathbf{A}} = \{(x_1, x_2, x_3, x_4): x_i = 1, 2, 3, 4, 5\}, \qquad \text{and} \qquad |\overline{\mathbf{A}}| = 5^4.$$

Thus,

$$P(\overline{\mathbf{A}}) = \frac{5^4}{6^4} = \tfrac{625}{1296} < \tfrac{1}{2}, \qquad \text{and so} \qquad P(\mathbf{A}) > \tfrac{1}{2},$$

confirming the Chevalier's observations.

2. Another very old problem involves conditional probabilities. Stated (somewhat archaically):

> Three chests, identical in appearance, each have two drawers. The first chest contains a gold coin in each drawer; the second contains a silver coin in each drawer; the third contains a gold coin in one drawer and a silver coin in the other. One of the chests is selected randomly.

We interrupt the statement to observe that the probability is $\tfrac{1}{3}$ that the selected chest will contain both a gold and a silver coin (since the chests are equally likely and one of the three contains coins of both kinds). The problem continues:

> One drawer in the selected chest is opened disclosing a gold coin. Now, what is the probability that the chest contains coins of both kinds?

Our initial reaction may be to reason as follows: Finding the gold coin effectively eliminates the possibility of the chest with a silver coin in each drawer. Among the two remaining chests, one has coins of both types, hence its probability should be $\tfrac{1}{2}$. Further, we are encouraged by the memory that probability often changes with the addition of new information. Being prudent, however, we decide to check our reasoning by what we have learned about conditional probabilities. Suppose we label the chests,

$$\mathbf{C}_1, (\mathrm{G, G}); \qquad \mathbf{C}_2, (\mathrm{S, S}); \qquad \mathbf{C}_3, (\mathrm{G, S});$$

and we denote by $\mathbf{B}$ the event that a gold coin is drawn. From the tree diagram in Figure 21.6, $P(\mathbf{B})$ is the sum of the probabilities at each point labeled G,

$$P(\mathbf{B}) = \tfrac{1}{3} + 0 + \tfrac{1}{6} = \tfrac{1}{2}.$$

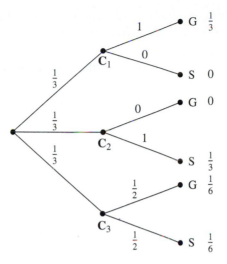

Figure 21.6

To find $P(C_3 \mid B)$, simply use the definition of conditional probability

$$P(C_3 \mid B) = \frac{P(C_3 \cap B)}{P(B)} = \frac{\frac{1}{6}}{\frac{1}{2}} = \frac{1}{3}.$$

3. Suppose that two families $\mathcal{F}_1$ and $\mathcal{F}_2$ have moved into your neighborhood recently. You know nothing about them except that each family has two children. (We will assume that children are equally likely to be male or female.) The next day you discover that there is a 6-year-old girl in each family; incidentally, you also learn that the other child in $\mathcal{F}_2$ is a baby. What is the probability (for each family) that both children are girls?

For $\mathcal{F}_1$ we are tempted to argue that the unknown child has a 50:50 chance of being a girl; hence the probability that $\mathcal{F}_1$ has two girls is $\frac{1}{2}$. In the same way, we argue that the probability also is $\frac{1}{2}$ that $\mathcal{F}_2$ has two girls. It turns out that the first probability is wrong and the second is right. To see this, return to the initial evidence that each family has two children (of unknown sex). The sample space then can be recorded as

$$S = \{(B, B), (B, G), (G, B), (G, G)\},$$

where the first coordinate represents the older child. Because children are equally likely to be male or female, these options also are equally likely. The new information about $\mathcal{F}_1$ eliminates the option (B, B), leaving the new sample space $\{(B, G), (G, B), (G, G)\}$. Thus, for $\mathcal{F}_1$

$$P(\text{both girls} \mid \text{at least one girl}) = \frac{1}{3}.$$

The new information about $\mathcal{F}_2$ not only eliminates (B, B) but also (B, G), leaving the new sample space {(G, B), (G, G)}. Thus, for $\mathcal{F}_2$

$$P(\text{both girls} \mid \text{older child a girl}) = \tfrac{1}{2}.$$

4. A (bridge) hand of 13 cards is randomly dealt from an ordinary deck of playing cards. Suppose we are told that this hand has at least one ace (A). Now let **T** be the event that the hand has at least two aces and **U** be the event that the hand has at least one ace. We will also let **A1** be the event that the hand has exactly one ace. As will be shown below,

$$P(\mathbf{T} \mid \mathbf{U}) = 0.37.$$

Suppose, however, we had been told that this hand held the ace of hearts (AH). Now, what is the probability that it holds at least two aces? Should it be different from 0.37? Perhaps you will consider it paradoxical that the answer is

$$P(\mathbf{T} \mid \text{AH}) = 0.56.$$

To determine the first of these probabilities, note that

$$P(\mathbf{T} \mid \mathbf{U}) = \frac{P(\mathbf{T} \cap \mathbf{U})}{P(\mathbf{U})},$$

and that

$$P(\mathbf{U}) = 1 - P(\text{no A}) = 1 - \frac{\binom{48}{13}}{\binom{52}{13}} = 0.70.$$

Also

$$P(\mathbf{T} \cap \mathbf{U}) = P(\mathbf{T}) = 1 - P(\text{no A}) - P(\mathbf{A1})$$

$$= (1 - P(\text{no A})) - \frac{4 \cdot \binom{48}{12}}{\binom{52}{13}}$$

$$= 0.70 - 0.44 = 0.26.$$

Hence,

$$P(\mathbf{T} \mid \mathbf{U}) = \frac{0.26}{0.70} = 0.37.$$

Now for the second, note that

$$P(T \mid AH) = \frac{P(T \cap AH)}{P(AH)},$$

and that

$$P(AH) = \frac{\binom{51}{12}}{\binom{52}{13}} = 0.25.$$

The event $T \cap AH$ consists of those hands that hold the ace of hearts and at least one other ace. The number of hands that hold the ace of hearts is $\binom{51}{12}$, and of these, $\binom{48}{12}$ hold no other aces.

Thus

$$|T \cap AH| = \binom{51}{12} - \binom{48}{12},$$

and so

$$P(T \cap AH) = \frac{\binom{51}{12} - \binom{48}{12}}{\binom{52}{13}} = 0.14.$$

Hence,

$$P(T \mid AH) = \frac{0.14}{0.25} = 0.56.$$

Problems such as the four we have presented above appear in various guises from time to time; a few, even, achieve notoriety. The problem quoted below was stated in the "Ask Marilyn" column of the Sunday supplement called *Parade* (Sept. 9, 1990). It was referred to in several later columns. The solution is discussed in an article called "The Car and the Goats" by L. Gillman in the *American Mathematical Monthly* (vol. 99, no. 1, pp. 3–7, 1992):

> Suppose you're on a game show, and you're given the choice of three doors: behind one door is a car; behind the others, goats. You pick a door, say No. 1, and the host, who knows what's behind the other doors, opens another door, say No. 3, which has a goat. He then says to you, "Do you want to pick door No. 2?" Is it to your advantage to take the switch?

Problems for Section 21

1. An urn contains 10 red balls and 12 green balls. Suppose that two balls are drawn one after another, without replacement. We use the notation G2, for example, to mean that the second draw results in a green ball. Find the probability indicated. (*a*) $P(G2 \mid R1)$, (*b*) $P(G2 \mid G1)$, (*c*) $P(R2 \mid G1)$.

2. Using the experiment in Problem 1, find
(a) $P(R2 \mid R1)$, (b) $P(G1 \cap G2)$,
(c) $P(R1 \cap G2)$.

3. The experiment in Problem 1 may be analyzed via the tree diagram:

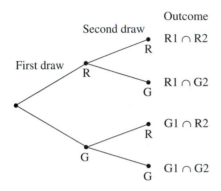

Give the probability assignment for each branch, and compute the probability of each outcome.

4. Repeat Problem 1 if the urn contains 8 red balls and 14 green balls.

5. Using the information in Problem 4, compute the probabilities in Problem 2.

6. Analyze Problem 4 with a tree diagram.

7. An urn contains 6 red balls, 8 green balls, and 10 blue balls. As in Problem 1, find the probability indicated. (a) $P(G2 \mid R1)$, (b) $P(G2 \mid G1)$, (c) $P(G2 \mid B1)$.

8. Using the information in Problem 7, find the indicated probabilities. (a) $P(R2 \mid R1)$, (b) $P(G1 \cap G2)$, (c) $P(R1 \cap B2)$.

9. Analyze Problem 7 with a tree diagram, giving the probability assignment for each branch, and computing the probability of each outcome.

10. Given an urn as in Problem 1, assume that three balls are drawn one after another without replacement. (a) Construct a tree diagram to illustrate this experiment. (b) What

is the probability that the second draw results in a green ball?

11. Repeat Problem 10 but with urn contents as in Problem 7.

12. Suppose that an unbiased pair of dice is tossed. Let **A** denote the event that the same number shows on each. Let **B** denote the event that the sum is greater than 7. Find (a) $P(\mathbf{A} \mid \mathbf{B})$, (b) $P(\mathbf{B} \mid \mathbf{A})$.

13. Consider the experiment and events given in Problem 12. Find (a) $P(\mathbf{A} \mid \overline{\mathbf{B}})$, (b) $P(\overline{\mathbf{B}} \mid \overline{\mathbf{A}})$.

14. Two cards are dealt from an ordinary deck of 52 playing cards. (a) What is the probability that both are spades? (b) Suppose that a third card is dealt before the two are replaced. What is the probability that it is a spade, given that the first two cards dealt are spades?

15. Two cards are dealt from an ordinary deck of 52 playing cards. What is the probability that (a) both cards are black, (b) both cards are of the same suit, (c) both cards have the same face value (rank)?

16. Three cards are dealt from an ordinary deck of 52 playing cards. What is the probability that (a) all three cards are spades, (b) all three cards are aces, (c) all three cards are face cards?

17. Three cards are dealt from an ordinary deck of 52 playing cards. What is the probability that (a) all three cards are the same suit, (b) all three cards have the same face value, (c) all three cards are red?

18. A box office has three tickets left for sale, and there are five individuals ($\mathcal{A}, \mathcal{B}, \mathcal{C}, \mathcal{D}, \mathcal{E}$) remaining in line. If these five are randomly arranged, then what is the probability that $\mathcal{A}$ and $\mathcal{B}$ fail to get tickets?

19. Assume that each month of the year is equally likely as a birth month and that individuals are selected randomly. (a) What is the probability that two individuals were born in the same month? (*b*) What is the probability that a third individual was born in a different month, given that the first two were born in April?

20. A box contains four tokens labeled 1, 1, 2, and 3. The tokens are indistinguishable except for their labels. Construct a tree diagram which describes the following experiment: (i) At the first step, one token is drawn (without replacement). (ii) At the second step, two tokens are drawn simultaneously (without replacement). (iii) At the third step, the last token is drawn. Assuming that the branches are equally likely, what is the probability that the first number drawn is 1, given that the last number drawn is 1?

21. An urn labeled I contains 10 red, 8 blue, and 7 white balls. Another urn labeled II contains 1 red, 2 blue, and 1 white ball. A ball of unobserved color is transferred from urn I to urn II. What is the probability that a ball drawn from urn II is blue? (*Note:* A tree diagram may be helpful.)

22. An urn labeled I contains three red and five blue balls. Two balls are randomly chosen from urn I and then dropped into an empty urn labeled II. A single ball is randomly drawn from urn II; what is the probability that it is red?

23. An urn labeled I contains m red and k blue balls. Two balls are randomly chosen from urn I and then dropped into an empty urn labeled II. A single ball is randomly drawn from urn II; what is the probability that it is red?

24. Four airlines service a certain city: A_1 schedules one-half the daily arrivals, A_2 schedules one-fourth the daily arrivals, and the other two (A_3 and A_4) share the remaining arrivals equally. Past experience suggests that 90 percent of both A_1 and A_2 arrivals are on time; 80 percent of A_3 arrivals are on time, and 70 percent of A_4 arrivals are on time. Compute the probability that an incoming passenger will be late.

25. For the experiment in Problem 1, verify that (*a*) $P(R2) = P(R1)$, (*b*) $P(G2) = P(G1)$.

26. For the experiment in Problem 7, verify that (*a*) $P(G2) = P(G1)$, (*b*) $P(B2) = P(B1)$, (*c*) $P(R2) = P(R1)$.

27. Three players ($\mathcal{A}, \mathcal{B}, \mathcal{C}$) compete against each other in a Frisbee tossing contest. Each tosses the Frisbee once, and a point is scored by that player whose Frisbee stops farthest from a base line. The player who first accumulates 4 points is declared the winner. Suppose that $\mathcal{A}$ has already won 3 points and that $\mathcal{B}$ and $\mathcal{C}$ each have won 2 points. Draw a tree diagram illustrating the possible ways in which the contest might proceed until one player wins.

28. In electing the chairman of a small committee, Candidate $\mathcal{A}$ receives four votes and Candidate $\mathcal{B}$ receives two votes. Draw a tree diagram to represent the possible orders in which the six ballots are counted. In what fraction of the cases is $\mathcal{A}$ ahead all the way?

29. Three current novels (A, B, and C) are popular on a certain campus. Thirty-five percent of the students have read at least two of them, and A has been read by 45 percent of the students. Fifteen percent of the students have read at least B and C, and 10 percent of the students have read all three. What is the probability that a randomly chosen student has read only A?

30. (*Conclusion of Problem 29.*). If 20 percent of the students have not read any one of the three, what is the probability that a randomly chosen student, who has read at least one of the books, has not read A?

Section 22.   Independent Events

Overview for Section 22

- Drawing with replacement as a model for independence
- Contrast between mutually exclusive events and independence
- Sample space as a Cartesian product, and definition of joint events

Key Concepts: independent events, mutually exclusive events, joint events

22.1

Multistaged experiments sometimes involve operations which have no discernible impact on one another. An experiment, for example, might consist of tossing a coin, then rolling a pair of dice, then drawing a card from a deck. There seems little reason to think that "heads" and "7" at the first two stages will have anything to do with what card is drawn at the third stage. Another experiment might consist of tossing two coins, one after the other. Again, it seems reasonable to assume that neither of the two tossed coins is affected by how the other coin falls. We might even agree that consecutive tosses of the *same* coin exhibit similar "independence." On the other hand, some might suspect a subtle connection between two such operations. In any event, our intuitive sense of "independence" among several operations needs to be formalized in a way that avoids dependence upon subjective judgment. It turns out that the desired objectivity is realized in an unexpected way: The formal definition of independence is based upon probability assignments. Example 1 explores the classical model of independent events. It suggests a rationale for the definition, which we will state following the example.

Example 1

Assume that an urn U contains five red, three white, and four blue balls. The experiment consists in drawing two balls sequentially from U. Designating the events of red on first draw by R1 and red on second draw by R2, then our interest is in the event R1 ∩ R2. By the multiplication rule [(2) in paragraph 21.2],

$$P(\text{R1} \cap \text{R2}) = P(\text{R1}) \cdot P(\text{R2} \mid \text{R1}). \tag{1}$$

Hence, we need to determine the conditional probability of R2 given R1. The tree diagram in Figure 22.1 indicates all possible histories of this experiment.

If the drawing is *without* replacement, then the conditional probabilities of red on the second draw depend upon the outcome of the first draw, as displayed in

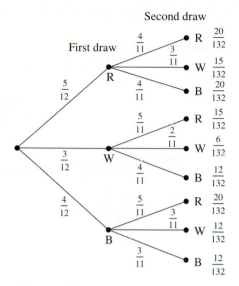

Figure 22.1

Figure 22.1. Since

$$P(\text{R2} \mid \text{R1}) = \tfrac{4}{11},$$

it follows that

$$P(\text{R1} \cap \text{R2}) = P(\text{R1}) \cdot P(\text{R2} \mid \text{R1}) = \tfrac{5}{12} \cdot \tfrac{4}{11} = \tfrac{20}{132}.$$

If, however, the drawing is *with* replacement, then the contents of U remain unchanged after the first draw and the conditional probability of red on the second draw is unaffected by the outcome of the first draw. Thus, it is reasonable to claim that

$$P(\text{R2} \mid \text{R1}) = P(\text{R2}) = \tfrac{5}{12},$$

and from (1), we obtain

$$P(\text{R1} \cap \text{R2}) = P(\text{R1}) \cdot P(\text{R2}) = \tfrac{5}{12} \cdot \tfrac{5}{12} = \tfrac{25}{144}. \tag{2}$$

This is the promised clue to our definition of independent events. Generalizing from (2), if $\mathscr{E}$ is any experiment with sample space **S**, and if **A** and **B** are any events in **S** for which

$$P(\mathbf{A} \cap \mathbf{B}) = P(\mathbf{A}) \cdot P(\mathbf{B}), \tag{3}$$

then **A** and **B** are called **independent events.** Assuming that neither $P(\mathbf{A})$ nor $P(\mathbf{B})$ is zero, it follows from (1) in paragraph 21.2 that

$$P(\mathbf{B} \mid \mathbf{A}) = P(\mathbf{B}) \qquad \text{and} \qquad P(\mathbf{A} \mid \mathbf{B}) = P(\mathbf{A}).$$

Thus under independence, the conditional probability of one event turns out to be unaffected by the occurrence or nonoccurrence of the other event.

Tutorial 22.1

a. Assuming that two successive tosses of a coin are independent, how should you assess the probability that the first toss is a "head" and the second toss is a "tail"?

b. Refer to Example I and let W2 denote white on second draw. Find $P(RI \cap W2)$ assuming that the draw is (i) without replacement, (ii) with replacement.

22.2

The definition of independence is not based upon some intrinsic property of events, as we might have expected, but depends upon the probability assignments. This turns out to be perfectly appropriate in the development of probability theory. But we should remember that in any "real world" experiment modeled by that theory, probability assignments are often unavoidably colored by subjective judgment. At least in the simpler situations such as coin tossing, however, it is reasonable to expect general agreement on the question of independence. But in other situations, the issue is not always clear-cut, as the following example illustrates.

Example 1

Let $\mathscr{E}$ be the experiment which consists of a single toss of a pair of dice. To analyze $\mathscr{E}$, it is helpful to think of the dice as being distinguished into a first die and a second die (perhaps by color: Think of the first die as red, the second die as green). For simplicity of notation, let xy indicate the outcome obtained by tossing the dice, where x is the number of dots showing on the first (red) die and y is the number of dots showing on the second (green) die. By FCP II, the number of outcomes is 36, since x and y must each be replaced by one of the six integers 1, 2, 3, 4, 5, 6. The sample space for this experiment is the set

$$\mathbf{S} = \{11, 12, 13, 14, 15, 16, 21, 22, \ldots, 66\}.$$

(Compare with Example 2 of paragraph 20.1, where the notation varies slightly from this.) Consider three events:

$$\begin{aligned}
\mathbf{E}_1 &= \{15, 24, 33, 42, 51\} &&\text{(the sum is 6),} \\
\mathbf{E}_2 &= \{16, 25, 34, 43, 52, 61\} &&\text{(the sum is 7),} \\
\mathbf{F} &= \{31, 32, 33, 34, 35, 36\} &&\text{(the red die shows a ``3'').}
\end{aligned}$$

The probabilities are

$$P(E_1) = \tfrac{5}{36}, \qquad P(E_2) = \tfrac{6}{36}, \qquad P(F) = \tfrac{6}{36}.$$

Before continuing, we ask, "Does it seem likely that some two of these events are independent?" Right away we observe that E_1 and E_2 seem *not* to be independent, since the occurrence of one precludes the occurrence of the other. But what about E_1 and F or E_2 and F? Suppose we refer each of the three cases to the definition of independence in (3) in paragraph 22.1.

a. Since $E_1 \cap E_2 = \varnothing$,

$$P(E_1 \cap E_2) = 0 \neq P(E_1) \cdot P(E_2) = \tfrac{5}{216},$$

which confirms our judgment that E_1 and E_2 are not independent.

b. Since $E_1 \cap F = \{33\}$,

$$P(E_1 \cap F) = \tfrac{1}{36} \neq P(E_1) \cdot P(F) = \tfrac{5}{216},$$

it follows that E_1 and F are not independent. On the surface, there seems little difference between this case and the final one. But, again, be cautious about jumping to conclusions.

c. Since $E_2 \cap F = \{34\}$,

$$P(E_2 \cap F) = \tfrac{1}{36} = P(E_2) \cdot P(F).$$

Thus, E_2 and F are independent according to our definition. We may rationalize this conclusion by the observation that our assessment of the probability that "7" is rolled is unaffected by our knowledge that the red die shows "3"; that is,

$$P(E_2 \mid F) = \frac{P(E_2 \cap F)}{P(F)} = \tfrac{1}{6} = P(E_2).$$

Tutorial 22.2

Refer to Example 1.
a. Show that $P(F \mid E_2) = P(F)$.
b. Show that $P(F \mid E_1) \neq P(F)$.
c. If **G** is the event that the sum is even, are **F** and **G** independent?

22.3

The preceding example also serves to illustrate a second source of potential uncertainty or confusion. It is easy to fall into the following trap: If two events are disjoint (often called **mutually exclusive**), then surely they have nothing to do with one another, hence should be considered independent. But, referring to part **a** in Example 1 of paragraph 22.2, we note that E_1 and E_2 *are* mutually exclusive and yet are *not* independent. Notice, for example, that $P(E_2) = \frac{1}{6}$ while $P(E_2 \mid E_1) = 0$; thus the occurrence of E_1 has a drastic impact on the possible occurrence of E_2. The general rule here is that "mutually exclusive" and "independent" are different characteristics of pairs of events and must be considered separately.

Formula (1) in paragraph 22.1 is a special case of the multiplication rule

$$P(A \cap B) = P(A) \cdot P(B \mid A).$$

This rule extends in a natural way to include more than two events:

$$\begin{aligned} P(A \cap B \cap C) &= P((A \cap B) \cap C) \\ &= P(A \cap B) \cdot P(C \mid (A \cap B)) \\ &= P(A) \cdot P(B \mid A) \cdot P(C \mid (A \cap B)). \end{aligned} \tag{1}$$

Referring to the sizes of the sets, note that

$$P(A) = \frac{|A|}{|S|}, \qquad P(B \mid A) = \frac{|A \cap B|}{|A|},$$

and

$$P(C \mid (A \cap B)) = \frac{|A \cap B \cap C|}{|A \cap B|};$$

hence,

$$P(A \cap B \cap C) = \frac{|A|}{|S|} \cdot \frac{|A \cap B|}{|A|} \cdot \frac{|A \cap B \cap C|}{|A \cap B|} = \frac{|A \cap B \cap C|}{|S|}.$$

The idea of independence can be extended, also, to more than two events. Intuitively, the intent is that no one of the events is dependent upon any combination of the others. Thus in the case of three events **A**, **B**, and **C**, we would have

$$P(A) = P(A \mid B) = P(A \mid C) = P(A \mid (B \cap C)),$$

and similarly for the other two events **B** and **C**. The multiplication rule in the case of independent events has the form

$$P(A \cap B \cap C) = P(A) \cdot P(B) \cdot P(C). \tag{2}$$

Tutorial 22.3

Let $\mathcal{E}$ be a three-stage experiment consisting of tossing a coin, rolling a pair of dice, and drawing a card from a deck. Compute the probability that $\mathcal{E}$ results in "heads," an "odd sum," and a "red card."

22.4   The use of (1) and (2) in paragraph 22.3 tends to disguise the underlying sample space. Consider the experiment mentioned at the very beginning of this section: Toss a coin, then roll dice, then draw a card. How are we to describe symbolically the sample space, or the events in the sample space? The answer is that we think of the experiment as a succession of simpler components. An outcome of the experiment can then be expressed as a joint outcome of the several components. In the illustration at hand, let $\mathbf{S}_1, \mathbf{S}_2, \mathbf{S}_3$ be sample spaces for the component experiments to be conducted in the indicated sequence. We can describe a sample space for the combined activity by

$$\mathbf{S} = \mathbf{S}_1 \times \mathbf{S}_2 \times \mathbf{S}_3.$$

A point (x_1, x_2, x_3) in $\mathbf{S}$ indicates that x_1 occurs in the first component experiment, x_2 occurs in the second, and x_3 in the third. Any subset of $\mathbf{S}$ is called a **joint event.** This notation makes a little more precise the language in which we describe experiments having multiple components. Typical points in the sample space of our illustration are (heads, 34, ace of spades) or (tails, 43, 2 of clubs), where "34" indicates that the red (first) die shows "3" and the green die shows "4". The size of $\mathbf{S}$ is

$$|\mathbf{S}| = |\mathbf{S}_1| \cdot |\mathbf{S}_2| \cdot |\mathbf{S}_3| = 2 \cdot 36 \cdot 52 = 3744.$$

As in Tutorial 22.3, let $\mathbf{A}$ be the event {heads, odd sum, red}. Then

$$|\mathbf{A}| = 1 \cdot 18 \cdot 26, \qquad \text{and} \qquad P(\mathbf{A}) = \frac{1 \cdot 18 \cdot 26}{2 \cdot 36 \cdot 52} = \frac{1}{8},$$

which is consistent with the calculation using (2) in paragraph 22.3:

$$P(\text{head}) = \tfrac{1}{2}, \qquad P(\text{odd}) = \tfrac{18}{36}, \qquad P(\text{red}) = \tfrac{26}{52},$$

and
$$P(\text{head, odd, red}) = \tfrac{1}{2} \cdot \tfrac{1}{2} \cdot \tfrac{1}{2} = \tfrac{1}{8}.$$

Example 1   Consider again the urn of Example 1 of paragraph 22.1, which contains five red, three white, and four blue balls. Let a joint experiment consist of drawing three balls in sequence from the urn with replacement. Each draw results in one of the 12 balls; thus $\mathbf{S}$ contains 12^3 points. The joint event consisting of red on first draw, white on second draw, and blue on third draw is represented by (R, W, B). These events are independent, and by (2) in paragraph 22.3 the probability of the joint event is the product

$$P(R, W, B) = \tfrac{5}{12} \cdot \tfrac{3}{12} \cdot \tfrac{4}{12} = \tfrac{60}{1728}.$$

This probability is associated with the specific order in which the colors occur. If we are interested in the event that all three colors are represented, then there is a corresponding probability for each of the 3! orders in which the three colors can be drawn. Thus,

$$P(\text{each color represented}) = 6 \cdot \tfrac{60}{1728} = \tfrac{360}{1728}.$$

Example 2   Consider an experiment similar to that in Example 1, except this time the drawing is without replacement. The picture must be modified, since no one of the 12 balls can be drawn more than once. The sample space actually is a subset of the Cartesian product, consisting of $12 \cdot 11 \cdot 10 = 1320$ points. These events are not independent; hence the probability of the event (R, W, B) is found by the product in (1), not by (2), in paragraph 22.1: $P(R, W, B) = \tfrac{5}{12} \cdot \tfrac{3}{11} \cdot \tfrac{4}{10} = \tfrac{60}{1320}$. Once again, if we want the probability that each of the three colors is represented, this number is multiplied by 3!,

$$P(\text{each color represented}) = \tfrac{360}{1320}.$$

22.5   ## Complement: An Application of Difference Equations and Generating Functions
Drawing from an urn with replacement is a classic example of independent events. Often, a real-life situation can be modeled by an extended succession of such drawings. In Section 26 this idea will be examined in some detail; for the moment we consider several approaches to one particular problem of this sort.

> Suppose that an urn contains a large number of balls, p percent of which are red. A **trial** consists of drawing a ball randomly from the urn, noting its color, and returning it to the urn. In a succession of n such trials, what is the probability that an even number of red balls has been drawn?

Immediately we think, the number of red balls must be either even or odd; hence the probability must be $\tfrac{1}{2}$. But, is it true that "even" and "odd" are equally likely? We try a quick test for small n, say $n = 1$ and $n = 2$. The tree diagrams are shown in Figure 22.5A. For the case $n = 1$, $P(\text{even}) = 1 - p$; and for the case $n = 2$, $P(\text{even}) = p^2 + (1 - p)^2$. Of course! The probability must depend on the given percentage of red balls in the urn. But the nature of that dependence is unclear from the evidence at hand. As usual, we must begin by agreeing on notation: We denote by $P(k)$ the probability that after exactly k trials the number of red balls drawn is even. For example, $P(0) = 1$ (since the number of red balls drawn is 0), and $P(1) = 1 - p$ (a red ball is not drawn at the first trial). The answer to our original question is $P(n)$,

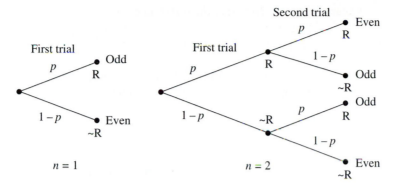

Figure 22.5A

and our problem is to evaluate this function in terms of the given parameters (in particular, p and n). The solutions to be presented depend upon recurrence relations (sometimes called recursion formulas), which describe $P(n)$ in terms of previous values, not the given parameters.

Solution I.   Difference Equations Technique. To find the proper recurrence relation, consider the tree diagram in Figure 22.5B which describes the transition from the $(k-1)$st trial to the kth trial. After $k-1$ trials the probability of an even number of red balls is $P(k-1)$, and the probability of an odd number of red balls is $1 - P(k-1)$. Thus the probability of an even number of red balls after k trials is the sum

$$P(k) = (1-p) \cdot P(k-1) + p \cdot (1 - P(k-1)),$$

which may be simplified to

$$P(k) - (1 - 2p) \cdot P(k-1) = p. \tag{1}$$

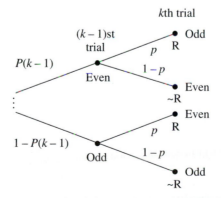

Figure 22.5B

We are fortunate: Note that the difference

$$P(k) - (1 - 2p) \cdot P(k - 1)$$

is a constant (independent of k). To simplify notation replace, temporarily, $1 - 2p$ with t, then construct the telescoping sequence:

$$P(n) - t \cdot P(n - 1) = p;$$

$$t \cdot P(n - 1) - t^2 \cdot P(n - 2) = t \cdot p, \qquad \text{since } P(n - 1) - t \cdot P(n - 2) = p;$$

$$t^2 \cdot P(n - 2) - t^3 \cdot P(n - 3) = t^2 \cdot p, \qquad \text{since } P(n - 2) - t \cdot P(n - 3) = p;$$

$$\cdots$$

$$t^{n-2} \cdot P(2) - t^{n-1} \cdot P(1) = t^{n-2} \cdot p, \qquad \text{since } P(2) - t \cdot P(1) = p;$$

$$t^{n-1} \cdot P(1) - t^n \cdot P(0) = t^{n-1} \cdot p, \qquad \text{since } P(1) - t \cdot P(0) = p.$$

Because of cancellations, the sum is

$$P(n) - t^n \cdot P(0) = p \cdot (1 + t + t^2 + \cdots + t^{n-1}).$$

Recall that $P(0) = 1$, and by Problem 18 in Section 13, the sum of the geometric sequence is

$$1 + t + t^2 + \cdots + t^{n-1} = \frac{1 - t^n}{1 - t}.$$

Hence, $\qquad P(n) = t^n + p \cdot \dfrac{1 - t^n}{1 - t} = (1 - 2p)^n + \dfrac{1 - (1 - 2p)^n}{2},$

and so $\qquad\qquad P(n) = \frac{1}{2}(1 + (1 - 2p)^n).$

Note that $P(1) = 1 - p$, as we had previously determined.

Solution II.   Generating Functions Technique. Let $f(x) = P(0) + P(1) \cdot x + P(2) \cdot x^2 + P(3) \cdot x^3 + \cdots$. Again, we must make use of the recurrence relation given in (1), and again for simplicity of notation let $t = 1 - 2p$. Then

$$t \cdot x \cdot f(x) = t \cdot P(0)x + t \cdot P(1)x^2 + t \cdot P(2)x^3 + \cdots.$$

Hence,

$$f(x) - t \cdot x \cdot f(x) = P(0) + (P(1) - t \cdot P(0))x + (P(2) - t \cdot P(1))x^2 + \cdots,$$

$$(1 - t \cdot x) \cdot f(x) = 1 + px + px^2 + \cdots,$$

$$f(x) = \frac{1}{1 - t \cdot x}(1 + px + px^2 + \cdots).$$

From (1) in paragraph 0.6,

$$\frac{1}{1-tx} = 1 + tx + t^2 x^2 + \cdots;$$

hence,

$$f(x) = (1 + tx + t^2 x^2 + \cdots) \cdot (1 + px + px^2 + \cdots).$$

Now using convolution, introduced in paragraph 19.3,

$$f(x) = 1 + (p + t)x + (p + pt + t^2)x^2 + \cdots.$$

Equating coefficients,

$$P(0) = 1, \qquad P(1) = p + t = 1 - p,$$

and, in general,

$$P(n) = p + pt + pt^2 + \cdots + pt^{n-1} + t^n$$
$$= p(1 + t + \cdots + t^{n-1}) + t^n$$
$$= p\left(\frac{1 - t^n}{1 - t}\right) + t^n,$$

which we obtained in Solution I.

To get a feeling for the numerical values involved, we list in Table 22.5 the probabilities $P(n)$ to two decimal places for several values of n and p. The property that seems to be most apparent from the table (although we have *not* proved it) is that for any p, $0 < p < 1$, $P(n)$ differs from 0.5 by successively smaller amounts as n increases. In fact, for the given values of p, $P(n)$ is essentially indistinguishable from 0.5 after about 10 trials. This is an example of predictable, asymptotic behavior. Here, "asymptotic" simply refers to large values of n, and "predictable" refers to an

p	1	2	3	4	5	10	20
$\frac{1}{4}$	.75	.62	.56	.53	.52	.50	.50
$\frac{1}{3}$	.67	.56	.52	.51	.50	.50	.50
$\frac{1}{2}$	.50	.50	.50	.50	.50	.50	.50
$\frac{2}{3}$	.33	.56	.48	.51	.50	.50	.50
$\frac{3}{4}$	.25	.62	.44	.53	.48	.50	.50

Table 22.5   Values of $P(n)$

observable pattern which allows us to closely approximate $P(n)$ for sufficiently large n. Note that if $p = 0$, then $P(n) = 1$, and if $p = 1$, then

$$P(n) = \begin{cases} 1, & \text{if } n \text{ is even,} \\ 0, & \text{if } n \text{ is odd.} \end{cases}$$

On the other hand, if $0 < p < 1$, then

$$-1 < 1 - 2p < 1.$$

For large values of n, $(1 - 2p)^n$ differs from 0 by only a small amount; hence $P(n) = \frac{1}{2} \cdot (1 + (1 - 2p)^n) \approx 0.5$. For example, with $p = 0.99$ and for $n \geq 228$, $-0.01 < (1 - 2p)^n < 0.01$. This means that if the urn contained 99 red balls and 1 green ball, then after 228 trials, the probability that an even number of red balls has been drawn deviates from 0.5 by less than 0.005.

Problems for Section 22

1. If two identical coins are tossed, then what is the probability that they match?

2. Suppose that a nickel and a dime are tossed and that you may keep any coin that falls heads. What is the probability that you get at least 10 cents? At most 10 cents?

3. Suppose that two nickels and one dime are tossed. Again, you may keep any coin that falls heads. What is the probability that you get exactly 10 cents?

4. Given the same experiment as in Problem 3. Let $\mathbf{A}$ denote the event that the dime falls heads and let $\mathbf{B}$ denote the event that you get exactly 15 cents. (a) Are the events $\mathbf{A}$ and $\mathbf{B}$ independent? (b) Are the events $\bar{\mathbf{A}}$ and $\mathbf{B}$ mutually exclusive?

5. In Example 1 of paragraph 22.2, we showed that events $\mathbf{E}_2$ and $\mathbf{F}$ are independent. Is it true that $\mathbf{E}_2$ and $\bar{\mathbf{F}}$ also are independent?

6. An urn contains 10 red and 12 green balls. Suppose that several balls are drawn, but each is replaced before the next one is selected. Find the probabilities: (a) $P(G3 \mid R1)$, (b) $P(G1 \cap G2)$, (c) $P(R1 \cap G2)$.

7. Analyze the experiment in Problem 6 using a tree diagram.

8. Consider Example 1 of paragraph 22.4. Sketch the tree diagram which describes this experiment. Confirm the probabilities given in that example.

9. Again, consider Example 1 of paragraph 22.4. Compute (a) $P(R1)$, (b) $P(R2)$, (c) $P(R3)$.

10. A target shooter fires one shot from each of two guns at a target. The probability of his hitting the bull's-eye with one gun is $\frac{1}{2}$ and with the other gun is $\frac{2}{5}$. What is the probability that the two shots result in (a) two bull's-eyes, (b) one bull's-eye, (c) no bull's-eye?

11. If the weather is too hot $\frac{2}{5}$ of the time, too cold $\frac{4}{7}$ of the time, too wet $\frac{5}{9}$ of the time, and too dry $\frac{1}{4}$ of the time, then assuming temperature and humidity are independent, what is the probability that on a given day the weather will be just right?

12. A spinner is used to select randomly one of the numbers 1, 2, 3, or 4. (For example, the card on which the spinner is mounted could be marked with a coordinate system, and the number obtained from the quadrant to which the spinner points.) (*a*) If *a* is determined by the spinner, what is the probability that the equation $ax - 8 = 0$ has an integer solution? (*b*) If *a* and *b* are determined by the spinner, what is the probability that the equation $ax + b = 0$ has an integer solution?

13. A pair of unbiased dice is thrown. Compute the probability for each of the possible sums that can show.

14. A single unbiased die is thrown twice in succession. What is the probability that the number showing on the second toss is greater than that on the first toss?

15. Consider the experiment described in Problem 14. What is the probability that at least one face shows a prime number? (*Hint:* Consider the complementary event.)

16. An urn contains five red balls and seven green balls. Three balls are drawn in succession. What is the probability that all three are red if (*a*) each ball is replaced before the next one is drawn, (*b*) none of the balls is replaced before the next draw, (*c*) only the first ball is replaced before the next draw?

17. A coin is tossed four times. Construct a tree diagram analyzing this experiment. Note that there are 16 possible outcomes; compute the probability of each.

18. Consider the experiment in Problem 17. Compute the probability that the experiment results in exactly (*a*) 4 heads, (*b*) 3 heads, (*c*) 2 heads, (*d*) 1 head, (*e*) 0 head.

19. If events **A** and **B** are mutually exclusive and $P(A) > 0$ and $P(B) > 0$, then can **A** and **B** be independent? Why or why not?

20. (*Refer to Problem 1.*) If four identical coins are tossed, then what is the probability that (*a*) all four match, (*b*) at least three match?

21. (*Conclusion of Problem 20.*) If five identical coins are tossed, then what is the probability

that (*a*) at least four match, (*b*) at least three match?

22. Team A and Team B are in the World Series. Assume that the probability of A winning a game is 0.55, denoted $P(A)$; hence $P(B) = 0.45$. Also, assume that the games are independent of each other (a huge assumption). For each team, what is the probability that it will win in four straight games?

23. (*Continuation of Problem 22.*) (*a*) In how many ways can A win the Series 4 games to 1? (*b*) What is the probability that A wins the Series in five games? [*Hint:* This is simply the answer to (*a*) multiplied by the probability that B wins the first game and A wins the next four games.]

24. (*Continuation of Problem 22.*) (*a*) In how many ways can A win the Series in six games? (*Hint:* Note that A must win the final game, and so B must win two of games 1, 2, 3, 4, or 5. How many ways can two of these five numbers be chosen?) (*b*) What is the probability that A wins the Series in six games?

25. (*Conclusion of Problem 22.*) What is the probability that A wins the Series in seven games?

26. Suppose that **A** and **B** are independent events for which $P(A) = 0.7$ and $P(B) = 0.5$. Evaluate (*a*) $P(A \cap B)$, (*b*) $P(A \cup B)$, (*c*) $P(B \mid A)$, (*d*) $P(\overline{A} \cap \overline{B})$. (*Hint:* Use a De Morgan Law.)

27. (*Conclusion of Problem 26.*) Show that $\overline{A}$ and $\overline{B}$ are independent.

28. Select a digit at random (i.e., each of the 10 digits has probability of $\frac{1}{10}$). Define the events $A = \{1, 2, 3, 4, 5\}$, $B = \{1, 2, 6, 7\}$, and $C = \{1, 2, 5, 7\}$. Show that **A** and **B** are independent, but that **A** and **C** are not independent.

29. Ten "true-false" questions appear on an examination; suppose that they are answered at random. What is the probability

that exactly seven of them are answered correctly?

30. (*Conclusion of Problem 29.*) (*a*) What is the probability that Question 4 is among the seven answered correctly? (*b*) What is the probability that Question 4 is answered correctly, given that exactly seven questions are answered correctly?

Section 23.   Bayes' Theorem

Overview for Section 23

- Introduction to "reverse" probabilities
- Partition of sample space into alternate hypotheses
- Probabilities of hypotheses and Bayes' Theorem
- Introduction to the problem of "false calls" in applications

Key Concepts: alternate hypotheses, Bayes' Theorem, prior and post probabilities, false calls

23.1   The familiar trail

$$\mathscr{E} \to \mathbf{S} \to \mathbf{A} \to P(\mathbf{A})$$

ends with a probability assignment which is a way of assessing the uncertainty of an event **A**. We begin with a body of information associated with an experiment and go toward a consequent event (and its probability).

$$\boxed{\text{Information}} \to \mathbf{A}.$$

Suppose, however, we are faced with a "reverse" trail: Given that **A** has occurred, what can that fact tell us about the nature of the initial information? In an important but specialized situation this question has an answer which sharpens our understanding of the sample space. As a matter of fact, our question, in its simplest version, was anticipated in Example 1 of paragraph 21.3 where a ball was drawn from a randomly selected urn and the observed color of the ball was used to predict which urn had been selected. To understand the more general situation, we now begin a detailed study of this "reverse" problem (which deals with what are aptly called "probabilities of hypotheses"). The fundamental result, due to Thomas Bayes (1702–1761), has become known as Bayes' Theorem (published posthumously in 1763). In rough outline, we suppose that an event **A** may occur as a consequence of any one of several possible hypotheses. An experiment is performed and **A** is observed to occur. Bayes' Theorem provides the tool needed to compute how likely each hypothesis is to be correct. The ideas involved are not difficult, but some preliminary machinery is necessary. It may also prove helpful if we relate our development to the following illustrative situation.

Quality control in a manufacturing process is sometimes erratic. Different machines, different workers, and different raw materials are some of the factors that tend to produce variability in product output. Suppose that a furniture manufacturing plant has contracted with four different machine shops to supply fine hinges required to meet rigid specifications. The plant has in stock a bin full of hinges supplied in various proportions by the four machine shops. The output of the shops is not perfect, and some small percentage of hinges supplied by each shop is defective. Now, suppose that one of the cabinetmakers selects a hinge at random and as he tries to fit it in place notices that it is defective. Pitching the hinge into the discard bin he exclaims, "I bet that one came from the new shop." The cabinetmaker's exasperation with the new supplier may or may not be justified, and there is very likely no way to tell with certainty which one of the shops supplied the defective hinge. But if certain records are available, then we can at least assess the likelihood that the new shop is guilty.

We begin the development by recalling from (3) in paragraph 21.2 that if **A** and **B** are two events in a sample space **S**,

$$P(\mathbf{B}) \cdot P(\mathbf{A} \mid \mathbf{B}) = P(\mathbf{A}) \cdot P(\mathbf{B} \mid \mathbf{A}).$$

On the assumption that $P(\mathbf{B}) \neq 0$, this can be restated

$$P(\mathbf{A} \mid \mathbf{B}) = \frac{P(\mathbf{A}) \cdot P(\mathbf{B} \mid \mathbf{A})}{P(\mathbf{B})}, \tag{1}$$

which turns out to be the key to our problem.

Let **S** be partitioned into n subsets:

$$\mathbf{S} = \mathbf{H}_1 \cup \mathbf{H}_2 \cup \cdots \cup \mathbf{H}_n. \tag{2}$$

It is traditional to refer to these subsets $\mathbf{H}_j$ as *alternate hypotheses*. For convenience, and to match our illustration, we will assume (temporarily) that $n = 4$; the general case, of course, is similar. The Venn diagram of this situation appears in Figure 23.1A. Suppose we label each machine shop in our illustration with the numbers 1, 2, 3, and 4 (new supplier), and let $\mathbf{H}_j$ be the hypothesis that the selected hinge was produced in shop j.

Next, let **B** be an event in **S**, and note that **B** also may be partitioned in a way consistent with the partition of **S** (see Figure 23.1B):

$$\mathbf{B} = (\mathbf{H}_1 \cap \mathbf{B}) \cup (\mathbf{H}_2 \cap \mathbf{B}) \cup (\mathbf{H}_3 \cap \mathbf{B}) \cup (\mathbf{H}_4 \cap \mathbf{B}). \tag{3}$$

The darkest shaded region in Figure 23.1B represents the joint event $\mathbf{H}_4 \cap \mathbf{B}$, and because the four joint events are mutually exclusive, we can add the probabilities of

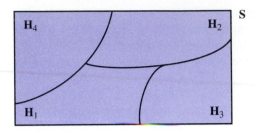

Figure 23.1A

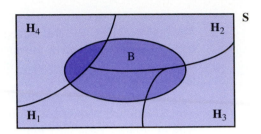

Figure 23.1B

each to obtain

$$P(\mathbf{B}) = P(\mathbf{H}_1 \cap \mathbf{B}) + P(\mathbf{H}_2 \cap \mathbf{B}) + P(\mathbf{H}_3 \cap \mathbf{B}) + P(\mathbf{H}_4 \cap \mathbf{B}). \qquad (4)$$

Returning to the illustration, let **B** represent the event that the selected hinge is defective. Then the joint event $\mathbf{H}_4 \cap \mathbf{B}$ asserts that the defective hinge was supplied by shop 4. By the multiplication rule,

$$P(\mathbf{H}_4 \cap \mathbf{B}) = P(\mathbf{H}_4) \cdot P(\mathbf{B} \mid \mathbf{H}_4) = P(\mathbf{B}) \cdot P(\mathbf{H}_4 \mid \mathbf{B}). \qquad (5)$$

What we seek is the conditional probability $P(\mathbf{H}_4 \mid \mathbf{B})$ that the selected hinge came from shop 4, *given* that the hinge is defective. We will return to this computation following the statement of Bayes' Theorem in paragraph 23.2.

Tutorial 23.1

Review briefly Example 1 of paragraph 21.4. Note that there are two alternate hypotheses: $\mathbf{H}_1$ (urn 1 was chosen), $\mathbf{H}_2$ (urn 2 was chosen).
a. What event corresponds to **B**?
b. Rewrite Formulas (3), (4), and (5) for this example (using $\mathbf{H}_1$, $\mathbf{H}_2$, and **B**).
c. What is $P(\mathbf{H}_1 \mid \mathbf{B})$?

23.2 The stage is now set, and we will state the theorem in generality. The proof, which depends upon the theoretical structure to be introduced in Section 24, follows identically the outline given below.

THEOREM 23.2

Bayes' Theorem. Let a sample space **S** be partitioned into n alternate hypotheses: $\mathbf{S} = \mathbf{H}_1 \cup \mathbf{H}_2 \cup \ldots \cup \mathbf{H}_n$.

Let **B** denote any event in **S** for which $P(\mathbf{B}) \neq 0$. Then for each integer j, $1 \leq j \leq n$,

$$P(\mathbf{H}_j \mid \mathbf{B}) = \frac{P(\mathbf{H}_j) \cdot P(\mathbf{B} \mid \mathbf{H}_j)}{\sum_{i=1}^{n} P(\mathbf{H}_i) \cdot P(\mathbf{B} \mid \mathbf{H}_i)}. \tag{1}$$

Outline of Proof

Modeled on (5) in paragraph 23.1, we can state for each j,

$$P(\mathbf{H}_j \mid \mathbf{B}) = \frac{P(\mathbf{H}_j) \cdot P(\mathbf{B} \mid \mathbf{H}_j)}{P(\mathbf{B})}.$$

By an extension of both (4) and (5) in paragraph 23.1,

$$P(\mathbf{B}) = \sum_{i=1}^{n} P(\mathbf{H}_i) \cdot P(\mathbf{B} \mid \mathbf{H}_i).$$

Substituting this summation for $P(\mathbf{B})$ in the preceding formula, we obtain the desired result (1). ∎

An application of this theorem is illustrated in the following example, which picks up our story of the furniture manufacturing plant.

Example 1

Suppose that the furniture manufacturing plant has in stock a large supply of hinges, of which 40 percent have been produced by shop 1, 25 percent by shop 2, 25 percent by shop 3, and 10 percent by shop 4. Based on past experience, we suppose also that:

- 0.7 percent of the hinges supplied by shop 1 are defective.
- 0.5 percent of the hinges supplied by shop 2 are defective.
- 0.4 percent of the hinges supplied by shop 3 are defective.
- 0.8 percent of the hinges supplied by shop 4 are defective.

Let the sample space **S** consist of the set of all hinges on hand, and let **S** be partitioned into subsets $\mathbf{H}_j$ of those hinges produced by shop j:

$$\mathbf{S} = \mathbf{H}_1 \cup \mathbf{H}_2 \cup \mathbf{H}_3 \cup \mathbf{H}_4.$$

The probability that a randomly selected hinge was supplied by shop j is $P(\mathbf{H}_j)$, and these are called **prior** probabilities:

$$P(\mathbf{H}_1) = \tfrac{40}{100}, \qquad P(\mathbf{H}_2) = \tfrac{25}{100}, \qquad P(\mathbf{H}_3) = \tfrac{25}{100}, \qquad P(\mathbf{H}_4) = \tfrac{10}{100}.$$

As before, **B** denotes the subset of **S** consisting of all defective hinges. When it is observed that the selected hinge is defective, then the conditional probabilities $P(\mathbf{H}_j \mid \mathbf{B})$ are called **post** probabilities, because they are computed *after* information about the event **B** is in hand. To calculate these post probabilities by (1), we must know the conditional probabilities $P(\mathbf{B} \mid \mathbf{H}_j)$, which are given at the beginning of this example:

$$P(\mathbf{B} \mid \mathbf{H}_1) = 0.007, \qquad P(\mathbf{B} \mid \mathbf{H}_2) = 0.005,$$

$$P(\mathbf{B} \mid \mathbf{H}_3) = 0.004, \qquad P(\mathbf{B} \mid \mathbf{H}_4) = 0.008.$$

The following tabulation offers a convenient organization for the calculation required in (1). Note that in the first three columns we list the alternate hypotheses, their prior probabilities, and the known conditional probabilities. From this point on, the computation is automatic: involving products, sum, and quotients (in that order). On each line the product produces $P(\mathbf{H}_j \cap \mathbf{B})$, the sum of the "product" column (denoted by Σ) is $P(\mathbf{B})$, and the quotients (of each product by Σ) are the desired post probabilities.

Alternate hypotheses	Prior probabilities	Conditional probabilities	Product $P(\mathbf{H}_i) \cdot P(\mathbf{B} \mid \mathbf{H}_i)$	Quotient $P(\mathbf{H}_i) \cdot P(\mathbf{B} \mid \mathbf{H}_i)/\Sigma$
$\mathbf{H}_1$	0.4	0.007	0.0028	0.48
$\mathbf{H}_2$	0.25	0.005	0.00125	0.21
$\mathbf{H}_3$	0.25	0.004	0.001	0.17
$\mathbf{H}_4$	0.1	0.008	0.0008	0.14
			$\Sigma = 0.00585$	1.00

A comparison of the final column with the second column shows how the new information relative to the event **B** has affected our assignment of probabilities to the alternate hypotheses. (Observe that the cabinetmaker's loyalty to the older suppliers seems to have been misplaced! Our best guess must be that shop 1 is guilty.) ●

Tutorial 23.2A

Convince yourself that the last four columns in the tabulation in Example I could be relabeled:

Prior probabilities	by $P(\mathbf{H}_i)$,
Conditional probabilities	by $P(\mathbf{B} \mid \mathbf{H}_i)$,
Product	by $P(\mathbf{H}_i \cap \mathbf{B})$,
Quotient	by $P(\mathbf{H}_i \mid \mathbf{B})$.

Example 2

The students in a certain class are distributed by major as follows: 30 percent in biology, 20 percent in economics, 25 percent in psychology, and 25 percent in sociology. Within each major the fraction of class members who are female is $\frac{1}{2}$ in biology, $\frac{1}{4}$ in economics, $\frac{1}{3}$ in psychology, and $\frac{1}{2}$ in sociology. The instructor calls on a student selected randomly from a roster of last names. The prior probability that the selected student is a biology major is 0.30. If the selected student is female, what is the post probability that she is a biology major? Suppose we designate the majors as follows: H_1 for biology, H_2 for economics, H_3 for psychology, and H_4 for sociology. Also, let B denote the event that the selected student is female. Now, we tabulate this situation:

Alternate hypotheses	Prior probabilities	Conditional probabilities	Product	Quotient
H_1	$\frac{3}{10}$	$\frac{1}{2}$	$\frac{3}{20}$	$\frac{18}{49}$
H_2	$\frac{1}{5}$	$\frac{1}{4}$	$\frac{1}{20}$	$\frac{6}{49}$
H_3	$\frac{1}{4}$	$\frac{1}{3}$	$\frac{1}{12}$	$\frac{10}{49}$
H_4	$\frac{1}{4}$	$\frac{1}{2}$	$\frac{1}{8}$	$\frac{15}{49}$

$$\Sigma = \frac{49}{120}$$

The required post probability is

$$P(H_1 \mid B) = \frac{18}{49}.$$

Note that the table provides all the post probabilities for the selected student. According to these figures, she is most likely to be a biology major, and least likely to be an economics major.

Example 3

An urn contains five red, three white, and four blue balls. Suppose that one ball is lost unnoticed from the urn. A ball is then drawn randomly from the urn and is observed to be red. What is the probability that the lost ball was white? Again, we must establish notation. Suppose we assume

H_1 :   lost ball is red,

H_2 :   lost ball is white,

H_3 :   lost ball is blue,

B :   selected ball is red.

Here is the complete tabulation:

Alternate hypotheses	Prior probabilities	Conditional probabilities	Product	Quotient
H_1	$\frac{5}{12}$	$\frac{4}{11}$	$\frac{20}{132}$	$\frac{20}{55}$
H_2	$\frac{3}{12}$	$\frac{5}{11}$	$\frac{15}{132}$	$\frac{15}{55}$
H_3	$\frac{4}{12}$	$\frac{5}{11}$	$\frac{20}{132}$	$\frac{20}{55}$
			$\Sigma = \frac{55}{132}$	

Hence, $P(H_2 \mid B) = \frac{15}{55} = \frac{3}{11}$, which is slightly larger than the prior probability of H_2.

Tutorial 23.2B

Note that in each table in Examples 2 and 3, two columns, prior probabilities and quotient (or post probabilities), sum to 1. Explain why this is to be expected.

23.3   Bayes' Theorem finds occasional application to a dilemma which plagues such varied segments of our society as product testing, aircraft safety, and medical diagnosis. The problem arises from uncertainties, such as those described in the following situation. Suppose that a commercial airliner is removed from service to undergo a periodic safety inspection. Using sophisticated electronic gear which can be difficult to interpret, an inspector examines a structural component. For simplicity, we assume that the inspector reaches one of two decisions: The component is flawed (F), or the component is not flawed ($\sim$F). Of course, the component *is* either flawed or not; hence the four possible combinations may be tabulated:

	Component	
Decision	F	$\sim$F
F	a	b
$\sim$F	c	d

By far, the majority of decisions fall in categories a and d which represent correct decisions: A flawed component is so identified, and a sound component is so identified. The trouble comes with b and c, which represent mistakes usually referred to as *false calls*. In category b, a sound component is misidentified as flawed (an error which results in the unnecessary time, labor, and cost of replacing the component). In category *c*, a flawed component is misidentified as sound (an error which may ultimately have serious safety implications). The dilemma is how best to minimize *b* without jeopardizing *c*.

The following example, using hypothetical data, illustrates an application of Bayes' Theorem to the problem of false calls in a medical context.

Example 1

An individual, identified as John Doe, is selected at random from a community in which 0.25 percent of the population has a disease (assume that its symptoms are not overt). The diagnostic test T used to detect presence of the disease is not totally accurate: It gives a positive result in 95 percent of the diseased cases and in 1 percent of the nondiseased cases. Suppose that John Doe is given the test and its result is positive. What is the probability that he actually has the disease?

Let the sample space **S** be the entire population of the given community. Let $\mathbf{H}_1$ be the subset of **S** consisting of those individuals who have the disease, and let $\mathbf{H}_2$ be all the others. Let **B** denote the subset of those who test positive. (In this simplistic situation, the tabulation is hardly necessary, but it remains a useful display.)

Alternate hypotheses	Prior probabilites	Conditional probabilities	Product	Quotient
$\mathbf{H}_1$	0.0025	0.95	0.002375	0.1923
$\mathbf{H}_2$	0.9975	0.01	0.009975	0.8077
			$\Sigma = 0.01235$	

The, perhaps unexpected, conclusion to draw from the given data is that only about 1 time in 5 does a positive test result correctly identify the disease. On the other hand, his positive test result does significantly raise John Doe's probability of having the disease.

Tutorial 23.3

Construct the tabulation, as above, for the data in Example I of paragraph 21.4.

Example 2

Consider again the data given in Example 1. There is an alternate technique of analysis which uses the ideas of "continuous" probability (see Example 1 of paragraph 20.1). Let the sample space be denoted by a square of area 1, as in Figure 23.3, partitioned into $\mathbf{H}_1$ and $\mathbf{H}_2$ (by the straight segment). Assume that the area of $\mathbf{H}_1$ is 0.0025 and that the area of $\mathbf{H}_2$ is 0.9975 (the figure is distorted for pictorial convenience). The event **B** covers 95 percent of $\mathbf{H}_1$ and 1 percent of $\mathbf{H}_2$; hence the area in $\mathbf{H}_1 \cap \mathbf{B}$ is $(0.95) \cdot (0.0025) = 0.002375$, and the area of $\mathbf{H}_2 \cap \mathbf{B}$ is $(0.01) \cdot (0.9975) = 0.009975$.

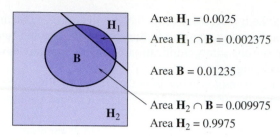

Figure 23.3

Since John Doe belongs to the subset **B**, his chance of belonging also to $\mathbf{H}_1$ is simply

$$P(\mathbf{H}_1 \mid \mathbf{B}) = \frac{\text{area } (\mathbf{H}_1 \cap \mathbf{B})}{\text{area } \mathbf{B}} = \frac{0.002375}{0.01235} \approx 0.1923.$$

23.4   Finally, we note that the new information provided by the event **B** affects the probability assignments to the various alternate hypotheses because **B** depends on those hypotheses. If, however, **B** is independent of $\mathbf{H}_i$, for each i, then Bayes' Theorem offers no help. This follows directly from (1) in paragraph 23.2, since $P(\mathbf{B} \mid \mathbf{H}_i) = P(\mathbf{B})$ by independence; therefore,

$$P(\mathbf{H}_j \mid \mathbf{B}) = \frac{P(\mathbf{H}_j) \cdot P(\mathbf{B})}{\displaystyle\sum_{i=1}^{n} P(\mathbf{H}_i) \cdot P(\mathbf{B})}.$$

Because $P(\mathbf{B})$ is a common factor in all terms of the denominator and because the sum of the probabilities of the alternate hypotheses must be 1,

$$P(\mathbf{H}_j \mid \mathbf{B}) = \frac{P(\mathbf{H}_j) \cdot P(\mathbf{B})}{P(\mathbf{B}) \cdot \displaystyle\sum_{i=1}^{n} P(\mathbf{H}_i)} = \frac{P(\mathbf{H}_j) \cdot P(\mathbf{B})}{P(\mathbf{B})} = P(\mathbf{H}_j).$$

Problems for Section 23

1. Let a single unbiased die be tossed two times in succession. Create a partition of the sample space based on whether the number showing on the second toss is less than, equal to, or greater than that showing on the first.

2. (*Conclusion of Problem 1.*) Let **B** denote the event that at least one of the numbers

showing is a prime. Create a partition of **B** consistent with the partition of the sample space given in Problem 1.

3. Let a penny, a nickel, and a dime be tossed simultaneously. Create a partition of the sample space according to the value of just those coins which show heads.

4. (*Continuation of Problem 3.*) If **B** is the event that the penny shows heads, create a partition of **B** consistent with the partition of the sample space given in Problem 3.

5. (*Conclusion of Problem 3.*) Let **A** denote the event that the coins which show heads add to exactly 15 cents. Compute (*a*) $P(\mathbf{A})$, (*b*) $P(\mathbf{A} \mid \mathbf{B})$.

6. Let five dimes be tossed simultaneously (hence the sample space consists of 2^5 five-tuples). Create a partition of the sample space according to the value of just those coins which show heads.

7. An urn labeled I contains 10 red, 8 blue, and 7 white balls. Another urn labeled II contains 1 red, 2 blue, and 1 white ball. A ball of unobserved color is transferred from urn I to urn II and then a ball is drawn from urn II. We want to compute the probability that if the ball drawn from urn II is blue, then the ball transferred was white. (*a*) What is the sample space **S** of this experiment? (*b*) The alternate hypotheses are $\mathbf{H}_1$: a white ball is transferred; $\mathbf{H}_2$: a red ball is transferred; $\mathbf{H}_3$: a blue ball is transferred. What are the prior probabilities of these hypotheses?

8. (*Continuation of Problem 7.*) For this problem, the event **B** will be drawing a blue ball from urn II. Compute the conditional probabilities $P(\mathbf{B} \mid \mathbf{H}_i)$ for $i = 1, 2, 3$ and create a table as in Example 1 of paragraph 23.2.

9. (*Continuation of Problem 7.*) Using the table computed in Problem 8, given that a blue ball was drawn from urn II, what color ball was most likely transferred?

10. (*Continuation of Problem 7.*) Letting $\overline{\mathbf{B}}$ be the event that either a white or red ball was drawn from urn II, compute the conditional probabilities $P(\overline{\mathbf{B}} \mid \mathbf{H}_i)$ for $i = 1, 2, 3$ and create a table as in Example 1 of paragraph 23.2.

11. (*Continuation of Problem 7.*) If the ball drawn from urn II is not blue, then what is the probability that the transferred ball was blue?

12. (*Conclusion of Problem 7.*) In Problems 10 and 11, why did we ask for $P(\overline{\mathbf{B}} \mid \mathbf{H}_i)$ and not for $P(\mathbf{R} \mid \mathbf{H}_i)$?

13. An urn labeled I contains three red and two blue balls. Two of these balls are transferred to an empty urn labeled II. One ball is then chosen from urn II. (*a*) What is the sample space of this experiment? (*b*) There are three alternate hypotheses: $\mathbf{H}_1$: both transferred balls are red; $\mathbf{H}_2$: both transferred balls are blue; $\mathbf{H}_3$: one transferred ball is red and the other is blue. What are the prior probabilities of each?

14. (*Continuation of Problem 13.*) For this problem, let **B** be the event that a blue ball is drawn from urn II. Compute the conditional probabilities $P(\mathbf{B} \mid \mathbf{H}_i)$ for $i = 1, 2, 3$ and create a table as in Example 1 of paragraph 23.2.

15. (*Conclusion of Problem 13.*) Using the table created in Problem 14, compute $P(\mathbf{H}_2 \mid \mathbf{B})$.

16. Referring to Problem 24 of Section 21, the probabilities that a randomly selected incoming passenger arrived on airlines A_1, A_2, A_3, A_4, are respectively, $\frac{1}{2}$, $\frac{1}{4}$, $\frac{1}{8}$, and $\frac{1}{8}$. Let **L** be the event that the incoming passenger is late. Compute $P(\mathbf{L} \mid A_i)$ for $i = 1, 2, 3, 4$.

17. (*Conclusion of Problem 16.*) Create a table and compute $P(A_i \mid \mathbf{L})$ for $i = 1, 2, 3, 4$.

18. Let **D** represent an ordinary deck of 52 playing cards. Draw a card randomly from **D** and discard it. If a second card drawn randomly from the 51 remaining cards is a spade, what is the probability that a spade was discarded? Before making any calculations, think about this problem. How will your calculated probability compare with $\frac{1}{4}$?

19. Suppose that urn I contains five red balls, four white balls, and three blue balls and that urn II contains one red ball, one white ball, and three blue balls. A single ball (of unobserved color) is transferred from urn I to urn II, and then a single ball is drawn randomly from urn II. (*a*) Draw a tree diagram of the experiment and put the probabilities on each branch. (*b*) What is the probability that a red ball is drawn from urn II? (*c*) What is the probability that a white ball was transferred, given that a red ball is drawn from urn II?

20. An urn contains four balls which are known (with equal probability) to be either all red or two red and two green. A ball is drawn at random and found to be red. What is the probability that all are red?

21. Suppose that you have three billfolds exactly alike, one containing a $1 bill and a $5 bill, another containing a $1 bill and a $10 bill, the third containing two $1 bills. You choose a billfold at random without noting the contents and remove a bill without noticing the one left. If the bill selected is a $1 bill, what is the probability that the one remaining in the billfold is the $10 bill?

22. In a certain college the geographical distribution of male students is 40 percent from the northeast (NE), 20 percent from the southeast (SE), 30 percent from the midwest (MW), and 10 percent from the far west (FW). Assume that the following proportions of these students wear beards: NE at 20 percent, SE at 25 percent, MW at 15 percent, and FW at 40 percent. If you meet at random a bearded student, what is the probability that he is a midwesterner?

23. Consider Example 1 in paragraph 23.2, and suppose that the percentage of defective hinges from shop 4 had been 1.6 rather than 0.8. Compute the post probabilities and compare $P(\mathbf{H}_1 \mid \mathbf{B})$ with $P(\mathbf{H}_4 \mid \mathbf{B})$.

24. (*Conclusion of Problem 23.*) To the nearest tenth, what percentage of defective hinges

from shop 4 is necessary if $P(\mathbf{H}_4 \mid \mathbf{B}) > P(\mathbf{H}_1 \mid \mathbf{B})$?

25. Bayes' Theorem may seem complicated, but it is really doing something quite simple. Given the data in Example 1 of paragraph 23.2, assume that the bin contains 10,000 hinges altogether. (*a*) Show that the bin contains about 28 defective hinges from shop 1, 12 defective hinges from shop 2, 10 defective hinges from shop 3, and 8 defective hinges from shop 4. (*b*) Show from (*a*) that the probability is about $\frac{1}{2}$ that a randomly drawn defective hinge is from shop 1.

26. Consider Example 2 of paragraph 23.2. Suppose that the number of students in the class is 120. Compute the number of female class members in each major. Confirm that $P(\mathbf{H}_1 \mid \mathbf{B}) = \frac{18}{49}$.

27. At State U., a class in advanced mathematics contains three juniors, ten seniors, and five graduate students. One of the juniors, four of the seniors, and three of the graduate students received an A in the course. If a student is chosen at random from this class and is found to have received an A, what is the probability that the student is a senior? Are you more confident that the student chosen is a senior *before* or *after* you know that the grade received is A?

28. A major cost in the supply budget of many academic departments is paper. Suppose that company A supplies 30 percent of the paper for the mathematics department, company B supplies 20 percent, and company C supplies 50 percent. Based on past experience, 0.1 percent of company A's paper is defective, 0.8 percent of company B's is defective, and 0.2 percent of company C's is defective. A randomly chosen ream of paper is found to be defective. What is the probability that company C supplied this paper?

29. Jane Doe is selected at random from a community in which 1 percent of the population has a disease that in its early stages can only

be detected by an expensive test. This test gives a positive result in 97 percent of the diseased cases but also gives a positive result in 5 percent of the nondiseased cases. The test is given to Jane Doe. (*a*) If the result is positive, then what is the probability that she does not have the disease? (*b*) If the result is negative, then what is the probability that she does have the disease?

30. The infamous "smoking gun" is left near the scene of a crime with enough blood so that there can be a DNA test. There are 50,000 people in the city whose blood type could match the blood on the gun. A suspect is arrested, and a forensic expert produces a DNA "fingerprint" that indicates a one in a million match between the suspect and the DNA fingerprint. Let H_1 be the hypothesis that the suspect is guilty and let H_2 be the hypothesis that the suspect is innocent. If the *only* evidence is the blood on the gun, then $P(H_1) = 1/50000$ and $P(H_2) = 49999/50000 \approx 1$. Let B be the event that the suspect's DNA fingerprint matches the blood on the gun. Hence, $P(B \mid H_1) \approx 1$ and $P(B \mid H_2) = 1/1000000$. Fill in the following table and decide if the suspect is guilty beyond a reasonable doubt.

Alternate hypotheses	Prior probabilities	Conditional probabilities	Product $P(H_i)P(B \mid H_i)$	Quotient $P(H_i)P(B \mid H_i)/\sum$
H_1	$\dfrac{1}{50,000}$	1	$\dfrac{1}{50,000}$	
H_2	1	$\dfrac{1}{1,000,000}$	$\dfrac{1}{1,000,000}$	
			$\sum = \dfrac{21}{1,000,000}$	

Section 24. Finite Probability Theory

Overview for Section 24

- Introduction of axiomatic structure to model probability
- Axioms and proofs of basic theorems
- Use of Venn diagrams to illustrate conditional probability
- Discussion of independence
- Pairwise-disjoint events and proof of Bayes' Theorem

Key Concepts: axioms and theorems, conditional probability, independence, pairwise-disjoint events, Bayes' Theorem

24.1

The numerical computations of the preceding four sections may be codified into a simple axiomatic structure which serves as the foundation for more advanced developments in probability and statistics. This axiomatic structure rests very heavily upon the basic concepts of set theory, logic, and functions. At the same time, applications of this structure rest equally heavily upon permutations, combinations, binomial coefficients, and, generally, upon the "art of counting." Thus finite probability theory is an area of mathematics in which essentially all the fundamental ideas of elementary discrete mathematics play a critically important role.

We assume the existence of a nonempty, finite set **S** called the **sample space;** any subset of **S** will be called an **event.** Further, we assume the existence of a function P which assigns to each event a real number called the **probability** of that event. Now, let **A** and **B** denote events in **S** and recall (since they are subsets of **S**) that

$$\mathbf{A} \cup \mathbf{B} = \mathbf{B} \cup \mathbf{A} \quad \text{and} \quad \mathbf{A} \cap \mathbf{B} = \mathbf{B} \cap \mathbf{A}.$$

Because P is a function, and therefore assigns a single value to each set in its domain,

$$P(\mathbf{A} \cap \mathbf{B}) = P(\mathbf{B} \cap \mathbf{A}) \quad \text{and} \quad P(\mathbf{A} \cup \mathbf{B}) = P(\mathbf{B} \cup \mathbf{A}).$$

It is acceptable, therefore, to be indifferent to the order in which a *union* or an *intersection* is written. Finally, we assume that the probability function P satisfies the following:

Axioms

I. If $\mathbf{A} \subseteq \mathbf{S}$, then $P(\mathbf{A}) \geq 0$.

II. $P(\mathbf{S}) = 1$.

III. If $\mathbf{A} \cap \mathbf{B} = \varnothing$, then $P(\mathbf{A} \cup \mathbf{B}) = P(\mathbf{A}) + P(\mathbf{B})$.

Based on these axioms we will derive theorems in the abstract. It may help, therefore, to keep a fixed experiment in mind (the simpler the better): The illustrations following most of the theorems below refer to the sample space

$$\mathbf{S} = \{1, 2, 3, 4, 5, 6\}$$

associated with the experiment of rolling a single (unbiased) die. Consider the following events in **S**:

$$\mathbf{A} = \{2, 4, 6\} \quad \text{(the outcome is even),}$$
$$\mathbf{B} = \{2, 3, 5\} \quad \text{(the outcome is a prime number),}$$
$$\mathbf{C} = \{5, 6\} \quad \text{(the outcome is greater than 4).}$$

It is clear that $P(\mathbf{A}) = \frac{1}{2}$, $P(\mathbf{B}) = \frac{1}{2}$, $P(\mathbf{C}) = \frac{1}{3}$, and $P(\mathbf{S}) = 1$.

**THEOREM
24.1A**

If $\overline{\mathbf{A}} = \mathbf{S} - \mathbf{A}$, then $P(\overline{\mathbf{A}}) = 1 - P(\mathbf{A})$.

Proof

From set theory we know that

$$\overline{\mathbf{A}} \cap \mathbf{A} = \varnothing \qquad \text{and} \qquad \overline{\mathbf{A}} \cup \mathbf{A} = \mathbf{S}.$$

By Axiom II, $\qquad\qquad P(\overline{\mathbf{A}} \cup \mathbf{A}) = P(\mathbf{S}) = 1,$

and by Axiom III, $\qquad\quad P(\overline{\mathbf{A}} \cup \mathbf{A}) = P(\overline{\mathbf{A}}) + P(\mathbf{A}).$

Thus $\qquad\qquad\qquad\quad P(\overline{\mathbf{A}}) + P(\mathbf{A}) = 1;$

hence, $\qquad\qquad\qquad\quad P(\overline{\mathbf{A}}) = 1 - P(\mathbf{A}).$ ■

ILLUSTRATION

$\overline{\mathbf{A}}$ is the event that the outcome is odd. Thus

$$P(\overline{\mathbf{A}}) = 1 - P(\mathbf{A}) = 1 - \tfrac{1}{2} = \tfrac{1}{2}.$$

**THEOREM
24.1B**

If $\varnothing$ denotes the empty event, then $P(\varnothing) = 0$.

Proof

From set theory, $\varnothing = \overline{\mathbf{S}}$. By Theorem 24.1A,

$$P(\varnothing) = P(\overline{\mathbf{S}}) = 1 - P(\mathbf{S}).$$

By Axiom II, $\qquad\qquad\qquad P(\varnothing) = 1 - 1 = 0.$ ■

ILLUSTRATION

$|\varnothing| = 0$; hence $P(\varnothing) = |\varnothing|/|\mathbf{S}| = 0$.

**THEOREM
24.1C**

For any event $\mathbf{A}$, $0 \le P(\mathbf{A}) \le 1$.

Proof

The left-hand inequality is simply Axiom I. From Theorem 24.1A,

$$P(\mathbf{A}) = 1 - P(\overline{\mathbf{A}}),$$

and by Axiom I, $\qquad\qquad\qquad P(\overline{\mathbf{A}}) \ge 0;$

hence $\qquad\qquad\qquad\qquad P(\mathbf{A}) \le 1.$ ■

In order that Axiom III apply, it is necessary that events **A** and **B** be disjoint. As in our illustration, however, events **A** and **B** often are not disjoint; hence we cannot expect that $P(\mathbf{A} \cup \mathbf{B})$ is the sum of $P(\mathbf{A})$ and $P(\mathbf{B})$. The problem is to avoid counting the intersection twice: Recall from (6) in paragraph 18.4 that

$$|\mathbf{A} \cup \mathbf{B}| = |\mathbf{A}| + |\mathbf{B}| - |\mathbf{A} \cap \mathbf{B}|.$$

The correct probability formula turns out to be remarkably similar to this one.

THEOREM 24.1D

For any events **A** and **B**,

$$P(\mathbf{A} \cup \mathbf{B}) = P(\mathbf{A}) + P(\mathbf{B}) - P(\mathbf{A} \cap \mathbf{B}).$$

Proof

From (3) and (4) in paragraph 18.4 we know that $\mathbf{A} \cup \mathbf{B} = \mathbf{A} \cup (\mathbf{B} \cap \overline{\mathbf{A}})$. Since $\mathbf{A} \cap (\mathbf{B} \cap \overline{\mathbf{A}}) = \varnothing$, by Axiom III,

$$P(\mathbf{A} \cup \mathbf{B}) = P(\mathbf{A} \cup (\mathbf{B} \cap \overline{\mathbf{A}})) = P(\mathbf{A}) + P(\mathbf{B} \cap \overline{\mathbf{A}}). \qquad (1)$$

From (5) in paragraph 18.4 we know that $\mathbf{B} = (\mathbf{B} \cap \mathbf{A}) \cup (\mathbf{B} \cap \overline{\mathbf{A}})$. Since $(\mathbf{B} \cap \mathbf{A}) \cap (\mathbf{B} \cap \overline{\mathbf{A}}) = \varnothing$, by Axiom III,

$$P(\mathbf{B}) = P((\mathbf{B} \cap \mathbf{A}) \cup (\mathbf{B} \cap \overline{\mathbf{A}})) = P(\mathbf{B} \cap \mathbf{A}) + P(\mathbf{B} \cap \overline{\mathbf{A}}),$$

and $$P(\mathbf{B} \cap \overline{\mathbf{A}}) = P(\mathbf{B}) - P(\mathbf{B} \cap \mathbf{A}). \qquad (2)$$

By substitution of (2) into (1),

$$P(\mathbf{A} \cup \mathbf{B}) = P(\mathbf{A}) + P(\mathbf{B}) - P(\mathbf{B} \cap \mathbf{A}) = P(\mathbf{A}) + P(\mathbf{B}) - P(\mathbf{A} \cap \mathbf{B}). \qquad \blacksquare$$

ILLUSTRATION

$P(\mathbf{A} \cup \mathbf{B}) = P(\mathbf{A}) + P(\mathbf{B}) - P(\mathbf{A} \cap \mathbf{B}) = \frac{1}{2} + \frac{1}{2} - \frac{1}{6}$, since $\mathbf{A} \cap \mathbf{B} = \{2\}$. Thus the probability of rolling either an even number or a prime is $\frac{5}{6}$.

Tutorial 24.1A

Draw the Venn diagrams which illustrate the following formulas:
a. $\mathbf{A} \cup \mathbf{B} = \mathbf{A} \cup (\mathbf{B} \cap \overline{\mathbf{A}})$.
b. $\mathbf{B} = (\mathbf{B} \cap \mathbf{A}) \cup (\mathbf{B} \cap \overline{\mathbf{A}})$.

**THEOREM
24.1E**

For any events **A**, **B**, and **C**,

$$P(\mathbf{A} \cup \mathbf{B} \cup \mathbf{C}) = P(\mathbf{A}) + P(\mathbf{B}) + P(\mathbf{C}) - P(\mathbf{A} \cap \mathbf{B}) - P(\mathbf{A} \cap \mathbf{C})$$
$$-P(\mathbf{B} \cap \mathbf{C}) + P(\mathbf{A} \cap \mathbf{B} \cap \mathbf{C}).$$

[Notice the similarity of this statement with (1) in paragraph 18.5. Of course, we cannot use that formula in this proof but must rely only on the current status of the theory.]

Proof

Let $\mathbf{D} = \mathbf{B} \cup \mathbf{C}$. By two applications of Theorem 24.1D,

$$P(\mathbf{A} \cup \mathbf{D}) = P(\mathbf{A}) + P(\mathbf{D}) - P(\mathbf{A} \cap \mathbf{D}),$$

and $\qquad\qquad P(\mathbf{D}) = P(\mathbf{B} \cup \mathbf{C}) = P(\mathbf{B}) + P(\mathbf{C}) - P(\mathbf{B} \cap \mathbf{C}).$

Thus, $P(\mathbf{A} \cup \mathbf{B} \cup \mathbf{C}) = P(\mathbf{A} \cup \mathbf{D})$, and by substitution

$$P(\mathbf{A} \cup \mathbf{B} \cup \mathbf{C}) = P(\mathbf{A}) + P(\mathbf{B}) + P(\mathbf{C}) - P(\mathbf{B} \cap \mathbf{C}) - P(\mathbf{A} \cap \mathbf{D}). \qquad \textbf{(3)}$$

By Theorem 18.3A, we know that

$$\mathbf{A} \cap \mathbf{D} = \mathbf{A} \cap (\mathbf{B} \cup \mathbf{C}) = (\mathbf{A} \cap \mathbf{B}) \cup (\mathbf{A} \cap \mathbf{C}).$$

Again, by Theorem 24.1D,

$$P(\mathbf{A} \cap \mathbf{D}) = P((\mathbf{A} \cap \mathbf{B}) \cup (\mathbf{A} \cap \mathbf{C}))$$
$$= P(\mathbf{A} \cap \mathbf{B}) + P(\mathbf{A} \cap \mathbf{C}) - P(\mathbf{A} \cap \mathbf{B} \cap \mathbf{C}). \qquad \textbf{(4)}$$

Hence, substituting (4) into (3),

$$P(\mathbf{A} \cup \mathbf{B} \cup \mathbf{C}) = P(\mathbf{A}) + P(\mathbf{B}) + P(\mathbf{C}) - P(\mathbf{B} \cap \mathbf{C})$$
$$- (P(\mathbf{A} \cap \mathbf{B}) + P(\mathbf{A} \cap \mathbf{C}) - P(\mathbf{A} \cap \mathbf{B} \cap \mathbf{C})),$$
$$= P(\mathbf{A}) + P(\mathbf{B}) + P(\mathbf{C}) - P(\mathbf{B} \cap \mathbf{C}) - P(\mathbf{A} \cap \mathbf{B})$$
$$- P(\mathbf{A} \cap \mathbf{C}) + P(\mathbf{A} \cap \mathbf{B} \cap \mathbf{C}). \qquad \blacksquare$$

ILLUSTRATION

$P(\mathbf{A} \cup \mathbf{B} \cup \mathbf{C}) = \frac{1}{2} + \frac{1}{2} + \frac{1}{3} - \frac{1}{6} - \frac{1}{6} - \frac{1}{6} + 0$, since $\mathbf{A} \cap \mathbf{C} = \{6\}$, $\mathbf{B} \cap \mathbf{C} = \{5\}$, $\mathbf{A} \cap \mathbf{B} \cap \mathbf{C} = \varnothing$. Thus the probability of rolling either an even number, a prime number, or a number greater than 4 is $\frac{5}{6}$.

**THEOREM
24.1F**

For any events **A** and **B**, if $\mathbf{A} \subseteq \mathbf{B}$, then $P(\mathbf{A}) \leq P(\mathbf{B})$.

Proof

Again using (5) in paragraph 18.4, we know that

$$\mathbf{B} = (\mathbf{B} \cap \mathbf{A}) \cup (\mathbf{B} \cap \overline{\mathbf{A}}) \qquad \text{and} \qquad \mathbf{B} \cap \mathbf{A} = \mathbf{A}.$$

By Axiom III,

$$P(\mathbf{B}) = P(\mathbf{B} \cap \mathbf{A}) + P(\mathbf{B} \cap \overline{\mathbf{A}}) = P(\mathbf{A}) + P(\mathbf{B} \cap \overline{\mathbf{A}}).$$

By Axiom I, $$P(\mathbf{B} \cap \overline{\mathbf{A}}) \geq 0;$$

hence $$P(\mathbf{B}) \geq P(\mathbf{A}). \qquad \blacksquare$$

ILLUSTRATION

Since $\mathbf{C} \subseteq \mathbf{A} \cup \mathbf{B}$, $P(\mathbf{C}) \leq P(\mathbf{A} \cup \mathbf{B})$; and, in fact, $\frac{1}{3} \leq \frac{5}{6}$.

THEOREM 24.1G

For any events **A** and **B**,

$$P(\mathbf{A} \cap \mathbf{B}) \leq P(\mathbf{A}) \leq P(\mathbf{A} \cup \mathbf{B}) \leq P(\mathbf{A}) + P(\mathbf{B}).$$

Proof

The first two inequalities come from Theorem 24.1F; the last one follows from Theorem 24.1D and Axiom I. $\qquad \blacksquare$

ILLUSTRATION

Since $\mathbf{A} \cap \mathbf{B} = \{2\}$ and $\mathbf{A} \cup \mathbf{B} = \{2, 3, 4, 5, 6\}$,

$$\tfrac{1}{6} \leq \tfrac{1}{2} \leq \tfrac{5}{6} \leq \tfrac{1}{2} + \tfrac{1}{2}.$$

Tutorial 24.1B

Give a more detailed proof of Theorem 24.1G by examining separately each of the following inequalities:

a. $P(\mathbf{A} \cap \mathbf{B}) \leq P(\mathbf{A})$.
b. $P(\mathbf{A}) \leq P(\mathbf{A} \cup \mathbf{B})$.
c. $P(\mathbf{A} \cup \mathbf{B}) \leq P(\mathbf{A}) + P(\mathbf{B})$.

24.2

The introduction of "conditional probability" and "independent events" follows the pattern described in preceding sections. For convenience we will include here a brief review of the rationale in each case. The idea of "conditional probability" may

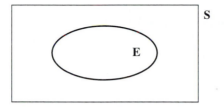

Figure 24.2A

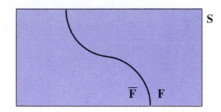

Figure 24.2B

be illustrated with a very simple Venn diagram. Let **S** denote the sample space and let **E** denote an event (see Figure 24.2A). The probability function assigns to **E** the value $P(\mathbf{E})$.

Now suppose that the experiment which has **S** as its sample space is performed, but the information we obtain about its outcome is incomplete. Assume, further, that the (incomplete) information obtained corresponds to an event which we will label **F** and which partitions **S** into the disjoint subsets **F** and $\overline{\mathbf{F}}$ (see Figure 24.2B). Because of our information we know that $\overline{\mathbf{F}}$ is impossible; hence we can think of cutting it away from **S** to obtain a new sample space consisting only of $\mathbf{S} \cap \mathbf{F} = \mathbf{F}$, as in Figure 24.2C. Our concern is still with the event **E**, and we need to know how the "incomplete information" **F** affects the probability assignment. The new probability assigned to **E** should reflect the relative likelihoods of the events $\mathbf{E} \cap \mathbf{F}$ and **F**, and this is measured by the ratio of their probabilities.

In general, if **F** is an event for which $P(\mathbf{F}) \neq 0$, we define the probability of the event **E** given that the event **F** has occurred by

$$P(\mathbf{E} \mid \mathbf{F}) = \frac{P(\mathbf{E} \cap \mathbf{F})}{P(\mathbf{F})}. \tag{1}$$

As in (1) in paragraph 21.2, we call $P(\mathbf{E} \mid \mathbf{F})$ the **conditional probability of E given F.** For a fixed event **F** with positive probability, we show in the next three theorems that conditional probability satisfies properties analogous to Axioms I, II, and III.

THEOREM 24.2A

$P(\mathbf{A} \mid \mathbf{F}) \geq 0.$

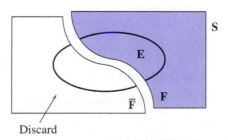

Figure 24.2C

Proof

$P(\mathbf{A} \cap \mathbf{F}) \geq 0$ by Axiom I. Since $P(\mathbf{F}) > 0$,

$$\frac{P(\mathbf{A} \cap \mathbf{F})}{P(\mathbf{F})} = P(\mathbf{A} \mid \mathbf{F}) \geq 0.$$

■

THEOREM 24.2B

$P(\mathbf{S} \mid \mathbf{F}) = 1.$

Proof

Since $\mathbf{F} \subseteq \mathbf{S}, \mathbf{S} \cap \mathbf{F} = \mathbf{F}$ and

$$P(\mathbf{S} \mid \mathbf{F}) = \frac{P(\mathbf{S} \cap \mathbf{F})}{P(\mathbf{F})} = \frac{P(\mathbf{F})}{P(\mathbf{F})} = 1.$$

■

THEOREM 24.2C

If $\mathbf{A} \cap \mathbf{B} = \varnothing$,

$$P((\mathbf{A} \cup \mathbf{B}) \mid \mathbf{F}) = P(\mathbf{A} \mid \mathbf{F}) + P(\mathbf{B} \mid \mathbf{F}).$$

Proof

By Theorem 18.3A, we know that

$$(\mathbf{A} \cup \mathbf{B}) \cap \mathbf{F} = (\mathbf{A} \cap \mathbf{F}) \cup (\mathbf{B} \cap \mathbf{F}),$$

and since $\mathbf{A} \cap \mathbf{B} = \varnothing$, $(\mathbf{A} \cap \mathbf{F}) \cap (\mathbf{B} \cap \mathbf{F}) = \varnothing$. Now by Axiom III,

$$P((\mathbf{A} \cap \mathbf{F}) \cup (\mathbf{B} \cap \mathbf{F})) = P(\mathbf{A} \cap \mathbf{F}) + P(\mathbf{B} \cap \mathbf{F}),$$

and so

$$P((\mathbf{A} \cup \mathbf{B}) \mid \mathbf{F}) = \frac{P((\mathbf{A} \cup \mathbf{B}) \cap \mathbf{F})}{P(\mathbf{F})}$$

$$= \frac{P(\mathbf{A} \cap \mathbf{F}) + P(\mathbf{B} \cap \mathbf{F})}{P(\mathbf{F})} = P(\mathbf{A} \mid \mathbf{F}) + P(\mathbf{B} \mid \mathbf{F}).$$

■

Tutorial 24.2

Show that in Theorem 24.2C the hypothesis $\mathbf{A} \cap \mathbf{B} = \varnothing$ can be replaced by the weaker condition $\mathbf{A} \cap \mathbf{B} \cap \mathbf{F} = \varnothing$.

With these three results we have actually gained much more than we expected, for each one of the earlier theorems has its counterpart in the language of conditional probability. For the proofs, simply replace any appeal to Axioms I, II, and III with reference to Theorems 24.2A, 24.2B, and 24.2C, respectively.

24.3

The formula defining conditional probability may be rewritten

$$P(E \cap F) = P(F) \cdot P(E \mid F), \tag{1}$$

and in this form it is valid (though not especially interesting) even in the case that $P(F) = 0$. This is called the **multiplication rule.** The information that a new event **F** has occurred usually leads to increased accuracy in our assessment of the probability assigned to **E**. This is accomplished via the reduction of the original sample space from **S** to **F**. But in some situations, this reduction in sample space does not affect the probability assignment at all, and this situation leads to the important special case

$$P(E \cap F) = P(E) \cdot P(F), \tag{2}$$

which we take to be the definition of the statement that **events E and F are independent.**

Example 1

The probability of drawing an ace from a well-shuffled deck of playing cards is $\frac{4}{52} = \frac{1}{13}$. Suppose now that a card is drawn and we are told only that it is black. The conditional probability is calculated as follows:

$$P(\text{ace} \mid \text{black}) = \frac{P(\text{black ace})}{P(\text{black})} = \frac{\frac{2}{52}}{\frac{26}{52}} = \frac{2}{26} = \frac{1}{13} = P(\text{ace}).$$

Thus, knowledge of the event "black" has had no effect on the probability assigned to the event "ace," and it follows that

$$P(\text{black and ace}) = P(\text{black}) \cdot P(\text{ace}),$$

which is the definition that the events "black" and "ace" are independent.

Once a given pair of events is known to be independent, there occurs the question about independence of related events, especially the complementary events. It is easy to show, in the example above, that "red" and "nonace" are also independent. The probabilities are

$$P(\text{nonace}) = \frac{48}{52} = \frac{12}{13}, \qquad P(\text{red}) = \frac{1}{2},$$

and

$$P(\text{nonace and red}) = \frac{24}{52} = \frac{6}{13}.$$

Thus,

$$P(\text{nonace and red}) = P(\text{nonace}) \cdot P(\text{red}).$$

In the following theorem we show that the result illustrated here is true in general.

THEOREM 24.3

If **A** and **B** are independent, then $\overline{\mathbf{A}}$ and $\overline{\mathbf{B}}$ are also independent.

Proof

We must show that $P(\overline{\mathbf{A}} \cap \overline{\mathbf{B}}) = P(\overline{\mathbf{A}}) \cdot P(\overline{\mathbf{B}})$. By one of the De Morgan Laws,

$$P(\overline{\mathbf{A}} \cap \overline{\mathbf{B}}) = P(\overline{\mathbf{A} \cup \mathbf{B}}),$$

and by Theorem 24.1A,

$$P(\overline{\mathbf{A}} \cap \overline{\mathbf{B}}) = 1 - P(\mathbf{A} \cup \mathbf{B}).$$

Thus, by Theorem 24.1D,

$$P(\overline{\mathbf{A}} \cap \overline{\mathbf{B}}) = 1 - (P(\mathbf{A}) + P(\mathbf{B}) - P(\mathbf{A} \cap \mathbf{B})).$$

By hypothesis, **A** and **B** are independent; hence

$$P(\mathbf{A} \cap \mathbf{B}) = P(\mathbf{A}) \cdot P(\mathbf{B}).$$

Substitute this into the preceding equation to obtain

$$P(\overline{\mathbf{A}} \cap \overline{\mathbf{B}}) = 1 - (P(\mathbf{A}) + P(\mathbf{B}) - P(\mathbf{A}) \cdot P(\mathbf{B}))$$
$$= 1 - P(\mathbf{A}) - P(\mathbf{B}) + P(\mathbf{A}) \cdot P(\mathbf{B}).$$

Finally, by factoring,

$$P(\overline{\mathbf{A}} \cap \overline{\mathbf{B}}) = (1 - P(\mathbf{A})) - P(\mathbf{B}) \cdot (1 - P(\mathbf{A}))$$
$$= (1 - P(\mathbf{A})) \cdot (1 - P(\mathbf{B}))$$
$$= P(\overline{\mathbf{A}}) \cdot P(\overline{\mathbf{B}}). \qquad \blacksquare$$

Example 2

Let **A** and **B** denote independent events. If $P(\mathbf{A}) = \frac{1}{3}$ and $P(\mathbf{B}) = \frac{3}{4}$, find $P(\overline{\mathbf{A}} \cup \overline{\mathbf{B}})$. There are several approaches; perhaps the most direct uses Theorems 24.1D, 24.1A, and 24.3:

$$P(\overline{\mathbf{A}} \cup \overline{\mathbf{B}}) = P(\overline{\mathbf{A}}) + P(\overline{\mathbf{B}}) - P(\overline{\mathbf{A}} \cap \overline{\mathbf{B}})$$
$$= \tfrac{2}{3} + \tfrac{1}{4} - P(\overline{\mathbf{A}}) \cdot P(\overline{\mathbf{B}})$$
$$= \tfrac{8}{12} + \tfrac{3}{12} - \tfrac{2}{12} = \tfrac{3}{4}.$$

Although we have not proved that **A** and $\overline{\mathbf{B}}$ are independent (given that **A** and **B** are independent), it happens to be true. We may use the data above to illustrate this fact. First,

$$P(\mathbf{A}) \cdot P(\overline{\mathbf{B}}) = \tfrac{1}{3} \cdot \tfrac{1}{4} = \tfrac{1}{12}.$$

Next, we must compute $P(\mathbf{A} \cap \bar{\mathbf{B}})$. Since $\mathbf{A} = (\mathbf{A} \cap \mathbf{B}) \cup (\mathbf{A} \cap \bar{\mathbf{B}})$,

$$P(\mathbf{A}) = P(\mathbf{A} \cap \mathbf{B}) + P(\mathbf{A} \cap \bar{\mathbf{B}}).$$

Hence,
$$P(\mathbf{A} \cap \bar{\mathbf{B}}) = \tfrac{1}{3} - P(\mathbf{A}) \cdot P(\mathbf{B})$$
$$= \tfrac{1}{3} - \tfrac{1}{4} = \tfrac{1}{12}$$
$$= P(\mathbf{A}) \cdot P(\bar{\mathbf{B}}).$$

Tutorial 24.3

If $\mathbf{A}$ and $\mathbf{B}$ are independent, show that $\mathbf{A}$ and $\bar{\mathbf{B}}$ also are independent:

a. Use $\mathbf{A} = (\mathbf{A} \cap \mathbf{B}) \cup (\mathbf{A} \cap \bar{\mathbf{B}})$ and Axiom III to show $P(\mathbf{A} \cap \bar{\mathbf{B}}) = P(\mathbf{A}) - P(\mathbf{A} \cap \mathbf{B})$.

b. Then use independence and Theorem 24.1A to show $P(\mathbf{A} \cap \bar{\mathbf{B}}) = P(\mathbf{A}) \cdot P(\bar{\mathbf{B}})$.

24.4 We come now to Bayes' Theorem, and to prove it we will need an extension of Axiom III to include more than two events. Three or more events are called **pairwise-disjoint** if no two of them have nonempty intersection. It may seem clear that if $\mathbf{A}$, $\mathbf{B}$, and $\mathbf{C}$ are pairwise-disjoint, then

$$P(\mathbf{A} \cup \mathbf{B} \cup \mathbf{C}) = P(\mathbf{A} \cup \mathbf{B}) + P(\mathbf{C}) = P(\mathbf{A}) + P(\mathbf{B}) + P(\mathbf{C}),$$

but what is needed, in general, is an application of mathematical induction. We will use PMI (see paragraph 12.1).

THEOREM 24.4A

For each positive integer n, let

$$\mathbf{A}_0, \mathbf{A}_1, \ldots, \mathbf{A}_n$$

be pairwise-disjoint events in a sample space $\mathbf{S}$. Then

$$P(\mathbf{A}_0 \cup \mathbf{A}_1 \cup \cdots \cup \mathbf{A}_n) = P(\mathbf{A}_0) + P(\mathbf{A}_1) + \cdots + P(\mathbf{A}_n). \qquad (1)$$

Proof
Let $\mathbf{M} = \{n \in \mathbb{N} : \text{the predicate in (1) is true}\}$.

a. When n is replaced by 1, (1) reduces to Axiom III; hence $1 \in \mathbf{M}$.

b. Assume that $k \in \mathbf{M}$; hence

$$P(\mathbf{A}_0 \cup \mathbf{A}_1 \cup \cdots \cup \mathbf{A}_k) = P(\mathbf{A}_0) + P(\mathbf{A}_1) + \cdots + P(\mathbf{A}_k).$$

Now consider the pairwise-disjoint events

$$\mathbf{A}_0, \mathbf{A}_1, \ldots, \mathbf{A}_k, \mathbf{A}_{k+1},$$

and put $\mathbf{B} = \mathbf{A}_0 \cup \mathbf{A}_1 \cup \cdots \cup \mathbf{A}_k$. Then $\mathbf{B} \cap \mathbf{A}_{k+1} = \varnothing$, and by Axiom III,

$$P(\mathbf{B} \cup \mathbf{A}_{k+1}) = P(\mathbf{B}) + P(\mathbf{A}_{k+1}).$$

Because $k \in \mathbf{M}$,

$$P(\mathbf{A}_0 \cup \mathbf{A}_1 \cup \cdots \cup \mathbf{A}_{k+1}) = P(\mathbf{A}_0) + P(\mathbf{A}_1) + \cdots + P(\mathbf{A}_{k+1});$$

hence $(k + 1) \in \mathbf{M}$. By PMI, $\mathbf{M} = \mathbb{N}$.   ∎

THEOREM 24.4B

Bayes' Theorem. Let a sample space **S** be partitioned into n alternate hypotheses

$$\mathbf{S} = \mathbf{H}_1 \cup \mathbf{H}_2 \cup \cdots \cup \mathbf{H}_n,$$

and let **B** denote any event in **S** for which $P(\mathbf{B}) \neq 0$. Then for each integer j, $1 \leq j \leq n$,

$$P(\mathbf{H}_j \mid \mathbf{B}) = \frac{P(\mathbf{H}_j) \cdot P(\mathbf{B} \mid \mathbf{H}_j)}{\displaystyle\sum_{i=1}^{n} P(\mathbf{H}_i) \cdot P(\mathbf{B} \mid \mathbf{H}_i)}. \tag{2}$$

Proof

Now **S** is partitioned by the alternate hypotheses, which are therefore pairwise-disjoint. Observe that

$$\begin{aligned}\mathbf{B} = \mathbf{B} \cap \mathbf{S} &= \mathbf{B} \cap (\mathbf{H}_1 \cup \mathbf{H}_2 \cup \cdots \cup \mathbf{H}_n) \\ &= (\mathbf{B} \cap \mathbf{H}_1) \cup (\mathbf{B} \cap \mathbf{H}_2) \cup \cdots \cup (\mathbf{B} \cap \mathbf{H}_n),\end{aligned}$$

and these events also are pairwise-disjoint. By Theorem 24.4A and by the multiplication rule (1) in paragraph 24.3,

$$P(\mathbf{B}) = \sum_{i=1}^{n} P(\mathbf{B} \cap \mathbf{H}_i) = \sum_{i=1}^{n} P(\mathbf{H}_i) \cdot P(\mathbf{B} \mid \mathbf{H}_i). \tag{3}$$

Since $P(\mathbf{B} \cap \mathbf{H}_j) = P(\mathbf{B}) \cdot P(\mathbf{H}_j \mid \mathbf{B}) = P(\mathbf{H}_j) \cdot P(\mathbf{B} \mid \mathbf{H}_j)$,

$$P(\mathbf{H}_j \mid \mathbf{B}) = \frac{P(\mathbf{H}_j) \cdot P(\mathbf{B} \mid \mathbf{H}_j)}{P(\mathbf{B})},$$

and from (3) we substitute for $P(\mathbf{B})$ to obtain the desired result (2).   ∎

Example 1

Suppose that a sample space **S** is partitioned into n alternate hypotheses. If these hypotheses are equally likely, then Bayes' Theorem has a somewhat simpler formulation: The post probabilities no longer depend upon the prior probabilities. Since $P(\mathbf{H}_1) = P(\mathbf{H}_2) = \cdots = P(\mathbf{H}_n) = 1/n$,

$$\sum_{i=1}^{n} P(\mathbf{H}_i) \cdot P(\mathbf{B} \mid \mathbf{H}_i) = \frac{1}{n} \cdot \sum_{i=1}^{n} P(\mathbf{B} \mid \mathbf{H}_i).$$

Thus for each j the post probability is

$$P(\mathbf{H}_j \mid \mathbf{B}) = \frac{(1/n) \cdot P(\mathbf{B} \mid \mathbf{H}_j)}{(1/n) \cdot \sum_{i=1}^{n} P(\mathbf{B} \mid \mathbf{H}_i)} = \frac{P(\mathbf{B} \mid \mathbf{H}_j)}{\sum_{i=1}^{n} P(\mathbf{B} \mid \mathbf{H}_i)}.$$

Referring to Tutorial 23.1 and Example 1 of paragraph 21.4,

$$P(\mathbf{H}_1 \mid \mathbf{B}) = \frac{P(\mathbf{B} \mid \mathbf{H}_1)}{P(\mathbf{B} \mid \mathbf{H}_1) + P(\mathbf{B} \mid \mathbf{H}_2)} = \frac{\frac{4}{7}}{\frac{4}{7} + \frac{4}{9}} = \frac{\frac{1}{7}}{\frac{16}{63}} = \frac{9}{16}.$$

Problems for Section 24

1. Explain how the following situation illustrates Theorem 24.1A: If four coins are tossed randomly, compute the probability that at least one of them shows heads.

2. Explain how the following situation illustrates Theorem 24.1B: From an urn containing four balls, one red, two white, and one blue, three balls are drawn successively without replacement. Compute the probability that a white ball is not drawn.

3. Explain how the following situation illustrates Theorem 24.1C: Two real numbers x and y are chosen randomly from the interval $0 \le t \le 1$. If the point (x, y) is plotted on a rectangular coordinate system, what is the probability that it lies below the line $y = x$?

4. Explain how the following situation illustrates Theorem 24.1D: Remove all the face cards and aces from an ordinary deck of 52 playing cards. If one card is drawn randomly from the diminished deck, compute the probability that it is either a spade or a 10.

5. Prove that if $P(\overline{\mathbf{A}}) < P(\mathbf{A})$, then $P(\mathbf{A}) > \frac{1}{2}$.

6. Prove that if $\mathbf{A} \subseteq \mathbf{B}$ and $P(\mathbf{A}) < P(\mathbf{B})$, then $\mathbf{A}$ is a proper subset of $\mathbf{B}$.

7. Prove that if $\mathbf{A} \cap \mathbf{B} = \varnothing$, then $P(\overline{\mathbf{A} \cup \mathbf{B}}) = P(\overline{\mathbf{A}}) - P(\mathbf{B})$.

8. Prove that if $\mathbf{A} \cap \mathbf{B} = \varnothing$, $\mathbf{B} \cap \mathbf{C} = \varnothing$, and $\mathbf{A} \cap \mathbf{C} = \varnothing$, then $P(\mathbf{A} \cup \mathbf{B} \cup \mathbf{C}) = P(\mathbf{A}) + P(\mathbf{B}) + P(\mathbf{C})$.

9. (*Continuation of Problem 8.*) Show by a counterexample that $P(\mathbf{A} \cup \mathbf{B} \cup \mathbf{C}) = P(\mathbf{A}) + P(\mathbf{B}) + P(\mathbf{C})$ is not necessarily true if we assume only that $\mathbf{A} \cap \mathbf{B} \cap \mathbf{C} = \varnothing$.

10. (*Conclusion of Problem 8.*) Prove that if $\mathbf{A} \cap \mathbf{B} = \mathbf{C}$ and $\mathbf{A} \cup \mathbf{B} = \mathbf{D}$, then $P((\mathbf{A} \cap \overline{\mathbf{B}}) \cup (\overline{\mathbf{A}} \cap \mathbf{B})) = P(\mathbf{D}) - P(\mathbf{C})$.

11. Let $\mathbf{A}_1$, $\mathbf{A}_2$, and $\mathbf{A}_3$ be any events in **S**. Let $\sum_{i<j} P(\mathbf{A}_i \cap \mathbf{A}_j)$ denote the sum of all probabilities corresponding to pairs $\mathbf{A}_i$ and $\mathbf{A}_j$ for which $1 \le i < j \le 3$. (*a*) Determine the other two terms in the sum

$\sum_{i<j} P(\mathbf{A}_i \cap \mathbf{A}_j) = P(\mathbf{A}_1 \cap \mathbf{A}_2) + ? + ?$.
(b) Show that Theorem 24.1E may be expressed as follows: $P(\mathbf{A}_1 \cup \mathbf{A}_2 \cup \mathbf{A}_3) = \sum_{i=1}^{3} P(\mathbf{A}_i) - \sum_{i<j} P(\mathbf{A}_i \cap \mathbf{A}_j) + P(\mathbf{A}_1 \cap \mathbf{A}_2 \cap \mathbf{A}_3)$.

12. To extend the formula in Theorem 24.1E, we introduce the notations: $\cup_{i=1}^{n} \mathbf{A}_i = \mathbf{A}_1 \cup \mathbf{A}_2 \cup \cdots \cup \mathbf{A}_n$ and $\cap_{i=1}^{n} \mathbf{A}_i = \mathbf{A}_1 \cap \mathbf{A}_2 \cap \cdots \cap \mathbf{A}_n$. Show that $P\left(\cup_{i=1}^{4} \mathbf{A}_i\right) = \sum_{i=1}^{4} P(\mathbf{A}_i) - \sum_{i<j} P(\mathbf{A}_i \cap \mathbf{A}_j) + \sum_{i<j<k} P(\mathbf{A}_i \cap \mathbf{A}_j \cap \mathbf{A}_k) - P\left(\cap_{i=1}^{4} \mathbf{A}_i\right)$.

13. Explain how the following situation illustrates Theorem 24.1E: If one card is drawn randomly from the diminished deck described in Problem 4, compute the probability that it is either a spade, an even number, or greater than 7.

14. Explain how the following situation illustrates Theorem 24.2C: Suppose that one penny, two nickels and three dimes are tossed simultaneously, and we are interested in the value of those coins that show heads. Let $\mathbf{F}$ be the event that the penny shows heads; let $\mathbf{A}$ be the event that the value of the coins showing heads is greater than 15 cents; and let $\mathbf{B}$ be the event that no dime shows heads. Compute $P(\mathbf{A} \cup \mathbf{B} \mid \mathbf{F})$.

15. Let $\mathbf{F}$ denote an event with nonzero probability. Prove the following: (a) $P(\overline{\mathbf{A}} \mid \mathbf{F}) = 1 - P(\mathbf{A} \mid \mathbf{F})$. (b) $P((\mathbf{A} \cup \mathbf{B}) \mid \mathbf{F}) = P(\mathbf{A} \mid \mathbf{F}) + P(\mathbf{B} \mid \mathbf{F}) - P((\mathbf{A} \cap \mathbf{B}) \mid \mathbf{F})$. (c) If $\mathbf{A} \subseteq \mathbf{B}$, then $P(\mathbf{A} \mid \mathbf{F}) \le P(\mathbf{B} \mid \mathbf{F})$.

16. Let $\mathbf{S} = \{0, 1, 2, 3, \ldots, 9\}$ and assign the probability $\frac{1}{10}$ to each digit. Show that the events $\mathbf{E} = \{1, 2, 3, 4, 5\}$ and $\mathbf{F} = \{1, 2, 6, 7\}$ are independent.

17. Let $\mathbf{S}$ be as in Problem 16. Are the events $\mathbf{E} = \{\text{primes in } \mathbf{S}\}$ and $\mathbf{F} = \{\text{perfect squares in } \mathbf{S}\}$ independent? Why or why not?

18. Suppose that $\mathbf{E}$ and $\mathbf{F}$ are independent events, each having nonzero probability. Show that $\mathbf{E}$ and $\mathbf{F}$ cannot be disjoint.

19. Show that $P(\mathbf{A} \cap \mathbf{B} \cap \mathbf{C}) = P(\mathbf{A}) \cdot P(\mathbf{B} \mid \mathbf{A}) \cdot P(\mathbf{C} \mid (\mathbf{A} \cap \mathbf{B}))$.

20. Suppose that $\mathbf{A}$ and $\mathbf{B}$ are independent events and $P(\mathbf{A}) = \frac{1}{6}$ and $P(\mathbf{B}) = \frac{1}{4}$. Determine $P(\mathbf{A} \cup \mathbf{B})$, $P(\overline{\mathbf{A}} \cup \mathbf{B})$, and $P(\overline{\mathbf{A}} \cap \overline{\mathbf{B}})$.

21. Suppose that $\mathbf{A}$ and $\mathbf{B}$ are independent events, and suppose that $P(\mathbf{A}) = \frac{1}{4}$ and $P(\mathbf{A} \cap \mathbf{B}) = \frac{1}{12}$. Find (a) $P(\mathbf{B})$, (b) $P(\mathbf{A} \cup \mathbf{B})$, (c) $P(\overline{\mathbf{A}} \cap \overline{\mathbf{B}})$.

22. Solve the problem in Example 2 of paragraph 24.3 by using a De Morgan Law on $\overline{\mathbf{A} \cup \mathbf{B}}$.

23. Consider the sample space of all five-card hands from a standard deck of 52 cards. Show that the following events are independent: having exactly one king and having more red cards than black.

24. Assume all data as in Example 2 of paragraph 23.2, except that distribution by major is uniform (that is, 25 percent each in biology, economics, psychology, and sociology). Now compute the post probabilities $P(\mathbf{H}_i \mid \mathbf{B})$.

25. A card of unknown suit has been lost from a deck of playing cards. Two cards are dealt randomly from the deck, and both turn out to be hearts. What is the probability that the lost card also is a heart?

26. Suppose that $\mathbf{A}$ and $\mathbf{B}$ are events in a sample space $\mathbf{S}$ and suppose that $P(\mathbf{A}) = P(\mathbf{B}) = \frac{2}{3}$. (a) Is it possible that $\mathbf{A} \cap \mathbf{B} = \varnothing$? (b) Assuming that $\mathbf{S} = \mathbf{A} \cup \mathbf{B}$, evaluate $P(\mathbf{A} \cap \mathbf{B})$. (c) Is it possible that $\mathbf{A}$ and $\mathbf{B}$ are independent?

27. Let $\mathbf{S}$ be a sample space and let it be partitioned into three events, $\mathbf{S} = \mathbf{A}_1 \cup \mathbf{A}_2 \cup \mathbf{A}_3$, each with positive probability. If $\mathbf{B}$ is any event in $\mathbf{S}$, show that (a) $\mathbf{B} = (\mathbf{B} \cap \mathbf{A}_1) \cup (\mathbf{B} \cap \mathbf{A}_2) \cup (\mathbf{B} \cap \mathbf{A}_3)$, (b) $P(\mathbf{B}) = P(\mathbf{A}_1)P(\mathbf{B} \mid \mathbf{A}_1) + P(\mathbf{A}_2)P(\mathbf{B} \mid \mathbf{A}_2) + P(\mathbf{A}_3)P(\mathbf{B} \mid \mathbf{A}_3)$. (c) If $P(\mathbf{A}_1) = P(\mathbf{A}_2) = P(\mathbf{A}_3) = \frac{1}{3}$, then find the post probabilities $P(\mathbf{A}_i \mid \mathbf{B})$.

28. Suppose that **A**, **B**, and **C** are events in a sample space, and suppose that $\mathbf{A} \cap \mathbf{B} \cap \mathbf{C} = \varnothing$. Prove that $P((\mathbf{A} \cup \mathbf{B}) \mid \mathbf{C}) = P(\mathbf{A} \mid \mathbf{C}) + P(\mathbf{B} \mid \mathbf{C})$.

29. (*Conclusion of Problem 28.*) Argue from a Venn diagram that if $\mathbf{A} \cap \mathbf{B} \cap \mathbf{C} \neq \varnothing$, then the formula in Problem 28 does not necessarily hold.

30. (This problem is taken from Mosteller's *Fifty Challenging Problems in Probability.* It is called Molina's Urns.) There are two urns with the same number of balls in each. Some of these balls are black and some are white, but it is not necessarily the case that there is the same number of black balls in each urn.

Let n be some positive integer greater than 2. The experiment is to draw from each urn n balls with replacement. We want the probability that all white balls are drawn from the first urn to be equal to the probability that the drawing from the second is either all whites or all blacks. Show that if z is the number of white balls in the first urn, x is the number of white balls in the second urn, and y is the number of blacks balls in the second urn, then the probabilities are $(z/(x + y))^n$ for the first urn and $(x/(x + y))^n + (y/(x + y))^n$ for the second urn. Conclude that if the probabilities are equal, then $z^n = x^n + y^n$. Ask your instructor why this is unlikely to happen.

Section 25.   Random Variables

Overview for Section 25

- Introduction to random variables
- Discussion of probability functions and distributions
- Expected value or mean of a random variable
- Variance and standard deviation of a random variable
- Computational formulas for variance

Key Concepts: random variable, probability function, distribution, mean, expected value, variance, standard deviation

25.1   Our discussion of probability has focused so far on the sequence of ideas displayed in Figure 25.1A. Perhaps the most important application of these ideas is to the concept

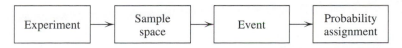

Figure 25.1A

of random variable. First, an illustration: Consider, as we have before, an urn which contains five red, three white, and four blue balls. This time, our experiment is to draw one ball at a time without replacement until a color repeats. For example, (R, R) might be an outcome, or (W, R, B, B) might be another outcome. The question is, "How many draws are required?" The answer must be one of the numbers 2, 3, or 4: Since there are only three colors available, it is easy to see that the fourth draw must result in a repetition (by the Pigeonhole Principle). The answer, of course, is a variable which depends upon the particular outcome of the experiment.

Formally, a **random variable** is a real-valued function defined on a sample space. It has become customary in probability theory to denote random variables by capital letters such as X, Y, etc., and values of a random variable by numbers or lowercase letters (subscripted, if necessary, to distinguish one value from another). In the illustration above, if X is the random variable denoting how many draws are required, then either $X = 2$, or $X = 3$, or $X = 4$.

Now consider the question, "What is the probability that $X = 2$?" Remember that "probability" is assigned to events, so we translate "$X = 2$" into the event consisting of all those points in the sample space of the experiment which correspond to 2 draws. These are the outcomes (R, R), (W, W), (B, B). The partial tree diagram containing these branches is shown in Figure 25.1B, and the sum of the three probabilities is $\frac{38}{132}$. Again, there is an unfamiliar custom regarding notation in probability theory: For the probability that X has the value 2 in a random performance of the experiment we write $P(X = 2)$. Hence

$$P(X = 2) = \tfrac{38}{132}.$$

In a similar way, we can compute the probability for each of the other two values of the random variable. The events corresponding to $X = 2$, $X = 3$, and $X = 4$ constitute a partition of the sample space, so

$$P(X = 2) + P(X = 3) + P(X = 4) = 1.$$

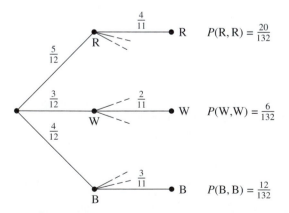

Figure 25.1B

Tutorial 25.1

a. Construct the partial tree diagram (similar to Figure 25.1B) which leads only to the event $X = 4$. (*Hint:* Note that once a color is drawn, it must not be repeated if an unused color remains available.)

b. Compute $P(X = 4)$.

25.2 Suppose, in general, that the random variable X may assume any of the distinct values $x_1, x_2, x_3, \ldots, x_n$. There exists a **probability function** f with domain $\{x_1, x_2, x_3, \ldots, x_n\}$, defined by

$$f(x_i) = P(X = x_i).$$

This function f distributes one unit of probability among the possible values of X, so a probability function is sometimes referred to as a **distribution.** Applications of probability occur primarily through concepts related to distributions, some of which are especially valuable as models of statistical behavior. In the next section, we will consider in some detail one of these special distributions. In Figure 25.2A we extend the outline in Figure 25.1A to include these new ideas.

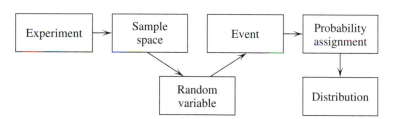

Figure 25.2A

Example 1 Roll a pair of fair dice and let X denote the sum of the faces showing. Thus X is a random variable which has as its values $2, 3, 4, \ldots, 12$. The probabilities are easy to calculate; for example,

$$f(4) = P(X = 4) = \text{probability that sum of two dice is } 4,$$
$$= P(\{(1, 3), (2, 2), (3, 1)\}) = \tfrac{3}{36}.$$

Similar computations lead us to the following tabulation of all the values of this probability function:

x	2	3	4	5	6	7	8	9	10	11	12
$f(x)$	$\frac{1}{36}$	$\frac{2}{36}$	$\frac{3}{36}$	$\frac{4}{36}$	$\frac{5}{36}$	$\frac{6}{36}$	$\frac{5}{36}$	$\frac{4}{36}$	$\frac{3}{36}$	$\frac{2}{36}$	$\frac{1}{36}$

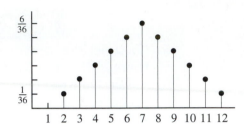

Figure 25.2B

Note that $\sum_{\text{all } x} f(x) = 1$. The graph of this function is shown in Figure 25.2B; it consists of only the 11 dots; we adjoin the vertical segments for clarity. ⬤

Example 2   Let two pennies and a nickel be tossed, and record the results as heads (H) or tails (T). We regard this as a succession of three experiments performed independently. Let $S_1 = S_2 = S_3 = \{H, T\}$, where S_1 and S_2 represent the toss of the pennies and S_3 the toss of the nickel. In every case we assign probability $\frac{1}{2}$ each to H and T. Then the joint sample space is

$$\mathbf{S} = \mathbf{S}_1 \times \mathbf{S}_2 \times \mathbf{S}_3 = \{(H, H, H), (H, H, T), (H, T, H), (T, H, H),$$
$$(H, T, T), (T, H, T), (T, T, H), (T, T, T)\}.$$

Because the tosses are presumed independent, we compute probabilities in $\mathbf{S}$ according to the multiplication rule (2) in paragraph 24.3. For example,

$$P(H, H, H) = P(H) \cdot P(H) \cdot P(H)$$
$$= \tfrac{1}{2} \cdot \tfrac{1}{2} \cdot \tfrac{1}{2}$$
$$= \tfrac{1}{8}.$$

(The seven other probabilities are similarly found to be $\frac{1}{8}$.) Now suppose X is the random variable which assigns to each outcome the total value of those coins which fall heads. Then for each point in the sample space the random variable values are

$$X(H, H, H) = 7 \qquad X(H, H, T) = 2$$
$$X(H, T, H) = 6 \qquad X(T, H, H) = 6$$
$$X(H, T, T) = 1 \qquad X(T, H, T) = 1$$
$$X(T, T, H) = 5 \qquad X(T, T, T) = 0.$$

We see that the range of X is the set $\{0, 1, 2, 5, 6, 7\}$, and this set is the domain of the corresponding probability function, denoted by f. The graph of f is displayed in Figure 25.2C (again, with vertical segments adjoined). From this data, we may compute, for example, the probability that the total value of the coins showing heads

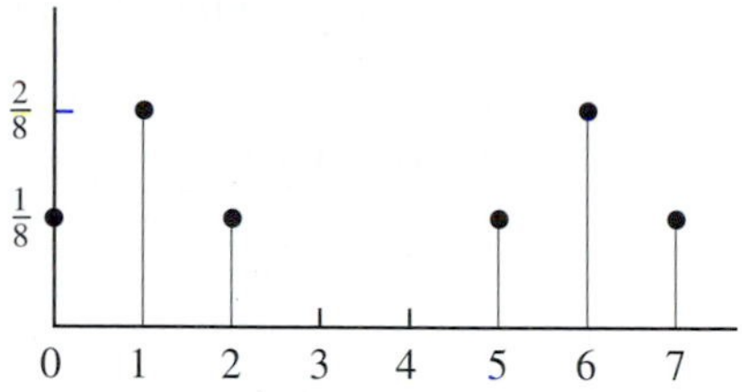

Figure 25.2C

is under 6 cents:

$$P(X < 6) = P(X = 0, 1, 2, \text{ or } 5)$$
$$= f(0) + f(1) + f(2) + f(5)$$
$$= \tfrac{1}{8} + \tfrac{2}{8} + \tfrac{1}{8} + \tfrac{1}{8}$$
$$= \tfrac{5}{8}.$$

Tutorial 25.2

a. Confirm the values of the probability function tabulated in Example 1.

b. In Example 2, find $P(1 < X < 7)$.

25.3

The graphs in the two preceding examples suggest that distributions have widely different appearances. Furthermore, statistical data can often be displayed in graphical form similar to a distribution. It is useful, then, to be able to compare one distribution with another, or a distribution with a statistical graph. To avoid relying on subjective judgment based on the appearance of the graphs, we introduce two numerically computed parameters which will offer a start toward an objectively based technique of comparison.

The first parameter is a number which measures (in some sense) the "middle" of the distribution. Let m denote this hypothetical middle. Recalling that each x_i denotes a value of the random variable, the numbers $x_i - m$ denote **deviations** of the values of X from m. Note that a deviation is positive when $x_i > m$ and is negative when $x_i < m$. Disregarding the probability function, for the moment, we want the sum of the deviations to be zero in order that those to the right will balance those to the left:

$$\sum_{i=1}^{n}(x_i - m) = 0.$$

Recalling properties of the summation notation from paragraph 10.3, note that

$$\sum_{i=1}^{n}(x_i - m) = \sum_{i=1}^{n} x_i - \sum_{i=1}^{n} m = \sum_{i=1}^{n} x_i - n \cdot m = 0.$$

Hence, solving for m,

$$m = \frac{1}{n} \cdot \sum_{i=1}^{n} x_i. \tag{1}$$

Therefore, m simply represents the arithmetic mean of the values of X. The situation, in general, is complicated by the probability function, but (1) offers a clue. By the distributive law of arithmetic, (1) can be rewritten as

$$m = \sum_{i=1}^{n}\left(x_i \cdot \frac{1}{n}\right). \tag{2}$$

If the n values of X are equally likely, then $f(x_i) = 1/n$ and (2) can be expressed as

$$m = \sum_{i=1}^{n} x_i \cdot f(x_i). \tag{3}$$

If, on the other hand, the values of X are not equally likely, then (2) is not appropriate but (3) is appropriate, and we use it to define the middle of the distribution. In general, then, the number computed by (3) is referred to as the **mean** of X, which is denoted by μ, or as the **expected value** of X, which is denoted by $E(X)$. These are simply different names and symbols for the same number; hence (3) can be expressed as

$$\mu = E(X) = \sum_{i=1}^{n} x_i \cdot f(x_i). \tag{4}$$

Example 1   Suppose that you are dealt a five-card hand from a well-shuffled deck of playing cards. Let X be the random variable which denotes the number of spades in your hand. Then X must have one of the values 0, 1, 2, 3, 4, 5, and the probabilities are calculated as follows:

$$P(X = j) = \frac{\binom{13}{j} \cdot \binom{39}{5-j}}{\binom{52}{5}}. \tag{5}$$

Approximating these probabilities to four decimal places, we tabulate the probability function:

x	0	1	2	3	4	5
$f(j)$	0.2215	0.4114	0.2743	0.0815	0.0107	0.0005

Calculating from (4) and (5), the expected number of spades in your hand is

$$E(X) = \sum_{j=0}^{5} j \cdot f(j) = \tfrac{5}{4} \qquad \text{(exactly)},$$

or from the table,

$$E(X) = 0 \cdot (0.2215) + 1 \cdot (0.4114) + 2 \cdot (0.2743) + 3 \cdot (0.0815)$$
$$+ \, 4 \cdot (0.0107) + 5 \cdot (0.0005) = 1.2498.$$

Tutorial 25.3

a. Compute the expected value $E(X)$ for the random variable defined in Example 1 of paragraph 25.2.

b. Compute the expected value $E(X)$ for the random variable defined in Example 2 of paragraph 25.2.

An important observation, illustrated in Example 1, is that the expected value (or the mean) of a distribution is not necessarily one of the possible random variable values. It is a (fictitious) value which represents the "middle" of the distribution in a sense illustrated by the following "mechanical" interpretation. Consider a horizontal bar of length 5 feet and marked at 1-foot intervals. Now place at each mark a weight proportional to the probability associated with that mark (see Figure 25.3). Although unrealistic, we will assume that the bar is rigid, and that its weight is negligible compared with the weights at each mark (perhaps the weights are given in fractions of a ton). Then, if a fulcrum is placed at the mark 1.25, this mechanical system will balance.

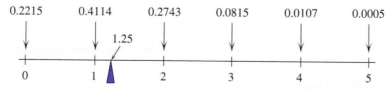

Figure 25.3

25.4

The second of our two parameters measures the "spread" of the distribution. If the values of X corresponding to the larger probabilities are grouped near the mean (as in Example 1 of paragraph 25.2), then the spread should be relatively small. But if much of the probability is grouped away from the mean (as in Example 2 of paragraph 25.2), then the spread should be relatively large. If we wish to find a single number which provides information about spread, then it must (somehow) depend upon the deviations, $x_i - \mu$, of the random variable values from the mean. But how? We simplify the discussion by temporarily assuming that the random variable values are equally likely, and as a first guess for our parameter we simply pick the average value of the deviations

$$\frac{1}{n} \cdot \sum_{i=1}^{n} (x_i - \mu).$$

This perfectly natural choice, however, leads into a blind alley. Note that

$$\frac{1}{n} \cdot \sum_{i=1}^{n}(x_i - \mu) = \frac{1}{n}\left(\sum_{i=1}^{n} x_i - \sum_{i=1}^{n} \mu\right) = \frac{1}{n}\left(\sum_{i=1}^{n} x_i - n \cdot \mu\right)$$

$$= \frac{1}{n} \cdot \left(\sum_{i=1}^{n} x_i\right) - \mu = \mu - \mu = 0;$$

hence no useful information about the distribution can come from this calculation. The sum is zero because the positive and negative deviations cancel out. The simple modification of squaring the deviations will avoid this cancellation, and the average value of these "squared deviations,"

$$\frac{1}{n} \cdot \sum_{i=1}^{n}(x_i - \mu)^2, \tag{1}$$

turns out to be a good relative measure of spread. As with the situation involving expected value, (1) is not a good measure when the values of X are not equally likely. In that case, we need to replace $1/n$ by the probability function values. Thus, the parameter we seek is

$$\sum_{i=1}^{n}(x_i - \mu)^2 \cdot f(x_i), \tag{2}$$

which is called the **variance** of X and is denoted by $\text{Var}(X)$, or by σ^2. Because of (2), the variance of X is measured in units which are squared relative to the units in which X is measured. By taking the square root, we obtain the **standard deviation** of X:

$$\sigma = \sqrt{\text{Var}(X)}. \tag{3}$$

Both the mean and the standard deviation of X are measured in units which are consistent with the values of X. We will return to this point in Sections 26 and 27, where σ turns out to be the length of an interval on the X axis (which has special significance in terms of the units in which X is measured).

Example 1
Consider again the data given in Example 1 of paragraph 25.3. The variance of the random variable X is defined by (2) to be

$$\text{Var}(X) = \sum_{i=0}^{5}(i - 1.25)^2 \cdot f(i).$$

Unless one has access to a programmable calculator or a computer, this computation is quite tedious. We organize it via Table 25.4 (retaining only two decimal places). Now, the sum of the right-hand column is the variance of X,

$$\text{Var}(X) = 0.83.$$

The standard deviation of X is

$$\sigma = \sqrt{0.83} = 0.91.$$

The graph of the probability function f is shown in Figure 25.4. On the X axis, both μ and σ (as a deviation from μ) are indicated. Notice that

i	$i - 1.25$	$(i - 1.25)^2$	$f(i)$	$(i - 1.25)^2 \cdot f(i)$
0	−1.25	1.56	0.22	0.34
1	−0.25	0.06	0.41	0.02
2	0.75	0.56	0.27	0.15
3	1.75	3.06	0.08	0.24
4	2.75	7.56	0.01	0.08
5	3.75	14.06	0.00	0.00

Table 25.4   0.83

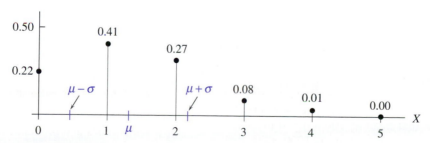

Figure 25.4

$$P(\mu - \sigma < X < \mu + \sigma) = P(X = 1) + P(X = 2) = 0.68.$$

It is an observed fact that for many distributions, the probability that the random variable assumes a value within one standard deviation of the mean is approximately $\frac{2}{3}$.

There is another formula for the calculation of $\text{Var}(X)$ which is often less tedious than using (2) directly as we did above. The proof will be sketched in Problem 25.

$$\text{Var}(X) = \left(\sum_{i=1}^{n} x_i^2 \cdot f(x_i) \right) - \mu^2. \tag{4}$$

We recommend using this formula in the following problem set; it can be remembered fairly easily as:

The mean of the squares minus the square of the mean.

Problems for Section 25

1. Let an integer between 1 and 20 (inclusive) be chosen at random, and let X denote the number of prime numbers less than it. Thus, for example, $X(1) = X(2) = 0$ and $X(9) = 4$. (*a*) What values may X assume? (*b*) Sketch the graph of its probability function. (*c*) Compute the mean of this distribution.

2. An urn contains three red balls and five blue balls. Four balls are drawn randomly and simultaneously from the urn. Let X denote the number of red balls drawn. (*a*) What are the possible values of X? (*b*) Sketch the graph of its probability function. (*c*) Compute the mean of this distribution.

3. Let X denote a random variable which assumes the values $x_1, x_2, \ldots, x_n$ with equal probability [that is, $P(X = x_i) = 1/n$]. A random variable with this property is said to have a **uniform distribution.** (*a*) If the sum of the random variable values is 100, show that $E(X) = 100/n$. (*b*) If the sum of the squared deviations is 1000, show that $\text{Var}(X) = 1000/n$.

4. (*Conclusion of Problem 3.*) Suppose that X is a random variable which can assume the values $-1, 0, 1, 2, 3, 4$. If X has a uniform distribution, calculate $E(X)$ and $\text{Var}(X)$.

5. Suppose that X and Y denote random variables on the same sample space which may assume the values X: 0, 1, 2, 3, and Y: 0, 1, 2. (*a*) What is the range of values of the random variable $W = X + Y$? (*b*) What is the range of values of the random variable $Z = X \cdot Y$?

6. Suppose that X and Y denote random variables on the same sample space which may assume the values X: 0, 1, 2, 3 and Y: 0, 1, 2. (*a*) What is the range of values of the random variable $W = X - Y$? (*b*) What is the range of values of the random variable $Z = X + 3 \cdot Y$?

7. Suppose that X and Y are random variables with values and probabilities as shown:

X	−1	1	2	3
P(X)	$\frac{1}{4}$	$\frac{1}{8}$	$\frac{1}{4}$	$\frac{3}{8}$

Y	−1	0	1	2
P(Y)	$\frac{1}{8}$	$\frac{1}{4}$	$\frac{1}{4}$	$\frac{3}{8}$

(a) Compute $E(X)$ and $\text{Var}(X)$. (b) Compute $E(Y)$ and $\text{Var}(Y)$.

8. (*Conclusion of Problem 7.*) Suppose that X and Y are "independent" in the sense that $P(X = i \text{ and } Y = j) = P(X = i)P(Y = j)$. (a) What are the possible values that $W = X + Y$ can assume? (b) Construct the probability function for the random variable W. (c) Compute $E(W)$, and compare with your expected values in Problem 7.

9. In your wallet there are eight bills: one $10, two $5, and five $1. You donate two of these bills (randomly chosen) to a worthy charity. Let Y denote the amount of your contribution. (a) What possible values might Y have? (b) Find $P(Y = 2)$ and $P(Y = 15)$.

10. In Problem 9, what is the expected value of your contribution?

11. You have a box containing 12 lightbulbs of which two are defective. Three lightbulbs are randomly drawn from the box (without replacement), and X denotes the number of defectives drawn. (a) What are the possible values of X? (b) Calculate the probability function (distribution). (c) Find the expected value $E(X)$.

12. In nine innings at bat, a baseball team scores, respectively, 4, 2, 0, 2, 3, 0, 0, 0, 1 runs. Let Z denote the number of runs per inning. (a) Compute the probability function for Z [assuming, for example, that $P(Z = 2) = \frac{2}{9}$]. (b) Find the expected number of runs per inning.

13. Let X be a random variable having the following probability distribution:

X	−1	0	1	2
P(X)	0.3	0.2	0.4	0.1

(a) Calculate $E(X)$. (b) Calculate $\text{Var}(X)$ and the standard deviation.

14. A fair coin is tossed successively until H or T appears a second time. Let X denote the number of tosses. (Note that X can have only two values.) Calculate the probability distribution, $E(X)$, and $\text{Var}(X)$.

15. Assume that the random variable Y has the following probability distribution:

Y	0	1	2	3
P(Y)	$\frac{1}{3}$	$\frac{1}{3}$	$\frac{1}{6}$	$\frac{1}{6}$

(a) Compute $E(Y)$. (b) Compute $\text{Var}(Y)$ and the standard deviation.

16. Let X be a random variable with possible values −1, 0, 1, 2, 4, and 8. Two of the following three fail to be probability distributions. Calculate the expected value for the one that is a probability distribution.

X	−1	0	1	2	4	8
(a)	$\frac{1}{6}$	$\frac{1}{6}$	$\frac{1}{4}$	$\frac{1}{2}$	$\frac{1}{8}$	$\frac{1}{8}$
(b)	$\frac{1}{12}$	$\frac{1}{3}$	$\frac{1}{12}$	$\frac{1}{8}$	$\frac{1}{8}$	$\frac{1}{4}$
(c)	$\frac{1}{16}$	$\frac{1}{32}$	$\frac{1}{16}$	$\frac{1}{2}$	$\frac{1}{4}$	$\frac{1}{8}$

17. Suppose that a class consists of 14 male and 12 female students. If three different students are selected randomly, let X be the number of females selected. (a) What are the values that X can assume? (b) Calculate the probability function. (c) Calculate $E(X)$, $\text{Var}(X)$, and the standard deviation.

18. Suppose that urn I contains four red and three green balls and that urn II contains four red and five green balls. Suppose that one ball is drawn randomly from each urn. Let X

denote the number of red balls drawn.
(a) Tabulate the probability function for X and draw its graph. (b) Calculate $E(X)$, $\text{Var}(X)$, and the standard deviation.

19. The Student Union rents bicycles and unicycles and currently has seven bicycles and three unicycles. Four of these cycles are rented at random. Let X be the number of wheels rented. (a) Tabulate the probability function for X and draw its graph. (b) Calculate $E(X)$, $\text{Var}(X)$, and the standard deviation.

20. A pet shop has a cat, a dog, a parakeet, two fish, and one octopus. Two of these animals are sold at random. Let X be the number of legs sold. (For this problem, assume that an octopus has eight "legs.") (a) Tabulate the probability function for X and draw its graph. (b) Calculate $E(X)$, $\text{Var}(X)$, and the standard deviation.

21. Suppose that wallet I contains two $5 bills and two $1 bills and that wallet II contains one $10 bill and three $1 bills. Suppose that one bill is randomly taken from each wallet. Let X denote the amount of money taken. (a) Tabulate the probability function for X and draw its graph. (b) Calculate $E(X)$, $\text{Var}(X)$, and the standard deviation.

22. Suppose that for $1 you can buy a state lottery ticket that allows you to choose without repetition 6 of 44 numbers. You win if your numbers match in any order those chosen. (a) What is your probability of winning if you buy one ticket? (b) If you don't win, then you have won (-1). What is the distribution function for the experiment of buying one lottery ticket if winning earns you $M ? (c) What is the expected value of this distribution if M = 1 million? [*Hint:* $\binom{44}{6} = 7{,}059{,}052$.]

23. A friend of yours wants you to invest $1000 in his band. He claims that within a year the band will sign a big recording contract and

he will pay you back $10,000. You estimate that the probability of this happening is $\frac{1}{50}$, but that there is a probability of $\frac{4}{5}$ that the band will break up and you will lose the entire $1000. There is also the chance that the band will continue to muddle along and you would just get your money back. (a) What is the distribution function for your return (which could be positive, negative, or zero)? (b) What is the expected value? (c) If you had a guaranteed investment that would return 5 percent in 1 year, would you invest in the band or take the guarantee?

24. For simplicity, let X be a random variable with three equally likely values x_1, x_2, and x_3. Suppose that the mean is 1. (a) Confirm that $f(x_1) = f(x_2) = f(x_3) = \frac{1}{3}$, and that $x_1 + x_2 + x_3 = 3$. (b) Show that the variance can be written as $\text{Var}(X) = \frac{1}{3}(x_1^2 - 2x_1 + 1) + \frac{1}{3}(x_2^2 - 2x_2 + 1) + \frac{1}{3}(x_3^2 - 2x_3 + 1)$.
(c) Collect terms of like power to show that $\text{Var}(X) = \frac{1}{3}(x_1^2 + x_2^2 + x_3^2) - \frac{2}{3}(x_1 + x_2 + x_3) + 1$.
(d) Finally, show that $\text{Var}(X) = \frac{1}{3}(x_1^2 + x_2^2 + x_3^2) - 1$.

25. Assume that X has n values with probabilities $f(x_i)$. In this problem, we show that

$$\text{Var}(X) = \left(\sum_{i=1}^{n} x_i^2 f(x_i) \right) - \mu^2.$$

(a) Using $\text{Var}(X) = \sum_{i=1}^{n}(x_i - \mu)^2 f(x_i)$, show that $\text{Var}(X) = \sum_{i=1}^{n}(x_i^2 - 2x_i\mu + \mu^2)f(x_i)$. (b) Now show that $\text{Var}(X) = \left(\sum_{i=1}^{n} x_i^2 f(x_i) \right) - 2\mu \cdot \left(\sum_{i=1}^{n} x_i f(x_i) \right) + \mu^2 \cdot \left(\sum_{i=1}^{n} f(x_i) \right)$. (c) Why does $\sum_{i=1}^{n} f(x_i) = 1$? (d) Using (4) in paragraph 25.3, show that $2\mu \cdot \sum_{i=1}^{n} x_i f(x_i) = 2\mu^2$.
(e) Show that $\text{Var}(X) = \left(\sum_{i=1}^{n} x_i^2 f(x_i) \right) - \mu^2$.

26. Suppose that a class consists of 9 men and 11 women. Two students are selected randomly to discuss problems in the homework assignment. Let X denote the number of men selected. (In the following calculations use at

most two decimal places.) (*a*) Construct the probability function for the random variable *X*. (*b*) Compute $E(X)$. (*c*) Compute $\text{Var}(X)$

in two ways: by its definition and by the formula in Problem 25. Observe that even in this simple case, the latter is slightly easier.

Section 26.   The Binomial Distribution

Overview for Section 26

- Definition and examples of a Bernoulli sequence of trials
- Derivation of the binomial distribution
- Mean and variance of the binomial distribution
- Applications of the binomial distribution
- Observed variability of important distributions, including the binomial

Key Concepts: trial, Bernoulli sequence, binomial distribution, mean, variance, standard deviation, variability of distributions

26.1

Let $\mathscr{E}$ denote an experiment which has a sample space **S** consisting of the possible outcomes of $\mathscr{E}$. Let **A** denote an event in **S** and let the complement of **A** be denoted by $\overline{\textbf{A}}$. It is customary to say $\mathscr{E}$ results in a **success** when **A** occurs and in a **failure** when $\overline{\textbf{A}}$ occurs.

Example 1

a. $\mathscr{E}:$ Toss a coin.

    S :   {H, T},

        $|\textbf{S}| = 2.$

    A :   {H},

        $P(\textbf{A}) = P(\text{success}) = \frac{1}{2}.$

b. $\mathscr{E}:$ Roll a pair of dice.

    S :   {(1, 1), (1, 2), (1, 3), . . . , (6, 6)},

        $|\textbf{S}| = 36.$

    A :   {(1, 6), (2, 5), (3, 4), (4, 3), (5, 2), (6, 1)},

        $P(\textbf{A}) = P(\text{success}) = \frac{1}{6}.$

c. $\mathscr{E}$:   From an urn with 5 red and 10 green balls, select 1 ball.

S :   {R, G},

$|\mathbf{S}| = 2$.

A :   {G},

$P(\mathbf{A}) = P(\text{success}) = \frac{2}{3}$.

In each of these experiments, respectively, the probability of failure is $\frac{1}{2}$, $\frac{5}{6}$, and $\frac{1}{3}$.

It is also customary to denote the probability of success by p and the probability of failure by q. Note that $p + q = 1$ by Theorem 24.1A. Now consider the following somewhat more complex situation. You wish to drive along part of a major boulevard which includes four traffic signals, each of which is set to give your direction of travel twice as long on green as the cross-traffic. We will assume that the timing of these signals is random (i.e., not adjusted for any particular speed). A reasonable question might be, "How many green lights do you expect to encounter?" The situation you face at each signal is modeled by $\mathscr{E}$ in part **c** of Example 1. Calling it a success if you encounter a green light, $p = P(\text{green light}) = \frac{2}{3}$, since the light is timed to stay green twice as long as red. Your drive, then, involves a sequence of four experiments, each just like $\mathscr{E}$. It is customary to call each experiment (in the sequence) a **trial,** and to think of the sequence itself as a new experiment $\mathscr{E}^*$ called a **Bernoulli sequence of trials** [named for Jakob Bernoulli (1654–1705)]. Because the number of trials is known to be 4 in this illustration, we may replace $\mathscr{E}^*$ by $\mathscr{E}^4$ to be consistent with the notation for the sample space, $\mathbf{S}^4 = \mathbf{S} \times \mathbf{S} \times \mathbf{S} \times \mathbf{S}$. Any outcome of $\mathscr{E}^4$ is an ordered quadruple, (x_1, x_2, x_3, x_4), in which each coordinate is either $\mathbf{A}$ or $\overline{\mathbf{A}}$ depending upon whether its trial results in success or failure. Note that in our example $\mathscr{E}^4$ has a sample space $\mathbf{S}^4$ consisting of 16 quadruples, since each coordinate has two possible replacements. A typical outcome might be $(\mathbf{A}, \overline{\mathbf{A}}, \mathbf{A}, \mathbf{A})$, which we interpret to mean that you are stopped by a red light only at the second traffic signal along your route.

In the general situation, a Bernoulli sequence of n trials, corresponding to an experiment $\mathscr{E}^n$, has these characteristics:

1. Each trial results in success or failure.

2. The probability of success p in each trial is constant.

3. The trials are independent: The outcome of an earlier trial has no effect on that of a later trial.

Given a Bernoulli sequence $\mathscr{E}^n$, a natural question to ask is, "How many successes are there in a given point $(x_1, x_2, \ldots, x_n)$ in $\mathbf{S}^n$?" The answer to this question must be one of the numbers $0, 1, 2, \ldots, n$. If we let X denote the number of successes in $\mathscr{E}^n$, then we can consider X to be a random variable; it is a function which assigns a real number value to each point in the sample space $\mathbf{S}^n$. The fact that the domain of X is a sample space allows us to compute probabilities corresponding to each of the possible values assumed by X, as was done in the preceding section. Recall that the notation $P(X = k)$ refers to the probability that X assumes the value

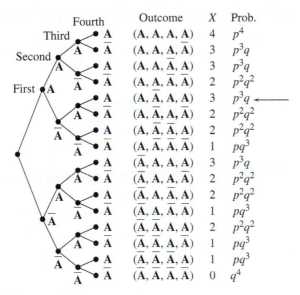

Figure 26.1

$k, 0 \leq k \leq n$. This means that in a performance of $\mathscr{E}^n$, $P(X = k)$ is the probability that the resulting point in $\mathbf{S}^n$ will have exactly k successes and $n - k$ failures among its n coordinates. To indicate how this probability is computed, we return to the "traffic signal" illustration. The tree diagram of all possibilities is displayed in Figure 26.1. Note that the probability on each rising branch is $P(G) = p = \frac{2}{3}$ and on each descending branch is $P(R) = q = \frac{1}{3}$.

The point $(\mathbf{A}, \overline{\mathbf{A}}, \mathbf{A}, \mathbf{A})$ in $\mathbf{S}^4$ has an X value of 3 and a probability of $(\frac{2}{3})^3 \cdot (\frac{1}{3})$, since $P(\mathbf{A}) = \frac{2}{3}$, $P(\overline{\mathbf{A}}) = \frac{1}{3}$, and the trials are independent (the marked path in Figure 26.1). But notice that there are three other points in $\mathbf{S}^4$ which also have an X value of 3: $(\mathbf{A}, \mathbf{A}, \mathbf{A}, \overline{\mathbf{A}})$, $(\mathbf{A}, \mathbf{A}, \overline{\mathbf{A}}, \mathbf{A})$, and $(\overline{\mathbf{A}}, \mathbf{A}, \mathbf{A}, \mathbf{A})$. The probability assignment to each of these points is $(\frac{2}{3})^3 \cdot (\frac{1}{3})$, also. Adding these numbers, by Theorem 24.4A, we obtain the probability function value

$$f(3) = P(X = 3) = 4 \cdot (\tfrac{2}{3})^3 \cdot (\tfrac{1}{3}).$$

In the same way, we find the remaining values in the probability function

$$f(0) = P(X = 0) = (\tfrac{1}{3})^4,$$

$$f(1) = P(X = 1) = 4 \cdot (\tfrac{2}{3}) \cdot (\tfrac{1}{3})^3,$$

$$f(2) = P(X = 2) = 6 \cdot (\tfrac{2}{3})^2 \cdot (\tfrac{1}{3})^2,$$

$$f(4) = P(X = 4) = (\tfrac{2}{3})^4.$$

In each case, the coefficient simply counts the number of ways we can choose k coordinates, from among the four available, to label success while the remainder are labeled failure. Thus, for $k = 0, 1, 2, 3, 4$ the probability of obtaining k successes is

$$P(X = k) = \binom{4}{k} \cdot \left(\frac{2}{3}\right)^k \cdot \left(\frac{1}{3}\right)^{4-k}.$$

Tutorial 26.1

Compute each of the probability values, above, to two decimal places and tabulate the distribution for this example.

k	0	1	2	3	4
$f(k)$					

26.2   Now return to the case of a general Bernoulli sequence of n trials with probability of success denoted by p and probability of failure denoted by q (recall that $p + q = 1$). For each integer k, $0 \le k \le n$,

$$f(k) = P(X = k) = \binom{n}{k} \cdot p^k q^{n-k}. \tag{1}$$

Referring to Theorem 17.2, we see that this probability is the kth term in the binomial expansion

$$(q + p)^n = \sum_{k=0}^{n} \binom{n}{k} \cdot p^k q^{n-k} = q^n + n \cdot p \cdot q^{n-1} + \cdots + p^n.$$

For this reason, the probability function f with domain $\{0, 1, 2, \ldots, n\}$ defined by $f(k)$ in (1) is called the **binomial distribution.** It distributes one unit of probability among the $n + 1$ possible values of the random variable X. The binomial distribution is uniquely determined by the parameters n and p, and for this reason the probability $P(X = k)$ is sometimes written in the notation $b(k; n, p)$.

As introduced in Section 25, there are two principal descriptive measures of any probability distribution: the **mean** (a measure of central tendency) and the **variance** (a measure of deviation from the mean). It happens that each of these measures has an especially simple form when applied to the binomial distribution.

THEOREM 26.2   For the binomial distribution with parameters n and p, the mean is

$$\mu = n \cdot p.$$

Proof

By definition

$$\mu = \sum_{k=0}^{n} k \cdot f(k) = \sum_{k=0}^{n} k \cdot \binom{n}{k} \cdot p^k q^{n-k}$$

$$= \sum_{k=1}^{n} k \cdot \frac{n!}{k! \cdot (n-k)!} \cdot p^k q^{n-k} = \sum_{k=1}^{n} \frac{n!}{(k-1)! \cdot (n-k)!} \cdot p^k q^{n-k}.$$

Now notice that both n and p appear as factors in each term; hence

$$\mu = n \cdot p \cdot \left(\sum_{k=1}^{n} \frac{(n-1)!}{(k-1)! \cdot (n-k)!} \cdot p^{k-1} q^{n-k} \right).$$

By the Binomial Theorem, the parenthetical summation, which we abbreviate by Z, has the value 1. To see this, change the index variables by putting $j = k - 1$ and $m = n - 1$. Then, since $j = 0$ when $k = 1$, $j = m$ when $k = n$, and $n - k = m - j$,

$$Z = \sum_{j=0}^{m} \frac{m!}{j! \cdot (m-j)!} \cdot p^j q^{m-j} = (q + p)^m.$$

Because $q + p = 1$, $Z = 1$, and therefore $\mu = np$.   ■

Tutorial 26.2

Follow through the proof of Theorem 26.2 step by step using $n = 4$ and $p = \frac{2}{3}$. Since there are so few terms, it may be best to write out each sum rather than use the sigma notation.

By an argument which is quite similar to the proof above, but a little more complicated, we can show that the variance, denoted by σ^2, is given by

$$\sigma^2 = n \cdot p \cdot q.$$

The proof of this result is outlined in the problem set.

26.3

Recall that our original question from the traffic signal illustration was, "How many green lights do you expect to encounter?" In the preceding section, it was observed that the mean of a distribution is often referred to as the expected value of the corresponding random variable. The answer to our question, then, is the mean of a binomial distribution with parameters $n = 4$ and $p = \frac{2}{3}$,

$$E(X) = \mu = \tfrac{8}{3} = 2.7 \qquad \text{(approx.)}.$$

As we observed following Example 1 of paragraph 25.3, the mean is not always one of the random variable values. In this case, of course, we cannot encounter 2.7 green lights! Since 3 is the nearest integer to $\frac{8}{3}$, we should expect (roughly) to hit 3 green lights and 1 red light on any given journey. A reasonable "frequency" interpretation of

$$E(X) = \tfrac{8}{3}$$

is that if we were to repeat this journey many times and keep a record of the number of green lights encountered each time, then we should expect the average number of green lights to be close to $\frac{8}{3}$.

Example 1

Consider a binomial distribution with parameters $n = 12$ and $p = 0.4$. By the preceding formulas (to two decimal places):

The expected value is $\qquad \mu = 12 \cdot (0.4) = 4.80.$

The variance is $\qquad \text{Var}(X) = 12 \cdot (0.4) \cdot (0.6) = 2.88.$

The standard deviation is $\quad \sigma = \sqrt{2.88} = 1.70.$

In the usual applications of probability theory, it makes little sense to retain probabilities beyond two decimal places. We will occasionally record more than that in order to give an indication of relative sizes of very small probabilities (that would otherwise be rounded to 0). A few of the probability function values in this example are

$$b(2; 12, 0.4) = \binom{12}{2} \cdot (0.4)^2 \cdot (0.6)^{10} = 0.06,$$

$$b(5; 12, 0.4) = \binom{12}{5} \cdot (0.4)^5 \cdot (0.6)^7 = 0.23,$$

$$b(11; 12, 0.4) = \binom{12}{11} \cdot (0.4)^{11} \cdot (0.6) = 0.00.$$

We should observe that a binomial probability is never 0. The event $X = 11$, in this example, may be highly unlikely, but it is not impossible; we would expect it to occur once in about 3300 repetitions of the experiment $\mathscr{E}^{12}$.

The graph of this distribution is shown in Figure 26.3. Note that the sum of the probabilities is 1. It is intuitively clear from the figure that $\mu = 4.8$ is a reasonable measure of the middle of the distribution. As in Example 1 of paragraph 25.4,

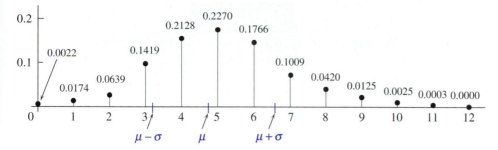

Figure 26.3

however, the interpretation of σ is a bit less apparent. By measuring $\sigma = 1.7$ units on either side of μ, we obtain the interval $(3.1, 6.5)$, and X will fall in this interval if $X = 4, 5,$ or 6. Hence,

$$P(\mu - \sigma < X < \mu + \sigma) = P(X = 4) + P(X = 5) + P(X = 6) = 0.62.$$

Similarly, by measuring $2\sigma = 3.4$ units on either side of μ we have

$$P(\mu - 2\sigma < X < \mu + 2\sigma) = P(X = 2) + P(X = 3) + \cdots + P(X = 8) = 0.97.$$

Finally, by measuring $3\sigma = 5.1$ units on either side of μ, we have

$$P(\mu - 3\sigma < X < \mu + 3\sigma) = 1 - P(X = 10) - P(X = 11) - P(X = 12)$$
$$= 1.00.$$

The figures in Example 1 are reasonably consistent with the important observation that for many distributions related to statistical analysis:

- Slightly more than 68 percent of the probability falls within 1 standard deviation of the mean.

- Slightly more than 95 percent of the probability falls within 2 standard deviations of the mean.

- Slightly more than 99 percent of the probability falls within 3 standard deviations of the mean.

These figures are based on a distribution which occurs in practice with such widespread regularity that it is called the *normal* distribution. It is more or less fully discussed in all textbooks on probability and statistics. Although it belongs to the realm of "continuous" mathematics, we will return to the normal distribution briefly in paragraph 27.7.

Tutorial 26.3

By using the probabilities shown in Figure 26.3, confirm the values given in Example 1 for:

a. $P(\mu - \sigma < X < \mu + \sigma)$.
b. $P(\mu - 2\sigma < X < \mu + 2\sigma)$.
c. $P(\mu - 3\sigma < X < \mu + 3\sigma)$.
d. Now, find $P(X \le 4)$.

Example 2

A hospital is searching for a donor to supply blood of a rare type which occurs in about 5.3 percent of the population. How many individuals, from its pool of volunteer donors, must it test before identifying an individual of the right blood type? This question cannot be answered precisely; the very first test might luckily result in the rare type needed. Presumably, the hospital must simply continue testing until it finds a donor. We can, however, get some idea of the magnitude of the project by using expected value. We will make the assumption that the rare blood type occurs in the donor pool in the same proportion as in the population, and that individuals are selected randomly for testing. We may think of the testing procedure as a Bernoulli sequence of n trials with probability of success being $\frac{53}{1000}$. If X denotes the number of successes (individuals with the rare blood type), then by Theorem 26.2,

$$E(X) = n \cdot (0.053) = \frac{53n}{1000}.$$

Since the hospital needs only one success, we put $E(X) \ge 1$, and find

$$\frac{53n}{1000} \ge 1 \quad \text{or} \quad n \ge \tfrac{1000}{53} = 18.9 \quad \text{(approx.)}.$$

Thus, it should come as no surprise that about 19 tests are required to find an appropriate donor.

Example 3

Based on past experience, a commercial landscape company estimates a 75 percent survival rate for newly planted dogwood saplings. The company has just completed a landscape project which includes eight dogwood saplings. We will assume that this project is a Bernoulli sequence of trials in which $n = 8$ and $p = \frac{3}{4}$. If X is a random variable denoting the number of successes (surviving trees), then it has the binomial distribution and the expected number of surviving trees is

$$E(X) = n \cdot p = 8 \cdot \tfrac{3}{4} = 6.$$

a. Suppose we wish to know the probability that at least six trees survive. Then we must compute

$$P(X \ge 6) = P(X = 6) + P(X = 7) + P(X = 8).$$

These numbers are:

$$b(6; 8, \tfrac{3}{4}) = \binom{8}{6} \cdot \left(\frac{3}{4}\right)^{6} \cdot \left(\frac{1}{4}\right)^{2} = \frac{28 \cdot 3^{6}}{4^{8}} = 0.31,$$

$$b(7; 8, \tfrac{3}{4}) = \binom{8}{7} \cdot \left(\frac{3}{4}\right)^{7} \cdot \left(\frac{1}{4}\right) = \frac{8 \cdot 3^{7}}{4^{8}} = 0.27,$$

$$b(8; 8, \tfrac{3}{4}) = \binom{8}{8} \cdot \left(\frac{3}{4}\right)^{8} = \frac{3^{8}}{4^{8}} = 0.10.$$

Thus, $$P(X \geq 6) = 0.68.$$

b. If we ask for the probability that at least two trees survive, then instead of computing $P(X \geq 2)$, it is much easier to compute the probability of the contrary event, $X \leq 1$, and make use of Theorem 24.1A.

$$P(X \leq 1) = P(X = 0) + P(X = 1)$$

$$= \binom{8}{0} \cdot \left(\frac{1}{4}\right)^{8} + \binom{8}{1} \cdot \left(\frac{3}{4}\right) \cdot \left(\frac{1}{4}\right)^{7} = 0.0004.$$

Hence, $P(X \geq 2) = 0.9996$, which implies that the survival of at least two trees is a virtual certainty.

26.4

Complement: Modes If an unbiased pair of dice is rolled, let X denote the sum of the points showing. The probability distribution is shown in Figure 25.2B, from which it is clear that $X = 7$ is the event with the greatest probability of occurrence. In general, a value of a random variable which has the highest probability is called a **mode** of the distribution. The mode corresponds to the most likely value of the *random variable*. Sometimes a probability distribution will have more than one mode. The most trivial example of this occurs when X denotes the number of heads showing after the toss of a single unbiased coin:

$$P(X = 0) = P(X = 1) = \tfrac{1}{2}.$$

Hence, both 0 and 1 are modes. A much more interesting example relates to the binomial distribution.

The probability distribution for a Bernoulli sequence with $n = 12$ and $p = \frac{2}{5}$ is displayed in Figure 26.3. Note that the most likely number of successes is 5, since $P(X = 5)$ is greater than any other of those probabilities. Thus, 5 is the unique mode for that distribution. From this example, several questions arise: "Is the mode of a binomial distribution always unique, or can there be two (or even more) modes?" "If there had not been a graph, could we have predicted the mode?" Both these questions can be answered for binomial distributions by making use of an interesting technique, which has application elsewhere in mathematics.

Note from Figure 26.3 that as X increases, the probabilities increase steadily to a maximum value, then decrease steadily. Certainly this property is not true of all distributions (see, for example, Figure 25.2C), but is it true for all binomial distributions? Suppose we consider the binomial probabilities for $k = 0, 1, 2, \ldots, n$, given in

$$f(k) = \binom{n}{k} \cdot p^k \cdot q^{n-k}. \tag{1}$$

Note that when the probabilities are increasing, then

$$f(k) < f(k+1) \qquad \text{which is equivalent to} \qquad \frac{f(k)}{f(k+1)} < 1,$$

and when the probabilities are decreasing, then

$$f(k) > f(k+1) \qquad \text{which is equivalent to} \qquad \frac{f(k)}{f(k+1)} > 1.$$

This observation suggests that we look at the ratio

$$r(k) = \frac{f(k)}{f(k+1)},$$

which is defined for $k = 0, 1, 2, \ldots, n-1$. Hence, from (1)

$$r(k) = \frac{\binom{n}{k} \cdot p^k q^{n-k}}{\binom{n}{k+1} \cdot p^{k+1} q^{n-k-1}} = \frac{\dfrac{n!}{k! \cdot (n-k)!}}{\dfrac{n!}{(k+1)! \cdot (n-k-1)!}} \cdot p^{-1} q$$

$$= \frac{(k+1)! \cdot (n-k-1)!}{k! \cdot (n-k)!} \cdot \frac{q}{p} = \frac{(k+1) \cdot q}{(n-k) \cdot p}.$$

First, $r(k) < 1$ implies

$$\frac{(k+1) \cdot q}{(n-k) \cdot p} < 1, \qquad \text{so} \quad kq + q < np - kp,$$

and

$$kp + kq < np - q,$$
$$k(p+q) < np - q,$$
$$k < np - q.$$

Next, $r(k) > 1$ implies

$$\frac{(k+1) \cdot q}{(n-k) \cdot p} > 1, \qquad \text{so} \quad kq + q > np - kp,$$

and
$$kp + kq > np - q,$$
$$k(p + q) > np - q,$$
$$k > np - q.$$

THEOREM 26.4A

If X is a binomial random variable with parameters n and p, then

$$f(k) < f(k + 1) \qquad \text{if } k < np - q,$$
$$f(k) = f(k + 1) \qquad \text{if } k = np - q,$$
$$f(k) > f(k + 1) \qquad \text{if } k > np - q.$$

Proof

For the binomial distribution, recall that

$$r(k) = \frac{f(k)}{f(k + 1)} = \frac{(k + 1)q}{(n - k)p}.$$

If, in fact, $k = np - q$, then since $p + q = 1$,

$$k(p + q) = np - q.$$

Hence,
$$kq + q = np - kp,$$
$$\frac{(k + 1) \cdot q}{(n - k) \cdot p} = 1.$$

Since this quotient is $r(k)$, we have $r(k) = f(k)/f(k + 1) = 1$; hence,

$$f(k) = f(k + 1).$$

The other two claims follow from the reversibility of the arguments preceding the theorem. ∎

The answers to our original questions are now at hand.

THEOREM 26.4B

If X is a binomial random variable with parameters n and p, then:

- k and $k + 1$ are the modes if $k = np - q$.
- $k + 1$ is the unique mode if k is the integer for which

$$k < np - q < k + 1.$$

Proof

Suppose first that $k = np - q$, which implies that $f(k) = f(k + 1)$ by Theorem 26.4A. For each $j = 0, 1, 2, \ldots, k - 1$, $f(j) < f(j + 1)$ (by Theorem 26.4A); hence

$$f(0) < f(1) < \cdots < f(k - 1) < f(k).$$

For each $j = k + 1, k + 2, \ldots, n - 1$, $f(j) > f(j + 1)$ (by Theorem 26.4A); hence,

$$f(k + 1) > f(k + 2) > \cdots > f(n).$$

Thus, $f(k) = f(k + 1)$ is the maximum probability.

Suppose next that $np - q$ is not an integer and that k satisfies $k < np - q < k + 1$. Again, by Theorem 26.4A,

$$f(k) < f(k + 1) \qquad \text{and} \qquad f(k + 1) > f(k + 2).$$

As before, for any appropriate integer $j < k$ or $j > k + 1$, similar inequalities hold; hence,

$$f(0) < f(1) < \cdots < f(k) < f(k + 1),$$

and

$$f(k + 1) > f(k + 2) > \cdots > f(n).$$

Thus, $f(k + 1)$ is the unique maximum probability. ∎

Example 1   By use of Theorem 26.4B we can predict the mode(s) of any binomial distribution. Note that the procedure holds even in the extreme cases of $p = 1$ or $p = 0$, if we recall that the mode must be one of the possible values of X. Also, note that k is the largest integer less than or equal to $np - q$, and so $k = \lfloor np - q \rfloor$.

(n, p)	$np - q$	k	Mode(s)
(12, 0.4)	4.2	4	5
(12, 0.5)	5.5	5	6
(7, 0.5)	3	3	3 and 4
(23, $\frac{1}{3}$)	7	7	7 and 8
(11, 1)	11	11	11
(10, 0)	-1	-1	0

Problems for Section 26

Unless indicated to the contrary, you may use the binomial distribution tables to approximate required probabilities.

1. Compute the following binomial probabilities from (1) in paragraph 26.2 and compare with the best available table entries. (*a*) For

$n = 6$ and $p = \frac{1}{3}$ find $f(2)$ and $f(5)$.
(b) For $n = 8$ and $p = \frac{1}{2}$ find $f(3)$. [*Reminder:* The alternate notation for these three probabilities is $b(2; 6, \frac{1}{3})$, $b(5; 6, \frac{1}{3})$, and $b(3; 8, \frac{1}{2})$.]

2. For the parameters $n = 10$ and $p = \frac{2}{5}$, compute from (1) in paragraph 26.2 and compare with the table entries: (a) $f(0)$, $f(1)$, $f(2)$; (b) $f(8)$, $f(9)$, $f(10)$; (c) $f(5)$.

3. In each of the following, express the probability as a formula and find its value in the table: (a) $b(8; 12, \frac{1}{4})$, (b) $b(4; 12, \frac{3}{4})$.

4. In each of the following, express the probability as a formula and find its value in the table: (a) $b(16; 20, \frac{1}{2})$, (b) $b(15; 18, \frac{1}{3})$, (c) $b(1; 15, \frac{1}{3})$.

5. For the binomial distribution with parameters $n = 12$ and $p = \frac{1}{2}$, use the table to evaluate (a) $P(10 \leq X \leq 12)$, (b) $P(3 < X < 6)$.

6. For the binomial distribution with parameters $n = 15$ and $p = \frac{1}{3}$, use the table to evaluate (a) $P(X \leq 3)$, (b) $P(X > 12)$.

7. Using (1) in paragraph 26.2, prove that $b(k; n, p) = b(n - k; n, 1 - p)$.

8. Using (1) in paragraph 26.2, prove that

$$b(k + 1; n, p) = \frac{p \cdot (n - k)}{(k + 1) \cdot (1 - p)} b(k; n, p).$$

9. (a) Compute $b(0; 15, 0.05)$. (b) Use Problem 8 to compute $b(k; 15, 0.05)$ for $k = 1, 2$. (c) If $b(12; 20, 0.35) = 0.0136$, then what is $b(k; 20, 0.65)$ for $k = 8, 9, 10, 11, 12$?

10. Using (1) in paragraph 26.2, show that if $p = \frac{1}{2}$, then $b(k; n, p) = b(n - k; n, p)$. (Note that this result also follows from Problem 7.)

11. Assume that 1 percent of all model airplane kits are sold with missing parts. If a child receives five model airplane kits at a birthday party, what is the probability that at least one of them has missing parts?

12. If the probability is 0.05 that a baseball game will go into an extra inning, find the probabilities that among 15 baseball games: (a) exactly one will go into extra innings; (b) at most two will go into extra innings; (c) at least two will go into extra innings.

13. If the probability that the Internal Revenue Service will audit an income tax return reporting gross income over $100,000 is 0.65, find the probabilities that among 20 such returns: (a) exactly 10 will be audited; (b) at least 10 will be audited; (c) between 8 and 12 (inclusive) will be audited. (*Hint:* Some of these probabilities have been computed in Problem 9.)

14. If one-third of the employees of a certain company bring their lunches to work, find the probabilities that among four such employees: (a) exactly two bring their lunches; (b) none of them bring their lunches; (c) more than one of them bring their lunches.

15. If a professional basketball player makes, on the average, 7 of 10 free throws, then what is the probability that he will make exactly five of his next six free throws?

16. If 10 percent of car accidents in Rockbridge County are caused by fatigue, then what is the probability that three of the next five car accidents in Rockbridge County will be caused by fatigue?

17. A test has eight multiple-choice questions each having a choice of three answers. A student rolls a die and chooses the first answer if a 1 or 2 appears, the second answer if a 3 or 4 appears, and the third answer if a 5 or 6 appears. What is the probability that exactly four of the answers are correct?

18. The probability of the Cubs winning any particular game is 0.6. If they play five

games, what is the probability that they will win fewer than three? What is the expected number of wins in 162 games?

19. What is the expected number of sixes in 30 rolls of a die? What is the variance?

20. Five percent of the people exposed to a certain contagious disease become infected. If 900 people are exposed, then what is the expected number that will become infected?

21. Teams A and B are playing in the World Series. Suppose that the probability of each team winning a game is $\frac{1}{2}$ and also suppose that the games are independent. (*a*) If Team A has won the first three games, then what is the probability that Team B will win the next two games? (*b*) What is the probability that A wins the first three games and B wins the next two games? (*c*) In 90 World Series, how many times would you expect the situation in part (*b*) to happen? (Note that this has never happened in World Series history.)

22. Suppose that the records of a large insurance company show that 5 percent of the accidents reported involve a fatality. What is the probability that exactly 2 of the next 15 accidents reported will involve fatalities?

23. (Do not use the table in this problem.) Suppose that a fair coin is tossed six times and that X denotes the number of heads obtained. (*a*) Find $P(X = 1)$ and $P(X > 1)$. (*b*) Compute the mean $E(X)$.

24. (*Conclusion of Problem 23; again, no tables.*) (*a*) Compute $\mathrm{Var}(X)$ and the standard deviation. (*b*) Compute $P(\mu - \sigma < X < \mu + \sigma)$.

25. (*a*) Using (1) in paragraph 26.2, find in simplest terms an algebraic expression for $f(k+1)/f(k)$. (*b*) Determine $f(4)/f(3)$ for the case $n = 6$ and $p = \frac{2}{3}$. (*c*) Determine $f(4)/f(3)$ for the case $n = 8$ and $p = \frac{2}{3}$.

26. For $k = 0, 1, \ldots, 6$, we have pictured in (*a*) below, $b(k; 6, 0.5)$ and in (*b*), $b(k; 6, 0.3)$. Do

likewise for $b(k; 8, 0.5)$ and $b(k; 8, 0.3)$ for $k = 0, 1, 2, \ldots, 8$.

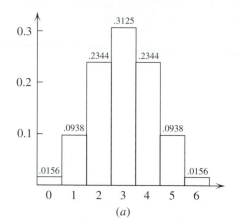

(*a*)

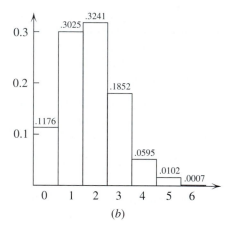

(*b*)

27. The special binomial distribution with $n = 1$ is sometimes called a Bernoulli distribution. Note that $P(X = 0) = q$ and $P(X = 1) = p$. In such a distribution, what must q be in order that $E(X) = \frac{3}{4}$?

28. Compute the variance for the binomial distribution with parameters n and p, using (4) in paragraph 25.4,

$$\sigma^2 = \mathrm{Var}(X) = \sum_{i=1}^{n} x_i^2 f(x_i) - \mu^2.$$

(*a*) Remembering that the random variable values are $0, 1, 2, \ldots, n$, show that this translates to $\sigma^2 = \sum_{k=0}^{n} k^2 f(k) - (np)^2$, where $f(k)$ is given by (1) in paragraph 26.2.

(b) Show that this can be rewritten (sequentially):

$$\sigma^2 + (np)^2$$

$$= \sum_{k=0}^{n} (k(k-1) + k) f(k)$$

$$= \left(\sum_{k=0}^{n} k(k-1) f(k) \right) + \left(\sum_{k=0}^{n} k f(k) \right)$$

$$= \left(\sum_{k=2}^{n} k(k-1) \frac{n!}{k! \cdot (n-k)!} \cdot p^k q^{n-k} \right) + np$$

$$= (n(n-1)p^2) \cdot$$

$$\left(\sum_{k=2}^{n} \frac{(n-2)!}{(k-2)!(n-k)!} \cdot p^{k-2} q^{n-k} \right) + np.$$

(c) Show that the summation at the end of (b) is $(q + p)^{n-2} = 1$. (*Hint:* Put $j = k - 2$ and $m = n - 2$.) (d) Show that $\sigma^2 = -(np)^2 + (np)^2 - np^2 + np = npq$.

29. As in Tutorial 26.2, for $n = 4$ and $p = \frac{2}{3}$, confirm the formula $\text{Var}(x) = npq$ by computing $\text{Var}(x)$ from (4) in paragraph 25.4.

30. For a binomial random variable with parameters $n = 12$ and $p = \frac{1}{4}$: (a) what are μ, σ^2, and σ? (b) Compute, using the table if necessary, $P(\mu - \sigma \leq X \leq \mu + \sigma)$.

31. In a Bernoulli sequence with $p = \frac{1}{3}$, find the probability that the first success occurs on the fourth trial. [*Hint:* The first three trials must include no success (with probability $b(0; 3, \frac{1}{3})$) and the fourth trial must be a success (with probability $\frac{1}{3}$). Now, remember independence.]

32. (*Continuation of Problem 31.*) What is the probability that the second success occurs on the fifth trial? [*Hint:* Consider $b(1; 4, \frac{1}{3})$.]

33. (*Continuation of Problem 31.*) Find an algebraic expression for the probability that the rth success occurs on the nth trial. [*Hint:* Consider the formula for $b(r - 1; n - 1, \frac{1}{3})$.]

34. (*Conclusion of Problem 31.*) Generalizing from the preceding three problems, show that in a Bernoulli sequence with probability of success p, the probability that the rth success occurs on the nth trial is given by

$$\binom{n-1}{r-1} p^r q^{n-r} = \frac{r}{n} \cdot b(r; n, p).$$

Section 27. Introduction to Statistics

Overview for Section 27

- Introduction to the concept of a statistical population
- Definitions of population parameters: measures of location, measures of dispersion
- Definition of percentiles (including quartiles)
- Random samples from populations
- Definitions of sample parameters
- Discussion of confidence intervals

Key Concepts: mean, median, mode, variance, standard deviation, quartiles, random samples, point estimates, confidence intervals

27.1 The practical importance of probability theory rests in large part upon its application in the area of statistical analysis. The goal of many such uses is to make predictions, and because predictions are rarely certain, probability theory measures the degree of confidence which should be attached to a given prediction. The problems of statistics, and the applications of probability theory to them, are far too broad for us even to summarize in a single section. Instead, we will look briefly at two of the important ideas (the first dealing with populations, the second with samples), and we will introduce some of the standard terminology and consider a few of the typical questions.

27.2 The word "population," as used in statistics, usually refers to a list in which the individual entries are related by some common property. We might, for example, be interested in the latest census report for the District of Columbia. Our statistical concern is likely not to be with the inhabitants, themselves, but with some numerical characteristic such as the age of individuals or the income of family units. We will agree that a **population** consists of a list of numbers, often referred to as **data,** on the basis of which it is necessary to evaluate or to predict some special factor. Such concerns are reported on frequently in the public media in relation to economic forecasts, weather predictions, election results, and the like. There are two especially important numerical measures, called *parameters,* which help to summarize the information in such populations. They are the *mean* and the *standard deviation,* corresponding to the same parameters defined in Section 25 for random variables. Again, the mean will be a *measure of location,* identifying the "middle" of the population; the standard deviation will be a *measure of dispersion*, indicating the "spread" of the population about the mean. The usefulness of these parameters becomes apparent when one tries to make sense out of the raw data, which often consists of a list of thousands of numbers. Even the relatively small population listed in Example 1, below, seems unmanageable at first glance. The goal of statistics, in part, is to bring order out of such chaos.

To begin our development, we assume that the given population may be denoted by the following list:

$$x_1, x_2, x_3, \ldots, x_n,$$

which is finite, but n may be quite large. The numbers in the list need not be different from one another, so it is not appropriate to call the list a set. The population **mean** is defined by

$$\mu = \frac{1}{n} \cdot \sum_{i=1}^{n} x_i. \qquad \textbf{(1)}$$

It is a measure of the "middle" of the list of numbers, and it is not necessarily one of the numbers in the list. Furthermore, its value may be significantly affected by just a few numbers in the population which chance to deviate widely from the majority (this is especially likely, for example, in populations which list family incomes). In some cases, therefore, the mean may not be a very good descriptive parameter for the population. In spite of this, it remains the most used and most useful of the numerical measures designed to identify the middle of a population. Two other such measures are of some value in special circumstances. To describe them, let us assume that the population has been arranged in numerically increasing order:

$$x_1 \leq x_2 \leq x_3 \leq \cdots \leq x_n. \tag{2}$$

If n is odd, say $n = 2k - 1$, then there is a middle item in the list, x_k. If n is even, say $n = 2k$, then there is a middle pair of items in the list, x_k and x_{k+1}. We define the **median** of the population to be

$$\begin{array}{ll} x_k, & \text{if } n = 2k - 1; \\[2mm] \dfrac{x_k + x_{k+1}}{2}, & \text{if } n = 2k. \end{array} \tag{3}$$

If, in (2), every inequality is strict, then the median splits the data so that exactly as many items appear before the median as after it. But, because many of the items of the data in the list may have the same value as x_k, we cannot claim that the median always splits the data in halves. What we *can* claim about the median is that both the following are true:

- At least 50 percent of the data is less than or equal to the median.

- At least 50 percent of the data is greater than or equal to the median.

Consider again the population as listed in (2). Some numbers may appear in the list more than once, and we may wish to identify those that appear most frequently. Any number is called a **mode** of the population if no other number appears more frequently in the list than it does. Thus the mode need not be unique. In fact, if in (2) all inequalities are strict, then every number in the list is a mode!

Neither the median nor the mode lends itself to numerical calculation as easily as does the mean. Certain numerical consequences of (1) in more advanced theory account for the importance of the mean in statistical analysis.

Example 1

Consider the following population of ages (in 1990) of U.S. senators:

$$\begin{aligned} &69,\ 56,\ 67,\ 57,\ 53,\ 54,\ 65,\ 56,\ 76,\ 57,\ 51,\ 50,\ 46,\ 48,\ 69,\ 48,\ 54, \\ &50,\ 52,\ 50,\ 66,\ 66,\ 52,\ 45,\ 63,\ 62,\ 58,\ 47,\ 57,\ 51,\ 67,\ 58,\ 66,\ 48, \\ &58,\ 46,\ 50,\ 57,\ 57,\ 54,\ 58,\ 47,\ 52,\ 56,\ 56,\ 53,\ 49,\ 54,\ 51,\ 49,\ 55, \\ &69,\ 47,\ 51,\ 53,\ 60,\ 49,\ 47,\ 66,\ 58,\ 47,\ 63,\ 53,\ 69,\ 73,\ 82,\ 42,\ 69, \\ &73,\ 49,\ 42,\ 68,\ 58,\ 52,\ 60,\ 72,\ 68,\ 88,\ 68,\ 48,\ 43,\ 54,\ 42,\ 69,\ 48, \\ &58,\ 56,\ 50,\ 56,\ 63,\ 51,\ 63,\ 62,\ 72,\ 53,\ 48,\ 55,\ 57,\ 59. \end{aligned} \tag{4}$$

The age of one senator is not known; hence there are 99 data items. It is a bit daunting to be faced with raw data such as this (although perhaps a hundred or a thousand times as large). Once, however, the data are entered into a computer, modern programs make short work of organization and computation. As a first step in this direction, we construct a frequency distribution in the form of a set of ordered pairs (a, b), where a denotes age and b denotes the number of senators of that age.

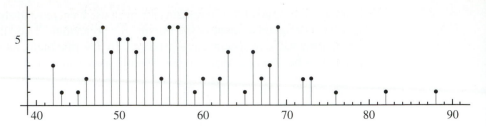

Figure 27.2

$$(42, 3), \ (43, 1), \ (45, 1), \ (46, 2), \ (47, 5), \ (48, 6), \ (49, 4), \ (50, 5),$$
$$(51, 5), \ (52, 4), \ (53, 5), \ (54, 5), \ (55, 2), \ (56, 6), \ (57, 6), \ (58, 7),$$
$$(59, 1), \ (60, 2), \ (62, 2), \ (63, 4), \ (65, 1), \ (66, 4), \ (67, 2), \ (68, 3), \qquad (5)$$
$$(69, 6), \ (72, 2), \ (73, 2), \ (76, 1), \ (82, 1), \ (88, 1).$$

Note that the sum of the second coordinates (the ordinates) must be the total number of data items. Now, one can plot these 30 points on a rectangular coordinate system to obtain a detailed picture of the distribution (Figure 27.2). Once again we have included vertical segments for clarity. From this figure it is easy to see that the bulk of the distribution falls between 50 and 60; hence we would not be surprised to discover that the "middle" of the distribution falls in that range. We will examine briefly each of the three defined measures of location.

a. First, note that the mode is 58, since that is the most frequently occurring age. It happens in this population that the mode is unique, but if the missing age were to be 48 or 56 or 57 or 69 (say it were 69), then the mode would not be unique (both 58 and 69 would be modes).

b. Next, since there is an odd number of data items and $99 = 2 \cdot 50 - 1$, the fiftieth item (in order of increasing age) is the median. To find it, simply add the ordinates from left to right in Figure 27.2 until the fiftieth item is reached. There are 48 items less than or equal to age 55; hence the fiftieth item is one of those corresponding to age 56. The median is 56. Note that about 54 percent of the data are less than or equal to the median, while about 51 percent are greater than or equal to the median. If the missing age had been included, then we would have identified the fiftieth and fifty-first items and computed the average. (It happens, in this situation, that the median would be unchanged.)

c. Finally, we compute the mean using (1):

$$\mu = \tfrac{1}{99} \cdot (5639) = 56.96.$$

Again, we don't know the missing age, but its presence would have little effect on the mean; even if it were as much as 90, the new value of μ would increase by only 0.33.

a. Find the mean, median, and mode of the following data (low temperatures in seven U.S. cities on Jan. 27, 1992): 30, 59, 16, 7, 30, 30, 20.
b. Suppose that Fairbanks, Alaska, is added to the list; its low temperature on that date was -23. Compute the new mean.

27.3

The second major characteristic of a population, involving spread, is important because it may be the determining factor in decision making. For example, a machine designed to produce ball bearings of a particular diameter may, as it ages, produce daily batches with the right mean diameter but with a spread which exceeds the allowed tolerance. When this happens, the machine must be either adjusted or replaced, and information about spread is crucial to that decision.

Again, as in Section 25, we define the population **variance** in terms of the squared deviations from the mean,

$$\sigma^2 = \frac{1}{n} \cdot \sum_{i=1}^{n} (x_i - \mu)^2, \tag{1}$$

and the **standard deviation** σ as its square root. From an arithmetic point of view, the computations are simple, and this measure is certainly the most used and most useful of its kind in statistics. But, as with measures of location, there are other, sometimes useful, measures of dispersion.

Consider again the population as ranked in (2) in paragraph 27.2. The least data item Q_1, such that the first 25 percent of the items in (2) in paragraph 27.2 are less than or equal to Q_1, is called the **lower quartile** of the population. The least data item Q_3, such that the first 75 percent of the items in (2) in paragraph 27.2 are less than or equal to Q_3, is called the **upper quartile.** The difference, $Q_3 - Q_1$, is called the **interquartile range,** and it sometimes is used as a measure of the spread of the population. In general, the interquartile range will include approximately 50 percent of the population.

We may extend this idea as follows. For any percentage, say t percent, the least data item T, such that the first t percent of the items in (2) in paragraph 27.2 are less than or equal to T, is called the *t*th **percentile.** If, for example, one of your College Board scores was reported at the 80th percentile, then your score was at least as good as approximately 80 percent of all scores in that population. If the median is unique, then it is the 50th percentile, as defined above. (In this case, the natural notation is Q_2, which is consistent with the quartile notation above.) If the median is not unique, then it is an interpolated value between the 50th and 51st percentiles. (It is possible to refine the definition of percentile to an interpolated value if there happens to be an appropriate break in the data. We will not do this here.)

Example 1

Consider again the data in Example 1 of paragraph 27.2, listing ages of U.S. senators. Since the mean is so close to 57, we will use that value to simplify the computation of the variance. By (1), the variance of this population is

$$\sigma^2 = \frac{1}{99} \cdot \sum_{i=1}^{99} (x_i - 57)^2 = 81.9.$$

The standard deviation, then, is $\sigma = \sqrt{81.9}$, which is about 9.05. As with random variables, we are interested in what proportion of the population falls within one standard deviation of the mean. Since

$$\mu - \sigma = 47.9 \qquad \text{and} \qquad \mu + \sigma = 66.1,$$

we must count the data items from age 48 to age 66 by summing the ordinates in Figure 27.2 for ages 48, 49, ..., 66. The total is 69, which represents about 70 percent of the population.

To determine the other measure of dispersion, we need to find both lower and upper quartiles. Again, summing the ordinates in Figure 27.2, we find that:

- About 22 percent of the data are less than or equal to 49.

- About 27 percent of the data are less than or equal to 50.

Hence, $\qquad\qquad\qquad\qquad\qquad\qquad\qquad Q_1 = 50.$

Similarly,

- About 73 percent of the data are less than or equal to 62.

- About 76 percent of the data are less than or equal to 63.

Hence, $\qquad\qquad\qquad\qquad\qquad\qquad\qquad Q_3 = 63.$

The interquartile range is $Q_3 - Q_1 = 13$. Thus, an interval of 13 years (encompassing the ages 51, 52, ..., 63) includes very close to 50 percent of the population.

Tutorial 27.3

Referring to the data on senatorial ages, find:
a. The 40th percentile.
b. The 85th percentile.

Returning to the most important measures, mean and standard deviation, we should remark that for many populations of large size (usually much greater than 99):

- Approximately 68 percent of the population lies within σ units of μ.

- Approximately 95 percent of the population lies within 2σ units of μ.

- Virtually all the population is between $\mu - 3\sigma$ and $\mu + 3\sigma$.

27.4

Suppose that a corporation plans to develop an advertising strategy for use in the District of Columbia. Although its product may have appeal to various age groups, the focus of the advertising campaign will depend upon the age distribution in the potential market. To help identify the right focus, corporate executives wish to know the mean and standard deviation of the ages of all D.C. residents. If that information were not readily available, an analysis of recent census data would be required. Often, a population is so huge that the expense in both time and money to analyze it is prohibitive. The next best thing is to select a relatively small fraction of the population, called a **sample,** compute the corresponding measures for the sample, and hope that these sample measures are reasonably close to the population measures which one is really interested in. It should not be expected that a sample can be chosen which exactly mirrors the population characteristics; it is critical, however, that the sample be chosen completely at random. So important is this idea that the word "sample" alone is always used in statistics to mean a *random sample.*

With the realization that population data must be replaced by sample data, two major problems need to be addressed. The first was referred to above: "How will a random sample be selected from the population?" The answer is not easy; the selection of an appropriate sample is often as much an art as a science. But, there *is* help. Extensive lists of random numbers are available in print, and most computers have available a program which generates random numbers. Such numbers may be used sequentially until a sample of the required size has been selected. There are precautions to be exercised in the use of such aids, and this issue is thoroughly explored in most textbooks and courses in applied statistics. Here, we will simply avoid this problem by assuming that our samples are random!

The second problem relates to the interpretation of sample characteristics as estimators of the desired population parameters. This one is subtle, and much of the theory of statistics is devoted to it. Once again we will be forced simply to indicate roughly what is going on.

Consider the question of estimating the population mean μ and the population standard deviation σ, making use of a sample of size m, which we denote by

$$x_1, x_2, x_3, \ldots, x_m. \tag{1}$$

As in the population list, sample items need not be different from one another. We will assume, in fact, that the entire population is available at each choice of a sample value. Statisticians have shown that, subject to quite reasonable criteria, each of these parameters μ and σ has a "best" *point estimate.* (The word "point" indicates that the estimated value is a single number, rather than an interval of values, to be defined shortly.) Given the sample data in (1), we first construct the sample mean, denoted by $\bar{x}$ to distinguish it from the population mean. The formula is just like (1) in paragraph 27.2:

$$\bar{x} = \frac{1}{m} \cdot \sum_{i=1}^{m} x_i. \tag{2}$$

As might be expected, this computed value is our best guess for the unknown population mean μ. We will return shortly to the question of assessing just how good this guess is likely to be.

Now, consider the unknown population variance σ^2. We can also compute from the sample data a sample variance, denoted by s^2 to distinguish it from the population variance, and s^2 is our best guess for σ^2. This time there is a small surprise: The formula isn't exactly like (1) in paragraph 27.3 but is

$$s^2 = \frac{1}{m-1} \cdot \sum_{i=1}^{m} (x_i - \bar{x})^2. \tag{3}$$

Of course, we will use the square root, denoted by s, as our estimate of the population standard deviation. These two numbers are very easy to calculate, and all seems to be well! Our corporate executives, who need those population parameters on which to base a business decision, commission the selection of a random sample, compute $\bar{x}$ and s^2, and use $\bar{x}$ and s as the estimated values for μ and σ.

Example 1

The following list is a random sample of size 7 drawn from the population in Example 1 of paragraph 27.2 (arranged in numerical order):

$$50, 50, 51, 56, 60, 67, 69.$$

The sample mean is

$$\bar{x} = \tfrac{1}{7} \cdot (403) = 57.6.$$

The sample variance is

$$s^2 = \tfrac{1}{6} \cdot (385.72) = 64.3;$$

hence the sample standard deviation is

$$s = 8.0.$$

The numbers 57.6 and 8.0 are the point estimates we would use for the population parameters μ and σ (if, in fact, they were unknown).

Tutorial 27.4

Assume that the temperatures in part **a** of Tutorial 27.2 are a sample randomly selected from a much larger population. Compute an estimate for the variance of that population, assuming that the sample mean is 27.

There is the usual undercurrent of uncertainty in the preceding discussion. We may have reason to believe that no other computed values are better estimators than the ones described above, but just how good are they? Close enough to justify what may be a substantial corporate investment? The answer, of course, is that we don't know! And that's the problem with point estimates: We have no basis for judging, in a particular case, how likely the estimates are to be "close" to μ and σ.

27.5 In spite of their suspect nature as estimators on which to base critical management decisions, point estimates turn out to have great value in more advanced statistical theory. We will return very briefly to this topic at the end of the section. But for the moment, how is the dilemma of estimating population parameters to be resolved? To simplify the development, we will restrict attention to one of the parameters only, the population mean. The procedure here will suggest the general approach to the problem.

Consider the following experiment: A sample of size m is selected from the given population, which we assume to be of size n and much larger than m. The sample space **S** of the experiment consists of all such samples of size m. (Perhaps this is the origin of that peculiar terminology "sample space.") Corresponding to each such selection, we compute the number $\bar{x}$. Thus many different numbers $\bar{x}$ are possible, and we may define a random variable $\overline{X}$ on **S** which takes as its values these numbers $\bar{x}$. As described in Section 25, we may define for the random variable $\overline{X}$ its mean, denoted by $\mu_{\bar{x}}$, and its standard deviation, denoted by $\sigma_{\bar{x}}$. Now, here is the interesting point. It is a theorem of statistics that if μ and σ are the population parameters, then

$$\begin{cases} \mu_{\bar{x}} = \mu, \\ \sigma_{\bar{x}} = \dfrac{1}{\sqrt{m}} \cdot \sigma. \end{cases} \tag{1}$$

That is, $\overline{X}$ may be used as a predictor of μ, and the computed sample means will cluster more closely about μ as the sample size m increases. As we will see next, this observation is the key to our problem.

From the information at the end of paragraph 27.3, we can claim that for many important populations

$$P(\mu_{\bar{x}} - \sigma_{\bar{x}} < \bar{x} < \mu_{\bar{x}} + \sigma_{\bar{x}}) = 0.68,$$

and from (1),

$$P\left(\mu - \frac{1}{\sqrt{m}} \cdot \sigma < \bar{x} < \mu + \frac{1}{\sqrt{m}} \cdot \sigma\right) = 0.68. \tag{2}$$

What is this formidable formula trying to tell us? To understand, suppose we first assume that both μ and σ are known. Now plot the numbers

$$\mu, \qquad \mu - \frac{1}{\sqrt{m}} \cdot \sigma, \qquad \mu + \frac{1}{\sqrt{m}} \cdot \sigma$$

on a horizontal axis of the random variable $\bar{X}$, as in Figure 27.5A. If we were to select many random samples, each of size m, and if we calculate $\bar{x}$ for each sample, then about 68 percent of these numbers, $\bar{x}$, will fall on the interval

$$\left(\mu - \frac{1}{\sqrt{m}} \cdot \sigma, \quad \mu + \frac{1}{\sqrt{m}} \cdot \sigma\right).$$

If the size of the original sample had been $4m$ instead of m, then the length of this interval would have been halved, which means that 68 percent of the sample means $\bar{x}$ (for the larger sample size) would lie only half as far from μ as before.

This interpretation is fairly straightforward, but if we knew μ and σ there would be no need to sample the population. We move a step closer to reality by remembering that our goal is to estimate the unknown population mean. This time we will assume that μ is *unknown* but that σ is *known*. Again, the selection of many random samples produces many sample means (one for each sample). For each of these numbers $\bar{x}$, we plot the points

$$\bar{x}, \qquad \bar{x} - \frac{1}{\sqrt{m}} \cdot \sigma, \qquad \bar{x} + \frac{1}{\sqrt{m}} \cdot \sigma$$

on the $\bar{X}$ axis, as in Figure 27.5B, and consider the interval

$$\left(\bar{x} - \frac{1}{\sqrt{m}} \cdot \sigma, \quad \bar{x} + \frac{1}{\sqrt{m}} \cdot \sigma\right). \tag{3}$$

There is an intimate connection between (3) and (2). By a little arithmetic, we will discover an equivalent form for the inequality

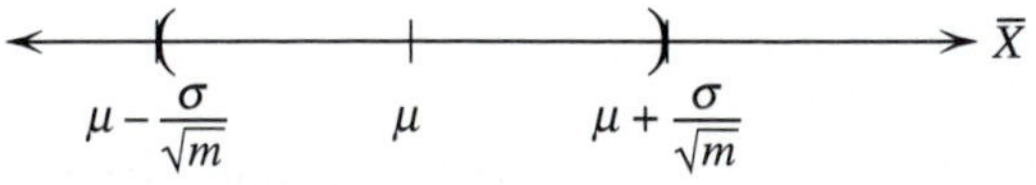

Figure 27.5A

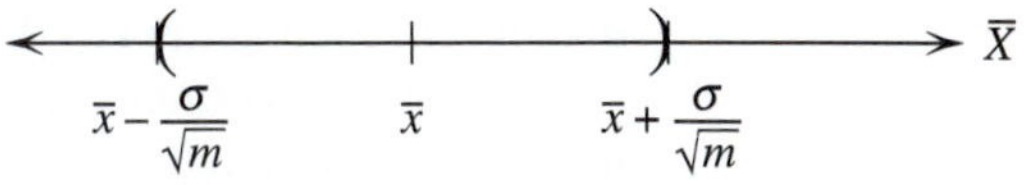

Figure 27.5B

$$\mu - \frac{1}{\sqrt{m}} \cdot \sigma < \bar{x} < \mu + \frac{1}{\sqrt{m}} \cdot \sigma.$$

Add $-\mu$ to each term:

$$-\frac{1}{\sqrt{m}} \cdot \sigma < \bar{x} - \mu < \frac{1}{\sqrt{m}} \cdot \sigma.$$

Add $-\bar{x}$ to each term:

$$-\bar{x} - \frac{1}{\sqrt{m}} \cdot \sigma < -\mu < -\bar{x} + \frac{1}{\sqrt{m}} \cdot \sigma.$$

Multiply each term by -1, remembering to reverse the inequalities:

$$\bar{x} + \frac{1}{\sqrt{m}} \cdot \sigma > \mu > \bar{x} - \frac{1}{\sqrt{m}} \cdot \sigma.$$

Finally, rewrite as

$$\bar{x} - \frac{1}{\sqrt{m}} \cdot \sigma < \mu < \bar{x} + \frac{1}{\sqrt{m}} \cdot \sigma.$$

Thus, (2) has the alternate form

$$P\left(\bar{x} - \frac{1}{\sqrt{m}} \cdot \sigma < \mu < \bar{x} + \frac{1}{\sqrt{m}} \cdot \sigma\right) = 0.68. \qquad (4)$$

The frequency interpretation of (4) is the following:

> For each of many random samples we compute $\bar{x}$ and plot the interval (3); then about 68 percent of all intervals so constructed will include μ.

In practice, of course, we don't select multitudes of samples; we simply select one sample, compute its mean, and then assert that the probability is 0.68 that the unknown μ actually falls on the interval

$$\left(\bar{x} - \frac{1}{\sqrt{m}} \cdot \sigma, \quad \bar{x} + \frac{1}{\sqrt{m}} \cdot \sigma\right).$$

Example 1   Assume again the population in Example 1 of paragraph 27.2 and the sample selected in Example 1 of paragraph 27.4. If we assume that μ is unknown but that $\sigma = 9.1$ (from Example 1 of paragraph 27.3), then the probability is about 0.68 that μ is on the interval

$$\left(57.6 - \frac{1}{\sqrt{7}} \cdot 9.1, \quad 57.6 + \frac{1}{\sqrt{7}} \cdot 9.1\right) = (54.2, 61.0).$$

Note that we have "lucked out," as will happen about two times in three, because the population mean is known to be 57.96, which lies in the computed interval. ●

27.6   The interval (3) in paragraph 27.5,

$$\left(\overline{x} - \frac{1}{\sqrt{m}} \cdot \sigma, \quad \overline{x} + \frac{1}{\sqrt{m}} \cdot \sigma\right),$$

is called an **interval estimate** for μ. More specifically, it is called a **confidence interval with coefficient** 0.68.

It most often happens in practice that sample sizes are much larger than 7 (as in Example 1 of paragraph 27.5) and that we can accept a wider deviation from μ than $(1/\sqrt{m}) \cdot \sigma$. We can increase the probable accuracy of our estimate significantly by doubling the allowed deviation. This follows from the remark at the end of paragraph 27.3, which implies that

$$P\left(\overline{x} - \frac{2}{\sqrt{m}} \cdot \sigma < \mu < \overline{x} + \frac{2}{\sqrt{m}} \cdot \sigma\right) = 0.95. \tag{1}$$

The interval

$$\left(\overline{x} - \frac{2}{\sqrt{m}} \cdot \sigma, \quad \overline{x} + \frac{2}{\sqrt{m}} \cdot \sigma\right)$$

is another example of an *interval estimate* for μ. More specifically, it is called a *confidence interval with coefficient* 0.95. Stated a little differently, if we select a random sample and calculate $\overline{x}$, then we may expect $\overline{x}$ to deviate from the population mean μ by more than $(2/\sqrt{m}) \cdot \sigma$ only one time in *twenty*. Note that there is a "trade-off" going on: The shorter the interval, the less confidence we have in it. In other words, the more accurate we require the estimate to be, the less confidence we can claim for that estimate!

Example 1   Again, consider the sample selected in Example 1 of paragraph 27.4 from a population with known standard deviation $\sigma = 9.1$. The sample size and mean are

$$m = 7, \qquad \overline{x} = 57.6.$$

Since $(1/\sqrt{7}) \cdot 9.1 = 3.4$, the confidence interval with coefficient 0.68 is

$$(54.2, \ 61.0).$$

Since $(2/\sqrt{7}) \cdot 9.1 = 6.9$, the confidence interval with coefficient 0.95 is

$$(50.7, \ 64.5).$$

We interpret these intervals as follows:

- The probability is 0.68 that the (unknown) population mean μ lies on the interval (54.2, 61.0).

- The probability is 0.95 that the (unknown) population mean μ lies on the interval (50.7, 64.5).

The blocks are in place now: The dilemma of estimating a parameter cannot be resolved with certainty. Those corporate executives must, in the final analysis, base their strategy upon probabilities. But the confidence interval estimate of a population parameter offers more information and, therefore, a more informed basis for judgment than the point estimate defined earlier.

So, we return to the concept of point estimate, as promised at the beginning of paragraph 27.5. To construct the interval estimate of μ, we not only need to select a sample and compute $\bar{x}$, but also need to know the population standard deviation σ. If we don't know the population mean, is it likely that we will know the standard deviation? There are, in fact, many instances in which a good estimate of σ is available from prior information. But, for the most part, σ is just as much a mystery as μ. Generally speaking, when the sample size is at least 30, it is reasonable to replace the unknown σ in the confidence interval formula with the point estimate s computed from the sample values only, via (3) in paragraph 27.4. Even with smaller sample sizes, statisticians have proved that with a relatively small change in the probabilities assigned, the sample value s can be used in place of σ. So, point estimates turn out to be critical in the computation of interval estimates. Again, we must leave a detailed study for specialized courses in statistics.

27.7 Complement: The Normal Approximation

Return to the data of Example 1 of paragraph 27.2, and group them into intervals of length 5 units along the X axis, as in Figure 27.7A. Note that the height of each bar is the frequency count for its interval of X values; thus, there are 24 ages in our list between 47.5 and 52.5 . Let us agree to identify each rectangle by its midpoint on the axis. From left to right these points are labeled 40, 45, 50, . . . , 85, 90. Such a diagram is called a **bar chart;** it describes the data somewhat less precisely than Figure 27.2. The sum of all bar heights must be the total number of items in the population, 99. Suppose we rescale these bar heights to represent *relative frequency* (i.e., frequency divided by 99). Thus, the height of the bar labeled 50 is $\frac{24}{99}$. The bar heights, now, can be taken to represent probability; for example, the probability is $\frac{24}{99}$ that a randomly chosen data item will fall on the interval labeled 50.

In more advanced statistics, it is most useful to rescale the heights one more time so that the heights remain proportional but the total area of the bars is one unit. Since all bars have the same width in this example, we need only divide each height by 5.

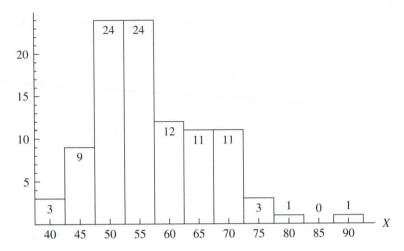

Figure 27.7A

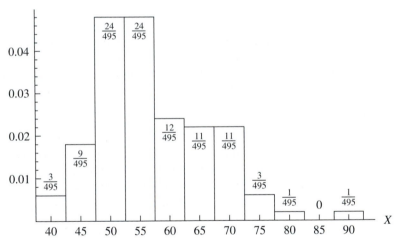

Figure 27.7B

This diagram is shown in Figure 27.7B. The area of the bar labeled 50 is now $\frac{24}{99}$. Such a diagram, often called a **histogram,** represents a major step in the transition from a discrete population to a continuous distribution, and the purpose is to bring the "heavy machinery" of calculus to bear on statistical problems. We intend here to indicate in only a very rough way how this can be done.

It is likely that the senatorial ages are not unbiased; in Figure 27.7B, there seems to be a clear propensity toward advanced age. You can probably think of a number of reasons; for example, incumbency may be a political advantage. Whatever the case, our purpose here is not to analyze the Senate but to illustrate the approximation of data by a very important continuous distribution. To simplify the arithmetic, we will impose an artificial upper bound on age by disregarding all data for ages greater than

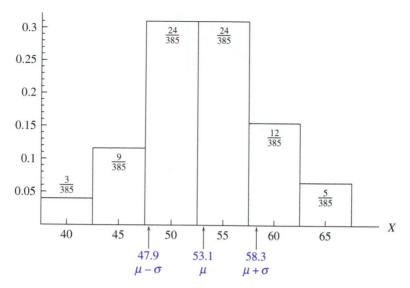

Figure 27.7C

65. (Please remember that what we do from this point on is no longer appropriate to the original population.)

The histogram corresponding to the new population is shown in Figure 27.7C; note that the new total number of data items is 77 and that the areas of all the rectangles sum to 1. The mean and standard deviation for the new population are $\mu = 53.1$ and $\sigma = 5.2$.

It is often the case that characteristics of two or more populations need to be compared. Such populations may have quite different means and standard deviations, complicating the task of comparison. The solution is to compare each to a known standard. Given a population, such as our new list of ages, let X denote the random variable for the population. We define a standardized random variable Z as follows:

$$Z = \frac{X - \mu}{\sigma}. \tag{1}$$

Note how X and Z are related:

X	μ	$\mu + \sigma$	$\mu - \sigma$	$\mu + 2\sigma$	$\mu - 2\sigma$
Z	0	1	-1	2	-2

It turns out that for many populations the standardized variable Z has a graph in the shape of a bell, as pictured in Figure 27.7D. This is called the **standard normal distribution.** Among its properties are:

1. It is symmetric about the vertical line $Z = 0$.

2. The total area between the curve and the horizontal axis is 1.

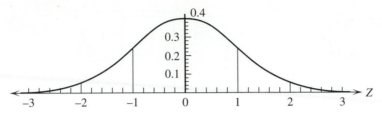

Figure 27.7D

3. The area above the interval $(-1, 1)$ is 0.68.

4. The area above the interval $(-2, 2)$ is 0.95.

5. The area above the interval $(-3, 3)$ is 0.997.

6. For any points a and b $(a < b)$ on the axis, the area above the interval (a, b) is the probability that a randomly determined value of Z will fall on that interval.

7. There is a (somewhat complicated) formula which has Figure 27.7D as its graph.

8. Areas under the curve can be expressed in the language of calculus and can be approximated very accurately.

9. This distribution occurs frequently in applications.

In large populations, it is observed that the distribution of ages is very nearly normal. In smaller populations, such as ours, the fit is not usually as good. If we standardize the population random variable X in our example,

$$Z = \frac{X - 53.1}{5.2},$$

then the approximation by the standard normal distribution, as shown in Figure 27.7E, seems to be reasonably close.

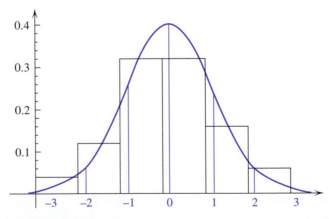

Figure 27.7E

It is possible to translate a probability statement about Z into a prediction about X. For example,

$$P(-1 < Z < 1) = 0.68 = P\left(-1 < \frac{X - 53.1}{5.2} < 1\right) = P(47.9 < X < 58.3).$$

Checking the latter probability against the actual data, we note that the area of the histogram in Figure 27.7C above the interval (47.9, 58.3) is 0.62 (which misses the predicted value of 0.68 by less than 10 percent).

Problems for Section 27

1. Find the mean, median, and mode of each list: (*a*) 14, 18, 10, 32, 4, 16; (*b*) 223, 236, 224, 223; (*c*) 69, 68, 71, 71, 72, 66, 72, 73.

2. The following list is a population of measurements of a certain astronomical constant by various techniques:

74 80 95 84 87 82 50 75 65
95 50 55 65 69 80 100 49 80

(*a*) Construct a frequency plot, as in Example 1 of paragraph 27.2. (*b*) Find the median and the mode(s). (*c*) Find the lower quartile and the upper quartile. (*d*) Find the 90th percentile.

3. (*Continuation of Problem 2.*) (*a*) Find the mean of this population. (*b*) Find the variance and the standard deviation of the population (assume that the mean is 74).

4. (*Conclusion of Problem 2.*) Using the information in Problems 2 and 3, find the interval $(\mu - \sigma, \mu + \sigma)$ and compare it with the interquartile range.

5. The following list is a population of measurements taken from a test of metal fatigue in various specimens:

40 35 35 45 30 30 40 40 30 40
30 30 30 30 30 25 30 35 40 35

(*a*) Construct a frequency plot, as in Example 1 of paragraph 27.2. (*b*) Find the upper

and lower quartiles. (*c*) How many items of data lie beyond the upper and lower quartiles? (*d*) Does this population have a unique mode; if so, what is it?

6. (*Continuation of Problem 5.*) (*a*) Compute the mean of this population. (*b*) Compute the variance and standard deviation.

7. (*Conclusion of Problem 5.*) (*a*) Find the 50th percentile, and compare with the mean. (*b*) The number 35 is at what largest percentile?

8. The following list is a population of playing times (to the nearest minute) of a collection of CDs:

53 56 47 55 59 53 53 57 71 74
73 58 65 70 52 66 51 71 60 62
71 78 72 68 74 55 56 50 54 38

(*a*) Construct a frequency plot, as in Example 1 of paragraph 27.2. (*b*) Find the mean, median, and mode of this population.

9. (*Continuation of Problem 8.*) (*a*) Find the upper and lower quartiles. (*b*) What is the interquartile range? (*c*) If you selected a CD at random from this collection, what is the probability that it lies strictly between the upper and lower quartiles?

10. (*Conclusion of Problem 8.*) (*a*) Calculate the variance and standard deviation of this population. (Tedious, by hand!) (*b*) Compare the

interval $(\mu - \sigma,\ \mu + \sigma)$ with the interquartile range. (c) If you selected a CD (with playing time T) at random from this collection, what is $P(\mu - \sigma < T < \mu + \sigma)$?

11. Given a population of the kind described at the end of paragraph 27.3, explain why you would expect the interquartile range to be shorter than the interval from $\mu - \sigma$ to $\mu + \sigma$?

12. Consider the following to be a random sample drawn from a much larger population: 17, 20, 20, 17, 21, 19. (a) Calculate the sample mean. (b) What estimates might you use for the population mean, variance, and standard deviation?

13. (a) Devise a way of selecting a random sample of size 6 from the data in Problem 2, and pick such a sample. (b) From your sample, estimate the mean and standard deviation of the population. Compare with the figures obtained earlier.

14. (a) Devise a way of selecting a random sample of size 6 from the data in Problem 5, and pick such a sample. (b) From your sample, estimate the mean and standard deviation of the population. Compare with the figures obtained earlier.

15. (a) Devise a way of selecting a random sample of size 6 from the data in Problem 8, and pick such a sample. (b) From your sample, estimate the mean and standard deviation of the population. Compare with the figures obtained earlier.

16. Five adult men, selected at random, weighed 163, 181, 152, 144, and 196 pounds. Find weight limits which include approximately 68 percent of the population from which the men were drawn (assuming that the population standard deviation is 20 pounds).

17. In Problem 16, suppose that the population standard deviation is unknown. Now answer the question as best you can. What assumption have you made?

18. Ten car engines, taken at random from an assembly plant, had tested horsepower as follows: 107, 112, 111, 115, 108, 110, 103, 111, 108, and 115. Give an interval which will include the horsepower of approximately 95 percent of all the car engines of this type. (Estimate mean and standard deviation from the sample.)

19. Four students picked at random from a local elementary school are 132, 120, 118, and 121 centimeters tall. Estimate the tallest and shortest students at this school. (Estimate mean and standard deviation from the sample.)

20. Given the data in Problem 19, would a student 106 centimeters tall be considered short? (Note that this is a subjective judgment.)

21. Pick a random sample of size 5 from the population in Example 1 of paragraph 27.2, and compute the sample mean and variance. How do these compare with the sample mean and variance of Example 1 of paragraph 27.4?

22. Using your sample from Problem 21, what is a confidence interval for μ with coefficient 0.68? (See Example 1 of paragraph 27.5.)

23. You own a small company that makes ball bearings. Before using a batch of 1-centimeter balls, you always take a random sample and compute the sample mean and variance of the diameters. Usually, the sample mean is very close to 1 centimeter, but if the sample standard deviation is too large, then you do not use the batch of balls. If "too large" is 0.005, then do you use the batch with the following sample diameters: 1.001, 1.005, 0.995, 0.990, 1.011, 1.0, 0.998?

24. Consider a large population of ball bearings manufactured by a certain process, and suppose that the population standard deviation is $\sigma = 0.042$. Suppose that a random sample

of size 200 is selected and its sample mean turns out to be $\bar{x} = 0.824$. As in paragraph 27.6, (*a*) construct a confidence interval for the population mean with coefficient 0.68, (*b*) construct a confidence interval for the population mean with coefficient 0.95.

25. In reference to the end of paragraph 27.6, find an elementary statistics textbook in your library, and look up the "Student's *t*" distribution. Observe that its graph differs only a little from that of the normal distribution.

CHAPTER 5

Relations and Matrices

Section 28.   Zero-One Matrices

Overview for Section 28

- The acquaintance problem expressed in terms of (0, 1)-matrices
- Definition of relation and its representation as a (0, 1)-matrix
- Matrix properties: reflexive, irreflexive, symmetric
- Enumeration of relations

Key Concepts: (0, 1)-matrix, relation, reflexive, irreflexive, symmetric, enumerations

28.1   Suppose that the mathematics club at your school sponsors a party to which each member may invite a number of friends. To be invited, of course, each guest must know at least one club member, but among the *guests* present, some may know one another and some may not. It may happen, in fact, that some guest knows none of the other guests, or that some guest knows all the other guests. Whatever the case, the question arises, "Is it possible that each guest at the party is acquainted with a different number of the other guests?" To answer this question, we must agree on what "acquaintance" means. We will assume that:

a. It takes two to be acquainted (acquaintance with oneself doesn't count).

b. Acquaintance is symmetric (two guests either know one another or not).

If there is only one guest present, then the answer to our question is "yes," since this guest has zero acquaintances, and there are no others to worry about. But if there is more than one guest present, then the (perhaps surprising) answer to our question is "no." We will examine this situation by organizing the data in a way which is often useful in discrete mathematics.

Let n denote any integer greater than 1 and assume that there are exactly n guests present, labeled as follows,

$$\mathbf{G} = \{g_1, g_2, g_3, \ldots, g_n\}.$$

Now construct a table with n rows and n columns numbered as shown in Table 28.1. For each pair of guests (g_i, g_j), consider the entry a_{ij} in the row numbered i and the column numbered j. Put

$$a_{ij} = \begin{cases} 1, & \text{if } g_i \text{ and } g_j \text{ are acquainted;} \\ 0, & \text{if } g_i \text{ and } g_j \text{ are not acquainted.} \end{cases} \tag{1}$$

Our earlier assumption **a** implies that

$$a_{ii} = 0 \qquad \text{for each } i,$$

and our assumption **b** implies that

$$a_{ij} = a_{ji} \qquad \text{for each } i \neq j.$$

Here are some observations about Table 28.1.

- If r_i denotes the sum of the entries in the row numbered i, then

$$r_i = \sum_{k=1}^{n} a_{ik}.$$

- If c_j denotes the sum of the entries in the column numbered j, then

$$c_j = \sum_{k=1}^{n} a_{kj}.$$

	1	2	3	$\cdots$	n
1	a_{11}	a_{12}	a_{13}	$\cdots$	a_{1n}
2	a_{21}	a_{22}	a_{23}	$\cdots$	a_{2n}
3	a_{31}	a_{32}	a_{33}	$\cdots$	a_{3n}
$\cdots$	$\cdots$	$\cdots$	$\cdots$	$\cdots$	$\cdots$
n	a_{n1}	a_{n2}	a_{n3}	$\cdots$	a_{nn}

Table 28.1

- For each i, $r_i = c_i$ because $a_{ik} = a_{ki}$ for each k.

- For each i, r_i is the number of guests with whom g_i is acquainted, so $0 \le r_i \le n - 1$.

In this model, our question asks whether it is possible that

$$r_i \ne r_j \qquad \text{for each } i \text{ and } j. \tag{2}$$

It will be helpful to consider separately the two possible cases:

I. Every guest knows at least one other guest present (that is, $r_i > 0$ for each i).

II. Some guest has no acquaintance among the other guests present (that is, $r_i = 0$ for some i).

Under case I, $1 \le r_i \le n - 1$ for each i and there are exactly $n - 1$ integers satisfying this condition. But there are n rows; hence by the Pigeonhole Principle at least two of these rows have the same row sum. Thus, condition (2) must fail.

Under case II, some row sum is zero. For convenience assume that $r_n = 0$ and that no other row sum is zero, else condition (2) already fails. Note that by symmetry $c_n = 0$ also; hence each row preceding the nth has at least two zeroes. Thus, $1 \le r_i \le n - 2$ for $i = 1, 2, \ldots, n - 1$. But now there are $n - 1$ rows with row sums from among only $n - 2$ available integers. Again, by the Pigeonhole Principle at least two rows have the same row sum; hence condition (2) must fail. Because no other alternatives are possible, we have shown that condition (2) fails and there must be at least two guests who have the same number of acquaintances.

We are accustomed to the idea of theorems in geometry and in arithmetic, but what we have just proved is a result which seems to be of a quite different sort. It can be stated as follows.

THEOREM 28.1

Within any given group of two or more people, at least two of them have exactly the same number of acquaintances among the members of the group.

Although expressed in terms of "people" and "acquaintance," Theorem 28.1 applies more generally to any structure in which there are "objects" related in some dichotomous fashion, as in the geometric example in Figure 28.1.

Example 1

On a sheet of paper place n points so that no three of them are collinear (points in a plane that are so placed are said to be in *general position*). There are $\binom{n}{2}$ pairs of points, and for each pair either (*a*) join the two points with a straight-line segment or (*b*) not (see Figure 28.1). Considering only the original n points, note that two of them lie on the same number of segments (Q and S are each on three segments). This situation is identical with the acquaintance problem: Simply refer to points as people

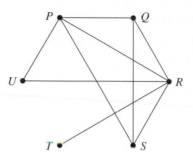

Figure 28.1

and segments as acquaintance. (In the figure, T is acquainted only with R; U with P and R; and so on.) Theorem 28.1, therefore, is true also in this geometric setting. Notice that the figure illustrates case I above: Each point is on at least one segment. If we were to erase the three segments joined at S, leaving the endpoints, then the resulting figure would illustrate case II. This time Q and U are on the same number of segments (two each).

Tutorial 28.1

Suppose that Figure 28.1 indicates the acquaintance pattern among the six guests at your party. Let P denote g_1, let Q denote g_2, and so on. Complete Table 28.1 for this situation, given that the first row is 0 1 1 1 0 1.

28.2   The proof which precedes Theorem 28.1 actually establishes a general result about the abstract mathematical structure described in Table 28.1 and (1) in paragraph 28.1. That structure happens to model precisely both the "acquaintance" problem and the "segment" problem. (We should note that it also models situations in other disciplines; hence without further proof a similar result will hold with respect to each of them.) We now turn our attention to a study of the abstract structure itself.

The square array in Table 28.1 may be abbreviated by

$$[a_{ij}], \qquad i = 1, 2, \ldots, n \quad \text{and} \quad j = 1, 2, \ldots, n,$$

or simply by $[a_{ij}]$ when the size is clear from context. It is called an **$n \times n$ matrix** (this is read "n by n matrix," indicating that there are n rows and n columns in the array). Because each entry in the matrix is either 0 or 1, it is also called a **(0, 1)-matrix.** Such matrices (the plural of matrix) have the following especially important interpretation.

Let $\mathbf{S} = \{s_1, s_2, \ldots, s_n\}$ be a finite set containing n elements. Recall that the Cartesian product $\mathbf{S} \times \mathbf{S}$ is, by definition,

$$\mathbf{S} \times \mathbf{S} = \{(s_i, s_j) : s_i \in \mathbf{S}, s_j \in \mathbf{S}\}.$$

By FCP II, $|\mathbf{S} \times \mathbf{S}| = n^2 = |\mathbf{S}|^2$. In analogy with this, and for abbreviation, we put

$$\mathbf{S} \times \mathbf{S} = \mathbf{S}^2.$$

Any subset of $\mathbf{S}^2$ is a **relation,** say $\mathbf{R}$, which has a convenient representation as an $n \times n$, $(0, 1)$-matrix $[a_{ij}]$ in which

$$a_{ij} = \begin{cases} 1, & \text{if } (s_i, s_j) \in \mathbf{R}; \\ 0, & \text{otherwise.} \end{cases} \tag{1}$$

It may be helpful to think of (1) as defining a characteristic function on $\mathbf{S}^2$ for the relation $\mathbf{R}$.

Example 1   If $\mathbf{V} = \{a, e, i, o, u\}$, then *any* subset of $\mathbf{V}^2$ is a relation, but here we want to construct a particular one. Do you notice anything slightly unusual about the word "equation"? Let $\mathbf{R}$ be the relation in $\mathbf{V}^2$ consisting of exactly those ordered pairs (s_i, s_j) for which s_i precedes s_j in the word "equation." Since "e" precedes each other vowel, "u" precedes each other vowel except "e", and so on,

$$\mathbf{R} = \{(e, a), (e, i), (e, o), (e, u), (u, a), (u, i), (u, o), (a, i), (a, o), (i, o)\}.$$

To find the matrix representation for $\mathbf{R}$, think of renaming the vowels: "a" by s_1, "e" by s_2, "i" by s_3, "o" by s_4, and "u" by s_5. Then fill in the matrix $[a_{ij}]$ by the use of (1). For example, $a_{24} = 1$ since $(s_2, s_4) = (e, o) \in \mathbf{R}$ and $a_{22} = 0$ since $(s_2, s_2) = (e, e) \notin \mathbf{R}$:

$$\begin{array}{c} & \begin{array}{ccccc} 1 & 2 & 3 & 4 & 5 \end{array} \\ \begin{array}{c} 1 \\ 2 \\ 3 \\ 4 \\ 5 \end{array} & \left[\begin{array}{ccccc} 0 & 0 & 1 & 1 & 0 \\ 1 & 0 & 1 & 1 & 1 \\ 0 & 0 & 0 & 1 & 0 \\ 0 & 0 & 0 & 0 & 0 \\ 1 & 0 & 1 & 1 & 0 \end{array} \right] \end{array}. \tag{2}$$

It is in this sense that we may think of (2) as a characteristic function on $\mathbf{V}^2$: It essentially picks out from among all elements in $\mathbf{V}^2$ those which belong to the subset $\mathbf{R}$. Note that in this matrix the row sum r_i counts how many other vowels s_i precedes; these row sums are (top to bottom) 2, 4, 1, 0, 3. Note, further, that

$$\sum_{i=1}^{5} r_i = |\mathbf{R}| = 10$$

is the sum of all entries in $[a_{ij}]$.

28.3

The row sums of the matrix displayed in (2) in paragraph 28.2 are different from one
another, which seems to be in violation of Theorem 28.1. But remember, a theorem
has hypotheses as well as a conclusion. The matrix in our example certainly satisfies
the hypothesis $a_{ii} = 0$, but it fails to satisfy the hypothesis that $a_{ij} = a_{ji}$ for $i \neq j$.
For example, "e" precedes "a" in the word "equation," but "a" does not precede "e".
Because of this we should not be surprised that the conclusion of the theorem fails.

The two hypotheses of Theorem 28.1 describe general properties that are important enough to have special names. The entries a_{ii} lie along what is called the
main diagonal of the matrix $[a_{ij}]$. A relation (as well as its corresponding matrix) is
called **reflexive** if each entry on the main diagonal is 1, and **irreflexive** if each entry
on the main diagonal is 0. The "acquaintance" relation of Table 28.1 is irreflexive;
so also is the matrix in paragraph 28.2. A relation (as well as its corresponding matrix) is called **symmetric** if for each i and j, $a_{ij} = a_{ji}$. In such a matrix, pairs of
entries which are symmetrically placed with respect to the main diagonal must be
the same. Geometrically speaking, the matrix is unchanged when rotated about its
main diagonal (Figure 28.3A illustrates the simple case in which $n = 2$). The matrix in paragraph 28.2 fails to satisfy this condition, but the acquaintance matrix does
satisfy the condition.

In the language of our abstract matrix structure, Theorem 28.1 has the following
form.

**THEOREM
28.1**

Alternate Form. If $[a_{ij}]$ is the relation matrix for an irreflexive, symmetric
relation with $n > 1$, then at least two rows have identical row sums.

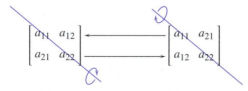

Figure 28.3A

$$\begin{bmatrix} 0 & 0 \\ 0 & 0 \end{bmatrix} \quad \begin{bmatrix} 1 & 0 \\ 0 & 0 \end{bmatrix} \quad \begin{bmatrix} 0 & 1 \\ 0 & 0 \end{bmatrix} \quad \begin{bmatrix} 0 & 0 \\ 1 & 0 \end{bmatrix} \quad \begin{bmatrix} 0 & 0 \\ 0 & 1 \end{bmatrix} \quad \begin{bmatrix} 1 & 1 \\ 0 & 0 \end{bmatrix} \quad \begin{bmatrix} 1 & 0 \\ 1 & 0 \end{bmatrix} \quad \begin{bmatrix} 1 & 0 \\ 0 & 1 \end{bmatrix}$$

(a)　　　(b)　　　(c)　　　(d)　　　(e)　　　(f)　　　(g)　　　(h)

$$\begin{bmatrix} 0 & 1 \\ 1 & 0 \end{bmatrix} \quad \begin{bmatrix} 0 & 1 \\ 0 & 1 \end{bmatrix} \quad \begin{bmatrix} 0 & 0 \\ 1 & 1 \end{bmatrix} \quad \begin{bmatrix} 1 & 1 \\ 1 & 0 \end{bmatrix} \quad \begin{bmatrix} 1 & 1 \\ 0 & 1 \end{bmatrix} \quad \begin{bmatrix} 1 & 0 \\ 1 & 1 \end{bmatrix} \quad \begin{bmatrix} 0 & 1 \\ 1 & 1 \end{bmatrix} \quad \begin{bmatrix} 1 & 1 \\ 1 & 1 \end{bmatrix}$$

(i)　　　(j)　　　(k)　　　(l)　　　(m)　　　(n)　　　(o)　　　(p)

Figure 28.3B

Example 1　Let $\mathbf{S} = \{1, 2\}$ and note that

$$\mathbf{S}^2 = \{(1, 1), (1, 2), (2, 1), (2, 2)\}.$$

To get some feel for the variety of relations (even for very small n), in Figure 28.3B we list the matrices for *all* relations in $\mathbf{S}^2$. Given the relation R, remember that its matrix

$$\begin{bmatrix} a_{11} & a_{12} \\ a_{21} & a_{22} \end{bmatrix}$$

is defined by $a_{ij} = 0$ if $(i, j) \notin \mathbf{R}$ and by $a_{ij} = 1$ if $(i, j) \in \mathbf{R}$. Among these relations:

- 4 are reflexive (h, m, n, p),
- 4 are irreflexive (a, c, d, i),
- 8 are neither reflexive nor irreflexive (b, e, f, g, j, k, l, o),
- 8 are symmetric (a, b, e, h, i, l, o, p),
- 2 are both reflexive and symmetric (h, p),
- 2 are both irreflexive and symmetric (a, i),
- 4 are neither reflexive nor irreflexive nor symmetric (f, g, j, k).

28.4　Questions relating to enumeration are always fun to play with, and it is not at all necessary to display and count as we did in Example 1 of paragraph 28.3. As we learned in Section 20, enumeration is essential in the calculation of probabilities, but there are other applications as well. For example, there may be many different "routes" by which a computer can be programmed to perform a required calculation. Time equals money in the real world; hence that program which accomplishes its mission via the most economical route is usually the best. Enumeration of computational steps is necessary to provide estimates of the comparative efficiency of programs.

Let $\mathbf{S} = \{s_1, s_2, \ldots, s_n\}$ denote an arbitrary set of size n. Recall that $\mathbf{S}^2$ contains n^2 ordered pairs. As indicated in paragraph 28.2, a relation in $\mathbf{S}^2$ is simply a subset of $\mathbf{S}^2$. The number of such subsets is just the number of characteristic functions on $\mathbf{S}^2$. Recall from Theorem 16.1 that if $\mathbf{B}$ is a set such that $|\mathbf{B}| = m$, then the number of subsets of $\mathbf{B}$ is 2^m; hence the number of relations in $\mathbf{S}^2$ is 2^{n^2}. When $n = 2$, this number is $2^4 = 16$, which we observed in Example 1 of paragraph 28.3.

How many of these relations are reflexive? From paragraph 28.3, a relation is reflexive if $a_{ii} = 1$ for $i = 1, 2, \ldots, n$. Since each other entry in the matrix can be either 0 or 1, the number of reflexive relations is $2^{n^2-n} = 2^{n(n-1)}$. This is also the number of irreflexive relations, for in this case $a_{ii} = 0$ for $i = 1, 2, \ldots, n$, and the other entries may be either 0 or 1. Again, when $n = 2$, this number is $2^2 = 4$, which we observed in Example 1 of paragraph 28.3.

Tutorial 28.4

Assume that $|\mathbf{S}| = 3$.
a. How many relations are there in $\mathbf{S}^2$?
b. How many irreflexive relations are there in $\mathbf{S}^2$?
c. Write in matrix form three different irreflexive and symmetric relations in $\mathbf{S}^2$.

To enumerate the symmetric relations bear in mind that if $i \neq j$, then $a_{ij} = a_{ji}$. This means that if a_{ij} is known, then a_{ji} is determined. If the following matrix is to be symmetric, then it is completely determined once the entries on and above the main diagonal are assigned:

$$\begin{bmatrix} a_{11} & a_{12} & a_{13} & \cdots & a_{1n} \\ & a_{22} & a_{23} & \cdots & a_{2n} \\ & & & \cdots & \\ & & & & a_{nn} \end{bmatrix}.$$

How many such entries are there? We know this already (Theorem 10.4A):

$$1 + 2 + 3 + \cdots + n = \frac{n(n + 1)}{2}.$$

We may choose either 0 or 1 for each of these entries; hence the number of symmetric relations in $\mathbf{S}^2$ is $2^{n(n+1)/2}$.

Finally, the number of reflexive and symmetric relations is the same as the number of irreflexive and symmetric relations. Because entries on the main diagonal are now determined, our only choices are in assigning the entries above the main diagonal. There are

$$1 + 2 + 3 + \cdots + (n - 1) = \frac{(n - 1)n}{2}$$

such entries. Hence the number of reflexive and symmetric relations in $\mathbf{S}^2$ is $2^{n(n-1)/2}$. It is interesting to note that this number is the square root of the number of reflexive relations in $\mathbf{S}^2$. We summarize all these results in the following theorem.

THEOREM 28.4

If **S** is a set with n elements, then in $\mathbf{S}^2$:

- The number of relations is 2^{n^2}.
- The number of reflexive relations is $2^{n(n-1)}$.
- The number of irreflexive relations is $2^{n(n-1)}$.
- The number of symmetric relations is $2^{n(n+1)/2}$.
- The number of relations that are both reflexive and symmetric is $2^{n(n-1)/2}$.
- The number of relations that are both irreflexive and symmetric is $2^{n(n-1)/2}$.

28.5

Complement: Stirling Numbers The relation concept may be generalized immediately to include the option that first and second coordinates belong to different sets. If $\mathbf{A} = \{a_1, a_2, \ldots, a_m\}$ and $\mathbf{B} = \{b_1, b_2, \ldots, b_n\}$, then a relation $\mathbf{R}$ in $\mathbf{A} \times \mathbf{B}$ is any subset of $\mathbf{A} \times \mathbf{B}$. Consider an $m \times n$ rectangle consisting of m rows and n columns. We label the rows by the elements in $\mathbf{A}$ and the columns by the elements in $\mathbf{B}$, as in Figure 28.5. Any selection of 0 or 1 in each blank leads to an $m \times n$, $(0, 1)$-matrix which we will denote by $[c_{ij}]$, where $i = 1, 2, \ldots, m$ and $j = 1, 2, \ldots, n$. The relation $\mathbf{R}$ is represented by that matrix $[c_{ij}]$ for which

$$c_{ij} = \begin{cases} 1, & \text{if } (a_i, b_j) \in \mathbf{R}; \\ 0, & \text{otherwise.} \end{cases} \tag{1}$$

Suppose we agree to limit our attention to a subset of the relations in $\mathbf{A} \times \mathbf{B}$ consisting of those for which each row sum is at least 1. This means, of course, that

Figure 28.5

each $a_i \in \mathbf{A}$ occurs at least once as a first coordinate among the ordered pairs in $\mathbf{R}$. We say, then, that

$$(\text{Domain } \mathbf{R}) = \mathbf{A}.$$

If we agree further that each row sum is exactly 1, then the relation $\mathbf{R}$ is a function (i.e., exactly one element in $\mathbf{B}$ corresponds to any given element in the domain). For example,

$$[c_{ij}] = \begin{bmatrix} 0 & 0 & 0 & 0 & 1 \\ 1 & 0 & 0 & 0 & 0 \\ 0 & 1 & 0 & 0 & 0 \end{bmatrix} \tag{2}$$

is the matrix representing a function

$$f: \mathbf{A} \rightarrow \mathbf{B}$$

(in our usual terminology), where $|\mathbf{A}| = 3$ and $|\mathbf{B}| = 5$. Explicitly,

$$f = \{(a_1, b_5), (a_2, b_1), (a_3, b_2)\}.$$

A different matrix

$$[c_{ij}] = \begin{bmatrix} 0 & 1 & 0 & 0 & 0 \\ 0 & 1 & 0 & 0 & 0 \\ 0 & 1 & 0 & 0 & 0 \end{bmatrix}, \tag{3}$$

represents a constant function, defined by $f(x) = b_2$. It is easy to see that (2) represents a one-to-one function.

Returning to the more general case in which $|\mathbf{A}| = m$ and $|\mathbf{B}| = n$, the total number of functions

$$f: \mathbf{A} \rightarrow \mathbf{B}$$

is just the number of $m \times n$, $(0, 1)$-matrices with exactly one 1 in each row. Since there are n choices for each of the m rows, that number is

$$n^m.$$

The number of one-to-one functions is just the number of $m \times n$, $(0, 1)$-matrices with exactly one 1 in each row *and* at most one 1 in each column. Thus, we must have $m \leq n$, and there are

$$n \text{ choices for the first row,}$$
$$n - 1 \text{ choices for the second row,}$$
$$n - 2 \text{ choices for the third row,}$$
$$\cdots$$
$$n - (m - 1) \text{ choices for the } m\text{th row.}$$

The number of one-to-one functions is

$$(n)_m = \frac{n!}{(n-m)!} = n(n-1)(n-2)\cdots(n-m+1).$$

These enumerations were computed in Theorem 15.5 (but with sizes of **A** and **B** reversed). Our purpose in reviewing these computations has been to motivate our main question, "Is there an equally simple formula for the number of onto functions?"

The number of onto functions is just the number of $m \times n$, $(0, 1)$-matrices with exactly one 1 in each row *and* at least one 1 in each column. The matrix in (2) illustrates the impossibility of an onto function if $m < n$. Hence, we assume that $m \geq n$, which means that $[c_{ij}]$ is either square or has more rows than columns. To have a concrete example for reference, consider the onto function with the 6×4 matrix

$$[c_{ij}] = \begin{bmatrix} 1 & 0 & 0 & 0 \\ 0 & 1 & 0 & 0 \\ 0 & 1 & 0 & 0 \\ 0 & 0 & 0 & 1 \\ 0 & 0 & 0 & 1 \\ 0 & 0 & 1 & 0 \end{bmatrix}. \tag{4}$$

Each column in $[c_{ij}]$ can be thought of as a characteristic function on the domain **A** which identifies the subset

$$\mathbf{A}_j = \{a_i \in \mathbf{A} : c_{ij} = 1\}.$$

For example, in (4)

$$\mathbf{A}_1 = \{a_1\}, \qquad \mathbf{A}_2 = \{a_2, a_3\}, \qquad \mathbf{A}_3 = \{a_6\}, \qquad \mathbf{A}_4 = \{a_4, a_5\}.$$

These subsets $\mathbf{A}_1, \mathbf{A}_2, \ldots, \mathbf{A}_n$ partition **A**:

$$\mathbf{A} = \mathbf{A}_1 \cup \mathbf{A}_2 \cup \cdots \cup \mathbf{A}_n, \tag{5}$$

where $\mathbf{A}_i \cap \mathbf{A}_j = \varnothing$ if $i \neq j$ and, further, $\mathbf{A}_i \neq \varnothing$ for all i. The number of such partitions depends upon m and n, and we denote it by $S(m, n)$. It is called a Stirling number of the second kind, named for James Stirling (1692–1770). Our goal is to evaluate these numbers.

Any onto function, as in (4), for example, generates a partition of **A**, and a given partition corresponds to exactly $n!$ onto functions which are obtained by permuting the n columns in $[c_{ij}]$. For example, one permutation of the columns in (4) leads to

$$\begin{bmatrix} 1 & 0 & 0 & 0 \\ 0 & 1 & 0 & 0 \\ 0 & 1 & 0 & 0 \\ 0 & 0 & 1 & 0 \\ 0 & 0 & 1 & 0 \\ 0 & 0 & 0 & 1 \end{bmatrix}. \tag{6}$$

This is a different function from that in (4): explicitly, the two functions are

$$\{(a_1, b_1), (a_2, b_2), (a_3, b_2), (a_4, b_4), (a_5, b_4), (a_6, b_3)\}, \tag{4}$$

$$\{(a_1, b_1), (a_2, b_2), (a_3, b_2), (a_4, b_3), (a_5, b_3), (a_6, b_4)\}. \tag{6}$$

Notice that these two functions generate the same partition of **A**, namely,

$$\mathbf{A} = \{a_1\} \cup \{a_2, a_3\} \cup \{a_4, a_5\} \cup \{a_6\}.$$

Thus, each of the $S(m, n)$ different partitions of **A** (into exactly n nonempty subsets) corresponds to $n!$ different functions; hence the number of onto functions $f: \mathbf{A} \to \mathbf{B}$ is

$$n! \cdot S(m, n).$$

There exists a complicated formula for the numbers $S(m, n)$, but rather than derive it we will consider an enumeration by recursion. For this, we must discover a relationship between $S(m + 1, n)$ and smaller Stirling numbers. Let

$$\mathbf{A}' = \mathbf{A} \cup \{a_{m+1}\} = \{a_1, a_2, \ldots, a_m, a_{m+1}\},$$

and partition $\mathbf{A}'$ into n subsets. The element a_{m+1} either is in a singleton subset in the partition (call this type I) or is in a subset with more than one element (call this type II). The number of partitions of type I is $S(m, n-1)$, since **A** must be partitioned into $n - 1$ subsets:

$$\mathbf{A}' = \underbrace{\mathbf{A}}_{\substack{n-1 \\ \text{subsets}}} \cup \{a_{m+1}\}.$$

The number of partitions of type II is

$$n \cdot S(m, n).$$

To see this, consider any partition of **A** into n (nonempty) subsets. For each one of these, a_{m+1} can be inserted into any one of the n subsets in the partition, creating a type II partition of $\mathbf{A}'$. Thus, the recurrence relation is

$$S(m + 1, n) = S(m, n - 1) + n \cdot S(m, n). \tag{7}$$

The initial conditions are

$$S(m, 1) = 1 = S(m, m),$$

since the only partition of **A** into one subset is **A** itself, and the only partition of **A** into m subsets is

$$\mathbf{A} = \{a_1\} \cup \{a_2\} \cup \cdots \cup \{a_m\}.$$

m	n					
	1	2	3	4	5	6
1	1					
2	1	1				
3	1	3	1			
4	1	7	6	1		
5	1	15	25	10	1	
6	1	31	90	65	15	1

Table 28.5A Stirling numbers (second kind)

m	n					
	1	2	3	4	5	6
1	1					
2	1	2				
3	1	6	6			
4	1	14	36	24		
5	1	30	150	240	120	
6	1	62	540	1560	1800	720

Table 28.5B Number of onto functions

Remembering that $m \geq n$, we may create a table of values of $S(m, n)$, very much like Pascal's triangle (see Table 28.5A). As shown earlier, we obtain the number of onto functions by multiplying the entries in Table 28.5A by $n!$ (see Table 28.5B). Matrices corresponding to the six onto functions $f: \mathbf{A} \rightarrow \mathbf{B}$ for $|\mathbf{A}| = 3$ and $|\mathbf{B}| = 2$ are

$$\begin{bmatrix} 1 & 0 \\ 1 & 0 \\ 0 & 1 \end{bmatrix} \quad \begin{bmatrix} 1 & 0 \\ 0 & 1 \\ 0 & 1 \end{bmatrix} \quad \begin{bmatrix} 1 & 0 \\ 0 & 1 \\ 1 & 0 \end{bmatrix} \quad \begin{bmatrix} 0 & 1 \\ 0 & 1 \\ 1 & 0 \end{bmatrix} \quad \begin{bmatrix} 0 & 1 \\ 1 & 0 \\ 1 & 0 \end{bmatrix} \quad \begin{bmatrix} 0 & 1 \\ 1 & 0 \\ 0 & 1 \end{bmatrix}.$$

Since Table 28.5A lists Stirling numbers of the *second* kind, it is fair to ask whether there are Stirling numbers of the *first* kind. These numbers are denoted by $s(m, n)$ and are given recursively by

$$s(m + 1, n) = s(m, n - 1) - m \cdot s(m, n),$$

with initial conditions

$$s(m, 0) = 0 \quad \text{and} \quad s(m, m) = 1.$$

A discussion of the combinatorial significance of these numbers is best postponed to a more advanced course. Similarly, we must postpone a discussion of alternate formulas related to the Stirling numbers.

A final observation, however, is in order. Stirling numbers of the second kind answer an occupancy question similar to that considered in paragraph 20.5. It turns out that $S(m, n)$ is the number of ways to distribute m distinguishable objects among n indistinguishable containers so that no container is empty. For example, with four objects (say a, b, c, d) and two containers (say ⌊___⌋, ⌊___⌋) the seven ways (from Table 28.5A) are

$$⌊\,a\,⌋ \quad ⌊\,bcd\,⌋, \quad ⌊\,b\,⌋ \quad ⌊\,acd\,⌋, \quad ⌊\,c\,⌋ \quad ⌊\,abd\,⌋, \quad ⌊\,d\,⌋ \quad ⌊\,abc\,⌋,$$

$$⌊\,ab\,⌋ \quad ⌊\,cd\,⌋, \quad ⌊\,ac\,⌋ \quad ⌊\,bd\,⌋, \quad ⌊\,ad\,⌋ \quad ⌊\,bc\,⌋.$$

Problems for Section 28

1. Let **S** be the set $\{1, 3, 6, 9, 12\}$. Let **R** be the subset of $\mathbf{S} \times \mathbf{S} = \mathbf{S}^2$, where $(a, b) \in R$ if a divides b. List the elements of **R** and its matrix representation. Is **R** reflexive, irreflexive, symmetric, or none of these?

2. Let $\mathbf{S} = \{-2, -1, 0, 1, 2\}$ and let $(a, b) \in \mathbf{R}$ if $|a| = |b|$. Answer each of the questions in Problem 1 for this **S** and **R**.

3. Let **S** be the set of the final 16 teams in the NCAA basketball tournament. Let **R** be the subset of $\mathbf{S}^2$ where $(a, b) \in \mathbf{R}$ if team a beats team b in any of the final four rounds. List the row sums of the matrix of **R** in increasing order. (*Note:* A team is eliminated after its first loss; hence eight teams have zero row sum.)

4. The **trace** of an $n \times n$ matrix A is defined by $\mathrm{Tr}(A) = \sum_{i=1}^{n} a_{ii}$. Give two examples of 5×5, $(0, 1)$-matrices whose traces are equal to 2.

5. (*Continuation of Problem 4.*) How many $n \times n$, $(0, 1)$-matrices are there with trace equal to 2 for $n = 3, 4, 5$?

6. (*Continuation of Problem 4.*) How many $n \times n$, $(0, 1)$-matrices are there with trace equal to 2?

7. (*Conclusion of Problem 4.*) Let A be an $n \times n$, $(0, 1)$-matrix. (*a*) If A is irreflexive, what is $\mathrm{Tr}(A)$? (*b*) If n is even, how many $n \times n$, $(0,1)$-matrices are there with trace equal to $n/2$?

8. A **tridiagonal** matrix, $A = [a_{ij}]$, is any $n \times n$ matrix, $n \geq 4$, for which $a_{ij} = 0$ whenever $|i - j| \geq 2$. Give three examples of (*a*) 4×4 tridiagonal, $(0, 1)$-matrices; (*b*) 8×8 tridiagonal, $(0, 1)$-matrices.

9. How many different $n \times n$, tridiagonal, $(0, 1)$-matrices are there?

10. A matrix A is **upper-triangular** if $a_{ij} = 0$ for $1 \leq j < i \leq n$. Give three examples of 5×5, $(0, 1)$-upper-triangular matrices.

11. How many different $n \times n$, upper-triangular, $(0, 1)$-matrices are there?

12. Let $\mathbf{S} = \{0, 1, \ldots, 10\}$. Let **R** be a relation on **S** with $(a, b) \in \mathbf{R}$ if the number of letters in the spelling of the number a is the number b. For example, $(7, 5) \in \mathbf{R}$. List the elements of **R** and give the matrix of **R**.

13. In Problem 12, it is easy to see that **R** is a function. What are the row sums of the matrix for any relation that is a function?

14. Let $\mathbf{S} = \{1, 2, 3, 4, 5\}$. Let **R** be the relation on **S** with $(a, b) \in R$ if $a^2 + b$ is divisible by 3. List the matrix for **R** and the elements of **R**. Does **R** possess any of the properties introduced in this section?

15. Give an example of a 3×3, $(0, 1)$-matrix whose row sums are all equal. How many such matrices are there?

16. How many 5×5, $(0, 1)$-matrices are there with identical row sums?

17. How many $n \times n$, $(0, 1)$-matrices are there (*a*) with all row sums equal to 1, (*b*) with all row sums equal to $n - 1$?

18. How many 3×3, $(0, 1)$-matrices have all row sums the same and all column sums the same?

19. Is it possible for an $n \times n$, $(0, 1)$-matrix to have all row sums equal to j and all column sums equal to k, with $j \neq k$?

20. How many $n \times n$, $(0, 1)$-matrices are there with every row sum and every column sum equal to 1?

21. Let $\mathbf{S} = \{2, 3, 4, 5, 6, 10\}$. Let $\mathbf{R} = \{(a, b) : a, b \in \mathbf{S}, \gcd(a, b) = 1\}$. (*a*) List the matrix of **R**. (*b*) What properties does **R** possess?

22. Give real-life examples of symmetric relations which are (a) reflexive, (b) irreflexive, (c) not reflexive and not irreflexive.

23. Let A denote an $n \times n$, $(0, 1)$-matrix which is symmetric. (a) Prove that if all row sums in A are the same, then all column sums are the same. (b) The two extreme examples are the matrix with every entry 0 and the matrix with every entry 1. Discover at least two other examples "between" these two.

24. Let $\mathbf{S} = \{-4, -3, -2, -1, 0, 1, 2, 3, 4\}$, and let A be the 9×9, $(0, 1)$-matrix defined by

$$a_{ij} = \begin{cases} 1, & \text{if } 3 \mid (a_i - a_j); \\ 0, & \text{otherwise.} \end{cases}$$

(a) Construct A. (b) Show that A is both reflexive and symmetric.

25. Let $\mathbb{R}$ be the real numbers and define a relation $\mathbf{R}$ on $\mathbb{R}$ in the same manner as in Problem 12. For instance, 596 is related to 20 for "five hundred ninety-six" has 20 letters. Also $\pi/2$, written as "pi divided by two," is related to 14. An amazing fact is that repeated application of this relation always leads to 4. Using 596, the relation first gives 20 and then 6, since 20 has 6 letters. Now 6 is related to 3 which is related to 5 which is related to 4. Find such a sequence for 1024, -373, and $\sin 30°$ (it does not matter how $\sin 30°$ is written; for example, "sine of thirty degrees").

Section 29. Matrix Operations

Overview for Section 29

- Operations on square matrices with real number entries
- Equality of matrices, sums, and scalar products
- Linear transformations, composites, and matrix multiplication

Key Concepts: matrix equality, sums and scalar products, linear transformation, system of linear equations, composite of transformations, matrix products

29.1 The present chapter focuses attention mainly upon relation matrices, but these, in fact, represent only one among many diverse applications of the matrix concept in mathematics, physics, economics, and other disciplines. Although less than two centuries old, matrix theory has developed into a dominant theme in many branches of mathematics including analysis, geometry, algebra, and applied mathematics. It is a generalized mathematical structure similar in richness to the real number system, yet with significant and surprising differences. To illustrate the power of matrix methods we will depart (in this section only) from our study of discrete structures: Variables may now represent any real numbers. Although we considered matrices of size $n \times n$ in the preceding section, it will be helpful in the first four paragraphs here to consider only 2×2 matrices, thus simplifying the geometric motivation which underlies much of this development. In more advanced mathematics, and in its applications, the theory is much enlarged beyond these introductory concepts.

We will be concerned with 2×2 matrices

$$[a_{ij}] = \begin{bmatrix} a_{11} & a_{12} \\ a_{21} & a_{22} \end{bmatrix} \qquad (1)$$

in which each entry is a real number. Two matrices $[a_{ij}]$ and $[b_{ij}]$ are said to be **equal** if the corresponding entries in each position are equal; thus, for each i and j, $a_{ij} = b_{ij}$. For example,

$$[a_{ij}] = \begin{bmatrix} 2 & -1 \\ \sqrt{2} & 0 \end{bmatrix} \neq \begin{bmatrix} 2 & 1 \\ \sqrt{2} & 0 \end{bmatrix} = [b_{ij}]$$

since $a_{12} = -1$ and $b_{12} = 1$.

The **sum** of two matrices $[a_{ij}]$ and $[b_{ij}]$ is the matrix $[c_{ij}]$ for which $c_{ij} = a_{ij} + b_{ij}$. Thus, to add two matrices we simply add the corresponding entries in each position. For example,

$$\begin{bmatrix} 2 & -1 \\ \sqrt{2} & 0 \end{bmatrix} + \begin{bmatrix} -4 & 2 \\ -\sqrt{2} & \sqrt{3} \end{bmatrix} = \begin{bmatrix} -2 & 1 \\ 0 & \sqrt{3} \end{bmatrix}.$$

Matrices can be multiplied by real numbers, and this operation is referred to as **scalar multiplication.** If t is any real number, then the **scalar product** is defined by

$$t \cdot [a_{ij}] = [t \cdot a_{ij}]. \qquad (2)$$

This means that each entry in $[a_{ij}]$ is multiplied by t; for example,

$$6 \cdot \begin{bmatrix} \frac{1}{3} & 0 \\ \frac{1}{2} & -1 \end{bmatrix} = \begin{bmatrix} 2 & 0 \\ 3 & -6 \end{bmatrix}.$$

Tutorial 29.1

Let

$$[a_{ij}] = \begin{bmatrix} 2 & 5 \\ -1 & 3 \end{bmatrix}.$$

a. Show that $2 \cdot [a_{ij}] + 5 \cdot [a_{ij}] = 7 \cdot [a_{ij}]$.

continued on next page

continued from previous page

b. Show that

$$[a_{ij}] + (-1) \cdot [a_{ij}] = \begin{bmatrix} 0 & 0 \\ 0 & 0 \end{bmatrix}.$$

Referring to paragraph 2.8, the set of matrices under addition shares the structural properties listed there for addition in the real number system, including commutativity, associativity, and so on. Scalar multiplication, however, is not an analog of real number multiplication: The real number t and the matrix $[a_{ij}]$ are different kinds of objects. Yet, scalar multiplication does behave in familiar ways; for example,

$$1 \cdot [a_{ij}] = [1 \cdot a_{ij}] = [a_{ij}].$$

Example 1   Another familiar real number property,

$$t(a + b) = ta + tb,$$

is shared also by addition and scalar multiplication of matrices.

$$t\left(\begin{bmatrix} a_{11} & a_{12} \\ a_{21} & a_{22} \end{bmatrix} + \begin{bmatrix} b_{11} & b_{12} \\ b_{21} & b_{22} \end{bmatrix}\right) = t\begin{bmatrix} a_{11} + b_{11} & a_{12} + b_{12} \\ a_{21} + b_{21} & a_{22} + b_{22} \end{bmatrix}$$

$$= \begin{bmatrix} t(a_{11} + b_{11}) & t(a_{12} + b_{12}) \\ t(a_{21} + b_{21}) & t(a_{22} + b_{22}) \end{bmatrix}$$

$$= \begin{bmatrix} ta_{11} + tb_{11} & ta_{12} + tb_{12} \\ ta_{21} + tb_{21} & ta_{22} + tb_{22} \end{bmatrix}$$

$$= \begin{bmatrix} ta_{11} & ta_{12} \\ ta_{21} & ta_{22} \end{bmatrix} + \begin{bmatrix} tb_{11} & tb_{12} \\ tb_{21} & tb_{22} \end{bmatrix}$$

$$= t\begin{bmatrix} a_{11} & a_{12} \\ a_{21} & a_{22} \end{bmatrix} + t\begin{bmatrix} b_{11} & b_{12} \\ b_{21} & b_{22} \end{bmatrix}.$$

29.2   Up to this point matrices appear not to be particularly different in behavior from real numbers. But the picture, so far, has been pretty sterile; we need geometry to breathe a little life into the ideas. Through this geometric interpretation, we will find a proper analog for multiplication. The surprise is, however, that the properties of matrix multiplication differ in some dramatic ways from those of real number multiplication. In particular, matrix multiplication is not necessarily commutative, and the multiplicative inverse fails to be a simple reciprocal. These differences are not germane to our immediate goal, but they will be explored briefly in the problems.

Figure 29.2A

We begin with the familiar concept of a function defined on the set $\mathbb{R}$ of all real numbers:

$$y = f(x)$$

means that f is a function which relates each element x in the domain with some element y in the range. For example, if f is defined by the expression

$$y = \tfrac{3}{2} \cdot (x + 1),$$

then a few of the ordered pairs (x, y) in f are

x	0	1	-1	$\frac{1}{3}$	$-\frac{1}{3}$
y	$\frac{3}{2}$	3	0	2	1

We may think geometrically of the function f moving the point labeled by 1 on the x axis to the point labeled by 3 on the y axis (as in Figure 29.2A), and similarly with the other pairs. In essence, f is moving the real numbers around in a prescribed way. The familiar plot of $y = f(x)$ in the Cartesian plane $\mathbb{R}^2$ gives a more direct image of this relationship. As in Figure 29.2B, a point (x, y) on the graph of f tells us that f moves the number x to the number y.

Because there is one independent variable x in $y = f(x)$, f is referred to as a function of a single variable. Consider next a function F of two variables, named x_1 and x_2, which relates an ordered pair (x_1, x_2) to another ordered pair (y_1, y_2). We may think geometrically of such a function moving the point labeled (x_1, x_2) in the Cartesian plane to a point labeled (y_1, y_2) in the Cartesian plane (as in Figure 29.2C).

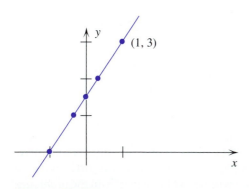

Figure 29.2B

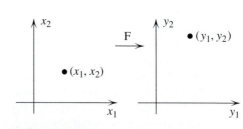

Figure 29.2C

In essence, F is moving points in the Cartesian plane around in a prescribed way. The description of F is complicated by the fact that it must tell how to compute both y_1 and y_2; hence two formulas are involved. For example, suppose we define a function by

$$F : \begin{cases} y_1 = 3x_1 + x_2; \\ y_2 = 2x_1 - x_2. \end{cases} \tag{1}$$

As before, we can compute a table of values:

(x_1, x_2)	$(0, 0)$	$(1, 1)$	$(-1, 2)$
(y_1, y_2)	$(0, 0)$	$(4, 1)$	$(-1, -4)$

This time there exists no picture comparable to Figure 29.2B (for it would require four dimensions and we have only three available). Nevertheless, "before" and "after" pictures like those in Figure 29.2C can be very instructive. Consider the straight-line segment from $(0, 0)$ to $(1, 1)$ in the (x_1, x_2)-coordinate system. The function F moves (or transforms) it into the straight-line segment from $(0, 0)$ to $(4, 1)$ in the (y_1, y_2)-coordinate system. In fact, F always moves straight lines into straight lines. Because of this, F is a special type of function referred to as a **linear transformation** [in (1) the formulas defining such a function are linear; only the first power of the variables appear].

Example 1 Any point on the segment shown in part (a) of Figure 29.2D has coordinates (t, t), where t is a real number satisfying $0 \le t \le 1$. It is easy to show that F transforms this point into one on the segment shown in part (b) of Figure 29.2D:

$$y_1 = 3x_1 + x_2 = 3t + t = 4t;$$

$$y_2 = 2x_1 - x_2 = 2t - t = t.$$

Thus for $0 \le t \le 1$,

$$0 \le y_1 \le 4 \qquad \text{and} \qquad y_2 = \tfrac{1}{4} \cdot y_1$$

which we recognize as the segment shown in part (b) of Figure 29.2D. ●

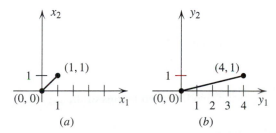

(a) $\qquad\qquad\qquad$ (b)

Figure 29.2D

Consider the function F in Example 1.
a. Sketch the line segment between $(0, 0)$ and $(-1, 1)$ in the domain of F [as in part (a) of Figure 29.2D].
b. On a coordinate system for the range of F [as in part (b) of Figure 29.2D], plot the points $F(0, 0)$, $F(-\frac{1}{2}, \frac{1}{2})$, and $F(-1, 1)$.

29.3

We observe from (1) in paragraph 29.2 that the distinguishing information about the function F resides in the coefficients and their relative locations; this information we may abstract in the form of a 2×2 matrix

$$\begin{bmatrix} 3 & 1 \\ 2 & -1 \end{bmatrix}.$$

Correspondingly, the matrix (1) in paragraph 29.1 simply represents the general linear transformation from $\mathbb{R}^2$ to $\mathbb{R}^2$:

$$y_1 = a_{11}x_1 + a_{12}x_2;$$
$$y_2 = a_{21}x_1 + a_{22}x_2.$$

(1)

   This is the geometric interpretation we have been looking for: A 2×2 matrix represents a transformation of the plane which takes straight lines in the domain to straight lines in the range (or, in some circumstances, to a single point, see Problem 31). You may, perhaps, recognize (1) from previous experience with *systems of linear equations* (a topic often included in secondary level algebra). Here is a typical example of the sort considered there.

Example 1

In the early part of this century buildings were often heated by coal-fired furnaces. Suppose that management bought a total of 120 tons in two different grades, which cost $4.50 per ton of soft coal and $7.00 per ton of hard coal. Assuming that the total bill was $640.00, how much of each grade was bought? From the information about tonnage,

$$x_1 + x_2 = 120,$$

and from the information about cost,

$$4.5x_1 + 7x_2 = 640.$$

Thus, we have a system of two linear equations of the type described in (1):

$$x_1 + x_2 = 120,$$
$$4.5x_1 + 7x_2 = 640.$$

The matrix defining the linear transformation is

$$\begin{bmatrix} 1 & 1 \\ 4.5 & 7 \end{bmatrix}$$

and our problem is to find that point (x_1, x_2) in the domain which is transformed under this matrix into the point $(120, 640)$ in the range. In this case, the solution by substitution is easy:

$$4.5(120 - x_2) + 7x_2 = 640,$$
$$2.5x_2 = 100;$$

hence $x_2 = 40$ tons and $x_1 = 80$ tons.   ●

29.4 Return briefly to linear functions of a single variable. Suppose that two such functions are defined by the formulas

$$y = f(x) \qquad \text{(compute } y \text{ given } x\text{),}$$
$$z = g(y) \qquad \text{(compute } z \text{ given } y\text{).}$$

Thus, z and x are related by

$$z = g(y) = g(f(x)),$$

which we usually denote by

$$z = (g \circ f)(x). \tag{1}$$

This defines a new linear function called the **composite** (or **composition**) of f and g. The composite, $g \circ f$, may be illustrated schematically as in Figure 29.4A. For

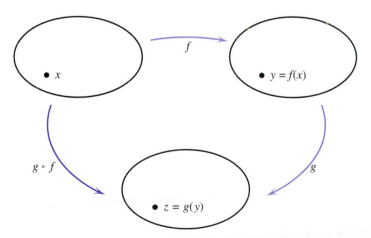

Figure 29.4A

example, if $y = ax + b$ and $z = cy + d$ (where a, b, c, d are real numbers), then

$$z = c(ax + b) + d = cax + cb + d,$$

which is in the form

$$z = Ax + B,$$

where A and B are the real numbers ca and $(cb + d)$, respectively.

Example 1

The international currency exchange rate is often reported in the daily paper. The following rates appear for Feb. 2, 1992:

$$1.7975 \text{ U.S. dollars per British pound,}$$
$$0.1832 \text{ U.S. dollars per French franc.}$$

If a Londoner, scheduled to travel to Paris on that date, converted 50 pounds to francs, how many francs were received? Schematically, we have Figure 29.4B. In this figure,

$$y = f(x) = 1.7975x \qquad \text{and} \qquad z = g(y) = \frac{1}{0.1832}y = 5.4585y.$$

The composite function is

$$z = (g \circ f)(x) = g(f(x)) = (5.4585)(1.7975x) = 9.8117x.$$

Hence, the Londoner receives (approximately)

$$(g \circ f)(50) = 9.8117 \cdot 50 = 491 \text{ francs.}$$

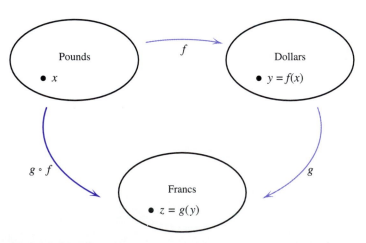

Figure 29.4B

Our problem now is to extend this important idea of the "composite" to functions of two variables. Suppose

$$(z_1, z_2) = G(y_1, y_2) \qquad \text{and} \qquad (y_1, y_2) = F(x_1, x_2)$$

are two linear transformations defined by

$$G: \begin{bmatrix} a_{11} & a_{12} \\ a_{21} & a_{22} \end{bmatrix} \qquad \text{and} \qquad F: \begin{bmatrix} b_{11} & b_{12} \\ b_{21} & b_{22} \end{bmatrix};$$

that is,

$$G: \begin{cases} z_1 = a_{11}y_1 + a_{12}y_2, \\ z_2 = a_{21}y_1 + a_{22}y_2, \end{cases} \qquad \text{and} \qquad F: \begin{cases} y_1 = b_{11}x_1 + b_{12}x_2, \\ y_2 = b_{21}x_1 + b_{22}x_2. \end{cases}$$

The schematic diagram of Figure 29.4C is similar to Figure 29.4A. Thus, $(G \circ F)(x_1, x_2) = G(F(x_1, x_2))$ which means that

$$z_1 = a_{11}(b_{11}x_1 + b_{12}x_2) + a_{12}(b_{21}x_1 + b_{22}x_2),$$
$$z_2 = a_{21}(b_{11}x_1 + b_{12}x_2) + a_{22}(b_{21}x_1 + b_{22}x_2),$$

and simplifying

$$z_1 = (a_{11}b_{11} + a_{12}b_{21})x_1 + (a_{11}b_{12} + a_{12}b_{22})x_2,$$
$$z_2 = (a_{21}b_{11} + a_{22}b_{21})x_1 + (a_{21}b_{12} + a_{22}b_{22})x_2.$$

Hence, the matrix defining $G \circ F$ is

$$G \circ F: \begin{bmatrix} (a_{11}b_{11} + a_{12}b_{21}) & (a_{11}b_{12} + a_{12}b_{22}) \\ (a_{21}b_{11} + a_{22}b_{21}) & (a_{21}b_{12} + a_{22}b_{22}) \end{bmatrix}.$$

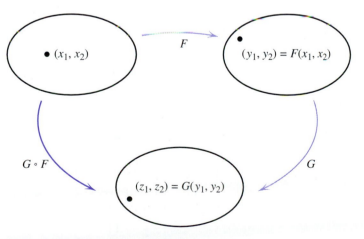

Figure 29.4C

This matrix is defined to be the **product** of the matrices for G and F (in that order):

$$\begin{bmatrix} a_{11} & a_{12} \\ a_{21} & a_{22} \end{bmatrix} \cdot \begin{bmatrix} b_{11} & b_{12} \\ b_{21} & b_{22} \end{bmatrix} = \begin{bmatrix} c_{11} & c_{12} \\ c_{21} & c_{22} \end{bmatrix},$$

where for each i and j,

$$c_{ij} = a_{i1}b_{1j} + a_{i2}b_{2j}.$$

This appears to be a complicated formula, but it is highly structured, hence easy to remember. To find the entry c_{ij} (on the ith row and jth column) in the product

$$[a_{ij}] \cdot [b_{ij}] = [c_{ij}],$$

simply pick the ith row from $[a_{ij}]$ and the jth column from $[b_{ij}]$, then multiply corresponding entries and add. For example, to find c_{21}, pick the second row from $[a_{ij}]$,

$$[a_{21} \quad a_{22}],$$

and the first column from $[b_{ij}]$,

$$\begin{bmatrix} b_{11} \\ b_{21} \end{bmatrix},$$

then compute the number

$$a_{21} \cdot b_{11} + a_{22} \cdot b_{21}.$$

The following "row by column" operation may be helpful:

$$\begin{bmatrix} a_{21} & a_{22} \end{bmatrix} \cdot \begin{bmatrix} b_{11} \\ b_{21} \end{bmatrix} \longrightarrow \begin{bmatrix} a_{21} & a_{22} \end{bmatrix} \cdot \begin{bmatrix} b_{11} \\ b_{21} \end{bmatrix} \longrightarrow \begin{bmatrix} b_{11} & b_{21} \\ a_{21} & a_{22} \end{bmatrix}.$$

Now form the product of the first two coordinates and add this product to the product of the two second coordinates to get

$$a_{21} \cdot b_{11} + a_{22} \cdot b_{21}.$$

Example 2

$$\begin{bmatrix} 3 & 0 \\ \frac{1}{2} & -2 \end{bmatrix} \cdot \begin{bmatrix} 1 & 4 \\ 2 & \frac{1}{2} \end{bmatrix} = \begin{bmatrix} 3 \cdot 1 + 0 \cdot 2 & 3 \cdot 4 + 0 \cdot \frac{1}{2} \\ \frac{1}{2} \cdot 1 + (-2) \cdot 2 & \frac{1}{2} \cdot 4 + (-2) \cdot \frac{1}{2} \end{bmatrix}$$

$$= \begin{bmatrix} 3 & 12 \\ -\frac{7}{2} & 1 \end{bmatrix}.$$

29.5   There is a very simple extension of the "matrix" ideas introduced in this section having to do with size. In general, a matrix may have any number of rows, say m, and any number of columns, say n, and is then referred to as an $m \times n$ matrix. In the special case $m = n$, the matrix is square, like those discussed above and in the preceding section. When $m \neq n$, the matrix is a rectangular array of numbers. With a little care, the matrix operations defined earlier (in the 2×2 case) carry over to the more general case. This means simply that the underlying arithmetic operations on entries must be meaningful. To be precise, the definitions are as follows.

Let $[a_{ij}]$ and $[b_{ij}]$ be any two matrices of the same size, say $m \times n$. The **sum** $[a_{ij}] + [b_{ij}]$ is the $m \times n$ matrix $[c_{ij}]$, where

$$c_{ij} = a_{ij} + b_{ij} \qquad (1)$$

for each $i = 1, 2, \ldots, m$ and $j = 1, 2, \ldots, n$.

Let $[a_{ij}]$ be any $m \times n$ matrix and let t be any real number. The **scalar product** $t \cdot [a_{ij}]$ is the $m \times n$ matrix $[c_{ij}]$, where

$$c_{ij} = t \cdot a_{ij} \qquad (2)$$

for each $i = 1, 2, \ldots, m$ and $j = 1, 2, \ldots, n$.

Let $[a_{ij}]$ be any $m \times n$ matrix and let $[b_{ij}]$ be any $n \times p$ matrix. The **(matrix) product** $[a_{ij}] \cdot [b_{ij}]$ is the $m \times p$ matrix $[c_{ij}]$, where

$$c_{ij} = a_{i1}b_{1j} + a_{i2}b_{2j} + \cdots + a_{in}b_{nj} = \sum_{k=1}^{n} a_{ik}b_{kj} \qquad (3)$$

for each $i = 1, 2, \ldots, m$ and $j = 1, 2, \ldots, p$. Note, especially, that the matrix product is not defined unless the number of columns in the left-hand matrix is the same as the number of rows in the right-hand matrix.

Example 1   Let $t = 3$ and let

$$A_1 = \begin{bmatrix} 1 & 4 \\ -1 & 2 \\ 0 & 1 \end{bmatrix}, \qquad A_2 = \begin{bmatrix} 2 & 3 & 1 \\ -1 & 0 & 2 \end{bmatrix}, \qquad A_3 = \begin{bmatrix} 1 & -1 \\ -1 & 1 \end{bmatrix}.$$

Then
$$t \cdot A_1 = \begin{bmatrix} 3 & 12 \\ -3 & 6 \\ 0 & 3 \end{bmatrix},$$

$A_1 + A_2$ is not defined, $A_2 + A_3$ is not defined,

$$A_2 \cdot A_1 = \begin{bmatrix} 2 & 3 & 1 \\ -1 & 0 & 2 \end{bmatrix} \begin{bmatrix} 1 & 4 \\ -1 & 2 \\ 0 & 1 \end{bmatrix} = \begin{bmatrix} -1 & 15 \\ -1 & -2 \end{bmatrix}, \qquad A_2 \cdot A_1 + A_3 = \begin{bmatrix} 0 & 14 \\ -2 & -1 \end{bmatrix},$$

$$A_1 \cdot A_3 = \begin{bmatrix} 1 & 4 \\ -1 & 2 \\ 0 & 1 \end{bmatrix} \cdot \begin{bmatrix} 1 & -1 \\ -1 & 1 \end{bmatrix} = \begin{bmatrix} -3 & 3 \\ -3 & 3 \\ -1 & 1 \end{bmatrix},$$

and $A_3 \cdot A_1$ is not defined.

29.6 Complement: Vectors

We are already familiar with the interpretation of an ordered pair (x_1, x_2) as the "address" of a point in a rectangular coordinate system. There is an important alternate interpretation of (x_1, x_2) as the endpoint of an arrow which begins at the origin (see Figure 29.6A). The arrow in this picture has both a direction and a length. In the special case $x_1 = x_2 = 0$, the arrow degenerates to a point (the origin) which has length 0 but has no defined direction. In all other cases the direction is along the ray from the origin to the point (x_1, x_2) and the length is given by the Pythagorean Theorem,

$$\sqrt{x_1^2 + x_2^2}.$$

(Think of the arrow as the hypotenuse of a right triangle having horizontal and vertical legs.)

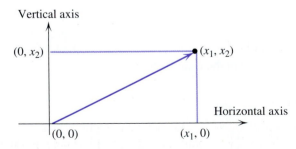

Figure 29.6A

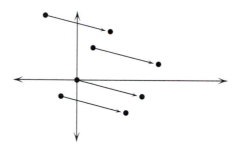

Figure 29.6B

Example 1   Consider the following arrows sketched in Figure 29.6B:

	Initial point	Terminal point	Length
A_1	$(0, 0)$	$(4, -1)$	$\sqrt{(4 - 0)^2 + (-1 - 0)^2} = \sqrt{17}$
A_2	$(-1, -1)$	$(3, -2)$	$\sqrt{(3 - (-1))^2 + (-2 - (-1))^2} = \sqrt{17}$
A_3	$(-2, 4)$	$(2, 3)$	$\sqrt{(2 - (-2))^2 + (3 - 4)^2} = \sqrt{17}$
A_4	$(1, 2)$	$(5, 1)$	$\sqrt{(5 - 1)^2 + (1 - 2)^2} = \sqrt{17}$

These arrows have a common direction (they point the same way along parallel lines), and they have a common length.

Arrows with a common direction and length represent a single mathematical object called a **vector,** which is subject to certain arithmetic operations to be defined shortly. To indicate a vector we usually represent it by the arrow with its initial point at the origin; then only the terminal point is necessary to fix direction and length. As a convention, we will enclose the coordinates of the terminal point in square brackets. It will sometimes be convenient to write the coordinates vertically rather than horizontally, the same vector being represented either way. We refer to

$$[x_1 \quad x_2]$$

as a **row vector,** and refer to

$$\begin{bmatrix} x_1 \\ x_2 \end{bmatrix}$$

as a **column vector.** A row vector may be thought of as a matrix with one row and two columns, thus a 1×2 matrix; a column vector may be thought of as a matrix with two rows and one column, thus a 2×1 matrix. Because of this, the operations of

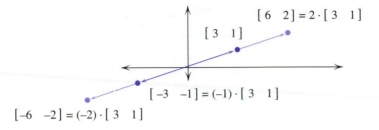

Figure 29.6C

addition, scalar multiplication, and matrix multiplication apply to vectors, and each has an important geometric interpretation. For simplicity we will use row vector notation for the most part; the results would be similar if column notation were used.

First, consider scalar multiplication:

$$t \cdot [x_1 \quad x_2] = [tx_1 \quad tx_2].$$

As indicated in Figure 29.6C, the orientation of the vector is reversed if $t < 0$ and is the same if $t > 0$. Also, the length of the vector is multiplied by the factor $\sqrt{t^2}$. Thus, if either $t = 2$ or $t = -2$ the length of $t \cdot [x_1 \quad x_2]$ is twice that of $[x_1 \quad x_2]$.

Second, consider addition:

$$[x_1 \quad x_2] + [y_1 \quad y_2] = [x_1 + y_1 \quad x_2 + y_2].$$

As indicated in Figure 29.6D, the sum of two vectors is (geometrically) the diagonal of a parallelogram.

Third, consider multiplication. There are two possibilities,

$$[x_1 \quad x_2] \cdot \begin{bmatrix} y_1 \\ y_2 \end{bmatrix} = [x_1 y_1 + x_2 y_2],$$

and

$$\begin{bmatrix} x_1 \\ x_2 \end{bmatrix} \cdot [y_1 \quad y_2] = \begin{bmatrix} x_1 y_1 & x_1 y_2 \\ x_2 y_1 & x_2 y_2 \end{bmatrix}.$$

The first of these products is the more useful for our purposes and is given a special name: the **inner product.** Because a 1×1 matrix offers no information beyond the

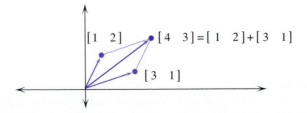

Figure 29.6D

entry itself, we simply consider it to be a real number and write

$$[x_1 \quad x_2] \cdot \begin{bmatrix} y_1 \\ y_2 \end{bmatrix} = x_1 y_1 + x_2 y_2.$$

Much of elementary plane geometry can be recast in the language of vectors, with two important consequences. The statement and proof of many results can be simplified, and geometry can be generalized in ways that Euclid (and his successors for two millennia) could not even imagine. We will end this introduction with a brief indication of how lines and perpendicularity may be expressed in terms of vectors.

Suppose we are given two vectors $V_1 = [x_1 \quad x_2]$ and $V_2 = [y_1 \quad y_2]$. Note that the terminal point of V_1 is (x_1, x_2). How can we determine the line which lies on the point (x_1, x_2) and is parallel to the direction of the vector V_2? The answer turns out to be strongly reminiscent of (1) in paragraph 1.4; it is, in fact, a significant generalization of that idea. Just as in the earlier formula, to determine an arbitrary point on the desired line, we must first "get to" (x_1, x_2), then move in the direction of V_2 some multiple of its length. This recipe has the very simple symbolic form

$$V_1 + tV_2. \tag{1}$$

Example 2   Let $V_1 = [1 \quad 2]$ and let $V_2 = [3 \quad 1]$. Now sketch the vectors $V_1 + tV_2$ corresponding to $t = 0, 1, -1, 2$ and -2, as in Figure 29.6E (note the similarity with Figure 29.6D). The terminal points of those vectors lie on the desired line. The coordinates of the corresponding points on the line may be tabulated as follows.

t	tV_2	$V_1 + tV_2$	*Coordinates*
0	[0 0]	[1 2]	(1, 2)
1	[3 1]	[4 3]	(4, 3)
−1	[−3 −1]	[−2 1]	(−2, 1)
2	[6 2]	[7 4]	(7, 4)
−2	[−6 −2]	[−5 0]	(−5, 0)

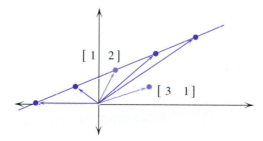

Figure 29.6E

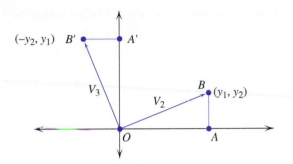

Figure 29.6F

Again, suppose we are given the two vectors $V_1 = [x_1 \quad x_2]$ and $V_2 = [y_1 \quad y_2]$. This time we want the line which lies on the point (x_1, x_2) and is perpendicular to the direction of the vector V_2. The first task is to determine a vector V_3 which is perpendicular to V_2. In Figure 29.6F, note that triangle $OA'B'$ is constructed to be congruent with triangle OAB. Thus, the coordinates of B' must be $(-y_2, y_1)$; hence the vectors $[-y_2 \quad y_1]$ and $[y_1 \quad y_2]$ are at right angles. In more advanced mathematics, this condition is described by calling the two vectors **orthogonal.** Thus $V_3 = [-y_2 \quad y_1]$ and V_2 are orthogonal, and by (1), the line on the point (x_1, x_2) perpendicular to V_2 has the vector form

$$V_1 + tV_3.$$

Typically, this might appear as in Figure 29.6G.

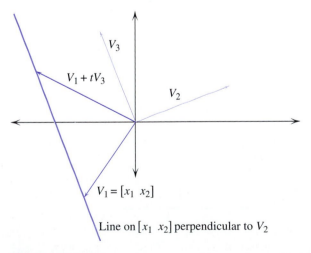

Figure 29.6G

As a final observation note that the inner product of V_2 and V_3 is

$$[y_1 \quad y_2] \cdot \begin{bmatrix} -y_2 \\ y_1 \end{bmatrix} = -y_1 y_2 + y_1 y_2 = 0.$$

Perhaps surprisingly, it would be difficult to overestimate the importance of the idea behind this simple equation. In many areas of mathematics, physics, and engineering, this concept is fundamental in both theory and applications.

Problems for Section 29

In Problems 1 through 7, let $A = \begin{bmatrix} 1 & 2 \\ -1 & 0 \end{bmatrix}$, $B = \begin{bmatrix} 2 & 3 \\ 0 & 1 \end{bmatrix}$, and $C = \begin{bmatrix} -1 & 0 \\ 2 & -1 \end{bmatrix}$.

1. Compute $A + B$, $A + C$, and $B + C$.

2. Compute $5 \cdot A$, $-3 \cdot B$, and $\frac{3}{4} \cdot C$.

3. Compute $5 \cdot A - 3 \cdot B$, $2 \cdot A + 4 \cdot B$, and $3 \cdot C - A$.

4. Compute $A \cdot A$, $B \cdot B$, and $C \cdot C$.

5. Compute $A \cdot B$ and $B \cdot A$. Note again that matrix multiplication is not commutative.

6. Compute $A \cdot C$ and $C \cdot A$.

7. (a) Compute $D = B + C$. (b) Compute $A + D$. (c) Compute $E = A + B$. (d) Compute $E + C$. (e) Compare your answer in parts (b) and (d).

8. Show that matrix addition is associative for $n \times n$ matrices; that is, $A + (B + C) = (A + B) + C$. [*Hint:* Think of each matrix as size $n \times n$ and consider the (i, j) entry in each matrix.]

9. Let $I_n = [a_{ij}]$ be the $n \times n$ **identity** matrix with

$$a_{ij} = \begin{cases} 1, & \text{if } i = j; \\ 0, & \text{otherwise.} \end{cases}$$

(a) What are $B \cdot I_3$ and $I_3 \cdot B$ for any 3×3 matrix B? (b) If B is any $n \times n$ matrix, then what are $B \cdot I_n$ and $I_n \cdot B$?

10. Let $H_n = [a_{ij}]$ be the $n \times n$ matrix with

$$a_{ij} = \begin{cases} 1, & \text{if } j = n + 1 - i; \\ 0, & \text{otherwise.} \end{cases}$$

(a) If B is any 3×3 matrix, then what are $B \cdot H_3$ and $H_3 \cdot B$? (b) If B is any $n \times n$ matrix, then what are $B \cdot H_n$ and $H_n \cdot B$?

11. We know that matrix multiplication is not necessarily commutative, and from Problem 8 we know that matrix addition is associative. Show that $A \cdot (B \cdot C) = (A \cdot B) \cdot C$ for the three matrices defined at the beginning of these problems.

12. The verification that matrix multiplication is associative, even for 2×2 matrices, is tedious. Assuming 2×2 matrices of the form $A = [a_{ij}]$, $B = [b_{ij}]$, and $C = [c_{ij}]$, calculate the first row and first column entry of $A \cdot (B \cdot C)$ and $(A \cdot B) \cdot C$, and show that they are the same.

13. Show that if A and B are $n \times n$, upper-triangular matrices, then $A \cdot B$ is upper-triangular. (See Problem 10 in Section 28.)

14. It is natural to let $A^2 = A \cdot A$. But should $A^3 = A^2 \cdot A$ or $A^3 = A \cdot A^2$? Assuming that matrix multiplication is associative, show that for a 2×2 matrix, $A^2 \cdot A = A \cdot A^2$.

15. Let A be any $n \times n$ matrix. For $n > 1$, define $A^n = A^{n-1} \cdot A$. Using mathematical induction and assuming that matrix multiplication is associative, show that $A^n = A \cdot A^{n-1}$.

16. For each of the following, write out the matrix $A = [a_{ij}]$. (a) $a_{ij} = i + j$: $1 \leq i \leq 5$, $1 \leq j \leq 5$. (b) $a_{ij} = i - j$: $1 \leq i \leq 5$, $1 \leq j \leq 5$. (c) $a_{ij} = i/j$: $1 \leq i \leq 5$, $1 \leq j \leq 5$.

17. Verify that the following matrices are equal:
$A = [a_{ij}]$, where $a_{ij} = \binom{i + j}{j}$ for $0 \leq i \leq 4, 0 \leq j \leq 4$, and $B = [b_{ij}]$, where $b_{0,k} = b_{k,0} = 1$ for $0 \leq k \leq 4$ and $b_{i,j} = b_{i-1,j-1} + b_{i-1,j}$ for $1 \leq i \leq 4$, $1 \leq j \leq 4$.

18. Recall that a matrix $A = [a_{ij}]$ is symmetric if $a_{ij} = a_{ji}$. Which of the matrices in Problems 16 and 17 are symmetric?

19. Find two symmetric matrices A and B such that $A \cdot B$ is not symmetric.

20. (*Continuation of Problem 19.*) Assume that A and B are symmetric matrices which commute. Show that $A \cdot B$ is symmetric.

21. (*Conclusion of Problem 19.*) Show that if A is symmetric, then A^n is symmetric.

22. Matrices behave differently than the real numbers in several ways. First, find a 2×2 matrix, A, such that $A^2 = A$ but A is neither $\begin{bmatrix} 1 & 0 \\ 0 & 1 \end{bmatrix}$ (the *identity matrix*) nor the matrix consisting of all zeroes.

23. (*Continuation of Problem 22.*) Find two 4×4, $(0, 1)$-matrices such that their product is the matrix consisting of all zeroes. Each matrix should have at least four 1s in it.

24. (*Conclusion of Problem 22.*) Find a 3×3 matrix A such that A^2 is not the all-zero matrix, but A^3 is the all-zero matrix.

25. If A is a 2×3 matrix, B is a 3×4 matrix, and C is a 4×3 matrix, then which of the following are valid products? (a) $A \cdot A$,

(b) $A \cdot B$, (c) $A \cdot C$, (d) $B \cdot A$, (e) $B \cdot B$, (f) $B \cdot C$, (g) $C \cdot A$, (h) $C \cdot B$, (i) $C \cdot C$.

For the next five problems, let

$$A = \begin{bmatrix} 1 & 0 & -2 & 3 \\ -1 & 4 & 2 & 5 \end{bmatrix}, B = \begin{bmatrix} 2 & 1 \\ -2 & 3 \\ -3 & 0 \\ 0 & 5 \end{bmatrix},$$

$$C = \begin{bmatrix} 3 & 1 & 1 \\ 0 & -2 & 3 \end{bmatrix}, \text{ and } D = \begin{bmatrix} 0 & 1 & -3 & 3 \\ 0 & 4 & -1 & 5 \end{bmatrix}.$$

26. Compute $A + D$ and $-5 \cdot C$.

27. Compute $A \cdot B$ and $B \cdot C$.

28. Compute $A \cdot (B \cdot C)$ and $(A \cdot B) \cdot C$.

29. Compute $B \cdot D$ and $D \cdot B$.

30. Compute $(B \cdot D)^2$.

31. Occasionally, a linear transformation takes a straight line into a single point. (a) Show that $\begin{bmatrix} 0 & 0 \\ 0 & 0 \end{bmatrix}$ takes all lines to the origin.

(b) Show that $\begin{bmatrix} 0 & 1 \\ 0 & 1 \end{bmatrix}$ takes the horizontal line $x_2 = 4$ to the point $(4, 4)$. (c) Show that $\begin{bmatrix} 3 & 1 \\ 3 & 1 \end{bmatrix}$ takes the line $x_2 = -3x_1 + 3$ to the point $(3, 3)$.

32. (*Conclusion of Problem 31.*) Show that the matrix $\begin{bmatrix} a & b \\ c & d \end{bmatrix}$ takes the line $x_2 = ux_1 + v$ to the point (bv, dv) provided that $a = -bu$ and $c = -du$ (in this problem both u and v represent real numbers).

33. If u and v are real numbers and if A is any 2×2 matrix, show that $(u + v)A = uA + vA$.

34. If u and v are real numbers and if A is any $n \times n$ matrix, show that $(u + v)A = uA + vA$.

Section 30. Special Matrices

Overview for Section 30

- Description of certain special relations:
  empty, full, identity
- Inverse of a relation and transpose of a matrix
- Operations on matrices and transposes
- The transpose of a product

Key Concepts: empty, full, identity relations, transpose, antisymmetry, transpose of a product

30.1

The preceding section introduced what is called the "algebra of matrices"; its structure is based upon the matrix operations of addition, multiplication, and scalar multiplication. Our primary concerns in that section were:

- To offer some hint of the widespread occurrence and applicability of matrices.

- To present just enough of the general theory so that the definition of matrix multiplication seems natural rather than contrived.

Students in either the social or the physical sciences are likely to find that the matrix concept will become an increasingly useful tool, not only for descriptive purposes but in the analysis of problems as well. We leave the further development of matrix theory in its general setting to other courses and return now to the somewhat more specialized concerns appropriate to discrete mathematics. What this means, in essence, is that matrix entries will be nonnegative integers having some sort of combinatorial significance.

For the remainder of the present chapter our concern remains with $n \times n$, $(0, 1)$-matrices, representing relations in $\mathbf{S}^2$ for some set

$$\mathbf{S} = \{s_1, s_2, \ldots, s_n\}.$$

It will be helpful to standardize notation: If $\mathbf{R} \subseteq \mathbf{S}^2$ is a relation, then the matrix for $\mathbf{R}$ is denoted by

$$M(\mathbf{R}) = [a_{ij}] = \begin{bmatrix} a_{11} & a_{12} & \cdots & a_{1n} \\ a_{21} & a_{22} & \cdots & a_{2n} \\ \cdots & \cdots & \cdots & \cdots \\ a_{n1} & a_{n2} & \cdots & a_{nn} \end{bmatrix}, \tag{1}$$

where

$$a_{ij} = \begin{cases} 1, & \text{if } (s_i, s_j) \in \mathbf{R}; \\ 0, & \text{otherwise.} \end{cases}$$

If the relation is clear from context, we will omit the $\mathbf{R}$ in the notation and refer to the matrix simply by M. Further, we will refer to the main diagonal of M by Δ (no matter what its specific entries may be),

$$\Delta = \{a_{ii} : i = 1, 2, \dots, n\}.$$

Recall from Section 28 that for each i:

- If $a_{ii} = 1$, then M is reflexive.
- If $a_{ii} = 0$, then M is irreflexive.

Among the set of all possible relations in $\mathbf{S}^2$ there are three unique ones that we will refer to from time to time:

1. The **empty** relation $\mathbf{R} = \varnothing$ which corresponds to the **zero** matrix in which each entry is 0 (denoted by O).

2. The **full** relation $\mathbf{R} = \mathbf{S}^2$ which corresponds to the **unit** matrix in which each entry is 1 (denoted by J).

3. The **identity** relation, which corresponds to the **identity** matrix in which

$$a_{ij} = \begin{cases} 1, & \text{if } j = i; \\ 0, & \text{if } j \neq i. \end{cases}$$

From an earlier course in mathematics you may be familiar with the concept of the identity function $f: \mathbb{R} \to \mathbb{R}$ defined by the condition

$$f(x) = x.$$

Thus, $f = \{(x, x): x \in \mathbb{R}\}$. The finite analog of f is the identity relation in $\mathbf{S}^2$ (in which each element in $\mathbf{S}$ is related to itself and to no other element). The notation we will use for the identity matrix is I, and a bold $\mathbf{I}$ will be used to denote the identity relation. Thus, I is a matrix in which each entry in Δ is 1 and each of the other entries is 0.

The size of these matrices may vary with context, and where it seems important for clarity we will subscript the symbol, using n to denote a matrix of size $n \times n$. For example, O_n, J_n, I_n are to be considered $n \times n$ matrices.

Example 1   If $\mathbf{S} = \{s_1, s_2, s_3\}$, then the zero matrix is

$$O_3 = \begin{bmatrix} 0 & 0 & 0 \\ 0 & 0 & 0 \\ 0 & 0 & 0 \end{bmatrix},$$

the unit matrix is

$$J_3 = \begin{bmatrix} 1 & 1 & 1 \\ 1 & 1 & 1 \\ 1 & 1 & 1 \end{bmatrix},$$

and the identity matrix is

$$I_3 = \begin{bmatrix} 1 & 0 & 0 \\ 0 & 1 & 0 \\ 0 & 0 & 1 \end{bmatrix}.$$

Note that the zero matrix is irreflexive and that each of the other two is reflexive.

Tutorial 30.1

Let $A = [a_{ij}] = \begin{bmatrix} 1 & 1 & 0 \\ 0 & 1 & 1 \\ 1 & 0 & 0 \end{bmatrix}.$

Compute the following matrix products.

a. $A \cdot O_3$.

b. $A \cdot J_3$.

c. $A \cdot I_3$.

d. Which of these products *is not* commutative?

30.2 Each of the matrices in Example 1 of paragraph 30.1 is symmetric: If each is rotated about Δ, the matrix is unchanged. But most relations are not symmetric; in the case $n = 3$, for example, there are $2^{3^2} = 2^9 = 512$ relations altogether, but of these only $2^6 = 64$ are symmetric (see Theorem 28.4).

Example 1 Let $S = \{1, 2, 3, 4, 5, 6\}$ and consider the following relation in $S \times S$:

$$R = \{(x, y) : x^y < y^x\}.$$

Some of the ordered pairs in R are

$$\{(1, 2), (1, 3), \ldots, (2, 3), \ldots, (6, 5)\}. \tag{1}$$

The matrix for R (in complete detail) is

$$M = \begin{bmatrix} 0 & 1 & 1 & 1 & 1 & 1 \\ 0 & 0 & 1 & 0 & 0 & 0 \\ 0 & 0 & 0 & 0 & 0 & 0 \\ 0 & 0 & 1 & 0 & 0 & 0 \\ 0 & 1 & 1 & 1 & 0 & 0 \\ 0 & 1 & 1 & 1 & 1 & 0 \end{bmatrix}.$$

If M is rotated about Δ, then the resulting matrix is denoted by M^t, which is clearly different from M,

$$M^t = \begin{bmatrix} 0 & 0 & 0 & 0 & 0 & 0 \\ 1 & 0 & 0 & 0 & 1 & 1 \\ 1 & 1 & 0 & 1 & 1 & 1 \\ 1 & 0 & 0 & 0 & 1 & 1 \\ 1 & 0 & 0 & 0 & 0 & 1 \\ 1 & 0 & 0 & 0 & 0 & 0 \end{bmatrix}.$$

Some of the ordered pairs in its corresponding relation are

$$\{(2, 1), (3, 1), \ldots, (3, 2), \ldots, (5, 6)\}. \tag{2}$$

The matrices M and M^t in this example are obtained from one another by simply interchanging rows and columns (this is what rotating the matrix about Δ does: The first row of M becomes the first column of M^t, and so on). In general, if $M = [a_{ij}]$, then the **transpose** of M is $M^t = [b_{ij}]$, where $b_{ij} = a_{ji}$ for each i and j. For example,

$$b_{11} = a_{11}, \ b_{21} = a_{12}, \ldots, \ b_{n1} = a_{1n}.$$

It is easy to see that the transpose of M^t brings us back to M. This is consistent with our (informal) geometric operations: A second rotation about Δ produces the original matrix (see Figure 30.2).

The relations corresponding to M and M^t share an important characteristic illustrated in (1) and (2): The ordered pairs in (2) are obtained from those in (1) simply by interchanging the coordinates. In general, if $\mathbf{R}$ is any relation in $\mathbf{S}^2$, then the **inverse** of $\mathbf{R}$, denoted by $\mathbf{R}^{-1}$, is

$$\mathbf{R}^{-1} = \{(x, y) \in \mathbf{S}^2 : (y, x) \in \mathbf{R}\}. \tag{3}$$

We note that the ordered pairs in (1) are obtained from those in (2) simply by interchanging the coordinates; hence the inverse of $\mathbf{R}^{-1}$ is again $\mathbf{R}$. Thus $(\mathbf{R}^{-1})^{-1} = \mathbf{R}$, and this corresponds with our earlier observation that

$$(M^t)^t = M.$$

Example 1 illustrates the following general observation: If a relation $\mathbf{R}$ has M as its matrix, then the inverse $\mathbf{R}^{-1}$ has M^t as its matrix.

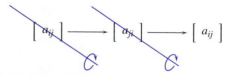

Figure 30.2

The matrix M in Example 1 is intended to illustrate nonsymmetry, but it happens to illustrate an even stronger property: There is no entry for which both a_{ij} and a_{ji} are 1. In general, a matrix $M = [a_{ij}]$, and its corresponding relation, is called **antisymmetric** if for each i and j, $i \neq j$,

$$a_{ij} = 1 \qquad \text{implies that} \qquad a_{ji} = 0.$$

Example 2

$\begin{bmatrix} 1 & 0 & 0 \\ 0 & 0 & 1 \\ 0 & 1 & 1 \end{bmatrix}$ is symmetric, $\begin{bmatrix} 1 & 0 & 0 \\ 0 & 0 & 1 \\ 1 & 0 & 1 \end{bmatrix}$ is antisymmetric, $\begin{bmatrix} 1 & 0 & 0 \\ 0 & 0 & 1 \\ 1 & 1 & 1 \end{bmatrix}$ is neither.   ●

Tutorial 30.2

Let $S = \{1, 2, 3, 4\}$, and consider the relation in $S \times S$ given by $R = \{(x, y) : (-2)^x < (-2)^y\}$.
a. Construct the matrix M corresponding to R.
b. Write the matrix M^t.
c. Is M symmetric, antisymmetric, or neither?

30.3

Generally speaking, the algebra of matrices plays a more central role in continuous than in discrete mathematics. Nonetheless, there are important points of contact, some of which are suggested in the following example.

Example 1

Return to the matrix M and its transpose M^t in Example 1 of paragraph 30.2. First, consider the sum

$$\begin{bmatrix} 0 & 1 & 1 & 1 & 1 & 1 \\ 0 & 0 & 1 & 0 & 0 & 0 \\ 0 & 0 & 0 & 0 & 0 & 0 \\ 0 & 0 & 1 & 0 & 0 & 0 \\ 0 & 1 & 1 & 1 & 0 & 0 \\ 0 & 1 & 1 & 1 & 1 & 0 \end{bmatrix} + \begin{bmatrix} 0 & 0 & 0 & 0 & 0 & 0 \\ 1 & 0 & 0 & 0 & 1 & 1 \\ 1 & 1 & 0 & 1 & 1 & 1 \\ 1 & 0 & 0 & 0 & 1 & 1 \\ 1 & 0 & 0 & 0 & 0 & 1 \\ 1 & 0 & 0 & 0 & 0 & 0 \end{bmatrix} = \begin{bmatrix} 0 & 1 & 1 & 1 & 1 & 1 \\ 1 & 0 & 1 & 0 & 1 & 1 \\ 1 & 1 & 0 & 1 & 1 & 1 \\ 1 & 0 & 1 & 0 & 1 & 1 \\ 1 & 1 & 1 & 1 & 0 & 1 \\ 1 & 1 & 1 & 1 & 1 & 0 \end{bmatrix}.$$

Because $M + M^t$ is symmetric, we are tempted to wonder whether the same might be true for other matrices. Furthermore, $M + M^t$ suggests a possible characterization of antisymmetry, since any symmetric pair of 1s in M must produce a 2 in $M + M^t$. These observations, in fact, lead to generalizations, to be proved shortly.

Second, consider the product $M \cdot M^t$,

$$\begin{bmatrix} 0 & 1 & 1 & 1 & 1 & 1 \\ 0 & 0 & 1 & 0 & 0 & 0 \\ 0 & 0 & 0 & 0 & 0 & 0 \\ 0 & 0 & 1 & 0 & 0 & 0 \\ 0 & 1 & 1 & 1 & 0 & 0 \\ 0 & 1 & 1 & 1 & 1 & 0 \end{bmatrix} \cdot \begin{bmatrix} 0 & 0 & 0 & 0 & 0 & 0 \\ 1 & 0 & 0 & 0 & 1 & 1 \\ 1 & 1 & 0 & 1 & 1 & 1 \\ 1 & 0 & 0 & 0 & 1 & 1 \\ 1 & 0 & 0 & 0 & 0 & 1 \\ 1 & 0 & 0 & 0 & 0 & 0 \end{bmatrix} = \begin{bmatrix} 5 & 1 & 0 & 1 & 3 & 4 \\ 1 & 1 & 0 & 1 & 1 & 1 \\ 0 & 0 & 0 & 0 & 0 & 0 \\ 1 & 1 & 0 & 1 & 1 & 1 \\ 3 & 1 & 0 & 1 & 3 & 3 \\ 4 & 1 & 0 & 1 & 3 & 4 \end{bmatrix}.$$

This time, also, the question of symmetry arises, and we will see that the generalization again is true. But there is another, more important property of the product which is (to some extent) disguised by the arithmetic. It has to do with "composition," not a great surprise given the motivation for the definition of matrix multiplication. We will return to this point in the next section after introducing a new (and "lean") version of arithmetic.

Tutorial 30.3

Let $A = \begin{bmatrix} 1 & 1 & 0 \\ 0 & 1 & 1 \\ 1 & 0 & 0 \end{bmatrix}$.

a. Compute $A \cdot A^t$.
b. Compute $A^t \cdot A$.
c. Are these products equal?

30.4

For the remainder of this section we will assume that $S = \{s_1, s_2, \ldots, s_n\}$ and that R is a relation in S^2. The matrix corresponding to R is denoted by $M = [a_{ij}]$, and for convenience we denote its transpose by $M^t = [b_{ij}]$.

THEOREM 30.4A

$M + M^t$ is symmetric.

Proof

For convenience, put $M + M^t = [c_{ij}]$. We must show that $c_{ij} = c_{ji}$. By definition,

$$c_{ij} = a_{ij} + b_{ij} = a_{ij} + a_{ji},$$

and

$$c_{ji} = a_{ji} + b_{ji} = a_{ji} + a_{ij};$$

hence

$$c_{ij} = c_{ji}. \qquad \blacksquare$$

THEOREM 30.4B

M is antisymmetric if and only if no entry off Δ in $M + M^t$ is greater than 1.

Proof

Suppose $c_{ij} = 0$ or 1 for each i and j, $i \neq j$. Since $c_{ij} = a_{ij} + b_{ij} = a_{ij} + a_{ji}$, it is clear that if $a_{ij} = 1$, then $a_{ji} = 0$. Thus M is antisymmetric.

Now, suppose that M is antisymmetric. Then for each i and j, $i \neq j$, $c_{ij} = a_{ij} + a_{ji}$, and if $a_{ij} = 1$, then $a_{ji} = 0$; hence $c_{ij} \leq 1$. $\qquad \blacksquare$

**THEOREM
30.4C**

$M \cdot M^t$ is symmetric.

Proof

For convenience, put $M \cdot M^t = [d_{ij}]$. We must show that $d_{ij} = d_{ji}$. By definition,

$$d_{ij} = \sum_{k=1}^{n} a_{ik} b_{kj} = \sum_{k=1}^{n} a_{ik} a_{jk} = a_{i1} a_{j1} + a_{i2} a_{j2} + \cdots + a_{in} a_{jn},$$

and

$$d_{ji} = \sum_{k=1}^{n} a_{jk} b_{ki} = \sum_{k=1}^{n} a_{jk} a_{ik} = a_{j1} a_{i1} + a_{j2} a_{i2} + \cdots + a_{jn} a_{in};$$

hence, $d_{ij} = d_{ji}$. ∎

We note that the matrix representation of symmetry is exceedingly simple, namely, $M^t = M$. By the definition of matrix equality, this is equivalent to the condition that $a_{ij} = b_{ij}$ for each i and j. A slight modification of this condition is that $M - M^t = O$, the zero matrix, where matrix "subtraction" is defined in a natural way by means of scalar multiplication and matrix addition,

$$[a_{ij}] - [b_{ij}] = [a_{ij}] + (-1)[b_{ij}] = [a_{ij}] + [-b_{ij}]$$
$$= [a_{ij} - b_{ij}]$$
$$= O.$$

One of the principal tools of the algebra of matrices, especially with respect to relations and their inverses, is the connection between products and transposes. In preparation for a more detailed study of relations in the next section, we prove the following very important property: The transpose of a product is the product of the transposes, *but in reverse order.*

**THEOREM
30.4D**

Let $A = [a_{ij}]$ and $B = [b_{ij}]$ be any two $n \times n$ matrices. Then

$$(A \cdot B)^t = B^t \cdot A^t.$$

Proof

Note first that all the indicated transposes and products are $n \times n$ matrices. To prove equality, we must show that corresponding entries on the left and on the right are the same. It will help to clarify the argument if we introduce some new notation:

$$[c_{ij}] = [a_{ij}] \cdot [b_{ij}] \qquad \left(c_{ij} = \sum_{k=1}^{n} a_{ik} b_{kj} \right), \tag{1}$$

$$[d_{ij}] = [a_{ij}]^t \qquad (d_{ij} = a_{ji}), \qquad (2)$$

$$[e_{ij}] = [b_{ij}]^t \qquad (e_{ij} = b_{ji}), \qquad (3)$$

$$[f_{ij}] = [c_{ij}]^t \qquad (f_{ij} = c_{ji}), \qquad (4)$$

$$[g_{ij}] = [e_{ij}] \cdot [d_{ij}] \qquad \left(g_{ij} = \sum_{k=1}^{n} e_{ik}d_{kj} \right). \qquad (5)$$

Assuming that i and j are any integers satisfying

$$1 \le i \le n \qquad \text{and} \qquad 1 \le j \le n,$$

our task is to prove that

$$f_{ij} = g_{ij}.$$

First, note that $f_{ij} = c_{ji}$ by (4) and that

$$c_{ji} = \sum_{k=1}^{n} a_{jk}b_{ki} \qquad \text{by (1)}.$$

Next, note that

$$g_{ij} = \sum_{k=1}^{n} e_{ik}d_{kj} \qquad \text{by (5)},$$

and that $e_{ik} = b_{ki}$ by (3) and $d_{kj} = a_{jk}$ by (2). Thus, by substitution and the commutativity of real number multiplication

$$g_{ij} = \sum_{k=1}^{n} b_{ki}a_{jk} = \sum_{k=1}^{n} a_{jk}b_{ki} = c_{ji}.$$

Hence, $\qquad\qquad\qquad f_{ij} = \sum_{k=1}^{n} a_{jk}b_{ki} = g_{ij}.$ ■

Example 1   It is possible to use Theorem 30.4D to give the following alternate proof of Theorem 30.4C. By Theorem 30.4D,

$$(M \cdot M^t)^t = (M^t)^t \cdot M^t = M \cdot M^t,$$

which is the condition that the matrix $M \cdot M^t$ be symmetric. ●

Problems for Section 30

In each of Problems 1 to 3, let $\mathbf{S} = \{0, 1, 2, 3\}$, and write out the matrix for each of the relations indicated.

1. (a) $\mathbf{R}_1 = \{(i, j): i + j = 3\}$, (b) $\mathbf{R}_2 = \{(i, j): i + j \leq 4\}$.

2. (a) $\mathbf{R}_1 = \{(i, j): |i - j| < 4\}$, (b) $\mathbf{R}_2 = \{(i, j): \max(i, j) = 3\}$.

3. (a) $\mathbf{R}_1 = \{(i, j): i \leq j\}$, (b) $\mathbf{R}_2 = \{(i, j): i \cdot j$ is spelt with three letters$\}$.

4. For each of the relations in Problem 1, determine which of the properties it has: reflexive, irreflexive, symmetric, or antisymmetric.

5. For each of the relations in Problem 2, determine which of the properties it has: reflexive, irreflexive, symmetric, or antisymmetric.

6. For each of the relations in Problem 3, determine which of the properties it has: reflexive, irreflexive, symmetric, or antisymmetric.

7. Are any of the relations in Problems 1 to 3 full, empty, or the identity?

8. Construct the matrix for the inverse of the relations given in (a) Problem 1, (b) Problem 2, (c) Problem 3.

9. Refer to the relations in Problem 1, and let M_1 be the matrix for $\mathbf{R}_1$ and M_2 be the matrix for $\mathbf{R}_2$. (a) Construct the product $M_1 M_2$. (b) Show that $(M_1 M_2)^t = M_2^t M_1^t$.

10. Repeat Problem 9 for the relations given in Problem 2.

11. Repeat Problem 9 for the relations given in Problem 3.

12. Suppose that $\mathbf{R}_1$ and $\mathbf{R}_2$ are symmetric relations on the set $\mathbf{S}$. (a) Is $\mathbf{R}_1 \cap \mathbf{R}_2$ also sym-

metric? Why or why not? (b) Is $\mathbf{R}_1 \cup \mathbf{R}_2$ also symmetric? Why or why not?

13. (a) Show that $\mathbf{R}$ is symmetric if and only if $\mathbf{R} = \mathbf{R}^{-1}$. (b) Show that $\mathbf{R}$ is antisymmetric if and only if $\mathbf{R} \cap \mathbf{R}^{-1} \subseteq \mathbf{I}$.

14. Show that if $\mathbf{R}_1$ and $\mathbf{R}_2$ are relations on $\mathbf{S}$, then (a) $(\mathbf{R}_1 \cup \mathbf{R}_2)^{-1} = \mathbf{R}_1^{-1} \cup \mathbf{R}_2^{-1}$, (b) $(\mathbf{R}_1 \cap \mathbf{R}_2)^{-1} = \mathbf{R}_1^{-1} \cap \mathbf{R}_2^{-1}$.

15. What is the inverse relation for the relation in Problem 12 of Section 28?

16. Show that if $M = [a_{ij}]$ and $M^t = [b_{ij}]$ are $(0, 1)$-matrices, then the matrix $H = [h_{ij}]$ given by $h_{ij} = a_{ij} \cdot b_{ij}$ is symmetric.

The next five problems introduce the important concept of matrix inversion. This concept must be distinguished from the inverse of a relation and the corresponding transpose of a matrix. Once again, traditional usage assigns different meanings to the same word and symbol; attention to the context will help minimize confusion. Given an $n \times n$ matrix A, the **inverse** of A, denoted by A^{-1}, is an $n \times n$ matrix such that $AA^{-1} = A^{-1}A = I$. Not every matrix has an inverse, but when one exists, it is unique.

17. If $A = \begin{bmatrix} 1 & 3 \\ 2 & 1 \end{bmatrix}$ and $B = \begin{bmatrix} -\frac{1}{5} & \frac{3}{5} \\ \frac{2}{5} & -\frac{1}{5} \end{bmatrix}$, verify that $A \cdot B = B \cdot A = I$.

18. (*Continuation of Problem 17.*) Find an inverse for $A = \begin{bmatrix} 1 & 1 \\ 1 & 2 \end{bmatrix}$. (*Hint:* Multiply A by $\begin{bmatrix} a & b \\ c & d \end{bmatrix}$ and equate the corresponding entries with those in I, then solve the four equations.)

19. (*Continuation of Problem 17.*) Show that $\begin{bmatrix} 1 & 2 \\ 3 & 6 \end{bmatrix}$ has no inverse. (*Hint:* Follow the hint in Problem 18 and show that the equations do not have a solution.)

20. (*Continuation of Problem 17.*) Show that
$$\begin{bmatrix} a & b \\ c & d \end{bmatrix} \cdot \begin{bmatrix} -d & b \\ c & -a \end{bmatrix} = \begin{bmatrix} bc - ad & 0 \\ 0 & bc - ad \end{bmatrix}.$$

21. (*Conclusion of Problem 17.*) Show that
$$\begin{bmatrix} a & b \\ c & d \end{bmatrix}$$
has an inverse if $ad - bc \neq 0$.

22. In arithmetic, if $a^2 = 1$, then either $a = 1$ or $a = -1$. The situation is different with respect to matrices. (*a*) Corresponding to real number arithmetic, show that
$$\begin{bmatrix} 1 & 0 \\ 0 & 1 \end{bmatrix}^2 = \begin{bmatrix} -1 & 0 \\ 0 & -1 \end{bmatrix}^2 = I_2.$$ (*b*) Now, however, find a 2×2 matrix A with no zero entry such that $A^2 = I$. (In the language of the preceding problems, A is its own inverse.)

23. (*Conclusion of Problem 22.*) Find a 3×3 matrix different from the identity for which

$A^2 = I$. [*Hint:* Use your answer to Problem 22(*b*)].

24. Find a 2×2 matrix with no zero entry for which $A^2 = O_2$.

25. A $(0, 1)$-matrix is a **permutation** matrix if each row and column contains exactly one 1. The identity matrix is an example of a permutation matrix. What is the other 2×2 permutation matrix?

26. (*Continuation of Problem 25.*) How many $n \times n$ permutation matrices are there? (*Hint:* Do this for $n = 3$ first and remember that they are called permutation matrices!)

27. (*Conclusion of Problem 25.*) Consider $A = \begin{bmatrix} 0 & 1 & 0 \\ 1 & 0 & 0 \\ 0 & 0 & 1 \end{bmatrix}$ and $B = \begin{bmatrix} a & b & c \\ d & e & f \\ g & h & i \end{bmatrix}$. Calculate AB and BA and see if you understand why A is a permutation matrix.

Section 31.   Relations and Boolean Arithmetic

Overview for Section 31

- Introduction to Boolean arithmetic
- Composition of relations in matrix language
- The inverse of the composition of matrices
- Definition of order between matrices

Key Concepts: Boolean arithmetic, composition, inverse of composition, order

31.1   We have already studied a number of special topics in relations, but they offer only a hint at the richness of the theory which pervades nearly all the broad subfields of mathematics and its applications. In the next few sections we will continue with a detailed investigation, relying heavily on the very descriptive language of relation matrices.

Let $\mathbf{S} = \{s_1, s_2, \ldots, s_n\}$ and let $\mathbf{R}$ be a relation in $\mathbf{S} \times \mathbf{S}$. Recall that the matrix corresponding to $\mathbf{R}$ is denoted by $M(\mathbf{R})$, or by M alone, and is defined to be the square matrix $[a_{ij}]$, where

$$a_{ij} = \begin{cases} 1, & \text{if } (s_i, s_j) \in \mathbf{R}; \\ 0, & \text{otherwise.} \end{cases}$$

Here, again, is the canonical picture for this situation:

$$\begin{array}{c c} & \begin{array}{cccc} s_1 & s_2 & \cdots & s_n \end{array} \\ \begin{array}{c} s_1 \\ s_2 \\ \cdots \\ s_n \end{array} & \left[\begin{array}{cccc} a_{11} & a_{12} & \cdots & a_{1n} \\ a_{21} & a_{22} & \cdots & a_{2n} \\ \cdots & \cdots & \cdots & \cdots \\ a_{n1} & a_{n2} & \cdots & a_{nn} \end{array}\right]. \end{array}$$

Because

$$\varnothing \subseteq \mathbf{R} \subseteq \mathbf{S} \times \mathbf{S},$$

$$0 \le |\mathbf{R}| \le n^2.$$

Note that the size of $\mathbf{R}$ is actually

$$|\mathbf{R}| = \sum_{i=1}^{n} \sum_{j=1}^{n} a_{ij}.$$

The meaning of this "double summation" is

$$\sum_{i=1}^{n} \left(\sum_{j=1}^{n} a_{ij} \right) = \sum_{i=1}^{n} (a_{i1} + a_{i2} + \cdots + a_{in})$$

$$= (a_{11} + a_{12} + \cdots + a_{1n}) + \cdots + (a_{n1} + a_{n2} + \cdots + a_{nn}).$$

This sum computes the number of 1s in $M(\mathbf{R})$, which is just the number of ordered pairs in $\mathbf{R}$. Also, note that this sum computes the number of 1s in the rows and then sums these row sums. Thus, this same sum can be computed by first counting the number of 1s in each column and then summing these column sums. Hence, we can reverse the summation:

$$|\mathbf{R}| = \sum_{i=1}^{n} \sum_{j=1}^{n} a_{ij} = \sum_{j=1}^{n} \sum_{i=1}^{n} a_{ij}.$$

For many purposes in relation theory, we are not concerned with enumerations of this sort but rather with the identification of ordered pairs belonging to relations. There is a very special "arithmetic" appropriate to this task called **Boolean arithmetic,** named for the logician George Boole (1815–1864). Only two elements appear in Boolean arithmetic, 0 and 1, and the "addition" and "multiplication" tables are exceedingly simple:

$\oplus$	0	1
0	0	1
1	1	1

$\otimes$	0	1
0	0	0
1	0	1

An easy way to remember this is to interpret 0 as the empty set $\varnothing$; 1 as any nonempty set $\mathbf{A}$; $\oplus$ as union $\cup$; and $\otimes$ as intersection $\cap$. As in ordinary arithmetic the operations are commutative, associative, and distributive, and we agree that $\otimes$ precedes $\oplus$.

Example 1

Compute the following matrix product using Boolean arithmetic.

$$\begin{bmatrix} 1 & 0 & 1 \\ 1 & 1 & 0 \\ 0 & 0 & 1 \end{bmatrix} \cdot \begin{bmatrix} 0 & 1 & 0 \\ 1 & 1 & 1 \\ 0 & 0 & 1 \end{bmatrix} = \begin{bmatrix} c_{11} & c_{12} & c_{13} \\ c_{21} & c_{22} & c_{23} \\ c_{31} & c_{32} & c_{33} \end{bmatrix}$$

$$c_{11} = (1 \otimes 0) \oplus (0 \otimes 1) \oplus (1 \otimes 0) = 0 \oplus 0 \oplus 0 = 0,$$

$$c_{22} = (1 \otimes 1) \oplus (1 \otimes 1) \oplus (0 \otimes 0) = 1 \oplus 1 \oplus 0 = 1,$$

$$c_{33} = (0 \otimes 0) \oplus (0 \otimes 1) \oplus (1 \otimes 1) = 0 \oplus 0 \oplus 1 = 1.$$

The remaining six entries are computed similarly, and the matrix product in full is

$$\begin{bmatrix} 0 & 1 & 1 \\ 1 & 1 & 1 \\ 0 & 0 & 1 \end{bmatrix}.$$

Tutorial 31.1

Compute the remaining six entries in the product shown in Example 1. To find c_{12}, for example, compute $(1 \otimes 1) \oplus (0 \otimes 1) \oplus (1 \otimes 0)$.

31.2

The matrix product immediately above has a valuable interpretation. Observe first that its two factor matrices correspond to the relations

$$\mathbf{R}_1 = \{(s_1, s_1), (s_1, s_3), (s_2, s_1), (s_2, s_2), (s_3, s_3)\},$$

$$\mathbf{R}_2 = \{(s_1, s_2), (s_2, s_1), (s_2, s_2), (s_2, s_3), (s_3, s_3)\}.$$

We may illustrate each relation by a diagram of arrows which link paired elements, shown in Figure 31.2. From this diagram we may construct a new relation, $\mathbf{R}_1 \circ \mathbf{R}_2$,

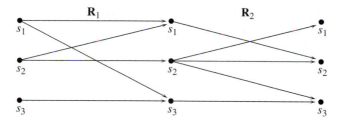

Figure 31.2

consisting of $\mathbf{R}_1$ followed by $\mathbf{R}_2$. Its pairs are linked by a two-step directed path from left to right (possibly by more than one such path). Thus, each of the following pairs belongs to $\mathbf{R}_1 \circ \mathbf{R}_2$:

$$(s_1, s_2), \quad \text{since } s_1 \longrightarrow s_1 \longrightarrow s_2;$$
$$(s_1, s_3), \quad \text{since } s_1 \longrightarrow s_3 \longrightarrow s_3;$$
$$(s_2, s_1), \quad \text{since } s_2 \longrightarrow s_2 \longrightarrow s_1;$$
$$(s_2, s_2), \quad \text{since } s_2 \longrightarrow s_2 \longrightarrow s_2;$$
$$(s_2, s_3), \quad \text{since } s_2 \longrightarrow s_2 \longrightarrow s_3;$$
$$(s_3, s_3), \quad \text{since } s_3 \longrightarrow s_3 \longrightarrow s_3.$$

Now, observe that the matrix corresponding to the new relation $\mathbf{R}_1 \circ \mathbf{R}_2$ is the matrix product displayed in Example 1 of paragraph 31.1.

The preceding discussion illustrates an important general property of relations, to be stated in Theorem 31.2. Let $\mathbf{R}_1$ and $\mathbf{R}_2$ be relations in $\mathbf{S} \times \mathbf{S}$. Corresponding to the *composition* of functions, defined in paragraph 29.4, the **composition** of $\mathbf{R}_1$ and $\mathbf{R}_2$, denoted by $\mathbf{R}_1 \circ \mathbf{R}_2$, is the relation in $\mathbf{S} \times \mathbf{S}$ defined by

$$\mathbf{R}_1 \circ \mathbf{R}_2 = \{(s_i, s_j): \text{there is an } s_k \text{ such that } (s_i, s_k) \in \mathbf{R}_1 \text{ and } (s_k, s_j) \in \mathbf{R}_2\}. \quad (1)$$

Note that the element s_k in (1) stands in the middle column of a diagram similar to that in Figure 31.2. Again, there may be several such elements; only one, however, is necessary. For simplicity of notation, in the following theorem and in succeeding calculations we will replace $\oplus$ and $\otimes$ by the standard usage for addition and multiplication, relying on a local reminder when the arithmetic is Boolean.

THEOREM 31.2

Let $\mathbf{R}_1$ and $\mathbf{R}_2$ be relations in $\mathbf{S} \times \mathbf{S}$. Then

$$M(\mathbf{R}_1 \circ \mathbf{R}_2) = M(\mathbf{R}_1) \cdot M(\mathbf{R}_2).$$

Proof

Note first that each matrix in question is of size $n \times n$; hence the operations are defined. Let

$$M(\mathbf{R}_1) = [a_{ij}], \qquad M(\mathbf{R}_2) = [b_{ij}],$$

and $[a_{ij}] \cdot [b_{ij}] = [c_{ij}]$, where

$$c_{ij} = \sum_{k=1}^{n} a_{ik}b_{kj} \qquad \text{(Boolean)}.$$

If $c_{ij} = 1$, then there is some k for which $a_{ik} = b_{kj} = 1$. But this means that $(s_i, s_k) \in \mathbf{R}_1$ and that $(s_k, s_j) \in \mathbf{R}_2$; hence $(s_i, s_j) \in \mathbf{R}_1 \circ \mathbf{R}_2$.

If $c_{ij} = 0$, then for every k, $a_{ik} \cdot b_{kj} = 0$; hence either $a_{ik} = 0$ or $b_{kj} = 0$. This means that for every $s_k \in \mathbf{S}$, either $(s_i, s_k) \notin \mathbf{R}_1$ or $(s_k, s_j) \notin \mathbf{R}_2$, so $(s_i, s_j) \notin \mathbf{R}_1 \circ \mathbf{R}_2$. ∎

Tutorial 31.2

In algebra, if two functions $f: \mathbf{A} \to \mathbb{R}$ and $g: \mathbf{A} \to \mathbb{R}$ are given, we can define two "algebraic" operations:

Sum : $(f + g)(x) = f(x) + g(x)$,

Product : $(f \cdot g)(x) = f(x) \cdot g(x)$.

Similarly, in Boolean arithmetic we can define the sum and product of functions. Let $\mathbf{V} = \{a, e, i, o, u\}$. The characteristic function $f = \{(a, 1), (e, 0), (i, 0), (o, 1), (u, 0)\}$ describes the subset $\{a, o\}$ of $\mathbf{V}$.
a. What characteristic function g describes the subset $\{a, e, u\}$ of $\mathbf{V}$?
b. Find the sum $f + g$ in Boolean arithmetic.
c. Find the product $f \cdot g$ in Boolean arithmetic.
d. For what subsets are $f + g$ and $f \cdot g$ characteristic functions?

Example 1   Let $\mathbf{S} = \{s_1, s_2, s_3\}$. Referring to Example 1 of paragraph 31.1, the relations are

$$\mathbf{R}_1 = \{(s_1, s_1), (s_1, s_3), (s_2, s_1), (s_2, s_2), (s_3, s_3)\},$$
$$\mathbf{R}_2 = \{(s_1, s_2), (s_2, s_1), (s_2, s_2), (s_2, s_3), (s_3, s_3)\},$$

and

$$\mathbf{R}_1 \circ \mathbf{R}_2 = \{(s_1, s_2), (s_1, s_3), (s_2, s_1), (s_2, s_2), (s_2, s_3), (s_3, s_3)\}.$$

The matrix product is

$$\begin{bmatrix} 1 & 0 & 1 \\ 1 & 1 & 0 \\ 0 & 0 & 1 \end{bmatrix} \cdot \begin{bmatrix} 0 & 1 & 0 \\ 1 & 1 & 1 \\ 0 & 0 & 1 \end{bmatrix} = \begin{bmatrix} 0 & 1 & 1 \\ 1 & 1 & 1 \\ 0 & 0 & 1 \end{bmatrix}.$$

Now we consider the transposes

$$(M(\mathbf{R}_1 \circ \mathbf{R}_2))^t = \begin{bmatrix} 0 & 1 & 0 \\ 1 & 1 & 0 \\ 1 & 1 & 1 \end{bmatrix} = (M(\mathbf{R}_1) \cdot M(\mathbf{R}_2))^t.$$

By Theorem 30.4D, this should be

$$(M(\mathbf{R}_2))^t \cdot (M(\mathbf{R}_1))^t,$$

which is confirmed by calculating (Boolean)

$$\begin{bmatrix} 0 & 1 & 0 \\ 1 & 1 & 0 \\ 0 & 1 & 1 \end{bmatrix} \cdot \begin{bmatrix} 1 & 1 & 0 \\ 0 & 1 & 0 \\ 1 & 0 & 1 \end{bmatrix} = \begin{bmatrix} 0 & 1 & 0 \\ 1 & 1 & 0 \\ 1 & 1 & 1 \end{bmatrix}.$$

31.3 We know that if M is the matrix corresponding to the relation $\mathbf{R}$, then M^t is the matrix corresponding to $\mathbf{R}^{-1}$. This can be denoted by

$$M(\mathbf{R}^{-1}) = (M(\mathbf{R}))^t.$$

If $\mathbf{R}_1$ and $\mathbf{R}_2$ are relations, then we also know that

$$M(\mathbf{R}_1 \circ \mathbf{R}_2) = M(\mathbf{R}_1) \cdot M(\mathbf{R}_2).$$

Now consider the transposes

$$(M(\mathbf{R}_1 \circ \mathbf{R}_2))^t = (M(\mathbf{R}_2))^t \cdot (M(\mathbf{R}_1))^t,$$

and restate this condition in terms of inverses

$$M(\mathbf{R}_1 \circ \mathbf{R}_2)^{-1} = M(\mathbf{R}_2^{-1}) \cdot M(\mathbf{R}_1^{-1}) = M(\mathbf{R}_2^{-1} \circ \mathbf{R}_1^{-1}).$$

In its role as a characteristic function on $\mathbf{S} \times \mathbf{S}$, M simply identifies the ordered pairs in its corresponding relation. Thus, from the preceding equation

$$(\mathbf{R}_1 \circ \mathbf{R}_2)^{-1} = \mathbf{R}_2^{-1} \circ \mathbf{R}_1^{-1}. \tag{1}$$

This rule states that the inverse of the composition of two relations is the composition of the inverses, but *in reverse order.* The similarity of this property with Theorem 30.4D is apparent.

Example 1

Consider again the relations $\mathbf{R}_1$, $\mathbf{R}_2$, and $\mathbf{R}_1 \circ \mathbf{R}_2$ in Example 1 of paragraph 31.2. Then

$$\mathbf{R}_1^{-1} = \{(s_1, s_1), (s_1, s_2), (s_2, s_2), (s_3, s_1), (s_3, s_3)\},$$

$$\mathbf{R}_2^{-1} = \{(s_1, s_2), (s_2, s_1), (s_2, s_2), (s_3, s_2), (s_3, s_3)\},$$

and

$$(\mathbf{R}_1 \circ \mathbf{R}_2)^{-1} = \{(s_1, s_2), (s_2, s_1), (s_2, s_2), (s_3, s_1), (s_3, s_2), (s_3, s_3)\}.$$

The "arrow diagram" for the composition $\mathbf{R}_2^{-1} \circ \mathbf{R}_1^{-1}$ is given in Figure 31.3. From this diagram we observe that $\mathbf{R}_2^{-1} \circ \mathbf{R}_1^{-1} = \{(s_1, s_2), (s_2, s_1), (s_2, s_2), (s_3, s_1), (s_3, s_2), (s_3, s_3)\}$, which is identical with $(\mathbf{R}_1 \circ \mathbf{R}_2)^{-1}$.   ●

Recall from paragraph 13.1 that the domain of a relation is the set of its first coordinates and that the range of a relation is the set of its second coordinates. The domain of $\mathbf{R}_1 \circ \mathbf{R}_2$ is always a subset of the domain of $\mathbf{R}_1$, but the two need not be equal. For example, if $s_i \in (\text{domain } \mathbf{R}_1)$, then there may be no element s_k such that $(s_i, s_k) \in \mathbf{R}_1$ and $s_k \in (\text{domain } \mathbf{R}_2)$. In some applications, it may be important that the domains of $\mathbf{R}_1 \circ \mathbf{R}_2$ and $\mathbf{R}_1$ be the same. To assure this, we simply adjoin the requirement that $(\text{domain } \mathbf{R}_2) \subseteq (\text{range } \mathbf{R}_1)$.

Boolean arithmetic has still another advantage. If $\mathbf{R}_1$ and $\mathbf{R}_2$ are again relations in $\mathbf{S} \times \mathbf{S}$, then to say that $\mathbf{R}_1 \subseteq \mathbf{R}_2$ means, of course, that each ordered pair in $\mathbf{R}_1$ is also an ordered pair in $\mathbf{R}_2$. As before, put

$$M(\mathbf{R}_1) = [a_{ij}] \qquad \text{and} \qquad M(\mathbf{R}_2) = [b_{ij}].$$

Now assuming that $0 < 1$, we may compare the two matrices by examining the entries term by term. Thus,

$$[a_{ij}] \leq [b_{ij}] \tag{2}$$

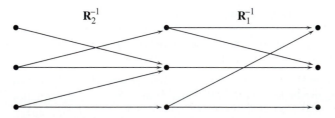

Figure 31.3

if for each i, j, $a_{ij} \leq b_{ij}$. This condition guarantees that if $a_{ij} = 1$, then $b_{ij} = 1$ also, which implies that if $(s_i, s_j) \in \mathbf{R}_1$, then $(s_i, s_j) \in \mathbf{R}_2$. Thus, this matrix condition (2) is equivalent to the inclusion $\mathbf{R}_1 \subseteq \mathbf{R}_2$.

Example 2

Let $\mathbf{S} = \{1, 2, 3, 4, 5, 6, 7\}$ and let $\mathbf{R}_1$ and $\mathbf{R}_2$ be relations in $\mathbf{S} \times \mathbf{S}$ defined by

$$\mathbf{R}_1 = \{(s_i, s_j): s_i \text{ is prime and } s_i \mid s_j\},$$
$$\mathbf{R}_2 = \{(s_i, s_j): s_i \mid s_j\}.$$

The corresponding matrices are

$$
\begin{bmatrix}
0 & 0 & 0 & 0 & 0 & 0 & 0 \\
0 & 1 & 0 & 1 & 0 & 1 & 0 \\
0 & 0 & 1 & 0 & 0 & 1 & 0 \\
0 & 0 & 0 & 0 & 0 & 0 & 0 \\
0 & 0 & 0 & 0 & 1 & 0 & 0 \\
0 & 0 & 0 & 0 & 0 & 0 & 0 \\
0 & 0 & 0 & 0 & 0 & 0 & 1
\end{bmatrix}
\qquad
\begin{bmatrix}
1 & 1 & 1 & 1 & 1 & 1 & 1 \\
0 & 1 & 0 & 1 & 0 & 1 & 0 \\
0 & 0 & 1 & 0 & 0 & 1 & 0 \\
0 & 0 & 0 & 1 & 0 & 0 & 0 \\
0 & 0 & 0 & 0 & 1 & 0 & 0 \\
0 & 0 & 0 & 0 & 0 & 1 & 0 \\
0 & 0 & 0 & 0 & 0 & 0 & 1
\end{bmatrix}
$$
$$\quad M(\mathbf{R}_1) \qquad\qquad\qquad M(\mathbf{R}_2)$$

Comparing each 1 in $M(\mathbf{R}_1)$ with the corresponding entry in $M(\mathbf{R}_2)$, it is easy to see that $M(\mathbf{R}_1) \leq M(\mathbf{R}_2)$. Notice also that $\mathbf{R}_1 \subseteq \mathbf{R}_2$, since any ordered pair in $\mathbf{R}_1$ satisfies the condition that it belongs to $\mathbf{R}_2$.

Tutorial 31.3

Given $[a_{ij}] = \begin{bmatrix} 1 & 0 & 1 \\ 0 & 1 & 0 \\ 1 & 1 & 0 \end{bmatrix}$ and $[b_{ij}] = \begin{bmatrix} 1 & 0 & \\ 0 & 1 & 0 \\ & & 1 \end{bmatrix}$.

a. Fill in the blanks in $[b_{ij}]$ so that $[a_{ij}] \leq [b_{ij}]$.
b. In part **a**, only one entry permitted a choice, b_{33}. How many $[b_{ij}]$ matrices are there satisfying $[a_{ij}] \leq [b_{ij}]$?
c. Consider that $[c_{ij}]$ is a 3 × 3 matrix with all blanks. How many different $[c_{ij}]$ matrices can you construct which satisfy $[a_{ij}] \leq [c_{ij}]$?

THEOREM 31.3

If $\mathbf{R}_1$ and $\mathbf{R}_2$ are relations in $\mathbf{S} \times \mathbf{S}$, then $\mathbf{R}_1 \subseteq \mathbf{R}_2$ if and only if $M(\mathbf{R}_1) \leq M(\mathbf{R}_2)$.

Proof

The argument preceding Example 2 suffices to prove that

$$M(\mathbf{R}_1) \le M(\mathbf{R}_2) \qquad \text{implies} \qquad \mathbf{R}_1 \subseteq \mathbf{R}_2.$$

Now assume that $\mathbf{R}_1 \subseteq \mathbf{R}_2$ and let

$$M(\mathbf{R}_1) = [a_{ij}] \qquad \text{and} \qquad M(\mathbf{R}_2) = [b_{ij}].$$

We must show that if $a_{ij} = 1$, then $b_{ij} = 1$ also. If $a_{ij} = 1$, then $(s_i, s_j) \in \mathbf{R}_1$. By hypothesis $\mathbf{R}_1 \subseteq \mathbf{R}_2$, so $(s_i, s_j) \in \mathbf{R}_2$. This means that $b_{ij} = 1$. ∎

31.4

In all the preceding discussion of composition, we have been careful with the order of the factors in a product. The reason is that matrix multiplication is not commutative; hence we should not expect

$$M(\mathbf{R}_1) \cdot M(\mathbf{R}_2) \qquad \text{and} \qquad M(\mathbf{R}_2) \cdot M(\mathbf{R}_1)$$

to be the same. Of course we should not expect the composition of relations to be commutative either.

Example 1

Refer once more to the relations in Example 1 of paragraph 31.2. We may use an arrow diagram to determine $\mathbf{R}_2 \circ \mathbf{R}_1$:

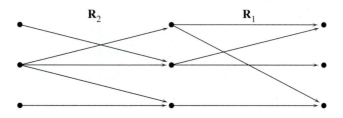

Each of the following pairs belongs to $\mathbf{R}_2 \circ \mathbf{R}_1$:

(s_1, s_1),	since	$s_1 \longrightarrow s_2 \longrightarrow s_1$;
(s_1, s_2),	since	$s_1 \longrightarrow s_2 \longrightarrow s_2$;
(s_2, s_1),	since	$s_2 \longrightarrow s_1 \longrightarrow s_1$;
(s_2, s_2),	since	$s_2 \longrightarrow s_2 \longrightarrow s_2$;
(s_2, s_3),	since	$s_2 \longrightarrow s_1 \longrightarrow s_3$;
(s_3, s_3),	since	$s_3 \longrightarrow s_3 \longrightarrow s_3$.

Thus

$$\mathbf{R}_2 \circ \mathbf{R}_1 = \{(s_1, s_1), (s_1, s_2), (s_2, s_1), (s_2, s_2), (s_2, s_3), (s_3, s_3)\} \ne \mathbf{R}_1 \circ \mathbf{R}_2. \quad \bullet$$

There is an important, although obvious, special case in which composition does commute: When the relations are the same,

$$\mathbf{R}_1 = \mathbf{R}_2 = \mathbf{R}.$$

In this case, the composition of $\mathbf{R}$ with itself, $\mathbf{R} \circ \mathbf{R}$, is often denoted by $\mathbf{R}^2$, which is consistent with the notation

$$M^2 = M \cdot M \qquad \text{(Boolean)}.$$

Example 2   Let $\mathbf{S} = \{s_1, s_2, s_3\}$ and let $\mathbf{R} = \{(s_1, s_1), (s_1, s_3), (s_2, s_1), (s_3, s_2)\}$. Then

$$M = \begin{bmatrix} 1 & 0 & 1 \\ 1 & 0 & 0 \\ 0 & 1 & 0 \end{bmatrix};$$

hence, by Boolean arithmetic,

$$M^2 = \begin{bmatrix} 1 & 0 & 1 \\ 1 & 0 & 0 \\ 0 & 1 & 0 \end{bmatrix} \cdot \begin{bmatrix} 1 & 0 & 1 \\ 1 & 0 & 0 \\ 0 & 1 & 0 \end{bmatrix} = \begin{bmatrix} 1 & 1 & 1 \\ 1 & 0 & 1 \\ 1 & 0 & 0 \end{bmatrix}.$$

It is easy to show that this is the matrix corresponding to $\mathbf{R} \circ \mathbf{R}$, using

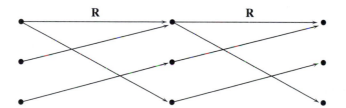

31.5   Complement: Closure of Relations Let $\mathbf{S} = \{s_1, s_2, \ldots, s_n\}$, let $\mathbf{R}$ be a relation in $\mathbf{S} \times \mathbf{S}$, and let M be the matrix for $\mathbf{R}$. Suppose it happens that $\mathbf{R}$ fails to satisfy some property $\mathcal{P}$ of interest to us, symmetry, for example. Then it may be possible to adjoin ordered pairs to $\mathbf{R}$, producing a new relation which does have property $\mathcal{P}$. The new relation obtained by adjoining as few ordered pairs as possible is called the $\mathcal{P}$ **closure** of $\mathbf{R}$. We can express this idea very simply in matrix terminology. If, for example, $\mathcal{P}$ denotes symmetry, then the symmetric closure of M is a symmetric matrix M_S such that:

1. $M \leq M_S$.

2. If M' is symmetric and $M \leq M'$, then $M_S \leq M'$.

It is not difficult, in this case, to show that

$$M_S = M + M^t \qquad \text{(Boolean)}. \tag{1}$$

The proof of Theorem 30.4A is equally valid in Boolean arithmetic; hence M_S is symmetric. It is clear that $M \leq M_S$. For convenience, let $M = [a_{ij}]$, $M_S = [b_{ij}]$, and $M' = [c_{ij}]$, where M' is symmetric and $M \leq M'$. We must show that $M_S \leq M'$. For each i, $b_{ii} = a_{ii} \leq a'_{ii}$. For $i \neq j$, if $b_{ij} = 0$, then $b_{ij} \leq a'_{ij}$, and if $b_{ij} = 1$, then either $a_{ij} = 1$ or $a_{ji} = 1$ and in each case $a'_{ij} = 1$ (remember that M' is symmetric). We have stated conditions **1** and **2** broadly enough so that any symmetric matrix is its own symmetric closure.

It is an almost immediate consequence of the definitions that the reflexive closure of any matrix M is

$$M_R = M + I_n \qquad \text{(Boolean).} \tag{2}$$

Essentially, this operation replaces any 0 in Δ (the main diagonal of M) by a 1 and leaves unchanged all other entries in M.

We will now introduce a new property of matrices for which the closure of a matrix M is a sum of powers:

$$M_T = M + M^2 + \cdots + M^n \qquad \text{(Boolean).} \tag{3}$$

We begin by considering the composition of **R** with itself k times:

$$\mathbf{R}^2 = \mathbf{R} \circ \mathbf{R}, \qquad \mathbf{R}^3 = \mathbf{R} \circ \mathbf{R} \circ \mathbf{R}, \qquad \text{and so on.}$$

In matrix terminology this is

$$M^2 = M \cdot M, \qquad M^3 = M \cdot M \cdot M, \qquad \text{and so on.}$$

Let **R** be the relation diagrammed as $\mathbf{R}_1$ in Figure 31.2, and consider the following diagram for $\mathbf{R}^2$:

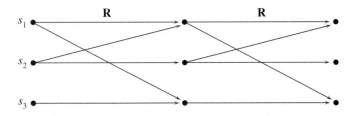

The composition $\mathbf{R} \circ \mathbf{R} = \mathbf{R}^2$ is really concerned with paths of length 2, from left to right along arrows linked at the intermediate points. A few of the paths of length 2 are

$$s_1 \longrightarrow s_1 \longrightarrow s_3,$$
$$s_2 \longrightarrow s_1 \longrightarrow s_3,$$
$$s_3 \longrightarrow s_3 \longrightarrow s_3.$$

Thus $\mathbf{R}^2$ consists of those ordered pairs (s_i, s_j) for which there exists a path of length 2 beginning at s_i and ending at s_j. For example,

$$(s_1, s_3) \in \mathbf{R}^2, \qquad (s_2, s_3) \in \mathbf{R}^2, \qquad (s_3, s_3) \in \mathbf{R}^2, \qquad (s_1, s_2) \notin \mathbf{R}^2.$$

In this simple diagram we could easily determine by inspection whether a path of length 2 exists, but the matrix product

$$M^2 \qquad \text{(Boolean)}$$

does so automatically:

$$M^2 = \begin{bmatrix} 1 & 0 & 1 \\ 1 & 1 & 0 \\ 0 & 0 & 1 \end{bmatrix} \cdot \begin{bmatrix} 1 & 0 & 1 \\ 1 & 1 & 0 \\ 0 & 0 & 1 \end{bmatrix} = \begin{bmatrix} 1 & 0 & 1 \\ 1 & 1 & 1 \\ 0 & 0 & 1 \end{bmatrix}.$$

This is the matrix for $\mathbf{R}^2$, and note that $a_{12} = 0$ since there is no path of length 2 from s_1 to s_2. Notice there may be several paths of length 2 linking s_i with s_j; for example, there are two such paths linking s_1 with s_3. The matrix M^2 does not count the number of paths—it merely indicates whether there is at least one such path.

We will need to consider paths of various lengths, so it is convenient to abbreviate "path of length 2" to "2-path," and similarly for paths of other lengths. A 1-path is simply a single arrow. The entries in M^2 indicate the existence of 2-paths in M, of which only one cannot be contracted to a 1-path. For example, corresponding to a 2-path from s_1 to s_3 there is a 1-path from s_1 to s_3; but there is a 2-path from s_2 to s_3 and no 1-path from s_2 to s_3. Thus if we want M to be closed under "contraction of 2-paths to 1-paths," then we must adjoin (s_2, s_3) to the relation $\mathbf{R}$. We indicate this by

$$M_T = M + M^2. \tag{4}$$

We are dealing here with the idea of "transitivity," mentioned briefly in paragraph 1.15, which accounts for our use of the subscript T. (This concept will be explored more fully in the following section.) In the remainder of this discussion we will continue to use the terminology of paths; in particular, we use "path closure" to indicate contraction of k-paths to 1-paths.

In the example discussed above, $M \le M^2$, but this need not happen in general; hence the sum indicated in (4) is necessary so that $M \le M_T$ (as required by condition **1** for a closure). Again, using the example above, M^3 indicates the existence of the 3-paths to be found in the diagram

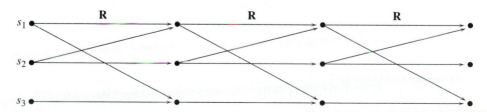

It turns out that $M^3 = M^2$; hence there are no 3-paths that are not also contractible to 2-paths or 1-paths.

In the more general situation in which $|\mathbf{S}| > 3$, additional powers of M may produce new connections via k-paths. But in no case will new connections be produced by powers of M greater than $|\mathbf{S}|$. We will not prove this fact here.

As a more elaborate example of path closure we consider the following relation on a set with four elements:

$$\mathbf{R} = \{(s_1, s_2), (s_1, s_3), (s_2, s_2), (s_3, s_1), (s_3, s_2), (s_3, s_4), (s_4, s_4)\}.$$

Its matrix and successive powers are

$$M = \begin{bmatrix} 0 & 1 & 1 & 0 \\ 0 & 1 & 0 & 0 \\ 1 & 1 & 0 & 1 \\ 0 & 0 & 0 & 1 \end{bmatrix}, \quad M^2 = \begin{bmatrix} 1 & 1 & 0 & 1 \\ 0 & 1 & 0 & 0 \\ 0 & 1 & 1 & 1 \\ 0 & 0 & 0 & 1 \end{bmatrix},$$

$$M^3 = \begin{bmatrix} 0 & 1 & 1 & 1 \\ 0 & 1 & 0 & 0 \\ 1 & 1 & 0 & 1 \\ 0 & 0 & 0 & 1 \end{bmatrix}, \quad M^4 = M^2.$$

By (3), the path closure of M is

$$M_T = M + M^2 + M^3 + M^4 = M + M^2,$$

since there are no 3-paths that are not contractible to 2-paths or 1-paths.

$$M_T = \begin{bmatrix} 0 & 1 & 1 & 0 \\ 0 & 1 & 0 & 0 \\ 1 & 1 & 0 & 1 \\ 0 & 0 & 0 & 1 \end{bmatrix} + \begin{bmatrix} 1 & 1 & 0 & 1 \\ 0 & 1 & 0 & 0 \\ 0 & 1 & 1 & 1 \\ 0 & 0 & 0 & 1 \end{bmatrix} = \begin{bmatrix} 1 & 1 & 1 & 1 \\ 0 & 1 & 0 & 0 \\ 1 & 1 & 1 & 1 \\ 0 & 0 & 0 & 1 \end{bmatrix}.$$

Problems for Section 31

1. How do the addition and multiplication tables for Boolean arithmetic differ from the corresponding tables for binary arithmetic? Can any Boolean sum ever be greater than 1?

2. In Boolean arithmetic, show that
(a) $1 \oplus (1 \oplus 0) = (1 \oplus 1) \oplus 0$, (b) $1 \otimes (1 \otimes 0) = (1 \otimes 1) \otimes 0$, (c) $(1 \oplus 1) \otimes 1 = (1 \otimes 1) \oplus (1 \otimes 1)$, (d) $(1 \otimes 1) \oplus 0 = (1 \oplus 0) \otimes (1 \oplus 0)$, (e) $(1 \otimes 1) \oplus 0 \neq (1 \oplus 1) \otimes 0$.

3. Let $\mathbf{S} = \{0, 1, 2, 3\}$, $\mathbf{R}_1 = \{(i, j): i + j = 3\}$, $\mathbf{R}_2 = \{(i, j): 3 \mid (i + j)\}$, $\mathbf{R}_3 = \{(i, j): \max\{i, j\} = 3\}$. Compute (a) $\mathbf{R}_1 \circ \mathbf{R}_3$, (b) $\mathbf{R}_3 \circ \mathbf{R}_1$, (c) $\mathbf{R}_2 \circ \mathbf{R}_2 = \mathbf{R}_2^2$.

4. Let $\mathbf{S} = \{0, 1, 2, 3, 4, 5, 6\}$, $\mathbf{R}_1 = \{(i, j): i \mid j\}$, $\mathbf{R}_2 = \{(i, j): 6 \mid (i + j)\}$, $\mathbf{R}_3 = \{(i, j): \max\{i, j\} = 3\}$. Compute (a) $\mathbf{R}_1 \circ \mathbf{R}_3$, (b) $\mathbf{R}_3 \circ \mathbf{R}_1$, (c) $\mathbf{R}_2 \circ \mathbf{R}_2 = \mathbf{R}_2^2$.

5. Draw the diagrams associated with the relations $\mathbf{R}_1$, $\mathbf{R}_2$, and $\mathbf{R}_3$ in Problem 3.

6. Draw the diagrams associated with the relations $\mathbf{R}_1$, $\mathbf{R}_2$, and $\mathbf{R}_3$ in Problem 4.

7. Draw the diagrams associated with the compositions in Problem 3.

8. Draw the diagrams associated with the compositions in Problem 4.

9. Let $\mathbf{S} = \{0, 1, 2, 3\}$ and let $\mathbf{R} = \{(i, j): i \le j\}$. (a) Show that $\mathbf{R}$ is reflexive. (b) Let $M(\mathbf{R}) = M$ and show that $M \le M^2$. (c) List the ordered pairs in $\mathbf{R} \circ \mathbf{R} = \mathbf{R}^2$.

10. Let $\mathbf{S} = \{1, 2, 3\}$. Find a relation $\mathbf{R}$ on $\mathbf{S}$ such that $|\mathbf{R}| \ge 4$, $\mathbf{R}$ is not reflexive, and $M(\mathbf{R}) \le (M(\mathbf{R}))^2$.

11. Let $n \ge 4$ and $\mathbf{S} = \{1, 2, \ldots, n\}$. Find a relation $\mathbf{R}$ on $\mathbf{S}$ such that $|\mathbf{R}| \ge n + 1$, $\mathbf{R}$ is not reflexive, and $M(\mathbf{R}) \le (M(\mathbf{R}))^2$.

12. Let

$$A = \begin{bmatrix} 1 & 0 & 0 & 1 \\ 0 & 1 & 1 & 0 \\ 1 & 0 & 1 & 0 \\ 0 & 0 & 1 & 1 \end{bmatrix}$$

and

$$B = \begin{bmatrix} 0 & 0 & 1 & 1 \\ 1 & 0 & 1 & 1 \\ 0 & 0 & 1 & 0 \\ 1 & 1 & 0 & 0 \end{bmatrix}.$$

Using Boolean arithmetic, compute (a) AB, (b) A^2, (c) BA, (d) B^2.

13. Let

$$A = \begin{bmatrix} 1 & 0 & 1 & 1 \\ 0 & 1 & 1 & 1 \\ 0 & 0 & 1 & 1 \\ 0 & 0 & 1 & 0 \end{bmatrix}$$

and

$$B = \begin{bmatrix} 0 & 1 & 1 & 0 \\ 1 & 0 & 0 & 1 \\ 0 & 0 & 1 & 0 \\ 1 & 0 & 0 & 1 \end{bmatrix}.$$

Using Boolean arithmetic, compute (a) AB, (b) A^2, (c) BA, (d) B^2.

14. (a) Find in regular arithmetic

$$\begin{bmatrix} 1 & 0 & 0 & 1 \\ 1 & 1 & 0 & 1 \\ 0 & 0 & 1 & 1 \end{bmatrix} \begin{bmatrix} 1 & 1 \\ 0 & 1 \\ 1 & 0 \\ 0 & 0 \end{bmatrix}.$$

(b) Find in Boolean arithmetic the product in part (a).

15. Compute

$$\begin{bmatrix} 1 & 1 & 0 \\ 1 & 0 & 0 \\ 0 & 1 & 1 \\ 0 & 1 & 0 \end{bmatrix} \begin{bmatrix} 1 & 0 \\ 0 & 1 \\ 1 & 1 \end{bmatrix}$$

in both regular and Boolean arithmetic.

16. In Boolean arithmetic, compute A^2 and $A^3 = A^2A$ for

$$A = \begin{bmatrix} 1 & 1 & 0 \\ 0 & 1 & 0 \\ 1 & 0 & 1 \end{bmatrix}.$$

Now compute A^n for successively higher values of n until you can predict the entries of A^n.

17. (*Conclusion of Problem 16.*) Using the matrix A from Problem 16 and using regular arithmetic, compute A^2 and A^3, and try to predict the entries for A^n.

18. Let $\mathbf{R}_1$, $\mathbf{R}_2$, $\mathbf{R}_3$ be relations on the set $\mathbf{S} = \{s_1, s_2, \ldots, s_n\}$. Let $(s_i, s_j) \in (\mathbf{R}_1 \circ \mathbf{R}_2) \circ \mathbf{R}_3$. Why is there an $s_m \in \mathbf{S}$ and an $s_k \in \mathbf{S}$ such that $(s_i, s_m) \in \mathbf{R}_1$, $(s_m, s_k) \in \mathbf{R}_2$, and $(s_k, s_j) \in \mathbf{R}_3$? From this, why does $(s_i, s_j) \in \mathbf{R}_1 \circ (\mathbf{R}_2 \circ \mathbf{R}_3)$? Conclude that $(\mathbf{R}_1 \circ \mathbf{R}_2) \circ \mathbf{R}_3 \subseteq \mathbf{R}_1 \circ (\mathbf{R}_2 \circ \mathbf{R}_3)$.

19. (*Continuation of Problem 18.*) Show that $\mathbf{R}_1 \circ (\mathbf{R}_2 \circ \mathbf{R}_3) \subseteq (\mathbf{R}_1 \circ \mathbf{R}_2) \circ \mathbf{R}_3$ and conclude that $\mathbf{R}_1 \circ (\mathbf{R}_2 \circ \mathbf{R}_3) = (\mathbf{R}_1 \circ \mathbf{R}_2) \circ \mathbf{R}_3$.

20. (*Conclusion of Problem 18.*) Let A_1, A_2, and A_3 be $n \times n$, $(0, 1)$-matrices and let $\mathbf{R}_1$, $\mathbf{R}_2$, and R_3 be relations on S such that $M(R_1) = A_1$, $M(R_2) = A_2$, and $M(R_3) = A_3$. Using Problem 19 and Theorem 31.2, show that $A_1(A_2A_3) = (A_1A_2)A_3$. Thus matrix multiplication is associative, at least for (0, 1)-matrices and Boolean arithmetic.

21. Let $S = \{a, b, c, d\}$ and let R be the relation in $S \times S$ having matrix

$$M = \begin{bmatrix} 0 & 1 & 1 & 0 \\ 1 & 1 & 1 & 0 \\ 0 & 0 & 1 & 1 \\ 1 & 0 & 1 & 0 \end{bmatrix}.$$

(a) Find M^2 in Boolean arithmetic. (b) Verify that M^2 is the matrix for the composition of R with itself.

22. Let $S = \{a, b, c, d\}$ and let the three relations R_1, R_2, R_3 in $S \times S$ have the matrices, respectively,

$$A = \begin{bmatrix} 1 & 0 & 0 & 1 \\ 0 & 1 & 1 & 0 \\ 1 & 0 & 1 & 0 \\ 0 & 0 & 1 & 1 \end{bmatrix},$$

$$B = \begin{bmatrix} 0 & 0 & 1 & 1 \\ 1 & 0 & 1 & 1 \\ 0 & 0 & 1 & 0 \\ 1 & 1 & 0 & 0 \end{bmatrix},$$

$$C = \begin{bmatrix} 0 & 1 & 0 & 0 \\ 1 & 0 & 1 & 0 \\ 0 & 0 & 0 & 1 \\ 0 & 1 & 1 & 1 \end{bmatrix}.$$

Using matrix multiplication in Boolean arithmetic, verify that $(R_1 \circ R_2) \circ R_3 = R_1 \circ (R_2 \circ R_3)$.

23. Let R denote a relation in $S \times S$, where $|S| = 5$, which has the matrix

$$M = \begin{bmatrix} 0 & 1 & 1 & 0 & 1 \\ 1 & 1 & 0 & 0 & 0 \\ 0 & 0 & 1 & 1 & 0 \\ 1 & 0 & 1 & 0 & 1 \\ 0 & 0 & 1 & 1 & 1 \end{bmatrix}.$$

(a) Using Boolean arithmetic compute M^2. (b) Is it true that $M^2 \leq M$? (c) Is it true that $M \leq M^2$?

24. For R_1 and R_2 in Problem 3, verify (1) in paragraph 31.3.

25. For R_2 and R_3 in Problem 3, verify (1) in paragraph 31.3.

26. For the relations described in Problem 22, compute $(R_1 \circ R_2)^{-1} \circ R_3$.

27. For the relations described in Problem 22, compute $R_1^{-1} \circ (R_2^{-1} \circ R_3^{-1})$.

28. Referring to paragraph 31.3, suppose that each of A and B is an $n \times n$, (0, 1)-matrix. If it is true that $A \leq B \leq A$, what can you claim about A and B? Give an argument in support of your claim.

29. (*Continuation of Problem 28.*) Suppose we were to define "$A < B$" to mean that $a_{ij} < b_{ij}$ for each i and j. Show that this would be an uninteresting situation in Boolean arithmetic.

30. (*Conclusion of Problem 28.*) A more interesting definition would be the following: "$A < B$" means $A \leq B$ and $a_{ij} < b_{ij}$ for some i and j. If B is the 3×3 identity matrix, how many 3×3 matrices A satisfy $A < B$ under this definition?

Section 32.   Transitivity and Orderings

32.1

In this section we continue the investigation of relations in $\mathbf{S} \times \mathbf{S}$ and their corresponding $n \times n$, $(0, 1)$-matrices. Again, Boolean arithmetic is used in computations, and we will remind you of this from time to time. Earlier we have seen examples in which matrix operations differ markedly from the familiar real number arithmetic. The following theorem, however, is quite similar to a property of the positive real numbers.

THEOREM 32.1A

Let $A = [a_{ij}]$, $B = [b_{ij}]$, and $C = [c_{ij}]$ be $n \times n$, $(0, 1)$-matrices for which $A \leq B$. Then,

$$A \cdot C \leq B \cdot C \qquad \text{and} \qquad C \cdot A \leq C \cdot B.$$

Proof

For convenience, let $A \cdot C = [d_{ij}]$ and $B \cdot C = [e_{ij}]$. We must show that for each i and j,

$$d_{ij} \leq e_{ij}.$$

If $d_{ij} = 0$, this inequality is obviously true; hence we need only prove that if $d_{ij} = 1$, then also $e_{ij} = 1$. Suppose, then, that (Boolean)

$$d_{ij} = \sum_{k=1}^{n} a_{ik} c_{kj} = a_{i1} c_{1j} + a_{i2} c_{2j} + \cdots + a_{in} c_{nj} = 1.$$

This means that for some k, $a_{ik} = c_{kj} = 1$ (otherwise the Boolean sum would be 0). Since $A \leq B$ by hypothesis,

$$a_{ik} \leq b_{ik} \qquad \text{and so} \qquad b_{ik} = 1.$$

This implies that $b_{ik}c_{kj} = 1$; hence

$$e_{ij} = \cdots + b_{ik}c_{kj} + \cdots = 1.$$

The proof of the second inequality is almost identical to this. ∎

Example 1 Let $A = \begin{bmatrix} 1 & 0 & 1 \\ 0 & 1 & 0 \\ 1 & 1 & 0 \end{bmatrix}$, $B = \begin{bmatrix} 1 & 0 & 1 \\ 0 & 1 & 0 \\ 1 & 1 & 1 \end{bmatrix}$, $C = \begin{bmatrix} 0 & 1 & 0 \\ 1 & 0 & 0 \\ 1 & 0 & 1 \end{bmatrix}$. Then, $A \cdot C = \begin{bmatrix} 1 & 1 & 1 \\ 1 & 0 & 0 \\ 1 & 1 & 0 \end{bmatrix}$

and $B \cdot C = \begin{bmatrix} 1 & 1 & 1 \\ 1 & 0 & 0 \\ 1 & 1 & 1 \end{bmatrix}$; therefore, $A \cdot C \le B \cdot C$.

Tutorial 32.1

Refer to Example 1.
a. Compute $C \cdot A$ and $C \cdot B$.
b. Show that $C \cdot A \le C \cdot B$.
c. Show that $C \cdot A \ne A \cdot C$ and $C \cdot B \ne B \cdot C$.

Both here and in Chapter 6 we will find that useful information about a relation can be obtained from powers of its matrix. In Example 2 of paragraph 31.4, we considered the matrix $M = \begin{bmatrix} 1 & 0 & 1 \\ 1 & 0 & 0 \\ 0 & 1 & 0 \end{bmatrix}$ and its square $M^2 = \begin{bmatrix} 1 & 1 & 1 \\ 1 & 0 & 1 \\ 1 & 0 & 0 \end{bmatrix}$. In real number arithmetic, we know that for any number x, either

$$x < x^2 \qquad \text{or} \qquad x^2 \le x.$$

From that, we might expect a similar property to hold among matrices. But for the matrices above,

$$M \nleq M^2 \qquad \text{(look at the (3, 2) entries),}$$

and $\qquad\qquad M^2 \nleq M \qquad$ (look at the (1, 2) entries).

Thus no general claim is possible. There is, however, an already familiar special case in which

$$M \le M^2.$$

THEOREM 32.1B If **R** is a reflexive relation in **S** $\times$ **S** with $M(\mathbf{R}) = M$, then $M \le M^2$.

Proof

Let $M = [a_{ij}]$ and note that $a_{ii} = 1$ for each i, since M is reflexive. Thus, $I \leq M$. Now, multiply each side of this inequality by M. It follows from Theorem 32.1A that

$$M \cdot I \leq M \cdot M \qquad \text{(Boolean)}.$$

The product on the left simply reproduces the columns of M one by one; hence

$$M \leq M^2. \qquad\qquad \blacksquare$$

The converse of Theorem 32.1B is *not* true. A trivial counterexample is provided by the matrix

$$M(\mathbf{R}) = \begin{bmatrix} 0 & 0 & 0 \\ 0 & 0 & 0 \\ 0 & 0 & 1 \end{bmatrix}.$$

Note that $\mathbf{R}$ is not reflexive, but

$$M^2 = \begin{bmatrix} 0 & 0 & 0 \\ 0 & 0 & 0 \\ 0 & 0 & 1 \end{bmatrix};$$

hence $M \leq M^2$. Because M^2 and M are actually the same in this case, it is also true that

$$M^2 \leq M.$$

Curiosity suggests the question, "Is there a special class of relations for which this latter inequality holds?" The answer will lead us to a result similar to Theorem 32.1B but even more satisfying in that it establishes a logical equivalence.

32.2

Suppose that $\mathbf{R}$ is a relation in $\mathbf{S} \times \mathbf{S}$ for which the matrix $M(\mathbf{R})$ (hereafter denoted by just M) satisfies

$$M^2 \leq M.$$

If we put $M = [a_{ij}]$ and $M^2 = [b_{ij}]$, then this inequality implies that for each i and j,

$$b_{ij} \leq a_{ij}.$$

Thus if $b_{ij} = 1$, then $a_{ij} = 1$ also. Since

$$b_{ij} = \sum_{k=1}^{n} a_{ik} a_{kj} \qquad \text{(Boolean)},$$

the following condition holds:

$$\text{If for any } k, a_{ik} = a_{kj} = 1, \text{ then } a_{ij} = 1. \tag{1}$$

In the language of relations, condition (1) has the form:

$$\text{If both } (s_i, s_k) \in \mathbf{R} \text{ and } (s_k, s_j) \in \mathbf{R}, \text{ then } (s_i, s_j) \in \mathbf{R}. \tag{2}$$

Any relation in $\mathbf{S} \times \mathbf{S}$ for which condition (2) holds is called **transitive.** Transitive relations were referred to briefly and informally in paragraph 1.15 in connection with the operation of "inclusion" among sets. For example, if **A**, **B**, and **C** are sets for which

$$\mathbf{A} \subseteq \mathbf{B} \text{ and } \mathbf{B} \subseteq \mathbf{C}, \qquad \text{then } \mathbf{A} \subseteq \mathbf{C}.$$

We will return to this example later; for the moment we consider a different example which involves divisibility.

Example 1   Let $\mathbf{S} = \{1, 2, 3, 4, 6, 12\}$ and consider the relation $\mathbf{R}$ in $\mathbf{S} \times \mathbf{S}$ defined by

$$(s_i, s_j) \in \mathbf{R} \text{ if } s_i \mid s_j \qquad (\text{that is, } s_i \text{ is a divisor of } s_j).$$

The matrix $M(\mathbf{R}) = M$ is

$$M = \begin{bmatrix} 1 & 1 & 1 & 1 & 1 & 1 \\ 0 & 1 & 0 & 1 & 1 & 1 \\ 0 & 0 & 1 & 0 & 1 & 1 \\ 0 & 0 & 0 & 1 & 0 & 1 \\ 0 & 0 & 0 & 0 & 1 & 1 \\ 0 & 0 & 0 & 0 & 0 & 1 \end{bmatrix}.$$

Computing M^2 we obtain

$$M^2 = \begin{bmatrix} 1 & 1 & 1 & 1 & 1 & 1 \\ 0 & 1 & 0 & 1 & 1 & 1 \\ 0 & 0 & 1 & 0 & 1 & 1 \\ 0 & 0 & 0 & 1 & 0 & 1 \\ 0 & 0 & 0 & 0 & 1 & 1 \\ 0 & 0 & 0 & 0 & 0 & 1 \end{bmatrix}.$$

Since $M^2 \leq M$, $\mathbf{R}$ is transitive by the argument preceding this example. (This confirms what we already know from arithmetic: If $s_i \mid s_k$ and if $s_k \mid s_j$, then $s_i \mid s_j$.)

Tutorial 32.2

Refer to Example 1. Consider the product M^2:

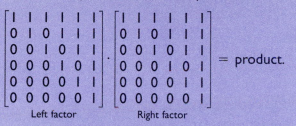

Left factor   Right factor   = product.

a. To find the first column in the product, choose the first column in the right factor. Note that only the first column in the left factor will contribute to the product, and it is reproduced.

b. To find the second column in the product, choose the second column in the right factor. Note that only the first and second columns in the left factor will contribute to the product. A 1 anywhere in those columns produces a 1 in the product. Compute the second column.

c. To find the third column in the product, choose the third column in the right factor. Note that only the first and third columns in the left factor will contribute to the product. A 1 anywhere in those columns produces a 1 in the product. Compute the third column.

d. Perhaps you have discovered already that matrix products in Boolean arithmetic are exceedingly simple. Identify which columns in the left factor contribute. A 1 in any one of those columns produces a 1 in the product. If there are no 1s on a given row in those columns, the corresponding entry in the product is 0. Compute the rest of the matrix product.

The inequality in Example 1 is stronger than we may have expected: M^2 and M are actually the same. This turns out to be no accident, as the next theorem shows.

THEOREM 32.2

The relation **R** in **S** $\times$ **S** with matrix M is transitive if and only if $M^2 \leq M$.

Proof

Our earlier argument has shown that

$$M^2 \le M \qquad \text{implies} \qquad \mathbf{R} \text{ is transitive.}$$

Assume now that $\mathbf{R}$ is transitive; hence (2) holds which means that (1) also holds. If $M = [a_{ij}]$ and $M^2 = [b_{ij}]$, then we must show that $b_{ij} \le a_{ij}$. If $b_{ij} = 0$, the inequality evidently is true, so we need only show that if $b_{ij} = 1$, so also is a_{ij}. Suppose that (Boolean)

$$b_{ij} = \sum_{k=1}^{n} a_{ik}a_{kj} = 1.$$

As in the proof of Theorem 32.1A, for some k, $a_{ik}a_{kj} = 1$; thus $a_{ik} = a_{kj} = 1$ and by (1), $a_{ij} = 1$. ∎

Because "divisibility " is a reflexive and transitive relation, we expect both

$$M \le M^2 \qquad \text{from Theorem 32.1B,}$$

and

$$M^2 \le M \qquad \text{from Theorem 32.2.}$$

The computed result in Example 1, namely, that

$$M^2 = M,$$

now comes as no surprise.

32.3

The relation of divisibility satisfies still another familiar property: It is antisymmetric (paragraph 30.2) which means that if $s_i \mid s_j$ and $s_i \ne s_j$, then $s_j \nmid s_i$. Thus, for any two different elements s_i and s_j in $\mathbf{S}$, exactly one of the following must occur:

$$(s_i, s_j) \in \mathbf{S} \qquad \text{and} \qquad (s_j, s_i) \notin \mathbf{S},$$
$$(s_j, s_i) \in \mathbf{S} \qquad \text{and} \qquad (s_i, s_j) \notin \mathbf{S},$$
$$(s_i, s_j) \notin \mathbf{S} \qquad \text{and} \qquad (s_j, s_i) \notin \mathbf{S}.$$

The last of these three conditions is illustrated in Example 1 of paragraph 32.2 by the fact that $2 \nmid 3$ and $3 \nmid 2$. In general, any relation $\mathbf{R}$ which is reflexive, transitive, and antisymmetric is called a **partial order.** The term "partial" is used in recognition of the possibility that some pairs of elements in $\mathbf{S}$ may not be comparable with respect to the relation. Any set $\mathbf{S}$ along with a partial order in $\mathbf{S} \times \mathbf{S}$ is called a **partially ordered set,** often abbreviated **poset.** The set $\mathbf{S}$ in Example 1 of paragraph 32.2 is a poset under the relation of divisibility. The importance of this concept in mathematics results from the many different structures which can be modeled as posets. Among the already familiar ones are the integers under "divisibility," the real numbers under "less than or equal to," and the power set of a given set under "inclusion." These relations and many others in mathematics are inherently orderly: They establish a precedence between some, if not all, elements in a set. The relations mentioned above have the traditional symbols $|$, $\leq$, and $\subseteq$. To investigate the properties of posets in general we will use $\lhd$ as a generic partial order symbol, $a \lhd b$ denoting that the element a precedes the element b.

Example 1

Let $\lhd$ represent the alphabetic order of words in a dictionary. Then

$$\text{animal} \lhd \text{tiger}, \qquad \text{graft} \lhd \text{graph}, \qquad \text{over} \lhd \text{overall}, \qquad \text{tall} \lhd \text{tall}. \quad \bullet$$

Example 2

From our earliest experience with numbers, the positive integers are inseparable from the "precedence" established by counting:

$$1 < 2 < 3 < 4 < \cdots.$$

So ingrained is this concept that it may be difficult to feel equally comfortable with any other "rule of precedence," even so simple a generalization as

$$1 \leq 2 \leq 3 \leq 4 \leq \cdots.$$

Beyond that, we are conditioned to believe that *every* pair of elements should be ranked, because that is how the positive integers work. (In Problem 25, we will introduce another ordering of the positive integers that arises in the study of "chaos.") $\bullet$

It may come as something of a shock to realize that a different concept of order, namely, partial order, is more important (perhaps, even, more natural) in mathematics than that illustrated by the "counting numbers." The difference, small but important, is referred to in Example 2. A partial order which has the additional property that no two elements fail to be related is called a **total order** or a **linear order.** Any set **S** along with a relation in $\mathbf{S} \times \mathbf{S}$ which is a total (or linear) order is called a **totally** (or **linearly**) **ordered set.** Thus, in a partially ordered set it is possible that

$$(s_i, s_j) \notin \mathbf{R} \qquad \text{and} \qquad (s_j, s_i) \notin \mathbf{R}, \tag{1}$$

but the impossibility of (1) distinguishes from among partial orders those that are also total orders. Any totally ordered set is also a poset, but any poset which has even one pair of elements satisfying (1) is not totally ordered.

Example 3

Let $\mathbf{S} = \{1, 2, 4\}$ and let $\mathbf{R}$ in $\mathbf{S} \times \mathbf{S}$ be defined by

$$(s_i, s_j) \in \mathbf{R} \qquad \text{if } s_i \mid s_j.$$

The matrix of this relation is

$$M = \begin{bmatrix} 1 & 1 & 1 \\ 0 & 1 & 1 \\ 0 & 0 & 1 \end{bmatrix}.$$

Compare this matrix with M in Example 1 of paragraph 32.2. Here, one of each pair of numbers in **S** divides the other; no two of them fail to be comparable with respect to divisibility. Thus, $\{1, 2, 4\}$ is totally ordered by divisibility, but $\{1, 2, 3, 4, 6, 12\}$ is not totally ordered by divisibility.

Tutorial 32.3

Let $\mathbf{S} = \{s_1, s_2, s_3, s_4\}$ and let $\mathbf{R} = \{(s_1, s_1), (s_2, s_1),$ $(s_2, s_2), (s_2, s_3), (s_2, s_4), (s_3, s_3), (s_3, s_4), (s_4, s_4)\}$.
a. Determine the matrix $M = [a_{ij}]$ for **R**.
b. Show that **R** is transitive (Theorem 32.2).
c. Show that **R** is a partial order, but not a linear order.

32.4   If $\mathbf{S} = \{s_1, s_2, \ldots, s_n\}$ and if **R** is an ordering denoted by the generic symbol $\lhd$, then to say that $\lhd$ is a total (or linear) order means that it is possible to list the elements of **S** sequentially with respect to $\lhd$:

$$s_1 \lhd s_2 \lhd \cdots \lhd s_n.$$

If, for example, $\mathbf{S} = \{4, 2, 12, 6, 36, 18, 114\}$ and if the order relation is $\leq$, then we can write

$$2 \leq 4 \leq 6 \leq 12 \leq 18 \leq 36 \leq 144.$$

This accounts for the use of the term "linear" to describe such an order. The other terminology, "total order," is suggested by the observation that

$$\mathbf{R} \cup \mathbf{R}^{-1} = \mathbf{S} \times \mathbf{S},$$

or in matrix language (Boolean),

$$M + M^t = J_n.$$

Perhaps the most fundamental example of a partial order in mathematics which is not also a linear order is that of a power set under inclusion.

Example 1   If $\mathbf{A} = \{x, y, z\}$, then the eight subsets of **A** are elements of the set $2^{\mathbf{A}}$. The relation $\subseteq$ in $2^{\mathbf{A}} \times 2^{\mathbf{A}}$ has the following matrix:

	∅	{x}	{y}	{z}	{x, y}	{x, z}	{y, z}	A
∅	1	1	1	1	1	1	1	1
{x}	0	1	0	0	1	1	0	1
{y}	0	0	1	0	1	0	1	1
{z}	0	0	0	1	0	1	1	1
{x, y}	0	0	0	0	1	0	0	1
{x, z}	0	0	0	0	0	1	0	1
{y, z}	0	0	0	0	0	0	1	1
A	0	0	0	0	0	0	0	1

It is easy to observe from this matrix that the relation is reflexive and antisymmetric. Transitivity is not so apparent (as is often the case). A proof using properties of the relation (if known) may be possible; otherwise, recourse to Theorem 32.2 is an option.

Detailed information about a poset contained in its matrix is not always easy to see at a glance; the matrix in Example 1 is a case in point. An alternate, and often more easily interpreted, way of depicting a poset is by use of what is called a **Hasse diagram,** named for Helmut Hasse (1898–1979). In such a diagram, the elements in the set are denoted by points arranged in levels so that a line segment drawn between a, in a lower level, and b, in a higher level, means that (a, b) is in the partial order, that is, $a \triangleleft b$. To keep the diagram as simple as possible a line segment implied by transitivity is omitted. For example, if $a \triangleleft b$ and $b \triangleleft c$, then no connection is drawn between a and c even though $a \triangleleft c$. These conventions reduce the diagram to the bare minimum necessary to convey all information about the poset. By reflexivity, if a is a point in the diagram, then $a \triangleleft a$; by antisymmetry, if a is below b in the diagram, then $b \ntriangleleft a$; by transitivity, if $a, b, c, \ldots, g$ are points on successively higher levels and if there are line segments between a and b, between b and c, etc., then $a \triangleleft g$. Returning to Example 1, the Hasse diagram is shown in Figure 32.4A.

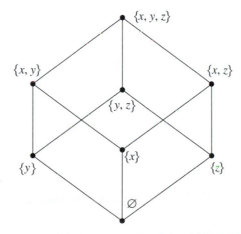

Figure 32.4A

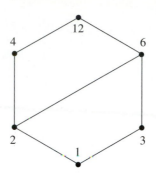

Figure 32.4B

The Hasse diagram in Figure 32.4B corresponds to the poset in Example 1 of paragraph 32.2 in which $\mathbf{S} = \{1, 2, 3, 4, 6, 12\}$ and the relation is divisibility. No line segment is necessary between 1 and 6, for example, because $1 \mid 3$ and $3 \mid 6$ imply $1 \mid 6$. Without the line segment between 2 and 6 we could not conclude from the diagram that $2 \mid 6$. Of course, the fact that 2 is below 6 implies that $6 \nmid 2$. Observe, also, that the connections between 1 and 2, 2 and 4, 4 and 12 imply that $1 \mid 12$. ⬤

32.5   **Complement: Chains and Antichains** Let $\mathbf{S}$ denote a set which is partially ordered by a relation $\mathbf{R}$ in $\mathbf{S} \times \mathbf{S}$. If $\mathbf{A}$ is any subset of $\mathbf{S}$, then $\mathbf{A}$ inherits a structure based on $\mathbf{R}$ restricted to the elements in $\mathbf{A}$,

$$\mathbf{R_A} = \mathbf{R} \cap (\mathbf{A} \times \mathbf{A}). \qquad (1)$$

We will show, now, that $\mathbf{A}$ is a poset with respect to this inherited structure.

THEOREM 32.5A   Let $\mathbf{S}$ be a poset with the partial order $\mathbf{R}$, and let $\mathbf{A} \subseteq \mathbf{S}$. Then $\mathbf{A}$ is a poset with partial order $\mathbf{R_A}$.

Proof
If $s_i \in \mathbf{A}$, then $(s_i, s_i) \in \mathbf{A} \times \mathbf{A}$. Since $\mathbf{R}$ is reflexive, $(s_i, s_i) \in \mathbf{R}$, and hence $(s_i, s_i) \in \mathbf{R_A}$. So $\mathbf{R_A}$ is reflexive.

If $s_i \neq s_j$ and if $(s_i, s_j) \in \mathbf{R_A}$, then $(s_i, s_j) \in \mathbf{R}$. Since $\mathbf{R}$ is antisymmetric, $(s_j, s_i) \notin \mathbf{R}$; hence $(s_j, s_i) \notin \mathbf{R_A}$. So $\mathbf{R_A}$ is antisymmetric.

If $(s_i, s_k) \in \mathbf{R_A}$ and if $(s_k, s_j) \in \mathbf{R_A}$, then both pairs are in $\mathbf{R}$. Since $\mathbf{R}$ is transitive, $(s_i, s_j) \in \mathbf{R}$. Because both ordered pairs belong to $\mathbf{A} \times \mathbf{A}$, $s_i \in \mathbf{A}$, $s_j \in \mathbf{A}$, and $(s_i, s_j) \in \mathbf{A} \times \mathbf{A}$. Hence $(s_i, s_j) \in \mathbf{R_A}$. So $\mathbf{R_A}$ is transitive. ∎

If $\mathbf{S}$ is a poset and if $\mathbf{A} \subseteq \mathbf{S}$, then $\mathbf{A}$ with the relation given in (1) will be called a **subposet.** We will be concerned, especially, with subposets at two extremes. Any subposet of $\mathbf{S}$ which is linearly ordered is called a **chain** in $\mathbf{S}$. A singleton subset of $\mathbf{S}$ is a trivial example of a chain. In general, a poset will have many chains, some intersecting one another. If **S** is written as a union of disjoint chains,

$$\mathbf{S} = \mathbf{C}_1 \cup \mathbf{C}_2 \cup \cdots \cup \mathbf{C}_m,$$

then these chains *partition* **S**.

Example 1

Consider the poset displayed in Figure 32.4A but relabeled as in Figure 32.5A. In Figure 32.5B, there are three partitions of **S** into chains.

It is clear that among all such partitions, some have the fewest chains. In Example 1, the minimum number of chains in a partition is 3, since (by inspection) no chain can contain any two of the elements b, c, d. To analyze a poset it is often desirable to partition it into the smallest possible number of chains. This number may not be known in general, but it is closely related to the second of the extreme subposets referred to earlier.

If a poset is not a chain, then it contains at least two elements x and y such that $x \ntrianglelefteq y$ and $y \ntrianglelefteq x$, and two such elements are termed **independent.** Any subset A

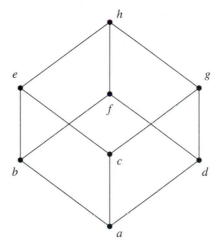

Figure 32.5A

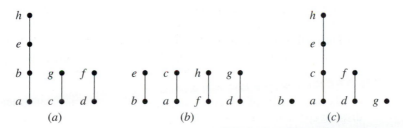

Figure 32.5B

of **S** consisting of pairwise-independent elements is called an **antichain.** Usually, a poset has many antichains, some having different numbers of elements. Among these antichains pick one having the maximum number of elements and let that number be k:

$$A = \{a_1, a_2, \ldots, a_k\}.$$

It is clear that no chain can contain two of the elements in **A**, since any two of them are independent. Thus any partition of **S** into disjoint chains must have *at least k* chains. A beautiful theorem of R. P. Dilworth (1914–1993) states that there always exists a partition which has exactly k chains. We will sketch here an adaptation of Dilworth's original argument for finite posets. It uses induction on k, the maximum size of any antichain in **S**.

THEOREM 32.5B

Let **S** denote any finite poset and let k be the maximum size of an antichain **A** in **S**,

$$A = \{a_1, a_2, \ldots, a_k\}.$$

Then there is a partition of **S** into k chains,

$$S = C_1 \cup C_2 \cup \cdots \cup C_k.$$

Remark.   By an easy argument, the elements in the antichain **A** must be distributed, one each, among the chains in the partition; for each element in **A** is in at least one chain and by independence no two elements in **A** can be in the same chain.

Proof

Assume the theorem is false. Then there must be a finite poset **S** which:

1. Has an antichain of maximum size k.

2. Has no partition into as few as k chains.

By WOA, we may assume that k is the smallest positive integer for which these conditions hold.

If the maximum size of any antichain in **S** is 1, then no two elements are independent, so **S** must be a chain itself. In this special case, the theorem is true; hence $k > 1$.

Dilworth's idea is the following: Given any union of k disjoint chains,

$$C = C_1 \cup C_2 \cup \cdots \cup C_k,$$

if x is an element of **S** not in that union, then we may construct a new union of k disjoint chains,

$$C' = C'_1 \cup C'_2 \cup \cdots \cup C'_k,$$

such that $\mathbf{C} \cup \{x\} \subseteq \mathbf{C}'$. If there remains an element of $\mathbf{S}$ not in $\mathbf{C}'$, simply repeat the construction. Because $\mathbf{S}$ is finite, this process results in the construction of a *partition* of $\mathbf{S}$ into exactly k chains; contradicting condition **1**, thus proving the theorem. We look now at his construction.

Suppose that $\mathbf{S}$ is a poset having an antichain of maximum size k. Let

$$\mathbf{C} = \mathbf{C}_1 \cup \mathbf{C}_2 \cup \cdots \cup \mathbf{C}_k$$

be a union of k disjoint chains in $\mathbf{S}$, and suppose $x \in \mathbf{S} - \mathbf{C}$. For each i, define

$$\mathbf{U}_i = \{r \in \mathbf{C}_i : x \lhd r\} \quad \text{and} \quad \mathbf{L}_i = \{r \in \mathbf{C}_i : r \lhd x\}.$$

Now observe that for each i and j,

$$\mathbf{L}_i \cup \{x\} \cup \mathbf{U}_j$$

is a chain in $\mathbf{S}$. Dilworth shows that there are subscripts p and q such that the poset $\mathbf{C} - \mathbf{L}_p - \mathbf{U}_q$ has an antichain of maximum size $k - 1$. (The proof of this claim is fairly intricate. For brevity we omit the proof, referring to Dilworth's paper for details.) Since $k - 1 < k$, there must exist a partition of $\mathbf{C} - \mathbf{L}_p - \mathbf{U}_q$ into $k - 1$ chains:

$$\mathbf{C} - \mathbf{L}_p - \mathbf{U}_q = \mathbf{C}_1' \cup \mathbf{C}_2' \cup \cdots \cup \mathbf{C}_{k-1}'.$$

If we put

$$\mathbf{C}_k' = \mathbf{L}_p \cup \{x\} \cup \mathbf{U}_q,$$

then

$$\mathbf{C}' = \mathbf{C} \cup \{x\} = \mathbf{C}_1' \cup \mathbf{C}_2' \cup \cdots \cup \mathbf{C}_k',$$

which is a union of disjoint chains. ∎

Problems for Section 32

1. Referring to Theorem 32.1A, prove that $CA \leq CB$.

2. Suppose that A, B, and C are 3×3, $(0, 1)$-matrices for which $A \leq B$, and C is not the zero matrix. If it is true that $CA \leq CB \leq CA$, is it necessarily true that $A = B$?

In each of Problems 3 to 5, let $\mathbf{S} = \{0, 1, 2, 3\}$, and determine which of the relations on $\mathbf{S}$ are transitive.

3. (a) $\mathbf{R}_1 = \{(i, j) : i + j = 3\}$, (b) $\mathbf{R}_2 = \{(i, j) : i + j \leq 4\}$.

4. (a) $\mathbf{R}_1 = \{(i, j) : 3 \mid (i - j)\}$, (b) $\mathbf{R}_2 = \{(i, j) : \max(i, j) = 3\}$.

5. (a) $\mathbf{R}_1 = \{(i, j) : i \leq j\}$, (b) $\mathbf{R}_2 = \{(i, j) : i \cdot j \text{ is spelt with three letters}\}$.

6. Which, if any, of the relations in Problem 3 are partial orders or linear orders?

7. Which, if any, of the relations in Problem 4 are partial orders or linear orders?

8. Which, if any, of the relations in Problem 5 are partial orders or linear orders?

9. Draw the Hasse diagram for the relation in Tutorial 32.3.

10. Draw the Hasse diagram for the relation in Problem 5(a).

11. Draw the Hasse diagram for the inclusion relation on subsets of $\{a, b, c, d\}$.

12. Suppose that $\mathbf{R}_1$ and $\mathbf{R}_2$ are transitive relations on the set $\mathbf{S}$. (a) Is $\mathbf{R}_1 \cap \mathbf{R}_2$ also transitive? Why or why not? (b) Is $\mathbf{R}_1 \cup \mathbf{R}_2$ also transitive? Why or why not?

13. Suppose that $\mathbf{R}_1$ and $\mathbf{R}_2$ are transitive relations in $\mathbf{S} \times \mathbf{S}$. Is the composition $\mathbf{R}_1 \circ \mathbf{R}_2$ also transitive? Why or why not?

14. Suppose that $\mathbf{R}$ is a transitive relation in $\mathbf{S} \times \mathbf{S}$. Is it true that $\mathbf{R}^{-1}$ is also transitive? If not, construct a 3×3 counterexample.

15. Let $\mathbf{S} = \{1, 2, 3, 4, 5, 6\}$. Define a relation $\mathbf{R}$ on $\mathbf{S}$ as follows: $(i, j) \in \mathbf{R}$ if $i + j$ is a divisor of 24. (a) Construct the $(0, 1)$-matrix M for $\mathbf{R}$. (b) Compute M^2 (in Boolean arithmetic), and use M and its square to determine whether or not $\mathbf{R}$ is transitive.

16. (*Conclusion of Problem 15.*) (a) Is the relation $\mathbf{R}$ a partial order? (b) If the element 5 were omitted from $\mathbf{S}$, would the resulting relation be a partial order?

17. If $\mathbf{R}$ is a total order on a set $\mathbf{S}$, then show that $\mathbf{R} \cup \mathbf{R}^{-1} = \mathbf{S} \times \mathbf{S}$.

18. If $\mathbf{R}$ is a total order and its matrix is M, then show that $M + M^t = J$ (Boolean).

19. In this problem, assume each order relation to be reflexive. Let $\mathbf{A}$ be the alphabet with $\lhd$ the usual alphabetic order. Define the relation $\lhd_*$ on $\mathbf{A} \times \mathbf{A}$ by $(x_1, y_1) \lhd_* (x_2, y_2)$ if $x_1 \neq x_2$ and $x_1 \lhd x_2$ or $x_1 = x_2$ and $y_1 \lhd y_2$. For example, $(t, m) \lhd_* (w, d)$; $(t, m) \lhd_* (t, n)$; and $(t, m) \lhd_* (t, m)$. Show that $\lhd_*$ is a total order.

20. In this problem, assume each order relation to be reflexive. Let $\mathbf{A}$ and $\mathbf{B}$ be sets with linear orders $\lhd_\mathbf{A}$ and $\lhd_\mathbf{B}$, respectively. Show that $\mathbf{A} \times \mathbf{B}$ can be linearly ordered by the relation $(a_1, b_1) \lhd_{\mathbf{A} \times \mathbf{B}} (a_2, b_2)$, if $a_1 \neq a_2$ and $a_1 \lhd_\mathbf{A} a_2$, or $a_1 = a_2$ and $b_1 \lhd_\mathbf{B} b_2$. This is called the **lexicographic** (or **dictionary**) order on $\mathbf{A} \times \mathbf{B}$.

21. The lexicographic order can be extended to three or more linearly ordered sets. Consider $\mathbf{A} \times \mathbf{B} \times \mathbf{C}$. What should it mean to say that $(a_1, b_1, c_1) \lhd_{(\mathbf{A} \times \mathbf{B} \times \mathbf{C})} (a_2, b_2, c_2)$?

22. Let $\mathbf{S} = \mathbf{A} \cup \{?, !\}$, where $\mathbf{A}$ represents the alphabet. Let an order on $\mathbf{S}$ be defined as follows: any two letters are ordered alphabetically, ? precedes any other symbol, and ! follows any other symbol. Arrange the following elements of $\mathbf{S} \times \mathbf{S} \times \mathbf{S} \times \mathbf{S}$ in lexicographic order: ABOA, BBOA, ABO?, A?OA, ??!!, A?!A.

23. Let $\mathbf{S}^*$ be $\mathbf{S}$ from Problem 22 but with @ added. The order on $\mathbf{S}^*$ is the same as $\mathbf{S}$ except that @ precedes any letter but follows ?. Arrange the following elements of $\mathbf{S}^* \times \mathbf{S}^* \times \mathbf{S}^* \times \mathbf{S}^*$ in lexicographic order: BAB@, @BAB, BA?@, BA@@, BAC@.

24. Let $\mathbf{S}$ be a poset with order relation indicated by $a \lhd b$. An element $z \in \mathbf{S}$ is called **maximal** if there is no other element $x \in \mathbf{S}$ such that $z \lhd x$. The poset $\mathbf{S}$ has a **greatest** element m if $x \lhd m$ for all other elements $x \in \mathbf{S}$. (a) Show that any greatest element is also maximal. (b) Partially order the set $\mathbf{S} = \{2, 3, 4, 6, 8\}$ by divisibility to show that a poset may have more than one maximal element but no greatest element. (c) Partially order the power set of $\{a, b, c\}$ by inclusion and find a greatest element. (d) Can a poset have more than one greatest element?

25. The following ordering, $\lhd_S$, of the positive integers is due to A. N. Sharkovsky (see *Encounters with Chaos* by Denny Gulick, p. 67). Let $m = 2^e x$ and $n = 2^f y$, $e \geq 0$, $f \geq 0$ with x and y both odd. Then if $x > 1$ and $y > 1$, $m \lhd_S n$ if $e < f$ or if $e = f$ and $x < y$. If $x > 1$ and $y = 1$, then $m \lhd_S n$.

If $y = x = 1$, then the larger power of two precedes the smaller. Note that all positive integers precede 1 in Sharkovsky's ordering and list 1, 2, 3, ..., 16 in order from smallest to largest.

26. Recall that if $A = [a_{ij}]$ and $B = [b_{ij}]$ are square matrices of the same size, then $A \leq B$ if $a_{ij} \leq b_{ij}$, for each i and j. List the 16 possible 2×2, $(0, 1)$-matrices. Three of them are $\begin{bmatrix} 0 & 0 \\ 0 & 0 \end{bmatrix}$, $\begin{bmatrix} 1 & 0 \\ 0 & 0 \end{bmatrix}$, and $\begin{bmatrix} 0 & 1 \\ 0 & 0 \end{bmatrix}$. This set of 16 matrices is partially ordered by $\leq$. Draw the Hasse diagram for the poset of 2×2, $(0, 1)$-matrices.

Section 33. Equivalence Relations

Overview for Section 33

- Introduction to equivalence relations through divisibility
- Equivalence classes and quotient sets
- Discussion of modular arithmetic and congruence

Key Concepts: equivalence relations, equivalence classes, quotient set, modular arithmetic, congruent elements

33.1

We return now to an idea introduced much earlier (in paragraph 5.3) and explore it from a new perspective. If $\mathbb{Z}$ denotes the set of all integers, we want to consider the question of divisibility, using divisibility by 5 for illustration. Some elements in $\mathbb{Z}$ are divisible by 5 and some are not, but in either case the division algorithm says that for any $x \in \mathbb{Z}$ we can write

$$x = 5 \cdot q + r, \qquad \text{where} \qquad 0 \leq r < 5.$$

Recall that $5 \mid x$ if $r = 0$ and $5 \nmid x$ if $0 < r < 5$. We construct five disjoint subsets of $\mathbb{Z}$ by assigning each integer to the subset identified by its remainder. As in paragraph 5.3, we denote the subsets by

$$[0]_5 = \{\ldots, -5, 0, 5, 10, \ldots\},$$
$$[1]_5 = \{\ldots, -4, 1, 6, 11, \ldots\},$$
$$[2]_5 = \{\ldots, -3, 2, 7, 12, \ldots\},$$
$$[3]_5 = \{\ldots, -2, 3, 8, 13, \ldots\},$$
$$[4]_5 = \{\ldots, -1, 4, 9, 14, \ldots\}.$$

Notice that if two elements x, y are in the same subset, then $x - y$ is divisible by 5. We will take this as the defining property for a relation **R** in $\mathbb{Z} \times \mathbb{Z}$:

$$(x, y) \in \mathbf{R} \qquad \text{if and only if} \qquad 5 \mid (x - y). \tag{1}$$

THEOREM 33.1

The relation **R** defined in (1) is reflexive, symmetric, and transitive.

Proof

For any integer x, $x - x = 0$ and 0 is divisible by 5. It follows that $(x, x) \in \mathbf{R}$, and **R** is reflexive.

If $(x, y) \in \mathbf{R}$, then $x - y$ is divisible by 5, and since $y - x = -(x - y)$, it also is divisible by 5. It follows that $(y, x) \in \mathbf{R}$, and **R** is symmetric.

Finally, if $(x, y) \in \mathbf{R}$ and $(y, z) \in \mathbf{R}$, then for some integers m and n,

$$x - y = 5m \qquad \text{and} \qquad y - z = 5n.$$

Hence, $$(x - y) + (y - z) = 5m + 5n,$$

$$x - z = 5(m + n).$$

It follows that $(x, z) \in \mathbf{R}$, and so **R** is transitive. ∎

The familiar "equals" relation as used in various parts of mathematics shares the three properties of **R** stated in Theorem 33.1. In the real number system, for example, any number x is equal to itself (reflexive), if x is equal to y, then y is equal to x (symmetric), and if x is equal to y and y is equal to z, then x is equal to z (transitive). Any relation, therefore, which satisfies these three properties defines a kind of generalized "equality" or "equivalence" among the elements in its set.

In general, if **S** is any set and if **R** is a relation in $\mathbf{S} \times \mathbf{S}$ which is reflexive, symmetric, and transitive, then **R** is called an **equivalence relation** on S. A frequently used symbol to denote equivalence is $x \sim y$ ($\sim$ is read "tilde"). Thus, given an equivalence relation **R**,

$$x \sim y \qquad \text{means} \qquad (x, y) \in \mathbf{R}$$

and the three defining properties can be expressed as follows:

Reflexive : $\forall x, x \sim x.$

Symmetric : $\forall x, y,$ if $x \sim y,$ then $y \sim x.$

Transitive : $\forall x, y, z,$ if $x \sim y$ and $y \sim z,$ then $x \sim z.$

If $x \sim y$, then x and y are called **equivalent,** and it has become customary to denote the set of all elements in **S**, each of which is equivalent to x, by $[x]$. Thus

$$[x] = \{y \in \mathbf{S} : y \sim x\}, \tag{2}$$

and this subset of **S** is called an **equivalence class.** We may choose any element in **S** as the representative of its class. For if $x \sim y$, then it follows easily from the properties of equivalence that $[x] = [y]$ as subsets of **S**.

Tutorial 33.1

Let **S** be a set and let $x \sim y$. To show that the equivalence classes $[x]$ and $[y]$ are equal, we must show $[x] \subseteq [y]$ and $[y] \subseteq [x]$.
  a. Let $p \in [x]$. Then by (2), $p \sim x$. Show that $p \in [y]$.
  b. Let $q \in [y]$. Show that $q \in [x]$.

As an example, in our earlier illustration the equivalence classes are:

$$[0]_5 = [0] = [5] = \cdots, \qquad [1]_5 = [1] = [6] = \cdots, \qquad [2]_5 = [2] = [7] = \cdots,$$

$$[3]_5 = [3] = [8] = \cdots, \qquad [4]_5 = [4] = [9] = \cdots.$$

33.2   It is reasonably clear from the example discussed in paragraph 33.1 that

$$\mathbb{Z} = [0] \cup [1] \cup [2] \cup [3] \cup [4],$$

and that no integer belongs to two different equivalence classes (after all, no integer has two different remainders when divided by 5). Thus the equivalence relation of divisibility by 5 has created a partition of the set $\mathbb{Z}$ (see paragraph 18.4). This is no accident; we prove next that this property holds for equivalence relations in general.

THEOREM 33.2   If $\sim$ denotes an equivalence relation on any set **S**, then the equivalence classes form a partition of **S**.

Proof
By the reflexive property of $\sim$, $x \in [x]$; hence every element of **S** is in some equivalence class. So, **S** is a union of (nonempty) equivalence classes, and we must now show that these classes are disjoint. We will do this by proving that if two equivalence classes have a nonempty intersection, then they are equal as subsets of **S**.

Suppose that $z \in [x] \cap [y]$. Then $z \sim x$ and $z \sim y$ and by symmetry $x \sim z$. By transitivity, $x \sim z$ and $z \sim y$ implies that $x \sim y$. If $p \in [x]$, then $p \sim x$, and again by transitivity, $p \sim y$. Hence $p \in [y]$, and $[x] \subseteq [y]$. If $q \in [y]$, then $q \in [x]$ by a similar argument, remembering that $y \sim x$ by symmetry. Hence, we conclude that $[x] = [y]$. ∎

The set of equivalence classes is called a **quotient set.** This terminology reflects the idea that we have "divided out" or "canceled out" differences in the elements that are irrelevant (with respect to the given equivalence relation). For example, in real number arithmetic the fractions

$$\frac{1}{2}, \quad \frac{-5}{-10}, \quad \frac{6}{12}, \quad \frac{50}{100}$$

are different as symbols, yet we are accustomed to recognize them as representatives of precisely the same rational number. (In fact, an axiomatic development of the number system will define a rational number as an equivalence class of fractions.) A quotient set is often denoted by **S**/~ (read this as "**S** mod tilde"). In our illustration in paragraph 33.1,

$$\mathbf{S}/{\sim} = \{[0], [1], [2], [3], [4]\}.$$

One of the differences between **S**/~ and **S** is that **S** has infinitely many elements, while $|\mathbf{S}/{\sim}| = 5$.

Example 1   Let $\mathbf{S} = \{0, 1, 2, 3, 4, 5, 6, 7, 8, 9, 10\}$, and consider the relation in $\mathbf{S} \times \mathbf{S}$ defined by

$$\mathbf{R} = \{(x, y): 5 \mid (x - y)\}.$$

We list a few of the ordered pairs in **R** and display its matrix in Table 33.2A: $\mathbf{R} = \{(0, 0), (0, 5), (0, 10), (1, 6), \ldots, (10, 10)\}$. The equivalence classes are $[0] = \{0, 5, 10\}$, $[1] = \{1, 6\}$, $[2] = \{2, 7\}$, $[3] = \{3, 8\}$, $[4] = \{4, 9\}$. The quotient set,

$$\mathbf{S}/{\sim} = \{[0], [1], [2], [3], [4]\},$$

provides a natural "grouping" of the elements of **S** into equivalence classes. We might wonder what appearance the matrix would have if its rows and columns were

	0	1	2	3	4	5	6	7	8	9	10
0	1	0	0	0	0	1	0	0	0	0	1
1	0	1	0	0	0	0	1	0	0	0	0
2	0	0	1	0	0	0	0	1	0	0	0
3	0	0	0	1	0	0	0	0	1	0	0
4	0	0	0	0	1	0	0	0	0	1	0
5	1	0	0	0	0	1	0	0	0	0	1
6	0	1	0	0	0	0	1	0	0	0	0
7	0	0	1	0	0	0	0	1	0	0	0
8	0	0	0	1	0	0	0	0	1	0	0
9	0	0	0	0	1	0	0	0	0	1	0
10	1	0	0	0	0	1	0	0	0	0	1

Table 33.2A

	(0	5	10)	(1	6)	(2	7)	(3	8)	(4	9)
0	1	1	1	0	0	0	0	0	0	0	0
5	1	1	1	0	0	0	0	0	0	0	0
10	1	1	1	0	0	0	0	0	0	0	0
1	0	0	0	1	1	0	0	0	0	0	0
6	0	0	0	1	1	0	0	0	0	0	0
2	0	0	0	0	0	1	1	0	0	0	0
7	0	0	0	0	0	1	1	0	0	0	0
3	0	0	0	0	0	0	0	1	1	0	0
8	0	0	0	0	0	0	0	1	1	0	0
4	0	0	0	0	0	0	0	0	0	1	1
9	0	0	0	0	0	0	0	0	0	1	1

Table 33.2B

"grouped" in this same way. This is illustrated in Table 33.2B. Note that the matrices in both tables represent the same relation; only the appearance is different because the row and column labels have been rearranged.

Again, this special case is not exceptional; the matrix for any equivalence relation can be arranged similarly to display this pattern of J-blocks (all 1s) centered on the main diagonal and 0s elsewhere. This is because each element in an equivalence class is related to each other element in that class and to no element in a different class. The two extreme matrices exhibiting this pattern are I_n and J_n. The n J-blocks in I_n are of size 1×1, and the one J-block in J_n is of size $n \times n$.

Tutorial 33.2

Let **S** $= \{a, b, c, d\}$ and let **R** $= \{(a, a), (a, c), (b, b),$
$(b, d), (c, a), (c, c), (d, b), (d, d)\}$.
a. Show that **R** is reflexive.
b. Show that **R** is symmetric.
c. Check each case to show that **R** is transitive.
d. Label rows and columns so that the matrix displays the pattern of J-blocks centered on the main diagonal.

33.3

It is obvious that any matrix of the form illustrated in Table 33.2B is both reflexive and symmetric. It is almost as obvious that any such matrix reproduces itself when squared, hence is transitive by Theorem 32.2. Such a matrix, therefore, must represent an equivalence relation. This observation has an interesting consequence.

THEOREM 33.3

Let the finite set **S** be partitioned into m nonempty subsets

$$\mathbf{S} = \mathbf{A}_1 \cup \mathbf{A}_2 \cup \cdots \cup \mathbf{A}_m.$$

This partition generates an equivalence relation **R** on **S**:

$$\mathbf{R} = \{(x, y)\colon \text{for some } i, x \in \mathbf{A}_i \text{ and } y \in \mathbf{A}_i\}.$$

Proof

Let $|\mathbf{S}| = n$ and construct the $n \times n$, $(0, 1)$-matrix M with rows and columns labeled (alike) by the elements in each $\mathbf{A}_i$ "grouped" together. Now put J-blocks corresponding to each subset $\mathbf{A}_i$ centered on the main diagonal, and put 0s elsewhere. The resulting matrix represents the relation **R** which is therefore reflexive, symmetric, and transitive. ∎

The enumeration of equivalence relations is a "nontrivial" problem. By Theorems 33.2 and 33.3, it reduces to the enumeration of partitions of a set **S**. We will avoid the general case (see paragraph 28.5), but for $n = 2$ and $n = 3$ we can easily list all the partitions.

Example 1   Let $\mathcal{P}$ designate a partition of a set **S**.

a. Let $\mathbf{S} = \{x, y\}$. The two partitions of **S** are

$$\mathcal{P}_1\colon \mathbf{S} = \{x\} \cup \{y\}, \qquad \mathcal{P}_2\colon \mathbf{S} = \{x, y\}.$$

The matrices are $I_2 = \begin{bmatrix} 1 & 0 \\ 0 & 1 \end{bmatrix}$ and $J_2 = \begin{bmatrix} 1 & 1 \\ 1 & 1 \end{bmatrix}$.

b. Let $\mathbf{S} = \{x, y, z\}$. The five partitions of **S** are

$$\mathcal{P}_1\colon \mathbf{S} = \{x\} \cup \{y\} \cup \{z\}, \qquad \mathcal{P}_2\colon \mathbf{S} = \{x, y\} \cup \{z\}, \qquad \mathcal{P}_3\colon \mathbf{S} = \{x, z\} \cup \{y\},$$

$$\mathcal{P}_4\colon \mathbf{S} = \{y, z\} \cup \{x\}, \qquad \mathcal{P}_5\colon \mathbf{S} = \{x, y, z\}.$$

The matrices are I_3, J_3, and three matrices of the form

$$\begin{bmatrix} 1 & 1 & 0 \\ 1 & 1 & 0 \\ 0 & 0 & 1 \end{bmatrix}$$

in which the rows and columns are labeled as in $\mathcal{P}_2$, $\mathcal{P}_3$, and $\mathcal{P}_4$.

Tutorial 33.3

Refer to part **b** of Example 1.

a. What are the matrices corresponding to $\mathcal{P}_1$ and $\mathcal{P}_5$?

b. If the rows are labeled x, y, z (top to bottom) and columns are labeled the same (left to right), then the matrix above corresponds to $\mathcal{P}_2$. Relabel the rows and columns so that same matrix corresponds to $\mathcal{P}_3$.

c. Relabel rows and columns so that same matrix corresponds to $\mathcal{P}_4$.

33.4

If **S** has an arithmetic structure, it is possible that **S**/~ will inherit a more or less similar structure. In our initial illustration, involving divisibility by 5, this results in what is called **arithmetic modulo 5**, in which addition and multiplication of equivalence classes are defined by

$$[x] + [y] = [x + y],$$

$$[x] \cdot [y] = [x \cdot y]. \tag{1}$$

Because each equivalence class has many representatives, it is necessary to prove that these operations are **well-defined.** That is, we want to be sure that if $x' \sim x$ and $y' \sim y$, then

$$[x] + [y] = [x'] + [y']$$

and

$$[x] \cdot [y] = [x'] \cdot [y'].$$

These definitions do turn out to be independent of the representatives chosen, as will be shown in the problem set. The resulting tables are:

+	[0]	[1]	[2]	[3]	[4]
[0]	[0]	[1]	[2]	[3]	[4]
[1]	[1]	[2]	[3]	[4]	[0]
[2]	[2]	[3]	[4]	[0]	[1]
[3]	[3]	[4]	[0]	[1]	[2]
[4]	[4]	[0]	[1]	[2]	[3]

·	[0]	[1]	[2]	[3]	[4]
[0]	[0]	[0]	[0]	[0]	[0]
[1]	[0]	[1]	[2]	[3]	[4]
[2]	[0]	[2]	[4]	[1]	[3]
[3]	[0]	[3]	[1]	[4]	[2]
[4]	[0]	[4]	[3]	[2]	[1]

It is customary, as we have done here, to use the same addition and multiplication symbols in the two sets **S** and **S**/~. A different symbol, however, is used for the generalization of "equality:"

$$x \equiv y \ (\text{mod } 5). \tag{2}$$

This means that x and y are in the same equivalence class, and in that case we say that x **is congruent to y modulo** 5. For example,

$$5 \equiv 0 \ (\text{mod } 5), \qquad 16 \equiv 1 \ (\text{mod } 5), \qquad -3 \equiv 2 \ (\text{mod } 5).$$

We have used divisibility by 5 here as a concrete illustration of these ideas. Other positive integers could be used as well, and the development would proceed along the same lines. An example often included in elementary courses is sometimes identified as *clock arithmetic*.

Example 1

Again, let $\mathbb{Z}$ be the set of all integers, and for any integers x and y we define $x \sim y$ if and only if $x - y$ is divisible by 12. Thus

$$\mathbf{S}/\!\sim \ = \{[0], [1], [2], \ldots, [11]\}.$$

Two numbers in the same equivalence class are congruent modulo 12; for example,

$$12 \equiv 0 \ (\text{mod } 12),$$

$$13 \equiv 1 \ (\text{mod } 12).$$

The addition and multiplication tables are constructed as shown in Tables 33.4A and 33.4B.

+	0	1	2	3	4	5	6	7	8	9	10	11
0	0	1	2	3	4	5	6	7	8	9	10	11
1	1	2	3	4	5	6	7	8	9	10	11	0
2	2	3	4	5	6	7	8	9	10	11	0	1
3	3	4	5	6	7	8	9	10	11	0	1	2
4	4	5	6	7	8	9	10	11	0	1	2	3
5	5	6	7	8	9	10	11	0	1	2	3	4
6	6	7	8	9	10	11	0	1	2	3	4	5
7	7	8	9	10	11	0	1	2	3	4	5	6
8	8	9	10	11	0	1	2	3	4	5	6	7
9	9	10	11	0	1	2	3	4	5	6	7	8
10	10	11	0	1	2	3	4	5	6	7	8	9
11	11	0	1	2	3	4	5	6	7	8	9	10

Table 33.4A

·	0	1	2	3	4	5	6	7	8	9	10	11
0	0	0	0	0	0	0	0	0	0	0	0	0
1	0	1	2	3	4	5	6	7	8	9	10	11
2	0	2	4	6	8	10	0	2	4	6	8	10
3	0	3	6	9	0	3	6	9	0	3	6	9
4	0	4	8	0	4	8	0	4	8	0	4	8
5	0	5	10	3	8	1	6	11	4	9	2	7
6	0	6	0	6	0	6	0	6	0	6	0	6
7	0	7	2	9	4	11	6	1	8	3	10	5
8	0	8	4	0	8	4	0	8	4	0	8	4
9	0	9	6	3	0	9	6	3	0	9	6	3
10	0	10	8	6	4	2	0	10	8	6	4	2
11	0	11	10	9	8	7	6	5	4	3	2	1

Table 33.4B

To simplify the notation in these tables we have omitted the brackets and indicated equivalence classes by the representatives

$$0, 1, 2, \ldots, 11.$$

The name "clock arithmetic" originates from the observation that clock faces are often marked off in 12 hours. In this structure 0 represents midday and midnight (these being congruent mod 12). ●

33.5

Arithmetic mod 5 and arithmetic mod 12 can each be proved to share many similarities with the usual real number arithmetic. In this brief introduction, we will accept without proof the associative, commutative, and distributive laws. But there *are* differences, and the detailed study of these differences has led mathematicians to the development of a number of abstract structures (studied in advanced courses with such titles as "abstract algebra" or "modern algebra").

Example 1

We illustrate, briefly, some of the similarities and differences referred to above by considering the problem of solving certain simple equations in each system:

a.
$$x + 3 = 2.$$

b.
$$3 \cdot x + 4 = 2.$$

In the usual real number arithmetic:

a.
$$x + 3 - 3 = 2 - 3,$$
$$x + 0 = x = -1.$$

b.
$$3 \cdot x + 4 - 4 = 2 - 4,$$
$$3 \cdot x + 0 = 3 \cdot x = -2,$$
$$x = -\tfrac{2}{3}.$$

In arithmetic mod 5 (remember, the brackets are omitted):

a.
$$x + 3 + 2 = 2 + 2,$$
$$x + 0 = x = 4.$$

b.
$$3 \cdot x + 4 + 1 = 2 + 1,$$
$$3 \cdot x + 0 = 3 \cdot x = 3,$$
$$2 \cdot 3 \cdot x = 2 \cdot 3,$$
$$x = 1.$$

Finally, in arithmetic mod 12 (remember, the brackets are omitted):

a.
$$x + 3 + 9 = 2 + 9,$$
$$x + 0 = x = 11.$$

b.
$$3 \cdot x + 4 + 8 = 2 + 8,$$
$$3 \cdot x + 0 = 3 \cdot x = 10,$$

which has *no* solution. To see this, divide 12 into $3 \cdot x - 10$ for $x = 0, 1, 2, \ldots, 11$, and a nonzero remainder will occur each time; or you may refer to the multiplication table to observe that 3 times any element can only be one of 0, 3, 6, or 9, hence cannot be 10.

33.6

Complement: What Day of the Week Was D Day?
Using arithmetic modulo 4, 7, 12, and 100, it is not difficult to compute the day of the week for any date in the nineteenth, twentieth, or twenty-first centuries. The algorithm is somewhat complicated, but with an hour of practice, it is easy to calculate mentally the day of the week for any date in this century.

To change the days of the week to numbers, we let the equivalence classes modulo 7 represent the days of the week:

$$0 = \text{Sunday}, \qquad 4 = \text{Thursday},$$
$$1 = \text{Monday}, \qquad 5 = \text{Friday},$$
$$2 = \text{Tuesday}, \qquad 6 = \text{Saturday}.$$
$$3 = \text{Wednesday},$$

Unfortunately, the numbers for the months are not as straightforward. A useful mnemonic device for these is given below. Note that the first triple of numbers is 12^2, the second is 5^2, the third is 6^2, and the last triple is $12^2 + 2$. For example, the number for August is 3 and the number for June is 5.

$(1, 4, 4) \leftrightarrow$ (January, February, March)

$(0, 2, 5) \leftrightarrow$ (April, May, June)

$(0, 3, 6) \leftrightarrow$ (July, August, September)

$(1, 4, 6) \leftrightarrow$ (October, November, December).

We will use D day, June 6, 1944, as one example to illustrate the algorithm. Let Y be the year (for our example, $Y = 1944$), and let D be the date ($D = 6$). Define

$$y \equiv Y \pmod{100} \quad \text{and} \quad r \equiv y \pmod{12},$$

and let q be the greatest integer less than or equal to $y/12$, denoted by

$$q = \lfloor y/12 \rfloor,$$

and finally, let s be the greatest integer less than or equal to $r/4$, again denoted by

$$s = \lfloor r/4 \rfloor.$$

Now if M is the number of the month ($M = 5$ in our example), then w, the day of the week, is given by

$$w \equiv (q + r + s + M + D + \varepsilon) \pmod{7}. \tag{1}$$

The ε is a correction determined by the century. For the 1800s, $\varepsilon = 1$; for the 1900s, $\varepsilon = -1$; and for the twenty-first century, $\varepsilon = -2$. Leap years, however, cause a problem if the month is January or February. For these two months *only*, the correct ε for a leap year is 1 less than those given. [Recall that Y is a leap year if $Y \equiv 0 \pmod{4}$, but that $Y = 1900$ and $Y = 1800$ were not leap years.] We illustrate this algorithm with D day. Here,

$$y = 44 \quad \text{and since} \quad 44 \equiv 8 \pmod{12},$$

$$r = 8.$$

Hence, $\qquad s = \lfloor 8/4 \rfloor = 2 \quad$ and $\quad q = \lfloor 44/12 \rfloor = 3.$

Since $Y = 1944$, $\varepsilon = -1$, and so

$$w \equiv (3 + 8 + 2 + 5 + 6 - 1) \equiv (11 + 7 + 5) \equiv 16 \equiv 2 \pmod{7}.$$

Hence, D day was on a Tuesday.

To show how to use the algorithm for a leap year, we will find the day of the week for Valentine's Day, 1952. Here,

$$y = 52 \quad \text{and since} \quad 52 \equiv 4 \pmod{12},$$

$$r = 4.$$

Hence, $s = \lfloor r/4 \rfloor = \lfloor 4/4 \rfloor = 1$ and $q = \lfloor 52/12 \rfloor = 4$.

Since $1952 \equiv 0 \,(\text{mod } 4)$, 1952 was a leap year and since Valentine's Day is in February, $\varepsilon = -1 - 1 = -2$. Now $D = 14$, $M = 4$ and hence,

$$w \equiv (4 + 4 + 1 + 4 + 14 - 2) \equiv 4 \,(\text{mod } 7).$$

Therefore, Valentine's Day in 1952 was on a Thursday.

Problems for Section 33

1. In Problem 3 of Section 32, which relations are equivalence relations?

2. In Problem 4 of Section 32, which relations are equivalence relations?

3. In Problem 5 of Section 32, which relations are equivalence relations?

4. Let **R** be a relation on $\mathbb{Z}$ defined by $\mathbf{R} = \{(m, n) : 3 \mid (m^2 - n^2)\}$. Show that **R** is an equivalence relation.

5. For the relation **R** in Problem 4, how many equivalence classes are there? List at least three elements in the equivalence classes [0] and [1].

6. Let **R** be a relation on $\mathbb{Z}$ defined by $\mathbf{R} = \{(m, n) : 3 \mid (m - n)\}$. (a) Show that **R** is an equivalence relation. (b) Construct the addition and multiplication tables for arithmetic modulo 3.

7. (*Conclusion of Problem 6.*) (a) Solve the equation $x^2 - 1 = 0$ in arithmetic modulo 3. (b) Does this equation have more than one solution modulo 3? (c) Show that the equation $x^2 + 1 = 0$ has no solution in arithmetic modulo 3.

8. Let $\mathbf{S} = \{0, 1, 2, \ldots\}$ and define the relation **R** on **S** by $(x, y) \in \mathbf{R}$ if and only if $7 \mid (x - y)$. (a) Show that **R** is an equivalence relation. (b) List the classes in **S/R**. (c) List five members of the equivalence class of 1.

9. Let $\mathbf{S} = \{0, 1, 2, 3, 4, 5\}$. Define a relation **R** on **S** by the condition: for each $x \in \mathbf{S}$, $(x, y) \in \mathbf{R}$ if y is the number of even integers in **S** which are less than x. Let M be the matrix for **R**. (a) Determine both M and M^t. (b) Compute the product MM^t (in Boolean arithmetic). (c) Show that MM^t is an equivalence relation.

10. Let **R** be a relation in $\mathbb{N} \times \mathbb{N}$ defined by $\mathbf{R} = \{((a, b), (c, d)) : a + d = b + c\}$. Show that **R** is an equivalence relation.

11. For the relation in Problem 10, list three elements in the equivalence class of $[(1, 5)]$, $[(2, 9)]$, and $[(7, 10)]$.

12. Let $\mathbb{Z}_0 = \mathbb{Z} - \{0\}$. Let **R** be a relation in $\mathbb{Z} \times \mathbb{Z}_0$ defined by $\mathbf{R} = \{((a, b), (c, d)) : ad = bc\}$. Show that **R** is an equivalence relation.

13. How many equivalence relations are there on a set (a) with three elements, (b) with four elements?

14. Which of the following are equivalence relations on $\mathbb{Z}$? Why? (a) $\mathbf{R}_1 = \{(m, n) : 4 \mid (n - m)\}$, (b) $\mathbf{R}_2 = \{(m, n) : m \cdot n > 0\}$.

15. Which of the following are equivalence relations on $\mathbb{Z}$? Why? (a) $\mathbf{R}_1 = \{(m, n) : m \cdot n = 0\}$, (b) $\mathbf{R}_2 = \{(m, n) : n \leq m\}$.

16. Each of the following is a relation on the real numbers. For each relation, decide if it is reflexive, symmetric, or transitive. (a) $\mathbf{R}_1 =$

$\{(x, y) : x \cdot y = 0\}$, (b) $\mathbf{R}_2 = \{(x, y) : x \cdot y \neq 0\}$, (c) $\mathbf{R}_3 = \{(x, y) : |x - y| < 5\}$.

17. Each of the following is a relation on $\mathbb{R}^+ = \{x \in \mathbb{R} : x > 0\}$. For each relation, decide if it is reflexive, symmetric, or transitive.
(a) $\mathbf{R}_1 = \{(x, y) : x/y \leq 1\}$,
(b) $\mathbf{R}_2 = \{(x, y) : x/(x + y) \leq \frac{1}{2}\}$,
(c) $\mathbf{R}_3 = \{(x, y) : \lfloor x \rfloor = \lfloor y \rfloor\}$. (Here $\lfloor x \rfloor$ is the greatest integer less than or equal to x.)

18. Let M be a matrix consisting of J-blocks centered on the diagonal. Show that $M^2 = M$ (in Boolean arithmetic).

19. In this problem, the equivalence classes are modulo 5. (a) Show that $[58] \cdot [19] = [1102] = [2]$. (b) Show that if $x \equiv 3 \pmod 5$ and $y \equiv 4 \pmod 5$, then $xy \equiv 2 \pmod 5$. (Hint: $x = 5m + 3$, $y = 5k + 4$.) (c) Let x and z be in $[3]$ and y and w be in $[4]$. Show that xy and zw both have a remainder of 2 when divided by 5 (so $[x] \cdot [y] = [z] \cdot [w] = [2]$).

20. (*Continuation of Problem 19.*) To show that multiplication modulo 5 is well-defined, let x and z be in $[a]$ and y and w be in $[b]$ (both $[a]$ and $[b]$ are classes modulo 5). Show that $[x] \cdot [y] = [z] \cdot [w]$.

21. (*Conclusion of Problem 19.*) Show that addition modulo 5 is well-defined.

22. Let m be a natural number greater than 1. Show that $\mathbf{R} = \{(x, y) : x, y \in \mathbb{Z}, m \mid (x - y)\}$ is an equivalence relation.

23. (*Continuation of Problem 22.*) Let $\mathbb{Z}_m = \mathbb{Z}/\mathbf{R}$ with the usual arithmetic operations. Show that addition in $\mathbb{Z}_m$ is well-defined.

24. (*Continuation of Problem 22.*) Show that multiplication in $\mathbb{Z}_m$ is well-defined.

25. (*Continuation of Problem 22.*) Show that addition in $\mathbb{Z}_m$ is commutative and associative.

26. (*Conclusion of Problem 22.*) Show that multiplication in $\mathbb{Z}_m$ is commutative and associative. Also, show that multiplication distributes over addition.

27. Does the equation $3x + 4 = 2$ have solutions in arithmetic mod 5? mod 12? If so, classify the solutions; if not, why not?

28. Arithmetic mod 2 is extremely interesting. Show that in arithmetic mod 2, $(a + b)^2 = a^2 + b^2$.

29. (a) Consider a 2-element set. What is the one nonempty equivalence relation that is also a partial order? (b) Consider an n-element set. What is the one nonempty equivalence relation that is also a partial order?

30. (*This question relates to the complement, paragraph 33.6.*) Using the algorithm in the complement: (a) compute the day of the week that Christmas was on in 1952; (b) compute the day of the week that New Year's Day was on in 1924. (c) Thanksgiving is usually on the fourth Thursday in November. What was the date of Thanksgiving in 1980? (d) Compute the day of the week on which you were born.

CHAPTER 6

Graph Theory

Section 34. Introduction to Graph Theory

34.1

As the term is used in this chapter, a "graph" is a mathematical object totally unlike the familiar graphs of functions such as those illustrated in Figures 1.1B and 13.2. We will see that the idea is very simple, yet its consequences are unexpectedly broad in both theory and application.

Example 1

Suppose that the New England Tourist Bureau wishes to reproduce in color the map shown in Figure 34.1A as the cover of its current brochure. For clarity, of course,

Figure 34.1A

it is necessary that states sharing a common boundary line be colored differently. Since only six states are involved, it would easily be possible to use a different color for each one. But it is not unreasonable, however, to ask whether fewer colors might suffice. Trial and error quickly leads to the observation that only three colors are required. Then, at its final planning meeting, the Bureau decides that coastal waters should be colored blue. Is it now possible that three colors will suffice to ensure different colorings for each two adjacent map regions? This time we observe that the answer must be "no"; four colors are necessary.   ●

A map, in general, may be far more complex than that in Figure 34.1A, and for more than a century it was a tantalizing open problem to decide whether there exists a plane map so complicated that five colors are necessary (to be certain of an appropriate coloring). The solution to this problem had to wait until the advent of high-speed computing *and* until the question could be recast into a more manageable mathematical format. The answer, due to K. Appel and W. Haken, came in 1977: Four colors are sufficient for every plane map. Their proof is an exhaustive survey of cases (perhaps one of the most complicated existing extensions of the idea discussed in paragraph 3.9). Clearly, the geographic representation of maps is not an especially helpful setting for this question. What, then, is?

Look again at Figure 34.1A, and suppose we replace each region by its name, as in Figure 34.1B. What is important to us is the existence of a common boundary line; these occur, for example, between Vermont and New Hampshire, but not between Vermont and the coastal waters. Suppose we simply draw a connecting line between the names of each pair of regions sharing a common boundary. Note that the absence of a line provides information just as the presence of a line does. Realizing that the "names" of the states are unimportant to our question, suppose we replace each name by a dot, as in Figure 34.1C. Our question now reduces to, "How many colors are required to paint each dot so that dots joined by a line are differently colored?" Looking just at the four dots labeled W, R, C, and Ma, we note that each one is connected by a line to each of the other three dots. Therefore, at least four distinct colors are required, and it follows easily that four colors are sufficient for the entire diagram, as we had seen earlier. The abstract object in Figure 34.1C illustrates what is commonly referred to in discrete mathematics as a "graph."

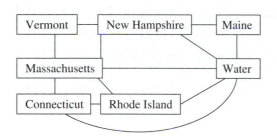

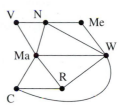

Figure 34.1B   **Figure 34.1C**

34.2

To describe a graph in this new context, we need two kinds of things: a finite set of elements called **vertices** and a set of **edges,** each of which is simply a 2-element subset of the set of vertices. We will denote the set of vertices, or **vertex set,** by **V** and the set of edges, or **edge set,** by **E**. It is customary to denote a graph by (**V, E**), or simply by **G** when specific reference to the vertex and edge sets is not important. In Figure 34.1C, the 7 dots correspond to vertices and the 12 lines joining pairs of dots correspond to edges.

Example 1

Let a vertex set be

$$\mathbf{V} = \{v_1, v_2, v_3, v_4, v_5, v_6, v_7\}.$$

If a 2-element subset of **V**, say $\{v_1, v_2\}$, is an edge, it is customary to abbreviate that subset notation to v_1v_2. Thus, we may indicate a particular edge set as

$$\mathbf{E} = \{v_1v_2, v_1v_5, v_1v_7, v_2v_4, v_2v_5, v_2v_6, v_2v_7, v_3v_4, v_3v_7, v_4v_6, v_4v_7, v_5v_7\}.$$

Notice how difficult it is to get a "feel" for the relationships among the vertices and edges simply from the list of elements in **V** and in **E**. The pictorial representation in Figure 34.1C displays far more clearly these exact relationships (the vertices in this example represent the regions in alphabetical order, $v_1 = C, v_2 = Ma, v_3 = Me, v_4 = N, v_5 = R, v_6 = V, v_7 = W$). ●

We will assume that the vertex set is nonempty and that, in general, it contains n vertices. Then, from paragraph 16.4, we know that altogether there are

$$\binom{n}{2} = \frac{n(n-1)}{2}$$

2-element subsets of **V**. For convenience of reference, we will denote this set by **T**; thus

$$\mathbf{T} = \{\mathbf{B} \subseteq \mathbf{V} : |\mathbf{B}| = 2\} \quad \text{and} \quad |\mathbf{T}| = \binom{n}{2}.$$

Formally, a **graph** is a finite, nonempty set **V** of vertices together with a set **E** of edges consisting of any subset of **T**. Thus a graph on n vertices may have any number of edges from 0 to $\binom{n}{2}$, inclusive. The graph $(\mathbf{V}, \varnothing)$, which has 0 edges, is called **null** (or **totally disconnected**); the graph $(\mathbf{V}, \mathbf{T})$, which has $\binom{n}{2}$ edges, is called **complete** and is denoted by $\mathbf{K}_n$. The number of edges in any other graph on **V** falls between these two extremes.

34.3

As remarked in Example 1 of paragraph 34.2, there is a conventional geometric representation of a graph, called its **diagram,** which often provides a quick and easy display of certain characteristics of the graph. On a sheet, mark n points, each representing an element in the vertex set; then connect the two vertices in each edge with a line segment (either straight or curved). Because full information about vertex and edge sets is displayed in the diagram, we will most often not distinguish between the graph and its diagram. But there is a warning to be observed here! Technically, a graph is determined solely by the elements in the vertex set and the connections between them given by the edge set. Because it is a geometric object, however, a diagram may provide extraneous information which is occasionally more useful than the underlying graph itself. An example of this is familiar to anyone who has seen diagrams of constellations in astronomy. The constellation Ursa Major contains an asterism popularly called the Big Dipper, which is suggestively indicated in Figure 34.3A as a graph on seven vertices. (The "star" named Mizar is actually a double star, visible to the naked eye on dark nights, but we will indicate it here as a single vertex.) Precisely the same graphical structure is indicated by the diagram in Figure 34.3B, which is now useless as an astronomical model.

Example 1

The graph diagram (Figure 34.3C) in this example consists of 10 vertices and 11 edges; it models a fragment of the interstate highway system. The vertex set is

{Big Springs, Billings, Buffalo, Cheyenne, Denver, Duluth, Fargo,

Grand Forks, Omaha, Sioux Falls}

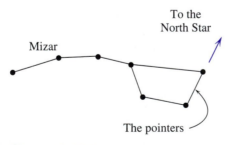

Figure 34.3A

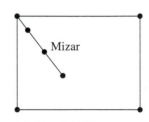

Figure 34.3B

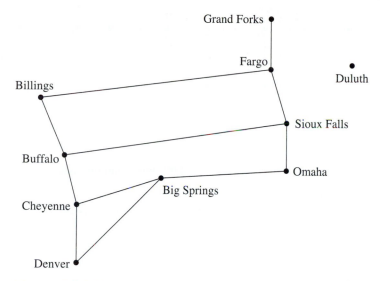

Figure 34.3C

and the edge set is

{{Big Springs, Cheyenne}, {Big Springs, Denver}, {Big Springs, Omaha},
   {Billings, Buffalo}, {Billings, Fargo}, {Buffalo, Cheyenne},
   {Buffalo, Sioux Falls}, {Cheyenne, Denver}, {Fargo, Grand Forks},
                 {Fargo, Sioux Falls}, {Omaha, Sioux Falls}}.

An edge joining two vertices indicates a direct interstate link between those localities. Notice that the diagram offers no editorial commentary on sizes of cities or towns, distances between them, or highway numbers. Although the diagram preserves rough geographic orientation, this is immaterial to the graph's purpose of indicating the fact of direct interstate connection (or lack of it) within this particular part of the system.

As illustrated in Figure 34.3C, not every vertex need be linked by an edge to other vertices. A vertex which belongs to no edge is called **isolated.** Any two vertices which *are* joined by an edge are called **adjacent,** and each is called an **end-vertex** of that edge. For example, the vertex labeled Duluth is isolated, whereas the vertices labeled Grand Forks and Fargo are adjacent. The vertices labeled Billings and Buffalo are end-vertices of the edge which joins them.

34.4

From its definition in terms of sets, a graph (as well as its diagram) must satisfy the following properties (compare with the "nongraph" in Figure 34.4B):

1. Any edge joins two distinct vertices; it cannot contain three vertices, nor can it consist of a loop at a single vertex.

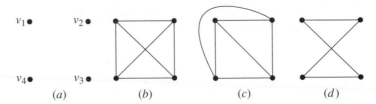

v_1 • v_2 •

v_4 • v_3 •

(a)   (b)   (c)   (d)

Figure 34.4A

2. Two vertices cannot be joined by more than one edge.

3. Edges intersect in a graph only at vertices; even though line segments denoting edges in a diagram may meet, such intersections are not in the graph unless they are end-vertices.

Example 1   Consider graphs on four vertices, with vertex set

$$\mathbf{V} = \{v_1, v_2, v_3, v_4\}.$$

Assume that the vertices in each diagram of Figure 34.4A are labeled as in part (a). The graph in part (a) is null, and the graph in part (b) is complete (note that the two diagonals do not meet in a vertex of the graph). The complete graph in part (b) may also be diagrammed differently, as in part (c), without the extra intersection. (It is an intersecting fact, to be discussed in Section 37, that the complete graph on five vertices cannot be diagrammed without at least one intersection which is not a vertex!) The graph in part (d) is one of the many graphs that are intermediate between the two extremes in parts (a) and (b).   ●

Tutorial 34.4

Let $\mathbf{V} = \{v_1, v_2, \ldots, v_n\}$.
a. Let $n = 3$. Construct the diagram of any graph $\mathbf{G} = (\mathbf{V}, \mathbf{E})$ for which $|\mathbf{E}| = 2$. What is its edge set?
b. Let $n = 4$. Construct the diagram of any graph $\mathbf{G} = (\mathbf{V}, \mathbf{E})$ for which $|\mathbf{E}| = 3$. What is its edge set?
c. Let $n = 5$. Construct the diagram of any graph $\mathbf{G} = (\mathbf{V}, \mathbf{E})$ for which $|\mathbf{E}| = 7$. Could there exist such a graph having an isolated vertex?

As suggested by the illustrations so far, graph diagrams come in a wide variety of patterns, but there *are* limitations. The diagram shown in Figure 34.4B, for example,

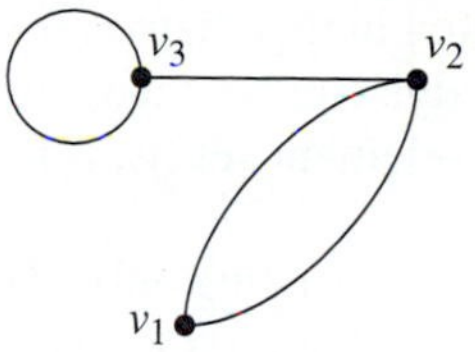

Figure 34.4B

fails to represent a graph for two reasons: There cannot be two edges joining a pair of vertices, as between v_1 and v_2, and an edge cannot consist of a loop at a single vertex, as at v_3. Such diagrams, however, are not devoid of interest: They are studied under the names of *multigraph* and *pseudograph* in more advanced courses in discrete mathematics. In this book, these more general objects will not be our primary concern.

34.5

Although graphs may be pictured very naturally in the form of diagrams, there is an alternate method of representing graphs which is especially helpful in answering certain kinds of questions. It is based upon the (0, 1)-matrix concept which was introduced in paragraph 28.2. Let **G** denote a graph with vertex set $\mathbf{V} = \{v_1, v_2, \ldots, v_n\}$ and edge set **E**. Corresponding to **G**, we construct an $n \times n$, (0, 1)-matrix

$$[a_{ij}], \qquad i = 1, 2, \ldots, n, \quad \text{and} \quad j = 1, 2, \ldots, n, \tag{1}$$

where we assign

$$a_{ij} = \begin{cases} 1, & \text{if } \{v_i, v_j\} \in \mathbf{E}; \\ 0, & \text{otherwise.} \end{cases}$$

This matrix is called the **adjacency matrix** of the graph **G**.

Example 1

Suppose we denote by $\mathbf{G}_1$ the graph which is diagrammed in part (*d*) of Figure 34.4A. Its vertex set is

$$\mathbf{V}_1 = \{v_1, v_2, v_3, v_4\}$$

and its edge set is

$$\mathbf{E}_1 = \{v_1 v_2, v_1 v_3, v_2 v_4, v_3 v_4\}.$$

Hence $\mathbf{G}_1$ has the adjacency matrix

$$[a_{ij}] = \begin{array}{c} \\ v_1 \\ v_2 \\ v_3 \\ v_4 \end{array} \begin{array}{cccc} v_1 & v_2 & v_3 & v_4 \\ \begin{bmatrix} 0 & 1 & 1 & 0 \\ 1 & 0 & 0 & 1 \\ 1 & 0 & 0 & 1 \\ 0 & 1 & 1 & 0 \end{bmatrix} \end{array}.$$

As illustrated in this matrix, the properties of a graph require that $a_{ii} = 0$ for each i (since no edge can be a loop at a vertex), and $a_{ij} = a_{ji}$ for each i and j (since each edge is a 2-element set $\{v_i, v_j\} = \{v_j, v_i\}$). ⬤

A matrix consisting only of 0 entries corresponds to a null graph; it has n vertices and no edges. A matrix consisting only of 1 entries (except, of course, on the main diagonal) corresponds to a complete graph; it has n vertices and $\binom{n}{2}$ edges. In general, any graph $\mathbf{G} = (\mathbf{V}, \mathbf{E})$ may be identified with an irreflexive, symmetric relation having the matrix representation given in (1). Notice that if $\mathbf{G}$ has m edges, then its matrix will contain $2m$ 1s.

The number of different graphs on n vertices is the same as the number of irreflexive, symmetric relations on a set of size n, and by Theorem 28.4 this number is

$$2^{n(n-1)/2}. \tag{2}$$

It is possible to confirm this enumeration directly from the definition of a graph. Suppose we are given a vertex set $\mathbf{V}$ with $|\mathbf{V}| = n$. Again, denoting by $\mathbf{T}$ the set of all 2-element subsets of $\mathbf{V}$, recall that $|\mathbf{T}| = \binom{n}{2}$. Graphs on $\mathbf{V}$ are distinguished by their edge sets, which are simply subsets of $\mathbf{T}$. Thus, each member of the power set of $\mathbf{T}$ determines a graph. From paragraph 16.1, the size of the power set is

$$2^{\binom{n}{2}},$$

which is the same as the enumeration given in (2). As shown in Table 34.5A, the number of graphs increases quite rapidly with n.

The set of all graphs may be conveniently partitioned by the number of edges. There is one graph with 0 edges (the null graph), and one graph with $\binom{n}{2}$ edges (the complete graph). If $0 < m < \binom{n}{2}$, then any selection of m elements of $\mathbf{T}$ produces a graph with m edges. Since $|\mathbf{T}| = \binom{n}{2}$, the number of such selections is

n	$\binom{n}{2}$	$2^{\binom{n}{2}}$
2	1	2
3	3	8
4	6	64
5	10	1024

Table 34.5A

n	0	1	2	3	4	5	6	7	8	9	10	Total
					m							
2	1	1										2
3	1	3	3	1								8
4	1	6	15	20	15	6	1					64
5	1	10	45	120	210	252	210	120	45	10	1	1024

Table 34.5B

$$\left(\binom{n}{2} \atop m \right).$$ (3)

Choosing $n = 4$ and $m = 3$, the number of graphs on 4 vertices with 3 edges is

$$\left(\binom{4}{2} \atop 3 \right) = \binom{6}{3} = 20.$$

The complete tabulation for $n = 2, 3, 4,$ and 5 is displayed in Table 34.5B (compare with Theorem 16.1).

Tutorial 34.5

a. How many graphs are there on the vertex set

$$V = \{v_1, v_2, v_3, v_4, v_5, v_6\}?$$

b. How many of the graphs in part **a** have exactly seven edges?

c. Sketch the diagram of any one of the graphs in part **b** which has no isolated vertex.

34.6 Now we consider in greater detail the matrix representation of a graph **G**. The row labeled v_i indicates by its 1s exactly those vertices which are adjacent to the vertex v_i. The row sum, therefore, counts vertices adjacent to v_i, and this sum is called the **degree** of v_i, denoted by $\deg(v_i)$. Each row sum in the adjacency matrix for the graph G_1 in Example 1 of paragraph 34.5 is 2; thus the degree of each vertex in that graph is 2. The diagram in part (d) of Figure 34.4A illustrates this fact clearly. Also illustrated in that figure are the general observations that $\deg(v) = 0$ for each vertex in a null graph, and $\deg(v) = n - 1$ for each vertex in a complete graph.

All graphs in Figure 34.4A have the property that the degree of every vertex is the same; such graphs are an important but very restricted class among all graphs. In general, if the degree of each vertex is the same number, say k, then the graph is called **regular** of degree k. Thus, the row sums (and column sums) in the matrix representation of a regular graph are the same. Note that the graph diagrammed in Figure 34.3C is not regular; it has vertices of degrees 0, 1, 2, and 3.

Since each edge in a graph contributes 1 to the degree count at each of its end-vertices, the sum of all degrees is twice the number of edges,

$$\sum_{i=1}^{n} \deg(v_i) = 2 \cdot |\mathbf{E}|. \tag{1}$$

For the graph diagrammed in Figure 34.3A,

$$\sum_{i=1}^{7} \deg(v_i) = 1 + 2 + 2 + 3 + 2 + 2 + 2 = 14 = 2 \cdot |\mathbf{E}|,$$

and we note that the graph has seven edges.

The following theorem is more important than might appear from its very simple proof. It is another one of those results, like the Pigeonhole Principle, at once obvious yet fundamental in ways that are not immediately apparent. We will meet it again in a later section.

THEOREM 34.6

If the graph $\mathbf{G} = (\mathbf{V}, \mathbf{E})$ is regular of degree k, then

$$k \cdot |\mathbf{V}| = 2 \cdot |\mathbf{E}|.$$

Proof

The sum of the degrees in $\mathbf{G}$ is simply k times the number of vertices; hence the result follows immediately from (1). ∎

A consequence of this theorem is the observation that there cannot exist a regular graph of degree 3 on 11 vertices. Why not? Because $3 \cdot 11$ is not an even number! More generally, there cannot exist a regular graph of odd degree on an odd number of vertices, for this would contradict Theorem 34.6.

34.7

Answers to the enumeration question for all graphs and for graphs with a given number of edges were obtained easily from (2) and (3) in paragraph 34.5. In each case, the formula involves only the most basic combinatorial facts. Lest this happy accident be perceived as the norm, we consider briefly the question, "Of the graphs on n vertices, how many are regular of degree k?" On the face of it, there seems little reason to consider this a more challenging question than the ones above. But the answer is far less clean and direct. In Table 34.7, answers are given for $n = 2$, 3, 4, and 5, and for $0 \le k \le n - 1$.

			k			
n	0	1	2	3	4	*Total*
2	1	1	—	—	—	2
3	1	0	1	—	—	2
4	1	3	3	1	—	8
5	1	0	12	0	1	14

Table 34.7

For convenience, suppose we let $r(n, k)$ denote the number of regular graphs of degree k on n vertices. Then $r(n, 0) = 1$ (the null graph) and $r(n, n - 1) = 1$ (the complete graph). By Theorem 34.6, $r(n, k) = 0$ if $n \cdot k$ is odd. Furthermore, Table 34.7 is "symmetric" in the following sense: If $0 \leq k \leq (n - 1)/2$, then $r(n, k) = r(n, n - 1 - k)$. This follows from the observation that if $[a_{ij}]$ is the matrix corresponding to a regular graph of degree k, then $[b_{ij}]$, where

$$b_{ij} = \begin{cases} 0, & \text{if } i = j; \\ 1 - a_{ij}, & \text{if } i \neq j, \end{cases} \tag{1}$$

is the matrix corresponding to a regular graph of degree $n - 1 - k$. (We will return to this idea in paragraph 37.4.)

Tutorial 34.7

a. Sketch diagrams for the eight regular graphs on $\mathbf{V} = \{v_1, v_2, v_3, v_4\}$.

b. Pair the diagrams in part **a** according to the observation recorded in (1).

The numbers $r(n, 3)$ for $n \geq 4$ and $r(n, 4)$ for $n \geq 5$ have been computed but require fairly sophisticated methods. For general k, it appears to be quite difficult to compute $r(n, k)$.

Graph theory as a structured subdiscipline of mathematics is of recent vintage; it is the subject of intense current research, much of it motivated by applications in such diverse fields as physics, chemistry, biology, computer science, economics, sociology, and psychology. But graph theory has its own inherent mathematical interest, which is quite independent of any practical application. Among its attractions are richness of detail, novelty of techniques, and diversity of problems. It is our hope that some of this will become apparent as we survey a few of its major themes in the remainder of this chapter.

Problems for Section 34

1. (*a*) By omitting the state of Vermont in Figure 34.1C, does the resulting map require four colors? (*b*) If the state of Connecticut were omitted (instead of Vermont), would the resulting map require four colors?

2. Suppose that the vertices in Figure 34.1C, except for Me, have been colored with the least number of colors. Without increasing the number of colors used, how many choices are there for the vertex Me?

3. The "four corners" area includes that region near the common point in which the states of Arizona, Colorado, New Mexico, and Utah meet. How many colors are required for a map of just that area? (Note that two states may share a common boundary point without requiring different colors.)

In the next seven problems, let $V = \{v_1, v_2, v_3, v_4, v_5\}$; draw a diagram and give the matrix for $G = (V, E)$.

4. $E = \{\{v_1, v_2\}, \{v_2, v_3\}, \{v_3, v_4\}, \{v_4, v_5\}, \{v_1, v_5\}\}$.

5. $E = \{\{v_1, v_2\}, \{v_1, v_3\}, \{v_1, v_4\}, \{v_1, v_5\}\}$.

6. $E = \{\{v_1, v_3\}, \{v_1, v_4\}, \{v_2, v_4\}, \{v_2, v_5\}, \{v_3, v_5\}\}$.

7. $E = \{\{v_1, v_5\}, \{v_2, v_3\}, \{v_2, v_5\}, \{v_3, v_4\}, \{v_4, v_5\}\}$.

8. $E = \{\{v_1, v_2\}, \{v_2, v_3\}, \{v_3, v_4\}, \{v_3, v_5\}, \{v_4, v_5\}\}$.

9. $E = \{\{v_1, v_2\}, \{v_1, v_3\}, \{v_1, v_4\}, \{v_2, v_3\}, \{v_2, v_4\}, \{v_3, v_4\}\}$.

10. $E = \{\{v_1, v_2\}, \{v_2, v_3\}, \{v_1, v_3\}, \{v_4, v_5\}\}$.

11. Consider the five Virginia cities Blacksburg, Charlottesville, Lexington, Richmond, and Roanoke. There is direct air service from Richmond to each city other than Lexington and a direct flight from Roanoke to Charlottesville. Using Example 1 in paragraph 34.3 as a guide, model this situation with a graph, and give its matrix.

12. (*a*) Redraw the diagrams in Problems 4 and 6 so that they "look the same," if possible. (This means that you can simply replace the labels on the same diagram.) (*b*) Try to redraw the diagrams in Problems 7 and 8 so that they "look the same."

13. How many edges are in the complete graph on five vertices? Draw its diagram with exactly one point in which two edges meet in a nonvertex.

14. What is the maximum degree of any vertex in the graph diagrammed in (*a*) Problem 5, (*b*) Problem 9, (*c*) Problem 10?

15. (*a*) Find the minimum and maximum number of edges that a graph on five vertices can have if exactly one vertex is isolated. (*b*) Repeat for a graph on six vertices.

16. Why is there no regular graph of degree 5 with 15 vertices?

17. Draw the graph in Problem 9 with no edges crossing.

18. Try to draw the two graphs,

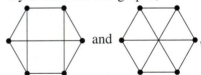

and

without any edges crossing. One is easy to do, and the other is impossible.

19. Show that each graph with more than one vertex has at least two vertices of the same degree. (*Hint:* Theorem 28.1.)

20. Draw all eight graphs with vertex set $\{v_1, v_2, v_3\}$.

21. How many graphs are there with 12 edges on a given 9-element vertex set? (Leave your answer in terms of a binomial coefficient.)

22. Draw the diagrams for 3 of the 15 graphs with two edges on the vertex set {a, b, c, d}.

23. (*Continuation of Problem 22.*) Let **T** be all the 2-element subsets of {a, b, c, d}. Using one of your graphs from Problem 22, draw a new graph with the same vertices but with edge set **T** minus the edges in the original graph. How many edges does this new graph have?

24. (*Continuation of Problem 22.*) Show that there must be the same number of graphs on the vertex set {a, b, c, d} with two edges as there are with four edges.

25. (*Conclusion of Problem 22.*) Show that there are the same number of graphs on an n-element vertex set with m edges as there are with $\binom{n}{2} - m$ edges.

26. My wife and I attended a party with four other couples. No one shook hands with his or her spouse. After some time, I asked each person (including my wife) with how many other people he/she had shaken hands. The answers I received from the nine people range from 0 to 8 with no number being repeated. How many hands did I shake? *Hint:* Think of the people as the vertices of a graph with the vertices adjacent if the corresponding people shook hands. First show that the spouse of the person who shook eight hands shook no one's hand. Next show that the spouse of the person who shook seven hands shook one hand. Continue in this manner. (*Note:* One of the authors first read this problem in an article by Prof. Paul Halmos.)

27. Find the adjacency matrix for the graph in Figure 34.1C.

28. What is the degree of each vertex in the graph of Figure 34.1C?

29. Sketch the floor plan of a one-story house which has a central hallway, a kitchen, a dining room, a living room, two bedrooms, and a connecting bath. Now model this plan as in Figure 34.1C. (There should be seven vertices.)

In each of the final two problems, draw diagrams in which the vertices are on a circle and the edges are drawn with a ruler. Consider only triangles with graph vertices.

30. Draw the graph given by

	v_1	v_2	v_3	v_4	v_5
v_1	0	1	0	1	1
v_2	1	0	1	0	1
v_3	0	1	0	1	1
v_4	1	0	1	0	0
v_5	1	1	1	0	0

and determine how many triangles it contains.

31. How many edges are there in a complete graph with six vertices, and how many triangles does it contain?

Section 35.   Subgraphs and Walks

Overview for Section 35

- Discussion of subgraphs, especially induced and spanning subgraphs
  - The degree sequence of a graph
  - Introduction to walks, trails, and paths
  - Connected graphs and components of disconnected graphs

Key Concepts: incidence, subgraphs, induced and spanning subgraphs, degree sequence, equality of graphs, walks and length of walks, trails, paths, triangles and cycles, connected graphs, and components of graphs

35.1   In Example 1 of paragraph 34.1, we considered the question of coloring a graph in such a way that no two adjacent vertices were assigned the same color. For the graph diagrammed in Figure 34.1C, this turned out to be impossible using a palette of just three colors. The reason is intimately related to that part of the graph involving just the vertices labeled C, Ma, R, and W. Very often, one part of a given graph may be especially useful in determining a property associated with the graph as a whole. For this reason we must be able to focus temporarily on parts of a graph, much as we focus on part of a given set when considering one of its subsets. The idea required is that of a "subgraph," but before giving a formal definition, we will adopt a useful abbreviation for an edge. Recall that in Example 1 of paragraph 34.2 we introduced $v_i v_j$ as a shorthand symbol for the edge $\{v_i, v_j\}$. Thus CR denotes the edge joining vertices representing the states of Connecticut and Rhode Island in Figure 34.1C. When the vertices of a graph are distinguished by numerical indices, we will use an even briefer notation: The edge $\{v_i, v_j\}$ is denoted by the symbol e_{ij}. Because an edge is a set, each of the symbols e_{ij} and e_{ji} denotes the same edge. We say that a vertex is **incident** with any edge to which it belongs, and any edge is **incident** with either of its two end-vertices. For example, in the graph diagrammed in part (a) of Figure 35.2A, the edge e_{24} is incident with each of the vertices v_2 and v_4 but is not incident with any other vertex. The vertex v_4 in that graph is incident with e_{24} and also with two other edges, e_{14} and e_{46}.

   If $\mathbf{G} = (\mathbf{V}, \mathbf{E})$ and $\mathbf{H} = (\mathbf{U}, \mathbf{D})$ are graphs, then $\mathbf{H}$ is a **subgraph** of $\mathbf{G}$ provided $\mathbf{U} \subseteq \mathbf{V}$ and $\mathbf{D} \subseteq \mathbf{E}$. It is essential to note that $\mathbf{H}$ must be a graph; this means that every vertex incident with an edge in $\mathbf{D}$ must belong to $\mathbf{U}$. Thus, the subsets $\mathbf{U}$ and $\mathbf{D}$ cannot be chosen arbitrarily. For example, if $\mathbf{G} = (\mathbf{V}, \mathbf{E})$ is the complete graph on the vertex set

$$V = \{v_1, v_2, v_3, v_4\},$$

then

$$U = \{v_1, v_2, v_3\} \subseteq V \quad \text{and} \quad D = \{e_{12}, e_{23}, e_{34}\} \subseteq E$$

cannot be the vertex and edge sets of a subgraph of **G** because e_{34} must have v_3 and v_4 as end-vertices, but $v_4 \notin U$. Note that the definition allows any graph to be a subgraph of itself; we say that **H** is a **proper** subgraph of **G** if either

$$U \neq V \quad \text{or} \quad D \neq E \quad \text{(or, of course, both).}$$

35.2

The definition of subgraph allows the widest possible latitude to the idea, but in practice two particular classes called "induced" and "spanning" are especially important.

If **U** is any subset of **V**, then **H** = (**U, D**) is the subgraph of **G** **induced** by **U** provided **D** contains every edge in **E** having end-vertices in **U**. This means that **H** is maximal in the sense that no subgraph of **G** with vertex set **U** can have an edge that is not in **H**. The other class consists of subgraphs **H** for which **U** = **V**, and in this case **H** is called a **spanning subgraph** of **G**. Note that a spanning subgraph **H** need not contain *all* the edges in **G**, but if **H** is both induced and spanning, then **H** = **G**.

Example 1

Let **G** = (**V, E**) be the graph on six vertices diagrammed in part (*a*) of Figure 35.2A. Then:

- H_1 in part (*b*) is a subgraph of **G**.

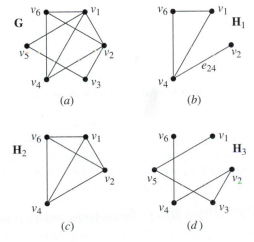

(*a*)   (*b*)

(*c*)   (*d*)

Figure 35.2A

Figure 35.2B

- **H$_2$** in part (*c*) is an induced subgraph of **G** with the same vertex set as **H$_1$**.

- **H$_3$** in part (*d*) is a spanning subgraph of **G**.

Tutorial 35.2

Consider the graph diagrammed in part (*a*) of Figure 35.2A.

a. Diagram any induced subgraph of **G** with five vertices.

b. Diagram any spanning subgraph of **G** with three edges.

If, in part (*b*) of Figure 35.2A, we were simply to erase the vertex v_2, then the resulting diagram, shown in Figure 35.2B, would *not be* a graph, because the vertex set is now $\{v_1, v_4, v_6\}$ and the segment labeled e_{24} no longer identifies a 2-element subset of this vertex set.

35.3   Given a graph **G** $= (\mathbf{V}, \mathbf{E})$, such as that shown in part (*a*) of Figure 35.2A, there is a technique for producing proper subgraphs of **G** based upon two operations:

1. Delete an edge from **E**.

2. Delete a vertex from **V** together with all its incident edges.

As an example of operation **1,** think of erasing the edge e_{24}, which leaves the proper, spanning subgraph shown in Figure 35.3A. As an example of operation **2,** think of erasing the vertex v_4 along with the remaining edges e_{14} and e_{46}, which leaves the proper induced subgraph shown in Figure 35.3B. These operations may be performed sequentially to produce various subgraphs, each a proper subgraph of the preceding one.

Because a graph may be identified with a relation (which is irreflexive and symmetric), a result like that in Theorem 31.3 holds for graphs also. Let **G** $= (\mathbf{V}, \mathbf{E})$ and **H** $= (\mathbf{U}, \mathbf{D})$ be graphs for which $\mathbf{U} \subseteq \mathbf{V}$, and construct the two $n \times n$, (0, 1)-matrices $[a_{ij}]$ and $[b_{ij}]$, respectively, with rows and columns labeled (alike) by the elements

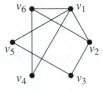
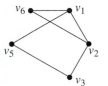

Figure 35.3A   **Figure 35.3B**

in **V**. An adjacency matrix serves to identify the edges in its graph; hence (under the conditions above)

H is a subgraph of **G** if and only if $[b_{ij}] \le [a_{ij}]$.

For example, the matrices for the graphs in Figures 35.3B and 35.3A satisfy

$$
\begin{bmatrix} 0 & 1 & 0 & - & 1 & 1 \\ 1 & 0 & 1 & - & 0 & 1 \\ 0 & 1 & 0 & - & 1 & 0 \\ - & - & - & - & - & - \\ 1 & 0 & 1 & - & 0 & 0 \\ 1 & 1 & 0 & - & 0 & 0 \end{bmatrix} \le \begin{bmatrix} 0 & 1 & 0 & 1 & 1 & 1 \\ 1 & 0 & 1 & 0 & 0 & 1 \\ 0 & 1 & 0 & 0 & 1 & 0 \\ 1 & 0 & 0 & 0 & 0 & 1 \\ 1 & 0 & 1 & 0 & 0 & 0 \\ 1 & 1 & 0 & 1 & 0 & 0 \end{bmatrix}. \quad (1)
$$

Notice that in constructing the matrix on the left for the graph in Figure 35.3B, we included a blank row and column for the "missing" vertex v_4. This is because only matrices of the same size can be compared by $\le$. Note that if the blank row and column were replaced with 0 entries, the resulting matrix would correspond to the graph in Figure 35.3B with the isolated vertex v_4 adjoined to its vertex set. The two "deletion" operations **1** and **2** have a simple matrix interpretation. If $[a_{ij}]$ is the matrix for **G** = (**V, E**), then:

1′. To delete the edge e_{ij} from **E**, simply replace by 0 the entries $a_{ij} = a_{ji} = 1$.

2′. To delete the vertex v_i from **V**, simply replace each entry in the row and column labeled v_i by a blank.

For simplicity of notation, we will indicate the spanning subgraph of **G** = (**V, E**) resulting from operation **1′** by (**V, E** − e_{ij}), and we will indicate the induced subgraph resulting from operation **2′** by (**V** − v_i, **E′**). Note that **E′** is the set of all edges in **G** except those incident with v_i.

Tutorial 35.3

a. Construct the matrix M for the graph **G** diagrammed in part (a) of Figure 35.2A.

continued on next page

continued from previous page

b. Construct the matrix for the subgraph of **G** obtained by deleting the edge e_{24}.

c. Construct the matrix for the subgraph of **G** obtained by deleting the vertex v_4.

d. Compare your matrices with those in (1).

35.4 Two graphs $\mathbf{G}_1 = (\mathbf{V}_1, \mathbf{E}_1)$ and $\mathbf{G}_2 = (\mathbf{V}_2, \mathbf{E}_2)$, are **equal** (or **identical**) if $\mathbf{V}_1 = \mathbf{V}_2$ and $\mathbf{E}_1 = \mathbf{E}_2$; hence two graphs are **different** if either the vertex sets differ or the edge sets differ. One of the major tasks in graph theory is the identification of properties which help to distinguish one graph from another, avoiding, if possible, a detailed examination of the vertex and edge sets. Size is one of the more primitive distinguishing properties: If either $|\mathbf{V}_1| \neq |\mathbf{V}_2|$ or $|\mathbf{E}_1| \neq |\mathbf{E}_2|$, then $\mathbf{G}_1$ and $\mathbf{G}_2$ are different. But size offers only the roughest of guides; from Table 34.5B, for example, there are 20 different graphs on the same vertex set $\mathbf{V}$ with $|\mathbf{V}| = 4$ and $|\mathbf{E}| = 3$.

Another property which is often useful in distinguishing among graphs on n vertices is called the **degree sequence.** This is an n-tuple in which the n coordinates are the degrees at the n vertices, customarily listed in nondecreasing order. For example, the degree sequence of the Big Dipper, Figure 34.3A, is

$$(1, 2, 2, 2, 2, 2, 3),$$

and the degree sequence of the graph **G** in Figure 35.2A is

$$(2, 2, 3, 3, 4, 4).$$

It is clear that two graphs on the same vertex set are different if their degree sequences differ (for one must have an edge, the other does not), but the graphs may differ even though the degree sequences coincide, as in Figure 35.4, in which both graphs have degree sequence (1, 1, 2, 2, 2).

One of the most important of all structural properties of a graph is particularly apparent in diagram form. In Figure 35.4, the graph in part (*a*) falls into two pieces,

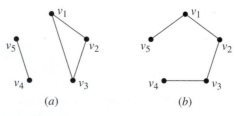

(*a*)   (*b*)

Figure 35.4

while that in part (*b*) does not; this intuitive distinction is referred to as "connectedness." To make the idea more precise, we will need to discuss some new and useful concepts.

35.5

Let **G** denote a graph with the vertex set

$$\mathbf{V} = \{v_1, v_2, v_3, \ldots, v_n\}.$$

A **walk** in the graph **G** is a k-tuple of vertices $(u_1, u_2, \ldots, u_k)$ selected from **V**, with repetition allowed, such that $\{u_i, u_{i+1}\}$ is an edge of **G** for $1 \leq i \leq k-1$. The **length** of the walk is $k - 1$, which is just the number of edges, including any repetitions. Although vertices and edges may be repeated in a walk, consecutive vertices must be distinct (because "loops" are not allowed as edges). A "walk" in **G** is a very general concept; its length may be 0 or any positive integer (perhaps greater than n). For example, in Figure 35.5,

$$(v_1, v_2, v_5, v_3, v_4, v_5, v_2, v_3, v_6, v_3)$$

is a walk of length 9. In a walk, if the first vertex u_1 and the last vertex u_k are distinct, then the walk is said to be **from** u_1 **to** u_k, or to **join** u_1 and u_k. If $u_1 = u_k$, then the walk is said to be **closed** and may be referred to as a closed walk **at** u_1.

Tutorial 35.5A

Refer to the graph **G** in Figure 35.2A.
a. Find two different walks of length 4 from v_1 to v_4.
b. Find walks from v_1 to v_6 of lengths 1, 2, 3, 4, and 5.
c. Find a closed walk of length 7 at v_3.

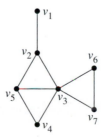

Figure 35.5

A walk in which no edge is repeated is called a **trail.** It is possible that a trail may contain a repeated vertex. For example, in Figure 35.5, $(v_1, v_2, v_5, v_3, v_4, v_5)$ is a trail of length 5 from v_1 to v_5, and $(v_2, v_5, v_3, v_6, v_7, v_3, v_2)$ is a closed trail of length 6 at v_2. It is clear that no trail can be longer than $|\mathbf{E}|$.

A trail in which no vertex is repeated is called a **path.** In Figure 35.5, $(v_1, v_2, v_5, v_3, v_4)$ is a path of length 4 from v_1 to v_4. Every path is also a trail, and every trail is also a walk, but these inclusions do not reverse: $(v_1, v_2, v_5, v_3, v_4, v_5, v_2)$ is a walk which is not a trail, and $(v_1, v_2, v_5, v_3, v_4, v_5)$ is a trail which is not a path. If a closed trail with more than one vertex has no repeated vertices (other than the first and last vertex), then the trail is called a **cycle.** In Figure 35.5, for example, $(v_2, v_3, v_4, v_5, v_2)$ is a cycle of length 4. A cycle of length 3 is called a **triangle;** again in that figure, (v_3, v_6, v_7, v_3) denotes a triangle.

Neither a walk nor a trail is necessarily a subgraph of $\mathbf{G}$ since vertices and edges may be repeated. We may, however, consider a path to be a subgraph having k vertices and $k - 1$ edges, and we say that the path **joins,** or is **between,** its two extreme vertices. In Figure 35.5, we consider either (v_1, v_2, v_5) or (v_5, v_2, v_1) to identify the same path between v_1 and v_5. Similarly, we may consider a cycle to be a subgraph having k vertices ($k \geq 3$) and k edges. Again in Figure 35.5, we consider either (v_3, v_6, v_7, v_3) or (v_6, v_7, v_3, v_6) to identify the same triangle.

If a walk has exactly two distinct vertices u_1 and u_2, then it may flip-flop any finite number of times; for example,

$$(u_1, u_2, u_1, u_2, u_1, u_2).$$

But if such a walk were also a trail, then it may only be of the form (u_1, u_2) and thus must also be a path. Notice that in Figure 35.4*b* there is a path of length 1 between the vertices v_1 and v_5, but in Figure 35.4*a* there is no path of any length between the same pair of vertices.

At last, the machinery is in place for the following simple but critically important definition. A graph is said to be **connected** if for any two of its vertices there is a path between them.

Example 1   Let $\mathbf{G}$ be the graph shown in Figure 35.5. Its vertex set is

$$\mathbf{V} = (v_1, v_2, v_3, v_4, v_5, v_6, v_7)$$

and its edge set is

$$\mathbf{E} = \{e_{12}, e_{23}, e_{25}, e_{34}, e_{35}, e_{36}, e_{37}, e_{45}, e_{67}\}.$$

This graph is connected because there is a path between any two of its vertices. For example, $(v_1, v_2, v_3, v_6, v_7)$ is a path of length 4 between v_1 and v_7. (Actually, there are six different paths joining these extreme vertices. Can you identify all of them?) Furthermore, $(v_2, v_5, v_4, v_3, v_2)$ is a cycle of length 4. If the edge between v_2 and v_3 in the cycle were deleted, the resulting trail is a path of length 3 between v_2 and v_3.

35.6

If a graph **G** $=$ (**V, E**) is not connected, then it can be expressed as the union of maximal connected subgraphs, each of which is called a **component** of **G**. "Maximality" implies that a component of **G** is not properly contained in any other connected subgraph of **G**. The graph in Figure 35.4a has 5 vertices and 4 edges and it can be expressed as the union of two components $\mathbf{G}_1 = (\mathbf{V}_1, \mathbf{E}_1)$ and $\mathbf{G}_2 = (\mathbf{V}_2, \mathbf{E}_2)$, where

$$\mathbf{V}_1 = \{v_1, v_2, \ldots\} \quad \text{and} \quad \mathbf{E}_1 = \{e_{12}, e_{13}, e_{23}\};$$
$$\mathbf{V}_2 = \{v_4, v_5\} \quad \text{and} \quad \mathbf{E}_2 = \{e_{45}\}.$$

Notice that each component is, itself, a graph and that it is an induced subgraph of **G**.

Example 1

Consider the connected graph **G** $=$ (**V, E**), diagrammed in Figure 35.6A, where

$$\mathbf{V} = \{v_1, v_2, v_3, v_4, v_5, v_6, v_7\}, \qquad \mathbf{E} = \{e_{12}, e_{23}, e_{25}, e_{34}, e_{35}, e_{36}, e_{45}, e_{67}\}.$$

By deleting a single edge from **G** we obtain a spanning subgraph (all the vertices remain), which may be connected or not. For example, $\mathbf{G}_1 = (\mathbf{V}, \mathbf{E} - e_{35})$ is connected, but $\mathbf{G}_2 = (\mathbf{V}, \mathbf{E} - e_{36})$ is not connected. On the other hand, we remind you that deleting just a single vertex from **G** may fail to leave a subgraph. For example, deleting the vertex v_3 leaves the vertex set $\mathbf{V}' = \{v_1, v_2, v_4, v_5, v_6, v_7\}$, and

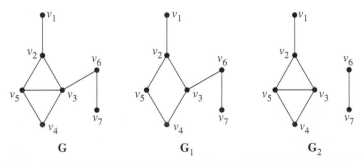

Figure 35.6A

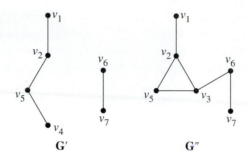

Figure 35.6B

we know that the edge set cannot be all of **E**. We will agree, as in condition **2** in paragraph 35.3, that deleting the vertex v_3 produces the subgraph of **G** *induced* by **V′**; that is, **G′** = (**V′**, **E′**) is the subgraph of **G** with vertex set **V′** and edge set **E′** = {e_{12}, e_{25}, e_{45}, e_{67}}. Again, removal of a single vertex may result in a subgraph which is either connected or not. The graph **G′** in Figure 35.6B is not connected, but notice that the graph **G″** = (**V** − v_4, **E″**) is connected.

35.7 **Complement: Hamiltonian Cycles and Paths** Let **G** = (**V**, **E**) denote a graph. Recall that a walk of length $k - 1$ in **G** can be represented as a k-tuple of vertices $(u_1, u_2, \ldots, u_k)$. If $u_1 = u_k$ and if no other vertices are repeated, then the walk is called a *cycle*. The length of the cycle is the length of the corresponding walk. In Figure 35.7A, for example, (R, Q, Z, X, W, R) is a cycle of length 5.

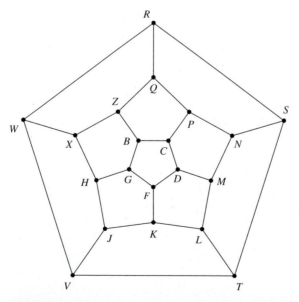

Figure 35.7A

In the mid-nineteenth century Sir William Rowan Hamilton (1805–1865) invented a game which he titled "The Icosian Game" (from the Greek word meaning "twenty"). It is based upon the graph shown in Figure 35.7A, which has 20 vertices and represents one of the five Platonic solids (to be discussed in Section 41). This solid, incidentally, was called by the Greeks a dodecahedron because it has 12 faces. One of the objects in Hamilton's game is to discover a cycle which includes all 20 of the vertices. One such, beginning and ending with Q, may be started as follows (complete it, if you can):

$$(Q, P, C, D, F, G, B, Z, \ldots, Q).$$

As the subject of graph theory matured, much work was done on questions, related to Hamilton's game, concerning the existence of a cycle of length n or a path which contains each vertex exactly once. In fact, any graph **G** on n vertices which contains a cycle of length n is now called **hamiltonian.** Any path in a graph that contains each vertex of the graph is called a **hamiltonian path,** and any graph which has a hamiltonian path is called **traceable.** Of course, any hamiltonian graph is traceable, but the converse is not true: a path of length $n - 1$ is traceable but has no cycle.

The problem of determining relatively simple characterizations of hamiltonian and traceable graphs seems to be quite difficult. Because such graphs have many applications, even partial results are useful, and hamiltonian theory remains an active field of research. We will consider, for example, two conditions relating to hamiltonian graphs, one of which is necessary and the other is sufficient.

Let v denote a vertex of the graph **G**, and let **G**$'$ denote the subgraph of **G** induced by the vertices **V** $- v$. Thus, to obtain **G**$'$ simply delete v and each edge incident with v. If **G** is a connected graph, then v is a **cut-vertex** of **G** if **G**$'$ is not connected. Notice that no vertex in the graph shown in Figure 35.7A is a cut-vertex. A proof of the following generalization is based simply on the observation that no hamiltonian path which contains a cut-vertex can be a cycle. The details of the argument are omitted.

THEOREM 35.7A

A hamiltonian graph has no cut-vertex.

Any complete graph on at least three vertices is hamiltonian. To find a hamiltonian cycle in a complete graph, begin at any vertex and proceed sequentially to each other vertex. This is possible since all the required edges are present. When the graph is not complete, however, the existence of a hamiltonian cycle is problematical. A sufficient condition for a graph to be hamiltonian was given by Gabriel A. Dirac (1925–1984) in 1952. (This Dirac is the stepson of the Dirac in paragraph 20.5.) It is based on the observation that one can delete many edges from a complete graph without destroying the hamiltonian property (but, it *requires* that deletions be "uniform" in the sense that no vertex may have degree less than $n/2$).

THEOREM 35.7B

Dirac's Theorem. Let **G** be a graph with $n \geq 3$ vertices. If $\deg(v) \geq n/2$ for all vertices v of **G**, then **G** is hamiltonian.

Proof

Notice that if the conditions of the theorem are satisfied for a graph G with $n = 3$ or $n = 4$ vertices, then G must be either the triangle or one of the following hamiltonian graphs:

Suppose the theorem is false. Then there is a least integer n such that there exists a non-hamiltonian graph G on n vertices for which $\deg(v) \geq n/2$ for all $v \in G$. Observe that $n > 4$ and that G is not complete. Hence, we can select such a G which has so many edges that the addition of any new edge produces a hamiltonian graph.

Consider such a graph $G = (V, E)$ and suppose that its vertices $V = \{v_1, v_2, \ldots, v_n\}$ are labeled so that $e_{1n} \notin E$. Denote by G'' the graph G with the edge e_{1n} adjoined to E. Then G'' has a hamiltonian cycle which we will assume to be $(v_1, v_2, v_3, \ldots, v_n, v_1)$. If for any k, $1 < k < n$, v_1 is adjacent to v_k and v_n is adjacent to v_{k-1}, then

$$(v_1, v_k, v_{k+1}, \ldots, v_{n-1}, v_n, v_{k-1}, \ldots, v_2, v_1)$$

is a hamiltonian cycle in G (see Figure 35.7B). This cannot be. Hence for each vertex v_k, adjacent to v_1, there is a vertex not adjacent to v_n. Now $\deg(v_1) \geq n/2$, and so there are at least $(n/2) - 1$ vertices among $\{v_2, \ldots, v_{n-1}\}$ which are not adjacent to v_n. Also, both v_1 and v_n are not adjacent to v_n in G, and hence there are at least $(n/2) + 1$ vertices not adjacent to v_n. Therefore, there are at most $n - ((n/2) + 1) = (n/2) - 1$ vertices adjacent to v_n, and so $\deg(v_n) < n/2$. But this is a contradiction; hence the theorem is true. ∎

The Dirac condition is by no means necessary: A cycle of length n is hamiltonian and is regular of degree 2; also the graph in Figure 35.7A is hamiltonian and is regular of degree 3. There exist other theorems which have less restrictive hypotheses (than in Dirac's Theorem), and they can be used to guarantee the existence of hamiltonian cycles in certain graphs to which Dirac's Theorem does not apply. Nevertheless, among conditions based upon degrees of vertices, Dirac's Theorem is, in a sense, the best possible; for $n/2$ cannot even be replaced by the greatest integer in $n/2, \lfloor n/2 \rfloor$. To see this, consider a graph with $2m+1$ vertices $\{u_1, \ldots, u_m, v_1, \ldots, v_{m+1}\}$ and edge set $\{\{u_i, v_j\}: 1 \leq i \leq m, 1 \leq j \leq m + 1\}$. This graph with $m = 4$ is illustrated in Figure 35.7C.

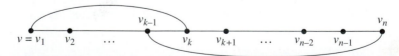

Figure 35.7B

Figure 35.7C

The degree of each of the m u_i-vertices is $m + 1$, and the degree of the $(m + 1)$ v_j-vertices is $m = \lfloor(2m + 1)/2\rfloor$. It is not hard to see that this graph fails to be hamiltonian; hence we cannot replace $n/2$ in Dirac's Theorem by $\lfloor n/2\rfloor$.

Problems for Section 35

1. Consider the Petersen graph [Julius Petersen (1839–1910)]

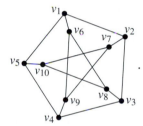

Sketch the subgraphs induced by the vertices (a) $\{v_1, v_5, v_6, v_9, v_{10}\}$, (b) $\{v_1, v_2, v_3, v_4, v_5\}$, (c) $\{v_6, v_7, v_8, v_9, v_{10}\}$.

2. Label the graph ⊓ so that it is a sub-

graph of 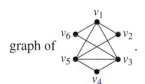 .

3. Draw all the spanning subgraphs of

v_3 — v_4
v_2 — v_1

that have 0 or 1 edges.

4. (*Continuation of Problem 3.*) Draw all the spanning subgraphs of the graph in Problem 3 that have 2 edges.

5. (*Continuation of Problem 3.*) Draw all the spanning subgraphs of the graph in Problem 3 that have 3 or 4 edges.

6. (*Conclusion of Problem 3.*) Considering your answers to Problems 3, 4, and 5, if a graph has n vertices and m edges, then how many spanning subgraphs does it have with k edges, $0 \leq k \leq m$?

7. (*a*) If **E** is the edge set of the labeled graph in Problem 2, draw the graphs with the same vertices but with edge sets $\mathbf{E} - e_{35}$ and $\mathbf{E} - \{e_{35}, e_{36}, e_{31}, e_{34}\}$. (*b*) Using this same graph, draw the induced graphs with vertex sets $\mathbf{V} - v_3$ and $\mathbf{V} - \{v_3, v_5\}$. (*c*) Is $\mathbf{V} - v_3$ the same graph as the final graph in part (*a*)?

8. Let $\mathbf{G} = $ (graph) $\begin{smallmatrix}v_1 & v_2 & v_3 & v_4\\ v_6 & & & v_5\end{smallmatrix}$. What are the components of the graphs with vertex sets $\mathbf{V} - v_i$ for $i = 1, 2, \ldots, 6$?

9. Let **G** be the graph in Problem 8. Sketch the components in the graphs with edge sets $\mathbf{E} - e_{12}$, $\mathbf{E} - e_{23}$, and $\mathbf{E} - \{e_{23}, e_{34}, e_{35}\}$.

10. Draw the graph represented by the matrix

$$\begin{array}{c} v_1 \\ v_2 \\ v_3 \\ v_4 \\ v_5 \\ v_6 \end{array} \begin{bmatrix} 0 & 1 & 1 & 0 & 0 & 0 \\ 1 & 0 & 0 & 1 & 0 & 0 \\ 1 & 0 & 0 & 1 & 1 & 0 \\ 0 & 1 & 1 & 0 & 0 & 1 \\ 0 & 0 & 1 & 0 & 0 & 1 \\ 0 & 0 & 0 & 1 & 1 & 0 \end{bmatrix}.$$

11. Give the matrix for the labeled graph in Problem 2.

12. Give the matrix for the graph **G** in Problem 8.

13. Determine the degree sequence for the graph in Figure 35.3a.

14. Determine the degree sequences for each of the graphs in Figure 35.2A.

15. What is unusual about the degree sequence for the Petersen graph (see Problem 1)?

16. Display a graph with degree sequence (2, 2, 2, 2, 3, 3, 3, 3).

17. Display a graph with degree sequence (1, 1, 1, 1, 1, 1, 1, 1, 4, 4).

18. Try briefly to construct a graph with degree sequence (1, 1, 2, 2, 3); then explain why it cannot be done.

19. In the labeled graph in Problem 2, find cycles of length 3, 4, 5, and 6.

20. List all the cycles of the graph in Problem 8.

21. How many trails are there from v_1 to v_5 in the graph in Problem 8? Are these trails all paths?

22. List the walks of length 3 from v_1 to v_4 in the labeled graph in Problem 2.

23. The **distance** between two vertices in a connected graph is the length of a shortest path connecting them. What is the distance between v_1 and v_i, $i = 2, 3, \ldots, 10$, in the Petersen graph of Problem 1?

24. What is the distance between any two vertices in a complete graph?

25. Show that in a connected graph any two longest paths must have a vertex in common.

26. Give an example of a graph with vertices u, v, and w such that u and v are on a common cycle, v and w are on a common cycle, but u and w are not on a common cycle.

27. Let **G** be a graph with distinct vertices u, v, and w. Is it true that if e_{uv} and e_{vw} are edges, then e_{uw} is an edge? If there is a path joining u and v and a path joining v and w, then is there a path joining u and w? Why or why not?

28. Let $(v_1, v_2, \ldots, v_k, v_1)$ be a closed trail in **G**. Does **G** necessarily include a cycle? Does **G** necessarily contain a cycle at v_1?

29. What is the maximum number of edges that a graph with four vertices and no triangles can have? Suppose the graph has no triangles and six vertices? (*Hint:* A graph with six vertices and no triangles can have at most nine edges.)

30. The **girth** of a connected graph with cycles is the length of a shortest cycle in the graph. What is the girth of a complete graph with more than two vertices? What is the girth of the Petersen graph?

31. Find a regular graph of degree 3 with 10 vertices that has girth 5. (This is called the **5-cage.**)

32. Find a regular graph of degree 3 with 14 vertices that has girth 6. [This is called the 6-cage (and named the Heawood graph) and is more difficult to find than the 5-cage.]

33. Find a regular graph of degree r with $2r$ vertices that has girth 4 for $r = 2, 3, 4$.

34. What is the maximum number of edges in a disconnected graph with n vertices? First, suppose a graph **G** has k components, $C_1, C_2, \ldots, C_k$. If $k > 2$, then show that adding an edge between C_2 and C_3 leaves a disconnected graph with one more edge than **G** and one less component. Conclude that a disconnected graph with a maximal number of edges has two components.

35. (*Continuation of Problem 34.*) Show that if a graph has k components and a maximal number of edges, then each component is a complete graph.

36. (*Continuation of Problem 34.*) Again, let **G** be a disconnected graph with a maximal number of edges. If **G** has n vertices and two components $\mathbf{C}_1$ and $\mathbf{C}_2$ with m and r vertices, respectively, $m \geq r$, show that $\mathbf{C}_1$ has $\binom{m}{2}$ edges and $\mathbf{C}_2$ has $\binom{r}{2}$ edges, and hence, $\mathbf{G}$ has $\binom{m}{2} + \binom{r}{2}$ edges. [If $r = 1$, recall that $\binom{1}{2} = 0$.]

37. (*Continuation of Problem 34.*) Let $\mathbf{G}$, m, and r ($r > 1$) be as in Problem 36. Suppose $\mathbf{G}_1$ is a graph with two components, one a complete graph with $m + 1$ vertices and the

other a complete graph with $r - 1$ vertices. Why does $\mathbf{G}_1$ have $\binom{m+1}{2} + \binom{r-1}{2}$ edges?

Show that $\binom{m+1}{2} + \binom{r-1}{2} - \binom{m}{2} - \binom{r}{2} = m - r + 1 > 0$. Conclude that $\mathbf{G}_1$ has more edges than $\mathbf{G}$.

38. (*Conclusion of Problem 34.*) Show that if $\mathbf{G}$ is a disconnected graph with a maximal number of edges and n vertices, then $\mathbf{G}$ has two components, one an isolated vertex and the other the complete graph on $n - 1$ vertices.

Section 36.   Graphs and Matrices

Overview for Section 36

- The adjacency matrix and its powers; the interpretation of entries
- Definition of the trace of a matrix
- Calculation of the number of triangles in a graph

Key Concepts: powers of an adjacency matrix, the trace of a matrix, the number of walks of given length, the number of triangles

36.1   If, in a graph, there is a walk from vertex u to vertex v and a walk from vertex v to vertex w, then there is a walk from vertex u to vertex w, another example of transitivity at work. This can be considered a generalization of the notion of adjacency (which is not transitive). In the graph of Figure 36.1, for example, v_1 is adjacent to v_2, v_2 is adjacent to v_3, but v_1 is not adjacent to v_3. There is, however, a walk joining v_1 and v_3; in fact, several walks of various lengths. For certain applications it may be useful to know the minimum length of a walk joining two vertices, or whether there exists a walk of a given length, or how many such walks there might be. Such information is "hard to read" from the diagram of any except a fairly simple graph, but it and more can be obtained from routine matrix calculations.

Let $\mathbf{G}$ be a graph with vertex set $\mathbf{V} = \{v_1, v_2, \ldots, v_n\}$, and let $A = [a_{ij}]$ denote its adjacency matrix, with rows and columns labeled in our customary manner. Consider now the square of A,

$$B = [b_{ij}] = A^2.$$

Our immediate goal is to discover what the entries in B can tell us about the graph $\mathbf{G}$. Recall from the definition of matrix multiplication that for any i and j,

$$b_{ij} = \sum_{k=1}^{n} a_{ik}a_{kj}. \tag{1}$$

(In this and later sections, computations will always be in ordinary arithmetic unless specifically referred to as Boolean.) Suppose that for some k in (1) the term $a_{ik}a_{kj} = 1$. Then $a_{ik} = a_{kj} = 1$, and this implies that both e_{ik} and e_{kj} are edges in the graph. Thus, as defined in paragraph 35.5, there is a walk of length 2 in $\mathbf{G}$ from v_i to v_j, namely, (v_i, v_k, v_j).

Example 1   Let $\mathbf{G} = (\mathbf{V}, \mathbf{E})$ be the graph shown in Figure 36.1. Specifically,

$$\mathbf{V} = \{v_1, v_2, v_3, v_4, v_5, v_6\},$$

$$\mathbf{E} = \{e_{12}, e_{14}, e_{15}, e_{16}, e_{23}, e_{24}, e_{25}, e_{34}, e_{45}, e_{56}\}.$$

The matrix $A = [a_{ij}]$ corresponds to $\mathbf{G}$, and the matrix $B = [b_{ij}]$ is A^2. Consider, for example, the entry

$$b_{15} = \sum_{k=1}^{n} a_{1k}a_{k5} = 3.$$

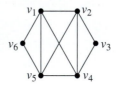

$$A = \begin{bmatrix} 0 & 1 & 0 & 1 & 1 & 1 \\ 1 & 0 & 1 & 1 & 1 & 0 \\ 0 & 1 & 0 & 1 & 0 & 0 \\ 1 & 1 & 1 & 0 & 1 & 0 \\ 1 & 1 & 0 & 1 & 0 & 1 \\ 1 & 0 & 0 & 0 & 1 & 0 \end{bmatrix}$$

$$B = A^2 = \begin{bmatrix} 4 & 2 & 2 & 2 & 3 & 1 \\ 2 & 4 & 1 & 3 & 2 & 2 \\ 2 & 1 & 2 & 1 & 2 & 0 \\ 2 & 3 & 1 & 4 & 2 & 2 \\ 3 & 2 & 2 & 2 & 4 & 1 \\ 1 & 2 & 0 & 2 & 1 & 2 \end{bmatrix}$$

Figure 36.1

This says that there must exist three vertices v_k such that $a_{1k} = a_{k5} = 1$, which implies that e_{1k} and e_{k5} are edges in **G**. From the diagram, these vertices are v_2, v_4, v_6. Thus, there are three walks of length 2 from v_1 to v_5:

$$(v_1, v_2, v_5), \qquad (v_1, v_4, v_5), \qquad (v_1, v_6, v_5).$$

By reversing these arrays, there are three walks of length 2 from v_5 to v_1. Thus, as we observe in the matrix,

$$b_{15} = b_{51} = 3,$$

and, in general, $b_{ij} = b_{ji}$; hence the matrix B is symmetric.

We note that B, unlike A, is not irreflexive. Consider the entry b_{11}. It is the number of walks of length 2 from v_1 to v_1. Since any such walk is of the form

$$(v_1, v_k, v_1)$$

with $e_{1k} \in \mathbf{E}$, it follows that b_{11} simply counts the number of vertices adjacent to v_1 and hence is the degree of v_1. It is also easy to see, arithmetically, why $b_{11} = \deg(v_1)$: b_{11} is the sum of the products of corresponding entries of row 1 and column 1 in A, and since A is symmetric, this simply gives the number of ones in row 1. ●

36.2

As we have just observed, entries on the main diagonal Δ of a square matrix have an important graph-theoretic interpretation. This is not the exception. Courses devoted to matrix theory put major emphasis on the study of Δ because of its fundamental significance in every area of application. Here, we will consider only one of its many facets; a more thorough study would carry us well beyond the introductory purposes of this text.

In applications, it is frequently useful to consider the sum of the entries on the main diagonal, which is given a special name. Thus, for any square matrix $A = [a_{ij}]$, the **trace** of A is

$$\mathrm{Tr}(A) = \sum_{i=1}^{n} a_{ii}. \qquad (1)$$

Referring to Example 1 in paragraph 36.1,

$$\mathrm{Tr}(A) = 0$$

because A is irreflexive, but

$$\mathrm{Tr}(A^2) = 20 = 2 \cdot |\mathbf{E}|,$$

because it is the sum of the degrees of the vertices in **G**, and, by (1) in paragraph 34.6, this is twice the number of edges.

An interesting consequence of this observation is the fact that in any graph **G**,

There is an even number of vertices with odd degree.   **(2)**

This result follows immediately from Theorem 5.6A, because the sum of the degrees is an even number.

Example 1   Figure 36.2A displays a plan of the main floor at Monticello (designed and built by Thomas Jefferson*). To focus attention on an application of (2), the schematic plan

Monticello Floor Plan

The shaded portions indicate the outline of the first house

Figure 36.2A†

*In his later years, Jefferson undertook the construction of a second home called Poplar Forest (near the present city of Lynchburg) where he and his family could enjoy greater privacy than at his much visited Monticello. He was a prolific correspondent and the following excerpt is from a letter dated August 17, 1811, written by Jefferson while at Poplar Forest to his friend Benjamin Rush.

I write to you from a place ninety miles from Monticello . . . which I visit three or four times a year, and stay from a fortnight to a month at a time. I have fixed myself comfortably, keep some books here, bring others occasionally, am in the solitude of a hermit. . . . Having to conduct my grandson through his course in mathematics, I have resumed that study with great avidity. It was ever my favorite one.

†Monticello/Thomas Jefferson Memorial Foundation, Inc.

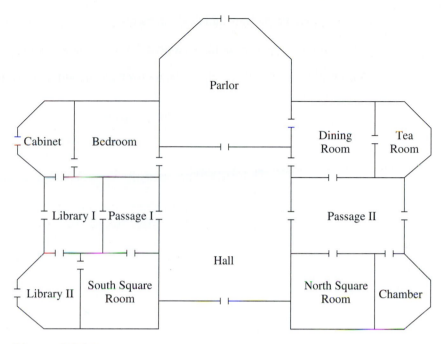

Figure 36.2B

in Figure 36.2B shows only rooms and doorways. Counting the exterior of the house as one (large) room, and including "passages," the plan contains 14 rooms and 22 doors. Now construct a graph, as in Figure 36.2C, having rooms as vertices and doors as edges: An edge joins two vertices if and only if there is a door between the two corresponding rooms. By (2) we claim that the number of vertices of odd degree

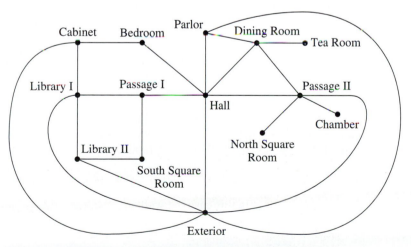

Figure 36.2C

is even, which translates into this statement:

The number of rooms in this floor plan that have an odd number of doors is even.

We observe, in fact, that eight of the rooms have an odd number of doors.   ⬤

Tutorial 36.2

a. Sketch a simplified floor plan of any dwelling that may be familiar to you. (Assume at most one door between any two rooms.)

b. Draw the graph corresponding to your floor plan, and verify the fact stated in (2).

36.3   We will now formalize some of the observations made in Example 1 of paragraph 36.1.

THEOREM 36.3

If the graph $\mathbf{G} = (\mathbf{V}, \mathbf{E})$ has matrix A and if $B = [b_{ij}] = A^2$, then

$$b_{ij} \text{ is the number of walks of length 2 from } v_i \text{ to } v_j.$$

If $i \neq j$, then each of these walks is also a path. For each i,

$$b_{ii} = \deg(v_i) \quad \text{and} \quad \text{Tr}(A^2) = 2 \cdot |\mathbf{E}|.$$

Proof

From (1) in paragraph 36.1, b_{ij} is the number of vertices v_k for which

$$a_{ik} = a_{kj} = 1.$$

Each of these vertices v_k corresponds to a walk

$$(v_i, v_k, v_j).$$

If $i \neq j$, these vertices are distinct and the walk is also a path. If $i = j$, then v_k is adjacent to v_i and, again, b_{ii} is the number of vertices adjacent to v_i. The trace is the sum of the degrees, so by (1) in paragraph 34.6,

$$\text{Tr}(A^2) = 2 \cdot |\mathbf{E}|.$$

Note, however, that in this case the walk

$$(v_i, v_k, v_i)$$

is neither a path nor a trail (for there is a repeated edge).   ◼

Recall that the product of matrices is not commutative, in general. It happens, however, that matrix products *are* associative; thus, if the products are defined,

$$(A \cdot B) \cdot C = A \cdot (B \cdot C). \tag{1}$$

We will omit a proof of this fact here, referring to any text on matrix theory or linear algebra. Powers of a square matrix may be defined inductively, as discussed in paragraph 13.4 (see also Problems 14 and 15 in Section 29):

$$\begin{aligned} A^1 &= A, \\ A^n &= A^{n-1} \cdot A, \qquad \text{for } n > 1. \end{aligned} \tag{2}$$

By (2),

$$\begin{aligned} A^3 &= A^2 \cdot A = A \cdot A^2, \\ A^4 &= A^3 \cdot A = A \cdot A^3, \end{aligned}$$

and so on. Leaving a proof of (3) to Problem 23, we simply remark:

If i and j are positive integers such that $i + j = n$, then

$$A^n = A^i \cdot A^j = A^j \cdot A^i. \tag{3}$$

If A is symmetric, so also is A^n. $\tag{4}$

[*Caution:* Do *not* assume that just because the matrices C and D are symmetric, that $C \cdot D$ is symmetric. See Problems 20 and 21 in Section 29 for a proof of (4).]

36.4

The result in Theorem 36.3 may be generalized to higher powers. For example, let **G** denote the graph in Example 1 of paragraph 36.1 with matrix A and consider the matrix

$$A^3 = A^2 \cdot A = B \cdot A = C = [c_{ij}]$$

computed and displayed in Figure 36.4. To obtain c_{13}, for example, we pick the first row in B and the third column in A, multiply corresponding entries, and add:

$$c_{13} = 4 \cdot 0 + 2 \cdot 1 + 2 \cdot 0 + 2 \cdot 1 + 3 \cdot 0 + 1 \cdot 0 = 4.$$

Now, consider the first term, $4 \cdot 0$. By Theorem 36.3, there are four walks of length 2 from v_1 to v_1; there is no edge between v_1 and v_3; hence there can be no walk of

$$
\begin{bmatrix}
4 & 2 & 2 & 2 & 3 & 1 \\
2 & 4 & 1 & 3 & 2 & 2 \\
2 & 1 & 2 & 1 & 2 & 0 \\
2 & 3 & 1 & 4 & 2 & 2 \\
3 & 2 & 2 & 2 & 4 & 1 \\
1 & 2 & 0 & 2 & 1 & 2
\end{bmatrix}
\cdot
\begin{bmatrix}
0 & 1 & 0 & 1 & 1 & 1 \\
1 & 0 & 1 & 1 & 1 & 0 \\
0 & 1 & 0 & 1 & 0 & 0 \\
1 & 1 & 1 & 0 & 1 & 0 \\
1 & 1 & 0 & 1 & 0 & 1 \\
1 & 0 & 0 & 0 & 1 & 0
\end{bmatrix}
=
\begin{bmatrix}
8 & 11 & 4 & 11 & 9 & 7 \\
11 & 8 & 7 & 9 & 11 & 4 \\
4 & 7 & 2 & 7 & 4 & 4 \\
11 & 9 & 7 & 8 & 11 & 4 \\
9 & 11 & 4 & 11 & 8 & 7 \\
7 & 4 & 4 & 4 & 7 & 2
\end{bmatrix}
$$

Figure 36.4

length 3 from v_1 to v_3 of the form

$$(v_1, v_k, v_1, v_3).$$

Next, consider the term $2 \cdot 1$. By Theorem 36.3, there are two walks of length 2 from v_1 to v_2; there is one edge e_{23}; hence there are two walks of length 3 from v_1 to v_3 of the form

$$(v_1, v_k, v_2, v_3).$$

Continuing, we see that there are two walks of length 3 from v_1 to v_3 of the form

$$(v_1, v_k, v_4, v_3).$$

Altogether, then, there are four walks of length 3 from v_1 to v_3:

$$(v_1, v_4, v_2, v_3), \qquad (v_1, v_5, v_2, v_3), \qquad (v_1, v_2, v_4, v_3), \qquad (v_1, v_5, v_4, v_3).$$

Thus, c_{13} has enumerated the walks of length 3 from v_1 to v_3.

Tutorial 36.4

For the graph in Example I of paragraph 36.1, display the seven walks of length 3 from v_1 to v_6. [*Hint:* One of them is (v_1, v_6, v_1, v_6).]

THEOREM 36.4

Let **G** be a graph with vertex set

$$\mathbf{V} = \{v_1, v_2, \ldots, v_n\},$$

let $A = [a_{ij}]$ denote its adjacency matrix, and for $m > 1$ let $A^{m-1} = [t_{ij}]$ and $A^m = [u_{ij}]$. Then for each i and j, u_{ij} is the number of walks of length m from v_i to v_j.

Proof

(By mathematical induction.) When m is replaced by 2, this theorem reduces to Theorem 36.3, which has already been proved. For $m > 2$, we assume that t_{ij} is the number of walks of length $m - 1$ from v_i to v_j. Now, we must consider

$$u_{ij} = t_{i1}a_{1j} + t_{i2}a_{2j} + \cdots + t_{in}a_{nj}.$$

As before, we analyze each term $t_{ik}a_{kj}$. Note that t_{ik} is the number of walks of length $m - 1$ from v_i to v_k. If $a_{kj} = 0$, then there can be no walk of length m from v_i to v_j

of the form

$$(v_1, \ldots, v_k, v_j).$$

On the other hand, if $a_{kj} = 1$, then e_{kj} is an edge in **G**; hence there are t_{ik} walks of length m from v_i to v_j of the form

$$(v_1, \ldots, v_k, v_j).$$

The entry u_{ij}, thus, enumerates all possible such walks. By PMI, the theorem is true.
∎

36.5

As was the case with A^2, each main diagonal entry in $A^3 = [c_{ij}]$ has an interesting graphical significance. For example, c_{33} is the number of closed walks of length 3 at v_3, each of which must be of the form

$$(v_3, v_k, v_m, v_3), \tag{1}$$

and must involve three different vertices (remember that consecutive vertices in a walk must be different). It corresponds, therefore, to a cycle of length 3 in **G** (i.e., a triangle). Referring to Figure 36.4, for example, $c_{33} = 2$, and the two closed walks are

$$(v_3, v_2, v_4, v_3) \qquad \text{and} \qquad (v_3, v_4, v_2, v_3).$$

Interchanging the middle two vertices does not produce a different triangle; hence $c_{33}/2$ is the number of triangles in **G** which have v_3 as a vertex. We are tempted, therefore, to conclude that $\sum_{i=1}^{n} c_{ii}/2$ is the number of triangles in **G**; but caution prevails. The triangle identified by the closed walk

$$(v_3, v_2, v_4, v_3)$$

is counted also in $c_{22}/2$ and $c_{44}/2$. Therefore, the sum must be divided by 3 to avoid this duplication. Since this special case is in no way exceptional, we will state the following theorem without a formal proof.

THEOREM 36.5A

If A is the adjacency matrix for a graph **G**, and if $A^3 = [c_{ij}]$, then the number of triangles in **G** is

$$\tfrac{1}{6} \cdot \mathrm{Tr}(A^3),$$

and the number of triangles in **G** which have v_i as a vertex is

$$\tfrac{1}{2} \cdot c_{ii}.$$

Consider the graph displayed in Figure 36.2C.
a. How many triangles do you observe in that graph?
b. If A is the matrix for that graph, and assuming that your answer to part **a** is correct, find $\text{Tr}(A^3)$. (*Hint:* Use Theorem 36.5A; do not find A or compute its cube.)
c. What is $\text{Tr}(A^3)$ if there were also a door between the Parlor and Jefferson's Bedroom?

For $m > 3$, the main diagonal of A^m provides additional information about the structure of the graph $\mathbf{G}$, but we will not examine the question beyond the special cases A^2 and A^3. When considering higher powers, it should not be assumed that a relationship such as

$$A^{m-1} \leq A^m$$

will hold. It is entirely possible that $\mathbf{G}$ may have a walk of length $m - 1$ from v_i to v_j, yet have no walk of length m from v_i to v_j. If we are interested in walks of any length ($\leq m$) from v_i to v_j, then we must construct the matrix sum

$$A^* = [s_{ij}] = A + A^2 + \cdots + A^m. \tag{2}$$

If $s_{ij} = 0$, then there exists no walk from v_i to v_j of any length less than $m + 1$; otherwise there are exactly s_{ij} walks from v_i to v_j of various lengths less than $m + 1$.

Any walk from v_i to v_j can be replaced by a path between v_i and v_j consisting of some of its vertices and edges. (This observation will be shown in the Problems.) The following characterization of connectedness is then evident.

THEOREM 36.5B

Let $\mathbf{G}$ be a graph with adjacency matrix A. Then $\mathbf{G}$ is connected if and only if for some positive integer m, the matrix A^*, defined in (2), satisfies

$$s_{ij} > 0 \qquad \text{for all } i \neq j.$$

36.6 **Complement: Bipartite Graphs** Some matrices occur so frequently that it is useful to denote them by special symbols. Recall from paragraph 30.1 that the $n \times n$ matrix of all ones is denoted by J_n, the $n \times n$ matrix with ones on its main diagonal and zeroes elsewhere is denoted by I_n, and that O_n denotes the $n \times n$ matrix with all entries zero.

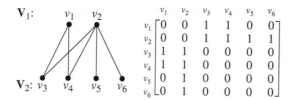

Figure 36.6A

A graph **G** is called **bipartite** if its vertex set **V** is the union of two nonempty disjoint sets $\mathbf{V}_1$ and $\mathbf{V}_2$ such that every edge of **G** has end-vertices in both $\mathbf{V}_1$ and $\mathbf{V}_2$. In Figure 36.6A, a bipartite graph is pictured along with its adjacency matrix. It is sometimes helpful to assume that the vertices in $\mathbf{V}_1$ are red and the vertices in $\mathbf{V}_2$ are blue. Hence, a graph is bipartite if each edge has one red end-vertex and one blue end-vertex.

The adjacency matrix in Figure 36.6A can be expressed conveniently by

$$\begin{bmatrix} O_2 & A \\ A^t & O_4 \end{bmatrix},$$

where A is the 2×4 submatrix

$$\begin{bmatrix} 1 & 1 & 0 & 0 \\ 1 & 1 & 1 & 1 \end{bmatrix}$$

and A^t is its transpose. This pattern is typical of bipartite graphs.

THEOREM 36.6A

A graph with n vertices is bipartite if and only if its vertices can be labeled so that its adjacency matrix is of the form

$$\begin{bmatrix} O_k & A \\ A^t & O_m \end{bmatrix}, \tag{1}$$

where $n = k + m$ and both k and m are positive integers.

Proof

Let the red vertices (the ones in $\mathbf{V}_1$) be $v_1, v_2, \ldots, v_k$, and let the blue vertices be $v_{k+1}, v_{k+2}, \ldots, v_{k+m} = v_n$. Let the rows and columns of the adjacency matrix be labeled sequentially by $v_1, v_2, \ldots, v_n$ (as usual). Clearly the adjacency matrix will be as in (1), since no two vertices in $\mathbf{V}_1$ are adjacent and no two vertices in $\mathbf{V}_2$ are adjacent.

Likewise, if the adjacency matrix is as in (1), then we simply let the red vertices be $v_1, \ldots, v_k$ and the blue vertices be $v_{k+1}, \ldots, v_{k+m}$. Again, all edges have one red end-vertex and one blue end-vertex. ∎

A bipartite graph need not be connected. Trivially, the null graph on two vertices is bipartite: If

$$\mathbf{V}_1 = \{v_1\} \quad \text{and} \quad \mathbf{V}_2 = \{v_2\},$$

then its adjacency matrix is of the form (1)

$$\begin{bmatrix} 0 & 0 \\ 0 & 0 \end{bmatrix} = \begin{bmatrix} O_1 & A \\ A^t & O_1 \end{bmatrix}$$

where $A = O_1 = A^t$. An isolated vertex (one adjacent to no edge) can be adjoined to a bipartite graph without compromising its "bipartiteness," so we will assume that none of the graphs to be considered in the rest of this complement have isolated vertices. Less trivially, the graph $\mathbf{G} = (\mathbf{V}, \mathbf{E})$ with three components shown in Figure 36.6B is bipartite. Each component has its own adjacency matrix of the form (1), as given. To show that the adjacency matrix for $\mathbf{G}$ can be put in the form (1), let $\mathbf{V} = \mathbf{V}_1 \cup \mathbf{V}_2$, where $\mathbf{V}_1 = \{v_1, v_2, v_3, v_4, v_5\}$ and $\mathbf{V}_2 = \{v_6, v_7, v_8, v_9, v_{10}\}$. Just as indicated here, a graph in general is bipartite if and only if each of its components is bipartite.

Given two distinct vertices v_1 and v_2 in the same component of a graph, there is at least one path between them, and there may be several of various lengths. The length of the shortest such path is called the **distance** between v_1 and v_2, which we will denote by $\text{dist}(v_1, v_2)$. In Figure 36.6B, for example, $\text{dist}(v_2, v_7) = 1$, $\text{dist}(v_2, v_3) = 2$, and $\text{dist}(v_8, v_{10}) = 2$. For convenience, we will agree that for any vertex v,

$$\text{dist}(v, v) = 0.$$

If a graph $\mathbf{G}$ has no cycles, then we will refer to this by the statement that $\mathbf{G}$'s cycles are of length 0 (an even number, recall). Note that the two smaller components of the graph in Figure 36.6B have cycles of length 0. More generally, bipartite graphs may have cycles of positive length, but there *is* a restriction. Consider any cycle in a bipartite graph $\mathbf{G}$. Let's start at a red vertex. Since all edges have end-vertices of

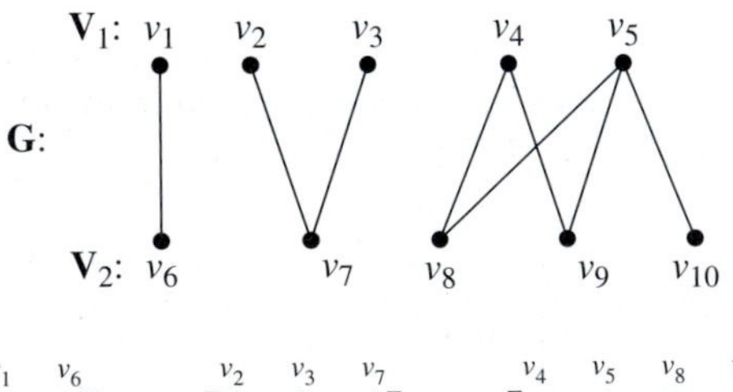

$$
v_1 \begin{array}{c} {}^{v_1 \; v_6} \\ v_6 \end{array}\begin{bmatrix} 0 & 1 \\ 1 & 0 \end{bmatrix}
\qquad
\begin{array}{c} {}^{v_2 \; v_3 \; v_7} \\ v_2 \\ v_3 \\ v_7 \end{array}\begin{bmatrix} 0 & 0 & 1 \\ 0 & 0 & 1 \\ 1 & 1 & 0 \end{bmatrix}
\qquad
\begin{array}{c} {}^{v_4 \; v_5 \; v_8 \; v_9 \; v_{10}} \\ v_4 \\ v_5 \\ v_8 \\ v_9 \\ v_{10} \end{array}\begin{bmatrix} 0 & 0 & 1 & 1 & 0 \\ 0 & 0 & 1 & 1 & 1 \\ 1 & 1 & 0 & 0 & 0 \\ 1 & 1 & 0 & 0 & 0 \\ 0 & 1 & 0 & 0 & 0 \end{bmatrix}
$$

Figure 36.6B

both colors, it is obvious that the cycle is as follows:

$$r \rightarrow b \rightarrow r \rightarrow b \rightarrow \cdots \rightarrow r \rightarrow b \rightarrow r,$$

where $r \rightarrow b$ means we have gone from a red vertex to a blue vertex (and similarly for $b \rightarrow r$). The length of this cycle is even since each red vertex is reached after an even number of edges have been selected. Thus, any cycle in a bipartite graph must have even length. It happens in this case that the converse is also true; hence bipartite graphs are characterized by the condition that all cycles are of even length.

THEOREM 36.6B

A graph is bipartite if and only if all its cycles have even length.

Proof

The "only if" part of the theorem follows from the argument in the preceding paragraph. Now, we assume that $\mathbf{G} = (\mathbf{V}, \mathbf{E})$ is a graph in which all cycles have even length. Choose any vertex, say v_1, in $\mathbf{G}$ and define

$$\mathbf{V}_1 = \{v_i : \text{dist}(v_1, v_i) \text{ is even}\}$$

$$\mathbf{V}_2 = \mathbf{V} - \mathbf{V}_1.$$

By our assumption that $\mathbf{G}$ has no isolated vertices, there exist edges joining vertices in $\mathbf{V}_1$ with vertices in $\mathbf{V}_2$. We will prove that there is no edge joining two vertices in $\mathbf{V}_1$; a similar argument will show that there is no edge joining two vertices in $\mathbf{V}_2$.

Suppose on the contrary that v_i and v_j are in $\mathbf{V}_1$ and that $e_{ij} \in \mathbf{E}$. Note, first, that if $v_i = v_1$, then $\text{dist}(v_1, v_j) = 1$, which contradicts the fact that $v_j \in \mathbf{V}_1$. Hence, $v_i \neq v_1$, and by the same argument $v_j \neq v_1$. Next, we note that there are positive integers p and q such that

$$\text{dist}(v_i, v_1) = 2p \qquad \text{and} \qquad \text{dist}(v_j, v_1) = 2q. \qquad (2)$$

Let $\mathbf{P}_i$ be a shortest path from v_i to v_1, and let $\mathbf{P}_j$ be a shortest path from v_j to v_1. There are two cases to consider.

Case 1. Suppose there is no vertex, except v_1, common to $\mathbf{P}_i$ and $\mathbf{P}_j$. Then the union of $\mathbf{P}_i$ and $\mathbf{P}_j$ together with e_{ij} forms a cycle of length $2p + 2q + 1$, which contradicts the hypothesis (that all cycles are even).

Case 2. Suppose there is a vertex different from v_1 which is common to $\mathbf{P}_i$ and $\mathbf{P}_j$. Then there is such a vertex, say v_k, which is closest to v_i and v_j. It is clear that

$$\text{dist}(v_i, v_1) = \text{dist}(v_i, v_k) + \text{dist}(v_k, v_1)$$

and

$$\text{dist}(v_j, v_1) = \text{dist}(v_j, v_k) + \text{dist}(v_k, v_1).$$

Thus there exists a cycle which includes v_i, v_j, and v_k of length

$$(\text{dist}(v_i, v_1) - \text{dist}(v_k, v_1)) + (\text{dist}(v_j, v_1) - \text{dist}(v_k, v_1)) + 1,$$

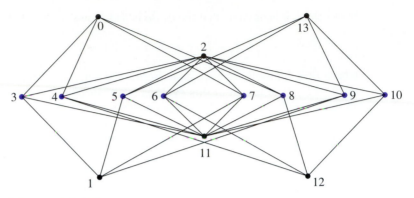

Figure 36.6C

where the 1 is for the edge e_{ij}. By (2) the length of this cycle is

$$2p + 2q + 1 - 2 \cdot \text{dist}(v_k, v_1),$$

which is odd, and, again, the hypothesis is contradicted.

Thus, the existence of the edge e_{ij} leads to a contradiction, and in the same way the existence of an edge between two vertices in $\mathbf{V}_2$ leads to a contradiction. Hence, the graph on the vertex set $\mathbf{V}_1 \cup \mathbf{V}_2$ must be bipartite.

Finally, we note that if the set $\mathbf{V}_1 \cup \mathbf{V}_2$ fails to exhaust $\mathbf{V}$, then the process continues beginning with a vertex in $\mathbf{V} - (\mathbf{V}_1 \cup \mathbf{V}_2)$ and produces a second component of $\mathbf{G}$. Finitely many repetitions suffice to prove that each component of $\mathbf{G}$ is bipartite; hence $\mathbf{G}$, itself, is bipartite. ∎

In paragraph 35.7, we defined a graph on n vertices as hamiltonian if it had a cycle of length n. From Theorem 36.6B, it is immediate that if a bipartite graph has an odd number of vertices, then it is not hamiltonian. But even if a bipartite graph has an even number of vertices, it cannot be hamiltonian unless it has equally many red and blue vertices. (Try to construct a hamiltonian cycle in a complete bipartite graph for which this condition fails!) With the above observations, it shouldn't take you long to show that "The Numbered Moth" in Figure 36.6C is not hamiltonian.

Problems for Section 36

1. Let $\mathbf{G} = \begin{array}{c} v_1 \quad v_2 \\ \diagdown\!\!\diagup \\ v_4 \quad v_3 \end{array}$. Find the adjacency matrix A for $\mathbf{G}$ and compute A^2.

2. (*Continuation of Problem 1.*) From A^2, find the number of walks of length 2 from (*a*) v_1 to v_1, (*b*) v_1 to v_3, (*c*) v_2 to v_2, (*d*) v_2 to v_3.

(*e*) Confirm these numbers by identifying the walks in $\mathbf{G}$.

3. (*Continuation of Problem 1.*) Using A and A^2, compute A^3.

4. (*Continuation of Problem 1.*) From A^3, find the number of walks of length 3 from (*a*) v_4

to v_4, (b) v_4 to v_3. (c) Confirm these numbers by identifying the walks in **G**.

5. (*Conclusion of Problem 1.*) From A^3, confirm that the number of triangles in **G** is 2 and that both of them contain v_2.

6. Let $\mathbf{G} = $

. Find the adjacency matrix A for **G** and compute A^2.

7. (*Continuation of Problem 6.*) Using A^2, determine the number of walks in **G** of length 2 from v_1 to each of the five vertices.

8. (*Continuation of Problem 6.*) Using A and A^2, compute A^3.

9. (*Continuation of Problem 6.*) Using A^3, determine the number of walks in **G** of length 3 from v_3 to v_4.

10. (*Conclusion of Problem 6.*) Using A^3, determine the number of triangles in **G**.

11. Let $\mathbf{G} = $

. Find the adjacency matrix A for **G** and compute A^2.

12. (*Continuation of Problem 11.*) Confirm the relationship between the entries on the main diagonal of A^2 and the degrees of the vertices in **G**.

13. (*Conclusion of Problem 11.*) Without computing the matrix A^3, find $\text{Tr}(A^3)$.

14. Let **G** be the graph with matrix

$$A = \begin{bmatrix} 0 & 1 & 1 & 0 & 1 & 1 & 0 \\ 1 & 0 & 0 & 1 & 1 & 0 & 1 \\ 1 & 0 & 0 & 1 & 0 & 1 & 1 \\ 0 & 1 & 1 & 0 & 1 & 1 & 0 \\ 1 & 1 & 0 & 1 & 0 & 0 & 1 \\ 1 & 0 & 1 & 1 & 0 & 0 & 1 \\ 0 & 1 & 1 & 0 & 1 & 1 & 0 \end{bmatrix}.$$

Draw the diagram for **G**. Without computing A^2, determine $\text{Tr}(A^2)$.

15. Using (2) in paragraph 36.2, show that at any party the number of people who shake an odd number of hands is even. [Because of this, (2) in paragraph 36.2 is often called the *Handshaking Lemma*.]

16. The adjacency matrix A_n for a complete graph on n vertices is $A_n = J_n - I_n$; i.e., it is all ones except for zeroes on the diagonal. Compute A_2^2, A_3^2, A_4^2, and A_5^2.

17. (*Continuation of Problem 16.*) Show that $A_n^2 = (n-2)J_n + I_n$ by first showing that for $i \neq j$, the number of paths of length 2 from v_i to v_j is $n-2$. Then observe that a complete graph is regular of degree $n-1$.

18. (*Continuation of Problem 16.*) Show that $A_n^2 = (n-2)J_n + I_n$ by showing that $(J_n - I_n)^2 = J_n^2 - J_nI_n - I_nJ_n + I_n^2$. (*Hint:* $J_n^2 = nJ_n$.)

19. (*Continuation of Problem 16.*) Compute A_2^3, A_3^3, and A_4^3.

20. (*Continuation of Problem 16.*) By using $(J_n - I_n)^3 = (J_n - I_n)(J_n - I_n)^2 = (J_n - I_n)((n-2)J_n + I_n)$, show $A_n^3 = (n^2 - 3n + 3)J_n - I_n$.

21. (*Continuation of Problem 16.*) Show that the diagonal entries of A_n^3 are $2\binom{n-1}{2}$ by observing that any three vertices of a complete graph form a triangle.

22. (*Conclusion of Problem 16.*) Let $A_n^3 = [c_{ij}]$. For $i \neq j$, c_{ij} is the number of walks of length 3 from v_i to v_j. There are four types of these walks. (a) (v_i, v_k, v_m, v_j), where all subscripts are different. To count the number of such walks, remember that (v_i, v_k, v_m, v_j) and (v_i, v_m, v_k, v_j) are counted as different walks and so we want the number of permutations of $n-2$ vertices taken two at a time. (b) (v_i, v_k, v_i, v_j), where k is not i or j. How many of these are there? (c) (v_i, v_j, v_m, v_j), where m is not i or j. How many of these are there? (d) (v_i, v_j, v_i, v_j). (e) Show that the

sum of the number of walks in parts (a), (b), (c), and (d) is $2\binom{n-1}{2} + 1$.

23. Using the Well-Ordering Axiom and the definition $A^n = A^{n-1}A$, show that if $i, j > 0$ and $i + j = n$, then $A^n = A^i A^j$.

24. If $W = (v_1, v_2, \ldots, v_m)$ is a walk in a graph, then the following algorithm will give a path $P = (u_1, u_2, \ldots, u_r)$ from $u_1 = v_1$ to $u_r = v_m$ using only vertices and edges in the walk W. **Step 1.** Let u_1 be v_1 and $i = 1$. **Step 2.** Find the largest subscript k such that $u_i = v_k$. (Note that k could be i.) **Step 3.** Let u_{i+1} be v_{k+1}. **Step 4.** If u_{i+1} is v_m, then we are done. Otherwise, increase i by 1 and go to step 2. ▲ Verify that this algorithm finds a path from v_1 to v_4 in the walk $(v_1, v_2, v_3, v_6, v_7, v_3, v_5, v_4, v_3, v_7, v_6, v_3, v_4)$ in the graph in Figure 35.5.

25. (*Continuation of Problem 24.*) To show that the algorithm in Problem 24 produces a path, first show that there is an edge of W between u_i and u_{i+1}; then show that all vertices in P are distinct.

26. (*Conclusion of Problem 24.*) The reverse of the walk given in Problem 24 is a walk from v_4 to v_1. Use the algorithm on the reverse walk to find a path from v_4 to v_1. Note that this is not the reverse of the path found from v_1 to v_4. In fact, the two paths are of different lengths!

27. The **incidence** matrix of a graph G with n vertices $\{v_1, \ldots, v_n\}$ and m edges $\{e_1, \ldots, e_m\}$ is an $n \times m$ matrix $B = [b_{ij}]$ with $b_{ij} = 1$ if v_i is incident with e_j and $b_{ij} = 0$ otherwise. What are the incident matrices for

$$G_1 = $$

and $G_2 = $

28. (*Conclusion of Problem 27.*) If B is the incidence matrix of $G = (V, E)$, $V = \{v_1, \ldots, v_n\}$, and $E = \{e_1, \ldots, e_m\}$, then what is the ith row sum of B and what is each column sum of B?

29. How many columns does an incidence matrix of a complete graph with n vertices have? How many columns does an incidence matrix of a cycle with n vertices have? Write out the incidence matrix for the cycle $(v_1, v_2, v_3, v_4, v_5, v_1)$ with $e_1 = e_{12}, e_2 = e_{23}, \ldots, e_5 = e_{51}$.

30. This problem generalizes the results found in Problems 16 to 22. (a) Show by induction on m that $J_n^m = n^{m-1}J_n$. (b) Since $J_nI_n = I_nJ_n = J_n$ and $I_n^k = I_n$, we can use the Binomial Theorem to expand $A_n^m = (J_n - I_n)^m$. Verify that

$$(J_n - I_n)^m = J_n^m + \left(\sum_{k=1}^{m-1}\binom{m}{k}J_n^k(-1)^{m-k}I_n^{m-k}\right)$$
$$+ (-1)^m I_n^m$$

$$= J_n\left(\sum_{k=1}^{m}(-1)^{m-k}n^{k-1}\binom{m}{k}\right)$$
$$+ (-1)^m I_n^m.$$

(c) Using the Binomial Theorem, verify that

$$(n-1)^m - (-1)^m = \sum_{k=1}^{m}(-1)^{m-k}n^k\binom{m}{k}.$$

(d) Conclude that the diagonal entries of A_n^m are

$$\frac{(n-1)^m - (-1)^m}{n} + (-1)^m$$

and the off-diagonal entries are

$$\frac{(n-1)^m - (-1)^m}{n}.$$

Section 37.   Isomorphism in Graph Theory

37.1   The map coloring problem, which initiated our study of graphs in paragraph 34.1, was reduced to a consideration of the diagram reproduced here in part (*a*) of Figure 37.1A. The solution to the problem (determining the minimum number of colors required) depended in no way on the names of the states or on their relative geographic orientation but only on the manner in which they were linked by common boundary lines. Both parts of Figure 37.1A contain exactly the same pertinent information. Thus, we could answer our question about the map of New England by examining the graph in part (*b*) of Figure 37.1A. It is this idea of "abstracting" only pertinent information that we now explore, and in this context graph theory *becomes* a search for patterns and for techniques of distinguishing among patterns.

In previous sections our concern has been with graphs identified by a vertex set

$$\mathbf{V} = \{v_1, v_2, \ldots, v_n\} \tag{1}$$

of distinguishable elements and a set **E** of edges determined by specified end-vertices. Such graphs are referred to as **labeled;** an example is the graph in Figure

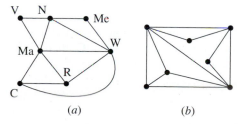

(*a*)   (*b*)

Figure 37.1A

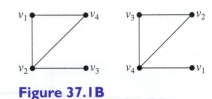

Figure 37.1B

36.2C which has vertices labeled by room names. Frequently, vertices are given labels which serve merely to distinguish one from another, as in (1). Equality of graphs, defined in Section 35, is dependent upon such labeling; the enumerations discussed in Section 34 also depend upon labeling. But many properties, like some of those related to coloring or connectedness, are independent of labeling. The two graphs shown in Figure 37.1B are different as labeled graphs, yet if the labels were erased, the two would be indistinguishable. In general, given a graph $G = (V, E)$, when the vertex labels are erased a structure remains which still has $|V|$ vertices and $|E|$ edges; it is called an **unlabeled** graph. In the remainder of this section the unmodified word "graph" will refer to an unlabeled graph (in which there is no intrinsic distinction among vertices). The graph diagram remains an important tool in communicating structural properties, but visual distinction must be employed cautiously, as illustrated in the following example.

Example 1

The graph displayed in part (*a*) of Figure 37.1C models a simple truss designed for a bridge across a small stream. The graph consists of 8 vertices and 13 edges with degree sequence (2, 2, 3, 3, 3, 4, 4, 5). As real structures, one could clearly distinguish the shape in part (*b*) of Figure 37.1C from that in (*a*), yet as unlabeled graphs, determined solely by vertices and edges, the two have essentially the same pattern. (The precise nature of this "sameness" is our next concern.)

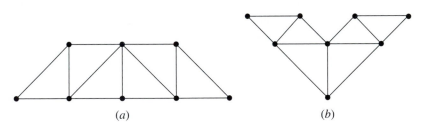

(*a*)   (*b*)

Figure 37.1C

37.2

Any unlabeled graph G can be converted into a labeled graph simply by assigning labels (say, $v_1, v_2, \ldots$) to its vertices. The edges of G, then, can be determined by the labels of the end-vertices. For each graph in Figure 37.1C, suppose we assign labels to each vertex (as in Figure 37.2A). As labeled graphs, the two now have the same vertex and edge sets

$$V = \{v_1, v_2, v_3, v_4, v_5, v_6, v_7, v_8\},$$

$$E = \{e_{12}, e_{13}, e_{18}, e_{23}, e_{34}, e_{38}, e_{45}, e_{48}, e_{56}, e_{57}, e_{58}, e_{67}, e_{78}\};$$

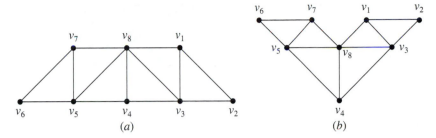

Figure 37.2A

hence they are identical. This is the key idea: Two graphs have the same **pattern** if the elements in each vertex set can be labeled with the same symbols so that the edge sets are identical. Mathematicians describe this situation by the word "isomorphism," derived from the Greek words "isos" (meaning "equal") and "morphe" (meaning "form").

More precisely, the technical definition of "sameness" is as follows:

Two graphs $G_1 = (V_1, E_1)$ and $G_2 = (V_2, E_2)$ are called **isomorphic** if there exists a one-to-one and onto correspondence $f: V_1 \rightarrow V_2$ such that $\{v_1, v_2\} \in E_1$ if and only if $\{f(v_1), f(v_2)\} \in E_2$.

This condition is often paraphrased by: G_1 and G_2 are isomorphic if there exists a one-to-one correspondence between the vertex sets which preserves adjacency.

Tutorial 37.2

Refer to the graphs in Figure 37.1B.
a. Give a one-to-one correspondence f between the vertices in these two graphs which shows that they are isomorphic.
b. Under this correspondence, is $f(v_i) = v_i$ for any i?
c. Sketch the diagram of the graph $G' = (V', E')$, where

$V' = \{v_1, v_2, v_3, v_4\}$ and $E' = \{e_{12}, e_{23}, e_{34}, e_{41}\}.$

d. Is G' isomorphic to the graph in Figure 37.1B?

Example 1   The two graphs diagrammed in Figure 37.1A are isomorphic. An appropriate one-to-one correspondence is indicated in Figure 37.2B.

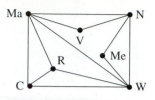

Figure 37.2B

37.3

The importance of "isomorphism" in graph theory rests upon the following fact.

THEOREM 37.3

Among all graphs, isomorphism is an equivalence relation.

Sketch of Proof

Using the symbol introduced in Section 33, we will write $\mathbf{G}_1 \sim \mathbf{G}_2$ to mean that the graphs $\mathbf{G}_1$ and $\mathbf{G}_2$ are isomorphic. The theorem is proved by showing that isomorphism is reflexive, symmetric, and transitive.

a. To show that $\mathbf{G}_1 \sim \mathbf{G}_1$, simply pick $f \colon \mathbf{V}_1 \to \mathbf{V}_1$ to be the identity function.

b. Suppose that $\mathbf{G}_1 \sim \mathbf{G}_2$ and that

$$f \colon \mathbf{V}_1 \to \mathbf{V}_2$$

is an appropriate one-to-one correspondence. By interchanging the coordinates of each ordered pair in f we obtain a one-to-one, onto correspondence

$$f^{-1} \colon \mathbf{V}_2 \to \mathbf{V}_1,$$

which preserves adjacency.

c. Suppose that $\mathbf{G}_1 \sim \mathbf{G}_2$ and $\mathbf{G}_2 \sim \mathbf{G}_3$, and let

$$f_1 \colon \mathbf{V}_1 \to \mathbf{V}_2, \qquad f_2 \colon \mathbf{V}_2 \to \mathbf{V}_3,$$

be appropriate one-to-one correspondences. Then $f_3 = f_2 \circ f_1$ is a one-to-one, onto correspondence

$$f_3 \colon \mathbf{V}_1 \to \mathbf{V}_3,$$

which preserves adjacency.   ∎

As noted earlier, one of our goals is to identify properties which distinguish between unlabeled graphs. For certain special types of graphs, the size of the vertex set

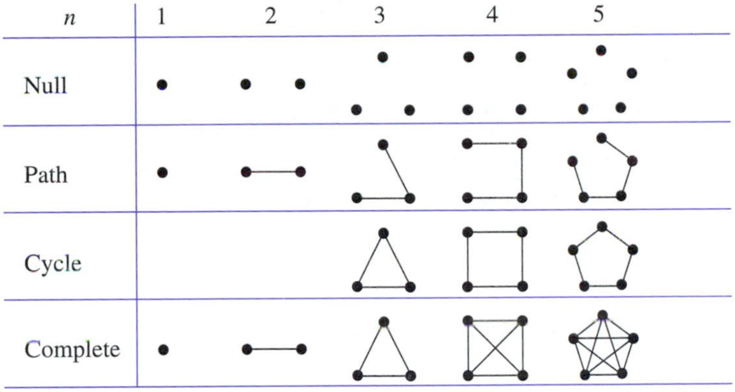

Figure 37.3A

determines the pattern completely. Among these are the null graphs, paths, cycles, and complete graphs (as illustrated in Figure 37.3A).

   The graphs shown in Figure 37.3A illustrate the observation that unlabeled graphs on different numbers of vertices are clearly different; no one-to-one correspondence can exist between V_1 and V_2 if $|V_1| \neq |V_2|$. On the other hand, there may be many different patterns on the same number of vertices. If we let $\mathcal{G}_n$ denote the set of all labeled graphs on n vertices, then $\mathcal{G}_n/\sim$ is the set of all equivalence classes (see Section 33). Two graphs in the same equivalence class are isomorphic and hence determine the same pattern. For this reason, we could define an equivalence class to be a pattern (this is essentially the same as our earlier use of the term). The problem of enumerating unlabeled graphs is the same as that of enumerating patterns, and it requires techniques beyond the level of this book. Of course, we would expect the number of labeled graphs to be much larger, in general, than the number of unlabeled graphs (since one unlabeled graph corresponds to a whole equivalence class of labeled graphs). For comparison, we list a few of these numbers in Table 37.3. With $|V| = n$, we let $l(n)$ denote the number of labeled graphs and let $u(n)$ denote the number of unlabeled graphs (patterns). Beyond $n = 7$, these numbers increase dramatically.

n	1	2	3	4	5	6	7
$l(n)$	1	2	8	64	1024	2^{15}	2^{21}
$u(n)$	1	2	4	11	34	156	1044

Table 37.3

Example 1   In Figure 37.3B we list (as diagrams) the eight labeled graphs with vertex set $\{v_1, v_2, v_3\}$ partitioned into the four equivalence classes (patterns) indicated in Table 37.3.

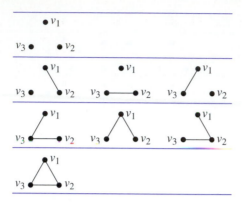

Figure 37.3B

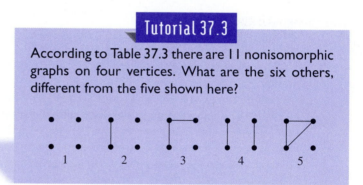

Tutorial 37.3

According to Table 37.3 there are 11 nonisomorphic graphs on four vertices. What are the six others, different from the five shown here?

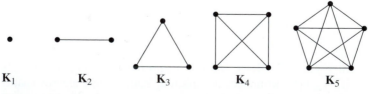

1   2   3   4   5

37.4

The complete, unlabeled graph on n vertices, often denoted by $\mathbf{K}_n$, contains $\binom{n}{2}$ edges; for $n = 1, 2, 3, 4,$ and 5, their graphs appear in Figure 37.4A.

Any graph $\mathbf{G} = (\mathbf{V}, \mathbf{E})$ on n vertices is a spanning subgraph of the complete graph $\mathbf{K}_n$ on the vertex set $\mathbf{V}$. Now imagine that each edge of $\mathbf{K}_n$ has been colored red or blue so that an edge is red if and only if it belongs to $\mathbf{E}$. Then the spanning subgraph of $\mathbf{K}_n$ with edge set consisting of the blue edges is called the **complement** of $\mathbf{G}$ and is denoted by $\overline{\mathbf{G}}$. There is a simple procedure for constructing the matrix corresponding to the complement of a graph $\mathbf{G}$ with adjacency matrix $[a_{ij}]$. We used

K_1 K_2 K_3 K_4 K_5

Figure 37.4A

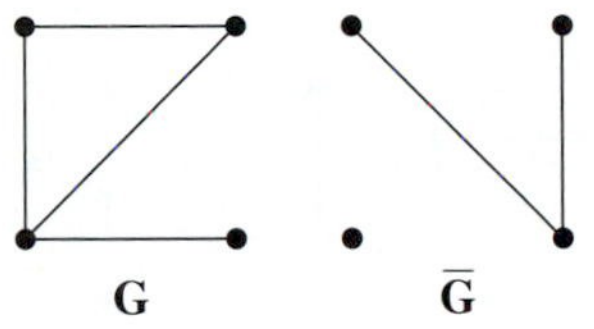

$$G \qquad \overline{G}$$

Figure 37.4B

this procedure in paragraph 34.7: The complement $\overline{G}$ of G has as its matrix $[b_{ij}]$, where

$$b_{ij} = \begin{cases} 0, & \text{if } i = j; \\ 1 - a_{ij}, & \text{if } i \neq j. \end{cases} \tag{1}$$

Of course, the rows and columns of $[a_{ij}]$ and $[b_{ij}]$ must correspond to the same vertices in $\mathbf{V}$.

Example 1 Consider the graphs $\mathbf{G}$ and $\overline{\mathbf{G}}$ given in Figure 37.4B. If

$$[a_{ij}] = \begin{bmatrix} 0 & 1 & 1 & 1 \\ 1 & 0 & 0 & 0 \\ 1 & 0 & 0 & 1 \\ 1 & 0 & 1 & 0 \end{bmatrix}$$

is a matrix for $\mathbf{G}$, then

$$[b_{ij}] = \begin{bmatrix} 0 & 0 & 0 & 0 \\ 0 & 0 & 1 & 1 \\ 0 & 1 & 0 & 0 \\ 0 & 1 & 0 & 0 \end{bmatrix}$$

is the corresponding matrix for $\overline{\mathbf{G}}$. (The reader should label the vertices of $\mathbf{G}$ to match the rows of the matrix $[a_{ij}]$.)

It is possible to construct a diagram for $\mathbf{K}_4$ which has no extra crossings (see Figure 37.4C), but this is not possible for $\mathbf{K}_5$. We can almost do it, as in Figure 37.4C, but there is no way to draw the final "shaded" edge without crossing one

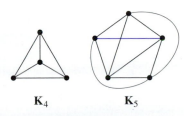

$$\mathbf{K}_4 \qquad\qquad \mathbf{K}_5$$

Figure 37.4C

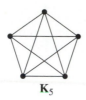
$\mathbf{K}_5$

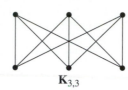
$\mathbf{K}_{3,3}$

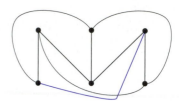

Figure 37.4D   **Figure 37.4E**

of the other edges already drawn. A graph, for example $\mathbf{K}_4$, which can be drawn on a page without extra crossings is called **planar.** One of the most famous and impressive theorems in graph theory characterizes a graph as planar provided it has no subgraph which, in a technical sense not described here, "looks like" either of the two graphs shown in Figure 37.4D. This theorem was published by Kazimierz Kuratowski (1896–1980) in 1930.

As with $\mathbf{K}_5$, the graph $\mathbf{K}_{3,3}$ as diagrammed in Figure 37.4D is almost planar (as shown in Figure 37.4E), but there is no way to make the shaded-line connection without crossing a previously drawn edge. We will postpone further consideration of planarity to Section 41; the concept is important in computer design and is studied in much greater detail in more advanced courses in graph theory.

The graph diagrammed in Figure 37.4E is of a type called **bipartite** in which the vertex set is partitioned into two nonempty subsets,

$$\mathbf{V} = \mathbf{V}_1 \cup \mathbf{V}_2, \qquad \text{with } |\mathbf{V}| = n = |\mathbf{V}_1| + |\mathbf{V}_2|,$$

and no edge joins two vertices in the same subset. Each of the following, for example, is a bipartite graph.

$\mathbf{V}_1$:

$\mathbf{V}_2$:

    (a)   (b)   (c)   (d)

If every possible edge joining vertices in $\mathbf{V}_1$ with those in $\mathbf{V}_2$ is in $\mathbf{G}$, then $\mathbf{G}$ is called a **complete bipartite** graph, denoted by $\mathbf{K}_{r,s}$ where $|\mathbf{V}_1| = r$ and $|\mathbf{V}_2| = s$. This is why the graph in Figure 37.4D is designated $\mathbf{K}_{3,3}$.

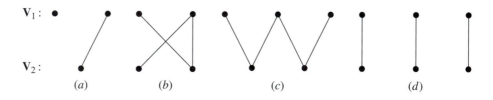

Tutorial 37.4

a. As with $K_{3,3}$ of Figure 37.4D, draw the diagram of $K_{3,2}$.
b. Show by a diagram that $K_{3,2}$ is planar.

37.5

We introduce the next theorem with a puzzle. Can you shade the edges of K_4 light and dark so that neither the light graph nor the dark graph contains a triangle (i.e., contains K_3 as a subgraph)? The answer is easy; by trial and error you can find several ways to do it, two of which are given in (a) of Figure 37.5A. Consider the similar puzzle for K_5. This time the search may not be so easy, but after a little trial and error you will discover the diagram illustrated in part (b) of Figure 37.5A. Note that this diagram has equal numbers of light and dark edges. Spend a few minutes thinking about this problem if the shades are not used equally.

For K_6 the situation abruptly changes! No matter how you shade the edges light or dark, it is impossible to avoid either a light triangle or a dark triangle. The precise statement is given in Theorem 37.5.

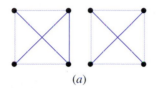

(a)   (b)

Figure 37.5A

Figure 37.5B

THEOREM 37.5

Let **G** be any spanning subgraph of K_6 and let $\overline{\mathbf{G}}$ denote its complement. Then either **G** or $\overline{\mathbf{G}}$ contains a triangle.

Proof

As in Figure 37.5B, let p denote any vertex of K_6 and note that $\deg(p) = 5$. Since these edges (at p) are divided between two graphs **G** and $\overline{\mathbf{G}}$, the average number of edges per vertex is $\frac{5}{2}$. But there cannot be fractional edges; hence $\deg(p) \geq 3$ in either **G** or $\overline{\mathbf{G}}$. The argument is similar in each case, so we may suppose that $\deg(p) \geq 3$ in **G**. Let **U** denote the set of vertices in **G** adjacent to p, and note that $|\mathbf{U}| \geq 3$. Let **H** denote the subgraph of **G** induced by **U**. Now the answer is at hand: Either **H** is a null graph [see part (a) of Figure 37.5C] or **H** contains at least one edge [see part (b) of Figure 37.5C]. In the first case, $\overline{\mathbf{G}}$ must contain a triangle (among the vertices in **H**), and in the second case, any edge in **H** together with the two edges between its end-vertices and p form a triangle in **G**. ∎

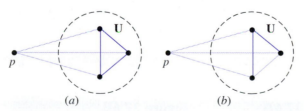

(a)   (b)

Figure 37.5C

From the discussion above, we may conclude the following: 6 is the smallest integer such that for any graph $\mathbf{G}$ on six vertices either $\mathbf{G}$ or $\overline{\mathbf{G}}$ *must* contain at least one $\mathbf{K}_3$ as a subgraph. This observation suggests a problem which is typical of a broad class of problems seeking to minimize some numerical characteristic of graphs. What is the smallest integer n such that no matter how $\mathbf{K}_n$ is partitioned into complementary subgraphs $\mathbf{G}$ and $\overline{\mathbf{G}}$, at least one of them contains a specified complete subgraph (say $\mathbf{K}_m$)? For $\mathbf{K}_3$, the answer is $n = 6$, for no matter how $\mathbf{K}_6$ is partitioned into complementary subgraphs $\mathbf{G}$ and $\overline{\mathbf{G}}$, at least one of them contains $\mathbf{K}_3$. In the case of $\mathbf{K}_4$, the answer is also known: 18 is the smallest number of vertices for which either $\mathbf{G}$ or $\overline{\mathbf{G}}$ must contain $\mathbf{K}_4$. The proof is difficult. In spite of continuing effort by many mathematicians, the answer corresponding to the case $\mathbf{K}_5$ (or any larger complete graph) has not yet been discovered. (Such numbers are referred to as **Ramsey numbers;** see paragraph 9.6 for additional discussion.)

37.6

Complement: Turán's Theorem Here is a problem: Begin with the null graph on five vertices (see Figure 37.6A), then adjoin as many edges as possible without creating a triangle. Of course, the first few edges are easy, but after five can you put another one in? How about after six? Now, experiment with smaller vertex sets.

Let $b_3(n)$ be the maximum number of edges in a graph on n vertices which fails to have $\mathbf{K}_3$ as a subgraph. By trial and error we begin the following tabulation.

n	3	4	5	6
$b_3(n)$	2	4	6	

(1)

It is clear that the addition of a single new edge to each of the graphs in Figure 37.6B will produce at least one triangle. Consider the next entry in our tabulation shown in (1); we are tempted to guess that $b_3(6) = 8$. But the diagrams in Figure 37.6B suggest trying the graph $\mathbf{G}$ in Figure 37.6C, which has no triangle.

Thus $b_3(6) \geq 9$. It is clear that no edge can be adjoined to $\mathbf{G}$ without creating a triangle, but perhaps some different configuration may have 10 edges without a triangle. We want to show that this is impossible, which means that $b_3(6) = 9$. Assume, therefore, that there is a graph $\mathbf{G} = (\mathbf{V}, \mathbf{E})$ for which $\mathbf{V} = \{v_1, v_2, v_3, v_4, v_5, v_6\}$, $|\mathbf{E}| = 10$, and $\mathbf{G}$ has no triangle. Let $e_{ij} \in \mathbf{E}$ and let $\mathbf{G}'$ be the subgraph of $\mathbf{G}$ induced by $\mathbf{V} - \{v_i, v_j\}$ (that is, simply delete v_i and v_j from $\mathbf{G}$); see Figure 37.6D. Since $\mathbf{G}$ contains no triangle, no vertex in $\mathbf{G}'$ is adjacent to both v_i and v_j. Along with v_i and

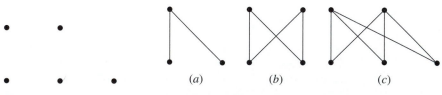

(a)   (b)   (c)

Figure 37.6A   **Figure 37.6B**

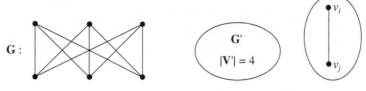

Figure 37.6C   **Figure 37.6D**

v_j we have deleted at most $4 + 1$ edges from $\mathbf{G}$. So $\mathbf{G}'$ is a graph on four vertices with at least $10 - 5 = 5$ edges. But $b_3(4) = 4$; hence $\mathbf{G}'$ must contain a triangle, which also is in $\mathbf{G}$. This contradiction proves that $b_3(6) \leq 9$, so we now conclude that $b_3(6) = 9$.

The pattern, perhaps, is beginning to emerge. We can construct a graph without triangles by partitioning the vertex set as nearly as possible into halves [$\mathbf{V} = \mathbf{V}_1 \cup \mathbf{V}_2$ and $|\mathbf{V}_1| = n/2$ or $(n - 1)/2$, whichever is an integer] and then adjoining all edges e_{ij} for which $v_i \in \mathbf{V}_1$ and $v_j \in \mathbf{V}_2$. These graphs are exactly the complete bipartite graphs $\mathbf{K}_{r,s}$, where r and s differ by at most 1. By FCP II, the number of edges in $\mathbf{K}_{r,s}$ is $r \cdot s$; so for our graphs the number of edges is

$$\frac{n}{2} \cdot \frac{n}{2} = \frac{n^2}{4}, \qquad \text{if } n \text{ is even};$$

$$\frac{n-1}{2} \cdot \frac{n+1}{2} = \frac{n^2 - 1}{4}, \qquad \text{if } n \text{ is odd}.$$

Using the "greatest integer" notation $[x]$ (or, as it is often called "the floor function," $\lfloor x \rfloor$), these two results can be combined into a single formula,

$$\left\lfloor \frac{n^2}{4} \right\rfloor = \left[\frac{n^2}{4} \right].$$

The same meaning is assigned to both notations: The greatest integer less than or equal to $n^2/4$. (See paragraph 6.8 for more detail.)

The graphs $\mathbf{K}_{r,s}$ show that for any $n \geq 3$, $b_3(n) \geq \lfloor n^2/4 \rfloor$. The proof that $b_3(n) \leq \lfloor n^2/4 \rfloor$ is by induction. If the inequality fails, then there is a graph $\mathbf{G} = (\mathbf{V}, \mathbf{E})$ without a triangle for which

$$|\mathbf{V}| = n \qquad \text{and} \qquad |\mathbf{E}| > \left\lfloor \frac{n^2}{4} \right\rfloor.$$

By the Well-Ordering Axiom, we may assume that n is the least integer for which this condition holds. Then, by (1), $n > 4$ (we know, actually, that $n > 6$). We don't know whether n is even or odd, but whichever the case

$$3 \leq n - 2 < n;$$

hence $b_3(n-2) = \lfloor (n-2)^2/4 \rfloor$. Now, by an argument almost identical to that given for the case $n = 6$, we can show that the graph $\mathbf{G}'$ obtained by deleting two vertices v_i and v_j from $\mathbf{G}$ has more than $\lfloor (n-2)^2/4 \rfloor$ edges, and hence must contain a triangle. Thus we have a contradiction which completes the proof of the following result.

THEOREM
37.6

For all $n \geq 3$, $b_3(n) = \lfloor n^2/4 \rfloor$.

This result is included in a paper published by Paul Turán (1910–1976) in 1941 and is one of the earliest theorems in "extremal graph theory."

Problems for Section 37

1. Which of the graphs

can be redrawn so that they are the same? Label the isomorphic graphs so that the edges are the same, and give a reason why the remaining graph is not isomorphic to the other two.

2. Which of the graphs

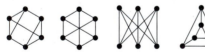

can be redrawn so that they are the same? Label the isomorphic graphs so that the edges are the same, and give a reason why the first two graphs are not isomorphic to each other.

3. Which of the graphs

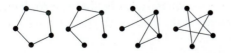

can be redrawn so that they are the same? Label the isomorphic graphs so that the edges are the same, and give a reason why the first two graphs are not isomorphic to each other.

In the remainder of this problem set, all graphs are considered unlabeled and when asked to draw a set of graphs, it is meant that all the graphs are to be nonisomorphic.

4. Draw all regular graphs with five vertices. There are three.

5. Draw all eight graphs with five vertices and three or fewer edges.

6. Draw all six graphs with five vertices and four edges.

7. Draw all six graphs with five vertices and five edges.

8. Draw all six graphs with five vertices and six edges.

9. Draw all eight graphs with five vertices and seven or more edges.

10. The numbers in the table are the number of graphs with n vertices and m edges. There is symmetry about the middle of each row. Why?

	m										
n	0	1	2	3	4	5	6	7	8	9	10
4	1	1	2	3	2	1	1				
5	1	1	2	4	6	6	6	4	2	1	1

11. Draw all regular graphs with six vertices. (There are eight. Three are not connected.)

12. Draw any three regular graphs of degree 2 with eight vertices.

13. Draw any three regular graphs of degree 3 with eight vertices.

14. Draw all regular graphs of degree 5 with nine vertices.

15. Find the graph with the least number of edges and minimum degree 3. Why is this graph the smallest?

16. Draw the complement of each graph in Problem 1.

17. Show that if **G** is isomorphic to **H**, then $\overline{\mathbf{G}}$ is isomorphic to $\overline{\mathbf{H}}$.

18. Draw the complement of each graph in Problem 3.

19. Draw the complement of each graph in Problem 2.

20. Prove that either a graph or its complement is connected.

21. A graph **G** is **self-complementary** if it is isomorphic to its complement. For example, the graphs   and   are self-complementary. Find the other self-complementary graph with five vertices.

22. Find any one of the 10 self-complementary graphs with eight vertices.

23. Show that every self-complementary graph has $4k$ or $4k + 1$ vertices.

24. If **G** is a bipartite graph, then show that **G** has no triangles.

25. For the complete bipartite graph $\mathbf{K}_{r,s}$, let the vertices be $\mathbf{V} = \{v_1, \ldots, v_r, u_1, \ldots, u_s\}$ with the edge set $\mathbf{E} = \{(v_i, u_j): 1 \le i \le r, 1 \le j \le s\}$. What is the matrix A of $\mathbf{K}_{2,2}$? What are A^2 and A^3?

26. (*Continuation of Problem 25.*) What is the matrix A of $\mathbf{K}_{2,3}$? What are A^2 and A^3?

27. (*Continuation of Problem 25.*) What is the matrix A of $\mathbf{K}_{3,3}$? What are A^2 and A^3?

28. (*Conclusion of Problem 25.*) Note that the matrix A in each of the above three problems is of the form

$$\begin{bmatrix} O & J \\ J & O \end{bmatrix}$$

where each entry of O is 0 and each entry of J is 1. In general, if A is the matrix of $\mathbf{K}_{r,s}$, then

$$A = \begin{bmatrix} O & J \\ J & O \end{bmatrix}.$$

What are the sizes of the matrices O and J? Note that the O's and J's may be of different sizes.

29. Imagine $\mathbf{K}_n$ with each edge colored red, green, or blue. Find in $\mathbf{K}_4$ and $\mathbf{K}_6$ a coloring so that the red, green, and blue subgraphs are isomorphic.

30. In $\mathbf{K}_8$ there is a coloring of the edges with four colors so that the subgraphs induced by each color are isomorphic. How many edges does each subgraph have? Find such a coloring.

31. How many triangles are in the complement of $\mathbf{K}_{1,6}$? How many triangles are in the complement of $\mathbf{K}_{1,n}$?

32. How many triangles are in the complement of $\mathbf{C}_6$, the cycle with six vertices? (Use Theorem 36.5A.) How many triangles are in the complement of $\mathbf{C}_n$, the cycle with n vertices?

Let $\mathbf{G}$ be a spanning subgraph of $\mathbf{K}_6$ and $\overline{\mathbf{G}}$ be its complement. In Theorem 37.5, we proved that either $\mathbf{G}$ or $\overline{\mathbf{G}}$ contained a triangle. We now will prove a slightly stronger result. Call a triangle in $\mathbf{K}_6$ **monochrome** if all of its three edges are in one or the other of $\mathbf{G}$ and $\overline{\mathbf{G}}$; otherwise it is **bichrome.** Our problem is to discover the maximum possible number of bichrome triangles in $\mathbf{K}_6$. Observe that a bichrome triangle has two edges either in $\mathbf{G}$ or $\overline{\mathbf{G}}$ and one edge in the other; thus, exactly two of its vertices are incident with an edge in $\mathbf{G}$ and with an edge in $\overline{\mathbf{G}}$. We call such vertices in a triangle **bichrome.**

33. Define the set of ordered pairs $\mathbf{W} = \{(\mathbf{B}, v): \mathbf{B}$ is a bichrome triangle and v is a bichrome vertex in $\mathbf{B}\}$. Argue that $|\mathbf{W}|$ is exactly twice the number of bichrome triangles.

34. (*Continuation of Problem 33.*) Consider a vertex $v \in \mathbf{K}_6$. If an edge e in $\mathbf{G}$ and an edge $\overline{e}$ in $\overline{\mathbf{G}}$ are incident with v, then v, e, and $\overline{e}$ belong to exactly one bichrome triangle. Show that the maximum possible number of bichrome triangles with vertex v is six. (*Hint:* The degree of v in $\mathbf{K}_6$ is 5; consider what happens if its degree in $\mathbf{G}$ is 0, 1, 2, 3, 4, or 5.)

35. (*Continuation of Problem 33.*) Show that $|\mathbf{W}| \le 36$.

36. (*Continuation of Problem 33.*) Compare the number of triangles in $\mathbf{K}_6$ with the maximum possible number of bichrome triangles in $\mathbf{K}_6$.

37. (*Conclusion of Problem 33.*) Construct a $\mathbf{K}_6$ with exactly two monochrome triangles.

Section 38.   Eulerian Graphs

Overview for Section 38

- The Königsberg bridges problem and multigraphs
- Definitions of eulerian trails and eulerian graphs
- Discussion and proof of Euler's Theorem
- Definition of a "bridge" and description of Fleury's Algorithm

Key Concepts: multigraph, eulerian trail, eulerian graph, bridge, Fleury's Algorithm

38.1   Many topics in mathematics have obscure beginnings, but this is not the case with graph theory. The first paper devoted exclusively to a problem in what we now call graph theory was published in 1736 by Leonhard Euler (1707–1783). Euler (pronounced oíl·er) is not so well known by the general public as Euclid or Newton, yet he was an astounding genius whose legacy includes seminal contributions to all areas

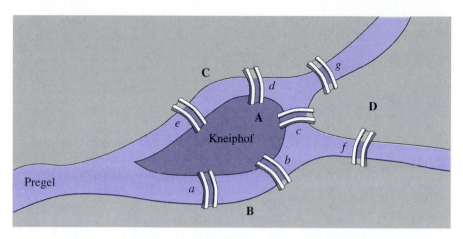

Figure 38.1A

of mathematics and to much of physics and engineering. Although troubled by partial and eventually total blindness, his "complete works" fill about 70 volumes. Euler's paper entitled "The Solution of a Problem Relating to the Geometry of Position" was written in Latin, but a translation and commentary can be found in *Graph Theory: 1736–1936* by Biggs et al. (It is an excellent example of a readable research paper by a great mathematician.)

This first paper on graph theory is about a puzzle concerning a city, an island, and seven bridges, as shown in Figure 38.1A. In Euler's day, this region belonged to the Kingdom of Prussia, the river was called the Pregel, and the city was known as Königsberg. Various parts of the city, including the island of Kneiphof, were joined by bridges named (*a*) Green, (*b*) Connecting, (*c*) Merchants, (*d*) Blacksmith, (*e*) Honey, (*f*) High, and (*g*) Wooden. The legend has it that the citizens would try to walk through town and return home by crossing each bridge exactly once. Every attempt resulted in the omission of some bridge or the multiple crossing of some bridge. The Seven Bridges of Königsberg problem achieved some notoriety and eventually attracted Euler's attention. His analysis reduced the problem to what is now called a **multigraph:** a structure like a graph except that more than one edge is permitted between vertices. The basic concepts defined in preceding sections extend in a natural way to multigraphs. Euler replaced land areas by vertices and bridges by edges, producing the multigraph **M** shown in Figure 38.1B. So the problem faced by the

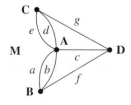

Figure 38.1B

citizens of Königsberg is simply this: Find a closed trail in the multigraph **M** which includes each edge precisely once. Euler's paper proved the impossibility of such a trail, but, beyond that, it answered a broad class of similar questions concerned with what is now referred to as "traversability."

38.2

In recognition, later mathematicians have used Euler's name in the description of traversability. To be explicit, if **G** is either a graph or a multigraph, then **T** is an **eulerian trail** of **G** if **T** is a trail that includes each edge of **G** exactly once; **G** is **eulerian** if it has a closed eulerian trail. Because an eulerian trail is defined in terms of edges, no isolated vertex can be touched by the trail. In this section we will exclude isolated vertices and multiple components by assuming that all graphs are connected. We now state Euler's Theorem and a corollary of it that characterize eulerian graphs, or those with an eulerian trail. In the following, it will be convenient to call a vertex **even** if its degree is even, and **odd** if its degree is odd.

THEOREM 38.2

Euler's Theorem. A connected graph is eulerian if and only if every vertex is even.

COROLLARY 38.2

A connected graph has an eulerian trail if and only if there are at most two odd vertices. If there are two odd vertices, then an eulerian trail must begin and end at those vertices.

Before we prove Euler's Theorem we note three things. First, these results are true for multigraphs as well as graphs. Second, the Königsberg multigraph **M** has more than two odd vertices and so has no eulerian trail. Third, Euler just proved the "only if" part of Theorem 38.2; the proof of the "if" part appeared in 1873 in a paper by Carl Hierholzer (1840–1871), who, apparently, had been unaware of Euler's paper.

Tutorial 38.2A

a. Construct a graph **G** on the vertex set **V** = $\{1, 2, 3, 4, 5, 6\}$ which is regular of degree 4.
b. Construct a closed eulerian trail in **G**.
c. Find two cycles which have no edge in common but which together include all edges in **G**.

Proof of Euler's Theorem

First we assume that **G** is eulerian and let **T** denote a closed eulerian trail in **G**. Each vertex v in **T** has an incident edge preceding it and an incident edge following it. All edges of **G** appear in **T** (each exactly once). Hence, deg(v) is twice the number of appearances of v in **T**. Therefore deg(v) is even.

Conversely, suppose that **G** is a connected graph with n vertices and that all vertices are even. If the converse is not true, then we may suppose that **G** is not eulerian and that it is as small as possible in the following sense: Any connected graph **H** with vertices of even degree must be eulerian if it has fewer than n vertices, or if it has n vertices but fewer edges than **G**. Note that n is greater than 3 since $\mathbf{K}_3$ is the smallest connected graph with all even vertices, and it is certainly eulerian.

Our first step is to find a closed trail in **G**. Because we are constructing a trail, keep in mind that vertices, but not edges, may repeat. For descriptive convenience, we label the vertices by $v_1, v_2, \ldots, v_n$. Begin with any vertex of **G**, say v_1. Next, select any edge e_{12} incident with v_1 and mark it as used. Now select any edge e_{23} incident with v_2 that has not already been marked and mark it as used. Continue this procedure until a vertex, say v_k, is chosen which has no unmarked edge incident with it. So the number of marked edges incident with v_k is the degree of v_k. We now have a trail $(v_1, v_2, \ldots, v_k)$ which includes the marked edges. To show that $v_k = v_1$, assume the contrary. Now, v_k may have appeared in this trail more than once, but each time it appeared prior to the final time, two edges incident with it were marked. Only one edge incident with it was marked at its final appearance in the trail, which implies that v_k is an odd vertex. But this contradicts our hypothesis. Hence this trail, call it **C**, is closed.

Let **H** be the spanning subgraph of **G** obtained by deleting each edge in **C**. If **H** has no edges, then **C** is a closed eulerian trail and **G** is eulerian. Otherwise, each nontrivial component of **H** is eulerian, because it is smaller than **G**. We may ignore any vertex of degree 0 in **H**.

Now, to form an eulerian trail in **G** simply start at v_1 and traverse **C** until a vertex with positive degree in **H** is encountered. Traverse the eulerian trail in this component of **H** and then continue on the trail **C** (see Example 1 below). This closed eulerian trail contradicts our assumption that **G** is not eulerian. Hence, every connected graph with all even vertices has a closed eulerian trail. ∎

Example 1 Consider the graph **G** shown in Figure 38.2A. Suppose that we have constructed in **G** the closed trail $\mathbf{C} = (v_1, v_2, v_3, v_1)$. Now delete the edges of **C** from **G** to obtain the spanning subgraph **H**, consisting of the vertex v_1 and the two nontrivial components $\mathbf{H}_1$ and $\mathbf{H}_2$ (shown in Figure 38.2B). The closed trails in these components are $\mathbf{C}_1 = (v_2, v_4, v_5, v_2, v_6, v_7, v_2)$ and $\mathbf{C}_2 = (v_3, v_8, v_9, v_3)$. The eulerian trail for **G** is, therefore,

$$(v_1, v_2, (\text{trail for } \mathbf{H}_1), v_2, v_3, (\text{trail for } \mathbf{H}_2), v_3, v_1),$$

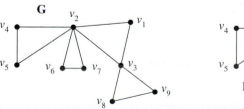

Figure 38.2A

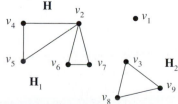

Figure 38.2B

which in full is

$$(v_1, v_2, v_4, v_5, v_2, v_6, v_7, v_2, v_3, v_8, v_9, v_3, v_1).$$

Tutorial 38.2B

Consider the graph **G** in Figure 38.2A.
a. Construct a new graph **G'** by deleting the edge e_{67} from **G** and adjoining two edges, one between v_5 and v_6 and one between v_7 and v_8.
b. Construct an eulerian trail in **G'**. (*Hint:* Refer to Corollary 38.2.)

We next prove Corollary 38.2: A connected graph **G** has an eulerian trail if and only if it has at most two odd vertices.

Proof of Corollary 38.2

Note that **G** has no odd vertices if and only if **G** has a closed eulerian trail. Thus we assume that **G** has odd vertices.

Suppose **G** has an eulerian trail which is not closed. Since each vertex in the middle of the trail is associated with two edges and since there is only one edge associated with each end-vertex of the trail, these end-vertices must be odd and the other vertices must be even.

By (2) in paragraph 36.2, **G** cannot have just one odd vertex. Hence, for the converse, let v_i and v_j be the only two odd vertices in the connected graph **G**. There are two cases. First, suppose v_i and v_j are not adjacent [see part (*a*) of Figure 38.2C]. If we adjoin e_{ij} to the edge set of **G**, then all vertices in the enlarged graph are even; hence it has a closed eulerian trail. Deleting e_{ij} from this closed trail gives an eulerian trail in **G** starting at v_i and ending at v_j. In the second case, suppose that v_i and v_j are adjacent [see part (*b*) of Figure 38.2B]. In this case, we adjoin to the vertex set of **G** a new vertex v_t and to the edge set of **G** two new edges e_{ti} and e_{tj}. All vertices in

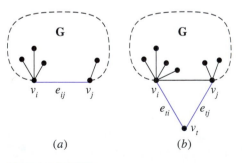

(*a*)   (*b*)

Figure 38.2C

the enlarged graph have even degree, and so it has a closed eulerian trail. Deleting v_t leaves **G** with an eulerian trail starting at v_i and ending at v_j. ∎

38.3

There exists an algorithm for finding the eulerian trails in graphs. It involves the sequential identification of edges which are then deleted from the graph. But the edges cannot be chosen randomly; we must avoid, to the extent possible, "disconnecting" the graph. An edge e_{ij} in a graph **G** (not necessarily connected) is called a **bridge** if its deletion creates a subgraph with more components than in the original. For example, each graph in Figure 38.3 has e_{34} as a bridge. After deletion of e_{34}, the graphs in parts (a) and (b) have two components while that in (c) has three components, one of which is a single vertex.

Let $\mathbf{G} = (\mathbf{V}, \mathbf{E})$ be a connected graph with all even vertices.

FLEURY'S ALGORITHM

Attributed to M. Fleury by Édouard Lucas (1842–1891) in *Récréations Mathématiques*, vol. 4.

Step 1. Choose any vertex of **G** and label it v_0. Let $\mathbf{T}_0 = (v_0)$ and $\mathbf{G}_0 = \mathbf{G} = (\mathbf{V}_0, \mathbf{E}_0)$.

Step 2. Select an edge of $\mathbf{G}_0$ incident with v_0, making sure that it is not a bridge unless there is no other choice, and label its other end-vertex v_1.

Step 3. Let $\mathbf{T}_1 = (v_0, v_1)$.

Step 4. Let $\mathbf{G}_1$ be the graph resulting from the deletion of the edge e_{01} from $\mathbf{G}_0$; that is, $\mathbf{G}_1 = (\mathbf{V}, \mathbf{E}_1 = \mathbf{E}_0 - e_{01})$.

Step 5. If $\mathbf{G}_1$ is not the null graph (a graph without edges), then we continue with the selection process.

The construction of the trail continues by recursion as follows.

Step 2'. Assuming that $\mathbf{T}_k = (v_0, v_1, \ldots, v_k)$ has been defined, select an edge of $\mathbf{G}_k$ incident with v_k, making sure that it is not a bridge unless there is no other choice, and label its other end-vertex v_{k+1}.

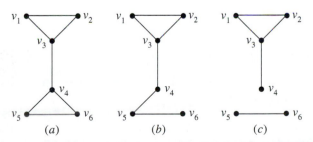

Figure 38.3

Step 3′. Let $\mathbf{T}_{k+1} = (v_0, v_1, \ldots, v_{k+1})$.

Step 4′. Let $\mathbf{G}_{k+1}$ be the graph resulting from the deletion of the edge $e_{k,k+1}$ from $\mathbf{G}_k$; that is, $\mathbf{G}_{k+1} = (\mathbf{V}, \mathbf{E}_{k+1} = \mathbf{E}_k - e_{k,k+1})$.

Step 5′. If $\mathbf{G}_{k+1}$ is not null, increase k by 1 and return to step 2′. Otherwise, the algorithm ends with the closed eulerian trail $\mathbf{C} = \mathbf{T}_{k+1}$. ▲

38.4

In the Problems we outline a proof to show that Fleury's Algorithm does indeed find an eulerian trail in a connected graph with all even vertices. As an example of Fleury's Algorithm, we find an eulerian trail in the graph in Figure 38.4A.

Example 1

Let $\mathbf{G}$ be the graph shown in Figure 38.4A, where the vertices are labeled merely for convenience of reference. Note first that every vertex is of even degree. Our choice of v_{k+1} will always be made by choosing the vertex (subject to the constraints of the algorithm) with the smallest numerical value. Recall, once again, that vertices may repeat but not edges. Our trail starts with the choice $v_0 = 1$ and continues with $v_1 = 2$ and $v_2 = 3$ (note that there is no other choice at this step). We next select $v_3 = 4$, and at this step the graph $\mathbf{G}_3$ is shown in Figure 38.4B. We cannot now select $v_4 = 5$, for the edge e_{45} is a bridge. Hence, we select $v_4 = 8$ and continue with $v_5 = 9$, $v_6 = 4$, $v_7 = 5$ (for there are no other choices at these steps). Because 1 is the least integer still adjacent to 5, we choose $v_8 = 1$, then continue with the algorithm. The closed eulerian trail is (using the original vertex labels)

$$\mathbf{C} = (1, 2, 3, 4, 8, 9, 4, 5, 1, 6, 3, 5, 6, 10, 11, 6, 12, 13, 6, 7, 1).$$

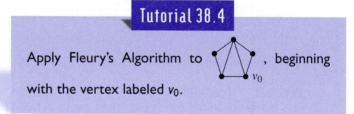

Tutorial 38.4

Apply Fleury's Algorithm to , beginning

with the vertex labeled v_0.

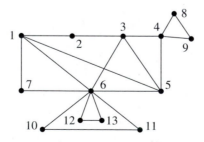

Figure 38.4A

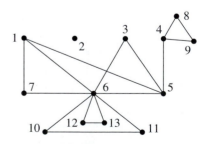

Figure 38.4B

As illustrated in the preceding tutorial, Fleury's Algorithm can be applied to graphs which satisfy the hypotheses of Corollary 38.2, if v_0 is chosen to be an odd vertex.

38.5 Complement: The Ubiquitous Eulerian Trail

The fundamental idea of an eulerian trail occurs in widely dispersed cultures and is likely to be quite ancient in origin. In this complement we present several examples described by anthropologists who have studied societies remote from European influence. As reported by Claudia Zaslavsky in *Africa Counts,* the two graphs in Figure 38.5A were used by Shongo children of the Congo as puzzles. The challenge was to discover an eulerian trail in each: A little experimentation will probably convince you of its difficulty (remember to look for the odd vertices, if any). The graph in Figure 38.5B, also taken from *Africa Counts,* represents God, man, the moon, and the sun. God is at the top, man is on the bottom, the moon is at the right, and the sun is on the left. This graph was drawn by the Jokwe of Angola, and the eulerian trail was used to illustrate some of their religious beliefs.

The graph in Figure 38.5C is the "Stone of Ambat." This is one of the many remarkable designs that artists of the New Hebrides (now Vanuatu) could trace in the sand from memory. These graphs were drawn with the restriction that "the finger should never be lifted from the ground, nor should any part of the line be traversed twice," another definition of eulerian graphs. There are over 50 such graphs pictured in "Geometrical Drawings from Malekula and other Islands of the New Hebrides" by A. Bernard Deacon. Some of these are more intricate than the "Stone of Ambat," and most are as beautiful.

Aside from their intrinsic recreational and/or cultural significance in various societies, graphical diagrams can be used to model traversability problems that are typical to our own society. These may be separated into two general classes:

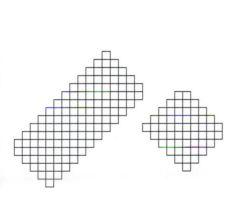

Figure 38.5A

Figure 38.5B

Figure 38.5C

- The "eulerian" problem which seeks a trail that includes each edge once, but may include vertices multiple times

- The "hamiltonian" problem (see paragraph 35.7) which seeks a cycle including each vertex once, but may not include all edges.

Despite their similarity, there appears to be little connection between them. Typical of the hamiltonian class is what has become popularly known as "the traveling salesman problem." A representative wishes to cover a territory which includes n cities, and there is a known cost associated with the trip between each pair of cities. The ideal solution is to visit each city exactly once before returning home, at a minimum expense for the entire journey. Surprisingly perhaps, this problem is quite difficult, is unsolved in general, and attracts much current study.

We will close by describing a situation which illustrates the "eulerian" class of traversability problems. Consider the street map of Smalltown in Figure 38.5D. The vertex labeled 1 is the office of the Street Department, and its chief is about to make his annual inspection of all the streets in Smalltown. To do this, he walks along the street and hence can inspect both sides of a street at one time, and he can also

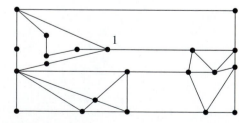

Figure 38.5D

walk against the traffic on one-way streets. He naturally does not want to walk along any street twice. Your task is to assure him that an eulerian trail exists, and then to find one.

Problems for Section 38

1. Restate Theorem 38.2 in terms of the row sums of an adjacency matrix of an eulerian graph.

2. For which n are the complete graphs $\mathbf{K}_n$ eulerian? Which have eulerian trails?

3. For which r and s are the complete bipartite graphs $\mathbf{K}_{r,s}$ eulerian? Which have eulerian trails?

4. If a graph has exactly two vertices of odd degree, then it has an eulerian trail beginning and ending with the odd vertices. What can be said about a graph with exactly four vertices of odd degree? ("Nothing" is not an acceptable answer.)

5. Can the edges of the following multigraph be traced without removing the pencil from the page? Why or why not?

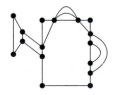

6. You are a street inspector and the street map of your town is shown below. Is there a way to inspect all these streets without having to drive over any twice?

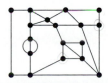

7. Use the algorithm in the text to find an eulerian trail in

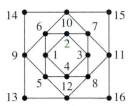

8. Suppose that the citizens of Königsberg had constructed two more bridges (indicated by the dashed lines). Would there then have been an eulerian trail through the city?

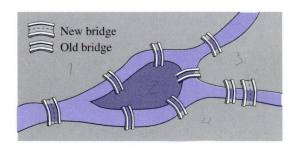

New bridge
Old bridge

9. Shown below is another city with a river and three islands. Can a citizen traverse each bridge once in a walk around this city?

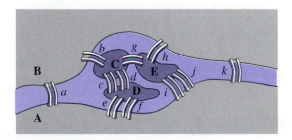

10. Is there a path through the following house which goes through each door exactly once? A door is represented by the parallel lines in the walls. (*Hint:* Let the rooms be vertices and the doors be edges.)

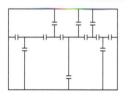

11. Is there a path through the following house which goes through each door exactly once?

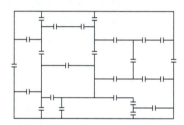

12. Show that if a graph has an eulerian trail and a bridge, then the end-vertices of the bridge are both odd.

13. Show that an eulerian graph has no bridges.

14. In the two drawings in Figure 38.5A, consider each intersection as a vertex of a graph. At which vertices must an eulerian trail start for each of these drawings?

15. Prove that any graph (the graph may not be connected) with exactly two odd vertices has a path between the odd vertices.

16. Let **G** be a connected graph with exactly $2k$ odd vertices. We use induction to show that there are k edge-disjoint paths joining these vertices. Let **M** be the set of all $k \in \mathbb{N}$ such that if **G** (not necessarily connected) has exactly $2k$ odd vertices, then there are k edge-disjoint paths joining these vertices. (*a*) Now $1 \in \mathbf{M}$ by which of the problems in this section? (*b*) Assume $k \in \mathbf{M}$ and suppose **G** has $2(k + 1)$ odd vertices. Show that

two of these odd vertices, u and v, are in the same component of **G**. Conclude that there is a path **P** joining u and v.

17. (*Conclusion of Problem 16.*) (*a*) Let **G**' be the graph **G** with the edges of **P** deleted. Show that the parity of every vertex in **G**' is the same as in **G**, except for u and v which are even in **G**'. (*b*) Since $k \in \mathbf{M}$, conclude that **G**' has k edge-disjoint paths joining its $2k$ odd vertices, and hence **G** has $k + 1$ edge-disjoint paths joining its $2(k + 1)$ odd vertices.

18. Can you trace a path that crosses each edge of 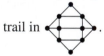 exactly once without lifting your pencil off the page? Why or why not?

19. It is obvious that $\mathbf{C}_n$ is eulerian, but what about $\overline{\mathbf{C}}_n$? For which n is $\overline{\mathbf{C}}_n$ eulerian? Why?

20. Suppose that **G** and $\overline{\mathbf{G}}$ are both connected and that **G** is eulerian. Is $\overline{\mathbf{G}}$ sometimes, never, or always eulerian? If $\overline{\mathbf{G}}$ is sometimes eulerian, is there an easy way to determine this?

21. Use Fleury's Algorithm to find an eulerian trail in [figure].

22. Find an eulerian trail in the graph in Figure 38.5D.

The answers to the next four problems show that Fleury's Algorithm terminates after finding an eulerian trail. Let $\mathbf{T}_k$ and $\mathbf{G}_k$ be as in the algorithm and suppose that at some step in the algorithm we have encountered a vertex that has degree zero after its edge has been deleted. Let this vertex be $v_m \in \mathbf{G}_m$.

23. (*a*) Why is the degree of v_i, $2 \le i \le m$, even in $\mathbf{T}_m$? (*b*) If $v_m \ne v_0$, then why is the degree of v_0 odd in $\mathbf{T}_m$? (*c*) Since $\mathbf{T}_m$ is itself a graph, it cannot have just one odd vertex. Conclude that $v_0 = v_m$, and hence $\mathbf{T}_m$ is a closed trail.

24. (*Continuation of Problem 23.*) We proceed by contradiction to show that $\mathbf{G}_m$ is the null graph, and hence $\mathbf{T}_m$ is an eulerian trail of $\mathbf{G}$. (*a*) Suppose $\mathbf{G}_m$ has an edge. Show that every vertex of $\mathbf{G}_m$ with positive degree has even degree in $\mathbf{G}_m$. (*b*) Let $\mathbf{G}'$ be a nontrivial component of $\mathbf{G}_m$, and show that at least one vertex of $\mathbf{G}'$ is also on the trail $\mathbf{T}_m$. (*Hint:* Since $\mathbf{G}$ is connected, there is a path in $\mathbf{G}$ between every pair of vertices.)

25. (*Continuation of Problem 23.*) Let r be the largest subscript such that v_r is on both $\mathbf{T}_m$ and $\mathbf{G}'$. Why is $r \neq m$? Verify that $\mathbf{G}$ can be pictured as follows, where e is an edge of $\mathbf{G}'$ incident with v_r.

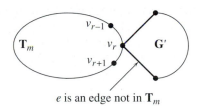

e is an edge not in $\mathbf{T}_m$

26. (*Conclusion of Problem 23.*) By Problem 24(*a*), $\mathbf{G}'$ has all even vertices and so is eulerian. (*a*) Conclude that e is not a bridge in $\mathbf{G}'$ (Problem 13), and hence e is not a bridge in $\mathbf{G}_r$. (*b*) For $s > r$, show that there is no path from v_s to any vertex of $\mathbf{G}_r$. Conclude that $e_{r,r+1}$ is a bridge in $\mathbf{G}_r$, and thus the edge e would have been chosen by Fleury's Algorithm instead of $e_{r,r+1}$. This is a contradiction, and so $\mathbf{G}_m$ is the null graph.

Section 39. Trees

Overview for Section 39

- Introduction to the idea of an acyclic graph
- Enumeration of trees (Cayley's Theorem)
- Existence of a spanning subtree of a graph
- Some characterizations of trees

Key Concepts: acyclic graph, tree, spanning subtree

39.1 In the late nineteenth century, Arthur Cayley (1821–1895) studied a special class of graphs related to certain chemical compounds, especially the hydrocarbons (see Figure 39.1A). Imagine that each of the letters (which represent either a carbon or a hydrogen atom) is a vertex and that each of the indicated connections (called bonds) is an edge; thus each compound is diagrammed as a graph. Cayley was interested in the difficult problem of enumerating such graphs. We observe, first, that these "hydrocarbon" graphs have an important property in common: They are **acyclic,** which means that no one of them contains a cycle. It should be clear that this property is hereditary; that is, any subgraph of an acyclic graph is also acyclic. It should also

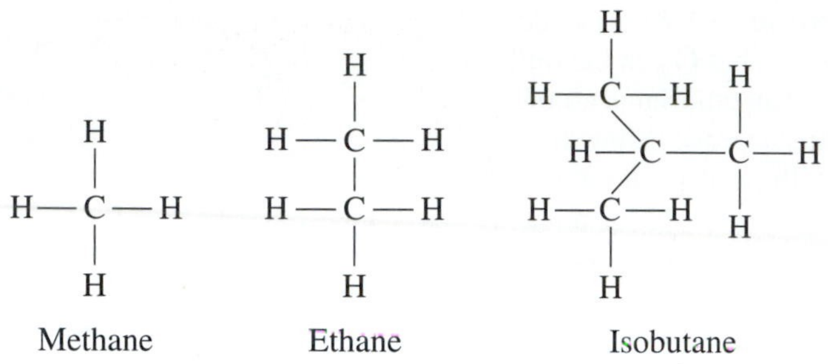

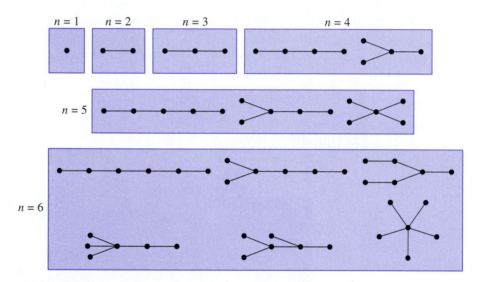

Figure 39.1A

Figure 39.1B

be clear that any acyclic graph is planar: Its diagram need not include any extraneous crossings.

Because of its similarity with the branching process of a tree, any connected, acyclic graph is called a **tree.** (Since an acyclic graph can be represented as a union of its components, each of which is a tree, it is not unnatural that we should call any acyclic graph a **forest.** But here we will restrict our attention solely to the concept of "tree.") It is not difficult to discover (simply by observation) all possible patterns of trees for small values of n; these are displayed in Figure 39.1B for $n < 7$. A generating function for the number of unlabeled trees exists, but its derivation is more appropriate to an advanced course. Here, we will merely indicate the first few terms:

$$f(x) = x + x^2 + x^3 + 2x^4 + 3x^5 + 6x^6 + 11x^7 + 23x^8 + \cdots. \qquad \textbf{(1)}$$

Tutorial 39.1

Three of the eleven unlabeled tree diagrams on seven vertices are

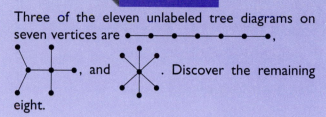

, and . Discover the remaining eight.

39.2

Cayley's concern was with trees having vertices of (possibly) different characteristics; hence he wanted to enumerate the labeled trees. This is also a difficult problem, but the final answer turns out to be expressed in a surprisingly simple form. We can begin to appreciate Cayley's formula by attempting to construct labeled trees for $n = 2, 3, 4$, and 5. Recall that graphs in general are distinguished from one another *only* by their vertices and the connections between them via the edges. It is irrelevant how the vertices may be situated spatially in the plane (on a sheet of paper). Thus, the labeled trees $v_2 \bullet\!\!-\!\!\bullet v_1$ and $v_1 \bullet\!\!-\!\!\bullet v_2$ are not to be considered different (each has the same vertex set and the same edge set). Hence, there is exactly one labeled tree on two vertices. Now look at $v_1 \bullet\ \bullet_{v_2}\ \bullet v_3$. The labels can be permuted in $3! = 6$ ways, so there are certainly *at most* six different labeled trees on three vertices. All have the same vertex set; hence differences must appear in the edge sets. Here are the edge sets for each of the six permutations:

Permutation	Edge set	
$(v_1\ v_2\ v_3)$	e_{12}	e_{23}
$(v_1\ v_3\ v_2)$	e_{13}	e_{23}
$(v_2\ v_1\ v_3)$	e_{12}	e_{13}
$(v_2\ v_3\ v_1)$	e_{23}	e_{13}
$(v_3\ v_1\ v_2)$	e_{13}	e_{12}
$(v_3\ v_2\ v_1)$	e_{23}	e_{12}

Now, note that $(v_1v_2v_3)$ and $(v_3v_2v_1)$ have the same edge set, $(v_1v_3v_2)$ and $(v_2v_3v_1)$ have the same edge set, and $(v_2v_1v_3)$ and $(v_3v_1v_2)$ have the same edge set. Hence, there are exactly $3!/2 = 3$ labeled trees on three vertices.

Next, we can show in a similar way that there are $4!/2$ labeled trees for the pattern

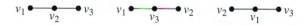

, and there are 4 labeled trees for the pattern , depending

upon the label assigned to the vertex of degree 3. Hence, there are $4!/2 + 4 = 16$ labeled trees on four vertices. Finally, we can show that there are $5!/2$ labeled trees for

the pattern ●——●——●——●, and there are 5 labeled trees for the pattern ⤬,

depending upon the label assigned to the vertex of degree 4, and there are $(5)_3 =$

$5 \cdot 4 \cdot 3$ labeled trees for the pattern ⤙——●——●, depending upon the labels assigned

to the three rightmost vertices. Hence, there are

$$\tfrac{1}{2} \cdot 5! + 5 + 5 \cdot 4 \cdot 3 = 125$$

labeled trees on five vertices. Denoting the number of labeled trees on n vertices by $l(n)$, we may tabulate these results as follows:

n	2	3	4	5
$l(n)$	1	3	16	125

Profiting from hindsight (namely, that there is a simple formula) we might guess that the results can be retabulated as follows:

n	2	3	4	5
$l(n)$	2^0	3^1	4^2	5^3

The evident generalization, n^{n-2}, turns out to be correct. A number of proofs are known; we will sketch one due to Ernst Paul Heinz Prüfer (1896–1934). Details can be found in *Graph Theory: 1736–1936* by Biggs et al., p. 52.

Tutorial 39.2

Let $l(n)$ denote the number of labeled trees on n vertices, and let $u(n)$ denote the number of unlabeled trees on n vertices.

a. Referring to (1) in paragraph 39.1 and to Theorem 39.2, complete the following table:

n	2	3	4	5	6	7
$l(n)$	1					
$u(n)$	1					

continued on next page

continued from previous page

b. Display the 12 labeled trees for the pattern

●——●——●——●.

THEOREM 39.2

There are exactly n^{n-2} labeled trees on the vertex set $\mathbf{V} = \{v_1, v_2, \ldots, v_n\}$.

Indication of Proof

Let $\mathbf{T} = (\mathbf{V}, \mathbf{E})$ be a tree with $|\mathbf{V}| = n > 2$. For notational convenience, we call a vertex of degree 1 an "end-vertex," and we put $\mathbf{V} = \{1, 2, 3, \ldots, n\}$. Now we apply the algorithm below to create an $(n-2)$-tuple

$$(t_1, t_2, \ldots, t_{n-2}), \tag{1}$$

in which each t_i is an integer satisfying $1 \leq t_i \leq n$.

PRÜFER'S ALGORITHM

To begin the construction, put $\mathbf{T} = \mathbf{T}_0$ and go to step 1 with $k = 0$.

Step 1. Let v be the end-vertex of $\mathbf{T}_k$ with smallest label, and suppose it is adjacent to the vertex u.

Step 2. Define t_{k+1} to be the label of the vertex u.

Step 3. Delete v (and its incident edge) from $\mathbf{T}_k$, leaving the subtree $\mathbf{T}_{k+1}$.

Step 4. If $\mathbf{T}_{k+1} = \mathbf{K}_2$, the algorithm ends; otherwise, return to step 1 with $\mathbf{T}_k$ replaced by $\mathbf{T}_{k+1}$. ▲

After the algorithm ends, note that (1) corresponds to a function from a set of size $n-2$ to a set of size n. By Theorem 15.5, the number of such functions is n^{n-2}. The proof is completed by showing that these functions correspond in a one-to-one manner with the labeled trees on n vertices. ∎

Example 1

We apply the algorithm to find the quadruple which corresponds to the labeled tree

$\mathbf{T}_0$:

First Loop

Step 1. $v = 1$.

Step 2. $u = t_1 = 3$.

Step 3. T_1:

Step 4. Return.

Second Loop

Step 1. $v = 2$.

Step 2. $u = t_2 = 3$.

Step 3. T_2:

Step 4. Return.

Third Loop

Step 1. $v = 3$.

Step 2. $u = t_3 = 5$.

Step 3. T_3:

Step 4. Return.

Fourth Loop

Step 1. $v = 4$.

Step 2. $u = t_4 = 5$.

Step 3. T_4:

Step 4. End.

Hence, the required quadruple is (3, 3, 5, 5).

39.3 In more recent years, trees have become useful models in disciplines other than chemistry, especially in the area of data structures in computer science, but we will leave such applications to other courses.

A connected graph, in general, may have many cycles, but it turns out that by selectively deleting edges we can break the cycles without destroying connectivity. Given an arbitrary connected graph **G**, we will refer to any subgraph of **G** which is spanning, connected, and acyclic as a **spanning subtree.** The following very general result is the basis for important applications in computer science.

**THEOREM
39.3**

Every connected graph has a spanning subtree.

Proof

We use induction on the number of vertices. Let $\mathbf{G} = (\mathbf{V}, \mathbf{E})$ denote a connected graph with $|\mathbf{V}| = n$. If $n = 1$ or $n = 2$, then $\mathbf{G}$ is a tree. Let's suppose that every connected graph on $k < n$ vertices has a spanning tree. We first let v be any vertex of $\mathbf{G}$, and we consider the components of the induced subgraph $\mathbf{G}' = (\mathbf{V} - v, \mathbf{E}')$. Each of these (there may be only one) is a connected graph on $k < n$ vertices. Hence each has a spanning tree. Now v must be connected to at least one vertex in each component, and we add to each of the component's spanning trees an edge from v to that component. Clearly this does not add any cycles, and it also produces a connected spanning subgraph of $\mathbf{G}$. ∎

Example 1

A cycle of length n, shown in part (a) of Figure 39.3A with $n = 6$, has a spanning subtree obtained by deleting any one of its n edges. In a more complicated graph such as that shown in part (b) of Figure 39.3A, a spanning subtree results from the sequential deletion of edges, subject to the requirement that no bridge be deleted. To illustrate this procedure, begin with part (b) and delete edges one by one as indicated in Figure 39.3B. Note that every edge in the final graph is a bridge; hence no further deletions can take place. So we have found a spanning subtree. An interesting observation is that spanning subtrees for the graphs in parts (a) and (b) of Figure 39.3A each have exactly five edges. We will discover in Theorem 39.4 that this result is to be expected.

Tutorial 39.3

As in Figure 39.3B, begin with the same graph, then sequentially delete edges to determine a different spanning subtree.

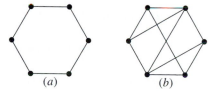

(a) (b)

Figure 39.3A

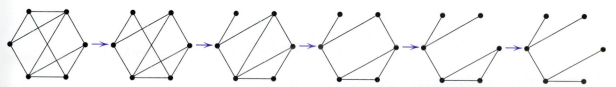

Figure 39.3B

39.4

We now prove a theorem of major importance, which establishes three characterizations of trees.

THEOREM 39.4

The following statements are equivalent for a graph **G** with n vertices and m edges.
A. G is a tree.
B. Every two vertices of **G** are joined by a unique path.
C. G is connected and $n = m + 1$.
D. G has no cycles and $n = m + 1$.

Proof

To prove a theorem like this, we show that

$$\mathbf{A} \to \mathbf{B}, \qquad \mathbf{B} \to \mathbf{C}, \qquad \mathbf{C} \to \mathbf{D}, \qquad \text{and} \qquad \mathbf{D} \to \mathbf{A}.$$

We can then conclude that these statements are logically equivalent.

$\mathbf{A} \to \mathbf{B}$. Assume that **G** is a tree, and so **G** is a connected graph with no cycles. Since **G** is connected, there is a path between any two vertices. Suppose now that there are vertices u and v which are joined by two paths,

$$(u = u_0, u_1, u_2, \ldots, u_r = v)$$

and

$$(u = v_0, v_1, v_2, \ldots, v_s = v).$$

At some point $u_i \neq v_i$, for otherwise the paths are the same. Let j be the smallest index for which $u_j \neq v_j$. (In Figure 39.4A, $j = 1$.) Since $u_r = v = v_s$, there is a smallest index larger than j, say k, for which $u_k = v_m$ for some $m \leq s$. (In Figure 39.4A, $k = 3$, $m = 4$.) Since $u_{j-1} = v_{j-1}$,

$$(u_{j-1}, u_j, u_{j+1}, \ldots, u_k(= v_m), v_{m-1}, \ldots, v_j, v_{j-1})$$

is a cycle in **G**. In Figure 39.4A, the cycle is

$$(u, u_1, u_2, u_3(= v_4), v_3, v_2, v_1, u).$$

But **G** is a tree, and it has no cycles. So we have a contradiction, and thus there is only one path between vertices u and v.

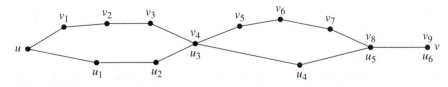

Figure 39.4A

B → **C**. We now assume every two vertices of **G** are joined by a unique path (but we are *not* assuming that **G** is a tree). We need to show that **G** is connected and that $n = m + 1$. It is immediate that **G** is connected since every two vertices are joined by a path. The proof that $n = m + 1$ is by induction on n. If **G** has $n = 2$ vertices, then **G** is K_2 and $n = m + 1$ $(2 = 1 + 1)$. Let n be the least integer for which there is a graph **G** on n vertices such that statement **B** is true for **G** but $n \neq m + 1$. Let e_{ij} be any edge in **G** joining vertices v_i and v_j. Let **G'** be the graph obtained by deleting e_{ij} from **G**. Then **G'** has two components since the edge e_{ij} was the unique path in **G** from v_i to v_j. (Why can't **G'** have more than two components? This is left as a problem.)

Each component satisfies the statement **B**, and since the number of vertices in each is less than n, statement **C** is also true. If n_1 and n_2 are the numbers of vertices in each component, then clearly $n_1 + n_2 = n$ and each component has $n_i - 1$ edges $(i = 1, 2)$. Thus, **G** has $(n_1 - 1) + (n_2 - 1) + 1$ edges (the final 1 was added to count the edge e_{ij}). So **G** has $n - 1$ edges, contradicting our original assumption. Hence, we conclude that **B** → **C**.

C → **D**. Let **G** be any connected graph for which $m = n - 1$. We use proof by contradiction to show that **G** cannot have a cycle. Assume that **G** has a cycle,

$$\mathbf{H} = (u_0, u_1, u_2, \ldots, u_{r-1}, u_r = u_0).$$

The u_i denote vertices of **G**, where none are the same except for u_0 and u_r. Let $\mathbf{V}_1$ denote the set of vertices in **H**, let $\mathbf{E}_1$ denote the set of edges in **H**, and observe that $|\mathbf{E}_1| = |\mathbf{V}_1| = r$. Our plan is to show that there are at least as many edges in **G** as there are vertices in **G**; for in that case $m \geq n$, which contradicts the hypothesis that $m = n - 1$. We construct an algorithmic proof.

a. If there is a vertex v in $\mathbf{V} - \mathbf{V}_1$, then (by connectedness) there is a path between v and some vertex in $\mathbf{V}_1$. Let u be a vertex in $\mathbf{V}_1$ such that the path $\mathbf{P}_1$ from u to v contains no other vertex in $\mathbf{V}_1$. In $\mathbf{P}_1$ there are exactly as many edges outside $\mathbf{E}_1$ as there are vertices outside $\mathbf{V}_1$. Let $\mathbf{V}_2$ be the union of $\mathbf{V}_1$ and the vertices in $\mathbf{P}_1$, and let $\mathbf{E}_2$ be the union of $\mathbf{E}_1$ and the edges in $\mathbf{P}_1$. Thus, $|\mathbf{V}_2| = |\mathbf{E}_2|$.

b. If there is a vertex v in $\mathbf{V} - \mathbf{V}_2$, then (by connectedness) there is a path between v and some vertex in $\mathbf{V}_2$. Let u be a vertex in $\mathbf{V}_2$ such that the path $\mathbf{P}_2$ from u to v contains no other vertex in $\mathbf{V}_2$. In $\mathbf{P}_2$ there are exactly as many edges outside $\mathbf{E}_2$ as there are vertices outside $\mathbf{V}_2$. Let $\mathbf{V}_3$ be the union of $\mathbf{V}_2$ and the vertices in $\mathbf{P}_2$, and let $\mathbf{E}_3$ be the union of $\mathbf{E}_2$ and the edges in $\mathbf{P}_2$. Thus, $|\mathbf{V}_3| = |\mathbf{E}_3|$.

c. Continue. After not more than $n - r$ steps we encounter the condition $\mathbf{V} - \mathbf{V}_k = \emptyset$. There may, of course, remain edges in $\mathbf{E} - \mathbf{E}_k$; thus, $|\mathbf{E}| \geq |\mathbf{V}|$. Hence **G** is acyclic.

D → **A**. Finally we assume **G** has no cycles and that $n = m + 1$. Because **G** is acyclic, we need only show that **G** is connected. Again, we use induction on n. For $n = 1$ and $n = 2$, it is obvious that **G** is connected. Suppose, for $k < n$, that any graph on k vertices with no cycles and with $k - 1$ edges is a tree. If **G** is not connected, then we will assume that it has r components, each of which is a tree.

But note that since $\mathbf{A} \rightarrow \mathbf{B}$ and $\mathbf{B} \rightarrow \mathbf{C}$, then $\mathbf{A} \rightarrow \mathbf{C}$, and so any tree has one more vertex than it has edges. If n_i is the number of vertices in the ith component, then $n_i - 1$ is the number of edges in the ith component. Thus,

$$n = \sum_{i=1}^{r} n_i,$$

and

$$m = \sum_{i=1}^{r} (n_i - 1) = \sum_{i=1}^{r} n_i - \sum_{i=1}^{r} 1 = n - r < n - 1,$$

which contradicts the hypothesis that $m = n - 1$. Therefore, $\mathbf{G}$ must be connected, so $\mathbf{D} \rightarrow \mathbf{A}$ and the theorem is proved. ∎

Example 1

We illustrate the argument $\mathbf{D} \rightarrow \mathbf{A}$ in Theorem 39.4. Consider the graph $\mathbf{G}$ in Figure 39.4B. It is acyclic, and each of its three components is acyclic. By the induction hypothesis, each component $\mathbf{G}_i$ is a tree and hence satisfies

$$n_i = m_i + 1$$

(that is, the number of vertices is 1 more than the number of edges). Thus,

$$n = \sum_{i=1}^{3} n_i = 4 + 5 + 6 = 15,$$

and

$$m = \sum_{i=1}^{3} m_i = \sum_{i=1}^{3} (n_i - 1) = 15 - 3 = 12 < 15 - 1.$$

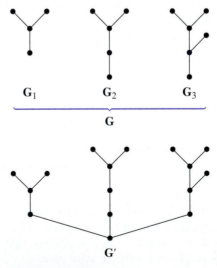

Figure 39.4B

By a similar argument, if **G** has any number of components greater than 1, then $n \neq m + 1$. If we insist that the graph be acyclic *and* have exactly one more vertex than edge, then it must have one component; hence it must be connected and, therefore, be a tree. Note that the graph **G'** in Figure 39.4B satisfies $n' = n + 1$ and $m' = m + 3$; hence $n' = 15 + 1 = m' + 1$. The graph **G'** is a tree, whereas the graph **G** is not a tree. (The latter is an example of what we referred to earlier as a "forest.")

39.5

A path of length $n - 1$ is perhaps the simplest of all trees on n vertices. Beyond the trivial case, in which $n = 1$, every path has two vertices of degree 1. Our final result shows that no tree can have fewer than two such vertices.

THEOREM 39.5

Every nontrivial tree has at least two vertices of degree 1.

Proof

By part **B** of Theorem 39.4, there are $\binom{n}{2}$ unique paths in a tree with n vertices. We can examine each of these paths and choose a path $\mathbf{P} = (u_1, u_2, \ldots, u_r)$ so that no other path is longer than $\mathbf{P}$. Since u_2 is adjacent to u_1, $\deg(u_1) \geq 1$. If $\deg(u_1) > 1$, then there is a vertex $w \neq u_2$ such that $\{w, u_1\}$ is an edge in the tree and therefore $(w, u_1, u_2, \ldots, u_r)$ is a path longer than $\mathbf{P}$. This is a contradiction; hence $\deg(u_1) = 1$. Similarly, it can be shown that $\deg(u_r) = 1$. ∎

39.6

Complement: The Matrix-Tree Theorem At the end of this discussion you may be inclined to think that the title should read, The Magic-Tree Theorem. It *is* magic in the sense that the connection leading from the input data through the intermediate operations to the output information is opaque to the point of disbelief. The proof, which offers assurance but little enlightenment, depends upon concepts not introduced in this textbook, and so is omitted. The best advice, perhaps, is to sit back and enjoy some bizarre intellectual scenery.

Our theorem appears to have originated with the work of G. Kirchhoff (1824–1887) on electric circuits. A modern treatment may be found in *Graph Theory* by Harary, p. 152, or in *Graphs, Networks, and Algorithms* by Swamy and Thulasiraman, p. 148. We must begin with a digression on "determinants," including only enough information for "brute-force" computations. Convenient shortcuts are derived in other courses which devote detailed attention to the solution of systems of linear equations.

A determinant is a number associated with a square matrix; it is defined, for our purposes, by the algorithm which computes it. To describe that procedure we need to introduce some new notation. Let us denote an $n \times n$ matrix with real number entries by

$$U = [u_{ij}] = \begin{bmatrix} u_{11} & u_{12} & \cdots & u_{1n} \\ u_{21} & u_{22} & \cdots & u_{2n} \\ \cdots & \cdots & \cdots & \cdots \\ u_{n1} & u_{n2} & \cdots & u_{nn} \end{bmatrix}.$$

It is traditional to denote the determinant of U by

$$\det(U) = \begin{vmatrix} u_{11} & u_{12} & \cdots & u_{1n} \\ u_{21} & u_{22} & \cdots & u_{2n} \\ \cdots & \cdots & \cdots & \cdots \\ u_{n1} & u_{n2} & \cdots & u_{nn} \end{vmatrix},$$

where the "brackets" in the matrix notation are replaced by "vertical bars." The determinant is said to be of **order** n if its matrix is of size $n \times n$. We will denote by U_{ij} the $(n-1) \times (n-1)$ submatrix obtained by eliminating the ith row and the jth column from U. Thus, for example,

$$U_{21} = \begin{bmatrix} u_{12} & u_{13} & \cdots & u_{1n} \\ u_{32} & u_{33} & \cdots & u_{3n} \\ \cdots & \cdots & \cdots & \cdots \\ u_{n2} & u_{n3} & \cdots & u_{nn} \end{bmatrix}.$$

Now, corresponding to any entry u_{ij} in U, denote by C_{ij} the number

$$C_{ij} = (-1)^{i+j} \cdot \det(U_{ij}).$$

Again, for example,

$$C_{21} = (-1)^3 \cdot \begin{vmatrix} u_{12} & u_{13} & \cdots & u_{1n} \\ u_{32} & u_{33} & \cdots & u_{3n} \\ \cdots & \cdots & \cdots & \cdots \\ u_{n2} & u_{n3} & \cdots & u_{nn} \end{vmatrix}.$$

The number C_{ij} is called the **cofactor** of the entry u_{ij} in U.

We are now in a position to describe the computation of determinants inductively, beginning with the 2×2 case.

If $U = \begin{bmatrix} u_{11} & u_{12} \\ u_{21} & u_{22} \end{bmatrix}$, then

$$\det(U) = u_{11} \cdot u_{22} - u_{12} \cdot u_{21}. \tag{1}$$

For example,

$$\begin{vmatrix} 2 & -1 \\ -1 & 2 \end{vmatrix} = 2 \cdot 2 - (-1) \cdot (-1) = 3.$$

If

$$U = \begin{bmatrix} u_{11} & u_{12} & u_{13} \\ u_{21} & u_{22} & u_{23} \\ u_{31} & u_{32} & u_{33} \end{bmatrix},$$

then

$$\det(U) = u_{11} \cdot C_{11} + u_{12} \cdot C_{12} + u_{13} \cdot C_{13}$$

$$= u_{11} \cdot (-1)^2 \cdot \begin{vmatrix} u_{22} & u_{23} \\ u_{32} & u_{33} \end{vmatrix} + u_{12} \cdot (-1)^3 \cdot \begin{vmatrix} u_{21} & u_{23} \\ u_{31} & u_{33} \end{vmatrix} + u_{13} \cdot (-1)^4 \cdot \begin{vmatrix} u_{21} & u_{22} \\ u_{31} & u_{32} \end{vmatrix}.$$

$$(2)$$

For example,

$$\begin{vmatrix} 3 & -1 & -1 \\ -1 & 2 & -1 \\ -1 & -1 & 2 \end{vmatrix} = 3 \cdot \begin{vmatrix} 2 & -1 \\ -1 & 2 \end{vmatrix} - (-1) \cdot \begin{vmatrix} -1 & -1 \\ -1 & 2 \end{vmatrix} + (-1) \cdot \begin{vmatrix} -1 & 2 \\ -1 & -1 \end{vmatrix}$$

$$= 3 \cdot 3 - 3 - 3 = 3.$$

If

$$U = \begin{bmatrix} u_{11} & u_{12} & u_{13} & u_{14} \\ u_{21} & u_{22} & u_{23} & u_{24} \\ u_{31} & u_{32} & u_{33} & u_{34} \\ u_{41} & u_{42} & u_{43} & u_{44} \end{bmatrix},$$

then

$$\det(U) = u_{11} \cdot C_{11} + u_{12} \cdot C_{12} + u_{13} \cdot C_{13} + u_{14} \cdot C_{14}. \qquad (3)$$

For example,

$$\begin{vmatrix} 1 & -1 & 0 & 0 \\ -1 & 3 & -1 & -1 \\ 0 & -1 & 2 & -1 \\ 0 & -1 & -1 & 2 \end{vmatrix} = 1 \cdot \begin{vmatrix} 3 & -1 & -1 \\ -1 & 2 & -1 \\ -1 & -1 & 2 \end{vmatrix} - (-1) \cdot \begin{vmatrix} -1 & -1 & -1 \\ 0 & 2 & -1 \\ 0 & -1 & 2 \end{vmatrix} + 0 + 0$$

$$= 1 \cdot 3 + \left((-1) \cdot \begin{vmatrix} 2 & -1 \\ -1 & 2 \end{vmatrix} + 0 + 0 \right) = 3 - 3 = 0.$$

As our special cases suggest, a determinant of order n may be computed in terms of its first row entries and cofactors. Given the $n \times n$ matrix $U = [u_{ij}]$, then

$$\det(U) = \sum_{j=1}^{n} u_{1j} \cdot C_{1j}. \qquad (4)$$

The arithmetic becomes exceedingly tedious for large n, but (theoretically) determinants of any order can be computed.

No magic so far! Just some sticky preliminaries to get us ready for the show. Now let $\mathbf{G} = (\mathbf{V}, \mathbf{E})$ be any connected, labeled graph with $\mathbf{V} = \{v_1, v_2, \ldots, v_n\}$, and let $A = [a_{ij}]$ be its $n \times n$, $(0, 1)$-adjacency matrix. We now construct a new matrix

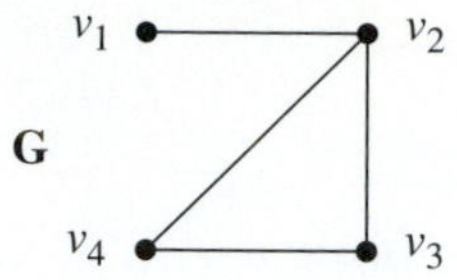

$$[a_{ij}] = \begin{bmatrix} 0 & 1 & 0 & 0 \\ 1 & 0 & 1 & 1 \\ 0 & 1 & 0 & 1 \\ 0 & 1 & 1 & 0 \end{bmatrix}$$

Figure 39.6A

$B = [b_{ij}]$ as follows:

$$b_{ij} = \begin{cases} \deg(v_i), & \text{if } j = i; \\ -a_{ij}, & \text{if } j \neq i. \end{cases} \tag{5}$$

For example, let **G** be the graph shown in Figure 39.6A with indicated adjacency matrix $[a_{ij}]$. Since $\deg(v_1) = 1$, $\deg(v_2) = 3$, and $\deg(v_3) = \deg(v_4) = 2$, the matrix defined by (5) is

$$B = \begin{bmatrix} 1 & -1 & 0 & 0 \\ -1 & 3 & -1 & -1 \\ 0 & -1 & 2 & -1 \\ 0 & -1 & -1 & 2 \end{bmatrix}.$$

This is the matrix used to illustrate (3), above; in it, the cofactor C_{11} has already been computed:

$$C_{11} = (-1)^2 \begin{vmatrix} 3 & -1 & -1 \\ -1 & 2 & -1 \\ -1 & -1 & 2 \end{vmatrix} = 3.$$

Suppose we compute a different cofactor, C_{42} for example,

$$C_{42} = (-1)^6 \begin{vmatrix} 1 & 0 & 0 \\ -1 & -1 & -1 \\ 0 & 2 & -1 \end{vmatrix} = \begin{vmatrix} -1 & -1 \\ 2 & -1 \end{vmatrix} + 0 + 0 = 1 + 2 = 3.$$

Notice that $C_{11} = C_{42}$. Can this be accidental? The answer is "no." And what about the common value, does it mean anything? The answer is given by the Matrix-Tree Theorem.

THEOREM 39.6

Matrix-Tree Theorem. Let A denote the adjacency matrix for a connected, labeled graph **G**, and let B denote the matrix defined in (5). Then:

a. All cofactors of B have a common value, say k.

b. k is the number of spanning trees of the graph **G**.

Look back at Figure 39.6A. The Matrix-Tree Theorem predicts that **G** has exactly three spanning trees. With vertices as labeled in Figure 39.6A, they are shown in

Figure 39.6B

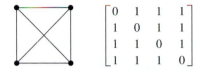

$$\begin{bmatrix} 0 & 1 & 1 & 1 \\ 1 & 0 & 1 & 1 \\ 1 & 1 & 0 & 1 \\ 1 & 1 & 1 & 0 \end{bmatrix}$$

Figure 39.6C

Figure 39.6B. We told you there was magic in this theorem. But the surprise is not yet over. Let's apply the Matrix-Tree Theorem to the complete graph $\mathbf{K}_4$, shown with its adjacency matrix $[a_{ij}]$ in Figure 39.6C. First, note that

$$B = \begin{bmatrix} 3 & -1 & -1 & -1 \\ -1 & 3 & -1 & -1 \\ -1 & -1 & 3 & -1 \\ -1 & -1 & -1 & 3 \end{bmatrix}.$$

Then,

$$C_{11} = \begin{vmatrix} 3 & -1 & -1 \\ -1 & 3 & -1 \\ -1 & -1 & 3 \end{vmatrix} = 3 \cdot \begin{vmatrix} 3 & -1 \\ -1 & 3 \end{vmatrix} + \begin{vmatrix} -1 & -1 \\ -1 & 3 \end{vmatrix} - \begin{vmatrix} -1 & 3 \\ -1 & -1 \end{vmatrix}$$

$$= 3 \cdot 8 - 4 - 4 = 16 = 4^2,$$

which is a special case of Cayley's result (Theorem 39.2).

In generality, the Matrix-Tree Theorem provides an alternate technique of proof for that theorem: Simply apply it to $\mathbf{K}_n$. The corresponding B matrix is of size $n \times n$:

$$B = \begin{bmatrix} n-1 & -1 & -1 & \cdots & -1 \\ -1 & n-1 & -1 & \cdots & -1 \\ -1 & -1 & n-1 & \cdots & -1 \\ \cdots & \cdots & \cdots & \cdots & \cdots \\ -1 & -1 & -1 & \cdots & n-1 \end{bmatrix};$$

hence the cofactor C_{11} is the $(n-1) \times (n-1)$ determinant

$$\begin{vmatrix} n-1 & -1 & \cdots & -1 \\ -1 & n-1 & \cdots & -1 \\ \cdots & \cdots & \cdots & \cdots \\ -1 & -1 & \cdots & n-1 \end{vmatrix}.$$

By simple manipulations (not proved here), C_{11} can be expressed differently as the following determinant of order $n - 1$, which can be computed (trivially) as the product of the entries on the main diagonal:

$$C_{11} = \begin{vmatrix} 1 & -1 & -1 & \cdots & -1 \\ 0 & n & 0 & \cdots & 0 \\ 0 & 0 & n & \cdots & 0 \\ \cdots & \cdots & \cdots & \cdots & \cdots \\ 0 & 0 & 0 & \cdots & n \end{vmatrix} = n^{n-2}.$$

Problems for Section 39

1. This problem is concerned with trees having exactly eight vertices, none of which has degree greater than 3. (*a*) Draw the only tree having each vertex of degree less than 3. (*b*) Draw the four trees having exactly one vertex of degree 3. (*c*) Draw the five trees having exactly two vertices of degree 3. (*d*) Draw the only tree having three vertices of degree 3.

2. Draw the six trees on eight vertices having exactly one vertex of degree 4.

3. Draw the six trees on eight vertices which have not been accounted for in Problems 1 and 2.

4. This problem is concerned with trees having exactly nine vertices, none of which has degree greater than 3. (*a*) Draw the only tree having each vertex of degree less than 3. (*b*) Draw the five trees having exactly one vertex of degree 3. (*c*) Draw the nine trees having exactly two vertices of degree 3.

5. Devise an algorithm to find a spanning tree in a connected graph.

6. Let $\mathbf{G} = (\mathbf{V}, \mathbf{E})$ be a graph with a bridge e. Show that $\mathbf{G}' = (\mathbf{V}, \mathbf{E} - e)$ has one more component than $\mathbf{G}$.

7. If $\mathbf{T}$ is a nontrivial tree, then show that deleting any edge of $\mathbf{T}$ results in a forest with two components.

8. The **diameter** of a tree is the length of a longest path in the tree. What are the diameters of

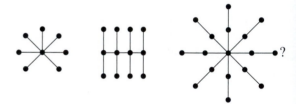

9. (*Conclusion of Problem 8.*) What is the diameter of

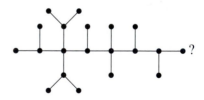

10. The **distance** between two vertices u and v, denoted dist(u, v), of a graph $\mathbf{G}$ is the length of a shortest path connecting u and v. What is the distance between u and v in the following graphs?

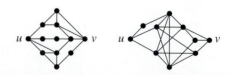

11. The **diameter** of a connected graph is the maximum of dist(u, v) for all pairs of vertices u and v in the graph. What is the diameter of $\mathbf{K}_n$ and $\mathbf{K}_{m,n}$? What is the diameter of a path with n vertices?

12. Construct a graph with eight vertices and diameter 5.

13. Which is larger: the number of labeled trees with six vertices or the number of labeled graphs with five vertices?

14. (*a*) Can a graph with $n \geq 3$ vertices have a cut-vertex and no bridge? If so, draw such a graph. If not, prove it. (*b*) Can a graph with $n \geq 3$ vertices have a bridge and no cut-vertex? If so, draw such a graph. If not, prove it.

15. Using Theorem 39.4, show that the following are equivalent for $\mathbf{G} = (\mathbf{V}, \mathbf{E})$ which has $n > 1$ vertices. (*a*) $\mathbf{G}$ is a tree. (*b*) $\mathbf{G}$ is connected, and if e is an edge of $\mathbf{G}$, then $\mathbf{G}' = (\mathbf{V}, \mathbf{E} - e)$ is not connected. (*c*) $\mathbf{G}$ has no cycles, and if e is not an edge in $\mathbf{G}$, then $\mathbf{G}'' = (\mathbf{V}, \mathbf{E} \cup \{e\})$ is a graph with at least one cycle.

16. Show that the following are equivalent for a graph $\mathbf{G} = (\mathbf{V}, \mathbf{E})$ which has $n > 1$ vertices and m edges. (*a*) $\mathbf{G}$ is connected and has exactly one cycle. (*b*) $\mathbf{G}$ is connected and $n = m$. (*c*) For some edge e of $\mathbf{G}$, the graph $\mathbf{G}' = (\mathbf{V}, \mathbf{E} - e)$ is a tree.

17. Let $\mathbf{G} = (\mathbf{V}, \mathbf{E})$ be a graph with $n > 2$ vertices. Show that the following are equivalent. (*a*) $\mathbf{G}$ is connected and regular of degree 2. (*b*) If e is any edge of $\mathbf{G}$, then $\mathbf{P}_n = (\mathbf{V}, \mathbf{E} - e)$ is the path on n vertices. (*c*) $\mathbf{G}$ is connected, has one cycle, and has no bridges. (Problem 15 of Section 36 and Theorem 39.4 can be used in this problem.)

18. Show that if $\mathbf{G}$ is a tree with n vertices, then the sum of the degrees of the vertices of $\mathbf{G}$ is $2n - 2$.

19. How many cycles does a connected graph have if the graph has n vertices and n edges? Why?

20. As in Example 1 of paragraph 39.2, apply the algorithm of Theorem 39.2 to find the 4-tuple which corresponds to the labeled tree

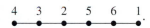

21. Repeat the previous problem with the tree

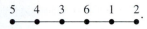

22. As in Example 1 of paragraph 39.2, apply the algorithm of Theorem 39.2 to find the 5-tuple which corresponds to the labeled tree

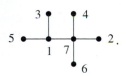

23. As in Example 1 of paragraph 39.2, apply the algorithm of Theorem 39.2 to find the 6-tuple which corresponds to the labeled tree

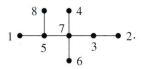

24. Find the tree corresponding to the 4-tuple $(1, 3, 3, 2)$.

25. Find the tree corresponding to the 4-tuple $(1, 1, 3, 1)$.

26. Find three spanning trees of $\mathbf{K}_5$.

27. Find a spanning tree of $\mathbf{K}_8$ with a vertex of degree 4.

28. Find a spanning tree of the Petersen graph (see Problem 1 of Section 35). How many vertices of degree 3 can your tree have?

Section 40.   Digraphs, Tournaments, and Networks

Overview for Section 40

- Introduction to the idea of directed graph (digraph)
- Nodes and arcs and the relationship between digraphs and irreflexive relations
- Enumeration of digraphs
- Definition of tournament and its score sequence
- Domination and in-degree and out-degree of a node
- Distinction between strongly and weakly connected digraphs
- Condition that a connected digraph be eulerian
- Brief discussion of a network

Key Concepts: node, arc, digraph, tournament, degree of a node, score sequence, walk, path, connectivity, cycle, eulerian property, weighted digraph, and source and sink

40.1   Suppose that the students of discrete mathematics field an intramural softball team which plays in a league with four other teams. If every team plays every other team once, a possible outcome is depicted in Figure 40.1A, where the vertices represent the teams and the arrows on the edges indicate which team won. For example, the discrete mathematics team D beat teams A, B, and E but lost to team C. A tournament in which each team plays every other team once is known as a **round-robin**

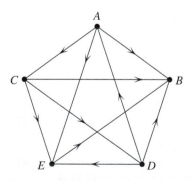

Figure 40.1A

tournament, and the "graph" used to represent the outcome of such a competition is called a "tournament." In more mathematical language, a **tournament** is a complete graph in which each edge is "directed" (has an arrow). We can be precise about what this condition means by first generalizing the concept of tournament to a new structure which models a great variety of interconnections, not readily described by our already familiar graphs. The structure is similar to a graph, but it assigns directions from some vertices to others. Throughout this section we will use different words for "vertex" and "edge" so as to minimize possible confusion.

Let $\mathbf{S} = \{s_1, s_2, \ldots, s_n\}$ be a (finite) set of objects called **nodes** (instead of vertices). Let $\mathbf{A}$ be any set of ordered pairs of different nodes called **arcs** (instead of edges). A **directed graph, D** = (**S, A**), is a set of nodes

$$\mathbf{S} = \{s_1, s_2, \ldots, s_n\}$$

and a set of arcs

$$\mathbf{A} \subseteq \{(s_i, s_j) \in \mathbf{S}^2 : s_i \neq s_j\}.$$

The two standard representations of a directed graph, as an $n \times n$, (0, 1)-matrix and as a diagram, are illustrated in Figure 40.1B using the following nodes and arcs:

$$\mathbf{S} = \{s_1, s_2, s_3, s_4\}$$

$$\mathbf{A} = \{(s_1, s_2), (s_1, s_3), (s_2, s_1), (s_2, s_3), (s_2, s_4), (s_4, s_3)\}.$$

Note that ordered pairs of the form (s_i, s_i) are not permitted as arcs, which is in conformity with our agreement to avoid "loops" at vertices of graphs. The matrix representation of **D** is irreflexive and is constructed (as for graphs) by the requirement

$$a_{ij} = \begin{cases} 1, & \text{if } (s_i, s_j) \in \mathbf{A}; \\ 0, & \text{otherwise.} \end{cases}$$

This representation is simply a relation matrix, as studied in the preceding chapter. It differs from the corresponding representation for graphs in that it is not necessarily symmetric. Thus, a directed graph, conveniently abbreviated **digraph,** is really nothing more than what we called in paragraph 28.3 an irreflexive relation in $\mathbf{S} \times \mathbf{S}$. The enumeration of digraphs on $\mathbf{S} = \{s_1, s_2, \ldots, s_n\}$ is given in Theorem 28.4;

$$[a_{ij}] = \begin{array}{c} \\ s_1 \\ s_2 \\ s_3 \\ s_4 \end{array} \begin{array}{cccc} s_1 & s_2 & s_3 & s_4 \\ \begin{bmatrix} 0 & 1 & 1 & 0 \\ 1 & 0 & 1 & 1 \\ 0 & 0 & 0 & 0 \\ 0 & 0 & 1 & 0 \end{bmatrix} \end{array}$$

(a)

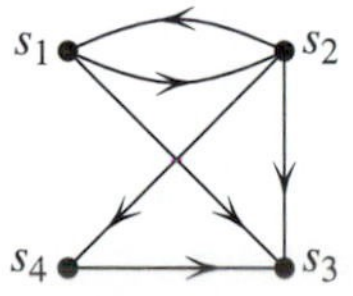

(b)

Figure 40.1B

that is,

$$2^{n(n-1)}. \tag{1}$$

The other standard representation of a digraph is shown in part (*b*) of Figure 40.1B. It is a diagram consisting of *n* points labeled by the nodes, in which there is an "arrow" from s_i to s_j if and only if $(s_i, s_j) \in \mathbf{A}$. The diagram allows for the possibility of two different arcs between the same pair of nodes. Observe, of course, that we consider $(s_i, s_j) \neq (s_j, s_i)$ if $i \neq j$.

Example 1

According to (1), the number of digraphs on 2 nodes is $2^2 = 4$. Their diagrams are:

$s_1 \bullet$ $\bullet s_2$ $s_1 \bullet \longrightarrow \bullet s_2$ $s_1 \bullet \longleftarrow \bullet s_2$ $s_1 \bullet \mathbin{<\!\!\!\!>} \bullet s_2$

The matrix representations are, respectively,

$$\begin{bmatrix} 0 & 0 \\ 0 & 0 \end{bmatrix}, \begin{bmatrix} 0 & 1 \\ 0 & 0 \end{bmatrix}, \begin{bmatrix} 0 & 0 \\ 1 & 0 \end{bmatrix}, \begin{bmatrix} 0 & 1 \\ 1 & 0 \end{bmatrix}.$$

The number of digraphs on 3 nodes is $2^6 = 64$. Of these, $\binom{6}{k}$ have exactly *k* arcs for each $0 \leq k \leq 6$. The reason follows most easily from the matrix representation

$$[a_{ij}] = \begin{bmatrix} 0 & & \\ & 0 & \\ & & 0 \end{bmatrix}. \tag{2}$$

Each entry off the main diagonal corresponds to a possible arc ($a_{ij} = 1$ indicating the presence of an arc, $a_{ij} = 0$ indicating the absence of an arc). To obtain a digraph with exactly two arcs, for example, we must place 1s in two of the six blanks and 0s elsewhere. These $\binom{6}{2} = 15$ digraphs have diagrams as shown in Figure 40.1C

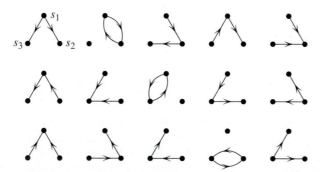

Figure 40.1C

(labels are as indicated in the first diagram). Any digraph on three nodes must have exactly k arcs for some $0 \le k \le 6$; hence the total number of digraphs is the sum of these enumerations:

$$2^6 = \sum_{k=0}^{6} \binom{6}{k} = \binom{6}{0} + \binom{6}{1} + \binom{6}{2} + \binom{6}{3} + \binom{6}{4} + \binom{6}{5} + \binom{6}{6}.$$

You may recognize this as the Binomial Theorem (Theorem 17.2) with $x = y = 1$ and $m = 6$. ●

Tutorial 40.1

a. Are you sure that the diagrams in Figure 40.1C are all different?
b. Referring to (2), discover the pattern which guided our arrangement of the diagrams in Figure 40.1C.
c. Use the corresponding pattern for digraphs on four nodes with two arcs to sketch the diagrams which should appear in the first, tenth, and twentieth positions.

THEOREM 40.1

The number of digraphs on a set of n nodes is $2^{n(n-1)}$, and the number of such digraphs having exactly k arcs, $0 \le k \le n(n-1)$, is $\binom{n(n-1)}{k}$.

Proof

The proof follows directly from (1) and the argument given in the example above. ■

40.2

We return now to the notion of "tournament" and refer to Figure 40.2. Two characteristics stand out: There is an arc between each pair of nodes, and no pair of nodes has an arc in each direction. In the matrix representation of this digraph, these properties are seen to correspond with relations which are, in the language of paragraph 32.3, both antisymmetric and total. For any symmetric pair of entries a_{ij} and a_{ji}, one of them is 1 and the other is 0. Here, then, is an alternate definition: A **tournament** on a set $\mathbf{S}$ of nodes is a digraph corresponding to a relation in $\mathbf{S}^2$ which is irreflexive, total, and antisymmetric. The enumeration of tournaments now follows easily. We need only determine the number of symmetric pairs a_{ij} and a_{ji} with $i \ne j$, then

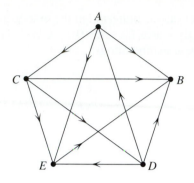

$$[a_{ij}] = \begin{array}{c} \\ A \\ B \\ C \\ D \\ E \end{array} \begin{array}{ccccc} A & B & C & D & E \\ \begin{bmatrix} 0 & 1 & 1 & 0 & 1 \\ 0 & 0 & 0 & 0 & 0 \\ 0 & 1 & 0 & 1 & 1 \\ 1 & 1 & 0 & 0 & 1 \\ 0 & 1 & 0 & 0 & 0 \end{bmatrix} \end{array}$$

Figure 40.2

choose one of the two entries in each pair to be assigned the value 1. Interestingly, this number is

$$2^{n(n-1)/2}, \tag{1}$$

which is just the number of graphs on n vertices; further, the number of tournaments on **S** is the square root of the number of digraphs on **S** since

$$2^{n(n-1)/2} \cdot 2^{n(n-1)/2} = 2^{n(n-1)}.$$

Notice that a tournament is not an "order relation," for transitivity may fail. Not infrequently in the real world, favorites are upset; because D beats A and A beats C, it is not assured that D beats C (Figure 40.2, for example).

40.3

In a digraph $\mathbf{D} = (\mathbf{S}, \mathbf{A})$, to say that $(s_i, s_j) \in \mathbf{A}$ means that there is an arrow pointing from node s_i to node s_j. We say, then, that node s_i **dominates** node s_j, and we write this as $s_i \rightarrow s_j$. The number of nodes dominated by s_i is the **out-degree** of s_i [denoted odeg(s_i)] and the **in-degree** of s_i is the number of nodes that dominate s_i [denoted ideg(s_i)]. It is immediate that for each node s_i in a tournament,

$$\text{odeg}(s_i) + \text{ideg}(s_i) = n - 1. \tag{1}$$

The out-degree of node s_i is also known as the **score** of s_i. The **score sequence** of a digraph is the n-tuple of scores, usually arranged in nondecreasing order.

Example 1   Refer in this example to the tournament described in Figure 40.2. The scores, or out-degrees, are

$$\text{odeg}(A) = 3, \quad \text{odeg}(B) = 0, \quad \text{odeg}(C) = 3, \quad \text{odeg}(D) = 3, \quad \text{odeg}(E) = 1.$$

Observe that the row sums in $[a_{ij}]$ of Figure 40.2 are the scores. By relabeling the rows and columns we can assure that the quintuple of row sums

$$(r_1, r_2, r_3, r_4, r_5)$$

is, in fact, the score sequence

$$(0, 1, 3, 3, 3).$$

Under this relabeling, the new matrix is

$$
\begin{array}{c}
 \\
B \\
E \\
A \\
C \\
D
\end{array}
\begin{array}{c}
\begin{array}{ccccc} B & E & A & C & D \end{array} \\
\left[
\begin{array}{ccccc}
0 & 0 & 0 & 0 & 0 \\
1 & 0 & 0 & 0 & 0 \\
1 & 1 & 0 & 1 & 0 \\
1 & 1 & 0 & 0 & 1 \\
1 & 1 & 1 & 0 & 0
\end{array}
\right]
\begin{array}{c}
0 \\
1 \\
3 \\
3 \\
3
\end{array}
\end{array} \text{ row sums .}
\tag{2}
$$

The score sequence of this tournament demonstrates that it may not be easy to determine a winner in a round-robin tournament. In this case B is a clear loser, but there is a three-way tie for first place.

Tutorial 40.3

a. In the matrix shown in (2), what do the column sums represent?

b. How is (1) related to (2)?

c. How many 1s are in a matrix corresponding to a tournament on four nodes, on five nodes, on n nodes?

40.4   As in the case of graphs, the idea of "connectedness" offers an important distinction among digraphs, but "direction" introduces a complication. Several types of paths (and, therefore, types of connectedness) have been found useful, but here we will restrict our attention to two types only.

A **walk** in a digraph is a sequence of nodes

$$s_1 \rightarrow s_2 \rightarrow s_3 \rightarrow \cdots \rightarrow s_k, \tag{1}$$

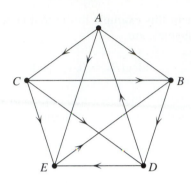

Figure 40.4

which implies that s_1 dominates s_2, s_2 dominates s_3, and so on. Note that nodes and arcs may be repeated. The walk is **closed** if $s_k = s_1$. A **path** is a walk in which $s_i \neq s_j$ for all i and j. The **length** of a walk is the number of arrows in it. A **cycle** is a walk in which $k > 2$ and all nodes are distinct except that $s_k = s_1$. If there is a path from any node of a digraph to any other, then the digraph is **strongly connected.** The digraphs in Figures 40.1A and 40.1B are *not* strongly connected, but the digraph in Figure 40.4 is strongly connected. It is the same tournament as the one in Figure 40.1A except that the outcome of one game is reversed.

In spite of the fact that they fail to be strongly connected, each of the digraphs in Figures 40.1A and 40.1B have diagrams which are linked together in one piece. If we were to erase the arrowheads, leaving the unordered arcs, it is clear that there is a path in the "graph" sense between any two nodes. We will refer to this property of a digraph as "connectedness" (it is essentially the same as that for a graph, being independent of the directions assigned to arcs). Thus, a digraph is **connected** (sometimes called **weakly connected**) if for any pair of nodes s_0 and s_k there is a list of distinct nodes

$$s_0, s_1, s_2, \ldots, s_k$$

such that consecutive nodes are joined by an arc (in either direction or both).

A digraph is an extremely general structure, so much so that the most useful concepts depend upon specializations of one sort or another. The enumerations in Theorem 40.1 are the only results we will state about digraphs in complete generality. On the other hand, many subfamilies of digraphs, such as tournaments, have properties which are both pretty (a subjective attribute) and easy to prove (an objective attribute at this point). Here is an example of what we mean; it shows that in any tournament, no matter how large its node set, there is at least one node which is "close" to every other node (specifically, within a path of length 2).

THEOREM 40.4   Let **T** be a tournament with n nodes and let s be the largest score of **T**. If v is a node with $\mathrm{odeg}(v) = s$, then for every other node $u \in$ **T**, either $v \to u$ or $v \to w \to u$ for some node $w \in$ **T**.

Proof

If v dominates every other node in **T**, then we are done. Hence, we assume that v dominates the nodes in $\mathbf{W} = \{w_1, w_2, \ldots, w_s\}$ and is dominated by the nodes in $\mathbf{U} = \{u_1, u_2, \ldots, u_m\}$. (Since **T** is a tournament, $s + m + 1 = n$.) Clearly, if for each $u \in \mathbf{U}$ there exists a $w \in \mathbf{W}$ such that $w \to u$, then $v \to w \to u$ and we are done. Recall from paragraph 9.2 the universal quantifier $\forall$ and the existential quantifier $\exists$ and note that the hypothesis in the previous sentence could be written as

$$\forall u \in \mathbf{U}, \exists w \in \mathbf{W}, w \to u. \tag{2}$$

The negation of this is

$$\exists u \in \mathbf{U}, \forall w \in \mathbf{W}, u \to w. \tag{3}$$

To finish the proof, we need only assume that the negation of (2) is true and then produce a contradiction. Thus we assume that there is a node $u \in \mathbf{U}$ such that for all $w \in \mathbf{W}$, u dominates w. Since **W** has s nodes and since $u \to v$, u dominates at least $s + 1$ nodes. But this contradicts the fact that s is the largest score of **T**. Hence, (2) must be true, as is the theorem. ∎

40.5

A tournament may very well have a node which is dominated by all the others (as is B in Figure 40.1A). This means that there is no path from that node to any other; hence the tournament cannot be strongly connected. It *is* true, however, that every tournament is connected, for there is an arc between any pair of nodes. But an even stronger statement holds: One can always find a path which includes every node. (In our tournament one such path is $A \to C \to D \to E \to B$.)

THEOREM 40.5

In any tournament there is a path containing all the nodes.

Proof

Let **T** be a tournament with n nodes. We use induction to show that there are paths of *all* lengths from 1 to $n - 1$. Any arc will serve as a path of length 1. Assume that there is a path of length k, $1 < k < n - 1$, namely,

$$v_1 \to v_2 \to \cdots \to v_{k+1}.$$

Our problem is to produce a path of length $k + 1$. Because **T** has n nodes, there exists a node w not on the given path of length k. If $w \to v_1$, then

$$w \to v_1 \to v_2 \to \cdots \to v_{k+1}$$

is a path of length $k + 1$ and we are done. Otherwise $v_1 \to w$, because in a tournament one or the other must be true. Let r be the greatest index such that $v_r \to w$. If $r = k + 1$ then

$$v_1 \to v_2 \to \cdots \to v_{k+1} \to w$$

is a path of length $k + 1$. On the other hand, if $r < k + 1$, then

$$v_1 \to \cdots \to v_r \to w \to v_{r+1} \to \cdots \to v_{k+1}$$

is a path of length $k + 1$. This follows since v_{r+1} does not dominate w; hence, $w \to v_{r+1}$. ■

Tutorial 40.5

Consider the tournament

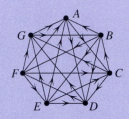

a. Find a node which is close to any other node (in the sense of Theorem 40.4).
b. Extend the path $A \to C \to B \to F \to E \to G$ (of length 5) to one of length 6 as in the proof of Theorem 40.5.

40.6

Turning our attention from nodes to arcs, we now extend the idea of an eulerian graph to digraphs. The definition of an eulerian digraph is similar to that of an eulerian graph, studied in Section 38. A connected digraph **D** is **eulerian** if there is a closed walk in **D**, called an **eulerian walk,** which contains every arc of **D** exactly once. This also implies that every node is included in an eulerian walk at least once. Recall that a connected graph is eulerian if the degree of each vertex is even. This ensured that upon entering a vertex on the walk there must be another edge incident to the vertex that had not yet been used in the walk. To have this happen in a digraph, each node of the digraph must have an arc leaving it for each arc entering it; that is, the in-degree of the node must be no greater than its out-degree. In fact, equality turns out to be essential.

THEOREM 40.6

A connected digraph is eulerian if and only if for every node v of **D**, $\mathrm{odeg}(v) = \mathrm{ideg}(v)$.

Proof
Suppose **D** is eulerian, and let **T** be an eulerian walk. Pick some node s_0 in **D**, and starting at s_0, traverse the walk **T**. For each vertex v in **D**, the in-degree and out-

degree of v increases by 1 each time v is encountered, except that the initial and terminal encounters with s_0 produce one of each. Since every arc incident to v is included exactly once in the walk, $\text{odeg}(v) = \text{ideg}(v)$.

Now suppose that for all nodes v in **D**, $\text{odeg}(v) = \text{ideg}(v)$. It is easily seen that if the arcs in a cycle of **D** are deleted from **D**, then the resulting digraph, or each of its nontrivial components, still has nodes with equal in- and out-degrees. So if we knew that every connected digraph in which each node has equal in- and out-degrees had a cycle, then we could use induction exactly as it was used in Theorem 38.2. The details are omitted here (see Problems 10 to 12).   ■

If one exists, an eulerian walk in a digraph can be identified by an algorithm similar to Fleury's Algorithm (see paragraph 38.3). The proof that the following algorithm is correct is given in the problems.

FLEURY'S ALGORITHM FOR DIGRAPHS

Step 1.   Begin at any node and traverse the digraph along arcs.

Step 2.   Mark each arc when used.

Step 3.   Only as a last resort, use an arc that disconnects (in the weak sense) the subdigraph consisting of unmarked arcs and their incident nodes.

Step 4.   Stop after entering a node that has no unmarked exit arc.   ▲

Example 1

A tournament on an even number of nodes can never be eulerian, since $\text{odeg}(v) + \text{ideg}(v)$ is odd. A tournament on an odd number of nodes, however, can be eulerian. The tournament displayed in Tutorial 40.5 is not eulerian because it fails to satisfy the condition stated in Theorem 40.6. If the direction is changed on each of the arcs (A, F), (B, D), and (E, G), then the resulting tournament is eulerian, and a possible eulerian walk begins

$$A \to C \to B \to A \to D \to B \to E \to \cdots.$$

More generally, consider the digraph shown in Figure 40.6. If the two arcs in the cycle $A \to D \to A$ are deleted, then each of the two remaining components is a digraph in which out-degrees equal in-degrees. Each is eulerian; hence the original digraph is eulerian, and a possible eulerian walk is $A \to D \to E \to F \to D \to A \to B \to C \to A$.   ●

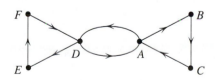

Figure 40.6

40.7

Return, once again, to the tournament in Figure 40.1A. If some of the games were rained out, then not all the arcs would exist and the resulting digraph would no longer be a tournament. In part (*a*) of Figure 40.7A, a digraph is shown in which the games between *A* and *C*, *A* and *E*, *B* and *D*, and *B* and *E* were rained out. Suppose that a number of games in this league were scheduled during the spring term, some of which were rained out. The results for the term might be as shown in part (*b*) of Figure 40.7A. Note that *C* beat *D* once, but that *D* beat *C* twice and *C* beat *E* three times. Evidently, *B* played only *A* in the spring term.

When each arc has a nonnegative number, called a **weight,** assigned to it the digraph is referred to as a **network.** Usually networks are assumed also to have one **source,** a node that is dominated by no node, and one **sink,** a node that dominates no node. A network with a source and sink is illustrated in Figure 40.7B.

There are many interpretations of such a network, based upon applications in various fields. A fairly obvious one is to imagine that the arcs of the network are pipelines carrying some commodity, such as oil. In this case, the weights would be the capacity of the pipeline (measured, perhaps, in thousands of barrels per hour). A natural problem might be to determine how much oil the network can deliver to a particular node. Another quite natural interpretation is to view the network as a map, with arcs representing roads and each weight representing the time required to travel the road. A typical problem here is to determine the quickest way to travel from the source to the sink. In the following example, we will consider in some detail a less evident interpretation of this network. It requires the additional information presented in Table 40.7A.

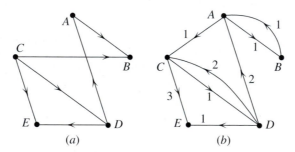

(a)   (b)

Figure 40.7A

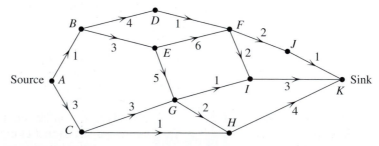

Figure 40.7B

Task	Time needed	Prerequisites	Arc
a	1	None	A → B
b	3	None	A → C
c	3	a	B → E
d	4	a	B → D
e	3	b	C → G
f	1	b	C → H
g	1	d	D → F
h	6	c	E → F
i	5	c	E → G
j	2	g, h	F → I
k	2	g, h	F → J
l	1	e, i	G → I
m	2	e, i	G → H
n	4	f, m	H → K
o	3	j, l	I → K
p	1	k	J → K

Table 40.7A

Example 1

Imagine that you are building a house. There are 16 tasks (labeled a to p) that must be performed before the house can be completed. Certain of these tasks can only be done after others have been completed; for example, task i must be finished before task m can begin. The natural question to ask is, "How quickly can the house be built?" To answer this, we convert Table 40.7A into the network of Figure 40.7B. The tasks are the arcs of the network, and the weight of an arc is the time required for that task. In the table, each arc corresponds to a given task, and the appropriate time is indicated. For example, we may assume that task b requires 3 weeks for completion and that tasks e and f can only begin after b is completed. Now, suppose we define the **capacity** of a path to be the sum of the weights of its arcs. To determine how quickly the house can be built, we must find the path with the *largest* capacity! In this example there are two such paths,

$$A \rightarrow B \rightarrow E \rightarrow F \rightarrow I \rightarrow K$$

and $$A \rightarrow B \rightarrow E \rightarrow G \rightarrow H \rightarrow K,$$

both 15 weeks long which, in our simple digraph, can be found by trial and error. The capacity, of course, tells us that we should not expect completion of the house in under 15 weeks.

Weeks														
1	2	3	4	5	6	7	8	9	10	11	12	13	14	15
I *a*	*c*						*h*				*j*		*o*	
II	*b*		*f*			*i*				*m*		*n*		
III		*d*				*g*	*e*		*l*		*k*			*p*

Table 40.7B

In an actual construction project, work may proceed simultaneously on tasks which are independent of one another. The scheduling required to achieve minimum construction time may be quite complicated, and contractors often use computer-based models to create job schedules. In Table 40.7B, we indicate one possible schedule which allows for completion of the entire project in the minimum time of 15 weeks. Note that no task begins before its prerequisite tasks have ended, but that for most of the period three crews must be at work concurrently.

Problems associated with this, and other, scheduling interpretations are sufficiently important that much effort has been devoted in recent years to the construction of algorithms which provide "best" answers. We will not pursue the matter in further detail here; two of the more accessible references are *Applied Combinatorics* by Tucker and *Graph Theory Applications* by Foulds. More advanced courses include the study of a technique called *critical path analysis,* which can be used to find paths of largest capacity in a network.

Finally, a distinction can be made between labeled and unlabeled digraphs, just as with graphs. The existence, for example, of an eulerian walk is independent of labels on the nodes. As is to be expected, the difference in enumeration is significant. Once again, advanced techniques are required to enumerate unlabeled digraphs. We defer the problem to a later course, simply listing in Table 40.7C a few of the known numbers. Let $ld(n)$ denote the number of labeled digraphs on n nodes (from Theorem 40.1), and let $ud(n)$ denote the number of unlabeled digraphs on n nodes.

40.8

Complement: Landau's Theorem A question that occurs with some relevance in digraph applications is, "Suppose we determine, from experimental data, a list of n nonnegative integers. Can we model our experiment as a digraph having the given n-tuple as its score sequence?" A biologist studying an animal community,

n	1	2	3	4	5
$ld(n)$	1	4	64	4096	1,048,576
$ud(n)$	1	3	16	218	9608

Table 40.7C

for example, may observe a social trait called "dominance" operating between each two individuals. Records maintained over a period of time may provide for each individual the number of others that it dominates, and these numbers constitute our list. From investigations of this type, the phrase "pecking order" has entered current usage. "Dominance" is a one-way relationship: If A dominates B, then B does not dominate A. We might expect, then, to represent dominance among members of the community by a tournament in which $A \rightarrow B$ indicates that A dominates B. Our problem is to investigate conditions under which a given n-tuple of nonnegative integers

$$(r_1, r_2, \ldots, r_n) \tag{1}$$

is the score sequence of some tournament. If there does exist such a tournament $\mathbf{T} = (\mathbf{S}, \mathbf{A})$, with matrix representation

$$[t_{ij}], \tag{2}$$

then the coordinates r_i in (1) are the row sums. We will not assume here that the coordinates are arranged in any particular order. The solution to this problem was given by Landau in a paper published in the *Bulletin of Mathematical Biophysics*.

It can be observed quickly that if (1) were the score sequence of a tournament, then it cannot be given arbitrarily. For example, if $r_i = r_j = 0$, then $t_{ij} = t_{ji} = 0$, and this violates the condition that there must be an arrow between the nodes s_i and s_j. Landau noted two important properties of a tournament on n nodes.

I. Since each 2-element subset of $\mathbf{S}$, say $\{s_i, s_j\}$, contributes a 1 and a 0 to the matrix $[t_{ij}]$, $t_{ij} + t_{ji} = 1$, and since the number of such subsets is $\binom{|\mathbf{S}|}{2}$, then

$$\sum_{k=1}^{n} r_i = \binom{n}{2}. \tag{3}$$

II. Consider, next, any two elements in $\mathbf{S}$, say s_i and s_j. Then $r_i + r_j \geq \binom{2}{2} = 1$, since $t_{ij} + t_{ji} = 1$. Again, consider any three elements in $\mathbf{S}$, say s_i, s_j, s_k. Then $r_i + r_j + r_k \geq \binom{3}{2} = 3$, since $t_{ij} + t_{ji} = 1$, $t_{ik} + t_{ki} = 1$, and $t_{jk} + t_{kj} = 1$. Hence, in general, if $\mathbf{Y}$ is any nonempty subset of $\mathbf{S}$, then

$$\sum_{s_k \in \mathbf{Y}} r_k \geq \binom{|\mathbf{Y}|}{2}. \tag{4}$$

Landau was able to show that (3) and (4) are the only conditions required to guarantee that (1) is the score sequence of a tournament. We will show that his theorem is a direct consequence of Hall's Theorem on systems of distinct representatives (see paragraph 11.6). This proof appears in the paper "Score Vectors of Tournaments" by Bang and Sharp.

Landau's Theorem. Let $\mathbf{S} = \{s_1, s_2, \ldots, s_n\}$ and let $(r_1, r_2, \ldots, r_n)$ be an n-tuple of nonnegative integers. There exists a tournament on $\mathbf{S}$ having the given n-tuple as its score sequence if and only if

$$\sum_{k=1}^{n} r_k = \binom{n}{2} \tag{3}$$

and for each nonempty subset $\mathbf{Y} \subseteq \mathbf{S}$, $\displaystyle\sum_{s_k \in \mathbf{Y}} r_k \geq \binom{|\mathbf{Y}|}{2}$. $\tag{4}$

Proof

By the arguments in properties I and II above, it follows that (3) and (4) hold for any score sequence of a tournament. To prove sufficiency of the given conditions, we assume that $(r_1, r_2, \ldots, r_n)$ is an n-tuple of nonnegative integers for which (3) and (4) are true. Our task is to construct a tournament with matrix $[t_{ij}]$ which has the given n-tuple as its score sequence.

For each $s_k \in \mathbf{S}$, let $\mathbf{G}_k$ be a set for which $|\mathbf{G}_k| = r_k$. Suppose we assume that the sets $\mathbf{G}_k$ are pairwise-disjoint and that $\mathbf{G} = \displaystyle\bigcup_{k=1}^{n} \mathbf{G}_k$. Thus $|\mathbf{G}| = \binom{n}{2}$, by (3). For each $\{s_i, s_j\} \subseteq \mathbf{S}$, we must assign 0 and 1 to t_{ij} and t_{ji} so that the row sums are correct. Here's how.

Let $\mathbf{B}$ denote the set of all 2-element subsets of $\mathbf{S}$; hence $|\mathbf{B}| = \binom{n}{2} = |\mathbf{G}|$. For each $\{s_i, s_j\} \in \mathbf{B}$, let $\mathbf{H}_{ij} = \mathbf{G}_i \cup \mathbf{G}_j$. Because $\mathbf{H}_{ij} = \mathbf{H}_{ji}$, we will assume from this point on that $i < j$. Let $\mathcal{H}$ be the family of all such sets $\mathbf{H}_{ij}$, and note that $\mathcal{H}$ is a family of subsets of $\mathbf{G}$ indexed by $\mathbf{B}$. We want to show that $\mathcal{H}$ satisfies the Hall condition, and hence has a system of distinct representatives.

Let $\mathbf{A}$ be any nonempty subset of $\mathbf{B}$ and let $\mathbf{Y}$ be a subset of $\mathbf{S}$ defined by

$$\mathbf{Y} = \{s_k \in \mathbf{S} : s_k \text{ belongs to any 2-element set in } \mathbf{A}\}.$$

Then by (4),

$$|\mathbf{A}| \leq \binom{|\mathbf{Y}|}{2} \leq \sum_{s_k \in \mathbf{Y}} r_k = \left| \bigcup_{s_k \in \mathbf{Y}} \mathbf{G}_k \right| = \left| \bigcup_{\mathbf{A}} \mathbf{H}_{ij} \right|.$$

Thus the Hall condition holds, and there exists a system of distinct representatives $\{h_{ij} \in \mathbf{H}_{ij} = \mathbf{G}_i \cup \mathbf{G}_j, i < j\}$.

Now construct the tournament $\mathbf{T} = [t_{ij}]$ as follows: Let $t_{ii} = 0$ for all i, and for all $i < j$ let

$$\begin{cases} t_{ij} = 1 & \text{and} & t_{ji} = 0, & \text{if } h_{ij} \in \mathbf{G}_i; \\ t_{ij} = 0 & \text{and} & t_{ji} = 1, & \text{if } h_{ij} \in \mathbf{G}_j. \end{cases}$$

From this it follows that for each k, the kth row sum is less than or equal to $|\mathbf{G}_k|$. But the sum of the 1s in $\mathbf{T}$ is $\binom{n}{2}$; hence each row sum must be equal to its corresponding $|\mathbf{G}_k| = r_k$. ∎

A formal proof sometimes obscures the underlying ideas which motivated the original discovery. The following remarks are intended to help you identify these ideas in the proof above. The key observation is that Landau's hypothesis (4) implies the Hall condition; after that, the argument simply puts the machinery in place in order to apply that theorem.

If $\mathbf{T} = [t_{ij}]$ is a tournament, then $t_{ii} = 0$ for all i and $t_{ji} = 1 - t_{ij}$ for all $i \neq j$. Thus, to construct $\mathbf{T}$ completely we need only assign a value (0 or 1) to each t_{ij} for $i < j$; that is, we must fill in $\binom{n}{2}$ blanks in the matrix, illustrated in Figure 40.8A with $n = 6$.

Now think of placing the set $\mathbf{H}_{ij} = \mathbf{G}_i \cup \mathbf{G}_j$ in the blank corresponding to t_{ij}, as in part (a) of Figure 40.8B.

$$[t_{ij}] = \begin{bmatrix} 0 & & & & & \\ - & 0 & & & & \\ - & - & 0 & & & \\ - & - & - & 0 & & \\ - & - & - & - & 0 & \\ - & - & - & - & - & 0 \end{bmatrix}$$

Figure 40.8A

$$\begin{bmatrix} \mathbf{H}_{12} & \mathbf{H}_{13} & \mathbf{H}_{14} & \mathbf{H}_{15} & \mathbf{H}_{16} \\ & \mathbf{H}_{23} & \mathbf{H}_{24} & \mathbf{H}_{25} & \mathbf{H}_{26} \\ & & \mathbf{H}_{34} & \mathbf{H}_{35} & \mathbf{H}_{36} \\ & & & \mathbf{H}_{45} & \mathbf{H}_{46} \\ & & & & \mathbf{H}_{56} \end{bmatrix} \qquad \begin{bmatrix} h_{12} & h_{13} & h_{14} & h_{15} & h_{16} \\ & h_{23} & h_{24} & h_{25} & h_{26} \\ & & h_{34} & h_{35} & h_{36} \\ & & & h_{45} & h_{46} \\ & & & & h_{56} \end{bmatrix}$$

(a)　　　　　　　　　　　　(b)

Figure 40.8B

Each $\mathbf{H}_{ij} \subseteq \mathbf{G}$, and we have already shown that the family of sets $\mathbf{H}_{ij}$ satisfies the Hall condition, namely, that the union of any m of the sets contains at least m elements. By Hall's Theorem there exists a selection of elements $h_{ij} \in \mathbf{H}_{ij}$, one for each of the sets without duplication. The picture is in part (b) of Figure 40.8B.

Notice that the h_{ij} include every element in $\mathbf{G}$, since $|\mathbf{G}| = \binom{n}{2}$, and this is exactly how many elements h_{ij} there are. Finally, we replace each h_{ij} by 1 if $h_{ij} \in \mathbf{G}_i$ and by 0 if $h_{ij} \in \mathbf{G}_j$. Thus, there is a 1 in any row, say the kth, if and only if either $h_{kl} \in \mathbf{G}_k$ or $h_{lk} \in \mathbf{G}_k$. For example, $t_{25} = 1$ if and only if $h_{25} \in \mathbf{G}_2$, and $t_{21} = 1$ if and only if $t_{12} = 0$, which means that $h_{12} \in \mathbf{G}_2$. Hence, the kth row sum in $[t_{ij}]$ is $|\mathbf{G}_k| = r_k$, and $\mathbf{T}$ is the required tournament.

Problems for Section 40

1. Let $\mathbf{D}$ be a digraph. Show that $\sum_{v \in \mathbf{D}} \text{odeg}(v) = \sum_{v \in \mathbf{D}} \text{ideg}(v)$.

2. If $\mathbf{T}$ is a tournament, then show that $\sum_{v \in \mathbf{T}}(\text{odeg}(v))^2 = \sum_{v \in \mathbf{T}}(\text{ideg}(v))^2$. [*Hint:* Note that $(\text{ideg}(v))^2 - (\text{odeg}(v))^2 = (\text{ideg}(v) - \text{odeg}(v)) \cdot (\text{ideg}(v) + \text{odeg}(v))$.]

3. Consider a digraph on n nodes, $\{v_1, v_2, \ldots, v_n\}$. For any one of the $\binom{n}{2}$ unordered pairs of nodes $\{v_i, v_j\}$ there are four possibilities: no arc, $v_i \to v_j$, $v_j \to v_i$, and both $v_i \to v_j$ and $v_j \to v_i$. Conclude that there are $4^{\binom{n}{2}}$ labeled digraphs on n nodes. Show that this is the same as (1) in paragraph 40.1.

4. The **converse $\mathbf{D}'$** of a digraph $\mathbf{D}$ is obtained by reversing every arc in $\mathbf{D}$. (a) Give the converse of the digraphs in Figures 40.1A and 40.1B. (b) Give an example of a digraph with $n \geq 4$ nodes that is isomorphic to its converse.

5. Show that a tournament with an even number of nodes cannot have each node having the same score.

6. A tournament is **transitive** if $u \to w$ whenever $u \to v$ and $v \to w$. (a) Give an example of a transitive tournament with five nodes. (b) Give an example of a nontransitive tournament with five nodes.

7. (a) Show that in a transitive tournament the nodes can be ranked so that each node dominates all the nodes that follow it in the ranking. (b) Show that a transitive tournament with $n > 2$ nodes is not strongly connected.

8. Show that a tournament with n nodes is transitive if and only if the score sequence is $(0, 1, 2, \ldots, n - 1)$.

9. Let $\mathbf{T}$ be a tournament with score sequence $(s_1, s_2, \ldots, s_n)$. (a) Show that
$$\sum_{i=1}^{n} s_i = \binom{n}{2}.$$
(b) Show that for $k < n$,
$$\sum_{i=1}^{k} s_i \geq \binom{k}{2}.$$

10. Show that if a digraph $\mathbf{D}$ is such that for all nodes v in $\mathbf{D}$, $\text{ideg}(v) = \text{odeg}(v)$, then $\mathbf{D}$ must have a cycle.

11. (*Continuation of Problem 10.*) Let $\mathbf{D}$ be a strongly connected digraph, let $\mathbf{C}$ be a cycle in $\mathbf{D}$, and let $\mathbf{D}'$ be the subgraph of $\mathbf{D}$ obtained by removing the arcs of $\mathbf{C}$. Show that if $\mathbf{D}'$ is eulerian, then $\mathbf{D}$ is eulerian.

12. (*Conclusion of Problem 10.*) To finish the proof of Theorem 40.6, show that the connected components of $\mathbf{D}'$ are strongly connected, eulerian, and hence $\mathbf{D}$ is eulerian.

13. Let $\mathbf{O}$ be the set of nodes of odd out-degree in a digraph $\mathbf{D}$ and let $\mathbf{I}$ be the set of nodes of odd in-degree in $\mathbf{D}$. Can $|\mathbf{O}| + |\mathbf{I}|$ be odd? Why or why not?

14. Show that a tournament has at most one source and one sink.

15. A **cyclic triple** in a tournament is a set of three nodes u, v, and w such that $u \to v \to w \to u$, and a **transitive triple** is a set of three nodes that is not a cyclic triple. (*a*) If u, v, and w is a transitive triple, then show that one of u, v, or w must dominate the other two nodes. (*b*) Show that if s_i is the score of node i, then $\binom{s_i}{2}$ is the number of transitive triples for which node i dominates each of the other two nodes in the triple.

16. (*Continuation of Problem 15.*) Show that the number of cyclic triples in a tournament is

$$\binom{n}{3} - \sum_{i=1}^{n} \binom{s_i}{2}$$

where $(s_1, s_2, \ldots, s_n)$ is the score sequence of the tournament.

17. (*Continuation of Problem 15.*) Let u be a node with score s, hence u dominates the other two nodes in $\binom{s}{2}$ transitive triples. Show that u is dominated by the other two nodes in $\binom{n-1-s}{2}$ transitive triples.

18. (*Continuation of Problem 15.*) Let n be odd. Show that u is in the smallest number of transitive triples when its score is $(n-1)/2$.

19. (*Conclusion of Problem 15.*) Show that the maximum number of cyclic triples in a tour-

nament with n nodes is $(n^3 - n)/24$ if n is odd and $(n^3 - 4n)/24$ if n is even.

20. Draw the network associated with the following tasks and find the path with the largest capacity.

Task	Time	Prerequisites
a	3	None
b	5	None
c	4	None
d	4	a
e	5	c
f	3	a
g	2	b, d
h	4	f, g
i	6	e

21. In this and the next three problems, we will separate the 64 labeled digraphs with three nodes into the 16 equivalence classes of unlabeled digraphs with three nodes. First observe that there is only one digraph with no arcs. Next, how many labeled digraphs have one arc? Note that all these are in the same equivalence class.

22. (*Continuation of Problem 21.*) (*a*) There are four digraphs with three nodes and two arcs. Draw them. (*b*) How many labeled digraphs are there in each of these equivalence classes?

23. (*Continuation of Problem 21.*) (*a*) There are four digraphs with three arcs. Draw them. (*b*) How many labeled digraphs are there in each of these equivalence classes?

24. (*Continuation of Problem 21.*) Using Problem 21, how many digraphs with three nodes are there with five and six arcs? How many labeled digraphs are there of each type?

25. (*Conclusion of Problem 21.*) Using Problem 22, how many digraphs are there with three nodes and four arcs? How many labeled digraphs are there of this type?

26. In the network in Figure 40.7B, find a path from the source to the sink with the smallest capacity.

27. To show that the algorithm given in this section finds an eulerian cycle, first show that each node in the walk (except the first and last) has the same in-degree as out-degree. Show that if the last node is not the same as the first, then its in-degree is 1 greater than its out-degree. Conclude that the walk is closed.

28. (*Conclusion of Problem 27.*) If not all arcs of **D** are on the walk $v_1 \to v_2 \to \cdots \to v_m = v_1$ generated by the algorithm, let **A'** be the set of arcs in **D** that are not on the walk. Let v_k be the node with the largest subscript that is incident with an arc in **A'**. Why does such a node exist? Show that the removal of the arc (v_k, v_{k+1}) increases the number of components in $\mathbf{D}_k$ which is the digraph **D** with the arcs $\{(v_i, v_{i+1}) : i = 1, 2, \ldots, k - 1\}$ deleted. Why is this a violation of the way the algorithm chose (v_k, v_{k+1})?

29. Apply Fleury's Algorithm to the graph in Figure 40.6.

30. How many digraphs (labeled and unlabeled) are there with four nodes and two arcs?

31. Change the fewest arcs possible in Figure 40.1A so that it is eulerian.

Section 41.   An Application in Geometry

Overview for Section 41

- Introduction to plane graphs and faces of plane graphs
- Euler's Formula for plane graphs
- Introduction to polyhedra
- Euler's Formula for polyhedra
- Definition and classification of the Platonic solids

Key Concepts: plane graphs, Euler's Formula, polyhedra, Platonic solids

41.1   The ideas to be discussed in this section will illustrate, once again, the unforeseen impact that one branch of mathematics sometimes has on another. Here, a discovery made in the mid-eighteenth century provides an easy solution to a question pondered by the ancient Greek mathematicians, and finally answered at considerable length in Books XI, XII, and XIII of Euclid's *Elements*. Our story begins with an observation about planar graphs; its relevance to geometry will be explained later in this section.

Denote by $\mathbf{G} = (\mathbf{V}, \mathbf{E})$ a planar graph which we will consider to be diagrammed so that no two edges intersect in a point other than a vertex. (Planar graphs diagrammed in this way are sometimes called **plane graphs.**) It should be clear that any subgraph of a planar graph is also planar, and that if each component of a graph is planar, then the graph itself is planar. In Figure 41.1, for example, we may consider

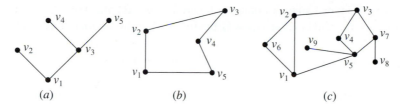

Figure 41.1

each part to be a separate connected planar graph or we may consider each to be a component of a single disconnected planar graph. In either case, think of the vertices and edges of the graph as subsets of the plane. The graph in Figure 41.1b is a cycle which, we will assume, separates the plane into two connected pieces: an "inside" or "bounded" part and an "outside" or "unbounded" part. It is traditional to call each of these two connected pieces a **face**. Heuristically, a face is a maximal subset **f** of the plane which is in the complement of the graph **G** and which has the property that any two points in **f** can be connected by a curved line entirely in **f**. "Maximal" means that no face is properly contained in another face. For example, the graph in Figure 41.1a is a tree, and *any* tree determines exactly one face (it is unbounded); the graph in Figure 41.1c determines exactly four faces (one of which is unbounded). Denoting the set of faces by **F**, we list in Table 41.1 the numbers of vertices, edges, and faces for each part of Figure 41.1 (considered to be a separate connected graph). The final column in that table is reserved for a discovery made by Leonhard Euler while studying geometric solids enclosed by plane faces. His result translates into a simple fact about planar graphs, which is easily verified in Table 41.1.

THEOREM 41.1A

Let the diagram of a connected plane graph $\mathbf{G} = (\mathbf{V}, \mathbf{E})$ determine the set **F** of faces. Then

$$|\mathbf{V}| - |\mathbf{E}| + |\mathbf{F}| = 2. \tag{1}$$

Proof

Observe first that if **G** is a tree, then by Theorem 39.4, $|\mathbf{V}| - |\mathbf{E}| = 1$; and since a tree determines exactly one face,

$$|\mathbf{V}| - |\mathbf{E}| + |\mathbf{F}| = 2.$$

	$\|\mathbf{V}\|$	$\|\mathbf{E}\|$	$\|\mathbf{F}\|$	*Euler number*
(a)	5	4	1	
(b)	5	5	2	
(c)	9	11	4	

Table 41.1

Now, suppose that the theorem fails. By the Well-Ordering Axiom, there is a connected planar graph **G** having the fewest number of edges for which

$$n - m + p \neq 2, \tag{2}$$

where n, m, and p arc, respectively, the numbers of vertices, edges, and faces determined by **G**. We know that **G** cannot be a tree; hence it contains at least one cycle. Let e be any edge in that cycle, and consider the graph **G′** obtained from **G** by deleting the edge e. Because the edge e is on a cycle, the two faces on either side merge into a single face when that edge is deleted. Thus in **G′**, the number of vertices is n, the number of edges is $m - 1$, and the number of faces is $p - 1$. Furthermore, **G′** is also planar and connected (again, because the deleted edge is on a cycle). Since **G′** has fewer edges than **G**,

$$n - (m - 1) + (p - 1) = 2,$$

which contradicts (2). ■

A simple modification of this theorem extends almost immediately to planar graphs which are not connected. If, for example, the planar graph **G** has two components **G₁** and **G₂**, then Euler's Formula, (1), applies separately to each component,

$$n_1 - m_1 + p_1 = 2$$

and

$$n_2 - m_2 + p_2 = 2.$$

Since **G₂** must be contained entirely in one face of **G₁**, we find for the graph **G** that $n = n_1 + n_2$, $m = m_1 + m_2$, but $p = p_1 + p_2 - 1$ (because one face is duplicated in the count). Hence,

$$\begin{aligned} n - m + p &= (n_1 + n_2) - (m_1 + m_2) + (p_1 + p_2 - 1) \\ &= (n_1 - m_1 + p_1) + (n_2 - m_2 + p_2) - 1 \\ &= 2 + 2 - 1 = 3. \end{aligned}$$

(Note that 3 is 1 more than the number of components.) An inductive argument like that for Theorem 41.1A confirms the following generalization.

THEOREM 41.1B

If **G** is a plane graph having k components, then

$$|\mathbf{V}| - |\mathbf{E}| + |\mathbf{F}| = 1 + k.$$

41.2

As mentioned earlier, Euler's concern was with three-dimensional geometric objects bounded by flat (plane) faces. As an example, consider the obelisk shown in Figure 41.2A, which is bounded by nine faces (a square base, four rectangular sides, and four triangles at the top). Two faces may adjoin along an edge, or at a vertex only, or not at all. Two or more edges may adjoin at a vertex, or not at all. Each of these situations occurs in the obelisk. Notice that there are 9 vertices and 16 edges. For this figure,

$$|\mathbf{V}| - |\mathbf{E}| + |\mathbf{F}| = 9 - 16 + 9 = 2.$$

This answer, identical to (1) in Theorem 41.1A, is surely no accident. But to establish the connection we need to introduce some new terminology.

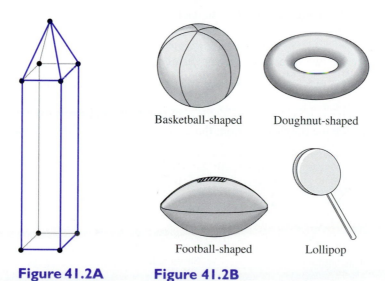

Basketball-shaped   Doughnut-shaped

Football-shaped   Lollipop

Figure 41.2A   **Figure 41.2B**

A three-dimensional (solid) object denoted by **P** is called **convex** if the straight-line segment joining any two points in **P** lies entirely in **P**. For example, a basketball-shaped object is convex and so is a football-shaped object, but a doughnut-shaped object is not convex, nor is an object shaped like a lollipop (see Figure 41.2B). We will be considering a special class of convex solids similar to that shown in Figure 41.2A.

Tutorial 41.2

a. Describe several familiar solids which are convex and several which are nonconvex.
b. Look up in your dictionary the word "parallelepiped."
c. Sketch a parallelepiped which has rectangles (not squares) as faces.

Suppose that k ($k > 2$) distinct vertices in the plane, denoted by $v_1, v_2, \ldots, v_k$, are so placed that no three consecutively labeled vertices are collinear. Now join these vertices sequentially by the edges $e_{12}, e_{23}, \ldots, e_{k1}$. Assume, further, that no two of the edges intersect in a point other than a common vertex. The figure so formed in the plane is called a k-**sided polygon;** note that it consists of k vertices and k edges, as in Figure 41.2C. We may consider this to be the diagram of a cycle, as defined in paragraph 35.5, which (as we assumed earlier) separates the plane into two faces, one of which is bounded (or finite in extent), the other one is unbounded (or infinite in extent).

Now suppose that some finite number of bounded faces, possibly of various sizes, can be fitted together so as to enclose a single convex solid which satisfies the conditions:

1. No two faces adjoin except at a common vertex or along a single common edge.

2. No two faces which share an edge are in the same plane.

Such a solid is known as a (convex) **polyhedron.** Its surface, which separates points inside the polyhedron from those outside, consists of the vertices, edges, and faces,

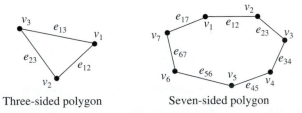

Three-sided polygon   Seven-sided polygon

Figure 41.2C

denoted as usual by **V**, **E**, and **F**. The obelisk in Figure 41.2A is an example of a convex polyhedron.

A fanciful thought experiment will suffice to relate convex polyhedra to planar graphs. Suppose that the surface of a convex polyhedron **P** is made of an elastic material. Place **P** so that one of its flat faces rests on a table (plane). Now cut out any one of the upper faces, say f_1, creating in the surface of **P** an opening bounded by a polygon. Next, grab the edges of that opening and stretch out the surface until it can be flattened into a plane, without either tearing the elastic material or overlapping it. All the vertices, edges, and faces of the surface now form a graph in the plane which retains the combinatorial properties (although not sizes and shapes) of the original polyhedron. The distorted surface of **P** sits inside the cycle into which the boundary of f_1 has been stretched. In our planar graph, the number of vertices is $|V|$, the number of edges is $|E|$, and the number of faces is $|F|$, including the unbounded region of the plane which corresponds to the "cut-out" face in the original polyhedron.

Thus, Euler's combinatorial formula is true equally for connected planar graphs and for convex polyhedra. Incidentally, Euler considered it surprising that this result had not been remarked on by earlier mathematicians. For such a simply stated property, Theorem 41.1A has turned out to be profound in its implications. As an illustration, we consider a question about "regular" polyhedra, which puzzled the ancient Greek geometers for centuries.

41.3

The philosopher Plato (ca. 427–347 B.C.) established a school in Athens called The Academy. Among the subjects studied there, geometry was one of the most important, but at that time Euclid, and the synthesis of geometry into a deductive system, was still a century in the future. Many of its results were "ad hoc," even experimental, in nature. The Greeks recognized, however, that certain convex polyhedra had properties of regularity which were considered aesthetically desirable. Perhaps the most familiar is the cube (see Figure 41.3), which is bounded by six flat faces each of which is a square. The **regularity** of a polyhedron means that:

1. Each single vertex is an end-vertex of the same number of edges (three in the case of the cube).

2. Each face is bounded by the same number of edges (four in the case of the cube).

Tetrahedron

Cube

Octahedron

Dodecahedron

Icosahedron

Figure 41.3

The Greeks also required that the faces of a regular polyhedron be congruent (as in the cube), and each of the solids pictured in Figure 41.3 is assumed to have this property. For our purposes, however, only the combinatorial properties **1** and **2** are relevant.

The cube is not the only simple solid possessing this property of regularity. For example, the tetrahedron (see Figure 41.3) is composed of four flat faces, each in the shape of a triangle, and it has four vertices and six edges. For it, each vertex is on three edges and each face is bounded by three edges. A natural question, long explored by the Greek mathematicians, asks, "Is it possible to construct other regular polyhedra?" They eventually discovered three others: the octahedron, the dodecahedron, and the icosahedron. These five, displayed in Figure 41.3, are now referred to as the **Platonic solids.**

> ### Tutorial 41.3
>
> Confirm Euler's Formula for each of the Platonic solids diagrammed in Figure 41.3

Despite their geometric inventiveness, the ancient Greeks could discover no other regular polyhedra. If any such existed, they would certainly be more complicated than those already known and, correspondingly, more difficult to find. By the time of Euclid, however, enough had been learned about geometry to prove that no others could exist. The proof which appears in Euclid's *Elements* is both long and involved; a much simpler, algebraic proof was published shortly after Euler's Formula became known.

THEOREM 41.3

There are exactly five regular polyhedra.

Proof

Let **P** represent any (convex) regular polyhedron, and suppose that exactly s edges meet at each vertex and that exactly t edges bound each face. Let the set of vertices be $\mathbf{V} = \{v_1, v_2, \ldots, v_p\}$, where $p = |\mathbf{V}|$, and let the set of edges be $\mathbf{E} = \{e_1, e_2, \ldots, e_q\}$, where $q = |\mathbf{E}|$. (Note that our notation here only distinguishes edges, it does not indicate the incident vertices.) We will make use here of the strategy described in (1) in paragraph 16.2: Identify a set, count it in two ways, then equate the counts.

Now, let **W** be the set of ordered pairs

$$\{(v_i, e_j): e_j \text{ has } v_i \text{ as one of its end-vertices}\}.$$

For each i, **W** contains exactly s ordered pairs (because s edges meet at each vertex); hence $|\mathbf{W}| = s \cdot |\mathbf{V}|$. For each j, **W** contains exactly two ordered pairs (because each edge has two endpoints); hence $|\mathbf{W}| = 2 \cdot |\mathbf{E}|$. Thus, $s \cdot |\mathbf{V}| = 2 \cdot |\mathbf{E}|$ from which $|\mathbf{V}| = 2 \cdot |\mathbf{E}|/s$. By listing the faces, and noting that each edge is common to exactly two faces, a similar argument shows that $t \cdot |\mathbf{F}| = 2 \cdot |\mathbf{E}|$ from which $|\mathbf{F}| = 2 \cdot |\mathbf{E}|/t$. By Theorem 41.1A,

$$|\mathbf{V}| - |\mathbf{E}| + |\mathbf{F}| = \frac{2 \cdot |\mathbf{E}|}{s} - |\mathbf{E}| + \frac{2 \cdot |\mathbf{E}|}{t} = 2.$$

Hence

$$\frac{1}{s} - \frac{1}{2} + \frac{1}{t} = \frac{1}{|\mathbf{E}|}.$$

From the requirements imposed on the construction of $\mathbf{P}$, each face is bounded by at least three edges, and at least three edges meet at each vertex; hence, $s \geq 3$ and $t \geq 3$. We show next that s and t cannot both be greater than 3. For suppose both $s \geq 4$ and $t \geq 4$. Then,

$$\frac{1}{|\mathbf{E}|} = \frac{1}{s} + \frac{1}{t} - \frac{1}{2} \leq \frac{1}{4} + \frac{1}{4} - \frac{1}{2} = 0.$$

This inequality contradicts the fact that $1/|\mathbf{E}| > 0$, since $|\mathbf{E}|$ must be some positive integer. Thus, one or the other of these cases must hold:

$$\text{Case 1:} \quad s = 3 \text{ and } t \geq 3,$$

or

$$\text{Case 2:} \quad t = 3 \text{ and } s \geq 3.$$

In case 1,

$$\frac{1}{3} - \frac{1}{2} + \frac{1}{t} = \frac{1}{t} - \frac{1}{6} = \frac{1}{|\mathbf{E}|} > 0.$$

So, the only possible values of t are 3, 4, and 5. In case 2,

$$\frac{1}{s} - \frac{1}{2} + \frac{1}{3} = \frac{1}{s} - \frac{1}{6} = \frac{1}{|\mathbf{E}|} > 0.$$

So, the only possible values of s are 3, 4, and 5. The solution $s = 3$ *and* $t = 3$ is common to both; hence there are only five different possibilities. Each of these five pairs of values of s and t corresponds to one of the Platonic solids. For example, if $s = 3$ and $t = 5$, then from the formula

$$\frac{1}{t} - \frac{1}{6} = \frac{1}{|\mathbf{E}|},$$

we find that $|\mathbf{E}| = 30$; hence $|\mathbf{V}| = (2 \cdot 30)/3 = 20$, and $|\mathbf{F}| = (2 \cdot 30)/5 = 12$. ■

s	t	$\|\mathbf{V}\|$	$\|\mathbf{E}\|$	$\|\mathbf{F}\|$	*Platonic solids*
3	3	4	6	4	Tetrahedron
3	4	8	12	6	Hexahedron
3	5	20	30	12	Dodecahedron
4	3	6	12	8	Octahedron
5	3	12	30	20	Icosahedron

Table 41.3

The five distinct cases are listed in Table 41.3. As a final note, the names of these solids are derived from the Greek words denoting the numbers of faces. The hexahedron corresponds to the "cube" referred to earlier.

41.4 **Complement: Hamiltonian Planar Graphs** As we have shown in paragraph 35.7, there are sufficient conditions for a graph to be hamiltonian. In this complement we give a necessary condition for a planar graph to be hamiltonian and use this condition to show that Tutte's Graph (Figure 41.4B) is not hamiltonian.

First, let **G** be a hamiltonian plane graph with n vertices and let **C** be a hamiltonian cycle of **G**. We denote the number of faces of **G** with exactly i edges and which are interior to **C** by r_i and the number of faces with exactly i edges which are exterior to **C** by s_i. In the graph in Figure 41.4A, faces 1, 2, 3, and 4 are interior to the cycle (indicated by the darker line) and faces 5, 6, and 7 (the infinite face) are exterior to the cycle. In this case $r_3 = 0$, $r_4 = 4$, $r_5 = 0$, $s_3 = 0$, $s_4 = 1$, and $s_5 = 2$.

THEOREM 41.4

Grinberg's Theorem. Let **G** be a hamiltonian plane graph with n vertices. Then with respect to some hamiltonian cycle **C**,

$$\sum_{i=3}^{n}(i - 2)(r_i - s_i) = 0.$$

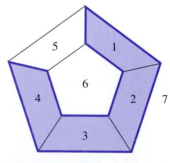

Figure 41.4A

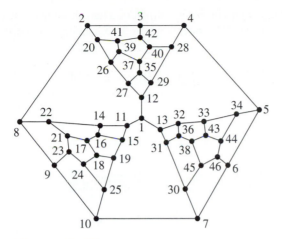

Figure 41.4B

We will not present the proof of Grinberg's Theorem but will illustrate its use in the proof that Tutte's Graph (shown in Figure 41.4B) is not hamiltonian. Before we do this, note that for the graph in Figure 41.4A,

$$(3-2)\cdot(r_3 - s_3) + (4-2)\cdot(r_4 - s_4) + (5-2)\cdot(r_5 - s_5)$$
$$= 0 + 2\cdot 3 + 3\cdot(-2) = 0,$$

as predicted by Grinberg's Theorem.

In Tutte's Graph there are three triangular-shaped faces, each containing 15 vertices. If this graph has a hamiltonian cycle, then the cycle must traverse each vertex in one of these triangles before exiting the triangle. Hence, each triangle has a hamiltonian path induced by the hamiltonian cycle. Since there are three triangles and only one vertex in the middle of Tutte's Graph (vertex 1), in at least one of these triangles the path induced by the cycle must start and end at the outside vertices. Without loss of generality, assume that it is the top triangle as shown in part (*a*) of Figure 41.4C. To this triangle we add the edge joining vertices 2 and 4, which, along

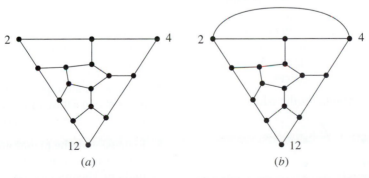

Figure 41.4C

with the hamiltonian path in this graph, gives a hamiltonian cycle in the graph shown in part (*b*) of Figure 41.4C. For this graph, by Grinberg's Theorem we must have

$$\sum_{i=3}^{8}(i-2)(r_i - s_i) = 0. \tag{1}$$

The infinite face has eight edges, and so $r_8 = 0$ and $s_8 = 1$. Also, there is only one face with three edges which must be inside the cycle since the edge $\{2, 4\}$ is on the cycle. (Note that each edge of the cycle has two adjoining faces, one inside and one outside the cycle, and the infinite face is always outside the cycle.) Hence $r_3 = 1$ and $s_3 = 0$. Plugging these facts into (1) yields

$$(3 - 2)(1 - 0) + (4 - 2)(r_4 - s_4) + (5 - 2)(r_5 - s_5) + (8 - 2)(0 - 1) = 0,$$

or
$$2(r_4 - s_4) + 3(r_5 - s_5) = 5. \tag{2}$$

Since vertex 12 has degree 2, both edges incident with it are in the cycle, and so the face containing vertex 12 borders the infinite face. Therefore, this face must be inside the cycle, and since there are only two faces with four edges, either $r_4 = 1$ or $r_4 = 2$. If $r_4 = 2$, then $s_4 = 0$, and (2) reduces to

$$3(r_5 - s_5) = 1,$$

an impossibility. If $r_4 = 1$, then $s_4 = 1$, and (2) becomes

$$3(r_5 - s_5) = 5,$$

another impossibility. Thus, this triangle has no hamiltonian path, and therefore Tutte's Graph cannot have a hamiltonian cycle.

Problems for Section 41

1. Verify Euler's Formula, (1) in paragraph 41.1, for the following graphs: (*a*) a path of length 5; (*b*) a cycle of length 5; (*c*) the complete graph on four vertices.

2. Verify Euler's Formula for the wheel:

3. Refer to part **C** of Theorem 39.4. Show how that condition is consistent with Euler's Formula.

4. Suppose that the planar graph **G** is actually a forest consisting of three trees. Verify the formula in Theorem 41.1B.

5. Suppose that the planar graph **G** is actually a forest consisting of *k* trees. Verify the formula in Theorem 41.1B.

6. Construct a proof by PMI that for any positive integer n, a cycle of length $n+2$ satisfies Euler's Formula.

7. Prove Theorem 41.1B by induction on the number k of components.

8. Let **G** be a connected plane graph with n vertices, $m \geq 3$ edges, and f faces. (*a*) Show that $3f \leq 2m$. (*b*) Combining the inequality in part (*a*) with Euler's Formula, show that $m \leq 3n - 6$.

9. Let **G** be a connected plane graph with n vertices, $m \geq 4$ edges, and no triangles. Show that $m \leq 2n - 4$.

10. Using Problem 8, show that $\mathbf{K}_5$ is not planar.

11. Using Problem 9, show that $\mathbf{K}_{3,3}$ is not planar.

12. Using Problem 8, show that every planar graph contains a vertex whose degree is at most 5.

13. The **girth** of a connected graph having at least one cycle is the length of a shortest cycle. Show that if the girth of a connected planar graph is 5, then $m \leq \frac{5}{3}(n - 2)$, where m is the number of edges and n is the number of vertices.

14. Using Problem 13, show that the Petersen graph is not planar.

15. Show that for a connected planar graph with at least one cycle, n vertices, m edges, and girth g:
$$m \leq \frac{g}{g - 2}(n - 2).$$

16. Find a graph **G** on eight vertices such that both **G** and $\overline{\mathbf{G}}$ are planar.

17. Let **G** be a graph with at least 11 vertices and let $\overline{\mathbf{G}}$ be its complement. Show that **G** and $\overline{\mathbf{G}}$ cannot both be planar. (This is also true for only nine vertices, but it is more difficult to prove.) Use Problem 8 and the fact that $\mathbf{K}_n$ has $\frac{1}{2}n(n - 1)$ edges.

18. Show that $\mathbf{C}_n$ and $\overline{\mathbf{C}}_n$ are planar for $3 \leq n \leq 6$ and draw each in the plane.

19. Show that $\overline{\mathbf{C}}_n$ is not planar for $n \geq 8$.

20. To show that $\overline{\mathbf{C}}_7$ is not planar, label it clockwise $1, 2, \ldots, 7$. Note that $\overline{\mathbf{C}}_7$ consists of two edge-disjoint cycles of length 7, (1, 3, 5, 7, 2, 4, 6, 1) and (1, 4, 7, 3, 6, 2, 5, 1). If $\overline{\mathbf{C}}_7$ is planar, then one of these is a face in a drawing of $\overline{\mathbf{C}}_7$ in the plane. Assume that it is the first cycle. Note that the edge e_{14} is either inside or outside the face. If it is inside, then e_{36} and e_{26} are both outside. Hence, e_{15} must be inside the face. Continue this case-by-case analysis to show that $\overline{\mathbf{C}}_7$ is not planar.

21. Let **G** be a connected plane graph that is regular of degree 3 and for which every face is polygonal. Let f_k be the number of faces of **G** with k edges and let r be the largest number of sides of any face of **G**. (*a*) Show that $3f_3 + 2f_4 + f_5 = 12 + f_7 + 2f_8 + \cdots + (r - 6)f_r$. (*b*) Show that one of f_3, f_4, or f_5 is not zero.

22. Blow up a balloon and with a felt tip pen mark 10 vertices on the surface of the balloon. Now, in some fashion, connect those vertices with lines which do not otherwise intersect, and let no vertex be isolated. Test Euler's Formula for your figure.

23. Find a soccer ball. Counting seams as edges and intersections of seams as vertices, test Euler's Formula.

24. Let **G** be a polyhedron, all of whose faces are pentagons or hexagons. (*a*) Use Euler's Formula to show that **G** must have at least 12 pentagonal faces. (*b*) If there are exactly three faces meeting at each vertex, show that **G** must have exactly 12 pentagonal faces. (*c*) What connection does this problem have with the preceding problem?

25. Discover an example of a nonconvex solid bounded by plane, polygonal faces, and test Euler's Formula for it.

26. Refer to Figure 39.3B, and note that the original graph can be drawn as a plane graph. Verify Euler's Formula at each step in the transition to a spanning tree.

Appendix Table

Selected Values of the Binomial Probability Distribution

$$b(k;n,p) = \binom{n}{k} p^k q^{n-k}$$

Example: If $p = .30$, $n = 5$, and $k = 2$, then $b(2;5,0.3) = .3087$. (When p is greater than .50, the value of $b(k;n,p)$ is found by locating the table for the specified n and using $n - k$ in place of the given k and $1 - p$ in place of the specified p.)

n	k	.01	.05	.10	.15	.20	.25	.30	.35	.40	.45	.50
1	0	.9900	.9500	.9000	.8500	.8000	.7500	.7000	.6500	.6000	.5500	.5000
	1	.0100	.0500	.1000	.1500	.2000	.2500	.3000	.3500	.4000	.4500	.5000
2	0	.9801	.9025	.8100	.7225	.6400	.5625	.4900	.4225	.3600	.3025	.2500
	1	.0198	.0950	.1800	.2550	.3200	.3750	.4200	.4550	.4800	.4950	.5000
	2	.0001	.0025	.0100	.0255	.0400	.0625	.0900	.1225	.1600	.2025	.2500
3	0	.9703	.8574	.7290	.6141	.5120	.4219	.3430	.2746	.2160	.1664	.1250
	1	.0294	.1354	.2430	.3251	.3840	.4219	.4410	.4436	.4320	.4084	.3750
	2	.0003	.0071	.0270	.0574	.0960	.1406	.1890	.2389	.2880	.3341	.3750
	3	.0000	.0001	.0010	.0034	.0080	.0156	.0270	.0429	.0640	.0911	.1250
4	0	.9606	.8145	.6561	.5220	.4096	.3164	.2401	.1785	.1296	.0915	.0625
	1	.0388	.1715	.2916	.3685	.4096	.4219	.4116	.3845	.3456	.2995	.2500
	2	.0006	.0135	.0486	.0975	.1536	.2109	.2646	.3105	.3456	.3675	.3750
	3	.0000	.0005	.0036	.0115	.0258	.0469	.0756	.1115	.1536	.2005	.2500
	4	.0000	.0000	.0001	.0005	.0016	.0039	.0081	.0150	.0256	.0410	.0625
5	0	.9510	.7738	.5905	.4437	.3277	.2373	.1681	.1160	.0778	.0503	.0312
	1	.0480	.2036	.3280	.3915	.4096	.3955	.3602	.3124	.2592	.2059	.1562
	2	.0010	.0214	.0729	.1382	.2048	.2637	.3087	.3364	.3456	.3369	.3125
	3	.0000	.0011	.0081	.0244	.0512	.0879	.1323	.1811	.2304	.2757	.3125
	4	.0000	.0000	.0004	.0022	.0064	.0146	.0284	.0488	.0768	.1128	.1562
	5	.0000	.0000	.0000	.0001	.0003	.0010	.0024	.0053	.0102	.0185	.0312

Source: Adapted from Donald H. Sanders, *Statistics: A First Course*, 5th ed., copyright ©1995 by The McGraw-Hill Companies, Inc. Used by permission of the McGraw-Hill Companies, Inc.

n	k	.01	.05	.10	.15	.20	p .25	.30	.35	.40	.45	.50
6	0	.9415	.7351	.5314	.3771	.2621	.1780	.1176	.0754	.0467	.0277	.0156
	1	.0571	.2321	.3543	.3993	.3932	.3560	.3025	.2437	.1866	.1359	.0938
	2	.0014	.0305	.0984	.1762	.2458	.2966	.3241	.3280	.3110	.2780	.2344
	3	.0000	.0021	.0146	.0415	.0819	.1318	.1852	.2355	.2765	.3032	.3125
	4	.0000	.0001	.0012	.0055	.0154	.0330	.0595	.0951	.1382	.1861	.2344
	5	.0000	.0000	.0001	.0004	.0015	.0044	.0102	.0205	.0369	.0609	.0938
	6	.0000	.0000	.0000	.0000	.0001	.0002	.0007	.0018	.0041	.0083	.0156
7	0	.9321	.6983	.4783	.3206	.2097	.1335	.0824	.0490	.0280	.0152	.0078
	1	.0659	.2573	.3720	.3960	.3670	.3115	.2471	.1848	.1306	.0872	.0547
	2	.0020	.0406	.1240	.2097	.2753	.3115	.3177	.2985	.2613	.2140	.1641
	3	.0000	.0036	.0230	.0617	.1147	.1730	.2269	.2679	.2903	.2918	.2734
	4	.0000	.0002	.0026	.0109	.0287	.0577	.0972	.1442	.1935	.2388	.2734
	5	.0000	.0000	.0002	.0012	.0043	.0115	.0250	.0466	.0774	.1172	.1641
	6	.0000	.0000	.0000	.0001	.0004	.0013	.0036	.0084	.0172	.0320	.0547
	7	.0000	.0000	.0000	.0000	.0000	.0001	.0002	.0006	.0016	.0037	.0078
8	0	.9227	.6634	.4305	.2725	.1678	.1002	.0576	.0319	.0168	.0084	.0039
	1	.0746	.2793	.3826	.3847	.3355	.2670	.1977	.1373	.0896	.0548	.0312
	2	.0026	.0515	.1488	.2376	.2936	.3115	.2965	.2587	.2090	.1569	.1094
	3	.0001	.0054	.0331	.0839	.1468	.2076	.2541	.2786	.2787	.2568	.2188
	4	.0000	.0004	.0046	.0185	.0459	.0865	.1361	.1875	.2322	.2627	.2734
	5	.0000	.0000	.0004	.0026	.0092	.0231	.0467	.0808	.1239	.1719	.2188
	6	.0000	.0000	.0000	.0002	.0011	.0038	.0100	.0217	.0413	.0403	.1094
	7	.0000	.0000	.0000	.0000	.0001	.0004	.0012	.0033	.0079	.0164	.0312
	8	.0000	.0000	.0000	.0000	.0000	.0000	.0001	.0002	.0007	.0017	.0039
9	0	.9135	.6302	.3874	.2316	.1342	.0751	.0404	.0207	.0101	.0046	.0020
	1	.0830	.2985	.3874	.3679	.3020	.2253	.1556	.1004	.0605	.0339	.0176
	2	.0034	.0629	.1722	.2597	.3020	.3003	.2668	.2162	.1612	.1110	.0703
	3	.0001	.0077	.0446	.1069	.1762	.2336	.2668	.2716	.2508	.2119	.1641
	4	.0000	.0006	.0074	.0283	.0661	.1168	.1715	.2194	.2508	.2600	.2461
	5	.0000	.0000	.0008	.0050	.0165	.0389	.0735	.1181	.1672	.2128	.2461
	6	.0000	.0000	.0001	.0006	.0028	.0087	.0210	.0424	.0743	.1160	.1641
	7	.0000	.0000	.0000	.0000	.0003	.0012	.0039	.0098	.0212	.0407	.0703
	8	.0000	.0000	.0000	.0000	.0000	.0001	.0004	.0013	.0035	.0083	.0176
	9	.0000	.0000	.0000	.0000	.0000	.0000	.0000	.0001	.0003	.0008	.0020
10	0	.9044	.5987	.3487	.1969	.1074	.0563	.0282	.0135	.0060	.0025	.0010
	1	.0914	.3151	.3874	.3474	.2684	.1877	.1211	.0725	.0403	.0207	.0098
	2	.0042	.0746	.1937	.2759	.3020	.2816	.2335	.1757	.1209	.0763	.0439
	3	.0001	.0105	.0574	.1298	.2013	.2503	.2668	.2522	.2150	.1665	.1172
	4	.0000	.0010	.0112	.0401	.0881	.1460	.2001	.2377	.2508	.2384	.2051
	5	.0000	.0001	.0015	.0085	.0264	.0584	.1029	.1536	.2007	.2340	.2461
	6	.0000	.0000	.0001	.0012	.0055	.0162	.0368	.0689	.1115	.1596	.2051

APPENDIX TABLE (Continued)

n	k	.01	.05	.10	.15	.20	.25	.30	.35	.40	.45	.50
							p					
10	7	.0000	.0000	.0000	.0001	.0008	.0031	.0090	.0212	.0425	.0746	.1172
	8	.0000	.0000	.0000	.0000	.0001	.0004	.0014	.0043	.0106	.0229	.0439
	9	.0000	.0000	.0000	.0000	.0000	.0000	.0001	.0005	.0016	.0042	.0098
	10	.0000	.0000	.0000	.0000	.0000	.0000	.0000	.0000	.0001	.0003	.0010
11	0	.8953	.5688	.3138	.1673	.0859	.0422	.0198	.0088	.0036	.0014	.0005
	1	.0995	.3293	.3835	.3248	.2362	.1549	.0932	.0518	.0266	.0125	.0054
	2	.0050	.0867	.2131	.2866	.2953	.2581	.1998	.1395	.0887	.0513	.0269
	3	.0002	.0137	.0710	.1517	.2215	.2581	.2568	.2254	.1774	.1259	.0806
	4	.0000	.0014	.0158	.0536	.1107	.1721	.2201	.2428	.2365	.2060	.1611
	5	.0000	.0001	.0025	.0132	.0388	.0803	.1321	.1830	.2207	.2360	.2256
	6	.0000	.0000	.0003	.0023	.0097	.0268	.0566	.0985	.1471	.1931	.2256
	7	.0000	.0000	.0000	.0003	.0017	.0064	.0173	.0379	.0701	.1128	.1611
	8	.0000	.0000	.0000	.0000	.0002	.0011	.0037	.0102	.0234	.0462	.0806
	9	.0000	.0000	.0000	.0000	.0000	.0001	.0005	.0018	.0052	.0126	.0269
	10	.0000	.0000	.0000	.0000	.0000	.0000	.0000	.0002	.0007	.0021	.0054
	11	.0000	.0000	.0000	.0000	.0000	.0000	.0000	.0000	.0000	.0002	.0005
12	0	.8864	.5404	.2824	.1422	.0687	.0317	.0138	.0057	.0022	.0008	.0002
	1	.1074	.3413	.3766	.3012	.2062	.1267	.0712	.0368	.0174	.0075	.0029
	2	.0060	.0988	.2301	.2924	.2835	.2323	.1678	.1088	.0639	.0339	.0161
	3	.0002	.0173	.0852	.1720	.2362	.2581	.2397	.1954	.1419	.0923	.0537
	4	.0000	.0021	.0213	.0683	.1329	.1936	.2311	.2367	.2128	.1700	.1204
	5	.0000	.0002	.0038	.0193	.0532	.1032	.1585	.2039	.2270	.2225	.1934
	6	.0000	.0000	.0005	.0040	.0155	.0401	.0792	.1281	.1766	.2124	.2256
	7	.0000	.0000	.0000	.0006	.0033	.0115	.0291	.0591	.1009	.1489	.1934
	8	.0000	.0000	.0000	.0001	.0005	.0024	.0078	.0199	.0420	.0762	.1208
	9	.0000	.0000	.0000	.0000	.0001	.0004	.0015	.0048	.0125	.0277	.0537
	10	.0000	.0000	.0000	.0000	.0000	.0000	.0002	.0008	.0025	.0068	.0161
	11	.0000	.0000	.0000	.0000	.0000	.0000	.0000	.0001	.0003	.0010	.0029
	12	.0000	.0000	.0000	.0000	.0000	.0000	.0000	.0000	.0000	.0001	.0002
13	0	.8775	.5133	.2542	.1209	.0550	.0238	.0097	.0037	.0013	.0004	.0001
	1	.1152	.3512	.3672	.2774	.1787	.1029	.0540	.0259	.0113	.0045	.0016
	2	.0070	.1109	.2448	.2937	.2680	.2059	.1388	.0836	.0453	.0220	.0095
	3	.0003	.0214	.0997	.1900	.2457	.2517	.2181	.1651	.1107	.0660	.0349
	4	.0000	.0028	.0277	.0838	.1535	.2097	.2337	.2222	.1845	.1350	.0873
	5	.0000	.0003	.0055	.0266	.0691	.1258	.1803	.2154	.2214	.1989	.1571
	6	.0000	.0000	.0008	.0063	.0230	.0559	.1030	.1546	.1968	.2169	.2095
	7	.0000	.0000	.0001	.0011	.0058	.0186	.0442	.0833	.1312	.1775	.2095
	8	.0000	.0000	.0001	.0001	.0011	.0047	.0142	.0336	.0656	.1089	.1571
	9	.0000	.0000	.0000	.0000	.0001	.0009	.0034	.0101	.0243	.0495	.0873
	10	.0000	.0000	.0000	.0000	.0000	.0001	.0006	.0022	.0065	.0162	.0349
	11	.0000	.0000	.0000	.0000	.0000	.0000	.0001	.0003	.0012	.0036	.0095

APPENDIX TABLE (Continued)

n	k	.01	.05	.10	.15	.20	*p* .25	.30	.35	.40	.45	.50
13	12	.0000	.0000	.0000	.0000	.0000	.0000	.0000	.0000	.0001	.0005	.0016
	13	.0000	.0000	.0000	.0000	.0000	.0000	.0000	.0000	.0000	.0000	.0001
14	0	.8687	.4887	.2288	.1028	.0440	.0178	.0068	.0024	.0008	.0002	.0001
	1	.1229	.3593	.3559	.2539	.1539	.0832	.0407	.0181	.0073	.0027	.0009
	2	.0081	.1229	.2570	.2912	.2501	.1802	.1134	.0634	.0317	.0141	.0056
	3	.0003	.0259	.1142	.2056	.2501	.2402	.1943	.1366	.0845	.0462	.0222
	4	.0000	.0037	.0349	.0998	.1720	.2202	.2290	.2002	.1549	.1040	.0611
	5	.0000	.0004	.0078	.0352	.0860	.1468	.1963	.2178	.2066	.1701	.1222
	6	.0000	.0000	.0013	.0093	.0322	.0734	.1262	.1759	.2066	.2088	.1833
	7	.0000	.0000	.0002	.0019	.0092	.0280	.0618	.1082	.1574	.1952	.2095
	8	.0000	.0000	.0000	.0003	.0020	.0082	.0232	.0510	.0918	.1398	.1833
	9	.0000	.0000	.0000	.0000	.0003	.0018	.0066	.0183	.0408	.0762	.1222
	10	.0000	.0000	.0000	.0000	.0000	.0003	.0014	.0049	.0136	.0312	.0611
	11	.0000	.0000	.0000	.0000	.0000	.0000	.0002	.0010	.0033	.0093	.0222
	12	.0000	.0000	.0000	.0000	.0000	.0000	.0000	.0001	.0005	.0019	.0056
	13	.0000	.0000	.0000	.0000	.0000	.0000	.0000	.0000	.0001	.0002	.0009
	14	.0000	.0000	.0000	.0000	.0000	.0000	.0000	.0000	.0000	.0000	.0001
15	0	.8601	.4633	.2059	.0874	.0352	.0134	.0047	.0016	.0005	.0001	.0000
	1	.1303	.3658	.3432	.2312	.1319	.0668	.0305	.0126	.0047	.0016	.0005
	2	.0092	.1348	.2669	.2856	.2309	.1559	.0916	.0476	.0219	.0090	.0032
	3	.0004	.0307	.1285	.2184	.2501	.2252	.1700	.1110	.0634	.0318	.0139
	4	.0000	.0049	.0428	.1156	.1876	.2252	.2186	.1792	.1268	.0780	.0417
	5	.0000	.0006	.0105	.0499	.1032	.1651	.2061	.2123	.1859	.1404	.0916
	6	.0000	.0000	.0019	.0132	.0430	.0917	.1472	.1906	.2066	.1914	.1527
	7	.0000	.0000	.0003	.0030	.0138	.0393	.0811	.1319	.1771	.2013	.1964
	8	.0000	.0000	.0000	.0005	.0035	.0131	.0348	.0710	.1181	.1647	.1964
	9	.0000	.0000	.0000	.0001	.0007	.0034	.0116	.0298	.0612	.1048	.1527
	10	.0000	.0000	.0000	.0000	.0001	.0007	.0030	.0096	.0245	.0515	.0916
	11	.0000	.0000	.0000	.0000	.0000	.0001	.0006	.0024	.0074	.0191	.0417
	12	.0000	.0000	.0000	.0000	.0000	.0000	.0001	.0004	.0016	.0052	.0139
	13	.0000	.0000	.0000	.0000	.0000	.0000	.0000	.0001	.0003	.0010	.0032
	14	.0000	.0000	.0000	.0000	.0000	.0000	.0000	.0000	.0000	.0001	.0005
	15	.0000	.0000	.0000	.0000	.0000	.0000	.0000	.0000	.0000	.0000	.0000
16	0	.8515	.4401	.1853	.0743	.0281	.0100	.0033	.0010	.0003	.0001	.0000
	1	.1376	.3706	.3294	.2097	.1126	.0535	.0228	.0087	.0030	.0009	.0002
	2	.0104	.1463	.2745	.2775	.2111	.1336	.0732	.0353	.0150	.0056	.0018
	3	.0005	.0359	.1423	.2285	.2463	.2079	.1465	.0888	.0468	.0215	.0085
	4	.0000	.0061	.0514	.1311	.2001	.2252	.2040	.1553	.1014	.0572	.0278
	5	.0000	.0008	.0137	.0555	.1201	.1802	.2099	.2008	.1623	.1123	.0667
	6	.0000	.0001	.0028	.0180	.0550	.1101	.1649	.1982	.1983	.1684	.1222
	7	.0000	.0000	.0004	.0045	.0197	.0524	.1010	.1524	.1889	.1969	.1746

APPENDIX TABLE (Continued)

n	k	.01	.05	.10	.15	.20	.25	.30	.35	.40	.45	.50
16	8	.0000	.0000	.0001	.0009	.0055	.0197	.0487	.0923	.1417	.1812	.1964
	9	.0000	.0000	.0000	.0001	.0012	.0058	.0185	.0442	.0840	.1318	.1746
	10	.0000	.0000	.0000	.0000	.0002	.0014	.0056	.0167	.0392	.0755	.1222
	11	.0000	.0000	.0000	.0000	.0000	.0002	.0013	.0049	.0142	.0337	.0667
	12	.0000	.0000	.0000	.0000	.0000	.0000	.0002	.0011	.0040	.0115	.0278
	13	.0000	.0000	.0000	.0000	.0000	.0000	.0000	.0002	.0008	.0029	.0085
	14	.0000	.0000	.0000	.0000	.0000	.0000	.0000	.0000	.0001	.0005	.0018
	15	.0000	.0000	.0000	.0000	.0000	.0000	.0000	.0000	.0000	.0001	.0002
	16	.0000	.0000	.0000	.0000	.0000	.0000	.0000	.0000	.0000	.0000	.0000
17	0	.8429	.4181	.1668	.0631	.0225	.0075	.0023	.0007	.0002	.0000	.0000
	1	.1447	.3741	.3150	.1893	.0957	.0426	.0169	.0060	.0019	.0005	.0001
	2	.0117	.1575	.2800	.2673	.1914	.1136	.0581	.0260	.0102	.0035	.0010
	3	.0006	.0415	.1556	.2359	.2393	.1893	.1245	.0701	.0341	.0144	.0052
	4	.0000	.0076	.0605	.1457	.2093	.2209	.1868	.1320	.0796	.0411	.0182
	5	.0000	.0010	.0175	.0668	.1361	.1914	.2081	.1849	.1379	.0875	.0472
	6	.0000	.0001	.0039	.0236	.0680	.1276	.1784	.1991	.1839	.1432	.0944
	7	.0000	.0000	.0007	.0065	.0267	.0668	.1201	.1685	.1927	.1841	.1484
	8	.0000	.0000	.0001	.0014	.0084	.0279	.0644	.1134	.1606	.1883	.1855
	9	.0000	.0000	.0000	.0003	.0021	.0093	.0276	.0611	.1070	.1540	.1855
	10	.0000	.0000	.0000	.0000	.0004	.0025	.0095	.0263	.0571	.1008	.1484
	11	.0000	.0000	.0000	.0000	.0001	.0005	.0026	.0090	.0242	.0525	.0944
	12	.0000	.0000	.0000	.0000	.0000	.0001	.0006	.0024	.0081	.0215	.0472
	13	.0000	.0000	.0000	.0000	.0000	.0000	.0001	.0005	.0021	.0068	.0182
	14	.0000	.0000	.0000	.0000	.0000	.0000	.0000	.0001	.0004	.0016	.0052
	15	.0000	.0000	.0000	.0000	.0000	.0000	.0000	.0000	.0001	.0003	.0010
	16	.0000	.0000	.0000	.0000	.0000	.0000	.0000	.0000	.0000	.0000	.0001
	17	.0000	.0000	.0000	.0000	.0000	.0000	.0000	.0000	.0000	.0000	.0000
18	0	.8345	.3972	.1501	.0536	.0180	.0056	.0016	.0004	.0001	.0003	.0010
	1	.1517	.3763	.3002	.1704	.0811	.0338	.0126	.0042	.0012	.0003	.0001
	2	.0130	.1683	.2835	.2556	.1723	.0958	.0458	.0190	.0069	.0022	.0006
	3	.0007	.0473	.1680	.2406	.2297	.1704	.1046	.0547	.0246	.0095	.0001
	4	.0000	.0093	.0700	.1592	.2153	.2130	.1681	.1104	.0614	.0291	.0117
	5	.0000	.0014	.0218	.0787	.1507	.1988	.2017	.1664	.1146	.0666	.0327
	6	.0000	.0002	.0052	.0301	.0816	.1436	.1873	.1941	.1655	.1181	.0708
	7	.0000	.0000	.0010	.0091	.0350	.0820	.1376	.1792	.1892	.1657	.1214
	8	.0000	.0000	.0002	.0022	.0120	.0376	.0811	.1327	.1734	.1864	.1669
	9	.0000	.0000	.0000	.0004	.0033	.0139	.0386	.0794	.1284	.1694	.1855
	10	.0000	.0000	.0000	.0001	.0008	.0042	.0149	.0385	.0771	.1248	.1669
	11	.0000	.0000	.0000	.0000	.0001	.0010	.0046	.0151	.0374	.0742	.1214
	12	.0000	.0000	.0000	.0000	.0000	.0002	.0012	.0047	.0145	.0354	.0708
	13	.0000	.0000	.0000	.0000	.0000	.0000	.0002	.0012	.0045	.0134	.0327
	14	.0000	.0000	.0000	.0000	.0000	.0000	.0000	.0002	.0011	.0039	.0117

n	k	.01	.05	.10	.15	.20	.25	.30	.35	.40	.45	.50
							p					
18	15	.0000	.0000	.0000	.0000	.0000	.0000	.0000	.0000	.0002	.0009	.0031
	16	.0000	.0000	.0000	.0000	.0000	.0000	.0000	.0000	.0000	.0001	.0006
	17	.0000	.0000	.0000	.0000	.0000	.0000	.0000	.0000	.0000	.0000	.0001
	18	.0000	.0000	.0000	.0000	.0000	.0000	.0000	.0000	.0000	.0000	.0000
19	0	.8262	.3774	.1351	.0456	.0144	.0042	.0011	.0003	.0001	.0000	.0000
	1	.1586	.3774	.2852	.1529	.0685	.0268	.0093	.0029	.0008	.0002	.0000
	2	.0144	.1787	.2852	.2428	.1540	.0803	.0358	.0138	.0046	.0013	.0003
	3	.0008	.0533	.1796	.2428	.2182	.1517	.0869	.0422	.0175	.0062	.0018
	4	.0000	.0112	.0798	.1714	.2182	.2023	.1491	.0909	.0467	.0203	.0074
	5	.0000	.0018	.0266	.0907	.1636	.2023	.1916	.1468	.0933	.0497	.0222
	6	.0000	.0002	.0069	.0374	.0955	.1574	.1916	.1844	.1451	.0949	.0518
	7	.0000	.0000	.0014	.0122	.0443	.0974	.1525	.1844	.1797	.1443	.0961
	8	.0000	.0000	.0002	.0032	.0166	.0487	.0981	.1489	.1797	.1771	.1442
	9	.0000	.0000	.0000	.0007	.0051	.0198	.0514	.0980	.1464	.1771	.1762
	10	.0000	.0000	.0000	.0001	.0013	.0066	.0220	.0528	.0976	.1449	.1762
	11	.0000	.0000	.0000	.0000	.0003	.0018	.0077	.0233	.0532	.0970	.1442
	12	.0000	.0000	.0000	.0000	.0000	.0004	.0022	.0083	.0237	.0529	.0961
	13	.0000	.0000	.0000	.0000	.0000	.0001	.0005	.0024	.0085	.0233	.0518
	14	.0000	.0000	.0000	.0000	.0000	.0000	.0001	.0006	.0024	.0082	.0222
	15	.0000	.0000	.0000	.0000	.0000	.0000	.0000	.0001	.0005	.0022	.0074
	16	.0000	.0000	.0000	.0000	.0000	.0000	.0000	.0000	.0001	.0005	.0018
	17	.0000	.0000	.0000	.0000	.0000	.0000	.0000	.0000	.0000	.0001	.0003
	18	.0000	.0000	.0000	.0000	.0000	.0000	.0000	.0000	.0000	.0000	.0000
	19	.0000	.0000	.0000	.0000	.0000	.0000	.0000	.0000	.0000	.0000	.0000
20	0	.8179	.3585	.1216	.0388	.0115	.0032	.0008	.0002	.0000	.0000	.0000
	1	.1652	.3774	.2702	.1368	.0576	.0211	.0068	.0020	.0005	.0001	.0000
	2	.0159	.1887	.2852	.2293	.1369	.0669	.0278	.0100	.0031	.0008	.0002
	3	.0010	.0596	.1901	.2428	.2054	.1339	.0718	.0323	.0123	.0040	.0011
	4	.0000	.0133	.0898	.1821	.2182	.1897	.1304	.0738	.0350	.0139	.0046
	5	.0000	.0022	.0319	.1028	.1746	.2023	.1789	.1272	.0746	.0365	.0148
	6	.0000	.0003	.0089	.0454	.1091	.1686	.1916	.1712	.1244	.0746	.0370
	7	.0000	.0000	.0020	.0160	.0545	.1124	.1643	.1844	.1659	.1221	.0739
	8	.0000	.0000	.0004	.0046	.0222	.0609	.1144	.1614	.1797	.1623	.1201
	9	.0000	.0000	.0001	.0011	.0074	.0271	.0654	.1158	.1597	.1771	.1602
	10	.0000	.0000	.0000	.0002	.0020	.0099	.0308	.0686	.1171	.1593	.1762
	11	.0000	.0000	.0000	.0000	.0005	.0030	.0120	.0336	.0710	.1185	.1602
	12	.0000	.0000	.0000	.0000	.0001	.0008	.0039	.0136	.0355	.0727	.1201
	13	.0000	.0000	.0000	.0000	.0000	.0002	.0010	.0045	.0146	.0366	.0739
	14	.0000	.0000	.0000	.0000	.0000	.0000	.0002	.0012	.0049	.0150	.0370
	15	.0000	.0000	.0000	.0000	.0000	.0000	.0000	.0003	.0013	.0049	.0148
	16	.0000	.0000	.0000	.0000	.0000	.0000	.0000	.0000	.0003	.0013	.0046
	17	.0000	.0000	.0000	.0000	.0000	.0000	.0000	.0000	.0000	.0002	.0011
	18	.0000	.0000	.0000	.0000	.0000	.0000	.0000	.0000	.0000	.0000	.0002
	19	.0000	.0000	.0000	.0000	.0000	.0000	.0000	.0000	.0000	.0000	.0000
	20	.0000	.0000	.0000	.0000	.0000	.0000	.0000	.0000	.0000	.0000	.0000

The First Thousand Primes

2	3	5	7	11	13	17	19	23	29	31	37
41	43	47	53	59	61	67	71	73	79	83	89
97	101	103	107	109	113	127	131	137	139	149	151
157	163	167	173	179	181	191	193	197	199	211	223
227	229	233	239	241	251	257	263	269	271	277	281
283	293	307	311	313	317	331	337	347	349	353	359
367	373	379	383	389	397	401	409	419	421	431	433
439	443	449	457	461	463	467	479	487	491	499	503
509	521	523	541	547	557	563	569	571	577	587	593
599	601	607	613	617	619	631	641	643	647	653	659
661	673	677	683	691	701	709	719	727	733	739	743
751	757	761	769	773	787	797	809	811	821	823	827
829	839	853	857	859	863	877	881	883	887	907	911
919	929	937	941	947	953	967	971	977	983	991	997
1009	1013	1019	1021	1031	1033	1039	1049	1051	1061	1063	1069
1087	1091	1093	1097	1103	1109	1117	1123	1129	1151	1153	1163
1171	1181	1187	1193	1201	1213	1217	1223	1229	1231	1237	1249
1259	1277	1279	1283	1289	1291	1297	1301	1303	1307	1319	1321
1327	1361	1367	1373	1381	1399	1409	1423	1427	1429	1433	1439
1447	1451	1453	1459	1471	1481	1483	1487	1489	1493	1499	1511
1523	1531	1543	1549	1553	1559	1567	1571	1579	1583	1597	1601
1607	1609	1613	1619	1621	1627	1637	1657	1663	1667	1669	1693
1697	1699	1709	1721	1723	1733	1741	1747	1753	1759	1777	1783
1787	1789	1801	1811	1823	1831	1847	1861	1867	1871	1873	1877
1879	1889	1901	1907	1913	1931	1933	1949	1951	1973	1979	1987
1993	1997	1999	2003	2011	2017	2027	2029	2039	2053	2063	2069
2081	2083	2087	2089	2099	2111	2113	2129	2131	2137	2141	2143
2153	2161	2179	2203	2207	2213	2221	2237	2239	2243	2251	2267
2269	2273	2281	2287	2293	2297	2309	2311	2333	2339	2341	2347
2351	2357	2371	2377	2381	2383	2389	2393	2399	2411	2417	2423
2437	2441	2447	2459	2467	2473	2477	2503	2521	2531	2539	2543

2549	2551	2557	2579	2591	2593	2609	2617	2621	2633	2647	2657
2659	2663	2671	2677	2683	2687	2689	2693	2699	2707	2711	2713
2719	2729	2731	2741	2749	2753	2767	2777	2789	2791	2797	2801
2803	2819	2833	2837	2843	2851	2857	2861	2879	2887	2897	2903
2909	2917	2927	2939	2953	2957	2963	2969	2971	2999	3001	3011
3019	3023	3037	3041	3049	3061	3067	3079	3083	3089	3109	3119
3121	3137	3163	3167	3169	3181	3187	3191	3203	3209	3217	3221
3229	3251	3253	3257	3259	3271	3299	3301	3307	3313	3319	3323
3329	3331	3343	3347	3359	3361	3371	3373	3389	3391	3407	3413
3433	3449	3457	3461	3463	3467	3469	3491	3499	3511	3517	3527
3529	3533	3539	3541	3547	3557	3559	3571	3581	3583	3593	3607
3613	3617	3623	3631	3637	3643	3659	3671	3673	3677	3691	3697
3701	3709	3719	3727	3733	3739	3761	3767	3769	3779	3793	3797
3803	3821	3823	3833	3847	3851	3853	3863	3877	3881	3889	3907
3911	3917	3919	3923	3929	3931	3943	3947	3967	3989	4001	4003
4007	4013	4019	4021	4027	4049	4051	4057	4073	4079	4091	4093
4099	4111	4127	4129	4133	4139	4153	4157	4159	4177	4201	4211
4217	4219	4229	4231	4241	4243	4253	4259	4261	4271	4273	4283
4289	4297	4327	4337	4339	4349	4357	4363	4373	4391	4397	4409
4421	4423	4441	4447	4451	4457	4463	4481	4483	4493	4507	4513
4517	4519	4523	4547	4549	4561	4567	4583	4591	4597	4603	4621
4637	4639	4643	4649	4651	4657	4663	4673	4679	4691	4703	4721
4723	4729	4733	4751	4759	4783	4787	4789	4793	4799	4801	4813
4817	4831	4861	4871	4877	4889	4903	4909	4919	4931	4933	4937
4943	4951	4957	4967	4969	4973	4987	4993	4999	5003	5009	5011
5021	5023	5039	5051	5059	5077	5081	5087	5099	5101	5107	5113
5119	5147	5153	5167	5171	5179	5189	5197	5209	5227	5231	5233
5237	5261	5273	5279	5281	5297	5303	5309	5323	5333	5347	5351
5381	5387	5393	5399	5407	5413	5417	5419	5431	5437	5441	5443
5449	5471	5477	5479	5483	5501	5503	5507	5519	5521	5527	5531
5557	5563	5569	5573	5581	5591	5623	5639	5641	5647	5651	5653
5657	5659	5669	5683	5689	5693	5701	5711	5717	5737	5741	5743
5749	5779	5783	5791	5801	5807	5813	5821	5827	5839	5843	5849
5851	5857	5861	5867	5869	5879	5881	5897	5903	5923	5927	5939
5953	5981	5987	6007	6011	6029	6037	6043	6047	6053	6067	6073
6079	6089	6091	6101	6113	6121	6131	6133	6143	6151	6163	6173
6197	6199	6203	6211	6217	6221	6229	6247	6257	6263	6269	6271
6277	6287	6299	6301	6311	6317	6323	6329	6337	6343	6353	6359
6361	6367	6373	6379	6389	6397	6421	6427	6449	6451	6469	6473
6481	6491	6521	6529	6547	6551	6553	6563	6569	6571	6577	6581
6599	6607	6619	6637	6653	6659	6661	6673	6679	6689	6691	6701
6703	6709	6719	6733	6737	6761	6763	6779	6781	6791	6793	6803
6823	6827	6829	6833	6841	6857	6863	6869	6871	6883	6899	6907
6911	6917	6947	6949	6959	6961	6967	6971	6977	6983	6991	6997
7001	7013	7019	7027	7039	7043	7057	7069	7079	7103	7109	7121

7127	7129	7151	7159	7177	7187	7193	7207	7211	7213	7219	7229
7237	7243	7247	7253	7283	7297	7307	7309	7321	7331	7333	7349
7351	7369	7393	7411	7417	7433	7451	7457	7459	7477	7481	7487
7489	7499	7507	7517	7523	7529	7537	7541	7547	7549	7559	7561
7573	7577	7583	7589	7591	7603	7607	7621	7639	7643	7649	7669
7673	7681	7687	7691	7699	7703	7717	7723	7727	7741	7753	7757
7759	7789	7793	7817	7823	7829	7841	7853	7867	7873	7877	7879
7883	7901	7907	7919								

Index of Names

Boldface double numbers refer to paragraph numbers; thus **3.9** refers to paragraph 3.9.

Index of Symbols

Boldface double numbers refer to paragraph numbers; thus **1.2** refers to paragraph 1.2.

References

Boldface double numbers refer to paragraph numbers; thus **34.1** refers to paragraph 34.1.

General References

1. Bell, E. T.: *Men of Mathematics.* New York: Simon & Schuster, 1937.

2. Biggs, Norman L., E. Keith Lloyd, and Robin J. Wilson: *Graph Theory: 1736–1936.* Oxford: Clarendon Press, 1976. This book contains extracts of Refs. 7, 14, 23, 25, 26, and 31 from the Works Cited.

3. Dantzig, Tobias: *Number, the Language of Science; A Critical Survey Written for the Cultured Nonmathematician,* 3d ed. New York: Macmillan, 1939.

4. Davis, Philip J., and Reuben Hersh: *The Mathematical Experience.* Cambridge, Mass.: Birkhäuser Boston, 1980.

5. Gessel, Ira, and Gian-Carlo Rota (Eds.): *Classic Papers in Combinatorics.* Cambridge, Mass: Birkhäuser Boston, 1987. This book contains the papers in Refs. 10, 19, 20, and 32 from the Works Cited.

6. Hardy, G. H.: *A Mathematician's Apology.* London: Cambridge University Press, 1967.

7. Katz, Victor J.: *A History of Mathematics: An Introduction.* New York: HarperCollins, ca. 1993.

8. Lipton, James: *An Exaltation of Larks.* New York: Grossman, 1968.

9. Newman, James Roy: *The World of Mathematics: A Small Library of the Literature of Mathematics from Ah-mose the Scribe to Albert Einstein.* New York: Simon & Schuster, 1956.

10. Parlett, David Sidney: *The Oxford Guide to Card Games.* New York: Oxford University Press, 1990.

11. Wilder, Raymond Louis: *Mathematics as a Cultural System.* New York: Pergamon, 1981.

General Mathematical References

1. Beckenbach, Edwin F., and Richard Bellman: *An Introduction to Inequalities.* New York: Random House, 1961.

2. Honsberger, Ross: *Mathematical Gems I.* Washington, D.C.: Mathematical Association of America, 1973.

3. ———: *Mathematical Gems II.* Washington, D.C.: Mathematical Association of America, 1976.

4. ———: *Mathematical Gems III.* Washington, D.C.: Mathematical Association of America, 1985.

5. ———: *Mathematical Morsels.* Washington, D.C.: Mathematical Association of America, 1978.

6. Niven, Ivan Morton: *Mathematics of Choice; or, How to Count Without Counting.* New York: Random House, 1965.

7. Ore, Oystein: *Number Theory and Its History.* New York: Dover, 1988.

8. Saaty, Thomas L., and Paul C. Kainen: *The Four-Color Problem: Assaults and Conquest.* New York: Dover, 1986.

9. Sloane, N. J. A., and Simon Plouffe: *The Encyclopedia of Integer Sequences.* San Diego: Academic, 1995.

Works Cited

1. Appel, Kenneth I., and Wolfgang Haken: *Every Planar Map Is Four Colorable.* Providence, R.I.: American Mathematical Society, 1989. **34.1.**

2. Bang, Chang M., and Henry Sharp, Jr.: Score Vectors of Tournaments. *J. Combinatorial Theory,* **B26** (1):81–84 (1979). **40.8.**

3. Biggs, Norman L., E. Keith Lloyd, and Robin J. Wilson: *Graph Theory: 1736–1936.* Oxford: Clarendon Press, 1976. **38.1, 39.2.**

4. Carroll, Lewis: *Alice's Adventures in Wonderland.* New York: Doubleday, 1907. **2.9.**

5. ———: *Symbolic Logic, Part I.* New York: Berkeley Enterprises, 1955. **2.9.**

6. ———: *Through the Looking Glass and What Alice Found There.* New York: Random House, 1946. **2.9.**

7. Cayley, Arthur: On the Theory of the Analytical Forms Called Trees. *Phil. Mag.,* **13** (4): 172–176 (1857). This paper can be found in Ref. 3, pp. 40–44, of the Works Cited. **39.1.**

8. Deacon, A. Bernard: Geometrical Drawings from Malekula and Other Islands of the New Hebrides. *J. Anthropol. Inst. Great Britain and Ireland,* **64**: 129–175 (1934). **38.5.**

9. Dilworth, R. P.: A Decomposition Theorem for Partially Ordered Sets. *Ann. Math.,* **51**: 161–166 (1950). This can be found in Ref. 5 of the General References. **32.5.**

10. Dirac, Gabriel Andrew: Some Theorems on Abstract Graphs. *Proc. London Math. Soc.*, **2** (3): 69–81 (1952). **35.7.**

11. Doyle, Sir Arthur Conan: *The Memoirs of Sherlock Holmes.* New York: Harper & Brothers, 1894. Problem 44, Sec. 17.

12. Eigeland, Tor: The Cuisine of Al-Andalus. *Aramco World*, **40** (5): 28–35 (1989). **4.7.**

13. Euclid: *The Elements.* See Ref. 22 below.

14. Euler, Leonhard: Solutio Problematis ad Geometriam Situs Pertinentis. *Comm. Acad. Sci. Imp. Petropol.*, **8**: 128–140 (1736). For an English translation of part of this paper, see Ref. 3, pp. 3–8, of the Works Cited. **38.1.**

15. Foulds, L. R.: *Graph Theory Applications.* New York: Springer-Verlag, 1991. **40.7.**

16. Fraenkel, A. A.: *Abstract Set Theory*, 2d ed. Amsterdam: North-Holland, 1961. **1.16.**

17. Gillman, L.: The Car and the Goats. *Am. Math. Monthly,* **99** (1): 3–7 (1992). **21.6.**

18. Gulick, Denny: *Encounters with Chaos.* New York: McGraw-Hill, 1992. Problem 25, Sec. 32.

19. Hall, P.: On Representatives of Subsets. *J. London Math. Soc.,* **10**: 26–30 (1935). This can be found in Ref. 5 of the General References. **11.6.**

20. Halmos, P. R., and H. E. Vaughan: The Marriage Problem. *Am. J. Math.,* **72**: 214–215 (1950). This can be found in Ref. 5 of the General References. **11.6.**

21. Harary, Frank: *Graph Theory.* Reading, Mass.: Addison-Wesley, 1972. **39.6.**

22. Heath, T. L. (Ed.): *The Thirteen Books of Euclid's Elements.* New York: Dover, 1956. **2.1., 3.9, 7.6.**

23. Hierholzer, Carl: Über die Möglichkeit, einen Linienzug ohne Wiederholung und ohne Unterbrechnung zu umfahren. *Math. Ann.*, **6**: 30–32 (1873). For an English translation of part of this paper, see Ref 3, pp. 11, 12, of the Works Cited. **38.2.**

24. Huntley, H. E.: *The Divine Proportion: A Study in Mathematical Beauty.* New York: Dover, 1970. **7.6.**

25. Kirchhoff, G. R.: Über die Auflösung der Gleichungen, auf welche man bei der Untersuchung der linearen Verteilung galvanischer Ströme geführt wird. *Ann. Phys. Chem.*, **72:** 497–508 (1847). For an English translation, see Ref. 3, pp. 133–135, of the Works Cited. **39.6.**

26. Kuratowski, K.: Sur le problème des courbes gauches en topologie. *Fund. Math.*, **15**: 271–283 (1930). For an English translation of part of this paper, see Ref. 3, pp. 146, 147, of the Works Cited. **37.4.**

27. Landau, H. G.: On Dominance Relations and the Structure of Animal Societies. III. The Condition for a Score Structure. *Bull. Math. Biophys.,* **15**: 143–148 (1953). **40.8.**

28. Lucas, Édouard: *Récréations mathématiques.* Paris: Gauthier-Villars, 1882–94. **38.3.**

29. Moser, Leo: On the Danger of Induction. *Mathematics Magazine,* **23**: 109 (1949). **14.2, 17.4.**

30. Mosteller, Frederick: *Fifty Challenging Problems in Probability with Solutions.* New York: Dover, 1987. Problem 30, Sec. 24.

31. Prüfer, H.: Neuer Beweis eines Satzes über Permutationen. *Arch. Math. Phys.*, **27** (3): 142–144 (1918). For an English translation of part of this paper, see Ref. 3, pp. 52–54, of the Works Cited. **39.2.**

32. Ramsey, F. P.: On a Problem of Formal Logic. *Proc. London Math. Soc.*, **30** (2): 264–286 (1928). This can be found in Ref. 5 of the General References. **9.6.**

33. Shakespeare, William: *Hamlet.* **1.5.**

34. ———: *Henry IV, Part I.* Problem 25, Sec. 5.

35. Stevick, Robert D.: *The Earliest Irish and English Bookarts: Visual and Poetic Forms before A. D. 1000.* Philadelphia: University of Pennsylvania Press, 1994. Problem 30, Sec. 11.

36. Swamy, M. N. S., and K. Thulasiraman: *Graphs, Networks, and Algorithms.* New York: Wiley, 1981. **39.6.**

37. Tucker, Alan: *Applied Combinatorics.* New York: Wiley, 1980. **40.7.**

38. Vajda, S.: *Fibonacci & Lucas Numbers, and the Golden Section: Theory and Application.* New York: Halsted Press, 1989. **13.5.**

39. Zaslavsky, Claudia: *Africa Counts; Number and Pattern in African Culture.* Boston: Prindle, Weber & Schmidt, 1973. **38.5.**

Specialized Mathematical Books

1. Bondy, J. A., and U. S. R. Murty: *Graph Theory with Applications.* New York: American Elsevier, 1976.

2. Brousseau, Alfred: *Linear Recursion and Fibonacci Sequences.* San Jose, Calif.: Fibonacci Association, 1971.

3. Cantor, Georg: *Contributions to the Founding of the Theory of Transfinite Numbers.* La Salle, Ill.: Open Court, 1952.

4. Chartrand, Gary, and Linda Lesniak: *Graphs & Diagraphs,* 3d ed. London: Chapman & Hall, 1996.

5. Fletcher, Peter, and C. Wayne Patty: *Foundations of Higher Mathematics.* Boston: PWS-Kent, 1988.

6. Fomin, S. V.: *Number Systems.* Chicago: University of Chicago Press, 1974.

7. Hall, Marshall: *Combinatorial Theory,* 2d ed. New York: Wiley, 1986.

8. Kazarinoff, Nicholas D.: *Geometric Inequalities.* New York: Random House, 1961.

9. Manber, Udi: *Introduction to Algorithms: A Creative Approach.* Reading, Mass.: Addison-Wesley, 1989.

10. Reingold, Edward M., Jurg Nievergelt, and Narsingh Deo: *Combinatorial Algorithms: Theory and Practice.* Englewood Cliffs, N.J.: Prentice-Hall, 1977.

11. Riordan, John: *An Introduction to Combinatorial Analysis.* Princeton, N.J.: Princeton University Press, 1980.

12. Roberts, Fred S.: *Applied Combinatorics.* Englewood Cliffs, N.J.: Prentice-Hall, 1984.

13. Ryser, Herbert John: *Combinatorial Mathematics.* New York: Mathematical Association of America; distributed by Wiley, 1963.

14. Stark, Harold M.: *An Introduction to Number Theory.* Cambridge, Mass.: MIT Press, 1978.

15. Uspensky, J. V., and M.A. Heaslet: *Elementary Number Theory.* New York: McGraw-Hill, 1939.

16. Wilder, Raymond Louis: *Introduction to the Foundations of Mathematics.* New York: Wiley, 1952.

17. Wilson, Robin J.: *Introduction to Graph Theory,* 3d ed. Essex, England: Longman, 1985.

Specialized Mathematical Articles

1. Campbell, D. M.: The Computation of Catalan Numbers. *Mathematics Magazine,* **57**: 191–208 (1984). **19.5.**

2. Coolidge, J. L.: The Story of the Binomial Theorem. *Am. Math. Monthly,* **56**: 147–157 (1949). **17.5.**

3. Hanson, D., K. Seyffarth, and J. H. Weston: Matchings, Derangements, Rencontres. *Mathematics Magazine,* **56**: 224–229 (1983). **18.6.**

4. Lagarias, J. C.: The $3x + 1$ Problem and Its Generalizations. *Am. Math. Monthly,* **92**: 29–42 (1985). **4.7.**

5. Manvel, B.: Counterfeit Coin Problems. *Mathematics Magazine,* **50**: 90–92 (1977). **3.9.**

6. Robinson, L. V.: Pascal's Triangle and Negative Exponents. *Am. Math. Monthly,* **54**: 540–541 (1947). **17.5.**

7. Smith, C. A. B.: The Counterfeit-Coin Problem. *The Mathematical Gazette,* **21**: 31–39 (1947). **3.9.**

8. Wilder, R. L.: The Nature of Mathematical Proof. *Am. Math. Monthly,* **51**: 309–323 (1944). **14.7.**

Electronic References

We have not included references from the World Wide Web because the addresses for such references tend to change frequently. One site that should be noted is the *Electronic Journal of Combinatorics*; in particular, its *Dynamic Surveys in Combinatorics.* The survey, "Small Ramsey Numbers" by Stanislaw Radziszowski, contains some of the information found in paragraph 9.6. Frank Ruskey's remarkable document "A Survey of Venn Diagrams," not only has a biography and picture of John Venn, but also much information on Venn diagrams. Professor Dymàček's web page is located at http://liberty.uc.wlu.edu/~wdymacek/ and there is a link from this page to the *Electronic Journal of Combinatorics*.

Answers to Tutorials and Selected Problems

Section 1. Answers to Tutorials

1.3. a. 6 **b.** $m = 0$

1.8. a. Yes, 0 **b.** $\{\pm 2, \pm 6, \pm 18, \pm 54\}$ **c.** $\mathbb{O} = \{x : x = 2k - 1, k \in \mathbb{Z}\}$

1.11. a. If **B** is a subset of **A**, then every element of **B** is an element of **A**. Since **B** − **A** contains only those elements of **B** that are not in **A**, and every element of **B** is in **A**, **B** − **A** must be $\varnothing$. **b.** If **A** − **B** is empty, then every element of **A** is also an element of **B**. Hence, **A** ⊆ **B**.

Section 1. Answers to Selected Problems

1. (a) $\frac{7}{4}$ (b) $\frac{3}{2}$ (c) $\frac{1}{2}$ (d) $-\frac{7}{2}$

3. (a) $\left(-\frac{15}{2}, \frac{5}{2}\right)$ (b) $\left(-\frac{11}{4}, -\frac{9}{4}\right)$

5. (a) $\frac{19}{8}$ (b) $\frac{9}{4}$ (c) $\frac{7}{4}$ (d) $-\frac{1}{4}$

7. The point u is two-fifths of the way from a to b.

9. $a = 2, b = 8$

13. (a) Yes (b) No

15. (a)

B	A − B	B	A − B
$\varnothing$	$\{w, x, y, z\}$	$\{x, y\}$	$\{w, z\}$
$\{w\}$	$\{x, y, z\}$	$\{x, z\}$	$\{w, y\}$
$\{x\}$	$\{w, y, z\}$	$\{y, z\}$	$\{w, x\}$
$\{y\}$	$\{w, x, z\}$	$\{w, x, y\}$	$\{z\}$
$\{z\}$	$\{w, x, y\}$	$\{w, x, z\}$	$\{y\}$
$\{w, x\}$	$\{y, z\}$	$\{w, y, z\}$	$\{x\}$
$\{w, y\}$	$\{x, z\}$	$\{x, y, z\}$	$\{w\}$
$\{w, z\}$	$\{x, y\}$		

(b) $\{\{w\}, \{w, x\}, \{w, y\}, \{w, z\}, \{w, x, y\}, \{w, x, z\}, \{w, y, z\}\}$

17. (*a*) $\frac{1}{2}$ (*b*) **A** has twice as many subsets as **M**.

19. (*a*) 0 (*b*) $x = 10$ or $x = 100$
(*c*) $x \in \{\ldots, -4, -3, 3, 4, \ldots\}$

21. (*a*) $\mathbf{V} - \mathbf{K} = \{a, e, i, o\}$ (*b*) $\mathbf{V} - \mathbf{K} = \{a, e, i, o\}$

23. (*a*) $\mathbf{A} - \mathbf{B} = \{2, 3, w, z\}$ (*b*) $\mathbf{B} - \mathbf{A} = \{\{2\}, \{3\}, \{w, z\}\}$

25. (*a*) $\{\{2\}, \{3\}, \{w, z\}\}$ (*b*) $\{\varnothing, \{1\}\}$

27. $\{\{a, b\}, \{a, c\}, \{a, d\}, \{a, e\}, \{b, c\}, \{b, d\}, \{b, e\}, \{c, d\}, \{c, e\}, \{d, e\}\}$

29. Since a is not a set and $\mathbf{2^V}$ contains only sets, $a \notin \mathbf{2^V}$.

31. Since $\mathbf{A} - \mathbf{B} = \{b\}$, $\mathbf{2^{A-B}} = \{\varnothing, \{b\}\}$. Now $\mathbf{2^A} - \mathbf{2^B} = \{\{b\}, \{a, b\}, \{b, 1\}, \mathbf{A}\}$.

33. Note that $\varnothing \in \mathbf{2^{A-B}}$ but that $\varnothing \notin \mathbf{2^A} - \mathbf{2^B}$ since $\varnothing \in \mathbf{2^A}$ and $\varnothing \in \mathbf{2^B}$. Hence, $\mathbf{2^{A-B}} \not\subseteq \mathbf{2^A} - \mathbf{2^B}$.

35. $1 < 9$

Section 2.   Answers to Tutorials

2.3.

a	b	c	$a < b$	$b < c$	$a < c$
2	0	1	False	True	False
-1	0	$-\frac{1}{2}$	True	False	True
$-\pi$	-3	$-\sqrt{2}$	True	True	True

2.6. a. If $a < b$, then $a + p = b$ for some positive number p. Thus $a \cdot c + p \cdot c = b \cdot c$. Since c is a positive number, $p \cdot c$ is also positive, and hence $a \cdot c < b \cdot c$. **b.** Some crustaceans have claws.

Section 2.   Answers to Complement Problems

1. Correct.

2. Wrong (no conclusion possible).

3. Correct.

4. Wrong (some tedious songs are not his).

5. Wrong (some vain persons are not professors).

6. Correct.

7. Correct.

8. Correct.

9. No banker fails to shun hyenas.

10. Some greyhounds are not fat.

11. Some things that are not umbrellas should be left behind on a journey.

12. Some judges do not exercise self-control.

13. Some lessons need attention.

14. No country infested by dragons fails to be fascinating.

15. Some ill-fed canaries are unhappy.

16. Some things that are meant to amuse are not Acts of Parliament.

17. Babies cannot manage crocodiles.

18. My poultry are not officers.

19. My gardener is very old.

20. All hummingbirds are small.

21. Guinea pigs never really appreciate Beethoven.

22. Wedding cake always disagrees with me.

23. No bird in this aviary lives on mince pies.

24. No kitten with green eyes will play with a gorilla.

25. Shakespeare was clever.

26. Donkeys are not easy to swallow.

Section 2. Answers to Selected Problems

1. (a) Statement (b) Not a statement (c) Statement

3. (a) Statement (b) Statement

5. 1(a) and 2(b) are true statements.

7. If $a < b$, then there is a positive number p such that $a + p = b$. Hence $(a + p) + k = b + k$ or $(a + k) + p = b + k$. Since $p > 0$, $a + k < b + k$.

9. Suppose that $0 < a < b$. Then there is a positive number p such that $a + p = b$. Thus $b/a = (a + p)/a = 1 + p/a$. Since a and p are positive, so is p/a. Hence, $1 < b/a$.

11. If $a < b$ and $c < d$, then there are positive numbers p and q such that $a + p = b$ and $c + q = d$. Thus $(a + p) + (c + q) = b + d$ or $(a + c) + (p + q) = b + d$. Since p and q are positive, $p + q$ is also positive, and hence $a + c < b + d$.

13. Let $0 < a < b$ and $0 < c < d$. Then there are positive numbers p and q such that $a + p = b$ and $c + q = d$. Now $b \cdot d = (a + p) \cdot (c + q) = a \cdot c + p \cdot c + a \cdot q + p \cdot q = a \cdot c + (p \cdot c + a \cdot q + p \cdot q)$.

15. Let $x \in \mathbf{L} - \mathbf{K}$. Thus $x \in \mathbf{L}$ and $x \notin \mathbf{K}$. Since $\mathbf{L} \subseteq \mathbf{M}$, $x \in \mathbf{M}$. So $x \in \mathbf{M}$ and $x \notin \mathbf{K}$. Hence $x \in \mathbf{M} - \mathbf{K}$. Therefore, $\mathbf{L} - \mathbf{K} \subseteq \mathbf{M} - \mathbf{K}$.

17. Let $x \in \mathbb{E} - (\mathbb{E} - \mathbf{D})$. So $x \in \mathbb{E}$ and $x \notin \mathbb{E} - \mathbf{D}$. Since $x \notin \mathbb{E} - \mathbf{D}$, either $x \notin \mathbb{E}$ or $x \in \mathbf{D}$. Since $x \in \mathbb{E}$, it must be that $x \in \mathbf{D}$, and so $\mathbb{E} - (\mathbb{E} - \mathbf{D}) \subseteq \mathbf{D}$. In fact, $\mathbb{E} - (\mathbb{E} - \mathbf{D}) = \{0, 2, 4, 8\}$.

19. Now $\mathbb{N} - \mathbb{E}$ is the set of positive odd numbers, and so $\mathbb{N} - (\mathbb{N} - \mathbb{E})$ is the set of positive even integers which is a proper subset of $\mathbb{E}$.

21. $\mathbf{A} \, \Delta \, \mathbf{B} = \{1, 3, 5, 7, 9\}$

24. $\mathbf{A} - \mathbf{B}$ is a subset of $\mathbf{A} \, \Delta \, \mathbf{B}$ because each element of $\mathbf{A} - \mathbf{B}$ is in $\mathbf{A}$ and not $\mathbf{B}$ and hence is in exactly one of $\mathbf{A}$ or $\mathbf{B}$.

25. This problem requires little effort.

27. The only time the answer will be "no" is when the first person is a liar and the second is a truthteller.

Section 3. Answers to Tutorials

3.1 Let x be an even integer. Then there is another integer k such that $x = 2k$. Hence, $x^3 = (2k)^3 = 2(4k^3)$. Since k is an integer, $4k^3$ is also. Thus, x^3 is even.

3.2

		Hypothesis	Conclusion
x	y	$(0 < x < y)$	$(0 < x^2 < y^2)$
-2	-1	False	False
-2	-4	False	True
2	3	True	True
0	9	False	False
5	3	False	False

3.4 a. If p is true, then $\sim(\sim p)$ is true. **b.** If p is false, then $\sim(\sim p)$ is false. **c.** If p is false, then $\sim(\sim(\sim(\sim p)))$ is false.

3.6 a. If $x^2 \leq 9$, then $x \leq 3$. **b.** $q \to p$

Section 3. Answers to Selected Problems

1. Let x be odd. Then there is an integer k such that $x = 2k + 1$. So $x^2 = (2k + 1)^2 = 4k^2 + 4k + 1 = 2(2k^2 + 2k) + 1$. Since k is an integer, $2k^2 + 2k$ is also an integer, and hence x^2 is odd.

3. Let x be odd. Then there is an integer k such that $x = 2k + 1$. So $x^3 = (2k + 1)^3 = 8k^3 + 12k^2 + 6k + 1 = 2(4k^3 + 6k^2 + 3k) + 1$. Since k is an integer, $4k^3 + 6k^2 + 3k$ is also. Therefore, x^3 is odd.

5. Let x and y be odd. Then there are integers k and m such that $x = 2k + 1$ and $y = 2m + 1$. Thus $xy = (2k + 1)(2m + 1) = 4km + 2k + 2m + 1 = 2(2km + k + m) + 1$. Since k and m are integers, so is $2km + k + m$. Hence, xy is odd.

9. Suppose a divides x and a divides $(x + y)$. Then there are integers k and m such that $x = ak$ and $x + y = am$. Hence $y = am - x = am - ak = a(m - k)$. Since m and k are integers, $m - k$ is also. Thus, a divides y.

11. (a) If x^2 is even, then x is even. (b) If x^3 is even, then x is even.

13. (a) Let y be any integer. If xy is odd, then x is odd. (b) If $x + y$ is odd, then either x or y is even.

15. If I will not get wet, then it is not raining.

17. (a) If $a > c$, then $ab > cb$. (b) Since $a > c$, there is a positive number p such that $a = c + p$. Hence, $ab = cb + pb$. But b is positive, so pb is positive and thus $ab > cb$.

19. (a) False, for $2 + 3 + 4 = 9$. (b) True. Among three consecutive integers, one will always be even; hence their product is even.

21. Let $2k + 1, 2k + 3, 2k + 5$ be three consecutive odd integers. Then their sum is $(2k + 1) + (2k + 3) + (2k + 5) = 6k + 9 = 3(2k + 3)$, which is divisible by 3.

23. (a) If $\mathbf{M} - \mathbf{B} \not\subseteq \mathbf{M} - \mathbf{A}$, then $\mathbf{A} \not\subseteq \mathbf{B}$. (b) If $\mathbf{M} - \mathbf{B} \not\subseteq \mathbf{M} - \mathbf{A}$, then there is an $x \in \mathbf{M} - \mathbf{B}$ such that $x \notin \mathbf{M} - \mathbf{A}$. Since $x \in \mathbf{M} - \mathbf{B}$, $x \in \mathbf{M}$ and $x \notin \mathbf{B}$. Since $x \notin \mathbf{M} - \mathbf{A}$, either $x \notin \mathbf{M}$ or $x \in \mathbf{A}$. But $x \in \mathbf{M}$, so $x \in \mathbf{A}$. Therefore, $\mathbf{A} \not\subseteq \mathbf{B}$.

25. The contrapositive is: If n is even, then n^5 is even. So assume that n is even. Hence there is an integer k such that $n = 2k$, and so $n^5 = (2k)^5 = 2(2^4 k^5)$. Since k is an integer, $2^4 k^5$ is an integer, and thus n^5 is even.

27. If $2 \nmid n$, then n is odd. Let $n = 2m + 1$. Thus $n^2 = 4m^2 + 4m + 1 = 4(m^2 + m) + 1$.

29. By Problem 28, the sum of any two squares is even or has a remainder of 1 when divided by 4. In neither case can the sum be of the form $4m + 3$.

31. The contrapositive is: If $2 \nmid m$, then $2 \nmid 3m$. Hence, we need to show that if m is odd, then $3m$ is odd. But this is true by Problem 5.

33. Let x be even. So $x = 2k$ and $x^{25} = 2^{25}k^{25} = 2(2^{24}k^{25})$. Therefore, x^{25} is even.

35. (a) If n is even, then there is an integer k such that $n = 2k$. Now either k is even or k is odd. So either $k = 2m$ or $k = 2m + 1$ for some integer m. Thus, either $n = 4m$ or

$m = 4m + 2$. (b) If n is odd, then there is an integer k such that $n = 2k + 1$. Now either k is even or k is odd. So either $k = 2m$ or $k = 2m + 1$ for some integer m. Thus, either $n = 4m + 1$ or $n = (4m + 2) + 1 = 4m + 3$.

37. The contrapositive is: If $x + y$ is odd, then xy is even. If $x + y$ is odd, then one of x or y is odd and the other is even. But the product of any integer with an even integer is even; hence xy is even.

Section 4. Answers to Tutorials

4.2. Step 1, $M = -1$; Step 2, $M = 18$; Step 3, $M = 18$; Step 4, $M = 19$; Step 5, $M = 19$; Step 6, $M = 21$.

4.4. **a.** $22 = 2 \cdot 11$; 23; $24 = 2^3 \cdot 3$; $25 = 5^2$; $26 = 2 \cdot 13$; $27 = 3^3$; $28 = 2^2 \cdot 7$; 29; $30 = 2 \cdot 3 \cdot 5$; 31 **b.** 24 **c.** 31

4.5. **Proof.** Assume, on the contrary, that the set of even positive integers is finite. Then by Theorem 4.2 there exists a largest even positive integer which we may call L. By the closure property of the integers, we know

that (1) $L + 2$ is again an even positive integer. Since 2 is a positive integer, we know, by the definition of order, that $L + 2 > L$. But, recall that L is the largest even positive integer; hence (2) $L + 2$ cannot be an even positive integer. Statements (1) and (2) are contradictory, and both are implied by the assumption that the set of even positive integers is finite. Hence, the assumption must be false, so the set of even positive integers is infinite. ■

Section 4. Answers to Selected Problems

1. Step 1, -15; Step 2, -15; Step 3, -13; Step 4, -13; Step 5, -13; Step 6, -12; Step 7, -12.

3. Step 1, -15; Step 2, -18; Step 3, -18; Step 4, -30; Step 5, -30; Step 6, -30; Step 7, -30.

5. Suppose L is the largest positive integer. Now $2L$ is an integer, and $2L$ is larger than L, a contradiction.

7. (a) $\{1, 2, 4, 8\}$ (b) Divide each number m from 1 to 8 into 8 and keep the divisors.

9. (a) $\{1, 2, 3, 6, 7, 14, 21, 42\}$
(b) $\{(1, 42), (2, 21), (3, 14), (6, 7)\}$

11. $\{2, 3, 5, 7, 11, 13, 17, 19, 23, 29, 31, 37, 41, 43, 47\}$

13. $\{(3, 5), (5, 7), (11, 13), (17, 19), (29, 31), (41, 43), (59, 61), (71, 73)\}$

15. 11

17. No, $\{151, 461, 971, 1601\}$ is a set of primes.

19. (a) $\{2, 3, 5, 7, 11, 13, 17\}$ (b) $\{2, 3, 5, 7, 11\}$

21. Since $306 = 2 \cdot 3^2 \cdot 17$ and $942 = 2 \cdot 3 \cdot 157$, the largest number dividing both is 6.

23. The contrapositive is: If $m \neq n$, then $m^2 \neq n^2$. If $m \neq n$, then $m < n$. Hence, there is a positive integer p such that $m + p = n$. Thus $(m + p)^2 = n^2$, or $m^2 + 2mp + p^2 = n^2$. Since m and p are positive, $2mp + p^2$ is also positive, and so $m^2 < n^2$. Thus, $m^2 \neq n^2$.

25. Let $x \mid y$ and $y \mid z$. Then $y = xk$ and $z = ym$. Hence $z = xkm = (km)x$. So $x \mid z$.

27. Suppose that $d \mid n$ and $d \mid (n + 1)$. By Prob. 9 in Sec. 3, $d \mid 1$. Hence $d = 1$.

29. Step 1. Let i be 1 and let registers D and L both be 0. Step 2. If $r \mid a_i$, then add 1 to D, and if $a_i < r$, then add 1 to L. Step 3. Add 1 to i and go to Step 2. Stop when i is $n + 1$.

31. If $0 < a < b$ and $a < d$, then there are positive numbers p and q such that $a + p = b$ and $a + q = d$. So $(a + p)(a + q) = bd$. Hence $a^2 + (a \cdot (p + q) + pq) = bd$, and since a, p, and q are positive, $a^2 < bd$.

33. Let p be a prime larger than 2. Now p is odd, and thus $p = 4k + 1$ or $p = 4k + 3$.

35. $\{3, 7, 11, 19, 23, 31, 43, 47, 59, 67\}$

37. Clearly $q > p_n$. Note that $q = 4m - 1 = 4m - 4 + 3 = 4(m - 1) + 3$.

39. If p is a prime larger than 3, then p is odd. So p is of the form $6k + 1$, $6k + 3$, or $6k + 5$. But $3 \mid (6k+3)$, and so p is of the form $6k+1$ or $6k + 5$.

41. The cells that are locked are the ones numbered by squares, 1, 4, 9, 16, etc. This happens because the jailer visits a cell once for each divisor of the cell number, and squares are the only numbers with an odd number of divisors.

43. Let P be a register containing the primes, let N be a register containing 1, and let k be 2. Start with 7 in P. Step 1. If $6k + 1$ is prime, then increase N by 1 and put $6k + 1$ into P. Step 2. If $N = 100$, then stop. Otherwise, increase k by 1 and go to Step 1.

Section 5. Answers to Tutorials

5.4 a. True, $18 = 3 \cdot 6$ **b.** False, $18 = 4 \cdot 4 + 2$ **c.** False, $18 = 4 \cdot 4 + 2$ **d.** True, $28 = 5 \cdot 5 + 3$ **e.** False, $82 = 5 \cdot 16 + 2$ **f.** True, $100 = 9 \cdot 11 + 1$ **g.** False, $89 = 9 \cdot 9 + 8$ **h.** False, $9 = 9 \cdot 1$ **i.** True, $1000 = 9 \cdot 111 + 1$

5.5. a. 10, 14, 18, 22 **b.** Each counterexample is of the form $4k + 2$.

5.6. a. e, o, o; o, e, e; o, e, o; o, o, e; o, o, o **b.** 7 **c.** o, o, o **d.** Remember that odd times odd is odd. So if all three integers are odd, the product is odd. **e.** If one of the integers is even, then since even times anything is even, the product is even.

Section 5. Answers to Selected Problems

1. Note that x^3 belongs to the same class as x.

3. $x \in [0]_4 \rightarrow x^2 \in [0]_4$; $x \in [1]_4 \rightarrow x^2 \in [1]_4$; $x \in [2]_4 \rightarrow x^2 \in [0]_4$; $x \in [3]_4 \rightarrow x^2 \in [1]_4$

5. $(b) x \in [2]_5 \rightarrow x^2 \in [4]_5; x \in [2]_5 \rightarrow x^3 \in [3]_5; x \in [2]_5 \rightarrow x^4 \in [1]_5$

7. If 8 divides x, then 8 divides x^2. Note that 8 divides $144 = 12^2$, but 8 does not divide 12. Hence, the claim is false.

9. (a) If I will get wet, then it is raining. (b) If $a - b < 0$, then $b - a \geq 0$.

11. (a) $q \rightarrow \sim p$ (b) $p \rightarrow \sim q$ (c) $p \rightarrow q$ (d) $\sim q \rightarrow p$

13. (a) 2 (this is the only one) (b) 307, 401 (c) None possible (d) 9, 15

15. (a) If 3 divides $2n$, then 3 divides n. (b) Yes

17. If m is odd, then m divides n if and only if m divides $2n$.

19. Suppose neither x nor y is divisible by 3. Then there are integers h and k such that $x = 3h + r, r = 1$ or 2, and $y = 3k + s$, $s = 1$ or 2. So $x + y = 3(h + k) + (r + s)$, and since 3 divides $x + y$, 3 divides $r + s$. But $r + s$ is either 2, 3, or 4, and so $r + s = 3$. Hence, either $r = 1$ and $s = 2$ or $r = 2$ and $s = 1$.

21. If p is a prime larger than 3, then p is not divisible by 3, so either (a) $p \in [1]_3$ or (b) $p \in [2]_3$. In case (a) $p + 2 \in [0]_3$ and $p + 4 \in [2]_3$. Thus only $p + 2$ is divisible by 3. In case (b) $p + 2 \in [1]_3$ and $p + 4 \in [0]_3$. Thus only $p + 4$ is divisible by 3.

23. To be a statement, the hypothesis and conclusion must both be statements, and "the shoe fits" is a subjective judgment.

25. (a) If I had not been attacked by 52 or 53 men, then I am not a two-legged creature. (b) If I am a two-legged creature, then I was attacked by 52 or 53 men. (c) If I were attacked by 52 or 53 men, then I am a two-legged creature.

27. If 12 divides n, then both 3 and 4 divide n. Conversely, suppose that both 3 and 4 di-

vide n. Then $n = 3k$ and $n = 4m$ for some integers k and m. Hence $3k = 4m$, and by Problem 18, 3 must divide either 4 or m. Since 3 does not divide 4, 3 divides m, and so $m = 3w$ for some integer w. Thus $n = 4m = 4(3w) = 12w$. Therefore, 12 divides n.

29. If x and y are even, then x^2 and y^2 are also even (Theorem 5.2). Since the product of any number with an even number is even and the sum of even numbers is even, $x^2 + 3y^2$ is even.

31. *Contrapositive:* If $x^2 + 3y^2$ is odd, then x and y are of opposite parity. *Converse:* If $x^2 + 3y^2$ is even, then x and y are of the same parity.

33. Suppose that x and y are both odd. Then by Prob. 5 in Sec. 3, xy is odd. To prove the converse, we will prove its contrapositive: If x or y is even, then xy is even. To this end, note that if x is even, then $x = 2k$ for some integer k, and thus $xy = (2k)y = 2(ky)$ and so xy is even. If x is odd, then y must be even, and so $y = 2m$ for some integer m. Hence $xy = x(2m) = 2(xm)$, and so xy is even.

35. If 2 divides k, then 2 divides mk. Suppose that 2 divides mk where m is odd. If k were also odd, then mk is odd. But mk is even, and so k also must be even.

37. If m is in $[2]_3$, then $m = 3r + 2$ for some integer r. Also, if 3 divides mk, then $mk = 3s$ for some integer s. Thus, $(3r + 2)k = 3s$ or $3(s - rk) = 2k$. So 3 divides $2k$, and by Prob. 30 in Sec. 4, 3 divides k.

39. If $n = 4$, $1 + (1 \cdot 2 \cdot 3 \cdot 4) = 1 + 24 = 25 = 5^2$, not prime. Try $n = 5$.

41. If $p = 11$, then $2^{11} - 1 = 2048 - 1 = 2047 = 23 \cdot 89$.

43. $n = 0, 3$; yes: $n = 1, 5$; yes: $n = 2, 17$; yes: $n = 3, 257$; yes: $n = 4, 65537$; yes

Section 6. Answers to Tutorials

6.2. a. $\frac{7}{8} = 0.875$, terminating **b.** $\frac{8}{45} = 0.177777\ldots$, periodic

6.3. There must be 43 class members.

6.4. $0.\overline{18} = \frac{2}{11}$

6.5. a. $1386 = 105 \cdot 13 + 21; 105 = 21 \cdot 5 + 0$; hence $\gcd(1386, 105) = 21$. **b.** $\frac{105}{1386} = \frac{5}{66}$

Section 6. Answers to Selected Problems

1. (a) $\frac{3}{5}$ (b) $\frac{2}{3}$ (c) $\frac{1}{3}$ (d) $\frac{2}{13}$ (e) $\frac{5}{9}$ (f) $\frac{17}{19}$

3. (a) $0.818181\ldots$, period 2 (b) $0.486486\ldots$, period 3 (c) $0.41212\ldots$, period 2 (d) $0.198198\ldots$, period 3

5. $\frac{1}{7} = 0.142857\ldots, \frac{2}{7} = 0.285714\ldots, \frac{3}{7} = 0.428571\ldots, \frac{4}{7} = 0.571428\ldots, \frac{5}{7} = 0.714285\ldots, \frac{6}{7} = 0.857142\ldots$; all have period 6.

7. (a) $\frac{13}{99}$ (b) $\frac{2389}{9900}$ (c) $\frac{123}{999} = \frac{41}{333}$ (d) $\frac{10}{909}$

9. (a) $0.012999\ldots$ (b) $0.20999\ldots$ (c) $0.374999\ldots$ (d) $0.819989999\ldots$

11. (a) $d = 3$ (b) $d = 1$

13. (a) No (b) Yes

15. 287

17. 1, 8, 10, 14, 16

19. 1, 7, 11, 13, 17, 19, 23, 29. All are prime, except 1.

21. $260 = 7 \cdot 33 + 29; 33 = 1 \cdot 29 + 4; 29 = 7 \cdot 4 + 1; 4 = 4 \cdot 1 + 0$; therefore, $\gcd(260, 33) = 1$.

23. $420 = 1 \cdot 270 + 150; 270 = 1 \cdot 150 + 120; 150 = 1 \cdot 120 + 30; 120 = 4 \cdot 30 + 0$; therefore, $\gcd(420, 270) = 30$. Note that any immediately apparent common factor (like 10) can be factored out to simplify the arithmetic.

25. By the Pigeonhole Principle at least two of the numbers must have the same units digit; their difference ends in 0 and thus is divisible by 10.

27. At least two of the seven numbers have units digit in the same set. If that set is a singleton, then both the sum and difference are divisible by 10, whereas for the other four, if the two digits are the same (e.g., two 3s), the difference is divisible by 10 and if different (for example, 3 and 7), the sum is divisible by 10.

29. Divide the triangle into four subtriangles, each of side 1 foot. The pigeonholes are the four small triangles, the pigeons are the five darts. Assuming all five darts hit the dart board, we know that at least two are in the same small triangle, hence are less than 1 foot apart.

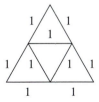

31. There are 100 different numbers of cents (pigeonholes) and 120 monthly statements (pigeons) in 10 years.

33. 11100011100011100011

35. The line contains alternately nine women and nine men.

37. $\frac{4901}{140}$

39. $\frac{242}{303} = 0.79867986\ldots$

41. (a) If $x = 0.b_1 b_2 \ldots b_r a_1 a_2 \ldots a_k a_1 a_2 \ldots a_k \ldots$, then
$$x = \frac{b_1 b_2 \ldots b_r a_1 a_2 \ldots a_k}{10^r(10^k - 1)}.$$

(b) If $x = 0.a_1 a_2 \ldots a_k$, then
$$x = \frac{a_1 a_2 \ldots a_k}{10^k}.$$

Section 7. Answers to Tutorials

7.1. a. $1.101001000100001000001\ldots$
b. $-0.101001000100001000001\ldots$
c. $0.202002000200002000002\ldots$

7.2A. a.

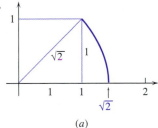

(a)

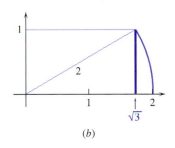

(b)

b.

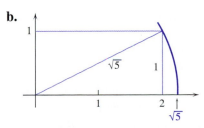

7.2B. Assume that $\sqrt{3}$ can be represented as a quotient of two integers p/q, where we assume

that (1) the integers p and q are relatively prime. Thus, by assumption, $\sqrt{3} = p/q$. Now apply simple arithmetic operations: $3 = p^2/q^2$, or $p^2 = 3q^2$. This says that p^2 is divisible by 3, and by Theorem 5.3, p must also be divisible by 3. So we can write $p = 3k$, or $p^2 = 9k^2$. But p^2 also equals $3q^2$, so $3q^2 = 9k^2$ from which $q^2 = 3k^2$. This says that q^2 is divisible by 3, and again by Theorem 5.3, q must also be divisible by 3. Hence it follows that p and q both have 3 as a common factor, and (2) the integers p and q are not relatively prime. Statements (1) and (2) are contradictory. The original assumption, therefore, must be false; hence $\sqrt{3}$ *cannot* be represented as a quotient of two integers.

7.3. a. $(1.73)^2 = 2.9929 < 3 < 3.0276 = (1.74)^2$ **b.** 1.73

7.5. Let x be any positive integer which has a prime factorization in which some prime number, say p, occurs an odd number of times, say $x = m \cdot p^{2k+1}$. Assume that $\sqrt{x}$ is a rational number. Then $\sqrt{x} = r/s$, and so $xs^2 = r^2$ or $m \cdot p^{2k+1}s^2 = r^2$. In the factorizations of s^2 and r^2, p must appear an even number of times. Thus p appears an odd number of times in the factorization of $m \cdot p^{2k+1}s^2$ and an even number of times in the factorization of r^2, a contradiction to the Fundamental Theorem of Arithmetic.

Section 7. Answers to Selected Problems

1. Assume $\sqrt{4}$ is rational; i.e., assume $\sqrt{4} = r/s$, where r, s are relatively prime. Then $r^2 = 4s^2$, and so $4 \mid r^2$. The next step would be to say that $4 \mid r$, but this does not follow (for example, $4 \mid 36$ but $4 \nmid 6$). The argument disintegrates here.

3. Suppose $\sqrt[3]{3}$ is rational; that is, $\sqrt[3]{3} = m/n$. Then $m^3 = 3n^3$. Let h be the number of 3s in m; then the number of 3s in m^3 is $3h$. Let k be the number of 3s in n; then the number of 3s in n^3 is $3k$, and the number of 3s in $3n^3$ is $3k + 1$. Now $3h = 3k + 1$ by FTOA, which cannot happen, for 3 divides $3h$ but not $3k + 1$.

5. Suppose $\sqrt[3]{4}$ is rational; that is, $\sqrt[3]{4} = m/n$. Then $m^3 = 4n^3 = 2^2 n^3$. Let h be the number of 2s in m; then the number of 2s in m^3 is $3h$. Let k be the number of 2s in n; then the number of 2s in n^3 is $3k$, and the number of 2s in $2^2 n^3$ is $3k + 2$. Now $3h = 3k + 2$ by FTOA, which cannot happen, for 3 divides $3h$ but not $3k + 2$.

7. If $0 < x < y$, then by Theorem 7.3, $0 < x^2 < y^2$. Multiplying this inequality by the positive number x gives $0 < x^3 < xy^2$, and multiplying $0 < x < y$ by y^2 gives $0 < xy^2 < y^3$. Combining these two inequalities yields $0 < x^3 < y^3$.

9. If $0 < x < y$, then $y^5 - x^5 = (y - x)(x^4 + x^3 y + x^2 y^2 + xy^3 + y^4)$. Since $x^4 + x^3 y + x^2 y^2 + xy^3 + y^4$ and $y - x$ are positive, $x^5 < y^5$.

11. 2.2360: $(2.2)^2 = 4.84$; $(2.3)^2 = 5.29$; $(2.23)^2 = 4.9729$, $(2.24)^2 = 5.0176$; $(2.236)^2 = 4.999696$, $(2.237)^2 = 5.004169$; $(2.2360)^2 = 4.999696$, $(2.2361)^2 = 5.00014321$

13. 1.442: $(1.4)^3 = 2.744$; $(1.5)^3 = 3.375$; $(1.44)^3 = 2.985984$; $(1.45)^3 = 3.048625$;

$(1.442)^3 = 2.998442888$; $(1.443)^3 = 3.004685307$

15. Yes. One possible pairing is $(1, 1^2), (2, 2^2), (3, 3^2), (4, 4^2), \ldots, (n, n^2), \ldots,$ for $n \in \mathbb{N}$.

17. $(-1, 2), (-2, 4), (-3, 6), \ldots, (-n, 2n), \ldots,$ for $n \in \mathbb{N}$

19. If $\mathbf{A}$ is a subset of $\mathbf{M}$ with an even number of elements, then $\mathbf{M} - \mathbf{A}$ (see paragraph 1.11) is a subset of $\mathbf{M}$ with an odd number of elements. Pair each set with an even number of elements with its complement.

21. Assume $\sqrt[4]{2}$ is rational; i.e., assume $\sqrt[4]{2} = r/s$. Then $r^4 = 2s^4$. Let h and k be the number of 2s in r and s, respectively. Then the numbers of 2s in r^4 and s^4, respectively, are $4h$ and $4k$, and the number of 2s in $2s^4$ is $4k + 1$ which is not divisible by 4, whereas $4h$ is divisible by 4. This contradicts FTOA, so $\sqrt[4]{2}$ is not rational.

23. Same proof as for Problem 21, using p in place of 2.

25. Same proof as for Problem 21, using n instead of 4.

27. Same proof as for Problem 21, using p in place of 2 and n instead of 4.

29. If $\log_{10} 3 = x$, then $10^x = 3$. If x is rational, then $x = m/n$, and so $10^{m/n} = 3$. Raising both sides to the nth power, $10^m = 3^n$, or $2^m \cdot 5^m = 3^n$. This equation is a contradiction (in several ways) of FTOA. Therefore, x is not rational.

31. Let $r = h/k$, with h and k integers. We assume rx is rational; that is, $rx = m/n$, or $(h/k) \cdot x = m/n$, or $x = (k \cdot m)/(h \cdot n)$, a rational number and a contradiction of the hypothesis that x is irrational.

33. Yes. Let $x = y = \sqrt{2}$, irrational. Then $xy = 2$, rational.

35. Assume $x = \log_2 10$ is rational; that is, $x = r/s$. Then $2^{r/s} = 10$, or $2^r = 10^s = 2^s 5^s$. This equation contradicts FTOA, so x is not rational.

37. $2, 8, 128, \frac{1}{4}, \frac{1}{16}, 2^r$ for r rational (for example, $\log_2 \sqrt{2}$ is rational; here $r = \frac{1}{2}$).

39. Represent a one-to-one correspondence between **A** and **B** by $\mathbf{E} = \{(a, b): a \in \mathbf{A}, b \in \mathbf{B}\}$. So for each $a \in \mathbf{A}$, there is a unique $b \in \mathbf{B}$ that corresponds to it. Likewise, let $\mathbf{F} = \{(b, c): a \in \mathbf{B}, b \in \mathbf{C}\}$ represent a one-to-one correspondence between **B** and **C**.

Consider $\mathbf{G} = \{(a, c): (a, b) \in \mathbf{E}, (b, c) \in \mathbf{F}\}$. This is a one-to-one correspondence between **A** and **C** since for each a, there is a unique b, and for this b, there is a unique c that is paired with b. Also, note that each c is paired with a unique b and this b is paired with a unique a.

41. Now $(2n+1, n)$, where $n \in \mathbb{Z}$ is a one-to-one correspondence between the odd integers $\mathbb{O}$ and all integers $\mathbb{Z}$. Also, (n, n^3), where $n \in \mathbb{Z}$ is a one-to-one correspondence between all integers and all cubes. By Problem 39, there must be a one-to-one correspondence between all odd integers and all cubes.

Section 8.   Answers to Tutorials

8.1. **a.** $y = 987,654,321$ **b.** $y - x = 864197532 = 9 \cdot 96,021,948$ **c.** Since the sum of the digits of y and x are the same, their difference is divisible by 9.

8.3A. **a.** $x = 2^0 + 2^3 + 2^5 + 2^6$ **b.** $x = 105$ **c.** No, because the only power of 2 that is odd is 2^0, and it is represented in the number.

8.3B. **a.** $88 = 2 \cdot 44 + 0; 44 = 2 \cdot 22 + 0; 22 = 2 \cdot 11 + 0; 11 = 2 \cdot 5 + 1; 5 = 2 \cdot 2 + 1; 2 = 2 \cdot 1 + 0; 1 = 2 \cdot 0 + 1.$ $88 = 1011000$ **b.** The binary representation will end in at least three zeroes.

8.4. If the hex representation ends in a 0, then the binary representation will end in at least four zeroes.

Section 8.   Answers to Selected Problems

1. For example, in (a) change 392 to 239; $392 - 239 = 153 = 9 \cdot 17$.

3. 2394

5. (a) sum of digits $= 8 = 0 \cdot 9 + 8$ (b) sum of digits $= 17 = 1 \cdot 9 + 8$ (c) sum of digits $= 26 = 2 \cdot 9 + 8$

7. $s(13638) = 21, s(948) = 21$

9. Yes. Referring to Prob. 6, let $n = s(n) + 9k$ and $m = s(m) + 9s$. So $n - m = s(n) - s(m) + 9(k - s)$ which is divisible by 9.

11. (a) 49 (b) 63 (c) 17 (d) 42

13. (a) 79 (b) 221

15. (a) $97 = (1100001)_2$ (b) $26 = (11010)_2$ (c) $321 = (101000001)_2$

17. $137 = (10001001)_2 = (89)_{16} = (211)_8$

19. In Prob. 17, grouping from the right $(10001001)_2$ into groups of four gives $(1000)_2 = 8$ and $(1001)_2 = 9$, and thus $(10001001)_2 = (89)_{16}$. Also, since $8 = 2^3$, we group the binary digits into groups of 3: $(010)_2 = 2$ (the first 0 is inserted to ensure that there are three digits), $(001)_2 = 1$, $(001)_2 = 1$, and so $(10001001)_2 = (211)_8$.

21. (a)

$$110001 = 49$$
$$10001 = 17$$
$$\underline{111111 = 63}$$
$$10000001 = 129$$

(b)

$$11 = 3$$
$$111 = 7$$
$$100 = 4$$
$$10 = 2$$
$$1 = 1$$
$$\underline{101 = 5}$$
$$10110 = 22$$

23. $(110001111)_2$

25. $(101011111001)_2$

27. $182 = (20202)_3$

29. $2^{20} = 1{,}048{,}576$

31. A positive integer n written in base 3 would be $n = (a_k a_{k-1} \ldots a_1 a_0)_3 = a_k 3^k + a_{k-1} 3^{k-1} + \cdots + a_1 \cdot 3 + a_0$, where $a_0, a_1, \ldots, a_k$ equal 0, 1, or 2. The a_i which are 0 are irrelevant. Since 3 is odd, 3^j is odd for all nonnegative j. Hence the only terms in the sum that are even are the ones

with $a_j = 2$. By Theorem 5.6A, n is odd if and only if there is an odd number of odd terms in the sum. Therefore, n is odd if and only if there is an odd number of times for which $a_j = 1$.

33. (a) $s_9(99) = 0$ (b) $s_9(10986) = 6$ (c) $s_9(1492) = 7$ (d) $s_9(198919896213) = 3$

35. (a) $s_9(253467) = 0$ (b) $s_9(909187) = 7$ (c) $s_9(357883) = 7$ (d) $s_9(42357871) = 1$

37. Since $s_9(1234567890) = 0$, any number using all ten distinct digits exactly once is divisible by 9.

39. $d = 3$

41. (a) $\frac{1}{4} = (0.01)_2$ (b) $\frac{1}{8} = (0.001)_2$ (c) $\frac{3}{4} = (0.11)_2$ (d) $13\frac{5}{8} = (1101.101)_2$

43. (a) $(3.7)_{16}$ (b) $(0.4E)_{16}$ (c) $(B6.6B)_{16}$

45. The odd bases.

Section 9. Answers to Tutorials

9.2. **a.** $\forall x \in \mathbb{E}, x^3 \in \mathbb{E}$. **b. Proof:** Let x be odd. Then there is an integer k such that $x = 2k + 1$. So $x^3 = (2k + 1)^3 = 2(4k^3 + 6k^2 + 3k) + 1$, which is odd. ∎

9.3. **a.** The negation is: There is an integer such that $1 - x^2 > 0$. The original statement is false. **b.** Some dog does not have its day.

9.4. If "$\exists x \in \mathbf{S}, \mathcal{P}(x)$" is false, then it is not the case that there is an x in $\mathbf{S}$ such that $\mathcal{P}(x)$ is true. Hence for all x in $\mathbf{S}$, $\mathcal{P}(x)$ is false. But this is the quantified statement "$\forall x \in \mathbf{S}, (\sim\mathcal{P}(x))$."

Section 9. Answers to Selected Problems

1. (a) $\{-1, 3\}$ (b) $\varnothing$ (c) $\{1\}$

3. If the set described is not $\mathbb{N}$, then there is a natural number larger than all primes. This implies that the number of primes is finite, contradicting Theorem 4.4.

5. (a) $\forall x \in \mathbb{P}$, x is odd. (b) $\forall x \in \mathbb{P}, x \leq 300$. (c) Neither is true.

7. (a) $\exists x \in \mathbb{R}, x \notin \mathbb{Q}$. (b) $\forall x \in \mathbb{R}, x \notin \mathbb{Q}$.

9. (a) No Senator is a lawyer. Or, every Senator is not a lawyer. (b) Some scientists do not enjoy mathematics.

11. (a) $\forall n \in \mathbb{E}$, $n + (n + 1) + (n + 2)$ is not divisible by 6. (b) $4 + 5 + 6 = 15$, $6 + 7 + 8 = 21$, $10 + 11 + 12 = 33$.

(c) If $x = 2k + (2k + 1) + (2k + 2)$, then $x = 6k + 3 = 3(2k + 1)$. Since $2k + 1$ is odd, x cannot be divisible by 6.

13. (a) $\forall n \in \mathbb{Z}, 6 \mid n(n+1)(n+2)$. (b) $1 \cdot 2 \cdot 3 = 6, 7 \cdot 8 \cdot 9 = 504, 51 \cdot 52 \cdot 53 = 6 \cdot 23426$. (c) To prove that $x = n(n+1)(n+2)$ is divisible by 6, we prove that it has both 2 and 3 as divisors. If n is odd, then $n + 1$ is even, so x is divisible by 2; and if n is even, then x is divisible by 2. Also, exactly one of three consecutive integers must be divisible by 3, so x is divisible by 3.

15. (a) $\forall p \in \mathbb{P}, \forall a \in \mathbb{N}, p \mid (a^p - a)$. (b) For some prime p and some natural number a, p does not divide the difference of a^p and a. $\exists p \in \mathbb{P}, \exists a \in \mathbb{N}, p \nmid (a^p - a)$.

17. (a) **S** is the universe of people. (b) $p(x)$: x will be admitted. (c) $q(x)$: x is over 18.

19. (a) Every natural number is odd. (b) Some natural numbers are odd.

21. (a) $\forall n \in \mathbb{N}', \exists p \in \mathbb{P}, p \mid n$. (b) $\exists n \in \mathbb{N}'$, $\forall p \in \mathbb{P}, p \nmid n$. Some natural number larger than 1 is not divisible by any prime.

23. For all natural numbers n, there is a real number x so that x^n is 1. The negation is "$\exists n \in \mathbb{N}, \forall x \in \mathbb{R}, x^n - 1 \neq 0$." The original statement is true.

25. For each real number e greater than 0, there is an s in **S** and a z not in **S** such that the absolute values of the differences $x - s$ and $x - z$ are both less than e.

Section 10.   Answers to Tutorials

10.1. a. $10 \in A$ **b.** The smallest element in **A** is 6.

10.3. a. $\sum_{i=1}^{9}(2i + 3) = 5 + 7 + 9 + 11 + 13 + 15 + 17 + 19 + 21; \sum_{i=1}^{3}(2i + 3) = 5 + 7 + 9;$ $\sum_{i=4}^{9}(2i + 3) = 11 + 13 + 15 + 17 + 19 + 21$ **b.** $a_1 + a_2 + a_3 + a_4 + a_5 + a_6 + a_7 + a_8 + a_9 = (a_1 + a_2 + a_3) + (a_4 + a_5 + a_6 + a_7 + a_8 + a_9)$

10.4. a. $t_5 = 15; t_6 = 21; t_7 = 28; t_8 = 36$
b.

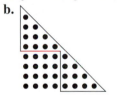

Section 10.   Answers to Selected Problems

1. (a) $\sum_{i=1}^{100} 2i$ (b) $\sum_{i=1}^{n} 2i$

3. (a) 4 (b) 64 (c) 63

5. (a) $\sum_{k=1}^{5} \frac{1}{2k}$ (b) $\sum_{k=1}^{4} \frac{1}{2^k}$

7. (a) $\sum_{i=1}^{6} i^2 = (1^2 + 2^2 + 3^2 + 4^2 + 5^2) + 6^2 = \left(\sum_{i=1}^{5} i^2\right) + 36$ (b) $\sum_{i=1}^{k+1} i^2 = (1^2 + 2^2 + 3^2 + \cdots + k^2) + (k + 1)^2 = \left(\sum_{i=1}^{k} i^2\right) + (k + 1)^2$

9. (a) $\sum_{i=1}^{5}(i + 2) = 25$ (b) $\sum_{i=1}^{5} i = 15$ (c) $\sum_{i=1}^{5} 2 = 10$

11. (a) $\sum_{i=1}^{20} \frac{1}{(4i^2 - 1)} = \sum_{i=1}^{19} \frac{1}{(4i^2 - 1)} +$

$\sum_{i=20}^{20} \frac{1}{4i^2 - 1} = \left(\sum_{i=1}^{19} \frac{1}{(4i^2 - 1)}\right) + \frac{1}{1599}$

(b) $\sum_{i=1}^{20} \frac{1}{(4i^2 - 1)} = \sum_{i=1}^{19} \frac{1}{(4i^2 - 1)} + \frac{1}{1599} =$

$\sum_{i=1}^{19} \frac{1}{(2i - 1)(2i + 1)} + \frac{1}{1599} = \frac{19}{39} + \frac{1}{1599},$

where the first "=" is by part (a), the second is by the hint, and the third is by (5) in paragraph 10.3.

13. (a) $\sum_{i=1}^{10}(-1)^i \cdot i = 5$ (b) $\sum_{i=1}^{1000}(-1)^i \cdot i = 500$ (note that each successive pair adds 1 to the sum)

15. 106

17. (a) 3825 (b) 110 (c) 140

19. (a) $\sum_{k=1}^{4}\dfrac{(-1)^{k+1}}{2^k}$ (b) $\sum_{i=0}^{5}(-1)^i \cdot \dfrac{1}{2^i}$

(c) $\sum_{i=0}^{3}(-1)^i \cdot \dfrac{1}{2^{2i}}$

21. Let $n = \sum_{i=0}^{k} d_i \cdot 10^i$, where $d_0, d_1, \ldots, d_k$ are the digits and $d_k \neq 0$. Since for each j, $10^j = 3h_j + 1$ (Prob. 20), we can write $n = \sum_{i=0}^{k} d_i \cdot (3h_i + 1) = 3 \cdot \sum_{i=0}^{k} d_i \cdot h_i + \sum_{i=0}^{k} d_i = 3m + s(n)$, where $s(n)$ is the sum of the digits of n.

23. No. Consider $10^2 = 100 = 7 \cdot 14 + 2$.

25. Now $1^2 = (1 \cdot 2 \cdot 3)/6$, or $1 = 1$; $1^2 + 2^2 = (2 \cdot 3 \cdot 5)/6$, or $5 = 5$; $1^2 + 2^2 + 3^2 = (3 \cdot 4 \cdot 7)/6$, or $14 = 14$, and so $\mathcal{P}(1)$, $\mathcal{P}(2)$, and $\mathcal{P}(3)$ are true. If $\mathcal{P}(n)$ is not true for all n, then by WOA, there is a smallest integer j for which $\mathcal{P}(j)$ is not true. Now

$$\sum_{i=1}^{j} i^2 = \sum_{i=1}^{j-1} i^2 + j^2$$

$$= \frac{(j-1)(j)(2(j-1)+1)}{6} + j^2$$

(since $\mathcal{P}(j-1)$ is true)

$$= \frac{j}{6} \cdot ((j-1)(2j-1) + 6j)$$

$$= \frac{j}{6} \cdot (2j^2 - 3j + 1 + 6j)$$

$$= \frac{j}{6} \cdot (2j^2 + 3j + 1)$$

$$= \frac{j(j+1)(2j+1)}{6}.$$

So $\mathcal{P}(j)$ is true, a contradiction. Hence, $\mathcal{P}(n)$ is true for all $n \in \mathbb{N}$.

27. Now $1/(1 \cdot 2) = \frac{1}{2}$, or $\frac{1}{2} = \frac{1}{2}$ and so $\mathcal{P}(1)$ is true. ($n = 2$, $\frac{2}{3} = \frac{2}{3}$; $n = 3$, $\frac{3}{4} = \frac{3}{4}$.) If $\mathcal{P}(n)$ is not true for all n, then by WOA, there is a smallest integer j for which $\mathcal{P}(j)$ is not true. Now

$$\sum_{i=1}^{j} \frac{1}{i \cdot (i+1)} = \sum_{i=1}^{j-1} \frac{1}{i \cdot (i+1)} + \frac{1}{j \cdot (j+1)}$$

$$= \frac{(j-1)}{(j-1)+1} + \frac{1}{j \cdot (j+1)}$$

($\mathcal{P}(j-1)$ is true)

$$= \frac{j-1}{j} + \frac{1}{j \cdot (j+1)}$$

$$= \frac{j^2 - 1 + 1}{j \cdot (j+1)}$$

$$= \frac{j^2}{j \cdot (j+1)} = \frac{j}{j+1}.$$

So $\mathcal{P}(j)$ is true, a contradiction. Hence, $\mathcal{P}(n)$ is true for all $n \in \mathbb{N}$.

29. Now $1 \cdot 2 = (1 \cdot 2 \cdot 3)/3$, or $2 = 2$, and so $\mathcal{P}(1)$ is true ($n = 2$, $8 = 8$; $n = 3$, $20 = 20$). If $\mathcal{P}(n)$ is not true for all n, then by WOA, there is a smallest integer j for which $\mathcal{P}(j)$ is not true. Now

$$\sum_{i=1}^{j} i \cdot (i+1) = \sum_{i=1}^{j-1} i \cdot (i+1) + j \cdot (j+1)$$

$$= \frac{(j-1) \cdot (j) \cdot (j+1)}{3} + j \cdot (j+1)$$

(since $\mathcal{P}(j-1)$ is true)

$$= \frac{j \cdot (j+1)}{3} \cdot (j-1+3)$$

$$= \frac{j \cdot (j+1) \cdot (j+2)}{3}.$$

So $\mathcal{P}(j)$ is true, a contradiction. Hence, $\mathcal{P}(n)$ is true for all $n \in \mathbb{N}$.

31. Now $(2-1)^2 = \dfrac{1 \cdot (4-1)}{3}$, or $1^2 = \dfrac{1 \cdot 3}{3}$,

and so $\mathcal{P}(1)$ is true. ($n = 2, 10 = 10; n = 3, 35 = 35$.) If $\mathcal{P}(n)$ is not true for all n, then by WOA, there is a smallest integer j for which $\mathcal{P}(j)$ is not true. Now

$$\sum_{i=1}^{j}(2i-1)^2$$

$$= \sum_{i=1}^{j-1}(2i-1)^2 + (2j-1)^2$$

$$= \frac{(j-1) \cdot (4 \cdot (j-1)^2 - 1)}{3} + (2j-1)^2$$

(since $\mathcal{P}(j-1)$ is true)

$$= \frac{(j-1) \cdot (4 \cdot (j-1)^2 - 1) + 3 \cdot (2j-1)^2}{3}$$

$$= \frac{(j-1) \cdot (2 \cdot (j-1) - 1)(2 \cdot (j-1) + 1) + 3 \cdot (2j-1)^2}{3}$$

$$= \frac{(j-1) \cdot (2j-3)(2j-1) + 3 \cdot (2j-1)^2}{3}$$

$$= \frac{(2j-1) \cdot ((j-1) \cdot (2j-3) + 3 \cdot (2j-1))}{3}$$

$$= \frac{(2j-1) \cdot (2j^2 - 5j + 3 + 6j - 3)}{3}$$

$$= \frac{(2j-1) \cdot (2j^2 + j)}{3}$$

$$= \frac{j \cdot (2j-1) \cdot (2j+1)}{3}$$

$$= \frac{j \cdot (4j^2 - 1)}{3}.$$

So $\mathcal{P}(j)$ is true, a contradiction. Hence, $\mathcal{P}(n)$ is true for all $n \in \mathbb{N}$.

Section 11.   Answers to Tutorials

11.1. **a.** 19 **b.** 1, 3, 6, 10, 15, 21, 28, 36, 45, 55
c. $100 = 45 + 55$. A square array of 100 objects can be partitioned along a diagonal into two pieces, one containing 45 objects and the other containing 55 objects.

11.2. **a.**

n	n^3	2^n	$n^3 < 2^n$
0	0	1	T
1	1	2	T
2	8	4	F
3	27	8	F
4	64	16	F
5	125	32	F
6	216	64	F
7	343	128	F
8	512	256	F
9	729	512	F
10	1000	1024	T

b. $\forall n \in \mathbb{W}_{10}, n^3 < 2^n$.

Section 11. Answers to Selected Problems

1. Now $4^1 - 1 = 3$ which is divisible by 3; $\mathcal{P}(1)$ is true. ($4^2 - 1 = 3 \cdot 5$, $4^3 - 1 = 3 \cdot 21$.) If $\mathcal{P}(n)$ is not true for some n, then by WOA, there is a smallest integer j for which $\mathcal{P}(j)$ is not true. Thus, $4^j - 1 = 4 \cdot 4^{j-1} - 1 = 4 \cdot (4^{j-1} - 1 + 1) - 1 = 4 \cdot (4^{j-1} - 1) + 4 - 1$. Since $\mathcal{P}(j - 1)$ is true, $4^{j-1} - 1 = 3m$ for some integer m. Hence, $4^j - 1 = 4(3m) + 3$, and so $\mathcal{P}(j)$ is true, a contradiction. Hence, $\mathcal{P}(n)$ is true for all $n \in \mathbb{N}$.

3. Now $3^{2 \cdot 1} - 1 = 8$ which is divisible by 8; $\mathcal{P}(1)$ is true. ($3^4 - 1 = 8 \cdot 10$, $3^6 - 1 = 8 \cdot 91$.) If $\mathcal{P}(n)$ is not true for some n, then by WOA, there is a smallest integer j for which $\mathcal{P}(j)$ is not true. Thus, $3^{2j} - 1 = 3^{2(j-1)+2} - 1 = 9 \cdot 3^{2(j-1)} - 1$ (since $3^{a+b} = 3^a \cdot 3^b$) $= 9(3^{2(j-1)} - 1 + 1) - 1 = 9(3^{2(j-1)} - 1) + 9 - 1$. Since $\mathcal{P}(j - 1)$ is true, $3^{2(j-1)} - 1 = 8m$ for some integer m. Hence, $3^{2j} - 1 = 9(8m) + 8 = 8(9m + 1)$, and so $\mathcal{P}(j)$ is true, a contradiction. Hence, $\mathcal{P}(n)$ is true for all $n \in \mathbb{N}$.

5. The predicate $\mathcal{P}(n)$ is that x^n is odd. Now $x^1 = x$ is given to be odd, and so $\mathcal{P}(1)$ is true. If $\mathcal{P}(n)$ is not true for some n, then by WOA, there is a smallest integer j for which $\mathcal{P}(j)$ is not true. But, $x^j = x^{j-1} \cdot x$ and x^{j-1} is odd since $\mathcal{P}(j - 1)$ is true. Thus x^j is the product of two odd numbers, which is odd. Hence, $\mathcal{P}(j)$ is true, a contradiction. Therefore, $\mathcal{P}(n)$ is true for all $n \in \mathbb{N}$.

7.

n	$5n + 3$	n^2	$5n + 3 < n^2$
1	8	1	F
2	13	4	F
3	18	9	F
4	23	16	F
5	28	25	F

n	$5n + 3$	n^2	$5n + 3 < n^2$
6	33	36	T
7	38	49	T
8	43	64	T
9	48	81	T
10	53	100	T

9. (*a*) See answer for Prob. 7. (*b*) By part (*a*), $6 \notin \mathbf{S}$, so $j > 6$ and $j - 1 > 5$; that is, $j - 1 \in \mathbb{W}_6$. Now $j \in \mathbf{S}$ means that $\mathcal{P}(j)$ is false, and $j - 1 \notin \mathbf{S}$ means that $\mathcal{P}(j - 1)$ is true.

11. Let $\mathcal{P}(n)$ be the statement $n^2 - n - 100 > 0$. Let $\mathbf{S} = \{n \in \mathbb{W}_{11} : \mathcal{P}(n) \text{ is false}\}$. If $\mathbf{S}$ is not empty, then by WOA, it has a least element j. Since $\mathcal{P}(11)$ is true ($10 > 0$), $j > 11$, and so $j - 1 \in \mathbb{W}_{11}$. Thus, $0 < (j-1)^2 - (j-1) - 100 = j^2 - 2j + 1 - j + 1 - 100 = j^2 - j - 100 - (2j - 2)$. Thus $2j - 2 < j^2 - j - 100$. Since $j \in \mathbb{W}_{11}$, $0 < 2j - 2$, and so $\mathcal{P}(j)$ is true, a contradiction. Hence $\mathbf{S}$ is empty.

13. The predicate $\mathcal{P}(n)$ is that $2^n > (n + 1)^2$. Now $2^6 = 64 > (6 + 1)^2 = 7^2 = 49$, and so $\mathcal{P}(6)$ is true. If $\mathcal{P}(n)$ is not true for some $n \in \mathbb{W}_6$, then by WOA, there is a smallest integer j for which $\mathcal{P}(j)$ is not true. But, $2^j = 2 \cdot 2^{j-1} > 2j^2$ since $\mathcal{P}(j - 1)$ is true. So $2^j > j^2 + j^2 > j^2 + 2j + 1$ by Prob. 12. Hence, $2^j > (j + 1)^2$. Thus, $\mathcal{P}(j)$ is true, a contradiction. Therefore, $\mathcal{P}(n)$ is true for all $n \in \mathbb{N}$.

15. (*a*) WOA (*b*) Now $j \in \mathbf{S}$ means $j \geq 8$ and $j \notin \mathbf{T}$; that is, $j \neq 2a + 5b$, for any a and b in $\mathbb{W}_0$. Since j is the smallest element in $\mathbf{S}$, $j - 1 \notin \mathbf{S}$; that is, $j - 1 = 2a' + 5b'$, for some a' and b' in $\mathbb{W}_0$.

17. (*a*) If $b' > 0$ (so $b' - 1 \geq 0$), let $a = a' + 3$, $b = b' - 1$. Then $2a + 5b = 2(a' + 3) + 5(b' - 1) = 2a' + 5b' + 6 - 5 = (j - 1) + 1 = j$.

(b) Since $j = 2a + 5b$, $j \in \mathbf{T}$, so $j \notin \mathbf{S}$.
(c) By definition, j is the smallest number in
$\mathbf{S}$. This contradicts the result in part (b), so
$\mathbf{S} = \varnothing$. (d) This follows from part (c) and
the answers to Prob. 14.

19. Now

$$\frac{2^2}{1 \cdot 3} = \frac{2 \cdot 2}{2 + 1},$$

or $\frac{4}{3} = \frac{4}{3}$, and so $\mathcal{P}(2)$ is true. If $\mathcal{P}(n)$ is not
true for some n, then by WOA, there is a
smallest integer j for which $\mathcal{P}(j)$ is not true.
Thus,

$$\frac{2^2}{1 \cdot 3} \cdot \frac{3^2}{2 \cdot 4} \cdots \frac{j^2}{(j-1) \cdot (j+1)}$$

$$= \left[\frac{2^2}{1 \cdot 3} \cdot \frac{3^2}{2 \cdot 4} \cdots \frac{(j-1)^2}{((j-1)-1) \cdot ((j-1)+1)} \right]$$

$$\cdot \frac{j^2}{(j-1) \cdot (j+1)}.$$

Since $\mathcal{P}(j-1)$ is true, this product is

$$\frac{2(j-1)}{(j-1)+1} \cdot \frac{j^2}{(j-1)(j+1)} = \frac{2j^2}{j(j+1)}$$

$$= \frac{2j}{j+1}.$$

Hence, $\mathcal{P}(j)$ is true, a contradiction. Therefore, $\mathcal{P}(n)$ is true for all $n \in \mathbb{N}$.

21. (a) By definition of r, $r < j$, and since j is
the smallest number in $\mathbf{S}$, $r \notin \mathbf{S}$. (b) Thus,
$r = 0$ and $a = q \cdot j$. Use the division algo-
rithm to compute $b = q_1 j + r, 0 \le r < j$.
Follow the argument in Prob. 20 and part (a)
of this problem. (c) Since j divides a and j
divides b, j is a common divisor of a and b.
But as d is the greatest common divisor of a
and b, $j \le d$.

23. $1729 = 1000 + 729 = 10^3 + 9^3$ and $1729 = 1728 + 1 = 12^3 + 1^3$

25. Sum of odds between 500 and 1000 is

$$\sum_{i=251}^{500} (2i-1) = \sum_{i=1}^{500}(2i-1) - \sum_{i=1}^{250}(2i-1)$$

$$= 500^2 - 250^2$$
$$= 250{,}000 - 62{,}500$$
$$= 187{,}500.$$

27. $\sum_{i=1}^{100} (-1)^i (2i-1) = -1 + 3 - 5 + 7 - \cdots$
$$- 197 + 199$$
$$= 2 + 2 + \cdots + 2$$
$$= 50 \cdot 2 = 100.$$

29. Theorem: For $n \in \mathbb{N}$, $\sqrt{n}$ can be constructed using only a straightedge and com-
pass (given a unit length). **Proof.** Since the
unit length is given, $\sqrt{1}$ can be constructed.
Suppose that j is the smallest positive integer so that $\sqrt{j}$ cannot be constructed. Now
$\sqrt{j-1}$ can be constructed, and so a rectangle with sides of 1 and $\sqrt{j-1}$ can be constructed. But the diagonal of this rectangle
is $\sqrt{j}$, a contradiction. Therefore, $\sqrt{n}$ can be
constructed for all $n \in \mathbb{N}$. ∎

Section 12. Answers to Tutorials

12.2. a. $a_n = 17$ **b.** $a_n = 136$ **c.** $a_n = \dfrac{n(n+1)}{2}$

12.3. a. $n = 1, \frac{2}{3}$; $n = 2, \frac{2}{3} + \frac{2}{15} = \frac{12}{15} = \frac{4}{5}$;
$n = 3, \frac{2}{3} + \frac{2}{15} + \frac{2}{35} = \frac{90}{105} = \frac{6}{7}$; $n = 4$,
$\frac{2}{3} + \frac{2}{15} + \frac{2}{35} + \frac{2}{63} = \frac{280}{315} = \frac{8}{9}$
b. $\displaystyle\sum_{i=1}^{n} \frac{2}{4i^2-1} = \frac{2n}{2n+1}$

12.4. a. $5^2 = 25 < 32 = 2^5$ **b.** If k is in $\mathbf{M}$, then
$2^{k+1} = 2^k 2 = 2^k + 2^k > k^2 + k^2 > k^2 + 2k + 1 = (k+1)^2$. Hence, $k + 1$ is in $\mathbf{M}$.

12.5. a. $7887/11 = 717$; $138831/11 = 12621$
b. The quotients are palindromes.
c. $210012/11 = 19092$. This quotient is not
a palindrome.

Section 12.   Answers to Selected Problems

1. Since $(2 \cdot 1 - 1) \cdot (2 \cdot 1) = (1 \cdot 2 \cdot 3)/3$, or
$2 = 2$, $\mathcal{P}(1)$ is true. Now

$$\sum_{i=1}^{k+1}(2i - 1) \cdot (2i)$$

$$= \left(\sum_{i=1}^{k}(2i - 1) \cdot (2i) \right)$$

$$+ (2(k + 1) - 1) \cdot (2(k + 1))$$

$$= \frac{k(k + 1)(4k - 1)}{3} + 2(k + 1) \cdot (2k + 1),$$

since $\mathcal{P}(k)$ is assumed true. So

$$\sum_{i=1}^{k+1}(2i - 1) \cdot (2i)$$

$$= (k + 1)\left[\frac{4k^2 - k}{3} + \frac{2 \cdot 3(2k + 1)}{3} \right]$$

$$= (k + 1)\frac{4k^2 - k + 12k + 6}{3}$$

$$= \frac{(k + 1)(4k^2 + 11k + 6)}{3}$$

$$= \frac{(k + 1)(4k + 3)(k + 2)}{3}$$

$$= \frac{((k + 1)(k + 1) + 1)(4(k + 1) - 1)}{3}.$$

Hence $\mathcal{P}(k + 1)$ is true.

3. Since $(2 \cdot 1)^3 = 2 \cdot 1^2(2)^2$, or $8 = 2 \cdot 4 = 8$,
$\mathcal{P}(1)$ is true. Now

$$\sum_{i=1}^{k+1}(2i)^3 = \left(\sum_{i=1}^{k}(2i)^3 \right) + (2(k + 1))^3$$

$$= 2k^2(k + 1)^2 + 2^3(k + 1)^3,$$

since $\mathcal{P}(k)$ is assumed true. So

$$\sum_{i=1}^{k+1}(2i)^3 = 2(k + 1)^2(k^2 + 4k + 4)$$

$$= 2(k + 1)^2(k + 2)^2$$

$$= 2(k + 1)^2((k + 1) + 1)^2.$$

Hence $\mathcal{P}(k + 1)$ is true.

5. Since

$$\frac{1}{(2 + 1)(2 + 3)} = \frac{1}{3(2 + 3)},$$

or

$$\frac{1}{3 \cdot 5} = \frac{1}{3 \cdot 5},$$

$\mathcal{P}(1)$ is true. Now

$$\sum_{i=1}^{k+1}\frac{1}{(2i + 1)(2i + 3)}$$

$$= \sum_{i=1}^{k}\frac{1}{(2i + 1)(2i + 3)}$$

$$+ \frac{1}{(2(k + 1) + 1)(2(k + 1) + 3)}$$

$$= \frac{k}{3(2k + 3)} + \frac{1}{(2k + 3)(2k + 5)},$$

since $\mathcal{P}(k)$ is assumed true. So

$$\sum_{i=1}^{k+1}\frac{1}{(2i + 1)(2i + 3)}$$

$$= \frac{1}{2k + 3}\left(\frac{k}{3} + \frac{1}{2k + 5} \right)$$

$$= \frac{1}{2k + 3}\left(\frac{2k^2 + 5k + 3}{3(2k + 5)} \right)$$

$$= \frac{(k + 1)}{3(2k + 5)}$$

$$= \frac{k + 1}{3(2(k + 1) + 3)}.$$

Hence $\mathcal{P}(k + 1)$ is true.

7. Since $1^5 - 1 = 0$ is divisible by 5, $\mathcal{P}(1)$ is true. Now $(k + 1)^5 - (k + 1) = (k^5 + 5k^4 + 10k^3 + 10k^2 + 5k + 1) - (k + 1) = (k^5 - k) + 5(k^4 + 2k^3 + 2k^2 + k) = 5m + 5(k^4 + 2k^3 + 2k^2 + k)$, since $\mathcal{P}(k)$ is assumed true. So $(k + 1)^5 - (k + 1) = 5(m + k^4 + 2k^3 + 2k^2 + k)$. Hence $\mathcal{P}(k + 1)$ is true.

9. Let $\mathcal{P}(n)$ be

$$\sum_{i=1}^{n}(3i) = \frac{3n(n + 1)}{2}.$$

Since $3 \cdot 1 = (3 \cdot 1 \cdot 2)/2$, or $3 = 3$, $\mathcal{P}(1)$ is true. Now

$$\sum_{i=1}^{k+1}(3i) = \left(\sum_{i=1}^{k}(3i)\right) + 3(k + 1)$$

$$= \frac{3k(k + 1)}{2} + 3(k + 1)$$

since $\mathcal{P}(k)$ is assumed true. So

$$\sum_{i=1}^{k+1}(3i) = \frac{3(k + 1)}{2}(k + 2)$$

$$= \frac{3(k + 1)((k + 1) + 1)}{2}.$$

Hence $\mathcal{P}(k + 1)$ is true.

11. Let $\mathcal{P}(n)$ be the statement "the maximum number of points in which n lines in the plane may intersect is $n(n - 1)/2$." Since one line intersects no other line and $(1 \cdot 0)/2 = 0$, $\mathcal{P}(1)$ is true. Now if there are $k(k - 1)/2$ intersections of k lines, then adding one more line can produce a maximum of k additional intersections (one for the intersection of the new line with each of the k original lines). Thus the total number is

$$\frac{k(k - 1)}{2} + k = k\left(\frac{k - 1}{2} + 1\right)$$

$$= k\left(\frac{k - 1 + 2}{2}\right)$$

$$= \frac{k(k + 1)}{2}$$

$$= \frac{(k + 1)((k + 1) - 1)}{2}.$$

Hence $\mathcal{P}(k + 1)$ is true.

13. Let $\mathcal{P}(n)$ be the statement "the number of diagonals in an n-sided polygon is $n(n - 3)/2$." Since a quadrilateral has two diagonals and $(4 \cdot 1)/2 = 2$, $\mathcal{P}(4)$ is true. Now, consider a polygon on a circle with k vertices numbered consecutively $1, 2, \ldots, k$. If we add a new vertex, numbered $k + 1$, between vertices k and 1, then we can add new diagonals from vertex 1 to vertex k and from vertex $k + 1$ to vertices $2, 3, \ldots, k - 1$; namely, we can add $1 + (k - 2) = k - 1$ *new* diagonals. Now if we assume $\mathcal{P}(k)$ is true, then the total number of diagonals will be $k(k - 3)/2 + (k - 1) = (k + 1)(k - 2)/2 = (k + 1)((k + 1) - 3)/2$. Hence $\mathcal{P}(k + 1)$ is true.

15. Since $2^5 = 32 > 25 = 5^2$, $\mathcal{P}(1)$ is true. Now $2^{(k+4)+1} = 2 \cdot 2^{k+4} > 2(k + 4)^2$, since $\mathcal{P}(k)$ is assumed true. But $2(k + 4)^2 = 2k^2 + 16k + 32 = k^2 + 10k + 25 + (k^2 + 6k + 7) > k^2 + 10k + 25 = (k + 5)^2 = ((k + 4) + 1)^2$. Hence $\mathcal{P}(k + 1)$ is true.

17. Since $7 + 1 = 8 = 4 \cdot 2$, $\mathcal{P}(1)$ is true. Now $7^{2(k+1)-1} + 1 = 7^{2k+1} + 1 = 7^{(2k-1)+2} + 1 = 7^2 \cdot 7^{2k-1} + 1 = 49(7^{2k-1} + 1 - 1) + 1 = 49(7^{2k-1} + 1) - 49 + 1 = 49(4m) - 48$, since $\mathcal{P}(k)$ is assumed true. So $7^{2(k+1)-1} + 1 = 4(49m - 12)$. Hence $\mathcal{P}(k + 1)$ is true.

19. Since $(1 + \frac{2}{3})^1 = 1 + \frac{2}{3}$, $\mathcal{P}(1)$ is true. Now $(1 + \frac{2}{3})^{k+1} = (1 + \frac{2}{3})^k(1 + \frac{2}{3}) \geq (1 + (2k/3))(1 + \frac{2}{3})$, since $\mathcal{P}(k)$ is assumed true. So $(1 + \frac{2}{3})^{k+1} \geq 1 + (2k/3) + \frac{2}{3} + (4k/9) = 1 + (2(k + 1)/3) + (4k/9) > 1 + (2(k + 1)/3)$, since $(4k/9) > 0$. Hence $\mathcal{P}(k + 1)$ is true.

21. Since $(1 + x)^1 = 1 + x$, $\mathcal{P}(1)$ is true. Now $(1 + x)^{k+1} = (1 + x)^k(1 + x) \geq (1 + kx)(1 + x)$, since $\mathcal{P}(k)$ is assumed true. So $(1 + x)^{k+1} \geq 1 + kx + x + kx^2 =$

$(1 + (k + 1)x) + kx^2 > 1 + (k + 1)x$, since $kx^2 > 0$. Hence $\mathcal{P}(k + 1)$ is true.

23. Since $f(1) = 1 \cdot f(1) = f(1)$, $\mathcal{P}(1)$ is true. Now f is additive and so $f(k + 1) = f(k) + f(1)$. Also, since $\mathcal{P}(k)$ is assumed true, $f(k + 1) = kf(1) + f(1) = (k + 1)f(1)$. Hence $\mathcal{P}(k + 1)$ is true.

25. Proof by PMI. Let $\mathcal{P}(n)$ be the statement that "a set with n elements has $(n(n - 1)/2)$ two-element subsets." If $n = 1$, then $(1 \cdot 0)/2 = 0$ which is the number of 2-element subsets of a set with one element. Consider now a set $\mathbf{A}$ with $j + 1$ elements, say $\mathbf{A} = \{a_1, a_2, \ldots, a_j, a_{j+1}\} = \{a_1, a_2, \ldots, a_j\} \cup \{a_{j+1}\} = \mathbf{A}_1 \cup \{a_{j+1}\}$, where $\mathbf{A}_1 = \{a_1, a_2, \ldots, a_j\}$. Now, since $\mathcal{P}(j)$ is true, $\mathbf{A}_1$ has $j(j - 1)/2$ two-element subsets. For $\mathbf{A}$, there will also be the 2-element subsets $\{a_1, a_{j+1}\}, \{a_2, a_{j+1}\}, \ldots,$ $\{a_j, a_{j+1}\}$, a total of j. These two collections constitute all the 2-element subsets of $\mathbf{A}$ (those *without* a_{j+1} and those *with* a_{j+1}); the total number is $j(j - 1)/2 + j = j(j + 1)/2$. But this says $\mathcal{P}(j + 1)$ is true. ∎

27. (*a*) $s^*(33) = 3 - 3 = 0$ (*b*) $s^*(286) = 6 - 8 + 2 = 0$ (*c*) $s^*(1234567) = 7 - 6 + 5 - 4 + 3 - 2 + 1 = 4$ (*d*) $s^*(7654321) = 1 - 2 + 3 - 4 + 5 - 6 + 7 = 4$ (*e*) $s^*(1819171625) = 5 - 2 + 6 - 1 + 7 - 1 + 9 - 1 + 8 - 1 = 29$ (*f*) $s^*(5261719181) = 1 - 8 + 1 - 9 + 1 - 7 + 1 - 6 + 2 - 5 = -29$

29. From Prob. 28, if

$$n = \sum_{i=0}^{k} d_i 10^i,$$

then

$$n = \sum_{i \text{ even}} d_i(10^i - 1) + \sum_{i \text{ odd}} d_i(10^i + 1)$$
$$+ \sum_{i=0}^{k} (-1)^i d_i$$
$$= \sum_{i \text{ even}} d_i(10^i - 1) + \sum_{i \text{ odd}} d_i(10^i + 1)$$
$$+ s^*(n);$$

see Prob. 27. Thus

$$n - s^*(n) = \sum_{i \text{ even}} d_i(10^i - 1) + \sum_{i \text{ odd}} d_i(10^i + 1)$$
$$= \sum_{i \text{ even}} d_i(11h_i) + \sum_{i \text{ odd}} d_i(11m_i)$$
$$= 11 \left(\sum_{i \text{ even}} d_i h_i + \sum_{i \text{ odd}} d_i m_i \right).$$

31. If $s_{11}(n) = n - 11m$, then $n = 11m + s_{11}(n)$. By its definition in the algorithm of Prob. 30, $s_{11}(n)$ satisfies $0 \leq s_{11}(n) < 11$, so $s_{11}(n)$ is the remainder when n is divided by 11.

35. (*a*) $8 \neq s_{11}(178)$ (*b*) $3 \neq s_{11}(249)$ (*c*) $7 \neq s_{11}(220)$

37. $z = 7$

39. No, since $1 + 3 + 5 + 7 = 16 \neq 22 = 4^3 - (5 \cdot 4^2) + (11 \cdot 4) - 6$.

41. $2^{11} = 2048$ and $12^3 = 1728$

Section 13.   Answers to Tutorials

13.2. a. $f = \{(-4, 16), (-3, 9), (-2, 4), (-1, 1),$ $(0, 0), (1, 1), (2, 4), (3, 9), (4, 16)\}$
b. $\{0, 1, 4, 9, 16, \ldots\}$

13.4. a. $8! - 5! = 40320 - 120 = 40200$; $(8 - 5)! = 3! = 6$ **b.** $(4!) \cdot (3!) = 144$; $(4 \cdot 3)! = 479{,}001{,}600$ **c.** $2^{10} \cdot 10!$

13.5. a. 1, 1, 2, 3, 5, 8, 13, 21, 34, 55, 89, 144, 233, 377, 610, 987, 1597, 2584, 4181, 6765
b. $\sum_{i=1}^{12} F_i = 376$

Section 13. Answers to Selected Problems

1. (a) $\mathbf{D} = \{0, 1, 2\}$, $\mathbf{E} = \{0, 1, 2\}$ (b) $\mathbf{D} = \{0, 1\}$, $\mathbf{E} = \{0, 1, -1, 2, -2, 3, -3\}$
(c) $\mathbf{D} = \{a, b, c, d, e\}$, $\mathbf{E} = \{0, 1\}$ (d) $\mathbf{D} = \mathbb{N}$,
$\mathbf{E} = \{2, 3, 4, \ldots\} = \mathbb{N} - \{1\}$

3. **1**(a). $\{(0, 0), (1, 0), (1, 1), (2, 1), (2, 2)\}$
1(b). $\{(0, 0), (1, 0), (-1, 1), (2, 0), (-2, 0), (3, 0), (-3, 0)\}$ **1**(c). $\{(1, a), (0, b), (0, c), (0, d), (1, e)\}$
1(d). $\{(x, y): x \in \mathbb{N}, y \in \mathbb{N}, y < x\}$
2. $\{(a, a), (a, b), (a, c), (a, d), (a, e), (e, e)\}$

5. (a) $\phi(5) = 4$, $\phi(6) = 2$, $\phi(7) = 6$, $\phi(8) = 4$, $\phi(9) = 6$, $\phi(10) = 4$ (b) Each of the numbers $1, 2, \ldots, p - 1$ is relatively prime to the prime p, and p is not relatively prime to p. Therefore, $\phi(p) = p - 1$. (c) $\phi(12) = 4 = 2 \cdot 2 = \phi(3) \cdot \phi(4)$, but $4 \neq 1 \cdot 2 = \phi(2) \cdot \phi(6)$; $\phi(20) = 8 = 2 \cdot 4 = \phi(4) \cdot \phi(5)$, but $8 \neq 1 \cdot 4 = \phi(2) \cdot \phi(10)$.

7. $\{(2, 1), (3, 2), (4, 3), (5, 1), (7, 3), (7, 6)\}$. **R** is not a function since $(7, 3)$ and $(7, 6)$ have the same first coordinate and different second coordinates.

9. (a) $1, 2, 3, 4, 5, 6, 7, 8, 9, 10$ (b) $3, 8, 13, 18, 23, 28, 33, 38, 43, 48, 53$ (c) $-5, -7, -9, -11, -13, -15, -17, -19, -21, -23$

11. Let $\mathcal{P}(n)$ be the statement that $f(n) = a + d(n - 1)$. Since $f(1) = a + d \cdot 0 = a$, $\mathcal{P}(1)$ is true. By definition of arithmetic progressions, $f(k + 1) = d + f(k)$, but since $\mathcal{P}(k)$ is assumed true, $f(k) = d + (a + d(k - 1))$, and so $f(k + 1) = a + dk$. Hence $\mathcal{P}(k + 1)$ is true.

13. (a) The first sum is from 0 to $n - 1$ and the second is from 1 to $n - 1$. (b) By Theorem 10.4A,

$$\sum_{k=1}^{n-1} k = \frac{n(n - 1)}{2}$$

and so

$$\sum_{k=1}^{n} f(k) = na + \frac{dn(n - 1)}{2}.$$

Simple algebra yields the expression in the problem.

15. (a) $15, 75, 375, 5859375$ (b) $f(n) = 3 \cdot 5^{n-1}$ (c) 2343

17. (a) $f(n) = 1$, sum is 5. (b) $f(n) = (\frac{1}{2})^{n-1}$, sum is $\frac{31}{16} = 2 - \frac{1}{16}$. (c) $f(n) = 3(-2)^{n-1}$, sum is 33. (d) $f(n) = (-1)^{n-1}$, sum is 1.

19. (a) $(1 - (-1)^n)/2$ (b) $2 - (1/2^{n-1})$ (c) Note that the sum starts at 1, not 0. The sum is $(1 - (1/3^{n-1}))/2$. (d) $(5 + (-\frac{1}{5})^{n-1})/6$

21. $1, 3, 7, 15, 31, 63, 127, 255, 511, 1023$; $g(n) = 2^n - 1$

23. The first five terms are $2, 4, 2, 4, 2$. Now $f(1) = 3 + (-1)^1$. If $f(k) = 3 + (-1)^k$, then $f(k + 1) = 6 - (3 + (-1)^k) = 3 - (-1)^k = 3 + (-1)^{k+1}$.

25. (a) $22{,}100$ (b) $270{,}725$ (c) $2{,}598{,}960$

27. $n! - (n - 2)! = n(n - 1)(n - 2)! - (n - 2)! = (n - 2)!(n(n - 1) - 1) = (n - 2)!(n^2 - n - 1)$

29. (a) $2^8 \cdot 8!$ (b) $\dfrac{15!}{2^7 \cdot 7!}$

31. Let $\mathcal{P}(n)$ be the statement that

$$\sum_{i=1}^{n} i(i!) = (n + 1)! - 1.$$

Since $1(1!) = 1 = 2! - 1$, $\mathcal{P}(1)$ is true. Now

$$\sum_{i=1}^{k+1} i(i!) = \sum_{i=1}^{k} i(i!) + (k + 1)(k + 1)!$$

$$= (k + 1)! - 1 + (k + 1)(k + 1)!$$

since $\mathcal{P}(k)$ is assumed true. So

$$\sum_{i=1}^{k+1} i(i!) = (k + 1)!(1 + k + 1) - 1$$

$$= (k + 1)!(k + 2) - 1 = (k + 2)! - 1.$$

Hence $\mathcal{P}(k + 1)$ is true.

33. By repeated use of (1) in par. 13.5: $F_{2n} = F_{2n-1} + F_{2n-2} = F_{2n-1} + (F_{2n-3} + F_{2n-4}) = F_{2n-1} + F_{2n-3} + (F_{2n-5} + F_{2n-6}) = \cdots = F_{2n-1} + F_{2n-3} + \cdots + F_5 + (F_3 + F_2) = F_{2n-1} + F_{2n-3} + \cdots + F_5 + F_3 + F_1$, since $F_2 = F_1 = 1$. (Note that there is a nice inductive proof of this.)

35. Since $f(1) = a = (a+b) - b = f(3) - f(2)$ and $f(1) + f(2) = a + b = (a + 2b) - b = f(4) - f(2)$, $\mathcal{P}(1)$ and $\mathcal{P}(2)$ are both true. Now

$$\sum_{i=1}^{k+1} f(i) = \sum_{i=1}^{k} f(i) + f(k+1)$$
$$= f(k+2) - f(2) + f(k+1),$$

since $\mathcal{P}(k)$ is assumed true. So

$$\sum_{i=1}^{k+1} f(i) = f(k+3) - f(2)$$
$$= f((k+1)+2) - f(2).$$

Hence $\mathcal{P}(k+1)$ is true.

37. $F_{n+1}^2 - F_n^2 = (F_{n+1} + F_n)(F_{n+1} - F_n) = F_{n+2}((F_n + F_{n-1}) - F_n) = F_{n+2}F_{n-1}$

39. (a) For $m = 1$, $F_{m-1}F_n + F_mF_{n+1} = F_0F_n + F_1F_{n+1} = 0 + F_{n+1} = F_{n+1}$.
(b) For $m = 2$, $F_{m-1}F_n + F_mF_{n+1} = F_1F_n + F_2F_{n+1} = F_n + F_{n+1} = F_{n+2}$.

41. Set $m = n + 1$ in (2) in Prob. 39. So $F_{n+(n+1)} = F_nF_n + F_{n+1}F_{n+1}$, or $F_{2n+1} = F_n^2 + F_{n+1}^2$.

43. Since $F_1^2 = 1^2 = F_1F_2$, $\mathcal{P}(1)$ is true. Now

$$\sum_{i=1}^{k+1} F_i^2 = \sum_{i=1}^{k} F_i^2 + F_{k+1}^2 = F_kF_{k+1} + F_{k+1}^2,$$

since $\mathcal{P}(k)$ is assumed true. So

$$\sum_{i=1}^{k+1} F_i^2 = F_{k+1}(F_k + F_{k+1}) = F_{k+1}F_{k+2}.$$

Hence $\mathcal{P}(k+1)$ is true.

45. $\frac{1}{1} = 1$; $\frac{2}{1} = 2$; $\frac{3}{2} = 1.5$; $\frac{5}{3} \approx 1.6667$; $\frac{8}{5} = 1.6$; $\frac{13}{8} = 1.625$; $\frac{21}{13} \approx 1.6154$; $\frac{34}{21} \approx 1.6190$; $\frac{55}{34} \approx 1.6176$; $\frac{89}{55} \approx 1.6181818$; $(1 + \sqrt{5})/2 \approx 1.61803398875$

Section 14. Answers to Tutorials

14.2. b. 31

14.4. a. False

14.5. If the column is F, F, then the following table results:

p	q	$p \rightarrow q$	$q \rightarrow p$	$(p \rightarrow q) \wedge (q \rightarrow p)$	$p \leftrightarrow q$
T	T	T	T	T	T
T	F	F	F	F	F
F	T	F	F	F	F
F	F	F	F	F	T

This shows that $(p \rightarrow q) \wedge (q \rightarrow p)$ has a different truth table than $p \leftrightarrow q$. If the column is T, F, then the following table results:

p	q	$p \to q$	$q \to p$	$(p \to q) \wedge (q \to p)$	$p \leftrightarrow q$
T	T	T	T	T	T
T	F	F	T	F	F
F	T	T	F	F	F
F	F	F	F	F	T

This also shows that $(p \to q) \wedge (q \to p)$ has a different truth table than $p \leftrightarrow q$.

Section 14.   Answers to Selected Problems

3. $1 = 2^0 = (1)_2; 1 + 2 = 3 = 2^4 - 1 =$
$(11)_2; 1 + 2 + 2^2 = 7 = 2^3 - 1 = (111)_2;$
$1 + 2 + 2^2 + 2^3 = 15 = 2^4 - 1 = (1111)_2.$
From the previous calculations, $\mathcal{P}(1)$ is true.
Now

$$\sum_{i=0}^{k+1} 2^i = \sum_{i=0}^{k} 2^i + 2^{k+1}$$
$$= (2^{k+1} - 1) + 2^{k+1}$$
$$= 2 \cdot 2^{k+1} - 1$$
$$= 2^{k+2} - 1 = 2^{(k+1)+1} - 1.$$

Hence $\mathcal{P}(k + 1)$ is true.

5. (a) "9 and 11 is a prime pair or $\sqrt{13}$ is an irrational number" and "9 and 11 is a prime pair and $\sqrt{13}$ is an irrational number"
(b) The first (disjunction) is true.

7. (a) $x > 3$ and x and $x + 2$ is a prime pair.
(b) Apparently. Can you prove it?

9.

p	q	$\sim q$	$p \wedge \sim q$	$\sim(p \wedge \sim q)$
T	T	F	F	T
T	F	T	T	F
F	T	F	F	T
F	F	T	F	T

11.

$(\sim p) \vee q$	$p \vee \sim q$	$((\sim p) \vee q) \wedge (p \vee (\sim q))$
T	T	T
F	T	F
T	F	F
T	T	T

13.

p	q	r	$\sim p$	$\sim q$	$\sim p \vee q$	$\sim q \vee r$	$(\sim p \vee q) \wedge (\sim q \vee r)$
T	T	T	F	F	T	T	T
T	T	F	F	F	T	F	F
T	F	T	F	T	F	T	F
T	F	F	F	T	F	T	F
F	T	T	T	F	T	T	T
F	T	F	T	F	T	F	F
F	F	T	T	T	T	T	T
F	F	F	T	T	T	T	T

15. (a) By a De Morgan Law, $\sim(\sim p \vee q) \leftrightarrow \sim(\sim p) \wedge (\sim q) \leftrightarrow p \wedge (\sim q)$. Therefore, $\sim(\sim p \vee q) \vee p \leftrightarrow (p \wedge (\sim q)) \vee p$. If p is T, then this disjunction is T; if p is F, then each part of the disjunction, hence the disjunction itself, is F. Thus the disjunction is T exactly when p is T.

(b)

p	q	$\sim p$	$\sim p \vee q$	$\sim(\sim p \vee q)$	$\sim(\sim p \vee q) \vee p$
T	T	F	T	F	T
T	F	F	F	T	T
F	T	T	T	F	F
F	F	T	T	F	F

17. First, $(\sim p \vee (\sim q)) \wedge r \leftrightarrow \sim(p \wedge q) \wedge r$. Next, $\sim((p \wedge q) \vee (\sim r)) \leftrightarrow \sim(p \wedge q) \wedge (\sim(\sim r)) \leftrightarrow \sim(p \wedge q) \wedge r$. Therefore, $(\sim p \vee (\sim q)) \wedge r \leftrightarrow \sim((p \wedge q) \vee (\sim r))$.

19.

p	q	$q \rightarrow p$	$(q \rightarrow p) \rightarrow p$	$p \vee q$
T	T	T	T	T
T	F	T	T	T
F	T	F	T	T
F	F	T	F	F

21. The statements (a) and (c) are true.

23. The statements (c), (d), and (e) are true.

25. (a) p (b) $\left[(\sqrt{2})^{\sqrt{2}}\right]^{\sqrt{2}} = (\sqrt{2})^2 = 2 \in \mathbb{Q}$

27. See below

29. (a) $(p \wedge q) \wedge r$ (b) $\sim q \wedge \sim r \wedge (p \vee \sim p)$

31. (a) 3, 7, 15, 31 (b) 4, 13, 40, 121 (c) 6, 31, 156, 781

33. The divisors are $1, p, p^2, \ldots, p^n$. Since the sum of these is a geometric progression, with initial value 1 and common ratio p, the sum is $\dfrac{p^{n+1} - 1}{p - 1}$.

35. (a) $1 + 2 + 4 + 8 + 16 + 32 + 37 + 74 + 148 + 296 + 592 = 1210$; $1 + 2 + 5 + 10 + 11 + 22 + 55 + 110 + 121 + 242 + 605 = 1184$ (b) $1 + 2 + 4 + 8 + 16 + 23 + 46 + 92 + 184 + 368 + 47 + 94 + 188 + 376 + 752 + 1081 + 2162 + 4324 + 8648 = 18416$; $1 + 2 + 4 + 8 + 16 + 1151 + 2302 + 4604 + 9208 = 17296$

37. Since $\gcd(F_1, F_2) = \gcd(1, 1) = 1$, $\mathscr{P}(1)$ is true. Now $F_{k+2} = F_k + F_{k+1}$, so any common divisor of F_{k+1} and F_{k+2} would have to be a common divisor of F_k and F_{k+1}. But, as $\mathscr{P}(k)$ is assumed true, $\gcd(F_k, F_{k+1}) = 1$. Thus $\gcd(F_{k+1}, F_{k+2}) = 1$ and hence, $\mathscr{P}(k + 1)$ is true.

39. (a) 2 (b) 1 (c) 3 (d) 2 (e) 8

27. (a)

q	s	$\sim q$	$q \rightarrow s$	$\sim q \rightarrow s$	$(q \rightarrow s) \wedge (\sim q \rightarrow s)$
T	T	F	T	T	T
T	F	F	F	T	F
F	T	T	T	T	T
F	F	T	T	F	F

Section 15. Answers to Tutorials

15.3A. **a.** Since every element of **A** is in **A** $\cup$ **B**, **A** $\subseteq$ **A** $\cup$ **B**. **b.** Note that **C** contains exactly those elements in **A** $\cup$ **B** that are not in **A**. Hence **C** contains exactly those elements of **B** that are not in **A**. So, **A** $\cup$ **C** = **A** $\cup$ **B**. **c.** **A** $\cap$ **C** = $\varnothing$. **d.** $|\,$**A**$\,| = |\,$**A** $\cup$ **B**$\,|$ whenever **B** $\subseteq$ **A**.

15.3B. a. $\mathbf{A} \times \mathbf{B} = \{(0, x), (0, y), (0, z), (1, x), (1, y),$ $(1, z)\}$ and $\mathbf{B} \times \mathbf{A} = \{(x, 0), (x, 1), (y, 0),$ $(y, 1), (z, 0), (z, 1)\}$. So $|\mathbf{A} \times \mathbf{B}| = |\mathbf{B} \times \mathbf{A}| = 6$.
b. $\mathbf{A} \times \mathbf{A} = \{(0, 0), (0, 1), (1, 0), (1, 1)\}$ and $\mathbf{B} \times \mathbf{B} = \{(x, x), (x, y), (x, z), (y, x), (y, y),$ $(y, z), (z, x), (z, y), (z, z)\}$. **c.** No.

15.5. a. $5^3 = 125$. A constant function is $\{(1, a), (2, a), (3, a)\}$ and a nonconstant function is $\{(1, a), (2, a), (3, u)\}$. **b.** $(5)_3 = 60$. Two examples are $\{(1, a), (2, e), (3, u)\}$ and $\{(1, a), (2, i), (3, u)\}$.

Section 15. Answers to Selected Problems

1. $\mathbf{A} = \{2, 3, 11, 13\}$ and $\mathbf{B} = \{2, 3, 7, 11\}$.
(a) $\{2, 3, 7, 11, 13\}$ (b) $\{2, 3, 11\}$ (c) $\{13\}$
(d) $\{7\}$

3. (a) $\mathbf{A} \times \mathbf{B} = \{(0, a), (0, b), (1, a), (1, b), (2, a),$ $(2, b)\}$ (b) $\mathbf{B} \times \mathbf{A} = \{(a, 0), (a, 1), (a, 2), (b, 0),$ $(b, 1), (b, 2)\}$

5. (a) (G, F) (b) (S, W) (c) $(\mathbf{A} \times \mathbf{B}) \cap (\mathbf{B} \times \mathbf{A}) =$ $\{(N, N), (N, O), (N, S), (O, N), (O, O), (O, S),$ $(S, N), (S, O), (S, S)\}$

7. $\mathbf{A} = \{s_2, s_4\}$, $\mathbf{B} = \{s_6, s_8\}$

9. (a) $\overline{\mathbf{A} \cup \mathbf{B}} = \{1, 2, 4, 5, 14, 16, 17, 19, 20\}$
(b) $\overline{\mathbf{A} \cap \mathbf{B}} = \{1, 2, 3, 4, 5, 6, 7, 8, 10, 11, 13,$ $14, 15, 16, 17, 18, 19, 20\}$
(c) $\overline{\mathbf{A}} \cup \overline{\mathbf{B}} = \{1, 2, 3, 4, 5, 6, 7, 8, 10, 11, 13,$ $14, 15, 16, 17, 18, 19, 20\}$
(d) $\overline{\mathbf{A}} \cap \overline{\mathbf{B}} = \{1, 2, 4, 5, 14, 16, 17, 19, 20\}$
(e) $\overline{\mathbf{A} \cup \mathbf{B}} = \overline{\mathbf{A}} \cap \overline{\mathbf{B}}, \overline{\mathbf{A} \cap \mathbf{B}} = \overline{\mathbf{A}} \cup \overline{\mathbf{B}}$

11. (a) $9 \cdot 4 = 36$ (b) $\mathbf{R} = \{(3, 2), (5, 8), (7, 6),$ $(9, 4), (11, 2), (13, 8), (15, 6), (17, 4), (19, 2)\}$
(c) Yes; no two pairs have the same first coordinate.

13. Since $\mathbf{A} \cap \mathbf{B} = \{2\}$, $\mathbf{A} \cap \mathbf{B} \neq \varnothing$, and so FCP I does not apply.

15. (a) $9 \cdot 10^3$ (b) 2^3 (c) $15 \cdot 16^3$ (d) $10^4 - 1 =$ $9999; 2^4 - 1 = 15; 16^4 - 1 = 65535$

17. $7! = 5040$

19. Define $\mathbf{A}_0 \times \mathbf{A}_1 = \{(a_0, a_1) : a_0 \in \mathbf{A}_0, a_1 \in \mathbf{A}_1\}$ and inductively let $\mathbf{A}_0 \times \mathbf{A}_1 \times \cdots \times \mathbf{A}_{n-1} \times \mathbf{A}_n = (\mathbf{A}_0 \times \mathbf{A}_1 \times \cdots \times \mathbf{A}_{n-1}) \times \mathbf{A}_n = \{(a_0, a_1, \ldots, a_{n-1}, a_n) : a_i \in \mathbf{A}_i, i = 0, 1, \ldots, n\}$. Let $\mathcal{P}(n)$ be the predicate,

$|\mathbf{A}_0 \times \mathbf{A}_1 \times \cdots \times \mathbf{A}_n| = p_0 p_1 \cdots p_n$. Since $|\mathbf{A}_0 \times \mathbf{A}_1| = p_0 p_1$ by FCP II, $\mathcal{P}(1)$ is true. By FCP II, $|\mathbf{A}_0 \times \mathbf{A}_1 \times \cdots \times \mathbf{A}_k \times \mathbf{A}_{k+1}| = |(\mathbf{A}_0 \times \mathbf{A}_1 \times \cdots \times \mathbf{A}_k) \times \mathbf{A}_{k+1}| = |\mathbf{A}_0 \times \mathbf{A}_1 \times \cdots \times \mathbf{A}_k| \cdot p_{k+1} = (p_0 p_1 \cdots p_k) p_{k+1}$, since $\mathcal{P}(k)$ is assumed true. So $|\mathbf{A}_0 \times \mathbf{A}_1 \times \cdots \times \mathbf{A}_k \times \mathbf{A}_{k+1}| = p_0 p_1 \cdots p_k p_{k+1}$. Hence, $\mathcal{P}(k + 1)$ is true.

21. (a) If p is prime, then its only divisors are 1 and p : $\tau(p) = 2$. (b) If p is prime, then the divisors of p^a are $1, p, p^2, p^3, \ldots, p^{a-1}, p^a$, and so $\tau(p^a) = a + 1$.

23. If $n = p_1^{e_1} p_2^{e_2} \cdots p_r^{e_r}$, where the p_i are distinct primes, then, as in Prob. 22, the divisors d of n are $\{d = p_1^{f_1} p_2^{f_2} \cdots p_r^{f_r} : 0 \le f_i \le e_i, i = 1, \ldots, r\}$. Let $\mathbf{A}_i = \{1, 2, \ldots, e_i\}$ for $i = 1, 2, \ldots, r$. Then $|\mathbf{A}_i| = e_i + 1$ and $(f_1, f_2, \ldots, f_r) \in \mathbf{A}_1 \times \mathbf{A}_2 \times \cdots \times \mathbf{A}_r$. Thus, by Prob. 19, $\tau(n) = |\mathbf{A}_1 \times \mathbf{A}_2 \times \cdots \times \mathbf{A}_r| = (e_1 + 1)(e_2 + 1) \cdots (e_r + 1)$.

25. (a) $9^3 = 729$ (b) $8^3 = 512$

27. (a) 0 (b) 1 (c) 2 (d) 3

29. (a) 5^{21} (b) No. Apply the Pigeonhole Principle.

31. There are 5 constant functions of the type in Prob. 29, and in Prob. 30 there are 10 of the type $f: \mathbf{A} \to \mathbf{D}$ and 26 of the type $f: \mathbf{D} \to \mathbf{A}$.

33. (a) (i) (b) (iii) (c) (ii)

35. We are given that $f: \mathbf{A} \rightarrow \mathbf{A}$ and $|\mathbf{A}| = n > 0$. (i) Hypothesis: f is one-to-one. By the definition, no second coordinate of f is repeated; therefore *all* elements of $\mathbf{A}$ must appear in the range of f, that is, f is onto. (ii) Hypothesis: f is onto. The hypothesis means that every element of $\mathbf{A}$ appears as a second element. This, in turn, means that no second coordinate can be repeated, for if it were, some element of $\mathbf{A}$ would not appear as a second coordinate. Thus, f is one-to-one.

37. (*a*) For f, 16; for g, 15. (*b*) For f, $(16)_{15}$; for g, none. (*c*) For f, 16^{15}; for g, 15^{16}.

39. $(2^{12} - 1) \cdot (2^6 - 1) = 257{,}985$

41. (*a*) $g(n, 1) = 1$, as the only way is to give all n \$1 bills to the one friend. (*b*) $g(1, k) = k$ since the one \$1 bill could be given to any of the k friends. (*c*) $g(n, 2) = n + 1$: for $j = 0, 1, 2, \ldots, n$, give j \$1 bills to the first friend and give the remaining $n - j$ \$1 bills to the second friend.

43. Now $(x, y) \in (\mathbf{A} \times \mathbf{B}) \cap (\mathbf{B} \times \mathbf{A})$ if and only if x and y are in both $\mathbf{A}$ and $\mathbf{B}$. Hence (x, y) is in $(\mathbf{A} \times \mathbf{B}) \cap (\mathbf{B} \times \mathbf{A})$ if and only if (x, y) is in $(\mathbf{A} \cap \mathbf{B}) \times (\mathbf{A} \cap \mathbf{B})$.

Section 16. Answers to Tutorials

16.3. a. $(x, y, z), (x, z, y), (y, x, z), (y, z, x), (z, x, y),$ (z, y, x) **b.** $(5)_3 = 60$ **c.** 36

16.4. a. $n = 2$, there are no 3-element subsets; $n = 3, \{a_1, a_2, a_3\}; n = 4,$ $\{a_1, a_2, a_3\}, \{a_1, a_2, a_4\}, \{a_1, a_3, a_4\}, \{a_2, a_3, a_4\};$ $n = 5, \{a_1, a_2, a_3\}, \{a_1, a_2, a_4\}, \{a_1, a_2, a_5\},$ $\{a_1, a_3, a_4\}, \{a_1, a_3, a_5\}, \{a_1, a_4, a_5\}, \{a_2, a_3, a_4\},$ $\{a_2, a_3, a_5\}, \{a_2, a_4, a_5\}, \{a_3, a_4, a_5\}$

b. $\binom{3}{3} = 1, \binom{4}{3} = 4, \binom{5}{3} = 10$

c. $\binom{15}{5} = \dfrac{15!}{(15 - 5)! \cdot 5!} = \dfrac{15!}{10! \cdot 5!}$

$$= \dfrac{15 \cdot 14 \cdot 13 \cdot 12 \cdot 11}{5 \cdot 4 \cdot 3 \cdot 2 \cdot 1}$$

$$= \dfrac{15}{5} \cdot \dfrac{12}{4 \cdot 3} \cdot 7 \cdot 13 \cdot 11$$

$$= 3 \cdot 1 \cdot 7 \cdot 13 \cdot 11 = 3003$$

16.5. a. $\binom{12}{4} = 495, \binom{11}{3} = 165, \binom{11}{4} = 330$

b. $\dfrac{11!}{8! \cdot 3!} + \dfrac{11!}{7! \cdot 4!} = \dfrac{11! \cdot 4}{8! \cdot 4!} + \dfrac{11! \cdot 8}{8! \cdot 4!}$

$$= \dfrac{11! \cdot 4 + 11! \cdot 8}{8! \cdot 4!}$$

$$= \dfrac{11! \cdot (4 + 8)}{8! \cdot 4!}$$

$$= \dfrac{11! \cdot 12}{8! \cdot 4!} = \dfrac{12!}{8! \cdot 4!}$$

Section 16. Answers to Selected Problems

1. (*a*) $\{(a, 0), (e, 1), (i, 0), (o, 0), (u, 0)\}$
(*b*) $\{(a, 0), (e, 0), (i, 1), (o, 1), (u, 1)\}$
(*c*) $\{(a, 0), (e, 0), (i, 0), (o, 0), (u, 0)\}$
(*d*) $\{(a, 1), (e, 1), (i, 1), (o, 1), (u, 1)\}$

3.

a	b	c	d	
0	0	0	0	$\varnothing$
1	0	0	0	$\{a\}$
0	1	0	0	$\{b\}$
0	0	1	0	$\{c\}$
0	0	0	1	$\{d\}$

3. *Continued*

a	b	c	d	
1	1	0	0	$\{a, b\}$
1	0	1	0	$\{a, c\}$
1	0	0	1	$\{a, d\}$
0	1	1	0	$\{b, c\}$
0	1	0	1	$\{b, d\}$
0	0	1	1	$\{c, d\}$
0	1	1	1	$\{b, c, d\}$
1	0	1	1	$\{a, c, d\}$
1	1	0	1	$\{a, b, d\}$
1	1	1	0	$\{a, b, c\}$
1	1	1	1	$\{a, b, c, d\}$

5. Let $\mathbf{A} = \{a_1, a_2, \ldots, a_n\}$ and let $\mathbf{B}$ be a subset of $\mathbf{A}$. Define $f: \mathbf{A} \to \{0, 1\}$ by $f(a_i) = 1$ if a_i is in $\mathbf{B}$, 0 otherwise. Hence f is a characteristic function on $\mathbf{A}$. Note that no subset of $\mathbf{A}$ other than $\mathbf{B}$ will produce this characteristic function. Also, given a characteristic function $g: \mathbf{A} \to \{0, 1\}$, define a subset $\mathbf{C}$ of $\mathbf{A}$ by $\mathbf{C} = \{x \in \mathbf{A}: g(x) = 1\}$. Note that no characteristic function on $\mathbf{A}$ other than g will produce this subset. Therefore, there is a one-to-one correspondence between the subsets of $\mathbf{A}$ and the characteristic functions on $\mathbf{A}$.

7. Upper: $(10)_3 = 10 \cdot 9 \cdot 8 = 720$; middle: $(9)_3 = 9 \cdot 8 \cdot 7 = 504$; lower: $(7)_3 = 7 \cdot 6 \cdot 5 = 210$

9. (a) $\binom{10}{2} \cdot (9 + 7) \cdot 3! = 45 \cdot 16 \cdot 6 = 4320$

(b) $\binom{9}{2} \cdot (10 + 7) \cdot 3! = 36 \cdot 17 \cdot 6 = 3672$

(c) $\binom{7}{2} \cdot (10 + 9) \cdot 3! = 21 \cdot 19 \cdot 6 = 2394$

11. $\binom{m}{k-1} + \binom{m}{k} = \dfrac{m!}{(k-1)!(m - (k-1))!}$

$+ \dfrac{m!}{k!(m - k)!}$

$= \dfrac{k \cdot m! + (m - k + 1)m!}{(m - k + 1)!k!}$

$= \dfrac{(m + 1)!}{k!(m + 1 - k)!}$

$= \binom{m + 1}{k}$

13. (a) $\binom{5}{2} = 10$ (b) $\binom{12}{2} = 66$

15. (a) $\binom{101}{4} = \dfrac{101!}{4!97!} = \dfrac{98}{98} \cdot \dfrac{101!}{4 \cdot 3!97!}$

$= \dfrac{98}{4}\binom{101}{3}$

(b) $\binom{n}{k + 1} = \dfrac{n!}{(k + 1)!(n - k - 1)!}$

$= \dfrac{n - k}{n - k} \cdot \dfrac{n!}{(k + 1)k!(n - k - 1)!}$

$= \dfrac{n - k}{k + 1} \cdot \dfrac{n!}{k!(n - k)!}$

$= \dfrac{n - k}{k + 1}\binom{n}{k}$

17. $(18)_2 = 306$

19. $\binom{12}{3} = 220$

21. (a) $6! = 720$ (b) $5! = 120$

23. (a) $\binom{10}{5} = 252$ (b) $\binom{8}{3} + \binom{8}{5} = 112$

25. (a) 2   (b) 4

27. $S = \binom{n}{0} + \binom{n + 1}{1} + \binom{n + 2}{2} - \binom{n + 3}{2} =$

$\binom{n + 1}{0} + \binom{n + 1}{1} + \binom{n + 2}{2} - \binom{n + 3}{2}$ since

$\binom{n}{0} = \binom{n + 1}{0} = 1$. Repeated use of (1) in par. 16.5 shows that

$S = \binom{n + 2}{1} + \binom{n + 2}{2} - \binom{n + 3}{2}$

$= \binom{n + 3}{2} - \binom{n + 3}{2} = 0.$

29. book, boko, bkoo, obok, obko, oobk, ookb, okbo, okob, kboo, kobo, koob

31. There are 4! arrangements of four letters, but if two are the same, then there are $\frac{4!}{2!}$ arrangements. Similarly, if a four-letter word consists of just two different letters, both appearing twice, then there are $\frac{4!}{2!2!}$ different arrangements.

33. $\dfrac{21!}{2!9!2!2!2!3!1!} = 1,466,593,128,000$

35. $\dbinom{10}{3} = 120$

37. (a) 24   (b) 48   (c) 100

39. $(5)_3(1)_1\dbinom{6}{3}(4)_3 = 28,800$

41. (a) $(4)_2\dbinom{13}{1}\dbinom{13}{4} = 111,540$

   (b) $(4)_2\dbinom{13}{2}\dbinom{13}{3} = 267,696$

   (c) $\dbinom{4}{1}\dbinom{13}{5} = 5148$

43. (a) 1,712,304 (b) 108,336

Section 17.   Answers to Tutorials

17.1. a. (i) $y^4 + 3y^3x + 3y^2x^2 + yx^3$, (ii) $xy^3 + 3y^2x^2 + 3yx^3 + x^4$, (iii) $y^4 + 4y^3x + 6y^2x^2 + 4yx^3 + x^4$ **b.** (i) 3, (ii) 1, (iii) 4

17.2. a. $y^2 + 2yx + x^2$ **b.** $y^3 + 3y^2x + 3yx^2 + x^3$ **c.** $y^4 + 4y^3x + 6y^2x^2 + 4yx^3 + x^4$

17.3. a. $15x^4$ **b.** $15x^4$

Section 17.   Answers to Selected Problems

1. 1
1   1
1   2   1
1   3   3   1
1   4   6   4   1
1   5   10   10   5   1
1   6   15   20   15   6   1
1   7   21   35   35   21   7   1
1   8   28   56   70   56   28   8   1
1   9   36   84   126   126   84   36   9   1
1   10   45   120   210   252   210   120   45   10   1

3. $(y + x)^6 = \sum_{k=0}^{6}\dbinom{6}{k}y^{6-k}x^k = y^6 + 6y^5x +$
$15y^4x^2 + 20y^3x^3 + 15y^2x^4 + 6yx^5 + x^6$

5. (a) $(1 + x)^2 = \sum_{k=0}^{2}\dbinom{2}{k}x^k = 1 + 2x + x^2$

   (b) $(1+x)^3 = \sum_{k=0}^{3}\dbinom{3}{k}x^k = 1+3x+3x^2+x^3$

   (c) $(1 + x)^7 = \sum_{k=0}^{7}\dbinom{7}{k}x^k = 1 + 7x + 21x^2 +$
   $35x^3 + 35x^4 + 21x^5 + 7x^6 + x^7$

   (d) $(1 + x)^8 = \sum_{k=0}^{8}\dbinom{8}{k}x^k = 1 + 8x + 28x^2 +$
   $56x^3 + 70x^4 + 56x^5 + 28x^6 + 8x^7 + x^8$

7. (c) $2^7 = 1 + 7 + 21 + 35 + 35 + 21 + 7 + 1$. The number of subsets of a set **A** with $|\mathbf{A}| = 7$ is 2^7.

9. $-21yx^{5/2}$

11. $(1 + x)^3 + 3(1 + x)^2 y + 3(1 + x)y^2 + y^3 =$
$1 + 3x + 3x^2 + x^3 + 3y + 6xy + 3x^2 y + 3y^2 +$
$3xy^2 + y^3$

13. 2.441

15. 2.594

17. (*a*) 20 (*b*) No

19. We have $(y - x)^6 = \sum_{k=0}^{6} \binom{6}{k} y^{6-k}(-x)^k$;

letting $x = y = 1$ gives $0 = \sum_{k=0}^{6} \binom{6}{k}(-1)^k$.

21. We have $(y - x)^n = \sum_{k=0}^{n} \binom{n}{k} y^{n-k}(-x)^k$;

letting $x = y = 1$ gives $0 = \sum_{k=0}^{n} \binom{n}{k}(-1)^k$.

23. 64

25. $\sum_{k=0}^{4} \binom{n-1}{k} = \binom{n-1}{0} + \binom{n-1}{1} + \binom{n-1}{2} +$

$\binom{n-1}{3} + \binom{n-1}{4} = \binom{n}{0} + \binom{n-1}{1} +$

$\binom{n-1}{2} + \binom{n-1}{3} + \binom{n-1}{4}$, since

$\binom{n-1}{0} = \binom{n}{0} = 1$. Using (1) in par. 16.5,

this can be written as $\binom{n}{0} + \binom{n}{2} + \binom{n}{4}$.

27.
```
        2
       2  2
      2  4  2
     2  6  6  2
    2  8  12  8  2
   2  10  20  20  10  2
```

The numbers will be twice the corresponding numbers in Pascal's triangle.

29. $n = 3, \sum_{k=0}^{m} \binom{3+k}{3} = \binom{m+4}{4}; m = 5,$

$\binom{3}{3} + \binom{4}{3} + \binom{5}{3} + \binom{6}{3} + \binom{7}{3} + \binom{8}{3} =$

$1 + 4 + 10 + 20 + 35 + 56 = 126 = \binom{9}{4}$

31. By Prob. 16, $\sum_{r=k}^{n} \binom{n}{r}\binom{r}{k} = \sum_{r=k}^{n} \binom{n}{k}\binom{n-k}{r-k}$

which is $\binom{n}{k} \sum_{r=k}^{n} \binom{n-k}{r-k}$ since $\binom{n}{k}$ is con-

stant with respect to r. Letting $r - k = h$, or

$r = k + h$, gives $\binom{n}{k} \sum_{h=0}^{n-k} \binom{n-k}{h}$ which is

$\binom{n}{k} 2^{n-k}$ by Theorem 16.7.

33. $\sum_{k=0}^{n} \binom{n}{k} 3^{2n} = \sum_{k=0}^{n} \binom{n}{k} 9^n = (1 + 9)^n = 10^n$

35. (*a*) $-2, 6, -24, 120$ (*b*) $\frac{1}{2}, -\frac{1}{4}, \frac{3}{8}, -\frac{15}{16}$
(*c*) $-\frac{1}{2}, \frac{3}{4}, -\frac{15}{8}, \frac{105}{16}$

37. $1, 1, 0, 0; 1, \frac{1}{2}, -\frac{1}{8}, \frac{1}{16}; 1, -1, 1, -1; 1, -\frac{1}{2},$
$\frac{3}{8}, -\frac{5}{16}$

39. (*a*) 4 does not divide $\binom{4}{2} = 6$ and 6 does not

divide $\binom{6}{2} = 15$. (*b*) 5 divides $\binom{5}{2} = 10$

and 11 divides $\binom{11}{6} = 462$. (*c*) Since

$\binom{p}{k} = \frac{(p)_k}{k!}$, we have $(p)_k = k!\binom{p}{k}$, or

$p(p - 1)_{k-1} = k!\binom{p}{k}$. This equation says that

p divides $k!\binom{p}{k}$; but p is a prime and $k < p$

implies that p does not divide $k!$; therefore p

must divide $\binom{p}{k}$.

41. Assume that 7 divides $n^7 - n$. Now $(n + 1)^7 -$

$$(n + 1) = n^7 + 7n^{7-1} + \binom{7}{2}n^{7-2} + \cdots +$$

$\binom{7}{7-2}n^2 + 7n - n$. By Prob. 39(c), 7 divides

$\binom{7}{k}$ for $0 < k < 7$. Since 7 also divides

$n^7 - n$, 7 divides $(n + 1)^7 - (n + 1)$.

43. By Prob. 15.42(c), $g(n, k) = g(n, k - 1) + g(n - 1, k)$. By Prob. 15.41(a), $g(n, 1) = 1$ and by Prob. 15.41(b), $g(1, k) = k$. But these three formulas for g produce the part of Table 17.3A below the diagonal of 1s. Therefore, $g(n, k) = \binom{n + k - 1}{n}$.

Section 18. Answers to Tutorials

18.2A. a. Let $x \in \overline{A \cap B}$. Hence $x \notin A \cap B$, and so either $x \notin A$ or $x \notin B$. Thus $x \in \overline{A}$ or $x \in \overline{B}$. Therefore, $x \in \overline{A} \cup \overline{B}$. **b.** $\overline{A} = \{w, z\}$, $\overline{B} = \{u, v\}$, $\overline{A} \cup \overline{B} = \{u, v, w, z\}$, $A \cap B = \{x, y\}$, and $\overline{A \cap B} = \{u, v, w, z\}$.

18.2B. We need to enumerate $\overline{A \cap B} = \overline{A} \cup \overline{B}$.

18.3. a. $A \cap C = A \cap C$ for Theorem 18.3A and $A \cup B = A \cup B$ for Theorem 18.3B.
b. Since $B \cup C = \{t, u, w, x, y, z\}$, $A \cap (B \cup C) = \{u, x, z\}$. Now $A \cap B = \{x, z\}$ and $A \cap C = \{u, x, z\}$, and so $(A \cap B) \cup (A \cap C) = \{u, x, z\}$. This verifies (2). Since

$B \cap C = \{x, z\}$, $A \cup (B \cap C) = \{u, v, x, z\}$. Now $A \cup B = \{u, v, w, x, y, z\}$ and $A \cup C = \{t, u, v, x, z\}$, and so $(A \cup B) \cap (A \cup C) = \{u, v, x, z\}$. This verifies (3).

18.5.

$A \cup B$	$A \cap \overline{B}$	$A \cap B$	$\overline{A} \cap B$
Add $|A|$	$+1$	$+1$	
Add $|B|$		$+1$	$+1$
Subtract $|A \cap B|$		-1	
Total	1	1	1

Section 18. Answers to Selected Problems

1. (a) $A \cap B = \{0, 2, 4, 6, 8\} \cap \{2, 3, 5, 7\} = \{2\}$, $A \cap \overline{B} = \{0, 4, 6, 8\}$, $(A \cap B) \cup (A \cap \overline{B}) = \{0, 2, 4, 6, 8\}$
(b) $\overline{A \cap B} = \{0, 1, 3, 4, 5, 6, 7, 8, 9\}$, $\overline{A} \cup \overline{B} = \{0, 1, 3, 4, 5, 6, 7, 8, 9\}$
(c) $A \cup B = \{0, 2, 3, 4, 5, 6, 7, 8\}$, $\overline{A \cup B} = \{1, 9\}$, $|\overline{A \cup B}| = 2$

3. (a) $A \cap B$ is the set of lattice points with both coordinates positive. (b) $A \cup B$ is the set of lattice points with at least one positive coordinate. (c) $\overline{A} \cap \overline{B}$ is the set of lattice points with both coordinates nonpositive (negative or zero). (d) Same as (c).

5. By a De Morgan Law, $\overline{A \cap \overline{B}} = \overline{A} \cup \overline{\overline{B}}$, and since $\overline{\overline{B}} = B$, $\overline{A \cap \overline{B}} = \overline{A} \cup B$.

7. By a De Morgan Law, $\overline{A \cap (B \cup C)} = \overline{A} \cup \overline{(B \cup C)}$, and by the other De Morgan Law, $\overline{A} \cup \overline{(B \cup C)} = \overline{A} \cup (\overline{B} \cap \overline{C})$.

9. (a) Let $A = \{1, 2, 3\}$, $B = \{3, 4\}$, $C = \{2, 4\}$.
(b) No. Let $A = \{1, 2, 3\}$, $B = \{1\}$, $C = \{2\}$.
(c) Yes

11. Let $x \in (A \cap B) \cup (A \cap C)$. Thus $x \in (A \cap B)$ or $x \in (A \cap C)$. Hence, either $x \in A$ and $x \in B$ or $x \in A$ and $x \in C$. In either case, $x \in A$ and also $x \in B$ or $x \in C$. Therefore, $x \in A \cap (B \cup C)$.

13.

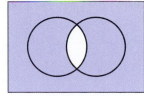

$\overline{\mathbf{A}} \cup \overline{\mathbf{B}}$ and $\overline{\mathbf{A} \cap \mathbf{B}}$ are the shaded region.

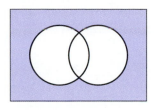

$\overline{\mathbf{A}} \cap \overline{\mathbf{B}}$ and $\overline{\mathbf{A} \cup \mathbf{B}}$ are the shaded region.

15.

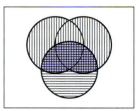

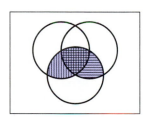

$(\mathbf{A} \cup \mathbf{B}) \cap \mathbf{C}$ and $(\mathbf{A} \cap \mathbf{C}) \cup (\mathbf{B} \cap \mathbf{C})$ are the shaded regions.

17.

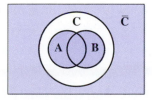

Note that the shaded regions do not overlap.

19. (*a*)

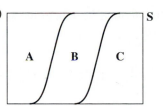

(*b*)

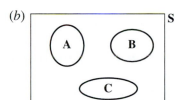

21. 4, 6, 8, 9, 10, 12, 14, 15, 16, 18

23. Since every integer has a remainder of 0, 1, 2, 3, or 4 when divided by 5, the union of these sets is $\mathbb{Z}$. Since no number can have two different remainders when divided by 5 (the division algorithm), these sets are disjoint, hence are a partition of $\mathbb{Z}$.

25. (*a*) No, because $\{(a, a), (b, b), (c, c)\}$ is in both $\mathbf{F}_a$ and $\mathbf{F}_b$. (*b*) 9

27. 600

29. (*a*) 494 (*b*) 390

31. (*a*) $\lfloor 276/3 \rfloor = 92$ (*b*) 130 (*c*) 275

33. 240

35. 52

37. 5

39. (*a*) $\mathbf{T} = \overline{\mathbf{A} \cap \mathbf{B} \cap \mathbf{C}}$ (*b*) $\overline{\mathbf{A} \cap \mathbf{B} \cap \mathbf{C}} = \overline{\mathbf{A}} \cup \overline{\mathbf{B}} \cup \overline{\mathbf{C}}$

41. (*a*) $|\mathbf{S}_p| = p^{a-1}$. (*b*) The only divisors of p^a are $1, p, p^2, \ldots, p^{a-1}, p^a$, all of which, excepting 1, are in $\mathbf{S}_p$. Thus, $\gcd(m, p^a) > 1$ if and only if $m \in \mathbf{S}_p$. (*c*) Since $\mathbf{S} = \mathbf{S}_p \cup \overline{\mathbf{S}}_p$, $|\overline{\mathbf{S}}_p| = |\mathbf{S}| - |\mathbf{S}_p|$, but, by part (*b*), the numbers in $\overline{\mathbf{S}}_p$ are exactly the numbers relatively prime to p^a; that is, $\phi(p^a) = |\overline{\mathbf{S}}_p| = |\mathbf{S}| - |\mathbf{S}_p|$. (*d*) By parts (*a*) and (*c*), $\phi(p^a) = |\mathbf{S}| - |\mathbf{S}_p| = p^a - p^{a-1} = p^a(1 - 1/p)$.

43. Make a suitable modification of the answer to Prob. 41(b).

45. (a) 8 (b) 16 (c) 40 (d) 800 (e) 48 (f) 448

Section 19. Answers to Tutorials

19.2. a. $F(x) = \sum_{i=0}^{\infty}(3x)^i = 1 + 3x + 9x^2 + 27x^3 + \cdots .G(x) = \sum_{i=0}^{\infty}(x^2)^i = 1 + x^2 + x^4 + x^6 + \cdots .H(x) = \sum_{i=0}^{\infty}(-x^2)^i = 1 - x^2 + x^4 - x^6 + \cdots$ **b.** $F(x) = 1 + 3x + 9x^2 + 27x^3 + \cdots$

19.3. a. $1 - 2x + 3x^2 - 4x^3 + \cdots$ **b.** $4x + 8x^3 + 12x^5 + \cdots = \sum_{i=1}^{\infty} 4ix^{2i-1}$

19.4. a.

1¢	5¢	10¢
2	0	2
2	2	1
2	4	0
7	1	1
7	3	0
12	0	1
12	2	0
17	1	0
22	0	0

Section 19. Answers to Selected Problems

1. (a) $1 - x + x^2 - x^3 + x^4 + \cdots + (-1)^n x^n + \cdots$

(b) $1 + \dfrac{x}{2} + \dfrac{x^2}{4} + \dfrac{x^3}{8} + \dfrac{x^4}{16} + \cdots + \dfrac{x^n}{2^n} + \cdots$

(c) $1 + (1 + a)x + (1 + a)^2 x^2 + (1 + a)^3 x^3 + (1 + a)^4 x^4 + \cdots + (1 + a)^n x^n + \cdots$

(d) $1 + x^2 + x^4 + x^6 + x^8 + \cdots + x^{2n} + \cdots$, $a_n = 0$ if n is odd and 1 if n is even.

(e) $1 + x^{1/2} + x + x^{3/2} + x^2 + \cdots + x^n + x^{(2n+1)/2} + \cdots$

3. (a) $1 + 3x + 6x^2 + 10x^3 + 15x^4 + \cdots$

(b) $\dfrac{(n + 1)(n + 2)}{2} = \dbinom{n + 2}{2}$

5. $\dbinom{n + m - 1}{m - 1} = \dbinom{m + n - 1}{n}$

7. $F(x) = x/(1 - x)^2$

9. $F(x) = x^k$

11. $a_n + 1$

13. $a_n - 2a_{n-1} - 1$

15. $F(x) = 1/(1 - x)^2$

17. $F(x) = (2 - x)/(1 + x - 2x^2)$

19. $G(x) = 0 + x + 1x^2 + 2x^3 + 3x^4 + 5x^5 + \cdots$

21. (a) $G(x) = \dfrac{x}{1 - x - x^2}$

(b) $\dfrac{\sqrt{5} - 1}{2}, \dfrac{-\sqrt{5} - 1}{2}$

23. (a) 6 (b) 36

25. (a) $\dbinom{n}{n}$ (b) $\dbinom{n + 1}{n}$ (c) $\dbinom{n + 2}{n}$

(d) $\dbinom{n + k}{n} = \dbinom{n + k}{k}$

27. $(1 + x)^n \dfrac{(1 + x)^{m+1} - 1}{x}$

29. The quotient in Prob. 28(d) is the same polynomial as the sum in this problem.

Section 20. Answers to Tutorials

20.3. a. $\mathcal{E}$: toss a pair of dice. **b. S** $= \{(x, y): x = 1, 2, \ldots, 6; y = 1, 2, \ldots, 6\}$ **c. A** $= \{(1, 1), (2, 2), \ldots, (6, 6)\}$ **d.** $P(\mathbf{A}) = \frac{6}{36} = \frac{1}{6}$

20.4. a. Approximately 0.97 **b.** If x and y are the number of dots on the faces, then $|x - y| \neq 1$.

$P(\overline{\mathbf{A}}) = (36 - 10)/36 = \frac{26}{36} = \frac{13}{18}$ **c.** The event $\overline{\mathbf{A}}$ is that at most one spade is drawn. Since $P(\mathbf{A}) = \frac{1}{17}$, $P(\overline{\mathbf{A}}) = 1 - \frac{1}{17} = \frac{16}{17}$.

Section 20. Answers to Selected Problems

1. S $= \{1, 2, 3, \ldots, 10\}$; 2, 9; $|\mathbf{S}| = 10$

3. S $= \{$red, not red$\}$; red ball, not red ball; $|\mathbf{S}| = 2$

5. S $= \{$January, February, $\ldots$, December$\}$; March, June; $|\mathbf{S}| = 12$

7. S is the set of states shown in Fig. 34.1A; Vermont, Maine; $|\mathbf{S}| = 6$

9. S is the set of all 3-card sets, each card an ace; $\{A\heartsuit, A\diamondsuit, A\clubsuit\}, \{A\spadesuit, A\heartsuit, A\diamondsuit\}$; $|\mathbf{S}| = 4$

11. S is the set of all 3-letter strings using a, b, and c, no letter being used more than once; abc, bca; $|\mathbf{S}| = 6$

13. All numbers are equally likely to be picked. $P(\text{prime}) = \frac{4}{10} = \frac{2}{5}$

15. All balls are equally likely to be drawn. $P(\text{not red}) = \frac{30}{50}$. (Note that the two elements in $\mathbf{S}$ are not equally likely.)

17. All months are equally likely to be named (this is a questionable assumption). $P(\text{month without an } r) = \frac{4}{12} = \frac{1}{3}$

19. States are equally likely to be named. $P(\text{state borders Canada}) = \frac{1}{2}$

21. All cards are equally likely to be drawn. $P(\text{two red cards}) = \frac{2}{4} = \frac{1}{2}$

23. All arrangements are equally likely. $P(\text{cab}) = \frac{1}{6}$

25. (a) $\mathbf{S} = \{\mathbf{B} \subseteq \mathbf{D} : |\mathbf{B}| = 3\}$ where $\mathbf{D}$ is the set of 52 playing cards. So $|\mathbf{S}| = \binom{52}{3} = 22{,}100$. ($b$) $\dfrac{\binom{4}{3} \cdot 13^3}{22100} = \dfrac{8788}{22100} \approx 0.40$

27. (a) Let $\mathbf{A}$ be the set of six chosen people, and let $\mathbf{M}$ be the set of months, $\{$Jan., Feb., $\ldots$, Dec.$\}$. So $\mathbf{S} = \{f : \mathbf{A} \to \mathbf{M}\}$ and $|\mathbf{S}| = 12^6$. (b) $P(\text{no month repeated}) = \dfrac{(12)_6}{12^6} = \dfrac{385}{1728} \approx 0.22$

29. $\dfrac{\binom{8}{3}\binom{4}{1}}{\binom{12}{4}} = \dfrac{224}{495} \approx 0.45$

31. Think of the people sitting in a row of six seats. The given pair can sit in $\binom{6}{2} = 15$ possible pairs of seats, with five of these being next to each other. Hence, the probability is $\frac{5}{15} = \frac{1}{3}$.

33. $\frac{1}{9}$

35. (a) $36^{24} \approx 2.25 \times 10^{37}$ (b) winners: $35^{24} \approx 1.14 \times 10^{37}$, losers: 1.10×10^{37} (c) 0.51

37. Consider the sample space as a 60×60 square with the area of interest being the area within 5 units of the diagonal. The area outside this is 55^2, and so the probability of meeting is $\frac{575}{3600} = \frac{23}{144} \approx 0.16$.

39. (a) 1 (b) $\frac{55}{72} \approx 0.76$

41. (a) For $n \geq 1$, $k \geq 1$, consider a fixed but arbitrary state; the a_{nk} ways can be divided into those for which the fixed state is empty and those for which it has at least one particle. If the fixed state is empty, then the k particles must go into the other $n-1$ states (in $a_{n-1,k}$ ways); the fixed state will have at least one particle if we put a particle in and then distribute the remaining $k-1$ particles into the n states (in $a_{n,k-1}$ ways). Thus $a_{nk} = a_{n-1,k} + a_{n,k-1}$. Part (b) goes as follows.

$$xG(x, y) = x\left[x + x^2 + \cdots + \sum_{n=1}\sum_{k=1} a_{nk}x^n y^k\right]$$

$$\text{from Prob. } 40(c)$$

$$= x^2 + x^3 + \cdots + \sum_{n=1}\sum_{k=1} a_{nk}x^{n+1} y^k$$

$$= x^2 + x^3 + \cdots + \sum_{i=2}\sum_{k=1} a_{i-1,k}x^i y^k$$

$$\text{letting } i = n+1$$

$$= x^2 + x^3 + \cdots + \sum_{n=2}\sum_{k=1} a_{n-1,k}x^n y^k$$

$$\text{letting } n = i$$

$$= x^2 + x^3 + \cdots + \sum_{n=1}\sum_{k=1} a_{n-1,k}x^n y^k$$

since $a_{0j} = 0$ [Prob. 40(a)].

(c) By Prob. 40(a), $yG(x, y) =$ $\sum_{i=0}\sum_{j=0} a_{ij}x^i y^{j+1} =$ $\sum_{i=1}\sum_{j=0} a_{ij}x^i y^{j+1}$. Letting $i = n$ and $j + 1 = k$ gives the desired result.
(d) From Probs. 40(c), 41(b), and 41(c),

$$G(x, y) - xG(x, y) - yG(x, y)$$

$$= \left[x + x^2 + x^3 + \cdots + \sum_{n=1}\sum_{k=1} a_{nk}x^n y^k\right]$$

$$- \left[x^2 + x^3 + \sum_{n=1}\sum_{k=1} a_{n-1,k}x^n y^k\right]$$

$$- \left[\sum_{n=1}\sum_{k=1} a_{n,k-1}x^n y^k\right]$$

$$= x + \sum_{n=1}\sum_{k=1}(a_{n,k} - a_{n-1,k} - a_{n,k-1})x^n y^k$$

$$= x \qquad \text{by Prob. } 41(a)$$

(e) From Prob. 41(d), $G(x, y)(1-x-y) = x$. Dividing both sides by $1 - x - y$ gives the desired result.

Section 21.   Answers to Tutorials

21.1. a. $P(\mathbf{B}) = \frac{26}{52} = \frac{1}{2}$ **b. F** = {J, Q, K} and $P(\mathbf{F}) = \frac{3}{13}$ **c.** No, because only the rank of the cards is of interest. **d.** $\mathbf{S}_5$, $\mathbf{S}_7$

21.2. a. $P(\mathbf{A} \cap \mathbf{B}) = \frac{1}{2} \cdot \frac{2}{3} = \frac{1}{3}$ **b.** To find $P(\mathbf{A} \cap \mathbf{B})$, you need either, both of $P(\mathbf{B})$ and $P(\mathbf{A} \mid \mathbf{B})$, or both of $P(\mathbf{A})$ and $P(\mathbf{B} \mid \mathbf{A})$. **c.** $P(\mathbf{A} \cap \mathbf{B}) = \frac{1}{3}$, and so $P(\mathbf{A}) = \frac{1}{3}/\frac{2}{5} = \frac{5}{6}$.

21.3. a. G = {IG, IIG} and $P(\mathbf{G}) = P(\text{IG}) + P(\text{IIG}) = \frac{3}{14} + \frac{5}{18} = \frac{31}{63}$ **b.** $P(\text{IIR}) =$

$P(\mathbf{II} \cap \mathbf{R}) = P(\mathbf{II}) \cdot P(\mathbf{R} \mid \mathbf{II}) = \frac{1}{2} \cdot \frac{4}{9} = \frac{4}{18}$, $P(\text{IIG}) = P(\mathbf{II} \cap \mathbf{G}) = P(\mathbf{II}) \cdot P(\mathbf{G} \mid \mathbf{II}) = \frac{1}{2} \cdot \frac{5}{9} = \frac{5}{18}$. **c.** Yes, since $\frac{4}{18} + \frac{5}{18} = \frac{1}{2}$.

21.4. a. $P(\mathbf{II} \mid \mathbf{R}) = P(\text{IIR})/P(\mathbf{R}) = \frac{4}{18}/\frac{32}{63} = \frac{7}{16}$ **b.** $P(\mathbf{I} \mid \mathbf{G}) = \frac{3}{14}/\frac{31}{63} = \frac{27}{62}$, $P(\mathbf{II} \mid \mathbf{G}) = \frac{5}{18}/\frac{31}{63} = \frac{35}{62}$ **c.** The branches must depict all that can happen, and the probability of all the possible events must be 1.

Section 21.   Answers to Selected Problems

1. $(a)\ \frac{12}{21}\ (b)\ \frac{11}{21}\ (c)\ \frac{10}{21}$

3. $P(R1 \cap R2) = \frac{10}{22} \cdot \frac{9}{21},\ P(R1 \cap G2) = \frac{10}{22} \cdot \frac{12}{21},$
$P(G1 \cap R2) = \frac{12}{22} \cdot \frac{10}{21},\ P(G1 \cap G2) = \frac{12}{22} \cdot \frac{11}{21}$

5. $(a)\ \frac{1}{3}\ (b)\ \frac{13}{33}\ (c)\ \frac{8}{33}$

7. $(a)\ \frac{8}{23}\ (b)\ \frac{7}{23}\ (c)\ \frac{8}{23}$

9.

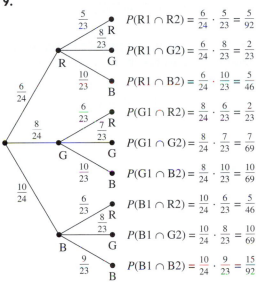

$$P(R1 \cap R2) = \frac{6}{24} \cdot \frac{5}{23} = \frac{5}{92}$$
$$P(R1 \cap G2) = \frac{6}{24} \cdot \frac{8}{23} = \frac{2}{23}$$
$$P(R1 \cap B2) = \frac{6}{24} \cdot \frac{10}{23} = \frac{5}{46}$$
$$P(G1 \cap R2) = \frac{8}{24} \cdot \frac{6}{23} = \frac{2}{23}$$
$$P(G1 \cap G2) = \frac{8}{24} \cdot \frac{7}{23} = \frac{7}{69}$$
$$P(G1 \cap B2) = \frac{8}{24} \cdot \frac{10}{23} = \frac{10}{69}$$
$$P(B1 \cap R2) = \frac{10}{24} \cdot \frac{6}{23} = \frac{5}{46}$$
$$P(B1 \cap G2) = \frac{10}{24} \cdot \frac{8}{23} = \frac{10}{69}$$
$$P(B1 \cap B2) = \frac{10}{24} \cdot \frac{9}{23} = \frac{15}{92}$$

11. $\frac{1}{3}$

13. $(a)\ \frac{1}{7}\ (b)\ \frac{3}{5}$

15. $(a)\ \frac{25}{102}\ (b)\ \frac{4}{17}\ (c)\ \frac{1}{17}$

17. $(a)\ \frac{22}{425}\ (b)\ \frac{1}{425}\ (c)\ \frac{2}{17}$

19. $(a)\ \frac{1}{12}\ (b)\ \frac{11}{12}$

21. $\frac{58}{125}$

23. The probability is really the same as the probability of choosing one red ball from urn I, $m/(m + k)$.

25. $(a)\ P(R2) = P(R1) = \frac{10}{22}\ (b)\ P(G2) = P(G1) = \frac{12}{22}$

27.

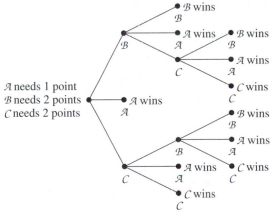

29. 0.15

Section 22.   Answers to Tutorials

22.1. a. The probability is $\frac{1}{4}$. **b.** $P(R1 \cap W2) = \frac{5}{12} \cdot \frac{3}{11} = \frac{15}{132}$ and $P(R1 \cap W2) = \frac{5}{12} \cdot \frac{3}{12} = \frac{5}{48}$

22.2. a. $P(F \mid E_2) = P(F) = \frac{1}{6}$ **b.** $P(F \mid E_1) = \frac{1}{5} \neq \frac{1}{6} = P(F)$ **c.** Since $P(F \cap G) = \frac{1}{12} = \frac{1}{6} \cdot \frac{1}{2} = P(F) \cdot P(G)$, **F** and **G** are independent.

22.3. The probability is $\frac{1}{2} \cdot \frac{1}{2} \cdot \frac{1}{2} = \frac{1}{8}$.

Section 22.   Answers to Selected Problems

1. $\frac{1}{2}$

3. $\frac{1}{4}$

5. Yes

7. The partial tree is

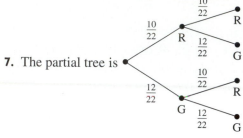

9. $P(R1) = P(R2) = P(R3) = \frac{5}{12}$

11. $\frac{1}{180}$

13. $P(2) = P(12) = \frac{1}{36}$, $P(3) = P(11) = \frac{2}{36}$, $P(4) = P(10) = \frac{3}{36}$, $P(5) = P(9) = \frac{4}{36}$, $P(6) = P(8) = \frac{5}{36}$, $P(7) = \frac{6}{36}$

15. $\frac{3}{4}$

17.

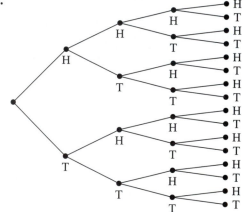

(*continuation of 17*)
Each edge has probability $\frac{1}{2}$, and the probability of each outcome is $\frac{1}{16}$.

19. No. If **A** and **B** are mutually exclusive, then $P(\mathbf{A} \cap \mathbf{B}) = 0$. Now $P(\mathbf{A}) > 0$ and $P(\mathbf{B}) > 0$ imply that $P(\mathbf{A}) \cdot P(\mathbf{B}) > 0$. Therefore, $P(\mathbf{A} \cap \mathbf{B}) \neq P(\mathbf{A}) \cdot P(\mathbf{B})$.

21. (*a*) There are two ways for all five to match and $2 \cdot \binom{5}{4}$ ways for exactly four to match.

The probability that at least four match is $\frac{12}{32} = \frac{3}{8}$. (*b*) By the Pigeonhole Principle, at least three must match, and so the probability is 1.

23. (*a*) 4 (*b*) $4(0.45)(0.55)^4 = 0.1647$

25. $\binom{6}{3}(0.45)^3(0.55)^4 = 0.1668$

27. $P(\overline{\mathbf{A}} \cap \overline{\mathbf{B}}) = 0.15 = 0.5 \times 0.3$

29. $\frac{15}{128}$

Section 23. Answers to Tutorials

23.1. **a.** The event **B** is that red was chosen.
b. $\mathbf{B} = (\mathbf{H}_1 \cap \mathbf{B}) \cup (\mathbf{H}_2 \cap \mathbf{B})$; $P(\mathbf{B}) = P(\mathbf{H}_1 \cap \mathbf{B}) + P(\mathbf{H}_2 \cap \mathbf{B})$; $P(\mathbf{H}_1 \cap \mathbf{B}) = P(\mathbf{H}_1) \cdot P(\mathbf{B} \mid \mathbf{H}_1) = P(\mathbf{B}) \cdot P(\mathbf{H}_1 \mid \mathbf{B})$
c. $P(\mathbf{H}_1 \mid \mathbf{B}) = \dfrac{P(\mathbf{H}_1)P(\mathbf{B} \mid \mathbf{H}_1)}{P(\mathbf{B})} = \dfrac{\frac{1}{2} \cdot \frac{4}{7}}{\frac{32}{63}} = \dfrac{\frac{4}{14}}{\frac{32}{63}} = \dfrac{9}{16}$

23.2B. The rows in each column represent all the possible outcomes; hence the sum of the probabilities must be 1.

Section 23.   Answers to Selected Problems

5. (a) $\frac{1}{8}$ (b) 0

7. (a) $\mathbf{S} = \{(E, F): E$ and F are either red, blue, or white$\}$ (b) $P(\mathbf{H_1}) = \frac{7}{25}$, $P(\mathbf{H_2}) = \frac{10}{25}$, $P(\mathbf{H_3}) = \frac{8}{25}$

9. Blue

11. $P(\mathbf{H_3} \mid \overline{\mathbf{B}}) = \frac{16}{67}$

13. (a) $\mathbf{S} = \{(RR, R), (RR, B), (BB, R), (BB, B), (RB, R), (RB, B)\}$ (b) $P(\mathbf{H_1}) = P(RR) = \frac{3}{10}$; $P(\mathbf{H_2}) = P(BB) = \frac{1}{10}$; $P(\mathbf{H_3}) = P(RB) = \frac{6}{10}$

15. $P(\mathbf{H_2} \mid \mathbf{B}) = \frac{1}{4}$

17.

Alternate hypotheses	Prior probabilities	Conditional probabilities	Product $P(\mathbf{H}_i)P(\mathbf{B} \mid \mathbf{H}_i)$	Quotient $P(\mathbf{H}_i)P(\mathbf{B} \mid \mathbf{H}_i)/\sum$
$\mathbf{A_1}$	$\frac{1}{2}$	$\frac{1}{10}$	$\frac{1}{20}$	$\frac{4}{11}$
$\mathbf{A_2}$	$\frac{1}{4}$	$\frac{1}{10}$	$\frac{1}{40}$	$\frac{2}{11}$
$\mathbf{A_3}$	$\frac{1}{8}$	$\frac{2}{10}$	$\frac{2}{80}$	$\frac{2}{11}$
$\mathbf{A_4}$	$\frac{1}{8}$	$\frac{3}{10}$	$\frac{3}{80}$	$\frac{3}{11}$
			$\sum = \frac{11}{80}$	

19. (b) $\frac{17}{72}$ (c) $\frac{4}{17}$

21. $\frac{1}{4}$

23. $P(\mathbf{H_1} \mid \mathbf{B}) = 0.42 > 0.24 = P(\mathbf{H_4} \mid \mathbf{B})$

25. $\frac{28}{58} \approx 0.48$

27. $P(\text{senior} \mid \text{A}) = \frac{1}{2}$. Before.

29. (a) $P(\overline{\mathbf{D}} \mid \text{positive}) = 0.836$
(b) $P(\mathbf{D} \mid \text{negative}) = 0.0003$

Section 24.   Answers to Tutorials

24.1A.

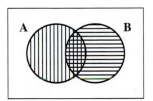

a. Since $\mathbf{A} = (\boxplus \cup \boxplus)$ and $\mathbf{B} = (\boxplus \cup \boxplus)$, $\mathbf{A} \cup \mathbf{B} = (\boxplus \cup \boxplus) \cup (\boxplus \cup \boxplus) = (\boxplus \cup \boxplus \cup \boxplus)$. Since $\mathbf{B} \cap \overline{\mathbf{A}} = \boxplus$, $\mathbf{A} \cup (\mathbf{B} \cap \overline{\mathbf{A}}) = ((\boxplus \cup \boxplus) \cup \boxplus) = \mathbf{A} \cup \mathbf{B}$.
b. Now $\mathbf{B} \cap \mathbf{A} = \boxplus$. But $\mathbf{B} = (\boxplus \cup \boxplus)$, and so $\mathbf{B} = (\mathbf{B} \cap \mathbf{A}) \cup (\mathbf{B} \cap \overline{\mathbf{A}})$.

24.1B. **a.** Since $\mathbf{A} \cap \mathbf{B} \subseteq \mathbf{A}$, by Theorem 24.1F, $P(\mathbf{A} \cap \mathbf{B}) \leq P(\mathbf{A})$. **b.** Since $\mathbf{A} \subseteq \mathbf{A} \cup \mathbf{B}$, by Theorem 24.1F, $P(\mathbf{A}) \leq P(\mathbf{A} \cup \mathbf{B})$.
c. By Theorem 24.1D, $P(\mathbf{A} \cup \mathbf{B}) = P(\mathbf{A}) + P(\mathbf{B}) - P(\mathbf{A} \cap \mathbf{B})$. By Axiom I, $0 \leq P(\mathbf{A} \cap \mathbf{B})$, and so $P(\mathbf{A} \cup \mathbf{B}) \leq P(\mathbf{A}) + P(\mathbf{B})$.

24.2. The fact that $\mathbf{A} \cap \mathbf{B}$ is empty is only used to show that $(\mathbf{A} \cap \mathbf{F}) \cap (\mathbf{B} \cap \mathbf{F}) = \varnothing$. But $(\mathbf{A} \cap \mathbf{F}) \cap (\mathbf{B} \cap \mathbf{F}) = \mathbf{A} \cap \mathbf{B} \cap \mathbf{F}$. So we only need the hypothesis that $\mathbf{A} \cap \mathbf{B} \cap \mathbf{F} = \varnothing$.

24.3. **a.** Now $\mathbf{A} = (\mathbf{A} \cap \mathbf{B}) \cup (\mathbf{A} \cap \overline{\mathbf{B}})$ and by Axiom III, $P(\mathbf{A}) = P(\mathbf{A} \cap \mathbf{B}) + P(\mathbf{A} \cap \overline{\mathbf{B}}) - P((\mathbf{A} \cap \mathbf{B}) \cap (\mathbf{A} \cap \overline{\mathbf{B}}))$. But $(\mathbf{A} \cap \mathbf{B}) \cap (\mathbf{A} \cap \overline{\mathbf{B}}) = \varnothing$. Hence, $P((\mathbf{A} \cap \mathbf{B}) \cap (\mathbf{A} \cap \overline{\mathbf{B}})) = 0$, and so $P(\mathbf{A}) = P(\mathbf{A} \cap \mathbf{B}) + P(\mathbf{A} \cap \overline{\mathbf{B}})$ or $P(\mathbf{A} \cap \overline{\mathbf{B}}) = P(\mathbf{A}) - P(\mathbf{A} \cap \mathbf{B})$. **b.** If $\mathbf{A}$ and $\mathbf{B}$ are independent, then $P(\mathbf{A} \cap \mathbf{B}) = P(\mathbf{A}) \cdot P(\mathbf{B})$. Now $P(\overline{\mathbf{B}}) = 1 - P(\mathbf{B})$ by Theorem 24.1A, and so $P(\mathbf{A}) \cdot P(\overline{\mathbf{B}}) = P(\mathbf{A})(1 - P(\mathbf{B})) = P(\mathbf{A}) - P(\mathbf{A}) \cdot P(\mathbf{B}) = P(\mathbf{A}) - P(\mathbf{A} \cap \mathbf{B})$. By part a, $P(\mathbf{A} \cap \overline{\mathbf{B}}) = P(\mathbf{A}) - P(\mathbf{A} \cap \mathbf{B}) = P(\mathbf{A}) \cdot P(\overline{\mathbf{B}})$. Therefore, $\mathbf{A}$ and $\overline{\mathbf{B}}$ are independent.

Section 24. Answers to Selected Problems

1. If **A** is the event that at least one coin shows heads, then $\overline{\mathbf{A}}$ is the event that no coin shows heads. Hence, $P(\mathbf{A}) = 1 - P(\overline{\mathbf{A}}) = 1 - \frac{1}{16} = \frac{15}{16}$.

3. Let **A** be the event that (x, y) lies below the line $y = x$. Hence, $P(\mathbf{A}) = \frac{1}{2}$ and $0 \le \frac{1}{2} \le 1$.

5. By Theorem 24.1A, $1 = P(\mathbf{A}) + P(\overline{\mathbf{A}}) < P(\mathbf{A}) + P(\mathbf{A})$. Hence, $1 < 2P(\mathbf{A})$ or $P(\mathbf{A}) > \frac{1}{2}$.

7. $P(\overline{\mathbf{A} \cup \mathbf{B}}) = 1 - P(\mathbf{A} \cup \mathbf{B})$

$$\text{(by Theorem 24.1A)}$$

$$= 1 - (P(\mathbf{A}) + P(\mathbf{B}))$$

$$\text{(since } \mathbf{A} \cap \mathbf{B} = \varnothing)$$

$$= (1 - P(\mathbf{A})) - P(\mathbf{B})$$

$$= P(\overline{\mathbf{A}}) - P(\mathbf{B})$$

$$\text{(by Theorem 24.1A)}$$

9. Choose **S**, **A**, **B**, and **C** as in the illustration preceding Theorem 24.1A. Then $\mathbf{A} \cup \mathbf{B} \cup \mathbf{C} = \{2, 3, 4, 5, 6\}$, $\mathbf{A} \cap \mathbf{B} \cap \mathbf{C} = \varnothing$, and $P(\mathbf{A} \cup \mathbf{B} \cup \mathbf{C}) = \frac{5}{6} \ne \frac{4}{3} = \frac{1}{2} + \frac{1}{2} + \frac{1}{3} = P(\mathbf{A}) + P(\mathbf{B}) + P(\mathbf{C})$.

11. (a) $P(\mathbf{A}_1 \cap \mathbf{A}_3)$ and $P(\mathbf{A}_2 \cap \mathbf{A}_3)$ (b) This follows from part (a).

13. $P(\mathbf{A} \cup \mathbf{B} \cup \mathbf{C}) = \frac{1}{4} + \frac{5}{9} + \frac{1}{3} - \frac{5}{36} - \frac{3}{36} - \frac{8}{36} + \frac{2}{36} = \frac{3}{4}$

15. (a) Since **F** is the union of the disjoint sets $\mathbf{F} \cap \mathbf{A}$ and $\mathbf{F} \cap \overline{\mathbf{A}}$, $P(\mathbf{F}) = P(\mathbf{F} \cap \mathbf{A}) + P(\mathbf{F} \cap \overline{\mathbf{A}})$. So $P(\mathbf{F} \cap \overline{\mathbf{A}}) = P(\mathbf{F}) - P(\mathbf{F} \cap \mathbf{A})$. The desired result follows by dividing by $P(\mathbf{F})$. (b) Since **B** is the disjoint union of $\overline{\mathbf{A}} \cap \mathbf{B}$ and $\mathbf{A} \cap \mathbf{B}$, $P(\mathbf{B} \mid \mathbf{F}) = P(\mathbf{A} \cap \mathbf{B} \mid \mathbf{F}) + P(\overline{\mathbf{A}} \cap \mathbf{B} \mid \mathbf{F})$ or $P(\overline{\mathbf{A}} \cap \mathbf{B} \mid \mathbf{F}) = P(\mathbf{B} \mid \mathbf{F}) + P(\mathbf{A} \cap \mathbf{B} \mid \mathbf{F})$. Substituting, $P(\mathbf{A} \cup \mathbf{B} \mid \mathbf{F}) = P(\mathbf{A} \cup (\overline{\mathbf{A}} \cap \mathbf{B}) \mid \mathbf{F}) = P(\mathbf{A} \mid \mathbf{F}) + P(\overline{\mathbf{A}} \cap \mathbf{B} \mid \mathbf{F})$ which is the desired result.

(c) If $\mathbf{A} \subseteq \mathbf{B}$, then $\mathbf{A} \cap \mathbf{F} \subseteq \mathbf{B} \cap \mathbf{F}$. Hence, $P(\mathbf{A} \cap \mathbf{F}) \le P(\mathbf{B} \cap \mathbf{F})$. Divide both sides by $P(\mathbf{F})$ to get the desired result.

17. No, because $\mathbf{E} \cap \mathbf{F} = \varnothing$, and so $P(\mathbf{E} \cap \mathbf{F}) = 0 \ne \frac{4}{10} \cdot \frac{3}{10} = P(\mathbf{E}) \cdot P(\mathbf{F})$.

19. Let $\mathbf{E} = \mathbf{A} \cap \mathbf{B}$. Then

$$P(\mathbf{A} \cap \mathbf{B} \cap \mathbf{C}) = P(\mathbf{E} \cap \mathbf{C})$$

$$= P(\mathbf{E}) \cdot P(\mathbf{C} \mid \mathbf{E})$$

$$\text{by (1) in par. 24.3}$$

$$= P(\mathbf{A} \cap \mathbf{B}) \cdot P(\mathbf{C} \mid (\mathbf{A} \cap \mathbf{B}))$$

$$= P(\mathbf{A}) \cdot P(\mathbf{B} \mid \mathbf{A}) \cdot P(\mathbf{C} \mid (\mathbf{A} \cap \mathbf{B}))$$

$$\text{by (1) in par. 24.3.}$$

21. (a) $\frac{1}{3}$ (b) $\frac{1}{2}$ (c) $\frac{1}{2}$

23. The probability of one king is

$$\frac{\binom{4}{1}\binom{48}{4}}{\binom{52}{5}}$$

and the probability of more red cards than black is $\frac{1}{2}$. To compute the probability of one king and more red than black cards, find the number of hands with k red cards and exactly one king for $k = 3, 4, 5$. For example, the number of hands with four red cards and exactly one king is

$$\binom{2}{1}\binom{24}{4} + \binom{24}{1}\binom{2}{1}\binom{24}{3}$$

where in each term, the black cards are chosen first.

25. $\frac{11}{50}$

27. (c) $\dfrac{P(\mathbf{B} \mid \mathbf{A}_i)}{3P(\mathbf{B})}$

Section 25.   Answers to Tutorials

25.1. b. $P(4) = \frac{3}{11}$

25.2. b. $P(1 < X < 7) = \frac{1}{2}$

25.3. a. $E(X) = \frac{252}{36} = 7$. **b.** $E(X) = \frac{7}{2}$. (*Note:* Each distribution is symmetric.)

Section 25.   Answers to Selected Problems

1. (*a*) 0, 1, 2, 3, 4, 5, 6, 7, 8 (*c*) $\frac{83}{20}$

3. (*a*) $E(X) = \sum \frac{x_i}{n} = \frac{1}{n} \sum x_i = \frac{100}{n} = \mu$

(*b*) $\mathrm{Var}(X) = \sum \frac{(x_i - \mu)^2}{n} =$

$\frac{1}{n} \sum (x_i - \mu)^2 = \frac{1000}{n}$

5. (*a*) $W = X + Y : 0, 1, 2, 3, 4, 5$ (*b*) $Z = X \cdot Y :$
0, 1, 2, 3, 4, 6

7. (*a*) $E(X) = \frac{3}{2}$ and $\mathrm{Var}(X) = \frac{5}{2}$ (*b*) $E(Y) =$
$\frac{7}{8}$ and $\mathrm{Var}(Y) = \frac{71}{64}$

9. (*a*) $Y : 2, 6, 10, 11, 15$ (*b*) $P(Y = 2) = \frac{5}{14}$,
$P(Y = 15) = \frac{1}{14}$

11. (*a*) $X : 0, 1, 2$ (*b*) $P(X = 0) = \frac{12}{22}$, $P(X = 1) =$
$\frac{9}{22}$, $P(X = 2) = \frac{1}{22}$ (*c*) $E(X) = \frac{1}{2}$

13. (*a*) $E(X) = 0.3$ (*b*) $\mathrm{Var}(X) = 1.01$,
$\sigma = 1.005$

15. (*a*) $E(Y) = \frac{7}{6}$ (*b*) $\mathrm{Var}(Y) = \frac{41}{36}$, $\sigma \approx 1.067$

17. (*a*) $X : 0, 1, 2, 3$ (*b*) $P(X = 0) = \frac{91}{650}$,
$P(X = 1) = \frac{273}{650}$, $P(X = 2) = \frac{231}{650}$,
$P(X = 3) = \frac{55}{650}$ (*c*) $E(X) = \frac{18}{13}$, $\mathrm{Var}(X) =$
$\frac{2898}{4225} \approx 0.6859$, $\sigma \approx 0.8282$

19. (*a*) $P(X = 5) = \frac{1}{30}$, $P(X = 6) = \frac{9}{30}$,
$P(X = 7) = \frac{15}{30}$, $P(X = 8) = \frac{5}{30}$
(*b*) $E(X) = \frac{34}{5}$, $\mathrm{Var}(X) = \frac{14}{25}$, $\sigma \approx 0.7483$

21. (*a*) $P(X = 2) = \frac{3}{8}$, $P(X = 6) = \frac{3}{8}$,
$P(X = 11) = \frac{1}{8}$, $P(X = 15) = \frac{1}{8}$ (*b*) $E(X) =$
$\frac{25}{4}$, $Var(X) = \frac{307}{16} = 19.1875$, $\sigma \approx 4.380$

23. (*a*) $P(X = -1000) = \frac{40}{50}$, $P(X = 0) = \frac{9}{50}$,
$P(X = 9000) = \frac{1}{50}$ (*b*) $E(X) = -\$620$
(*c*) The guarantee

Section 26.   Answers to Tutorials

26.1.

k	0	1	2	3	4
$f(k)$	0.01	0.10	0.30	0.40	0.20

26.2. $\mu = 4 \cdot \frac{2}{3^4} + 2 \cdot 6 \cdot \frac{2^2}{3^4} + 3 \cdot 4 \cdot \frac{2^3}{3^4} + 4 \cdot \frac{2^4}{3^4} =$
$4 \cdot \frac{2}{3} \left(\frac{1}{3^3} + 3 \cdot \frac{2}{3^3} + 3 \cdot \frac{2^2}{3^3} + \frac{2^3}{3^3} \right) = \frac{8}{3}$

26.3. a. 0.6156 **b.** 0.9651 **c.** 0.9972 **d.** 0.4382

Section 26.   Answers to Selected Problems

1. (*a*) 0.3292, 0.0165 (*b*) 0.2188

3. (*a*) 0.0024 (*b*) 0.0024

5. (*a*) 0.0193 (*b*) 0.3142

7. Recall that $\binom{n}{k} = \binom{n}{n-k}$. So

$b(k; n, p)$

$$= \binom{n}{k} q^{n-k} p^k$$

$$= \binom{n}{k}(1-p)^{n-k}(1-(1-p))^k$$

$$= \binom{n}{n-k}(1-(1-p))^{n-(n-k)}(1-p)^{n-k}$$

$$= b(n-k; n, 1-p).$$

9. (a) $(0.95)^{15} = 0.4633$ (b) $0.3658, 0.1348$
(c) Now $b(8; 20, .65) = b(12; 20, .35) = 0.0136$. Using the formula from Prob. 8, $b(9; 20, .65) = 0.0337, b(10; 20, .65) = 0.0688, b(11; 20, .65) = 0.1162, b(12; 20, .65) = 0.1619$. The correct values are: $b(9; 20, .65) = 0.0336, b(10; 20, .65) = 0.0686, b(11; 20, .65) = 0.1158, b(12; 20, .65) = 0.1614$.

11. $1 - b(0; 5, 0.01) = 1 - (0.99)^5 = 0.0490$

13. (a) 0.0686 (b) 0.9468 (c) 0.3930

15. 0.3025

17. 0.1707

19. $\mu = 5, \sigma^2 = \frac{25}{6}$

21. (a) $\frac{1}{4}$ (b) $1/2^5 = 0.03125$ (c) $\mu = np = 90(0.03125) \approx 3$

23. (a) $\frac{3}{32}$ and $\frac{57}{64}$ (b) 3

25. (a) $\dfrac{n-k}{k+1} \cdot \dfrac{p}{q}$ (b) $\frac{3}{2}$ (c) $\frac{5}{2}$

27. $\frac{1}{4}$

29. $\text{Var}(X) = \frac{648}{81} - \left(\frac{8}{3}\right)^2 = \frac{8}{9}$

31. $\frac{8}{81}$

33. $\binom{n-1}{r-1} \cdot \dfrac{2^{n-r}}{3^n}$

Section 27. Answers to Tutorials

27.2. a. The mean is 27.4°, the median is 30°, and the mode is 30°. **b.** 21.1°

27.3. a. 53 **b.** 68

27.4. $s^2 = \frac{1}{6}(1621) = 270.17$

Section 27. Answers to Selected Problems

1. (a) 15.67, 15, every number (b) 226.5, 223.5, 223 (c) 70.25, 71, 71, and 72

3. (a) 74.17 (b) 240.28, 15.5

5. (b) $Q_1 = 30, Q_3 = 40$ (c) 2 (d) Yes, 30

7. (a) The mean is 34 and the 50th percentile is 30. (b) 70th

9. (a) $Q_3 = 71, Q_1 = 53$ (b) 18 (c) $\frac{14}{30}$

11. The interquartile range generally contains fewer than 68% of the population.

17. (145.9, 188.5)

19. Tallest: 141.6 cm, shortest: 103.9 cm

23. No, $0.0068 > 0.005$

Section 28. Answers to Tutorials

28.1.

$$\begin{bmatrix} 0 & 1 & 1 & 1 & 0 & 1 \\ 1 & 0 & 1 & 1 & 0 & 0 \\ 1 & 1 & 0 & 1 & 1 & 1 \\ 1 & 1 & 1 & 0 & 0 & 0 \\ 0 & 0 & 1 & 0 & 0 & 0 \\ 1 & 0 & 1 & 0 & 0 & 0 \end{bmatrix}$$

One such word is *facetious*. Note that in *facetiously*, even the "vowel" *y* is in proper order.

28.4. a. $2^{3^2} = 2^9 = 512$ **b.** $2^6 = 64$

c. $\begin{bmatrix} 0 & 0 & 0 \\ 0 & 0 & 0 \\ 0 & 0 & 0 \end{bmatrix}, \begin{bmatrix} 0 & 0 & 1 \\ 0 & 0 & 0 \\ 1 & 0 & 0 \end{bmatrix}, \begin{bmatrix} 0 & 1 & 1 \\ 1 & 0 & 1 \\ 1 & 1 & 0 \end{bmatrix}$

28.2. R $= \{(a, e), (a, i), (a, o), (a, u), (e, i), (e, o),$
$(e, u), (i, o), (i, u), (o, u)\};$

$$\begin{bmatrix} 0 & 1 & 1 & 1 & 1 \\ 0 & 0 & 1 & 1 & 1 \\ 0 & 0 & 0 & 1 & 1 \\ 0 & 0 & 0 & 0 & 1 \\ 0 & 0 & 0 & 0 & 0 \end{bmatrix}.$$

Section 28. Answers to Selected Problems

1. R $= \{(1, 1), (1, 3), (1, 6), (1, 9), (1, 12), (3, 3),$
$(3, 6), (3, 9), (3, 12), (6, 6), (6, 12), (9, 9),$
$(12, 12)\},$

$$M(\mathbf{R}) = \begin{bmatrix} 1 & 1 & 1 & 1 & 1 \\ 0 & 1 & 1 & 1 & 1 \\ 0 & 0 & 1 & 0 & 1 \\ 0 & 0 & 0 & 1 & 0 \\ 0 & 0 & 0 & 0 & 1 \end{bmatrix}, \quad \mathbf{R} \text{ is reflexive.}$$

3. 0, 0, 0, 0, 0, 0, 0, 0, 1, 1, 1, 1, 2, 2, 3, 4

5. $n = 3, 3 \cdot 2^6; n = 4, 6 \cdot 2^{12}; n = 5, 10 \cdot 2^{20}$

7. (a) 0 (b) $\dfrac{n!}{((n/2)!)^2} \cdot 2^{n(n-1)}$

9. 2^{3n-2}

11. $2^{n(n+1)/2} = 2^{(n^2+n)/2}$

13. At most 1. (The domain may not be all of **S**.)

15. $1 + 3^3 + 3^3 + 1 = 56$

17. (a) n^n (b) n^n, just interchange zeroes and ones.

19. No

21. R $= \{(2, 3), (2, 5), (3, 2), (3, 4), (3, 5), (3, 10),$
$(4, 3), (4, 5), (5, 2), (5, 3), (5, 4), (5, 6),$
$(6, 5), (10, 3)\},$
R is irreflexive and symmetric.

$$M(\mathbf{R}) = \begin{bmatrix} 0 & 1 & 0 & 1 & 0 & 0 \\ 1 & 0 & 1 & 1 & 0 & 1 \\ 0 & 1 & 0 & 1 & 0 & 0 \\ 1 & 1 & 1 & 0 & 1 & 0 \\ 0 & 0 & 0 & 1 & 0 & 0 \\ 0 & 1 & 0 & 0 & 0 & 0 \end{bmatrix}$$

23. (a) Since $a_{ij} = 1$ if and only if $a_{ji} = 1$,
$\sum_{j=1}^{n} a_{ij} = \sum_{j=1}^{n} a_{ji}$ for $1 \leq i \leq n$.

25. Write 1024 as "one thousand twenty-four," and so the first pair is (1024, 21). Write 21 as "twenty-one" and so the remaining pairs are (21, 9) and (9, 4).

Section 29. Answers to Tutorials

29.2. b. $(0, 0)$, $(-1, -\frac{3}{2})$, $(-2, -3)$

29.4. a. $\begin{bmatrix} 1 & 4 \\ 2 & \frac{1}{2} \end{bmatrix} \begin{bmatrix} 3 & 0 \\ \frac{1}{2} & -2 \end{bmatrix} = \begin{bmatrix} 5 & -8 \\ \frac{25}{4} & -1 \end{bmatrix}$

Section 29. Answers to Selected Problems

1. $A + B = \begin{bmatrix} 3 & 5 \\ -1 & 1 \end{bmatrix}$, $A + C = \begin{bmatrix} 0 & 2 \\ 1 & -1 \end{bmatrix}$,

$B + C = \begin{bmatrix} 1 & 3 \\ 2 & 0 \end{bmatrix}$

3. $5 \cdot A - 3 \cdot B = \begin{bmatrix} -1 & 1 \\ -5 & -3 \end{bmatrix}$, $2 \cdot A + 4 \cdot B =$

$\begin{bmatrix} 10 & 16 \\ -2 & 4 \end{bmatrix}$, and $3 \cdot C - A = \begin{bmatrix} -4 & -2 \\ 7 & -3 \end{bmatrix}$

5. $A \cdot B = \begin{bmatrix} 2 & 5 \\ -2 & -3 \end{bmatrix}$, $B \cdot A = \begin{bmatrix} -1 & 4 \\ -1 & 0 \end{bmatrix}$

7. (a) $\begin{bmatrix} 1 & 3 \\ 2 & 0 \end{bmatrix}$ (b) $\begin{bmatrix} 2 & 5 \\ 1 & 0 \end{bmatrix}$ (c) $\begin{bmatrix} 3 & 5 \\ -1 & 1 \end{bmatrix}$

(d) $\begin{bmatrix} 2 & 5 \\ 1 & 0 \end{bmatrix}$ (e) Equal

9. (a) B (b) B

11. $A(BC) = \begin{bmatrix} 1 & 2 \\ -1 & 0 \end{bmatrix} \begin{bmatrix} 4 & -3 \\ 2 & -1 \end{bmatrix} = \begin{bmatrix} 8 & -5 \\ -4 & 3 \end{bmatrix}$

and $(AB)C = \begin{bmatrix} 2 & 5 \\ -2 & -3 \end{bmatrix} \begin{bmatrix} -1 & 0 \\ 2 & -1 \end{bmatrix} =$

$\begin{bmatrix} 8 & -5 \\ -4 & 3 \end{bmatrix}$

13. Consider $c_{ij} = \sum_{k=1}^{n} a_{ik} b_{kj}$ for $i > j$.
If $k < i$, then $a_{ik} = 0$ and if $k \geq i$, then
$b_{kj} = 0$.

15. For $n = 2$, $A^2 = A \cdot A$. Let $k > 2$ and assume that $A^k = A \cdot A^{k-1}$. So $A^k \cdot A = (A \cdot A^{k-1}) \cdot A$. By associativity, $(A \cdot A^{k-1}) \cdot A = A \cdot (A^{k-1} \cdot A)$ which is $A \cdot A^k$ by definition. But $A^{k+1} = A^k \cdot A$ by definition; hence, $A^{k+1} = A \cdot A^k$.

17. $A = B = $

	0	1	2	3	4
0	1	1	1	1	1
1	1	2	3	4	5
2	1	3	6	10	15
3	1	4	10	20	35
4	1	5	15	35	70

19. $\begin{bmatrix} 0 & 0 \\ 0 & 1 \end{bmatrix}$ and $\begin{bmatrix} 0 & 1 \\ 1 & 0 \end{bmatrix}$

21. Since $A \cdot A = A \cdot A$, A^2 is symmetric if A is symmetric (Prob. 20). Now use induction. Assume that A^k is symmetric. Then $A^{k+1} = A^k \cdot A = A \cdot A^k$ (Prob. 15), and by Prob. 20, A^{k+1} is symmetric.

23. $\begin{bmatrix} 1 & 0 & 0 & 1 \\ 0 & 0 & 0 & 0 \\ 0 & 0 & 0 & 0 \\ 1 & 0 & 0 & 1 \end{bmatrix}$ and $\begin{bmatrix} 0 & 0 & 0 & 0 \\ 1 & 0 & 0 & 1 \\ 1 & 0 & 0 & 1 \\ 0 & 0 & 0 & 0 \end{bmatrix}$

25. (a) No (b) Yes (c) No (d) No (e) No (f) Yes (g) No (h) Yes (i) No

27. $A \cdot B = \begin{bmatrix} 1 & 0 & -2 & 3 \\ -1 & 4 & 2 & 5 \end{bmatrix} \begin{bmatrix} 2 & 1 \\ -2 & 3 \\ -3 & 0 \\ 0 & 5 \end{bmatrix} =$

$\begin{bmatrix} 8 & 16 \\ -16 & 36 \end{bmatrix}$ and $B \cdot C =$

$\begin{bmatrix} 2 & 1 \\ -2 & 3 \\ -3 & 0 \\ 0 & 5 \end{bmatrix} \begin{bmatrix} 3 & 1 & 1 \\ 0 & -2 & 3 \end{bmatrix} = \begin{bmatrix} 6 & 0 & 5 \\ -6 & -8 & 7 \\ -9 & -3 & -3 \\ 0 & -10 & 15 \end{bmatrix}$

29. $B \cdot D = \begin{bmatrix} 2 & 1 \\ -2 & 3 \\ -3 & 0 \\ 0 & 5 \end{bmatrix} \begin{bmatrix} 0 & 1 & -3 & 3 \\ 0 & 4 & -1 & 5 \end{bmatrix} =$

$\begin{bmatrix} 0 & 6 & -7 & 11 \\ 0 & 10 & 3 & 9 \\ 0 & -3 & 9 & -9 \\ 0 & 20 & -5 & 25 \end{bmatrix}$ and $D \cdot B =$

$\begin{bmatrix} 0 & 1 & -3 & 3 \\ 0 & 4 & -1 & 5 \end{bmatrix} \begin{bmatrix} 2 & 1 \\ -2 & 3 \\ -3 & 0 \\ 0 & 5 \end{bmatrix} = \begin{bmatrix} 7 & 18 \\ -5 & 37 \end{bmatrix}$

31. (a) Now $F(x_1, x_2) = (0, 0)$ since $y_1 = 0x_1 + 0x_2 = 0$ and $y_2 = 0x_1 + 0x_2 = 0$. (b) Now $F(x_1, 4) = (4, 4)$ since $y_1 = 0x_1 + x_2 = x_2$ and $y_2 = 0x_1 + x_2 = x_2$. (c) Since $y_1 = 3x_1 + x_2$ and $y_2 = 3x_1 + x_2$, $F(x_1, -3x_1 + 3) = (3x_1 + (-3x_1 + 3), 3x_1 + (-3x_1 + 3)) = (3, 3)$.

Section 30. Answers to Tutorials

30.1. a. $A \cdot O_3 = O_3$ **b.** $A \cdot J_3 = \begin{bmatrix} 2 & 2 & 2 \\ 2 & 2 & 2 \\ 1 & 1 & 1 \end{bmatrix}$

c. $A \cdot I_3 = A$ **d.** The product in part **b** since

$J_3 \cdot A = \begin{bmatrix} 2 & 2 & 1 \\ 2 & 2 & 1 \\ 2 & 2 & 1 \end{bmatrix}$.

30.2. a. $M = \begin{bmatrix} 0 & 1 & 0 & 1 \\ 0 & 0 & 0 & 1 \\ 1 & 1 & 0 & 1 \\ 0 & 0 & 0 & 0 \end{bmatrix}$

b. $M = \begin{bmatrix} 0 & 0 & 1 & 0 \\ 1 & 0 & 1 & 0 \\ 0 & 0 & 0 & 0 \\ 1 & 1 & 1 & 0 \end{bmatrix}$ **c.** Antisymmetric

30.3. a. $A \cdot A^t = \begin{bmatrix} 2 & 1 & 1 \\ 1 & 2 & 0 \\ 1 & 0 & 1 \end{bmatrix}$ **b.** $A^t \cdot A = \begin{bmatrix} 2 & 1 & 0 \\ 1 & 2 & 1 \\ 0 & 1 & 1 \end{bmatrix}$

c. No

Section 30. Answers to Selected Problems

1. (a) $M_1 = \begin{bmatrix} 0 & 0 & 0 & 1 \\ 0 & 0 & 1 & 0 \\ 0 & 1 & 0 & 0 \\ 1 & 0 & 0 & 0 \end{bmatrix}$

(b) $M_2 = \begin{bmatrix} 1 & 1 & 1 & 1 \\ 1 & 1 & 1 & 1 \\ 1 & 1 & 1 & 0 \\ 1 & 1 & 0 & 0 \end{bmatrix}$

3. (a) $M_1 = \begin{bmatrix} 1 & 1 & 1 & 1 \\ 0 & 1 & 1 & 1 \\ 0 & 0 & 1 & 1 \\ 0 & 0 & 0 & 1 \end{bmatrix}$

(b) $M_2 = \begin{bmatrix} 0 & 0 & 0 & 0 \\ 0 & 1 & 1 & 0 \\ 0 & 1 & 0 & 1 \\ 0 & 0 & 1 & 0 \end{bmatrix}$

5. (a) M_1 is reflexive and symmetric. (b) M_2 is symmetric.

7. J_4 in Prob. 2(a) is full.

9. (a) $M_1 M_2 = \begin{bmatrix} 0 & 0 & 0 & 1 \\ 0 & 0 & 1 & 0 \\ 0 & 1 & 0 & 0 \\ 1 & 0 & 0 & 0 \end{bmatrix}\begin{bmatrix} 1 & 1 & 1 & 1 \\ 1 & 1 & 1 & 1 \\ 1 & 1 & 1 & 0 \\ 1 & 1 & 0 & 0 \end{bmatrix}$

$= \begin{bmatrix} 1 & 1 & 0 & 0 \\ 1 & 1 & 1 & 0 \\ 1 & 1 & 1 & 1 \\ 1 & 1 & 1 & 1 \end{bmatrix}$

(b) $M_2^t M_1^t = \begin{bmatrix} 1 & 1 & 1 & 1 \\ 1 & 1 & 1 & 1 \\ 1 & 1 & 1 & 0 \\ 1 & 1 & 0 & 0 \end{bmatrix}\begin{bmatrix} 0 & 0 & 0 & 1 \\ 0 & 0 & 1 & 0 \\ 0 & 1 & 0 & 0 \\ 1 & 0 & 0 & 0 \end{bmatrix}$

$= \begin{bmatrix} 1 & 1 & 1 & 1 \\ 1 & 1 & 1 & 1 \\ 0 & 1 & 1 & 1 \\ 0 & 0 & 1 & 1 \end{bmatrix} = (M_1 M_2)^t$

11. (a) $M_1 M_2 = \begin{bmatrix} 1 & 1 & 1 & 1 \\ 0 & 1 & 1 & 1 \\ 0 & 0 & 1 & 1 \\ 0 & 0 & 0 & 1 \end{bmatrix}\begin{bmatrix} 0 & 0 & 0 & 0 \\ 0 & 1 & 1 & 0 \\ 0 & 1 & 0 & 1 \\ 0 & 0 & 1 & 0 \end{bmatrix}$

$= \begin{bmatrix} 0 & 2 & 2 & 1 \\ 0 & 2 & 2 & 1 \\ 0 & 1 & 1 & 1 \\ 0 & 0 & 1 & 0 \end{bmatrix}$

(b) $M_2^t M_1^t = \begin{bmatrix} 0 & 0 & 0 & 0 \\ 0 & 1 & 1 & 0 \\ 0 & 1 & 0 & 1 \\ 0 & 0 & 1 & 0 \end{bmatrix}\begin{bmatrix} 1 & 0 & 0 & 0 \\ 1 & 1 & 0 & 0 \\ 1 & 1 & 1 & 0 \\ 1 & 1 & 1 & 1 \end{bmatrix}$

$= \begin{bmatrix} 0 & 0 & 0 & 0 \\ 2 & 2 & 1 & 0 \\ 2 & 2 & 1 & 1 \\ 1 & 1 & 1 & 0 \end{bmatrix} = (M_1 M_2)^t$

13. (a) Suppose **R** is symmetric. So $(x, y) \in \mathbf{R}$ if and only if $(y, x) \in \mathbf{R}$ if and only if $(x, y) \in \mathbf{R}^{-1}$. Thus $\mathbf{R} = \mathbf{R}^{-1}$. Conversely, suppose $\mathbf{R} = \mathbf{R}^{-1}$. Now if $(x, y) \in \mathbf{R}$, then $(x, y) \in \mathbf{R}^{-1}$ or $(y, x) \in \mathbf{R}$. Hence, **R** is symmetric. (b) Suppose that **R** is antisymmetric. So, if $x \neq y$ and $(x, y) \in \mathbf{R}$, it follows that $(y, x) \notin \mathbf{R}$ or $(x, y) \notin \mathbf{R}^{-1}$. Thus the only possible elements of $\mathbf{R} \cap \mathbf{R}^{-1}$ are those for which $x = y$. Conversely, suppose that $\mathbf{R} \cap \mathbf{R}^{-1} \subseteq \mathbf{I}$. If $x \neq y$ and $(x, y) \in \mathbf{R}$, then $(x, y) \notin \mathbf{R}^{-1}$, since $\mathbf{R} \cap \mathbf{R}^{-1} \subseteq \mathbf{I}$. Hence, $(y, x) \notin \mathbf{R}$; that is, **R** is antisymmetric.

15. $\mathbf{R}^{-1} = \{(3, 1), (3, 2), (3, 6), (3, 10), (4, 0), (4, 4), (4, 5), (4, 9), (5, 3), (5, 7), (5, 8)\}$

19. If $AB = I$ where $B = \begin{bmatrix} a & b \\ c & d \end{bmatrix}$, then $a + 2c = 1$, $3a + 6c = 0$, $b + 2d = 0$, and $3b + 6d = 1$. Multiplying the first equation by 3 and subtracting it from the second gives $0 = -3$, an impossibility. So A has no inverse.

21. If $D = -(ad - bc)$, then the inverse of A is $\dfrac{1}{D}\begin{bmatrix} -d & b \\ c & -a \end{bmatrix}$.

23. $\begin{bmatrix} 2 & 3 & 0 \\ -1 & -2 & 0 \\ 0 & 0 & 1 \end{bmatrix}$

25. $\begin{bmatrix} 0 & 1 \\ 1 & 0 \end{bmatrix}$

27. $AB = \begin{bmatrix} d & e & f \\ a & b & c \\ g & h & i \end{bmatrix}$ and $BA = \begin{bmatrix} b & a & c \\ e & d & f \\ h & g & i \end{bmatrix}$.

Note that multiplication on the left by A permutes rows 1 and 2 of B and multiplication on the right by A permutes columns 1 and 2 of B.

Section 31. Answers to Tutorials

31.1. $c_{12} = 1$, $c_{13} = 1$, $c_{21} = 1$, $c_{23} = 1$, $c_{31} = 0$, $c_{32} = 0$

31.2. **a.** $g = \{(a, 1), (e, 1), (i, 0), (o, 0), (u, 1)\}$
b. $f + g = \{(a, 1), (e, 1), (i, 0), (o, 1), (u, 1)\}$

c. $f \cdot g = \{(a, 1), (e, 0), (i, 0), (o, 0), (u, 0)\}$
d. The union and intersection of $\{a, o\}$ and $\{a, e, u\}$

31.3. a. $\begin{bmatrix} - & - & 1 \\ - & - & - \\ 1 & - & 0/1 \end{bmatrix}$ **b.** 2 **c.** 16

Section 31. Answers to Selected Problems

1. Only that $1 \oplus 1 = 1$ while $1 + 1 = 10$. No Boolean sum can be greater than 1.

3. (a) $\mathbf{R}_1 \circ \mathbf{R}_3 = \{(0, 0), (0, 1), (0, 2), (0, 3), (1, 3),$
$(2, 3), (3, 3)\}$ (b) $\mathbf{R}_3 \circ \mathbf{R}_1 =$
$\{(0, 0), (1, 0), (2, 0), (3, 0), (3, 1), (3, 2), (3, 3)\}$
(c) $\mathbf{R}_2^2 = \{(0, 0), (0, 3), (1, 1), (2, 2), (3, 0), (3, 3)\}$

5.

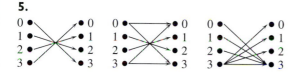

7.

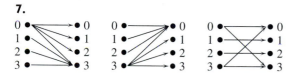

9. (a) Since $i \leq i$ for each $i \in S$, $\mathbf{R}$ is reflexive.

(b) $M = \begin{bmatrix} 1 & 1 & 1 & 1 \\ 0 & 1 & 1 & 1 \\ 0 & 0 & 1 & 1 \\ 0 & 0 & 0 & 1 \end{bmatrix} \leq \begin{bmatrix} 1 & 1 & 1 & 1 \\ 0 & 1 & 1 & 1 \\ 0 & 0 & 1 & 1 \\ 0 & 0 & 0 & 1 \end{bmatrix}$

$= M^2$

(c) $\mathbf{R} = \mathbf{R}^2 = \{(0, 0), (0, 1), (0, 2), (0, 3),$
$(1, 1), (1, 2), (1, 3), (2, 2), (2, 3), (3, 3)\}$

11. $\mathbf{R} = \{(1, 1), (1, n), (2, 2), (3, 3), \ldots,$
$(n - 1, n - 1), (n, 1)\}$

13. (a) $\begin{bmatrix} 1 & 1 & 1 & 1 \\ 1 & 0 & 1 & 1 \\ 1 & 0 & 1 & 1 \\ 0 & 0 & 1 & 0 \end{bmatrix}$ (b) $\begin{bmatrix} 1 & 0 & 1 & 1 \\ 0 & 1 & 1 & 1 \\ 0 & 0 & 1 & 1 \\ 0 & 0 & 1 & 1 \end{bmatrix}$

(c) $\begin{bmatrix} 0 & 1 & 1 & 1 \\ 1 & 0 & 1 & 1 \\ 0 & 0 & 1 & 1 \\ 1 & 0 & 1 & 1 \end{bmatrix}$ (d) $\begin{bmatrix} 1 & 0 & 1 & 1 \\ 1 & 1 & 1 & 1 \\ 0 & 0 & 1 & 0 \\ 1 & 1 & 1 & 1 \end{bmatrix}$

15. In regular arithmetic, $\begin{bmatrix} 1 & 1 \\ 1 & 0 \\ 1 & 2 \\ 0 & 1 \end{bmatrix}$;

in Boolean, $\begin{bmatrix} 1 & 1 \\ 1 & 0 \\ 1 & 1 \\ 0 & 1 \end{bmatrix}$

17. $A^2 = \begin{bmatrix} 1 & 2 & 0 \\ 0 & 1 & 0 \\ 2 & 1 & 1 \end{bmatrix}, A^3 = \begin{bmatrix} 1 & 3 & 0 \\ 0 & 1 & 0 \\ 3 & 3 & 1 \end{bmatrix},$

$A^4 = \begin{bmatrix} 1 & 4 & 0 \\ 0 & 1 & 0 \\ 4 & 6 & 1 \end{bmatrix},$ and $A^n = \begin{bmatrix} 1 & n & 0 \\ 0 & 1 & 0 \\ n & \binom{n}{2} & 1 \end{bmatrix}$

19. Let $(s_i, s_j) \in \mathbf{R}_1 \circ (\mathbf{R}_2 \circ \mathbf{R}_3)$. Hence, there exists s_m and s_k such that
$(s_i, s_m) \in \mathbf{R}_1, (s_m, s_k) \in \mathbf{R}_2,$ and
$(s_k, s_j) \in \mathbf{R}_3$. Thus, $(s_i, s_k) \in \mathbf{R}_1 \circ \mathbf{R}_2$ and
$(s_i, s_j) \in (\mathbf{R}_1 \circ \mathbf{R}_2) \circ \mathbf{R}_3$.

21. (a) $M^2 = \begin{bmatrix} 1 & 1 & 1 & 1 \\ 1 & 1 & 1 & 1 \\ 1 & 0 & 1 & 1 \\ 0 & 1 & 1 & 1 \end{bmatrix}$

23. (a) $M^2 = \begin{bmatrix} 1 & 1 & 1 & 1 & 1 \\ 1 & 1 & 1 & 0 & 1 \\ 1 & 0 & 1 & 1 & 1 \\ 0 & 1 & 1 & 1 & 1 \\ 1 & 0 & 1 & 1 & 1 \end{bmatrix}$ (b) No (c) No

27. $\begin{bmatrix} 1 & 1 & 1 & 1 \\ 0 & 0 & 1 & 1 \\ 1 & 1 & 1 & 1 \\ 1 & 1 & 1 & 1 \end{bmatrix}$

29. Since $0 < 1$ is the only possible strict inequality in Boolean arithmetic, $A = O_n$ and $B = J_n$.

Section 32. Answers to Tutorials

32.1. a. $CA = CB = \begin{bmatrix} 0 & 1 & 0 \\ 1 & 0 & 1 \\ 1 & 1 & 1 \end{bmatrix}$ **b.** $CA = CB$

32.2. $\begin{bmatrix} 1 & 1 & 1 & 1 & 1 & 1 \\ 0 & 1 & 0 & 1 & 1 & 1 \\ 0 & 0 & 1 & 0 & 1 & 1 \\ 0 & 0 & 0 & 1 & 0 & 1 \\ 0 & 0 & 0 & 0 & 1 & 1 \\ 0 & 0 & 0 & 0 & 0 & 1 \end{bmatrix}$

32.3. a. $M = \begin{bmatrix} 1 & 0 & 0 & 0 \\ 1 & 1 & 1 & 1 \\ 0 & 0 & 1 & 1 \\ 0 & 0 & 0 & 1 \end{bmatrix}$ **b.** $M^2 = M$ and

so $M^2 \le M$. **c.** Now $a_{ii} = 1$ for each i and $a_{ij}a_{ji} = 0$ for $i \ne j$. Note that $a_{13} = a_{31} = 0$.

Section 32. Answers to Selected Problems

1. Let $D = [d_{ij}] = CA$ and $E = [e_{ij}] = CB$. If $d_{ij} = 1$, then there is a k such that $c_{ik} = a_{kj} = 1$. Since $A \le B$, $b_{kj} = 1$. Hence, $e_{ij} = \cdots + c_{ik}b_{kj} + \cdots = 1$.

3. (*a*) Not transitive (*b*) Not transitive

5. (*a*) Transitive (*b*) Not transitive

7. Neither of the relations in Prob. 4 are partial or linear orders.

9.

11.

```
              {a, b, c, d}
            /    |    |    \
  {a, b, c} {a, b, d} {a, c, d} {b, c, d}
  {a, b} {a, c} {a, d} {b, c} {b, d} {c, d}
        {a}   {b}   {c}   {d}
                  ∅
```

13. No. For example, $\begin{bmatrix} 1 & 0 & 0 \\ 0 & 0 & 1 \\ 0 & 0 & 0 \end{bmatrix}$ and $\begin{bmatrix} 0 & 1 & 0 \\ 0 & 0 & 0 \\ 0 & 0 & 1 \end{bmatrix}$

are transitive, but their composition,

$\begin{bmatrix} 0 & 1 & 0 \\ 0 & 0 & 1 \\ 0 & 0 & 0 \end{bmatrix}$ is not transitive.

15. $M = \begin{matrix} & \begin{matrix} 1 & 2 & 3 & 4 & 5 & 6 \end{matrix} \\ \begin{matrix} 1 \\ 2 \\ 3 \\ 4 \\ 5 \\ 6 \end{matrix} & \begin{bmatrix} 1 & 1 & 1 & 0 & 1 & 0 \\ 1 & 1 & 0 & 1 & 0 & 1 \\ 1 & 0 & 1 & 0 & 1 & 0 \\ 0 & 1 & 0 & 1 & 0 & 0 \\ 1 & 0 & 1 & 0 & 0 & 0 \\ 0 & 1 & 0 & 0 & 0 & 1 \end{bmatrix} \end{matrix}$ and $M^2 =$

$\begin{bmatrix} 1 & 1 & 1 & 1 & 1 & 1 \\ 1 & 1 & 1 & 1 & 1 & 1 \\ 1 & 1 & 1 & 0 & 1 & 0 \\ 1 & 1 & 0 & 1 & 0 & 1 \\ 1 & 1 & 1 & 0 & 1 & 0 \\ 1 & 1 & 0 & 1 & 0 & 1 \end{bmatrix}$. Since $M^2 \nleq M$, M is

not transitive.

17. If $a \in S$, then $(a, a) \in R$. If $a \ne b$, then either $(a, b) \in R$ or $(b, a) \in R$, but not both. If $(a, b) \notin R$, then $(b, a) \in R$ which means that $(a, b) \in R^{-1}$. Thus, $S \times S \subseteq R \cup R^{-1}$.

19. As defined, $\lhd_*$ is reflexive. Suppose that $(x_1, y_1) \lhd_* (x_2, y_2)$ and $(x_2, y_2) \lhd_* (x_3, y_3)$. Since $x_1 \lhd x_2$ and $x_2 \lhd x_3$, $x_1 \lhd x_3$. If $x_1 = x_3$, then $x_1 = x_2 = x_3$, and hence $y_1 \lhd y_2$ and $y_2 \lhd y_3$ implies $y_1 \lhd y_3$. If $x_1 \ne x_3$, then $x_1 \lhd x_3$. In either case, $(x_1, y_1) \lhd_* (x_3, y_3)$ and $\lhd_*$ is transitive.

Suppose that $(x_1, y_1) \ne (x_2, y_2)$ and suppose that $(x_1, y_1) \lhd_* (x_2, y_2)$. If $x_1 \lhd x_2$, then $(x_2, y_2) \cancel{\lhd}_* (x_1, y_1)$. If $x_1 = x_2$, then $y_1 \lhd y_2$ (and $y_1 \ne y_2$), and hence $(x_2, y_2) \cancel{\lhd}_* (x_1, y_1)$. Therefore, $\lhd_*$ is antisymmetric.

Suppose that $(x_1, y_1) \cancel{\lhd}_* (x_2, y_2)$. If $x_1 \ne x_2$, then $x_2 \lhd x_1$ and $(x_2, y_2) \lhd_* (x_1, y_1)$. If $x_1 = x_2$, then $y_2 \lhd y_1$ and $(x_2, y_2) \lhd_* (x_1, y_1)$. Therefore, $\lhd_*$ is full.

21. Again, assume reflexivity. Then $(a_1, b_1, c_1) \lhd_{(A \times B \times C)} (a_2, b_2, c_2)$ if $a_1 \lhd_A a_2$, or $a_1 = a_2$ and $b_1 \lhd_B b_2$, or $a_1 = a_2$ and $b_1 = b_2$ and $c_1 \lhd_C c_2$.

23. @BAB, BA?@, BA@@, BAB@, BAC@

25. $3 \lhd_S 5 \lhd_S 7 \lhd_S 9 \lhd_S 11 \lhd_S 13 \lhd_S 15 \lhd_S 6 \lhd_S 10 \lhd_S 14 \lhd_S 12 \lhd_S 16 \lhd_S 8 \lhd_S 4 \lhd_S 2 \lhd_S 1$

Section 33. Answers to Tutorials

33.1. a. Since $p \sim x$ and $x \sim y$, $p \sim y$ (transitivity). Hence, by (2), $p \in [y]$. **b.** Since $q \in [y]$, $q \sim y$ by (2). Thus $y \sim x$ by symmetry and $q \sim x$ by transitivity. Again, by (2), $q \in [x]$.

33.2. a. Note that $(x, x) \in \mathbf{R}$ for each $x \in S$. Hence $\mathbf{R}$ is reflexive. **b.** Since both (a, c) and (c, a) and both (b, d) and (d, b) are in $\mathbf{R}$, $\mathbf{R}$ is symmetric. **d.**

$$
\begin{array}{c c}
 & \begin{array}{cccc} a & c & b & d \end{array} \\
\begin{array}{c} a \\ c \\ b \\ d \end{array} &
\left[\begin{array}{cccc}
1 & 1 & 0 & 0 \\
1 & 1 & 0 & 0 \\
0 & 0 & 1 & 1 \\
0 & 0 & 1 & 1
\end{array}\right]
\end{array}
$$

33.3. a. I_3 and J_3 **b.**

$$
\begin{array}{c c}
 & \begin{array}{ccc} x & z & y \end{array} \\
\begin{array}{c} x \\ z \\ y \end{array} &
\left[\begin{array}{ccc}
1 & 1 & 0 \\
1 & 1 & 0 \\
0 & 0 & 1
\end{array}\right]
\end{array}
$$

c.

$$
\begin{array}{c c}
 & \begin{array}{ccc} y & z & x \end{array} \\
\begin{array}{c} y \\ z \\ x \end{array} &
\left[\begin{array}{ccc}
1 & 1 & 0 \\
1 & 1 & 0 \\
0 & 0 & 1
\end{array}\right]
\end{array}
$$

Section 33. Answers to Selected Problems

1. Neither

3. Neither

5. There are exactly two equivalence classes, $[0] = \{0, 3, -3, \ldots\}$ and $[1] = \{1, -1, 2, -2, \ldots\}$.

7. (a) $x = 1$ or $x = 2$ (b) Yes (c) If $x \in [0]$, then $x^2 \in [0]$ and $x^2 + 1 \ne 0$. If $x \notin [0]$, then $x^2 \in [1]$ and $x^2 + 1 \ne 0$.

9. (a) $M =$
$$
\begin{bmatrix}
1 & 0 & 0 & 0 & 0 & 0 \\
0 & 1 & 0 & 0 & 0 & 0 \\
0 & 1 & 0 & 0 & 0 & 0 \\
0 & 0 & 1 & 0 & 0 & 0 \\
0 & 0 & 1 & 0 & 0 & 0 \\
0 & 0 & 0 & 1 & 0 & 0
\end{bmatrix},
$$

$$
M^t =
\begin{bmatrix}
1 & 0 & 0 & 0 & 0 & 0 \\
0 & 1 & 1 & 0 & 0 & 0 \\
0 & 0 & 0 & 1 & 1 & 0 \\
0 & 0 & 0 & 0 & 0 & 1 \\
0 & 0 & 0 & 0 & 0 & 0 \\
0 & 0 & 0 & 0 & 0 & 0
\end{bmatrix}
$$

(b) $MM^t = \begin{bmatrix} 1 & 0 & 0 & 0 & 0 & 0 \\ 0 & 1 & 1 & 0 & 0 & 0 \\ 0 & 1 & 1 & 0 & 0 & 0 \\ 0 & 0 & 0 & 1 & 1 & 0 \\ 0 & 0 & 0 & 1 & 1 & 0 \\ 0 & 0 & 0 & 0 & 0 & 1 \end{bmatrix}$

(c) The matrix MM^t has J-blocks along its main diagonal.

11. $[(1, 5)] = \{(1, 5), (2, 6), (3, 7), \ldots\}$, $[(2, 9)] = \{(2, 9), (1, 8), (3, 10), \ldots\}$, $[(7, 10)] = \{(7, 10), (1, 4), (2, 5), \ldots\}$

13. (a) 5 (see Example 1, par. 33.3) (b) 15

15. Neither

17. (a) Reflexive and transitive (b) Reflexive and transitive (c) Reflexive, symmetric, and transitive

19. (a) Now $[58] = [3]$ and $[19] = [4]$, and so $[3] \cdot [4] = [12] = [2]$. (b) Since $x = 5m + 3$

and $y = 5k + 4$, $xy = 25mk + 20m + 15k + 12 = 5(5mk + 4m + 3k + 2) + 2$. Therefore, $xy \in [2]$. (c) Let $x = 5m + 3$, $y = 5j + 4$, $z = 5k + 3$, and $w = 5i + 4$. So $xy = 5M + 12 = 5M' + 2$ and $zw = 5K + 12 = 5K' + 2$.

21. Now $x = 5m + a$, $z = 5m' + a$, $y = 5k + b$, and $w = 5k' + b$. Thus, $x + y = 5M + (a + b)$ and $z + w = 5M' + (a + b)$. Hence, $[x + y] = [z + w]$.

23. This is exactly like Prob. 21, except that the divisor is m instead of 5.

27. The equation mod 5 is $3x = 3$, and so $x \in [1]$. The equation mod 12 is $3x = 10$, but $3x$ is never 10 mod 12.

29. (a) **I** (b) **I**

Section 34.   Answers to Tutorials

34.4. a. $v_2 \prec \begin{smallmatrix} v_1 \\ v_3 \end{smallmatrix}$ $\mathbf{E} = \{(v_1, v_2), (v_2, v_3)\}$

b. $v_2 \longleftarrow v_4 \prec \begin{smallmatrix} v_1 \\ v_3 \end{smallmatrix}$ $\mathbf{E} = \{(v_1, v_2), (v_2, v_3), (v_2, v_4)\}$

c. graph with v_1, v_5, v_2, v_4, v_3 No

c. graph with $v_5, v_3, v_4, v_1, v_6, v_2$

34.7.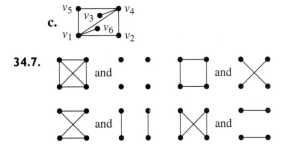

34.5. a. $2^{15} = 32{,}768$ **b.** $\binom{15}{7} = 6435$

Section 34.   Answers to Selected Problems

1. (a) Yes (b) No

3. Two

5. graph with v_2, v_3, v_1, v_4, v_5 $\begin{bmatrix} 0 & 1 & 1 & 1 & 1 \\ 1 & 0 & 0 & 0 & 0 \\ 1 & 0 & 0 & 0 & 0 \\ 1 & 0 & 0 & 0 & 0 \\ 1 & 0 & 0 & 0 & 0 \end{bmatrix}$

7.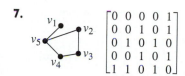

$$\begin{bmatrix} 0 & 0 & 0 & 0 & 1 \\ 0 & 0 & 1 & 0 & 1 \\ 0 & 1 & 0 & 1 & 0 \\ 0 & 0 & 1 & 0 & 1 \\ 1 & 1 & 0 & 1 & 0 \end{bmatrix}$$

9.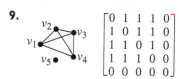

$$\begin{bmatrix} 0 & 1 & 1 & 1 & 0 \\ 1 & 0 & 1 & 1 & 0 \\ 1 & 1 & 0 & 1 & 0 \\ 1 & 1 & 1 & 0 & 0 \\ 0 & 0 & 0 & 0 & 0 \end{bmatrix}$$

11.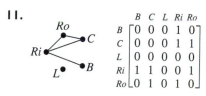

	B	C	L	Ri	Ro
B	0	0	0	1	0
C	0	0	0	1	1
L	0	0	0	0	0
Ri	1	1	0	0	1
Ro	0	1	0	1	0

13. There are 10 edges.

15. (*a*) 2 and 6 (*b*) 3 and 10

17.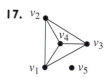

19. The matrix of a graph is a matrix for an irreflexive, symmetric relation. If the graph

has more than one vertex, then by the alternate form of Theorem 28.1 (found in par. 28.3), at least two row sums of the matrix are the same. Therefore, two vertices have the same degree.

21. $\dbinom{\binom{9}{2}}{12} = \dbinom{36}{12}$

23. Four

25. Any graph **G** on n vertices with m edges has exactly $\dbinom{n}{2} - m$ (possible) nonedges. Simply pair with **G** the graph $\overline{\textbf{G}}$ on the same vertex set in which $(v_i, v_j) \in \overline{\textbf{G}}$ if and only if $(v_i, v_j) \notin \textbf{G}$.

27.

	V	N	Me	W	R	C	Ma
V	0	1	0	0	0	0	1
N	1	0	1	1	0	0	1
Me	0	1	0	1	0	0	0
W	0	1	1	0	1	1	1
R	0	0	0	1	0	1	1
C	0	0	0	1	1	0	1
Ma	1	1	0	1	1	1	0

31. $\dbinom{6}{2} = 15$ edges and $\dbinom{6}{3} = 20$ triangles

Section 35.   Answers to Tutorials

35.2. a. 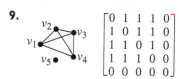 **b.**

35.3. a.
$$\begin{bmatrix} 0 & 1 & 0 & 1 & 1 & 1 \\ 1 & 0 & 1 & 1 & 0 & 1 \\ 0 & 1 & 0 & 0 & 1 & 0 \\ 1 & 1 & 0 & 0 & 0 & 1 \\ 1 & 0 & 1 & 0 & 0 & 0 \\ 1 & 1 & 0 & 1 & 0 & 0 \end{bmatrix}$$

b.
$$\begin{bmatrix} 0 & 1 & 0 & 1 & 1 & 1 \\ 1 & 0 & 1 & 0 & 0 & 1 \\ 0 & 1 & 0 & 0 & 1 & 0 \\ 1 & 0 & 0 & 0 & 0 & 1 \\ 1 & 0 & 1 & 0 & 0 & 0 \\ 1 & 1 & 0 & 1 & 0 & 0 \end{bmatrix}$$

c.
$$\begin{bmatrix} 0 & 1 & 0 & - & 1 & 1 \\ 1 & 0 & 1 & - & 0 & 1 \\ 0 & 1 & 0 & - & 1 & 0 \\ - & - & - & - & - & - \\ 1 & 0 & 1 & - & 0 & 0 \\ 1 & 1 & 0 & - & 0 & 0 \end{bmatrix}$$

35.5A. a. $(v_1, v_5, v_3, v_2, v_4)$, $(v_1, v_4, v_2, v_6, v_4)$
  b. (v_1, v_6), (v_1, v_4, v_6), (v_1, v_5, v_1, v_6),
  $(v_1, v_2, v_4, v_2, v_6)$, $(v_1, v_2, v_3, v_5, v_1, v_6)$
  c. $(v_3, v_2, v_1, v_6, v_4, v_1, v_5, v_3)$

35.5B. a. $(v_6, v_7, v_3, v_5, v_4, v_3, v_6)$; v_3 is repeated.
  b. $\mathbf{U} = \{v_1, v_2, v_3, v_6, v_7\}$, $\mathbf{D} =$

$\{e_{12}, e_{23}, e_{36}, e_{67}\}$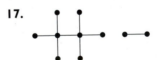

c. The subgraph induced by $\{v_2, v_3, v_5\}$. The subgraph induced by $\{v_3, v_6, v_7\}$. The subgraph induced by $\{v_3, v_4, v_5\}$.

Section 35. Answers to Selected Problems

1.

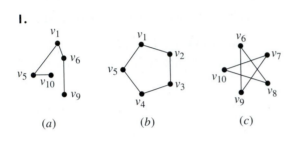

(a) *(b)* *(c)*

3. $v_3\bullet \quad \bullet v_4$

$v_2\bullet \quad \bullet v_1$

5. $v_3 \bullet\!\!-\!\!\bullet v_4$

$v_2 \bullet\!\!-\!\!\bullet v_1$

7.
(a)

(b) *(c)* No

9. $v_1\bullet \quad v_2 \quad v_3 \quad \bullet v_4$
$v_6\bullet \qquad\qquad \bullet v_5$

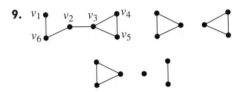

11. $\begin{bmatrix} 0 & 1 & 1 & 0 & 1 & 1 \\ 1 & 0 & 0 & 0 & 1 & 0 \\ 1 & 0 & 0 & 1 & 1 & 1 \\ 0 & 0 & 1 & 0 & 1 & 0 \\ 1 & 1 & 1 & 1 & 0 & 0 \\ 1 & 0 & 1 & 0 & 0 & 0 \end{bmatrix}$

13. $(2, 2, 2, 3, 3, 4)$

15. It is regular of degree 3.

17.

19. (v_1, v_3, v_5, v_1), $(v_1, v_3, v_4, v_5, v_1)$,
  $(v_1, v_2, v_5, v_3, v_6, v_1)$, $(v_1, v_2, v_5, v_4, v_3, v_6, v_1)$

21. Four, yes

23.

v_i	2	3	4	5	6	7	8	9	10
Distance	1	2	2	1	1	2	2	2	2

25. Suppose not. Let $\mathbf{P} = (v_1, v_2, \ldots, v_r)$ and $\mathbf{Q} = (u_1, u_2, \ldots, u_r)$ be longest paths in a connected graph $\mathbf{G}$. Since $\mathbf{G}$ is connected, there are paths $\mathbf{P}_{ij}$ between v_i and u_j for $1 \leq i, j \leq r$. Let $\mathbf{P}_{i_0 j_0} =$

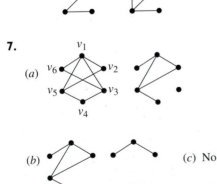

$(v_{i_0}, w_2, w_3, \ldots, w_k, v_{j_0})$ be a shortest such path. (Note that there may be only an edge between these paths and so there may be no w's.) None of the w's can be in either $\mathbf{P}$ or $\mathbf{Q}$ for otherwise, $\mathbf{P}_{i_0 j_0}$ is not the shortest such path. A path in $\mathbf{G}$ that is longer than $\mathbf{P}$ can be constructed by starting at whichever vertex v_1 or v_r is farther from v_{i_0}, following $\mathbf{P}$ to v_{i_0}, following $\mathbf{P}_{i_0 j_0}$ to u_{j_0}, and then following $\mathbf{Q}$ to whichever of u_1 or u_r is farther away from u_{j_0}.

27. No. Yes; for if the u, v and v, w paths have no vertex in common, then they jointly form a path from u to w. Otherwise, let t be a vertex common to the two paths (closest to u). Then the two subpaths joined at t form a path from u to w.

29. Consider the graph with $2n$ vertices u_i and v_j for $1 \le i \le n, 1 \le j \le n$, and edge set $\mathbf{E} = \{(u_i, v_j) : 1 \le i \le n, 1 \le j \le n\}$. This graph has $2n$ vertices, no triangles, and n^2 edges.

31. The Petersen graph from Prob. 1.

33. Consider the graphs described in the answer to Prob. 29.

35. If a component is not complete, then there are two vertices in it that are not joined by an edge. This contradicts the maximality of the edge set of $\mathbf{G}$.

37. A complete graph on n vertices has $\binom{n}{2}$ edges. So $\mathbf{G}_1$ has $\binom{m+1}{2} + \binom{r-1}{2}$ edges. Now

$$\binom{m+1}{2} + \binom{r-1}{2} - \binom{m}{2} - \binom{r}{2}$$

$$= \frac{(m+1)m - m(m-1)}{2}$$

$$+ \frac{(r-1)(r-2) - r(r-1)}{2}$$

$$= \frac{m(m+1-m+1) + (r-1)(r-2-r)}{2}$$

$$= \frac{2m - 2r + 2}{2} = m - r + 1 > 0,$$

since $m \ge r$.

Section 36.   Answers to Tutorials

36.4. $(v_1, v_6, v_1, v_6), (v_1, v_5, v_1, v_6), (v_1, v_4, v_1, v_6),$
$(v_1, v_2, v_1, v_6), (v_1, v_6, v_5, v_6), (v_1, v_2, v_5, v_6),$
(v_1, v_4, v_5, v_6)

36.5. a. 6 **b.** $\mathrm{Tr}(A^3) = 36$ **c.** $\mathrm{Tr}(A^3) = 42$

Section 36.   Answers to Selected Problems

1. $A = \begin{bmatrix} 0 & 1 & 1 & 0 \\ 1 & 0 & 1 & 1 \\ 1 & 1 & 0 & 1 \\ 0 & 1 & 1 & 0 \end{bmatrix}, A^2 = \begin{bmatrix} 2 & 1 & 1 & 2 \\ 1 & 3 & 2 & 1 \\ 1 & 2 & 3 & 1 \\ 2 & 1 & 1 & 2 \end{bmatrix}$

3. $A^3 = \begin{bmatrix} 2 & 5 & 5 & 2 \\ 5 & 4 & 5 & 5 \\ 5 & 5 & 4 & 5 \\ 2 & 5 & 5 & 2 \end{bmatrix}$

5. Note that $\frac{1}{6}\text{Tr}(A^3) = \frac{1}{6} \cdot 12 = 2$. The (v_2, v_2) entry in A^3 is 4, and $\frac{1}{2} \cdot 4 = 2$ is the number of triangles containing v_2.

7.

From v_1 to	v_1	v_2	v_3	v_4	v_5
No. of walks	3	2	1	2	1

9. 3

11. $A = \begin{bmatrix} 0 & 1 & 0 & 1 & 1 & 1 \\ 1 & 0 & 0 & 1 & 1 & 0 \\ 0 & 0 & 0 & 1 & 1 & 1 \\ 1 & 1 & 1 & 0 & 0 & 0 \\ 1 & 1 & 1 & 0 & 0 & 0 \\ 1 & 0 & 1 & 0 & 0 & 0 \end{bmatrix}$ and

$A^2 = \begin{bmatrix} 4 & 2 & 3 & 1 & 1 & 0 \\ 2 & 3 & 2 & 1 & 1 & 1 \\ 3 & 2 & 3 & 0 & 0 & 0 \\ 1 & 1 & 0 & 3 & 3 & 2 \\ 1 & 1 & 0 & 3 & 3 & 2 \\ 0 & 1 & 0 & 2 & 2 & 2 \end{bmatrix}$

13. $\text{Tr}(A^3) = 6 \cdot 2 = 12$

15. Designate each person by a vertex. Let an edge between vertices exist if and only if that pair of individuals shook hands. The degree of each vertex is the number of hands shaken by that person. Thus, an even number of persons shook an odd number of hands.

17. If $i \neq j$, then there is a path from v_i to v_j of length two via each *other* vertex; hence, there are $n - 2$ of them. Each entry on the main diagonal is the degree of its vertex, hence is $n - 1$. Thus, if $A_n^2 = [b_{ij}]$, then

$$b_{ij} = \begin{cases} n - 2 & \text{if } i \neq j \\ n - 1 & \text{if } i = j. \end{cases}$$

Section 37.   Answers to Tutorials

37.2. a. $f = \{(v_1, v_3), (v_2, v_4), (v_3, v_1), (v_4, v_2)\}$

19. $A_2^3 = \begin{bmatrix} 0 & 1 \\ 1 & 0 \end{bmatrix}$, $A_3^3 = \begin{bmatrix} 2 & 3 & 3 \\ 3 & 2 & 3 \\ 3 & 3 & 2 \end{bmatrix}$,

$A_4^3 = \begin{bmatrix} 6 & 7 & 7 & 7 \\ 7 & 6 & 7 & 7 \\ 7 & 7 & 6 & 7 \\ 7 & 7 & 7 & 6 \end{bmatrix}$

21. If A_n is the matrix of the complete graph, then $\text{Tr}(A^3) = 6\binom{n}{3}$. The n diagonal entries are identical; hence each entry on the main diagonal is

$$\frac{1}{n} \cdot 6 \cdot \frac{n(n-1)(n-2)}{6} = (n-1)(n-2)$$
$$= 2\binom{n-1}{2}.$$

27. The matrix for $\mathbf{G}_1$ is $\begin{array}{c} \\ v_1 \\ v_2 \\ v_3 \end{array}\begin{array}{c} e_1 \quad e_2 \end{array}\begin{bmatrix} 1 & 0 \\ 1 & 1 \\ 0 & 1 \end{bmatrix}$,

and the matrix for $\mathbf{G}_2$ is

$\begin{array}{c} \\ v_1 \\ v_2 \\ v_3 \\ v_4 \\ v_5 \end{array}\begin{array}{c} e_1 \;\; e_2 \;\; e_3 \;\; e_4 \;\; e_5 \;\; e_6 \;\; e_7 \end{array}\begin{bmatrix} 1 & 1 & 0 & 0 & 0 & 0 & 0 \\ 1 & 0 & 0 & 1 & 1 & 0 & 0 \\ 0 & 0 & 1 & 1 & 0 & 1 & 0 \\ 0 & 1 & 1 & 0 & 0 & 0 & 1 \\ 0 & 0 & 0 & 0 & 1 & 1 & 1 \end{bmatrix}$.

29. $\binom{n}{2}$, n, $\begin{array}{c} \\ v_1 \\ v_2 \\ v_3 \\ v_4 \\ v_5 \end{array}\begin{array}{c} e_1 \;\; e_2 \;\; e_3 \;\; e_4 \;\; e_5 \end{array}\begin{bmatrix} 1 & 0 & 0 & 0 & 1 \\ 1 & 1 & 0 & 0 & 0 \\ 0 & 1 & 1 & 0 & 0 \\ 0 & 0 & 1 & 1 & 0 \\ 0 & 0 & 0 & 1 & 1 \end{bmatrix}$

b. No **c.**

d. No

37.3.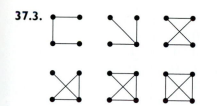

37.4. a. [figure] **b.** Move one of the two bottom vertices above the top three. [figure]

Section 37.   Answers to Selected Problems

1. Any labeling of the second and third is an isomorphism. The first graph is regular of degree 2, and the last two are regular of degree 3; hence the first cannot be isomorphic to either of the last two.

3. The middle two graphs cannot be isomorphic to the first and last since the first and last are regular of degree 2 and the middle two are not regular. The first and last are isomorphic to each other, and the middle two are isomorphic to each other.

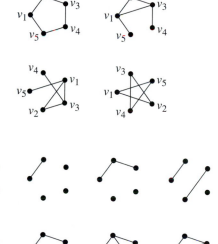

5.

7.

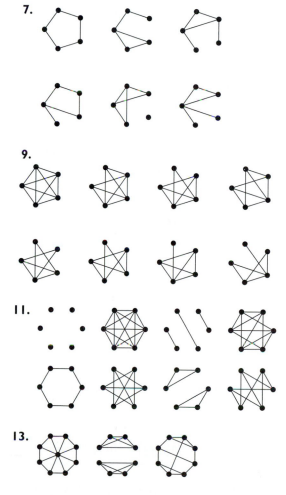

9.

11.

13.

15. If a graph has minimum degree 3, then it must have four vertices and at least six edges. Note that K_4 meets these conditions, and hence it is the graph we seek.

17. The same one-to-one correspondence between the vertex sets will do.

19. The complement of the first graph in Prob. 2 is C_6, for if the vertices are labeled v_1 to v_6 starting in the upper-left corner, then the complement is $(v_1, v_3, v_6, v_4, v_2, v_5, v_1)$. Since the first and fourth graphs in Prob. 2 are isomorphic, their complements are isomorphic (see Prob. 17). For the two middle graphs in Prob. 2, the complement is two disjoint copies of K_3. If the second graph is labeled as the first, then (v_1, v_3, v_5) and (v_2, v_4, v_6) are the K_3's.

21.

23. A graph with n vertices can be self-complementary only if the edge set of K_n can be partitioned into two subsets of equal size. Hence, the total number of edges in K_n must be even. Now K_n has $\binom{n}{2} = \dfrac{n(n-1)}{2}$ edges which is even when $n = 4k$ or $n = 4k+1$ and which is odd otherwise.

25. $A = \begin{array}{c} \\ v_1 \\ v_2 \\ u_1 \\ u_2 \end{array} \begin{array}{cccc} v_1 & v_2 & u_1 & u_2 \\ \begin{bmatrix} 0 & 0 & 1 & 1 \\ 0 & 0 & 1 & 1 \\ 1 & 1 & 0 & 0 \\ 1 & 1 & 0 & 0 \end{bmatrix} \end{array}, A^2 =$

$\begin{bmatrix} 2 & 2 & 0 & 0 \\ 2 & 2 & 0 & 0 \\ 0 & 0 & 2 & 2 \\ 0 & 0 & 2 & 2 \end{bmatrix}, A^3 = \begin{bmatrix} 0 & 0 & 4 & 4 \\ 0 & 0 & 4 & 4 \\ 4 & 4 & 0 & 0 \\ 4 & 4 & 0 & 0 \end{bmatrix}$

27. $A = \begin{bmatrix} 0 & 0 & 0 & 1 & 1 & 1 \\ 0 & 0 & 0 & 1 & 1 & 1 \\ 0 & 0 & 0 & 1 & 1 & 1 \\ 1 & 1 & 1 & 0 & 0 & 0 \\ 1 & 1 & 1 & 0 & 0 & 0 \\ 1 & 1 & 1 & 0 & 0 & 0 \end{bmatrix},$

$A^2 = \begin{bmatrix} 3 & 3 & 3 & 0 & 0 & 0 \\ 3 & 3 & 3 & 0 & 0 & 0 \\ 3 & 3 & 3 & 0 & 0 & 0 \\ 0 & 0 & 0 & 3 & 3 & 3 \\ 0 & 0 & 0 & 3 & 3 & 3 \\ 0 & 0 & 0 & 3 & 3 & 3 \end{bmatrix},$

$A^3 = \begin{bmatrix} 0 & 0 & 0 & 9 & 9 & 9 \\ 0 & 0 & 0 & 9 & 9 & 9 \\ 0 & 0 & 0 & 9 & 9 & 9 \\ 9 & 9 & 9 & 0 & 0 & 0 \\ 9 & 9 & 9 & 0 & 0 & 0 \\ 9 & 9 & 9 & 0 & 0 & 0 \end{bmatrix}$

29.   In each graph, the black edges form a subgraph isomorphic to each of the two shaded subgraphs.

31. There are 10 triangles in $\overline{K}_{1,6}$. There are $\binom{n-1}{3}$ triangles in $\overline{K}_{1,n}$.

37.

Section 38. Answers to Tutorials

38.2B. a.

b. $(v_5, v_6, v_2, v_5, v_4, v_2, v_1, v_3, v_9, v_8, v_3, v_2, v_7, v_8)$

38.4. Labeling the graph counterclockwise, v_0, $v_1, v_2, v_3,$ and v_4, a possible eulerian trail is $(v_0, v_1, v_2, v_3, v_4, v_0, v_3, v_1)$.

Section 38. Answers to Selected Problems

1. Let **G** be a connected graph with adjacency matrix M. If each row sum of M is even, then **G** is eulerian.

3. $\mathbf{K}_{r,s}$ is eulerian if both r and s are even. $\mathbf{K}_{r,s}$ has an eulerian trail if $r = 2$ and s is odd (or vice versa).

5. No, it has more than two odd vertices.

7. One of many solutions is (1, 2, 3, 4, 1, 5, 4, 8, 3, 7, 2, 6, 9, 5, 12, 8, 11, 7, 10, 14, 9, 13, 12, 16, 11, 15, 10, 6, 1). Note that at the first appearances of 6 and 10, one must avoid using a bridge prematurely.

9. Our model is a multigraph with degree sequence (4, 4, 4, 4, 6). Hence there is a closed eulerian trail starting at any vertex.

11. In each room record the number of its doors, remembering to include the outside as a "room." Because exactly two vertices (rooms) are of odd degree, there is a path through the house (including the outside "room") beginning in one of the rooms of odd degree and ending in the other.

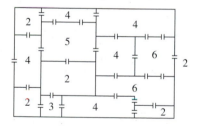

13. An eulerian graph has no odd vertices. Hence, by Prob. 12, an eulerian graph cannot have a bridge.

15. Note first that the two odd vertices must belong to the same component for the sum of the degrees of the vertices in any component must be even. Since these two odd vertices are in the same component, there is a path between them.

17. (*a*) Deleting a path from a graph leaves the parity of each vertex unchanged except for the end-vertices of the path. The parity of these two vertices changes. (*b*) In **G'**, the parity of all the vertices are the same as in **G**, except for u and v, both of which are even vertices in **G'**. Hence, **G'** has k edge-disjoint paths joining its $2k$ odd vertices.

19. For $n > 3$ with n odd, $\overline{\mathbf{C}}_n$ is eulerian since $\overline{\mathbf{C}}_n$ is regular of degree $n - 3$.

Section 39. Answers to Tutorials

39.1.

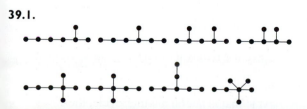

39.2. a.

n	2	3	4	5	6	7
$l(n)$	1	3	16	125	1296	16807
$u(n)$	1	1	2	3	6	11

b. Vertex subscripts in sequence: $(1, 2, 3, 4)$, $(1, 2, 4, 3)$, $(1, 3, 2, 4)$, $(1, 3, 4, 2)$, $(1, 4, 2, 3)$, $(1, 4, 3, 2)$, $(2, 1, 3, 4)$, $(2, 1, 4, 3)$, $(2, 3, 1, 4)$, $(2, 4, 1, 3)$, $(3, 1, 2, 4)$, $(3, 2, 1, 4)$

Section 39.   Answers to Selected Problems

1.

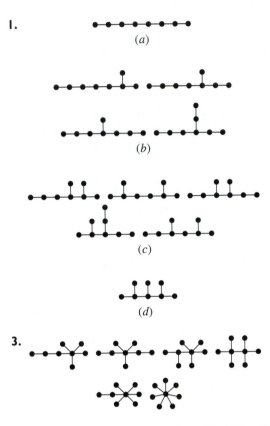

(a)

(b)

(c)

(d)

3.

5. Let **G** be a connected graph and let **T** be **G**. **Step 1.** Check **T** for cycles. **Step 2.** If **T** has a cycle, then let e be an edge of the cycle, let **T** be **T** $- e$, and go to **Step 1**. If **T** has no cycle, then stop. ▲

7. Since **T** contains no cycle, deleting an edge e of **T** must disconnect **T**. Replacing e in **T** $- e$ results in the connected graph **T**; hence, **T** $- e$ has two components.

9. 7

11. The diameter of $\mathbf{K}_n$ is 1, the diameter of $\mathbf{K}_{m,n}$ is 2, and the diameter of $\mathbf{P}_n$ is $n - 1$.

13. The number of labeled graphs with five vertices is $2^{10} = 1024$, which is smaller than the number of labeled trees with six vertices, namely, $6^4 = 1296$.

15. $(a) \rightarrow (b)$. Assume (a). So **G** is connected with $n - 1$ edges. Now **G'** has $n - 2$ edges and no cycles. By Theorem 39.4, **G'** is not a tree and hence cannot be connected.
$(b) \rightarrow (a)$ and (c). Assume (b). Since a graph cannot be disconnected by the removal of an edge of a cycle, **G** cannot have a cycle. Thus **G** is a tree, and by Theorem 39.4, **G** has $n - 1$ edges. Now **G''** is connected (since **G** is) and has n edges. Thus **G''** is not a tree, and, therefore, it must have a cycle.
$(c) \rightarrow (a)$. Assume (c). Suppose **G** is not connected. Let u and v be in different components of **G** and let $e = e_{uv}$. Since deleting e from **G''** results in more components, e cannot be on a cycle, a contradiction. So **G** is connected and is therefore a tree.

17. $(a) \rightarrow (b)$. Now **G** has n edges since it is regular of degree 2. Let $e = e_{uv}$ be an edge of **G** and **G'** $= (\mathbf{V}, \mathbf{E} - e)$. Note that **G'** has $n - 1$ edges, $\deg(u) = \deg(v) = 1$, and all other vertices have degree 2 in both **G** and **G'**. By Prob. 15 in Sec. 36, there is a path **P** in **G'** between u and v. Thus **G'** is connected, for any path using e in **G** can use **P** in **G'**. If w is a vertex not on **P**, then let x be the closest vertex on **P** to w. So x has degree 3, a contradiction. So **G'** $=$ **P**.
$(b) \rightarrow (c)$. Since $\mathbf{P}_n$ is connected, so is **G**. Since the removal of any edge of **G** results in $\mathbf{P}_n$, **G** has no bridges. Suppose that **G** has more than one cycle. If e is an edge on one cycle that is not on another cycle, then

removing e from **G** leaves a graph that still has a cycle. So **G** has only one cycle. Since $\mathbf{P}_n$ has $n - 1$ edges, **G** has n edges, and by Theorem 39.4, **G** must have a cycle (it is not a tree).

$(c) \rightarrow (a)$. Suppose that **G** is not $\mathbf{C}_n$. Let e' be an edge not on the cycle of **G**, let e'' be an edge on the cycle, let **G'** be **G** with e' removed, and let **G''** be **G** with e'' removed. Now **G''** is connected, has no cycles, and hence, by Theorem 39.4, is a tree. So **G** has n edges. Thus **G'** is connected with $n - 1$ edges and is also a tree. But **G'** has a cycle. Therefore, each edge of **G** is on the cycle and $\mathbf{G} = \mathbf{C}_n$.

19. A connected graph with n vertices and edges has exactly one cycle. It must have one, for

otherwise it is a tree and trees have $n - 1$ edges. It cannot have more than one, for removing an edge on one cycle that is not on another leaves a connected graph with a cycle and $n - 1$ edges, which implies that it is a tree.

21. $(1, 6, 4, 3)$

23. $(5, 3, 7, 7, 7, 5)$

25.

27.

Section 40. Answers to Tutorials

40.1. a.

40.3. a. The number of nodes that dominate the column node. **b.** Corresponding row and

column sums add to $n - 1$ (four, in this case).

c. 6; 10; $\dbinom{n}{2}$

40.5. a. F **b.** $A \rightarrow C \rightarrow B \rightarrow F \rightarrow E \rightarrow D \rightarrow G$

Section 40. Answers to Selected Problems

1. Each arc in **D** adds exactly 1 to the out-degree total and exactly 1 to the in-degree total.

3. $4^{\binom{n}{2}} = (2^2)^{\frac{n(n-1)}{2}} = 2^{n(n-1)}$

5. If a tournament has $2k$ nodes, then

$$\sum s_i = \binom{2k}{2} = k(2k - 1)$$

and this number is not divisible by $2k$.

7. (a) This is true for any transitive tournament with two nodes. Assume that it is true for

any transitive tournament with k nodes. Let **T** be a transitive tournament with $k + 1$ nodes, let v be a node in **T** with lowest score, and let **T'** be **T** with v removed. Now **T'** is also transitive and has k nodes. Let $v_1 \rightarrow v_2 \rightarrow \cdots \rightarrow v_k$ be a ranking of its nodes. Since every node before v_k dominates v_k, the score of v_k in **T'** must be 0. So the score of v in **T** is either 0 or 1. It cannot be 1, for then the score of v_k in **T** is 0. Hence every node of **T** dominates v. (b) There is no path from a lower-ranked node to a higher-ranked node.

9. (a) There are $\binom{n}{2}$ edges in $\mathbf{K}_n$, and each of these edges is an arc in the tournament.
(b) Consider the subtournament induced by any k of the nodes of $\mathbf{T}$. The score of each node in the subtournament is at most the score of the node in $\mathbf{T}$; hence,

$$\sum_{i=1}^{k} s_i \geq \binom{k}{2}.$$

11. If $\mathbf{D}'$ is eulerian, then let $\mathbf{W}$ be the eulerian trail in $\mathbf{D}'$. Now $\mathbf{W}$ must contain a node of $\mathbf{C}$ and at that node, traverse $\mathbf{C}$ and continue along $\mathbf{W}$.

13. Now $\sum \text{odeg} = \sum \text{ideg}$, and so $\sum_{\text{even}} \text{odeg} + \sum_{\text{odd}} \text{odeg} = \sum_{\text{even}} \text{ideg} + \sum_{\text{odd}} \text{ideg}$. If $|\mathbf{O}|$ is odd, then the left-hand side of the preceding equation is odd, and so $|\mathbf{I}|$ also must be odd. Hence, $|\mathbf{O}| + |\mathbf{I}|$ is even. Likewise, if $|\mathbf{O}|$ is even, then $|\mathbf{I}|$ is even, so $|\mathbf{O}| + |\mathbf{I}|$ is even. Thus, the sum can never be odd.

15. (a) If u, v, and w is a transitive triple, then the pattern of arrows is $\alpha \rightarrow \beta \rightarrow \gamma \leftarrow \alpha$. Note that the node in position α dominates the nodes in positions β and γ. (b) If s_i is the score of node i, then choosing any two of the nodes that i dominates determines a transitive triple. There are $\binom{s_i}{2}$ ways of doing this.

17. Now $n - 1 - s$ is the number of nodes that dominate u. Each pair of these nodes identifies a transitive triple in which u is dominated by both nodes.

19. If n is odd, then consider the tournament with nodes labeled $1, 2, \ldots, n$ and arcs $\{(i, i + j) : 1 \leq j \leq (n - 1)/2\}$. Each node has score $(n - 1)/2$, and so there are

$$\binom{n}{3} - n\binom{(n-1)/2}{2} = \frac{n^3 - n}{24}$$

cyclic triples.

Section 41. Answers to Tutorials

41.1. a. $|\mathbf{V}| - |\mathbf{E}| + |\mathbf{F}| = 10 - 15 + 7 = 2$
b. $|\mathbf{V}| - |\mathbf{E}| + |\mathbf{F}| = 19 - 20 + 5 = 4$

41.2. c.

41.3. Tetrahedron: $4 - 6 + 4 = 2$; cube: $8 - 12 + 6 = 2$; octahedron: $6 - 12 + 8 = 2$; dodecahedron: $20 - 30 + 12 = 2$; icosahedron: $12 - 30 + 20 = 2$

Section 41. Answers to Selected Problems

1. (a) ●—●—●—●—●—● $6 - 5 + 1 = 2$ (b)

$5 - 5 + 2 = 2$ (c) $4 - 6 + 4 = 2$

3. For a tree, $(m + 1) - m + 1 = 2$.

5. For each tree, $|\mathbf{V}| - |\mathbf{E}| = 1$. So for the graph having the k trees for components, $|\mathbf{V}| - |\mathbf{E}| = k$. Hence, $|\mathbf{V}| - |\mathbf{E}| + |\mathbf{F}| = 1 + k$.

7. By Theorem 41.1A, Theorem 41.1B is true for $k = 1$. Assume true for $k - 1$ components ($k > 1$). Let **G** be a planar graph with k components, $|\mathbf{V}|$ vertices, $|\mathbf{E}|$ edges, and $|\mathbf{F}|$ faces. Let **G'** be the graph obtained by connecting two components of **G** with an edge. Thus **G'** has $k - 1$ components, $|\mathbf{V}|$ vertices, $|\mathbf{E}| + 1$ edges, and $|\mathbf{F}|$ faces. Hence, $|\mathbf{V}| - (|\mathbf{E}| + 1) + |\mathbf{F}| = 1 + (k - 1) = k$. Therefore, $|\mathbf{V}| - |\mathbf{E}| + |\mathbf{F}| = 1 + k$, which is what we wished to show.

9. Now each face has at least four edges, and each edge is on, at most, two faces. Hence, $4f \leq 2m$. But $f = 2 + m - n$ by Euler's Formula, and so $4(2 + m - n) \leq 2m$ or $2m \leq 4n - 8$. Thus, $m \leq 2n - 4$.

11. Now $\mathbf{K}_{3,3}$ has no triangles, $n = 6$ vertices, and $m = 9$ edges. But $2n - 4 = 8$ which is less than m, and so by Prob. 9, $\mathbf{K}_{3,3}$ is not planar.

13. Now each face has at least five edges, and each edge is on at most two faces. Hence, $5f \leq 2m$. But $f = 2 + m - n$ by Euler's Formula, and so $5(2 + m - n) \leq 2m$ or $3m \leq 5n - 10$. Thus, $m \leq \frac{5}{3}(n - 2)$.

15. Now each face has at least g edges, and each edge is on, at most, two faces. Hence, $gf \leq 2m$. But $f = 2 + m - n$ by Euler's Formula,

and so $g(2 + m - n) \leq 2m$ or $(g - 2)m \leq g(n - 2)$. Thus, $m \leq \dfrac{g}{g - 2}(n - 2)$.

17. If **G** has $n \geq 11$ vertices, then either **G** or $\overline{\mathbf{G}}$ has at least $\frac{1}{4}n(n - 1)$ edges since $\mathbf{K}_n$ has $\frac{1}{2}n(n - 1)$ edges. Without loss of generality, assume that **G** has at least $\frac{1}{4}n(n - 1)$ edges. So if **G** is planar, then by Prob. 8, $3n - 6 \geq \frac{1}{4}n(n - 1)$, and so $0 \geq n^2 - 13n + 24$. But $n^2 - 13n + 24 = (n - 12)(n - 2) + n$ which is greater than 0 for $n \geq 11$. Therefore, **G** is not planar.

19. By Prob. 17, we have that since $\mathbf{C}_n$ is planar, $\overline{\mathbf{C}}_n$ is not planar for $n \geq 11$. For $n = 8$, $\overline{\mathbf{C}}_8$ has 20 edges, and so it cannot be planar using the formula from Prob. 8. Similarly, $\overline{\mathbf{C}}_9$ is not planar.

21. (a) Note that $\sum f_k = f$ and $\sum k f_k = 2m = 3n$, where m is the number of edges and n is the number of vertices. Multiplying Euler's Formula by 6 gives $6n - 6m + 6f = 12$, and substituting the preceding three equations yields $2 \sum k f_k - 3 \sum k f_k + 6 \sum f_k = 12$ or $\sum (6 - k) f_k = 12$. Hence, $3f_3 + 2f_4 + f_5 = 12 + \sum_{k>5}(k - 6)f_k$. (b) Since the right-hand side of the preceding equation is positive, so is the left-hand side. Therefore, at least one of f_3, f_4, or f_5 is positive.

Index

Boldface double numbers following page numbers refer to paragraph numbers; thus **28.1** refers to paragraph 28.1.